TOXICS AND TRANSNATIONAL LAW: INTERNATIONAL AND EUROPEAN REGULATION OF TOXIC SUBSTANCES AS LEGAL SYMBOLISM

This book analyses the development and effectiveness of transnational toxics law through two case studies: one dealing with the European regional regime for the control of toxic discharges in the aquatic environment and the other looking at the emerging global regime for the regulation of international trade in hazardous pesticides. The author shows that international normative efforts in these two fields have proved much more productive in establishing procedural obligations for states than in laying down actual substantive standards to govern their conduct, and argues that transnational environmental law may be valued by governments more for its symbolic, value-expressive function, than for any real problem-solving capacity.

Volume 2 in the series, Studies in International Law

Studies in International Law

Volume 1: Between Light and Shadow: The World Bank, the International Monetary Fund and International Human Rights Law *Mac Darrow*

Volume 2: Toxics and Transnational Law: International and European Regulation of Toxic Substances as Legal Symbolism *Marc Pallemaerts*

Toxics and Transnational Law: International and European Regulation of Toxic Substances as Legal Symbolism

MARC PALLEMAERTS

·HART·
PUBLISHING
OXFORD – PORTLAND OREGON
2003

Published in North America (US and Canada) by
Hart Publishing
c/o International Specialized Book Services
5804 NE Hassalo Street
Portland, Oregon
97213-3644
USA

Hart Publishing is a specialist legal publisher based in Oxford, England.
To order further copies of this book or to request a list of other publications please write to:

Hart Publishing, Salters Boatyard, Folly Bridge,
Abingdon Rd, Oxford, OX1 4LB
Telephone: +44 (0) 1865 245533 Fax: +44 (0) 1865 794882
email: mail@hartpub.co.uk
WEBSITE: http//:www.hartpub.co.uk

British Library Cataloguing in Publication Data
Data Available

ISBN 1-84113-129-6 (hardback)

Typeset by SNP Best-set Typesetter Ltd., Hong Kong
Printed and bound in Great Britain by Biddles Ltd, www.biddles.co.uk

Preface

This book is the product of a personal journey which took me into the fascinating world of international environmental policy-making in several different capacities and allowed me to observe and experience the international normative process both from the inside and from the outside—as a non-governmental activist, as an academic researcher and as a government official. The general subject matter—the regulation of toxic substances—goes to the very core of environmental policy. The two case studies in transnational regulation—emissions of hazardous substances in the aquatic environment and international trade in banned and severely restricted pesticides—involve fundamental issues concerning the social governance of industrial production processes and international trade which are at the centre of current policy debates about the necessary transformation of unsustainable patterns of production and consumption. Through these case studies, my research addresses the question of the function and effectiveness of transnational law as an instrument of international environmental governance at the European and global level. The empirical evidence from two specific issue areas may not be sufficiently broad and representative to substantiate theoretical conclusions of general validity for the wide-ranging and diverse field of international environmental policy and law as a whole, but it certainly raises questions whose relevance transcends the subject matter of the case studies.

This is a revised version of a doctoral dissertation in law defended at the Vrije Universiteit Brussel in January 1999 and subsequently updated to January 2002. It is based not only on scholarly research but also on my experience as a practitioner and 'participant observer' in some of the international normative processes analysed here. Between 1981 and 1991, I attended many meetings on the regulation of international trade in banned and severely restricted chemicals in the framework of the European Parliament, the United Nations Environment Programme and the Food and Agriculture Organization of the United Nations, as a representative of the Pesticides Action Network and Greenpeace International. As a legal and policy adviser to successive environment ministers in Belgium, I participated in the Fourth International Conference on the Protection of the North Sea in 1995, followed the negotiations on the European Community's IPPC Directive and Water Framework Directive between 1993 and 1999 and served as head of the Belgian delegation to the International Negotiating Committee which elaborated the Rotterdam Convention on Prior Informed Consent between 1996 and 1998. As this personal involvement inevitably influenced my perception, I mention it for the sake of transparency. It is, however, my conviction as a social scientist that the interpretations and views expressed in this work are adequately substantiated by the documentary evidence cited in the footnotes. Needless to say, these interpretations and views are entirely my own, and should not in any way be attributed to any of the organisations or institutions with which I have been associated.

Many people contributed to this endeavour in different ways, some even without being aware of it. Not all of them would care to be acknowledged and it would be impossible to mention them all anyway. But I am especially indebted to the co-supervisors of my dissertation, Professors Marc Maresceau and Johan Lammers, for the interest they took in the subject, for their advice and for their patience in seeing it through to its completion, and to the National Fund for Scientific Research, which made it possible for me to undertake this research by awarding me a research fellowship during its initial years. Thanks are also due to the chair and other members of the doctoral committee, Professor Bart De Schutter, who encouraged my research efforts from the very start, and the late Ambassador Winfried Lang, Dr Ludwig Krämer and Professor Gabriel Wilner, whose comments were most helpful during the final stage. I would like to express my special gratitude to friends and colleagues in the environmental movement and academia who provided precious help and intellectual support by sharing their thoughts and information with me, commenting on drafts or assisting in other ways: Tony Joris, Serge Gutwirth, Nicolas de Sadeleer, Frank Maes, Gretta Goldenman, Abou Thiam, Veerle Heyvaert, Catherine Wattiez, Topsy Jewell, and many others. Among them, I am particularly grateful to Susan Leubuscher for editing my dense prose. Most of all, of course, I am indebted to Karen, Sara, Lynn, and Nele, who endured the unpleasant consequences of this exercise for so many years. To them I dedicate this book.

Brussels,
January 2002.

Marc Pallemaerts

Contents

Part III. Toxic Substances in International Trade: The Regulation of International Trade in Pesticides

Part IV. Overview and Conclusions

Table of Abbreviations

ACP	African, Caribbean and Pacific
BAT	best available technology/techniques
BATNEEC	best available technology not entailing excessive cost
BEP	best environmental practice
CITES	Convention on International Trade in Endangered Species
COD	chemical oxygen demand
CRC	Chemical Review Committee
CSD	UN Commission on Sustainable Development
DDT	dichloro-diphenyl-dichloroethane
DG XI	Directorate General for Environment and Nuclear Safety, European Commission
EAEC	European Atomic Energy Community
EC	European Community
ECE	UN Economic Commission for Europe
ECJ	European Court of Justice
ECOSOC	Economic and Social Council
ECR	European Court Reports
ECSC	European Coal and Steel Community
EEA	European Economic Area
EEC	European Economic Community
EP	European Parliament
EPA	US Environmental Protection Agency
EQO	environmental quality objective
EQS	environmental quality standard
EU	European Union
FAO	Food and Agriculture Organization of the United Nations
FIFRA	Federal Insecticide, Fungicide and Rodenticide Act
GAO	US General Accounting Office
GATS	General Agreement on Trade in Services
GATT	General Agreement on Tariffs and Trade
GESAMP	Joint Group of Experts on the Scientific Aspects of Marine Pollution
GIFAP	International Group of National Associations of Manufacturers of Agrochemical Products
GTZ	Gesellschaft für Technische Zusammenarbeit
HCB	hexachlorobenzene
HCBD	hexachlorobutadiene
HCE	hexachloroethane

HCH	hexachlorocyclohexane
HELCOM	Baltic Marine Environment Protection Commission (Helsinki Commission)
IAEA	International Atomic Energy Agency
ICP	Industry Cooperative Programme
ICPR	International Commission for the Protection of the Rhine
IFCS	Intergovernmental Forum on Chemical Safety
ILM	International Legal Materials
ILO	International Labour Organization
IMM	Intermediate Ministeral Meeting
INC	Intergovernmental Negotiating Committee
INDSEC	Working Group on Industrial Sectors (Paris Commission)
INSC	International North Sea Conference(s)
IPC	integrated pollution control
IPPC	integrated pollution prevention and control
IRPTC	UNEP International Register of Potentially Toxic Chemicals
JCP	Joint Cooperative Programme
NGO	non-governmental organisation
NSC	North Sea Conference
OECD	Organisation for Economic Cooperation and Development
OJ	Official Journal of the European Communities
OSCOM	Oslo Commission
OSPAR	Oslo and Paris Commissions
OSPARCOM	Oslo and Paris Commissions
PAH	polycyclic aromatic hydrocarbons
PAN	Pesticides Action Network
PARCOM	Paris Commission
PCBs	polychlorinated biphenyls
PCP	pentachlorophenol
PCTs	polychlorinated terphenyls
PIC	prior informed consent
PNS	Provisional Notification Scheme
POPs	persistent organic pollutants
PREPCOM	Preparatory Committee of the United Nations Conference on Environment and Development
QSR	North Sea Quality Status Report
RAP	Rhine Action Programme
SEA	Single European Act
TBT	Technical Barriers to Trade
TEU	Treaty on European Union
TREMs	trade-related environmental measures
TWG	Technical Working Group (Paris Commission)
UES	uniform emission standards

UNCED	United Nations Conference on Environment and Development
UNCLOS	United Nations Convention on the Law of the Sea
UNCTC	United Nations Centre on Transnational Corporations
UNEP	United Nations Environment Programme
UNICE	Union des Industries de la Communauté européenne
UNTS	United Nations Treaty Series
USC	United States Code
Vr en Antw	Bulletin van Vragen en Antwoorden
WCED	World Commission on Environment and Development
WHO	World Health Organization
WTO	World Trade Organization

Table of Community Instruments

Table of Treaties

Part I

Introduction

1

Toxic Substances as an Object of Transnational Environmental Regulation

CONTROLLING THE SPREAD throughout the environment of toxic substances resulting from human activities has been a central concern of modern environmental policy ever since its emergence in the late 1960s. Indeed, public concern about the harmful consequences of toxic substances for ecosystems and human health is closely associated with the development of the environmental movement and governmental policies for environmental management in industrialised societies. This growing public awareness of what he terms the 'toxic environment' has been described by the leading American environmental historian Samuel Hays as 'a major political influence'.[1] Environmental contamination by toxic pollutants takes many different forms, and has only recently come to be recognised as a single complex of interrelated problems of chemical risk management resulting from prevailing production and consumption patterns. Like scientific knowledge, the perception and management of toxic risks developed only gradually, in an incremental way, and gave rise to many discrete strands of environmental policy and regulation at both the national and international level long before a more integrated perspective on this issue began to emerge.

This book does not aim to address the transnational legal aspects of the control of toxic chemicals in an exhaustive manner, but rather deals with transnational regulatory responses to two specific problems of chemical risk management: the control of discharges of toxic effluents in the aquatic environment and the control of risks associated with the trade and use of a particular category of toxic products, chemical pesticides. These two distinct issues were singled out as case studies because they have both become the focus of transnational regulatory efforts in a variety of international fora. As they developed independently of each other in different political and institutional contexts, involving different groups of state and non-state

[1] Hays (1987), p 177.

actors, different substantive issues, and different legal instruments, each of these normative regimes constitutes a self-contained object of study in its own right. But at the same time, they are both symptomatic of a wider crisis that has been described as the 'toxification' of the global environment by industrial activity[2] and exemplary of the general problems involved in the use of international and European Community law as an instrument to control the transboundary effects of industrial production on the environment and human health in a globalising economy. For that reason, this study also attempts to place these two regimes in a comprehensive perspective that considers the general legal and political issues they raise. This introduction serves to articulate the overall conceptual approach to these two case studies.

Toxic water pollutants and pesticides are both long-standing objects of environmental regulation. Their more or less contemporaneous emergence on the public policy agenda in the 1960s is directly related to the overall development of public concern about toxic risks in the environment generally. Two historical events played a seminal role in this respect.

In 1962, marine biologist Rachel Carson published her best-selling essay *Silent Spring*, in which she denounced the harmful effects of synthetic pesticides on human health, wildlife and ecosystems. Though highly controversial at the time of its publication, this book received considerable media attention, raised public awareness about the hazards of pesticides and toxic substances generally in the environment, both in the United States and later worldwide, and succeeded in putting the issue of pesticide regulation on the political agenda. It was, according to US Vice-President Al Gore, a 'brilliantly written argument that changed the course of history.'[3] Despite a vigorous counter-offensive by the chemical industry and agricultural interests, *Silent Spring* and the debate it provoked completely changed the then-prevailing, largely positive public perception of chemical pest control. As a political scientist who analysed the evolution of pesticide policy in the United States put it, Rachel Carson's book overturned the dominant 'pesticides paradigm' and 'defined pesticides as an environmental issue.'[4] Though it took many years for the US political system to digest the implications, especially given the scientific controversy and the powerful economic interests at stake, the movement triggered by *Silent Spring* eventually resulted in lasting policy changes and legislative reforms. More stringent environmental regulations were adopted, some of the most hazardous pesticide compounds were banned and control of pesticides was removed

[2] World Resources Institute, *World Resources 1994–95* (Oxford University Press, Oxford/ New York 1994), pp 213–222.

[3] A Gore, Introduction to 1994 edition of R Carson's *Silent Spring*. Carson (1994), p xv.

[4] Bosso (1987), p 120.

from the Department of Agriculture and transferred to the newly created Environmental Protection Agency.[5]

The arguments and evidence articulated in Carson's book focused mainly on the environmental and health effects of the persistent organochlorine insecticides widely used in the 1950s and 1960s. But the implications of *Silent Spring* and the problems it brought to the attention of public opinion extended far beyond the specific issues related to these particular pesticides. Through the example of pesticides, the book addressed a number of generic issues of environmental toxicology, such as the persistence of synthetic compounds, water and soil contamination and other pathways of dispersion in the environment, the mechanism of bio-accumulation in the food chain, carcinogenicity and other forms of chronic toxicity to humans, and the disruption of ecosystems through effects on other living organisms, and thus raised general awareness of the range of potential hazards of toxic chemicals released in the environment.

Another, dramatic event in the 1960s that was instrumental in focusing public and political attention on the potentially devastating effects of the toxic by-products of industrial production concerned the discharge of hazardous substances into the aquatic environment. From 1953 to 1960, a large number of residents of fishing communities along the shore of Minamata Bay in Southern Japan were diagnosed as suffering from a mysterious, crippling and often fatal disease of the central nervous system. It took medical researchers several years to establish the cause of this disease, which was eventually found to be mercury poisoning due to the consumption of heavily contaminated fish and shellfish from the bay. The origin of the mercury pollution was traced to the wastewater from the production of acetaldehyde discharged directly and indirectly into the sea by the Chisso corporation's chemical plant at Minamata. Mercury used as a catalyst in the production process formed a water-soluble and highly toxic organic compound, methyl mercury, which was discharged into the aquatic environment with the factory's effluent. This substance was absorbed by marine organisms and bio-accumulated in the food chain, causing very high mercury concentrations in the tissue of fish and shellfish consumed by the victims of the disease, which became known as 'Minamata disease'. This causal mechanism was discovered by scientists in 1962 but officially recognised by the Japanese government only in 1968, after another outbreak of Minamata disease occurred at Niigata in the North of the country in 1965. In this instance, the victims were

[5] The EPA was established in December 1970 and an overall reform of federal pesticide legislation enacted in October 1972. It took until December 1973 for a full ban on the use of DDT, one of the main substances whose effects were exposed in *Silent Spring*, to become effective in the United States, following protracted administrative and judicial proceedings. For a detailed account of the political debate and ensuing policy changes in the US in the 1960s and 1970s, see Bosso (1987), chs 6 & 7, and Dunlap (1981), ch 5 *et seq.*

contaminated by eating fish from the Agano River, which was polluted by similar discharges of methyl mercury from an acetaldehyde plant operated by the Showa Denko corporation. Both chemical companies were found liable and ordered to compensate the victims in the early 1970s. A third case of severe health damage caused by heavy metal pollution which was revealed in Japan during the 1960s, and eventually resulted in litigation and compensation, involved chronic cadmium poisoning among farming communities whose rice paddies and crops had been contaminated by irrigation water polluted by mining effluents discharged into the Jintsu River.[6]

This succession of incidents of serious pollution dramatically demonstrated the hazards, not only to ecosystems but also to human health, of industrial emissions of heavy metals into the aquatic environment and of bio-accumulation of toxic substances in the food chain, and had a strong impact on the development of environmental policy and law in Japan as well as internationally. The initial reaction of public authorities was to monitor the presence of heavy metals in the environment and establish maximum admissible concentrations in foodstuffs such as fish and shellfish. They also became aware of the need to regulate industrial discharges of toxic effluents into the freshwater and marine environment. 'Black lists' of hazardous substances to be controlled were established on the basis of evolving knowledge in aquatic ecotoxicology, the main pollution sources identified and emission standards laid down in most industrialised countries. More structural changes in production processes to avoid the use of toxic substances were sometimes encouraged, but seldom enforced.[7]

Since the 1960s, many other forms and sources of toxic threats to the environment and human health have surfaced as issues on the environmental policy agenda and prompted a variety of regulatory responses by governments: soil and groundwater contamination as a result of disposal of hazardous wastes, emissions of toxic substances in the atmosphere, the use of new synthetic chemicals whose risks have not been adequately assessed in industrial processes and products, the disruption of endocrine processes in living organisms by chemicals mimicking natural hormones, etc. While these are often regarded and addressed as distinct problems, chemical pollution issues involve a number of common, characteristic features that contribute to their perception as aspects of an overarching 'toxics' question: the ubiquity and persistence of toxic substances in the environment, the variety and complexity of pathways of dispersion and exposure, the role of biological processes of transformation and accumulation, and

[6] See Gresser, Fujikura & Morishima (1981), pp 55–105.

[7] As a result of the Minamata disease incidents the Japanese government issued 'administrative guidance' to induce the chemical industry to switch to mercury-free production processes, but this met with strong resistance. *Ibid*, p 66.

the long-term, insidious and often irreversible nature of many effects. Though it would be premature to speak of an integrated 'toxics policy', the term 'toxics' is increasingly being used as a convenient shorthand form to refer generically, in a non-technical sense, to a broad category of chemical pollutants, viz those which are toxic to living organisms, persistent in the environment or liable to bio-accumulate. In policy documents and legal instruments, this category of chemicals is most frequently referred to as 'toxic chemicals', 'toxic substances' or 'hazardous substances', sometimes as 'dangerous' or 'harmful' substances.[8] Pesticides and toxic water pollutants are part of this overall category and, in this book, I will use the term 'toxics' to denote them collectively. It should be stressed, however, that the notion of toxicity is defined technically as 'the capacity to cause injury to a living organism'[9] and thus encompasses a broad range of very different hazardous properties, of an acute as well as chronic nature, including mutagenicity, carcinogenicity and the capacity to disrupt reproductive or endocrine-related functions. Toxicity, environmental persistence and the tendency to bio-accumulate, though often mentioned together, are also distinct properties, which may, but do not necessarily, occur simultaneously in the same chemical. Where it does occur, however, their coincidence of course increases the hazardous nature of a substance.

Initial policy responses to the environmental and health problems caused by chemical water pollution and pesticides developed at the national level. Governments were responding to domestic political demands and dealing with what they at first perceived as essentially domestic issues. They established national administrative agencies, procedures and regulatory systems to address them. But soon it was recognised that chemical safety is an environmental issue that clearly transcends national boundaries. Toxics migrate across national boundaries as a result of both ecological and economic processes, through water and air but also through international trade. As Samuel Hays has noted, the mobility and ubiquity of toxic risks creates a transboundary community of interests in their control: 'the world of toxic transmission extended that sense of a common fate and interest to a wide range of people and places.'[10] In order to manage chemical risks effectively, it appeared early on that international cooperation and transnational normative efforts were necessary. Governments resorted to international law and institutions for this purpose. As early as 1972, the United Nations Conference on the Human Environment in Stockholm called for

[8] These different terms, which are used rather unsystematically in legal instruments, policy documents and the social science literature, will also be used indiscriminately as interchangeable synonyms in this study. Unless the context otherwise indicates, no particular technical meaning or distinction is implied by the choice of any one of these terms over the others.

[9] International Programme on Chemical Safety, Glossary of terms on chemical safety for use in IPCS publications, Doc WHO/ICS/89.27, Geneva, 1989, p 34.

[10] Hays (1987), p 173.

international cooperation in the regulation of discharges of toxic chemicals and the identification of 'pollutants of international significance'[11]; one year later, the European Community's First Environmental Action Programme already envisaged the establishment of common quality objectives and emission standards for hazardous substances in the aquatic environment and the harmonisation of pre-marketing controls for synthetic chemicals.[12]

The two issues chosen for the case studies in this book are both eminently transnational in nature. Toxic emissions in the aquatic environment are of international concern owing to their contribution to transboundary water pollution in international river basins and to pollution of the marine environment. In this case, the transnational character of the issue is the result of ecological processes: pollutants are transported across national boundaries and into the marine area beyond the limits of national jurisdiction through the natural mechanisms of the hydrological cycle and atmospheric circulation (when they reach the marine environment through the atmosphere). The transnational dimension of the issue is not merely physical and ecological, however, but also economic and technological, as regulations imposing emission reduction measures have an impact on the competitive position of the industries and national economies concerned in globalised markets. Awareness of these cross-border implications and the resulting need for international cooperation is particularly strong in Europe, where freshwater resources are largely shared in international river basins extending across many national boundaries, where an important number of coastal states border on semi-enclosed and ecologically vulnerable seas, and where efforts at economic integration are most advanced. This led to the development of an elaborate European regional regime for the control of toxic discharges in the aquatic environment, both inland and marine, consisting of partly overlapping and interlocking legal instruments and political arrangements concluded in a variety of institutional frameworks and comprising elements of both classical international law and European Community law. This regime will be the focus of the first case study.

In the second case, that of the pesticides trade, the element of extraneity that makes it into an object of transnational regulation is primarily linked to economic processes: these products move across national frontiers as a result of international trade patterns and thus cause environmental and human health effects outside the countries where they have been produced. The legal and political context of the issue of international trade in hazardous chemicals differs from that of transboundary water pollution in that there is a potential conflict of jurisdiction between exporting and

[11] Stockholm Conference, Recommendations for Action, paras 48(b) & 85(a).

[12] Declaration of the Council of the European Communities and of the Representatives of the Governments of the Member States meeting in the Council of 22 Nov 1973 on the programme of action of the European Communities on the environment, OJ No C112, 20.12.1973, pp 14, 20, 21.

importing countries and that the movement of the chemicals across national boundaries is not unintentional. Even though some of their effects, such as acute effects on human health, may be of a strictly local nature, pesticides which are traded internationally on a large scale must be regarded as chemicals of global environmental significance according to the criteria developed by UNEP.[13] Cross-border 'spillover' effects of pesticide use due to environmental phenomena are also known to occur. Spraying in border areas may locally result in contamination of transboundary aquifers in neighbouring countries, while large-scale agricultural use generally may contribute to the diffuse-source pollution of international rivers and the marine environment by pesticide compounds. Some persistent organochlorine pesticides have even been found to be subject to long-range atmospheric transport and accumulation in polar regions. Moreover, pesticides banned or severely restricted in producing countries but exported to other countries may come back to 'haunt' the exporting countries in the form of residues on imported agricultural products, a phenomenon sometimes referred to as the 'circle of poison.'[14] But the emerging global regime for the regulation of international trade in hazardous pesticides, which is the subject of the second case study in this book, was formed principally in response to international concern about the local health and environmental risks of these pesticides in importing developing countries rather than in order to control the potential transboundary effects of their use. This transnational regulatory regime also consists of both legally binding and non-binding norms elaborated in a variety of international fora, including the European Community.

The two issues which form the focus of this study are not normally considered jointly in the legal literature. This is because most scholarly perspectives on international environmental law mirror the compartmentalised, sectoral structure of the law itself. This structure, which is the result of unplanned incremental growth rather than deliberate design, reflects a primarily effects-based rather than source-oriented approach. The law developed in response to particular forms of pollution affecting different environmental media: air pollution, freshwater pollution, marine pollution, groundwater and soil pollution as a result of waste disposal, etc. Through this process, separate legal instruments and institutional fora evolved for each of these major sectors. On top of this underlying, medium-based structure, special regulatory regimes were developed to deal with particular activities presenting special environmental risks, such as nuclear energy, biotechnology or the management of hazardous chemicals. The subject-matter of this book would more traditionally be addressed partly as a

[13] Earthwatch/United Nations Environment Programme, *Chemical Pollution: A Global Overview*, UNEP, Geneva, 1992, p 2.

[14] Weir & Shapiro (1981).

sub-topic of freshwater and marine pollution control law, and partly as a sub-topic of chemicals management law. But it is necessary to transcend these artificial divisions and bring out the cross-sectoral linkages in environmental policy and law.

Though seemingly far apart, the two problem areas under study share a number of common features other than their transnational character and their relation with toxic chemicals. First, the chemical industry is a major actor in both issues, respectively as a major source of toxic emissions into the aquatic environment and as producer of pesticides. Though not the only source of water pollution, the chemical industry and its products are the target of a large part of international regulatory efforts to curb toxic emissions. The direct and indirect emissions of the pesticides industry, as a subcategory of the chemical industry, are the subject of specific measures with respect to both *emission* standards for pesticide production and formulation plants and standards relating to the *use* of pesticides designed to reduce diffuse source pollution of the aquatic environment. The products of the agrochemical industry are also the main target of international efforts to regulate international trade in hazardous chemicals. Secondly, the substances causing problems and subject to regulatory controls are partly the same. Some pesticides are regulated both under the legal regime for the control of toxic discharges and under that for the control of international trade in banned and severely restricted chemicals.

Finally, and most importantly, both problems under consideration are ultimately caused by industrial production and can be viewed as part of the overarching issue of the environmental regulation of industrial activity. Although their actual release into the environment at the place of use is not directly connected to industrial production but generally linked to local agricultural practices, it is in fact possible to regard international trade in hazardous pesticides as an *indirect* consequence of a particular mode of production in the agrochemical industry and the international markets on which it relies. As for toxic emissions in the aquatic environment, they mostly originate either directly from industrial process sources or are caused by the use or disposal of industrial products.

Industrial production has an impact on the environment in three ways: through its demand for raw materials and energy, through the distribution and use of its products, and through the various forms of waste resulting from its processes. It can be conceptualised as an open system which interacts with its environment through both its inputs and outputs, which 'takes in materials and energy, transforms them into products and wastes, and then excretes the products and wastes.'[15] The concept of 'waste', in this

[15] Frosch (1996), p 199. The term 'industrial metabolism' has recently been coined to describe this systemic view of industrial production in its interaction with the environment. See Ayres & Simonis (1994).

context, comprises all by-products of an industrial production process, in whatever form, which cannot be used in the process itself and hence are disposed of either as atmospheric emissions, as liquid effluents discharged into surface waters or as solid or liquid waste destined for specialised disposal operations such as landfilling or incineration. At the end of their economic life-cycle, the products of industrial production also end up as waste materials, which may or may not be recycled in other industrial processes or are otherwise dispersed in the environment.

Measures to reduce the environmental impact of industrial production can address either the input side of the above equation, through changes in the use of raw materials and energy, or the output side, through action to prevent, control or mitigate the environmental effects of products and production residues. The two case studies in this book both deal with problems linked to the output side of the industrial production system—the first with an essentially process-related problem and the second with a product-related one.

Initially, national and international environmental policy and law focused almost exclusively on the output end of industrial systems and, more specifically, on reducing the impact of their residues. This was to be achieved essentially through a curative approach based on the development and use of add-on, 'end-of-pipe' pollution control technology designed to prevent or reduce the release of wastes into the environment or mitigate their effects. This involved such devices as effluent treatment plants, flue gas scrubbers, and even higher smokestacks or longer and deeper discharge outfalls to ensure a better dispersion and dilution of pollutants in the receiving environment and thus mitigate acute environmental effects. It also involved the development of techniques for off-site disposal and management of hazardous wastes such as 'controlled' landfilling and high-temperature incineration. But the basic production processes which are the actual source of waste generation remained largely unchanged.

Emission standards evolved as the main legal technique used to control process-related industrial pollution; they were normally fixed on the basis of the emission levels achievable through the application of commercially available add-on pollution control technology. Separate standards and systems of regulation developed to control different forms of pollution affecting different environmental media. Consequently, transfers of pollution from one medium to another were not uncommon.

Product-related regulatory measures were not initially conceived as part of an integrated strategy for the control of industrial pollution but primarily designed to protect users against harmful health effects associated with the use of particular products. They included such measures as mandatory classification and labelling requirements and use restrictions based on potential hazards to human health. They were not intended to affect the production or marketing of the product per se, but only to regulate the *use* that may be made of it following its placing on the market.

In the field of chemicals, there was a gradual evolution towards a preventive regulatory approach based on pre-market control systems, which make market access for new products conditional on preliminary risk assessment. Mechanisms like pre-marketing notification requirements for new chemicals and registration requirements for pesticides are designed to allow potential risks to both human health and the environment to be screened by public authorities before the products concerned enter the market. Post-market regulatory measures may also be taken to remove products from the market when previously unsuspected effects or risks are discovered. Most existing systems of product regulation consider the product in isolation from the production process in which it originates and do not address production as such.[16]

There is, however, a growing awareness that symptom-oriented, curative strategies of pollution control, dealing only with the output side of industrial production, are ultimately self-defeating:

> Since pollution is *inherent in the very design of the production technologies*, once the technological choice is made, regulation can have only a limited effect, addressing the symptom instead of the disease.[17]

Therefore, in order to prevent environmental degradation at its source, the choice of products and production technologies must be re-oriented. This choice cannot be made exclusively by the private sector on the basis of private, short-term economic interests but must also be compatible with the long-term public interest in environmental quality and sustainability. As the well-known American environmental scientist and advocate Barry Commoner argues, 'substantial environmental improvement can occur only when the choice of production technology is open to social intervention.'[18] In order to achieve sustainable development, fundamental changes will be required in the system of industrial production and in the mechanisms of social choice determining *what* products are to be produced and *how*. Environmental law can be truly effective only if it compels or at least encourages such changes, if it functions as an instrument of what Commoner calls 'the social governance of production.'[19]

In recent years, there has been a trend in industrial pollution control policy towards a more integrated approach which takes into account the combined impact of products and processes on the environment as a whole and aims to develop sustainable modes of production and consumption.

[16] For an overview of various forms of pre-market and post-market regulation of chemicals, see Micklitz (1992a).

[17] Commoner (1990), p 173 (emphasis added).

[18] *Ibid*, p 217.

[19] *Ibid*.

This holistic approach, for which the United Nations Environment Programme (UNEP) has coined the term 'cleaner production', seeks to reduce environmental impacts through preventive measures in the design of both products and production processes and in the choice of raw materials and energy sources. Cleaner production, as defined by UNEP, "is the continuous application of an integrated preventive environmental strategy to processes, products and services to increase eco-efficiency and reduce risks for humans and the environment.'[20] In its application to production processes, cleaner production implies not only the reduction of the volume and toxicity of production residues but also the elimination of toxic raw materials and a more efficient use of raw materials and energy. For products, it requires a systematic reduction of negative environmental impacts throughout their life-cycle.[21] In terms of the development of environmental law, the integrated approach implies a shift away from the mere regulation of the disposal of production wastes and the use of products, toward the regulation of *material flows* in the economy.[22]

Ultimately, the achievement of sustainable and environmentally sound development requires nothing less than an 'ecological restructuring of industrial society',[23] a process which has also been described as 'ecological modernisation'. Such modernisation implies that production and consumption processes which hitherto 'have traditionally been dominated by economic rationality'[24] are redesigned and reorganised in a manner consistent with an emerging new form of rationality, ie 'ecological rationality'. This transformation of industrial production is 'no longer limited to the introduction of add-on technologies or process-integrated adaptations, but include[s] changes in product chains, technological systems and economic sectors/clusters'.[25] Despite increasing rhetorical support for a more integrated approach to environmental management, no comprehensive, cross-sectoral legal regime covering both the process- and product-related environmental effects of industrial production has thus far emerged.[26] As

[20] UNEP, 'Sustainable production and consumption', (1996) *Industry and Environment* 19/3 (1996), 4–5.

[21] One of the early legal manifestations of the life-cycle approach, albeit an extremely 'soft' one, is the EC ecolabelling regulation. Council Regulation (EEC) No 880/92 of 23 Mar 1992 on a Community eco-label award scheme, OJ No L99, 11.4.1992, p 1.

[22] See Rehbinder (1994).

[23] Mol (1995), p 3.

[24] *Ibid*, p 31.

[25] *Ibid*, p 58.

[26] In this context, it is necessary to note the important recent development of a legal regime covering both process and product emissions as well as production of one particular category of toxic substances, namely persistent organic pollutants (POPs). This development started at the regional level, in the framework of the UN Economic Commission for Europe (ECE), with the adoption, in June 1998, of a Protocol on POPs to the 1979 Geneva Convention on Long-Range Transboundary Air Pollution. Protocol to the Convention on Long-Range Transboundary Air Pollution on Persistent Organic Pollutants, Aarhus, 24 June 1998, UN Doc

this study will show, the regulatory regimes which seek to control toxic emissions and toxic trade appear to have only a marginal impact on established patterns of industrial production. It remains to be seen whether the ongoing transnational normative processes aimed at addressing transboundary environmental problems caused by toxic substances will eventually induce more fundamental changes towards cleaner production. Ultimately, what is at issue is the capacity of transnational law to function as an effective instrument of ecological modernisation while the regulatory power of the sovereign state is continually being eroded by globalisation.[27]

EB.AIR/1998/2, 31 Mar 1998. This instrument requires its parties to 'eliminate the production and use' of 12 persistent organic substances, to restrict the use of three others and to reduce total annual emissions, mainly from process sources, of dioxins, PAHs and hexachlorobenzene, inter alia through the application of best available techniques and limit values. Three years later, a global, legally binding instrument, similar in scope, was adopted under the auspices of UNEP. Stockholm Convention on Persistent Organic Pollutants, Stockholm, 23 May 2001. UN Doc UNEP/POPS/CONF/2, 9 Mar 2001. The Stockholm Convention provides for the elimination of the production and use of nine substances, restrictions on the production and use of DDT and for measures to reduce unintentional releases of dioxins, PCBs and hexachlorobenzene. As a global instrument, this convention applies to fewer substances and allows for more exemptions than the Aarhus Protocol. Both the Stockholm Convention and the Aarhus Protocol partly overlap the subject matter of the present study, since some POPs are persistent organochlorine pesticides banned or severely restricted in many countries, while others are toxic pollutants whose emission into the aquatic environment is already subject to regulation under international and/or European Community law. An innovative aspect of the new instruments is that they address production and use of some chemicals in an integrated way. However, the number and scope of derogations allowed is such that they stop short of effectively prescribing a total phase-out.

[27] See generally Falk (1995).

2

Law as an Instrument of International Environmental Policy

PARTS II AND III of this study will provide an in-depth analysis of the transnational normative prescriptions, both legally binding and non-binding, with respect to the management of the transboundary environmental and health effects of toxic substances in two different issue-areas: emissions into the aquatic environment and international trade. These two case studies, which respectively form chapters 3–9 and 10–16 of this book, focus on the development, substantive content and application of norms purposefully elaborated through international decision-making processes as a means of achieving certain collectively defined policy objectives. International environmental governance seeks to realise specific policy ends in an international community which lacks centralised institutional authority, through the establishment of mechanisms of coordination and cooperation and the elaboration of internationally agreed normative prescriptions that can guide the behaviour of relevant state and non-state actors with a view to optimising collective outcomes. This governance process involves both institutional and substantive elements, which together constitute what international relations theorists refer to as international regimes governing specific issue-areas. This study describes and analyses two such regimes in the field of international environmental policy, with a specific emphasis on the function of law as a policy instrument in a transnational context.

As sovereign states still constitute the primary actors and norm-addressees in the international community, as well as crucial intermediaries in influencing the behaviour of non-state actors subject to their territorially fragmented rule-making and enforcement authority, international law is inevitably regarded by policy-makers as an indispensable instrument of international environmental governance. It serves as the medium both for the formalisation of the necessary institutional and procedural arrangements at the intergovernmental or supranational level, and for the establishment, through consensual mechanisms, of substantive constraints on the conduct of states in the exercise of their domestic legislative authority. Thus, the development of international environmental cooperation, both within and outside the framework of intergovernmental organisations, has coincided with the steady expansion of an ever-growing body of international legal instruments aimed at the protection of the environment. It is estimated that there are over 500 multilateral treaties and other international agreements related to the environment today, nearly 60 per cent of which have been negotiated since 1972.[1] International environmental law is one of the most obvious manifestations of the internationalisation of environmental policy-making and a key element of the growing number of international regimes in this area. It is also perceived by policy-makers as one of the principal *instruments* of international environmental policy. As an authoritative observer and commentator puts it, 'national and international law are *both expressions and tools* of international environmental policy.'[2]

The study of international environmental regimes has been a prolific field of academic enquiry in recent years, especially from the angle of international relations theory. Regime theorists have shown a strong interest in international environmental governance as an area of international relations in which a functional perception of shared needs and interdependent interests by states as autonomous, rational utility-maximisers has brought about more or less permanent cooperative arrangements based on common norms and institutions. They have mainly studied the structural conditions under which obstacles to coordination and joint action between sovereign states can be overcome and opportunities for mutually beneficial cooperation arise, focusing on political processes for the creation and transformation of international regimes, and the shaping of common normative expectations in the international community, rather than on the actual substantive normative content of individual regimes themselves. Mainstream regime theory tends to conflate norms and institutions, substance and process, into a single subject of inquiry, and, in doing so, to disregard the actual international normative process itself and its substantive outcomes. It has in fact been observed by Thomas Gehring that all of the component elements of the classical definition of international regimes used in international relations theory are norms *sensu lato* and that, consequently, according to this definition, 'international regimes are institutions entirely composed of norms.'[3] Positivist legal scholarship, for its part, when addressing international environmental regimes, focuses on an abstract substantive and procedural analysis of legal norms, in isolation from the policy context in which they arise and are intended to function.

This study analyses the substantive normative content of two toxics-related international regimes from a policy perspective. It examines the role of transnational law and other normative prescriptions as an instrument for

[1] International Environmental Governance: Multilateral Environmental Agreements (MEAs), UN Doc UNEP/IGM/1/INF/3, 6 Apr 2001, para 4.

[2] Caldwell (1990), p 117 (emphasis added).

[3] Gehring (1994), p 44.

the achievement of stated objectives of international environmental governance. In doing so, it seeks to combine classical forms of legal analysis with policy-oriented insights from regime theory. The transnational normative process will be judged against the background of its instrumental ambitions. The emphasis will be on the process of substantive normative development and implementation and its effectiveness in influencing the behaviour of states and non-state actors, rather than on the structural and institutional aspects of regime-building and the motives and conditions of interstate cooperation.

This study takes a comprehensive view of the international normative process,[4] examining this process *as a whole*, from norm-creation through implementation to goal achievement. It shares with regime analysis its focus on specific issue-areas, its process-oriented perspective and its broad approach to the range of relevant normative prescriptions. Inspiration from international relations theory is indeed useful to transcend the doctrinal limitations of positivist international legal scholarship. The study of international regimes provides interesting opportunities for cross-fertilisation between the two disciplines,[5] though differences in vocabulary and analytical framework may create confusion and require conceptual clarification. This appears already from the very definition of the 'regime' concept itself. One political scientist proposes the following definition of regimes:

> For a defined issue-area, they are international institutions comprising both an accepted body of normative prescriptions and an organized process for the making and application of these prescriptions.[6]

According to an international lawyer, regimes are

> conglomerates of hard law rules (treaties), soft law instruments (declarations and recommendations) and institutions that are indispensable for the effective working of hard and soft law.[7]

The first definition looks upon regimes as 'institutions' consisting of both substantive and procedural norms and emphasises their dynamic nature as a continuous process for the elaboration and implementation of rules. The second definition places more emphasis on the formal nature of the rules themselves and views the institutional framework essentially as an instrumentality of the rules. One may note here that regime theorists do not ascribe

[4] This concept—intentionally broader than the treaty-making process *sensu stricto*—is borrowed from Slouka (1982), pp 137–139. Other authors use terms such as 'international legislative process' or 'international norm-making process' to denote essentially the same concept. See Szasz (1992), pp 41, 42. On the international normative process in the specific field of environmental protection, see generally Szasz (1992); Beyerlin & Marauhn (1997); Palmer (1992b); Lang (1992); Handl (1990), esp pp 5–16; Skala (1982); Birnie & Boyle (1992), pp 9–31; Sands (1995), pp 103–140; Kiss & Shelton (1991), pp 95–113.

[5] See generally Slaughter Burley (1993).

[6] Gehring (1990), p 56.

[7] Lang (1992), p 110.

the same meaning as lawyers to the concept of 'institution'. The latter clearly distinguish rules from institutions; from the former's perspective, institutions are more than just forms of organisation and also encompass substantive normative expectations. Political scientists attach little importance to the formal nature of regime norms. From their perspective, international regimes and the international legal system are not co-extensive. The concept of 'normative prescriptions', as used in the first definition, comprises all norms, whatever their legal nature, which are regarded as relevant by the actors concerned and influence their behaviour. International law usually forms the core of international regimes, but their scope generally extends beyond it to include all kinds of norms which, though formally not legally binding on states, nevertheless guide their conduct. Lawyers, as appears from the second definition, will tend to distinguish regime norms according to their legal or non-legal character, while at the same time also recognising that soft law constitutes an integral part of international regimes.

Though this study adopts a regime perspective, its vocabulary and conceptual framework will remain closer to that of legal studies than regime theory. The notion of institution will be used in its narrow, technical sense, as it usually is by lawyers. The term 'regime' will be used to denote a body of substantive normative prescriptions, which, depending on the context, may be of a different nature. While the concept of 'regulatory regime' includes both hard and soft law, considered as a single 'conglomerate' of rules, as in the above definition, 'legal regime' refers specifically to hard law rules and 'voluntary regime' to soft law rules. The substantive scope of the concept may also vary according to the context: 'regime' may refer to the system of rules established by one specific instrument or related to a particular subject or, alternatively, to a conglomerate of several instruments relating to a broader issue area or geographical area.[8]

In this study, rules of public international law and European Community law will be considered together with soft law as part of one and the same international normative process, as inseparable elements of integrated international regulatory regimes. This should not be taken to imply that the distinction between soft law and hard law has become irrelevant.[9] The equal attention given to soft and hard law simply reflects the fact that, in the field of environmental regulation, soft law functions both as a precursor and complement of hard law.[10] Therefore, one cannot be properly studied separately from the other. As an authoritative practitioner and observer of the development of international environmental law puts it, in this field,

[8] The notion of regime is, after all, quite elastic since, as Gehring has noted, issue areas are not determined by any objective structures, but by actors' perceptions. See Gehring (1994), p 43.

[9] Although that distinction is often overdrawn. See Bothe (1980).

[10] Dupuy (1991); Beyerlin & Marauhn (1997), pp 7–12.

treaty-making cannot be viewed in isolation from the making of instruments which have not yet attained the binding force of international law, but which reflect a certain degree of political commitment and thus generate expectations for certain future behaviour.[11]

Soft law is of particular importance in its relation to classical international law. But even the European Community, though a producer of supranational hard law *par excellence*, increasingly has recourse to soft law regulatory techniques.[12] The case studies will therefore explore the interactions between soft and hard law in the specific issue areas under consideration and attempt to draw some conclusions as to their relative effectiveness. It should be stressed, however, that this book has no particular theoretical ambitions as regards the relationship between soft law and hard law. It is not a book about the sources of international law, but rather about the effectiveness of international regulatory processes in the field of environmental protection.

The term 'transnational law' is used in this study as a generic term encompassing both public international law and European Community law. As defined by Jessup, transnational law refers generally to 'all law which regulates actions or events that transcend national frontiers.'[13] Jessup's definition also includes certain areas of private law relating to international transactions. In the present analysis, however, I shall concentrate on regulatory law, ie rules of public law developed and used to control certain forms of economic activity in the public interest. Private law issues, such as civil liability for harm caused by hazardous substances, will not be considered.[14] As Peter Sand has observed, the use of the term 'transnational law' is particularly appropriate in the context of international environmental regulation, since, even though the instrument used may be public international law, the actual object of regulation is not intergovernmental relations per se, but, through governments, the environmentally harmful activities of private entities.[15] Moreover, the qualification 'transnational' becomes increasingly pertinent to denote not only the object of regulation, but also the normative process from which such regulation emanates, a process which has been described as 'non-statist',[16] as the relevant actors are no longer exclusively states, but have come to include an expanding range of non-state actors such as

[11] Lang (1992), p 109.
[12] See Snyder (1993a), pp 31–36; Snyder (1993b).
[13] PC Jessup, as quoted in Steiner & Vagts (1986), p xix.
[14] There is already plenty of literature on this subject. On liability for toxic emissions, see, eg Van Dunné (1991). On liability for toxic products in international trade, see, eg Jasanoff (1985); Baughen (1995).
[15] Sand (1990), p 4.
[16] Koh (1996), p 184.

international organisations, multinational corporations and non-governmental organisations.[17]

INSTRUMENTAL VIEWS OF TRANSNATIONAL ENVIRONMENTAL LAW

Underlying the use of transnational law as a tool of environmental policies at the international level is an instrumental model of the international normative process, of how transnational law is supposed to function. The premises on which this model is based are articulated more or less explicitly in political documents and statements by policy-makers. Many politicians and international officials have inordinately high expectations of the instrumental power of international law to effectuate their policy objectives. A few quotes will serve to illustrate this point. Then Senator and vice-presidential candidate Al Gore, for one, in his bestselling environmental manifesto *Earth in the Balance* calls for 'an entirely new generation of international treaties and agreements aimed at protecting the environment' and goes on to assert:

> Just as democracy and market economics are important to a successful effort to restore the earth's ecological balance, so is a further extension of the rule of law.[18]

A few months earlier, the Secretary-General of the United Nations Conference on Environment and Development (UNCED) stressed that 'the power of international law as a regulatory and preventive tool *cannot be overestimated, nor the need for it.*'[19] According to the Executive Director of the United Nations Environment Programme (UNEP), international environmental law

> has shown itself to be one of the most effective instruments in building and enhancing a consensus in the world community in addressing the most pressing global environmental and developmental issues of the day.[20]

And the former Prime Minister of New Zealand, Sir Geoffrey Palmer, concluded an assessment of the international community's progress towards sustainable development since the Stockholm Conference with the following call to action:

[17] However, the term 'transnational environmental law' is not used in this book as in Brown Weiss (1998), p 7, where it refers to standards and management practices developed primarily by private sector organisations and semi-private institutions, as opposed to 'intergovernmental environmental law'.

[18] Gore (1993), p 352. The original hardcover edition of this book was published in early 1992, in the run-up to the Rio Conference. *Ibid*, p xi.

[19] M Strong, in his foreword to Kiss & Shelton (1991), p xxxiii (emphasis added).

[20] Dowdeswell (1994), pp 65–72.

We have had plenty of rhetoric—the time for rhetoric is past. The time for *binding international instruments that actually produce change* has arrived.[21]

But does the actual performance of international environmental law as a policy instrument bear out such unreserved confidence in its capacities? Is it effective in shaping the behaviour of states and, through them, non-state actors, or is it in the end merely another form of rhetoric? That is the question I intend to address in this book.

The conventional view of international environmental law, its potential and its limitations is well exemplified by the conclusions of the 1990 Siena Forum on International Law of the Environment,[22] a meeting of academics and policy-makers convened with the support of the Italian government as a contribution to the preparatory process of the Rio Conference. These conclusions start with a diagnosis of the state of international environmental law and formulate a number of recommendations for its improvement. According to the Siena Forum, the 'abundance of conventions and other international instruments' in the field of environmental protection, which 'constitute an impressive network of rights and obligations of states', should be regarded as 'a successful achievement of contemporary international law'.[23] There are, however, 'certain gaps' in the existing body of international environmental law.[24] Substantive gaps result from its sectoral, incremental and reactive mode of development. There is also a serious gap in the implementation and enforcement of international environmental law, 'both domestically and internationally.'[25] A number of 'treaty devices' of a procedural and institutional nature are suggested, through which 'problems relating to non-compliance or lack of effectiveness could be addressed.'[26]

The instrumental view of international environmental law also pervades the policy discourse of United Nations bodies. Although it had not, upon its establishment by the United Nations General Assembly in December 1972,[27] received any express mandate in this field, the Governing Council of the United Nations Environment Programme (UNEP), noting that 'the solutions to many environmental problems are dependent on adequate law relating to the environment,'[28] decided in 1974 that the new organisation should become involved in promoting the development of national and international environmental law. UNEP Secretariat soon established an

[21] Palmer (1992a), p 1028 (emphasis added).
[22] Conclusions of the Siena Forum on International Law of the Environment, reprinted in (1990), *Yearbook of International Environmental Law* 696–703.
[23] *Ibid*, para 1.
[24] *Ibid*, paras 2, 8.
[25] *Ibid*, para 2.
[26] *Ibid*, para 12.
[27] UNGA Res. 2997 (XXVII), 15 Dec 1972.
[28] UNEP Governing Council Decision 8(II), 22 Mar 1974, part III, 5, para (a).

'Environmental Law and Machinery Unit', which played an important catalytic role and assisted governments in the negotiation of numerous international environmental agreements under UNEP's auspices as well as in the development of environmental legislation at the national level.[29]

The unswerving faith of policy-makers in international law as an instrument of social engineering is almost ritually reiterated at every major juncture in the development of international environmental policy. In its widely-publicised 1987 report *Our Common Future*, the World Commission on Environment and Development (WCED) recognised the importance of legal and institutional change as a precondition of a successful transition to sustainable development, stressing that 'the international legal framework must . . . be significantly strengthened in support of sustainable development.'[30] The Commission recommended the elaboration of a universal declaration and convention laying down basic norms of state conduct with respect to environmental protection and sustainable development.[31]

The 'further development of international environmental law' was one of the many objectives explicitly assigned to UNCED by the General Assembly in 1989.[32] Three years later, the Rio Conference itself again called on states to 'cooperate in good faith and in a spirit of partnership . . . in the further development of international law in the field of sustainable development'[33] and devoted a full chapter to 'international legal instruments and mechanisms' in the section on 'means of implementation' of *Agenda 21*, a bulky and verbose programme of action for the international community adopted by the conference and later endorsed by the General Assembly.[34] Although UNCED did not achieve the codification of the general principles of international environmental law in the form of a universal, legally binding instrument, as recommended by the WCED, the development of this law has continued to progress steadily since 1992.

The dedication of policy-makers to the international normative process was reiterated by the Global Ministerial Environment Forum convened by UNEP in Malmö, Sweden, in May 2000. In their Malmö Declaration, ministers described 'the evolving framework of international environmental law' as '*a sound basis for addressing the major environmental threats of the day*', while at the same time stressing the need far 'a more coherent

[29] This unit was later renamed 'Environmental Law and Institutions Unit', presumably to dissipate the somewhat mechanistic connotation of the term 'machinery', used in a social and policy context.

[30] WCED (1987), p 312.

[31] *Ibid*, pp 332–333.

[32] UNGA Res. 44/228, 22 Dec 1989.

[33] Rio Declaration on Environment and Development, UN Doc A/CONF.151/5/Rev. 1, 13 June 1992, reprinted in 31 ILM 874 (1992), Principle 27.

[34] UNGA Res. 47/190, 22 Dec 1992.

and coordinated approach' and the importance of 'compliance, enforcement and liability'.

As appears from these statements, the prevailing view among policy-makers is that law is an effective regulatory instrument and a necessary 'basis' of international environmental governance, which not only serves to 'build consensus' in the international community but can actually 'produce change', and therefore needs to be further 'developed' and 'strengthened'. Overall, the development of international environmental norms is perceived as a success story, though further efforts are required to fill 'gaps', ensure more coherence and coordination and improve compliance.

A similar discourse on the instrumental role of law has accompanied the development of the European Community's environmental policy. In view of the supranational legislative powers conferred on EC institutions, law has traditionally played a key role in all Community policies. It has been noted that law 'has always been a basic instrument and central symbol of European integration.'[35] In this respect, environmental policy is no exception.

The European Commission's public information material on EC environmental policy typically contains a statement measuring the success of this policy by the number of Community legal instruments adopted within its framework:

> The European Community's environment policy has achieved notable results. In all, over 100 pieces of environmental legislation have been passed under the three four-year action programmes since 1973.[36]

As time goes by and this material is re-edited, the number of legislative instruments adopted grows and the figures in the brochures are adjusted to reflect the inexorable progress of the Community's environmental policy. In his preface to a compilation of EC environment legislation published by the Commission in 1992, Carlo Ripa di Meana, then Commissioner for the Environment, boasted:

> Over the past five years alone, the volume of Community environmental legislation has almost doubled as the Community moved into new areas and began to develop new instruments of environmental policy.[37]

Since law is undeniably the prime instrument of EC environmental policy, it is tempting, particularly for politicians, to resort to such quantitative metaphors to describe its achievements. In view of the Commission's

[35] Snyder (1993a), p 19.

[36] Commission of the European Communities, *The European Community and the Environment*, 3rd edn (European Documentation Series, Office for Official Publications of the European Communities, Luxembourg, 1987) p 29.

[37] Commission of the European Communities, *European Community Environment Legislation*, vol 1 (Office for Official Publications of the European Communities, Luxembourg, 1992) p vii.

inclination to give priority to the elaboration of new environmental legislation rather than ensuring the implementation of the existing one,[38] it is not surprising that the quantitative growth of secondary law is considered an indicator of institutional performance. But from an environmental point of view, what matters is not the volume of the Community institutions' normative output but the extent to which EC law effectively results in environmental improvement. The instrumental power of Community environmental law is routinely asserted to justify major new policy initiatives. For instance, in presenting the Commission's Sixth Environmental Action Programme, Commissioner Margot Wallström stated:

> Environment policy is one of the EU's success stories—*thanks to EU legislation we have seen big improvements* in cleaning up the air and our rivers, to take an example.[39]

It should be noted, however, that the instrumental discourse has become somewhat less self-confident since the rise of the ideology of subsidiarity and deregulation in the early 1990s. In tune with this general political climate, recent Community environmental policy has tended to de-emphasise legislation as its primary tool and profess a commitment to 'broadening the range of instruments.'[40] While EC legislative activity has somewhat slowed down, however, law remains an important instrument of European environmental policy.

As we have seen, transnational law is perceived and portrayed by policymakers as one of the key instruments of international environmental policies. Governments and international organisations invest considerable resources and energy in formulating and negotiating international environmental treaties and EC environmental directives; so do representatives of various interest groups which try to influence this activity in one way or other. Every year a few dozen bilateral and multilateral treaties and EC directives are added to a growing body of environmental law. But the growing discrepancy between this ever-increasing volume of transnational law and the still deteriorating state of the environment cries out for an inquiry into the effectiveness of the international normative process. All this law-making begs a legitimate question: what is the ultimate net result of this normative activity? What effect does it have in the real world? Are the instrumental promises of international environmental law fulfilled? To what extent does it actually achieve the objectives it purports to pursue? Is EC environmental law an effective instrument of environmental protection or a mere symbol of European integration?

[38] As deplored by Krämer (1992), p 219.
[39] European Commission, Press Release IP/01/102, 24 Jan 2001 (emphasis added).
[40] See generally Pallemaerts (1999).

THE INSTRUMENTAL MODEL ANALYSED: DETERMINANTS OF EFFECTIVENESS

This study will take a critical look at the international normative process in two issue areas related to chemical safety. The development, substantive content and function of norms in the two areas under consideration will be assessed against the background of the instrumental model which serves to justify the process of norm-creation. The normative force and effectiveness of the prescriptions resulting from this process, their likely impact on the behaviour of states and non-state actors and their adequacy in terms of environmental goal achievement will be evaluated to provide an indication of the extent to which the actual function of norms matches the instrumental assumptions on which the development of transnational environmental law is explicitly or implicitly based.

In recent years, we have witnessed an increasing interest in the issue of effectiveness of international environmental regimes, but most of the academic and political debate has focused on problems of *enforcement*, with a narrow focus on legal mechanisms and procedures to promote compliance with international and EC environmental law.[41] This is a reductionist approach to the issue of effectiveness, which takes the outcome of the normative process itself—the norms to be enforced—for granted. This study takes a broader view of the effectiveness issue: rather than take international norms for granted, it starts with an analysis of the normative process itself and the social context in which it operates—all the way from norm creation through implementation to goal achievement. Effectiveness cannot simply be equated with formal compliance with international norms or the availability of enforcement mechanisms. The effectiveness of norms is to be measured in terms of their impact on social reality. The effectiveness of international regulatory efforts depends on how norms shape the behaviour of the regulated target group and on ultimate goal achievement.

The first determinant of effectiveness is the *normative force* of the norms, ie their intrinsic capacity to influence behaviour in the context of the overall normative system of which they are part.[42] This depends on the formulation of the norm—its determinacy, specificity, prescriptive quality—and on the legal and institutional context in which it operates—the availability of mechanisms for further elaboration and specification of the norms, their binding or non-binding nature. The instrumental power of the normative

[41] See, inter alia, Boyle (1991); Nollkaemper (1990b); Sachariew (1991); Sands (1993); Boisson de Chazournes (1995); Handl (1997); Handl (1994); Sand (1996); Cameron, Werksman & Roderick (1996); Schally (1996); Somsen (1996); Krämer (1988); Krämer (1992), pp 209–228; Krämer (1995), pp 135–144; Wägenbaur (1991); Macrory (1992); Macrory (1996); Reitzes (1992).

[42] For a general theoretical articulation of this concept, see Van Dijk (1987).

process is contingent on a combination of conditions with respect to the operation of the normative system, from the elaboration and formalisation of norms all the way through their application. In order to assess the effectiveness of transnational normative processes, one needs a theoretical model of how they are supposed to work, an abstract standard against which they can be evaluated. The remainder of this chapter therefore seeks to articulate the instrumental models on which the use of international law and European Community law as a tool of environmental policy is implicitly based.

The prevailing instrumental perspective on the development and operation of international environmental law as the instrument of international regulatory policies can be roughly outlined as follows. Typically, the international normative process involves a series of sequential stages. As political consensus develops within the international community on the need for regulation of particular activities whose environmental effects transcend national boundaries, the international normative process will usually be set in motion through a decision of a political organ of an intergovernmental organisation or some other international body, defining in general terms the subject matter to be addressed and the objectives to be pursued and setting out the procedural and institutional framework for the formulation of norms. The actual process of norm-creation consists in deriving, through negotiation and further consensus-building, concrete rules and standards of state behaviour from vaguely defined policy objectives and principles. In this process, both the form and substance of the emerging norm are at stake.

The main issue of form is the legal status of the norm, its binding or non-binding nature. Very often, the first stage in the normative process proper consists in the elaboration of legally non-binding international norms, ie 'soft law'. Soft law can serve different purposes: it can be designed to influence the behaviour of states or non-state actors directly, or to provide a consensual basis for the subsequent development of legally binding norms at the international level, or both. Generally, soft law instruments are not viewed by policy-makers as the endpoint of the international normative process, but only as a stepping-stone for its continuation. To put it more graphically, soft law serves as 'the thin end of the normative wedge of international environmental law.'[43] This gradual transformation of soft law into hard law has been described as a process of 'juridification' of international environmental policy.[44]

Apart from this formal process of juridification, international norm-making also involves an important substantive dimension: the specification of behavioural prescriptions, through which general objectives and princi-

[43] Handl (1990), p 7.
[44] See generally Lang (1984).

ples are transformed into concrete rules of conduct for specific norm addressees. The potential effectiveness of a norm is not merely a function of its legal form, but also depends on its substantive content, on what Van Dijk[45] calls its *normative force*, ie its intrinsic capacity to determine the behaviour of its addressees by limiting their room for discretionary judgement and precluding alternative options. Such normative force is dependent on the norm's specificity and determinacy. In Thomas Franck's terms, the 'compliance pull'[46] exerted by a norm is inversely proportional to its ambiguity.

Normative ambiguity may, however, be compensated by the existence of some procedural mechanism whereby the agreed meaning and implications of an initially ambiguous norm may gradually be further elaborated and made explicit and such a norm may eventually acquire a measure of 'process determinacy.'[47] Where they exist, dispute settlement mechanisms may serve this function. Another technique which is frequently used is that of the open-ended framework convention, which establishes only vague objectives and general principles and an institutional framework but provides for the subsequent development of more specific rules in the form of additional protocols.[48] At any rate, the conventional model of direct regulation through international law is premised on the assumption that for an international norm to be fully effective, it must ideally be legally binding and impose on its primary addressees, ie states, specific and unambiguous obligations.

One further premise on which this model is based is that, once states have ultimately consented to be bound by such international obligations, they will take whatever domestic action is required to fulfil them. Of course, treaty provisions can be self-executing and thereby have direct effects in the internal legal order of contracting parties, but self-executing provisions will rarely be found in environmental treaties. In the field of environmental policy, international legal norms generally impose obligations to legislate on states primarily with a view to influencing, through them, the behaviour of non-state entities. Usually, national legislative and administrative action will be required to implement the obligations imposed on the state party

[45] Van Dijk (1987).

[46] Franck (1990), p 42.

[47] *Ibid*, p 64.

[48] This particular technique has been elevated to the status of a reference model by both practitioners and academic commentators. Thus, for example, Lang suggests that the 'step-wise approach', which he describes as 'a minimum of political consensus-building first, leading to a soft law instrument, to be followed by a treaty of the framework convention type, which again would be supplemented by one or more protocols', is the 'wisest course of action' in environmental regime-building. Lang (1992), p 119. In the end, the actual impact of such a regime will depend on how successful the treaty institutions have been in fulfilling their role to 'continuously work towards reducing ambiguity'. *Ibid*, p 115. On the 'framework convention and protocol approach', see also Beyerlin & Marauhn (1997), pp 28–33.

by the international norm. Through such action, these international obligations will be transposed into concrete behavioural prescriptions, binding under national law, for the ultimate, individual legal subjects whose activities the international normative process seeks to influence.[49] Eventually, goal achievement will thus be a function of the compliance of those secondary addressees with these prescriptions. At this point, however, the determinants of the effectiveness of international regulation become indistinguishable from those of any other regulatory law at the national level.

The functioning of the legislative process in the European Community's legal order differs from this general model of the international normative process in a number of significant respects. The Community normative process is initiated by the Commission, an independent supranational body which has a monopoly on the right of initiative. Soft law does not as frequently function as a precursor of hard law at the Community level as it does internationally, though its importance seems to be increasing.[50] Article 249 of the EC Treaty specifically provides for two soft law instruments, recommendations and opinions, which 'shall have no binding force', but their use in the field of environmental policy is very rare. The Treaty on European Union formalised an additional soft law instrument which had already been used in institutional practice since the very beginning of the Community's environmental policy, viz 'general action programmes setting out priority objectives to be attained'.[51] Such action programmes are elaborated regularly by the Commission to test the political ground for legislative initiatives; since the entry into force of the TEU, they are formally adopted by the Council and the Parliament under the co-decision procedure,[52] but they still have no legal effects. The Commission enjoys full political discretion in the exercise of its right of initiative, but can of course be prompted to act by resolutions of the Council or the European Parliament, or even by recommendations of intergovernmental organisations or other international soft law texts.

The further course of the Community normative process depends on the type of legislative instrument used. In the environmental policy area, the instrument most frequently utilised is the directive, which must be transposed into domestic law by the member states. In transposing a directive, member states have some discretion as to the means to be used to achieve

[49] The crucial role of national law in international environmental governance and the question of what he terms the 'compatibility' of international and national environmental law has been extensively studied by Ebbeson (1996).

[50] See generally Wellens & Borchardt (1989); Snyder (1993b).

[51] Art 175, para 3 EC.

[52] Prior to the TEU, the Council used to 'approve' these programmes or merely 'note' them through a 'Resolution of the Council of the European Communities and of the representatives of the governments of the Member States meeting within the Council'. See, eg, the 4th Environmental Action Programme (1987–1992), OJ No C 328, 7.12.1987, p 1.

the result required by the directive. The extent of this discretion depends on the specificity of the terms in which this result is formulated in the directive. The greater the indeterminacy of those terms, the greater the member states' discretion and, consequently, the lower the directive's normative force and potential effectiveness in achieving harmonisation of national legislation in the member states. Transposition into national law is only the first step of the implementation process of directives. Practical application and enforcement are equally necessary steps, but in this respect the implementation of EC directives does not really differ from that of international normative instruments generally, except to the extent that certain provisions of unimplemented directives may have *direct effect* under Community law and be capable of judicial enforcement through national courts, and that a member state's failure to implement a directive can lead to state liability,[53] as well as infringement proceedings before the Court of Justice under Article 226 EC.

Where Community regulations are used as a legislative instrument, the likelihood of effectiveness is theoretically higher, since regulations require no transposition into domestic law but are directly applicable in all the member states and can impose obligations directly on individual legal subjects under their jurisdiction. Nevertheless, the effectiveness of an EC regulation, like that of a directive or of any other legally binding international instrument, is not determined solely by its legal force but ultimately also depends on the *normative force* of its substantive provisions. However, what does distinguish the regulation from other instruments in this respect is that those provisions are normally not addressed to states, but to non-state actors, and that their normative force must therefore be judged from the perspective of these individual norm addressees. It should be noted, though, that some form of governmental action at the member state level, such as the establishment of the necessary administrative structures for implementation and the provision of sanctions and supervision and enforcement mechanisms, will generally be required to make an EC regulation fully effective.

The ultimate purpose of transnational environmental law is to regulate the behaviour of private actors, not that of states. Especially in the field of toxics regulation, most of the environmentally damaging activities which are the target of the regulatory process are not undertaken by governments, but by private corporate entities or individuals, though often with the express or tacit authorisation of public authorities. In order to control such activities, international environmental law must necessarily operate through the medium of domestic environmental law. The same applies to European Community environmental law in so far as it has recourse to the

[53] For an analysis of this doctrine of state liability in the specific context of EC environmental law, see Lefevere (1996); Somsen (1996), pp 135–150.

instrument of directives, as it mostly does. As a consequence, the effectiveness of transnational environmental regulation is closely linked to that of national environmental regulation. The effectiveness of environmental law in a domestic context has been the subject of considerable research from various social science perspectives. Although this level of the normative process is beyond the scope of this study, it should be noted that much of this research also tends to call into question many assumptions of legal instrumentalism.[54]

If we take the model described above as a point of departure for our analysis, assessing the effectiveness of international normative processes entails looking at each of these successive 'links' in the 'regulatory chain'. Where the normative process has only produced soft law, its effectiveness is to be measured in terms of the direct influence of the soft law norms on national policies and legislation and on the behaviour of non-state actors. Often, the normative process will not proceed beyond the development of soft law because, although there is a certain measure of substantive agreement among governments, the political will to assume international legal obligations remains absent.[55] Where soft law is, however, intended as a precursor of international hard law, the effectiveness of the normative process will be a function of the extent to which soft law prescriptions have actually 'matured' into rules which are legally binding on states under international law, the extent to which those rules substantively constrain these states' discretion and, where necessary, are transposed into domestic law by them, and the extent to which this domestic legislation is implemented in administrative practice and enforced through the national legal system and ultimately succeeds in regulating the behaviour of those private entities causing the environmental problem that the international normative process seeks to address. Where European Community law is involved, its effectiveness will depend on the normative force of the relevant Community norms, their transposition into domestic law by the member states (except in the case of regulations), their practical application in the member states and their enforcement at both the national and Community level.

I have chosen to focus my analysis mostly on the initial phases of the normative process, and particularly on the *normative force* of international norms; as we have seen above, this is a crucial determinant of the effectiveness of any such norms, whatever their legal nature. Normative force is a relevant parameter for soft law as well as hard law norms, and for norms of conventional international law as well as norms of European Community law. Thus, in the two case studies in Parts II and III of this book, I will analyse the process of formulation of international norms, from policy

[54] See, eg Yeager (1991); Aalders (1984); Hawkins (1984).

[55] Lang (1984), p 285, refers to this situation as '*Substanzkonkordanz*' in conjunction with a '*voluntaristisches Defizit*'.

declarations through soft law to hard law, from policies through principles to specific rules, and the extent to which these norms impose effective constraints on the discretion of their primary addressees, sovereign states. This part of the evaluation, which concentrates on substantive normative content, is essentially a matter of legal analysis. So is, one step further 'downstream' of norm-creation, the assessment of the *formal compliance* by these addressees with their legal obligations or, in the case of soft law, political commitments.

Ultimately, testing the validity of the instrumental hypothesis would involve verifying the *normative effectiveness*[56] of international environmental norms, ie finding out not only whether or not the behaviour of the norm addressees conforms to the norms, but also, in the affirmative, whether it does so *because* of them. In other terms: can it be shown that the international normative process in and of itself actually *causes* behavioural change? Demonstrating this is obviously extremely difficult, because of the multiplicity of variables other than norms which influence the behaviour of states and non-state actors, and the difficulty of identifying and ascribing subjective *intent* to these subjects of law. Thus, while it is possible to verify *empirical* effectiveness, ie whether the behaviour of the norm addressees complies with the relevant normative prescriptions, it seems nearly impossible to prove that such compliance is actually *caused by, and only by*, the force of these prescriptions.[57] At any rate, positively demonstrating such causation would require skills in areas such as social psychology which go well beyond the qualifications of most lawyers and regime theorists.

This is why this study concentrates on what Van Dijk has termed *internal effectiveness*, ie the *intrinsic capacity and adequacy* of international norms, within the overall normative system of which they are part, to influence behaviour in such a way as to achieve the purpose for which they have been created, rather than attempting to systematically assess their *external effectiveness*, ie their *actual impact* on social reality. Apart from its primary purpose of analysing the intrinsic normative force of the relevant international norms, this study also attempts, in a subsidiary and tentative manner, to ascertain their *empirical effectiveness*, which itself has several dimensions.

The first is that of *formal rule compliance*: does the behaviour of the relevant subject correspond with the behavioural prescriptions addressed to it? The second, and ultimately most important dimension when assessing effectiveness from an instrumental perspective, is *goal achievement*: has the environmental policy objective which the norm purports to achieve

[56] For a more detailed discussion of this concept, see Van Dijk (1987), p 22.

[57] Cf the distinction between 'first-order compliance' and 'treaty-induced compliance' made by Mitchell (1996).

actually been realised? In evaluating goal achievement, I shall take into account both the *stated objective* of the norm, where there is one, and my own view of how the problem in question should be addressed. Of course, as pointed out above, neither compliance nor goal achievement per se are conclusive evidence of normative effectiveness, but if both of them can be empirically verified, some measure of correlation with the norm is not unlikely.

The evidence from both case studies suggests that the actual development of the international normative process does not match the instrumentalist model on which it is implicitly based. The evidence casts doubt on the presumed inexorable progress from soft law to hard law and from general principles to specific rules acting to gradually reduce the room for national discretion and thus effectuate common international policy goals. It calls into question the effectiveness of transnational law as an instrument of international policies to regulate toxics.

Its ineffectiveness is not just a matter of inadequate implementation and enforcement, as is often suggested, but is as much rooted in the inherent dynamics and constraints of the international normative process itself, in which regulators are constantly forced to accommodate national economic and political imperatives with international environmental aspirations through half-hearted compromises and ambiguous language. The logic of consensus diplomacy and the political need for achievement encourage constant recourse to functional ambiguity as a drafting technique and explain the low normative force of many international norms. The development and use of vaguely circumscribed normative concepts makes it possible for states to agree on basic principles and objectives of international regulation while at the same time retaining a substantial measure of national discretion in determining their actual substantive reach. International and supranational institutional mechanisms for translating vague policies and principles into concrete rules have on the whole failed to produce the requisite level of norm specification for the instrumental model to work. The lack of visible results of many hard law instruments has provoked a flight into soft law: not as a precursor of, but rather as a convenient substitute for, hard law.

But despite the failure of legal instrumentalism, international normative activity does not seem to be on the wane and the development of transnational environmental law, both hard and soft, continues unabated. This suggests that it fulfils other than instrumental functions and may be valued by governments more for its symbolic, value-expressive function than for any real problem-solving capacity. While it may fail in its instrumental function, the normative process may nevertheless be effective in its symbolic function, by giving symbolic satisfaction to pressing political demands expressed in the international community.

Part II

Toxic Substances in International Waters: The Regulation of Toxic Emissions in the Aquatic Environment

3

Transboundary Pollution of the Aquatic Environment by Toxic Substances from Industrial Processes and Products: The Problem and Its Perception

IT HAS BECOME commonplace to start any discussion of water pollution by recognising that water is essential to life itself and that its pollution can threaten human life or health and that of other living organisms, as well as the functioning of vital ecosystems. As the Council of Europe put it in its 1968 European Water Charter: 'To pollute water is to harm man and other living creatures which are dependent on water.'[1] The Charter furthermore stresses that 'water is a common heritage', that it 'knows no frontiers' and that 'as a common resource it demands international cooperation.'[2] In nature, fresh water and sea water, linked through the water cycle, are part of a single system, referred to as the hydrosphere. As a result of this natural cycle, pollutants can be widely dispersed throughout the hydrosphere and across national boundaries: 'The common global hydrologic cycle dynamically links many watersheds, airsheds, estuaries, and coastal and marine waters through transboundary movement of water, pollutants, and living resources.'[3] Therefore, the pollution of the aquatic environment, especially the marine environment, by toxic substances has long been a cause of international concern and a focus of transnational normative efforts.

There are many different forms of water pollution, but this study will focus on one of them: the pollution of the aquatic environment by substances which are toxic, persistent and bio-accumulative, ie that have a tendency to accumulate in living organisms through the food chain. Most of this pollution originates directly or indirectly from industrial production,

[1] European Water Charter of the Council of Europe, Strasbourg, 6 May 1968, para III.
[2] *Ibid*, paras X & XII.
[3] Global Environment Facility, *Operational Strategy*, Washington, 1996, p 48.

either in the form of direct discharges of waste products from production processes or as a result of inputs from diffuse sources caused by the use of products containing toxic substances. The former are sometimes referred to as process sources or point sources, the latter as product sources or non-point sources.

The development of international law in the field of water pollution control, like the development of international environmental law generally, has occurred in a fragmented and incremental manner, as new forms and pathways of pollution are discovered and policy-makers are forced to respond to successive 'pollution crises' and the resulting pressure from public opinion for regulatory action. International policies for the control of marine pollution and freshwater pollution have mainly been developed in distinct international fora.[4] Both forms of pollution are generally subject to separate international legal instruments, although there is a growing recognition of the need for a more integrated approach, consistent with the basic unity of the hydrosphere.

The problem of transboundary pollution of the aquatic environment by hazardous substances was recognised early in the development of international environmental policy and law. This recognition first materialised in the international law relating to the protection of the marine environment. It was in the run-up to the Stockholm Conference that international law-making first focused on toxic substances as one of the main targets to be addressed by international regulatory efforts for the control of marine pollution. The earliest source of toxic inputs into the marine environment to become the subject of international regulation—albeit a minor one—was the dumping of industrial wastes at sea. In the early 1970s, international legal instruments were negotiated at both the global and regional level to prohibit the dumping of certain hazardous pollutants and strictly regulate that of others. These instruments were the first to establish internationally agreed lists of substances hazardous to the marine environment. Toxic pollutants were originally identified as a legal category in the annexes to the 1972 Oslo Convention and classified in two lists on the basis of the environmental hazards they pose. These 'black' and 'grey' lists, based on the scientific knowledge of the late 1960s and early 1970s, served as a model which later inspired many other multilateral conventions for the protection of the aquatic environment.

In the initial marine pollution conventions, however, no generic term was coined to encompass all the pollutants whose dumping was made subject to regulation. The main operative provisions of the Oslo Convention merely refer to 'substances listed' in its annexes,[5] while in the global London

[4] For an excellent historical overview of the development of international marine pollution control law, see Johnston (1981).

[5] Convention for the Prevention of Marine Pollution by Dumping from Ships and Aircraft, Oslo, 15 Feb 1972, 11 ILM 262 (1972), Arts 5 & 6. Art 3, however, which prohibits the diversion of dumping to areas outside the geographical scope of application of the Oslo

Dumping Convention, which was concluded less than a year later, the pollutants covered by the annexes are designated in the most general of terms as 'wastes or other matter.'[6] But it appears from the provisions of both conventions that some measure of consensus had already emerged on the main *criteria* to be used for identifying marine pollutants of special concern that should be subject to the regulatory regime for the regulation of dumping at sea. These criteria were toxicity, persistence and the potential for accumulation in biological material or sediments and transformation as a result of environmental processes.[7] The Stockholm Declaration, an important soft law instrument adopted the same year, also singles out 'the discharge of toxic substances' generally,[8] as well as 'pollution of the seas by *substances that are liable to create hazards* to human health [or] to harm living resources and marine life,'[9] as issues of international concern requiring concerted action by governments.

But waste dumping at sea, though a spectacular and early target of public concern, was by no means the most significant source of marine pollution by toxic substances. Sea dumping has been described as 'a tempting target for politicians', as 'a discrete and easily regulated source' of marine pollution 'with no important special interests to be offended by regulation.'[10] Toxic emissions from land-based sources, however, are an altogether different matter. When the conventions to regulate dumping were concluded, their signatories did recognise that pollution from land-based sources was, quantitatively speaking, a much more important cause of contamination of the marine environment by dangerous substances. This awareness resulted in the negotiation in the mid-1970s of the first international legal instruments for the control of marine pollution from land-based sources, which focused on essentially the same hazardous pollutants as the ocean dumping conventions, and covered not only direct discharges of effluents from land into the sea but also indirect inputs of pollutants through rivers and estuaries. At about the same time, work started on the elaboration of rules of international and European Community law relating to discharges of hazardous substances in inland waters, and especially to the pollution of

Convention, uses the term 'harmful substances' for this purpose, though it is unclear from the context whether this term is intended as a generic term referring to all the substances listed in annexes I and II, or as a broader, not specifically defined, category of pollutants.

[6] Convention on the Prevention of Marine Pollution by Dumping of Wastes and Other Matter, London, Mexico City, Moscow, Washington, 29 Dec 1972, 1046 UNTS 120, Art IV.

[7] Oslo Convention, Annex III part 1 items (e)–(h); London Dumping Convention, Annex III part A items 4–7.

[8] Stockholm Declaration, Principle 6. See also the Stockholm Conference's 'Recommendations for Action', para 71, calling for action 'to minimize the release to the environment of *toxic or dangerous substances, especially if they are persistent* substances such as heavy metals and organochlorine compounds' (emphasis added).

[9] Stockholm Declaration, Principle 7 (emphasis added). See also para 48(b) of the 'Recommendations for Action', referring to 'the discharge of toxic chemicals, heavy metals, and other wastes' as a threat to marine living resources.

[10] McManus (1983), p 121.

international watercourses by such substances. From a substantive point of view, as pollution prevention and reduction measures moved further 'upstream', the legal regime for the control of marine pollution from land-based sources and that for freshwater pollution became almost indistinguishable. That is why they will be considered together in this work.

Initially, the main source of land-based pollution to be tackled by these emerging international legal regimes was discharges of effluent from industrial point sources, and the primary means used to control such pollution was 'end-of-pipe' waste water treatment technology. The main legal instrument for water pollution control was the establishment of prior authorisation regimes for discharges combined with the imposition of legally binding emission standards and/or water quality standards for specific pollutants. International standard-setting efforts focused on a substance-by-substance, sector-by-sector approach, seeking to reach agreement on the identification of hazardous water pollutants of international concern and on internationally harmonised emission limit values and environmental quality objectives for the substances identified.

But it soon became clear that industrial point sources were not the only, or even—for certain pollutants—the main cause of pollution by toxic substances from land-based activities, and that releases from diffuse sources such as agricultural or consumer use of products containing such substances, as well as their subsequent disposal, also contribute substantially to water pollution. Consequently, international regulatory efforts for the reduction of toxic inputs into the aquatic environment also had to address the marketing and use of products likely to cause water pollution, and other diffuse sources. More recently, there has been a shift in pollution control policies from an approach focusing on specific environmental media (such as water, air and soil) towards a more integrated approach addressing all emissions and releases of hazardous substances into the environment jointly, regardless of their form, and focusing on the prevention of pollution at its source through changes in production processes and products, rather than on end-of-pipe remedial measures to remove pollutants from effluents or mitigate their environmental effects.

In the following chapters, I analyse the norms of international and European Community law that have been elaborated and are still being developed specifically to control emissions of toxic substances in the aquatic environment, primarily from point sources, and attempt to assess their effectiveness. The focus is on those rules which are relevant to the European Community and its member states. This enables us to study the interplay between European Community law and international law. Geographically, special attention is paid to the regime for the control of pollution in the North Sea, which is composed of elements of both international law and European Community law, supplemented and influenced by a growing body of soft law. However, the analysis is not limited to the

North Sea, but also covers other regional seas and international watercourses, such as the Baltic Sea, the Mediterranean and the Rhine, which are the subject of conventional regimes to which the European Community and/or some of its member states are parties.

Chapters 4 to 7 look at the regulation of emissions of toxic substances under multilateral conventions for the protection of the marine environment from pollution from land-based sources and for the protection of international rivers. A special effort is made to look beyond the general rules and principles of law laid down in these conventions themselves,[11] at the way in which they have been interpreted and implemented by the regulatory bodies established by them. This inquiry reveals the inherent indeterminacy and flexibility of the basic substantive rules laid down in the conventions, and the many mechanisms through which national regulatory discretion is preserved and a balance struck between environmental imperatives and economic interests. The analysis does not focus exclusively on binding rules of international law but also addresses the norms laid down in non-binding instruments, such as the North Sea Ministerial Declarations and the Rhine Action Programme, in their interaction with and influence upon binding rules.

Chapter 8 examines the role of European Community law. It explores both the general framework of European Community law for the control of water pollution and the specific rules relating to the control of emissions of toxic substances. Finally, chapter 9 addresses the participation of the European Community in various international conventions and the interaction between the development of European Community law and international law. This brings to the fore the striking similarities in the development of law at these two levels and the strong influence of the European Community on normative efforts in other international fora.

[11] For a more comprehensive analysis of the general principles, see Nollkaemper (1993a).

4

The Land-Based Sources Regime for the North Sea and North East Atlantic

HISTORY AND BACKGROUND OF THE CONVENTIONAL REGIME

The 1974 Paris Convention for the Prevention of Marine Pollution from Land-Based Sources[1] was the second regional convention for the control of marine pollution concluded by the coastal states of the North-East Atlantic. It was the outcome of a process of regime formation which started in 1971 at the initiative of the Scandinavian states.[2] The early negotiations among the states bordering the North-East Atlantic dealt with different sources of marine pollution in a piecemeal fashion and first led to the conclusion of the Convention for the Prevention of Marine Pollution by Dumping from Ships and Aircraft, signed in Oslo on 15 February 1972.[3] This Convention established a system for the regulation of the dumping of wastes at sea, based on two lists of substances deemed hazardous for the marine environment due to their toxicity, persistence and tendency to accumulate in living organisms, the so-called 'black list' of pollutants whose dumping was altogether prohibited, except as 'trace contaminants', and the 'grey list' of substances considered less dangerous, which initially were still allowed to be dumped under certain conditions. The 'black list'/'grey list' system first introduced by the Oslo Convention established an internationally recognised categorisation of marine pollutants which served as a model for many subsequent conventions for the protection of the marine environment, including the 1974 Paris Convention.[4]

In the preamble of the Oslo Convention, the contracting parties, 'noting that [marine] pollution has many sources, including dumping from ships

[1] Convention for the Prevention of Marine Pollution from Land-Based Sources, Paris, 4 June 1974, 13 ILM 352 (1974) (hereafter referred to as 1974 Paris Convention).

[2] See Van der Burgt (1984), pp 1–5.

[3] Convention for the Prevention of Marine Pollution by Dumping from Ships and Aircraft, Oslo, 15 Feb 1972, 11 ILM 262 (1972), 932 UNTS 3.

[4] For a general, comparative discussion of the 'black list'/'grey list' approach in regional marine environment protection conventions, see Meng (1987), pp 122–131.

and aircraft and discharges through rivers, estuaries, outfalls and pipelines within national jurisdiction', recognised that the control of waste dumping was only a first step towards effective control of marine pollution and that 'this action should not preclude discussion of measures to control other sources of marine pollution as soon as possible'. In order to build on the momentum created by the Oslo Convention negotiations and to continue the discussions among the signatories on measures to deal with other sources of marine pollution, the French government offered to host a diplomatic conference to address the issue of pollution from land-based sources.[5] Thus, negotiations on an additional convention were opened in 1973[6] and successfully concluded in June 1974 with the signing in Paris of the Convention for the Prevention of Marine Pollution from Land-Based Sources, which entered into force in May 1978.[7]

However, at the diplomatic conference which adopted the Paris Convention, the signatory states had already agreed to initiate discussions on the implementation of the Convention even prior to its entry into force. For this purpose, they established an Interim Commission whose task it was to prepare the work of the Commission which would be formally constituted following the entry into force of the Convention. The first formal meeting of the Paris Commission (PARCOM) was held in November 1978. The Commission subsequently met on an annual basis, normally back-to-back with the annual meetings of the Oslo Commission (OSCOM) established under the 1972 Oslo Convention. Though the Oslo and Paris Conventions were distinct treaties, their contracting parties were largely the same[8] and the respective Commissions, though formally two discrete institutions,[9] were served by a common secretariat based in London and have effectively operated as one integrated marine pollution control regime. The 1974 Paris Convention was amended in 1986 to extend its scope of application to

[5] Oslo and Paris Commissions, *Les Commissions d'Oslo et de Paris—La première décennie: Coopération internationale pour la protection de notre environnement marin*, London, p 8, para 1.2.2.

[6] Three negotiating meetings were held in Paris between September 1973 and February 1974, followed by a diplomatic conference for the formal adoption and signing of the convention in June 1974. The most detailed published account of the negotiations by one of the participants is to be found in De Yturriaga Barberan (1975). A shorter account by the same author but in English appears in De Yturriaga Barberan (1979).

[7] The exact date of entry into force is 6 May 1978, ie 30 days after the date of deposit of the 7th instrument of ratification.

[8] Finland was a contracting party to the Oslo Convention but not to the Paris Convention, and the European Community vice versa. The European Commission's proposal that the EC should seek accession to the Oslo Convention was never adopted by the Council.

[9] The back-to-back meetings of PARCOM and OSCOM were generally also accompanied by a joint meeting of both commissions to discuss general policy issues and administrative matters common to both Conventions. Documents from these joint meetings carried the code 'OSPAR' and this acronym was later adopted to designate the integrated 1992 Paris Convention and the new Commission resulting from the merger of the 1972 Oslo and 1974 Paris Conventions and their respective commissions.

pollution from land-based sources reaching the marine environment through the atmosphere.[10]

In 1990, the Oslo and Paris Commissions decided to revise both the Oslo and Paris Conventions and combine them in a single, integrated instrument. This revision process resulted in the adoption, at the first ministerial-level joint meeting of both Commissions, held in Paris in September 1992, of a new 1992 Paris Convention for the Protection of the Marine Environment of the North-East Atlantic,[11] designed to replace the 1974 Paris Convention and 1972 Oslo Convention upon its entry into force.[12] With the simultaneous adoption of a ministerial declaration[13] and of an Action Plan[14] establishing priorities for the future work of the Oslo and Paris Commissions, both before and after the entry into force of the 1992 Convention, the Paris high-level meeting also marked an important political step in the further development of the North-East Atlantic land-based sources regime and in the process of implementation of the 1974 Paris Convention and the measures adopted pursuant to it by the Paris Commission.

The parties agreed to meet again at ministerial level following the entry into force of the new Convention, and at regular intervals thereafter, to assess progress in its implementation. This conference, which was initially scheduled to be held no later than 1997, had to be postponed due to delay in the ratification process.[15] OSPAR Convention eventually entered into force on 24 March 1998, and the first ministerial meeting of OSPAR Commission was held in Sintra, Portugal, at the end of July 1998. It adopted a new Annex V to the Convention, on the protection of marine ecosystems and biological diversity,[16] the first series of formal decisions and recommendations under the provisions of the 1992 Convention, and a number of important policy documents, including a ministerial

[10] Protocol amending the Convention for the Prevention of Marine Pollution from Land-Based Sources, Paris, 26 Mar 1986, 27 ILM 625 (1988), OJ No L 24, 27.1.1987, p 49.

[11] Convention for the Protection of the Marine Environment of the North-East Atlantic, Paris, 22 Sept 1992, 32 ILM 1068 (1993) (hereafter referred to as 1992 Paris Convention or OSPAR Convention). For a general discussion of the new Convention in all its aspects, see Hey, IJlstra & Nollkaemper (1993), Juste (1993) and Hilf (1995).

[12] 1992 Paris Convention, Art 31.

[13] Final Declaration of the Ministerial Meeting of the Oslo and Paris Commissions, 21–22 Sep 1992, in: Oslo and Paris Commissions, *Ministerial Meeting of the Oslo and Paris Commissions, Paris, 21–22 September 1992*, London, 1993 (hereafter referred to as 'Paris Ministerial Meeting Proceedings'), p 115.

[14] Action Plan for the Oslo and Paris Commissions, 1992, *ibid*, p 123.

[15] According to its Art 29, the new Convention could only enter into force after having been ratified, accepted or approved by *all* the contracting parties to *both* the 1974 Paris Convention and the Oslo Convention, including the European Community.

[16] Annex V on the Protection and Conservation of the Ecosystems and Biological Diversity of the Maritime Area, Sintra, 23 July 1998. In accordance with Art 15 of the Convention, this new Annex entered into force on 30 Aug 2000 for Finland, Spain, Switzerland, Luxembourg, the European Community, the United Kingdom and Denmark and has since also been ratified by Sweden, Iceland, Norway and the Netherlands.

statement,[17] a new Action Plan for the period 1998–2003,[18] and an OSPAR Strategy with regard to hazardous substances.[19]

In this chapter, I will first analyse the provisions of the original 1974 Convention. I shall then look successively at the practice under that Convention with respect to the control of toxic emissions in the marine environment, at the influence of the International North Sea Conference process on this practice, at the provisions of the 1992 Convention and their likely implications for toxics reduction policies in the future, and at the results of the 1998 ministerial meeting and the early practice under the provisions of the 1992 Convention with respect to emissions of dangerous substances.

THE 1974 PARIS CONVENTION FOR THE PREVENTION OF MARINE POLLUTION FROM LAND-BASED SOURCES

Analysis of the Convention

In Article 1 of the Convention, the contracting parties, in very general terms, 'pledge themselves to take all possible steps to prevent pollution of the seas' and, more specifically, undertake to 'adopt individually and jointly measures to combat marine pollution from land-based sources in accordance with the provisions of the present Convention' and to 'harmonize their policies in this regard'.

Marine pollution is defined in the Convention as:

> the introduction by man, directly or indirectly, of substances or energy into the marine environment (including estuaries) *resulting in such deleterious effects* as hazards to human health, harm to living resources and to marine eco-systems, damage to amenities or interference with other legitimate uses of the sea.[20]

This definition is largely inspired by the classical definition of marine pollution adopted in 1969 by the Group of Experts on the Scientific Aspects of Marine Pollution (GESAMP).[21] The wording used assumes that marine pollution only exists where there is evidence of specific harm causally linked to the introduction of substances or energy into the marine environment. It must be positively shown that such introduction results in 'deleterious

[17] Sintra Statement of the Ministerial Meeting of OSPAR Commission, Sintra, 23 July 1998.

[18] OSPAR Action Plan 1998–2003, OSPAR Doc MMC 98/7/1–E, July 1998.

[19] OSPAR Strategy with Regard to Hazardous Substances, OSPAR Doc MMC 98/6/1–E, July 1998.

[20] 1974 Paris Convention, Art 1, para 1 (emphasis added).

[21] See Tomczak (1984), pp 317–318. See also Meng (1987), pp 3–5.

effects' before it can be considered as 'marine pollution' within the meaning of the Convention.[22]

Following the example set by the Oslo Convention, the Paris Convention classifies pollutants in lists according to the potential hazard they are considered to present for the marine environment. Substances are allocated to the different lists based on three criteria: persistence, toxicity, and tendency to bio-accumulate. Part I of Annex A, the so-called 'black list', lists organohalogen compounds, mercury and cadmium and their compounds, persistent synthetic materials and persistent oils and hydrocarbons.[23] According to the explanatory language in Annex A, these substances are included in the black list in essence 'because they are not readily degradable or rendered harmless by natural processes', because they may 'give rise to dangerous accumulation of harmful material in the food chain', and 'because it is considered that pollution by these substances necessitates urgent action'. The second list, Part II of Annex A, unofficially termed 'grey list', contains a number of substances which 'although exhibiting similar characteristics to the substances in Part I and requiring strict control ... seem less noxious or are more readily rendered harmless by natural processes'. The main substances on this list are organic compounds of phosphorus, silicon and tin, elemental phosphorus, non-persistent oils and hydrocarbons and six additional heavy metals and their compounds.[24] Finally, Annex A comprises a third category of substances, 'radioactive substances, including wastes', which are made subject to a special regime under Part III of Annex A and Article 5 of the Convention. As radioactive pollution falls outside the scope of this study, this regime will not be further examined here.

The measures to be taken by the contracting parties with respect to the two main categories of substances are further specified in Article 4 of the

[22] De Yturriaga Barberan (1979), p 332, notes that according to this definition pollution consists of two elements: the introduction of pollutants and harm to the marine environment. However, he elsewhere considers that the Paris Convention definition is open to interpretation and does not necessarily imply actual damage. *Ibid* at p 390.

[23] There are a few differences between Part I of Annex A to the Paris Convention and Annex I to the Oslo Convention. Organosilicon compounds, which are considered black list substances under the latter Convention, are not listed in Part I of Annex A to the Paris Convention. Neither are 'substances which have been agreed between the Contracting Parties as likely to be carcinogenic under the conditions of disposal'. However, the black list of the Paris Convention includes 'persistent oils and hydrocarbons of petroleum origin', which are not mentioned in Annex I to the Oslo Convention.

[24] The grey list in Annex II to the Oslo Convention is much shorter. It does not include organic phosphorus, silicon and tin compounds, elemental phosphorus, or hydrocarbons, whether persistent or not. It only covers four heavy metals and their compounds (arsenic, lead, copper and zinc) instead of six. However, the Oslo grey list includes two specific categories of pollutants not mentioned in the Paris Convention ('pesticides and their by-products' and 'cyanides and fluorides') and one open-ended category: 'Substances which, though of a non-toxic nature, may become harmful due to the quantities in which they are dumped, or which are liable to seriously reduce amenities.'

Convention. In general terms, the contracting parties undertake 'to eliminate, if necessary by stages, pollution of the maritime area' by black list substances, and 'to limit strictly' pollution by grey list substances.[25] More specifically, it is provided that, in order to carry out this general undertaking, the contracting parties '*jointly or individually as appropriate*, shall implement programmes and measures.'[26] This formula is a compromise between the concerns of those contracting parties wishing to leave it to the discretion of each individual party to decide what measures to take to comply with its general commitments under the Convention, and those which were proponents of a more international approach whereby specific joint measures binding on each contracting party would be elaborated through the organs created by the Convention.[27] The wording of Article 4, paragraph 2 juxtaposes joint and individual action without giving more prominence to either one and leaves it to contracting parties to choose one or the other 'as appropriate'. No explicit mention is made in Article 4 of the role of the Commission established by the Convention in the elaboration of 'programmes and measures', though such a role is clearly envisaged in Article 16 (d), which defines the powers of the Commission.[28]

The objective of the 'programmes and measures' to be implemented 'jointly or individually' by the contracting parties shall be 'the *elimination*, as a matter of urgency' of pollution by black list substances and 'the *reduction* or, as appropriate, elimination' of pollution by grey list substances.[29] These provisions further clarify the meaning of the general obligation respectively 'to eliminate' and 'to limit strictly' pollution by certain substances. The term 'to eliminate' was laid down in the Convention as a compromise between diverging viewpoints. Some parties favoured an outright prohibition of pollution by black list substances, while others considered that a reduction of such pollution was sufficient. Finally, agreement was reached on the objective 'to eliminate, *if necessary by stages*' pollution by black list substances, implying that, if elimination of pollution is the ultimate objective, it is recognised that it can be reached only gradually.[30] However, this concept of gradual elimination is somewhat counterbalanced

[25] 1974 Paris Convention, Art 4, para 1.

[26] *Ibid*, para 2 (emphasis added).

[27] De Yturriaga Barberan (1979), pp 356–357 and 391–392.

[28] According to De Yturriaga Barberan (1975), pp 55, 62, any reference to the Commission was deliberately omitted from Art 4 to stress that 'fundamental decisions' with respect to pollution measures remained in the hands of the parties, even where they chose to act 'jointly'. This was a compromise between those who wished to confine the Commission to a mere administrative role, and those who were in favour of giving it broader powers.

[29] 1974 Paris Convention, Art 4, para 2 (emphasis added).

[30] De Yturriaga Barberan (1979), p 389. The use of the verb 'eliminate' was proposed by the United Kingdom, as a compromise between 'prohibit' and 'reduce'. However, the UK initially proposed to refer to it as a 'common objective' only. De Yturriaga Barberan (1975), p 55.

by the language in Article 4, paragraph 2 referring to elimination 'as a matter of urgency'.

As regards grey list substances, the provisions of Article 4, paragraph 2 indicate that the obligation in paragraph 1 'to limit strictly' pollution by such substances is not to be interpreted as a mere standstill obligation. Article 4, paragraph 2 makes clear that the objective of the measures to be taken under the Convention is at least the *reduction* of pollution by grey list substances, or even 'as appropriate', its eventual elimination, as for black list substances. Unlike for black list substances, the Convention specifies the conditions under which grey list substances may be discharged:

> These substances shall be discharged only after approval has been granted by the appropriate authorities within each Contracting State. Such approval shall be periodically reviewed.[31]

Thus, the continued discharge of grey list substances in the marine environment is tolerated under the Convention, provided discharges are adequately controlled nationally and subjected to a periodical review, presumably with a view to making discharge conditions gradually more stringent in order to reduce pollution.

The Convention contains no similar provisions with respect to discharges of black list substances. Even though the ultimate objective of the Convention is to eliminate discharges of black list substances, it is nevertheless implicit that discharges may be allowed to continue for some time, since the Convention recognises that the elimination of pollution is to be achieved gradually, 'if necessary by stages'. The absence of any explicit reference to an authorisation system for discharges of black list as opposed to grey list substances could nevertheless be seen as reflecting the intent of the contracting parties not to legitimise such discharges in any way, especially in view of some parties' original aim of prohibiting them altogether.

Article 4, paragraph 3 elaborates on the scope of the 'programmes and measures' to be implemented under the Convention. It provides that those measures:

> shall include, as appropriate, specific regulations or standards governing the quality of the environment, discharges into the maritime area, such discharges into watercourses as affect the maritime area, and the composition and use of substances and products.

In fact, three types of measures are envisaged under the Convention, reflecting the different policy approaches of contracting parties to the pollution problem. The first is the setting of *environmental quality standards*

[31] 1974 Paris Convention, Art 4, para 2 *in fine*.

determining the concentrations of pollutants in the marine environment deemed to be acceptable but leaving it to individual contracting parties to appreciate what pollution control measures are required to achieve the set result in terms of environmental quality. The second type of measure referred to is the setting of *emission standards* for discharges into the maritime area or affecting that area through watercourses. The third type of measure relates to products and substances whose use is likely to lead to pollution of the marine environment.

This latter provision should be seen in the light of the proposal made by Norway during the negotiation of the Convention that the measures to be adopted by the Commission established under the Convention ought to include the prohibition of the *use and/or production* of certain substances.[32] This proposal was apparently deemed too far-reaching,[33] but the idea that product-related measures may have to be taken was not rejected altogether. The Convention does not explicitly refer to prohibition measures but includes 'specific regulations or standards governing . . . the composition and use of substances and products' within the range of possible measures. This wording does not necessarily rule out prohibition measures, but it should be noted that, contrary to the Norwegian proposal, no reference is made to restrictions on the *production* of certain substances, only to regulations governing the *use* of substances or *composition* of products. Finally, Article 4, paragraph 3 provides that the programmes and measures 'shall take into account the latest technical developments' and 'shall contain time limits for their completion.'

In addition to the provisions of Article 4 concerning black and grey list substances, the Convention contains a number of provisions laying down obligations which do not specifically relate to the listed substances. Article 4, paragraph 4 provides for the possibility of joint or individual action against pollution by substances which are not listed in Annex A 'if scientific evidence has established that a serious hazard may be created in the maritime area by that substance and if urgent action is necessary'. Article 6 elaborates on the general obligation of contracting parties 'to combat marine pollution from land-based sources', as spelled out in Article 1, paragraph 2, by stipulating in general terms that contracting parties 'shall endeavour', on the one hand, 'to reduce *existing* pollution from land-based sources' and, on the other, 'to forestall any *new* pollution from land-based sources, including that which derives from new substances.'[34] This shall be done 'with a view to preserving and enhancing the

[32] De Yturriaga Barberan (1979), p 392.

[33] Spain, in particular, objected vigorously to this proposal, on the grounds that it would confer on an international body the power to prohibit, by a majority decision, the use or production by a sovereign state of particular substances, including a number of essential metals. De Yturriaga Barberan (1975), p 57.

[34] 1974 Paris Convention, Art 6, para 1 (emphasis added).

quality of the marine environment' and 'without prejudice to the provisions of Article 4'.

This provision imposes on contracting parties a dual general obligation which could be described as a 'standstill' and 'rollback' obligation. The quality of the marine environment must be 'preserved' and 'enhanced'. This implies that any new pollution, ie any increase in pollution by substances which are already present in the marine environment as well as any pollution from new substances, must be prevented and that existing levels of pollution must be reduced. However, this obligation is somewhat qualified by the proviso that, in implementing their undertaking, contracting parties shall take account of, inter alia, 'the absorptive capacity of the receiving waters of the maritime area,'[35] which can be interpreted as legitimating the introduction of pollutants into the marine environment as long as the 'absorptive capacity' is not exceeded and implies that the notion of pollution is a relative one. The Convention not only imposes a standstill obligation in respect of pollution of the maritime area from land-based sources, it also provides that measures taken to combat pollution from land-based sources may not result in any increase in pollution of the area from other sources, nor in increased pollution of the seas outside the Paris Convention area.[36] In other terms, reduction of land-based marine pollution shall not be achieved at the expense of a transfer of pollution to other sources or other areas.

As the above review of the main substantive provisions of the Convention indicates, the implementation of the 1974 Paris Convention presupposes both individual action by each of the contracting parties and joint action by all contracting parties through the institutional framework established by the Convention. The mechanisms for joint action are laid down in Articles 15 to 18 of the Convention. The Convention establishes a Commission composed of representatives of the contracting parties, known as the Paris Commission, on which specific powers are conferred for the implementation of the Convention. The most important of these powers is that 'to draw up, in accordance with Article 4 of the present Convention, programmes and measures for the elimination or reduction of pollution from land-based sources.'[37] The procedure for the adoption of these programmes and measures is laid down in Article 18, paragraph 3, which provides that they shall in principle be adopted 'by unanimous vote' but that, 'should unanimity not be attainable', they may nevertheless be adopted by a three quarters majority vote, in which case, however, they will only be binding on those contracting parties that voted for them.

[35] *Ibid*, Art 6 para 2 (c).
[36] *Ibid*, Art 7.
[37] *Ibid*, Art 16 (d).

Legal Status of Commission Decisions under the 1974 Convention

The Convention does not actually use the term 'binding', but provides that measures adopted unanimously '*shall commence for and be applied by* all Contracting Parties two hundred days after their adoption, unless the Commission specifies another date', whereas measures adopted by a three quarters majority 'shall commence *for those Contracting Parties which voted for them*' within the same timeframe.[38] In such case, the measures shall 'commence' for the contracting parties which did not vote in favour only after they have 'explicitly accepted' them, which the Convention provides they may do 'at any time'. The imperative language used and the consensual model for their entry into force may be taken to indicate that the measures adopted pursuant to the Paris Convention are intended to have a legally binding effect, although this is not entirely undisputed by some contracting parties.

The practice of the Commission with respect to the legal status of its decisions can be described as one of deliberate ambiguity. First of all, it should be noted that, especially during its first years of activity, the Commission acted rather casually in terms of the way in which decisions were formulated and recorded. Decisions taken pursuant to Article 16 (d) of the Convention were simply recorded in the summary record of the meetings in the same format as the minutes of discussions, without any explicit reference to their legal basis. Recurring discussions within the Paris Commission about the legal status of decisions and how to record them led to some formalisation of procedures but did not altogether remove ambiguities and disagreements among contracting parties.

In 1980, the Paris Commission 'considered whether there was any uncertainty with regard to the legal status of the decisions . . . or to the point of time when such decisions become legally binding on Contracting Parties' and 'concluded that at present there was no ambiguity'. The Commission noted that decisions relating to implementation of the Convention 'become binding on the Contracting Parties once they have been adopted by the Commission' and decided that a more formal system of recording decisions was not required.[39] While recognising that its decisions made pursuant to Article 16 (d) of the Convention were legally binding, the Commission at the same time developed a practice of adopting mainly non-binding 'recommendations' on the implementation of the Convention, thus circumventing the legal effect ascribed to 'programmes and measures' under Article 18, paragraph 3.

[38] 1974 Paris Convention, Art 18, para 3 (emphasis added).

[39] Second Annual Report on the Activities of the Paris Commission, para 54, in *First and Second Annual Reports on the Activities of the Paris Commission*, London, 1981, p 80.

It should be noted that the Convention does not actually explicitly confer on the Commission the power to adopt non-binding recommendations for the implementation of Article 4. Article 16 provides for 'recommendations' of the Commission only in two specific cases: recommendations for amendments to Annex A (which are subject to approval by the governments of the contracting parties) and recommendations made pursuant to Article 9, paragraph 2 relating to bilateral or multilateral co-operation among contracting parties in special circumstances.[40] As regards the implementation of Article 4, the Convention only knows 'programmes and measures' which 'shall be applied' by contracting parties. The reluctance of the Commission to make formal use of its power to adopt binding 'programmes and measures' no doubt reflects the long-standing differences among contracting parties as to the extent of the role of the Commission, which some parties, during the negotiations leading up to the conclusion of the Convention, wished to confine to a purely administrative and recommendatory function.[41]

The schizophrenic attitude of the Commission remains apparent throughout the reports of its successive meetings. In 1984, the Commission, at a joint meeting with the Oslo Commission, agreed that 'as a general rule, binding legal Decisions, where open to the Commissions, were to be preferred to Recommendations to Contracting Parties', but a few years later, in 1987, it concluded that 'in many cases' it might be 'more practicable' to adopt recommendations, which 'might prove sufficient in terms of tangible benefits for the marine environment'. At the same time, however, the Commission 'recalled that all PARCOM Decisions are legally binding and have to be implemented by Contracting Parties in national legislation.'[42] A formal numbering system for the identification of decisions and recommendations was adopted in 1985.

At the 11th Joint Meeting of the Oslo and Paris Commissions in Dublin in 1988, the Secretariat presented a detailed paper on the 'Legal status of OSCOM and PARCOM Decisions and Recommendations', which reviewed past practice and attempted to draw some conclusions from it. In this paper, the Secretariat strongly argued that the Paris Commission does have the power to take decisions which are legally binding on contracting parties and had, in fact, repeatedly taken such decisions, which were perfectly valid notwithstanding the rather informal procedures followed by the Commission in the past.[43] The Secretariat took issue with 'the opinion of some Contracting Parties' that there is no distinction between decisions and recommendations and invited the Commissions

[40] 1974 Paris Convention, Art 16 (e) and (g).
[41] De Yturriaga Barberan (1979), p 357.
[42] Paris Commission, *Procedures and Decisions Manual*, C1/89–E, 2/6.
[43] OSPAR Doc 11/10/1–E, June 1989, para 23.

to confirm clearly and unambiguously that it is within the scope of the Commissions to take Decisions which, if agreed by Contracting Parties, bind those Parties to implement those Decisions

and:

to confirm that it is helpful to retain the present distinction between Decisions *which create binding obligations* on those Contracting Parties which accept them, and Recommendations which, *although not legally binding*, nevertheless create an expectation that the provisions of the Recommendation will be observed by those Contracting Parties which accept it.[44]

The Commissions refused to endorse the conclusions put forward by the Secretariat, but instead preferred to recognise that there were 'differences of interpretation' as to the powers of the Commissions and that it would 'not be fruitful' to examine the matter further.[45] However, even those contracting parties which objected most strongly to the Secretariat's proposals did not explicitly deny the power of the Paris Commission to take legally binding decisions in accordance with Article 18, paragraph 3 of the Convention.[46]

The debate on this question within the Paris Commission remained inconclusive for as long as the 1974 Convention was in force. From time to time, individual parties have put statements on record which highlight persisting disagreement and maintain the 'constructive ambiguity' in Commission practice. At the 1989 meeting of the Commission, for instance, France expressed its opinion 'that the Paris Commission is only empowered to draw up recommendations' and reminded other parties of its 'general reservation on all draft Decisions submitted to the Commission.'[47] The Netherlands, for its part, submitted a document to the 1991 Commission meeting in which it stated that it 'considers all Decisions and Recommendations of the Paris Commission as binding, *even though they do not have such legal status*.'[48] This latter statement is particularly confusing, because it could be taken to imply that even decisions do not have a legally binding character. This could hardly have been the intention of the Netherlands, which probably only wanted to put on record that it considers itself equally bound—in a political sense—by decisions and recommendations, even though *the latter* are not binding from a legal viewpoint.

The question of the legal status of PARCOM decisions was again discussed in the context of the renegotiation of the 1974 Convention in

[44] OSPAR Doc 11/10/1–E, June 1989, para 35 (emphasis added).

[45] OSPAR Doc 11/16/1–F, June 1989, para 10.4.

[46] Spain, Portugal and France formally objected to the Secretariat's proposals, though it seems that their objections primarily concerned the fact that the Secretariat had equated the powers of the Oslo and Paris Commissions, notwithstanding significant differences in the text of both conventions. See OSPAR Doc 11/16/1–F, June 1989, para 10.2.

[47] PARCOM Doc 11/9/1–E, June 1989, para 4.27.

[48] 'Binding Character of Decisions and Recommendations', PARCOM Doc 13/INFO.14–E, June 1991, para 1 (emphasis added).

1991–1992. While the legally binding nature of decisions, as opposed to recommendations, was unequivocally affirmed in the provisions of the 1992 Convention, these provisions apply only to decisions adopted after the entry into force of the new Convention. In the transitional provisions of that Convention, as we shall see below, the question of the legal effect of decisions adopted under the 1974 Paris Convention was once more quite deliberately left unsettled.

THE PRACTICE OF THE PARIS COMMISSION UNDER THE 1974 CONVENTION: ADOPTION OF PROGRAMMES AND MEASURES

The Interim Commission established by the signatories started its activities in 1974 and set up a Technical Working Group (TWG) which was given the task to advise the Interim Commission on the technical and scientific aspects of the implementation of the Convention. This group, whose establishment and terms of reference were confirmed by the Paris Commission at its first formal meeting in 1978, started considering measures which could be taken jointly by the contracting parties to combat pollution by listed substances. The initial focus was on black list substances, in particular mercury, followed, in a later stage, by cadmium and various individual organohalogen compounds. In recent years, the Commission has moved away from this initial substance-by-substance approach towards the development of more comprehensive regulatory measures, targetting entire industrial sectors which are recognised to be important land-based sources of marine pollution or other land-based activities involving the use of particular products which lead to diffuse pollution of the marine environment. These various kinds of 'programmes and measures' within the meaning of the 1974 Convention will be analysed below.

Mercury

The discussions on the regulatory approach to the problem of mercury pollution from the chlor-alkali industry revealed a deep rift between contracting parties, which has pervaded the Commission's work on the regulation of discharges of hazardous substances for many years. The majority of contracting parties favoured a policy of setting 'uniform emission standards' (UES) for discharges of mercury from this industry, based on the best technical means available and to be applied by all contracting parties throughout the Convention area, whereas the United Kingdom and Portugal advocated an approach based on 'environmental quality objectives' (EQO) whereby the Commission would only determine the water quality standards to be achieved but would leave the contracting parties free to regulate the actual discharges as they deemed fit, provided the quality standards were complied with.[49]

Both approaches were possible under Article 4, paragraph 3, of the Convention, which provides that the 'programmes and measures' may include standards relating both to 'the quality of the environment' as well as to 'discharges into the maritime area', without expressing any preference as to either approach. The contracting parties, which had already been unable to solve their differences on this question during the drafting of the Convention, chose to compromise once more by elaborating a formula which enabled both regulatory approaches to co-exist. At its first official meeting in 1978, the Paris Commission, on the grounds 'that there were insufficient data to make a conclusive comparison of the merits of the two approaches', endorsed the so-called 'dual approach', whereby it decided to set both UES and EQO, leaving it to individual contracting parties to decide which approach to adopt.[50] The 'dual approach' was originally intended as a temporary compromise solution. It was decided that the Commission would 'compare the consequences of both approaches for the marine environment, on the basis of measurements' and would review the decision after a period of five years.[51] The Commission also recommended that no new waste-brine chlor-alkali plants—the most polluting type of such plants—should be built.[52]

Once the Commission had decided on the 'dual approach' as the line of action to be followed, it still had to set the actual values of the UES and EQO. In doing so, it proceeded in what it itself termed a 'piece-meal fashion,'[53] adopting different UES for different types of chlor-alkali plants and setting different EQO for different components of the environment. Successive compromises were reached on partial aspects of the mercury pollution problem. In 1980, the Commission adopted a UES for brine-recirculation chlor-alkali plants to be applied by contracting parties from 1 July 1983, subject to agreement being reached before that date on a similar standard for waste-brine plants.[54] At the next meeting in 1981, the Commission indeed adopted limit values for discharges from waste-brine chlor-alkali plants, also to be applied by 1 July 1983.[55] One year later, the

[49] First Annual Report on the Activities of the Paris Commission, paras 12–13, in *First and Second Annual Reports on the Activities of the Paris Commission*, London, 1981, p 3. For a political analysis of the UES/EQO debate in the Paris Commission, see Skjaerseth (1999), pp 211–217.

[50] *Ibid*, para 15, p 4 & Annex III, p 23.

[51] *Ibid*, para 16.

[52] *Ibid*, Annex III, para (b).

[53] Second Annual Report on the Activities of the Paris Commission, para 12, in *First and Second Annual Reports on the Activities of the Paris Commission*, London, 1981, p 71.

[54] *Ibid*, para 13.

[55] *Third Annual Report on the Activities of the Paris Commission*, London, 1982, para 29, p 8.

Commission discussed whether the construction of new chlor-alkali plants using mercury cells should be prohibited altogether but could not reach agreement on such a decision. Instead it adopted a 'decision' which basically allows each contracting party to continue to freely determine its own policy in this regard. The decision in principle requires contracting parties only to grant authorisations for new chlor-alkali plants using mercury cells 'if such authorisations contain a reference to the standards corresponding to the best technical means available for preventing discharges of mercury' but at the same time allows parties to provide 'justification' to the Commission 'where for technical reasons the intended measures do not conform to the best technical means available.'[56] This 'decision' must be applied by contracting parties using the EQO approach as well as those using the UES approach,[57] but it is formulated sufficiently vaguely to accommodate as much national discretion as the 'dual approach' itself.

In fact, the Paris Commission merely endorsed the terms of the EEC Directive on mercury discharges by the chlor-alkali electrolysis industry, which had been adopted by the Council of the EC a few months earlier and contained exactly the same language on the use of 'best technical means available' in new plants.[58] The limit values for discharges in the EEC Directive were, in turn, based on those previously agreed within the Paris Commission. Thus the regulatory process in the Paris Commission was intertwined with that in the EEC and constrained by it. When the TWG in 1985 proposed more stringent limit values for existing brine-recirculation plants, the Commission could not adopt them in the form of a legally binding decision because of EEC objections on the grounds that the proposed new standards were more stringent than those in the EEC Directive. The new standards were merely recommended to contracting parties.[59] The Commission's early decisions on UES for mercury have remained unchanged to date.[60]

It proved equally difficult for the Commission to reach agreement on an EQO for mercury. The contracting parties differed on the question of how an EQO should be formulated: should it be expressed in terms of mercury concentrations in water, living organisms or sediments? When it agreed on the 'dual approach' in 1979, the Commission had requested the TWG to

[56] *Fourth Annual Report on the Activities of the Paris Commission*, London, 1983, para 8, p 2.

[57] *Ibid*, para 9.

[58] Council Dir 82/176/EEC of 22 March 1982 on limit values and quality objectives for mercury discharges by the chlor-alkali electrolysis industry, OJ No L81, 27.3.1982, p 29, Art 3, para 3.

[59] *Seventh Annual Report on the Activities of the Paris Commission*, London, 1985, para 43

[60] They are listed as still applicable within the framework of OSPAR Convention in a 1998 Secretariat paper. OSPAR Doc MMC 98/2/2–E, July 1998, Annex.

formulate proposals for quality objectives 'for organisms, as soon as possible for water and, if appropriate, for sediments.'[61] However, at the next meeting the Commission could only adopt an EQO expressed in terms of mercury concentrations in fish flesh. The TWG had been 'unable to make progress on an environmental standard for water or on whether an environmental standard for sediments was appropriate'. As a substitute for such standards, the Commission chose to endorse a 'standstill principle' for mercury concentrations in water 'as an interim step.'[62] What was supposed to be an 'interim step' has effectively remained a final step. When the Commission again considered the issue in 1979, it did not take any decision other than to keep the matter 'under review', on the grounds that there was 'a lack of sufficient scientific and technical data to set an environmental standard for water.'[63]

As a consequence, the only standard that the parties applying the EQO approach are bound to comply with remained the standard for mercury concentrations in fish flesh. According to the terms of the 1978 Commission decision, they do not have to apply the UES set by the Commission if they can 'prove' that the fish flesh standard is 'being met and continuously maintained throughout the area which might be affected by the discharges'. Some parties felt that the 'dual approach', in the absence of fully elaborated EQO for water, introduced an imbalance in terms of the parties' obligations under the Convention. France, for instance, objected to the lack of progress in setting EQO, on the grounds that there was no equivalence between the UES approach and the EQO approach as long as no standards were set for water and sediments in addition to those for living organisms.[64]

Even the application of the 'standstill' principle as an 'interim step' proved controversial. There was disagreement among the parties as to whether all contracting parties should have the obligation to respect this principle. While the Netherlands pointed out that this principle was already contained in Article 6, paragraph 1 (b) of the Convention, and Portugal and the UK insisted that it should be applied by all contracting parties, France expressed its opposition to a general 'standstill' obligation on the grounds that the principle should apply only to contracting parties applying the EQO approach.[65] In fact, the discussion on the EQO for mercury

[61] First Annual Report on the Activities of the Paris Commission, Annex III, para (c), in *First and Second Annual Reports on the Activities of the Paris Commission*, London, 1981, p 23.

[62] Second Annual Report on the Activities of the Paris Commission, paras 15–16, in *First and Second Annual Reports on the Activities of the Paris Commission*, London, 1981, p 71.

[63] *Fourth Annual Report on the Activities of the Paris Commission*, London, 1982, p 3, para 13.

[64] *Ibid*, para 14.

[65] *Third Annual Report on the Activities of the Paris Commission*, London, 1982, paras 35–37, p 10.

was symptomatic of the minimalist interpretation given by some contracting parties to their obligation under Article 4 of the Convention to 'eliminate' mercury pollution. It is significant that it proved impossible to reach unanimous agreement on the principle that mercury concentrations in water should not be allowed to increase anywhere in the Convention area, a principle which falls far short of the undertaking to 'eliminate' pollution by mercury and is already explicitly laid down in Article 6 of the Convention itself.

When the 'dual approach' was first adopted by the Commission in 1978, it was conceived as a temporary solution which was to be re-evaluated after five years, based on an assessment of the respective effectiveness of the UES and EQO approaches in terms of their consequences for the marine environment. While extensive discussions on the comparative merits of both approaches continued within PARCOM, these discussions never actually led to any formal change in Commission policy. In 1983, the first review effort concluded that the available data were insufficient to compare the consequences of the two approaches and that both should therefore 'continue to be permitted at least until a proper evaluation has been made at an appropriate future time.'[66] A second review effort was conducted by an *ad hoc* working group specifically established for the purpose of evaluating the EQO and UES approaches in 1984. Although this group actually showed that the parties applying the UES approach had achieved substantially greater reductions in mercury emissions from the chlor-alkali industry than those applying the EQO approach, ie that the UES approach was more effective than the EQO approach in terms of reducing pollution,[67] the Commission, at its 1985 meeting, chose not to draw any political conclusions from this embarrassing finding, instead confining itself to 'noting' the diverging views of contracting parties and calling for additional data to be submitted.[68] The 'dual approach' policy was never formally revoked, but quietly abandoned in the wake of the London North Sea conference and the resulting consensus on a precautionary approach to toxic pollutants, as we shall see below. The Commission implicitly recognised its inability to bring the scientific review effort to its logical conclusion by acknowledging that the controversy about UES versus EQO, although presented as a scientific and technical controversy, was in fact eminently political and based on different philosophies of risk assessment:

[66] *Fifth Annual Report on the Activities of the Paris Commission*, London, 1984, para 35, p 26.

[67] The group noted inter alia that chlor-alkali plants situated in continental countries applying the UES approach, with a combined production capacity 3 times greater than plants in the United Kingdom, discharged 3 times less mercury. PARCOM Doc 7/13/1–E, June 1985, para 7.6.5.

[68] *Ibid*, paras 7.5, 7.7 & 7.8. See Skjaerseth (1999), pp 213–214.

Contracting Parties have different views on what is 'acceptable risk'. Decisions on what is acceptable are not only based on scientific evaluation but are *ultimately the subject of political decisions*.[69]

Since 1985, the Paris Commission has adopted one further decision relating to the control of mercury emissions from the chlor-alkali industry, this time focusing on *atmospheric* emissions, which were found also to constitute a significant source of indirect mercury inputs into the marine environment. PARCOM Decision 90/3 on the reduction of atmospheric emissions from existing chlor-alkali plants sets a binding standard for atmospheric emissions of mercury which existing plants '*shall* be required to meet by 31 December 1996 . . . *unless* there is a firm commitment that the plant will be converted to mercury-free technology by the year 2000'. Furthermore, the contracting parties '*recommend* that existing mercury cell chlor-alkali plants be phased out *as soon as practicable*. The objective is that they *should* be phased out completely by 2010.'[70]

The wording of the 'decision', which, in view of its somewhat hybrid nature might perhaps more appropriately be called a 'decision-recommendation,'[71] is taken *verbatim* from the Hague North Sea Declaration,[72] with the significant difference that the phrase 'should be required' in the paragraph relating to emission standards has been replaced by 'shall be required', as is indeed more appropriate for a legally binding decision. However, the Commission was apparently unable to confer the same 'added value' to the more substantive paragraph on the *phase-out* of mercury-cell technology by adopting the same imperative form and removing all qualifications. It should also be noted that, according to the record of the meeting, the EC 'adopted the Decision subject to approval by the Council of Ministers.'[73]

While most of the Commission's work regarding pollution by mercury has focused on the chlor-alkali industry, which was singled out as responsible for 40 per cent of total mercury inputs in the marine environment,[74] measures with respect to other land-based sources of mercury pollution have also been adopted. When it adopted its first decision on emissions from the chlor-alkali industry in 1978, the Commission already stressed that 'members should have regard to the importance of reducing mercury discharges from all sources.'[75] However, this question was essentially left at the

[69] PARCOM Doc 7/13/1–E, para 7.4.4. (emphasis added).

[70] PARCOM Decision 90/3 on reducing atmospheric emissions from existing chlor-alkali plants, 14 June 1990, PARCOM Doc 12/13/1–E, Annex 8 (emphasis added).

[71] To use a term invented by the Organization for Economic Cooperation and Development.

[72] Hague Declaration, Annex 1B, part (a). See below.

[73] PARCOM Doc 12/13/1, June 1990, para 5.42. To date, the EU Council has not yet taken any formal decision to approve PARCOM Decision.

[74] *Les Commissions d'Oslo et de Paris: La première décennie*, London, 1984, p 28.

[75] First Annual Report on the Activities of the Paris Commission, Annex III, para (h), in *First and Second Annual Reports on the Activities of the Paris Commission*, London, 1981, p 24.

discretion of each contracting party. In 1982, the Commission again urged contracting parties to 'assess the possibilities of taking action' at the national level with respect to a number of sources of mercury pollution,[76] but no joint action in the form of 'programmes or measures' was envisaged until 1985. The first formal decision of the Commission prescribing specific measures in respect of other land-based sources of mercury pollution was taken in 1985, but only after agreement on the subject had already been reached within the EEC. PARCOM Decision 85/1 merely reproduces verbatim the provisions of Directive 84/156/EEC.[77]

Having first concentrated its activities on industrial point sources of mercury, the Paris Commission later decided that joint action was also required with respect to diffuse sources. At its 1989 meeting, the Commission adopted a recommendation 'on programmes and measures for reducing mercury discharges from various sources,'[78] which is intended to deal with those sources of mercury pollution, like agrochemicals, electrical equipment, dentistry and laboratories, which are not already covered by the earlier Commission decisions relating to the chlor-alkali industry and other mercury-emitting industrial sectors. Every single concrete measure in this recommendation is qualified by phrases like 'where suitable alternatives are available', 'where practicable', 'whenever suitable replacements are available at comparable cost', 'where appropriate and where excessive cost can be avoided'—phrases which leave almost total discretion to the contracting parties in deciding what action to take. As such, the 1989 recommendation is not a radical departure from the Commission's earlier exhortations to contracting parties to consider taking national measures.

A proposal for a binding decision on the reduction of mercury discharges from batteries failed to be adopted by the Commission at the same meeting due to 'waiting reservations' expressed by EEC member states.[79] The proposal was then submitted to contracting parties for a written vote but again failed to obtain the three quarter majority vote required by Article 18, paragraph 3 of the Convention.[80] The Commission considered the matter again at its 1990 meeting, where the scope of the discussion was expanded to include cadmium, another black list metal which is also used in batteries. Finally, the Commission 'accepted in principle' a decision on 'programmes and measures for mercury and cadmium containing batteries'[81] which prescribes a set of recovery and disposal measures for batteries and prohibits

[76] *Fourth Annual Report on the Activities of the Paris Commission*, London, 1982, p 3, para 16.

[77] Council Dir 84/156/EEC of 8 March 1984 on limit values and quality objectives for mercury discharges by sectors other than the chlor-alkali electrolysis industry, OJ No L74, 17.3.1984, p 49.

[78] PARCOM Recommendation 89/3, PARCOM Doc 11/9/1–E, June 1989, Annex 8.

[79] PARCOM Doc 11/9/1-E, June 1989, para 4.26 & Annex 7.

[80] PARCOM Doc TWG 17/20/1–E, March 1990, para 5.1.

[81] PARCOM Decision 90/2 on programmes and measures for mercury and cadmium containing batteries, 14 June 1990, PARCOM Doc 12/13/1–E, Annex 6.

the marketing of certain mercury-containing batteries. The decision could not be formally adopted due to 'waiting reservations' entered by the United Kingdom and the EC, which was in the process of elaborating its own Directive on the subject.

The UK has meanwhile lifted its reservation, but the EC informed the Paris Commission at its 1991 meeting that the Community's reservation could only be lifted by a formal decision of the EC Council of Ministers due to 'discrepancies' between PARCOM Decision 90/2 and the EEC Directive on batteries adopted in March 1991.[82] This example again illustrates how the decision-making process within the Paris Commission is often subordinated, not only implicitly but even explicitly, to that of the EC. The European Commission never made any proposals to the Council for measures to remove the 'discrepancies' it saw between PARCOM Decision and Directive 91/157/EEC, in order to enable the Community to lift its reservation.[83]

Since 1991, the Paris Commission has adopted only one further measure to address other diffuse sources of mercury pollution. PARCOM Recommendation 93/2 provides that special equipment should be installed in dental practices before 1 January 1997 to separate mercury-containing amalgam from waste water and enable the collection of such amalgam and thus to ensure its environmentally sound disposal.[84] However, three contracting parties—France, Portugal and Spain—entered formal reservations to this recommendation,[85] which is in fact the result of the consideration by the Paris Commission of a list of possible 'product control measures' adopted by the Hague North Sea Conference in 1990.[86] Other restrictions on the use and discharge of mercury were considered by PARCOM in 1993 and at subsequent meetings, but the Commission eventually decided in 1996 not to adopt a draft recommendation on this issue which had been elaborated by its subsidiary bodies because 'there was very little added value to be derived' by adopting it and 'this was clearly an area of EU competence.'[87] However, in a rather unusual move, PARCOM explicitly 'requested the EC to initiate appropriate actions, in line with the Esbjerg declaration, with a view to limiting effectively the marketing and use' of certain batteries, thermometers, leg bands and

[82] PARCOM Doc 13/9/1-E, June 1991, para 4.23. Cf Council Dir 91/157/EEC of 18 Mar 1991 on batteries and accumulators containing certain dangerous substances, OJ No L78, 26.3.1991, p 38.

[83] Though the EC reservation is not mentioned in a 1995 overview document (OSPAR Doc 95/15/1–E, June 1995, Annex 10), no trace can be found in the summary records of PARCOM and OSPAR meetings since 1991 of any formal withdrawal of this reservation.

[84] PARCOM Recommendation 93/2 on further restrictions on the discharge of mercury from dentistry, OSPAR Doc 15/13/1–E, June 1993, Annex 10.

[85] OSPAR Doc 15/13/1–E, June 1993, para 4.38.

[86] See Hague Declaration, Annex 1B, Part (b).

[87] OSPAR Doc 96/17/1–E, June 1996, para 3.75.

executive toys containing mercury.[88] No such action has yet been taken by the EC.

Cadmium

The Paris Commission has shown even greater indecision in dealing with cadmium, the second heavy metal on the black list, than with mercury. A Working Group on Cadmium Pollution was set up in the early 1980s to propose measures for consideration by the Commission. It was only in 1984 that the Commission adopted a first set of recommendations on the subject, which are noteworthy only as an indicator of the problem areas, but not for their specificity in terms of actual action to address those problem areas. The Commission in fact recognised implicitly that the most effective way of eliminating cadmium pollution was to substitute other materials for cadmium in those industrial applications which are the greatest sources of cadmium pollution. But it stopped short of actually making a firm recommendation to that effect, let alone a legally binding decision. In 1984 the Commission chose to leave action in this field at the discretion of individual contracting parties and merely recommended that they 'should take into account the scope which exists for the substitution of cadmium by other materials particularly in the fields of electroplating, pigments and stabilizers.'[89] Nor did the Commission recommend specific measures to deal with cadmium in batteries other than calling for research into substitutes and requesting contracting parties to report on national recycling programmes. No joint measures were envisaged at that time.

In 1985, when the Commission adopted a first legally binding decision on cadmium, it emphasised end-of-pipe pollution controls at the expense of cadmium substitution. PARCOM Decision 85/2 on 'programmes and measures on limit values and quality objectives for cadmium discharges' is based on the same 'dual approach' as the Commission decisions with respect to mercury discharges and reproduces *verbatim* the provisions of an earlier EEC Directive.[90] It sets emission standards for industrial cadmium producers and users as well as environmental quality objectives for waters affected by their discharges. The industries regulated include manufacturers of stabilisers and pigments as well as electroplating, precisely those industries for which the Commission had recognised the 'scope' for cadmium substitution. By setting emission standards for those industries based on end-of-pipe effluent treatment rather than cadmium

[88] *Ibid*, para 3.76.

[89] Paris Commission, *Procedures and Decisions Manual*, C8/88–E, 2/13, para 2.

[90] Council Dir 83/153/EEC of 26 Sept 1983 on limit values and quality objectives for cadmium discharges, OJ No L291, 24.10.1983, p 1.

substitution, the Commission actually legitimated continued cadmium pollution.

It was only six years after the initial recognition of the problem of cadmium in batteries that the Commission managed to agree on measures to address this problem. In 1990 the Commission 'accepted in principle' a decision which provides for a number of technical and information measures to promote the separate collection and recycling of cadmium contained in batteries. However, the wording of the decision is rather non-committal with respect to the objectives to be achieved. The contracting parties merely agree to '*aim for* the collection and recycling of all batteries larger than 500g and for the collection of at least 80 per cent of smaller batteries' and to 'promote the development and use of cadmium-free batteries and accumulators.'[91]

The Paris Commission has made little progress since 1984 on measures for the substitution of cadmium in industrial processes. It refrained from adopting a draft decision on the phasing out of cadmium use at its 1990 meeting 'because of divergences of opinion especially over the kind of approach to be used.'[92] It appeared that many contracting parties, especially the EC and some of its member states, were still unwilling to accept the principle of a general cadmium phase-out and were only prepared to consider banning particular cadmium applications as and when they regard it as technically and economically feasible. The Scandinavian countries, in particular, expressed their strong disappointment at the Commission's indecision. It should be noted that Sweden banned the use of cadmium for surface treatment, as well as in pigments and stabilisers, as long ago as 1979.[93] Though PARCOM recognised 'that further substantial reductions of cadmium emissions could not be achieved without reducing emissions from processes and products', it admitted its impotence by further deferring to EC initiative in the field.[94] As it happened, in June 1991 the EC Council did in fact adopt a directive banning the use of cadmium in a number of industrial applications,[95] including its use as a colouring agent in various plastic products and paints, as a stabiliser in PVC products, and for the coating of certain metallic products, subject to a variety of safety-related exceptions. These prohibitions were to come into effect gradually at different dates between 1992 and 1995. Following the adoption of this directive, PARCOM decided at its 1992 meeting that, in view of the EC legislation and of the fact that the non-EC contracting parties to the Paris Convention 'had adopted regulations which were at least as strict', there

[91] PARCOM Decision 90/2 on programmes and measures for mercury and cadmium containing batteries, 14 June 1990, PARCOM Doc 12/13/1–E, Annex 6 (emphasis added).

[92] PARCOM Doc 12/13/1–E, June 1990, para 5.33.

[93] *Ibid*, para 5.34.

[94] *Ibid*, para 5.35.

[95] Council Dir 91/338/EEC of 18 June 1991, OJ No L186, 12.7.1991, p 59.

was no need for it to pursue its regulatory efforts in this field 'for the time being.'[96]

It should be noted that the same year, notwithstanding a reservation from Spain, the ministerial-level meeting of the Oslo and Paris Commissions adopted a PARCOM Recommendation[97] which defines what constitutes best available technology (BAT) for the electroplating industry, a major source of emissions of cadmium and other heavy metals into the aquatic environment. This recommendation provides that 'waste water should only be discharged if its volume and pollutant load are kept at low levels' through a number of measures, such as, inter alia, the substitution of cadmium as a process agent by less hazardous substances 'if technically possible.'[98] However, the contracting parties implicitly recognised that such substitution was not always 'possible', as the recommendation also lays down requirements for the treatment of waste water from electroplating processes, including a limit value of 0.2 mg/l for the concentration of cadmium in 'specific waste water streams.'[99] Given the 1991 EEC ban on the use of cadmium for the electroplating of certain products, the effect of the 1992 PARCOM Recommendation on cadmium emissions from the electroplating industry will be limited to those applications which are not covered by that ban.

Organohalogen Compounds

The Paris Commission has so far failed to draw up anything like a comprehensive programme to eliminate land-based pollution by chlorinated organic compounds. The first efforts to deal with organohalogen compounds in a generic manner were made in the late 1980s, when the Commission started developing measures to address discharges of chlorinated organic compounds from the pulp and paper industry. Before then, the Paris Commission had taken decisions only concerning a few individual substances belonging to this group. These measures were all very narrow in their scope and sometimes rather ambiguous in their formulation.

Even before the Paris Convention entered into force, it was widely recognised that the so-called 'drins', a group of persistent organochlorine pesticides, constituted a serious threat to the marine environment. As early as its first meeting, the Commission considered the problem of marine pollution from these substances and recommended:

[96] PARCOM Doc 14/10/1–E, Sept 1992, para 3.5.

[97] PARCOM Recommendation 92/4 on the reduction of emissions from the electroplating industry, Sept 1992, in: *Paris Ministerial Meeting Proceedings*, *o.c.*, above n 13, p 161.

[98] *Ibid*, para 3(a).

[99] *Ibid*, para 4.2.

that aldrin, dieldrin and endrin should all be phased out of use *as soon as ecologically less harmful substitutes were available for each of the present uses of these substances.*[100]

The wording of this non-binding recommendation left considerable room for interpretation and for discussion as to the availability of 'ecologically less harmful substitutes'. In fact, reports of later Commission meetings show that contracting parties differed as to the feasibility and 'ecological harmlessness' of using particular substitutes.[101]

Little substantive progress was made over the years, notwithstanding the adoption in 1985 of a binding decision providing 'that all Contracting Parties will phase out the use of aldrin, dieldrin and endrin *as soon as practicable*.'[102] This decision is not only just as vaguely worded as the earlier recommendation but is even further qualified by a statement in the report of the meeting to the effect that:

those Contracting Parties which *had not yet agreed* to phase out the uses of aldrin, dieldrin and endrin expressed *their determination* to do so and would *continue their efforts to find acceptable substitutes.*[103]

This statement makes clear that, notwithstanding their unanimous 'decision' to phase out aldrin, dieldrin and endrin, the parties to the Paris Convention intended to preserve their full discretion in determining *how soon* this phasing out would be considered 'practicable'. One may even ask whether a unanimous, legally binding phase-out decision was actually taken by the Paris Commission, since the report of the meeting explicitly notes that there are parties 'which [have] not yet agreed to phase out the uses' of the three substances in question but have only expressed their 'determination' to do so, conditional on the availability of 'acceptable substitutes'. No firm, unambiguous decision to set a deadline for the phase-out was ever taken by the Commission.[104] Moreover, both the 1978 recommendation and

[100] PARCOM Doc I/17/1, para 42(d) (emphasis added).

[101] *Cf Third Annual Report on the Activities of the Paris Commission*, London, 1982, para 28, p 8.

[102] PARCOM Doc 7/13/1, June 1985, para 6.10 (emphasis added).

[103] *Ibid* (emphasis added).

[104] In fact, the 1978 PARCOM recommendation on phasing out drins was even explicitly *revoked* by OSPAR in 1998, presumably because parties felt it was no longer relevant in view of the fact that those pesticides are no longer produced. See OSPAR Decision 98/1 concerning the status of decisions, recommendations and other agreements adopted under the former Oslo Convention and Paris Convention within the framework of OSPAR Convention, 23 July 1998, OSPAR Doc MMC 98/2/1/–E. In the European Community, the *marketing* of drins was banned for virtually all uses by Council Dir 79/117/EEC of 21 Dec 1978 prohibiting the placing on the market and use of plant protection products containing certain active substances, OJ No L 33, 8.2.1979, p 36. Their *production* has now also been banned by the Protocol to the 1979 ECE Convention on Long-Range Transboundary Air Pollution on Persistent Organic Pollutants, signed in Aarhus on 24 June 1998, UN Doc EB.AIR/1998/2, 31 Mar 1998, Art 3, para 1(a) & Annex I.

the 1985 decision referred only to phasing out the use, but not the *production*, of drins.

Another group of chlorinated organic compounds identified early on as particularly hazardous to the marine environment are PCBs and PCTs, yet it took the Commission years to agree on a phase-out schedule. In 1983, the Commission first recommended that 'all Contracting Parties should take measures to phase out the use of PCBs and PCTs in new equipment'. The following year, a 'declaration of intent' was adopted in which 'the Commission agrees that the use of PCBs and PCTs in new equipment shall be prohibited as from 1 July 1985', but the adoption of a formal, legally binding decision to this effect was deferred.[105] As a matter of fact, such a formal decision was never taken because of parallel negotiations within the EEC which eventually led to the adoption of an EEC Directive.[106] In 1986, the Paris Commission decided that it would 'not be profitable' to elaborate a formal legal instrument due to the adoption of the EEC Directive.[107] Thus PARCOM again allowed its regulatory work to be pre-empted by that of the EEC.

The problem of phasing out *existing* uses of PCBs and PCTs, as opposed to their use in new equipment, remained on the agenda of the Paris Commission for a much longer time. In 1983, the Commission had agreed that 'Contracting Parties should be encouraged to embark at once upon plans for phasing out their use,'[108] but it took until 1990 before agreement could be reached on a formal decision setting a deadline for this phase-out. PARCOM Decision 90/4 lays down different timeframes for North Sea riparian states, in accordance with a political agreement reached at the Third North Sea Ministerial Conference in The Hague, and for the other contracting parties to the Paris Convention.[109] In doing so, the Commission gave effect to the political agreement reached at its 1988 meeting and recognised that these contracting parties may have 'different needs' and that 'different measures' and 'different timetables for compliance' may be appropriate for them. In this case, the political agreement on the phasing out of PCBs reached at the Hague Conference appears

[105] Paris Commission, *Procedures and Decisions Manual*, C6/89, 3/4.

[106] Dir 85/467/EEC of 1 Oct 1985, OJ No L269, 11.10.1985, p 56. This directive prohibited all use of PCBs and PCTs throughout the Community from 1 July 1986, except where 'solely intended, in the normal conditions of maintenance of equipment, to supplement the level of liquids containing PCBS in properly functioning existing plant' purchased prior to its entry into force.

[107] Paris Commission, *Procedures and Decisions Manual*, C6/89–E, 4/4.

[108] *Ibid*, 2/4.

[109] PARCOM Decision 90/4 on the phasing out of PCBs, 14 June 1990, PARCOM Doc 12/13/1–E, Annex 11. According to this decision, PCBs are to be phased out 'by 1995 and the end of 1999 at the latest' for Iceland and the riparian states of the North Sea and 'by 2005 and by the end of 2010 at the latest' for the other contracting parties of the Convention.

to have been instrumental in breaking an earlier stalemate in the Paris Commission.[110]

Apart from the measures relating to drins, PCBs and PCTs, which address pollution from diffuse sources through product control measures, the Commission has also taken a few measures concerning discharges of organohalogen pollutants from industrial point sources. The first such measure was the decision taken by the Commission at its 8th meeting in 1986, whereby it 'adopted' the standards laid down in the 1984 EEC directive on HCH[111] through a 'simplified procedure'. At that meeting, Sweden said it was 'favourable to the adoption by the Paris Commission of the basic principles and the limit values of EEC Directives which are relevant to its work' and suggested that 'the non-EEC countries could adopt the measures of the relevant EEC Directive by a simplified procedure consisting of a declaration of acceptance in the summary record of the meeting.'[112]

The Commission agreed on the 'simplified procedure' and Sweden and Norway, at that time the only two non-EC members of the Paris Commission, subsequently made a formal statement, recorded in the minutes of the meeting, to the effect that 'they accepted *the basic principles and the limit values* specified in EEC Directive 84/491/EEC on hexachlorocyclohexane.'[113] These limit values apply to discharges from plants producing HCH and its derivative lindane. Ironically, the report of the meeting explicitly recognises the purely symbolic significance of the Paris Commission 'decision', noting that: 'The actual environmental improvement resulting from the adoption of the measures for hexachlorocyclohexane (HCH), however, was likely to be low, since the non-EEC countries have no production of HCH.'[114]

In the late 1980s, PARCOM started addressing the issue of emissions of organochlorine compounds into the aquatic environment from the paper pulp industry. These emissions result from the use of chlorine as a bleaching agent in pulp production. Chlorine reacts with the organic substances in the wood used as raw material for the production of paper pulp and thus forms a variety of chlorinated organic compounds, including highly toxic ones such as dioxins, which are discharged with the effluent from pulp mills.

110 When consensus could not be reached on a similar draft decision at the 1989 meeting of the Commission, the chairman, referring to the then forthcoming Hague Ministerial Conference, concluded that the question of phasing out existing PCB uses 'would require a decision at a higher political level'. See PARCOM Doc 11/9/1–E, June 1989, para 4.72.

111 Council Dir 84/491/EEC of 9 Oct 1984 on limit values and quality objectives for discharges of hexachlorocyclohexane, OJ No L274, 17.10.1984, p 11.

112 PARCOM Doc 8/12/1–E, June 1986, paras 4.7–4.8.

113 *Ibid*, para 4.9 (emphasis added). It is somewhat unclear exactly *what* Sweden and Norway accepted: all the provisions of Dir 84/491/EEC, or only the limit values for emission standards? What are the 'basic principles' of the Directive? Did Sweden and Norway also accept the quality objectives for HCH laid down in the Directive? Overall, the legal formulation and precision of Paris Commission 'decisions' leaves much to be desired.

114 PARCOM Doc 8/12/1–E, June 1986, para 4.7.

Thus the pulp and paper industry is a major source of inputs of organohalogens in the riverine and marine environment.

The first PARCOM decision on the subject was adopted at the first Commission meeting following the Third North Sea Conference in The Hague, which had formulated recommendations on the reduction of emissions from the pulp and paper sector. Decision 90/1 'on the reduction of discharges of chlorinated organic substances from the production of bleached kraft pulp and sulphite pulp'[115] was of particular significance, both legally and politically. For the first time in its history, the Paris Commission actually adopted a binding decision by a three-quarter majority vote of its members, pursuant to Article 18, paragraph 3 of the Convention, instead of by consensus. The decision was adopted against the dissenting vote of three contracting parties, France, Norway and Portugal,[116] who, as provided in Article 18, paragraph 3, are not bound by it. Decision 90/1 was also politically significant in that the Paris Commission actually went *beyond* what was agreed at the Hague North Sea Conference, by setting a more stringent limit value for discharges from the bleaching of softwood kraft pulp than recommended by that Conference.[117] This is ostensibly why France and Norway refused to accept the decision, invoking the need to 'consider its technical implications'.[118]

The 1990 PARCOM decision set emission limit values which 'the discharges of chlorinated organic substances *should* not, *as an annual average*, exceed'. These limit values, which were explicitly labelled 'a first step', were to be complied with 'immediately' for any new mills, while existing mills were required to comply from 1 January 1995.[119] The decision also recommended a limit on the amount of chlorine which may be used in the bleaching process, in order specifically to reduce the formation of dioxins and furans, a related group of toxic organochlorine compounds.[120]

The 1990 decision was soon to be superseded, however, by a new PARCOM decision, adopted at the 1992 ministerial-level meeting,[121] which

[115] PARCOM Decision 90/1 on the reduction of discharges of chlorinated organic substances from the production of bleached kraft pulp and sulphite pulp, 14 June 1990, PARCOM Doc 12/13/1–E, Annex 5.

[116] PARCOM Doc 12/13/1–E, June 1990, para 5.16.

[117] See Hague Declaration, Annex 1B, part (a).

[118] PARCOM Doc 12/13/1–E, June 1990, para 5.15.

[119] PARCOM Decision 90/1, above n 115, para 1 (emphasis added). The use of the verb 'should' instead of 'shall' is puzzling, since it clearly seems to have been the intention of the Commission to adopt a binding decision, given the reference to Art 18 of the Convention and the voting procedure used. Moreover, the standards set by the decision are further qualified by the provision that contracting parties may use 'any other equivalent limit value if more suitable parameter(s) have been identified'. With respect to the 'annual average', it is specified that this 'should, as a minimum, be based on one analysis a month'.

[120] PARCOM Decision 90/1, above n 115, para 3.

[121] PARCOM Decision 92/1 on the reduction of discharges of chlorinated organic substances from the production of bleached kraft and sulphite pulp, Sept 1992, in: *Paris Ministerial Meeting Proceedings*, *o.c.*, above n 13, p 132.

postponed the dates of entry into force of the standards for both new and existing mills until 1 January 1993 and 1 January 1996, respectively. It should nevertheless be noted that PARCOM Decision 92/1 did actually further specify and tighten the limits on the use of molecular chlorine in new installations, although it failed to transform the recommendatory language of the 'decision' into mandatory language.[122] This time, Norway voted in favour of the decision, but France and Portugal confirmed their earlier reservations and, surprisingly, were joined by the EEC, as the European Commission also entered a formal reservation on behalf of the Community.[123]

Since 1992, the Paris Commission has continued its work on the reduction of emissions from the pulp and paper industry. At its 1994 meeting, it adopted two separate recommendations on BAT and best environmental practice (BEP) for the two main paper pulp production processes, the sulphite process and kraft process.[124] Both recommendations list a set of technical measures and operational practices which the parties deem should be regarded as BAT and BEP for both sectors. The use of these measures—which are formulated as process standards rather than emission limit values and are designed to limit both aquatic and atmospheric emissions not only of organohalogens but of other pollutants as well[125]—'or equally effective measures' is recommended to all contracting parties. The use of chlorine as a bleaching agent is not explicitly addressed. A footnote to both recommendations states that this matter is 'dealt with' in PARCOM Decision 92/1, thus indicating that the 1994 recommendations are intended as complementary to this earlier decision. Both recommendations do, however,

[122] Again, the language used is equivocal. Paras 1 and 2 use the 'should' form, but para 3 then goes on to state that the 'objectives' in both these paras 'shall' apply or be attained by a certain date.

[123] PARCOM Doc 14/10/1–E, Sept 1992, para 5.11.

[124] PARCOM Recommendation 94/2 on best available techniques and best environmental practice for the integrated and non-integrated sulphite paper pulp industry, OSPAR Doc 16/13/1–E, June 1994, Annex 6; PARCOM Recommendation 94/3 on best available techniques and best environmental practice for the integrated and non-integrated kraft pulp industry, *ibid*, Annex 7.

[125] It should be noted that, in 1995, PARCOM further supplemented its Decision 92/1 and Recommendations 94/2 and 94/3 with two decisions setting emission limit values for discharges of organic substances and suspended solids in effluent and atmospheric emissions of sulphur dioxide, other gaseous sulphur compounds and nitrogen oxides from existing and new sulphite and kraft pulp mills. These limit values are formulated in mandatory terms, but as they are not directly relevant to organohalogen emissions they will not be further analysed here. Reservations were entered by the EC, France and Portugal. *See* PARCOM Decision 95/2 on discharge and emission limit values for the integrated and non-integrated sulphite paper pulp industry, June 1995, OSPAR Doc 95/15/1–E, Annex 7; PARCOM Decision 95/3 on discharge and emission limit values for the integrated and non-integrated kraft pulp industry, *ibid*, Annex 8.

contain a general clause worded as follows:

> The principle of substitution should be followed. This principle means that if there is a choice between different products the one which is less hazardous to man and the environment should be used.[126]

This clause could be interpreted as recommending the substitution of molecular chlorine by other, less hazardous bleaching agents. This may explain why the United Kingdom and France entered reservations to both recommendations.[127]

While Decision 92/1 stopped short of prohibiting the use of chlorine as a bleaching agent, but merely called for limitations on its use and on resulting emissions of organochlorine substances, and Recommendations 94/2 and 94/3 did not directly address the bleaching process, the Paris Commission took an additional step in 1996 by adopting PARCOM Decision 96/2 on the phasing-out of chlorine-based bleaching processes in the kraft and sulphite pulp industry, notwithstanding the reservations of France and Spain.[128] This decision provides that 'processes using molecular chlorine (Cl_2) in the bleaching of kraft and sulphite pulp *shall be phased-out*'. Though somewhat ambiguously worded, the requirement imposed on contracting parties by this decision seems to be that the use of chlorine processes shall be stopped in new mills as from 1 January 1997 and in existing mills one year later. Parties are not explicitly required to *prohibit* the use of such processes by legislative or administrative action but may also implement the decision through voluntary agreements concluded with industry.[129]

Another source of organohalogen emissions reaching the marine environment which was identified in the 1980s is the use of hexachloroethane (HCE) as a degasifier in the non-ferrous metal industry. At its 1992 ministerial-level meeting, the Paris Commission, having found that 'other systems and alternative substances already exist, capable of attaining similar, or even superior, technical efficiency and performance', adopted a decision according to which the contracting parties to the Paris Convention '*agree* that . . . all uses of hexachloroethane in the Secondary Aluminium Industry . . . *shall be phased out* by 31 December 1994.'[130] The use of HCE

[126] PARCOM Recommendation 94/2 on BAT and BEP for the integrated and non-integrated sulphite paper pulp industry, June 1994, OSPAR Doc 16/13/1–E, Annex 6, para 10; PARCOM Recommendation 94/3 on BAT and BEP for the integrated and non-integrated kraft pulp industry, June 1994, *ibid*, Annex 7, para 12.

[127] OSPAR Doc 16/13/1–E, June 1994, paras 3.21 & 3.22.

[128] PARCOM Decision 96/2 on the phasing-out of processes using molecular chlorine (Cl_2) in the bleaching of kraft and sulphite pulp, June 1996, OSPAR Doc 96/17/1–E, Annex 10.

[129] Cf *ibid*, Appendix ('Implementation Reporting Format').

[130] PARCOM Decision 92/4 on the phasing out of the use of hexachloroethane (HCE) in the secondary aluminium industry and in the primary aluminium industry with integrated foundries, Sept 1992, *Paris Ministerial Meeting Proceedings*, *o.c.*, above n 13, p 143 (emphasis added).

was also to be phased out in non-integrated aluminium casting foundries two years later. PARCOM Decision 93/1 extends the HCE phase-out to the entire non-ferrous metal industry by 31 December 1997, subject to one exception for the production of special magnesium alloys.[131]

These decisions are significant in that they not only restrict the use of a particular product, HCE, but also have the effect of prohibiting a particular degasification *process* which was widely used in the non-ferrous metal industry. In this respect they are quite similar to the 1996 PARCOM decision phasing-out the use of molecular chlorine as a bleaching agent in the pulp industry. The adoption of the HCE decisions by the Paris Commission was not unanimous. The EC accepted the 1992 decision only *ad referendum* and entered a formal reservation to the 1993 decision, together with Germany and the UK. The decisions raised problems relating to the respective competences of the EC and its member states, which will be further analysed below in chapter 9.

Similar measures to eliminate the use of particular organohalogen compounds in industry were taken at the 1995 meeting of PARCOM, which adopted a decision on the phasing out of short-chained chlorinated paraffins.[132] These substances are used for different purposes in the production of certain paints, coatings, sealants, metal working fluids, rubber, plastic and textiles, resulting in diffuse pollution of the marine environment from the use of these products. As chlorinated paraffins have been shown to be persistent in the aquatic environment and toxic to aquatic organisms, the Paris Commission, having found that 'less environmentally hazardous substitutes are available for most major applications of these chlorinated paraffins', decided that their use for the purposes in question is to be phased out by 31 December 1999, subject to an exception for two special applications for which they may continue to be used until 31 December 2004. However, the UK and Portugal objected to this decision and entered formal reservations to it. Again, conflicts of competence with the EC were invoked as an argument against PARCOM action, as the UK delegation argued that 'controls on the marketing and use [of chlorinated paraffins] were better addressed at the Community level.'[133] This question will be examined extensively in chapter 9.

As the above analysis has demonstrated, these few Paris Commission decisions concerning organohalogen compounds are very far from achieving the objective of eliminating land-based pollution by these substances as laid down in the 1974 Paris Convention. Until the early 1990s, PARCOM had taken measures only with respect to a small number of indi-

[131] PARCOM Decision 93/1 on the phasing out of the use of hexachloroethane (HCE) in the non-ferrous metal industry, June 1993, OSPAR Doc 15/13/1–E, Annex 7.

[132] PARCOM Decision 95/1 on the phasing out of short-chained chlorinated paraffins, June 1995, OSPAR Doc 95/15/1–E, Annex 6.

[133] OSPAR Doc 95/15/1–E, June 1995, para 4.29.

vidual substances or groups of substances and had failed to address diffuse-source pollution and pollution from industrial point sources in any coherent manner. It had refrained from regulating the *production* of any organohalogen compound and moved only hesitantly in regulating the *use* of particular compounds in industrial processes and products. In recent years, partly as a result of the influence of the North Sea Conferences, the Paris Commission started addressing industrial production processes causing important emissions of organohalogen pollutants in a more systematic and comprehensive fashion, starting with the pulp and paper industry, and then moving on to other sectors.

Industrial Sectors Approach

The integrated sector-oriented regulatory strategy which developed in the late 1980s and became dominant in the 1990s was not confined to sources of organohalogen emissions. The Commission's *Working Group on Industrial Sectors* (INDSEC), established on an *ad hoc* basis in 1988 and made permanent in 1989,[134] became the main forum for the elaboration of programmes and measures and started addressing pollution from industrial point sources in an integrated way, tackling all emissions and discharges of pollutants likely to contribute significantly to marine pollution, both via aquatic and atmospheric pathways.

The regulatory work of this group has focused on the development of draft recommendations and decisions fleshing out the general concept of BAT for particular industrial sectors. This is done on the basis of a comparative analysis of the various technologies and practices used under the jurisdiction of the contracting parties, in order to identify those that constitute the 'best available techniques', as first generally defined in PARCOM Recommendations 88/3[135] and 89/2[136] adopted under the 1974 Paris Convention and subsequently codified in Appendix 1 to the 1992 Paris Convention. The preparatory work is usually done by a contracting party that has volunteered to act as the 'lead country' for a particular industrial sector, ie to compile and analyse the information collected from all the parties and, based on this analysis, to elaborate proposals for consideration by INDSEC.

The working group has developed a practice of working in stages. The first stage is the 'definition' of BAT in a technical form: detailed technical descriptions of best available techniques are elaborated. Based on these

[134] PARCOM Doc 11/9/1–E, June 1989, para 4.8 and Annex 4.

[135] PARCOM Recommendation 88/3 as a first approach to the use of best available technology, June 1988. See below.

[136] PARCOM Recommendation 89/2 on the use of best available technology, June 1989. See below.

descriptions, draft recommendations on BAT for the sector in question are formulated by the INDSEC for adoption by the Commission. In a final stage, which is not always reached, emission limit values for aqueous discharges and atmospheric emissions, based on the agreed BAT, and time-scales for their implementation in new and existing plants, are proposed for adoption in the form of another formal recommendation or decision.[137]

When initially established, the Working Group on Industrial Sectors was given a mandate to review ten sectors which had been identified as requiring priority action in view of their contribution to marine pollution, but was also authorised to recommend other sectors for consideration by the Commission if appropriate.[138] The list of priority sectors was later extended following the Third North Sea Conference in 1990 and the Ministerial Meeting of the Oslo and Paris Commissions in 1992. Since the establishment of the INDSEC, a substantial number of PARCOM recommendations, but only a few decisions, on BAT for specific industrial sectors have been adopted. Most of them are of a highly technical nature, and it would be beyond the scope of this study to analyse them in detail. I shall only point out a number of general trends which seem to be relevant from a legal and political viewpoint.

A typical case is that of the iron and steel industry. At its 1990 and 1991 meetings, PARCOM adopted recommendations on the definition of BAT for, respectively, the secondary[139] and primary[140] iron and steel industry. These recommendations do not contain a single quantified target or standard. They merely list a series of technical measures which can and should be taken to prevent or reduce emissions in different kinds of iron and steel production processes and are deemed to 'constitute' BAT. Quite often those measures are not exclusively based on the best available option but also include, as an alternative, a 'second-best' option, to be applied if the first option is 'not possible'. Thus, for example, PARCOM Recommendation 91/2 provides that waste water from rinsing and gas treatment 'should preferably not be produced' but goes on to specify what measures are to be taken to recirculate and treat waste water 'if dry methods are not possible.'[141] Other recommended measures are qualified by open-ended language as 'whenever possible', 'as much as possible', 'if feasible', 'generally'[142] or use vague and surprisingly non-technical concepts like 'good

[137] For a description of this practice by the Chairman of INDSEC, see PARCOM Doc 12/13/1–E, June 1990, para 5.2.

[138] PARCOM Doc 11/9/1–E, June 1989, Annex 4, paras 1 & 2.

[139] PARCOM Recommendation 90/1 on the definition of the best available technology for secondary iron and steel plants, 14 June 1990, PARCOM Doc 12/13/1–E, Annex 4.

[140] PARCOM Recommendation 91/2 on the definition of best available technology in the primary iron and steel industry, 20 June 1991, PARCOM Doc 13/9/1–E, Annex 7.

[141] *Ibid*, para 3. See also para 13: 'Dry quenching is *preferred. If wet quenching is applied*, . . .' (emphasis added).

[142] *Ibid*, paras 1, 4, 5.

housekeeping.'[143] A draft decision concerning the limitation of emissions from secondary iron and steel production, which did contain a number of quantified standards for both atmospheric emissions and aqueous discharges, was not adopted due to lack of 'unanimous support.'[144] The Commission did, however, adopt a second recommendation calling for further studies to be carried out on possible pollution reduction measures in this sector.[145]

In subsequent years, the INDSEC continued its efforts to further specify the technical standards for emission reduction in the iron and steel industry. These efforts did not result in the adoption of any PARCOM decision, but only of three recommendations, the first applying to new installations for primary iron and steel production licensed after 1 January 1993,[146] the second to existing primary plants which were in operation before that date[147] and were to comply with the standards only from 1 January 2000, and the third to new secondary steel production plants built after 1 January 1993.[148] These recommendations do contain quantified emission standards for a number of processes and pollutants, but it is striking that in many respects they fall short of actually prescribing, even in recommendatory terms, the application of the BAT which PARCOM itself 'defined' in its Recommendation 91/2.

For example, where Recommendation 91/2 provides that dust emissions should be prevented by the use of fabric filters and that wet 'scrubbing should be avoided wherever possible', Recommendation 92/2 lays down 'general requirements' for the recirculation and treatment of 'waste water used for scrubbing'. Where the former Recommendation prescribes 'polycyclic aromatic hydrocarbon removal' for waste water from coke ovens, a major source of PAH emissions in the marine environment, the latter Recommendation fails to lay down an actual limit value for PAH discharges, as for other pollutants, but merely stipulates in a footnote that 'the PAH content of the effluent should also be controlled' and 'preferably' be limited to a particular concentration. Though Recommendation 91/2 recommends specific treatment methods for waste

[143] *Ibid*, para 11.

[144] PARCOM Doc 13/9/1–E, June 1991, para 4.55. It should be noted that lack of unanimity should not necessarily prevent the Commission from acting, since decisions can be adopted by a three-fourths majority vote of the contracting parties.

[145] PARCOM Recommendation 91/3 on measures to be taken and investigations to be carried out in order to reduce pollution from secondary iron and steel production, 20 June 1991, PARCOM Doc 13/9/1–E, Annex 9.

[146] PARCOM Recommendation 92/2 concerning limitation of pollution from new primary iron and steel production installations, September 1992, *Paris Ministerial Meeting Proceedings*, above n 13, p 149.

[147] PARCOM Recommendation 93/1 concerning limitation of pollution from existing primary iron and steel production installations, June 1993, OSPAR Doc 15/13/1–E, Annex 6.

[148] PARCOM Recommendation 92/3 concerning limitation of pollution from new secondary steel production and rolling mills, Sept 1992, *Paris Ministerial Meeting Proceedings*, above n 13, p 153.

water from blast furnaces,[149] no emission limit values are prescribed for these effluents in Recommendation 92/2, which simply provides that 'waste water discharges should be minimized.'[150] Efforts to prevent emissions of hazardous substances from secondary steel production mills by avoiding the presence of heavy metals and chlorinated compounds in steel scrap through 'upstream' measures[151] seem to have been abandoned, as PARCOM Recommendation 92/3 only provides for process and emission standards based on dust collection and waste water recirculation and treatment systems.

Similar recommendations 'defining' BAT for broad sectors of the chemical industry, such as the organic chemical industry and the pharmaceutical manufacturing industry, have been adopted in recent years. Their prescriptions are of such a level of generality that their normative value appears very limited. PARCOM Recommendation 92/5 'qualitatively describes'[152] BAT for the pharmaceutical industry, focusing on chemical synthesis and biological extraction processes. PARCOM Recommendation 94/4[153] applies to the organic chemical industry as a whole, defined as 'all production processes using chemical synthesis of derivatives of hydrocarbons', ranging from the production of commodity organic chemicals to the production of specialty chemicals. Both recommendations enumerate a set of preventive, in-process and add-on or 'end-of-pipe' measures for application in the chemical plants concerned. It is not always clear whether these measures are intended to be applied cumulatively or whether the recommendation merely provides a 'menu' from which industry and regulatory officials are free to choose the measures they consider most appropriate in their particular circumstances. Recommendation 92/5, however, does indicate in an explanatory note that the three categories of measures are 'classified according to decreasing sustainability, and hence according to decreasing preferability.'[154]

The preventive measures include general exhortations to the effect that 'those production processes should be selected that have the best environmental performance' and 'waste minimization programmes should be undertaken.'[155] The recommendations further list a series of in-process technical measures that can be taken to minimise emissions to water and air, such as, eg making processes and equipment 'as closed as

[149] PARCOM Recommendation 91/2, above n 140, para 17.
[150] PARCOM Recommendation 92/2, above n 146, para 9.
[151] This was the main thrust of PARCOM Recommendation 91/3, above n 145.
[152] PARCOM Recommendation 92/5 concerning best available technology in the pharmaceutical manufacturing industry, Sept 1992, *Paris Ministerial Meeting Proceedings*, above n 13, p 167, Explanatory note, para 1.
[153] PARCOM Recommendation 94/4 on best available techniques for the organic chemical industry, OSPAR Doc 16/13/1–E, June 1994, Annex 8.
[154] PARCOM Recommendation 92/5, above n 152, Explanatory note, para 3.
[155] PARCOM Recommendation 94/4, above n 153, paras 2 and 4.

possible'[156] by ensuring recirculation of water and in-process recovery of certain production residues. The end-of-pipe measures are aimed at adequate biological or chemical treatment of any effluents which cannot be avoided and environmentally sound recovery or disposal of any solid and liquid wastes generated.[157] Sometimes, specific techniques are recommended for the treatment of particular waste streams, but the prescriptive force of such provisions is qualified by a note specifying that 'where specific technologies are mentioned, the use of at least equally effective alternative technologies is not excluded.'[158]

For the purposes of our study, the most relevant provisions are those relating to preventive measures to reduce emissions of hazardous substances from the industrial processes concerned. PARCOM Recommendation 94/4 addresses the selection of 'auxiliary chemicals' such as solvents, catalysts and cleaning agents used in the organic chemical industry. It enunciates as a general principle that those auxiliary chemicals should be used which 'pose the least risk to the environment' and, more specifically, that 'the use of hazardous substances, in particular hazardous organohalogens, as auxiliary chemicals, should be avoided *or minimized*', avoidance being the preferred option for new processes.[159] A footnote specifies that the term 'hazardous substances' is to be understood as referring to the substances mentioned in Appendix 2 of the 1992 Paris Convention, 'with particular attention to substances that are toxic, persistent and liable to bio-accumulate'. Thus, the Recommendation indicates that measures to curb emissions of hazardous substances to the marine environment must start in the design stage of production processes. However, it leaves contracting parties and industry considerable discretion in identifying the least-risk auxiliary chemicals and in opting between avoidance and minimisation. Moreover, the Recommendation contemplates continued use of hazardous substances in the organic chemical industry, prescribing various in-process and 'end-of-pipe' measures to prevent or minimise emissions of such substances when they are used.

Similar provisions can be found in other BAT recommendations. The 1992 PARCOM Recommendation on the pharmaceutical industry does not refer to hazardous substances generally, but specifically provides that 'the use of *halogenated solvents* should be minimized *or eliminated*' in existing processes and that, 'for new products and processes, the use of halogenated *and aromatic* hydrocarbons should be *avoided* where possible.'[160] At the

[156] *Ibid*, para 6. Cf PARCOM Recommendation 92/5, above n 152, para 1.2.
[157] PARCOM Recommendation 94/4, above n 153, paras 6, 8, 9 and 11.
[158] PARCOM Recommendation 92/5, above n 152, Explanatory note, para 6.
[159] PARCOM Recommendation 94/4, above n 153, para 5(a) (emphasis added).
[160] PARCOM Recommendation 92/5, above n 152, para 1.1 (emphasis added). See also Explanatory note, para 4, which specifies that these recommendations apply only to the use of halogenated and aromatic hydrocarbons *as solvents*, not as reagents. The requirements for new plants are effective from 1 Jan 1994, while existing plants should be in compliance by 31 Dec 1998.

same meeting, PARCOM adopted a recommendation on BAT for the electroplating industry,[161] another major user of, and source of water and air pollution by, organic solvents, which enunciates as a general principle that 'the use of chlorinated solvents should be avoided as far as possible' and that such solvents 'should be replaced by water-based systems or non-halogenated organic solvents.'[162] Only where it is proved that substitution is technically not possible may specific chlorinated solvents[163] continue to be used for degreasing in enclosed systems, subject to adequate treatment of any waste gas and liquid effluents, for which specific emission limit values are recommended.[164]

By contrast, the 1994 BAT recommendations for the textile processing industry are much less specific; they only provide for 'banning of the use of *substitutable* hazardous or dangerous substances.'[165] As regards organic solvents, the technical description of BAT annexed to PARCOM recommendation, which lists 'concrete elements' whose application should be 'considered' by operators,[166] merely indicates that 'use of halogenated solvents *in open systems* should cease', except when used 'in small quantities' for specific cleaning purposes, and goes on to stress that such solvents 'should only be used when their overall environmental impact is considered less damaging than other methods for grease removal.'[167] This ambiguous wording seems intended to imply that the use of halogenated solvents in closed systems is still considered acceptable in some circumstances.

The recommendations and decisions on industrial pollution control adopted by the Paris Commission since the establishment of the INDSEC Working Group in 1988, and especially since the Third North Sea Conference in 1990, certainly represent a more comprehensive and integrated approach to the prevention of marine pollution from land-based activities than the earlier piecemeal approach focusing on emission limit values for discharges of particular substances into the aquatic environment from industrial point sources. However, the new approach has also resulted in a loss of focus and normative force, as the detailed technical 'descriptions' and 'definitions' of 'best available techniques', mostly contained in non-binding PARCOM recommendations, in the final analysis impose few cat-

[161] PARCOM Recommendation 92/4 on the reduction of emissions from the electroplating industry, *Paris Ministerial Meeting Proceedings*, above n 13, p 161.

[162] *Ibid*, para 2.1.

[163] The recommendation specifically lists three substances which are 'the only volatile chlorinated hydrocarbons which should be used' and stresses that 'the use of other halogenated solvents is not necessary for technical reasons'. *Ibid*, para 2.2.

[164] *Ibid*, para 2.2 *in fine*.

[165] PARCOM Recommendation 94/5 concerning best available techniques and best environmental practice for wet processes in the textile processing industry, June 1994, OSPAR Doc 16/13/1–E, Annex 9, setion 4, para A.1.

[166] *Ibid*, s 5.

[167] *Ibid*, Annex 1, s 2.1, para 15 (emphasis added).

egorical obligations on contracting parties. Also, the initial emphasis on addressing sources of black list substances seems lost or at least diluted in the comprehensiveness of the new focus on integrated pollution control.

In recent years, there has been a tendency to compensate this deficit in the actual normative output of PARCOM by a new political discourse on hazardous substances, materialising in increasing recourse to new kinds of instruments of a purely declaratory nature. This trend was initiated by the 1992 ministerial-level meeting of the Oslo and Paris Commissions, which, in addition to signing the new OSPAR Convention, also adopted a Final Declaration and endorsed an Action Plan, designed to be reviewed by the Commissions on an annual basis. These texts have been at the centre of the policy debate on toxics reduction at the annual meetings of PARCOM since 1992, a debate which culminated in the adoption of an 'OSPAR Strategy with regard to hazardous substances' by the ministerial meeting held in July 1998 to mark the long-awaited entry into force of OSPAR Convention.

In the following sections of this chapter on the evolution of the North Sea and North-East Atlantic land-based sources regime, I shall first examine the influence of another series of soft law instruments, the declarations adopted by the successive ministerial conferences of the North Sea states since 1984 and then analyse the provisions of the 1992 OSPAR Convention and the line of non-binding instruments spawned by the 1992 Paris meeting and their implications for future policies and normative efforts in the field of hazardous substances.

SOFT LAW TO THE RESCUE: THE INTERNATIONAL CONFERENCES ON THE PROTECTION OF THE NORTH SEA

Origin and Purpose of the North Sea Conference Process

In 1984, the Federal Republic of Germany took the initiative of convening, in Bremen, the first 'International Conference on the Protection of the North Sea' (INSC). The conference for the first time brought together in a single forum the ministers responsible for environmental protection of the riparian states of the North Sea, as well as the EC Commissioner responsible for environmental policy, specifically to discuss all policy issues related to the protection of the marine environment of the North Sea in a comprehensive manner. The conference was held outside any existing formal institutional framework.

Several factors seem to have motivated the German initiative. Despite the existence of a number of conventions covering the North Sea area and addressing sectoral aspects of the marine pollution problem, the measures taken in the framework of these conventions were not perceived as constituting an adequate and comprehensive response to the pollution problems of the North Sea.[168] The lack of a single, high-level political forum with a specific mandate to address North Sea issues was hampering the development of a coordinated policy. Moreover, the diverse nature of the contracting parties to the Oslo and Paris Conventions and the fact that they covered a wider geographical area than the North Sea proper made it rather difficult to use these instruments to conduct a policy tailored to the specific needs of a subregion such as the North Sea. It was felt that it would be easier to do so in a more limited forum involving only the riparian states of the North Sea.

Moreover, the rather arcane activities of 'technical' bodies like the Paris Commission did not have sufficient public visibility to be perceived by the public at large as an adequate political response to the growing concern about the pollution of the North Sea. The publication, in 1980, of a rather alarming report by an official scientific advisory body of the German government had led to increased public concern about the state of the North Sea. German policymakers apparently felt that this situation necessitated a higher-profile political response. Thus, given the context in which the German government took the initiative of organising the first North Sea Conference, it is quite evident that, to use the words of an authoritative commentator, 'the primary reason for the initiation and continuation of the INSCs is the political motivation.'[169] However, the INSC did not remain a one-time political initiative in response to ephemeral political circumstances. As it apparently met a real need, it developed into a lasting political process which acquired a certain continuity and autonomous dynamics. After the first conference in Bremen in 1984, follow-up conferences were held in London in 1987, The Hague in 1990 and Esbjerg in 1995, and two 'Intermediate Ministerial Meetings' (IMMs) in Copenhagen in 1993 and Bergen in 1997.[170] It is anticipated that the INSC will continue to meet at three- to five-year intervals in the future. The next conference is scheduled to be held in Norway in 2002.

It was clear from the start that the aim of the INSC would not be to substitute itself for existing regulatory bodies or to develop any new legal instruments.[171] The INSC was not envisaged as a rule-making forum, but

[168] Wettestad (1989), p 179.

[169] Hayward (1990), p 92.

[170] The Bergen meeting focused on the integration of environmental concerns in fisheries policies and did not specifically address toxics reduction issues, beyond 'reaffirming' the 'political commitments' made at earlier North Sea Conferences. The conclusions of this meeting will therefore not be discussed below. See Statement of Conclusions of the Intermediate Ministerial Meeting on the Integration of Fisheries and Environmental Issues, Bergen, Norway, 13–14 Mar 1997, Ministry of Environment, Oslo, 1997, p 15, para 10.

[171] The existing legal instruments dealing with sectoral aspects of the marine pollution problem were generally perceived by most riparian states as providing an adequate legal frame-

as a political forum. As one commentator closely associated with the German initiative put it:

> It would not be the aim of the Conference to create a new set of international agreements. On the contrary, it would *provide political impetus* for the intensification of the work of the competent international commissions and bodies, and for the *more efficient implementation*, in all the neighbouring states, *of the existing international rules*.[172]

Thus described, the aim of the INSC process is to enhance the effectiveness of the existing legal instruments bearing on the protection of the North Sea, by promoting their implementation both at the international and national level. While commentators agree that 'the main *raison d'être* of the INSCs is political'[173] and the governments participating in the INSCs clearly view those conferences primarily as a political exercise as well,[174] the conferences were nevertheless intended to achieve more tangible results than mere political statements.[175]

The mechanism through which this is to be achieved is the provision of overall policy guidance and 'political impetus' to the regulatory efforts of the competent international bodies. While the INSC itself does not actually purport to create law directly, its proclaimed intent is to lay down general policy objectives which are then to be implemented through the development of legal norms at the national level and at the international level, in the forum of international organisations and regulatory commissions whose explicit mandate it is to develop such norms.

Indeed, the successive INSC declarations constantly refer to the Oslo and Paris Commissions and the European Community as the fora through

work for measures to protect the marine environment of the North Sea, and there was not much support for the development of a specific North Sea convention covering all aspects of marine pollution, modelled on the Barcelona Convention and other UNEP Regional Seas Conventions. For a French government official's arguments against a North Sea convention, see Massin (1990).

172 Ehlers (1990), p 5 (emphasis added).

173 Hayward (1990), p 93.

174 Referring to the INSC process initiated in Bremen in 1984, the Hague Declaration notes with apparent satisfaction: 'The *political work* regarding the protection of the North Sea environment has taken place within what has become an effective international framework.' Final Declaration of the Third International Conference on the Protection of the North Sea, The Hague, 8 Mar 1990, in: *International Conferences on the Protection of the North Sea—Ministerial Declarations*, Ministry of the Environment and Energy, Copenhagen, 1995 (hereafter referred to as *Ministerial Declarations*), pp 67–98 (hereafter referred to as Hague Declaration), preamble, at p 68 (emphasis added).

175 There has been some discussion in the literature about the legal status of the INSC declarations. While some authors are of the opinion that some provisions of the ministerial declarations create legal obligations, others argue that the participants in the INSC clearly have no intention of assuming such obligations and that the declarations therefore cannot be regarded as legally binding instruments. For a detailed articulation of these two diverging views, see respectively Somers & Maes (1989), pp 3–8, and Van der Mensbrugghe (1990). I rather tend to agree with the latter view.

which the commitments contained in the North Sea declarations will have to be translated into legally binding international measures.

The Bremen Declaration expresses the conviction of the signatories

> that it is important to lay down early priorities in *the competent international bodies for reduction measures* (in particular setting emission and environmental quality standards) for substances which are or could be harmful to the marine environment,

and further records their 'firm determination . . . to make highly effective use of the possibilities offered by international agreements on the prevention of marine pollution and *to develop them to the extent required*.'[176] An annex to the Bremen Declaration contains numerous recommendations and exhortations addressed to 'the EEC, the Oslo and Paris Commissions as well as River Commissions whose regulations may also have a bearing on the quality of the North Sea.'[177]

In London, the ministers of the North Sea states reiterated that '*building on the broad policy guidelines* adopted at the First International Conference on the Protection of the North Sea, *specific policy measures* are required by specific dates including *both national programmes and joint actions* by the North Sea states.'[178] As regards those 'joint actions', the North Sea states specifically 'invite *the appropriate international bodies* to undertake the *relevant measures*' proposed in the London Declaration.[179]

The Hague Declaration again contains an explicit, though cautious, reference to the need for implementation of its provisions in national and European Community law, as it notes that 'the North Sea States and the Commission of the European Communities declare their intention to implement, *where appropriate*, the . . . Declaration into *national or EEC legislation*.'[180] Though noting in its introduction that 'substantial further progress has been made in converting the political initiatives launched by the Bremen, London and Hague Declarations into compulsory provisions of international and European Union law,'[181] the Esbjerg Declaration, unlike its predecessors, contains no general provision explicitly calling for its recommendations to be translated into legally binding instruments by the Paris Commission and the European Community. Apart from a vague exhorta-

[176] Declaration of the International Conference on the Protection of the North Sea, Bremen, 1 Nov 1984, in: *Ministerial Declarations*, pp 19–41 (hereafter referred to as Bremen Declaration), at pp 23, 26, paras A 14, B 14 (emphasis added).

[177] *Ibid*, Annex, p 36, para (4)2.

[178] Ministerial Declaration, Second International Conference on the Protection of the North Sea, London, 25 November 1987, in: *Ministerial Declarations*, pp 45–64 (hereafter referred to as London Declaration), at p 47, para XIV (emphasis added).

[179] *Ibid*, p 50, para XVI.9 (emphasis added).

[180] Hague Declaration, p 81 (emphasis added).

[181] Ministerial Declaration of the Fourth International Conference on the Protection of the North Sea, Esbjerg, 9 June 1995, Ministry of the Environment and Energy, Copenhagen, 1995 (hereafter referred to as Esbjerg Declaration), p 12 (Introduction).

tion to make 'as much use as possible' of the 'new machinery' created by the 1992 Paris Convention,[182] there are merely scattered provisions throughout the Declaration inviting the Paris Commission and the EC to take particular action, though not necessarily of a regulatory nature.

In the final analysis, the effectiveness of the North Sea declarations ultimately depends on the extent to which other bodies than the INSC actually act upon the recommendations and statements of intent laid down in them. The irony is that the decision-making organs of those other organisations, which possess actual normative powers, are to a large extent composed of representatives of the same governments that make up the INSC. In one sense, the North Sea ministers are involved in a bizarre and surrealist process of addressing recommendations to themselves.

To make an overall assessment of the effectiveness of the INSC process, it would be necessary to examine, for each of the policy areas addressed by the North Sea Conferences, the extent to which the recommendations contained in the ministerial declarations have actually been followed up by action at the national or international level. Over the years, the successive Conferences have dealt with a broad range of subjects, including dumping and incineration at sea, inputs of nutrients, operational and accidental pollution from ships, pollution from offshore installations, disposal of radioactive waste, protection of habitats and species, fisheries, protection of the Wadden Sea, cooperation in marine scientific research, as well as inputs of hazardous substances from land-based sources. In some of these areas, the political decisions reached at the INSC have indeed been translated into legally binding agreements by the competent international bodies. For instance, the decisions to phase out incineration and dumping in the North Sea, initially taken by the INSC, were later adopted and made legally binding by the Oslo Commission. Thus the INSC was indeed effective in giving 'political impetus' to the work of the Oslo Commission.[183]

It is, however, beyond the scope of the present study to attempt to make a comprehensive evaluation of the effectiveness of the INSC process in all policy areas. In this chapter, I will carry out only a partial assessment of the results of the INSC in the one policy area that is of direct relevance to the subject of this book: the input of hazardous substances into the marine environment from land-based sources, directly, through rivers and estuaries as well as through the atmosphere. I shall first review and critically assess the provisions of the successive North Sea declarations relating to hazardous substances, and the international action taken to implement them. This review will show that the INSC process has not been particularly effective. However, it is obvious that an analysis of a single

[182] *Ibid.*
[183] For a detailed assessment, see Wettestad & Andresen (1991), pp 46–54.

policy area affords no basis for general conclusions on the effectiveness of the INSC process as a whole. It should be borne in mind that my purpose in this chapter is not to reach a judgment on the INSC process as such, but to evaluate the effectiveness of the INSC only in furthering international regulatory efforts to control emissions of hazardous substances.

The main international legal instruments relevant to the land-based pollution of the North Sea by dangerous substances are the 1974 and 1992 Paris Conventions, discussed elsewhere in this chapter, and Directives 76/464/EEC and 96/61/EC, which will be analysed in chapter 8 below. These instruments contain a number of general obligations with respect to the control of marine pollution from land-based sources and provide a legal framework within which binding measures can be taken to implement the decisions of the INSCs on the reduction of inputs of dangerous substances. Thus, these decisions must first of all be evaluated against the background of the pre-existing, legally binding commitments made by the riparian states of the North Sea in the 1974 Paris Convention and in the 1976 EEC Directive. Apart from the framework provisions of the Convention and Directive themselves, the decisions taken by the Paris Commission pursuant to the 1974 and 1992 Conventions and the implementing Directives adopted by the Council of the EU under Directive 76/464/EEC will be taken into account. Indeed, they are the means through which the North Sea states can translate into legally binding terms the political undertakings made in the forum of the INSC, and the extent to which this has actually happened will provide an indication of the effectiveness or lack thereof of the INSC process.

In this chapter, I will analyse the provisions of the successive North Sea ministerial declarations relating to inputs of hazardous substances and their implications in terms of regulatory action. This will be followed by a brief assessment of the implementation of those provisions by the Paris Commission. Their effect on the law and practice of the European Community will be discussed in chapter 8.

The Bremen Declaration

The declaration adopted by the first North Sea Conference in Bremen in 1984 is rather short on the subject of hazardous substances. The Bremen Declaration enunciates a number of general principles with respect to the prevention of North Sea pollution by dangerous substances but contains hardly any substantive commitments. The 'firm determination' of the North Sea ministers 'to prevent or at least reduce the input of hazardous substances into waste water' is qualified by the phrase 'as far as possible' and tempered by the recognition that this may not be 'practicable', in which case waste water treatment 'aiming at preventing *or at least reducing, as far as possible*' discharges of such substances into the aquatic environment will be considered sufficient.[184]

This statement of intent merely amounts to a reiteration of prevailing regulatory policies based on the 'best technical means available', where national governments have full discretion in deciding what pollution control measures are considered as 'best available' or 'practicable'. But it was precisely the elasticity of the concept of 'best technical means available' and the diverging views of governments as to what measures are economically feasible which were holding up agreement on implementing measures within the framework of the Paris Convention and Directive 76/464/EEC.

In this perspective, the fact that all 'specific measures' referred to in the Bremen Declaration for the reduction of North Sea pollution by substances of the black and grey lists are only exhortations to the EC and Paris Commission to adopt 'mandatory regulations' for specific substances 'rapidly, if possible as early as 1985', to 'intensify without delay' their activities and to 'examine more intensively' new compounds with a view to their inclusion in the lists[185] does not give the INSC process great credibility. Indeed, the Bremen Declaration sounds like an endorsement of the prevailing regulatory approach to the control of hazardous substances and contains no new ideas which could provide real political impetus to the standard-setting work of the Paris Commission and the EC. The Bremen Conference failed in an attempt to solve the lingering UES/EQO controversy at the political level.[186]

The London Declaration

Compared to the noncommittal language of the Bremen Declaration, the provisions of the subsequent London Declaration with respect to inputs of hazardous substances appear more substantive. The Second North Sea Conference has been widely hailed for its endorsement of what has become known as 'the principle of precautionary action', which is spelled out in the London Declaration as:

> the principle of safeguarding the marine ecosystem of the North Sea by reducing polluting emissions of substances that are persistent, toxic and liable to bioaccumulate at source by the use of the best available technology and other appropriate measures . . . *even where there is no scientific evidence to prove a causal link between emissions and effects*.[187]

[184] Bremen Declaration, para B9 (emphasis added).
[185] *Ibid*, paras C1–3.
[186] Skjaerseth (1999), p 213.
[187] London Declaration, para XVI.1 (emphasis added).

The London Declaration is more specific than the Bremen Declaration in that it sets out a quantitative target and deadline for the reduction of inputs of hazardous substances: the signatory governments agree 'to take measures to reduce urgently and drastically the total quantity of such substances reaching the aquatic environment of the North Sea, with the aim of achieving *a substantial reduction (of the order of 50%) in total inputs from these sources between 1985 and 1995*.'[188]

However, a closer reading indicates that these sweeping commitments still conceal many ambiguities and areas of substantive disagreement among the governments concerned. As in the Bremen Declaration, the standard for national and international regulatory measures remains 'best available technology', which, according to a footnote to the London Declaration, 'is understood to take into account economic availability', a qualification which leaves intact the existing room for national discretion in regulatory policies. The reduction target set out for hazardous substances does not apply to inputs into rivers and estuaries but to 'the total quantity of such substances *reaching the aquatic environment of the North Sea*', though baseline data on this quantity are lacking for most substances. The formulation of this reduction target in terms of quantities reaching the North Sea, in the absence of sufficient scientific information on those quantities, in fact leaves the riparian states a lot of flexibility in implementing their commitments.

Finally, the London Declaration does not specify *which* substances are to be covered by reduction measures, thus leaving it up to the individual governments to determine the substances which are 'persistent, toxic and liable to bioaccumulate' within the meaning of the declaration. This is not an innocent omission, given that the adoption of concrete measures to implement the 1974 Paris Convention and Directive 76/464/EEC has been hampered precisely by disagreement over the identification of individual substances that possess these hazardous properties and should be priority targets for specific reduction measures. While the 'black list' of the Directive, for instance, mentions a number of individual substances such as mercury and cadmium, it also includes general categories such as 'substances in respect of which it has been proved that they possess carcinogenic properties in or via the aquatic environment', which leave a lot of room for interpretation.

In the London Declaration, the North Sea states once again 'invite the appropriate international bodies to undertake the relevant measures,'[189] but they also seem to recognise that immediate action is required at the national level, irrespective of any progress or lack thereof in the adoption of binding

[188] London Declaration, para XVI.2 (emphasis added).
[189] *Ibid*, para XVI.9.

measures at the international level. The London Declaration is not very specific, however, as to the nature of those national measures. The signatory governments only agree to 'intensify . . . measures in hand' to reduce inputs of a limited number of substances which are already the subject of EEC directives or decisions or recommendations of the Paris Commission, and to 'take positive action by setting concrete targets to reduce inputs of other significant pollutants of the North Sea.'[190]

The declaration enumerates in very general terms a number of actions to be taken with respect to point and diffuse sources of pollution, but these measures do not go much beyond what EC member states, for example, are already committed to under Directive 76/464/EEC. The signatories agree to 'make every effort' to ensure the use of 'best available technology' in the construction of new installations as well as to reduce pollution from existing installations, but at the same time recognise that the 'best available technology' is yet to be 'identified' for many processes giving rise to emissions of hazardous substances.[191] It is further provided that 'strict environmental quality standards' are to be defined and measures taken to 'control the production, sale and use' of substances giving rise to diffuse source pollution.[192] The governments concerned undertake to 'urgently prepare plans of action' to achieve the goals set out in the declaration.[193]

All this sounds more like a reaffirmation of good intentions than a new and serious commitment. Indeed, those North Sea states that are also members of the EC, have been under a legal obligation to establish national programmes to reduce pollution by particular substances or groups of substances from new and existing installations since 1976.[194] According to Directive 76/464/EEC, these programmes shall include 'quality objectives for water' and emission standards based on those quality objectives, 'shall take into account the latest economically feasible technical developments' and shall 'set deadines for their implementation.'[195] Like the provisions of the London Declaration concerning the control of pollution from diffuse sources, the Directive too refers to the need for 'specific provisions governing the composition and use of substances or groups of substances and products.'[196]

[190] *Ibid*, para XVI.3.
[191] *Ibid*, para XVI.3 (a), (d), (e).
[192] *Ibid*, para XVI.3 (c), (f).
[193] *Ibid*, para XVI.7.
[194] Council Dir 76/464/EEC of 4 May 1976 on pollution caused by certain dangerous substances discharged into the aquatic environment of the Community, OJ No L 129, 18.5.1976, p 24, Art 7, para 1. This provision applies to the substances 'within List II', which includes the grey list substances plus those black list substances for which Community limit values have not yet been determined, which in practice covers most black list substances, since Community limit values have only been adopted for very few black list substances. See below ch 8.
[195] Dir 76/464/EEC, Art 7, paras 2–4.
[196] *Ibid*, Art 7, para 4.

The Hague Declaration

The Hague Declaration reiterates the general commitments contained in the London Declaration and supplements them with a number of 'additional measures'. The most notable new element is the selection of 'priority substances . . . which are presently considered to contribute most to the pollution of the North Sea'. The London commitment to achieve a 'substantial reduction' of inputs of hazardous substances is made more specific by referring to an agreed list of 36 'priority hazardous substances' and by requiring a reduction 'of 50% or more' instead of a reduction 'of the order of 50%.'[197] In addition, a further commitment is made to achieve reductions of total inputs 'of the order of 70% or more' between 1985 and 1995 'for substances that cause a major threat to the marine environment, and at least for dioxins, mercury, cadmium and lead', but this commitment is substantially qualified by the proviso 'provided that the use of Best Available Technology or other low waste technology measures enables such reductions.'[198]

The Hague Declaration also singles out pesticides as requiring special attention and commits the signatories 'to aim for a substantial reduction in the quantities of pesticides reaching the North Sea.'[199] However, it appears clearly from the further text of this paragraph as well as the wording of the relevant annexes that the North Sea states are not in agreement on the measures to be taken to achieve such a reduction and are not equally committed to the ultimate objective of reduction itself. The undertaking 'to control strictly the use and application of pesticides' by 31 December 1992 and to 'establish approval systems specifying permitted pesticides and permitted uses' was hardly revolutionary, given that all the states concerned already had national legislation providing for registration or approval of pesticides for specified uses, and would argue that their legislation was sufficient to 'control strictly the use and application of pesticides'. What is really required to achieve the objective of substantially reducing inputs of pesticides into the North Sea is a drastic reduction of pesticide production and use, but the signatories of the Hague Declaration only timidly agree 'to reduce, *where necessary*, emissions to the environment.'[200]

[197] Hague Declaration, para 2.

[198] *Ibid*, para 3.

[199] *Ibid*, para 4. It should be noted that the list of 36 priority substances, for which a quantified reduction target is set in para 3 of the declaration, also includes a number of substances used as pesticides for agricultural and/or non-agricultural uses: drins, HCH, DDT, pentachlorophenol, hexachlorobenzene, trifluralin, endosulfan, simazine, atrazine, azinphos-ethyl, azinphos-methyl, fenitrothion, fenthion, malathion, parathion, parathion-methyl, and dichlorvos.

[200] *Ibid* (emphasis added).

The measures to reduce pesticide inputs listed in an annex to the declaration are only 'examples' to which the ministers agree to pay 'special attention'. They amount to little more than a very mixed and open-ended shopping list of measures reflecting different and sometimes even plainly inconsistent policy approaches. It is impossible to comprehend how, for example, 'provisional approval of pesticides, including testing of their effectiveness as a pesticide'[201] can contribute to a reduction of pesticide inputs into the aquatic environment. The only really substantive commitment contained in the Hague Declaration with respect to pesticides is the undertaking to phase out a number of pesticides 'which are the most persistent, toxic and liable to bioaccumulate' and which are listed in an annex to the declaration.[202] It should be noted, however, that the list of pesticides to be phased out includes a great number of substances which are 'not currently in use as pesticides' or which have already been banned in most North Sea states either as a result of national measures or in implementation of an EC Directive.[203] Moreover, the commitment to 'phase out' those pesticides in the actual text of the declaration is somewhat qualified by the heading of the relevant annex, which provides that 'the use of the following substances as pesticides must be *strictly limited or banned*.'[204] Obviously, a limitation of the use of certain pesticides, however strict, is not quite the same thing as a complete phase-out and ban.

As regards specific measures to be taken in order to achieve the reduction targets for hazardous substances, the Hague Declaration is somewhat more specific than the London Declaration for some substances and sources, but equally noncommittal with respect to others. An annex to the declaration lists 'agreed measures' for a limited number of industrial sectors, which the signatory governments agree 'to implement', and 'examples of product control measures' intended to reduce inputs from diffuse sources of various heavy metals, which they only agree 'to consider further.'[205] However, these specified measures cover only a very small number of the 'priority hazardous substances' identified in Annex 1A and of their sources.

To be sure, the declaration also includes a much longer 'reference list of priority activities'[206] covering a larger number of sources and substances, but the obligations of the signatories with respect to these 'priority activities' do not go beyond the vague commitment to reduce emissions from those activities

[201] *Ibid*, Annex 1B, Part (d), no 9.

[202] *Ibid*, Annex 1B, Part (c).

[203] Half the substances listed were already banned throughout the EC under Council Dir 79/117/EEC of 21 Dec 1978 prohibiting the placing on the market and use of plant protection products containing certain active substances, OJ No L33/36, 8.2.1979, p 36.

[204] Hague Declaration, Annex 1B, Part (c).

[205] *Ibid*, para 5 and Annex 1B, Part (a) & (b).

[206] *Ibid*, Annex 1C.

by defining the Best Available Technology and applying it to specified point sources, and by defining and applying the Best Environmental Practice to specified diffuse sources.[207]

The novel concept of 'best environmental practice' (BEP) was coined in The Hague as a counterpart, for the control of releases from non-point sources, of the long-established notion of 'best available technology' for point sources. The text of the relevant annex to the Hague Declaration makes it clear that the signatories' commitment is only 'to apply at the national level the Best Available Technology and Best Environmental Practice *as defined by the Paris Commission*.'[208] Thus the actual substantive measures to be taken were yet to be 'defined' by an international body in which each of the North Sea riparian states retained a virtual veto power, a very time-consuming process which was not completed before the initial 1995 target date and is unlikely to be completed in the near future. A general, abstract definition of BEP was first formulated in a 1991 PARCOM recommendation.[209]

While earlier North Sea declarations did not identify specific substances to be reduced, but only referred to the general and sometimes ill-defined categories of the 1974 Paris Convention and 1976 EEC Directive, the Hague Declaration, as mentioned above, contains a clear list of 'priority substances'. This has the advantage of at last adding some specificity to the perpetually reiterated but conveniently vague general reduction commitments made by the riparian states of the North Sea, by focusing attention on a set of well-defined pollutants on whose environmentally hazardous properties an international consensus has emerged, and pre-empting further dilatory controversies as to their actual impact on the marine environment. On the other hand, the identification of a limited number of substances as priority targets for reduction measures also has the effect of distracting attention from the thousands of other substances which are probably equally hazardous for the marine environment and whose input should also be reduced or eliminated by virtue of the principle of precautionary action.

The signatories of the Hague Declaration seem aware of this problem when they state that '*as a matter of principle*, *all substances* that are persistent, toxic and liable to bioaccumulate should, regardless of their anthropogenic sources, be covered by reduction measures as required in the London Declaration,'[210] but they seem as yet unable to face the implications of this principle and adapt their policies to it. Indeed, while the experience in the Paris Commission and the EC clearly indicated the limitations

[207] Hague Declaration, para 6.
[208] *Ibid*, Annex 1C, para 2 (emphasis added).
[209] PARCOM Recommendation 91/1 on the definition of best environmental practice, see below n 275.
[210] Hague Declaration, para 1 (emphasis added).

of a substance-by-substance approach, the Hague Declaration signalled the intent of the signatories to pursue this approach into the future by welcoming, as an initiative 'to improve the setting of priorities for taking future measures', a programme of the European Commission 'to develop internationally and regionally applicable criteria for the identification of substances dangerous to the aquatic environment with the aim of achieving a selection scheme.'[211] If the ultimate objective of eliminating discharges of substances which are persistent, toxic and liable to bioaccumulate is ever to be achieved, a more generic approach to the problem, addressing particular groups of substances or waste streams as a whole, will inevitably be called for.

The Conclusions of the Copenhagen Intermediate Ministerial Meeting

In December 1993, midway between the Hague Conference and the next INSC scheduled for 1995, Denmark hosted an 'Intermediate Ministerial Meeting' (IMM) of the North Sea states. This was not a fully fledged conference, but a shorter, lower-key meeting with a limited agenda. The main issue on that agenda was the implementation of the INSC declarations with respect to inputs of nutrients and pesticides. In view of the importance of pollution from agricultural sources, ministers of agriculture of the riparian states were invited to attend the IMM together with their environmental colleagues, but very few of them actually did. I shall not discuss the results of the IMM with respect to pollution by nutrients, a subject which falls outside the scope of this thesis, but focus on the conclusions of the meeting relevant to toxics reduction, and in particular the reduction of pesticide inputs.[212]

In the part of their 'Statement of Conclusions'[213] relating to pesticides, the ministers start off on a self-congratulatory note by concluding, on the basis of data compiled by PARCOM, that 'progress has been made towards achieving the targets agreed in 1990 for reduced inputs via rivers and estuaries,'[214] as well as 'in strictly limiting or banning the use(s) of pesticides listed in the Hague Declaration.'[215] However, they also recognise in a subsequent paragraph 'that insufficient progress has been achieved in the

[211] *Ibid*, para 7 and Annex 1D, para C.1 (i).

[212] For a more comprehensive and highly critical assessment of the outcome of the Copenhagen meeting, see IJlstra (1994).

[213] Statement of Conclusions from the Intermediate Ministerial Meeting, Copenhagen, 8 Dec 1993, in: *Ministerial Declarations*, pp 101–25 (hereafter referred to as Copenhagen Statement), para 43.1.

[214] Copenhagen Statement, para 43.1. This refers to the pesticides listed in Annex 1A of the Hague Declaration. See above n 173.

[215] *Ibid*, para 43.2. This refers to the pesticides listed in Annex 1B, part (c) of the Hague Declaration.

reduction of the use' of a number of specific pesticides listed in the 1990 Declaration and 'agree to increase efforts aimed at reaching the goals set in the Hague Declaration.'[216]

As for the policy instruments to be used to achieve these goals, the Copenhagen statement contains references to restrictions on the marketing and/or use of specific substances and measures to achieve quantitative reductions in the *amounts* of active substances released into the environment. Such reductions are described as one of the 'key strategies' to be used.[217] As to marketing and use restrictions, the IMM reiterates the earlier commitment of the North Sea states to 'limit strictly or ban the use(s) of pesticides causing environmental harm' and specifies some of the means to be used to this end, namely 'substitution with less harmful pesticides, non-chemical methods [of pest control] or other strategies, where alternatives are available.'[218] Of particular importance is the new commitment

> to ensure that future mechanisms for authorization and regulation of both agricultural and non-agricultural uses of pesticides give adequate protection to the marine environment, taking into account atmospheric pathways.[219]

In chapter 8 below, I shall examine to what extent the recent Community legislation on the authorisation of agricultural and non-agricultural pesticides can be said to comply with this requirement. Furthermore, the IMM conclusions recommend 'agricultural codes of practice aimed at environmental protection'[220] and, in very cautious terms, invite North Sea states to 'consider . . . economic instruments for reducing the environmental impacts of pesticide usage.'[221] Finally, the Copenhagen meeting invited the Paris Commission to identify additional pesticides 'which are not covered by the Hague Declaration . . . but which pose a threat to the marine environment.'[222] In doing so, PARCOM 'should take account of the progress achieved in the framework of the EEC.'[223]

It is not clear exactly what 'progress' this refers to. The IMM's Statement of Conclusions mentions specific action to be taken by the EC with respect to pesticides only in two places, where it notes that the Community is 'studying' BAT for pesticide production and formulation plants[224] and

[216] Copenhagen Statement, para 45. The pesticides in question, listed in the Hague Declaration, are atrazine, azinphos-methyl, copper compounds, dichlorvos, endosulfan, lindane (ie gamma-HCH), simazine and trifluralin.
[217] *Ibid*, para 44.1.
[218] *Ibid*, para 44.2.
[219] *Ibid*, para 44.5.
[220] *Ibid*, para 44.3. This paragraph refers explicitly to the concept of 'Best Environmental Practice', as elaborated by the Paris Commission in PARCOM Recommendation 93/3 on the elaboration of national action plans and BEP for the reduction of inputs to the environment of pesticides from agricultural use, June 1993, OSPAR Doc 15/13/1–E, Annex 12.
[221] Copenhagen Statement, para 44.6.
[222] *Ibid*, para 47 (i).
[223] *Ibid*, para 47 (ii).
[224] *Ibid*, para 42.3.

where it 'looks forward to' the results of the European Commission's work on the 'ranking of substances by risk category', which were to be presented at the Fourth North Sea Conference.[225] The latter provision presumably refers to the Commission's initiative to develop a methodology for the identification of additional 'priority substances' based on their risk to the aquatic environment, which was announced and 'welcomed' at the Hague Conference.[226] But the 'progress' referred to in the Copenhagen statement could also be the adoption, in 1991, of Directive 91/414/EEC,[227] which aims to harmonise regulatory policies with respect to the registration of agricultural pesticides in the Community, although, as we shall see in chapter 8, that directive contains no specific provisions designed to protect the marine environment from pollution by pesticides.

In addition to these rather detailed recommendations on the reduction of inputs of pesticides, the IMM conclusions also contain a number of provisions regarding hazardous substances generally. The IMM agreed 'to review at the 4NSC the strategy needed to reach the goal' set in the Hague Declaration as well as in the declaration adopted by the ministerial-level meeting of the Oslo and Paris Commissions in September 1992[228] and requested PARCOM to provide 'advice' on this subject to the Esbjerg North Sea Conference in 1995.[229] It also gave the political go-ahead to the Paris Commission for the development of programmes and measures designed to achieve 'significant reductions of anthropogenic inputs of the order of 50% or more between 1985 and 2000 from all sources of PAHs of concern to the marine environment', thus targetting a new group of hazardous substances not specifically listed among the 'priority substances' of the Hague Declaration.[230]

The Esbjerg Declaration

The prevention of pollution by hazardous substances is again a prominent subject in the Esbjerg Declaration, which, somewhat paradoxically, recognises that the toxics reduction objectives agreed at the earlier North Sea Conferences have not been achieved but at the same time sets even more ambitious targets for the future. The Esbjerg Declaration notes that the reduction targets laid down in the Hague Declaration for a number of hazardous substances 'are not expected to be fully met'[231] and quite candidly

[225] *Ibid*, para 46.2.
[226] Hague Declaration, para 7 and annex 1D, part C.
[227] Dir 91/414/EEC of 15 July 1991 concerning the placing of plant protection products on the market, OJ No L230, 19.8.1991, p 1. For a detailed analysis of the provisions of this directive, see below ch 15.
[228] See below n 268 and accompanying text.
[229] Copenhagen Statement, para 4.7.
[230] *Ibid*, para 4.6.
[231] Esbjerg Declaration, para 20.

admits the gap between rhetoric and action, by expressing the ministers' concern

> that although the previous conferences in principle have dealt with all substances which are toxic, persistent and liable to bioaccumulate, *the concrete decisions on measures have only dealt with a limited number of such substances.*[232]

Though obviously aware of the weaknesses and limitations of the INSC process, the Esbjerg Conference did not recommend any radical departure from the established approach to toxics reduction but merely shifted the time horizon by proclaiming an additional, far-reaching long-term goal, while at the same time reaffirming the North Sea states' commitment to the Hague objectives which, though not achieved by their original deadline of 1995, are now to be reached 'as soon as possible.'[233]

The new long-term objective is 'to ensure a sustainable, sound and healthy North Sea ecosystem' which, more specifically, is to be achieved

> by continuously reducing discharges, emissions and losses of hazardous substances thereby *moving towards the target of their cessation within one generation (25 years)* with the *ultimate aim* of concentrations in the environment near background values for naturally occurring substances and *close to zero concentrations for man-made synthetic substances.*[234]

With these striking references to a 'zero emission'/'zero concentration' objective, the Esbjerg Declaration introduces a novel theme in the international political debate on toxics reduction, one that will no doubt appeal to environmentalists. Presented respectively as a 25-year target and an 'ultimate aim', these twin objectives, though distant, add a new sense of purpose to this debate. While the London and Hague Declarations spoke of reductions of *inputs* of hazardous substances *reaching the marine environment*, the Esbjerg Declaration for the first time calls for the *cessation* of *emissions* in whatever form. Long dismissed as an environmental utopia, the zero emission objective now enters mainstream policy discourse, albeit not to everyone's satisfaction. The United Kingdom felt compelled to put on record, in a footnote to the Esbjerg Declaration, that it 'shares the ideal of these aims, but does not accept that they are currently practicable.'[235] Effectively restoring the marine environment of the North Sea to a condition as close as possible to its natural state (with concentrations of hazardous substances close to natural background levels or zero level for xenobiotic ones) by reducing emissions of toxic substances to zero is of course a policy objec-

[232] Esbjerg Declaration, para 19 (emphasis added).

[233] *Ibid*, para 21. In Annex 2 to the Declaration, the ministers agree that the Hague reduction targets which have not yet been met should be achieved 'by the year 2000'.

[234] Esbjerg Declaration, para 17 (emphasis added).

[235] *Ibid*, footnote to para 17.

tive way beyond the environmental quality standards approach to marine pollution control long advocated by the UK.

It should be noted that the ambitious objective set out in the Esbjerg Declaration is implicitly qualified by a number of references to the need for 'priority setting' in toxics reduction measures.[236] In this context, the emphasis on *risk assessment* is a novelty. The paragraph on 'continuously reducing' emissions of hazardous substances is immediately followed by a clause in which 'the Ministers agree that in this work [ie emission reduction] scientific assessment of risks is a tool in setting priorities and developing action programmes.'[237] This clause implies that the risks associated with particular emissions should be assessed before phase-out action is taken. Since risk assessment is normally carried out on a substance-by-substance basis and involves an elaborate and time-consuming procedure, it seems inevitable that, as in the past, only a limited number of substances will be the subject of concrete measures at the international and national level. As a matter of fact, the inadequacy of existing risk assessment methodologies is duly recognised in an annex to the Declaration, which invites a host of 'competent international bodies' to 'develop further tools for assessing environmental risks of emissions and effluents containing complex mixtures of substances.'[238] The ultimate objective may be ambitious, but dilatory arguments about risks and priorities will delay its achievement just as much as, if not more than, that of previous, less ambitious emission reduction targets.

The Esbjerg Declaration is not particularly innovative in terms of the instruments it recommends for achieving its long-term goal. The tools proposed do not quite seem to match the goal. Basically, the Declaration reiterates the familiar exhortations about the development of BAT, BEP, clean technology, environmentally sound products, and the substitution of hazardous substances. It reaffirms the North Sea states' faith in the BAT and BEP concepts as 'the main instruments for translating their goals into operational and enforceable requirements,'[239] but—in tune with the now fashionable scepticism about the effectiveness of command-and-control regulation—also mentions, in very general terms, other instruments that may complement the traditional regulatory approach, such as economic instruments and voluntary agreements.[240]

More specific recommendations can be found in Annex 2 to the Declaration, which lists a number of follow-up actions, including 'urgent measures to be implemented by the year 2000'. Most of these recommendations are addressed to OSPAR and the European Commission and relate

[236] *Ibid*, paras 18, 23(ii)(b) and 25(iii).
[237] *Ibid*, para 18.
[238] *Ibid*, Annex 2, para 3.1.
[239] *Ibid*, para 25.
[240] *Ibid*, para 25(ii).

to the development of BAT and BEP. OSPAR is invited to continue its work in this field in what seems like a business-as-usual fashion. Significantly, preference is given to a soft law approach, as OSPAR is urged to adopt *recommendations* on BAT/BEP by the year 2000 for the sectors and activities already identified and for such other sectors and activities as it may later decide to include in its action plan.[241] In this field, the INSC also sees a role for the European Commission, when it implements the provisions of the IPPC Directive which provide for exchanges of information on BAT between the member states and direct it to draw up comparative notes on BAT as a form of 'soft' alternative to binding harmonisation measures.[242]

The 'urgent measures' also include a commitment by the North Sea ministers

> to ensure that *by the year 2000 at the latest*, all relevant permits covering hazardous substances are at least in accordance with internationally agreed BATs . . . or BEPs . . . *to the extent adopted by the North Sea States.*[243]

Basically, this amounts to little more than a commitment to implement existing PARCOM recommendations on BAT and BEP by those riparian states which have not objected to them. It should be pointed out that this provision, in its generality, is in fact inconsistent with the explicit terms of many of those recommendations, which lay down *earlier deadlines* for implementation than the year 2000. It could be interpreted as an implicit legitimation of non-compliance with these deadlines.

Both OSPAR and the European Commission are invited to 'review' their existing BAT and BEP at least every 10 years 'in so far it is not inconsistent with existing EU law.'[244] This qualification, which effectively subordinates the standard-setting work of OSPAR to EC law, is somewhat puzzling. There are no provisions of Community law which would prevent a review of emission limit values based on BAT for a particular sector at 10-year intervals. As we shall see in chapter 8, all daughter directives of Directive 76/464/EEC provide for a review of *individual authorisations* granted by the member states every four years, and some of them require the Commission to submit proposals to the Council for tightening BAT-based Community emission limit values at some particular time, generally less than 10 years after the adoption or transposition date of the directive in question. As a matter of fact, no such proposals have ever been made by

[241] Esbjerg Declaration, Annex 2, para 4.1 (iii).

[242] *Ibid*, Annex 2, para 4.1 (iv). Art 16, para 2 of Dir 96/61/EC, below n 244, provides for the 'results of the exchanges of information' on BAT to be published by the Commission every three years. In the Esbjerg Declaration, the Commission is invited to take into account the work of OSPAR 'in its forthcoming work on BAT'.

[243] *Ibid*, Annex 2, para 4.1 (ii) (emphasis added).

[244] *Ibid*, Annex 2, para 4.1 (v).

the Commission. The IPPC Directive, for its part, requires the competent national authorities to 'reconsider' *permit conditions* 'periodically'[245] and contains no provisions relating to the review of any Community emission limit values which may later be set pursuant to its Article 18.

It is thus hard to see how the INSC recommendation that BAT and BEP should be reviewed '*at least* every 10 years' could be inconsistent with EC law. There seems to have been some confusion in the minds of the Esbjerg Declaration's drafters between the review of *individual permit conditions*—for which a shorter periodicity has been laid down—and that of *general standards*—for which no periodicity has been imposed by EC law and in respect of which the Commission is entirely free to exercise its right of initiative at any time anyway. But even if the INSC recommendation were to apply to the former, there would still be no conflict, as the Esbjerg language allows for a periodicity shorter than 10 years.

With respect to hazardous substances, Annex 2 to the Esbjerg Declaration in fact contains few recommendations addressed directly to the North Sea states, as opposed to OSPAR or the European Commission. Thus, it is striking that one of the most substantive provisions of Annex 2, calling for 'a substantial reduction of the order of 50% or more, between 1985 and 2000, of the discharges, emissions and losses of [polycyclic aromatic hydrocarbons] of concern to the marine environment'[246] is worded in the form of an invitation to OSPAR 'to take further action', whereas the earlier toxics reduction objectives agreed in London and The Hague were formulated not only as recommendations to other international bodies, but also as commitments of the individual signatory states.

Similarly, wherever measures are recommended to restrict the marketing and use of hazardous substances, the INSC merely invites the European Commission to 'consider' such measures,[247] ie to make use of its right of initiative to submit the necessary proposals for Community action to the Council. Measures for the control of pesticides hazardous to the North Sea environment are also envisaged as measures to be taken primarily within the framework of Community law, as the Esbjerg Declaration records the agreement of the ministers of EU member states 'to give priority to review pesticides that have been detected in the North Sea or might pose a risk to the marine environment' within the framework of Directive 91/414/EEC and 'to carry through any action thus indicated.'[248] Thus, the INSC implicitly recognises that the appropriate forum for concerted international action to control the marketing and use of products containing hazardous

[245] Council Dir 96/61/EC of 24 Sept 1996 concerning integrated pollution prevention and control, OJ No L257, 10.10.1996, p 26, Art 3, para 1.

[246] Esbjerg Declaration, Annex 2, para 4.1 (vi).

[247] *Ibid*, Annex 2, para 4.1 (vii)(c) and (ix)(b).

[248] *Ibid*, para 27. This paragraph refers to App 1 of Annex 2, which lists 16 pesticides detected in the North Sea.

substances is the European Community and not OSPAR. As a matter of fact, France even objected to the inclusion in the Esbjerg Declaration of such invitations to the European Commission to consider taking regulatory action against particular products which are not yet subject to restrictions under EC law and registered its dissent in a footnote to the declaration, stressing that 'France would wish the Member States of the European Union not to embark in denigration campaigns on products for which use and marketing have not been banned.'[249]

THE IMPACT OF THE NORTH SEA CONFERENCE PROCESS ON THE WORK OF THE PARIS COMMISSION

As the foregoing analysis has demonstrated, the provisions of the INSC declarations with respect to emissions of hazardous substances add little to the existing legal framework for the regulation of these emissions. The declarations certainly do not represent a radical departure from the prevailing regulatory approach, as reflected in the provisions of the 1974 Paris Convention and not substantially altered by the 1992 OSPAR Convention. In a way, the widely publicised 'decisions' of the INSC with respect to emission reduction measures amount to little more than a reaffirmation of principles and general obligations already laid down in the Paris Convention since 1974.

However, the North Sea declarations contain some new elements which may contribute to the implementation of those obligations by interpreting them in a more focused and specific way. These new elements are the quantitative reduction targets, timetables and priority lists of hazardous substances to be reduced. In addition, the endorsement by the INSC of the precautionary principle as a guiding principle for the control of marine pollution introduces a new concept in the regulatory equation. Taken together, these few innovative political orientations resulting from the INSC process could indeed have provided some new direction and impetus to the implementation of the Paris Convention. However, there is little evidence that the Paris Commission has moved away from its piecemeal, incremental approach to the control of hazardous substances, towards a more vigorous and comprehensive approach designed to achieve the objectives agreed by the INSC.

In the previous section, I have reviewed in detail the 'programmes and measures' for the reduction of pollution by black and grey list substances adopted by the Paris Commission in implementation of the Convention, both before and after the initiation of the INSC process. This analysis has shown that PARCOM has adopted programmes and measures only for a

[249] Esbjerg Declaration, Annex 2, n 14 to para 4.1 (ix).

limited number of substances, that it has generally been inclined to adopt non-binding recommendations rather than binding decisions and that, on the whole, the measures taken by the Commission leave a lot of discretion to individual contracting parties in their implementation.

In the immediate aftermath of the first North Sea Conference, no significant change in Commission practice could be noticed. There was no noticeable increase in the speed of decision-making or in the number of legally binding decisions on the reduction of inputs of dangerous substances, relative to that of recommendations. Yet the Commission did consider the implications of the INSC process as early as in 1985. At its first meeting after the Bremen Conference, it discussed a paper prepared by the Secretariat on the 'outcome of the Bremen Conference'[250] but did not seem particularly moved by the ministers' exhortation to 'intensify without delay' its regulatory activities and to adopt binding rules for black and grey list substances 'rapidly, if possible as early as 1985.'[251] In fact the Commission decided to continue its business-as-usual approach with respect to black list substances and, as regards grey list substances, merely initiated a timid data-gathering effort; 'several delegations' stressed that, in view of the 'heavy workload' of the Commission, 'it could be unproductive to attempt to push ahead too quickly in this area.'[252]

Until 1990, the Paris Commission did not actually adopt a single specific emission reduction measure which can clearly be ascribed to the political impetus from the INSC. The few decisions on measures for the control of black list substances were the result of EC initiatives or of work initiated in the Paris Commission before the INSC. In 1985 and 1986, the Commission adopted only an ambiguous 'decision' on the phase-out of aldrin, dieldrin and endrin and emission limit values and quality standards for discharges of mercury, cadmium and HCH based on earlier EEC directives. The legal significance of the latter decisions is limited to the non-EC member states of the Paris Commission, since those standards were already legally binding on EC member states anyway.

The Bremen Conference had no visible impact at all on the decisions of the Paris Commission. The London Conference prompted the Paris Commission to re-examine its role and consider explicitly the political implications of the INSC process. At the 1988 Commission meeting in Lisbon, the first following the London North Sea Conference, the Commission examined the London Declaration and discussed its implications. The Netherlands presented a discussion paper in which it suggested that 'the Paris Commission provided a suitable framework for furthering the effective implementation of many of the decisions of the Second North

250 PARCOM Doc 7/10/1–E, June 1985.
251 Cf above n 184.
252 PARCOM Doc 7/13/1–E, June 1985, para 10.2.

Sea Conference', while at the same time recognising that the geographical scope of the Paris Convention extended beyond the North Sea and that the Convention had contracting parties which were not riparian states of the North Sea.[253]

Following discussion, the Commission agreed on a set of principles which were basically designed to safeguard the interests of the non-North Sea states within the Paris Commission. The Commission stressed the importance of 'common goals' and 'consensus among all Contracting Parties' and recognised

> that other parts of the Convention area may have *different needs* from the North Sea owing to geographical, hydrographic and ecological circumstances, and that they may consequently require *different measures*.

Accordingly, it was agreed that the decisions and recommendations of the Commission 'should, where necessary, reflect the fact that *different routes and different timetables for compliance may be acceptable in other parts of the Convention area*.'[254] Through this arrangement, which recognises the interests of non-North Sea states in the Paris Commission, the Commission was apparently seeking to ensure that the implementation of the measures agreed by the North Sea Conferences would not be hampered by the difference in membership between the INSC and the Paris Convention.

However, this arrangement did not have any immediate effect on the standard-setting work of the Commission and did not result in speeding up the implementation of INSC recommendations by the Paris Commission. In terms of legally binding pollution reduction measures, the London Conference did not have more influence on the Paris Commission than the Bremen Conference. Contrary to what the discussion at the 1988 meeting suggests, the problem does not lie as much with the contracting parties which are not riparian states of the North Sea as with the North Sea states themselves. The evidence rather suggests that the North Sea states are not as ready to commit themselves to legally binding measures within the framework of the Paris Commission as they are to endorse political statements of intent at the North Sea ministerial conferences. No legally binding decisions resulting from the work of the INSC were taken at the 1988 or 1989 Paris Commission meetings.

Up until the Hague Conference, the only clearly visible result of the 'political impetus' from the INSC in the work of the Paris Commission was the adoption of two recommendations of a general political nature, with no immediate legal implications whatsoever, on the 'principle of precautionary action' and the 'use of best available technology'. Instead of furthering the implementation of the INSC declarations in any material way,

[253] PARCOM Doc 10/10/1–E, June 1988, para 4.2.
[254] *Ibid*, para 4.6 (emphasis added).

the debate on these recommendations rather revealed political disagreements among North Sea states about the interpretation of the ministerial declarations.

At its 1988 Lisbon meeting, under the agenda item 'implications of the Second International Conference on the Protection of the North Sea', the Commission considered a proposal from the Secretariat for a recommendation 'on the use of best available technology,'[255] based on one of the preambular paragraphs of the London Declaration. The stated purpose of the proposed recommendation was to extend the validity of principles agreed by the North Sea states to the entire Paris Convention area and to give guidance to contracting parties on the interpretation of the term 'best available technology' (BAT) as used in various previous recommendations and decisions of the Commission.[256] However, it is hard to escape the impression that the real intent of the advocates of this recommendation was to highlight certain provisions of the London Declaration at the expense of others.

The proposal was 'strongly supported' by France, Denmark and the UK, but met with opposition from the FRG and, to a lesser extent, Iceland and Norway. According to the record of the meeting, Germany felt that the text 'was insufficient and represented no advance on the situation reached by Ministers at the London Conference', while Norway observed 'that the proposed Recommendation might be misleading if taken out of the total context of the Ministerial Declaration.'[257] After the title of the proposed recommendation was amended to read 'a first approach on the use of best available technology', Norway and Iceland withdrew their reservations and the proposal was formally adopted.[258] The FRG, however, entered a formal reservation 'because [the Recommendation] *does not reflect 'the principle of precautionary action'* contained in paragraph XVI, 1 of the London Conference Declaration.'[259]

Indeed, the recommendation as adopted, paraphrasing the text of paragraph X of the London Declaration, provides that best available technology

> should be applied in such a way as to prevent any *increase* in pollution in Convention waters, in other sea areas, or in other parts of the environment, or any risk to the health of industrial workers or the general population.[260]

More significantly, however, the recommendation gives great prominence to the notion of 'economic availability' which was hidden in a footnote to

[255] PARCOM Doc 10/4/1–E, June 1988.
[256] *Ibid*, para 3; *see also* PARCOM Doc 10/10/1–E, June 1988, para 4.7.
[257] PARCOM Doc 10/10/1–E, paras 4.7–4.10.
[258] PARCOM Recommendation 88/3 as a first approach on the use of best available technology, 17 June 1988, PARCOM Doc 10/10/1–E, Annex 15.
[259] *Ibid* (emphasis added).
[260] *Ibid* (emphasis added).

the London Declaration: 'The term "best available technology" *should be understood in the Paris Commission context to take into account economic availability*.'[261]

Clearly, the recommendation quotes very selectively from the London Declaration and, as Germany quite pertinently noted, fails to mention the key passage in that declaration establishing a link between the use of BAT and the precautionary principle.[262] At the same time, it upgrades the proviso on 'economic availability' from a mere footnote to a ministerial declaration to a fundamental principle applying to all decisions and recommendations made 'in the Paris Commission context'. There can be little doubt that this recommendation was a regressive move, insidiously re-interpreting the notion of BAT which, in previous decisions and recommendations of the Commission, was not always explicitly conditioned on economic feasibility.[263] Moreover, the link established by the recommendation between the application of BAT and the standstill principle was quite redundant, since that principle is implicitly contained in the Paris Convention itself.[264]

The fact that this 'revisionist' recommendation was the main political conclusion drawn by the Paris Commission from the London Declaration in 1988 threatened to harm the credibility of the institution. This is why PARCOM Secretariat, presumably after extensive consultations, acted to repair the damage at the following meeting of the Commission held in Dublin in 1989, by proposing two new recommendations, one on the 'principle of precautionary action' and another on the 'use of best available technology', which were intended to 'supersede' the controversial Recommendation 88/3. Both proposals were adopted by the Commission but not without considerable discussion and a number of substantive amendments.

In Recommendation 89/1, 'considering that it may be necessary to act upon the scientifically based presumption of a causal link between emissions and effects even if no definitive evidence of such a link has been established' and 'wishing to extend the principle adopted for the protection of the North Sea to the whole Convention area', the contracting parties to the

[261] PARCOM Recommendation 88/3 as a first approach on the use of best available technology, 17 June 1988, PARCOM Doc 10/10/1–E, Annex 15 (emphasis added). As a matter of fact, very similar language was already adopted by the Commission at its 1985 meeting, though not as a formal Recommendation. The summary record of that meeting notes, with respect to this 'semantic point', that 'the Commission confirmed that, because of the legal interpretations which have been given to these terms in other fora, the terms "best technical means available", "best available technology" and "best practicable means" *should all be understood in the Paris Commission context to take into account the economic availability of these means*.' PARCOM Doc 7/13/1–E, June 1985, para 7.10 (emphasis added).

[262] London Declaration, para XVI, 1. See above n 177 and accompanying text.

[263] See eg the 1982 decision on new chlor-alkali plants using mercury cells, PARCOM Doc 4/9/1–E, June 1982, paras 3.5–3.8.

[264] See Art 6, para 1 (a), which enjoins contracting parties to 'endeavour . . . to forestall any new pollution from land-based sources, including that which derives from new substances'.

Paris Convention 'accept' the 'principle of precautionary action' as enunciated in the London Declaration.[265] In attempting to explain the significance of this recommendation in its progress report to the Hague Conference, the secretariat of the Paris Commission noted that, by adopting the recommendation, 'the Commission recognised that the principle [of precautionary action] was consistent with the Paris Convention', and claimed that 'the Recommendation will give the principle a stronger legal status under international law.'[266]

Lawyers will no doubt have some trouble understanding exactly how a non-binding recommendation can give the principle of precautionary action 'a stronger legal status under international law', but who cares? The Paris Commission, after all, is not a lawyers' forum. The authors of the above-cited progress report probably meant that a formal recommendation of an intergovernmental commission established under an international convention carries more legal weight than a political statement adopted by a ministerial conference taking place outside any formal legal framework. That is questionable, all the more so since the 1974 Paris Convention did not actually provide a clear legal basis for the adoption of such 'recommendations'.

Moreover, the claim that the precautionary principle was 'consistent with the Paris Convention', as it then stood, is equally disputable. To be sure, the first preambular paragraph of the recommendation tries to give it some legal grounding in the provisions of the Convention, by referring 'to the objectives as stated in Article 1 of the Paris Convention, to take all possible steps to prevent pollution of the sea from land-based sources', but it carefully fails to quote the definition of 'pollution' in the very same provision, which implicitly requires the establishment of a causal link between the 'introduction of substances or energy into the marine environment' and specific 'deleterious effects.'[267]

It seems that the contracting parties to the Paris Convention attempted, through a rather ill-drafted but certainly politically expedient recommendation, to re-interpret the provisions of the 1974 treaty to bring them more

[265] PARCOM Recommendation 89/1 on the principle of precautionary action, June 1989, PARCOM Doc 11/9/1–E, Annex 5. The fifth preambular paragraph of the recommendation explicitly refers to para XVI, 1 of the London Declaration, which was omitted from the text of PARCOM Recommendation 88/3 and whose provisions are now reproduced *verbatim* in the operational paragraph of the recommendation.

[266] 'Progress Report of the Oslo and Paris Commissions', in: *The Implementation of the Ministerial Declaration of the Second International Conference on the Protection of the North Sea*, The Hague, Feb 1990, pp 485–525, at p 487. The Secretariat had already made the same optimistic claim in presenting its proposal for what eventually became PARCOM Recommendation 88/3. *See* PARCOM Doc 10/4/1–E, June 1988, para 3.

[267] Similarly, Art 4, para 4 of the Convention seems inconsistent with the precautionary principle where it provides for measures to reduce pollution by substances not listed in Annex A to the Convention to be implemented only 'if scientific evidence has established that a serious hazard may be created and if urgent action is necessary'.

in tune with current knowledge and political concerns. However, they realised a revision of the Convention itself would eventually be necessary. When the Paris Commission agreed at its 12th meeting in 1990 to establish an *ad hoc* working group to prepare amendments 'to bring the Paris Convention and its Annexes in line with the developments since 1974', this group's terms of reference from the outset included a specific mandate to incorporate in the revised Convention provisions recognising 'the risks of pollution and . . . the prevention of such risks on the basis of the precautionary principle', with an explicit reference to PARCOM Recommendation 89/1.[268]

The other major political recommendation adopted by the Paris Commission at its 1989 meeting concerns 'the use of best available technology'. It superseded the controversial recommendation on the same subject adopted at the previous meeting pursuant to the London Declaration.[269] This recommendation, which is also in the nature of an interpretative statement, refers in a general way to earlier decisions and recommendations of the Commission in which the term 'best available technology' is used and attempts to define the concept.[270] The contracting parties 'agree' that the term:

> is taken to mean the latest stage of development (state of the art) of processes, of facilities or of methods of operation which indicate the practical suitability of a particular measure for limiting emissions.

The recommendation then lists a whole range of factors to which 'special consideration' is to be given in determining what constitutes BAT 'in general or individual cases', including 'economic feasibility' and the precautionary principle.

The various factors listed are not prioritised in any way and may well point to contradictory conclusions. Thus, where a strict application of the precautionary principle may call for the application of the most advanced technology in a particular case, economic considerations may be invoked to argue that such technology is not 'feasible'. So the consensus reached on the recommendation did not pre-empt further controversies over the definition and application of BAT in particular sectors; it only defined the parameters of future debate. But it was significant that Recommendation 89/2 gave less prominence to the requirement of 'economic availability' of BAT than did Recommendation 88/3.

[268] PARCOM Doc 12/13/1-E, June 1990, Annex 16, para 2.

[269] PARCOM Recommendation 89/2 on the use of best available technology, June 1989, PARCOM Doc 11/9/1-E, Annex 6. The third preambular paragraph of the recommendation refers specifically to para X of the London Declaration.

[270] Throughout the London Declaration the term 'best available technology' is used without any definition. However, a footnote to the declaration specifies that the term 'is understood to take into account economic availability'.

Perhaps the most important consequence of the adoption of the 1989 PARCOM recommendations on the precautionary principle and BAT prompted by the INSC process was that it implicitly laid to rest the dispute on UES versus EQO which had seriously hampered the implementation of the Convention in the previous decade. By accepting those recommendations, the UK and Portugal effectively agreed to give the Commission a mandate to further develop BAT-based emission standards as a means of minimising inputs of dangerous substances into the marine environment without awaiting conclusive scientific evidence of harmful effects. Without formally renouncing its commitment to EQO as a basic instrument of water pollution control policy, the UK had indicated at an *ad hoc* technical meeting of the Paris Commission in November 1988 that it now accepted the need to minimise emissions of the most dangerous toxic, persistent and bio-accumulative pollutants through the application of strict technology-based effluent standards for precautionary reasons.[271] This cleared the air after the acrimonious debate at the 1988 Commission meeting and paved the way for the adoption of Recommendations 89/1 and 89/2 at the next plenary meeting.

While the London Declaration provoked a useful political discussion within the Paris Commission and led to the adoption of a number of political recommendations further elaborating on those of the INSC, the Commission did not immediately adopt any measures of a legally binding nature designed to implement the ambitious objectives for the reduction of inputs of hazardous substances set forth in London. It was only after the Third North Sea Conference in The Hague in 1990 that the Paris Commission at last started moving in a substantive though still hesitant fashion to translate some of the political commitments made in the INSC forum into legally binding decisions.

The 1990 meeting of the Commission actually adopted three decisions based on political commitments made by North Sea states at the Hague Conference. The most significant of these is no doubt the decision on the reduction of discharges of chlorinated organic substances from the pulp industry,[272] which was adopted by a three-fourths majority vote, and set even more stringent emission standards than those agreed by the INSC. Additionally, the Commission adopted decisions on the reduction of atmospheric emissions of mercury from chlor-alkali plants[273] and on the phasing out of PCBs,[274] both of them translating into legally binding instruments political decisions reached at the INSC. The decision on PCBs sets different phase-out deadlines for North Sea states and other contracting parties,

[271] Skjaerseth (1999), p 215.
[272] PARCOM Decision 90/1, above n 115.
[273] PARCOM Decision 90/3, above n 70.
[274] PARCOM Decision 90/4, above n 109.

thus giving effect to the political understanding reached at the 1988 meeting as to the 'different needs' of those parties.

The question of the phasing out of PCBs had been under discussion within the Commission for a long time, even prior to the first North Sea Conference, and it seems that here, indeed, the political agreement reached at The Hague was instrumental in breaking the deadlock in the Paris Commission. However, the case of the decision on the reduction of heavy metals in batteries, adopted 'in principle' at the 1990 Commission meeting, shows that the 'political impetus' from the INSC was not sufficient to speed up decision-making in the Commission. Despite the agreement reached at the Hague Conference on measures to reduce the mercury and cadmium content of batteries and promote their recovery, the proposed decision on this subject could not be formally adopted by the Paris Commission due to EC reservations. Thus it seems that the influence of the EC on the decisions of the Paris Commission was stronger than that of the INSC.

In its progress report to the Hague Conference, the Paris Commission secretariat proudly mentioned the recommendations on the precautionary principle and BAT as

> an important shift in the philosophy behind the Commission's work [which] means that the piecemeal substance-by-substance, sector-by-sector approach will have to be supplemented, and in some cases replaced, by a more holistic view.[275]

There was, however, little evidence in the decisions of the Paris Commission of this 'more holistic view'. There had certainly not been any radical departure from the substance-by-substance, sector-by-sector approach, since most of PARCOM decisions and recommendations still related either to particular substances or limited groups of substances or to specific industrial sectors. The Commission continued its practice of piecemeal, incremental regulation and did not adopt any binding measures of a more comprehensive nature pursuant to the recommendations of the INSC. Even the adoption of sectoral measures was still proceeding extremely slowly, and the apparent momentum gained at the 1990 Commission meeting in the wake of the Hague Conference did not continue in 1991.

The 1991 PARCOM meeting did not adopt a single binding decision, but only a few recommendations on the definition of BAT for specific sectors, as well as a recommendation of a more general policy nature on the definition of 'best environmental practice' (BEP),[276] a concept first mentioned in the Hague Declaration as the recommended regulatory approach to deal with inputs of hazardous substances resulting from diffuse sources.[277]

[275] 'Progress Report of the Oslo and Paris Commissions', above n 265, p 486.

[276] PARCOM Recommendation 91/1 on the definition of best environmental practice, 20 June 1991, PARCOM Doc 13/9/1–E, Annex 6.

[277] Hague Declaration, para 6.

This recommendation is a counterpart to Recommendation 89/2 on the definition of best available technology, to which it is quite comparable in terms of format and purpose. It gives a definition of BEP which leaves a lot of discretion to contracting parties in its application to specific cases. The 'best environmental practice' is defined as the 'most appropriate combination of measures', to be selected from a 'graduated range of measures' from consumer education, through 'codes of good environmental practice' and application of economic instruments, to licensing systems, bans and restrictions. The recommendation then lists a series of factors to which consideration must be given in determining BEP in 'general or individual cases'. These factors are so diverse and potentially conflicting that they do not provide clear guidance. Indeed, the application of the precautionary principle is likely to justify a different set of measures than consideration of 'social and economic implications'.

The recommendation itself explicitly recognises that BEP is a flexible concept that 'will change with time'. It is clear, however, that the concept will not only evolve in time but also vary according to each contracting party's interpretation of the recommendation. As a matter of fact, the wording of the recommendation indicates that there are significant differences of opinion among contracting parties as to what, concretely, constitutes the 'best' environmental practice to deal with specific pollution problems. The controversy centres particularly around the issue of product substitution. Some contracting parties wished to see the principle of substitution of hazardous substances by less hazardous chemicals recognised as a key element of BEP. Sweden proposed to include this 'principle of substitution' explicitly in the definition of BEP.[278] Other contracting parties, however, were apparently reluctant to see this recognised as a general policy principle.

It is significant that the recommendation, as finally adopted, does not mention product substitution explicitly among the range of *measures* whose combination *constitutes* BEP, but only refers to 'substitution by less polluting activities or substances' as one of the many *factors* to be *'considered'* in determining BEP. Recommendation 91/1, though purporting to define a concept put forward in the Hague Declaration, is so open-ended in its wording that its capacity to contribute effectively to the further specification of INSC commitments is limited. It seems that the adoption of this recommendation, like the earlier recommendation on the definition of BAT, essentially served a political purpose.

Both the detailed analysis of the measures to reduce emissions of hazardous substances adopted by the Paris Commission before and after the initiation of the INSC process, and the above review of the debate in the Commission on the general policy implications of the INSC declarations,

[278] PARCOM Doc 13/9/1–E, June 1991, para 4.46.

leads to the conclusion that, while the INSC process has certainly had a substantial *political* impact on the regulatory *debate* in the Paris Commission, its impact on the actual *practice* of the Commission in terms of the adoption of legally binding emission reduction measures has been minimal. Only a few decisions taken by the Commission since 1985 are the result of the 'political impetus' from the INSC. The Paris Commission can hardly be said to have diligently fulfilled the role of implementing body assigned to it by the INSC. It did not really 'intensify' its regulatory work as recommended by the North Sea Conferences and, with a few exceptions, did not actually translate the recommendations of the INSC into binding decisions. On the whole, the regulatory process within PARCOM remained very slow; it is therefore not surprising that this body did not succeed in taking the decisions required to achieve the ambitious toxics reduction objectives laid down by the INSC by the initial 1995 deadline. As we shall see in the remainder of this chapter, the full-scale revision of the 1974 Paris Convention, which was completed in 1992, did not change this picture in any significant way.

THE 1992 PARIS CONVENTION FOR THE PROTECTION OF THE MARINE ENVIRONMENT OF THE NORTH-EAST ATLANTIC AND SUBSEQUENT DEVELOPMENTS

Analysis of the Convention

The overall structure of the new Paris Convention[279] is modelled on that of UNEP regional seas conventions, such as the Barcelona Convention, which will be discussed in chapter 6 below. Its body consists of a number of articles setting out in very general terms the obligations of the parties with respect to the control of various forms of marine pollution, followed by other general provisions of a substantive, procedural or institutional nature. The more specific obligations of the contracting parties with respect to the main sources of marine pollution regulated under the Convention are laid down in three annexes, covering pollution from land-based sources, pollution by dumping or incineration of wastes at sea, and pollution from offshore activities. A fourth annex deals with scientific cooperation between the parties for the monitoring and assessment of the quality of the marine environment. Finally, there are two 'appendices' containing provisions 'of a scientific, technical or administrative nature.'[280]

[279] Convention for the Protection of the Marine Environment of the North-East Atlantic, Paris, 22 Sept 1992, 32 ILM 1068 (1993) (hereafter referred to as 1992 Paris Convention or OSPAR Convention).

[280] 1992 Paris Convention, Art 14, para 2. A fifth annex, on 'the Protection and Conservation of the Ecosystems and Biological Diversity of the Maritime Area', was adopted in July 1998. See above n 16.

The essential distinction between the annexes and appendices lies in the procedural requirements for their adoption or amendment: the adoption of new annexes or amendment of existing ones requires formal ratification, acceptance or approval by the contracting parties,[281] whereas amendments to existing appendices can be adopted by a three-fourths majority vote and automatically become binding on all contracting parties which have not availed themselves of an 'opting-out' procedure within a certain time period following their adoption.[282]

Our analysis of the new Convention will be confined to those provisions which are relevant to the control of toxic emissions from land-based sources, ie the general provisions, Annex I, which specifically relates to land-based sources, and Appendices 1 and 2, which contain criteria for, respectively, the definition of 'best available techniques' and 'best environmental practices', and the selection of the priority pollutants to be addressed by pollution prevention and control programmes and measures.[283]

The new definition of marine pollution in Article 1 of the 1992 Convention takes account of the implications of the precautionary principle,[284] by no longer requiring positive evidence, but only likelihood of harm:

> 'Pollution' means the introduction by man, directly or indirectly, of substances or energy into the maritime area which results, *or is likely to result*, in hazards to human health, harm to living resources and marine ecosystems, damage to amenities or interference with other legitimate uses of the sea.[285]

As a matter of fact, the precautionary principle, which was not enshrined in the provisions of the 1974 Convention but had nevertheless been 'accepted' by its contracting parties in a non-binding recommendation of the Paris Commission adopted in 1989,[286] is now given legal recognition and features prominently in Article 2 of the 1992 Convention as a fundamental principle to be implemented by the contracting parties. This provision stipulates that the parties

[281] *Ibid*, Art 16–17.

[282] *Ibid*, Art 19. The procedure for the adoption of new appendices which are not related to an amendment to the Convention itself or to one of its annexes, nor to a proposed new annex, is not clearly spelled out in the Convention. Those which are thus related follow the same procedure as applies to the adoption of the amendment or new annex itself, ie require ratification.

[283] For a comprehensive discussion of the full Convention, including the other three annexes, the reader is referred to the articles by Hey, IJlstra & Nollkaemper (1993), Juste (1993), and Hilf (1995).

[284] Hey, IJlstra & Nollkaemper (1993), p 8, consider that the precautionary principle has only been 'partly' incorporated into the new definition of pollution, but do not explain why. The fact that the new definition still presupposes the introduction of substances or energy into the marine environment does not as such seem to be in conflict with the precautionary principle.

[285] 1992 Paris Convention, Art 1(d) (emphasis added).

[286] PARCOM Recommendation 89/1, see above n 264.

> *shall* apply . . . the precautionary principle, by virtue of which preventive measures are to be taken when there are *reasonable grounds for concern* that substances or energy introduced, directly or indirectly, in the marine environment *may* bring about hazards to human health, harm living resources and marine ecosystems, damage amenities or interfere with other legitimate uses of the sea, *even when there is no conclusive evidence of a causal relationship between the inputs and the effects.*[287]

Another fundamental principle which the contracting parties are now legally required to apply is 'the polluter pays principle, by virtue of which the costs of pollution prevention, control and reduction measures are to be borne by the polluter.'[288] However, as we shall now see, these strong provisions on principles are not really matched by the other substantive provisions of the Convention spelling out in more precise terms the actual obligations of the contracting parties with respect to the control of pollution from land-based sources.

Like the 1974 Convention, the 1992 Convention starts with an article laying down the general obligations of the contracting parties. Article 2, paragraph 1, provides that the parties

> shall, *in accordance with the provisions of the Convention*, take *all possible steps to prevent and eliminate pollution* and shall take the necessary measures to protect the maritime area against the adverse effects of human activities so as to safeguard human health and to conserve marine ecosystems and, when practicable, restore marine areas which have been adversely affected.[289]

The next paragraph specifies the means to be used for this purpose in similar terms as in the 1974 Convention: the parties 'shall, individually and jointly, adopt programmes and measures and shall harmonise their policies and strategies.'[290] There are, however, a number of differences in the wording of the 1992 Convention as compared to the corresponding provisions of the 1974 Convention.

As regards pollution, the terms used to denote the contracting parties' obligations have changed. In the 1974 Convention, the parties 'pledge[d] themselves to take all possible steps to *prevent* pollution of the sea' generally and undertook to adopt 'measures to *combat* marine pollution *from land-based sources*' specifically.[291] The standard phrase now used in for-

[287] 1992 Paris Convention, Art 2, para 2(a) (emphasis added). This 'mandatory prescription' of the precautionary principle is seen by commentators as 'an important achievement' of the new Convention. Hey, IJlstra & Nollkaemper (1993), p 11. However, the same authors question whether Art 2, para 2(a) of the Convention imposes obligations on contracting parties independently of other provisions. *Ibid*, pp 11–12.

[288] *Ibid*, Art 2, para 2(b). For a discussion of the legal implications of this provision, see Hey, IJlstra & Nollkaemper (1993), pp 13–15.

[289] 1992 Paris Convention, Art 2, para 1(a) (emphasis added).

[290] *Ibid*, Art 2, para 1(b). Cf 1974 Paris Convention, Art 1, para 2.

[291] 1974 Paris Convention, Art 1, paras 1 and 2 (emphasis added).

mulating the general obligations of the parties in Article 2 and the other substantive provisions throughout the 1992 Convention is 'to *prevent and eliminate* pollution', whereas in the 1974 Convention, as we saw above, the term 'eliminate' was used only to denote a specific obligation of the parties with respect to pollution by certain hazardous substances.[292]

In the original Paris Convention, the obligations to 'eliminate' pollution by black list substances,[293] to 'limit strictly',[294] 'reduce' or, 'as appropriate, eliminate' pollution by grey list substances,[295] to 'forestall, reduce or eliminate' pollution by other hazardous substances,[296] to 'forestall and, as appropriate, eliminate' pollution by radioactive substances,[297] and to 'reduce' existing pollution[298] and 'forestall' any new pollution from land-based sources generally,[299] were all specific and distinct modalities of the parties' general obligation to 'combat' marine pollution from land-based sources, itself a specification of their overall 'pledge' to 'prevent' marine pollution in general. In the new Paris Convention, the same terms, 'prevent and eliminate', are now used to denote both the general and specific obligations of the contracting parties, resulting in a loss of specificity of the latter. The generalised use of the term 'eliminate', which in the 1974 Convention was reserved to denote only the most far-reaching of the parties' duties, that to be fulfilled 'as a matter of urgency,'[300] tends to devalue it and dilute its concrete meaning.

This becomes all the more obvious when reading another provision of the 1992 Convention which stipulates that the 'programmes and measures' to be adopted by the parties shall merely '*take full account*' of 'the latest technological developments and practices designed to prevent and eliminate pollution *fully*.'[301] This provision implies *a contrario* that the parties' general obligation 'to prevent and eliminate pollution' through the adoption and implementation of 'programmes and measures' which 'ensure the application of *best available techniques* and *best environmental practice*' does not go as far as to actually *require* them to 'eliminate pollution *fully*' by imposing the use of the '*latest* technological developments and practices.'[302]

In fact, the 1992 Convention's specific provisions on land-based sources are so disappointingly general that their added value over and above those

[292] 1974 Paris Convention, Art 4, paras 1(a), 2(a) and (b) and 4, and Art 5, para 1.
[293] *Ibid*, Art 4, paras 1(a) and 2(a).
[294] *Ibid*, Art 4, para 1(b).
[295] *Ibid*, Art 4, para 2(b).
[296] *Ibid*, Art 4, para 4.
[297] *Ibid*, Art 5.
[298] *Ibid*, Art 6, para 1(a).
[299] *Ibid*, Art 6, para 1(b).
[300] *Ibid*, Art 4, para 2(a).
[301] 1992 Paris Convention, Art 2, para 3(a).
[302] Cf also the discussion of the difference between BAT and 'clean' or 'non-waste' technology, below nn 310–313 and accompanying text.

of the earlier Convention is far from obvious.[303] As for all other forms of marine pollution, the contracting parties, in Article 3 of the new Convention, have committed themselves to 'take, individually and jointly, all possible steps to *prevent and eliminate* pollution from land-based sources'. They shall do so 'in accordance with the provisions of the Convention, in particular as provided for in Annex I.' So the only provision in the main body of the Convention which deals specifically with land-based pollution effectively has no other function than to refer the reader to Annex I.

Of the three annexes addressing specific sources of marine pollution, Annex I 'on the prevention and elimination of pollution from land-based sources' is the shortest one, consisting of no more than three articles. The first of them basically reiterates, in their application to land-based sources, the 'general obligations' laid down in Article 2 of the Convention. In their 'programmes and measures' for the control of land-based pollution

> the Contracting Parties shall require . . . the use of
> —best available techniques for point sources
> —best environmental practice for point and diffuse sources including, where appropriate, clean technology.[304]

Thus the key notions determining the parties' substantive obligations are 'best available techniques' and 'best environmental practice', which, as stipulated in Article 2 of the Convention, are to be 'defined' by the contracting parties themselves, 'taking into account the criteria set forth in Appendix 1.'[305] Thus, when trying to ascertain the material content of the obligations of the parties with respect to pollution from land-based sources, the reader is referred back from Annex 1 to Article 2 of the Convention and from there back again to Appendix 1, which, according to its heading, lists 'criteria for the definition of practices and techniques mentioned in paragraph 3(b)(i) of Article 2 of the Convention'.

The wording of several of the Convention's provisions implies that a distinction should be drawn between the *definition* and *application* of 'best available techniques' (BAT) and 'best environmental practice' (BEP).[306] While the latter is necessarily the responsibility of individual contracting parties, the former seems to be the concurrent responsibility of the individual contracting parties and of the Paris Commission. This implies that, in the absence of decisions or recommendations of the Commission defin-

[303] Thus also Juste (1993), pp 381, 391 (arguing that Annex I 'à certains égards . . . est un instrument moins complet que la Convention actuelle. La montagne tellurique a ainsi finalement accouché d'une souris!').

[304] 1992 Paris Convention, Annex I, Art 1, para 1.

[305] *Ibid*, Art 2, para 3(b)(i).

[306] Cf Art 2, para 3(b), which stipulates that contracting parties shall successively 'define . . . the application of' BAT and BEP and 'ensure the application of' BAT and BEP 'as so defined' in 'carrying out' the 'programmes and measures' which they are to adopt 'individually and jointly', as required by Art 2, para 1(b).

ing what constitutes BAT or BEP for a particular activity, each contracting party will itself effectively determine the extent of its substantive obligations under the Convention, subject only to the rather vague obligation to give 'special consideration' to a set of factors laid down in an appendix to the Convention.[307]

In the context of the 1974 Paris Convention, the concept of 'best available technology', which does not appear in the provisions of the Convention itself, was first defined in a PARCOM Recommendation of June 1989, which describes it as 'the latest stage of development (state of the art) of processes, of facilities or of methods of operation which indicate the practical suitability of a particular measure for limiting emissions' and lists a series of factors to which 'special consideration' should be given by the contracting parties and by the Paris Commission itself, when determining what constitutes BAT 'in general or individual cases.'[308] In the process of transforming this 1989 soft-law definition into hard-law conventional provisions, the contracting parties to the Paris Convention made a number of changes in wording.

First of all, the term 'best available technology' itself was changed into 'best available *techniques*', which is more appropriate to denote not only the technological 'hardware' but also the 'methods of operation' to which the definition refers. A new clause was also added in Appendix 1 which specifies that ' "Techniques" include both the technology used and the way in which the installation is designed, built, maintained, operated and dismantled.'[309] Secondly, the terms 'emissions and discharges concerned' were substituted for 'effluents concerned', which could have been mistaken as referring only to emissions in liquid form. The precautionary principle, which was originally listed in the 1989 definition as one of the factors to be taken into consideration, is no longer mentioned in the definition of BAT, as it is now included in the general provisions of the 1992 Convention as one of the basic principles which the contracting parties 'shall apply' in all aspects of the Convention's implementation.[310] Not surprisingly, 'economic feasibility' continues to feature prominently among the factors relevant to the definition and application of BAT.

Two altogether new concepts introduced in the 1992 Convention are 'clean technology'[311] and 'non-waste technology.'[312] Neither of these is defined, but we may assume that, for all practical purposes, they can be

[307] *Ibid*, App 1, para 2. As regards BEP, this obligation is formulated even more softly: 'particular consideration *should* be given' to the factors listed in para 7 of App 1 (emphasis added).

[308] PARCOM Recommendation 89/2 on the use of best available technology, see above n 268.

[309] 1992 Paris Convention, App 1, para 5.

[310] *Ibid*, Art 2, para 2(a).

[311] *Ibid*, Art 2, para 3(b)(i) and (ii) *in fine* and Annex I, Art 1 *in fine*. See also Annex III, Art 2, para 1 *in fine*.

[312] *Ibid*, App 1, para 1.

considered as synonymous. The only thing we can be sure of is that both of them are different from 'best available techniques'. If not, the clause in Appendix 1 to the effect that 'the use of best available techniques shall *emphasise* the use of non-waste technology, *if available*'[313] would not make any sense from a legal perspective. The references in Article 2 of the Convention to 'the application of . . . clean technology' are similarly qualified by the proviso 'where appropriate'. The wording of these provisions clearly indicates the scepticism of many contracting parties as to the availability of 'non-waste' or 'clean' technology and the desirability of imposing the use of such technology even where it *is* actually available.

The explicit recognition of the use of 'clean technology' as a binding objective to be achieved by the parties over time was one of the main demands of the environmental movement in its lobbying efforts during the negotiation of the 1992 Convention. It is quite obvious from the treaty provisions which were eventually adopted that the contracting parties deliberately stopped short of legally committing themselves to such an objective. While the mandatory use of BAT is formulated as a rule, the use of 'clean technology' or 'non-waste technology', where it is referred to, seems to be considered as an optional exception to the actual rule, albeit a desirable one. While some contracting parties may consider that, taking into account all the relevant factors listed in Appendix 1, clean technology which is 'practically suitable' exists for a particular activity and therefore 'constitutes' BAT for the activity in question, either in 'general' or 'individual' cases, others, interpreting the Convention's ambiguous provisions differently in their specific situation, will consider that the same technology is not 'economically feasible' or 'practically suitable' and that it is therefore 'inappropriate' to impose its application. In other terms, the mandatory use of clean or non-waste technology goes one step *beyond* what the parties are actually under a legal obligation to ensure, ie the application of 'best available techniques'. To quote the terms of Appendix 1, while the use of BAT 'shall *emphasise* the use of non-waste technology, *if available*', it does *not* automatically imply it.[314]

In the provisions of the 1992 Convention a distinction is made between the obligations of parties with respect to point sources and diffuse sources of pollution from land-based activities.[315] While the concept of 'best available techniques' applies to point sources only, that of 'best environmental practice' applies to both point and diffuse sources.[316] The BEP concept was

[313] 1992 Paris Convention (emphasis added).

[314] Hey, IJlstra & Nollkaemper (1993), p 17, are of the same view: 'The legal implications of the reference to clean technology appear to be limited.'

[315] The concept of 'land-based sources' is itself defined in Art 1(e) of the 1992 Paris Convention as '*point and diffuse sources on land* from which substances or energy reach the maritime area by water, through the air or directly from the coast.'

[316] *Ibid*, Annex I, Art 1, para 1.

first introduced in political discourse by the ministerial declaration of the 1990 North Sea Conference in The Hague and subsequently further defined in a recommendation adopted by the Paris Commission the following year.[317] This recommendation, however, explicitly linked this concept to prevention of pollution from *diffuse* sources only.

Like BAT, BEP is defined in Appendix 1 to the 1992 Convention. But more substantial changes were made to the initial non-binding PARCOM definition of BEP than to that of BAT. BEP is defined in extremely vague and non-prescriptive terms as 'the application of the most appropriate combination of environmental control measures and strategies'. In determining this 'appropriate combination' for 'individual cases', contracting parties *should* 'at least' *consider* a 'graduated range of measures' set out in paragraph 6 of Appendix 1, while giving 'particular consideration' to a set of factors enumerated in the following paragraph. The measures to be considered—apparently ranked in order of increasing severity—range from the provision of information to users and the development of presumably non-binding codes of good practice to the application of economic instruments and licensing systems 'involving a range of restrictions or a ban'. Two measures not mentioned in the 1991 PARCOM Recommendation but included in the provisions of the 1992 Convention are 'saving resources, including energy'[318] and 'avoiding the use of hazardous substances or products and the generation of hazardous waste.'[319]

Some of the measures listed explicitly relate to products or substances, but others seem to have been deliberately formulated in a vague and abstract way, without identifying their precise object. For instance, in which practices should resources or energy be saved and how is this supposed to reduce marine pollution from diffuse sources? Or does this recommended measure address point sources? What if less energy- or resource-intensive products appear to be more toxic for the marine environment? What exactly is to be recycled, recovered or re-used? Can hazardous substances continue to be used provided they are recycled or recovered after use, even if this inevitably leads to some releases into the aquatic environment and if less hazardous substitutes are available? What exactly is to be subject to licensing, restriction or prohibition: certain *activities* or *products*? The *production* of hazardous substances or products or only their *use*?

One has the impression that the crux of the matter has, not by accident, been submerged in a conceptual muddle. This impression is reinforced by the fact that the most pertinent measure, the substitution of polluting

[317] PARCOM Recommendation 91/1 on the definition of best environmental practice, 20 June 1991, PARCOM Doc 13/9/1–E, Annex 6.

[318] 1992 Paris Convention, App 1, para 6(d).

[319] *Ibid*, para 6(f).

activities and products by less polluting ones, is not actually listed among the 'graduated range of measures', but rather mentioned in the next paragraph as one of the items deserving 'particular consideration', along with, inter alia, 'the potential environmental benefits or penalty of substitute materials or activities' and 'social and economic implications.'[320] As in the definition of BAT, the precautionary principle, which was explicitly mentioned as the first of the items to be taken into consideration in the 1991 PARCOM Recommendation, is not mentioned in the provisions of Appendix 1 relating to BEP. As noted above, an explicit reference to this principle in Appendix 1 had become redundant because of its prominent place in Article 2 of the 1992 Convention.

Appendix 2 of the Convention contains the 'criteria' which, according to Article 1, paragraph 2 of Annex I, shall be 'used' by the contracting parties 'when setting priorities and in assessing the nature and extent of the programmes and measures and their time scales'. It seems that the term 'criteria' has been chosen somewhat indiscriminately to designate a variety of items lumped together under the same heading, some of which are dangerous intrinsic *properties* of pollutants,[321] others potential *effects* of pollutants[322] and others still *methods* for evaluating or predicting actual or potential effects of marine pollution.[323] Although this is by no means obvious from the unclear wording of the relevant provisions, these 'criteria' seem to be primarily intended for the purpose of identifying the priority pollutants whose emissions are to be addressed by both national and international 'programmes and measures' within the meaning of the Convention and for determining the time scales within which the latter are to be implemented.

The number and variety of the 'criteria' involved is such that the result of their application by the contracting parties seems largely indeterminate. The parties' margin of discretion is accentuated by the proviso that 'these criteria are not necessarily of equal importance for the consideration of a particular substance or group of substances.'[324] However, as if to compensate for this relative indeterminacy, the final paragraph of Appendix 2 contains a non-exhaustive list of categories of substances 'which *shall* be subject to programmes and measures.'[325] This list is essentially a combina-

[320] 1992 Paris Convention, para 7(b).

[321] Such as, eg 'persistency', 'toxicity or other noxious properties', 'tendency to bioaccumulation' and 'radioactivity'. *Ibid*, App 2, para 1(a), (b), (c) and (d).

[322] Such as, eg 'anthropogenically caused risk of eutrophication' or 'risk of undesirable changes in the marine ecosystem'. *Ibid*, para 1(f) and (g).

[323] Such as, eg 'the ratio between observed or . . . predicted concentrations and no observed effect concentrations' or 'non-fulfilment of environmental quality objectives'. *Ibid*, para 1(e) and (l).

[324] *Ibid*, para 2. This provision was copied almost verbatim from the *chapeau* of Annex A to the 1974 Paris Convention.

[325] *Ibid*, para 3 (emphasis added).

tion of the black and grey lists laid down in the annexes of the 1974 Paris Convention.[326]

The replacement of the black and grey lists by a single list of priority pollutants, without any differentiation of the parties' obligations with respect to specific substances or groups of substances, is undoubtedly an important change in the regime for the control of pollution from land-based sources in the North-East Atlantic region. The main substantive provision of the 1992 Convention concerning land-based sources can be found in Article 2 of Annex I, which provides:

> Point source discharges to the maritime area, and releases into water or air which reach and may affect the maritime area, *shall be strictly subject to authorisation or regulation* by the competent authorities of the Contracting Parties. Such authorisation or regulation *shall, in particular, implement relevant decisions of the Commission* which bind the relevant Contracting Party.[327]

Parties are also required to establish a monitoring and inspection system to 'assess compliance with authorisations and regulations of releases into water or air.'[328] Finally, Article 3 provides that it shall be the duty of the Paris Commission 'to draw up . . . *plans for the reduction and phasing out* of substances that are toxic, persistent and liable to bioaccumulate arising from land-based sources.'[329] This is the only remaining provision in the Convention which specifically addresses emissions of hazardous substances from land-based sources.[330] It is worth noting that it does not impose obligations directly on the individual contracting parties, but only *on the Commission* established by the Convention. It is also significant that it does not explicitly refer to the hazardous substances listed in paragraph 3 of Appendix 2.

Under the 1974 Convention, contracting parties had a variety of specific obligations with respect to particular categories of dangerous substances, such as, for instance, the obligation to 'eliminate' pollution by black list substances[331] and to 'periodically review' authorisations for the discharge of grey list substances.[332] Under the 1992 Convention, these specific obligations are subsumed under the general obligation of contracting parties to

[326] The main differences are that *all* 'heavy metals and their compounds' are now covered, that 'biocides' and 'radioactive substances, including wastes' have been added as new categories, and that the reference to elemental phosphorus has been replaced by a reference to 'nitrogen and phosphorus compounds', consistently with the new Convention's provisions prescribing specific action 'for the reduction of inputs of nutrients'. *Ibid*, Annex I, Art 3(b).

[327] *Ibid*, Annex I, Art 2, para 1 (emphasis added).

[328] *Ibid*, para 2.

[329] *Ibid*, Art 3(a) (emphasis added).

[330] Specific obligations with respect to hazardous substances can also be found in Annex III, which deals with pollution from offshore activities. Cf Annex III, Art 10(b).

[331] 1974 Paris Convention, Art 4, para 1(a).

[332] *Ibid*, Art 4, para 2(b).

'prevent and eliminate' pollution from land-based sources,[333] to require the use of BAT and BEP[334] and to ensure that point source discharges 'shall be strictly subject to authorisation or regulation.'[335] These new provisions imply that express authorisation of individual discharges is no longer mandatory, since the control of emissions by means of general regulations is also allowed. The Paris Commission, for its part, is now under an obligation to draw up 'plans'[336] for the reduction and phasing out of hazardous substances. The extent and specificity of the individual parties' obligations with respect to emissions of such substances will thus depend on the actual content of these plans and the legal form in which they will be laid down by the Commission.

A positive feature of the 1992 Convention is that it makes explicit the legal nature of the Paris Commission's decisions and recommendations. As noted earlier in this chapter, the question of the legal effect of decisions was a contentious issue under the provisions of the 1974 Convention. Article 13 of the new Convention now explicitly distinguishes between both categories of acts. It provides that decisions shall be binding for the contracting parties that have voted for them and have not used the 'opting-out' possibility which allows parties not to be bound by a particular decision by notifying the Commission's secretariat within a period of 200 days following its adoption.[337] Another provision stipulates that the Commission's recommendations 'shall have no binding force.'[338] The binding character of *decisions* is underscored in Annex I, which contains a clause to the effect that authorisations or regulations for discharges from point sources '*shall*, in particular, *implement* relevant decisions of the Commission *which bind* the relevant Contracting Party.'[339]

In the political declaration of the ministerial-level meeting of the Oslo and Paris Commissions which adopted the new Convention in September 1992 the ministers 'recognise the improvement in the decision-making process that *will result* from the competence of the Commission to take legally binding decisions.'[340] This statement is quite remarkable since it suggests that, under the 1974 Convention, the Paris Commission did *not* have the competence to take legally binding decisions, but that it will

[333] 1992 Paris Convention, Art 3.
[334] *Ibid*, Annex I, Art 1, para 1.
[335] *Ibid*, Annex I, Art 2, para 1.
[336] It is striking that the standard term 'programmes and measures' is not used here, as in the following subparagraph relating to the reduction of inputs of nutrients.
[337] 1992 Paris Convention, Art 13, para 2.
[338] *Ibid*, Art 13, para 5.
[339] *Ibid*, Annex I, Art 2, para 1 *in fine* (emphasis added).
[340] Final Declaration of the Ministerial Meeting of the Oslo and Paris Commissions, Paris, 21–22 Sept 1992, in: *Paris Ministerial Meeting Proceedings*, *o.c.*, above n 13, p 115, Part II, 7th para (emphasis added) (hereafter referred to as Paris Declaration).

acquire this power as a result of the entry into force of the 1992 Convention.[341] During the negotiations on the ministerial declaration, Belgium, which disagreed with this 'revisionist' re-interpretation of the 1974 Convention, proposed to add the words 'unequivocally established' before 'competence of the Commission' to avoid implying that PARCOM decisions taken pursuant to the provisions of the original convention were not legally binding.[342]

It is highly significant that no consensus could be reached on this proposed amendment. As the summary record of the preparatory meeting for the ministerial conference notes, 'some delegations pointed out that it would be unhelpful to reopen the debate about the legally binding character of Decisions under the present Conventions', and the meeting therefore decided 'not to pursue the proposal.'[343] The majority of the parties preferred to preserve the existing ambiguity, as appears clearly from Article 31, paragraph 2 of the new Convention, which provides that 'decisions, recommendations and all other agreements adopted under the Oslo Convention and [1974] Paris Convention shall continue to be applicable, *unaltered in their legal nature*' unless they are 'explicitly terminated' by a decision taken under the 1992 Convention.[344] This language effectively leaves the contentious issue of the 'legal nature' of existing decisions undecided and enables the contracting parties to stick to their established positions on this matter.

An interesting new feature of the 1992 Paris Convention is that it confers on the Paris Commission certain powers to deal with instances of non-compliance by contracting parties. According to Article 22 of the new Convention, parties are required to report regularly to the Commission 'the legal, regulatory, or other measures taken by them for the implementation of the provisions of the Convention and of decisions and recommendations adopted thereunder.'[345] On the basis of those reports from contracting parties, the Commission is mandated to 'assess their compliance with the Convention and the decisions and recommendations' of the Commission[346] and, 'where appropriate, decide upon and call for steps to bring about *full*

[341] Even some scholarly commentators have uncritically subscribed to this thesis. See Hilf (1995), p 583.

[342] See OSPAR Doc 14/12/3–E, Sept 1992.

[343] OSPAR Doc 14/14/1–E, Sept 1992, para 12.4.

[344] At its first meeting following the entry into force of the 1992 Convention, OSPAR Commission adopted a decision formally 'revoking' a whole series of decisions, recommendations and other agreements adopted under the 1974 Convention, which it considered obsolete or superseded by the provisions of the new Convention. See OSPAR Decision 98/1 concerning the status of decisions, recommendations and other agreements adopted under the former Oslo Convention and Paris Convention within the framework of OSPAR Convention, 22 July 1998, OSPAR Doc MMC 98/2/1–E.

[345] 1992 Paris Convention, Art 22(a).

[346] *Ibid*, Art 23(a).

compliance with the Convention, and decisions adopted thereunder, and *promote the implementation* of *recommendations.*'[347] The language chosen underscores the difference in legal nature between decisions and recommendations: whereas the former require 'full compliance', the implementation of the latter is only to be 'promoted'.

It is also significant that the compliance provisions of Article 23 refer only to decisions 'adopted under' the 1992 Convention, which seems to rule out the use of these new Commission powers to enforce compliance with decisions adopted pursuant to the provisions of the 1974 Convention. This, too, is probably a manifestation of the persisting reluctance of some contracting parties to accept the legally binding nature of those decisions. It should be noted that, while Article 23 is indicative of the current trend in international environmental law, initiated by the Montreal Protocol,[348] to give preference to 'soft', 'non-confrontational' methods for 'assessing' and 'promoting' compliance over classical methods for binding, third-party settlement of disputes, the new Convention in fact still contains, in addition to the new procedures of Article 23, provisions for binding arbitration identical to those of the 1974 Convention.[349] Thus, parties are given the option of either using the non-confrontational, multilateral process of Article 23 or having recourse to arbitration in the event of a dispute relating to the interpretation or application of the Convention. The signatory states ostensibly have high expectations with respect to the new provisions of Article 23, as their ministerial declaration 'emphasise[s] the importance of the new compliance procedure in ensuring the effectiveness of the measures taken by the Contracting Parties.'[350]

It is too early to judge what the full impact will be of the new provisions of the 1992 Convention on the actual practice of the Paris Commission and individual contracting parties with respect to the regulation of toxic emissions from land-based activities. While there is nothing in the new Convention that would *prevent* the Commission and the parties from adopting more stringent measures than under the 1974 Convention, the wording of its provisions on land-based sources does not indicate any clear intention to make radical changes in existing practices. As other commentators point out, these provisions 'essentially codify practice developed within the Paris Commission' under the 1974 Convention,[351] though the signatories 'have deemed it desirable to codify *only a limited amount* of existing practice.'[352]

347 1992 Paris Convention, Art 23(b) (emphasis added).

348 On this trend, see Koskenniemi (1992).

349 1992 Paris Convention, Art 32. Cf 1974 Paris Convention, Art 21 and Annex B.

350 Paris Declaration, above n 340, Part II, 8th para. For a more detailed discussion of the compliance procedure, see Hilf (1995), pp 591–594.

351 Hey, IJlstra & Nollkaemper (1993), p 22.

352 *Ibid*, p 47 (emphasis added). *Contra* Hilf (1995), p 602 (asserting that the parties 'succeeded in codifying recent political developments and technical advances to a large extent').

The absence of any quantitative targets and specific deadlines in the 1992 Convention, of any transformation into hard law of the political commitments made in the framework of the INSC, is also highly significant in this respect.

The 1992 Ministerial Declaration and OSPAR Action Plans

The declaration adopted by the ministerial-level meeting of the Oslo and Paris Commissions in Paris on 22 September 1992, in addition to rather self-congratulatory sections stressing 'the achievements of the Oslo and Paris Commissions'[353] and welcoming the formal adoption of the new OSPAR Convention,[354] lays down a number of 'priorities and objectives for future work,'[355] both for continuing the implementation of the existing conventions as long as they remained in force and for carrying out the new provisions of the 1992 Convention after its entry into force. The most significant passage in this part of the declaration is that in which the ministers

> agree that, *as a matter of principle* for the whole Convention area, discharges and emissions of substances which are toxic, persistent and liable to bio-accumulate, *in particular organohalogen substances*, and *which could reach the marine environment* should, regardless of their anthropogenic source, be reduced, *by the year 2000*, to levels that are not harmful to man or nature *with the aim of their elimination.*[356]

This ambitious political objective, which is supposed to guide the work of OSPAR into the new millennium, is not without ambiguities. Due to the lack of a comma after 'as a matter of principle', it is unclear whether this qualification applies only to the phrase delineating the geographical scope of the objective or to the paragraph as a whole. Secondly, it is disputed whether the particular reference to organohalogen substances covers all halogenated organic compounds or only those 'which are toxic, persistent and liable to bio-accumulate'. Finally, while the ultimate aim seems to be the complete elimination of emissions of toxic substances which may reach the marine environment, an objective proceeding logically from a strict application of the precautionary principle as laid down in the new Convention, the assimilative capacity approach implied by the reference to 'levels that are not harmful to man or nature' as an intermediate target

353 Paris Declaration, above n 340, Part I.
354 *Ibid*, Part II.
355 *Ibid*, Part III.
356 *Ibid*, Part III, 4th indent (emphasis added).

to be reached by the year 2000 appears rather inconsistent with that principle.[357]

The declaration goes on to specify to some extent the measures to be taken to achieve this objective: 'substantial reductions' in discharges and emissions of toxic substances are to be implemented and supplemented, 'where appropriate', with 'programmes to *phase out the use* of such substances.'[358] While the toxics phase-out, together with measures addressing eutrophication, oil pollution and dumping, is clearly identified in the declaration as one of the 'priorities' in the implementation of OSPAR Convention, the ministers chose to leave it to the Commission itself to 'adopt *specific objectives and timetables* for the programmes and measures for the prevention and elimination of pollution by substances.'[359] Thus, the general phase-out objective laid down in the ministerial declaration is to be translated into 'specific objectives', each with its own 'timetable' for implementation, which, in turn, should form the basis for the adoption of actual 'programmes and measures' in the form of decisions or recommendations of the Commission pursuant to the relevant provisions of the Convention.

One of the new tools to be used by the Oslo and Paris Commissions and subsequently the new OSPAR Commission in carrying out this mandate is the Action Plan which was first 'endorsed' by the ministerial meeting in 1992[360] and has been 'reviewed' and 'updated' by the Commissions on an annual basis since then. The 'Action Plan for the Oslo and Paris Commissions, 1992' is the result of a drafting process that took place in parallel with the negotiation of OSPAR Convention and the 1992 ministerial declaration. The political significance of the document is underscored by the fact that, in view of the political priorities identified in that declaration, a number of last-minute amendments to the draft were agreed at the joint meeting of the Commissions which immediately preceded the ministerial meeting in Paris, 'in order to reflect the priority to be given to organohalogen substances.'[361] A section entitled 'Objectives' was inserted in the Action Plan before the sections outlining the specific actions to be taken by the Commissions in their various fields of activity:

[357] Moreover, it is worth noting here that the INSC's scientific North Sea Task Force, in its 1993 Quality Status Report on the state of the marine environment of the North Sea, in what sounds like an implicit rejoinder to the language used in the Paris Declaration, pointed out that an 'appropriate methodology is lacking by which to assess whether contaminant concentrations in the various parts of the North Sea . . . will have reached levels by the year 2000 that are no longer harmful to man or nature'. See Copenhagen Statement, above n 212, Annex 2, Recommendations from the North Sea Quality Status Report, para 10.

[358] Paris Declaration, above n 340, Part III, 4th indent (emphasis added).

[359] *Ibid*, Part III, 2nd indent (emphasis added).

[360] Action Plan, in: *Paris Ministerial Meeting Proceedings*, above n 13, p 123.

[361] OSPAR Doc 14/14/1–E, para 5.2.a.

The Commissions will . . . establish priorities in the light of the following, *in particular giving priority to* the substantial reduction of inputs to the maritime area of organohalogen substances *which are toxic, persistent and liable to bioaccumulate*, with the aim of their elimination.[362]

Read in conjunction with the above-quoted paragraph of the ministerial declaration itself, and with further, related provisions in the section on land-based sources of the Action Plan, which also call for special attention to be given to activities resulting in inputs of 'substances which are toxic, persistent and liable to bioaccumulate *(especially organohalogen substances)*,'[363] this somewhat convoluted language seems to indicate that the contracting parties have mandated the Paris Commission to determine more specific priorities within the general priority phase-out objective set forth in the ministerial declaration and, at the same time, that they disagree on the extent to which the specific measures to be taken within this framework should address organohalogen substances generically or only such particular halogenated organic compounds as have been specifically determined to be toxic, persistent and liable to bio-accumulate. The language in the 'Objectives' section of the Action Plan rather seems to support the latter interpretation, whereas that in the subsequent paragraphs on point and diffuse sources could be read as supporting the former.

In many respects, the provisions of the 1992 Action Plan are hardly more specific than those of OSPAR Convention itself. They amount to little more than a codification of established Commission practice, where they provide for the development of 'further agreed descriptions' of BAT and BEP 'for particular sectors' and for the adoption of 'further measures', based on the application of BAT and BEP, for the reduction or elimination of emissions from 'specific industrial sectors' listed in an appendix to the Action Plan. This list is not intended as an exhaustive one, since the Action Plan also mandates the Commission 'to identify further sectors for such action.'[364] The provisions relating to diffuse sources are a mirror image of those concerning point sources, merely calling for the adoption of 'further measures, including best environmental practice, for the reduction or elimination of inputs to the maritime area of hazardous substances from diffuse sources' caused by activities specifically listed in another appendix to the Action Plan, and for the identification of 'further hazardous substances and diffuse sources for such action.'[365]

Finally, both the section on point sources and that on diffuse sources contain a similarly worded clause providing for

[362] Action Plan, in: *Paris Ministerial Meeting Proceedings*, above n 13, p 123 (emphasis added).
[363] *Ibid*, paras B.1.2 and B.2.2 (emphasis added).
[364] *Ibid*, para B.1.3.
[365] *Ibid*, paras B.2.1 and B.2.2.

further measures for the prohibition of the use of organohalogen substances *which are unnecessary* for the intended use or process, *and do not therefore need to be substituted for*, and to compile a list of processes and substances which are suitable for use as substitutes.'[366]

This wording apparently reflects an uncertain compromise between opposing views on substitution as a strategy for emission prevention, which already clashed during PARCOM debate on the definition of 'best environmental practice' in the aftermath of the Third North Sea Conference.[367] One view holds that the use of hazardous, and in particular organohalogen, substances in production processes or in activities leading to diffuse pollution should be avoided as a matter of principle, while the other stresses that the use of such substances is in many cases a necessary evil for which no technically and economically feasible alternative exists.

In essence, this remarkable provision of the 1992 Action Plan says that the use of organohalogen substances should be prohibited where it is 'unnecessary', but this is about as far as the consensus goes, as the contracting parties seem to have quite different views on when the use of these substances may be necessary or not. In particular, the wording used may be taken to imply that the mere existence of a suitable substitute does not automatically make the use of an organohalogen substance unnecessary, and that prohibition is only warranted where such use does not actually '*need* to be substituted for' because it is *truly* 'unnecessary for the intended use or process'. The subtle semantic function of the phrase 'and do not therefore need to be substituted for' seems to be to underscore that superfluousness, not substitutability, is the real and proper basis for banning the use of a substance.

This implication appears more clearly from the wording used in the section on diffuse sources, where the two concepts are actually juxtaposed as distinct and alternative clauses:[368] prohibition where the substance is unnecessary and there is consequently no need for substitution; '*otherwise*' the Commission should compile a list of suitable substitutes, and, by implication, refrain from imposing a prohibition.[369] In the corresponding passage of the section on point sources, the compilation of a list of substitutes may seem to be intended as *additional* to the prohibition, but such interpretation appears upon analysis to be absurd. Indeed, why should the Commission bother to produce a list of substitutes for substances which do not actually need to be substituted for? But, conversely, one might just as well wonder why any industrialist would bother to use, and pay for, a substance

366 Action Plan, in: *Paris Ministerial Meeting Proceedings*, para B.1.4 (emphasis added). Cf para B.2.3.

367 See above n 277.

368 Action Plan, above n 361, para B.2.3.

369 The fact that the word 'otherwise' was added in para B.1.4 of the Action Plan in 1994 confirms this interpretation.

which is effectively *unnecessary* for his production process, and why there would be any need at all for public authorities to step in and prohibit such economically irrational behaviour. I have dwelt on these semantic issues at length to demonstrate the ambiguity of some provisions of the 'Action Plan' which were carefully drafted so as to conceal the lack of consensus on what action should actually be taken by the Paris Commission.

In view of the underlying disagreement, it is not surprising that the annual 'review' of the Action Plan has turned out to be little more than a ritual exercise. In 1993 and 1994, no substantive changes were made in the provisions of the Action Plan on land-based sources which I have analysed above. Only the appendices were modified to add some new industrial sectors or sources of diffuse pollution for which measures should be considered and target dates for action by the Commission. In 1994, the section entitled 'Objectives' was reformulated to reproduce verbatim the overall objective laid down in the 1992 ministerial declaration and to add, as a specific objective additional to the substantial reduction of inputs of organohalogen substances, the development of measures 'to make significant reductions of anthropogenic inputs of the order of 50% or more between 1985 and 2000 from all sources of PAHs of concern to the marine environment.'[370] The 1995 Commission meeting was unable to agree on a revised Action Plan in the wake of the Fourth North Sea Conference held a few weeks earlier in Esbjerg.[371]

At the 1996 meeting, however, agreement was reached on a revised 1996/1997 Action Plan[372] which provides for the development of 'a *strategy* . . . for the further reduction of discharges, emissions and losses of hazardous substances in order to implement the Commissions' objective in this respect.'[373] This objective was itself to be 'reviewed' as part of the preparatory process for the first ministerial meeting of OSPAR Commission, initially scheduled for 1997, but eventually held in July 1998. In developing this new 'strategy' and reviewing their objective with respect to toxics reduction, the Commissions pledged to 'take into account' both the 1995 Esbjerg Declaration, 'tailored if necessary to reflect possible differences in conditions in the maritime area,'[374] and 'the use of tools for the *evaluation of the risks* of hazardous substances in the environment *in order to set priorities*.'[375] In the long run, the introduction of risk assessment as an instrument for priority-setting may well prove to have a more lasting influence

[370] Summary Record of the 16th Joint Meeting of the Oslo and Paris Commissions, OSPAR Doc 16/13/1–E, June 1994 Annex 20.

[371] Summary Record of the 17th Joint Meeting of the Oslo and Paris Commissions, OSPAR Doc 95/15/1–E, June 1995, Annex 17.

[372] Summary Record of the 18th Joint Meeting of the Oslo and Paris Commissions, OSPAR Doc 96/17/1–E, June 1996, Annex 26.

[373] *Ibid*, para A.1 (emphasis added).

[374] *Ibid*, footnote 1.

[375] *Ibid*, para A.1 (emphasis added).

on practice under OSPAR Convention than the sweeping statements contained in that ministerial declaration.[376]

As we have seen, the Final Declaration of the Paris ministerial-level meeting set in motion a new policy-making process on hazardous substances in the Paris Commission, which initially focused on the formulation of the relevant provisions of the Commission's Action Plan, and subsequently on the negotiation of new policy statements to be submitted for approval to the next ministerial meeting. The 1996 Commission meeting decided that the 'Objectives' section of the Action Plan would be reviewed and that a 'strategy' would be developed to operationalise the objective relating to hazardous substances, as eventually revised.

The 1998 OSPAR Hazardous Substances Strategy, Sintra Statement and Action Plan

The results of this process were formally adopted by the first ministerial meeting of the new OSPAR Commission which was held in Sintra, Portugal, in July 1998, a few months after the entry into force of the 1992 Convention. They include a rather elaborate policy document entitled 'OSPAR Strategy with regard to Hazardous Substances', a relatively short ministerial declaration known as the 'Sintra Statement' and the first Action Plan for the new Commission, designed to guide its work for a five-year period commencing in 1998. The Sintra Statement and the Action Plan of course address all matters covered by OSPAR Convention and deal only in part with the subject of toxics reduction. The key document is the new 'Strategy'.

It starts off by stating the specific 'objective' to be pursued by the Commission in relation to hazardous substances, 'in accordance with the general objective' laid down in Article 2, paragraph 1(a) of the Convention.[377] This specific objective, which supersedes that laid down in the 1992 Paris Declaration and subsequent Action Plans, is a watered-down version of paragraph 17 of the 1995 Esbjerg Declaration:

> the objective of the Commission with regard to hazardous substances is to prevent pollution of the maritime area by continuously reducing discharges, emissions and

[376] It should be noted that the paragraph in the Action Plan dealing with the identification of additional hazardous substances from diffuse sources which should be the subject of programmes and measures was also amended in 1996 to reflect the importance of priority-setting based on risk assessment and now reads 'to identify *and prioritise* further hazardous substances . . .'. *Ibid*, para D.2.4 (emphasis added).

[377] Surprisingly, the Strategy contains no explicit reference at all to Art 3 (a) of the Land-Based Sources Annex to the OSPAR Convention, which specifically mandates the Commission 'to draw up . . . *plans for the reduction and phasing out*' of hazardous substances from land-based sources. Cf above n 329 and accompanying text.

losses of hazardous substances . . . , with the ultimate aim of achieving concentrations in the marine environment near background values for naturally occurring substances and close to zero for man-made synthetic substances.[378]

No target date by which this 'ultimate aim' should be reached is mentioned in this paragraph. The key phrase of the Esbjerg language referring to 'the target of . . . cessation *within one generation* (25 years)' of discharges, emissions and losses was omitted, as was the phrase in the Paris Declaration which referred to the goal of reducing discharges and emissions '*by the year 2000*, to levels that are not harmful to man or nature'. However, the Strategy contains another, separate provision, which purports to lay down a 'timeframe' for the implementation of the objective set forth at the outset of the document, but in fact does more than that. It provides:

Following on from the commitment in the [Paris] Declaration . . . that . . . the Commission should continue to work towards the reduction, *by the year 2000*, of discharges, emissions and losses of hazardous substances *which could reach the marine environment*, to levels that are not harmful to man or nature *with the aim of their elimination*, the Commission will implement this strategy *progressively* by *making every endeavour to move towards the target of* the cessation of discharges, emissions and losses of hazardous substances *by the year 2020*.[379]

In an apparent compromise between the North Sea states and OSPAR contracting parties which are not riparian states of the North Sea, the drafters of the Strategy have merged language from the 1992 Paris and 1995 Esbjerg declarations into an elegant new formula, which conveys an image of both continuity and movement but, upon closer scrutiny, at the same time creates a sense of confusion as to the actual objective that parties have agreed upon.

The first part of the sentence merely recalls the earlier 'commitment' made by ministers in 1992, in terms identical to those of the Paris Declaration, while the second part, in terms inspired by paragraph 17 of the Esbjerg INSC declaration, enunciates what is a new political commitment in OSPAR framework. While the signatories of OSPAR Convention had already agreed in Paris that their ultimate aim was the elimination of inputs of toxic substances in the marine environment, no target date by which this aim should be achieved was set forth. The year 2000 was mentioned only in relation to the interim objective of reducing discharges and emissions 'to levels that are not harmful to man or nature'. In Sintra, OSPAR parties subscribed to a target date for the 'cessation of discharges, emissions and losses of hazardous substances', viz 2020. Although they refrained from using the INSC wording 'within one generation', the timeframe referred to—25 years from

378 OSPAR Doc 98/14/1–E, July 1998, Annex 34, p 1, para 1.
379 *Ibid*, p 3, para 4.1 (emphasis added).

1995—actually coincides with that laid down for the North Sea in the Esbjerg Declaration.

While the reference to the Paris commitment seems designed to stress the continuity in the development of the parties' toxics reduction policy, the Strategy actually stops short of formally *reiterating* that commitment with its initial 2000 deadline. In view of the scant progress made by PARCOM between 1992 and 1998 towards reducing toxic emissions 'to levels that are not harmful to man or nature', a reiteration of the intention to reach that aim 'by the year 2000'—which was actually included in earlier drafts of the Strategy[380]—would not have sounded very credible. By enouncing not only a new aim—'following on from' the earlier one but not in fact consecutive upon its achievement—but also, and above all, a new and comfortably remote deadline, OSPAR states have surreptitiously granted themselves a reprieve while maintaining the illusion of movement.

The parties' new commitment, however, is a rather soft one: they have only agreed to '*make every endeavour to move towards the target*' of zero emissions. And, contrary to both the medium-term and long-term aims of the Paris Declaration, the actual *objective* of OSPAR Strategy is formulated not in terms of *emission levels* (or inputs in the marine environment), but of *ambient concentrations* of toxic substances in the marine environment. In the Esbjerg Declaration, low ambient concentrations are referred to as a *consequence* of the cessation of emissions, rather than as a primary objective in itself. In the Sintra Strategy, however, the direct link between the ultimate objective in terms of environmental quality and the elimination of inputs as a prerequisite has been weakened, as the latter is referred to only in very qualified terms in the 'timeframe' section of the document. Finally, the 'timeframe' section emphasises that the Strategy is to be implemented 'progressively'.

The Strategy also sets out a number of 'guiding principles' to guide the Commission in its work to achieve the objective with regard to hazardous substances. The first, referring to application of the precautionary principle, the polluter pays principle and BAT and BEP, is merely a restatement of the provisions of Article 2 of OSPAR Convention. The other principles, which are not laid down as such in the Convention itself, are more significant. Indeed, the second 'guiding principle' deals with the controversial issue of substitution of hazardous substances in the following terms:

> *in addition*, the principle of substitution, ie the substitution of hazardous substances by less hazardous substances or preferably non-hazardous substances *where such alternatives are available*, *is a means* to reach this objective.[381]

[380] See eg OSPAR Doc HOD 97/6/1–E, May 1997, p 1, Part I, para 2.

[381] OSPAR Doc 98/14/1–E, July 1998, Annex 34, p 1, para 2.1.b (emphasis added).

The use of the words 'in addition' suggests that 'the principle of substitution' is not an integral part of the application of BAT and BEP as defined in the Convention, but merely *an* additional means to reach the toxics reduction objective, whose use is not actually mandatory under the provisions of the Convention.[382] Another, related provision, enunciates the principle that 'emissions, discharges and losses of new hazardous substances shall be avoided except where these are justified by the application of the principle of substitution'.

The last of the 'guiding principles' states, as a general rule for the Commission's work to implement the strategy and achieve the objective, that 'the *scientific assessment of risks* . . . is a tool for setting priorities and developing action programmes.'[383] Although it is stipulated that the instrument of risk assessment is to be used 'in connection with the criteria stipulated at Appendix 2' of OSPAR Convention, the effect of this new 'guiding principle' may well be to make assessed risk the overriding criterion for determining which hazardous substances and emission sources should be the subject of OSPAR measures, although the 'risk of undesirable changes in the marine ecosystem' is only one of *twelve* criteria listed in Appendix 2 of the Convention.[384] This particular emphasis is quite surprising in view of the contracting parties' explicit recognition, elsewhere in the Strategy, of the 'limited experience with the scientific assessment of the risk of potential hazardous substances in the marine environment.'[385]

Beyond the 'objective', 'timeframe' and 'guiding principles', the Strategy contains elaborate operative provisions describing in minute detail the process for its implementation. It would take us well beyond the scope of this study to undertake a detailed analysis of these highly technical provisions on such matters as the identification and classification of hazardous substances requiring regulatory action, risk assessment and priority

[382] For a further discussion of the issue of substitution under the provisions of the 1992 Convention, see above n 320 and accompanying text.

[383] OSPAR Doc 98/14/1–E, July 1998, Annex 34, p 2, para 2.1.d (emphasis added).

[384] 1992 Paris Convention, App 2, para 1(h). It should, however, be noted that a reference to 'progressive risk assessment strategies' can also be found in Art 2(c) of Annex IV of the Convention, which deals with the monitoring and assessment of the quality of the marine environment.

[385] OSPAR Doc 98/14/1–E, July 1998, Annex 34, p 4, para 5.4. In those circumstances, and in view of a large measure of scientific uncertainty, one may wonder whether the formal risk assessment requirement is in fact consistent with the principle of precautionary action. This was apparently the concern of Germany when it proposed to add to the paragraph referring to the selection scheme and assessment criteria a sentence stipulating that 'the application of this selection scheme should take due account of the precautionary principle'. OSPAR Doc HOD 97/6/1–E, May 1997, p 8, Annex, para 2.1, n 27. As a matter of fact, an early draft of the Strategy's provisions on priority setting, using language which can only be interpreted as an implicit reference to the definition of the precautionary principle in Art 2, para 2(a) of the OSPAR Convention, expressly recognised that 'establishing whether there are *reasonable grounds for concern* can be difficult when there is a lack of relevant risk assessment or monitoring data.' *Ibid*, p 9, Annex, para 2.6 (emphasis added).

setting. I will restrict my comments to a number of points of legal and political relevance.

In the operative part of the Strategy, the contracting parties describe OSPAR's task as follows:

> The Commission will develop programmes and measures to identify, *prioritise*, monitor and *control* (ie to prevent *and/or* reduce *and/or* eliminate) the emissions, discharges and losses of hazardous substances *which reach, or could reach, the marine environment.*[386]

This approach to the future development of toxics reduction measures implies that, before any emission control action is effectively taken, a number of procedural steps will have to be fulfilled. The Commission will first have to identify and, above all, *prioritise* the substances and sources to be controlled. This also involves a positive determination that hazardous substances from the sources concerned actually reach, or are likely to reach, the marine environment.[387]

The priority-setting as envisaged would occur at two different levels. In the first place, the Commission will 'complete the development of a *dynamic selection and prioritisation mechanism*' for hazardous substances.[388] This mechanism will be based on risk assessment methods[389] still largely to be developed.[390] The second level at which priorities will be set is that of the selection of the *sources* to be controlled and the *control measures* to be taken. Indeed, the Strategy provides that 'the most cost-effective measures should have the highest priority' and that these measures are to be selected 'in the light of the requirements laid down in the definitions of BAT and BEP in OSPAR Convention.'[391] Finally, the ultimate aim of the control measures is formulated in weaker terms in the Strategy than in the provisions of the 1992 Convention itself. Whereas the latter requires contracting parties to take 'all possible steps to prevent *and eliminate* pollution,'[392] the former

[386] OSPAR Doc 98/14/1–E, July 1998, Annex 34, p 2, para 3.1 (emphasis added).

[387] *Ibid*, para 3.1.a(iv). See also *ibid*, p 4, para 5.3.a, which stipulates that action should include 'identifying the sources of hazardous substances *and their pathways to the marine environment*' (emphasis added).

[388] *Ibid*, p 2, para 3.1.a (emphasis added).

[389] Para 5.3 explicitly provides that 'the identification of relevant measures' should be the result of a process which includes 'establishing with the help of an appropriate combination of monitoring, modelling, *risk characterisation and risk assessment* techniques, whether these sources represent either a widespread problem or a problem restricted to regional or local environments within the maritime area' (emphasis added).

[390] Indeed, para 5.4.a of the Strategy states that the Commission will 'as a matter of urgency' address 'the development of the relevant scientific tools for assessing risks of potential hazardous substances in the marine environment'.

[391] OSPAR Doc 98/14/1–E, July 1998, Annex 34, p 4, para 5.5. The latter is a specific reference to the provisions of App 1 of the 1992 Paris Convention, with their emphasis on 'economic feasibility' and 'social and economic implications'. See above nn 310 and 320 and accompanying text.

[392] 1992 Paris Convention, Art 2, para 1(a) and Art 3 (emphasis added).

provides that emissions, discharges and losses of hazardous substances shall be 'controlled', a generic term which, as defined, may refer to mere emission *reduction* as well as elimination.[393]

The 'dynamic selection and prioritisation mechanism', once developed, is to be applied to a long list of 'candidate substances' annexed to the Strategy. This list is essentially a compilation of existing, and partly overlapping, lists of hazardous substances which have already been identified earlier as targets for regulatory action either by PARCOM or in other fora. It includes the INSC list of priority substances annexed to the 1990 Hague Declaration and the list of pesticides 'that have been detected in the North Sea or might pose a risk to the marine environment' annexed to the 1995 Esbjerg Declaration. It also comprises two lists of persistent organic pollutants (POPs), one developed within the framework of the ECE Convention on Long-Range Transboundary Air Pollution for the purpose of the implementation of elimination or reduction measures under the provisions of the 1998 Aarhus Protocol to that Convention, and another, shorter one, drawn up by UNEP for the purpose of negotiations on a global convention for the phase-out of POPs. Substances subject to risk assessment and risk management programmes within the framework of the OECD or the WHO-ILO-UNEP International Programme on Chemical Safety are also listed. In view of the fact that OSPAR list of candidate substances was produced by compiling a series of existing lists, one is justified in wondering why the list of 129 candidate 'black list' substances drawn up by the European Commission in the context of Directive 76/464/EEC, and endorsed by the EC Council in 1982, was not added to the 'cocktail' as well.

The longest list of candidate substances was taken from Annex 1D to the Hague Declaration, which, as we have seen above, contains a 'common reference list' of substances which was the result of work undertaken by the European Commission in the late 1980s, in the context of Directive 76/464/EEC, with a view to 'compil[ing] a draft list of additional priority substances hazardous to the aquatic environment'[394] through the application of a 'selection scheme' based on the development of 'internationally and regionally applicable criteria for the identification of substances dangerous to the aquatic environment.'[395] It was then anticipated that this selection scheme would produce a 'draft list of additional priority substances' in time for consideration by the Fourth North Sea Conference in 1995 and that this list would serve 'to improve the *setting of priorities for taking future measures* with regard to the reduction of inputs of hazardous substances' in the INSC context.[396] In other terms, the European Commission, with the endorsement of the INSC, in 1990 already proposed to do exactly

[393] OSPAR Doc 98/14/1–E, July 1998, Annex 34, p 2, para 3.1.
[394] Hague Declaration, Annex 1D, para C.1 (ii).
[395] *Ibid*, para C.1 (i).
[396] Hague Declaration, para 7 (emphasis added).

what OSPAR again decided should be done eight years later, ie develop a science-based scheme for the selection and prioritisation of hazardous substances that should be the target of international emission reduction measures. Largely the same list of candidate substances that had already been identified eight years earlier again received political endorsement as a basis for a similar exercise in a different forum. Back to square one after all these years? On reading the 1998 OSPAR Strategy, it is hard to escape a strong feeling of *déjà vu*.

While the INSC's Intermediate Ministerial Meeting in 1993 still 'look[ed] forward to' the results of the European Commission's risk assessment and prioritisation initiative announced at the Hague Conference,[397] no trace of these results can be found in the texts adopted by the Fourth North Sea Conference in Esbjerg in 1995. The 'Progress Report' to the Esbjerg Conference in fact notes that, although a computer model for 'Integrated Priority Setting' had been developed by EC consultants by 1994, it was subsequently discovered that insufficient data were available for most of the 93 substances on the reference list to be able to apply the complex model to them. The European Commission merely reported that it intended to improve the data sets and 'to continue development to improve the selectivity of the prioritization process.'[398] The Esbjerg Declaration did no more than 'invite' various international bodies, including the European Commission and OSPAR, 'to develop further and use tools for the evaluation of the risks of hazardous substances in the environment in order to set priorities', without any specific reference to Annex 1D of the Hague Declaration and the Commission's ongoing efforts based on that list.[399] The new Hazardous Substances Strategy can be regarded as OSPAR's response to this invitation—as another remarkable example of policy continuity in the North Sea and North-East Atlantic land-based sources regime, albeit continuity in recourse to further process as a substitute for action.

It should be noted, though, that the Strategy's list of candidate substances is not entirely devoid of innovative elements. A list of potential endocrine disruptors, developed within the framework of OSPAR in response to growing scientific and public concern about the presence in the environment of synthetic compounds which, by 'mimicking' natural hormonal substances, could disrupt the functioning of the endocrine system in humans and animals, was also included among the substances to be reviewed by the 'dynamic mechanism'. Accordingly, the Strategy expands the traditional definition of toxicity to include 'adverse effects as a result of endocrine disruption.'[400] An annex to the Strategy also lists a number of 'priority research

[397] Copenhagen Statement, para 46.2.

[398] *Progress Report—4th International Conference on the Protection of the North Sea*, Ministry of the Environment and Energy, Copenhagen, 1995, p 76.

[399] Esbjerg Declaration, Annex 2 ('Follow-up actions related to the strategy on the prevention of pollution by hazardous substances'), para 3.1 ('List of tools').

[400] OSPAR Doc 98/14/1–E, July 1998, Annex 34, p 20, Annex 5, para 1.c.

and development actions' to be undertaken to further develop scientific knowledge about the risks of endocrine disruptors.[401] The Strategy further broadens the concept of 'hazardous substances' by redefining it as encompassing substances which, although they do not meet all the criteria for toxicity, persistence and bioaccumulation, 'give rise to an equivalent level of concern' and are therefore 'assessed by the Commission as requiring a similar approach' as substances which meet these criteria.[402]

In addition to the long list of candidate substances to be subjected to the selection, assessment and prioritisation process, a much shorter 'OSPAR List of Chemicals for Priority Action' is also annexed to the Strategy.[403] These are chemicals which were identified as being of concern in the past and which were either already subject to regulatory action decided by PARCOM prior to the entry into force of the 1992 Convention but for which further measures are being envisaged, or which are currently under consideration within OSPAR with a view to the development of programmes and measures. The Strategy directs OSPAR to 'carry forward the drawing up of programmes and measures' for these substances without awaiting the outcome of the application of the selection and prioritisation mechanism to the list of candidate substances.[404] This 'dynamic mechanism' is ostensibly not designed to interfere with the ongoing regulatory work on industrial sectors and diffuse sources, but only to identify *additional* hazardous substances for priority action. Its application is intended to result in a regular review of the 'List of Chemicals for Priority Action'; and in the 'rank[ing of] these substances in order of priority.'[405]

OSPAR Action Plan 1998–2003, adopted by the Sintra ministerial meeting simultaneously with the Hazardous Substances Strategy, and similar strategies covering the other areas of OSPAR's remit, specifies in operational and procedural terms the activities to be undertaken by the Commission and its various subsidiary bodies in the next five years to implement those strategies with a view to achieving their objectives. Unlike the annual action plans adopted since the first ministerial-level meeting in 1992, this new Action Plan is intended to span a five-year period and will only be reviewed and updated 'as necessary'.[406] With the adoption of the strategies laying down detailed policy guidelines for the Commission, the political significance of the Action Plan was substantially downgraded, as appears from the fact that ministers simply 'took note' of it, whereas they had formally 'endorsed' the 1992 Action Plan in Paris. In contrast with its predecessors, the new Action Plan lays down no deadlines for the adoption of 'urgent' measures. Hardly any new items have been added to the lists of

[401] *Ibid*, p 19, Annex 4.
[402] *Ibid*, p 8, Annex 1, para 1.a(ii).
[403] *Ibid*, p 9, Annex 2.
[404] *Ibid*, p 2, para 3.1.b.
[405] *Ibid*, p 2, para 3.1.c.
[406] *Ibid*, p 3, para 3.a.

industrial sectors and pollutants from diffuse sources for which programmes and measures are to be developed, in comparison to the previous Action Plan; in fact these lists seem to be shrinking. The need for future OSPAR regulatory action in a number of sectors is being called into question in view of the elaboration of non-binding BAT 'reference documents' for these sectors by the European Commission in the framework of the 1996 IPPC Directive.[407] The special emphasis on organohalogens as a generic category of substances requiring priority attention—a constant feature of earlier action plans—has vanished.

In their Sintra Statement, however, the ministers did put forward some 'intermediate targets' and target dates for the implementation of the Hazardous Substances Strategy. Programmes and measures for the agreed 'OSPAR List of Chemicals for Priority Action' are to be drawn up by 2002. The list itself is to be updated by 2000 with the use of the 'dynamic selection and prioritisation mechanism'. And, as a general rule, the necessary programmes and measures are to be developed by the Commission 'within three years after agreeing on the need for OSPAR action on a substance or group of substances.'[408] The drafters of the Sintra Statement apparently struck a political compromise between proponents of early regulatory action and advocates of rigorous application of the risk assessment and prioritisation process. Nevertheless, the different texts adopted by the Sintra ministerial meeting make quite plain the extent to which future OSPAR regulatory action in the field of toxics reduction hinges on the implementation of the agreed risk assessment and prioritisation mechanism, which has in fact resulted in an unprecedented formalisation of working procedures and decision-making processes for the development of programmes and measures under OSPAR Convention.

Since the adoption of the Hazardous Substances Strategy in 1998, the actual regulatory output of OSPAR with respect to toxic emissions from point and diffuse sources has considerably slowed down, as virtually all the resources and attention of the parties and their experts have been absorbed by the implementation of the 'dynamic mechanism'. Already at its 1999 regular meeting, the Commission noted difficulties in carrying forward the development of measures to address priority substances already identified and concluded that:

> without additional resources, it would be difficult for Contracting Parties to fulfil their commitments set out in OSPAR strategy and to act in accordance with the aspirations and expectations declared by Ministers at OSPAR/MMC 1998.[409]

[407] OSPAR Doc 98/14/1–E, July 1998, p 19, Annex 3. On the IPPC Dir and the role of BAT 'reference documents', see below ch 8.

[408] *Ibid*, Annex 45, p 2.

[409] OSPAR Doc 99/15/1–E, paras 3.33(f) and 3.34.

After two years of work, the expert group tasked with the assessment and prioritisation of substances submitted to the Commission a 'pragmatically' derived 'selection box' of 80 substances, and recommended that 12 of them, with the highest priority ranking based on their toxicity, persistence, and tendency to bioaccumulate, as well as production and use patterns, should immediately be added to the 'OSPAR List of Chemicals for Priority Action', while further data should be collected on the remaining substances, grouped in various categories.[410] The Commission adopted these recommendations and updated its priority list accordingly.[411] One year later, OSPAR decided to revise the list once more by adding a further 16 substances.[412] Ironically, there is consensus that 14 of those substances, though highly hazardous to the marine environment in terms of their intrinsic properties, do not in fact require any priority action as they are not currently being produced nor used in any of the states parties to OSPAR Convention. The need for any future action is to be reviewed every five years based on information voluntarily supplied by the chemical industry.[413]

For the other chemicals on the priority list, whether originally listed in 1998 or added in a subsequent revision, the only action taken so far for most of them has been the designation of a 'lead country' in charge of elaborating a 'background paper' for review by the Commission. This paper is to identify and quantify sources and pathways to the marine environment, evaluate available monitoring data, propose the desired level of reduction of emissions, discharges and losses, assess the effectiveness of any existing reduction measures and identify possible additional measures.[414] Since the launch of the Hazardous Substances Strategy, OSPAR has adopted background papers for nine priority substances and endorsed the recommendations for action contained in them.[415] However, no OSPAR decisions or recommendations on regulatory programmes and measures with respect to these substances under the 1992 Paris Convention have yet been adopted by the Commission.

It is striking that most of the recommendations for action endorsed by OSPAR are actually in the form of requests addressed to other organisations, mainly the European Community.[416] As regards product standards

[410] Briefing Document on the Work of DYNAMEC and the DYNAMEC Mechanism for the Selection and Prioritisation of Hazardous Substances, OSPAR Doc 00/5/2–E.

[411] OSPAR Doc 00/20/1–E, para 5.8 and Annex 6.

[412] OSPAR Doc 01/18/1–E, para 4.12 and Annex 7.

[413] *Ibid*, para 4.13.

[414] Interim Guidance how to address hazardous substances for priority action, OSPAR Doc 99/15/1–E, Annex 7.

[415] OSPAR Doc 00/20/1–E, para 5.14(b); OSPAR Doc 01/18/1–E, para 4.17(d) and Annex 9.

[416] See eg Table of Proposed Actions to Be Taken following the Adoption at OSPAR 2001 of OSPAR Background Documents for Hazardous Substances Identified for Priority Action, OSPAR Doc 01/18/1–E, Annex 9.

to address pollution from diffuse sources, a consensus seems to have developed within OSPAR that, because of the implications for the internal market, any regulatory action would more appropriately be taken by the EC under Directive 76/769/EEC. Where pesticides for agricultural use are concerned, the appropriate framework for action is considered to be Directive 91/414/EEC. So, in most cases, the only action taken by OSPAR is to send a letter to the European Commission inviting it to propose marketing and use restrictions under Directive 76/769/EEC or to refrain from including a particular pesticide in the Community list of active substances authorised under Directive 91/414/EEC. Even the mere act of formally sending such a communication to the European Commission was controversial, as the United Kingdom raised legal objections on the grounds that it might be inconsistent with the duty of Community loyalty laid down in Article 10 of the EC Treaty

> for a group of some Member States to join with non-Member States to make representations to the European Community which might result in legally binding provisions that would affect the Community as a whole. [417]

Eventually, these objections were set aside and the Commission decided at its 2001 meeting to mandate its Chairman to send the message in question to the European Commission,[418] whose representative in OSPAR had in fact indicated no objections to this procedure and informed the contracting parties of its intention to take these OSPAR recommendations into account anyway.[419]

OSPAR seems to have abdicated its regulatory responsibility to the EC not only for diffuse sources, but also for point sources. The argument here is the ongoing work within the framework of the IPPC Directive to develop non-binding BAT reference documents (BREFs) for all major industrial processes. Rather than proceeding independently with the further elaboration of decisions or recommendations on BAT for sectors emitting priority hazardous substances, OSPAR prefers to review the reference documents developed by the EC to examine whether its specific concerns regarding emissions and discharges of hazardous substances to the marine environment are adequately met and to determine whether there is any need for further OSPAR measures. The fact that BREFs are merely technical reference documents which are not binding on national permitting authorities in EC member states and have no status at all under OSPAR Convention seems to be no objection from OSPAR's perspective and no sufficient reason for the adoption of binding measures pursuant to the Convention.

[417] OSPAR Doc 00/20/1–E, para 5.18.
[418] OSPAR Doc 01/18/1–E, para 4.19.
[419] OSPAR Doc 00/20/1–E, paras 5.19(a) and 5.21.

In retrospect, the Sintra ministerial meeting seems to have marked the endpoint of OSPAR's standard-setting work with respect to industrial point source emissions rather than a new beginning. At Sintra itself, the Commission adopted a number of decisions and recommendations concerning BAT and emission limit values for existing aluminium electrolysis plants,[420] the primary non-ferrous metal industry[421] and the PVC sector and related processes in the organic chemical industry,[422] which were the outcome of the work on specific industrial sectors initiated prior to 1998. Since then, however, only two more OSPAR recommendations on point sources have been adopted, both of them completing the ongoing work on the PVC industry,[423] but not a single decision or recommendation directly arising from the Hazardous Substances Strategy has seen the light of day. Ironically, when OSPAR adopted its most recent recommendation setting emission limit values for the manufacture of PVC, a statement made by the representative of the European Commission underscored the waning importance of OSPAR as a rule-making forum. He announced that since the EU Council had declined to approve the earlier OSPAR decisions on emission limit values for the PVC sector, adopted in 1998, the Commission did not intend to submit the new recommendation to the Council for approval. 'Consequently,' he stressed for the record, 'this Recommendation and the ELVs set out therein, would not (i) apply to the European Community, (ii) have any status at Community level and (iii) be enforceable at EC level.'[424] In this context, and in view of the work carried out so far, it seems extremely unlikely that OSPAR will be able to develop programmes and measures for all the hazardous substances on its priority list by 2002, as mandated by ministers in their Sintra Statement.

The adoption in 1992 of a ministerial declaration setting forth an ambitious toxics phase-out objective and its subsequent elaboration in action plans, further objectives and strategies, endorsed by another ministerial conference in 1998, has no doubt heightened the political profile of OSPAR

[420] OSPAR Recommendation 98/2 on Emission and Discharge Limit Values for Existing Aluminium Electrolysis Plants.

[421] OSPAR Recommendation 98/1 concerning Best Available Techniques and Best Environmental Practice for the Primary Non-Ferrous Metal Industry (Zinc, Copper, Lead and Nickel Works).

[422] OSPAR Decision 98/4 on Emission and Discharge Limit Values for the Manufacture of Vinyl Chloride Monomer (VCM) including the Manufacture of 1,2-dichloroethane (EDC); OSPAR Decision 98/5 on Emission and Discharge Limit Values for the Vinyl Chloride Sector, Applying to the Manufacture of Suspension-PVC (s-PVC) from Vinyl Chloride Monomer (VCM).

[423] OSPAR Recommendation 99/1 on the Best Available Techniques for the Manufacture of Emulsion PVC (e-PVC); OSPAR Recommendation 2000/3 on Emission and Discharge Limit Values for the Manufacture of Emulsion PVC (e-PVC) from Vinyl Chloride Monomer, OSPAR Doc 00/20/1–E, Annex 10. VCM, the main organohalogen compound for which limit values are set by this recommendation, is not in fact included in the OSPAR List of Chemicals for Priority Action.

[424] OSPAR Doc 00/20/1–E, para 5.27.

Convention and its Commission. Whether this new approach will effectively result in stronger normative action within the framework of the Convention and enhance the effectiveness of international regulatory efforts for the control of toxic emissions in the aquatic environment seems doubtful. The original, rather straightforward legal mandate for toxics reduction of the 1974 Convention has now been replaced by less explicit treaty provisions and several layers of interpretative political discourse (ministerial declaration, objective, strategy, action plan) and procedures which tend to qualify the mandate and delay rather than speed up implementing action. It comes as no surprise, therefore, that the European chemical industry association CEFIC, in its statement to the Sintra meeting, warmly welcomed the new Strategy and its emphasis on science-based risk assessment, which 'will replace the formerly undefined ways of selecting substances and processes for OSPAR working plans.'[425]

[425] CEFIC, Comments on the OSPAR Strategy with regard to Hazardous Substances, OSPAR Doc MMC 98/6/NGO.1–E, July 1998, p 1.

5

The Baltic Land-Based Sources Regime: The 1974 and 1992 Helsinki Conventions on the Protection of the Marine Environment of the Baltic Sea Area

HISTORY AND BACKGROUND OF THE CONVENTIONS

The Convention on the Protection of the Marine Environment of the Baltic Sea Area, concluded in Helsinki on 22 March 1974[1] between the riparian states of the Baltic Sea, differed from the 1974 Paris Convention in that it was a comprehensive agreement covering all sources of marine pollution, and not focused specifically on pollution from land-based sources. In its comprehensiveness, it was quite similar to the Barcelona Convention for the Protection of the Mediterranean Sea against Pollution, which was concluded two and a half years later, although it was more than a mere framework convention. The 1974 Helsinki Convention and its annexes contained detailed provisions on dumping, pollution from ships and pollution from land-based sources. In a way, it prefigured the approach of the various 'Regional Seas Conventions' which were later negotiated under the auspices of UNEP, starting with the Barcelona Convention signed in 1976. From a substantive point of view, it could be considered as a Baltic equivalent of the Barcelona Convention and its Protocols combined in a single instrument. The ratification process of the 1974 Convention proved slow, and the instrument only entered into force in May 1980.[2] It served as the legal

[1] The original text of the Convention was published in 13 ILM 544 (1974). A consolidated text, including amendments made since entry into force, can be found in *Baltic Sea Environment Proceedings*, No 56, p 107. On the 1974 Helsinki Convention, see generally Fitzmaurice (1992), Boczek (1978) & Tulokas (1981).

[2] Fitzmaurice (1992), p 50. Surprisingly, the last of the signatories to ratify was the Federal Republic of Germany, which deposited its instrument of ratification on 3 Mar 1980. *Ibid*, n 10.

framework for the Baltic marine environment protection regime for 20 years, until its replacement by a new instrument.

In February 1990, ten years after its entry into force, the contracting parties decided to initiate negotiations on a full-scale revision of the 1974 Convention, 'in order to extend, strengthen and modernize the legal regime for the protection of the marine environment of the Baltic Sea Area,'[3] and established a special working group to that effect.[4] These negotiations were successfully concluded in 1992, resulting in a comprehensive new Convention intended to replace the earlier one. The 1992 Baltic Convention was formally adopted at a ministerial conference held in Helsinki on 9 April 1992, a few months before a similar, ministerial-level meeting of the Oslo and Paris Commissions which endorsed the new Paris Convention. Again, some signatories were slow to ratify, so that the new Convention only entered into force and formally replaced the previous one on 17 January 2000.

In this chapter, I shall examine in detail the provisions of the successive Helsinki Conventions relating to pollution from land-based sources, the practice of the Baltic Marine Environment Protection Commission, generally referred to as the Helsinki Commission (HELCOM), established under the 1974 Convention, and political developments in other regional fora which are relevant to the formulation and implementation of toxics reduction policies.

ANALYSIS OF THE 1974 HELSINKI CONVENTION

The fundamental obligation of the contracting parties, as laid down in Article 3 of the 1974 Baltic Convention, is to 'individually or jointly take all appropriate . . . measures in order to prevent and abate pollution'. Specific obligations with respect to emissions of dangerous substances into the Baltic marine environment are to be found in Articles 5 and 6. In Article 5, the contracting parties undertake to 'counteract the introduction, whether airborne, waterborne or otherwise' of certain hazardous substances into the Baltic Sea. The list of 'hazardous substances' within the meaning of Article 5, as laid down in Annex I of the Convention, is very limited, much shorter than the black lists of the other conventions. Originally, it contained only DDT and PCBs. In 1983, it was amended to include PCTs.[5]

[3] Intergovernmental Activities in the Framework of the Helsinki Convention 1974–1994, *Baltic Sea Environment Proceedings*, No 56, p 8.

[4] Fitzmaurice (1992), p 93.

[5] HELCOM Recommendation 4/1 concerning amendment of Annex I of the Helsinki Convention, 1 Feb 1983, *Baltic Sea Environment Proceedings*, No 8, p 37.

The term 'counteract' is somewhat ambiguous and opinions differ as to its interpretation. Some authors consider that the obligation imposed on contracting parties by Article 5 of the 1974 Helsinki Convention is stricter than the corresponding obligations to 'eliminate' pollution by black list substances under the 1974 Paris Convention and the 1980 Athens Protocol. In their view, Article 5 prohibits the introduction of these substances into the marine environment per se.[6] Others, however, are of the opinion that the undertaking to 'counteract the introduction' of those substances does *not* include the duty to eliminate pollution by them since it only applies to substances introduced after the entry into force of the Convention.[7] In fact, the question is rather academic, since it appears that, notwithstanding the specific wording of the Helsinki Convention, contracting parties have not interpreted their obligations with respect to hazardous substances under that Convention any differently than under the other relevant conventions.

The measures adopted by contracting parties to the Helsinki Convention to 'counteract the introduction' of PCBs, for instance, are not significantly different from those adopted by contracting parties to the Paris Convention to 'eliminate pollution' by PCBs. Both provide for a phased reduction of PCB emissions through different measures for new and existing sources. Although the preambular paragraphs of the Helsinki Commission's recommendation refer to the objective of 'accelerating the elimination of pollution by PCBs', its operative provisions fall short of what is required to achieve this objective.[8] Likewise, in its recommendation 'regarding the elimination of discharges of DDT', the Commission, though 'mindful of accelerating a total stop for the introduction of DDT . . . into the Baltic Sea Area', still allowed contracting parties to continue 'limited production' of DDT for 'special purposes.'[9]

In addition to the obligations with respect to the 'hazardous substances' in Article 5, Article 6 of the Convention lays down more general obligations concerning the control of pollution from land-based sources. In general terms, Article 6, paragraph 1 imposes on contracting parties the duty to 'take all appropriate measures to control and minimize' such pollution. More specifically, Article 6, paragraph 2 provides that measures must be taken 'in particular' to 'control and strictly limit' pollution by 'noxious substances', which are listed in Annex II. Annex II contains a much longer list of substances than Annex I, including most substances on the black and grey lists of the 1974 Paris Convention, plus a few additional ones.

[6] Kuwabara (1984), pp 55–57; De Yturriaga Barberan (1979), p 388; Boczek (1978), p 805.
[7] Meng (1987), p 123. See also Hakapää (1981), p 102.
[8] HELCOM Recommendation 3/1 regarding the limitation of the use of PCBs, 17 Feb 1982, *Baltic Sea Environment Proceedings*, No 7, p 46.
[9] HELCOM Recommendation 3/2 regarding the elimination of discharges of DDT, 17 Feb 1982, *ibid*, p 48.

Article 6, paragraph 2 further specifies the measures to be taken to control pollution by these substances. It provides for the adoption of 'specific programmes, guidelines, standards or regulations concerning discharges, environmental quality, and products containing such substances and materials and their use'. As in the 1974 Paris Convention, both emission standards and environmental quality standards as well as product standards are envisaged. The procedure for the adoption of such standards is not specified in Article 6, which only provides that contracting parties shall 'co-operate' to this effect. However, Article 13, paragraph b) confers on the Commission established under the Convention recommendatory powers which can be used for this purpose. Furthermore, Article 6 provides that the substances in Annex II shall not be discharged in 'significant quantities' without a 'prior special permit' issued by the appropriate national authority and 'which *may* be periodically reviewed'[10] and that contracting parties 'shall endeavour to establish and adopt common criteria for issuing permits for discharges.'[11]

It should be noted that the scope of application of the 1974 Convention's provisions on land-based sources is limited by Article 4, paragraph 3, which stipulates in general terms that its provisions 'do not apply to internal waters which are under the sovereignty of each Contracting Party', though it also contains a soft 'undertaking' of the parties to ensure that the 'purposes' of the Convention 'will be obtained' in their internal waters. This provision was originally interpreted by the Soviet Union and its allies in the Helsinki Commission as implying that discharges into internal waters were, as such, not directly subject to the provisions of the Convention relating to land-based sources, thus effectively excluding most of these sources from their scope. According to this interpretation, only fluxes of pollutants crossing the baseline which separates internal waters from the territorial sea and having an impact in the actual 'Baltic Sea Area', as defined in Article 1, are of legitimate concern to other parties and can be subject to international obligations under the Convention.[12]

In addition to the specific measures concerning 'hazardous substances' in Article 5 and 'noxious substances' in Article 6, a number of general measures for the prevention of land-based pollution by 'harmful substances' in general are laid down in Annex III. Article 6, paragraph 6 provides that the contracting parties 'shall aim at attaining the goals and applying the criteria' enumerated in Annex III. The wording used in this provision, as well as in the provisions of Annex III, does not impose very precise obligations on contracting parties. Annex III lays down a few general principles for the treatment of municipal sewage and industrial wastes which are not more

[10] Helsinki Convention, Art 6, para 3 (emphasis added).
[11] *Ibid*, Art 6, para 5.
[12] See Roginko (1998), p 586.

specific than, eg 'The polluting load of industrial wastes shall be minimized in an appropriate way in order to reduce the amount of harmful substances, organic matter and nutrients.'[13] While Annex III does not itself contain specific emission standards or pollution reduction objectives, it provides a basis for the adoption of more specific provisions by the Commission established under the Convention, which is given the mandate to 'define pollution control criteria, objectives for reduction of pollution and objectives concerning measures . . . to reduce pollution of the Baltic Sea Area.'[14] However, it is clear from the context that such criteria and objectives, which contracting parties would 'aim' to apply or attain, would be in the nature of recommendations only.[15]

In 1998, the Helsinki Commission, pursuant to Article 24 of the 1974 Convention, adopted amendments to Annex III, supplementing it with additional provisions on the prevention of pollution from agricultural sources.[16] The bulk of these new provisions deals with measures to reduce inputs of nutrients, which are not directly relevant to the subject of this study. However, some very general provisions on the use of pesticides are also included, which require parties to elaborate 'national risk reduction strategies' based on 'best environmental practice.'[17] Due to delays in the approval by contracting parties, these amendments did not become effective prior to the entry into force of the 1992 Convention.[18]

ANALYSIS OF THE 1992 HELSINKI CONVENTION

The 1992 Helsinki Baltic Convention was negotiated in parallel with the 1992 Paris Convention and displays striking similarities with it. There seems to have been some concern on the part of the participants involved in both negotiations simultaneously (Denmark, Sweden, Germany and the EC) to ensure the greatest possible harmonisation of the North Sea and Baltic Sea marine pollution regimes. However, in view of the specific political and geographical context of international environmental cooperation

[13] *Ibid*, Annex III, para 3.
[14] *Ibid*, Annex III, para 6.
[15] On the recommendatory nature of HELCOM decisions, see generally Ehlers (1993), pp 192–93.
[16] HELCOM Recommendation 19/6 concerning amendments to Annex III of the Helsinki Convention concerning regulations on prevention of pollution from agriculture, 26 Mar 1998. According to Art 24, para 2 of the Convention, these amendments shall be deemed to have been accepted on 1 Jan 1999 unless any contracting party formally objects to them prior to that date.
[17] 1974 Helsinki Convention, Annex III (as amended by HELCOM Recommendation 19/6), Part II, Regulation 3.
[18] See HELCOM Recommendation 21/1 concerning amendments to Annex III 'Criteria and measures concerning the prevention of pollution from land-based sources' of the 1992 Helsinki Convention, 20 Mar 2000, 4th preambular para.

in the Baltic region, the different partners involved and the particular character of the Baltic marine environment, it is only logical that a number of differences between the two instruments persist. In the field of pollution from land-based sources, as we shall see, these differences appear to be of a more formal and terminological than substantive nature.

Article 3 of the new Helsinki Convention, which lays down the 'fundamental principles and obligations' of the parties, is very similar in content to Article 2 of the 1992 Paris Convention. Whereas the 1974 Helsinki Convention committed its contracting parties 'to prevent *and abate* pollution and to protect and enhance the marine environment of the Baltic Sea Area,'[19] the general objective fixed by the 1992 Convention is considerably more ambitious: the contracting parties undertake 'to take all appropriate . . . measures to prevent *and eliminate* pollution in order to promote *the ecological restoration of the Baltic Sea Area and the preservation of its ecological balance*.'[20] Thus, as in the 1992 Paris Convention, the standard phrase used in the new Helsinki Convention to describe the parties' obligations with respect to marine pollution has become 'prevent and eliminate'. This seems consistent with the explicit objective of 'ecological restoration', an objective first enunciated in a 1988 ministerial declaration which shall be discussed below. The provisions of the new Convention transposed this objective into hard law.

Like the 1992 Paris Convention, the 1992 Helsinki Convention provides that its contracting parties 'shall apply' the precautionary principle[21] and the polluter pays principle.[22] However, the content of the latter is not made at all explicit, while that of the former is described in slightly different terms than in the new Paris Convention. According to Article 3, paragraph 2 of the 1992 Helsinki Convention, the precautionary principle is to be understood as the obligation

> to take preventive measures *when there is reason to assume* that substances or energy introduced, directly or indirectly, into the marine environment *may create* hazards to human health, harm living resources and marine ecosystems, damage amenities or interfere with other legitimate uses of the sea even when there is no conclusive evidence of a causal relationship between inputs and *their alleged* effects.[23]

It has been argued by some commentators that this definition of the precautionary principle 'is more objective and therefore more desirable'[24] than that in the 1992 Paris Convention. This argument hinges on the difference

[19] 1974 Helsinki Convention, Art 3, para 1 (emphasis added).
[20] 1992 Helsinki Convention, Art 3, para 1 (emphasis added).
[21] *Ibid*, Art 3, para 2. Cf 1992 Paris Convention, Art 2, para 2(a).
[22] 1992 Helsinki Convention, Art 3, para 4. Cf 1992 Paris Convention, Art 2, para 2(b).
[23] 1992 Helsinki Convention, Art 3, para 2 (emphasis added).
[24] Fitzmaurice (1993), p 26.

between the phrase 'when there is reason to assume' and the phrase 'when there are reasonable grounds for concern', which, according to Hey, IJlstra and Nollkaemper, 'introduces extremely subjective elements into the definition of the precautionary principle.'[25] It seems to me that the difference is marginal: the notion 'reason to assume' is hardly more objective than 'reasonable grounds for concern'. After all, assumptions are by definition subjective. As I have pointed out elsewhere,[26] whatever efforts may be made to 'objectify' the precautionary principle, arguments about scientific uncertainty are likely to re-emerge in other forms and will continue to feature prominently in policy debates on international environmental regulation.

The 1992 Helsinki Convention imposes on its contracting parties a general obligation with respect to the use of BAT and BEP, though formulated in softer terms than its counterpart provision in the 1992 Paris Convention:

> In order to prevent and eliminate pollution of the Baltic Sea Area the Contracting Parties shall *promote* the use of Best Environmental Practice and Best Available Technology.[27]

The parties' obligations regarding pollution from land-based sources, as laid down in Article 6 of the new Convention, are hardly more specific:

> The Contracting Parties undertake to prevent and eliminate pollution of the Baltic Sea Area from land-based sources by using, *inter alia*, Best Environmental Practice for all sources and Best Available Technology for point sources.[28]

Thus, as in the 1992 Paris Convention, the definition of the concepts of BAT and BEP is pivotal in ascertaining the content of the Helsinki parties' substantive obligations with respect to the control of marine pollution from land-based sources. The relevant definitions can be found in Annex II to the new Convention.

The 1992 Convention, like its predecessor, also provides for specific measures with respect to particular categories of pollutants. While the 1974 Convention contained a general definition of 'harmful substances', its substantive provisions specifically addressed two sub-categories referred to in this definition, namely 'hazardous substances' and 'noxious substances'. The introduction of the former into the marine environment was to be 'counteracted', while pollution by the latter was to be 'controlled and

[25] Hey, IJlstra & Nollkaemper, (1993), p 12.

[26] Pallemaerts (1995a), p 200; Pallemaerts (1996), p 650.

[27] 1992 Helsinki Convention, Art 3, para 3 (emphasis added). Cf 1992 Paris Convention, Art 2, para 3(b)(ii), which requires contracting parties to '*ensure* the application of' BAT and BEP. It should also be pointed out that the 1992 Helsinki Convention uses the term 'best available *technology*' instead of 'best available *techniques*', though there is no substantive difference in the definition of the two concepts.

[28] 1992 Helsinki Convention, Art 6, para 1.

strictly limited'. The 1992 Convention defines two different categories of substances: the general category of 'harmful substances', which includes 'any substance, which, if introduced into the sea, is liable to cause pollution,'[29] and a sub-category thereof, 'hazardous substances', which comprises 'any harmful substance which due to its intrinsic properties is persistent, toxic or liable to bio-accumulate.'[30] The concept of 'noxious substances' is no longer used. The specific obligations of parties mostly relate to 'harmful substances' generally; the 1992 Convention contains very few provisions relating to 'hazardous substances' specifically and one may wonder whether these provisions really warranted the need for a separately defined category of substances. I shall now examine the different obligations of contracting parties relevant to the control of toxic inputs, ie their general obligations with respect to pollution from land-based sources and their specific obligations with respect to 'harmful substances' and 'hazardous substances'.

As regards pollution from land-based sources, apart from the general duty prescribed by Article 6, paragraph 1 to 'prevent and eliminate' such pollution through the application of BAT and BEP, Article 6, paragraph 2 refers the reader to the 'procedures and measures' laid down in the new Convention's Annex III, whose implementation is mandatory. This annex is an updated and expanded version of Annex III to the 1974 Convention, dealing with pollution from industrial and municipal waste water. Administrative authorisation systems remain the main regulatory instrument for discharges of 'harmful substances' from land-based sources, as they were for 'noxious substances' under the 1974 Convention. Article 6, paragraph 3 of the 1992 Convention provides that

> harmful substances from point sources shall not, *except in negligible quantities*, be introduced directly or indirectly into the marine environment of the Baltic Sea Area, without a *prior special permit*, which *may* be periodically reviewed.

A number of substantive changes were made compared to the corresponding provisions of the 1974 Convention. Whereas, under that Convention, the requirement of a 'prior special permit' applied only to 'noxious substances' discharged 'in significant quantities,'[31] it has now been extended to all discharges of 'harmful substances' as defined in the new Convention, except those which are deemed 'negligible' by the parties. While the 1974 Convention only provided that the contracting parties would 'endeavour to establish and adopt common criteria' for discharge permits,[32] the 1992 Convention explicitly requires national permitting authorities to comply with a

[29] 1992 Helsinki Convention, Art 2, para 7.
[30] *Ibid*, Art 2, para 8.
[31] 1974 Helsinki Convention, Art 6, para 3 and Annex II.
[32] *Ibid*, Art 6, para 5.

set of common principles laid down in Annex III to the Convention and to 'ensure that authorized emissions to water and air are monitored and controlled.'[33]

The 'criteria and measures' laid down in Annex III shall be applied by the contracting parties 'in the whole catchment area' of the Baltic Sea.[34] The provisions of Annex III are generally more detailed than those of its 1974 counterpart. There are, however, a number of significant ambiguities. For instance, Regulation 1 of Annex III seems to contradict Article 6, paragraph 1 of the Convention where it provides that the contracting parties shall only 'take into account' BEP and BAT in applying the measures set out in the other provisions of Annex III. As regards emissions from industrial point sources, Annex III prescribes that the 'special permits' referred to in Article 6, paragraph 3 shall 'state' limit values for emissions to water and air containing harmful substances[35] and that 'industrial plants should aim at closed water systems or at a high rate of circulation in order to avoid waste water wherever possible.'[36] It also provides that 'industrial plants and other point sources *connected to municipal treatment plants* shall use Best Available Technology.'[37] But no explicit, general and unequivocal obligation for *all* industrial point sources to apply BAT can be found in Annex III. This is all the more surprising in view of the restatement in this Annex of the general requirement to eliminate pollution from diffuse sources 'by promoting and implementing Best Environmental Practice'. It could be argued that such a restatement is redundant in view of the general provisions in Article 3, paragraph 3 and Article 6, paragraph 1 of the Convention, but the fact that these general provisions are *selectively* restated in Annex III can hardly be coincidental.

The bulk of Annex III is made up of purely *procedural* obligations with respect to the issuing of permits for industrial plants in accordance with Article 6, paragraph 3 of the Convention. Regulation 3 of Annex III sets out the principles and procedures to be applied by the contracting parties in this respect. The information to be submitted in applications for permits is spelled out in great detail. The competent national permitting authorities are put under an obligation to 'evaluate the present status and potential impact of the planned activities on the environment' and to issue a permit only 'after comprehensive assessment'. Regulation 3 further specifies the items to be laid down in the permit, including, inter alia, 'instructions concerning . . . production processes and/or agents' and 'limit values for amount and quality . . . of direct and indirect discharges and emissions,'[38]

[33] 1992 Helsinki Convention, Art 6, para 3 and Annex III, Reg 3.
[34] *Ibid*, Annex III, Reg 1.
[35] *Ibid*, Reg 2, para 5.
[36] *Ibid*, para 2.
[37] *Ibid*, para 6 (emphasis added).
[38] *Ibid*, Reg 3, para 3, 2nd and 3rd indent.

but contains no explicit reference to the requirement to implement BAT. Finally, it imposes on national authorities a duty to monitor discharges and their impacts after authorisation has been granted and to 'review the permit where necessary.'[39]

As was mentioned above, the Helsinki Commission in 1998 adopted amendments to Annex III of the 1974 Convention to supplement it with regulations on the prevention of pollution from agricultural sources, focusing on nutrients and pesticides, but these amendments did not enter into force before the 1974 Convention was formally superseded by its successor instrument in 2000. As had been agreed at the time of adoption of the 1998 amendments, the same provisions were again adopted as amendments to Annex III of the 1992 Convention, and are due to become effective on 31 December 2000 in accordance with the relevant provisions of that convention.[40]

Article 5 of the 1992 Convention puts the contracting parties under a general obligation 'to prevent and eliminate pollution of the marine environment of the Baltic Sea Area caused by harmful substances *from all sources*,'[41] by implementing a number of 'procedures and measures' which are further spelled out in Annex I to the Convention. This Annex, which bears the heading 'Harmful substances', is made up of three distinct parts, one on 'general principles', one on 'banned substances' and one on pesticides. Part I lists a set of criteria to be used by the contracting parties 'in identifying and evaluating harmful substances' and further enumerates a number of 'priority groups' of substances 'which are generally recognized as harmful substances'. Both the criteria and the list of priority substances are essentially the same as in Appendix 2 of the 1992 Paris Convention.[42] Though Article 5 of the 1992 Convention, in referring to Annex I, speaks of 'procedures *and measures*', it is striking that Part I of this Annex, which relates to 'harmful substances' in general, does not actually state any specific measures to be taken by the contracting parties to address inputs of those substances. It only provides that they 'shall, *in their preventive measures*'—which are otherwise unspecified—'give priority to' the harmful

[39] 1992 Helsinki Convention, Annex III, Reg 3, para 4.

[40] HELCOM Recommendation 21/1 concerning amendments to Annex III 'Criteria and measures concerning the prevention of pollution from land-based sources' of the 1992 Helsinki Convention, 20 Mar 2000. It should be noted, however, that the recommendation specifies that Denmark, Finland, Germany and Sweden are to implement the new provisions of Annex III by 1 Jan 2002, whereas the other contracting parties are granted an additional period of nine years to comply. Thus, without any explicit legal basis in the Convention, the Commission effectively introduced a system of differentiated obligations for countries in transition.

[41] 1992 Helsinki Convention, Art 5 (emphasis added).

[42] The only significant differences are that 'proven carcinogenic, teratogenic or mutagenic properties in or through the marine environment' are included as an additional criterion in the Helsinki Convention and 'other organic compounds especially harmful to the marine environment' as an additional priority group of pollutants, while organic compounds of silicon are not explicitly mentioned in Helsinki's Annex I, contrary to Paris' App 2.

substances belonging to the priority groups listed. Parts 2 and 3 of Annex I, which address particular categories of 'hazardous substances' that may originate from diffuse sources, are more specific. Part 2, which is entitled 'Banned substances', is the equivalent in the 1992 Convention of Annex I to the 1974 Convention. It requires the contracting parties to 'prohibit, totally or partially, the use . . . in the Baltic Sea Area and its catchment area' of DDT and its derivatives, PCBs and PCTs and 'organotin compounds for antifouling paints for pleasure craft under 25 m and fish net cages'.

DDT, PCBs and PCTs were already mentioned in the 1974 Convention as hazardous substances whose introduction into the environment had to be 'counteracted'. As we have seen above, the 1974 provisions fell short of totally prohibiting the production and use of these pollutants. The 1992 provisions now amount to a virtually complete ban on their *use*, except (as regards PCBs and PCTs) in 'existing closed system equipment until the end of service life'. *Production*, however, is once again left unregulated as a matter of hard law, a surprising omission in view of a recommendation adopted by the Helsinki Commission in 1985, calling for all production of PCBs and PCTs to be stopped from 1987.[43] As regards the new addition to the list of hazardous substances, organotin compounds, it is stressed that these substances are banned 'for certain applications' only.[44] The ban on their use as antifouling paints for pleasure craft under 25 m and fish net cages amounts to a partial codification and translation into hard law of another HELCOM recommendation, adopted in 1988.[45] Indeed, at that time HELCOM had recommended that not only the use but also the *retail sale* of these paints be banned, and had referred to their use on pleasure boats generally, not just those under a certain size.

The list of pesticides in Part 3 of Annex I is a new feature of the 1992 Convention. The contracting parties have undertaken to '*endeavour to minimize and, wherever possible, to ban* the use . . . as pesticides in the Baltic Sea Area and its catchment area' of 26 substances or groups of substances which have been identified as hazardous to the marine environment.[46] This list of pesticides had already been agreed by the Helsinki Commission in a recommendation adopted in February 1992, which referred to them as 'banned pesticides' and provided unequivocally that they 'shall not be used.'[47] The provisions of Annex I thus amount to a

[43] HELCOM Recommendation 6/1 regarding the elimination of the use of PCBs and PCTs, 13 Mar 1985, *Baltic Sea Environment Proceedings*, No 15, p 35.

[44] 1992 Helsinki Convention, Annex I, Part 2, para 2.3.

[45] HELCOM Recommendation 9/10 concerning antifouling paints containing organotin compounds, 17 Feb 1988, *Baltic Sea Environment Proceedings*, No 26, p 63.

[46] All of the substances mentioned in Part 3 of Annex I of the 1992 Helsinki Convention are also listed in Part (c) of Annex IB to the 1990 Hague INSC Declaration, cf above ch 4.

[47] HELCOM Recommendation 13/13 concerning approval of pesticides for use in the catchment area of the Baltic Sea, 6 Feb 1992, Appendix and 1st operational para, item (f).

significantly watered-down version of the unconditional ban called for in this recommendation. It should be noted, however, that the measures to be taken by contracting parties to reduce inputs of pesticides into the marine environment are not confined to the specific substances identified in Part 3 of Annex I. Another clause, in Annex III of the 1992 Convention, stipulates that all pesticides used in the Baltic's catchment area 'shall comply with the criteria established by the Commission,'[48] thus providing a basis for further action by the Helsinki Commission to regulate the use of pesticides generally. The criteria referred to in Annex III were adopted by HELCOM in 1999[49] and will be discussed below.

The measures with respect to DDT, PCBs, PCTs, organotin compounds and pesticides in Annex I are specifically prescribed 'in order to protect the Baltic Sea area from *hazardous substances*.'[50] The only other provisions of the 1992 Convention referring to hazardous substances are to be found in Annex II and Annex III, in the definition of 'Best Environmental Practice' and in two of the 'specific requirements' for the prevention of pollution from land-based sources, respectively. 'Avoiding the use of hazardous substances' is one of the options in the 'graduated range of measures' which makes up BEP.[51] Annex III, for its part, prescribes separate treatment for waste waters containing hazardous substances and the use of BAT in industrial plants and other point sources connected to municipal sewage treatment plants 'in order to avoid hazardous substances which cannot be made harmless in the municipal sewerage treatment plant or which may disturb the process in the plant.'[52]

In view of these provisions, the exact purpose of the distinction between 'harmful substances' and 'hazardous substances' in Article 2 is unclear, all the more so since the criteria laid down in Part 1 of Annex I for the identification of 'harmful' substances include the three 'intrinsic properties' which are used in the definition of Article 2, paragraph 7 to differentiate the sub-category of 'hazardous' substances from 'harmful' substances in general. The conceptual basis and function of the distinction between the two categories is unclear. At any rate, it appears to have little significance in the context of the Convention's operative provisions. Though the 1974 Helsinki Convention never knew a clear semantic and operational distinction between black list and grey list substances similar to that in the 1974 Paris Convention, its 1992 revised version suffers from the same general 'blurring' of categories as the 1992 Paris Convention.

[48] 1992 Helsinki Convention, Annex III, Reg 2, para 9.

[49] HELCOM Recommendation 20/2 concerning approval of pesticides ('plant protection products') for use in the catchment area of the Baltic Sea, 23 Mar 1999.

[50] *Ibid*, Annex I, Parts 2 and 3, introductory phrase (emphasis added).

[51] *Ibid*, Annex II, Reg 2, 7th indent.

[52] *Ibid*, Annex III, Reg 2, paras 4 and 6.

IMPLEMENTATION OF THE CONVENTIONS: THE PRACTICE OF THE HELSINKI COMMISSION

A glance at the list of recommendations adopted by the Helsinki Commission since its first formal meeting in 1980 reveals that its activities were initially strongly focused on the regulation of vessel-source pollution. Up to 1984, the Commission adopted only four recommendations dealing with hazardous substances. It is only in 1985 that the Commission started devoting more attention to land-based pollution and adopting more frequent recommendations on the subject.

Yet discussions on the regulation of pollution from land-based sources started as early as the mid-70s in the framework of the Interim Commission established by the signatories of the Convention to prepare its entry into force. An ad hoc working group was established to examine the issue of land-based pollution and, more specifically, the possibility of developing 'common criteria for issuing permits for discharges', as provided in Article 6, paragraph 5 of the Convention. The signatories exchanged information on their national policies regarding discharge permits and discussed the respective merits of approaches based on emission standards and water quality standards. This led to the conclusion that 'both these approaches must simultaneously be taken into consideration' in the development of common criteria.[53] Thus the debate in the Interim Commission of the Helsinki Convention was very similar to that in the early years of the Paris Commission, and equally inconclusive.[54] In fact, the work of the Interim Commission did not initially result in actual proposals for 'common criteria' as envisaged in the Convention, but only in a few draft recommendations relating to the use of the 'hazardous substances' DDT and PCBs and efforts to formulate guidelines for water quality and emission standards for some of the 'noxious substances' emitted by certain pollution sources.

Product Control Measures

The first recommendations relating to land-based pollution adopted by the Helsinki Commission were those concerning PCBs and DDT, already

[53] Report of the Interim Commission (IC) to the Baltic Marine Environment Protection Commission, *Baltic Sea Environment Proceedings*, No 2, pp 9–10.

[54] The slow pace of progress on land-based sources during the 1970s and 1980s is attributed by observers to the preference of the USSR and its allies for an EQO-based approach and their general perception of any international standards relating to emissions from land-based sources as impinging upon their sovereignty over their territory and internal waters. See Greene (1998), pp 190–191. Greene considers that it is only after 1989 that the scope of the Baltic Sea pollution control regime in fact 'expanded' to include land-based sources. *Ibid*, p 204. From a legal perspective this is of course incorrect, as land-based sources were covered by the 1974 Convention from the outset.

mentioned above. In 1982, the Commission recommended measures to limit the use of PCBs and reduce their emission into the marine environment. The recommendation calls for national regulations to prohibit the introduction of new products containing PCBs but allows for exemptions to be granted for most of the major uses of PCBs. No measures are recommended to restrict the *production* of PCBs. National regulations to reduce discharges from existing sources of PCBs are also recommended, but the actual measures to be taken to this effect are not specified.[55] Stronger measures for the elimination of the use of PCBs and PCTs were recommended in 1985, after Annex I of the Convention had been amended to include PCTs. Contrary to the 1982 recommendation, the new recommendation adopted in 1985 actually recommends that production of PCBs and PCTs be stopped from 1987 and that the marketing of equipment containing PCBs and PCTs be prohibited from the same date. Exceptions are possible only for research purposes. Finally, measures are also recommended for the collection and disposal of existing PCB-containing equipment.[56] However, unlike the Paris Commission, the Helsinki Commission has laid down no timetable for the elimination of PCBs in existing equipment. The 1982 recommendation on DDT calls for the use *and production* of DDT to be 'abandoned', but allows 'limited production' to continue for 'special purposes.'[57] Unlike the recommendation on PCBs, this recommendation has not been revised since 1982 and the exceptions are thus technically still in force.[58]

In addition to the recommendations on DDT and PCBs discussed above, the Helsinki Commission has adopted a few other recommendations regarding the use of particular substances where such use is likely to lead to marine pollution. Thus, in 1985, the Commission adopted a recommendation on the reduction of mercury use in dentistry, which calls for measures to ensure the collection of mercury-containing waste from dental clinics and for the development of mercury-free materials for tooth fillings.[59] The same year, the Commission also recommended measures to reduce mercury and cadmium pollution resulting from the use of those substances in batteries. These measures, however, unlike those adopted by the Paris Commission and the EC, did not initially go so far as to prohibit or regulate the use of mercury and cadmium in certain batteries, but only provided for the

[55] HELCOM Recommendation 3/1 regarding the limitation of the use of PCBs, 17 Feb 1982, *Baltic Sea Environment Proceedings*, No 7, p 46.

[56] HELCOM Recommendation 6/1, above n 43.

[57] HELCOM Recommendation 3/2 regarding the elimination of discharges of DDT, 17 Feb 1982, *Baltic Sea Environment Proceedings*, No 7, p 48.

[58] As of 21 Mar 2000, Recommendation 3/2 was still listed in the 'List of valid HELCOM recommendations' available on HELCOM Internet site (http://www.helcom.fi/reclist.html).

[59] HELCOM Recommendation 6/4 concerning measures aimed at the reduction of mercury resulting from dentistry, 13 Mar 1985, *Baltic Sea Environment Proceedings*, No 15, p 41.

labelling and collection of batteries and the recovery and 'safe disposal' of mercury and cadmium in used batteries.[60]

In 1993, HELCOM adopted a new recommendation on the reduction of diffuse emissions of heavy metals from used batteries, addressing not only mercury- and cadmium-, but also lead-containing batteries.[61] It recommends that

> batteries containing heavy metals should be substituted by less hazardous batteries *to the extent possible* aiming at, *in the long run*, a complete ceasing of the use of such metals.

It is significant that, whereas the 1993 recommendation's provisions relating to the labelling, collection, recovery and disposal of batteries were to be implemented no later than by the end of 1994, no deadline has been fixed for the complete phase-out of the use of heavy metals in batteries. For some contracting parties, this phase-out apparently remains a long-term objective.

Lead, another 'noxious substance' listed in Annex II of the 1974 Convention, is also the subject of other HELCOM recommendations. In 1988, the Commission, 'recognizing that a considerable amount of lead enters the Baltic Sea via the atmosphere', recommended that 'lead content in gasoline as an automobile fuel should be reduced considerably step by step in an appropriate time-scale.'[62] Although this recommendation is significant as the first recommending specific measures to deal with a form of marine pollution through the atmosphere, it is equally noteworthy for its failure to establish quantitative reduction targets and precise deadlines. It is only in a later recommendation, addressing overall emissions from the transport sector and adopted in 1996,[63] that the Commission called for a reduction of the lead content in petrol to a maximum concentration of 0.15 g/l, followed by a total phase-out of leaded petrol accross the whole Baltic Sea Region 'as soon as possible but not later than the year 2000.'[64]

Another diffuse source of pollution of the Baltic Sea by heavy metals is the use of mercury in light sources and electrical equipment. Measures to address this source were adopted by HELCOM in 1997.[65] The

[60] HELCOM Recommendation 6/5 concerning safe handling of used mercury- and cadmium-containing batteries, 13 Mar 1985, *Baltic Sea Environment Proceedings*, No 15, p 42.

[61] HELCOM Recommendation 14/5 on the reduction of diffuse emissions from used batteries containing heavy metals (mercury, cadmium and lead), 3 Feb 1993, *Baltic Sea Environment Proceedings*, No 52, p 49. This Recommendation supersedes the earlier Recommendation 6/5.

[62] HELCOM Recommendation 9/4 concerning reduction of emissions of lead from combustion of leaded gasoline, 15 Feb 1988, *Baltic Sea Environment Proceedings*, No 26, p 46.

[63] HELCOM Recommendation 17/1 on the reduction of emissions from the transport sector affecting the Baltic Sea, 13 Mar 1996, *Baltic Sea Environment Proceedings*, No 62, p 38.

[64] *Ibid*, operative paras III.5 and III.6.

[65] HELCOM Recommendation 18/5 concerning measures aimed at the reduction of mercury pollution resulting from light sources and electrical equipment, 11 Mar 1997.

Commission recommends the substitution of mercury-containing light sources by 'energy-efficient mercury-free light sources' by 2000 in the Western riparian states of the Baltic, and five years later in the countries in transition. Likewise, mercury-containing electrical equipment is to be substituted by mercury-free equipment, though no specific target date is recommended in this instance. However, these recommendations are not entirely unqualified, as they also recognise that there are cases in which mercury-free alternatives may not be available and where the use of mercury is to be minimised rather than substituted.

In 1988, the Commission recommended restrictions on the use of antifouling paints containing organotin compounds, urging contracting parties, 'as a first step', to ban the 'retail sale or use' of organotin paints for pleasure boats and fish net cages, and to 'consider the need for restrictions on other uses' eg on sea-going vessels.[66] The ban on the *use* of organotin antifouling paints for pleasure craft under 25 m and fish net cages in the Baltic Sea area was formalised in 1992 by its inclusion in Annex I of the revised Helsinki Convention and became legally binding upon its entry into force in 2000. Oddly, however, one year before the entry into force of the 1992 Convention, HELCOM adopted a new recommendation concerning organotin paints,[67] superseding the earlier one, but whose operative provisions are worded in almost identical terms. Although its preamble refers to the relevant legal and political developments in the Baltic sea regime since 1988, which, as we shall see below, strengthened the commitment of the parties to toxics reduction, there is no substantive progress at all vis-á-vis the 1988 recommendation. The main operative paragraph merely reiterates the recommendation that parties 'take effective measures to eliminate' organotin pollution, without specifying any deadline,[68] and the specific recommendations with respect to restrictions on particular uses in exactly the same terms as in 1988, as though the context had not changed. The only substantive change is that parties are requested to report on implementation every three instead of five years, and that a final paragraph urges reconsideration of the issue 'as soon as possible taking into account the development in other international fora'. One is left wondering what purpose this new instrument serves, especially in view of the relevant provisions of the 1992 Convention. If its aim is to recall and confirm the terms

[66] HELCOM Recommendation 9/10, above n 45.

[67] HELCOM Recommendation 20/4 concerning antifouling paints containing organotin compounds, 23 Mar 1999.

[68] Ironically, a footnote to this paragraph simply recalls that HELCOM Recommendation 9/10 *did* in fact state a timeframe for taking such measures, viz 'as soon as possible but not later than 1991'. One would rather have expected an operative provision urging parties which had not yet implemented the measures recommended 11 years earlier to do so without any further delay, all the more so in view of the imminent entry into force of the 1992 Convention.

of the 1988 recommendation, in so far as they were more demanding than the prohibition laid down in the new Convention's annex—by applying to all pleasure boats, not just those under 25 m, and calling not only for a ban on the use but also on the sale of organotin paints—one would have expected that to be stated explicitly.

To complete the overview of product control measures, it should be mentioned that HELCOM has also adopted a number of recommendations of a general nature regarding pollution by pesticides. They concern both non-substance-related, practical measures that can be taken by users to reduce the need for pesticides and minimise pollution during application, in the form of a 'code of best environmental practices,'[69] and recommendations to governments on the regulation of the supply of pesticides. In the latter category, the Commission first recommended, in 1992, the basic principle that all pesticides marketed and used in the catchment area of the Baltic Sea should be subject to prior registration by governmental authorities and that such registration should not be granted for substances or products which are 'especially dangerous to health or especially harmful to the environment.'[70] This 1992 recommendation also contained a list of some 25 substances whose use as pesticides was to be banned by all contracting parties. Finally, it provided that 'basic criteria', relevant to the Baltic Sea Area, for the approval of pesticides were to be elaborated by HELCOM within two years. As mentioned above, this list of pesticides to be banned, as well as a reference to the future approval criteria, were incorporated in the provisions of the revised 1992 Convention.[71] Some basic provisions on 'best environmental practices' and registration of pesticides were incorporated in the amendments to Annex III of the 1974 Convention adopted by HELCOM in 1998,[72] but the criteria for approval were only established by the Commission one year later.[73]

The relevant recommendation specifies that '*no approval* for the use in the catchment area of the Baltic Sea *shall be granted* to pesticides identified as problematic according to the Criteria' set out in an appendix.[74] In contrast with the imperative form used in the operative provisions of the recommendation itself, the formulation of the actual 'Criteria for identification of problematic pesticides' in its appendix is much less prescriptive. It states

[69] HELCOM Recommendation 16/11 concerning measures to reduce pollution by pesticides from agriculture, forestry and horticulture, 15 Mar 1995.

[70] HELCOM Recommendation 13/13 concerning approval of pesticides for use in the catchment area of the Baltic Sea, 6 Feb 1992.

[71] 1992 Helsinki Convention, Annex I, Part 3 and Annex III, Reg 2, para 9.

[72] HELCOM Recommendation 19/6 concerning amendments to Annex III of the Helsinki Convention concerning regulations on prevention of pollution from agriculture, 26 Mar 1998.

[73] HELCOM Recommendation 20/2 concerning approval of pesticides ('plant protection products') for use in the catchment area of the Baltic Sea, 23 Mar 1999. This Recommendation supersedes Recommendation 13/13.

[74] HELCOM Recommendation 20/2, 1st operative para (emphasis added).

that these criteria '*may* include' hazardous properties entailing a 'general threat to the aquatic environment', 'indications of risk for the marine environment' or a danger to human health through the consumption of seafood, as well as evidence that the pesticides 'reach, or are likely to reach the marine environment' or have been found in one of its compartments.[75] It goes on to stipulate that 'full compliance' with the requirements of Directive 91/414/EEC[76] 'has to be assured.'[77] The 'relevant paragraphs' of Annex VI of that directive are then reproduced verbatim. What is remarkable about this reference to EC law is that the directive in question contains no explicit requirement, let alone method, to specifically assess the effects of a pesticide on the marine environment. It only requires a general evaluation of toxicity to aquatic organisms. Shall all pesticides which comply with the requirements of Directive 91/414/EEC automatically be presumed not to be 'problematic' for use in the Baltic Sea catchment area, or are contracting parties to the Helsinki Convention expected not to approve substances which meet any of the specific, marine-environment-related criteria spelled out in the appendix to HELCOM Recommendation itself? The wording of the recommendation is, perhaps deliberately, ambiguous in this respect.

Emission Control Measures for Industrial Pollution Sources

On the issue of emission standards for industrial pollution sources, the Helsinki Commission has moved rather slowly. It is only in 1992, ie 12 years after the 1974 Convention came into force, that the Commission eventually managed to agree on the 'common criteria' for industrial discharge permits referred to in Article 6 of that Convention.[78] These criteria, or rather 'principles of permitting', as they are called in the recommendation itself, are of a purely procedural nature. They establish a common list of the basic information to be included by operators in their permit applications, so as to enable the competent authority to 'evaluate the present status and the potential impact of the planned activities on the environment', as well as, in general terms, of the nature of the requirements to be laid down by public authorities in any permits granted, including, eg 'limit values for amount and quality . . . for direct and indirect discharges and emissions'.

[75] HELCOM Recommendation 20/2, App 1, para 4 (emphasis added).

[76] Council Dir 91/414/EEC of 15 July 1991 concerning the placing of plant protection products on the market, OJ No L230, 19.8.1991, p 1.

[77] HELCOM Recommendation 20/2, App 1, para 4.

[78] HELCOM Recommendation 13/5 concerning principles for permitting waste water discharge and emissions from industrial plants, 5 Feb 1992. The first preambular para of this recommendation refers explicitly to the provisions of Art 6 of the Convention calling for the establishment of 'common criteria'.

The competent authorities of the contracting parties are also urged to monitor compliance with permit conditions and 'review the permit when necessary'. It is clear that these recommendations do not substantially limit the discretion of national permitting authorities.

However, over the years, HELCOM has also adopted more detailed recommendations setting emission standards and recommending specific pollution control measures based on BAT for a number of individual branches of industry, such as oil refineries, the chlor-alkali industry, cadmium-discharging industries, the pulp and paper industry, the agrochemical industry, the glass industry, the leather industry, the textile industry, hard coal cokeries, the metal surface treatment industry and the iron and steel industry. The first HELCOM recommendations addressing discharges of particular hazardous substances from specific industrial sectors were adopted in 1985. The sector-oriented approach, which gradually became more integrated and started addressing multiple pollutants and atmospheric emissions as well as effluent discharges, developed into the mainstream of HELCOM's normative output with respect to land-based sources in the late 1980s and early 1990s. The most important recommendations relevant to this study will be analysed below.

In 1985, the Commission adopted a recommendation on the reduction of mercury discharges from the chlor-alkali electrolysis industry, which calls for 'best technical means' to be used in new plants and recommends an emission standard for existing plants which is equivalent to that laid down in Directive 82/176/EEC.[79] Similarly, the recommendation on cadmium discharges adopted at the same meeting is directly inspired by Directive 83/513/EEC. It recommends the same emission standards for the same industrial sectors and with the same exceptions as the EEC Directive. In addition, however, it calls for national regulations to limit the use of cadmium 'to a strict minimum' in three industrial sectors.[80]

Pulp and Paper Industry

The Helsinki Commission was faster than the Paris Commission in dealing with pollution from the pulp and paper industry, which is indeed a major source of pollution in the Baltic Sea area. The first recommendation on the subject was adopted in 1988. The contracting parties agreed on recommended emission standards for chemical and biochemical oxygen demand and phosphorus from the pulp industry as well as on the principle that the

[79] HELCOM Recommendation 6/3 concerning measures aimed at the reduction of discharges of mercury from chloralkali industry, 13 Mar 1985, *Baltic Sea Environment Proceedings*, No 15, p 39.

[80] HELCOM Recommendation 6/6 concerning limitation of discharges of cadmium from land-based sources, 13 Mar 1985, *Baltic Sea Environment Proceedings*, No 15, p 43.

load of chlorinated organic substances 'should be reduced considerably'. However, they could not reach consensus on specific emission standards and timetables for the reduction of discharges of chlorinated organic compounds, but agreed to keep the matter under consideration with a view to formulating recommendations on numerical values at a later meeting.[81] This was achieved at the 1990 meeting, where new recommendations were adopted setting annual mean limit values for the aggregate discharges of chlorinated organic substances and phosphorus per ton of pulp produced by each contracting party's sulphite and kraft pulp mills situated within the catchment area of the Baltic Sea, to be achieved by 1995 'as a first step', and stricter limits to be complied with from the year 2000.[82] It is important to note that these were not emission limit values to be respected by each individual plant, but industry-wide national averages. It was agreed that these standards would be re-evaluated in 1994 and that standards on a 'plant by plant' basis would then be considered by the Commission.

As a matter of fact, it took the Helsinki Commission until 1996 to reach agreement on discharge limit values for individual pulp and paper plants. Two recommendations adopted in March 1996 define BAT for sulphite and kraft pulp mills and lay down limit values for aquatic discharges of organic compounds, nitrogen and phosphorus from these mills.[83] As a compromise between the contracting parties, existing plants in countries in transition were given more time to comply with these standards. The strictest BAT-based emission limits must be respected by new mills in all riparian states from 1 January 1997, while mills in operation before that date must achieve less stringent standards by 2000 only, or even 2005 in countries in transition. The recommendations also provide that molecular chlorine should not be used for pulp bleaching after 1 January 1997 except in countries in transition, where such use may be continued until 1 January 2000. Unlike the Paris Commission, the Helsinki Commission did not make any distinction between new and existing plants in this respect.[84] Contrary to the 1996 PARCOM decision, however, HELCOM recommendations to phase out chlorine bleaching are not binding on contracting parties. To complete this overview of HELCOM measures relating to the pulp and paper industry, it should be noted that limit values for atmospheric emissions of nitro-

[81] HELCOM Recommendation 9/6 concerning restriction of discharges from the pulp and paper industry, 17 Feb 1988, *Baltic Sea Environment Proceedings*, No 26, p 53.

[82] HELCOM Recommendation 11/3 on restriction of discharges from the sulphite pulp industry and HELCOM Recommendation 11/4 on restriction of discharges from the kraft pulp industry, 14 Feb 1990, *Baltic Sea Environment Proceedings*, No 33, pp 33–37.

[83] HELCOM Recommendation 17/8 on reduction of discharges from the kraft pulp industry and HELCOM Recommendation 17/9 on reduction of discharges from the sulphite pulp industry, 13 Mar 1996. These recommendations superseded the two earlier ones.

[84] Cf PARCOM Decision 96/2 on the phasing-out of chlorine-based bleaching processes in the kraft and sulphite pulp industry, above ch 4.

gen and sulphur compounds from pulp and paper mills were adopted in 1995.[85]

Iron and Steel Industry

In 1990, the Commission adopted recommendations setting emission limit values for discharges of heavy metals, oil and cyanides from the iron and steel industry, both in effluents and atmospheric emissions. These recommendations call for the application of best available technology, which is 'understood to take into account technical and economic feasibility.'[86] It is interesting to note that the emission limit values for oil and heavy metals are formulated not in terms of maximum concentrations of these substances in effluents, but, as in the above-mentioned recommendations on the pulp and paper industry adopted at the same HELCOM meeting, in terms of limits on *total national emissions* from the iron and steel sector, in this case to be calculated by multiplying national production with 'specific discharge coefficients' expressed in grammes per ton of steel production.[87]

In 1996, the 1990 HELCOM recommendation on waste water discharges from the iron and steel industry was replaced by a new one which spells out in more detail what is to be regarded as BAT in this sector.[88] It lays down both 'general requirements' regarding processes and modes of operation to minimise waste water discharges, such as the use of dry operations and 'closed water systems', and emission limit values to be observed for any effluent which is discharged 'after having fulfilled the general requirements'. These limit values, which are now expressed in terms of annual mean values for *individual plants*, are to be complied with from 1 January 1998 for new plants, and from 2002 for existing plants (2005 for existing plants in countries in transition). It is surprising that, while the 1990 recommendation also established a limit value for total discharges of zinc and lead in effluent from blast furnaces, the 1996 recommendation lays down no requirements at all for heavy metal emissions, but merely recommends that such requirements 'should be examined in 2000'.

The 1990 recommendation on atmospheric emissions, which is still partly in force, prescribes detailed technical measures to minimise dust emissions from various processes in the iron and steel industry, which is an

[85] HELCOM Recommendation 16/4 on the reduction of emissions into the atmosphere from the pulp and paper industry, 15 Mar 1995, *Baltic Sea Environment Proceedings*, No 60, p 43.

[86] This was a standard footnote in HELCOM recommendations on BAT for particular sectors prior to the adoption of HELCOM Recommendation 12/3 on the generic 'definition' of best available technology, see below, n 115.

[87] HELCOM Recommendation 11/5 on the restriction of discharges from the iron and steel industry, 14 Feb 1990, *Baltic Sea Environment Proceedings*, No 33, p 39.

[88] HELCOM Recommendation 17/5 on the restriction of discharges from the iron and steel industry, 12 Mar 1996.

important source of airborne contamination of the marine environment by heavy metals. It also sets limit values or 'guiding values' for emissions of particulate matter from certain processes.[89] At the time of its adoption, this recommendation was the most detailed one in the area of airborne pollution, a form of pollution which was dealt with only in very general terms in the 1974 Convention itself. Indeed, Article 6, paragraph 8 only provides that contracting parties 'shall endeavour to use *best practicable means* in order to minimise the airborne pollution of the Baltic Sea Area by noxious substances.'[90] The 1990 HELCOM recommendation specifies what those 'best practicable means' are in the context of the iron and steel industry.

A complementary recommendation on 'upstream' preventive measures to minimise atmospheric emissions of heavy metals and dioxins from the secondary iron and steel industry using scrap as a raw material was adopted in 1992.[91] It recommends to contracting parties that 'measures should be taken to avoid cadmium and mercury in all products that can end up as scrap' and also requests them to present proposals to HELCOM 'to minimize the amount of chlorinated compounds in used scrap' resulting from the use of chlorinated oils and emulsions in metal-working and of chlorinated plastic in conjunction with steel products, in order to reduce dioxin emissions. In 1996, the Helsinki Commission adopted another recommendation on both atmospheric emissions and waste water discharges from coke plants,[92] a sector initially also covered by the 1990 recommendation on atmospheric emissions from the iron and steel industry. This new recommendation defines BAT for hard coal cokeries and sets limit values for dust emissions and for a number of water pollutants such as polycyclic aromatic hydrocarbons (PAHs), phenol and cyanides.

Other Industrial Sectors

The examples of the pulp and paper and iron and steel industry were analysed in some detail because they were among the earliest sectors to be regulated by the Helsinki Commission and have been addressed most comprehensively by two successive 'generations' of recommendations. Other industrial sectors that are important sources of pollution by haz-

[89] HELCOM Recommendation 11/7 on measures aiming at the reduction of emissions to the atmosphere from the iron and steel industry, 14 Feb 1990, *Baltic Sea Environment Proceedings*, No 33, p 47.

[90] It should be recognised, however, that the 1974 Helsinki Convention was the first treaty for the protection of the marine environment to explicitly address pollution through the atmosphere. On the issue of airborne pollution, see generally Brunnée (1992).

[91] HELCOM Recommendation 13/4 on atmospheric pollution related to the use of scrap materials in the iron and steel industry, 5 Feb 1992.

[92] HELCOM Recommendation 17/4 on the restriction of atmospheric emissions and waste water discharges from hard coal cokeries, 12 Mar 1996. This recommendation supersedes a number of specific provisions on coke plants contained in Recommendation 11/7.

ardous substances, nutrients and organic matter have also been tackled. I will mention only those that are relevant because of their emissions of hazardous substances. Discharges of heavy metals are addressed, mostly through emission limit values, in HELCOM recommendations concerning the textile industry (chromium, copper, zinc),[93] household waste incinerators (cadmium, mercury, lead, cobalt, copper, chromium, nickel and zinc),[94] pestidices production and formulation plants (copper, chromium, zinc and arsenic),[95] the fertilizer industry (cadmium, mercury and zinc),[96] the leather industry (chromium),[97] metal surface treatment plants (cadmium, mercury, lead, copper, chromium, nickel, silver and zinc),[98] and the glass industry (lead and arsenic).[99] Emissions of organohalogen compounds are addressed in various ways in different recommendations. Aggregate emission limit values for organohalogens as a group are prescribed for effluents from the pesticides industry,[100] the textile industry,[101] the metal surface treatment industry[102] and the chemical industry as a whole.[103] Atmospheric emissions of dioxins from household waste incinerators are also addressed through emission standards.[104]

Most recent HELCOM recommendations, however, do not use emission limit values as the only regulatory technique. They also contain more or less detailed prescriptions for particular treatment methods for effluents and waste gases or changes in production processes and inputs, which are deemed to constitute BAT for the sectors concerned. Thus, for example, the recommendation concerning the glass industry prescribes 'avoidance of heavy metal compounds in the raw materials as far as possible,'[105] while

[93] HELCOM Recommendation 16/10 on the reduction of discharges and emissions from production of textiles, 15 Mar 1995, *Baltic Sea Environment Proceedings*, No 60, p 75.

[94] HELCOM Recommendation 16/8 on the limitation of emissions into atmosphere and discharges into water from the incineration of household waste, 17 Feb 1988, *Baltic Sea Environment Proceedings*, No 60, p 65.

[95] HELCOM Recommendation 14/2 on the limitation of discharges into water and emissions to the atmosphere from production and formulation of pesticides, 3 Feb 1993, *Baltic Sea Environment Proceedings*, No 52, p 39.

[96] HELCOM Recommendation 17/6 on reduction of pollution from discharges into water, emissions into the atmosphere and phosphogypsum out of the production of fertilizers, 12 Mar 1996, *Baltic Sea Environment Proceedings*, No 62, p 58.

[97] HELCOM Recommendation 16/7 on basic principles in waste water management in the leather industry, 15 Mar 1995, *Baltic Sea Environment Proceedings*, No 60, p 59.

[98] HELCOM Recommendation 16/6 on the restriction of discharges and emissions from metal surface treatment, 15 Mar 1995, *Baltic Sea Environment Proceedings*, No 60, p 53.

[99] HELCOM Recommendation 14/3 on the limitation of emissions to the atmosphere and discharges into water from the glass industry, 3 Feb 1993, *Baltic Sea Environment Proceedings*, No 52, p 43.

[100] HELCOM Recommendation 14/2, above n 95.

[101] HELCOM Recommendation 16/10, above n 93.

[102] HELCOM Recommendation 16/6, above n 98.

[103] HELCOM Recommendation 16/5 on requirements for discharging of waste water from the chemical industry, 15 Mar 1995, *Baltic Sea Environment Proceedings*, No 60, p 47.

[104] HELCOM Recommendation 16/8, above n 94.

[105] HELCOM Recommendation 14/3, above n 99.

that for the metal surface treatment sector recommends as a general rule 'if technically possible, substitution of hazardous substances . . . by substances which are readily biodegradable, non-bioaccumulating and non-mutagenic and have a low toxicity' and specifies this further by urging the replacement of chlorinated solvents by 'water-based systems or non-halogenated organic solvents' unless 'it is proven that substitution is technically not possible.'[106]

Another regulatory instrument used in some HELCOM recommendations is an overall ecotoxicity standard for waste water. This technique, developed in Sweden, involves the determination of the toxic effect on aquatic organisms such as fish, daphnia, algae or bacteria of the effluent from a particular production process *as a whole*, rather than the effect of individual polluting *substances*. This method is of special interest for waste water which contains a great number of different pollutants, because it avoids the need to determine the concentration and test the effects of, and set an emission limit value for, each substance individually, and also takes into account synergetic effects which are otherwise difficult to assess. The recommendations relating to discharges from the pesticide industry,[107] the textile industry[108] and the chemical industry[109] prescribe that whole effluent toxicity testing should be carried out on two out of the four above-mentioned groups of aquatic organisms. Ironically, only the first recommendation actually stipulates a toxicity limit value which must be complied with. The other two, though they recommend testing, do not in fact specify what *conclusions* are to be drawn from these tests . . .

Other Measures

Apart from the recommendations on pollution control measures and emission standards for specific branches of industry, the Helsinki Commission has also adopted a number of recommendations of a more general policy nature, laying down general principles for the reduction of industrial emissions generally or across broad sectors like the chemical industry as a whole. In a general recommendation adopted in 1988, the Commission recommended 'that industrial discharges containing persistent organic substances or toxic metals should be carefully evaluated with a view to reduction' using

[106] HELCOM Recommendation 16/6, above n 98. If so, the recommendation provides that only three specific chlorinated solvents should be used and that the waste water from this process should be subject to separate treatment so as to comply with an emission limit value.

[107] HELCOM Recommendation 14/2, above n 95.

[108] HELCOM Recommendation 16/10, above n 93.

[109] HELCOM Recommendation 16/5, above n 103.

'best available technology.'[110] Apart from its reference to 'best available technology' as a general prescription for pollution control, this recommendation did not really add much to the general terms of the 1974 Convention itself. Later recommendations, however, expand on it by defining the concept of 'best available technology' and by further specifying principles for the management of industrial effluents. For instance, another general HELCOM recommendation of relevance to the reduction of pollution by hazardous substances urged contracting parties in 1991 to ensure that industrial effluents are not discharged into municipal sewage treatment plants without adequate pretreatment, because such plants are not equipped to reduce pollution by harmful substances.[111]

As a general principle to be applied throughout the chemical industry, the Commission recommended in 1990 that a selection of harmful chemicals drawn from the list of 'noxious substances' in Annex II of the 1974 Convention, which are used in industrial processes, 'should be substituted by less harmful chemicals or subjected to requirements which will provide at least as good a result from an environmental standpoint'. It also recommended that 'chemical factories should aim at closed water systems' and that any waste water containing such harmful substances should be separately treated using BAT.[112] The most significant aspect of this recommendation was no doubt the substitution of harmful substances in industrial processes, since this actually called for a modification of existing production processes and not merely for the application of end-of-pipe pollution control technology.

Based on a review of reports on the implementation of this recommendation which contracting parties were to submit in 1994, the Commission adopted a new general recommendation on waste water from the chemical industry in 1995, further specifying the BAT to be used to minimise the volume and pollutant load of waste water and also laying down emission limit values for chemical oxygen demand (COD), organohalogen compounds and heavy metals.[113] However, the most striking feature of this 1995 recommendation, which superseded its 1990 predecessor, was that, while it provided for many in-process technical measures for the recirculation of

[110] HELCOM Recommendation 9/8 concerning measures aimed at the reduction of discharges from industry, 17 Feb 1988, *Baltic Sea Environment Proceedings*, No 26, p 59.

[111] HELCOM Recommendation 12/4 on industrial connections to municipal sewerage networks, 20 Feb 1991, *Baltic Sea Environment Proceedings*, No 37, p 2. This recommendation was replaced one year later by HELCOM Recommendation 13/2 on industrial connections and point sources other than household to municipal sewerage systems, without any substantive change other than the specification of the reference to other point sources as referring to sources 'other than household'.

[112] HELCOM Recommendation 11/6 on basic principles in wastewater management in chemical industry, 14 Feb 1990, *Baltic Sea Environment Proceedings*, No 33, p 41.

[113] HELCOM Recommendation 16/5, above n 103.

process water and minimisation and end-of-pipe treatment of waste water, it no longer prescribed as a general rule the substitution of hazardous substances in chemical production processes, but merely recommended that 'raw materials and auxiliaries should be selected with environmental aspects taken into consideration'.

When these provisions were reconsidered and in turn replaced by a new recommendation in 1999,[114] the principle of substitution was re-introduced as a general prescription. It is referred to in the preamble of the recommendation together with the precautionary principle, and the vague provision concerning the selection of raw materials was rephrased in more explicit terms, calling for 'substitution of the use of hazardous substances by less hazardous substances or preferably non-hazardous substances where such alternatives are available'. No list of hazardous substances to be substituted is appended as in the 1990 recommendation. The term 'hazardous substances' presumably should be taken to refer to the entire category of toxic, persistent and bio-accumulative substances as defined in the 1992 Convention. The emission limit values laid down in the 1995 recommendation are confirmed and further emission standards are prescribed for total organic carbon, phosphorus and nitrogen. As one can see, progress in the specification of requirements for the chemical industry is slow and incremental.

The notion of 'best available technology', though used in a number of sectoral recommendations since the mid-1980s, was only first generally defined by the Helsinki Commission in a recommendation adopted in 1991,[115] which seems strongly inspired by an earlier Paris Commission recommendation on the same subject.[116] Using wording virtually identical to that used by the Paris Commission, the Helsinki Commission defines BAT as:

> the latest stage of development (state of the art) of processes, of facilities or of methods of operation which indicate the practical suitability of a particular measure for limiting discharges

and lists a series of factors, including 'economic feasibility' and the 'precautionary principle', which must be taken into account in determining what constitutes BAT in particular cases. These factors leave a lot of room for subjective judgement, and the recommendation in fact recognises that BAT is a flexible and evolving concept, which 'will change with time in the light of technological advances, economic and social factors, as well as changes in scientific knowledge and understanding.'

[114] HELCOM Recommendation 20E/6 on requirements for discharging of waste water from the chemical industry, 7 Sep 1999.

[115] HELCOM Recommendation 12/3 on definition of best available technology, 20 Feb 1991, *Baltic Sea Environment Proceedings*, No 37, p 25.

[116] PARCOM Recommendation 89/2 on the use of best available technology, see above ch 4.

A similar recommendation defining the related concept of 'best environmental practice' (BEP) was adopted by the Commission in 1992, equally inspired by a Paris Commission precedent.[117] Together with the 1991 recommendation on BAT, this recommendation served as a basis for the definitions of both concepts which were incorporated in the revised 1992 Convention.

After a period of intensive normative activity, especially from 1990 to 1996, which resulted in the adoption of numerous BAT and BEP recommendations addressing many different sources of pollution by toxic substances—though not of a comprehensive and coherent programme for the elimination of such pollution—the regulatory efforts of the Helsinki Commission in the area of industrial emissions and product standards have recently appeared to be slowing down. Since 1996, HELCOM did not adopt a single new recommendation on the reduction of industrial pollution, with the exception of a few amendments to an earlier recommendation on the chemical industry, and only a few recommendations on the regulation of products containing hazardous substances. Since Sweden and Finland joined the European Community and the Community itself became a contracting party to the Helsinki Convention, HELCOM seems increasingly preoccupied with the consistency of its activities with the environmental policy of the EU. Thus, for instance, the technical work on BAT 'reference documents' for various industrial sectors initiated by the European Commission within the framework of the IPPC Directive prompted HELCOM to suspend its own work on further refining standards for the iron and steel industry. At its March 1998 meeting, the Helsinki Commission decided to undertake an analysis of differences between HELCOM Recommendations and EU Directives with a view to harmonising them.[118] The stagnation of efforts to eliminate pollution by organotin compounds, where HELCOM prefers to await 'the development in other international fora', as well as the deference to EC law in the field of pesticide regulation, may well be evidence of a 'chilling effect' on HELCOM's independent regulatory initiatives.

At the same time, as we shall see below, the Commission is reconceptualising its policy with respect to hazardous substances on the basis of a risk assessment and priority-setting approach. The evolution of HELCOM's regulatory policy in relation to toxic emissions should be analysed against the background of a broader ministerial-level environmental policy-making process which developed in Baltic fora from 1988, and which will be addressed in the final section of this chapter.

[117] PARCOM Recommendation 91/1 on the definition of best environmental practice, 20 June 1991, PARCOM Doc 13/9/1, Annex 6.

[118] *Baltic Sea Environment Proceedings*, No 73, p 10.

NEW DIRECTIONS IN POLICY-MAKING: FROM THE BALTIC SEA MINISTERIAL DECLARATIONS TO HELCOM HAZARDOUS SUBSTANCES STRATEGY

Throughout the second half of the 1970s and most of the 1980s, the work on the implementation of the 1974 Helsinki Convention was carried out exclusively by experts in low-profile technical bodies and attracted little political attention.[119] In the last decade, efforts have been made, through a number of high-level meetings, to provide stronger overall political guidance and develop a more comprehensive approach for the implementation of the Convention. The introduction of regular ministerial gatherings as a new feature of the Baltic marine environment protection regime, inspired by the example of the North Sea conferences, is regarded by practitioners and observers alike as a turning point in the development of this regime.[120] According to HELCOM's Executive Secretary, the first ministerial meeting on Baltic environmental cooperation, organised in 1988 within the framework of the Helsinki Commission, laid 'the cornerstone for a notable change in political motivation for the control of marine pollution.'[121]

At that meeting, the ministers responsible for environmental protection of the Baltic Sea states adopted a 'Declaration on the Protection of the Marine Environment of the Baltic Sea Area,'[122] designed to give political impetus to the implementation of the 1974 Convention. In this declaration, the ministers expressed their conviction that:

> Contracting Parties to the Convention must adopt a precautionary approach and not wait for full and undisputed scientific proof of harmful effects before taking action to prevent and abate pollution.

They thus paved the way for the endorsement of the precautionary principle by the Helsinki Commission in its 1991 recommendation on best available technology and for its subsequent codification in the 1992 Convention.

Setting Toxics Reduction Targets

The main political feature of the 1988 declaration, however, was the establishment of a quantitative target and timetable for further efforts to reduce

[119] Ringius (1995), pp 2–3.
[120] Haas (1993), pp 173, 177; Greene (1988), p 180.
[121] *Baltic Sea Environment Proceedings*, No 71, p 3.
[122] Declaration on the Protection of the Marine Environment of the Baltic Sea Area, Helsinki, 15 Feb 1988, reprinted in: Intergovernmental Activities in the Framework of the Helsinki Convention 1974–1994, *Baltic Sea Environment Proceedings*, No 56, Annex 3, pp 187–193.

pollution by harmful substances from land-based sources. The ministers called for a 'substantive reduction' of the load of pollutants 'most harmful to the ecosystem of the Baltic Sea', especially heavy metals, toxic or persistent organic substances and nutrients, '*for example* in the order of 50 per cent of the total discharges . . . as soon as possible but not later than 1995.'[123] The wording of this political commitment is strikingly similar to that made by North Sea states in October 1987 at the London North Sea Conference, but the 50 per cent reduction target is formulated in even less imperative terms, and without stating any baseline against which emission reductions are to be measured.

Even more ambitious targets were laid down at a still higher political level two years later in a 'Baltic Sea Declaration'[124] adopted by the Heads of Government of the Baltic Sea states at a conference on environmental cooperation in the Baltic Sea region. This summit meeting, held in Ronneby, Sweden, in September 1990, in the wake of the wave of political change that swept through Eastern Europe, was convened jointly by the Swedish and Polish prime ministers. Two non-riparian states whose territory is partly situated in the catchment area of the Baltic Sea, Norway and Czechoslovakia, were also invited. Although the conference was held outside the formal framework of the Helsinki Commission, the Ronneby declaration contains many recommendations which bear directly on the implementation of the Helsinki Convention. The ultimate objective of the Baltic Sea states, as proclaimed in the declaration, is nothing less than 'the ecological restoration of the Baltic Sea.'[125] The signatories undertook to elaborate 'a *joint comprehensive programme* for decisive reduction of emissions in order to restore the Baltic Sea to a sound ecological balance' and decided to establish a 'high level task force' within the framework of the Helsinki Commission for this purpose.[126]

As regards toxics reduction, the 1990 declaration expands on the objectives laid down in the 1988 declaration by calling for emissions of harmful substances to be reduced 'to levels that are in accordance with a restored ecological balance'. The 'existing commitments' to a reduction 'in the order of 50%' by 1995, which were not unequivocal in the 1988 declaration, are now given an explicit baseline (1987) and unambiguously reaffirmed as 'a first step' towards this more ambitious, long-term objective.[127] Such reduction is to be achieved inter alia by the 'development and use of cleaner

[123] *Ibid*, 1st operative para (emphasis added).

[124] Baltic Sea Declaration by Heads of Governments and High Political Representatives of the Baltic Sea States, Norway, the Czech and Slovak Federal Republic and the Representative of the Commission of the European Communities assembled at Ronneby, Sweden, 2–3 Sep 1990, reprinted in *Yearbook of International Environmental Law* 1 (1990), p 424.

[125] *Ibid*, para 1.

[126] *Ibid*, para 2 (emphasis added).

[127] *Ibid*, para 3.

technologies, including low-waste and non-waste processes and environmentally non-hazardous products.'[128] The political leaders also declared their 'firm determination' to strengthen the Helsinki Convention and its institutions 'with a view to accelerating the implementation of existing commitments'[129] and thus expressed their support for the revision of the 1974 Convention which had been initiated by the Helsinki Commission a few months earlier.

The 1988 and 1990 political declarations had the effect of refocusing HELCOM's agenda on the central issue of toxics reduction. In the ensuing years, the Commission saw it as its main task to 'translate the overall 50 per cent goal into sector-wise pollution abatement recommendations', recommendations which it describes as the 'conventional tools' for achieving its objectives.[130] Though HELCOM adopted a substantial number of recommendations on BAT for specific industrial sectors in the late 1980s and 1990s, these measures, as we have seen above, fall short of what would be required to effectively achieve the ambitious pollution reduction goals proclaimed by ministers. The Baltic political leaders were apparently aware of the limitations of these 'conventional tools' when they called on the Commission to develop the 'joint comprehensive programme' as a new policy instrument in 1990.

The Joint Comprehensive Environmental Action Programme

The next meeting at ministerial level was the Diplomatic Conference on the Protection of the Marine Environment of the Baltic Sea Area, which was held in Helsinki on 9 April 1992 for the adoption of the revised Helsinki Convention and of the 'Baltic Sea Joint Comprehensive Environmental Action Programme' (JCP) which had been elaborated pursuant to the 1990 Baltic Sea Declaration. As a matter of fact, the JCP was not completely finalised at the time of the conference, which therefore was only able to 'approve the *strategic approach and principles* reflected in' a preliminary version of the programme. However, the JCP was subsequently completed later the same year[131] by a 'Programme Implementation Task Force' established by a resolution of the Diplomatic Conference[132] within the institu-

[128] Baltic Sea Declaration by Heads of Governments and High Political Representatives of the Baltic Sea States, para 4.

[129] *Ibid*, para 7.

[130] Final Report on the Implementation of the 1988 Ministerial Declaration, *Baltic Sea Environment Proceedings*, No 71, p 41.

[131] See *Baltic Sea Environment Proceedings*, No 52, p 9. The final version of the JCP was published as: The Baltic Sea Joint Comprehensive Environmental Action Programme, *Baltic Sea Environment Proceedings*, No 48, 1993.

[132] Final Act of the Diplomatic Conference on the Protection of the Marine Environment of the Baltic Sea Area, Resolution No 5, reprinted in: Intergovernmental Activities in the Framework of the Helsinki Convention 1974–1994, *Baltic Sea Environment Proceedings*, No 56, p 223.

tional framework of HELCOM. Apart from the political endorsement of the JCP, the 'Baltic Sea Environmental Declaration' adopted by the conference[133] contains little more than a ritual reaffirmation of the signatories' commitment to the precautionary principle, BAT and BEP, and a solemn undertaking to 'take action to promote implementation of the Programme in the entire catchment area of the Baltic Sea' and to 'assure that measures to implement the Programme will cause decisive reduction of the pollution load on the Baltic Sea Area'.

The JCP is not a hortatory instrument formulating recommendations of a general nature. It is conceived as a practical, operational action programme which identifies 132 environmental 'hot spots', ie major point and non-point sources of pollution, in the Baltic Sea catchment area and outlines, 'in realistic technical and financial terms',[134] the investments required for remedial measures, both of a preventive and curative nature, totalling 18 billion ECU over a 20 year period. Or, as the authors of the programme themselves eloquently put it, the JCP aims to present 'a comprehensive but implementable and affordable series of activities to promote environmentally sustainable development in an era of severe resource constraints.'[135] The programme is designed to be used as a planning tool and as an instrument for mobilising financial support at the national and international level, especially for the necessary environmental investments in the countries in transition of the eastern and southern parts of the Baltic region. In fact, international financial institutions such as the World Bank, the European Bank for Reconstruction and Development and the European Investment Bank were closely involved in its elaboration and have pledged support for its implementation.[136]

Ostensibly, the JCP purports to complement and support the regulatory activities of the Helsinki Commission:

> The Programme has also been designed to *support implementation of existing commitments* of the Contracting Parties to the Helsinki Convention, HELCOM Recommendations, and especially the priorities established in the Declaration on the Protection of the Marine Environment of the Baltic Sea, which was adopted by the Ministers of Environment of the Contracting Parties in 1988.[137]

Yet in a way, the JCP could also be seen as an implicit admission of the partial failure of the regulatory approach developed by HELCOM within

[133] *Ibid*, p 211.

[134] As HELCOM puts it in its overview of intergovernmental activities. *Ibid*, p 17.

[135] The Baltic Sea Joint Comprehensive Environmental Action Programme, *Baltic Sea Environment Proceedings*, No 48, pp 5–4.

[136] Ringius (1995), p 7, views the extension of the range of participants, the financial aspect of the JCP and what he terms its 'multilayered approach to regional cooperation on environmental protection' as a fundamental change in the Baltic Sea regime.

[137] *Ibid*, pp 5–2 (emphasis added). Another section of the JCP states that the 'ultimate goal' of the transition countries in implementing the programme should be compliance with EC environmental standards 'or, where applicable, with other stricter standards.' *Ibid*, pp 5–8.

the framework of the 1974 Helsinki Convention. According to one commentator, 'preparatory work for the JCP . . . was mainly carried out on the basis of a common understanding of how poor environmental performance had been.'[138] Indeed, the JCP notes, in its review of the causes of environmental degradation of the Baltic Sea, that a 'serious effort . . . should be made to implement HELCOM recommendations concerning product control' in all the countries of the region,[139] implying that these recommendations have not been taken seriously so far. The programme announces measures to 'promote the adoption' of BEP and BAT, in order 'to prevent pollution at source, consistent with the 1992 Helsinki Convention and HELCOM Recommendations',[140] while at the same time stressing that 'regulatory measures, including environmental standards, *such as those adopted in HELCOM Recommendations*, should be enforceable and realistic under prevailing economic conditions.'[141] It is clearly assumed that, without external financial and technical assistance, some riparian states will fail to fulfil their 'existing commitments' with respect to emission reduction and pollution prevention, some of which are implicitly criticised for being 'unrealistic'. In a summary of the JCP, HELCOM describes the investment activities as the core element of the programme and refers to other elements, including policies, laws and regulations, as 'chiefly . . . complementary and supportive.'[142] Does this not amount to an implicit recognition of the limited relevance of hard and soft law as an instrument for the achievement of its environmental objectives?

At any rate, the next ministerial meeting within the framework of HELCOM in 1994 refrained from adopting any new high-profile political declarations, but simply resulted in a number of 'ministerial decisions', recorded in the minutes of the regular Commission meeting, urging the contracting parties

> to implement effectively HELCOM decisions and recommendations . . . , to accelerate national measures concerning eg the implementation of 50% reduction of emissions . . . and the implementation of the Joint Comprehensive Environmental Action Programme.

The Commission's claim, in a document especially prepared for this 1994 meeting, that the introduction of ministerial-level meetings 'produced a

[138] Greene (1998), p 194. This author provides a detailed analysis of how the ministerial conferences and the activities set in motion by them resulted in the development of various mechanisms for implementation review in the Baltic Sea environmental regime.

[139] The Baltic Sea Joint Comprehensive Environmental Action Programme, *Baltic Sea Environment Proceedings*, No 48, pp 3–20.

[140] *Ibid*, pp 5–8.

[141] *Ibid*, pp 5–7 (emphasis added).

[142] Intergovernmental Activities in the Framework of the Helsinki Convention 1974–1994, *Baltic Sea Environment Proceedings*, No 56, p 95.

notable change in the effectiveness of a regional marine pollution control regime,'[143] appears rather optimistic.

New Hazardous Substances Strategy

A further step was taken in 1996. In a manifest desire to emulate the 1995 Esbjerg North Sea Conference, another high-level meeting within the framework of the Council of the Baltic Sea States, held in Kalmar, Sweden, called on HELCOM to develop an action programme for phasing out discharges, emissions and losses of hazardous substances 'towards the target of their cessation within one generation (25 years)'. The ministers also endorsed the 'ultimate aim', first proclaimed by the Esbjerg Conference, of 'concentrations in the environment near background values for naturally occurring substances and close to zero concentrations for man-made synthetic substances.'[144] This prompted a new round of policy-making on toxics reduction within the Helsinki Commission, in parallel with the development of the Hazardous Substances Strategy in OSPAR. In fact, this policy-making process in HELCOM completely mirrored that in OSPAR and almost simultaneously led to the same result: the adoption of an 'objective' and 'strategy' for phasing out toxic inputs through an elaborate process of risk assessment, selection and prioritisation of hazardous substances with a view to the implementation of emission reduction measures. Although formally the political decision-making on this new toxics reduction policy was completed in HELCOM a few months earlier than in OSPAR,[145] it was the work in the North Sea/North-East Atlantic forum that inspired the developments in the Baltic regime, rather than the other way round.

The new policy on hazardous substances was laid down in the form of a HELCOM recommendation adopted at a ministerial session of the Helsinki Commission in March 1998.[146] Though the recommendation was, technically, adopted on the basis of Article 13(b) of the 1974 Convention, as the 1992 Convention had not yet entered into force, it nevertheless refers in its preamble to Article 5 of the latter Convention, which, as we have seen above, sets out the general commitment of the parties to prevent and eliminate pollution of the Baltic marine environment by harmful substances. The operative provisions of the recommendation itself are rather short, merely

[143] *Ibid*, p 16.

[144] Action Programme for the Baltic Sea States Co-operation, adopted by the Fifth Ministerial Session of the Council of the Baltic Sea States, Kalmar, 2–3 July 1996, para 3.3.

[145] This was due to the routine scheduling of the respective plenary meetings rather than to deliberate design.

[146] HELCOM Recommendation 19/5 on HELCOM objective with regard to hazardous substances, 26 Mar 1998.

enunciating the actual objective and the timeframe for its achievement and further referring to more detailed provisions on implementation, contained in a document attached to the recommendation and entitled 'Strategy to implement HELCOM Objective with regard to hazardous substances'. Though their form is somewhat different, the language and substance of HELCOM instruments is very close to that of the 1998 OSPAR Hazardous Substances Strategy, which is not surprising in view of the preambular reference to 'the need for harmonization of principal approaches applied within HELCOM and OSPAR with regard to hazardous substances'. Like OSPAR, HELCOM now formally subscribes to the 'ultimate aim' first proclaimed by the Esbjerg North Sea Conference and subsequently endorsed by the Baltic Sea states' Kalmar Action Programme, that of 'concentrations in the environment near background values for naturally occurring substances and close to zero for man-made synthetic substances.'[147] The Commission recommends to governments of contracting parties to continue their emission reduction efforts 'in a stepwise process and time-frame' and, more specifically, to 'make every endeavour to move towards the target of cessation of discharges, emissions and losses of hazardous substances . . . by the year 2020.'[148]

This is to be done by applying HELCOM Strategy, which provides for the identification, prioritisation and control of hazardous substances through a similar process as OSPAR Strategy that was extensively analysed and discussed in the previous chapter. Notwithstanding some differences in formulation and emphasis, HELCOM Strategy's approach to toxics reduction is in essence the same as that of its OSPAR counterpart and its implementation is likely to prove equally cumbersome. To be sure, the criteria for the selection of substances have been formulated by HELCOM in less restrictive terms than in OSPAR Strategy, as they refer simply to 'hazardous properties' and 'indications of risk' instead of '*highly* hazardous properties' and '*strong* indications of risk', and do not explicitly require that substances be 'widespread' in the marine environment, thus apparently setting a lower threshold for action.[149] HELCOM is also mandated to take into account 'the specific conditions in the Baltic Sea' and to be guided 'in particular' by the precautionary principle.[150] But it seems rather doubtful that these nuances will make much difference in actual practice, in terms of the number and nature of the pollutants selected as targets for priority action.[151]

147 HELCOM Recommendation 19/5 on HELCOM objective with regard to hazardous substances, 26 Mar 1998, 1st operative para.

148 *Ibid*, 2nd and 3rd operative para.

149 *Ibid*, Attachment, para 3.1. Cf OSPAR Strategy, para 3.1.a.

150 HELCOM Recommendation 19/5, Attachment, para 3.

151 Like OSPAR Strategy, HELCOM Strategy provides for the development and regular updating of a 'HELCOM List of Chemicals for Priority Action', ranked in order of priority, which is to serve as a basis for the implementation of regulatory measures. This list is to be

No regulatory measures targetting specific substances have yet been adopted by the Helsinki Commission as a result of the implementation of the 1998 HELCOM Hazardous Substances Strategy. In view of the notable slowdown of HELCOM normative activities since the mid-1990s and of the 'chilling' effect of the accession of Sweden and Finland to the EU on the work of the Commission, as noted above, the prospects for ambitious measures within the framework of the 1992 Helsinki Convention seem rather slim. It is symptomatic that in a recent address to the Helsinki diplomatic corps, the Chairman of HELCOM openly questioned the role of the institution as an independent regulatory forum in view of the future further enlargement of the EU to the Baltic states. He argued that regional environmental bodies such as HELCOM would still have a role in an enlarged EU to respond to specific needs and 'make progress without waiting for agreements which cover the whole European area' but at the same time speculated that 'maybe the functions of HELCOM will change from a regulatory body to a task force defining problems, demands, incentives and voluntary measures, but leaving the final legislation to others.'[152]

drawn up through the application of selection and prioritisation mechanisms to a long 'list of potential substances of concern' laid down in App 2 to the Strategy. The latter list, like the corresponding OSPAR list of candidate substances with which it substantially coincides, is a compilation of earlier lists of hazardous substances established in different international fora, including OSPAR and the INSC, which again illustrates the strong influence of the North Sea regime on the Baltic regime. It also includes a list of substances identified as being 'of concern' by HELCOM in 1991, and amended two years later, as well as pesticides and other substances listed in Parts 2 and 3 of Annex 1 to the 1992 Helsinki Convention. The Strategy makes it clear, however, that further HELCOM regulatory action with respect to hazardous substances is not to be suspended until completion of the selection and prioritisation process it provides for. It stipulates that, 'notwithstanding' this process, HELCOM will, 'on an interim basis', continue to take action with respect to a shortlist of 'selected substances for immediate priority action', laid down in App 3 to the Strategy. Also, contracting parties are expected to continue their work on 'those substances for which a 50% reduction goal was set up by the Commission' in 1991 and 1993, pursuant to the 1988 ministerial declaration. See HELCOM Recommendation 19/5, Attachment, para 3.4.

[152] Statement by Dr Peter Ehlers, Chairman of HELCOM, to HELCOM Diplomatic Working Lunch 2001, Helsinki, 13 Nov 2001.

6

The Mediterranean Land-Based Sources Regime: The 1976 Barcelona Convention for the Protection of the Mediterranean Sea Against Pollution and Its Protocols

HISTORY AND BACKGROUND OF THE BARCELONA CONVENTION AND ITS PROTOCOLS

The Convention for the Protection of the Mediterranean Sea against Pollution was negotiated under the auspices of the United Nations Environment Programme (UNEP) and concluded in Barcelona in 1976, as the legal framework for the implementation of UNEP's Mediterranean Action Plan, a policy document approved by a regional intergovernmental conference one year earlier.[1] The mere fact of having succeeded in convincing all the riparian states of the Mediterranean, in spite of the deeply-rooted antagonisms and hostile relations between some of them, to sign on to a legally binding, multilateral instrument providing for cooperative action for the protection of their common marine environment represented a true diplomatic achievement for the new United Nations body, then hardly four years old.[2]

The Barcelona Convention was conceived as a framework convention covering all sources of marine pollution through general provisions, but intended to be supplemented by protocols laying down more specific rules for dealing with particular sources of pollution. During the negotiations which led to the conclusion of the Convention, it was already recognised

[1] See Report of the Intergovernmental Meeting on the Protection of the Mediterranean, Barcelona, 28 Jan–4 Feb 1975, reprinted in 14 ILM 464 (1975). For a detailed analysis, from an international relations perspective, of the development and implementation of the MAP and the Barcelona Convention, see Haas (1990). See also Déjeant-Pons (1990), pp 85–128; Raftopoulos (1990); Raftopoulos (1992).

[2] For the sake of accuracy, it should be mentioned that some riparian states, like Syria, Algeria and Albania, initially did not sign the Convention, but acceded to it later on.

that a protocol on pollution from land-based sources would have to be elaborated to lay down more precise obligations in this important field. The intergovernmental conference which adopted the Barcelona Convention in 1976 at the same time instructed the Executive Director of UNEP to continue the preparatory work for a protocol on land-based sources.[3] Accordingly, an 'intergovernmental consultation' was convened in Athens in February 1977 to initiate negotiations on the basis of a document prepared by UNEP Secretariat. Further meetings were held in 1977, 1978 and 1979 and the Protocol for the Protection of the Mediterranean Sea against Pollution from Land-Based Sources was finally adopted and opened for signature at a diplomatic conference in Athens in May 1980.

In the wake of the Rio Conference, and following the example set by the development of second-generation conventions for the North-East Atlantic and the Baltic Sea, the meeting of the parties to the Barcelona Convention in 1993 initiated a review process with a view to 'adapting the texts of the Barcelona Convention and its related Protocols to the latest developments in international environmental law.'[4] This process resulted in the adoption, by a diplomatic conference held in Barcelona in June 1995, to mark the twentieth anniversary of the launch of the Mediterranean Action Plan, of amendments to the Convention and a number of its Protocols on other matters than land-based sources.[5] The negotiations for the revision of the Athens Protocol were completed later, with the adoption of extensive amendments by a conference of plenipotentiaries, which met in Syracuse in March 1996.[6] Neither the amendments to the Convention itself, nor those to the Athens Protocol, have entered into force at the time of writing. Only a small number of contracting parties have so far notified their formal acceptance to the depositary, among them the European Community.[7]

In this chapter, I will examine the legal regime for the control of marine pollution from land-based sources as it developed within the framework of the Barcelona Convention system. This first entails an analysis of the provisions of the Convention itself, both in their original form and as amended in 1995, which lay down the overall framework and basic principles of marine pollution control in the region. Then I shall consider the more

[3] Kuwabara (1984), p 46.

[4] UN Doc UNEP(OCA)/MED IG.3/5, 15 Oct 1993, p 25, para 139.

[5] *Final Act of the Conference of Plenipotentiaries on the Amendments to the Convention for the Protection of the Mediterranean Sea against Pollution, to the Protocol for the Prevention of Pollution of the Mediterranean Sea by Dumping from Ships and Aircraft and on the Protocol concerning Specially Protected Areas and Biological Diversity in the Mediterranean*, Barcelona, 9–10 June 1995, UN Doc UNEP(OCA)/MED IG.6/7.

[6] *Final Act of the Conference of Plenipotentiaries on the Amendments to the Protocol for the Protection of the Mediterranean Sea against Pollution from Land-Based Sources*, Syracuse, 6–7 March 1996, UN Doc UNEP(OCA)/MED IG.7/4.

[7] Council Decision 1999/801/EC of 22 Oct 1999 on accepting the amendments to the Protocol for the protection of the Mediterranean Sea against pollution from land-based sources (Barcelona Convention), OJ No L322, 14.12.1999, p 18.

specific obligations of the riparian states with respect to land-based pollution by hazardous substances, as they were first spelled out in the 1980 Athens Protocol, and the common measures adopted by the contracting parties pursuant to the provisions of this protocol. To conclude, I will address the most recent developments in the regime: the 1996 Amendments to the Athens Protocol, which, though they have not yet entered into force, have already influenced the practice of the parties, which has taken a new direction with the adoption in 1997 of the Strategic Action Programme (SAP) to Address Pollution from Land-based Activities.

THE FRAMEWORK PROVISIONS OF THE BARCELONA CONVENTION

The obligations of the contracting parties under the Barcelona Convention itself are formulated in very general terms. Article 4, which lays down the 'general undertakings', commits the contracting parties to:

> individually or jointly take all appropriate measures in accordance with the provisions of this Convention and those protocols in force to which they are party, to prevent, abate and combat pollution of the Mediterranean Sea Area.

As in the other conventions on marine pollution concluded in the 1970s, the initial definition of 'pollution' in the Barcelona Convention follows the traditional harm-based model, referring to the introduction of substances or energy '*resulting in* . . . deleterious effects.'[8]

With respect specifically to land-based sources, Article 8 of the Convention provides:

> The Contracting Parties shall take all appropriate measures to prevent, abate and combat pollution of the Mediterranean Sea Area caused by discharges from rivers, coastal establishments or outfalls, or emanating from any other land-based sources within their territories.

These and other provisions were significantly amended in 1995. The general obligations of the parties in Article 4 of the Convention were strengthened and further elaborated, and now include specific commitments to 'apply, in accordance with their capabilities, the precautionary principle'[9] and the polluter pays principle[10] and to:

[8] Barcelona Convention, Art 2 (a) (emphasis added).

[9] *Ibid*, Art 4, para 3(a) (as amended, 1995). It should be noted that, notwithstanding the fact that the original Barcelona Convention contained no provision to this effect and defined 'pollution' in a way inconsistent with the precautionary principle, the contracting parties had already agreed, at their 1989 meeting, ie long before the revision of the Convention, 'to fully adopt the principle of precautionary approach regarding the prevention and elimination of contamination in the Mediterranean Sea area'. UN Doc UNEP(OCA)/MED IG.1/5, 1 Nov 1989, Annex V, p 2, para 3.6.

[10] Barcelona Convention, Art 4, para 3(b) (as amended, 1995).

utilize the best available techniques and the best environmental practices and to promote the application of, *access to and transfer of* environmentally sound technology, including clean production technologies, *taking into account the social, economic and technological conditions.*[11]

The similarities with the provisions of the 1992 Paris and Helsinki Conventions are striking, but there are a number of significant differences, which can be ascribed to the fact that the Barcelona Convention includes a considerable number of developing countries among its contracting parties, which quite successfully sought to ensure that its new provisions adequately reflect the South's post-Rio agenda. This explains, for instance, the references to technology transfer[12] and socio-economic conditions in conjunction with BAT and BEP, two concepts which the Convention does not actually attempt to define. It also explains why the precautionary principle is described in similar terms as in Principle 15 of the Rio Declaration, with an emphatic reference to the parties' 'capabilities', as the principle

by virtue of which where there are *threats of serious or irreversible damage*, lack of full scientific certainty shall not be used as a reason for postponing *cost-effective* measures to prevent environmental degradation.[13]

This formulation of the precautionary principle implies a higher threshold for preventive action than that in the 1992 Paris and Helsinki Conventions, in which 'reasonable grounds for concern' and 'reason to assume' that hazards may exist, respectively—instead of 'threats of serious or irreversible damage'—are sufficient to trigger the duty to take preventive measures. Also, the Paris and Helsinki versions contain no reference to the cost-effectiveness of preventive measures. As a considerable degree of scientific certainty is in fact required to assess the risk of damage, its possible irreversibility and the potential effectiveness of any measures that may be envisaged, the watered-down formulation of the precautionary principle in the Rio Declaration and Barcelona Convention may in effect seriously mitigate its actual impact on the parties' obligations and the Convention's implementation. It should, however, be mentioned that the definition of 'pollution' in the revised Barcelona Convention has been amended in line with the precautionary principle and now covers not only inputs of pollutants which demonstrably result in harmful effects, but also those which are merely '*likely* to result' in such effects.[14]

The general obligations of the parties in Article 4 have also been extended to encompass, in addition to their initial duty 'to prevent, abate and combat'

[11] Barcelona Convention, Art 4, para 4(b) (emphasis added).

[12] See also *ibid*, Art 13, para 2.

[13] *Ibid*, Art 4, para 3(a) (emphasis added).

[14] *Ibid*, Art 2 (a) (as amended, 1995) (emphasis added). Similar wording can be found in the 1992 Paris Convention.

marine pollution, the duty to *eliminate* it 'to the fullest possible extent'.[15] Similarly, the Convention's provisions on land-based sources have been reworded and thereby strengthened. Article 8 now provides:

> The Contracting Parties shall take all appropriate measures to prevent, abate, combat *and to the fullest possible extent eliminate* pollution of the Mediterranean Sea Area and *to draw up and implement plans for the reduction and phasing out of substances that are toxic, persistent and liable to bioaccumulate* arising from land-based sources.[16]

In the amended Convention, the phrase 'prevent, abate, combat and to the fullest possible extent eliminate' has become the standard language to describe the parties' obligations with respect to all sources of marine pollution[17] and thus its use in Article 8 does not imply any special treatment for pollution from land-based sources. As we have already seen above, similar changes in language, albeit without any qualification of the term 'eliminate', have also occurred in the Paris and Helsinki Conventions. The new, explicit obligation to draw up and implement toxics reduction and phase-out plans, however, seems to be a change of a more substantive nature. It implies the existence of more onerous obligations with respect to pollution by hazardous substances and explicates the meaning to be given to the term 'eliminate' as it applies to such substances. Apparently, elimination 'to the fullest possible extent' in this context ultimately means nothing less than a total phase-out of the substances in question, though the above-quoted provision does not actually specify *what* is to be phased out: their production, use or emission or merely the pollution caused by them?

To fully appreciate their meaning and scope, it is of course necessary to examine the Convention's provisions on land-based sources in conjunction with those of the relevant protocol. Hence, I shall first analyse the original provisions of the Athens Protocol, still currently in force, and the measures taken by the meeting of the contracting parties for their implementation, before discussing the implications of the Syracuse Amendments adopted in 1996 and the latest developments since their adoption.

ANALYSIS OF THE 1980 ATHENS PROTOCOL

The Athens Protocol is quite similar in structure to the 1974 Paris Convention, by which many of its provisions were apparently inspired. Like the Paris Convention, the Protocol lists pollutants in two distinct lists, for which

[15] Barcelona Convention, Art 4, para 1 (as amended, 1995).
[16] *Ibid*, Art 8 (emphasis added).
[17] Cf *ibid*, Art 5, 6, 7 and 11 (as amended, 1995).

different obligations are imposed on contracting parties. The 'black list' in Annex I is more extensive than that in Part I of Annex A to the Paris Convention: in addition to the substances and groups of substances which can be found in the black list of the Paris Convention it also contains two additional ones which in that Convention are on the grey list, viz organophosphorus and organotin compounds. Moreover, radioactive substances, which under the Paris Convention are treated as a separate category different from both the black and grey lists, are included in the black list of the Athens Protocol, at least 'when their discharges do not comply with the principles of radiation protection as defined by the competent international organizations, taking into account the protection of the marine environment'. Thus, while the contracting parties to the Athens Protocol have not gone as far as those of the Paris Convention in giving differential treatment to radioactive pollution, they have nevertheless shown deference to the 'competent international organizations', though implicitly recognising that the principles defined by them may not necessarily be sufficient for the protection of the marine environment. Compared to that of the Paris Convention, the grey list (Annex II) of the Athens Protocol is also much more comprehensive, comprising 13 categories of substances as opposed to five.

The contracting parties' substantive obligations with respect to black list substances are laid down in Article 5 of the Protocol, which, using the same terms as the 1974 Paris Convention, provides that they 'undertake to *eliminate* pollution' from land-based sources by those substances.[18] It is further provided that 'to this end' contracting parties 'shall elaborate and implement, jointly or individually, as appropriate, the necessary programmes and measures', which 'shall include, in particular, common emission standards and standards for use.'[19] Again, the wording is strikingly similar to that of the Paris Convention. The Athens Protocol is more explicit in its reference to 'common emission standards and standards for use' than the Paris Convention, which does not prescribe the use of any particular instrument but leaves it up to contracting parties to choose from a range of options 'as appropriate'.

The 'standards for use' referred to in Article 5, paragraph 3 of the Protocol are presumably standards relating to the use of black list substances and can be equated with the 'standards governing the composition and use of substances and products' in Article 4, paragraph 3 of the 1974 Paris Convention. It is noteworthy that Article 5 of the Athens Protocol, unlike the provisions of the Paris Convention relating to black list substances, contains no reference to environmental quality standards as a measure for the control of pollution by those substances. However, EQS are not altogether excluded from the Protocol, since Article 7 provides in

[18] Athens Protocol, Art 5, para 1 (emphasis added).
[19] *Ibid*, Art 5, paras 2 and 3.

general terms for the formulation of standards relating to 'the quality of sea-water used for specific purposes'.

The 'programmes and measures' for the elimination of pollution by black list substances are to be elaborated both at the national level by the parties individually and at the international level by the meeting of the contracting parties. The latter is explicitly provided for in Article 5, paragraph 4, which stipulates that 'the standards and time-tables for the implementation of the programmes and measures' are to be 'fixed' and 'periodically reviewed' by the parties 'for each of the substances listed in annex I', in accordance with the decision-making procedure laid down in Article 15 of the Protocol. This provision specifies that the programmes and measures shall be adopted by the meeting of the contracting parties by a two-thirds majority vote.

The Protocol does not explicitly provide that the 'programmes and measures' adopted by the meeting of the parties pursuant to Article 15 are binding on the contracting parties, although it could be understood by implication from Article 5, paragraphs 2 and 4 that the implementation of these programmes and measures is mandatory. Moreover, Article 15, paragraph 2, which institutes a special reporting procedure on alternative action taken and a possibility of delayed consent for contracting parties 'which are not able to accept a programme or measures', ie which have voted against their adoption, *a contrario* could be taken to imply that parties which have consented to a particular measure are bound to implement it.

At one time during the drafting of the Protocol, it was proposed that the programmes and measures be adopted 'in accordance with the procedure prescribed in Article 17 of the Convention', ie in the form of annexes to the Protocol which are to be regarded as 'an integral part' of it and thus legally binding.[20] According to Article 17 of the Barcelona Convention, new annexes or amendments to annexes may be adopted by a three-quarters majority vote and shall become effective for all contracting parties which have not submitted a notification of non-acceptance within a specified period. The negotiators of the Athens Protocol eventually opted for a less formal procedure for the adoption of 'programmes and measures', specifying only that they shall be adopted by a two-thirds majority vote and refraining from making any explicit provision with respect to their legal effect.

As regards the grey list substances of Annex II, Article 6 of the Protocol, again using wording inspired by the Paris Convention, provides that the parties shall 'strictly limit' pollution by them through the elaboration and implementation of 'suitable programmes or measures', both 'jointly and individually', as for black list substances. The provision does not, however,

[20] UN Doc UNEP/WG.17/6, 9 July 1979, Annex IV, Art 15, para 1.

specify what kinds of standards are to be included in those programmes or measures. But Article 6, paragraph 3 imposes on contracting parties a special obligation with respect to discharges of grey list substances, which, somewhat paradoxically, does not apply to discharges of black list substances: a requirement of prior authorisation by a competent national authority. Annex III to the Protocol lists a series of factors which national authorities are to take 'due account' of when issuing such authorisations, including the characteristics, composition and harmfulness of the effluent, the characteristics of the discharge site and receiving marine environment, the availability of alternative disposal methods and the potential impairment of the marine ecosystem. The fact that a similar authorisation requirement is not imposed on contracting parties for discharges of black list substances is qualified as an 'important omission' by one commentator, who speculates that it was not included because contracting parties did not wish to appear to legitimise the discharge of black list substances which, in principle, should be prohibited altogether.[21] Yet the reference in Article 5, paragraph 3 to 'common emission standards' for these substances indicates that contracting parties implicitly recognised that continued discharges would have to be accepted, for some time at least.

It should be noted that the Protocol contains a clause which somewhat qualifies the ambitious objectives laid down in Articles 5 and 6 by subordinating the implementation of the programmes and measures envisaged in those articles to economic considerations. Article 7, paragraph 3 provides that those programmes and measures

> shall be adopted by taking into account, for their *progressive implementation*, the capacity to adapt and reconvert existing installations, the *economic capacity* of the Parties and their *need for development*.[22]

Thus it is recognised that any measures to eliminate or limit pollution will have to be implemented progressively, taking into account economic realities. The special reference to 'the economic capacity of the Parties and their need for development' is intended to accommodate the concerns of the developing countries of the Mediterranean basin, who fear that pollution control measures may hamper their economic development.[23] This concern also finds expression in the preamble of the Protocol, which contains a phrase 'recognizing the differences in levels of development between the coastal States, and taking account of the economic and social imperatives of the developing countries'. One commentator sees in these provisions 'a disclaimer of uniform obligations', in the sense that the Protocol does not impose on developing coastal states the same burden as on

[21] Kuwabara (1984), p 56.
[22] Athens Protocol, Art 7, para 3 (emphasis added).
[23] On the positions and concerns of developing countries during the negotiation of the Athens Protocol, see Haas (1990), pp 110–115.

developed ones.[24] Indeed, during the drafting of the Protocol, some parties objected to the reference to 'economic capacity' on the grounds that this 'would lead to undesirable disparities in the application of the Protocol.'[25] There is, however, no evidence in the measures adopted by the meeting of contracting parties of preferential treatment for developing countries.

Special emphasis is put in Article 7, paragraph 3 on the difficulty of adapting existing industrial installations. At one time during the negotiations, it was proposed to include in the Protocol separate provisions dealing with pollution from existing and new installations, recognising that a different approach may be necessary for each.[26] Later, the legal experts drafting the Protocol suggested incorporating in Articles 5 and 6 a clause to the effect that 'time-limits for the implementation of . . . programmes and measures may differ depending on whether existing or new installations are concerned', but this suggestion was objected to by negotiators from a number of developing countries.[27] The final wording of Article 7, paragraph 3 makes reference to the problem of reconversion of existing installations as one factor to be taken into account, without specifying exactly what consequences are to be drawn from it.

In addition to the 'programmes and measures' for black and grey list substances to be elaborated pursuant to Articles 5 and 6, Article 7 of the Protocol also provides for contracting parties to 'formulate and adopt . . . common guidelines and, as appropriate, standards or criteria'. The matters which are to be the subject of such guidelines, standards or criteria are enumerated in a non-exhaustive way in Article 7, paragraph 1. Some of them can be viewed as a further specification of the 'programmes and measures' referred to in the previous articles, such as 'specific requirements concerning the quantities of the substances listed in annexes I and II discharged, their concentration in effluents and methods of discharging them.'[28] This provision indicates in somewhat greater detail than those of Articles 5 and 6 the kinds of common measures which may be envisaged for the purpose of limiting or eliminating pollution from land-based sources by black and grey list substances. Other items are of a more general nature, such as 'the control and progressive replacement of products, installations and industrial and other processes causing significant pollution of the marine environment', 'the length, depth and position of pipelines for coastal outfalls', 'special requirements for effluents necessitating separate treatment' and 'the quality of sea-water used for specific purposes that is necessary for the protection of human health, living resources and ecosystems.'[29]

[24] Kuwabara (1984), p 48. Or, to use post-Rio jargon, this would be a case of 'common but differentiated responsibilities' *avant la lettre*.
[25] UN Doc UNEP/IG.9/5, 28 Oct 1977, p 5, para 30.
[26] See, eg *ibid*, Annex III, Art 5 and 6.
[27] UN Doc UNEP/WG.17/6, 9 July 1979, Annex IV, Art 5, para 4 and Art 6, para 3.
[28] Athens Protocol, Art 7, para 1 (d) and (e).
[29] *Ibid*, Art 7, para 1 (a), (b) and (c).

The latter provision gives the meeting of the contracting parties a basis for adopting general environmental quality standards, which are not mentioned in Articles 5 and 6 as a measure for dealing with black or grey list substances. Article 7, paragraph 2 lists a number of factors which are to be taken into account in drawing up common guidelines, standards or criteria. In addition to 'the economic capacity of the Parties and their need for development', this provision also refers to 'local ecological, geographical and physical characteristics' and 'the level of existing pollution and the real absorptive capacity of the marine environment'. The reference to the 'absorptive capacity' of the marine environment, which is also to be found in the 1974 Paris Convention,[30] is indicative of some influence of the proponents of the EQO approach to controlling marine pollution,[31] an influence which other parties apparently felt the need to counterbalance by a clause stipulating that these factors shall be 'without prejudice to the provisions of Article 5', ie the objective of eliminating pollution by black list substances.

As to the legal effect of the 'common guidelines, standards or criteria' to be adopted pursuant to Article 7, the text of the Protocol is again not explicit. Early drafts of the Protocol provided that these guidelines, standards or criteria would be adopted by the meeting of contracting parties 'in the form either of recommended practices or of provisions incorporated in annexes to the Protocol.'[32] Thus they could either be non-binding or binding depending on the form chosen by the parties. The final text of Article 14 of the Protocol, defining the functions of the meeting of contracting parties, merely provides that common guidelines, standards or criteria in accordance with Article 7 may be adopted by the meeting 'in any form decided upon by the Parties.'[33] It could be inferred from this provision that the guidelines, standards or criteria adopted pursuant to this provision are of a recommendatory nature unless the meeting adopting them decides to give them another status. The Protocol does not specify under what procedure and by what majority 'common guidelines, standards or criteria' are to be adopted.[34] This lack of a formal procedure could be seen as another indication of their non-binding nature, unlike the 'programmes and measures', for which a formal procedure is prescribed in Article 15.

[30] 1974 Paris Convention, Art 6, para 2(c).

[31] For an ardent advocacy of the 'absorptive capacity' approach, as laid down in Art 7, para 2 of the Protocol, by a Yugoslav marine scientist, see Pravdic (1988), pp 259–261. This author, who describes this approach as the 'most advanced' strategy for marine pollution control, was Chairman of the UN expert group GESAMP in the 1980s, and presumably had an influence on his country's position in the Protocol negotiations.

[32] See UN Doc UNEP/IG.9/5, 28 Oct 1977, Annex III, Art 17, para 2 (d).

[33] Athens Protocol, Art 14, para 2 (d).

[34] See also Kuwabara (1984), p 69.

The above analysis has focused on those provisions of the Protocol which directly concern the regulation of emissions of hazardous substances and lay down the international legal framework for regulatory decisions at the national and international level. In addition, the Protocol contains many other provisions relating to other aspects of interstate cooperation, such as monitoring, scientific and technical research, technical assistance, consultations regarding specific instances of pollution affecting the interests of individual parties, and exchange of information, which will not be further discussed in this study.[35] Instead, I shall now examine the common measures adopted by the contracting parties for the implementation of the provisions of the Protocol relating to hazardous substances.

IMPLEMENTATION OF THE 1980 ATHENS PROTOCOL: ADOPTION OF COMMON MEASURES

The Athens Protocol entered into force on 17 June 1983 and the first meeting of its contracting parties was held the same year, within the framework of the ordinary meeting of the parties to the Barcelona Convention. Until 1995, all of the common measures concerning hazardous substances adopted by the parties dealt exclusively with pollutants on the black list. It is only in 1996 that the meeting of the parties adopted the first measures addressing pollution by grey list substances in accordance with Article 6 of the Protocol. The pollution control measures taken jointly by the parties have routinely been based on the results of a cooperative programme for the assessment of the state of pollution of the Mediterranean commonly known as 'MED POL'. This environmental assessment programme, coordinated by UNEP, was initiated together with the Mediterranean Action Plan in 1975 to develop a consensual scientific basis for MAP activities. It was institutionalised in Article 10 of the Barcelona Convention and, building on this existing framework, Article 8 of the Athens Protocol specifically requires its parties to cooperate in the systematic monitoring and assessment of marine pollution by black and grey list substances.

Environmental Quality Criteria

As appears from the above overview, the provisions of the Protocol afford the contracting parties a rather wide choice of instruments for the implementation of common policies for the control of pollution from land-based sources. It is quite remarkable that, in adopting their first international measures under the Athens agreement, they have shown a marked

[35] For further details, see Kuwabara (1984).

preference for environmental quality standards not only for water used for specific purposes as explicitly provided in Article 7, paragraph 1(c) of the Protocol, but also as an instrument to control black list substances. Indeed, the first two measures approved by the contracting parties in 1985 were 'interim environmental quality criteria for bathing waters' and 'interim environmental quality criteria for mercury'.

The quality criteria for bathing water are exactly the kind of measure envisaged in Article 7, paragraph 1(c) of the Protocol, since they relate to sea-water used for a specific purpose and are intended for the protection of human health. According to the decision taken at the 1985 meeting, the contracting parties undertake to 'take measures for a transition period that will ensure as minimum common requirements that the quality of bathing waters will conform' to a particular standard expressed in terms of concentrations of faecal coliforms in sea-water.[36] However, the decision does not really lay down 'common criteria' within the meaning of Article 7 of the Protocol, since it is expressly provided that contracting parties which already have different national standards may continue to apply them. The adoption of true 'Mediterranean common criteria' is deferred until 'comparative studies' have been completed.[37] Since these EQS for bathing water are not relevant to the issue of emissions of dangerous substances, as they relate only to bacteriological pollution, I will not analyse them in more detail. Neither will I discuss the 'environmental quality criteria for shellfish waters' adopted in 1987,[38] which likewise are based only on bacteriological parameters.

The decision taken at the 1985 meeting concerning 'interim environmental quality criteria for mercury'[39] is based on a preliminary assessment of mercury concentrations in Mediterranean seafood and is also intended for the protection of human health. Contrary to what its title indicates, it is a decision *not* to establish a common EQS for mercury in seafood. Indeed, the contracting parties, on the basis of the evidence available to them, have come to the conclusion that observed mercury concentrations in seafood do not present any risk for human health and that 'the adoption of upper limits for mercury concentrations in seafood on a

[36] United Nations Environment Programme, *Common Measures for the control of pollution adopted by the Contracting Parties to the Convention for the Protection of the Mediterranean Sea against Pollution*, MAP Technical Reports Series No 95, UNEP, Athens, 1995, p 1 (hereafter referred to as UNEP, *Common Measures*).

[37] *Ibid.* In 1991, the meeting of the contracting parties agreed that the adoption of firm criteria was 'premature'. *Ibid*, p 23, para (d). It is only in 1996 that it decided that 'there is now sufficient data on the basis of which criteria and standards of a more permanent nature than the interim ones adopted in 1985 can be developed', though without as yet fixing a deadline for the adoption of such new standards. UN Doc UNEP(OCA)/MED IG.8/7, 2 Aug 1996, Annex IV, p 16.

[38] UNEP, *Common Measures*, pp 7–8.

[39] *Ibid*, pp 3–4.

common regional basis would not be *a priori* justified.'[40] Instead, the contracting parties merely 'take note' of an interim criterion for tolerable intake of mercury determined by an FAO/WHO expert committee[41] and commit themselves to 'take into consideration' this criterion to establish national standards for mercury concentrations in marine organisms '*if national circumstances so require*.'[42] Furthermore, the contracting parties undertake to '*limit* anthropogenic discharges of mercury into the Mediterranean Sea pending the eventual formulation of emission standards for mercury' and to 'commence as early as possible, the elaboration of the necessary programmes and measures with respect to mercury' as mandated by Article 5 of the Protocol.[43] Thus, contracting parties recognised that they are under an obligation to take measures to control mercury emissions notwithstanding the absence of a perceived risk to human health, although their undertaking to 'limit' discharges was indicative of a rather minimalistic interpretation of the obligation to 'eliminate' mercury pollution under Article 5 of the Protocol and the adoption of specific joint standards was postponed.

Control Measures for Black List Substances

Further measures 'to prevent mercury pollution' were taken at the following meeting of the contracting parties in 1987, which adopted an actual 'common emission standard' for mercury in accordance with Article 5, paragraph 3 of the Protocol. The decision provides that

> the Contracting Parties shall . . . ensure a maximum concentration (to be calculated as a monthly average) of 50 μg mercury per litre . . . for all effluent discharges before dilution into the Mediterranean Sea, in terms of Article 5 and annex I of the Protocol.'[44]

This standard corresponds to the limit values established by two earlier EEC Directives relating to mercury discharges[45] and is based on what can be achieved by end-of-pipe effluent treatment. In addition to this emission standard, the decision prescribes certain measures relating to the design and construction of outfalls for new mercury discharges in order to ensure

[40] *Ibid*, p 3, para 2.
[41] *Ibid*, p 3, para 3(a).
[42] *Ibid*, p 3, para 3(b) (emphasis added).
[43] *Ibid*, p 3, para 3(e) (emphasis added).
[44] *Ibid*, p 5, para (a).
[45] Council Dir 82/176/EEC of 22 Mar 1982 on limit values and quality objectives for mercury discharges by the chlor-alkali electrolysis industry, OJ No L81, 27.3.1982, p 29; Council Dir 84/156/EEC of 8 Mar 1984 on limit values and quality objectives for mercury discharges by sectors other than the chlor-alkali electrolysis industry, OJ No L74, 17.3.1984, p 49.

'suitable effluent dilution.'[46] Thus, notwithstanding their obligation to 'eliminate' mercury pollution, the contracting parties actually accept new discharges of mercury provided the common emission standard is complied with and the effluent is 'suitably' diluted. The emission standard applies to all discharges, both new and existing, from 1 July 1989, but a 10-year transition period is provided for existing discharges to be 'adjusted' so as to comply with the measures for outfalls.[47] Notwithstanding the terms of Article 5, paragraph 4 of the Protocol, these standards and timetables have not been reviewed since their adoption in 1987.

Further measures relating to black list substances were adopted at the 1989 meeting of the contracting parties. The 'measures for the control of pollution by used lubricating oil'[48] are quite faithful to the objective of elimination of pollution by black list substances as laid down in the Protocol. The contracting parties 'adopt the principle' that no wastes containing such oils should be discharged directly or indirectly[49] and undertake to 'progressively implement' this principle through measures at the national level 'to ensure the eventual realisation of this principle *as early as possible to the extent dictated by national circumstances and not later than 1 January 1994*.'[50] Thus, while due allowance is made for 'national circumstances', a firm deadline is set for the eventual elimination of discharges.

The same is not true of the 'measures for control of pollution by cadmium and cadmium compounds.'[51] which are quite similar to those relating to mercury. In this decision, the contracting parties adopt a limit value for cadmium concentrations in industrial effluents, which, as for mercury, is identical to that laid down by an earlier EEC Directive.[52] Like the EEC limit value, the emission standard adopted under the Athens Protocol does not apply to the phosphate fertiliser industry, one of the main sources of cadmium pollution of the marine environment. With respect to this industry, the decision merely provides that each party 'should fix its national value pending a new decision by the Contracting Parties.'[53] No such decision has thus far been taken.

In addition to a common emission standard, the decision also contains measures concerning outfalls and effluent dilution similar to those in the earlier decision on mercury, and 'an *eventual* water quality objective of 0.5 μg cadmium per litre in marine waters' which, however, is adopted 'in

[46] UNEP, *Common Measures*, p 5, para (c).
[47] *Ibid*.
[48] *Ibid*.
[49] *Ibid*, para (b).
[50] *Ibid*, para (c) (emphasis added).
[51] *Ibid*, pp 11–12.
[52] Council Dir 83/513/EEC of 26 Sept 1983 on limit values and quality objectives for cadmium discharges, OJ No L291, 24.10.1983, p 1.
[53] UNEP, *Common Measures*, p 11, para (a).

principle' only.[54] As for mercury, no standard is set for cadmium concentrations in marine organisms, but contracting parties are invited to consider imposing one nationally 'if national or local circumstances so dictate.'[55] Finally, contracting parties undertake to monitor cadmium pollution and to 'encourage the development of substitutes and alternative technologies leading to the reduction of cadmium pollution.'[56] No date is set for the eventual elimination of cadmium discharges, which does not seem to be envisaged, or for review of the emission standard.

The 'measures for the control of pollution by organohalogen compounds', adopted in 1989,[57] fall even shorter of the objectives laid down in the Athens Protocol than the measures relating to cadmium and mercury. In fact, the decision of the meeting of the parties contains no concrete measures to reduce, let alone eliminate, the emission of organohalogen compounds into the marine environment. It merely lays down an environmental quality objective for DDT in coastal waters which, ironically, is claimed to be adopted 'in terms of Article 5 and Annex I of the Protocol,'[58] although, as pointed out above, Article 5 does not provide for the adoption of environmental quality objectives but of 'common emission standards and standards for use' for Annex I substances, which is quite different. Far from eliminating marine pollution by DDT, this measure merely legitimates the presence of this compound in the marine environment. Furthermore, the contracting parties 'agree to use' the FAO International Code of Conduct on the Distribution and Use of Pesticides,[59] a non-binding instrument which does not deal directly with water pollution resulting from the use of pesticides and contains no specific measures regulating the use of organohalogen compounds.[60] Finally, the 1989 decision calls on contracting parties to monitor levels of organohalogen compounds and to provide information on any national measures relating to them.

The contracting parties revisited the issue of organohalogen compounds at their 1993 meeting, which recommended in very general terms that they:

> reduce and phase out by the year 2005 inputs to the marine environment of toxic, persistent and bioaccumulative substances listed in the [Athens] Protocol, in particular organohalogen compounds *having those characteristics*.[61]

This recommendation was apparently inspired by a similar provision in the declaration adopted by the ministerial-level meeting of the contracting

[54] *Ibid*, p 11, para (c) (emphasis added).
[55] *Ibid*, para (e).
[56] *Ibid*, p 12, para (g).
[57] *Ibid*, p 15.
[58] *Ibid*, para (a).
[59] *Ibid*, para (b).
[60] For a detailed analysis of the FAO Code of Conduct, see below, ch 12.
[61] UN Doc UNEP(OCA)/MED IG.3/5, 15 Oct 1993, Annex IV, p 5 (emphasis added).

parties to the Oslo and Paris Conventions, held in Paris one year earlier.[62] It is more specific than its Paris counterpart, in that it sets a target date for a complete phase-out of inputs (five years later than the Paris target date for a *reduction* of inputs to non-harmful levels) and clearly applies only to those organohalogen compounds which have been shown to be toxic, persistent or liable to bio-accumulate. The 1993 recommendation calls for 'high priority' to be given both to diffuse sources and industrial point sources of organohalogens, without however identifying any specific sources nor recommending specific measures. Its implementation is to be assessed by the year 2000.

There are only two decisions of the contracting parties which actually set a 'standard for use' of black list substances within the meaning of Article 5. The first is the decision on 'measures for the control of pollution by organotin compounds' in which contracting parties agree not to allow the use of anti-fouling paints containing organotin compounds on small boats and equipment used in mariculture from 1 July 1991.[63] Like the Paris and Helsinki Commissions, the contracting parties to the Athens Protocol refrained from banning the use of organotin-based paints on larger vessels, which quantitatively is a much more important source of pollution than the uses which they decided to prohibit. Also, contracting parties which do not have 'access' to substitutes are allowed to derogate from the prohibition for a period of two years.[64]

The second measure purporting to regulate the use of a category of black list substances was taken at the 1991 meeting of the contracting parties. It addresses organophosphorus pesticides, which were found to be a diffuse source of marine pollution.[65] In this decision the parties

> taking into account the precautionary principle, . . . agree to *promote* measures to reduce inputs into the marine environment and to *facilitate* the progressive elimination by the year 2005 of organophosphorus compounds *hazardous to human health and the environment.*[66]

This decision contrasts with the previous ones in that it actually sets a target date for the *elimination* of a category of black list substances. However, the language used stops short of imposing an obligation of result on the parties, which have merely agreed to 'promote' measures and 'facilitate' elimination. Moreover, the parties' commitment does not relate to all organophosphorus compounds, but only to those that are positively found to constitute a health or environmental hazard. Thus, as long as there is no international consensus on a list of compounds which meet this qualification, parties

[62] See above ch 4.
[63] UNEP, *Common Measures*, p 13, para (a).
[64] *Ibid*, para (a) *in fine*.
[65] UN Doc UNEP(OCA)/MED IG.2/4, 11 Oct 1991, Annex IV, p 18, para 9(i)(3).
[66] UNEP, *Common Measures*, p 17, para (a) (emphasis added).

retain a considerable measure of discretion in the implementation of this decision. It is questionable whether this approach is in fact fully consistent with the precautionary principle, which the contracting parties claim to be 'taking into consideration'.

Though the decision does not specify *what* exactly is to be eliminated, it appears from the context that it is not the production but rather the *use* of such compounds in agriculture that is primarily targetted, in so far as this results in inputs into the marine environment. Indeed, the specific measures recommended to achieve the elimination objective all relate to pest control practices and, like the earlier decision on organohalogen compounds, include a reference to the FAO Code of Conduct on the Distribution and Use of Pesticides. One of the specific measures which parties agree to take immediately is a pre-marketing control system of the kind that most countries already apply to regulate the use of pesticides, which should:

> ensure that products containing organophosphorus compounds shall not be used in their territory unless they have been authorized and unless it has been proved that there is:
> —no direct effect on human and animal health and;
> —no unacceptable impact on the environment.[67]

This provision, which lays down a 'standard for use' within the meaning of Article 5, paragraph 3 of the Protocol, introduces a tautogical circularity in the text of the decision. Indeed, in those countries where such a pre-marketing control system exists, the authorisation of a pesticide is, normally, legally conditioned on the fulfilment of similarly worded health and environmental requirements, and, consequently, any pesticide which has thus been authorised must logically be deemed to meet them, ie not to be hazardous to either health or the environment. Any party which applies such a system would claim that it guarantees the protection of health and the environment and may argue that 'hazardous' organophosphorus compounds have already been 'eliminated' as a result of its application.

The practice of setting target dates for 'progressive elimination' of black list substances was continued in 1993, when the meeting of the parties adopted a decision on the control of pollution by carcinogenic, teratogenic and mutagenic substances.[68] This decision is similar in structure and language to the earlier one on organophosphorus compounds. The contracting parties agree to:

> *facilitate* the progressive elimination by the year 2005 of substances having *proven* carcinogenic, teratogenic and/or mutagenic properties in or through the marine environment.[69]

[67] *Ibid*, para (b)(ii).
[68] *Ibid*, p 25.
[69] *Ibid*, para (a) (emphasis added).

The wording of the decision is consistent with that of the corresponding entry in Annex I of the Protocol, which also refers to 'proven' properties.[70] This of course considerably qualifies the commitment of the parties, as the decision itself underscores 'the present state of uncertainty regarding risks'[71] and 'the complexity of the situation, both in terms of data required and in terms of implementation of measures.'[72] The preambular reference to the precautionary principle hardly compensates the substantive indeterminacy of that commitment. Contrary to the earlier decision on organohalogen compounds, this decision mentions no concrete measures to be taken by the parties, other than monitoring and data gathering. A 'comprehensive review of the situation', apparently on the basis of any new information that may be acquired, was planned for the year 2000.[73]

Control Measures for Grey List Substances

The most recent common measures adopted under the original provisions of the Protocol provide for action to limit pollution by substances or groups of substances mentioned in Annex II, ie the grey list. They were endorsed by the meeting of the contracting parties in July 1996, a few months after the diplomatic conference that concluded the revision of the Athens Protocol, and are still part of the implementation work initiated before this process. In fact they are very similar in substance and form to some of the earlier regulatory action taken with respect to black list substances.

The 'measures for the control of pollution by zinc, copper and their compounds,'[74] adopted with explicit reference to Article 6 of the Protocol, set both water quality objectives and emission limit values for these two grey list heavy metals. Though the assessment of the state of pollution by these substances in the Mediterranean has shown no risk to human health, the establishment of environmental quality objectives for coastal waters was found necessary 'for the protection of marine organisms, communities and ecosystems'. A uniform emission standard for all effluent discharges into the Mediterranean sea, from whatever source, of 1 mg/l for zinc and 0.5 mg/l for copper, as a monthly average concentration, is established 'as a step towards the achievement of the . . . quality objectives.'[75] Concentrations of both metals in marketed seafood are to be monitored by the parties and further action taken at the national or local level to protect human health as and when required.

70 Athens Protocol, Annex I, part A, item 8.
71 UNEP, *Common Measures*, p 25, preamble.
72 *Ibid*, para (b).
73 *Ibid*.
74 UN Doc UNEP(OCA)/MED.IG.8/7, 2 Aug 1996, Annex IV, p 11.
75 *Ibid*, p 12.

The other common measures adopted in 1996 under Article 6 of the Protocol concern pollution by detergents, which are also listed in Annex II. They set a product standard rather than an environmental quality standard, by urging parties to 'promote' measures to reduce pollution generally 'by restricting the use of detergents to those which are reasonably (90%) biodegradable', as well as to take further action 'to reduce the input of detergents in identified hot-spot areas.'[76]

The ministerial conference held in Barcelona in June 1995 to commemorate the twentieth anniversary of the launch of the Mediterranean Action Plan and adopt amendments to the Barcelona Convention and a number of its Protocols marks a political turning point in the development of the Mediterranean land-based sources regime. The first two phases of the MED POL programme have been completed and 'common measures' have been adopted under the Athens Protocol for all of the categories of black list substances enumerated in its Annex I, although these measures fall far short of what would be required to really operationalise the provisions of the Protocol and achieve its objective of eliminating pollution by these substances. The amendments to Article 8 of the Barcelona Convention approved by the conference apparently seek to reinvigorate the parties' toxics reduction policies by laying the basis for a more purposeful, programmatic approach through 'plans for the reduction and phasing out of substances that are toxic, persistent and liable to bioaccumulate arising from land-based sources.'[77] A revision of the Protocol along similar lines is under way, although not yet completed. At the Barcelona conference, ministers endorsed a new political agenda for the 'second phase' of Mediterranean environmental cooperation, in the form of a 'Barcelona Resolution on the Environment and Sustainable Development in the Mediterranean Basin', accompanied by an 'action plan' and a list of 'priority fields of activities' containing more detailed provisions for its implementation.

Toxics Reduction Objective

One of the priority objectives to which this Barcelona Resolution seeks to give political impetus is the phasing out of inputs of hazardous substances in the Mediterranean marine environment. In the resolution, ministers

> agree to the reduction by the year 2005 of discharges and emissions which could reach the marine environment, of substances which are toxic, persistent and liable

[76] *Ibid*, p 14.
[77] Barcelona Convention, Art 8 (as amended, 1995).

to bioaccumulate, *in particular the organohalogens*, to levels that are not harmful to man or nature, *with a view to* their *gradual* elimination.[78]

This language reaffirms, in general though not unequivocal terms, the earlier commitments made in various recommendations on the control of pollution by organohalogen, organophosphorus and carcinogenic compounds adopted by the meeting of the parties to the Athens Protocol in 1991 and 1993, which all mentioned the year 2005 as a target date. This time, the reduction objective is formulated in a generic manner, applying to all hazardous substances, though organohalogens are still specially targetted. They are now referred to as a general, unqualified category, implying that reduction measures should address all organohalogen compounds and not just those which have been positively demonstrated to have hazardous characteristics, as in the 1993 recommendation. While the scope of application of the reduction objective has thus been broadened, however, its formulation could be interpreted as a subtle retreat from earlier recommendations. The objective to be achieved by the year 2005 no longer appears to be full elimination, but rather a *reduction* of inputs to 'levels that are not harmful to man or nature, *with a view to* their *gradual* elimination', a longer-term objective to be reached at some later, unspecified date. This wording is obviously inspired by the language of the 1992 Paris Declaration, which was watered down by stressing the gradual nature of the elimination process.

The ambiguity of the phase-out objective is further highlighted by the subsequent phrase, in which the Mediterranean states pledge 'to implement *substantial reductions* of such discharges and emissions, and, *if necessary*, to *supplement the reduction measures* with programmes aiming at *banning the use* of such substances.'[79] This seems to indicate that the objective of 'gradual elimination' of inputs of hazardous substances does not necessarily imply a total ban on their use, but could also be achieved by 'substantial' emission reductions, while a ban is a 'supplementary' measure which would only have to be contemplated in certain cases.

The Barcelona Resolution and its appendices are not very specific as to how its objective is to be achieved. The resolution calls for further consultations on 'the definition of methods, programmes and timetables' and suggests that these be developed 'by categories of substance and by industrial branches.'[80] The elaboration of a 'regional action plan' against land-based pollution, laying down 'quantitative objectives and a calendar of implementation' is also envisaged.[81] I shall now examine how these new

[78] Barcelona Resolution on the Environment and Sustainable Development in the Mediterranean Basin, UN Doc UNEP(OCA)/MED.IG.6/7, 1 July 1995, p 98, para 6 (emphasis added).
[79] *Ibid.* (emphasis added).
[80] *Ibid.*
[81] *Ibid*, App I, p 119.

political directions have been translated in the amendments to the Athens Protocol, which were formally adopted less than one year after the Barcelona conference, and in the regional action programme which was drawn up one year later.

THE 1996 SYRACUSE AMENDMENTS TO THE ATHENS PROTOCOL

The amendments to the Athens Protocol adopted in Syracuse in March 1996 are in line with the 1995 amendments to the Barcelona Convention itself. They build on and complement the amendments to the general provisions of the Convention and are similar in thrust to the provisions on land-based sources of the 1992 Paris and Helsinki Conventions.

The Protocol, as amended, starts off with a 'general provision' which, in the same terms as Article 8 of the amended Convention, now requires the parties not only to 'prevent', 'abate' and 'combat' pollution from land-based sources, but also to 'eliminate' it 'to the fullest possible extent' and, in slightly different terms, to 'giv[e] priority to the phasing out of inputs of substances that are toxic, persistent and liable to bioaccumulate.'[82] These obligations are further specified in Article 5 of the amended Protocol, in which the parties

> undertake to *eliminate pollution* from land-based sources and activities, in particular to *phase out inputs* of the substances that are toxic, persistent and liable to bioaccumulate listed in annex I.[83]

Whereas the original Annex I to the Athens Protocol covered black list substances only, with grey list substances listed in a separate Annex II to which different obligations applied, the amended Protocol, like the 1992 Paris and Helsinki Conventions, no longer differentiates between black and grey list substances. The new Annex I contains a single list of pollutants which includes more than just toxic, persistent and bioaccumulative substances, as well as a broader list of environmental characteristics and criteria for the selection of pollutants and a new list of the main economic sectors contributing to marine pollution.

The revised Article 5 seems to spell out two different obligations: on the one hand, an obligation to 'eliminate pollution' from land-based sources generally, without the qualification 'to the fullest possible extent' which is found in Article 1 of the Protocol and Article 8 of the Convention, and, on the other hand, a specific obligation to 'phase out inputs' of particular substances. The relationship between the general obligation laid down in Article 1 of the Protocol and that in Article 5 is not entirely clear, nor is it

[82] Athens Protocol, Art 1 (as amended, 1996).
[83] *Ibid*, Art 5, para 1 (emphasis added).

obvious whether any legal consequences must be inferred from the omission of the qualifier 'to the fullest possible extent' in the latter provision. This phrase may have been omitted because its inclusion might have appeared as a regressive change from the original language of Article 5, paragraph 1, which provides for an unqualified obligation to 'eliminate pollution' by black list substances. Or did the parties really intend to commit themselves to eliminate pollution from land-based sources altogether, recognising that it may be possible to do so for the pollutants listed in Annex I other than those which are toxic, persistent and liable to bioaccumulate, such as eg nutrients, without totally phasing out all inputs into the marine environment?

At any rate, the new language of Article 5 of the Protocol makes it clear that the obligation to 'phase out' toxic, persistent and bioaccumulative substances referred to in the amended Article 8 of the Convention is indeed to be understood as an obligation to eliminate all *inputs* of those substances into the marine environment.[84] While the obligation itself may be clear, its *object* is not circumscribed without ambiguity: it does not comprise all substances listed in Annex I, but only those 'that are toxic, persistent and liable to bioaccumulate'. Whereas the original wording of Annex I implied that all substances or groups of substances on this black list were deemed to be toxic, persistent or bioaccumulative, no such implication can be drawn from the new, comprehensive list of pollutants in section C of the revised Annex I, and parties will have discretion in selecting substances from this list based on their own interpretation of the scientific evidence.

The Syracuse Amendments also affect the nature of the instruments to be used by the contracting parties in fulfilling their obligations under the Protocol. In line with the amended provisions of the Barcelona Convention itself and the recommendations for action contained in the Barcelona Resolution, the rather vague notion of 'programmes and measures' has been replaced by a reference to 'national and regional action plans and programmes, containing measures and timetables for their implementation.'[85] The Protocol no longer provides for 'common emission standards and standards for use' to be established as the main feature of such programmes. The reference to these instruments has been deleted altogether. Instead, the amended Protocol refers to the 'best available techniques' and 'best environmental practices', which the parties are required to 'take into account' when adopting their plans and programmes.[86] A new Annex IV to the Protocol, copied *verbatim* from Appendix 1 of the 1992 Paris Convention,[87] sets out 'criteria for the definition' of BAT and BEP, thus filling a lacuna in

[84] In this respect, the amended provisions of the Protocol are more explicit than those of the Barcelona Resolution. Cf above n 78.
[85] *Ibid*, Art 5, para 2.
[86] *Ibid*, Art 5, para 4.
[87] See UN Doc UNEP(OCA)/MED WG.92/4, 11 May 1995, p 3, para 15.

the amended Barcelona Convention, which, as we saw above, already provided for the 'utilization' of BAT and BEP, without however defining those concepts.

As a matter of fact, the working group which drafted the Syracuse Amendments considered that it would have been more 'opportune' to include these definitions as annexes to the revised Convention itself, but since that was not possible due to reasons of timing and coordination of the negotiations, eventually decided to annex them to the Protocol.[88] What is puzzling, however, is that the reference to BAT and BEP in the substantive provisions of the Protocol stops short of actually requiring the parties to *apply* these techniques and practices, unlike the corresponding provisions of the Convention, in which they undertake to 'utilize' them. It almost seems as though some parties, upon seeing the Paris Convention's definitions of BAT and BEP, felt inclined to renege on that earlier commitment, although it is hard to see how these 'definitions', indeterminate as they are,[89] could be perceived as threatening any contracting party's discretion.

Authorisation or regulation systems are another instrument to be used by the parties. Originally, the Athens Protocol imposed a prior authorisation requirement only for discharges of grey list substances.[90] The amended Protocol now requires that all point sources, both those discharging directly into the Protocol area and other sources whose emissions into water or air may reach and affect that area, be made 'strictly subject to authorization *or regulation* by the competent authorities of the Parties.'[91] This provision does not necessarily require an individual administrative authorisation for every point source; discharges may also be controlled through generally applicable administrative regulations. In issuing authorisations and regulations, the competent authorities of each contracting party should take 'due account' of the relevant decisions or recommendations of the meeting of the parties and the criteria laid down in Annex II of the Protocol.[92] Parties are also under an obligation to 'provide for systems of inspection . . . to assess compliance with authorizations and regulations'[93] and for 'appropriate sanctions in case of non-compliance.'[94]

Finally, the Syracuse Amendments clarify the scope and legal implications of the decisions which may be made by the meeting of the parties, as well as the procedure for their preparation and adoption. The 'regional action plans and programmes' referred to in Article 5 are to be adopted by a

[88] *Ibid.*
[89] See above ch 4.
[90] Athens Protocol, Art 6, para 3.
[91] *Ibid*, Art 6, para 1 (as amended, 1996) (emphasis added).
[92] *Ibid*, Annex II of the amended Protocol is the former Annex III, which remains substantively unchanged.
[93] *Ibid*, Art 6, para 2 (as amended, 1996).
[94] *Ibid*, Art 6, para 4.

two-thirds majority of the meeting of the parties, on the basis of proposals to be formulated by the secretariat for consideration and approval by a technical subsidiary body of that meeting within one year of the entry into force of the Amendments.[95] The revised provisions now unambiguously stipulate that the measures and timetables in such programmes shall be legally binding for those contracting parties which have not objected to them through a formal 'opting out' procedure.[96] The action plans, programmes and measures 'will aim to cover' the sectors of activity and groups of substances listed in the revised Annex I to the Protocol, which enumerates the 'elements to be taken into account' in their preparation.[97]

THE STRATEGIC ACTION PROGRAMME TO ADDRESS POLLUTION FROM LAND-BASED ACTIVITIES

Background and Purpose of the Strategic Action Programme

The Syracuse Amendments will not enter into force until three-fourths of the contracting parties to the Protocol have formally notified their acceptance of these amendments to the depositary. As was already pointed out above, this threshold was far from being reached at the time of writing. However, the contracting parties have decided not to await entry into force to start implementing the revised provisions of the Athens Protocol, especially those concerning the establishment of a regional action plan. In July 1996, a few months after the adoption of the Syracuse Amendments, an extraordinary meeting of the contracting parties to the Barcelona Convention, held in Montpellier, instructed the secretariat to organise an expert meeting for the purpose of preparing what it called 'the Regional Action Plan for the control and elimination of pollution by land-based sources and activities.'[98] The meeting also endorsed the third phase of the MED POL programme, which reflects 'the shift of the emphasis from pollution assessment to pollution control'[99] and refers to the formulation of such a regional action plan as one of its immediate priorities.[100] A special grant from the Global Environment Facility (GEF) enabled the secretariat to work very expeditiously.[101] The first draft of the action plan was presented to a meeting of government-designated experts less than one year later and, after one further expert meeting, a final draft was submitted for approval at the next meeting of the contracting parties. The document, which eventually became

95 Athens Protocol, Art 15, paras 1–2 (as amended, 1996).
96 *Ibid*, Art 15, para 3.
97 *Ibid*, Annex I, 2nd introductory para and ss A and C.
98 UN Doc UNEP(OCA)/MED IG.8/7, 2 Aug 1996, Annex IV, p 9.
99 *Ibid*, Annex IV, App, p 6, para 2.8.
100 *Ibid*, p 28, para 8.2(a).
101 UN Doc UNEP(OCA)/MED IG.11/10, 3 Dec 1997, p 22, para 105.

known as the 'Strategic Action Programme to Address Pollution from Land-based Activities' (SAP), was formally adopted by the parties at their Tunis meeting in November 1997.[102]

The early adoption of the SAP surely confirms the riparian states' intention to initiate the practical implementation of the amended Protocol prior to its entry into force, but, as a result, the legal status of the programme remains somewhat uncertain. Under the new provisions of the Protocol, the 'measures and timetables' contained in the regional action plans it provides for shall be binding on the parties. However, the SAP was not adopted in accordance with the special procedure laid down in these as yet ineffective provisions, but under the existing provisions of Articles 5, 6 and 7 of the Athens Protocol. In their decision adopting the SAP, the contracting parties pledge 'to *make every effort* to implement it in the framework of the objectives and principles of the LBS Protocol,'[103] suggesting a less than unequivocal commitment. Referring to the target dates for the implementation of certain actions contained in the SAP, a number of parties at the Tunis meeting raised questions 'as to the status of such dates and their binding force' and 'called for specific reference to be made in the SAP to the possibility for it to be revised, if necessary, upon the coming into force of the new LBS Protocol.'[104] To reassure those parties, the document was amended accordingly and the meeting agreed that the SAP would be 'resubmitted for adoption' under Article 15 of the amended Protocol upon its entry into force, thus providing a possibility for review of target dates and other provisions before the programme would become legally binding.[105] The contents of the document should be examined against the background of this rather tentative and provisional commitment.

Though entitled 'Strategic Action Programme to Address Pollution from Land-based Activities', the SAP is in fact broader in scope than its title indicates. It does not exclusively address marine pollution from land-based sources but also covers the protection of the marine environment from other harmful effects of land-based activities, such as the physical alteration of habitats, as well as some environmental management issues in the coastal area which have no direct relationship with the marine environment at all, or at most a very remote one, such as urban air pollution and the disposal of municipal waste.[106] As regards air pollution, its main goal is the protection of human health. The attention given to the human environment and

[102] *Ibid*, Annex IV, App II. It was later published as UNEP, *Strategic Action Programme to Address Pollution from Land-based Activities/Programme d'actions stratégique visant à combattre la pollution due à des activités menées à terre,* Athens, 1999 (hereafter referred to as SAP).

[103] UN Doc UNEP(OCA)/MED IG.11/10, 3 Dec 1997, Annex IV, p 4, para 8 (emphasis added).

[104] *Ibid*, p 23, para 109.

[105] *Ibid*.

[106] One may even wonder whether the Athens Protocol provides a sufficient legal basis for such measures.

integrated coastal zone management reflects the primary concerns of the developing country parties and the recognition of sustainable development as a new objective of the Barcelona Convention system in 1995. It is also linked with the fact that the SAP is more than a set of policy recommendations of a general nature.

The programme is essentially conceived as a framework for the further elaboration of operational projects to address the problems it identifies, with a view to mobilising national and international financial resources for their implementation. In this respect, it is somewhat similar in purpose and format to the 'Joint Cooperative Programme' (JCP) of the Baltic Sea states, which was also developed with the involvement of international financial institutions. Like the JCP, the SAP is based on a survey of the main pollution 'hot-spots' and 'sensitive areas' in the marine region it covers and contains an 'investment portfolio' of priority actions to be undertaken to address the key problems identified. Preliminary cost estimates are provided for these actions. The SAP is also designed to set out guidelines for the elaboration of national action plans by each of the parties, as provided in the amended Athens Protocol, to further operationalise its objectives at the country level, and includes capacity-building measures to help developing country parties in this exercise.

For the purposes of this study, it is not necessary to dwell on these operational, project-oriented aspects of the SAP. Our concern is with the impact of this new programmatic approach on the normative system of the Athens Protocol and on its implications for the interpretation and implementation of the Protocol's provisions. These will be assessed by analysing the general targets, measures and timetables laid down in the SAP, in so far as they relate to emissions of hazardous substances from land-based activities. The programme explicitly states that it is aimed at 'facilitating the implementation by the Contracting Parties of the LBS Protocol'[107] and that its priorities were determined taking into account the 'elements' set out for this purpose in Annex I of the amended Protocol, which lists the sectors of economic activity and the categories of substances to be covered by regional and national action plans.

What is most striking is that the SAP was drafted as though regional cooperation for the control of marine pollution from land-based sources only started in 1995. Even though it was formally adopted under the provisions of the 1980 Protocol, it contains hardly any reference to those provisions, to the existing commitments of the parties and to the common measures already adopted pursuant to them. The 1995 Barcelona Resolution and the 1996 Amendments to the Protocol serve as the SAP's only frame of reference, as if the drafters of the programme were anxious to start with a clean slate, thereby discounting 15 years of earlier cooperation as

[107] SAP, p 4.

effectively irrelevant. One would have expected the new programme to start from an assessment of the existing normative framework and its state of implementation. The fact that it does not may well be taken as an implicit admission of failure.

Specific Measures Concerning Toxics Reduction

The basic objective with respect to toxics reduction spelled out in the amended Protocol and reiterated in the SAP is that of 'phasing out inputs' of substances that are toxic, persistent and liable to bioaccumulate. No target date for achieving this objective is stated in the provisions of the Protocol itself, which leave it to the parties to adopt appropriate 'timetables' in the action plans to be drawn up for its implementation. Some guidance, however, can be inferred from the Barcelona Resolution, which is described in the introductory section of the SAP as 'an agreement made at ministerial level aiming at the *elimination* by the year 2005 of the greatest number of substances which are are toxic, persistent and bioaccumulable.'[108] In fact, as we have seen above, the language of the Barcelona Resolution is more qualified than this summary suggests. It only calls for a *reduction* of discharges to non-harmful levels by 2005, '*with a view to* their gradual elimination' by a later, unspecified date. The year 2005 had, however, been referred to as a target date for the elimination of hazardous organohalogen, organophosphorus and carcinogenic substances in earlier recommendations adopted by the contracting parties under the provisions of the Athens Protocol in 1991 and 1993. The targets and timetables laid down in the SAP for different categories of hazardous substances must be analysed against this background.

Though it is claimed that the Barcelona Resolution 'was fully taken into account in the preparation of the SAP,'[109] the overall target formulated by the SAP for inputs of toxic, persistent and bioaccumulable substances from industrial installations is considerably less ambitious than that agreed to by ministers in 1995: the parties shall seek to achieve a 50 per cent reduction of discharges, emissions and losses 'over a period of 10 years.'[110] At the regional level, 'guidelines for industrial waste water treatment and disposal' are to be adopted by 2005 and 'emission limit values for point source discharges into water and air' by 2010.[111] Given the late date envisaged for their adoption, it is hard to see how these measures could effectively contribute to achievement of the overall objective.

108 *Ibid*, pp 4–5 (emphasis added).
109 *Ibid*, p 5.
110 *Ibid*, p 11.
111 *Ibid*, pp 11–12.

More specific targets and measures are, however, laid down in the SAP for particular categories of hazardous substances. The first of these categories is that of a number of organochlorine compounds identified as persistent organic pollutants (POPs) of global concern by UNEP in 1995. In accordance with the terms of the Athens Protocol, the contracting parties agree to 'phase out inputs' into the Mediterranean of the pesticides DDT, aldrin, dieldrin, endrin, chlordane, heptachlor, mirex, toxaphene and hexachlorobenzene, as well as PCBs, by 2010.[112] By contrast, the ultimate objective for the other POPs, dioxins and furans, as well as for hexachlorobenzene, in so far as it is not used as a pesticide but emitted as an unwanted by-product of certain industrial processes, is formulated in terms which deviate from those of the Protocol, as parties are not expected to 'phase out' or 'eliminate' inputs of these substances altogether, but only to '*reduce* [them] *to the fullest possible extent*.'[113] An interim objective of a 50 per cent reduction of inputs of all priority POPs is to be achieved by the year 2005.[114] Specifically, the measures to be taken by parties to achieve these objectives include phasing out the use of the nine POP pesticides and prohibiting the manufacture, trade and new use of PCBs by the year 2000. Emissions of HCB, dioxins and furans are to be reduced by the application of BEP and 'if possible' BAT to the processes which produce these compounds.[115]

As regards heavy metals, the SAP aims to phase out discharges, emissions and losses of mercury, cadmium and lead into the Mediterranean 'to the fullest possible extent' by 2025.[116] The interim targets to be achieved are a 25 per cent reduction of inputs by 2000 and a 50 per cent reduction by 2005.[117] The objectives to be pursued with respect to the other heavy metals zinc, copper and chromium are much less precise. No target date is set for the elimination 'to the fullest possible extent', not of inputs, but of '*pollution* of the Mediterranean Sea caused by' these substances,[118] language which seems more in tune with the original provisions of the Athens Protocol than with the Syracuse Amendments. Discharges, emissions and losses of these metals are to be 'reduced' by 2010, but the SAP does not state to what extent.[119] Timetables and quantitative reduction objectives are laid down for organometallic compounds, inputs of which are to be reduced by 50 per cent by the year 2010.[120] In what seems to be a more specific, albeit apparently inconsistent objective, inputs of organic mercury compounds

[112] SAP, p 15.
[113] *Ibid* (emphasis added).
[114] *Ibid.*
[115] *Ibid.*
[116] *Ibid*, p 17.
[117] *Ibid.*
[118] *Ibid*, p 20 (emphasis added).
[119] *Ibid.*
[120] *Ibid*, p 19.

shall be 'phased out' and those of organolead and organotin compounds 'reduced', both 'to the fullest possible extent', by the same year.[121]

The measures to be taken to achieve these objectives are not spelled out in great detail. Again, the SAP provides for the formulation and adoption at the regional level of environmental quality criteria and emission standards for point source discharges of the pollutants in question, but not before 2010. Guidelines for the application of BAT and BEP are also to be prepared. In a rare reference to earlier measures adopted pursuant to the Athens Protocol, the SAP urges parties to 'adopt at the national level and apply' the common measures for the reduction of pollution by mercury, cadmium and cadmium compounds and organotin compounds agreed by the meeting of the contracting parties in 1987 and 1989.[122] In doing so, it elegantly glosses over the fact that these measures should already have been applied by parties years ago. The emission limit values for mercury and cadmium were intended to be enforced by contracting parties from as early as July 1989 and January 1991 respectively, while the restrictions on the use of organotin paints on boats and mariculture equipment were to be applied at the national level from July 1991. The only immediate added value of the SAP is that it also provides for the phasing out of organotin compounds as anti-fouling agents in cooling systems,[123] a measure not yet included in the 1989 recommendation, and complements the existing effluent standard for mercury with an additional emission standard for chlor-alkali plants, expressed in grams of mercury released per tonne of installed chlorine production capacity.[124]

Finally, the SAP establishes a series of targets and timetables for the reduction of discharges of organohalogen compounds other than POPs. The overall objective in this respect is 'to eliminate to the fullest possible extent pollution of the Mediterranean Sea caused by discharges, emissions and losses of organohalogen compounds' and to 'reduce' such discharges, emissions and losses by the year 2010,[125] an objective well in retreat from that formulated by the contracting parties in their 1993 decision on the subject. According to that decision, *inputs* of organohalogens, at least those with persistent, toxic and bioaccumulative properties, were to be *phased out by 2005*. From this perspective, it is striking that the SAP lays down no deadline for elimination, nor even a quantitative reduction target, as it does for other categories of hazardous substances. While its objectives with respect to organohalogens as a group are vague, the SAP does contain a number of more explicit recommendations concerning specific substances or

[121] *Ibid.*
[122] *Ibid*, p 18.
[123] *Ibid*, p 19.
[124] *Ibid*, p 18. This standard, however, like the existing one, is inspired by the provisions of a 1982 EEC Directive.
[125] SAP, p 23.

processes. It urges parties to regulate releases of organochlorines from the pulp and paper industry, by applying an emission limit value equivalent to that recommended by the Paris Commission in 1992 and promoting alternatives to the use of molecular chlorine as a bleaching agent.[126] It further recommends reductions in the use of short-chain chlorinated paraffins and calls on parties to 'reduce and control the manufacture and use' of certain polybrominated flame retardants and chlorinated pesticides, such as lindane, 2,4–D, 2,4,5–T and chlorophenols.[127] Further measures are to be elaborated based on national inventories and action programmes.

As noted above, an important portion of the SAP consists of guidelines for the preparation by contracting parties of national action plans to address pollution from land-based sources. Such national action plans are required under the provisions of the amended Protocol. The SAP supplements these provisions with a timeframe by urging parties to draw up such plans within five years of its adoption or review them where they already exist,[128] and provides a broad outline of what they should contain. One point of legal interest concerns the implementation of the provisions of Article 6 of the amended Protocol regarding the requirement of regulation or authorisation of emissions. These provisions apply to both effluent discharges and atmospheric emissions likely to reach the marine environment, and leave contracting parties a choice of applying either an administrative permit system or another form of regulation. The SAP interprets the provisions of Article 6 in a rather restrictive way, by establishing 'criteria to decide which industrial plants and which specific urban settlements generate precise discharges which should merit a permit or regulation' and differentiating between discharges from existing and new installations.[129] The actual language of Article 6 does not seem to leave parties such discretion and provides no legal basis for treating new and existing plants differently, unless one assumes that the reference to 'the relevant decisions or recommendations of the meetings of the Contracting Parties' is intended to allow the meeting of the parties to further define and, if appropriate, restrict the scope of application of the regulation and authorisation requirement.

At any rate, the provisions of the SAP indicate that contracting parties intend to follow a flexible, pragmatic approach rather than ensuring that all emissions are 'strictly subject' to authorisation or regulation as the Protocol itself requires. They recommend that the authorisation system should apply to new industrial installations with more than 50 employees selected from those listed in Annex I to the Protocol and that 'national regulations

126 SAP, p 24.
127 *Ibid.*
128 *Ibid*, p 38.
129 *Ibid*, p 41.

should be gradually adapted' to deal with existing installations.[130] The target is that 50 per cent of discharges 'shall be in conformity with national and international regulations' by the year 2010.[131] This approach, which is apparently intended to ensure that developing country parties focus their administrative resources primarily on the main point sources of pollution to gradually achieve compliance with the amended provisions of the Protocol, implicitly tolerates a considerable measure of non-compliance with explicit obligations arising from it. Moreover, it completely disregards the existing commitments of the parties under the original 1980 provisions, which already required them to subject all discharges of grey list substances to prior authorisation.

Though regional action plans are intended to have a binding status under the amended Protocol, the SAP as adopted in 1997 was clearly not drafted as a legal instrument specifying detailed measures to be implemented by parties within a given timetable. It is a programmatic document setting forth generally phrased medium- and long-term objectives and procedures for their further elaboration and operationalisation at the regional and national level. Some of the activities it provides for are of a normative nature, but on the whole it seems that spelling out the international legal obligations of the parties to the Protocol is not its main concern and that law is not intended to be a major instrument of the strategy it articulates. In fact, the legal provisions of the Protocol, both in their original and amended form, and the formal recommendations already adopted pursuant to it, appear to serve only as a loose conceptual and institutional backdrop for devising a more practical, project-oriented approach to pollution control which is more likely to attract support from public and private investors and international financial institutions. The parties' new-found pragmatism apparently proceeds from an awareness of the limitations of a purely normative approach and is not particularly scrupulous in adhering to the actual legal prescriptions and established policies of the regime. Although the Protocol strongly emphasises a preventive approach, most of the investments proposed in the SAP are in end-of-pipe pollution control projects. As the Programme itself candidly notes:

> Despite widespread awareness of the importance of prevention measures to reduce pollution, it is surprising that actions to improve the application of Best Available Techniques (BAT) and Best Environmental Practices (BEP) are not proposed.[132]

Of course, as the concluding section of the document makes abundantly clear, the SAP, as adopted by the meeting of the contracting parties in 1997, was elaborated within a very short timeframe and 'represents only the

[130] *Ibid.*
[131] *Ibid.*
[132] *Ibid*, p 52.

starting point of the process' of implementation of the amended Athens Protocol.[133] As has already been mentioned, a review of the Programme is scheduled to be undertaken after the entry into force of the Syracuse Amendments. It will be interesting to see what changes, if any, will be made at that time in the measures and timetables which are then intended to become legally binding on the parties.

133 SAP, p 79.

7

The Regulation of Emissions of Dangerous Substances in International Watercourses

DUE TO THE large number of international river basins and the high level of industrial development in Europe, transboundary pollution of international watercourses became a subject of intergovernmental cooperation of regional interest in the 1960s. An institutional framework for cooperative action to cope with the pollution of Western Europe's most important international river, the International Commission for the Protection of the Rhine against Pollution (ICPR), was established by the riparian states as early as 1963.[1] The activities of this Commission resulted in the conclusion of the Bonn Convention for the protection of the Rhine against chemical pollution in 1976. In 1999, a new, more comprehensive Convention on the Protection of the Rhine was signed in Berne.

International cooperation between European states on issues of freshwater pollution also developed on a more general level in two regional organisations, the Council of Europe and the United Nations Economic Commission for Europe (ECE), long before the first EEC directive on the subject was adopted. These two bodies elaborated a substantial number of soft law instruments on the protection and management of water resources.[2] However, it is only in 1992 that the normative activities of one of these organisations resulted in the adoption of a legally binding international framework agreement not specifically designed for a particular river, the ECE Convention on the Protection and Use of Transboundary Watercourses and International Lakes, which was opened for signature at a pan-European ministerial meeting in Helsinki on 17 March 1992.[3] Earlier efforts by the Council of Europe to elaborate a general European Convention for the protection of international watercourses against pollution were aborted in the 1980s.[4]

[1] Agreement Concerning the International Commission for the Protection of the Rhine against Pollution, Berne, 29 Apr 1963, 994 UNTS 3, OJ No L240, 19.9.1977, p 35.
[2] See Lammers (1984), pp 256–258.
[3] 31 ILM 1312 (1992).
[4] See Lammers (1984), p 8, n 1.

In this chapter I will discuss the Rhine pollution regime and the provisions of the Helsinki Convention in so far as they relate specifically to hazardous substances. The legal and institutional implications of the EC's status as a contracting party to the Bonn and Helsinki Conventions and a number of less important river basin agreements will be discussed in chapter 9.

THE 1976 BONN CONVENTION ON THE PROTECTION OF THE RHINE AGAINST CHEMICAL POLLUTION

History and Background of the Bonn Convention

In 1976, the riparian states of the Rhine and the then EEC concluded a Convention for the protection of the Rhine against chemical pollution which lays down a legal framework for cooperative efforts for the reduction of the pollution of the Rhine by dangerous substances.[5] The Convention was agreed a few months after the adoption by the EC Council of Directive 76/464/EEC, on whose provisions it is closely modelled. After having reached agreement internally within the EEC on the basic principles of a legal regime for the control of emissions of dangerous substances, the riparian states of the Rhine which are members of the EEC apparently sought to extend this regime to the entire Rhine basin by concluding a convention with the only non-EC riparian state, Switzerland. The Convention came about in the context of the activities of the International Commission for the Protection of the Rhine against Pollution (ICPR) and of the Ministerial Conferences on the Protection of the Rhine against Pollution which have been meeting regularly since 1972.

Analysis of the Bonn Convention

The regulatory regime instituted by the Convention, like that of the Paris Convention and Directive 76/464/EEC, is based on a listing of 'dangerous substances' in two lists: a black list (Annex I) of toxic, persistent and bioaccumulative substances, and a grey list (Annex II) comprising substances which, though not considered as hazardous as those of the black list, also cause 'deleterious effects' on the aquatic environment. The black and grey lists of the Bonn Convention are actually identical to those of Directive 76/464/EEC. The basic obligation of contracting parties under the Con-

[5] Convention for the Protection of the Rhine against Chemical Pollution, Bonn, 3 Dec 1976, OJ No L 240, 19.9.1977, p 37 (hereafter cited as Bonn Convention). Luxembourg, though not a riparian state of the Rhine proper, is also a party to the Convention, as its territory is almost entirely situated in the Rhine basin.

vention is to 'eliminate' pollution of the Rhine by black list substances and to 'reduce' pollution by grey list substances.

Unlike the Paris Convention and Directive 76/464/EEC, the Bonn Convention does not define 'pollution'. But its provisions seem to put more emphasis on actual emissions of pollutants into the aquatic environment than on effects. Indeed, the parties' obligations with respect to elimination of pollution by black list substances are further specified as follows:

> The purpose of the measures is to effect the gradual elimination of *discharges* of these substances, taking into account the findings of investigations carried out by experts separately for each one of them and the available technical means.[6]

It thus appears that the ultimate objective of the Convention is to achieve zero emissions of black list substances into the waters of the Rhine basin, rather than just eliminating their harmful effects.

It is to be noted that the parties' obligations with respect to black and grey list substances do not have the same geographical scope. Whereas the obligation to eliminate pollution by black list substances applies to all 'surface waters of the Rhine basin', ie the Rhine and its tributaries, the duty to reduce pollution by grey list substances applies only to the Rhine itself. There were differences between contracting parties as to whether the Convention should apply only to the Rhine proper or to its entire basin, and a compromise was reached by differentiating the obligations according to the nature of the pollutants involved.[7]

Article 1, paragraph 2 provides that the measures taken under the Convention 'shall take into reasonable account' the various uses of Rhine water, ranging from 'the production of drinking water for human consumption' to 'the production of water for industrial purposes'. It is not clear exactly what guidance should be inferred from this provision, since the various listed uses may well be conflicting.

The Convention imposes on contracting parties the duty to establish 'for their own use' a national inventory of discharges which may contain black list substances, to be updated regularly, and to communicate the 'contents' of their inventories to the International Commission for the Protection of the Rhine against Pollution. It is noteworthy that there is a significant difference between the information which parties are to include in their national inventories 'for their own use', which shall comprise information on individual points of discharge, and the information which they shall transmit to the Commission, which 'shall include the total quantities of each of the various substances set out in Annex I', ie consist of aggregate information without any details on individual discharges.[8] Apparently there was

[6] Bonn Convention, Art 1, para 1(a) (emphasis added).
[7] Lammers (1984), pp 182–183.
[8] Bonn Convention, Art 2 & Annex III.

a reluctance on the part of some contracting parties to make available information on individual pollution sources to an international body.[9]

For the regulation of discharges of black list substances, the Convention prescribes a system of emission standards identical to that of Directive 76/464/EEC. All discharges containing black list substances shall be subject to authorisation, which may be granted only for a limited period of time. The authorisation shall fix emission standards which shall be complied with by existing discharges within a given time limit. The emission standards fixed in the authorisation by the responsible national authorities shall not exceed the limit values agreed by contracting parties and laid down in Annex IV of the Convention. All contracting parties are committed to applying the limit values laid down pursuant to the Convention for the control of black list substances. The Convention does not give parties the option to apply an alternative approach based on environmental quality objectives. Indeed, the riparian states are in agreement that the UES approach is the most appropriate method for reducing emissions of black list substances. Unlike the 1974 Paris Convention and Directive 76/464/EEC, the Bonn Convention did not have to accommodate conflicting approaches to pollution control.

The procedure for the establishment of limit values, as set out in Articles 5 and 14 of the Convention, involves the International Commission for the Protection of the Rhine against Pollution. This Commission, however, is not vested with autonomous regulatory authority. Indeed, under the provisions of the 1963 Agreement establishing it, the Commission is only empowered to '*propose* to Contracting Parties measures capable of protecting the Rhine against pollution.'[10] Accordingly, Article 5, paragraph 1 of the Bonn Convention only mandates the Commission to 'propose' limit values, which are then formally adopted and included in Annex IV to the Convention in accordance with the provisions of Article 14, which provides that any changes to annexes 'shall enter into force following unanimous acceptance by the Contracting Parties'. The adoption of limit values thus actually requires double unanimity. First, unanimity is required within the Interna-

[9] It was Germany which refused to provide information on specific industrial point sources to the ICPR, on the grounds that this would result in the disclosure of confidential information on production processes. See Lammers (1984), p 183. In 1988, the ministerial conference of the Rhine states, recognising that 'exchange of information on actual discharges within the [ICPR] is of particular importance' to the implementation of the RAP, instructed the Commission to examine how 'transparency of data' could be achieved. See Communiqué of the 9th Conference of Ministers for the Protection of the Rhine against Pollution, Bonn, 11 Oct 1988, para VI.5. At their next meeting, the ministers agreed on a set of detailed guidelines regarding the exchange of information on permits and actual discharges between the parties. See Communiqué de la 10ème Conférence des Ministres sur la protection du Rhin contre la pollution, Brussels, 30 Nov 1989, s VI.

[10] Agreement concerning the International Commission for the Protection of the Rhine against Pollution, Berne, 29 Apr 1963, Art 2 (b) (emphasis added). English translation in *Selected Multilateral Treaties in the Field of the Environment* (UNEP, Nairobi, 1983), p 176.

tional Commission for the decision to 'propose' the limit values to the contracting parties.[11] Then, each contracting party shall individually notify its formal acceptance of the limit values to the depositary government.

The measures prescribed by the Convention for the reduction of pollution by grey list substances are also very similar to those of Directive 76/464/EEC. Article 6, paragraph 1 of the Convention stipulates as a general principle:

The discharge of any Annex II substance likely to affect the quality of Rhine water must be regulated by the national authorities with a view to limiting it strictly.

As for black list substances, the Convention imposes a requirement of prior authorisation laying down emission standards for discharges of grey list substances. This requirement is part of a more general obligation imposed on contracting parties to draw up 'national programmes for the reduction of the pollution of the Rhine' by grey list substances, including water quality objectives and deadlines for implementation. Emission standards shall be fixed nationally by each contracting party with reference to the quality objectives laid down in its pollution reduction programmes. No provision is made for limit values to be proposed by the International Commission, as for black list substances.

However, the Convention envisages another role for the Commission with respect to pollution by grey list substances. Article 6, paragraph 3 provides that contracting parties shall 'confer' within the Commission before drawing up their pollution reduction programmes and that the Commission 'shall regularly compare the draft national programmes in order to ensure that their aims and means coincide' and may 'submit proposals for achieving, *inter alia*, common goals in reducing pollution of the Rhine'. Such proposals are to be adopted unanimously by the contracting parties 'by applying the procedure laid down in Article 14'. The legal status of these 'common goals' is somewhat unclear. The reference to the formal procedure for the adoption of amendments or additions to annexes, which applies to limit values for black list substances, suggests that such measures are intended to bind the contracting parties. However, no provision is made for including them in the annexes to the Convention; technically, they are not amendments or additions to annexes and do not form an 'integral part' of the Convention within the meaning of Article 14.

Implementation of the Bonn Convention

The Rhine Chemical Pollution Convention entered into force on 1 February 1979, following ratification by the signatory states and conclusion by

[11] *Ibid*, Art 6, para 3.

the EEC.[12] Even before the Convention's entry into force, a working group on chemical pollution (Working Group B) was established within the framework of the International Commission for the Protection of the Rhine to prepare measures for its implementation. This working group was put in charge of elaborating proposals for limit values for discharges of black list substances recommended for inclusion in Annex IV of the Convention.

Selection of Individual Black List Substances

In discharging this task, which as a first step involved the selection of individual pollutants belonging to the groups of substances on the black list for which it was considered necessary to fix limit values, the group collected and reviewed the available scientific and technical data to evaluate whether particular substances met the criteria for inclusion in the black list and were a significant source of pollution of the Rhine basin. Contracting parties were requested to submit available information and, where necessary, additional studies were commissioned. In view of the lack of information and the scientific uncertainty involved in ecotoxicological evaluations, the selection of substances for priority attention involved substantial discretion and was often plagued by the conflicting views and interests of the parties. These difficulties were compounded by the procedural requirement of unanimity. Once the preparatory work had been concluded and a consensus reached within the working group, proposals for limit values could be submitted to the plenary meeting of the Commission for approval.[13]

As the terms of the Bonn Convention are very similar to those of Directive 76/464/EEC and its Annexes I and II identical to Lists I and II of the Directive, the process of selection of individual black list substances for priority attention was carried out in parallel with that under the EC Directive and in close cooperation with the European Commission, which participated in the activities of the working group. As a matter of fact, the same basic inventory of 1500 potential black list substances was used both by the EC and the Rhine Commission as a basis for their standard-setting work.[14] However, the Rhine Commission working group used somewhat different selection criteria from those applied by the Commission of the EC, and identified 83 substances as falling within the scope of the black list (17 of them requiring priority attention), whereas the EC Commission, for

[12] The Convention was concluded by the Community by virtue of Council Decision 77/586/EEC of 25 July 1977, OJ No L 240, 19.9.1977, p 35.

[13] Commission Internationale pour la Protection du Rhin contre la Pollution, *Rapport d'activité 1987*, Koblenz, 1988, p 55.

[14] Vennekens-Capkova (1990), p 154. The inventory referred to is that mentioned in the Commission Communication of 22 June 1982, OJ No C 176, 14.7.1982, p 3.

its part, arrived at a list of 129 candidate substances for inclusion in the black list.[15]

Emission Control Measures for Black List Substances

Notwithstanding the fact that the initial screening process in the Rhine Commission and EC led to different priority lists, the eventual results of the two organisations' parallel efforts to establish limit values for discharges of dangerous substances are strikingly similar. With one exception, all the substances for which the Rhine Commission has recommended limit values are also covered by EEC directives laying down the same limit values.[16] The implementation of the Bonn Convention has not proceeded any faster than that of Directive 76/464/EEC; on the contrary, the work of the Rhine Commission has effectively been conditioned by the pace of legislative activity in the EC. Comparing the provisions and procedures for implementation of the Bonn Convention with those of Directive 76/464/EEC, prior to the Convention's entry into force, Menno Kamminga had somewhat optimistically speculated that, since the Convention did not incorporate the 'dual approach' of the Directive, the setting of limit values under the Convention would not be delayed by discussions about the respective merits of the UES versus the EQO approach.[17] However, experience shows that implementation of the Rhine Convention has been just as slow, if not slower, than that of the EEC Directive. As a senior Dutch official put it, 'cooperation within the ICPR developed into a slow, bureaucratic process of struggling over detailed figures, which did not keep up with the continuous generation of new hazardous compounds.'[18] The hope that it would be possible to make faster progress on setting standards for emissions of dangerous substances in the smaller, relatively homogenous group of Rhine states than in the broader, more diverse framework of the EC has not materialised.

In the very beginning of the Convention's implementation, there were some indications that the Rhine Commission might move faster in its regulatory work than the EC and set more stringent standards, and that this pilot role would even be encouraged by the EC Commission. Indeed, the International Commission for the Protection of the Rhine, as early as its first meeting following the entry into force of the Bonn Convention, already recommended limit values for mercury discharges from the chloralkali industry, while the Commission of the EC had only just managed to submit a proposal to this effect to the EC Council.[19] Moreover, the

[15] Vennekens-Capkova (1990), p 154; Kiss (1987a), p 66.

[16] For a full list of IRC recommendations and corresponding EEC directives, see Nollkaemper (1990c), pp 136–138.

[17] Kamminga (1978), p 70.

[18] De Villeneuve (1996), p 450.

[19] OJ No C 169, 6.7.1979, p 2.

standards recommended by the Rhine Commission were more stringent than those proposed by the European Commission. Nevertheless, the latter Commission did not wait until the Council of the EC had adopted its proposal for an EEC directive setting limit values for mercury emissions to propose that the Community approve the limit values recommended by the Rhine Commission. In June 1980, while the Council was still bogged down in difficult negotiations due to the differences between proponents of the UES and EQO approach,[20] it submitted to the Council a formal proposal for a decision approving the supplement to Annex IV of the Bonn Convention recommended by the International Commission.[21]

In its explanatory memorandum to the Council, the Commission explained that, in participating in the work of the Rhine Commission, it had sought to ensure that the results of this work would be 'consistent with the implementation of Council Directive 76/464/EEC'. It noted that the standards recommended by the Rhine Commission were 'compatible' with those it had proposed in implementation of Directive 76/464/EEC, apart from the time limits for compliance with the limit values, which were shorter in the Rhine proposal. However, the Commission did not object to these shorter time limits, arguing that they were compatible with Article 10 of the EEC Directive, which allows for 'more stringent measures' to be taken 'individually or jointly' by member states.[22] This attitude is quite remarkable in view of the position the Commission has taken in the Paris Commission, where it has consistently opposed the adoption of more stringent measures than laid down in EEC directives.[23] In this case, the Commission apparently used the stronger ICPR recommendation as a tactical tool to put pressure on the Council to speed up the negotiations on the proposed EC chlor-alkali directive. This strategy seems to have worked, perhaps even better than the Commission anticipated, since, in the event, the Council adopted the same time limits as those recommended by the Rhine Commission in Directive 82/176/EEC on limit values and quality objectives for mercury discharges by the chlor-alkali electrolysis industry.[24] After adopting this directive, the Council formally accepted the Rhine Commission recommendation in accordance with Article 14 of the Bonn Convention.[25]

In this instance, a recommendation of the ICPR actually influenced the decision-making process in the EC. As later experience has shown, the

[20] On these negotiations, see Guruswamy, Papps & Storey (1983) & Haigh (1990), pp 87–89.

[21] Proposal for a Council Decision supplementing Annex IV to the Convention on the Protection of the Rhine against Chemical Pollution, EC Doc COM(80) 319 final. The text of the ICPR recommendation is reproduced in this document.

[22] *Ibid*, p 6. See also Scheuer (1981), p 321.

[23] See below ch 9.

[24] OJ No L 81, 27.3.1982, p 29.

[25] Council Decision 82/460/EEC of 24 June 1982, OJ No L 210, 19.7.1982, p 8.

reverse is generally the rule. The standard-setting work in the Rhine Commission has not developed autonomously, but has to a large extent mirrored the legislative activity of the EC. Since 1979, the Rhine Commission has adopted recommendations for inclusion of limit values in Annex IV of the Convention for mercury, cadmium, carbon tetrachloride, aldrin, dieldrin, endrin, isodrin, chloroform, hexachlorobenzene and hexachlorobutadiene.[26] All these black list substances have also been the subject of EEC directives, and the limit values and time limits recommended by the ICPR are invariably the same as those laid down in the corresponding EEC directives.[27] As a matter of fact, agreement on these limit values within the Rhine Commission proved to be possible only *after* they had already been adopted by the Council of the EC. In all these cases it was necessary for the EC to reach agreement internally before consensus could be achieved in the Rhine forum.

Thus, the weaknesses and lacunae of the EEC directives were almost automatically transposed into the ICPR recommendations. For example, when recommending limit values for cadmium emissions, the Rhine Commission, like the EC, could not lay down any standards for discharges from the phosphate industry. As in Directive 83/513/EEC, a footnote to the recommendation attempts to justify this by the lack of economically feasible emission control methods for this sector, but at the same time quite candidly admits the importance of this regulatory lacuna by announcing the Commission's intention, 'in view of the large quantities of cadmium discharged' by the phosphate sector, to propose limit values 'as soon as appropriate methods are available.'[28] However, no further progress has since been made on this question, either in the ICPR or in the EC.

Pollution Reduction Measures for Grey List Substances

The Rhine Commission has also rather sparingly used its powers with respect to grey list substances. The limited activity in this field can be explained by the fact that, in the scheme of Article 6 of the Convention, the right of initiative as regards the elaboration of measures for the control of these substances lies with the individual contracting parties, not with the Commission. It is the contracting parties who must take the initiative to develop national pollution reduction programmes for grey list substances

26 See Lammers (1989b), p 446; Dekker & De Villeneuve (1995), p 269 (table 1).

27 It should be noted that the Rhine Commission has not blindly copied *all* limit values adopted by the EEC. In some instances, after reviewing black list substances for which EEC directives had been agreed, the Commission decided that there was no need to set limit values for those substances under the Bonn Convention, as they are not produced in the Rhine basin. This was the case inter alia for HCH and DDT. The Commission's decisions with respect to those substances can be found in: Commission Internationale pour la Protection du Rhin contre la Pollution, *Rapport d'activité 1986*, Koblenz, 1987, pp 121–123.

28 See the text of the recommendation in OJ No L 175, 5.7.1985, p 36.

and to 'confer' on this subject within the Commission. The Commission is only empowered to 'compare' the 'draft national programmes' of the parties and to elaborate proposals for 'common goals' on this basis. In principle, the Commission can take no action unless and until the contracting parties submit their 'draft national programmes' to it. However, the parties have not been very forthcoming in complying with their obligations under Article 6 and communicating proposed national measures to the Commission. If it had strictly interpreted Article 6, paragraph 3, the ICPR might very well not have been able to take any action at all.

Nevertheless, it did adopt a recommendation on the reduction of pollution by chromium, a heavy metal on the grey list, in June 1982,[29] and the wording of that recommendation indicates that it had to stretch the provisions of Article 6, paragraph 3 rather far in order to do so. Instead of comparing and harmonising existing draft programmes, it turned the procedure on its head and actually anticipated programmes which it obviously had not yet received and which probably did not even exist. In its recommendation, the Commission 'requests' contracting governments to submit their draft national programmes in accordance with Article 6, paragraph 3, and at the same time 'proposes' detailed 'aims and means' to be 'taken into account' by contracting parties in elaborating these programmes. Not only did the Commission formulate its recommendations *before* receiving draft programmes from the parties, it also indicated that, if its recommendations were complied with by the parties in their national programmes, there would be no need for the contracting parties to 'confer' any further within the Commission *after* submitting these programmes, as required by Article 6, paragraph 3.

The 'aims' recommended by the Commission are specific water quality objectives to be achieved in the Rhine by 1 January 1984, while the 'means' are formulated in terms of emission limit values for different industrial sectors discharging chromium which shall not be exceeded by the emission standards laid down in the authorisations to be granted pursuant to Article 6, paragraph 4. Apparently, the Commission interpreted not only the procedural provisions of Article 6 very liberally, but also its substantive provisions. Indeed, the fixing of limit values by the Commission is provided for in Article 5 of the Convention, which applies to black list substances, but is not explicitly envisaged in Article 6, which speaks only of 'common goals' for the reduction of pollution by grey list substances. Whatever may be said of its consistency with the provisions of the Bonn Convention, the recommendation on chromium is probably the only example of original norm-setting work by the ICPR, independently of the EC.[30] However, this

[29] The recommendation is published in Leopold (1990), pp 120–123.

[30] The EC has not adopted any directives relating to grey list substances. The European Commission only submitted a proposal for a directive on water quality objectives for chromium to the Council in 1985. See EC Doc COM(85) 733 final, OJ No C 351, 31.12.1985.

bold initiative was not particularly successful, since the recommendation has not been formally accepted by all contracting parties and consequently has not entered into force.[31]

Problems of Implementation

The Rhine Commission's apparent lack of independent initiative and real decision-making autonomy has been ascribed by commentators to the reluctance of some riparian states, notably Germany, to commit themselves to specific, more stringent rules for discharges of dangerous substances into the Rhine than are applicable throughout the EC. This explains why the Rhine Chemical Pollution Convention only came into being after the EC had adopted a directive which provided a framework for the harmonisation of emission standards in the common market in order to avoid distortions of competition.[32] The dependence of the ICPR on the decision-making process within the EC, both procedurally and substantively, has for all practical purposes transformed the Commission into a kind of 'ratification chamber' for EC directives by Switzerland, its only non-EC member.

However, it does not even fulfil that role effectively. Indeed, most of the limit values for black list substances recommended for inclusion in Annex IV of the Convention have not actually entered into force, as they have not been formally 'accepted' by all contracting parties as required by Article 14, paragraph 3 of the Convention.[33] Thus, Switzerland so far has not become legally bound to apply the standards laid down by the ICPR, which are already binding on EC member states by virtue of their inclusion in EEC directives anyway. The net result of the activities of the ICPR in terms of the development of legally binding environmental standards is clearly very limited. This has even led some authors to question the significance of the Rhine Commission as a rule-making forum and to advocate its abolition.[34]

The Commission itself is painfully aware of the fact that its credibility suffers from this situation. In 1988, it noted that the 'need to take into account the limit values fixed by the EC' had created 'problems' and instructed its legal working group to elaborate proposals for the 'optimization' of procedures in order to create 'favourable conditions' to enable

[31] De Villeneuve (1996), p 450.

[32] Jessurun d'Oliveira (1987), p 26. See also Scheuer (1981), p 321.

[33] Lammers (1989b), p 446. The EEC has only formally accepted two ICPR recommendations, that relating to mercury discharges from the chlor-alkali industry and that relating to cadmium discharges, respectively by Council Decision 82/460/EEC (above, n 25) and Council Decision 85/336/EEC (OJ No L75, 5.7.1985, p 36). The Commission has not found it necessary to submit later recommendations to the Council for approval.

[34] Jessurun d'Oliveira (1987), p 36.

the Commission to adopt limit values for at least three substances annually.[35] The problem was addressed at a higher political level by the 9th Conference of Ministers for the Protection of the Rhine against Pollution, held in Bonn in October 1988, which decided that decision-making and adoption procedures in the ICPR 'should be accelerated'[36] and agreed that there was no need for the Rhine Commission 'to await decisions of the EC Council of Ministers . . . before setting limit values pursuant to the Rhine Chemical Convention'.[37]

Yet, at the same time, the ministerial conference made another recommendation which, though ostensibly intended to accelerate the regulatory work in the Rhine Commission, quite explicitly and paradoxically underscores its political dependence on internal decision-making within the EC, in terms which acknowledge the independence of Switzerland vis-a-vis the Community almost as if it were only a formality. The ministers agreed that when limit values or other legally binding measures adopted by the EC are more stringent than the corresponding measures recommended by the ICPR, the latter would automatically agree with 'the most stringent rules, *subject to express approval by Switzerland*.'[38] How this recommendation can be squared with the idea that the Rhine Commission should play a lead role does not seem to have been of particular concern to ministers.

THE RHINE ACTION PROGRAMME: SOFT LAW TO THE RESCUE

In November 1986, a fire in a pesticides warehouse of the Sandoz corporation near Basel caused massive accidental pollution of the Rhine, affecting all downstream states. Though the quantities of toxic substances released by this accident were small in comparison with the amounts of pollutants emitted in the Rhine as a result of 'normal' structural pollution from point and diffuse sources, the accidental nature of the pollution and its spectacular ecological effects provoked considerable public concern about the state of the Rhine and led to an immediate political response by the Conference of Ministers of the riparian states. There was a widespread perception that international efforts to control Rhine pollution lacked credibility. The lingering frustration over the near-paralysis of the regulatory activities of the Rhine Commission was strengthened by the failure of the early warning system for accidental pollution set up under the Bonn Convention

[35] Commission Internationale pour la Protection du Rhin contre la Pollution, *Programme d'action 'Rhin'—Plan de travail pour la mise en oeuvre*, Koblenz, 10 Oct 1988, p 35.

[36] Communiqué of the 9th Conference of Ministers for the Protection of the Rhine against Pollution, Bonn, 11 Oct 1988, para VII.1.

[37] *Ibid*, para VII.3.

[38] *Ibid*, para VII.4 (emphasis added). See also Lammers (1989b), p 455.

to work effectively.[39] As one commentator notes: 'The political need to provide an adequate answer to the Sandoz disaster was felt to be inescapable.'[40] The events following the Sandoz accident are symptomatic of the tendency of international environmental policy-making to flourish in the wake of ecological catastrophes.

The Conference of Ministers for the Protection of the Rhine against Pollution, which had not met since 1981, was convened in emergency session in Zürich barely two weeks after the accident. The Conference mainly discussed measures for the prevention of accidental pollution and instructed the ICPR to study the question further. To keep up the political momentum generated by the Sandoz disaster, the ministers resolved to meet again in Rotterdam one month later to adopt additional measures based on the proposals of the ICPR.[41] The Rotterdam Conference again focused on the prevention of accidental pollution, but also considered the long-term objectives of environmental cooperation among the riparian states. While the bulk of the recommendations adopted at the Rotterdam meeting deal with measures for accident prevention and emergency preparedness, as well as compensation for damage caused by the Sandoz accident—topics which are outside the scope of this study—the ministers also took a number of policy decisions concerning the reduction of non-accidental emissions of dangerous substances. They declared that the pollution load of hazardous substances in the Rhine must be 'further reduced' and stressed the need to 'intensify the implementation' of the Bonn Convention. More specifically, however, they proclaimed as a 'long-term objective' the restoration of the Rhine ecosystem to such a state as to allow the return of salmon in the river 'by the year 2000'. They instructed the ICPR to prepare a proposal for a 'programme of action' to this effect and to submit it to the next ministerial conference.[42] This is how the Sandoz disaster eventually gave birth to what became known as the 'Rhine Action Programme' (RAP).

In requesting the ICPR to prepare a comprehensive action programme for the restoration of the Rhine ecosystem, which was clearly intended to be broader in scope than the mere implementation of the Bonn Convention, the member states of the Commission decided to transcend the

[39] Art 11 of the Bonn Convention, which imposes a duty to inform all riparian states and the Rhine Commission 'without delay' in the event of 'an accident which could seriously threaten the quality of Rhine water', was not complied with by Switzerland. See Kiss (1987), p 723; Jessurun d'Oliveira (1987), p 21.

[40] Nollkaemper (1990c), p 125.

[41] Déclaration commune des ministres compétents des pays riverains du Rhin et du représentant de la Commission des Communautés européennes, Zurich-Glattbrugg, 12 Nov 1986, in Commission Internationale pour la Protection du Rhin contre la Pollution, *Rapport d'activité 1986*, Koblenz, 1987, pp 159–161.

[42] Communiqué de la 7e Conférence des ministres sur la pollution du Rhin, Rotterdam, 19 Dec 1986, *ibid*, pp 163–183, para F.1–2. For a more detailed critical analysis of the political response to the Sandoz disaster, see Jessurun d'Oliveira (1987).

existing legal framework of their cooperation and to make use of the possibility, laid down in Article 2, paragraph 2 of the 1963 Agreement, to entrust additional tasks to the Commission 'by common agreement'. From the start, the Rhine Action Programme was conceived as a *political* instrument, which would mobilise national action, give new impetus and a renewed sense of purpose to the ongoing cooperation within the Rhine Commission, and appeal to public opinion through a highly symbolic long-term objective, the return of salmon by the year 2000. It was intended to dispel the negative perception of stagnation of international cooperative efforts to control Rhine pollution resulting from the slow progress of work in the ICPR. The existing legal instruments were criticised as being too 'rigid' to achieve rapid results in emission reduction and the main quality of the RAP was perceived to be its 'flexibility.'[43] According to a senior Dutch official, who saw this flexibility as a distinct advantage, the ministers recognised that 'more flexible international policy instruments [were] required to deal with the serious problems we face', and the RAP 'introduced a degree of flexibility in European water quality policy that was hitherto unknown.'[44] Academic observers, too, view the programmatic, informal nature of the RAP as 'an improvement over the cumbersome, legalistic approach of the 1976 Chemical Convention.'[45]

Acting on the mandate received from the Rotterdam ministerial conference, the ICPR elaborated a draft action programme in the course of 1987,[46] which was approved by the 8th Conference of Ministers for the Protection of the Rhine against Pollution in Strasbourg on 1 October 1987.[47] In their communiqué, the ministers reiterated their 'firm determination' to achieve a rapid reduction in Rhine pollution and endorsed the objectives of the RAP as proposed by the International Commission. The objectives to be achieved 'by the year 2000' are threefold: to enable indigenous higher species, such as salmon, to re-establish themselves in the Rhine, and to ensure that the use of Rhine water for drinking water production will remain possible in the future, and that its sediments are not contaminated by toxic substances.

While the first two objectives, the conservation and development of the natural fauna and the production of drinking water for human consump-

[43] Plate (1991), p 567.

[44] *Ibid*, pp 567–568.

[45] Gurtner-Zimmermann (1998), p 251.

[46] Commission Internationale pour la Protection du Rhin contre la Pollution, *Programme d'action 'Rhin'*, Strasbourg, 1987 (hereafter cited as Rhine Action Programme). A Dutch translation of the RAP appears in Leopold (1990), pp 123–139.

[47] Communiqué de la 8e Conférence des ministres sur la protection du Rhin contre la pollution, Strasbourg, 1 Oct 1987, in Commission Internationale pour la Protection du Rhin contre la Pollution, *Rapport d'activité 1987*, Koblenz, 1988, pp 77–93 (hereafter cited as Strasbourg Communiqué). The general objectives, timetable and summary of the proposed measures are stated in para 1 of the communiqué. The measures are elaborated in more detail in the document approved by the ICPR, above n 46.

tion, were already explicitly laid down in the Bonn Convention, albeit in general terms,[48] the special attention to sediment pollution is new and reflects a particular concern of the Netherlands, where the disposal of contaminated dredging spoils from the harbour of Rotterdam poses serious environmental problems and entails considerable expense.[49] The fact that a reduction in sediment pollution is now recognised as an objective in its own right represents a shift away from an exclusive policy focus on water quality towards a more comprehensive concern with the river ecosystem as a whole. The measures envisaged in the RAP to achieve these long-term objectives fall into three categories: the 'accelerated reduction' of pollution from direct and diffuse emissions, the reduction of pollution risks from accidents, and the improvement of hydrological and biological conditions. Only the first category is relevant to this study and will be further analysed here.

List of Priority Substances

The RAP is to be carried out in three stages, according to a precise timetable agreed by the ministers, which is to be 'scrupulously observed.'[50] During the first, preparatory stage, from 1987 to 1989,[51] further information was to be gathered and the objectives of the programme were to be 'concretized'. To this end, a list of priority substances and industrial sectors which are to be the main target of emission reduction measures was established by the ICPR. A list of 27 substances drawn up by Working Group B of the ICPR was annexed to the Rhine Action Programme as a proposed 'first list', to be updated in the course of the implementation of the RAP.[52] In addition, a provisional list of 12 industrial sectors requiring priority attention was also agreed.[53] In 1988, the RAP Coordination Group decided that both these lists were a 'sufficient basis' for the implementation of the programme. It was also decided that the list of priority substances would be completed as necessary, taking into account the list of priority sectors.[54] Consequently, 18 more substances were added to the RAP priority list by the 10th Ministerial Conference one year later.[55]

The revised RAP priority list of 45 substances contains 14 black and grey list substances for which limit values or other measures have already been

[48] Bonn Convention, Art 1, para 2 (a) and (c).

[49] On the question of sediment pollution, see generally Grijns & Mostert (1991); Van Dunné (1991).

[50] Strasbourg Communiqué, para 1.7.

[51] The second stage covered the years 1990–1995, while the third stage ended in 2000.

[52] Rhine Action Programme, Annex B.

[53] *Ibid*, Annex C.

[54] Commission Internationale pour la Protection du Rhin contre la Pollution, *Programme d'action 'Rhin'—Plan de travail pour la mise en oeuvre*, Koblenz, 10 Oct 1988, p 9, para A.3.

[55] See Communiqué de la 10ème Conférence des Ministres sur la protection du Rhin contre la pollution, Brussels, 30 Nov 1989, para III.4 and Annex 1.

agreed under the Bonn Convention, plus another 28 black list substances which were under consideration by the ICPR for the purpose of establishing emission limit values but for which no values had yet been recommended. The list also includes phosphates and ammonia, two substances which are covered by the grey list of the Bonn Convention but for which no international measures had yet been agreed by the Commission. Finally, the list mentions the group of 'adsorbable organohalogen compounds', designated by the sum parameter AOX, as another priority category. 'Organohalogen compounds' as such were already mentioned in Annex I of the Bonn Convention as one of the families of substances from which black list substances are to be selected. But the approach in the RAP differs from that in the Convention in that it implies that the full group of adsorbable organohalogen compounds, which can be quantified more easily than individual organohalogen substances, will be targetted for emission reduction *as a group*, without the need to address each substance belonging to this group individually. This reflects an awareness, on the part of the member states of the Rhine Commission, of the limitations of the substance-by-substance approach to the control of hazardous substances which has prevailed in all international fora so far.

Inventories of Discharges

During the preparatory stage of the RAP, the riparian states were to establish national inventories of discharges of priority substances and update their inventories of major emitters. To a certain extent, the RAP merely reiterates pre-existing obligations, since the contracting parties to the Bonn Convention were already required to establish 'national inventories' of discharges of black list substances 'for their own use' and to communicate aggregate information from these inventories to the ICPR.[56] However, the inventories to be drawn up pursuant to the RAP are wider in scope, as they also cover discharges of a number of grey list and black list substances for which no limit values have been recommended by the ICPR. An annex to the RAP gives an outline of the information which the inventories shall contain, which includes details about discharges from individual firms.[57] While the RAP provides that the participating governments shall communicate to the ICPR 'all necessary elements' of their national inventories,[58] it does not, unlike the Bonn Convention,[59] specify *which* elements are to be made available to the Commission.

[56] Bonn Convention, Art 2, para 2 and Annex III.
[57] Rhine Action Programme, Annex D.
[58] *Ibid*, paras 2.3.1. and 3.1.A.6.
[59] Bonn Convention, Annex III, para 2.

As we have seen above, it is clear from the relevant provisions of the Bonn Convention that there is no obligation to communicate information about individual emitters, but only information about 'total quantities' of substances discharged. The provisions of the RAP are more ambiguous in this respect, as they do not explicitly exclude information about individual sources, which could well be regarded as a 'necessary element' for the implementation of the programme. However, the wording of the RAP still reflects a reluctance on the part of some riparian states to provide such information. Indeed, the participating governments pledge to observe 'the greatest possible transparency with respect to the communication to the ICPR of data on discharges of pollutants *per country and per sector*.'[60] The fact that this commitment to 'transparency' apparently does not extend to discharges *per firm* is certainly not without significance.[61]

Emission Reduction Measures

During the second, operational stage of the RAP, which ran until 1995, the riparian states were to implement emission reduction measures aimed at 'reducing drastically (in the order of 50%)' the total quantities of priority substances discharged into the Rhine between 1985 and 1995. These measures are to be based on the 'state of the art', which shall be applied to all effluents containing priority substances.[62] Additionally, the member states undertook to 'study' the possibility of introducing effluent charges as an economic incentive for the reduction of emissions of dangerous substances.[63] Measures to reduce pollution caused by diffuse sources were also to be taken, though within a timeframe to be agreed later and subject to further elaboration by the ICPR.[64] Finally, the RAP provided that, during its third stage, ie before the year 2000, 'additional measures', including, 'if necessary', a ban on the use of certain dangerous substances, might be taken, if the evaluation of the results of the first and second stages indicated that the intended emission reduction had not been fully achieved.[65]

There can be little doubt that this ambitious programme of 'drastic' pollution reduction through the application of 'state of the art' technology has a higher public visibility and more political appeal than the arduous

60 Rhine Action Programme, para 3.2.1. (emphasis added).

61 It probably reflected Germany's long-standing opposition to disclosure of emission data on individual sources on grounds of industrial secrecy. However, it should be noted that the Rhine ministers agreed two years later on a set of guidelines providing for information exchange on individual sources subject to certain conditions. See above n 9.

62 Rhine Action Programme, para 3.1.B.2.

63 *Ibid*, para 3.1.B.7.

64 *Ibid*, para 3.1.B.6.

65 *Ibid*, para 3.1.C.1.

technocratic exercise of setting emission limit values pursuant to the Chemical Pollution Convention. At any rate, the approach of the RAP differs significantly from that of other applicable instruments such as the Bonn Convention and Directive 76/464/EEC. The RAP is both more focused and more flexible at the same time. It is more focused in that it applies to a well-defined list of priority substances, instead of the more comprehensive, yet open-ended and conveniently vague categories of substances of the black and grey lists. The RAP can be implemented without any immediate need for further negotiations on the identification of individual target substances.

The RAP is more flexible than the other instruments, not only because of its non-binding nature, but also because it lays down only general objectives, without specifying the means through which these objectives are to be achieved at the national level other than by referring to the vague and elastic concept of 'state of the art'. It is obvious that this approach leaves the signatory states considerable discretion.[66] As a matter of fact, the emission reduction objective itself is formulated in rather vague terms. The quantitative target, 'in the order of 50%', is indicative only. Setting a quantitative target without really committing oneself to it was apparently found very attractive for political declarations of this kind, since it inspired the London North Sea Conference to adopt a similar target.

There is a manifest link both conceptually and politically between the RAP toxics reduction objective and the provisions of the London Declaration on the reduction of inputs of dangerous substances into the marine environment of the North Sea. The 1987 London Declaration, adopted only a few weeks after the RAP, contains a similarly formulated reduction objective 'of the order of 50%' between 1985 and 1995. Thus, the political formula invented by the riparian states of the Rhine was emulated by the broader North Sea forum.

Initially, however, the reduction of marine pollution was not among the stated objectives of the RAP, although the Bonn Convention did recognise a decade earlier that chemical pollution of the Rhine 'has undesirable effects on sea water' and explicitly mentioned 'the need to preserve an acceptable quality of sea water' as one of the factors to be 'taken into reasonable account' in developing and implementing measures under the Convention.[67] Following the 1987 London Conference, which had 'generalized the approach of the RAP to all watercourses flowing into the North Sea,'[68] the 9th Conference of Ministers of the riparian states of the Rhine in 1989 called for further coordination of the measures agreed in the framework of

[66] See Lammers (1989b), p 450; Nollkaemper (1990c), pp 125, 128.
[67] Bonn Convention, 2nd preambular para and Art 1, para 2.
[68] Nollkaemper (1990c), p 130.

the INSC and the RAP and decided formally to add the protection of the marine environment to the objectives of the RAP.[69]

It should be noted, however, that the commitments made in the INSC declarations and RAP, though both tending towards the same aim, are not materially identical. The RAP, consistent in this respect with the Chemical Pollution Convention, calls for a reduction of *discharges* of priority dangerous substances into the Rhine, while the London Declaration recommends an equivalent reduction of the quantity of dangerous substances *reaching the marine environment of the North Sea.*[70] Thus, as pointed out in chapter 4, the London Declaration did not in fact require a 50 per cent reduction of *discharges* of dangerous substances into the Rhine and other rivers flowing into the North Sea, since a substantial proportion of the substances emitted into rivers accumulate in sediment and do not actually reach the marine environment. If fully implemented, the objective laid down in the RAP would result in a more substantial reduction of inputs into the North Sea from the Rhine than formally required by the London Declaration and subsequent Hague Declaration. Apart from this, the provisions of the RAP are both more determinate and more narrow in scope than those of the London Declaration, in that they apply to a well-defined list of priority substances. It is only at the Hague Conference in 1990 that priority substances were also identified in the INSC framework.[71]

Exactly *what* is to be reduced by 50 per cent in the Rhine basin? The riparian states have committed themselves to reducing the '*total quantity* of discharges of priority substances.'[72] Thus it appears that they have not actually undertaken to reduce by half the emissions of *each individual* priority substance. The reduction target applies to the *aggregate* amount of discharges of all priority substances taken together, which is to be reduced by about 50 per cent *on the average.*[73] This is clearly implied in the clause of the RAP which stipulates that for some priority substances whose emissions have already been considerably reduced as a result of past measures, a further 50 per cent reduction may not be feasible, while for other substances reductions of *more* than 50 per cent may actually be possible in view of the 'state of the art'.[74] Consequently, riparian states have

[69] *Ibid*, pp 125, 130. See Communiqué de la 10ème Conférence des Ministres sur la protection du Rhin contre la pollution, Brussels, 30 Nov 1989, para II.5. See also Communiqué on the Ninth Conference of Ministers on the Protection of the Rhine against Pollution, Bonn, 11 Oct 1988, s X.

[70] London Declaration, para XVI.2.

[71] Hague Declaration, Annex 1A. This list includes 36 substances and overlaps to a large extent with the list of priority substances in Annex B of the RAP. However, a number of substances in the RAP list, such as benzene and chloroanilines, are not included in the North Sea list.

[72] Rhine Action Programme, para 3.1.B.2 (emphasis added). The original French text speaks of 'la quantité globale des rejets de substances prioritaires'.

[73] Thus also Lammers (1989b), p 450; De Villeneuve (1996), p 452.

[74] Rhine Action Programme, para 3.1.B.2, *in fine*.

considerable latitude in determining exactly to what extent they will reduce emissions of individual priority substances.

In fact, it could even be argued that the commitment to reduce emissions is *conditioned* by the 'state of the art,'[75] a rather indeterminate concept whose actual meaning will effectively be determined by each state for itself. The Rhine Commission has made this quite clear in a document on the implementation of the RAP:

> La fixation et l'application de l'état de la technique dans les différents secteurs industriels est une tâche *relevant de chaque Etat membre.*[76]

The interpretation and application of the concept of 'state of the art' in concrete situations leaves a lot of room for national discretion. The RAP does not give any precise definition of what is to be understood by 'state of the art'; it only states a few general 'principles' which are to be taken into account by the riparian states in applying the concept. The original German text of the RAP refers to '*Stand der Technik*', which is a regulatory concept developed in German environmental law.[77] Although it seems to place more emphasis on technological as opposed to economic factors than the corresponding concept of 'best available technology' as defined by the Paris Commission and subsequently laid down in the 1992 OSPAR Convention, the principles outlined in the RAP as a basis for determining what constitutes 'state of the art' leave just as much room for economic considerations as the Paris Commission definition of BAT.[78] Indeed, the RAP provides that 'the *practical applicability* of the measures is *decisive*' in determining the 'state of the art.'[79] Obviously, the riparian states may have different views as to the 'practical applicability' of particular measures.

To be sure, the ICPR was given an express mandate to 'harmonize' the 'state of the art' and the timetables for its application at the international level. But, oddly enough, this harmonisation effort is to be undertaken only *after* the 'state of the art' for the different industrial sectors has been defined and introduced at the national level.[80] This certainly does not facilitate the task of the Commission to reach an international consensus on what is to be regarded as the 'state of the art', since member states are likely to find

[75] Lammers (1989b), p 450.

[76] Commission Internationale pour la Protection du Rhin contre la Pollution, *Programme d'action 'Rhin'—Plan de travail pour la mise en oeuvre*, Koblenz, 10 Oct 1988, p 29 (emphasis added).

[77] See generally Wolf (1986).

[78] It should be noted that some authors treat the two concepts as synonymous. Nollkaemper (1990c), p 128, for instance, translates 'Stand der Technik' in the RAP as 'best available technology' (BAT).

[79] Rhine Action Programme, Annex E, para 3 (emphasis added).

[80] *Ibid*, para 2.4.

themselves negotiating from entrenched positions, having already taken policy decisions and made difficult compromises with industry at the national level which they will be reluctant to change for the sake of international harmonisation. The ICPR, in its discussions on the implementation of the RAP, apparently recognised this problem, since it stressed that harmonisation 'doit être engagée suffisamment tôt pour pouvoir avoir encore un effet sur les fixations nationales.'[81] There is, however, no intrinsic reason why harmonisation of the 'state of the art' in the context of the RAP should prove any easier than the setting of emission limit values under the Bonn Convention, especially in view of the requirement of unanimity which also applies to the work within the framework of the RAP.[82] Indeed, the experience with similar harmonisation exercises in other international fora, such as the work of the Paris Commission on the definition of BAT for specific sectors, indicates that this process may be just as slow and cumbersome.

Relationship Between the Rhine Action Programme and the Bonn Convention

While the more 'flexible' approach of the RAP to the reduction of pollution by dangerous substances is different from that of the Chemical Pollution Convention, the member states of the IPCR did not initially intend to break completely with their previous regulatory efforts under the Convention. Indeed, the contrary is implied in a provision of the RAP and the Strasbourg Communiqué which confirms their intent, already expressed at the Rotterdam ministerial conference, to 'intensify the implementation' of the Convention and declares that, during the implementation of the RAP, the harmonisation of emission limit values must be considered as a 'permanent task' of the Commission.[83] Thus, in 1987, the two instruments were apparently regarded as complementary. In principle, indeed, there is no incompatibility between their respective approaches to emission reduction. It would be possible to link them by fixing the emission limit values pursuant to Article 5, paragraph 1 in accordance with the 'state of the art' as determined under the RAP and systematically tightening them in pace with the evolution of technology.[84] In this way, the Bonn Convention could have been used as a legal framework to formalise the results of the 'state of the art' harmonisation exercise provided for in the RAP. In practice, however,

[81] Commission Internationale pour la Protection du Rhin contre la Pollution, *Programme d'action 'Rhin'—Plan de travail pour la mise en oeuvre*, Koblenz, 10 Oct 1988, p 29.
[82] *Ibid*, p 30, para 4.
[83] Rhine Action Programme, para 3.1 *in fine*; Strasbourg Communiqué, para 1.6.
[84] As suggested by Nollkaemper (1990c), p 128.

no such harmonisation efforts were undertaken by the ICPR in the context of the RAP.

It should be noted, though, that some form of 'juridification' of the RAP seems to have been initially envisaged, as the 1988 ministerial conference instructed the Rhine Commission to examine

> whether and to what extent the Chemical Convention should be amended in view of the requirements of effective water protection . . . or new legal bases should be established *in order to convert the provisions of the Rhine Action Programme into a legally binding form*.[85]

Apparently, the parties considered that the existing provisions of the Bonn Convention were not entirely adequate and sufficient as a legal basis for transforming *all* the measures laid down in the RAP into a legally binding form. For instance, the Bonn Convention does not provide for the adoption of *process* regulations as opposed to emission standards, for the use of sum parameters as a substitute for limit values for individual substances, or for the use of sectoral regulations of general application as an alternative to individual discharge permits for point sources. However, the idea of converting the RAP into a legally binding instrument was quietly abandoned—as were, for that matter, all further efforts to formulate emission limit values under the Bonn Convention.

Indeed, the very adoption of the RAP reflects a recognition by the riparian states of the failure of the traditional standard-setting regulatory approach and their preference for a non-legal approach based on general objectives, leaving plenty of room for national discretion in their implementation. In this perspective, the professed intent of the signatories of the RAP to 'intensify' the implementation of the Bonn Convention did not appear very credible. Indeed, shortly after the adoption of the RAP, one commentator noted that:

> some of the riparian states of the Rhine have shown a decreased interest in the elaboration of limit values for specific chemical substances in accordance with the Chemical Pollution Convention.[86]

There certainly is no evidence of any 'intensification' of the implementation of the Convention since the adoption of the RAP, any more than there is evidence that the regulatory work of the Paris Commission has been substantially accelerated as a result of the 'political impetus' of the North Sea Conferences. As a matter of fact, the ICPR has not adopted any further emission limit values for individual substances since 1988.[87] The

[85] Communiqué on the Ninth Conference of Ministers on the Protection of the Rhine against Pollution, Bonn, 11 Oct 1988, para VII.6 (emphasis added).

[86] Lammers (1989b), p 450.

[87] See Dekker & De Villeneuve (1995), p 269 (table 1).

Commission's standard-setting activities pursuant to Article 5 of the Bonn Convention seem to have come to a complete standstill after the adoption of the RAP.

The 1994 Ministerial Conference: Towards a New Rhine Convention

The 11th Rhine Ministerial Conference was held in Berne in December 1994 to take stock of the implementation of the RAP during its second stage. The ministers issued a self-congratulatory statement 'noting with satisfaction' that, as regards point sources, the input reduction targets for most priority substances had already been reached in 1992, ie three years before the original deadline.[88] The water quality objectives for two-thirds of these substances had also been achieved throughout the Rhine by 1993. However, in some areas, water quality did not yet conform to these objectives for a number of heavy metals and three persistent organic compounds: hexachlorobenzene, PCBs and lindane. The remaining pollution by these compounds is mainly due to contaminated sediments and diffuse sources.[89] The ICPR is instructed to consider, based inter alia on a cost-effectiveness assessment, what additional measures, such as, for example, removal of polluted sediments, could be taken with respect to these problem substances.[90]

The ministerial conference recognised that, while considerable progress had been achieved with respect to the reduction of toxic emissions from point sources, there were still important 'lacunae' with respect to inputs from diffuse sources.[91] Indeed, the Berne Communiqué, in laying down priorities for the third stage of the RAP, signals a shift of attention from point to diffuse sources, especially agricultural run-off.[92] The ministers called for a 'strong reduction' of pollution by nutrients and pesticides from agricultural sources,[93] but the concrete measures envisaged by the Bern Conference do not quite seem to match this ambitious objective. The Rhine states have not thus far decided that the use of any pesticide or, for that matter, any other dangerous substance should be

[88] Communiqué de la 11ème Conférence des Ministres sur la protection du Rhin, Bern, 8 Dec 1994, paras I.2 and II.2.

[89] *Ibid*, paras II.2 and II.5. The data on which the ministerial statement is based can be found in two ICPR reports published in 1994: Commission Internationale pour la Protection du Rhin contre la Pollution, *Programme d'action Rhin—Inventaire des rejets ponctuels de substances prioritaires 1992*, Koblenz, Aug 1994; *id., Programme d'action Rhin—Comparaison entre la qualité des eaux du Rhin et les objectifs de référence 1990–1993—Bilan intermédiaire*, Koblenz, Dec 1994.

[90] Bern Communiqué paras II.4 and II.5.

[91] *Ibid*, para II.1.

[92] *Ibid*, para VIII.2.

[93] *Ibid*, para III.2.

prohibited pursuant to the relevant provisions on 'additional measures' to be taken during the third stage of the RAP.[94] At their Berne meeting, the ministers merely instructed the ICPR to establish a new list of those pesticides, both for agricultural and non-agricultural use, which are a 'significant' source of pollution of the Rhine basin, and to prepare proposals for reduction measures,[95] and called on all Rhine states to establish 'codes of good agricultural practices' for application at the national level.[96]

No regulatory measures to phase out the production and use of particular pesticides in the framework of the ICPR are announced. The member states of the ICPR merely refer to existing or pending EC legislation on plant protection products and biocides for non-agricultural use and apparently have implicitly agreed to rely entirely on the European Commission's regulatory initiatives in this field.[97] The Rhine ministers 'expect' that these measures will be sufficient to reach the RAP reduction targets for agricultural pesticides.[98] However, as a 'preventive' measure, they did mandate the ICPR to consider what complementary regulatory instruments, such as, eg economic instruments, *could* be introduced to reduce pesticide and fertilizer use in the event that the RAP objectives are not achieved.[99]

From a legal point of view, the most important decision taken at the Berne conference was the launching of negotiations within the framework of the ICPR on a new, integrated and forward-looking convention for the protection of the Rhine, designed to enter into force by the year 2000.[100] The ministers did more than set out general terms of reference for the negotiators; they agreed on a set of rather detailed 'guidelines' regarding the scope, objectives, principles and institutional aspects of the new convention, which effectively predetermined the outcome of the negotiations to a considerable extent. In fact, the Berne Communiqué already contained the basic outline of the new Rhine Convention, which, it was understood from the outset, was to provide a single institutional and legal framework not just for pollution control but for an integrated overall approach to the sustainable management, protection and improvement of the Rhine ecosystem, incorporating new issues such as flood prevention and the conservation of biological diversity in the Rhine basin.

[94] Rhine Action Programme, para 3.1.C.1.
[95] Bern Communiqué, para II.8.
[96] *Ibid*, paras III.2, III.4 and VIII.2.
[97] *Ibid*, para II.7.
[98] *Ibid*, para III.5.
[99] *Ibid*, para III.6.
[100] Or, to quote the official French version of the Berne Communiqué, 'une nouvelle convention pour la protection du Rhin tournée vers l'avenir.' *Ibid*, para VII.

REFORM OF THE RHINE REGIME: THE 1999 BERNE CONVENTION ON THE PROTECTION OF THE RHINE

The text of the new Convention on the Protection of the Rhine[101] was formally adopted at the 12th Ministerial Conference in Rotterdam on 22 January 1998, but the instrument was not signed until more than one year later, following completion of internal procedures in some parties. The signing ceremony took place in Berne on 12 April 1999. The initial target of entry into force by the year 2000, somewhat optimistically proclaimed by ministers at their earlier meeting in the Swiss capital in 1994, was not achieved, but the ICPR was instructed in 1998 to start working immediately according to the provisions of the new Convention, without awaiting its formal entry into force.[102]

Though primarily designed to replace both the 1963 Agreement which established the ICPR and the 1976 Chemical Pollution Convention, the 1999 Rhine Convention is much broader in scope than those earlier instruments, which focused exclusively on the control of surface water pollution. Pollution control has become only one of several aims, subsumed under the overarching objective of the Convention, which is described in Article 3 as the 'sustainable development of the Rhine ecosystem.'[103] Under the same umbrella, a number of new goals for the ICPR are set out, alongside its long-established goal of protecting and improving water quality. They include the ecologically sound and rational quantitative management of water resources and the protection and restoration of biological diversity and natural habitats. Taking into account human needs and interests, the parties have also recognised 'general flood prevention and protection' and safeguarding the use of the Rhine as a source of drinking water as special goals of their cooperation. Finally, the protection of the marine environment of the North Sea is now also explicitly mentioned as an objective of the Rhine Convention, whose preamble notes 'that the restoration of the Rhine is also necessary to conserve and improve the ecosystem of the North Sea' and refers inter alia to the 1992 Paris Convention.

In tune with a recent trend in international environmental law, the new Rhine Convention contains an article entirely devoted to 'principles'. Article 4 enumerates no fewer than nine principles by which the contracting parties

[101] Convention on the Protection of the Rhine, Berne, 12 Apr 1999, OJ No L289, 16.11.2000, p 31 (hereafter referred to as 1999 Rhine Convention).

[102] Ministerial Declaration of the 12th Conference of Ministers on the Protection of the Rhine, Rotterdam, 22 Jan 1998, s II.4.

[103] 1999 Rhine Convention, Art 3, para 1. The concept of 'Rhine ecosystem' covers more than the river itself. According to Art 2, 'ground water interacting with the Rhine' and 'aquatic and terrestrial ecosystems which interact or could interact with the Rhine' also fall within the scope of the convention.

shall be 'guided'. These principles seem inspired by a variety of sources. Some, like the precautionary principle and the polluter pays principle, are recognised both as principles of EC environmental law and international environmental law and have been enshrined in other second-generation water pollution conventions such as OSPAR Convention and the 1992 Helsinki Rivers Convention, both of which are mentioned in the preamble to the new Convention. Others have long been familiar as principles of EC environmental law, either laid down in Article 174, paragraph 2 of the EC Treaty, such as the the principle of preventive action and the principle that environmental damage shall be rectified at source, or in secondary legislation, such as the standstill principle and the principle that pollution should not be transferred to other environmental media. Others are less well-established as general principles, and the legal implications of their elevation to that status in the Rhine Convention seem debatable. What exactly is the normative content of the 'principle of sustainable development'? Can the 'application and development of the state of the art and best environmental practice' really be considered as a 'principle'? The parties seem to be rather content with the indeterminate nature of most of the principles enumerated in Article 4, as they have made no attempt to define any of them.

In stark contrast with the elaborate provisions on objectives and principles, the actual obligations of contracting parties are spelled out in rather rudimentary terms. In the entire Convention, there is in fact only a single article, Article 5, which directly enunciates obligations for the parties. All the other articles either state objectives and principles or contain provisions of an institutional nature governing the functions of the ICPR.

The obligations of parties with respect to discharges of hazardous substances are considerably less detailed and specific than those laid down in the 1976 Bonn Convention, which will be terminated upon entry into force of the 1999 Rhine Convention.[104] One of the objectives of the new convention is that of 'preventing, reducing or eliminating *as far as possible* pollution caused by noxious substances . . . from point sources . . . and diffuse sources.'[105] The only specific obligation of the parties with respect to hazardous substances is to ensure that 'discharges of hazardous substances are gradually reduced *with a view to* complete elimination.'[106] Thus, elimination of discharges is little more than an objective to be pursued. The convention contains no definition or list of hazardous substances.

[104] 1999 Rhine Convention, Art 19, para 1(b). The same applies to the 1963 Agreement establishing the ICPR. However, decisions, recommendations, limit values and other agreements adopted by the ICPR pursuant to those earlier instruments shall remain applicable, 'without any change to their legal nature', as long as they are not explicitly repealed by the Commission. *Ibid*, Art 19, para 2.

[105] *Ibid*, Art 3, para 1(a) (emphasis added).

[106] *Ibid*, Art 5, para 4(b) (emphasis added).

As regards the instruments to be used for the control of effluent discharges in general, the 1999 Rhine Convention is hardly more specific. Article 5, paragraph 4(a) imposes on parties a general obligation to ensure that waste water discharges are 'subject to prior authorisation or to general rules laying down emission limits', without specifying on what basis emission limits are to be established. Unlike the Bonn Convention, the new treaty does not provide for the establishment of harmonised, BAT-based emission standards by the ICPR. While Article 4 provides that the parties shall be 'guided' by 'the application and development' of 'state of the art' technology, there is no provision which explicitly *requires* them to impose the use of 'state of the art' or BAT when authorising discharges. An implicit obligation to do so could arguably be inferred from Article 5, paragraph 4(d), which stipulates that parties have a duty to regularly review discharge permits and regulations and to 'adjust' them in so far as this is made possible by 'substantial improvements in the state of the art'. But, at any rate, the rather circuitous way in which the provisions relating to BAT are formulated is striking. The convention itself contains no definition of BAT and BEP, but a 'Protocol of signature' annexed to it records the agreement of the heads of delegation to the ICPR that '"state of the art" and "best available techniques" are synonymous expressions' which, within the framework of the Rhine Convention, are to be understood in the same way as they are defined in the 1992 Helsinki Rivers Convention and OSPAR Convention.[107]

In addition to the few specific obligations of contracting parties spelled out in Article 5, the same article also contains a general clause which requires parties to take the necessary measures in their territory to implement decisions of the ICPR in accordance with Article 11.[108] Viewed in isolation, this provision could be interpreted as implying that ICPR decisions are binding. But it appears from other provisions of the convention that this is not the case. In Article 8, the Commission is given a mandate to 'make *proposals* for individual measures and programmes of measures' to achieve the objectives laid down in Article 3.[109] Article 11 further stipulates that decisions on such measures shall be 'in the form of *recommendations*' addressed to the contracting parties, to be implemented by them in accordance with their national law.[110] The same article provides that each party shall report regularly to the ICPR on the implementation of its decisions and inform the Commission in the event it finds itself unable to implement any decision, in which case other parties may request that consultations be held, and the Commission may decide on measures to 'assist' the

[107] *Ibid*, Protocol of signature, para 2.
[108] *Ibid*, Art 5, para 5. Under the new convention, unanimity will continue to be required for the adoption of Commission decisions. *Ibid*, Art 10, para 1.
[109] *Ibid*, Art 8, para 1(b) (emphasis added).
[110] *Ibid*, Art 11, para 1 (emphasis added).

implementation of the decision in question.[111] These provisions indicate that, although ICPR decisions technically are not legally binding, there is nevertheless a strong expectation of compliance and parties will be exposed to institutional and peer pressure to comply.

The scant substantive obligations of the parties under the 1999 Convention and its almost total reliance on non-binding ICPR recommendations as the main instrument for collective action reflect the declining role of law in the Rhine regime. In this respect, the provisions of the new convention are no more than a confirmation of the *de facto* situation since the advent of the RAP and the demise of binding emission standards as a regulatory technique. The drafters of the Rhine Convention have essentially codified existing practice in the ICPR as it has developed over the last decade. The new instrument legitimates the extension of the Commission's jurisdiction to deal with all aspects of integrated water management in the Rhine basin and provides a legal and institutional framework for the continuation and further development of its current programmatic approach to international environmental cooperation, which is widely perceived as a success.[112]

THE 1992 HELSINKI CONVENTION ON THE PROTECTION AND USE OF TRANSBOUNDARY WATERCOURSES AND INTERNATIONAL LAKES

General Analysis of the Convention

The 1992 Helsinki Rivers Convention is essentially a framework convention, designed to apply to transboundary watercourses and international lakes generally, instead of a single, specific international river, like the Rhine Conventions discussed in the previous section. It contains two categories of provisions: provisions of a general nature which apply directly to all contracting parties in whose territory *any* transboundary waters as defined by the Convention[113] are situated, and provisions relating to riparian parties in their relations with respect to *specific* transboundary waters. The latter provisions are intended as a framework for bilateral or multilateral agreements or 'other arrangements' to be concluded by the riparian parties concerned 'in order to define their mutual relations and conduct regarding the prevention, control and reduction of transboundary impact' in specific international rivers or lakes. The parties' main obligation under

[111] 1999 Rhine Convention, Art 11, para 4.

[112] For an analysis of the perceptions of the various actors involved in the management of the Rhine, see generally Gurtner-Zimmermann (1998).

[113] Art 1, para 1 defines transboundary waters as 'any surface or ground waters which mark, cross or are located on boundaries between two or more States'.

these provisions is to conclude such agreements or arrangements 'where they do not yet exist, or adapt existing ones, where necessary to eliminate the contradictions with the basic principles of [the Helsinki] Convention.'[114] These agreements or arrangements 'shall provide for the establishment of joint bodies' which shall be entrusted with a number of tasks relating to cooperative management of the waters concerned.[115]

These tasks are formulated in general and non-exhaustive terms 'without prejudice to relevant existing agreements or arrangements'. This phrase in Article 9, paragraph 2, read in conjunction with the provisions of paragraph 1 of the same article, indicates that these framework provisions are not intended to affect any specific existing provisions relating to the functions of 'joint bodies' established prior to the adoption of the Helsinki Convention, subject however to the parties' general obligation to 'adapt' such provisions should they be 'in contradiction with the basic principles' of the Convention. The tasks listed in Article 9, paragraph 2 relevant to the control of discharges of hazardous substances include, inter alia, the elaboration of 'emission limits for waste water', the development of 'concerted action programmes for the reduction of pollution loads from both point sources . . . and diffuse sources' and the promotion of 'cooperation and exchange of information on the best available technology.'[116] Part II of the Convention, however, contains no provisions referring specifically to hazardous substances.

Such provisions are only to be found in Part I, which contains the provisions 'relating to all Parties', ie not specifically addressed to 'Riparian Parties'. The basic general obligation of the parties is 'to take all appropriate measures *to prevent, control and reduce* pollution of waters *causing or likely to cause* transboundary impact.'[117] Interestingly, the Convention contains no definition of 'pollution'. It is equally striking that the ECE Rivers Convention, contrary to many other international legal instruments discussed in this study, does not provide for the *elimination* of any form of water pollution. The standard wording describing the obligations of the

[114] Helsinki Rivers Convention, Art 9, para 1. While the Convention prescribes bilateral or multilateral cooperation between riparian states within the framework of 'joint bodies', it also imposes on them a number of duties independently of the existence of such bodies. Most of the obligations imposed by the second part of the Convention are either to be fulfilled through a common institutional structure, where one exists, or, alternatively, through non-institutionalised, direct cooperation on an ad hoc basis in accordance with the general provisions laid down in the Convention itself. Some of these provisions contain no reference at all to 'joint bodies' and are sufficiently detailed to be capable of direct application (eg Art 14 (warning and alarm systems), Art 15 (mutual assistance in the event of a 'critical situation'), Art 16 (public access to information).

[115] *Ibid*, Art 9, para 2. The term 'joint body' is defined in Art 1, para 5 as 'any bilateral or multilateral commission or other appropriate arrangements for cooperation between the Riparian Parties'.

[116] *Ibid*, Art 9, para 2 (d), (f) and (i).

[117] *Ibid*, Art 2, para 2(a) (emphasis added).

parties requires them only to 'prevent, control and *reduce*', but not to eliminate, water pollution or transboundary impacts.[118]

The concept of 'transboundary impact', which plays a material role in the description of many of the parties' obligations, is defined as:

> any *significant adverse effect* on the environment *resulting from* a change in the conditions of transboundary waters caused by a human activity, the physical origin of which is situated wholly or in part within an area under the jurisdiction *of a Party*, within an area under the jurisdiction of *another Party*.[119]

The threshold for an environmental interference to qualify as a 'transboundary impact' seems rather high, compared to the standard definition of pollution found in other relevant conventions concluded in the 1990s, such as the 1992 Paris Convention, the 1992 Helsinki Baltic Convention, or the 1995 amendments to the Barcelona Convention. Indeed, the existence of a 'transboundary impact' within the meaning of the Helsinki Rivers Convention apparently requires positive evidence of a causal link ('resulting from') between an anthropogenic change in the conditions of transboundary waters and a 'significant adverse effect'. The definition further lists some examples of 'adverse effects', but provides no clues as to what is to be considered 'significant'.

This restrictive way of defining 'transboundary impact' and, consequently, circumscribing the preventive obligations of the parties, might seem contrary to the now widely recognised precautionary principle. Paradoxically, however, this principle is explicitly endorsed by the Helsinki Convention as one of the principles by which the parties 'shall be guided' in implementing their general obligations set forth in Article 2, paragraphs 1 and 2. It is formulated as follows:

> The precautionary principle, by virtue of which action to avoid the *potential* transboundary impact of the release of *hazardous substances* shall not be postponed on the ground that scientific research has not *fully* proved a causal link between those substances, on the one hand, and the *potential* transboundary impact, on the other.[120]

[118] Ironically, a Protocol on Water and Health to the 1992 Helsinki Rivers Convention, adopted in 1999 'to complement that Convention with further measures to strengthen the protection of public health', goes beyond the Convention itself in providing that measures to be taken by the parties for the protection of water resources used as sources of drinking water 'shall aim at the effective reduction *and elimination* of discharges and emissions of substances judged to be hazardous to human health and water ecosystems'. Protocol on Water and Health to the 1992 Convention on the Protection and Use of Transboundary Watercourses and International Lakes, London, 17 June 1999, UN Doc MP.WAT/2000/1, 18 October 1999, Art 4, para 2(c) (emphasis added). However, the Protocol contains no further operational provisions for this purpose. Since its main focus is on the prevention of water-related diseases through measures in the area of drinking water supply and sanitation, it will not be further examined here.

[119] Helsinki Rivers Convention, Art 1, para 2 (emphasis added).

[120] *Ibid*, Art 2, para 5(a) (emphasis added).

This formulation differs from that in recent marine pollution conventions in that it applies only to releases of hazardous substances (as opposed to substances or energy generally) which may cause transboundary impacts, ie 'significant adverse effects' (as opposed to mere 'hazards' to human health or harm to living resources and ecosystems).[121] However, even in its weakened form, the principle implies that, with respect to emissions of hazardous substances, the existence of a *potential* transboundary impact is sufficient to trigger the parties' duty to 'prevent, control and reduce' water pollution, notwithstanding the lack of 'full' scientific proof that such emissions and potential impact are causally linked. This interpretation is confirmed by the wording of Article 2, paragraph 2(a), which refers to water pollution 'causing *or likely to cause* transboundary impact'. Thus, the reference to the precautionary principle has the effect of mitigating the restrictive nature of the general definition of 'transboundary impact', but only in so far as it relates to hazardous substances.

Generally speaking, the definition of 'transboundary impact' in the Helsinki Convention is both more comprehensive and more restrictive than the current standard definition of pollution. It is more comprehensive in that the concept of 'impact' comprises other adverse effects than those caused by changes in water *quality*; any change in the *condition* of transboundary waters, such as for instance a reduction in water *quantity* due to abstraction of water, which gives rise to 'adverse effects', is covered by the definition of 'transboundary impact', which is logical in view of the Convention's integrated approach to the management of water resources. On the other hand, it appears clearly from the provision referring to 'pollution of waters *causing or likely to cause transboundary impact*'[122] that there is a difference in scope between the two concepts. Not all pollution—not even all *transboundary* pollution—qualifies as a 'transboundary impact' within the meaning of the Convention. It must either cause or be likely to cause '*significant* adverse effects' on the environment in an area under the jurisdiction of another *contracting party* to the Convention than the party in whose territory the pollution originates. Adverse effects on the marine environment of the high seas, or on the territory of a non-party state, even if deemed 'significant', could not legally be regarded as a 'transboundary impact' under the Convention.

Other provisions of the Helsinki Rivers Convention do, however, explicitly recognise the link between the pollution of transboundary watercourses and that of the marine environment.[123] Article 9, paragraph 3 provides for cooperation between 'joint bodies' constituted by riparian states and any similar international bodies established by coastal states for the protection

[121] Cf 1992 Paris Convention, Art 2, para 2(a).
[122] Helsinki Rivers Convention, Art 2, para 2(a) (emphasis added).
[123] See generally Boyle (1990).

of the marine environment which may be directly affected by a 'transboundary impact' as defined in the Convention. In non-imperative terms, Article 9, paragraph 4, for its part, provides for the *possibility* of inviting *individual* coastal states which are not riparian states of the international river concerned but which are 'directly and significantly affected by transboundary impact' caused by pollution from such river 'to be involved in an appropriate manner' in the activities of the 'joint body' established by its riparian states. Significant adverse environmental effects occurring in the territorial waters or exclusive economic zones of coastal states would fall within the ambit of the definition of 'transboundary impact'.

Specific Provisions with Respect to Hazardous Substances

As we have seen, hazardous substances, though not the central focus of the Helsinki Convention, are one of the many objects of the regulatory regime established by it. This raises two questions. How exactly is the concept of 'hazardous substances' to be understood within the framework of the Convention? And what are the specific obligations of the contracting parties with respect to pollution of transboundary waters by hazardous substances?

Hazardous substances are generally defined in Article 1, paragraph 6 of the Helsinki Convention as 'substances which are toxic, carcinogenic, mutagenic, teratogenic or bio-accumulative, especially when they are persistent.' Though Germany proposed in the course of the negotiations to attach to the Convention an annex listing 'hazardous substances, whose introduction into transboundary waters shall be prohibited or prevented',[124] and the negotiating text at one point included operative provisions and a draft annex to this effect,[125] no consensus on this proposal could eventually be reached. As a result, the Convention contains no list of substances but merely provides that existing lists 'in international conventions or regulations, which are applicable in the area covered' by it, shall be 'taken into account.'[126] Since the signing of the Convention, however, the ECE Committee on Environmental Policy has drawn up 'Recommendations to ECE Governments on the prevention of water pollution from hazardous substances', which include 'indicative lists' of priority substances and of industrial sectors for which emission standards based on BAT should be established.[127] These recommendations were explicitly 'endorsed' by the first Meeting of the Parties to the Helsinki Convention, which was held

[124] UN Doc ENVWA/WP.3/R.18, 16 Aug 1990, pp 23–24.

[125] Albeit one entitled 'indicative list of hazardous substances'. See UN Doc ENVWA/WP.3/R.19, 31 Jan 1991, p 8, Art 3, para 2 & p 23, Annex II. See also the report of the second negotiating session, UN Doc ENVWA/WP.3/10, 15 Nov 1990, p 2, para 8.

[126] *Ibid*, Art 3, para 2 *in fine*. This would include the lists laid down in such other instruments as Dir 76/464/EEC, Dir 96/61/EC, the 1974 and 1992 Paris Conventions, etc.

[127] *See* Economic Commission for Europe, *Protection and Sustainable Use of Waters—Recommendations to ECE Governments*, UN Doc ECE/CEP/10 (1995), p 23.

in Helsinki in July 1997. In doing so, the meeting expressly noted that the various recommendations on water pollution adopted by the Committee on Environmental Policy since 1994 'further substantiate the Convention.'[128]

Hazardous substances are addressed in a few scattered provisions in Part I of the Convention and in its annexes. Waste-water discharges in transboundary waters shall be made subject to 'prior licensing' and permits shall impose emission limits for hazardous substances which are to be 'based on the best available technology', as defined in Annex I to the Convention.[129] These emission limits may not only be set in permits but also through regulations 'which are specifically applicable to individual industrial sectors or industries from which hazardous substances derive.'[130] Apart from the use of emission limit values, the Convention also provides for the adoption by the parties, at the national level, of water quality 'objectives' and 'criteria' aiming at, inter alia, 'the reduction of average pollution loads (in particular hazardous substances) to a certain degree within a certain period of time.'[131]

The parties, moreover, have the duty to implement 'appropriate measures and best environmental practices' for the reduction of inputs of hazardous substances from diffuse sources.[132] Unlike the above-mentioned concept of 'best available technology', the concept of 'best environmental practices' (BEP) is not, technically speaking, defined in the Convention. It is a notion to be 'developed' by individual contracting parties, but Annex II of the Convention contains a set of non-binding[133] 'guidelines for developing best environmental practices', to be used by parties 'in selecting for individual cases'. These guidelines, which list a 'graduated range of measures' and a set of factors to be given 'particular consideration',[134] are largely the same as the 'definition' of BEP in related international instruments.[135] One significant difference, however, is the conspicuous absence in the list of measures of a reference to 'avoiding the use of hazardous substances or products and the generation of hazardous waste.'[136]

[128] UN Doc ECE/MP.WAT/2, 12 Aug 1997, p 7, para 21(c) & Annex VIII.

[129] Helsinki Rivers Convention, Art 3, para 1(b) and (c). The definition of 'best available technology' in Annex I is almost literally the same as in App 1 of the 1992 Paris Convention. See above ch 4.

[130] Helsinki Rivers Convention, Art 3, para 2.

[131] *Ibid*, Art 3, para 3 and Annex III.

[132] *Ibid*, Art 3, para 1(g).

[133] The reference to Annex II in Art 3, para 1(g) is formulated in non-prescriptive terms: '*guidelines . . . are given in annex II*'. There is no reference to Annex II in the Convention's article on 'Definitions', which does however contain an entry on BAT referring to the 'definition' contained in Annex I. *Ibid*, Art 1, para 7.

[134] *Ibid*, Annex II, paras 1 and 2.

[135] Cf. 1992 Paris Convention, App 1.

[136] Cf. 1992 Paris Convention, App 1, para 6(f). 'Substitution by *less polluting* processes or *substances*' is, however, mentioned as one of the *factors* to be taken into consideration in Annex II, para 2(b) of the Helsinki Rivers Convention.

There are other provisions in the Convention reflecting a certain lack of consistency in dealing with the prevention of pollution by hazardous substances.[137] For instance, Article 3 specifies that the measures to be taken by parties with respect to both point sources and diffuse sources '*may*, *inter alia*, include total or partial *prohibition of the production or use* of such substances,'[138] while another clause in Article 5 provides for cooperative research and development programmes on such matters as 'the assessment of the toxicity of hazardous substances'[139] and 'environmentally sound methods of *disposal* of hazardous substances.'[140] At the same time, these provisions on research and development refer explicitly to 'the *phasing out and/or substitution* of substances likely to have transboundary impact.'[141] These various provisions seem somewhat contradictory, indicating that some parties consider that the production and use of hazardous substances needs to be phased out, while others prefer to focus on improving disposal and risk assessment methods. Finally, yet another provision stipulates that 'the emission of pollutants is [to be] prevented, controlled and reduced *at source* through the application of, *inter alia*, *low- and non-waste technology*.'[142] This reference to source reduction and 'low- and non-waste technology', a notion different from 'best available technology', appears to serve essentially the same hortatory purpose as the reference to 'clean technology' in the 1992 Paris Convention.[143]

As appears from the above analysis of its provisions, the Helsinki Rivers Convention is essentially a codification of existing practice in the ECE region. Its main value is that it establishes the skeleton of a basic regime for the protection and management of transboundary waters that potentially applies to the whole of Europe, subject of course to its ratification by all the member states of the ECE, but it does not add anything of great substantive significance to the transnational legal framework for the control of emissions of toxic substances in the aquatic environment.

[137] The inconsistency between the provisions of the Convention and those of its 1999 Protocol on Water and Health in this respect has already been noted in n 118 above.
[138] Helsinki Rivers Convention, Art 3, para 2 (emphasis added).
[139] *Ibid*, Art 5 (a).
[140] *Ibid*, Art 5(e) (emphasis added).
[141] *Ibid*, Art 5(d) (emphasis added).
[142] *Ibid*, Art 3, para 1(a) (emphasis added).
[143] Cf above ch 4.

8

The Regulation of Emissions of Dangerous Substances into the Aquatic Environment under European Community Law

THE GENERAL FRAMEWORK OF EUROPEAN COMMUNITY LAW AND POLICY FOR THE CONTROL OF WATER POLLUTION

The First Environmental Action Programme (1973–1976)

The struggle against water pollution is one of the earliest and most prolific areas of legislative activity in the European Community's environmental policy.[1] In its early years, the primary objective of EC environmental policy, as laid down in the First Environmental Action Programme, adopted by the Council on 22 November 1973,[2] was to 'prevent, reduce and as far as possible eliminate pollution and nuisances.'[3] From its inception, this policy thus placed great emphasis on combating water pollution and, to this end, developed a set of essentially remedial measures for the 'reduction' of pollution. These measures were based on a variety of policy approaches.

In the first place, the Action Programme provided for the establishment of quality objectives for water intended for specific uses, focusing on fresh water and sea water, as priority measures to be taken at Community level.[4]

[1] For a general overview of Community water pollution legislation, see Lavrysen (1992); Kromarek (1988); Cashman (1991); Howarth (1992) & Krämer (1993a).

[2] Declaration of the Council of the European Communities and of the Representatives of the Governments of the Member States meeting in the Council of 22 Nov 1973 on the programme of action of the European Communities on the environment, OJ No C112, 20.12.1973, p 1 (hereafter referred to as the First Environmental Action Programme). Since the amendment of the EEC Treaty by the Single European Act, the objectives of Community environmental policy are laid down in Art 130r (now Art 174), para 1 of the Treaty, and the objective of pollution control has been subsumed under the more general objective of 'preserving, protecting and improving the quality of the environment'.

[3] *Ibid*, p 5.

[4] First Environmental Action Programme, pp 9, 13–17.

Additionally, the setting of standards for emissions of hazardous substances in the aquatic environment and specific, source-oriented measures aimed at reducing pollution caused by certain highly polluting sectors of industry[5] were also envisaged in the Programme, though not given as much emphasis as the quality objectives. The document acknowledged the existence of gaps in scientific knowledge and stressed the need for any Community standards to be based on 'objective knowledge.'[6] It also contained a list of priority substances to be covered by Community standards.[7]

Pursuant to the First Environmental Action Programme, the Council first adopted two directives laying down quality objectives for surface water intended for the production of drinking water[8] and for bathing water.[9] These directives set water quality standards for water intended for specific uses but allow the member states considerable flexibility in their implementation as they do not specifically determine *where* these quality standards apply[10] nor *what measures*, other than monitoring, are to be taken by the member states to ensure compliance.

Under Directive 75/440/EEC, member states 'shall take all necessary measures to ensure that surface water conforms' to the quality standards laid down by the directive[11] and, furthermore, 'shall take the necessary measures to ensure *continuing improvement* of the environment' and 'shall draw up a *systematic plan of action* including a timetable for the improvement of surface water.'[12] The directive does not specify what constitutes 'continuing improvement' nor what measures a 'systematic plan of action' should comprise,[13] but merely indicates that 'considerable improvements are to be achieved under the national programmes over the next 10 years.'[14]

A similar timeframe is laid down in Directive 76/160/EEC, which provides that 'Member States shall take all necessary measures to ensure that,

[5] First Environmental Action Programme, pp 20–21.

[6] *Ibid*, p 12.

[7] *Ibid*, pp 13, 14.

[8] Council Dir 75/440/EEC of 16 June 1975 concerning the quality required of surface water intended for the abstraction of drinking water in the Member States, OJ No L194, 25.7.1975.

[9] Council Dir 76/160/EEC of 8 Dec 1975 concerning the quality of bathing water, OJ No L31, 5.2.1976.

[10] The discretion of member states with respect to the identification and monitoring of bathing waters is, however, limited by a more or less objective general definition of such waters in Dir 76/160/EEC. This was recognised by the Court of Justice in Case C–56/90, *Commission v United Kingdom*, [1993] ECR I–4109.

[11] Dir 75/440/EEC, Art 4, para 1.

[12] *Ibid*, Art 4, para 2 (emphasis added).

[13] It is in fact the Court of Justice which, in a number of judgments on the implementation of Dir 75/440/EEC, has tried to flesh out this notion. See Case C–290/89, *Commission v Belgium*, [1991] ECR I–2851, at para 7. Case C–58/89, *Commission v Germany*, [1991] ECR I–4983, at para 25.

[14] Dir 75/440/EEC, Art 4, para 2.

within 10 years following notification of this Directive, the quality of bathing water conforms' to the standards set by each member state in accordance with the directive.[15]

In line with the stated objective of the First Environmental Action Programme to 'prevent, reduce and as far as possible eliminate' water pollution, these directives view quality standards as an instrument of a Community policy aimed at achieving a gradual improvement in water quality.[16] However, the Action Programme also recognises that the implementation of such a policy requires source-oriented measures and, though the wording of the relevant provisions of the programme indicates a certain reluctance on the part of the member states to contemplate Community action in this respect, reference is made to the possible need for harmonisation of national pollution control measures beyond the mere establishment of Community water quality objectives.

It is in this context that the legal framework for the control of water pollution by dangerous substances in the Community was established in 1976 by the adoption of Directive 76/464/EEC.[17] This directive supplements the earlier two directives on water quality with a system for regulating discharges of certain specific water pollutants perceived as particularly hazardous. It lays down ambitious objectives for the protection from toxic emissions of water resources throughout the Community, initially covering both surface waters and groundwater. It requires member states to 'eliminate' pollution of surface waters by the most hazardous pollutants, the so-called 'black list' substances, and to 'reduce' pollution of the same waters by other toxic pollutants featuring on its 'grey list.'[18] In its original form, it also required no less than the application of 'a system of zero-emission to discharges into groundwater' of black list substances.[19] The directive's special 'programmatic' quality makes it heavily loaded with symbolic significance.[20] Yet for all its symbolic meaning, it was structurally flawed from the outset by its attempt to accommodate in one and the same legal instrument two fundamentally opposed approaches to water pollution control policy, as we shall see in the detailed analysis below.

[15] Dir 76/160/EEC, Art 4, para 1.

[16] On the function of water quality objectives as an instrument of water pollution control policy, see generally Jadot (1991).

[17] Council Dir 76/464/EEC of 4 May 1976 on pollution caused by certain dangerous substances discharged into the aquatic environment of the Community, OJ No L 129, 18.5.1976, p 24 (hereafter referred to as Dir 76/464/EEC).

[18] Dir 76/464/EEC, Art 2.

[19] *Ibid*, Art 4, para 1.

[20] According to Brusasco & Kiss (1978), p 314, the adoption of Dir 76/464/EEC 'avait une importance politique considérable; elle établit un programme aussi progressiste qu'ambitieux pour la réglementation des pollutions particulièrement dangereuses'.

The Second Environmental Action Programme (1977–1981)

Whereas early Community water policy focused mainly on control of freshwater pollution, Directive 76/464/EEC signalled a shift towards a combined approach to freshwater and marine pollution. This increased attention to marine pollution was confirmed in the Community's Second Environmental Action Programme.[21] Referring to both freshwater and marine pollution, this Programme notes that 'a number of important provisions already adopted or contemplated constitute the basis for a coherent policy designed to prevent and reduce this type of pollution at Community level' and announces that further action in this field 'will therefore be directed towards the continued implementation of these provisions.'[22] It is questionable whether the three water directives adopted in 1975 and 1976, which deal only with sectoral aspects of the water pollution problem, really constituted a legal framework for a 'coherent policy' for the control of water pollution. Instead of attempting to develop such a framework, the Commission chose to continue its legislative work in a rather opportunistic and incoherent fashion.

The fields of action outlined in the First Environmental Action Programme are reiterated in the Second, without any attempt to set clear priorities.[23] However, with respect to concrete action to be undertaken by the Commission, the Second Action Programme focuses essentially on the implementation of the three water directives adopted under the First Action Programme.[24]

Thus, for example, the programme provides for 'an examination of national plans for the improvement of surface water,'[25] plans which member states are required to draw up pursuant to Article 4, paragraph 2 of Directive 75/440/EEC. Nothing was ever heard of this effort again. As regards Directive 76/464/EEC, the Commission's programme for implementation during the 1977–1981 period included the submission of a proposal for a directive on the protection of groundwater,[26] the submission of proposals for limit values and quality objectives for black list substances, 'regular

[21] Resolution of the Council of the European Communities and of the Representatives of the Governments of the Member States meeting within the Council of 17 May 1977 on the continuation and implementation of a European Community policy and action programme on the environment, OJ No C139, 13.6.1977, p 1, especially paras 30–33 (hereafter referred to as the Second Environmental Action Programme).

[22] *Ibid*, para 33.

[23] *Ibid*, para 34. See also para 48.

[24] *Ibid*, paras 35–39.

[25] *Ibid*, para 36, 1st indent.

[26] Indeed, the 'zero-emission' principle laid down in Art 4, para 1 of Dir 76/464/EEC was conceived as a provisional rule only, as Art 4, para 4 explicitly provides that the provisions of that directive relating to groundwater 'shall no longer apply upon the implementation of a separate Directive on ground water'.

comparisons of programmes concerning [grey list substances] in order to ensure adequate coordination in their implementation', the examination of evidence submitted by those member states wishing to rely on the quality objectives approach, and 'where necessary' the submission of proposals for the revision of the black and grey lists 'on the basis of experience.'[27]

The only part of this legislative programme which was successfully completed within the period of the Second Action Programme was the adoption of the Directive on groundwater protection, which in fact relaxed the 'zero-emission' regime initially laid down in Directive 76/464/EEC and instituted different controls on direct and indirect discharges of black and grey list substances.[28] From 1977 to 1981 the Commission managed to submit to the Council no more than three proposals for limit values and quality objectives for black list substances, and not a single one of them was adopted during that period. As for grey list substances, the Commission was unable to undertake any meaningful examination of national reduction programmes, let alone any 'regular comparisons', due to the member states' failure to submit such programmes in due time. No proposals for revisions of the black or grey list were formulated; these lists have remained unchanged to date.

The Second Action Programme, like the first, provides that 'the setting of quality objectives for water' is a priority area for Community action and specifically calls for the completion of the work in this area as initiated and planned by the First Action Programme.[29] This resulted in the adoption by the Council of two further directives setting water quality standards, one for the protection of freshwater fish[30] and another relating to shellfish waters.[31] Again the impact of those directives on the member states' freedom of action is minimal.

Directive 78/659/EEC applies 'to those waters *designated by the Member States as* needing protection or improvement in order to support fish life.'[32] Member states are required by the Directive to 'designate salmonid and cyprinid waters' within two years from its notification, but the Directive does not specify the number or extent of the areas to be designated, leaving this entirely to national discretion.[33] For the designated waters, the member

[27] Second Environmental Action Programme, para 38.

[28] Council Dir 80/68/EEC of 17 Dec 1979 on the protection of groundwater against pollution caused by certain dangerous substances, OJ No L20, 26.1.1980, p 43.

[29] Second Environmental Action Programme, para 48, 2nd indent.

[30] Council Dir 78/659/EEC of 18 July 1978 on the quality of fresh waters needing protection or improvement in order to support fish life, OJ No L222, 14.8.1978, p 1.

[31] Council Dir 79/923/EEC of 30 Oct 1979 on the quality required of shellfish waters, OJ No L281, 10.11.1979, p 47.

[32] Dir 78/659/EEC, Art 1, para 1 (emphasis added).

[33] It should be noted, however, that national discretion does not extend as far as to allow member states to refrain from designating *any* waters as subject to the regime laid down in the directive. See Case 322/86, *Commission v Italy*, [1988] ECR 3995. The extent of member

states shall set quality standards which shall not be less stringent than those imperative values laid down in the Directive, and 'shall endeavour to respect' a number of non-imperative guiding values. The number of parameters for which imperative values are laid down is extremely small. The Directive does not specify what emission control measures should be taken by national authorities in order to ensure compliance with the quality standards. It only provides that 'Member States shall establish *programmes in order to reduce pollution and to ensure that designated waters conform* within five years following designation.'[34]

Similar provisions are to be found in Directive 79/923/EEC on the quality of shellfish waters. The directive applies only to those coastal and brackish waters designated by the member states as shellfish waters and does not impose any particular pollution control measures other than the establishment of 'programmes to reduce pollution and to ensure that designated waters conform within six years following designation.'[35]

Somewhat apart from the mainstream of Community water policy, based essentially on the setting of quality objectives for water intended for specific uses and of emission standards for discharges of selected dangerous substances, a third line of action, announced cautiously in the First Action Programme, was also mentioned again in the Second Action Programme: 'action specific to certain industrial sectors.'[36] This is probably the most ill-fated aspect of Community environmental policy. In the First Environmental Action Programme, a full chapter was devoted to this sector-based approach and, in a 'first stage', studies and proposals were announced for three sectors: the pulp and paper industry, the iron and steel industry and the titanium dioxide industry.[37] The corresponding chapter in the Second Environmental Action Programme is surprisingly succinct and merely notes that the Commission 'will continue with the tasks' assigned to it in the first programme.

In 1975, the Commission submitted to the Council proposals for two sectors: titanium dioxide[38] and paper pulp.[39] During the period of the Second Programme, the sector-oriented legislative work came to a virtual

state discretion was further circumscribed by the Court of Justice in a recent case concerning the implementation of a similar provision of Dir 79/923/EEC, in which the same member state was condemned for not having designated *a sufficient number* of shellfish waters in all its coastal regions. Case C–225/96, *Commission v Italy*, [1997] ECR I–6887. On the general issue of member state discretion with respect to the implementation of directives providing for a regime of localised environmental protection obligations, see Pallemaerts (1994).

[34] Dir 78/659/EEC, Art 5 (emphasis added).

[35] Dir 79/923/EEC, Arts 1 & 5.

[36] Second Environmental Action Programme, para 34, 6th indent. Cf First Environmental Action Programme, Part II, Title I, ch 5.

[37] First Environmental Action Programme, p 21. Additional sectors of industry were listed for consideration in a 'second stage'.

[38] OJ No C 99, 2.5.1975, p 2.

[39] OJ No C 222, 29.9.1975, p 110.

standstill. The only Commission proposal which was adopted by the Council is the one on waste from the titanium dioxide industry.[40]

The proposal relating to paper pulp mills was rejected by the Council in June 1977.[41] These were the only two formal proposals ever made by the Commission. The work on the steel industry was apparently quietly abandoned. Faced with clear opposition in the Council to the sector-based approach, the Commission 'stated in 1980 that in view of differences in the Council they saw no point in continuing activities in this sector and presenting specific proposals for other branches of industry.'[42]

Furthermore, the Second Action Programme also contained a long list of international conventions and conferences on the control of marine pollution and pollution of international watercourses in which the Commission intended to participate on behalf of the Community. The Commission's main intention in participating in these international regulatory efforts was to seek international recognition of the Community's external competence in the field of environmental protection and to ensure that any rules agreed in international fora 'are in conformity with the rules in the Treaties and with the environmental protection measures taken at Community level.'[43]

The Third Environmental Action Programme (1982–1986)

The Third Environmental Action Programme, covering the period 1982–1986 but endorsed by the Council only in 1983,[44] though in general placing great emphasis on the development of an overall environmental strategy and the strengthening of the preventive approach to environmental policy, does not indicate any significant shift in Community water policy but simply confirms previous policy orientations.

[40] Council Dir 78/176/EEC of 20 Feb 1978 on waste from the titanium dioxide industry, OJ No L 54, 25.2.1978, p 19. This directive deals with the dumping of such waste at sea. In 1983, the Commission proposed an additional directive addressing, in a comprehensive fashion, all forms of waste and pollution caused by this sector, which was adopted by the Council no less than six years later. Council Dir 89/428/EEC of 21 June 1989 on procedures for harmonising the programmes for the reduction and eventual elimination of pollution caused by waste from the titanium dioxide industry, OJ No L201, 14.7.1989, p 56. This directive became a *cause célèbre* when it was annulled by the Court of Justice as a result of a dispute between the Commission and the Council about its legal basis. Case C–300/89, *Commission v Council*, [1991] ECR I–2867. Following this annulment, an almost identical directive was adopted on the proper legal basis. Council Dir 92/112/EEC of 15 Dec 1992, OJ No L409, 31.12.1992, p 11.

[41] Johnson (1983), p 74.

[42] *Ibid.*

[43] Second Environmental Action Programme, para 45.

[44] Resolution of the Council of the European Communities and of the Representatives of the Governments of the Member States meeting within the Council of 7 Feb 1983 on the continuation and implementation of a European Community policy and action programme on the environment (1982 to 1986), OJ No C46, 17.2.1983, p 1 (hereafter referred to as Third Environmental Action Programme).

The Commission signals its intention to 'continue with the measures begun under the first two programmes' inter alia with respect to the control of pollution by dangerous substances under Directive 76/464/EEC, noting that 'it is essential to adopt the first implementing measures as soon as possible.'[45] The programme calls for 'the careful selection of priorities and the use of simplified procedures' with respect to black list substances and for 'particular attention' to be paid to 'harmonizing programmes for reducing pollution' by grey list substances. Finally, it provides for the Commission to 'review measures for reducing indirect or dispersed discharges of certain substances' and 'if necessary' to submit 'appropriate proposals' to the Council.[46] No further action with respect to the setting of quality objectives for water intended for specific uses is announced.

The period covered by the Third Programme indeed saw the adoption by the Council of the first implementing measures of Directive 76/464/EEC, ie 'daughter directives' setting limit values and quality objectives for a small number of black list substances.[47] A number of general provisions for the implementation of Directive 76/464/EEC were laid down in Directive 86/280/EEC, but other than that the procedures for the regulation of dangerous substances were not 'simplified' in any way. As for grey list substances, it is only in 1985 that the Commission managed to formulate its first proposal for harmonising national reduction programmes—a proposal which was never adopted by the Council.[48]

The Council has been equally reluctant to accept any measures to deal with 'indirect or dispersed discharges', ie diffuse sources, of dangerous substances. The principle that measures should be taken to this effect was not accepted by the Council when it adopted implementing directives for mercury in 1982, for cadmium in 1983 and for hexachlorocyclohexane in 1984. It is only in another implementing directive for mercury adopted in 1984 and in Directive 86/280/EEC that the need for 'specific programmes' to reduce pollution from 'multiple sources' was first explicitly recognised by the Council.

The Fourth Environmental Action Programme (1987–1992)

In October 1987, the Council approved the 'general approach' of the Fourth Environmental Action Programme,[49] in which the Commission takes stock

[45] OJ No C46, 17.2.1983, paras 16–17.

[46] *Ibid.*

[47] For a detailed analysis of these daugther directives, see below.

[48] Proposal for a Council Directive on water quality objectives for chromium, OJ No C 351, 31.12.1985, p 33.

[49] Resolution of the Council of the European Communities and of the Representatives of the Governments of the Member States meeting within the Council of 19 Oct 1987 on the continuation and implementation of a European Community policy and action programme on the environment, OJ No C 328, 7.12.1987, p 1 (hereafter referred to as Fourth Environmental Action Programme).

of the various approaches to the prevention and control of pollution developed under the previous Action Programmes. It notes that environmental policy and legislation, including that for the control of water pollution, has largely been based on a sectoral approach, whereby discharges of specific substances into a specific environmental medium have been regulated in isolation from emissions into other media. The Commission analyses the limitations of this approach, noting that 'the approach so far adopted to pollution in the different environmental sectors has not always been entirely consistent,'[50] and calls for 'a general review of the value and efficacy of the approaches to standard setting adopted to date.'[51] The Fourth Action Programme announces the development of a more integrated approach to pollution prevention and control, based on the development of cross-media controls, both substance-oriented and source-oriented.

The most interesting aspect of the Fourth Action Programme is the Commission's announced intent to revive the 'source-oriented' approach to specific industrial sectors which was launched in the First Action Programme but aborted after a few years. In the Fourth Programme, the Commission affirms that notwithstanding the negative experience so far, the source-oriented industrial sector approach 'may be worth considering again.'[52]

With respect specifically to the control of freshwater and marine pollution, the Fourth Action Programme confirms that the priorities laid down in the Third Programme 'remain valid.'[53] It somewhat optimistically claims that, with the adoption of Directive 86/280/EEC, the task of setting limit values and quality objectives for black list substances 'can be much accelerated' and announces the Commission's intention to formulate proposals for 'many' black list substances during the period of the Fourth Programme, as well as proposals for quality objectives for a number of grey list substances.[54] At the same time, however, the Commission seems to recognise the limitations imposed on its regulatory efforts by the legal framework of Directive 76/464/EEC where it calls for the development of 'a more coherent pollution control policy' covering both point and diffuse sources of dangerous substances.[55] The Fourth Action Programme also contains a number of ideas for 'new actions' to complete the existing legal framework with directives on water pollution resulting from certain agricultural practices and with additional directives on quality standards for various types of water.[56]

[50] *Ibid*, p 19, para 3.3.1.
[51] *Ibid*, p 21, para 3.6.2.
[52] *Ibid*, p 20, para 3.4.2.
[53] *Ibid*, p 23, para 4.2.2.
[54] *Ibid*, p 24, para 4.2.4.
[55] *Ibid*, p 23, para 4.2.3.
[56] *Ibid*, p 24, para 4.2.5.

The 1988 Ministerial Seminar on Community Water Policy

The future orientations of Community water policy were further elaborated at a Ministerial Seminar on 'Community Water Policy for the Nineties' held in Frankfurt in June 1988 at the invitation of the German government, which then held the presidency of the Council. This was an informal ministerial meeting, taking place outside any institutional context, which was not intended to take any formal decisions. The purpose of the meeting was to identify 'the key issues to be addressed by the European Community in the 90s.'[57] The meeting called for the development of a Community policy for rational use of water resources and, more specifically, for the elaboration of 'guidelines for integrated water management'.

As regards the control of water pollution by dangerous substances, the seminar hardly broke any new ground. It merely restated a number of generalities, like the need for 'addressing [all sources of water pollution by] dangerous substances simultaneously and in a complementary way, by the quality objective and emission standard approaches', the point 'that, ultimately, the aim should be the elimination of certain dangerous substances from waste water' and that, meanwhile, emission norms should continue to be based on best available technology, which 'is understood to mean technology not entailing excessive costs.'[58] With respect to the implementation of Directive 76/464/EEC, 'most delegations' expressed support for the limit values and quality objectives for dangerous substances to be adopted by qualified majority pursuant to Article 130s, 2nd indent, of the EEC Treaty in the future.[59] Finally, the ministers expressed support for the development of Community legislation on waste water treatment and the 'ecological quality of surface water.'[60]

The Council Resolution of 28 June 1988 on the Protection of the North Sea and the Directives on Urban Waste Water Treatment and Nitrate Pollution from Agricultural Sources

Responding to public concern about a massive number of seal deaths in the North Sea in May–June 1988, the Council on 28 June 1988 adopted a resolution[61] in which it invited the Commission to submit proposals for Com-

[57] Conclusions of the Ministerial Seminar on the Community Water Policy, Frankfurt/Main, 27–28 June 1988, para 2.

[58] *Ibid*, paras 9–10 and note 1.

[59] *Ibid*, para 11. At that time, Art 130s, 1st indent of the Treaty still required unanimity for the adoption of environmental measures.

[60] *Ibid*, paras 6 and 13.

[61] Council Resolution of 28 June 1988 on the protection of the North Sea and other waters in the Community, OJ No C209, 9.8.1988, p 3.

munity measures to tackle the problem of eutrophication through a reduction of inputs of nutrients in the aquatic environment. More specifically, referring to the conclusions of the Second International Conference on the Protection of the North Sea held in London in November 1987, the resolution calls for proposals regarding 'the reduction of nutrients from diffuse sources particularly from agriculture' and 'for the treatment of municipal sewage and as regards industrial waste waters'.

The Council resolution marks the start of a new legislative programme to deal with forms of water pollution which had hitherto been disregarded by the Community's environment policy and signals a shift in the Community's water policy away from its initial focus on discharges of toxic substances from industrial point sources to increased attention for nutrient emissions from both point and diffuse sources.

As a matter of fact, legislative action with respect to toxic emissions virtually came to a standstill during the period of the Fourth Action Programme: far from proposing measures for 'many' black list substances, as announced in that Programme, the Commission actually only managed to submit a single proposal for emission limit values and quality objectives, covering four substances, to the Council in 1988. Acting on this proposal, as well as on earlier Commission proposals still pending, the Council during this period adopted only two directives, laying down standards for 11 black list substances in all. The Commission's stated intention to propose quality objectives for grey list substances and sector-oriented measures did not materialise. The last Commission proposal for measures to implement Directive 76/464/EEC was made in February 1990 but was never adopted by the Council. Towards the end of the period covered by the Fourth Action Programme, the attention of Commission and Council had shifted entirely to other aspects of water pollution control.

As called for by the Council in its resolution of 28 June 1988, the Commission elaborated proposals for legislation on the treatment of urban waste water and on the prevention of pollution by nitrates from agricultural sources, which were both adopted by the Council in 1991. Directive 91/271/EEC on urban waste water treatment[62] imposes substantial obligations on member states to ensure proper treatment throughout the Community of municipal sewage and certain industrial waste waters similar in composition and environmental effects, by ensuring, in accordance with a specified timetable, that all agglomerations above a certain size are provided with waste water collecting systems and that waste waters entering those systems shall at least be subject to secondary or equivalent treatment. Sewage treatment plants discharging their effluent in 'sensitive areas' or in the catchment areas of waters designated as sensitive by the member states

[62] Council Dir 91/271/EEC of 21 May 1991 concerning urban waste water treatment, OJ No L135, 30.5.1991, p 40.

according to criteria spelled out in the Directive must apply tertiary treatment, ie special techniques for the removal of nitrogen and phosphorus. There can be little doubt that Directive 91/271/EEC has far-reaching implications for the direction of water pollution control policy and investments throughout the Community and imposes onerous obligations on member states with respect to the development of infrastructure for the collection and treatment of urban waste water. However, it is striking that this directive, like most of those discussed above, has virtually no immediate impact on the conditions of industrial production.[63] The burden of implementing its requirements falls almost entirely on public authorities, and the cost of the necessary investments is likely to be borne by water users or taxpayers generally.

Since measures to deal with eutrophication of the Community's aquatic environment could not be effective without tackling agricultural pollution as well, the adoption of a directive addressing nutrient pollution from agriculture was a necessary complement to the directive on urban waste water. Directive 91/676/EEC on water pollution caused by nitrates from agricultural sources[64] relies mostly on a voluntary approach to the reduction of agricultural pollution through 'codes of good agricultural practice', to be drawn up by each member state and applied nationally. However, it also provides for a system of 'vulnerable zones' to be designated by the member states similar to that of the 'sensitive areas' under Directive 91/271/EEC. For those vulnerable zones, member states are required to draw up 'action programmes' consisting of binding measures of a more detailed and stringent nature than the voluntary codes of practice. It is to be noted that Directive 91/676/EEC, like Directive 91/271/EEC, is not likely to have much of an impact on industry. Its primary addressee, through the member states, is the agricultural sector. Any possible effect on the production and use of chemical fertilisers, and on water pollution caused by them, would be indirect.[65]

As pollution by nutrients as such falls outside the scope of this study, the provisions of Directives 91/271/EEC and 91/676/EEC need not be analysed in more detail.

[63] Only those industries discharging their effluents into public sewerage systems—mostly small or medium-sized entreprises—and some industries belonging mainly to the food and agro-industrial sectors and discharging directly biodegradable effluents into surface waters, causing pollution problems similar to those from urban sewage, will be affected, as the Directive requires member states to take complementary measures with respect to these sources. However, its wording leaves ample discretion to the member states in determining the actual conditions to be imposed on such discharges and does not directly mandate specific restrictions with respect to emissions of hazardous substances.

[64] Council Dir 91/676/EEC of 12 Dec 1991 concerning the protection of waters against pollution caused by nitrates from agricultural sources, OJ No L375, 31.12.1991, p 1.

[65] Although it nominally applies to both manure and nitrogen-containing chemical fertilisers, the only quantified use restrictions provided for in the Directive relate solely to manure. *Ibid*, Annex III, para 2.

The Fifth Environmental Action Programme (1992–2000)

The Commission's Fifth Environmental Action Programme, submitted to the Council a few months before the international community gathered in Rio for the United Nations Conference on Environment and Development, is no doubt the most ambitious and widely publicised so far. It covers a longer period than the four previous ones and is centred on the new paradigm of 'sustainable development'. Its content also seems to have been strongly influenced by the political debate on subsidiarity which dominated the negotiation and ratification process of the Treaty on European Union. Contrary to its predecessors, the Fifth Action Programme does not focus on Community legislative action as the main instrument to achieve its objectives, but seeks to 'broaden the range of instruments' of the Community's environmental policy. It recognises that these objectives 'cannot be met by action at Community level alone, but rather on the basis of a sharing of responsibility at all levels of society.'[66] In accordance with this new concept of 'shared responsibility', the Programme not only spells out the Commission's legislative agenda, but also contains many recommendations for action addressed directly to member states, regional and local authorities, industry and other economic sectors and individual citizens. This approach tends to downplay the role of legislation and to dilute the responsibility of public authorities—both at Community and national level—in the formulation and implementation of environmental policy.

The Fifth Programme's chapter on 'the management of water resources' is not very specific as to the future direction of Community policy with respect to toxic emissions in the aquatic environment. The objectives of Community water policy are formulated in the most general of terms, and for the first time refer not only to water quality, but also to *quantitative* water resource management, as suggested by the 1988 Frankfurt ministerial seminar. The Commission announces its intention to propose measures for 'integrated water management and protection' and a directive on the ecological quality of surface waters, thus acting on another recommendation of the Frankfurt meeting.[67] The only reference to emissions of dangerous substances is to be found in the objectives relating to marine pollution control, which calls for such discharges to be reduced 'to levels which are not harmful to a high standard of ecological quality'. This ambiguous language could be interpreted as signalling a shift away from an approach based on emission standards to one based on quality objectives, were it not

[66] *Towards Sustainability: A European Community Programme of Policy and Action in relation to the Environment and Sustainable Development*, EC Doc COM(92) 23 final, 27 Mar 1992, vol II, p 19.

[67] *Ibid*, p 50, table 11.

for another provision in the same table referring to the 'elaboration of further specific emission standards encouraging the development of production processes and performance standards for products to prevent foreseeable negative effects on water.'[68] However, no express reference to Directive 76/464/EEC is to be found anywhere in the Fifth Action Programme.

The Commission apparently no longer regards that Directive as one of the main instruments for the harmonisation of industrial pollution control standards in the Community. As already announced in the Fourth Action Programme, the Commission is now turning to a more integrated, cross-media approach to industrial emissions. This new policy orientation—which the Commission somewhat pompously claims will give 'a new sense of direction and thrust . . . to the environment/industrial policy interface'—is confirmed in the Fifth Action Programme. Among the various planned measures listed in its industry chapter, 'improved management and control of production processes including a system of licensing linked to integrated pollution prevention and control' features prominently.[69] Further implementation of Directive 76/464/EEC is no longer on the agenda, as legislative developments since the publication of the Fifth Action Programme have confirmed.

A new directive on integrated pollution prevention and control (IPPC) was proposed to the Council in 1993 and adopted in 1996. Its implications for the control of aquatic emissions of toxic substances from industrial point sources will be examined in detail in a subsequent section of this chapter, following an in-depth analysis of the regulatory regime of Directive 76/464/EEC itself. The Commission's main legislative initiative in the field of water pollution announced in the Fifth Action Programme, the 1994 proposal for a directive on ecological water quality, which was not adopted by the Council, did however provoke a new round of intense political debate on the objectives, principles and legal framework of the Community's water policy.

The Proposed Directive on the Ecological Quality of Water

In July 1993, the Commission submitted to the Council its long-awaited proposal for a directive on the ecological quality of water.[70] This important new Commission initiative in the area of water policy took years to mature; it had first been called for by the Frankfurt informal ministerial meeting as long ago as June 1988.

[68] EC Doc COM(92) 23 final, p 50, table 11.
[69] *Ibid*, p 29.
[70] Proposal for a Council Directive on the ecological quality of water, EC Doc COM(93) 680 final, 15 June 1996.

The stated aim of the proposal is 'to simplify and increase the consistency of Community surface water legislation'[71] and to establish a 'general and comprehensive mechanism'[72] for the maintenance and improvement of the quality of all surface waters throughout the Community. This mechanism is designed to supplement existing Community legislation in the field of water pollution control, which, as described above, addresses only specific sources of pollution and lays down quality standards only for particular surface waters which have been designated for specific uses. By contrast, the proposed new directive would apply to all surface waters, regardless of use, and would require member states to take measures for the control of all sources of water pollution.

The draft directive describes its 'ultimate aim' as the achievement of 'good ecological water quality' in all Community surface waters.[73] The central concept of 'good ecological water quality' is defined as 'the quality which is suitable for the needs of the ecosystem, taking into account the need to maintain the capacity for self-purification.'[74] The different elements of the notion of water quality are further spelled out in annexes to the proposal.[75] They include physical and chemical properties as well as biological and ecological criteria related mainly to the composition and diversity of the biotic communities associated with the water system. It should be noted that none of the criteria used are quantified in any way. The proposed directive would leave it to the member states to translate these general criteria into quantified 'operational targets' for the surface waters in their territory.[76]

Having fixed these operational targets, member states would then be required to 'adopt, publish and implement integrated programmes' aimed at reaching them.[77] The elements to be included in the integrated programmes are listed in Annex VI to the draft directive. The programmes shall specify the necessary reductions in pollution and the measures planned for achieving them as well as a timetable for their execution. Apart from 'compliance with any existing legal obligations under relevant Community law,'[78] the specific measures to be implemented include the use of 'best available techniques' (BAT) for point sources[79] and 'best environmental practices' (BEP) for non-point sources 'where necessary.'[80] The proposed directive leaves it up to the member states to define what constitutes BAT

71 *Ibid*, Explanatory memorandum, p 2.
72 *Ibid*, p 4.
73 *Ibid*, Art 1, para 1.
74 *Ibid*, Art 2, para 2.
75 *Ibid*, Annexes I and II.
76 *Ibid*, Art 5, para 1.
77 *Ibid*, Art 6, para 1.
78 *Ibid*, Annex VI, para 2.1.
79 *Ibid*, para 2.2.
80 *Ibid*, para 2.3.

or BEP for any particular source whenever 'there are no requirements under Community law concerning the pollution in question.'[81]

The requirements referred to are those laid down by existing directives for specific sources of water pollution, such as, for example, the emission limit values based on BAT for emissions of certain dangerous substances established pursuant to Directive 76/464/EEC and the codes of good agricultural practice to reduce water pollution by nitrates required under Directive 91/676/EEC. Thus the effect of the proposed directive would be to introduce a general requirement to apply BAT and BEP to all relevant sources of water pollution, to supplement the more specific requirements for particular sources established by existing Community legislation. However, the member states would retain almost unfettered discretion in determining what constitutes BAT or BEP for any particular source, since the annexes to the proposal which purport to 'define' BAT and BEP only list a set of general criteria prone to divergent interpretations.[82]

In addition to the obligations regarding 'operational targets' and 'integrated programmes', which constitute the core of the proposed directive, the Commission's proposal also provides a number of ancillary obligations on matters such as water quality monitoring systems, detection of pollution sources, public information and consultation, the use of economic instruments, consultations between member states in cases of transboundary pollution, inspection and reporting.

The draft directive on the ecological quality of water is symptomatic of a recent trend in Community environmental policy towards the increased use of framework legislation which maximises member state discretion in implementation, in accordance with the Commission's reading of the principle of subsidiarity. It is striking that the proposal, in contrast with earlier Community water legislation, does not contain a single quantified obligation of result. It would impose mainly procedural, rather than substantive, obligations on the member states. In its explanatory memorandum, the Commission itself stresses that this is a deliberate policy choice, where it points out that 'a procedural approach has been chosen rather than a traditional regulatory approach' for reasons of subsidiarity, proportionality and cost-effectiveness.[83] The Commission claims that 'it is not possible to establish a precise, quantified definition of ecological quality applicable to all Community waters'[84] and that this is why the directive should only fix general objectives, 'leav[ing] it to Member States to decide, in accordance with regional and local conditions . . . which action is necessary to improve water quality.'[85]

[81] Proposal for a Council Directive on the ecological quality of water, EC Doc COM(93) 680 final, 15 June 1996 p 7, paras 2.2 and 2.3.

[82] *Ibid*, Annexes III and IV.

[83] *Ibid*, Explanatory memorandum, p 11, para 2.7.

[84] *Ibid*, para 2.8.

[85] *Ibid*, para 2.4.

In justifying its proposal, the Commission starts from the premise that water quality throughout the Community remains unsatisfactory despite the existence of a considerable amount of Community legislation on water pollution.[86] The proposal is presented as designed 'to ensure the overall efficiency of Community water policy'[87] by requiring member states to take 'additional action'[88] to ensure that good ecological water quality will ultimately be achieved. The Commission places all its confidence in the 'integrated programmes' to be drawn up by the member states as the most appropriate instrument to attain this objective. However, the experience so far with existing Community water legislation gives grounds for scepticism as to the effectiveness of this instrument. As a matter of fact, there is nothing really new about national pollution reduction programmes. Under existing Community law, member states are already required to draw up no less than 21 different kinds of 'programmes' or 'plans' for the control of various forms of water pollution.[89] However, member states' compliance with these existing 'programmatic' requirements is notoriously poor. It is hard to see how the imposition on member states of a new requirement to develop and implement water pollution reduction 'programmes', albeit 'integrated' ones, and giving them another three years to do so, could achieve anything that could not be achieved through proper implementation and enforcement of existing provisions.

Both the Council and the European Parliament found the 1994 Commission proposal inadequate. Following an initial round of discussions on the proposal, the Council adopted conclusions on 23 June 1995 in which it implicitly reprimanded the Commission, stressing 'the need to better define and develop the principles of Community water policy' and inviting it to provide guidance for a precise definition of those principles 'in order to establish coherence in present and future legislative instruments.' Although the Council conclusions envisaged this exercise to be carried out 'in parallel with consideration of the directive on the ecological quality of water', the Council effectively suspended consideration of the Commission's proposal pending the submission by the Commission of a

[86] *Ibid*, p 3.

[87] *Ibid*, p 7.

[88] *Ibid*, p 6.

[89] Ie a 'systematic plan of action' for the improvement of surface water quality under Dir 75/440/EEC; 'programmes' for the reduction of pollution by grey list substances and black list substances for which no Community emission standards have yet been established under Dir 76/464/EEC; 'specific programmes' to avoid or eliminate pollution from mercury discharges by multiple sources under Dir 84/156/EEC, and from discharges of 14 other black list substances from 'significant' multiple and diffuse sources under Dir 86/280/EEC; 'programmes' in order to reduce pollution of waters designated as needing protection in order to support fish or shellfish life under, respectively, Dir 78/659/EEC and Dir 79/923/EEC; 'programmes' for the implementation of requirements in respect of the treatment of urban waste water under Dir 91/271/EEC; and, finally, 'action programmes' to reduce pollution by nitrates in vulnerable areas designated under Dir 91/676/EEC.

communication outlining a strategy for the future development of Community water policy.

In a parallel move, the European Parliament's Environment Committee organised a public hearing on Community water policy on 20 June 1995 and, based on the results of this hearing, proposed a series of 'common principles' to guide this policy. The Committee noted that the existing system of water quality directives, which developed in an incremental and incoherent way, has proved insufficient to effectively prevent further deterioration of water quality and called for a better integration of water policy into overall environmental policy. More specifically, it urged the Commission to take a number of basic principles into account in preparing its communication, such as the need to formulate a clear hierarchy of priorities in the field of water policy, to avoid any lowering of the existing level of protection and to ensure consistency in definitions and comparability of data in order to allow effective monitoring of implementation. The Committee did not, however, make any specific recommendations with respect to future policy regarding emissions of dangerous substances.[90]

The Seville Informal Environment Council Meeting and the Council Conclusions of 19 December 1995

The political debate within the Council on the future direction of Community water policy, provoked by the 1994 Commission proposal on ecological water quality, continued through 1995. The Spanish presidency chose to make it one of the central themes of its agenda by selecting it as the topic of the informal meeting of the Environment Council held in Seville in October 1995. By convening this meeting in drought-stricken Andalusia, Spain's political objective was to focus the Council's attention on the acute water supply problems faced by Mediterranean member states and to rebalance the objectives of Community water policy, long dominated by Northern concerns about water quality. Based on a discussion paper submitted by the Commission and on the presidency's conclusions of the Sevilla meeting, formal Council conclusions on EC water policy were adopted in December 1995.

In these conclusions, the Council affirms that 'the European Union needs a new approach to water policy' and calls for 'the drawing up of a new framework Directive establishing the basic principles of sustainable water policy in the European Union *starting with* the proposal for a Directive on ecological water quality'. This wording seems to indicate that the latter proposal need not be jettisoned altogether but can serve as a basis for the elaboration of the framework directive. The Council conclusions go on to draw

[90] See the conclusions of the hearing in EP Doc PE 214.005, 7 July 1995.

the outlines of the 'new approach' that is to be embodied in the framework directive, which is presented as the core of 'a more consistent and coherent body of legislation'. Upon analysis, it appears that some elements of the approach envisaged by the Council hardly deserve the qualification 'new' but simply reflect in different terms recommendations already made seven years earlier at the 1988 Frankfurt seminar.

Echoing the theme of the Sevilla meeting but also the Frankfurt seminar's earlier call for a Community role in the promotion of 'integrated water management', the Council conclusions state that the framework directive 'should follow an integrated approach' and 'consider interactions between quality and quantity'. Echoing another long-standing theme of the debate on water policy, they further stipulate that 'the emission limit values approach and the quality objectives approach should be combined as appropriate to define *a common level of protection* whilst allowing Member States to establish a higher level of protection'. The notion of 'a common level of protection' implies that achieving some measure of harmonisation will continue to be a goal of Community water policy, but at the same time that the existence of different levels of protection from member state to member state is legitimate, as emphatic references to subsidiarity and to the 'diversity of natural and socio-economic conditions' indicate. Harmonisation of standards is to be justified not so much on environmental grounds, but rather 'where necessary . . . for a good functioning of the single market'.

In their only explicit reference to the control of toxic emissions, the Council conclusions specify that Community water policy 'should continue to be based on the principle of progressive reduction of the use of dangerous substances'. An implicit reference can also be found in the often-reiterated but never-materialising plea for Community action to 'focus on industrial sectors without disregarding individual substances'. The Council recognises that existing Community legislation may have to be amended or even repealed, but, like the European Parliament, stresses that this 'should not lead to a reduction in the current level of environmental protection'.

The 1996 Commission Communication on Water Policy

Responding to the call for the formulation of an overall policy framework, made by both the Council and the Parliament in 1995, the Commission issued a communication on European Community water policy in early 1996.[91] In this communication, it articulates its view of the objectives,

[91] EC Doc COM(96) 59 final, 21 Feb 1996.

principles and instruments of water policy and confirmed its intention to submit to the Council a proposal for a framework directive on water resources, which would 'absorb' the 1994 draft directive on ecological water quality. The communication is introduced as 'a development of the water protection elements of the Commission's 5th Environment Action Programme', elements which, as we have seen above, were only most summarily outlined in the Programme itself.

In defining the objectives of what it calls 'a sustainable water policy', the Commission points out the need to achieve 'a sensible balance' between environmental objectives and other requirements. The first objective of water policy should be to ensure a secure supply of safe drinking water. Guaranteeing the availability of water resources of a sufficient quantity and quality to meet other economic requirements, such as those of industry, agriculture and transport, ranks second. Environmental protection as such, or, more specifically, the protection of the good ecological state and functioning of aquatic ecosystems, is only the third objective, albeit one which, according to the Commission 'is particularly vulnerable and in need of special attention'. Finally, a sustainable water policy should also aim at the prevention of droughts and floods.

The communication's chapter on 'the principles of Community water policy' is hardly more than a restatement of the principles of Community environmental policy as laid down in Article 174, paragraph 2 of the Treaty, with a few elaborations on their particular relevance in the context of water management. It is particularly striking how much emphasis is placed on the subsidiarity principle and in general on the need to ensure a considerable measure of 'flexibility' for the member states. In the Commission's view, the variability of environmental conditions in the various regions of the Community 'argues against uniform controls applicable in all circumstances and in all places.'[92] Accordingly, 'Community water policy must be sufficiently flexible to avoid the imposition of inappropriate or unnecessarily strict requirements simply for the sake of "harmonisation".'[93] The Commission takes a rather minimalist view of the reasons which may justify Community, as opposed to national, action in the field of water policy. While the need to avoid 'market distortions' is mentioned as the first reason for Community action, the achievement of a common, high level of water protection is not mentioned at all in this context. Even where Community action is deemed necessary, the Commission wonders 'how much of the details of implementation should be left to the Member States.'[94] Much of the communication can in fact be read as an implicit, sometimes even explicit, indictment of what had in effect been the *Leitmotiv* of Community water

[92] EC Doc COM(96) 59 final, 21 Feb 1996, p 11.
[93] *Ibid*, p 7.
[94] *Ibid*, p 8.

policy for the past 20 years: the harmonisation at Community level of emission standards and quality objectives.

In the Commission's new philosophy of water pollution control, uniform standards, either for emissions or water quality, are as a rule no longer regarded as a desirable policy objective. They are considered to be justified only in exceptional cases:

> Where it is necessary for the protection of human health or *where particularly dangerous or persistent pollutants are concerned*, it is clear that common Community standards must apply.[95]

In other instances, flexibility should prevail, taking into account the variability of environmental conditions throughout the Community. Thus, for instance, the Commission considers that the first generation of water quality directives adopted in the 1970s and setting common water quality objectives for water destined for specific uses, as discussed above, is now outdated. The Commission no longer considers it necessary to set 'common parametric values at a Community level'. Its 'preferred approach' now is to fix only unquantified 'common criteria' for water quality, leaving it to the member states to determine specific parameters and actual limit values at the national level, as proposed in the draft directive on ecological water quality.[96]

As to industrial effluent standards, the communication notes that 'a strict emission limit values approach based on BAT can in some circumstances lead to unnecessary investment without significant benefits to the environment'[97] and praises the flexibility provided by the new IPPC Directive which, as a rule, leaves it to the permitting authorities in the member states to fix emission limit values based on their own interpretation of BAT and, in doing so, allows them to take into account local environmental conditions. The need for 'common Community standards' for emissions of particularly dangerous or persistent pollutants, referred to elsewhere in the communication, is not mentioned in this context. By announcing a 'review' of Directive 76/464/EEC in the light of the IPPC Directive, the Commission makes it clear that the establishment of Community-wide emission standards for discharges of dangerous substances will no longer be a principal feature of Community water policy in the future.

The New Framework Directive on Community Water Policy

In February 1997, the Commission, as announced in its 1996 communication, approved and transmitted to the Council a proposal for a directive

[95] *Ibid*, p 7 (emphasis added).
[96] *Ibid*, p 11.
[97] *Ibid*, p 10.

establishing a framework for Community action in the field of water policy.[98] The Council reached a common position in October 1999[99] and Directive 2000/60/EC was eventually adopted in October 2000, following a protracted conciliation procedure with the European Parliament.[100] The adoption of the Framework Directive entails a fundamental reform of Community water legislation, as the new instrument is designed ultimately to replace most existing water directives. Indeed, it provides for the repeal, gradually during the course of a 13-year transitional period, of all existing directives laying down environmental quality objectives for surface waters destined for particular uses (with the exception of Directive 76/160/EEC on the quality of bathing water, which, according to the explanatory memorandum 'makes a distinct Community contribution to the integration of environment policy and tourism policy and . . . benefits from having a clear, separate identity'[101]) as well as Directive 80/68/EEC on groundwater and, most importantly for our purposes, Directive 76/464/EEC.

According to its preamble, Directive 2000/60/EC is designed to lay down 'a transparent, efficient and coherent legislative framework' for the Community's water policy, in response to both the Council's and the European Parliament's call for such a framework instrument. To a large extent, the Framework Directive proceeds from the same regulatory philosophy as that which underlay the ecological quality proposal: it imposes essentially procedural obligations on member states and leaves most of the concrete, substantive measures to be taken in pursuit of its vaguely defined objectives to their discretion. Important new elements, however, are the river basin approach to water policy, the provisions relating to the quantitative management of water resources, the requirements regarding the recovery of costs for water services, and the integrated approach to both surface water and groundwater within a single legal framework.

In essence, Directive 2000/60/EC introduces an overall conceptual and organisational framework for integrated water management with the lofty objective of preventing further deterioration of and protecting and enhancing aquatic ecosystems throughout the Community. At this point, it is sufficient to describe in general terms how the regulatory scheme instituted by

[98] EC Doc COM(97) 49 final, 26 Feb 1997, OJ No C184, 17.6.1997, p 20. In the explanatory memorandum, the Commission announces its intention to withdraw the 1994 ecological water quality proposal upon adoption of the new proposed framework directive, which is clearly intended as a substitute for it.

[99] Common Position (EC) No 41/1999 adopted by the Council on 22 Oct 1999 with a view to the adoption of a Dir 1999/ . . . /EC of the European Parliament and the Council establishing a framework for Community action in the field of water policy, OJ No C343, 30.11.1999, p 1.

[100] European Parliament and Council Dir 2000/60/EC of 23 Oct 2000 establishing a framework for Community action in the field of water policy, OJ No L327, 22.12.2000, p 1 (hereafter referred to as Dir 2000/60/EC or Framework Directive).

[101] EC Doc COM(97) 49 final, 26 Feb 1997, p 8, para 2.5.4.

the Framework Directive is intended to operate, reserving a more detailed analysis of its implications for the future regulation of toxic emissions for a later section of this chapter.

The basic organisational unit for water management purposes is the 'river basin district'. Member states shall ensure that all river basins and groundwaters in their territory are assigned to a river basin district in which appropriate administrative structures and arrangements for the implementation of the Directive are established. Though the system is obviously designed primarily for the management of freshwater resources, the scope of application of the Directive also covers coastal waters, which are to be assigned to 'the nearest or most appropriate' river basin district.[102] Where a river basin covers the territory of more than one member state, an international river basin district shall be established. Though each member state shall retain responsibility for administrative arrangements in its territory, co-ordination in the implementation of the Directive shall be ensured. Within each river basin, areas requiring 'special protection' for the conservation of their surface and ground water resources and biological diversity are to be identified and registers of such 'protected areas' drawn up by the member states.

The second task falling upon the member states is an analytical one. They shall, for planning purposes, undertake an analysis of each river basin district's characteristics, conduct a 'review of the impact of human activity' on the status of water in the district and perform an 'economic analysis of water use' in each district at the latest four years after the entry into force of the Directive. Technical specifications for these analyses and reviews are provided in annexes to the Directive. The characterisation of water bodies is to be carried out according to ecological criteria and includes the establishment of 'type-specific reference conditions' at high ecological status. Member states are to collect and maintain information on the 'significant anthropogenic pressures' to which water quality is exposed in the river basin district. This includes the identification and estimation of significant point and diffuse source pollution, inter alia by hazardous substances. The economic analysis of water use is designed to gather information on the cost of water services with a view to applying the principle of cost recovery, and also to determine the cost-effectiveness of management measures that may be taken.

Member states shall follow up on the initial characterisation by establishing monitoring programmes for each river basin district in order to maintain a comprehensive overview of water status, including the 'chemical status' of all water bodies, again according to the technical specifications laid down in an annex to the Directive.

[102] Framework Directive, Art 3, para 1.

This elaborate administrative and analytical apparatus is to be put to use for the achievement of a set of 'environmental objectives', formulated in very general terms in Article 4 of Directive 2000/60/EC, through the implementation of 'programmes of measures' to be drawn up by the member states for each river basin district and laid down in a 'river basin management plan'. In the Framework Directive, these 'environmental objectives' and 'programmes of measures' are very much the equivalent of the 'operational targets' and 'integrated programmes' which constituted the essence of the draft directive on ecological water quality proposed by the Commission in 1994.

The general objectives with respect to surface water quality that member states are expected to pursue 'in making operational the programmes of measures' are, in the first place, 'to prevent deterioration of the status of all bodies of surface water'[103] and, secondly, to 'protect, enhance and restore all bodies of surface water . . . with the aim of achieving *good surface water status* at the latest 15 years after the entry into force' of the Directive.[104] An additional 'environmental objective' for surface waters is the implementation of a number of specific measures 'with the aim of progressively reducing pollution from priority substances and ceasing or phasing out emissions, discharges and losses of priority hazardous substances,'[105] which will be examined in detail later in this chapter. Similar objectives are laid down for groundwater. They refer, in general terms, to the protection, enhancement and restoration of all bodies of groundwater, to the prevention of their deterioration and to the aim of achieving 'good groundwater status' and, more specifically, to the implementation of measures 'to ensure a balance between abstraction and recharge of groundwater', to 'prevent or limit the input of pollutants into groundwater' and 'to reverse any significant and sustained upward trend in the concentration of any pollutant resulting from the impact of human activity.'[106] It should be noted that the general objectives, both for surface water and groundwater, are subject to possibilities for derogations and extensions of the deadline for specific bodies of water in certain circumstances. These will not be further analysed here. Instead, given our primary interest in surface water pollution, I shall focus on the substantive content of the central notion of 'good surface water status'.

The overall status of a body of surface water is determined by both its 'ecological status' (referring to 'the quality of the structure and functioning of aquatic ecosystems'[107]) and its 'chemical status' (referring to the presence of certain pollutants). 'Good surface water status' is defined as 'the status

[103] Framework Directive, Art 4, para 1(a)(i).
[104] *Ibid*, Art 4, para 1(a)(ii).
[105] *Ibid*, Art 4, para 1(a)(iv).
[106] *Ibid*, Art 4, para 1(b).
[107] *Ibid*, Art 2 (18).

achieved by a surface water body when both its ecological status and its chemical status are at least "good"'. 'Good chemical status', one of the component notions of 'good surface water status', is further defined, in a rather circular way, by reference to the 'environmental objectives' laid down in Article 4 of Directive 2000/60/EC and, more specifically, to environmental quality standards established at Community level by earlier Community legislation or later to be established for certain substances under the provisions of the Framework Directive itself.[108]

The other component notion, 'good ecological status', is specified in Annex V of the Directive. This annex provides, in tabular form, extensive technical definitions of the concepts of 'high, good and moderate ecological status' for each type of water body. These 'normative definitions of ecological status classifications' cover biological elements and hydromorphological and physico-chemical quality elements 'supporting the biological elements'. The tables in Annex V read like a hydrobiologist's wet dream, but the 'normative definitions' they list contain no quantified descriptors and are so open-ended that they leave member states considerable freedom of interpretation and have little normativity in the legal sense of the term. As far as the chemical quality elements are concerned, Annex V requires member states to set environmental quality standards for unspecified synthetic and non-synthetic pollutants 'identified as being discharged in significant quantities into the body of water' in accordance with a risk assessment procedure it spells out. These standards may be set, at the member states' discretion, for either water, sediment or biota, and shall be derived from available data relating to acute and chronic toxicity to aquatic oganisms representative for the type of water body concerned, while applying an adequate safety factor. Ironically, while these standards relate to concentrations of pollutants and are referred to in one part of Annex V as 'chemical quality standards', they are legally relevant only for the purpose of determining the *ecological* status of a water body and not its *chemical* status as technically defined. The latter is established by reference only to pollutants for which environmental quality standards have been established at *Community* level. Compliance with the standards established at member state level pursuant to Annex V is to be monitored as one element of ecological status, together with other physico-chemical and biological elements. A water body where concentrations of synthetic and non-synthetic pollutants are not in excess of those standards will be classified as having achieved 'good ecological status', provided it also meets other relevant physico-chemical and biological criteria.

The 'programmes of measures' required to be drawn up for each river basin district as part of its overall 'river basin management plan' constitute the heart of the regulatory system established by Directive 2000/60/EC. It

[108] *Ibid*, Art 2 (24).

is in these programmes that the actual measures to be taken by member states in order to achieve the 'environmental objectives' as laid down in Article 4 are to be spelled out. According to Article 11 of the Directive, these measures fall into two categories: 'basic measures', which must mandatorily be included in every individual programme, and 'supplementary measures', which may be implemented in addition to the basic measures 'where necessary'. As in the 1994 ecological quality proposal, the 'basic measures' with respect to emission controls proposed in the new Framework Directive add little to the obligations of member states under existing Community law. They consist, in the first place, of 'those measures required to implement Community legislation for the protection of water', including, more specifically, measures required under a series of existing directives listed in Annex VI. In other words, member states have to draw up programmes in which they re-commit themselves to implement measures which they are already legally required to take under existing Community legislation. Other 'basic measures' of a more substantive nature include whatever measures member states 'deem appropriate' for the implementation of the principle of recovery of costs for water uses; unspecified measures to safeguard and improve the quality of water bodies used for the abstraction of drinking water; controls over the abstraction of fresh surface water and groundwater and the artificial recharge or augmentation of groundwater bodies, including a requirement for prior authorisation; emission controls for 'point source discharges liable to cause pollution', which may take the form of either prior regulation, authorisation or registration; unspecified measures to 'prevent or control the input of pollutants' from diffuse sources; a prohibition of direct discharges of pollutants into groundwater subject to some exceptions; specific measures to 'eliminate pollution of surface waters' by a number of priority substances to be specified by subsequent Community legislative action; and measures to prevent accidental pollution. Some of these measures, like those relating to cost recovery or the control of water abstraction, are new. Others are little more than a reiteration, albeit often in less precise terms, of existing requirements under legislation which will be repealed by the Framework Directive, such as Directives 75/440/EEC, 76/464/EEC and 80/68/EEC. On the whole, the provisions on 'basic measures' are formulated in such general terms, or explicitly leave member states such a wide range of options, that the concrete content of the programmes of measures is left largely at their discretion and will tend to vary substantially from river basin to river basin.

Back in 1975, the very first Community directive on water pollution control, Directive 75/440/EEC concerning the quality required of surface water intended for the abstraction of drinking water, already required member states to draw up 'a systematic plan of action' to ensure 'considerable improvements' in the quality of surface waters within a 10-year period, ie by 1985. A string of judgments of the Court of Justice attests that this obligation was not complied with by most member states. Directive 2000/60/EC, using an approach that has already proved unsuccessful, albeit augmented with considerable procedural detail, now seems to be giving member states a fresh start. They are granted nine years from the date of entry into force of the Framework Directive to establish a 'programme of measures' for each river basin district. The measures themselves must be 'made operational' at the latest 12 years after that date, and the 'environmental objectives' laid down in Article 4 of the Directive in principle achieved three years later. And, at the end of this long process, the results to be expected are quite uncertain, as the wording of the Framework Directive is ambiguous as to whether member states actually have an unconditional obligation to achieve 'good surface water status' after 15 years. Significantly, the Directive contains a provision stipulating that 'steps must be taken to ensure that the application of the new provisions . . . guarantee at least the same level of protection as the existing Community legislation,'[109] as if the Council and the Parliament themselves were in doubt as to the effectiveness of these new provisions.

Lack of a Coherent Legislative Policy

As the above overview has shown, European Community policy and law for the control of water pollution developed in a fragmented and rather haphazard manner. For most of its history, a comprehensive approach to water pollution problems, dealing with inputs from point as well as non-point sources in a coherent and systematic fashion, was lacking.

Most existing Community legislation attempts to tackle problems of water pollution either through the setting of water quality standards or emission standards or both. Initially, the emphasis was on the establishment of common water quality objectives for surface waters destined for specific uses, leaving both the designation of the waters concerned and the choice of the measures to be taken to ensure compliance with the water quality standards at the discretion of individual member states. As we have seen above, these water quality directives left national sovereignty virtually intact and had no immediate impact on national policies with respect to the regulation of polluting emissions. A second, more ambitious line of legislative activity was aimed at curbing industrial emissions of dangerous substances through a combination of emission standards and water quality objectives, to be set both at Community and national level and to be implemented through a system of discharge permits and national pollution reduction programmes. The third wave of water legislation dealt with nutrient emissions

[109] *Ibid*, Art 4, para 8.

from urban waste water and agriculture, relying on member states to draw up and carry out action programmes to achieve common pollution control objectives established at Community level. In a fourth and thus far final stage, a fundamental overhaul of Community water law was undertaken, purportedly to establish a comprehensive and coherent legal framework for water policy, integrating and replacing much of the existing legislation adopted during the first two phases. In fact, this legislative reform, in tune with the new imperatives of subsidiarity and deregulation, involves a retreat from the long-standing objective of harmonising standards into a more 'flexible' strategy maximising national discretion with respect to both water quality objectives and emission standards within an 'integrated' Community legal framework consisting only of general principles and procedural obligations.

In the remainder of this chapter, we will examine in detail the provisions of EC law specifically addressing emissions of toxic substances in the aquatic environment. Directive 76/464/EEC, with its daughter directives, is the first EC legal instrument dealing with this issue. For a long time, it was also the only EC legislation in the field of water pollution which directly affected the conditions of industrial production.[110] Even though it is now scheduled for repeal, this Directive has been the cornerstone of Community policy in this area for over 20 years and is still to remain largely in force for years to come. The following section will therefore focus on a detailed analysis of its provisions and implementation. As the future regulation of toxic emissions to water is to be governed by the IPPC Directive and the Water Framework Directive, whose provisions will gradually supplant those of Directive 76/464/EEC, the implications of these new instruments will be discussed in the final section of this chapter.

DIRECTIVE 76/464/EEC: A FRAMEWORK FOR REGULATING EMISSIONS OF TOXIC SUBSTANCES INTO THE AQUATIC ENVIRONMENT

Background and General Analysis

The Commission initiative which led to the adoption of the 1976 Directive on pollution caused by certain dangerous substances discharged into the

[110] Except for Dir 89/428/EEC, above n 40, which, as the Court of Justice has duly noted, aims 'to approximate national laws on the *conditions of production in a given industrial sector* for the purpose of eliminating distortions of competition in this particular sector'. Case C–155/91, *Commission v Council*, [1993] ECR I–939, at para 20. See also Case C–300/89, *Commission v Council*, [1991] ECR I–2867, at para 12. The same of course applies to this annulled directive's successor, Dir 91/112/EEC, above n 40. However, as these sectoral directives regulate not only process discharges of dangerous substances into the aquatic environment, but also other pollutants and forms of pollution, such as waste dumping at sea and atmospheric emissions, they will not be further considered in this study.

aquatic environment[111] was taken in direct response to the development of international norms regarding pollution of the aquatic environment. Indeed, the preamble of the Directive refers to three international conventions which had either recently been concluded or were at that time under negotiation in different fora: the Paris Convention for the Prevention of Marine Pollution from Land-Based Sources,[112] the Convention for the Protection of the Rhine against Chemical Pollution[113] and the Council of Europe's draft Convention for the Protection of International Watercourses against Pollution.[114] These three conventions had in common that they all dealt with discharges of toxic substances into the aquatic environment, that they involved different member states of the Community and that the Commission had participated or was participating in the negotiations on behalf of the Community itself.[115] The preamble of Directive 76/464/EEC stresses that 'it is important to ensure the coordinated implementation of these conventions'. As explained in the explanatory memorandum of the Commission's proposal,[116] since, under these various conventions, member states are to assume international obligations to reduce discharges of dangerous substances, it is necessary for the Community to intervene in order to 'harmoniz[e] the approach of Member States to their obligations in one or other framework' and to 'ensure that the actual pollution-abatement programmes that are proposed are consistent with each other.'[117]

To this end, the Commission initially submitted to the Council a proposal for a Council Decision 'on the reduction of pollution caused by certain dangerous substances discharged into the aquatic environment of the Community'. The type of legal instrument proposed by the Commission, a Decision, was somewhat unusual for this kind of environmental policy measure. The proposal was based only on Article 235 of the Treaty and the Commission apparently did not aim for harmonisation of national legislation, but only intended to impose on member states obligations which could be complied

[111] Council Dir 76/464/EEC of 4 May 1976 on pollution caused by certain dangerous substances discharged into the aquatic environment of the Community, OJ No L 129, 18.5.1976, p 24 (hereafter referred to as Dir 76/464/EEC).

[112] Cf above ch 4.

[113] Cf above ch 7.

[114] This Convention was never adopted by the Committee of Ministers of the Council of Europe due to French opposition. However, as late as 1985, the Commission still expected the negotiations in the framework of the Council of Europe 'to culminate in the signature of the European Convention for the Protection of International Watercourses against Pollution'. See Answer by the Commission to Written Question No 330/85, OJ No C248, 30.9.1985, p 21. Eventually, the work of the UN Economic Commission for Europe in this field proved more fruitful than that of the Council of Europe. See above ch 7.

[115] See Answer by the Commission to Written Question No 800/85, OJ No C276, 28.10.1985, p 19.

[116] Proposal for a Decision of the Council on the reduction of pollution caused by certain dangerous substances discharged into the aquatic environment of the Community, EC Doc COM (74) 1706 final, 21 Oct 1974.

[117] *Ibid*, p 2.

with by mere administrative action.[118] Another reason for the Commission's caution may have been the fact that there was still a strong feeling on the part of some members of the Council at that time that environmental protection was a matter for intergovernmental cooperation rather than Community action. However, it appears that the Commission was excessively cautious, since the Council eventually opted for a Directive based jointly on Articles 100 and 235 EEC: that is, a legal instrument which is aimed explicitly at approximation of laws and provides greater legal certainty, while at the same time affording member states some flexibility in the implementation of their obligations.

Nevertheless, the Directive as finally adopted by the Council still contains many features of the originally proposed Decision. An analysis of the original proposal is useful in order to place the provisions of Directive 76/464/EEC in a proper perspective. The original proposal did not explicitly mention as its ultimate objective the elimination of pollution by certain substances. It only required member states 'to take all the measures needed *to forestall or reduce* pollution of the aquatic environment' by substances listed in its annex. As a first step, the draft Decision imposed upon member states the obligation to 'draw up an inventory of discharges into the aquatic environment of the Community' containing listed substances exceeding certain 'threshold levels' to be established by the Council within a period of 18 months following the adoption of the Decision. It further stipulated that 'limiting values' would also be fixed by the Council for all discharges of such substances, and that discharges of black list substances would require 'prior administrative authorization'. As regards discharges of grey list substances, the draft Decision required that they 'be reduced to limiting values to be fixed', without specifying the means of ensuring such reductions.

Like the initial Commission proposal, Directive 76/464/EEC distinguishes two different categories of 'dangerous substances', to which different regulatory measures apply. The first category of substances, listed in List I of the annex to the Directive, generally referred to as the 'black list', consists of:

> certain individual substances . . . selected mainly on the basis of their toxicity, persistence and bioaccumulation, with the exception of those which are biologically harmless or are rapidly converted into substances which are biologically harmless.

The Directive proclaims in its preamble the objective that water pollution by these substances 'must be eliminated'. The second category of substances, as laid down in List II, which is commonly known as the 'grey list', are described as substances

[118] In this respect there is a certain analogy with the Council Decision 93/389/EEC of 24 June 1993 for a monitoring mechanism of Community CO_2 and other greenhouse gas emissions, OJ No L167, 9.7.1993, p 31.

which have a deleterious effect on the aquatic environment, which can, however, be confined to a given area and which depends on the characteristics and location of the water into which they are discharged.

The preambular language is less categorical with respect to these substances, stating only that 'it is necessary to reduce' water pollution caused by them.

It is to be noted that the identification of black and grey list substances is not completed in the Directive itself but is in fact deferred to a later process of 'selection' based on general criteria laid down in the Directive. The annex to the Directive contains only a limited number of individual substances. It mainly enumerates 'families and groups of substances' from which 'certain individual substances' are later to be 'selected'. These families and groups of substances are defined in terms of general categories such as 'organohalogen compounds and substances which may form such compounds in the aquatic environment' or 'substances in respect of which it has been proved that they possess carcinogenic properties in or via the aquatic environment'.

The obligations of the member states with respect to black and grey list substances are formulated in general terms in Article 2 of Directive 76/464/EEC and spelled out in more detail in subsequent provisions. Article 2 requires the member states to 'take the appropriate steps to eliminate' pollution by black list substances and 'to reduce' pollution by grey list substances. The regime of prior authorisation of discharges constitutes the cornerstone of the Directive and has been extended to cover not only discharges of black list substances but also of grey list substances. The main distinction between member states' obligations with respect to the two categories of substances is that Directive 76/464/EEC, unlike the original draft Decision, provides for the establishment of Community-wide 'limit values' for emission standards, which must be respected by national authorities when delivering discharge permits, for black list substances only.

The minimum requirements of the administrative mechanism for the control of discharges[119] of black list substances to be instituted by the

[119] In two recent cases referred to it by the Dutch Council of State, the Court of Justice has had the opportunity to clarify the meaning of the notion of 'discharge', which is defined in the Directive itself only as the 'introduction' of substances into water. In both these cases the Court was asked to answer the question whether particular activities constituted 'discharges' within the meaning of the Directive. In the first case, the activity at issue was the placing in surface water, in order to shore up river banks, of wooden posts treated with creosote, a substance containing polycyclic aromatic hydrocarbons (PAHs) and thus belonging to the groups of substances in the black list. As a result of this activity, PAH-containing particles are released into surface waters. Case C–232/97, *L. Nederhoff & Zn. v Dijkgraaf en hoogheemraden van het Hoogheemraadschap Rijnland*, [1999] ECR I–6385. The other case involved an industrial process for wood impregnation with the use of steam. In this process steam is used to fix a solution containing the grey list heavy metals arsenic, copper and chromium onto the wood for the purpose of its preservation. Some of this polluted steam escapes from the plant and

member states are set forth in Article 3. The Directive requires the member states to subject all discharges 'which are liable to contain' black list substances to a system of prior authorisation. Authorisations may only be granted for a limited period of time and must lay down emission standards to be complied with within a timeframe to be determined by the authorisation. These standards may not be less stringent than the applicable 'limit values' established at Community level. A similar permit system is also mandatory for discharges of grey list substances under Article 7, paragraph 2 of the Directive. Though no Community 'limit values' are to be established for emissions of grey list substances, member states are nevertheless under an obligation to lay down 'emission standards' for such discharges in the individual permits themselves. These standards must be based on 'quality objectives for water' to be established at the national level by each member state, within the framework of its pollution reduction programmes. The requirement of an inventory of discharges, which was part of the Commission's initial proposal, was retained in the Directive,[120] though only for black list substances and not as a precondition for the application of emission standards.

Overall, the substantive provisions of Directive 76/464/EEC appear to have been somewhat strengthened vis-à-vis those of the original Commission proposal. The original proposal contained no explicit statement that the ultimate objective of the Community measure was the total elimination of pollution by black list substances. The shift in emphasis from a mere reduction of pollution towards its elimination probably reflects the expectations of certain member states. However, the apparent strengthening of these provisions is compensated by a deliberate ambiguity in the notion of 'pollution', which is the subject of such 'elimination'. At one stage during the negotiations, according to some authors, the result to be achieved by the member states was formulated in even stronger terms than those of the eventual directive. An amended draft of what eventually became Directive 76/464/EEC in fact called for the elimination of the *discharge* of black list substances.[121]

reaches surface waters, either directly by precipitating into a neighbouring ditch, or indirectly via a storm water drain following precipitation on to land and roofs. Case C–231/97, *AML van Rooij v Dagelijks bestuur van het waterschap de Dommel*, [1999] ECR I–6355. The Court gave an extensive interpretation of the concept of 'discharge', holding that it must be 'understood as referring to *any act attributable to a person* by which one of the dangerous substances listed in List I or List II of the Annex to the directive is *directly or indirectly* introduced into the waters to which the directive applies.' Case C–232/97, para 37; Case C–231/97, para 22 (emphasis added). A polluting act will be attributable to a person whenever it is 'foreseeable according to general experience' that it is likely to cause water pollution. Case C–231/97, para 32. The dangerous substances discharged do not necessarily have to be in the liquid state. *Ibid*, para 29. Accordingly, both activities at issue were held to be subject to the prior authorisation requirement of Dir 76/464/EEC.

[120] Dir 76/464/EEC, Art 11.

[121] Taylor, Diprose & Duffy (1986), p 232, citing EC Doc R/345/76(ENV 14).

The final wording of Directive 76/464/EEC does not go that far and could well be interpreted as deliberately falling short of requiring the total elimination of all discharges, as it refers only to elimination of 'pollution' by black list substances. 'Pollution' is defined in Article 2 as:

> the discharge by man, directly or indirectly, of substances or energy into the aquatic environment, *the results of which are such as to cause hazards to human health, harm to living resources and to aquatic ecosystems....*

A restrictive interpretation of this definition would imply that pollution is to be eliminated only to the extent that it causes harm to human health or the environment. As we shall see below, this question of interpretation is of largely theoretical interest, as the action taken by the Commission, the Council and the individual member states pursuant to the legislative mandate of Directive 76/464/EEC falls well short of total elimination of pollution, let alone of emissions per se.[122]

The 'Dual Approach': Emission Standards vs Quality Objectives

As pointed out above, specific Community implementing action with respect to emission standards for black list substances is provided for in Article 6 of Directive 76/464/EEC, which stipulates that the Council shall lay down 'the limit values which the emission standards [laid down in the discharge permits by the competent national authorities] shall not exceed'. It is further specified that the limit values for List I substances shall be laid down 'taking into account the best technical means available'. However, the water pollution control policy prescribed by the directive is not based exclusively on emission standards. The directive provides that, in addition to determining limit values for emission standards, the Council shall also establish 'quality objectives' for black list substances. The dual system[123] established by the directive represents a compromise between the divergent positions of the member states.[124] It is in fact an attempt to accommodate

[122] This general goal of 'elimination' of pollution, formulated, to quote the words of one commentator, 'in such clear, urgent, absolute and sweeping terms', was perceived by British policymakers as a significant departure from established policy in the UK at that time. See Guruswamy (1982), p 620. However, it is not obvious that by accepting this far-reaching objective, as enunciated in Art 2 of Dir 76/464/EEC, the UK really 'conceded' on a fundamental issue of substantive law, as Guruswamy asserts, given the qualified terms in which 'pollution' is defined in Art 1.

[123] Rehbinder and Stewart refer to this system as 'a strategy of alternative harmonization', but it seems questionable whether there really is harmonisation at all. See Rehbinder & Stewart (1985), p 67.

[124] For an unusually candid account of the negotiations within the Council, see Commission des Communautés européennes, *L'état de l'environnement: Premier rapport*, Luxembourg, 1977, pp 39–41 (hereafter referred to as '*Premier rapport*').

within a single legal instrument two fundamentally opposed philosophies of water pollution control.[125]

The first considers that emissions of pollutants must be minimised at their source by the imposition of uniform emission standards (UES).[126] It emphasises the use of the best available technology and the equal treatment of all pollution sources regardless of their location, in order to avoid distortions of competition. The second philosophy, advocated by the United Kingdom,[127] holds that pollution control measures must be based on environmental quality objectives (EQOs),[128] which are to be set taking into account the nature and use of the receiving waters. Thus emission standards may vary from individual emitter to individual emitter as a function of the location, absorptive capacity and intended use of the receiving waters.

[125] On this question, see generally Boehmer-Christiansen (1990a); Rehbinder & Stewart (1985), pp 216–20.

[126] It should be noted that the term 'uniform emission standards' is not used in Dir 76/464/EEC, nor in any of its daughter directives or any other Community legal instrument on water pollution control. However, it has somehow become the 'term of the art' used in most policy documents and in the literature to denote the primary regulatory mechanism instituted by the directive, though the Commission has gone out of its way to stress that it is technically incorrect. According to the Commission, 'there is no provision in the Directive for the application of uniform emission standards' (Answer by the Commission to Written Question No 489/82, OJ No C198, 2.8.1982, p 39), since member states are free to fix more stringent emission standards in their national legislation or in individual permits than the 'limit values' laid down at Community level. However, such emission limit values could be regarded as 'uniform' in the sense that they apply to all discharges from a particular category of point sources, without regard to each source's location and to the specific environmental conditions prevailing at that location.

The terminology used in the 1976 Directive and its subsequent daughter directives makes a clear distinction between 'emission standards', which are to be laid down in individual discharge authorisations by the competent authorities *of the member states* pursuant to Art 3(1) and Art 7, para 2, and 'limit values', which are to be fixed *at Community level* by the Council pursuant to Art 6, para 1. The Commission therefore prefers to speak of the 'limit values approach'. (See Answer by the Commission to Written Question No 1694/81, OJ No C98, 19.4.1982, p 14).

Though not actually defined in Art 1, the notion of 'emission standards' is further elaborated in terms of its technical meaning in Art 5, para 1 of the Directive. In another, though non-binding Community instrument, 'emission standards' are defined as standards 'which set levels for pollutants or nuisances not to be exceeded in emissions from fixed installations'. (Council Recommendation of 3 Mar 1975 regarding cost allocation and action by public authorities on environmental matters (75/346/Euratom, ECSC, EEC), OJ No L 194, 25.7.1975, p 1, Annex, para 4(a)(iii)(a)).

[127] The Commission refers to the UK's negotiating position as 'le problème essentiel' in what it describes as 'un débat long et parfois échauffé'. *Premier rapport, o.c.*, above n 124, p 40. For an articulate scholarly analysis and critique of the British position, see Guruswamy (1982) & Guruswamy (1984).

[128] As pointed out by Guruswamy (1984), pp 466–68, though the term used in Dir 76/464/EEC and its daughter directives is 'quality objectives', the 'objectives' in question are actually environmental quality *standards*, as defined in the 1975 Council Recommendation, ie 'standards which, with legally binding force, prescribe the levels of pollution or nuisance not to be exceeded in a given environment or part thereof' (Council Recommendation of 3 Mar 1975, above n 126, at para 4(a)(i)). We shall leave this semantic question aside, and use the terms 'quality objectives' and 'quality standards' as synonyms.

Water quality objectives should be based on scientific evidence as to the environmental effects of each pollutant.[129]

It has been noted about the debate over the choice between quality objectives and emission standards that 'the controversy over their respective uses was never primarily technical, but political.'[130] At issue is the extent to which environmental regulation should interfere with the processes of production. Under the environmental quality approach, emissions from individual sources are regulated only to the extent necessary to achieve a certain level of environmental quality, which is determined on the basis of an at best incomplete scientific understanding of dose-effect relationships. Emissions are not reduced beyond the level which is held to be 'acceptable', regardless of technological and economic feasibility.

Under the emission standards approach, the policy objective is to reduce emissions at source as much as is technologically feasible even where there is no conclusive scientific evidence of environmental harm. In order to achieve this objective, uniform technology-based standards are set on the basis of an evolving concept of 'best technical means available'. Regulatory policy is aimed at reducing the overall release of pollutants into the environment, not at mitigating their effects through dispersion and dilution. It has been said that the environmental quality standards approach is a 'science-driven' one, whereas the emission standards approach is 'technology-driven.'[131]

It rather seems, however, that in the environmental quality standards approach, science is used primarily as a means of justifying political and economic choices based on entirely non-scientific considerations.[132] As

[129] It should be noted that this approach was not inconsistent with the international consensus prevailing in the early 1970s, as reflected in Principle 7 of the Stockholm Declaration: 'The discharge of toxic substances . . . , *in such quantities or concentrations as to exceed the capacity of the environment to render them harmless*, must be halted in order to ensure that serious or irreversible damage is not inflicted upon ecosystems.' Stockholm Declaration on the Human Environment, UN Doc A/CONF.48/14 (1972), reprinted in 11 ILM 1416 (1972).

[130] Boehmer-Christiansen (1990a), p 139. It has even been suggested by some in the United Kingdom that the debate can be explained in terms of the different legal traditions in civil law and common law countries, that 'the "rule orientation" and "certainty" of the civil law tradition is embodied in the UES approach', while 'EQOs are the natural outcome of the common law system' with its preference for pragmatic and casuistic reasoning. See Guruswamy (1982), pp 624–27. After careful consideration of this argument, however, Guruswamy himself also concludes that the two approaches are motivated by policy reasons rather than differences in legal culture. *Ibid*, p 634.

[131] Boehmer-Christiansen (1990a), p 141.

[132] It is well-known that the imposition of uniform emission standards through regulation has traditionally been criticised by economists on grounds of economic inefficiency. See, eg Ashworth & Papps (1992). As this study is primarily concerned with the *effectiveness*, not the efficiency of transnational normative efforts, it will not address this issue. Whether or not uniform emission standards are justified from an economic viewpoint, it is clear that they are more prescriptive and hence have a stronger normative force from the perspective of the state as norm addressee. The Commission's assumption that the harmonisation of emission standards at the European level is necessary for market integration is challenged by Faure (1999), who argues for differentiation and flexibility on economic and environmental grounds.

Lomas points out: 'Whatever the merits of the two approaches in environmental terms, it is clear that at the heart of the dispute lay economic considerations.'[133] Economic self-interest was undoubtedly a powerful motive on both sides of the debate: the UK did not want to impose strict emission standards on its industry, but to rather allow it to benefit from the environmental 'comparative advantage' of its insular situation, whereas Germany, France and the other continental member states were primarily interested in avoiding distortions of competition and ensuring a 'level playing field' for their industries in the Community by harmonising emission standards.[134]

Political concerns about the preservation of national sovereignty were equally manifest, at a time when many member states were still reluctant to accept the legitimacy of Community action in the environmental field.[135] As a regulatory tool, environmental quality objectives are much more flexible than uniform emission standards, leaving national regulatory authorities a wide range of policy options with respect to measures to be applied to individual point sources. As Sonja Boehmer-Christiansen notes,

EQO, because of their less direct effect on emission regulation, do in fact *maximize national sovereignty or discretion* with respect to any [emission standards] actually set, and by whom.[136]

In Directive 76/464/EEC, the quality objectives approach is presented as an alternative to the emission standards approach. The member states are given the option of adopting either approach in dealing with black list substances. Indeed, Article 6, paragraph 3 provides that the limit values shall not apply

in the cases where a Member State can prove to the Commission . . . that the quality objectives . . . are being met and continuously maintained throughout the area which might be affected by the discharges because of the action taken, among others, by that Member State.

Thus there is a presumption that the emission standards approach applies, unless the member state concerned proves to the Commission that it complies with the quality objectives for all discharges of a substance on the black list. As stipulated in the preamble of all 'daughter directives'[137] of

[133] Lomas (1988), p 518.

[134] Lomas goes as far as to assert that the history of Dir 76/464/EEC 'shows that environmental considerations were largely secondary and incidental and that economic considerations were allowed to predominate'. *Ibid*, p 519.

[135] On this question, see generally Golub (1996) and, as regards the UK's concerns specifically, Golub (1994).

[136] Boehmer-Christiansen (1990a), p 147 (emphasis added).

[137] This is the unofficial generic term most frequently used to denote the implementing directives adopted pursuant to Art 6 of the framework directive and laying down emission limit values and quality objectives for specific black list substances. Some authors also speak of 'subsidiary' or 'offspring' directives. Guruswamy (1984), p 466.

Directive 76/464/EEC, 'Member States are required to apply the limit values except in the cases where they may employ quality objectives.'[138] While the burden of proof to demonstrate compliance is on the member state, the relative indeterminacy of how compliance is to be established in practice gives member states a substantial measure of discretion.

Indeed, there is considerable flexibility in the determination of the 'area which might be affected by the discharges', the choice of the place and frequency of sampling and the interpretation of monitoring results. While Directive 76/464/EEC provides that compliance is to be demonstrated 'in accordance with a monitoring procedure set up by the Council on a proposal from the Commission', the quality objectives and 'monitoring procedures' which have actually been laid down by the Council in subsequent implementing directives do not significantly restrict member state discretion.

To be sure, the Commission initially tried to specify some requirements to be observed by member states in monitoring discharges, but the Council watered down the provisions of daughter directives relating to monitoring procedures to such an extent that member states are given almost complete freedom. In its proposal for the first mercury directive, the Commission had outlined a detailed monitoring procedure which would have imposed certain constraints on member states. It would have required the competent national authority to determine for each point of discharge a 'diffusion zone' in which a network of 'statistically representative' sampling points was to be established. Mercury concentrations in the receiving waters were to be measured at least every six months and the 'dilution factor' calculated on that basis. Additionally, the mercury concentration in the actual effluent was to be measured on a daily basis and compliance with the quality objective established by dividing that concentration by the 'dilution factor.'[139]

Instead of imposing any of these constraints on member states, the Council in fact altogether delegated its power to determine the actual 'monitoring procedure' pursuant to Article 6, paragraph 3 of Directive 76/464/EEC to the 'competent [national] authority.'[140] Member states are only required to 'report' to the Commission 'the area in which the quality objective is applied, . . . the location of sampling points, the frequency of sampling, . . . the results obtained.'[141] Quality objectives are formulated in

[138] Dir 82/176/EEC, preamble, 8th recital. The preambles of Dirs 83/513/EEC, 84/156/EEC, 84/491/EEC, 86/280/EEC, 88/347/EEC and 90/415/EEC each contain an identically worded clause.

[139] Proposal for a Council Directive on the quality objectives for the aquatic environment into which mercury is discharged by the chlor-alkali electrolysis industry, OJ No C 169, 6.7.1979, p 8, Annex II.

[140] Dir 82/176/EEC, Annex IV, para 1.

[141] *Ibid*, para 2.

terms of the 'arithmetic mean of the [monitoring] results obtained over a year,'[142] but the daughter directives leave it to each member state to determine the frequency of sampling, provided only that this shall be 'sufficient to show any changes in the aquatic environment.'[143] These criteria are so vague and unenforceable that it would theoretically be possible for a member state to demonstrate compliance with a quality objective by taking a single sample in a period of one year at a point sufficiently remote from the point of discharge for the pollution to be diluted below the level of the quality standard and by claiming that no change is occurring in the aquatic environment.

When these highly flexible provisions were first laid down in Directive 82/176/EEC, some member states only reluctantly agreed to them. France even entered a statement in the Council minutes putting on record its position that

> the solution adopted for the monitoring and limitation of discharges *can in no way constitute a precedent* for any other Directives the Commission might propose on the basis of Directive 76/464/EEC.[144]

Notwithstanding these initial reservations, the provisions in question *did* in fact set a precedent, as they later became standard clauses for all daughter directives of 76/464/EEC and were eventually codified as such in the general application directive, Directive 86/280/EEC.[145]

The quality standards approach also forms the basis of the Directive's policy with regard to grey list substances. Article 7 requires the member states to 'establish programmes' for the reduction of pollution by List II substances, which 'shall set deadlines for their implementation'. All discharges containing such substances shall, like those containing black list substances, be made subject to 'prior authorization'. The emission standards laid down in the authorisations shall be based on water quality objectives determined by the member states in their reduction programmes. Unlike the regime applying to black list substances, the Directive's provisions on grey list substances do not provide for the setting of uniform Community emission limit values and Community quality objectives for grey list substances, thus leaving the member states full discretion in the establishment of both emission and quality standards. In addition to measures for the reduction of pollution from point sources, the member states' programmes 'may', according to Article 7, paragraph 4, also

142 Dir 82/176/EEC, Annex II, para 1.

143 *Ibid*, Annex IV, para 3.

144 Statement for entry in the minutes, as quoted in Guruswamy (1984), p 472, n 36 (emphasis added).

145 Dir 86/280/EEC, Annex I, Heading B. The only significant difference is the requirement that 'samples must be taken at a point sufficiently close to the discharge point to be representative of the quality of the aquatic environment in the area affected by the discharges'.

include provisions to curb pollution from non-point sources, such as product standards.

While grey list substances are to be dealt with primarily through national measures, Community measures are not altogether excluded. Article 7, paragraph 7 provides that the Commission shall undertake 'regular comparisons' of the member states' programmes 'to ensure sufficient co-ordination in their implementation'. If it deems it necessary to ensure such coordination, the Commission may submit harmonisation proposals to the Council for this purpose. As a matter of fact, Article 12, paragraph 2 stipulates that the Commission shall forward the first proposals under Article 7, paragraph 7 'where possible within 27 months following notification' of the Directive.

THE IMPLEMENTATION OF DIRECTIVE 76/464/EEC: A COMPLEX PROCESS

Directive 76/464/EEC is very much a framework directive. While it does enunciate ambitious substantive objectives, their achievement is contingent on the successful completion of a complex regulatory process, involving a large number of measures and decisions both at national and Community level. Indeed, it has been described by some commentators as 'un programme pour la législation communautaire à venir.'[146] Under the regulatory regime established by the Directive, before the discharge of any black list substance into the aquatic environment is actually reduced as a result of the application of Community law, the Commission shall first of all submit to the Council a proposal for limit values and quality objectives for this substance. That proposal must then be adopted by the Council. Although under Article 12, paragraph 1 of the Directive the Council has committed itself to take a decision on any Commission proposal within nine months, experience has shown that it can take several years for the Council to agree on a single daughter directive.

The adoption of a daughter directive setting emission and quality standards for a particular substance is only the first step in a process which eventually may lead to a reduction of discharges. Member states must then identify all discharges 'which are liable to contain' the substance in question and lay down emission standards complying with Community limit values for each such discharge in an individual discharge permit. Existing

[146] Brusasco & Kiss (1978), pp 315–316. Another commentator labels the framework directive as 'declaratory' and 'an uncertain foundation' for the establishment of a regime for the control of emissions of toxic substances into the aquatic environment. Simmonds (1989), p 77. German authors, with a preference for national public law metaphors and an undeniable feeling for bombast, have proclaimed Dir 76/464/EEC the 'Grundgesetz des westeuropäischen Gewasserschutzes'. Möbs (1978), p 18.

discharges must comply with emission standards only within a certain period of time specified in the implementing directive. Assuming that the emission standards laid down in the authorisation are adequately enforced by national authorities and are in fact more stringent than the standards, if any, previously applied to the same pollution source, a reduction in emissions will actually be achieved.

Whether the application by a member state of the quality objectives approach allowed under Article 6, paragraph 3 of the Directive will actually result in any reduction, let alone elimination, of discharges of black list substances is an even more open question. The member state must first determine the area of the aquatic environment which is 'affected' by discharges of a given black list substance for which quality objectives have been laid down in a Community Directive. It must then translate those quality objectives into binding water quality standards under national law and verify whether those standards are being met in the affected areas.

In establishing the actual quality standards against which compliance with the requirements of the Directive will be judged, member states have substantial discretion. Often, the implementing directive for a particular substance gives the competent national authority ample discretion to select from a range of different quality objectives, relating, for instance, to concentrations of the pollutant in water, in sediments, or in fish, 'the objective or objectives that it deems appropriate having regard to the intended use of the area affected.'[147]

Finally, the national authority must establish emission standards for individual discharges and 'ensure [they] are applied' so that the quality objectives it has itself selected are complied with. It is quite unlikely in this situation that a national authority, when given the option, would actually select a quality objective which would compel it to strengthen emission standards for particular sources.

The Legal Effect of the Framework Directive in the Absence of Daughter Directives

As we have just seen, the effectiveness of Directive 76/464/EEC depends to a large extent on the adoption of daughter directives for specific substances and their implementation by the member states. This does not imply, however, that Directive 76/464/EEC is completely devoid of any legal effect in the absence of implementing directives. The exact nature of the member states' obligations resulting from the general provisions of the directive may vary according to different interpretations.

[147] Dir 82/176/EEC, Annex II.

The Commission has made a number of interpretative statements with respect to the legal effect of Directive 76/464/EEC, which tend to confuse rather than clarify the issue. In response to a written question from a member of the European Parliament, the Commission stated that it

> regards part of Directive 76/464/EEC . . . as a framework Directive to be implemented by specific Directives. . . . It is true, however, that *other parts of the Directive lay down binding rules.*[148]

This statement may be interpreted *a contrario* to mean that, in the Commission's opinion, those parts of the Directive which call for implementing Directives do *not* lay down binding rules. Such an interpretation would seem to be in conflict with the binding nature of Directives as affirmed in Article 249 EC.

The most relevant question as to the legal effect of Directive 76/464/EEC is that of the respective status of List I and List II substances. Under the directive, a different legal regime applies to the two categories. Pollution by black list substances is to be 'eliminated', inter alia by means of the application of Community limit values, whereas pollution by grey list substances is to be 'reduced' through the implementation of national programmes comprising quality objectives and emission standards. By virtue of the provisions of List II, however, substances belonging to the families and groups referred to in List I for which Community limit values have not been established are provisionally to be treated as List II substances.

Of special interest are those 129 substances which the Commission has proposed for inclusion in List I. According to a communication it submitted to the Council in 1982,[149] the Commission has determined that those substances 'might' be included in List I. The Commission's determination, however, is not sufficient to actually include those substances in List I. That is a decision to be made by the Council. Although the Commission in and of itself is unable to include any substance in List I, the list of 129 substances has a special status by virtue of a Council resolution in which

> the Member States recognise the list of 129 substances as a provisional basis for any national measures to combat pollution of water by these substances, when applying the measures provided for in Directive 76/464/EEC.[150]

[148] Answer by the Commission to Written Question No 1649/87, OJ No C 195, 25.7.1988, p 8 (emphasis added).

[149] Communication of the Commission to the Council of 22 June 1982 on dangerous substances which might be included in List I of Council Dir 76/464/EEC, OJ No C176, 14.7.1982, p 3 (hereafter referred to as Commission Communication of 22 June 1982).

[150] Council Resolution of 7 Feb 1983 concerning the combating of water pollution, OJ No C46, 17.2.1983, p 17. This special status is recognised, for instance, in the national policy of the Netherlands, which provisionally treats the 129 substances on the EEC list as black list substances. See *Indicatief Meerjaren Programma Water*, Tweede Kamer, 1984–1985, Doc 19 153, nrs 1–2, p 14.

The Commission is of the opinion that those provisions of Directive 76/464/EEC 'which create specific legal obligations without the necessity of daughter-Directives are chiefly to be found in Article 7.'[151] Indeed, the regime of Article 7 applies to all substances for which daughter directives have not yet been adopted, by virtue of the provision which specifies that substances belonging to the groups and families of substances in List I for which Community limit values have not yet been established are to be treated as List II substances. Article 2 of Directive 76/464/EEC, according to the Commission, 'creates a general obligation to reduce pollution by list II substances.'[152] More specifically, Article 7 requires member states to establish programmes comprising quality objectives, prior authorisation of all discharges of list II substances and emission standards for such discharges. Finally, the Commission has also identified the standstill obligations laid down in Articles 8 and 9 as belonging to the provisions imposing 'specific legal obligations' on member states independently of the adoption of implementing directives.[153]

Directive 76/464/EEC is an unusual directive in that it does not specify a date by which its provisions must be transposed by the member states and does not require the member states to communicate to the Commission the provisions of national implementing legislation.[154] However, the Commission has indicated that this does not detract from the binding force of the directive and has stressed, specifically with regard to Article 7 relating to national pollution reduction programmes for grey list substances, that this provision 'would be pointless if not implemented within a reasonable time', while 'reserv[ing] the right to take appropriate action', which, as we shall see below, it eventually did, albeit years later.[155]

[151] Answer by the Commission to Written Question No 441/88, OJ No C114, 8.5.1989, p 34.

[152] *Ibid.* See also the Answer by the Commission to Written Question No 1779/88, OJ No C151, 19.6.1984, p 34, in which the Commission implies that the British government's decision to relax discharge conditions for certain municipal sewage treatment works with a view to their privatisation is inconsistent with the general requirement to eliminate or reduce pollution by dangerous substances as laid down in Art 2 of Dir 76/464/EEC. However, in a recent judgment, while dismissing on factual grounds a Commission plea that Greece had infringed the provisions of Art 2, the Court of Justice observed in obiter dictum that it is 'not impossible to construe the wording of that provision as meaning that the obligation laid down in Article 2 of Dir 76/464 is restricted to measures provided for by the directive itself', ie that Art 2 does not impose on member states independent substantive obligations additional to those resulting from the other provisions of the Directive. Joined Cases C–232/95 and C–233/95, *Commission v Hellenic Republic*, [1998] ECR I–3343, para 47.

[153] Answer by the Commission to Written Question No 441/88, OJ No C114, 8.5.1989, p 34.

[154] As noted by the Commission in its Answer to Written Question No 332/82, OJ No C198, 2.8.1982, p 26.

[155] Answer by the Commission to Written Question No 1036/84, OJ No C123, 20.5.1985, p 2.

National and Community Measures with Respect to Grey List Substances

The implementation of Article 7 by the member states has proceeded very slowly. In a letter addressed to all member states on 3 November 1976, the Commission requested them to establish the reduction programmes required under Article 7 by 15 September 1981 and to implement them by 15 September 1986.[156] Notwithstanding the Commission's request, member states have been reluctant to elaborate pollution reduction programmes and establish quality objectives for grey list substances and communicate them to the Commission. By 1981, the Commission had not received all the information on national programmes it had requested. It therefore tried to speed up implementation by convening a meeting of national experts to set priorities for comparing national programmes. A 'priority list' of six heavy metals on List II was agreed at that meeting.[157] The Commission later again specifically requested member states to communicate their national programmes for chromium, one of the heavy metals on the grey list. By the end of 1983, all the member states had complied with this request.[158] In 1986, the Commission noted that six member states had also sent in their programmes for reducing emissions of copper, lead, nickel and zinc.[159] But two years later, addressing the implementation of Article 7 generally, the Commission pointed out that 'not one Member State has completely fulfilled its obligations under this Article.'[160]

Notwithstanding the incomplete information received from the member states, the Commission announced in July 1982 that it had initiated 'a comparative study of the programmes in existence in the Member States for reducing discharges of List II heavy metals,'[161] in order to evaluate the need for 'coordination' of these programmes within the meaning of Article 7, paragraph 7. However, in 1985, the Commission noted that while all the

[156] Answer by the Commission to Written Question No 295/85, OJ No C255, 7.10.1985, p 36.

[157] Answer by the Commission to Written Question No 1023/82, OJ No C305, 22.11.1982, p 8. These priorities were 'confirmed' at another meeting of national experts in July 1983. Answer by the Commission to Written Question No 1218/83, OJ No C31, 6.2.1984, p 12.

[158] *Ibid.* See also Answer by the Commission to Written Question No 295/85, OJ No C255, 7.10.1985, p 36; Answer by the Commission to Written Question No 1023/82, OJ No C305, 22.11.82, p 8.

[159] Answer by the Commission to Written Question No 524/86, OJ No C31, 9.2.1987, p 10.

[160] Answer by the Commission to Written Question No 441/88, OJ No C114, 8.5.1989, p 34. See also Answer by the Commission to Written Question No 718/92, OJ No C283, 20.10.1993, p 7. In view of this information, the Commission's earlier statement that it had 'established that the Member States have complied with the main provisions' of Dir 76/464/EEC, including those relating to 'pollution-reduction programmes', appears puzzling. See Answer by the Commission to Written Question No 332/82, OJ No C198, 2.8.1982, p 26.

[161] Answer by the Commission to Written Question No 653/82, OJ No C232, 6.9.82, p 17.

member states had provided 'some information . . . in most cases this was insufficient to identify possible methods of harmonization.'[162] This probably explains why the Commission's study first focused on chromium, apparently the pollutant for which most information had been provided, and led to a proposal for a directive laying down uniform quality objectives for chromium in water.[163] Having noted that, with one or two exceptions, the national programmes for the reduction of pollution by this heavy metal did not fully comply with the requirements of Article 7,[164] the Commission concluded that there was a need for coordination[165] and to this end submitted a draft directive to the Council. This proposal initially provided only for *quality objectives* to be laid down at Community level. However, in response to the European Parliament's opinion, the Commission later amended its proposal to include limit values for industrial emissions of chromium.[166]

It is clear from the wording of Article 7 of Directive 76/464/EEC, as compared with the provisions relating to black list substances, that member states were to be granted a greater measure of discretion in applying the directive to grey list substances than to black list substances. Article 7 does not explicitly provide for limit values and quality objectives to be set at Community level. The determination of both emission standards and water quality standards is left to the member states. Where Article 7, paragraph 3 provides that national quality objectives 'shall be laid down in accordance with Council Directives, where they exist', the Council probably did not have in mind directives it would later adopt in implementation of Directive 76/464/EEC, but rather other Council directives defining quality objectives for water intended for specific uses, such as it had already adopted prior to Directive 76/464/EEC.[167]

However, the wording of Article 7 does not preclude the Commission from proposing to the Council the adoption of Community quality objectives or even emission limit values for grey list substances, where that is required 'to ensure sufficient coordination' as provided in Article 7, para-

[162] Answer by the Commission to Written Question No 295/85, above n 158.

[163] Proposal for a Council Directive on water quality objectives for chromium, OJ No C351, 31.12.1985, p 33.

[164] *Ibid*, Explanatory memorandum, EC Doc COM(85) 733 final, 18 Dec 1985, p 1.

[165] *Ibid*, p 2.

[166] Amended proposal for a Council Directive on water quality objectives for chromium and limits for chromium in water, OJ No C43, 16.2.1988, p 6.

[167] Namely, Dir 75/440/EEC and Dir 76/160/EEC. The former establishes quality objectives for surface water intended for the abstraction of drinking water, and the latter quality objectives for bathing water. Many of the parameters for which standards must be set and monitored by the member states pursuant to Dir 75/440/EEC, and some of the relevant parameters in Dir 76/160/EEC, are either grey list substances or candidate black list substances subject to the provisions of Art 7 of Dir 76/464/EEC.

graph 7. Nevertheless, the fact that the Council, in adopting Directive 76/464/EEC, did not include in it the provision of the Commission's original proposal which would explicitly have required that Community 'limiting values' be determined for emissions of grey list substances,[168] indicates the member states' great reluctance to contemplate Community interference with their emission control policies for grey list substances.

The draft directive on chromium is the only Commission proposal relating to grey list substances submitted pursuant to Article 7, paragraph 7 of Directive 76/464/EEC. In 1982, the Commission had announced that 'the programmes for the other priority substances will be compared later'[169] but, 10 years later, it declared that it 'feels it must wait for [the proposed chromium directive] to be adopted so as to have a model on which to base subsequent proposals regarding the five other priority heavy metals' referred to above.[170] However, the chromium proposal was never adopted by the Council; in fact, negotiations on it were effectively suspended in 1988 due to persistent disagreement among the member states. According to the Council, which last considered the proposal at its meeting of 21 March 1988, agreement could not be reached because some member states objected to the proposed introduction of Community limit values for chromium emissions, in addition to water quality objectives. Moreover, the desirability of taking measures at Community level with respect to grey list substances as long as all necessary measures have not been taken to deal with the more hazardous black list substances was also questioned in the Council.[171]

In 1993, the Commission finally decided to withdraw its 1985 proposal,[172] ostensibly conceding that it was 'inconsistent with the objectives of framework Directive 76/464/EEC' in that the latter only provides for *national* measures to deal with grey list substances.[173] This political decision in effect marked the end of any Community efforts to 'coordinate' national measures with respect to reduction of pollution by such substances.

[168] Proposal for a Decision of the Council on the reduction of pollution caused by certain dangerous substances discharged into the aquatic environment of the Community, EC Doc COM (74) 1706 final, 21 Oct 1974, Art 4.

[169] Answer by the Commission to Written Question No 1023/82, OJ No C305, 22.11.82, p 8.

[170] Answer by the Commission to Written Question No 1493/91, OJ No C183, 20.7.1992, p 3.

[171] Answer by the Council to Written Question No 1499/91, OJ No C38, 15.2.1992, p 30. See also Answer by the Commission to Written Question No 1493/91, OJ No C183, 20.7.1992, p 3.

[172] Withdrawal of certain proposals and drafts from the Commission to the Council, OJ No C228, 24.8.1993, p 12.

[173] Answer by the Commission to Written Question No 887/95, OJ No C209, 14.8.1995, p 29.

Community Measures with Respect to Black List Substances

The Selection of Black List Substances for Regulation

The first step in the process of implementation of Directive 76/464/EEC is the selection of individual substances belonging to List I and the formulation of proposals for limit values and quality objectives for submission to the Council. The use by the Commission of its right of initiative in this field involves a substantial measure of political discretion, since the framework directive gives only general guidance as to the selection criteria and basis for standard-setting. Though the 1976 Directive does not prescribe any particular procedure for the preparation of Commission proposals pursuant to its Article 6, the Commission has interpreted the provisions of this Article as implying that 'in-depth studies of the ecotoxicity of the substances concerned, of the available pollution abatement technologies and of the likely economic implications of the legislation *must* be completed before the Commission *can* submit proposals' for daughter directives.[174] Consequently, it has developed a quasi-formal process of fact-finding and consultation preceding the submission of any proposals for emission limit values and quality objectives to the Council.

From the start, member states have been closely involved in this process through an informal 'group of national experts' which is regularly consulted by the Commission. In addition, the Commission in 1978 established a Scientific Advisory Committee for research on the toxicity and ecotoxicity of chemicals,[175] composed of independent scientific experts appointed by it, which is also called upon to advise the Commission on the scientific basis for the selection of substances to be regulated and the setting of standards. The complex process for the elaboration of norms for specific black list substances, which involves formal and informal mechanisms for the balancing of environmental and economic concerns and the accommodation of divergent national interests, and the permanent interplay of technical-scientific and legal discourse, is analysed below.

Criteria for the Selection of Substances

The three basic criteria for the selection of black list substances as well as for the establishment of limit values and quality objectives are toxicity, persistence and bioaccumulation. List I provides that individual substances

[174] Answer by the Commission to Written Question No 1255/83, OJ No C38, 13.2.1984, p 20 (emphasis added). Some British authors consider that the Commission is actually under a 'legal duty' to carry out a 'full investigation'. Guruswamy (1984), p 476.

[175] Commission Decision of 28 June 1978, OJ No L198, 22.7.1978, p 17.

shall be selected 'mainly' on the basis of these criteria.[176] All three criteria do not necessarily have to be fulfilled cumulatively. Though many black list substances for which limit values and quality objectives have been set display all three properties, others which have been selected do not meet all three criteria.[177] On the other hand, substances meeting one or several of the criteria will not be included in the black list when they are 'biologically harmless or . . . are rapidly converted into substances which are biologically harmless'. The concept of toxicity includes chronic forms of toxicity such as carcinogenicity, since List I also comprises the category of 'substances in respect of which it has been proved that they possess carcinogenic properties in or via the aquatic environment.'[178]

This emphasis on scientific proof indicates that the regulatory philosophy underlying Directive 76/464/EEC predates the emergence of the precautionary approach. The same emphasis can be found in another provision with respect to the application of bioaccumulation as a criterion for laying down quality objectives, which refers to 'accumulation of the said substances in living organisms and in sediment, as indicated by the latest *conclusive* scientific data.'[179] Indeed, as a rule, the Commission and the national experts have interpreted Directive 76/464/EEC as requiring positive evidence that a substance which belongs to the families or groups of substances in List I actually constitutes a hazard for the aquatic environment because of its toxicity, persistence or tendency to bioaccumulate, before any proposal for limit values and quality objectives for this substance can be submitted to the Council. Insisting on scientific certainty in a field like ecotoxicology which is characterised by substantial uncertainty is a way of masking political value judgements and maximising discretion in the interpretation of scientific data.

The Selection Procedure: the Role of the Commission and the Member States

Shortly after the adoption of Directive 76/464/EEC, the Commission initiated the process of selecting black list substances and preparing proposals for submission to the Council, in close consultation with a group of national experts designated by the member states.[180] This group has no formal

[176] See also Dir 76/464/EEC, Art 1, paras 1 and 2. The latter paragraph provides that quality objectives shall be laid down 'principally' on the basis of the same criteria.

[177] According to a senior German official, member of the committee of national experts, toxicity is a necessary condition in all cases, but persistence and bio-accumulation are alternate criteria which need not necessarily be met simultaneously. See Möbs (1978), pp 22–23. Rehbinder and Stewart, for their part, consider this question of interpretation 'unsettled', Rehbinder & Stewart (1985), p 65.

[178] *Ibid*, Annex, List I, para 4.

[179] *Ibid*, Art 6, para 2 (emphasis added).

[180] Answer by the Commission to Written Question No 5/78, OJ No C175, 24.7.1978, p 32.

existence in the Directive. It has not been established by authority of the Council but only upon the initiative of the Commission, as an informal forum to sound out the views of the member states and test the political feasibility of proposals relating to particular substances before their formal submission to the Council. Though designated by the member states, the national experts are consulted in their personal capacity and are not presumed to express the official positions of their respective governments. Therefore, the discussions in the group of national experts have been described as 'uncommitting' by one Commission official.[181]

Indeed, there have sometimes been discrepancies between the views expressed by national experts and the positions later taken by the representatives of the same member states during the official discussions in Council.[182] Nevertheless, it seems that the opinions expressed by experts in the informal group have generally been regarded by the Commission as indicative of member state positions and have strongly influenced the Commission's policy on the implementation of Directive 76/464/EEC. In fact, the Commission has explicitly admitted in reply to a parliamentary question that its choice of black list substances for which draft directives are submitted to the Council 'depend[s] on the selection made in the meetings with the national experts, where the priorities are set.'[183]

The group of national experts is consulted at different stages of the process of preparing implementation measures. The first stage is the selection of substances to be studied for the purpose of assessing their toxicity, persistence and tendency to bioaccumulate and confirming their black list status. The national experts have been closely involved in this initial selection from the start. The Commission has routinely submitted its proposals to the group for advice and has deferred to this advice in drawing up the priority lists of substances for further study.

At the group's first meeting, agreement was reached on a first series of five substances to be considered for regulation as a matter of priority: mercury, cadmium, aldrin, dieldrin and endrin. The choice of the first two heavy metals was undisputed and not in fact discretionary, since they were already explicitly mentioned as individual substances in List I of Directive 76/464/EEC. The other three substances are persistent organochlorine insecticides whose environmental hazards were already widely documented. However, a sixth substance proposed by the Commission, 3,4-benzopyrene, was not considered a priority by the expert group and removed from the list.[184]

[181] Vennekens-Capkova (1990), p 152.

[182] Interview with Belgian member of the group of national experts, 6 June 1991.

[183] Answer by the Commission to Written Question No 1492/91, OJ No C89, 9.4.1992, p 10. See also Answer by the Commission to Written Question No 1022/82, OJ No C 312, 29.11.1982, p 13.

[184] Dekker (1983), p 276.

In consultation with the group of national experts, which met more or less on an annual basis from 1977 to 1980 to consider lists of substances proposed by the Commission, additional series of substances were selected for priority attention, mostly organochlorine compounds and a number of suspected carcinogens.[185] Initially, it was relatively easy to reach consensus within the group of national experts on priority substances whose hazardous properties were already quite well known internationally. However, as the work progressed, the need was felt for a more systematic procedure based on objective criteria to determine further priorities for the implementation of Directive 76/464/EEC.[186]

Consequently, the Commission established a procedure to review systematically substances which are candidates for inclusion in List I.[187] A comprehensive study was carried out by scientific consultants, who identified 1,500 substances which, by reason of their chemical structure, belong to the groups or families of substances referred to in List I. Of this group, the Commission selected for further review those substances which are produced and used in quantities of more than 100 tonnes per year throughout the Community and consequently may reach the aquatic environment in amounts sufficient to constitute a potential hazard. The magnitude of this potential hazard for human health and the environment was then evaluated by means of a mathematical model.

This evaluation produced a list of 122 substances, which was examined by the group of national experts at its fifth meeting in 1981. The group again successfully wielded its influence, since it selected only 108 out of those 122 substances as qualifying for further study, in addition to the 21 substances which had already been selected at previous meetings.[188] At the conclusion of this selection process, the Commission, in accordance with the opinion of the national experts, had identified 129 substances which it deemed worthy of further study with a view to their eventual inclusion in the black list. This list was officially communicated to the Council on 22 June 1982[189] and endorsed by the Council in its resolution of 7 February 1983 'as a basis for further work on the implementation of Directive 76/464/EEC.'[190]

It should be stressed that, by doing so, the Council did not *ipso facto* include these 129 substances in the black list. For this purpose, and to

[185] See Table I in the Commission Communication of 22 June 1982, above n 37; see also Table I in Dekker (1983), p 276.

[186] *Ibid*, p 276.

[187] For a full description of the procedure, see Commission Communication of 22 June 1982, above n 149.

[188] Dekker (1983), p 277; Vennekens-Capkova (1990), p 153.

[189] Commission Communication of 22 June 1982, above n 149.

[190] Council Resolution of 7 Feb 1983 concerning the combating of water pollution, OJ No C46, 17.2.1983, p 17.

trigger the application of Articles 3 and 5 of Directive 76/464/EEC, a directive of the Council laying down limit values and quality objectives for each individual substance remained necessary. It should also be noted that the endorsement of the list of 129 substances by the Council does not necessarily reflect the unconditional agreement of the member states with the selection criteria used and the result of the preliminary selection process nor a clear common understanding as to the status of the list. Indeed, one Commission official has observed that 'the status of the List and the foundation of the selection criteria used remains a permanent item of discussion.'[191]

The second phase in the preparatory process for daughter directives could be described as a research phase. During this phase, consultants are commissioned to carry out studies on the substances selected for priority consideration in order to provide a factual basis for the Commission to elaborate eventual regulatory proposals.[192] Three kinds of studies are normally required: an ecotoxicological study, a technical study and an economic study.[193] The ecotoxicological study is designed to evaluate the environmental properties of the substance concerned in order to determine whether it meets the criteria for inclusion in List I and to establish a scientific basis for setting water quality objectives. The technical study examines the production, use and discharges of the substance and the technical means available for reducing emissions, and thus provides a technical basis for laying down emission standards. Finally, the economic study assesses the economic feasibility of different emission reduction measures in the sectors concerned, which is also to be factored into the interpretation of the concept of 'best technical means available', which Article 6, paragraph 1 of Directive 76/464/EEC provides shall be taken into account in laying down emission limit values.

The results of these studies are communicated to the member states and again submitted to a consultative process. It is here that the Scientific Advisory Committee established by the Commission[194] enters into the fray. This Committee is officially consulted by the Commission on the results of the ecotoxicological study and asked to give a scientific opinion on two questions: whether the substance examined meets the criteria of Directive 76/464/EEC and qualifies for inclusion in List I and, if so, what water

[191] Vennekens-Capkova (1990), p 153.

[192] Concerted action was also undertaken within the framework of the Community's research policy to promote research on some of the pollutants listed in List I. See Council Decision 78/888/EEC of 9 Oct 1978 adopting a European Economic Community concerted project in the field of analysis of organic micropollutants in water, OJ No L311, 4.11.1978, p 6.

[193] The technical and economic aspects are often combined into a single study.

[194] Commission Decision of 28 June 1978, above n 175.

quality objectives should be proposed by the Commission to protect the aquatic environment. It is to be noted that the Committee advises the *Commission*,[195] not the Council or the group of national experts. Initially, the Committee's opinions were not even made available to the member states or to the national experts, but treated as confidential by the Commission. It is only in the face of protests from the member states that the Commission later reluctantly agreed to make them available to national experts.[196]

The group of national experts is, in turn, consulted by the Commission on the results of the ecotoxicological, technical and economic studies, and on the desirability of proceeding with a formal proposal for a directive establishing limit values and quality objectives. During the course of these consultations, national experts may provide the Commission with additional information available from national sources. The Commission will also have a first exchange of views with the national experts on the possible content of an eventual draft directive, in terms of sectors to be covered and values to be laid down. This informal round of consultations is used by the Commission to test the political feasibility of the regulatory proposals it intends to make and has considerable influence on the Commission's policy. It is at this stage that political conclusions must be drawn from the results of the studies commissioned and a decision made whether or not to initiate the actual legislative process with respect to particular substances. The opinion of the group of national experts appears to play a crucial role in this decision, which from an institutional point of view in fact is for the Commission to take in the sovereign exercise of its right of initiative under the Treaty.

Contrary to what might be inferred from a strict reading of Directive 76/464/EEC, the criteria of persistence, toxicity and bioaccumulation laid down in the directive are not the only factors which are taken into account by the national experts and the Commission in determining the Community's standard-setting policy for emissions of dangerous substances. Much of the debate has revolved around diverging and ever-shifting perceptions of 'priorities', in which economic and political factors and various other considerations of national interest have played a more or less overt role. The national experts, in their consultations with the Commission, not only address the question whether a particular substance meets the explicit criteria for inclusion in the black list, but also express an opinion on whether or not fixing Community limit values and quality objectives for the substance in question can be considered a 'priority', taking into account the relative 'significance' of the environmental risk involved, the volume

[195] *Ibid*, Art 2, para 1.
[196] Interview with Belgian member of the group of national experts, 6 June 1991.

and pattern of emissions, technical feasibility, costs and benefits of emission reduction measures, etc.[197]

Obviously, the Commission and the national experts prefer to legitimise their decision not to take further regulatory action with respect to particular pollutants on grounds of scientific rationality rather than overtly recognising that it is based on political or economic considerations. The discussion therefore first focuses on the scientific criteria for inclusion of substances in the black list and on the interpretation of the results of ecotoxicological studies. In view of the extent of scientific uncertainty involved, member states have considerable room for manoeuvering and national experts tend to differ on the conclusions to be drawn from the available ecotoxicological evidence. The national experts do not automatically defer to the opinion of the Scientific Advisory Committee on this question. The group of national experts extensively debates the necessity of laying down Community standards and thus conferring black list status on particular substances. If a consensus against further legislative action emerges within the group, this will normally be decisive. If the debate at this 'pre-legislative' stage is not conclusive, it is often carried forward into the formal negotiations in the Council, when the Commission, notwithstanding the disagreement among national experts, decides to go ahead and try out a formal proposal for a daughter directive anyway.

The case of carbon tetrachloride and chloroform, two chlorinated organic compounds, illustrates the controversial nature of the criteria and the interpretation of the ecotoxicological data. These two substances had been selected for priority attention by the Commission in agreement with the group of national experts as early as 1980,[198] and the Scientific Advisory Committee, based on the results of studies performed, had recommended that these substances be included on the black list in view of their carcinogenic properties.[199] However, the United Kingdom, which has consistently tried to limit the number of substances on the black list,[200] argued that there was no

[197] It seems as though the group of national experts, in its policy with respect to emissions of hazardous substances, in fact applied the factors which the Treaty provides should be taken into account in the development of Community action relating to the environment *avant la lettre*. The cost/benefit approach and the balancing of economic and environmental interests practiced by the group had no explicit legal basis in Dir 76/464/EEC but was later institutionalised as a basic tenet of EC environmental law in Art 174, para 3 of the Treaty. Similarly, in deciding whether or not Community regulatory action with respect to particular pollutants was appropriate, the experts were in fact debating the relative effectiveness of Community action as opposed to national action, thus in a way prefiguring the subsidiarity principle first codified by the SEA in what was then Art 130r, para 4 EEC.

[198] Dekker (1983), p 276, Table I, nos 17–18.

[199] Proposal for a Council Directive on limit values and quality objectives for discharges of certain dangerous substances included in List I in the Annex to Dir 76/464/EEC, OJ No C70, 18.3.1985, p 15. See the explanatory memorandum in EC Doc COM(84) 772 final, 17 Jan 1985, paras 3.2.1.1. & 3.2.1.4.

[200] At the Council meeting of 30 June 1980, the British Minister of Environment reportedly made the 'strongest possible appeal . . . that the priority list *should be reduced to the absolute minimum*'. Statement of the Rt Hon Tom King, quoted by Guruswamy (1984), p 465.

basis for conferring List I status on the two substances in question owing to their high volatility, which prevented them from being present in the aquatic environment in concentrations posing any risk.[201] The Commission nevertheless included chloroform and carbon tetrachloride in a draft daughter directive submitted to the Council in 1984,[202] but was eventually forced, in the face of continuing opposition from the UK in the Council, to request a second opinion from the Scientific Advisory Committee.[203] It is only after the Committee had confirmed its earlier opinion and the Council had agreed, as a political compromise, that in future proposals priority should be given to substances causing 'particularly important environmental problems', that the United Kingdom finally accepted the fixing of Community limit values and quality objectives for the two substances in question.[204]

There are also instances in which the Commission, following consultation with the group of national experts, decided *not* to propose limit values and quality objectives for certain substances *even though* the scientific evidence as to their toxicity, persistence and tendency to bioaccumulate was conclusive and their black list status undisputed. In two of these instances, the Commission made an effort to justify its decision in a formal communication to the Council. In 1980, the Commission informed the Council that it had determined that it would not be 'useful' to elaborate a daughter directive setting limit values and quality objectives for chlordane and heptachlor, two highly toxic and persistent organochlorine insecticides, because this would 'not lead to a significant reduction of the pollution of the aquatic environment' by these substances. The group of national experts, at its 1979 meeting, had recommended that although these compounds 'in principle' qualified for inclusion in List I, they should not be the subject of further regulatory efforts in the framework of Directive 76/464/EEC, because they were not being produced in the Community and their emissions in the aquatic environment were 'insignificant.'[205]

[201] Haigh (1990), p 109.

[202] Proposal for a Council Directive on limit values and quality objectives for discharges of certain dangerous substances included in List I in the Annex to Dir 76/464/EEC, above n 199. This proposal led to the adoption of Dir 86/280/EEC, but only after the proposed limit values and quality objectives for chloroform had been dropped from the draft directive to overcome the UK's objections. Although the Commission, invoking its 'obligation of professional secrecy', declined to answer a parliamentary question as to the identity of the member states opposing the inclusion of chloroform in this directive, it is a matter of common knowledge that the UK was one of them. See Answer by the Commission to Written Question No 109/86, OJ No C214, 25.8.1986, p 38.

[203] Interview with former Commission official, 20 Jan 1992.

[204] Haigh (1990), p 111. Carbon tetrachloride was regulated by Dir 86/280/EEC and chloroform by Dir 88/347/EEC. For a further analysis of the debate on the priorities for the implementation of Dir 76/464/EEC triggered by the controversy about those substances, see below.

[205] Communication from the Commission to the Council concerning the elaboration of directives with respect to heptachlor and chlordane pursuant to Council Dir 76/464/EEC, EC Doc COM(80) 433 final, paras 12–13. See also Answer by the Commission to Written Question No 686/87, OJ No C86, 4.4.1988, p 16.

The Commission, in a similar move, also decided not to take any further action with respect to arsenic and its compounds, though for different reasons. In 1982, arsenic had been listed in the priority list of 129 substances to be considered for inclusion in the black list, drawn up by the Commission in consultation with the group of national experts.[206] One year later, however, the Commission sent a communication to the Council in which it announced that it did not consider it 'necessary' to adopt a daughter directive setting limit values and quality objectives for arsenic.[207] The Commission came to this conclusion notwithstanding the fact that the studies carried out had demonstrated that arsenic has carcinogenic properties in or via the aquatic environment and therefore must be included in List I.[208] Even though the studies had confirmed that arsenic belongs in the black list, the Commission decided that a daughter directive was not required, because arsenic concentrations in the aquatic environment present no hazard to human health and most of the arsenic in the Community's waters originates from natural and diffuse sources instead of industrial point sources.[209] The Commission concludes that arsenic, even though a confirmed black list substance, will continue to be covered by the regime applying to grey list substances.[210] This is indeed an automatic consequence of the decision not to set Community limit values.

The attitude of the Commission and the group of national experts with respect to substances they had initially identified as worthy of inclusion in the black list is rather equivocal. Having spent six years following the adoption of Directive 76/464/EEC to agree on a priority list of substances for further study and consideration, the Commission and the national experts then started arguing about new priorities for legislative action within their initial 'priority list.' These 'priorities within the priorities' appeared to be shifting as the debate evolved and member states changed their dilatory tactics. While the lack of data and the need for detailed study of all potential black list substances could easily be invoked as a pretext for slowing down the standard-setting process in its early stage, other arguments had to be found when the ecotoxicological, technical and economic studies had been completed for virtually all 129 substances on the 1982 list, plus three others which were subsequently added.

Shortly following the adoption of the list of 129 substances, the group of national experts, at its meeting in October 1982, noting that it was impossible to study all 129 substances simultaneously, had selected a series

[206] Commission Communication of 22 June 1982, p 7, no 4.

[207] Communication from the Commission to the Council concerning the preparation of directives with respect to arsenic within the framework of Council Dir 76/464/EEC, EC Doc COM(83) 306 final, 2 June 1983, para 7.

[208] *Ibid*, para 3.

[209] *Ibid*, paras 5–6.

[210] *Ibid*, para 8.

of 11 substances from the list to be examined as a matter of priority.[211] This 'shortlist' had been endorsed by the Council in its resolution of 7 February 1983 as requiring 'special attention.'[212] Though the required studies have long been completed for all 11 substances and opinions of the Scientific Advisory Committee are available for most of them,[213] the Commission did not submit a proposal for limit values and quality objectives to the Council for a single one of these substances. When questioned about this in the European Parliament, the Commission admitted that when the 11 substances listed in the 1983 Council resolution 'were examined by the national experts . . . *none of them were found to have absolute priority*, with the exception of parathion.'[214] In other words, the national experts, who had first identified these substances as being of priority concern, had later changed their minds. The Commission does not explain *why*; it does not claim that the results of the ecotoxicological studies have indicated that these substances do *not* qualify for inclusion in the black list; and it has not submitted any formal communication to the Council explaining the reasons for its inaction.

The group of national experts subsequently became embroiled in a new discussion on 'priorities' as a result of differences over the criteria for selection of black list substances which became evident in the British opposition to the inclusion of carbon tetrachloride and chloroform in List I. The United Kingdom only accepted the fixing of limit values and quality objectives for carbon tetrachloride in Directive 86/280/EEC as a compromise, subject to the inclusion of a formal statement in the Council minutes urging the Commission to 'give priority to substances which are likely to be present in Community waters at levels which cause particularly important environmental problems' in submitting future proposals to the Council.[215] Britain continued to oppose the setting of Community standards for chloroform until 1988 and eventually dropped its opposition only on the understanding that a new priority list of substances would be agreed as a basis for further regulatory proposals.[216]

When it reached agreement on Directive 88/347/EEC, which lays down limit values and quality objectives inter alia for chloroform, at its meeting

[211] Dekker (1983), p 276, Table I.

[212] Council Resolution of 7 Feb 1983 concerning the combating of water pollution, OJ No C46, 17.2.1983, p 17.

[213] See, eg the opinions published in Commission of the European Communities, *Scientific Advisory Committee to examine the toxicity and ecotoxicity of chemical compounds—Activity Report 1984–88*, Report EUR 12964 EN, Luxembourg, 1990, pp 67–198; *id., Scientific Advisory Committee to examine the toxicity and ecotoxicity of chemical compounds—Activity Report 1992–93*, Report EUR 15674 EN, Luxembourg, 1993, pp 15–65.

[214] Answer by the Commission to Written Question No 1492/91, OJ No C89, 9.4.1992, p 10 (emphasis added).

[215] Haigh (1990), p 111.

[216] Interview with former Commission official, 20 Jan 1992.

in March 1988, the Council formally requested the Commission to prepare a new list of priority substances.[217] A list of 20 priority substances was 'unanimously agreed' by the group of national experts in June 1988.[218] Four substances were removed from the list in 1989, two due to 'insufficient ecotoxicological evidence' and two others in view of the fact that they were already included in a Commission proposal which was under discussion in Council.[219] The resulting list of 16 substances was given official status by the Commission in a proposal submitted to the Council in March 1990, which provided that they 'will be considered on a priority basis for the purpose of fixing limit values and quality objectives.'[220]

It is noteworthy that only one substance from the priority list agreed by the national experts in 1982 and endorsed by the Council in 1983 (parathion) also occurs on the new priority list proposed to the Council in 1990. While it is true that the earlier list, unlike the latter one, was drawn up *prior* to the completion of detailed ecotoxicological studies, the fact that the Commission and the national experts' perception of 'priorities' had changed so radically since 1983 suggests that these shifting 'priorities' are probably due as much to opportunistic political motives as to factual reasons. It is certainly no coincidence that most of the substances on the new priority list are also on the United Kingdom's 'Red List', a national priority list of hazardous substances whose emissions are to be reduced, drawn up in response to the recommendations of the London North Sea Conference as an alternative to the EEC list of 129 substances. Another striking feature of the new priority list of 16 substances is that most of these substances are pesticides, whose input into the aquatic environment principally originates from *diffuse sources* and whose emissions cannot adequately be regulated within the framework of Directive 76/464/EEC, a legal instument primarily designed to control emissions from industrial *point sources*. Thus, the implementation of Directive 76/464/EEC was put on another 'dead end' track.

As the foregoing analysis has shown, the 'pre-legislative' procedure involving the selection of substances, research, informal consultations with national experts, and the elaboration of regulatory proposals already takes several years before the Commission is able to formally submit any proposal for a directive establishing limit values and quality objectives for a particular black list substance to the Council. The Council, in turn, will typically take another few years to reach a decision on the Commission proposal.

[217] EC Doc XI/651/88, Explanatory memorandum, p 3.

[218] *Ibid.*

[219] *Ibid.* The Commission proposal referred to was eventually adopted as Dir 90/415/EEC.

[220] Proposal for a Council Directive amending Dir 76/464/EEC on pollution caused by certain dangerous substances discharged into the aquatic environment of the Community, OJ No C55, 7.3.1990, p 7, Art 2.

The slow decision-making process in the Council can be explained by a variety of factors. The first was obviously the requirement of unanimity laid down in Article 12, paragraph 1 of Directive 76/464/EEC and in the EEC Treaty itself, before its amendment by the SEA. Another factor is that the technical-scientific discussion conducted in the group of national experts may 'spill over' into the Council negotiations, especially when no agreement was reached at the earlier stage. The national experts who participated in informal consultations with the Commission often also take part in formal negotiations as members of their country's delegation in the Council's Environment Working Party. However, this does not necessarily guarantee consistency in national positions. The fact that consensus was reached on a certain substance in the group of national experts does not automatically mean that unanimity will also easily be achieved within the Council. It sometimes occurs that a member state takes a position during the formal negotiations different from that taken by its national expert during the informal consultations.[221]

Finally, the basic differences in regulatory philosophy which were allowed to co-exist side by side in Directive 76/464/EEC continued to plague the implementation process as proponents of the EQO and UES approach again clashed in the Council negotiations over implementing measures for specific substances.[222] A number of efforts were made by the Commission to attempt to solve these problems and speed up the implementation process of Directive 76/464/EEC. The first of these efforts was the codification of a number of general provisions applicable to limit values and quality objectives for all black list substances, so that these provisions would not have to be renegotiated for each individual daughter directive. The second Commission initiative, more fundamental in nature but unsuccessful, was a proposal to remove the requirement of unanimity. Both are discussed below.

THE 'DAUGHTER DIRECTIVES' OF DIRECTIVE 76/464/EEC

Directive 86/280/EEC: the General Application Directive

In order to avoid covering the same ground time and time again, the Council, 10 years after adopting Directive 76/464/EEC, in 1986 agreed on a 'general application directive' which lays down the basic legal provisions applying to all List I substances and provides for specific limit values and quality objectives to be laid down in the form of

221 Interview with former Commission official, 20 Jan 1992.

222 See Guruswamy, Papps & Storey (1983), pp 71–100, for a discussion of this problem in the negotiation of Dir 82/176/EEC.

technical annexes.[223] In its preamble, the directive reiterates the objectives of Directive 76/464/EEC, by stressing that:

> the purpose of the limit values and quality objectives is to eliminate pollution of the various parts of the aquatic environment which might be affected by discharges of these substances.[224]

This is not insignificant, especially in view of the opinion expressed by the European Parliament, which, apparently influenced by industry lobbyists, had called upon the Commission to reformulate the purpose of quality objectives as 'to limit pollution . . . *wherever this is technically and economically feasible*.'[225]

The general application directive lays down a number of general provisions relating to technical definitions, application of emission standards and quality standards and monitoring requirements. In doing so it establishes a legal framework for the implementation of certain provisions of Directive 76/464/EEC. However, it also supplements the provisions of the framework directive in some respects. Directive 86/280/EEC introduces a general requirement to use the 'best technical means available' in any new plants 'when that is necessary for the elimination of pollution in accordance with Article 2' of Directive 76/464/EEC 'or for the prevention of distortions of competition.'[226] In this provision, the regulatory philosophy underlying the emission standards approach seems to have prevailed, though the formulation leaves some room for proponents of the quality objectives approach to argue that the use of the best available technology is not 'necessary for the elimination of pollution', in that the emissions of the plant in question have not been shown to cause harm to the aquatic environment. Indeed, the same provision explicitly envisages the possibility 'where for technical reasons the measures envisaged do not correspond to the best technical means available', in which case the member state shall inform the Commission prior to granting an authorisation for the plant.

Another innovative feature of the Directive is that it requires member states to eliminate pollution by black list substances by regulating all sources of pollutants, not just point sources as provided in Directive 76/464/EEC. Thus, as the Court of Justice has noted, Directive 86/280/EEC does more than simply implementing Directive 76/464/EEC; it 'also contains rules not provided for in that directive.'[227] Indeed, with respect to all

[223] Council Dir 86/280/EEC of 12 June 1986 on limit values and quality objectives for discharges of certain dangerous substances included in List I of the Annex to Dir 76/464/EEC, OJ No L181, 1986, p 16 (hereafter referred to as Dir 86/280/EEC).

[224] *Ibid*, 10th preambular para.

[225] OJ C120, 20.5.1986, p 164 (emphasis added).

[226] Dir 86/280/EEC, Art 3, para 4.

[227] Case C–232/97, *L. Nederhoff & Zn. v Dijkgraaf en hoogheemraden van het Hoogheemraadschap Rijnland*, [1999] ECR I–6385, para 9.

black list substances for which emission limit values and quality objectives are set under Directive 86/280/EEC, Article 5 prescribes that:

> Member States shall draw up specific programmes to avoid or eliminate pollution from significant sources of these substances (including multiple and diffuse sources) other than sources of discharges subject to Community limit value rules or national emission standards.

The sources subject to 'national emission standards' are industrial point sources other than those for which limit values have been established. The directive clarifies the status of those sources by providing that 'Member States will independently set, in accordance with Directive 76/464/EEC, emission standards' for such discharges.[228] This provision makes clear that the provisions of Articles 3 and 5 of Directive 76/464/EEC apply to all industrial discharges of black list substances, including those discharges for which specific Community limit values have not been established. Even in the absence of such limit values, Article 3 requires member states to 'lay down emission standards' when authorising such discharges.[229]

The directive further provides a number of criteria to guide member states in the setting of national emission standards: 'Such standards must take into account the best technical means available and must not be less stringent than the most nearly comparable limit value.'[230] Though there can be some discussion as to whether there really is such a thing as 'the most nearly comparable limit value' when comparing two completely different production processes, this is probably intended to provide a point of reference in order of magnitude only.

The provisions of Article 5 of Directive 86/280/EEC on 'multiple and diffuse sources' fill a regulatory gap left by the prior authorisation system of Directive 76/464/EEC. By its very nature, this system can only be applied where the emission of hazardous substances can be traced to an identifiable person. The 1986 Directive therefore introduces a complementary scheme of 'specific programmes' which covers 'cases where the pollution, precisely because of its diffuse nature, cannot be attributed to a person and therefore cannot be the subject of prior authorisation.'[231] Thus, as the Court of Justice has observed, 'Community law has established two distinct systems for combating pollution of surface water by dangerous substances', which apply to the exclusion of each other.[232]

[228] Dir 86/280/EEC, Annex I, Heading A, para 3.

[229] The ambiguity of Dir 76/464/EEC in this respect had been duly noted by Dekker, who already suggested in 1983 that the relevant provisions of the directive should be interpreted as applying to all discharges of black list substances, including those from sectors for which no Community limit values have been set. Dekker (1983), p 275.

[230] Dir 86/280/EEC, Annex I, Heading A, para 3.

[231] Case C–232/97, *L. Nederhoff & Zn. v Dijkgraaf en hoogheemraden van het Hoogheemraadschap Rijnland*, [1999] ECR I–6385, para 40.

[232] *Ibid*, para 42.

Daughter Directives for Selected Black List Substances

The first implementing directive of Directive 76/464/EEC relates to mercury discharges from the chlor-alkali electrolysis industry.[233] It took three years for the Council to reach agreement on the proposal submitted by the Commission. The negotiations were again marked by controversy over the ultimate objective of the measures with respect to black list substances and the means of achieving them. The preamble of the directive reiterates that 'the purpose of . . . quality objectives must be to eliminate mercury pollution of the various parts of the aquatic environment which might be affected'. Yet for all its rhetorical emphasis on the ultimate objective of eliminating pollution, the actual provisions of the directive relating both to quality objectives and limit values fall short of achieving that objective. As some observers note, 'despite the claim of the preamble . . . , there remains considerable uncertainty as to whether the actual provisions of the Mercury Directive create such a legal regime' aimed at eliminating mercury pollution.[234]

Directive 82/176/EEC lays down different environmental quality objectives for mercury expressed in terms of mercury concentrations in water and fish flesh. It is up to the member state concerned to select the quality objective which it 'deems appropriate having regard to the intended use of the area affected' and demonstrate that it is complied with. As one British author put it, it would thus be possible for the competent authority to select an 'EQO for fish, knowing full well that this could be satisfied as no fish ever ventured into that stretch of water.'[235] Indeed, the UK opposed the formulation of EQOs for mercury concentrations in water and sediment, arguing that it would be unnecessary and costly to monitor mercury concentrations in those segments of the environment,[236] since 'fish are a very effective "sampler" of mercury in the water and a reliable indicator of the condition of the water', to quote the words of a British minister addressing the House of Lords during the negotiations on Directive 82/176/EEC.[237] The compromise reached in the Council was to fix EQOs for all relevant components of the aquatic environment but to leave member states free to choose from this 'menu' those EQOs which they 'deem appropriate'.

All of the quality objectives laid down in the directive in practice tolerate the presence of some level of mercury in the aquatic environment. Nevertheless the directive's provisions with respect to quality objectives

[233] Council Dir 82/176/EEC of 22 Mar 1982 on limit values and quality objectives for mercury discharges by the chlor-alkali electrolysis industry, OJ No L 81, 27.3.1982, p 29 (hereafter referred to as Dir 82/176/EEC).

[234] Guruswamy, Papps & Storey (1983), p 94.

[235] Guruswamy (1982), p 632.

[236] *Ibid*, pp 622–23.

[237] Statement by Lord Mowbray and Stourton, 17 Apr 1980, quoted by Guruswamy (1982), p 623.

stress that the objectives are set 'in order to eliminate pollution as defined in Directive 76/464/EEC, and pursuant to Article 2 of that Directive' and require member states, when selecting quality objectives, to take 'account of the fact that the purpose of this Directive is to eliminate all pollution'. It is as though the Council had sought to conceal with symbolic rhetoric the fact that the directive, far from eliminating mercury pollution, actually legimates it.

The reference to the definition of 'pollution' in Directive 76/464/EEC and to Article 2 of that directive is open to a variety of interpretations. The intent of the drafters may have been to stress that, under Directive 76/464/EEC, pollution need only be 'eliminated' in so far as it causes 'harm', which is how 'pollution' is defined in Article 1 of the Directive. The reference to Article 2 may be intended to imply that the application of the quality objectives for mercury laid down in Directive 82/176/EEC constitutes the full measure of the member states' obligations with respect to pollution by mercury. Compliance with those quality objectives would thus be equated with full compliance with Article 2 of Directive 76/464/EEC. On the other hand, the explicit reference to the 'fact that the purpose of this Directive is to eliminate all pollution' may be intended to emphasise that the quality objectives approach does not detract from the ultimate objective of Directive 76/464/EEC although the actual application of the mercury directive itself falls far short of achieving that objective of eliminating *all* pollution.

This applies not only to the quality objectives, but also to the limit values established by the directive. The directive provides that the emission standards shall be strengthened after a number of years. However, while the application of those stricter emission standards may lead to a reduction of mercury discharges, no further progress towards the eventual elimination of discharges is provided for. The directive implicitly tolerates the level of mercury pollution corresponding to what is defined as 'best available' technology.

In the 25 years that have elapsed since the adoption of Directive 76/464/EEC, the Council has succeeded in adopting limit values and quality objectives only for a very limited number of black list substances. In all, no more than six daughter directives have been approved by the Council, setting standards for only 17 different chemical substances belonging to List I. At this average speed of implementation it would take 150 years for the Council to set standards for the 129 black list substances identified by the Commission.[238] Even for those few substances for which standards have

[238] The slow pace of implementation of Dir 76/464/EEC was criticised by the Court of Auditors in a 1992 special report on Community environment policy. OJ No C245, 23.9.1992, p 18, para 4.11. According to one senior Commission official, too, 'the result is not impressive'. This same author wonders 'whether a total prohibition to discharge all the 129 substances . . . into water would not have been more efficient, with possibilities for derogation where no alternative for elimination on land existed.' Krämer (1989), p 5.

been set, the Community regulatory measures are far from comprehensive, since they apply only to a limited number of industrial sectors, which are not necessarily the most important sources of water pollution by the substance in question. Thus, it appears that the effectiveness of Community environmental law in achieving its stated objective to eliminate pollution by black list substances is virtually nil.

For example, Directive 83/513/EEC, the directive setting limit values and quality objectives for discharges of cadmium, does not apply to the most important industrial source of cadmium pollution of the aquatic environment in the Community, the phosphate industry. A footnote to Annex I of this directive simply notes that 'at present there are no economically feasible technical methods for systematically extracting cadmium' from the phosphate industry's effluents and that no Community limit values can therefore be fixed for such discharges. Any measures to limit cadmium discharges from this sector are left entirely at the discretion of individual member states, which, as the note recalls, have an 'obligation under Directive 76/464/EEC to fix emission standards for these discharges.'[239] Another footnote recognises that, apart from the phosphate industry, there are other industrial sectors discharging cadmium for which no limit values are set by the Directive. It is provided that such limit values shall 'if necessary' be fixed by the Council at a later date and that, meanwhile, member states shall set cadmium emission standards for these industries 'autonomously in accordance with Directive 76/464/EEC.'[240]

The scope of application of the measures prescribed by other daughter directives of 76/464/EEC is also often extremely limited. Sometimes the limit values established by those directives apply only to a handful of production units within the Community. This is the case for the directives setting standards for discharges of DDT, pentachlorophenol (PCP) and dieldrin, aldrin and endrin. The limit values for DDT apply only to plants producing and formulating DDT on the same site.[241] According to the Commission's explanatory memorandum, there were only two such plants in the entire Community at the time of the proposal, and they were responsible for only some 10 per cent of DDT discharges into the aquatic environment. More than 90 per cent of the discharges originate from DDT formulation plants, which are more numerous but for which the directive sets no limit values.[242]

[239] Council Dir 83/513/EEC of 26 Sept 1983 on limit values and quality objectives for cadmium discharges, OJ No L291, 24.10.1983, Annex I, note 6. It is difficult to understand why the absence of 'economically feasible technical methods' should prevent the Council from fixing Community limit values, whereas, in the Council's view, it should not actually prevent member states from fixing national emission standards for the very same cadmium discharges from the phosphate industry.

[240] *Ibid*, n 1.

[241] Dir 86/280/EEC, Annex II, item II, Heading A(46).

[242] EC Doc COM(84) 772 final, 17 Jan 1985, p 22, para 3.2.2.5.

The limit values for PCP discharges[243] apply to a type of industrial plant of which there appears to be only one in the EEC.[244] As for the 'drins', Directive 88/347/EEC establishes limit values for the single plant in the Community producing these persistent insecticides[245] but sets no standards for emissions from the textile industry, which uses them as a mothproofing agent and is responsible for 95 per cent of their total discharge into the aquatic environment.[246] The Commission was quite aware of the importance of the discharges from this sector and had included relevant limit values in its original proposal to the Council.[247]

The Problem of Diffuse Sources

On the whole, the Community has made only haphazard efforts to deal with other than industrial point sources of pollution by black list substances. The Commission has been aware of the need to regulate what it variously described as 'indirect discharges', 'multiple sources' or 'diffuse sources' of pollution from the beginning, but the Council has been extremely hesitant to follow suit. In its first proposal for a daughter directive relating to mercury, the Commission recognised that measures would be required not only to control mercury discharges from the chlor-alkali electrolysis industry, but also to address what it termed 'indirect discharges' from other sources. It therefore included in its proposal a provision requiring member states to establish 'programmes for the gradual reduction' of such 'indirect discharges.'[248] This provision was rejected by the Council, which chose to limit the scope of the directive strictly to the chlor-alkali electrolysis industry, while awaiting further proposals from the Commission before dealing with other sources.

The Commission subsequently proposed another directive relating to mercury discharges from sectors other than the chlor-alkali electrolysis industry, which would set emission standards for other major industrial point sources of mercury, while requiring member states to draw up

243 Dir 86/280/EEC, Annex II, item III, Heading A(102).

244 EC Doc COM(84) 772 final, 17 Jan 1985, p 24, para 3.2.3.2.

245 Council Dir 88/347/EEC of 16 June 1988 amending Annex II to Dir 86/280/EEC, OJ No L158, 25.6.1988, p 35, Art 1, item IV.

246 Johnson & Corcelle (1990), p 76.

247 OJ No C146, 12.6.1979, p 5. It is worth noting that in this proposal, the first proposal for a daughter directive submitted to the Council pursuant to Dir 76/464/EEC, the Commission, more faithful to the stated intent of Dir 76/464/EEC of 'eliminating' pollution by black list substances than in later proposals, proposed that a *zero emission level* should apply to any new plant producing 'drins' or using them as a mothproofing agent.

248 Commission proposal for a Council directive on the limit values applicable to discharges of mercury into the aquatic environment by the chlor-alkali electrolysis industry, OJ No C169, 6.7.1979, p 2, Art 4.

'specific programmes for the gradual elimination of certain discharges of mercury into the public sewerage system.'[249] In Directive 84/156/EEC, which it adopted as a result of this proposal, the Council included a more general provision which endorsed the concept of 'specific programmes' to deal with 'mercury discharges by multiple sources which are not industrial plants and for which the emission standards . . . cannot be applied in practice.' It is specified that 'the purpose of these programmes shall be to avoid or eliminate pollution' through measures for the 'replacement, retention and recycling of mercury.'[250]

This provision on discharges of mercury by 'multiple sources' is rather an exception in terms of the early daughter directives of Directive 76/464/EEC. Until the adoption of Directive 86/280/EEC, Directive 84/156/EEC was the only daughter directive to contain such a provision. Neither the cadmium directive[251] nor the HCH directive[252] requires any measures to deal with indirect discharges, though diffuse sources contribute significantly to pollution of the aquatic environment by both substances. It was only in 1986 that the Council agreed that 'specific programmes' were required to 'avoid or eliminate' pollution from 'multiple or diffuse sources' of all black list substances.[253]

Since the introduction of a general provision on diffuse sources by Directive 86/280/EEC, the Council has paid more attention to this question. In Directive 90/415/EEC, which regulates emissions of four chlorinated organic solvents,[254] several references are made to Article 5 of Directive 86/280/EEC, the provision laying down the general obligations of member states with respect to emissions of black list substances from diffuse sources.

[249] Commission proposal for a Council Directive on limit values and quality objectives for mercury discharges by sectors other than the chlor-alkali electrolysis industry, OJ No C20, 25.1.1983, p 5, Art 4, para 1.

[250] Council Dir 84/156/EEC of 8 March 1984 on limit values and quality objectives for mercury discharges by sectors other than the chlor-alkali electrolysis industry, OJ No L74, 17.3.1984, Art 4.

[251] Council Dir 83/513/EEC of 26 Sept 1983 on limit values and quality objectives for cadmium discharges, OJ No L291, 24.10.1983.

[252] Council Dir 84/491/EEC of 9 Oct 1984 on limit values and quality objectives for discharges of hexachlorocyclohexane, OJ No L274, 17.10.1984. The Commission was aware of the importance of indirect emissions resulting from the use of lindane in agriculture and the timber industry, but did not consider it necessary to propose specific measures for these emissions. See the explanatory memorandum of the Proposal for a Council Directive on limit values and quality objectives for discharges of hexachlorocyclohexane, and in particular lindane, EC Doc COM(83) 422 final, 7 July 1983, p 14, para 5.

[253] Dir 86/280/EEC, Art 5, para 1. In 1998, Portugal was condemned by the Court of Justice for having failed, inter alia, to establish such specific programmes. Case C-213/97, *Commission v Portuguese Republic*, [1998] ECR I-3289.

[254] Council Dir 90/415/EEC of 27 July 1990 amending Annex II to Dir 86/280/EEC on limit values and quality objectives for discharges of certain dangerous substances included in list I of the Annex to Dir 76/464/EEC, OJ No L219, 14.8.1990, p 49 (hereafter referred to as Dir 90/415/EEC).

In fact, the Council agreed to treat small point sources of certain solvents as diffuse sources for the purposes of the application of Community law. The preamble of this directive states that 'it is appropriate that small discharges *which are subject to the provisions of Article 5 of Directive 86/280/EEC* may be exempted from the requirements of Article 3 of Directive 76/464/EEC,'[255] which requires an authorisation laying down emission standards for each individual discharge.

It is specified in the annex that certain small-scale industrial applications of 1,2-dichloroethane, trichloroethylene and perchloroethylene, causing annual discharges of less than 30 kg/year, 'may be exempted from the requirements of Article 3 of Directive 76/464/EEC' but will be subject instead to the provisions of Article 5 of Directive 86/280/EEC.[256] In effect, this provision amounts to an implicit amendment of Article 3 of Directive 76/464/EEC, which in principle requires any direct discharge of a black list substance, however small, to be covered by a 'prior authorisation' whenever it is 'attributable to a person.'[257] Even when no Community limit values have been established for the sector concerned, member states must lay down national emission standards.[258] However, Directive 90/415/EEC indicates that member states consider this emission control method to be rather inappropriate for small point sources and prefer the regime of Article 5 of Directive 86/280/EEC, which leaves them full discretion as to the measures to be applied. This approach is inconsistent with the provisions of Article 5 of the 1986 Directive as subsequently interpreted by the Court of Justice, which has held that this particular regime applies exclusively to diffuse sources proper, ie to 'cases where the pollution . . . *cannot* be attributed to a person and therefore *cannot* be the subject of prior authorisation.'[259]

Neither the administrative authorisation system of Directive 76/464/EEC nor the vague provisions on 'specific programmes' of Directive 86/280/EEC seem fully adequate to deal with large-scale pollution of surface waters by hazardous substances from diffuse sources. The instrument of *product control* measures, directly addressing the marketing and use of substances themselves is potentially much more effective. This instrument has occasionally been used by the Community legislator for this purpose. The legal framework for such product control measures is Directive 76/769/EEC,[260]

[255] Dir 90/415/EEC, 10th preambular para (emphasis added).

[256] *Ibid*, Annex, para 2, items VIII, IX and X.

[257] Case C–232/97, *L. Nederhoff & Zn. v Dijkgraaf en hoogheemraden van het Hoogheemraadschap Rijnland*, [1999] ECR I–6385, para 37.

[258] This is actually confirmed by the wording of Art 5, para 1 of Dir 86/280/EEC itself.

[259] Case C–232/97, para 40 (emphasis added).

[260] Council Dir 76/769/EEC of 27 July 1976 on the approximation of the laws, regulations and administrative provisions of the Member States relating to restrictions on the marketing and use of certain dangerous substances and preparations, OJ No L 262, 27.9.1976, p 201.

which serves to harmonise restrictions on the marketing and use of certain dangerous substances and preparations in the internal market. This Directive was initially adopted to implement an OECD decision on the prohibition of the use of PCBs and PCTs in the European Community and was later frequently amended to make additional toxic substances or products subject to harmonised regulatory controls. Most of the product control measures taken within the framework of Directive 76/769/EEC are primarily aimed at the protection of users and consumers and are based on human health grounds, but some of them are taken for environmental reasons, including the control of water pollution. According to its preamble, the Directive is designed, inter alia, to 'contribute to the protection of the environment from all substances and preparations which have characteristics of ecotoxicity or which could pollute the environment'. It requires member states to 'take all necessary measures to ensure that the dangerous substances and preparations listed in [its] Annex may only be placed on the market or used subject to the conditions specified therein.'[261] The Annex was amended several times to impose restrictions on the marketing and use of substances and products contributing to the pollution of the aquatic environment, such as anti-fouling paints for ships and underwater equipment containing mercury, arsenic and organic tin compounds,[262] the biocide pentachlorophenol (PCP),[263] several PCB substitutes which were found to be persistent, bio-accumulative and ecotoxic,[264] and a number of chlorinated organic solvents.[265] The measures concerning PCP and some chlorinated solvents are in fact complementary to measures taken within the framework of Directive 76/464/EEC with respect to point source emissions of the same substances. Some other measures under Directive 76/769/EEC directly restrict the use of certain hazardous substances in industrial processes, such as the use of cadmium as a stabilizer in the manufacture of PVC products

[261] Council Dir 76/769/EEC of 27 July 1976, Art 2.

[262] Council Dir 89/677/EEC of 21 Dec 1989 amending for the eighth time Dir 76/769/EEC on the approximation of the laws, regulations and administrative provisions of the member states relating to restrictions on the marketing and use of certain dangerous substances and preparations, OJ No L 398, 30.12.1989, p 19.

[263] Council Dir 91/173/EEC of 21 Mar 1991 amending for the ninth time Dir 76/769/EEC on the approximation of the laws, regulations and administrative provisions of the Member States relating to restrictions on the marketing and use of certain dangerous substances and preparations, OJ No L 85, 5.4.1991, p 34. The restrictions on PCP were tightened by Commission Dir 1999/51/EC of 26 May 1999, OJ No L142, 5.6.1999, p 22.

[264] Council Dir 91/339/EEC of 18 June 1991 amending for the 11th time Dir 76/769/EEC on the approximation of the laws, regulations and administrative provisions of the Member States relating to restrictions on the marketing and use of certain dangerous substances and preparations, OJ No L186, 12.7.1991, p 64.

[265] Commission Dir 96/55/EC of 4 Sept 1996 adapting to technical progress for the 2nd time Annex I to Council Dir 76/769/EEC on the approximation of the laws, regulations and administrative provisions of the Member States relating to restrictions on the marketing and use of certain dangerous substances and preparations (chlorinated solvents), OJ No L231, 12.9.1996, p 20.

or for the coating of metallic products,[266] and the use of hexachloroethane (HCE) as a degasifier in the non-ferrous metal industry.[267]

The Concept of 'Best Technical Means Available'

Ever since the adoption of Directive 76/464/EEC, the Council has had a rather equivocal attitude with respect to the application of the concept of 'best technical means available', which, the directive provides, are to be 'taken into account' by the Council when fixing limit values for emission standards pursuant to Article 6, paragraph 1. This concept is nowhere defined in Directive 76/464/EEC. It appears, however, from the Council's subsequent practice with respect to the adoption of limit values, that the Council has applied this notion in a rather flexible way. First of all, it should be noted that the concept of 'best technical means available' was qualified by a statement of the Commission recorded in the minutes of the Council meeting of 4 May 1976, at which Directive 76/464/EEC was adopted. According to a former Commission official: 'The Commission stated that the concept of "the best technical means available" took into account the economic availability of those means.'[268]

Moreover, the provision of Directive 76/464/EEC referring to the 'best technical means available' is somewhat ambiguous. Strictly speaking, Article 6, paragraph 1 of the directive does not require that limit values fixed by the Council actually be based on the 'best technical means available' for reducing emissions of black list substances—that is, that the Council only establish limit values corresponding to state-of-the-art technology. It just requires the 'best technical means available' to be 'taken into account', which is not necessarily the same thing.

There are indications in several daughter directives of 76/464/EEC that the limit values laid down by the Council do *not* actually reflect the 'best technical means available'. When adopting Directive 82/176/EEC, the Council resorted to an unusual quasi-legislative technique to specify the meaning of the term 'best technical means available' used in Article 3, paragraph 3 of that directive, with the manifest intent of avoiding the legal consequences of including a definition of the term in a provision of the directive itself. A published 'statement' is appended to the directive according to which

266 Council Dir 91/338/EEC of 18 June 1991 amending for the 10th time Dir 76/769/EEC on the approximation of the laws, regulations and administrative provisions of the Member States relating to restrictions on the marketing and use of certain dangerous substances and preparations, OJ No L186, 12.7.1991, p 59.

267 Dir 97/16/EC of the European Parliament and of the Council of 10 Apr 1997 amending for the 15th time Dir 76/769/EEC on restrictions on the marketing and use of certain dangerous substances and preparations, OJ No L 116 , 6.5.1997, p 31.

268 Johnson (1983), p 57.

the Council and the Commission state that the application of the best technical means available makes it possible to limit discharges of mercury from the site of a new industrial plant using the recycled-brine process to *less* than

the limit value laid down in Annex I of the directive for plants using this process.[269] This statement implicitly recognises that the limit value fixed by the directive is not as stringent as technically possible.

Similarly, Directive 88/347/EEC, contains a footnote which states that 'the use of best technical means *already makes it possible to apply in some cases much more stringent values*' for emissions of hexachlorobenzene and hexachlorobutadiene than those laid down in the directive.[270] For this reason the footnote further provides that the Council shall fix 'more stringent limit values' before 1995. The acknowledgement that '*much* more stringent' limit values are already technically possible may well be taken as a straight admission that the Council did not duly 'take into account' the 'best technical means available' when adopting Directive 88/347/EEC, as it was required to do according to the provisions of Directive 76/464/EEC.[271]

The application of the concept of 'best technical means available' is clearly most controversial with respect to new plants. The Commission has consistently proposed that the daughter directives contain a provision requiring any new plants to use the 'best technical means available'. The Council, however, has been reluctant to include in the daughter directives unambiguous provisions to this effect. The first mercury directive, Directive 82/176/EEC, provides that:

Member States may grant authorisations for new plants only if such authorisations *contain a reference to* the standards corresponding to the best technical means available.[272]

The effectiveness of this provision is hampered not only by the lack of any definition of 'best technical means available,'[273] but also by its ambiguous wording: the directive does not actually say that the authorisations shall *impose* the use of the best technical means for new plants, but only that they shall 'contain a reference' to the corresponding emission standards.

As some British authors have noted:

It could be argued that a mere 'reference' to the best technical means in any instrument of authorisation *may constitute a recommendation but certainly not an obligation* to comply with those standards.[274]

[269] Statement on Article 3 (3), OJ No L81, 27.3.1982, p 34 (emphasis added).
[270] Dir 88/347/EEC, Art 1, para 2, item V, heading A(83), n 3 and item VI, heading A(84), n 3 (emphasis added).
[271] See also Dir 86/280/EEC, Annex II, item II, heading A(46), n 1.
[272] Dir 82/176/EEC, Art 3, para 3 (emphasis added).
[273] This is notwithstanding the 'Statement on Article 3(3)' discussed above.
[274] Guruswamy, Papps & Storey (1983), p 97 (emphasis added).

As a matter of fact, the directive also contains an explicit escape clause permitting member states to derogate from the use of the 'best technical means available':

> Whatever the method it adopts, the Member State, where for technical reasons the intended measures *do not conform to the best technical means available*, shall provide the Commission, before any authorisation, with the justifications for these reasons.[275]

It should be noted that such derogations are not made subject to the *consent* of the Commission, which is only called upon to give its 'opinion' in a report to the member states.[276] The escape clause gives virtually unfettered discretion to the member states in determining emission standards for new plants. It is quite likely that proponents of the quality objectives approach would invoke 'technical reasons' to derogate from the application of the 'best technical means available.'[277]

In subsequent daughter directives, the intentional ambiguity surrounding the application of the 'best technical means' is perpetuated through other means. In the cadmium directive, the relevant provision has been reworded to stipulate that authorisations for new plants may be granted:

> only if those plants *apply the standards corresponding to* the best technical means available *when that is necessary for the elimination of pollution* in accordance with Article 2 of [Directive 76/464/EEC] *or for the prevention of distortion of competition.*[278]

The same provision has been included in all subsequent daughter directives[279] and 'codified' in the general application directive of 1986.[280]

So, while the member states' obligation with respect to emission standards for new plants has been formulated more precisely to the effect that the best technical means available shall not merely be 'referred to' in the authorisation but actually 'applied' in such plants, the obligation is at the same time substantially qualified by the addition of the proviso 'when that is necessary.' This convoluted formulation performs the same artful balancing act between policies based on emission standards and quality standards as the provision instituting the 'parallel approach' in Directive 76/464/EEC.

Member states favouring the quality objectives approach will no doubt argue that the application of the best technical means by new plants is not 'necessary for the elimination of pollution' within the meaning of Article 2

[275] Dir 82/176/EEC, Art 3, para 3 (emphasis added).
[276] *Ibid.*
[277] Thus Guruswamy, Papps & Storey (1983), p 98.
[278] Dir 83/513/EEC, Art 3, para 4 (emphasis added).
[279] Dir 84/156/EEC, Art 3, para 4; Dir 84/491/EEC, Art 3, para 4.
[280] Dir 86/280/EEC, Art 3, para 4.

of Directive 76/464/EEC when pollution originating from a new plant does not result in an infringement of the applicable water quality standards. Proponents of the uniform emission standards approach may, in turn, attempt to counter that assertion with the argument that application of the best technical means by new plants wherever located is necessary 'for the prevention of distortions of competition.' The wording of the provision deliberately leaves room for both interpretations without deciding the issue either way. It would be most interesting to see how the Court of Justice would interpret this language, but it is to be doubted that it will ever have an opportunity to do so.

Both the Council and the Commission recognise that the concept of 'best technical means available' is an evolving one. Most daughter directives provide for a phased reduction in emissions by setting two series of limit values to be applied by successive deadlines.[281] However, as pointed out above, the lowest limit value, to be achieved in the second stage, does not necessarily correspond to what is technically feasible. Nevertheless the Council seems eager to convey the image of progressive regulation evolving in tune with technological development towards gradual reduction and eventual elimination of pollution. Indeed, all daughter directives contain a standard clause providing for adaptation of their provisions to technical and scientific progress.

The first such clause is to be found in Directive 82/176/EEC. It stipulates that 'in the event of a change in scientific knowledge' or 'in the event of an improvement in the best technical means available' the Commission shall 'submit appropriate proposals to the Council with the aim of *reinforcing, if necessary*, the limit values and the quality objectives.'[282] The same provision, with minor changes in wording,[283] can be found in subsequent directives and is 'codified' in the general application directive, which speaks of 'the aim of making the limit values and the quality objectives *more stringent*, *if appropriate*, or of establishing *new limit values and additional quality objectives*.'[284]

The wording of these provisions leaves ample room for political discretion both for the Commission and the Council in deciding whether strength-

[281] This is the case for mercury (Dir 82/176/EEC, Annex I; Dir 84/156/EEC, Annex I), cadmium (Dir 83/513/EEC, Annex I), HCH (Dir 84/491/EEC, Annex I), and DDT (Dir 86/280/EEC, Annex II, item II, heading A(46)), but not for carbon tetrachloride (Dir 86/280/EEC, Annex II, item I, heading A(13)), PCP (Dir 86/280/EEC, Annex II, item III, heading A(102)), drins, hexachlorobenzene, hexachlorobutadiene and chloroform (Dir 88/347/EEC, Art 1, para 2). In some of these cases the Commission had actually proposed two series of limit values, but was not followed by the Council. (See for carbon tetrachloride, PCP, and chloroform: EC Doc COM(84) 772 final, 17 Jan 1985; for HCB and HCBD: EC Doc COM(87) 457 final, OJ No C314, 6.11.87, p 5.)

[282] Dir 82/176/EEC, Art 5, para 2 (emphasis added).

[283] Probably due to translation reasons only.

[284] Dir 86/280/EEC, Art 6, para 3 (emphasis added).

ening the limit values and quality objectives is 'necessary' or 'appropriate'. Some daughter directives actually mention a date by which new, more restrictive limit values should enter into force[285] and call on the Commission to submit proposals to this effect 'in due course'[286] or 'in good time.'[287] Despite this, the Commission has thus far not submitted a single proposal to this effect to the Council, even though the earliest limit values and quality objectives have already been in force for more than 15 years.

THE EFFECT OF SOFT LAW: THE INFLUENCE OF THE NORTH SEA MINISTERIAL DECLARATIONS ON THE LEGISLATIVE ACTIVITY OF THE EUROPEAN COMMUNITY

The legislative process in the European Union is not determined exclusively by internal factors but is also subject to external political influences. With the exception of Norway, all the riparian states of the North Sea are also member states of the EU. The INSC process, initiated by Germany, an important EU member, from the outset sought to influence the agenda of the Community's environmental policy. The European Commission has participated in the INSC process since its inception, represented by the Commissioner responsible for the environment, who is one of the signatories of the INSC declarations.[288] In fact, the North Sea Conferences have viewed the European Community as one institutional channel for translating their policy guidelines into legally binding measures.

The Community has the capacity to make an important contribution to the implementation of INSC recommendations, especially with respect to emissions of hazardous substances from both point and diffuse sources. Directive 76/464/EEC provides a legal framework for binding measures for the reduction of industrial emissions of black and grey list substances. Directive 76/769/EEC, for its part, can serve as a legal instrument for Community-wide measures to restrict the placing on the market and use of hazardous substances, or products containing such substances, in order to prevent or reduce releases into the aquatic environment from non-point sources.

However, an examination of the record of the European Commission and the Council of the European Union in proposing and adopting legally

[285] See Dir 83/513/EEC, Annex I, para 1, n 2 ('by 1992'); Dir 84/156/EEC, Annex I, para 1, n 2 ('10 years after the notification of this Directive'); Dir 86/280/EEC, Annex II, item II, heading A(46), n 2 ('by 1994'); Dir 88/347/EEC, Art 1, para 2, item V, heading A(83), n 3 and item VI, heading A(84), n 3 ('by 1 January 1995').

[286] Dir 83/153/EEC, Annex I, para 1, n 2.

[287] Dir 86/280/EEC, Annex II, item II, heading A(46), n 2.

[288] On the participation of the Community in the INSC process and the development of a Community policy on the protection of the North Sea, see generally Prat (1990).

binding measures for the control of inputs of toxic substances in the aquatic environment indicates that the effect of the INSC has at best been minimal, if not entirely non-existent in some areas. Since the Bremen Declaration, the Council has adopted no more than three Directives setting emission limit values and water quality objectives for hazardous substances pursuant to Directive 76/464/EEC.[289] These directives set standards for only 14 organohalogen compounds[290] out of the priority list of 129 black list substances identified by the European Commission and endorsed by the Council in 1982.[291] Only one of these directives was enacted after the Hague Conference, which itself adopted a list of 36 priority hazardous substances whose inputs into the North Sea were to be drastically reduced by 1995.

To be sure, the European Community has not been inactive since Bremen and London. At the Hague Conference, the Commission of the EC presented a 'progress report' giving an overview of the 'main actions and measures taken at Community level' since the Second North Sea Conference.[292] Ironically, the first part of this report is entitled 'political impetus' and describes no concrete, legally binding measures, but what the Commission terms 'main events' relating to Community water policy. These 'events' are purely of a political nature, viz a vague political statement from the June 1988 European Council meeting in Hannover inviting the Commission and the Council 'to intensify efforts to improve the means to combat and prevent air and water pollution,'[293] a resolution of the Council urging the Commission to submit proposals concerning the reduction of inputs of nutrients into the aquatic environment and municipal sewage treatment,[294]

[289] Council Dir 86/280/EEC of 12 June 1986 on limit values and quality objectives for discharges of certain dangerous substances included in List I of the Annex to Dir 76/464/EEC, OJ No L181, 4.7.1986, p 16; Council Dir 88/347/EEC of 16 June 1988 amending Annex II to Dir 86/280/EEC on limit values and quality objectives for discharges of certain dangerous substances included in List I of the Annex to Dir 76/464/EEC, OJ No L158, 25.6.1988, p 35; Council Dir 90/415/EEC of 27 July 1990 amending Annex II to Dir 86/280/EEC on limit values and quality objectives for discharges of certain dangerous substances included in List I of the Annex to Dir 76/464/EEC, OJ No L219, 14.8.1990, p 49.

[290] Carbon tetrachloride, DDT, pentachlorophenol, aldrin, dieldrin, endrin, isodrin, hexachlorobenzene, hexachlorobutadiene, chloroform, 1,2-dichloroethane, trichloroethylene, perchloroethylene, and trichlorobenzene.

[291] See Commission Communication to the Council of 22 June 1982 concerning dangerous substances which might be included in List I of Dir 76/464/EEC, OJ No C176, 14.7.1982, p 3.

[292] 'Progress Report of the Commission of the European Communities', in: *The Implementation of the Ministerial Declaration of the Second International Conference on the Protection of the North Sea*, The Hague, February 1990, pp 479–83.

[293] Conclusions of the Hannover European Council, 27–28 June 1988, *Bulletin of the European Communities* 1988/6, p 164, at p 165.

[294] Council Resolution of 28 June 1988 on the protection of the North Sea and of other waters in the Community, OJ No C209, 9.8.1988, p 3.

and a 'Ministerial Seminar' on Community water policy held in Frankfurt in June 1988.[295]

This seminar, already discussed in the introductory section of this chapter, was convened at the initiative of the German presidency a few months after the London Conference and dealt with a variety of issues, some of which were entirely unrelated to the INSC agenda. However, the decisions of the London Conference on the reduction of inputs of hazardous substances were clearly on the ministers' minds when they discussed the Community's policy with regard to the implementation of Directive 76/464/EEC and expressed their wish to 'speed up' the setting of emission standards and quality objectives for black list substances. In a somewhat optimistic assessment of the political results of the Frankfurt seminar, the Commission saw this support as evidence that the 'spirit' of the London North Sea conference was 'carried over' to Frankfurt.[296] However, when the Commission submitted to the Council, a few weeks before the Hague Conference, a formal proposal to amend Directive 76/464/EEC in order to accelerate the standard-setting process through qualified majority decision-making,[297] it appeared that the unanimity that would have been required at that time for its adoption under Article 130s of the EEC Treaty, as it then stood, was manifestly lacking.

Notwithstanding the political commitments made in London, and reiterated in The Hague and Frankfurt, there has clearly been no speeding up of the EC's regulatory efforts with respect to dangerous substances as a result of the 'political impetus' from the INSC. Since the Frankfurt seminar, only a single new Commission proposal for limit values and quality objectives, relating to four organochlorine substances, has been submitted to the Council.[298] This proposal was adopted by the Council in July 1990,[299] after two years of deliberations, bringing the total number of new substances regulated since the Bremen Conference to 14. The Community simply pursued its 'business-as-usual' approach to the regulation of industrial emissions of dangerous substances, and made no significant contribution to the implementation of the INSC recommendations in this field. Since 1990, Community standard-setting efforts for black list substances under Directive 76/464/EEC have come to a complete standstill.

[295] 'Progress Report of the Commission of the European Communities', *o.c.*, above n 292, p 480.

[296] Byrne (1989), p 5.

[297] For a detailed analysis of this proposal, see below.

[298] Commission proposal for a Council Directive amending Annex II to Dir 86/280/EEC, OJ No C253, 29.9.1988, p 4. The 4 substances are 1,2-dichloroethane, trichloroethylene, tetrachloroethylene and trichlorobenzene.

[299] Dir 90/415/EEC, above n 289.

In the area of product regulation, some influence of the INSC process on EC legislative activity can be noticed. In 1984, the Bremen Declaration called for measures aiming at a phasing out of the use of PCBs to be 'intensified without delay.'[300] An EEC Directive banning all new uses of PCBs and terminating earlier exceptions which allowed certain existing uses to continue was adopted in 1985.[301] Five years later, at their Hague conference, North Sea ministers, in view of the evidence that PCBs from existing equipment and waste disposal continue to enter the marine environment despite the ban on new PCB uses, decided

> to take measures to phase out and destroy in an environmentally safe manner all identifiable PCBs as soon as possible with the aim of complete destruction . . . by 1995 and by the end of 1999 at the latest.[302]

Although the Commission had already submitted to the Council a proposal for a new directive on the disposal of PCBs and PCTs in October 1988,[303] it is only in 1996 that the Council adopted this directive,[304] notwithstanding the Hague conference's 1990 call for urgent action in this field. The 1996 Directive, which was to be transposed by member states by 1998, provides for complete destruction of all PCBs before the end of 2010, a target date well beyond that recommended by the Third North Sea Conference.

Batteries containing heavy metals are another product source of pollution of the aquatic environment by black list substances. The 1990 Hague Declaration recommended a limit on the mercury content of alkaline manganese batteries.[305] In 1991, the Council adopted a directive, based on Article 100a of the Treaty, laying down product standards for the mercury and cadmium content of certain batteries and accumulators and prescribing other measures for the recovery or environmentally sound disposal of used batteries containing mercury, cadmium and lead.[306] The provisions of this directive go beyond the Hague recommendations in that they apply not only to mercury but also to cadmium and lead-containing batteries, although in certain respects they are less specific than those of PARCOM Decision 90/2, which was adopted by the Paris Commission a few months after the Hague Conference.[307] In transposing the INSC recommendations

[300] Bremen Declaration, para C2.

[301] Dir 85/467/EEC of 1 Oct 1985, OJ No L269, 11.10.1985, p 56.

[302] Hague Declaration, para 9(1)(i).

[303] EC Doc COM(88) 559 final, 18 Oct 1988.

[304] European Parliament and Council Dir 96/59/EC of 16 Sept 1996 on the disposal of polychlorinated biphenyls and polychlorinated terphenyls, OJ No L243, 24.09.1996, p 31.

[305] Hague Declaration, Annex 1B, Part (a).

[306] Council Dir 91/157/EEC of 18 Mar 1991 on batteries and accumulators containing certain dangerous substances, OJ No L78, 26.3.1991, p 38.

[307] It should be recalled that the EC entered a formal reservation to the adoption of this decision by the Paris Commission. Cf above ch 4. Some provisions of Dir 91/157/EEC, eg Art 3, para 1, are, however, copied verbatim from PARCOM Decision.

and PARCOM Decision, the EC apparently struck a different balance between environmental and economic concerns. Indeed, the directive set later deadlines for the introduction of recycling systems than laid down in the Paris Commission decision.

The use of hexachloroethane (HCE) in aluminium scrap smelting is a process source of emissions of dioxins and other halogenated organic compounds. The Hague Declaration called on the North Sea states to 'reduce the use of hexachloroethane in aluminium smelters with a view to its elimination by the end of 1992', albeit 'to the extent that Best Available Technology allows it.'[308] This proviso indicated that there was not yet full consensus, even among the Northern member states of the EU, about the economic feasibility of this phase-out. As a matter of fact, the deadline set in The Hague was extended until the end of 1994 by the Paris Commission in 1992.[309] In 1993, PARCOM decided to phase out the use of HCE throughout the non-ferrous metal industry by the end of 1997, though the EC and two of its member states formulated reservations against this decision.[310] It is only in 1997 that Directive 76/769/EEC was amended to incorporate in Community law the ban on the use of HCE as a degasifier in the non-ferrous metal industry,[311] after the EC had convinced the Paris Commission to amend its earlier decision to allow for more derogations for small foundries.[312]

The successive North Sea Conferences have also recommended action to reduce inputs of pesticides into the marine environment. The EC is an increasingly important actor in the regulation of market access for pesticides for both agricultural and non-agricultural use. But there is little evidence so far that the development of Community law in this field has been influenced by the INSC recommendations. Directive 91/414/EEC,[313] which regulates the placing on the market of plant protection products, ie pesticides for agricultural use, contains no specific reference to the necessity to prevent the use of pesticides which may contaminate the marine environment. Notwithstanding the commitment made by North Sea states at the 1993 Copenhagen Intermediate Ministerial Meeting to ensure that authorisation mechanisms for pesticides 'give adequate protection to the marine

[308] Hague Declaration, Annex 1B, Part (a).

[309] PARCOM Decision 92/4 on the phasing out of the use of hexachloroethane (HCE) in the secondary aluminium industry and in the primary aluminium industry with integrated foundries, Sept 1992, in: Oslo and Paris Commissions, *Ministerial Meeting of the Oslo and Paris Commissions, Paris, 21–22 September 1992*, London, 1993.

[310] PARCOM Decision 93/1 on the phasing out of the use of hexachloroethane (HCE) in the non-ferrous metal industry, OSPAR Doc 15/13/1–E, June 1993, Annex 7.

[311] European Parliament and Council Dir 97/16/EC of 10 Apr 1997 amending for the 15th time Dir 76/769/EEC on restrictions on the marketing and use of certain dangerous substances and preparations, OJ No L116, 6.5.1997, p 31.

[312] See below ch 9.

[313] Council Dir 91/414/EEC of 15 July 1991 concerning the placing of plant protection products on the market, OJ No L 230, 19.8.1991, p 1.

environment,'[314] the 'uniform principles' for the authorisation of plant protection products under Directive 91/414/EEC adopted in 1994[315] do not provide for a specific evaluation of the risks of such products for the marine environment as part of the authorisation process. However, a more recent, similar harmonisation directive governing the marketing of biocides,[316] ie mainly pesticides for non-agricultural use, incorporates explicit provisions requiring an assessment of the risk of harmful effects on the estuarine and marine environment before the placing on the market of such products is authorised.[317]

While the INSC process has not accelerated the implementation of Directive 76/464/EEC, and the Commission's claim to exclusive Community jurisdiction over certain product- and process-related measures for the protection of the marine environment has even slowed down the implementation of certain INSC recommendations by the Paris Commission, as we shall see in the following chapter, it would be inaccurate to say that the INSC has had no impact at all on the development of European Community environmental law. In the field of the reduction of inputs of nutrients, as opposed to that of hazardous substances, substantial legislative progress was made with the adoption of a Directive concerning urban waste water treatment,[318] which is inspired by the recommendations of the Hague Conference.[319] This subject, however, is outside the scope of this study.

THE DEMISE OF DIRECTIVE 76/464/EEC

An Aborted Proposal for Speeding Up the Implementation Process

In the late 1980s, political dissatisfaction with the slowness of the implementation process of Directive 76/464/EEC led to proposals for reform. The impetus for those proposals came from an informal 'Ministerial Seminar on Community Water Policy for the Nineties' convened in Frankfurt by the German Council presidency in June 1988 to evaluate past policy and to

[314] See above ch 4.

[315] Council Dir 94/43/EC of 27 July 1994 establishing Annex VI to Dir 91/414/EEC concerning the placing of plant protection products on the market, OJ No L227, 1.9.1994, p 31, later replaced by Council Dir 97/57/EC of 22 Sept 1997 establishing Annex VI to Dir 91/414/EEC concerning the placing of plant protection products on the market, OJ No L265, 27.9.1997, p 87. The evaluation of risks to surface waters required under para B.2.5.1.3 of Annex VI focuses on the freshwater environment.

[316] European Parliament and Council Dir 98/8/EC of 16 Feb 1998 concerning the placing of biocidal products on the market, OJ No L123, 24.4.1998, p 1. For a more detailed analysis of the provisions of this directive, see below ch 15.

[317] Dir 98/8/EC, Annex VI, para 81.

[318] Council Dir 91/271/EEC of 21 May 1991 concerning urban waste water treatment, OJ No L135, 30.5.1991, p 40

[319] Hague Declaration, paras 11–12.

identify political priorities to guide the Commission in its future work. This seminar, which took place outside the formal institutional framework of the Council, is described by a Commission official as:

> a unique event in the history of European Community Water Policy as it brought Ministers together, in an informal atmosphere, in order to discuss priorities for the future. It offered them a chance for a frank and open debate without the responsibility of defending their entrenched national positions.[320]

It seems that the political, non-committal nature of the meeting did indeed enable ministers to recognise the problems affecting the regulatory work relating to emissions of dangerous substances in the aquatic environment. This did not, however, indicate a real willingness to take the necessary formal decisions within the Council, as later developments showed.

As regards the regulation of emissions of dangerous substances under Directive 76/464/EEC, the Commission's unofficial report of the ministerial seminar notes with satisfaction that 'Ministers wished to see a speeding up of measures to deal with the control of discharges of dangerous substances.'[321] The official 'conclusions' of the seminar adopted by the Ministers in fact reflect disagreement on this question:

> *Most delegations* urged that, in order to speed up progress, the identification of substances to be included in the black list should be decided by unanimity and that the values to be subsequently applied should be decided by qualified majority

on the basis of Article 130s, second indent, of the EEC Treaty, as amended by the Single European Act.[322]

The Commission official optimistically claimed that the 'spirit' of the London North Sea Conference was 'carried over' to the Frankfurt ministerial seminar.[323] The Commission certainly tried to cash in on the 'spirit of London' by seeking ministerial endorsement for its proposal to 'fast-track' decision-making on daughter directives of Directive 76/464/EEC through the application of the procedure provided in the second indent of Article 130s of the EEC Treaty, as it stood following the entry into force of the SEA. But if that much-hailed 'spirit of London' was ever present in Frankfurt, its presence was highly ephemeral, because the Commission in fact failed to obtain the *unanimous* support that would have been required to activate the qualified majority decision-making procedure of Article 130s, second indent. So the optimistic gloss put on the Frankfurt meeting by the Commission was not quite warranted.

[320] Byrne (1989), pp 5–6.
[321] *Ibid*, p 7.
[322] Conclusions of the Ministerial Seminar on 'The Community Water Policy', Frankfurt/Main, 27–8 June 1988, para 11 (emphasis added).
[323] Byrne (1989), p 5.

In fact, events since Frankfurt demonstrate that, as far as dangerous substances are concerned, the 'spirit of London', if it ever existed, has completely evaporated in the Council. Acting on the less-than-unanimous conclusions of the Frankfurt seminar, on 14 February 1990, a few weeks before the Hague North Sea Conference, the Commission submitted to the Council a proposal for a directive amending Directive 76/464/EEC.[324] The preamble of the proposed directive states that

> it is necessary to make the procedure establishing limit values and quality objectives for dangerous substances more efficient in order to achieve quickly common Community-wide standards for those substances belonging to List I in the Annex to Directive 76/464/EEC

and that:

> the setting of limit values and quality objectives should, for reasons of time and efficiency, be carried out by the Council acting by qualified majority pursuant to the second paragraph of Article 130S.

Accordingly, the Commission proposed to amend Article 12, paragraph 1 of Directive 76/464/EEC to enable the Council to act by qualified majority on any Commission proposal for the setting of limit values and quality objectives made pursuant to Article 6 of that Directive.[325] Furthermore, the Commission proposal lists 16 'substances belonging to List I of the Annex to Directive 76/464/EEC' which are to 'be considered on a priority basis for the purpose of fixing limit values and quality objectives.'[326] According to the Commission's explanatory memorandum, this proposal was intended to introduce a two-stage procedure. In the first stage, the Council would decide on the principle of setting Community limit values and quality objectives for a given substance. This decision would still require unanimity. However, in the second stage, the decision on the actual values of the standards for agreed substances would be taken by qualified majority.

On its face, however, the Commission proposal went beyond the intent stated in its explanatory memorandum and what 'most' member states tentatively agreed to in Frankfurt. Indeed, it would not have introduced a *two-stage procedure* whereby the substances to be regulated would be selected by unanimity while the actual standards for these substances would be set by qualified majority, but would have provided for a *single decision* of the Council acting by qualified majority pursuant to Article 130s. Directive 76/464/EEC itself provides no legal basis for a two-stage procedure; it does not distinguish between the identification of the individual substances on

[324] Proposal for a Council Directive amending Dir 76/464/EEC on pollution caused by certain dangerous substances discharged into the aquatic environment of the Community, OJ No C55, 7.3.1990, p 7.

[325] *Ibid*, Art 1.

[326] *Ibid*, Art 2.

the 'black list' for which limit values and quality objectives are to be set and the actual setting of the standards themselves. Both are performed by the same formal act of the Council, the adoption of a daughter directive as provided in Article 6 of Directive 76/464/EEC.

To be sure, the priority list of substances proposed by the Commission was part of a formal proposal for a Council directive based on Article 130s of the Treaty and thus would, at that time, have had to be adopted by a unanimous Council decision. But the wording of Article 2 of the Commission proposal is such that it has no legal implications: it only provides that the 16 listed substances 'will be considered on a priority basis for the purpose of fixing limit values and quality objectives'. Unlike Article 1, it is not formulated in terms of an amendment to Directive 76/464/EEC, and thus it could not restrict the power of the Council pursuant to Article 12, paragraph 1 of Directive 76/464/EEC, as amended according to Article 1 of the Commission proposal, to set standards for any substance proposed by the Commission *by qualified majority decision*. So the Commission's proposal, if it had been adopted prior to the amendment of Article 130s by the TEU, could have had far-reaching implications for the development of EC law with respect to emissions of dangerous substances, significantly accelerating the implementation process of Directive 76/464/EEC.

However, notwithstanding the solemn, albeit not unambiguous, commitments made in London and reiterated in The Hague to translate the measures recommended by the INSC into EC legislation, and notwithstanding the ministerial desire expressed at the Frankfurt seminar for a 'speeding up' of the EC's regulatory efforts with respect to dangerous substances, the Commission's proposal for a new decision-making procedure was never seriously taken into consideration by the Council and lost its relevance as a result of the amendment of Article 130s of the EC Treaty by the TEU, which abolished the requirement of unanimity.[327]

The Freezing of the Implementation of Directive 76/464/EEC

Since 1990, Community legislative activity for the implementation of Directive 76/464/EEC has come to a complete standstill. No further emission limit values and quality objectives for black list substances have been set by the Council following the adoption of Directive 90/415/EEC. As a matter of fact, no further proposals for daughter directives have been submitted to the Council by the Commission since the ill-fated proposal of March 1990 to amend the decision-making procedure in Directive 76/464/EEC for

[327] In 1992, the Commission noted that the proposal had 'not been examined by the Council since March 1990'. Answer by the Commission to Written Question No 1491/91, OJ No C 242, 21.9.1992, p 4.

the adoption of emission limit values and quality objectives. The Commission has refrained from exercising its right of initiative ever since the Council refused to consider that proposal, which has meanwhile been formally withdrawn.[328]

Yet in a recent paper, the Commission ironically sought to blame the Council for the lack of progress since 1990, arguing that '[f]urther attempts to introduce Community limit values and quality objectives were blocked by Council.'[329] This spurious argument glosses over the fact that the Commission has not actually made any 'further attempts' to implement Directive 76/464/EEC by proposing standards for additional black list substances, and that the requirement of unanimity for the adoption of such standards, which it had always depicted as the main impediment to implementation, no longer exists since the entry into force of the TEU. While it is true that the Council blocked the 1990 proposal, the amendment of Article 130s by the TEU in 1993, which introduced qualified majority decision-making as the rule for all environmental measures under Article 130s, paragraph 1, in effect made that proposal redundant.

The expectations of some that Community standards for 'many more substances will follow in the near future'[330] as a result of this change in legislative procedure have proved to be entirely unfounded. The fact is that the Commission has not taken advantage of this Treaty modification to make new proposals for the further implementation of Directive 76/464/EEC; this indicates that its inactivity is a matter of deliberate political choice. Since the early 1990s, the Commission has been pursuing a different legislative agenda, an agenda which entails a gradual dismantling and eventual repeal of Directive 76/464/EEC. Recent legislative developments and their implications are analysed below. But to conclude the discussion of Directive 76/464/EEC, I shall first examine the Commission's use of its supervision and enforcement powers to promote the implementation of this legislation.

COMMISSION ACTION FOR THE ENFORCEMENT OF DIRECTIVE 76/464/EEC AND ITS DAUGHTER DIRECTIVES

Having analysed the Commission's and Council's legislative policies and practice for the implementation of the framework provisions of Directive 76/464/EEC, I shall now examine the Commission's policy and practice with respect to monitoring the application of the framework directive and

[328] Withdrawal of certain proposals and drafts from the Commission to the Council, OJ No C228, 24.8.1993, p 13.

[329] *A Community strategy for the integrated control of emissions of dangerous and long range effects substances from smaller installations*, Consultation Paper of the Commission Services, 1996, p 17.

[330] Somsen (1991), p 233.

its daughter directives and taking enforcement action against the member states under Articles 211 and 226 of the Treaty. This policy and practice are equally relevant to an overall assessment of the effectiveness of Community legislation regulating toxic emissions in the aquatic environment.

Reading the official annual reports on the monitoring of the application of Community law, issued by the Commission every year since 1984, one might get the impression that there are no serious problems of implementation of Directive 76/464/EEC.[331] Indeed, before 1991, this directive was not mentioned at all in the tables presenting a synopsis of infringement proceedings relating to directives.[332] The infringements listed with respect to a number of daughter directives mainly concerned failures to notify national implementing measures. In 1982, the Commission complacently stated that although Directive 76/464/EEC does not actually require member states to communicate these measures, it had 'established that the Member States have complied with the main provisions of this Directive'.[333]

It was apparently only in the late 1980s, probably in response to complaints and parliamentary questions as well as a resolution of the European Parliament on the matter,[334] that the Commission started taking a hard look at the conformity of national legislation with Community requirements and initiating Article 226 proceedings against a number of member states for inadequate transposition and application of Directive 76/464/EEC and its daughter directives. In 1992, the Commission, somewhat surprisingly in view of its earlier complacency, suddenly reported that it was 'aware of numerous cases of infringement throughout the Community' and that, as of July 1991, no fewer than 40 proceedings had:

> been initiated against Member States for failing to comply, in various ways, with the provisions of the Community Directives concerning the discharge of dangerous substances into the aquatic environment.[335]

[331] For a general critical assessment of the Commission's reporting practice on its environmental enforcement policy, see Williams (1994). The European Parliament, too, in a 1988 resolution 'on the implementation of European Community legislation relating to water', noted that there were 'inconsistencies between the infringement proceedings recorded in annual reports on the application of Community law and those actually in progress'. OJ No C94, 11.4.1988, p 155, para 4.

[332] See 1st Annual Report, EC Doc COM(84) 181 final; 2nd Annual Report, EC Doc COM(85) 149 final, p 76; 3rd Annual Report, OJ No C220, 1.9.1986, p 66; 4th Annual Report, OJ No C 338, 16.12.1987, p 70; 5th Annual Report, OJ No C310, 5.12.1988, p 87; 6th Annual Report, OJ No C330, 30.12.1989, p 105; 7th Annual Report, OJ No C232, 17.9.1990; 8th Annual Report, OJ No C338, 31.12.1991, p 151. Dir 76/464/EEC is mentioned for the first time in the table annexed to the 9th Annual Report, OJ No C250, 29.8.1992, p 117.

[333] Answer of the Commission to Written Question No 332/82, OJ No C198, 2.8.1982, p 26.

[334] EP Resolution of 10 Mar 1988 on the implementation of European Community legislation relating to water, OJ No C94, 11.4.1988, p 155.

[335] Answer of the Commission to Written Question No 1496/91, OJ No C202, 10.8.1992, p 7.

Commission Monitoring of the Application of the Directives

In its original version, Article 13, paragraph 1 of Directive 76/464/EEC required the member states to supply to the Commission at its request certain information relating to measures taken for the application of the directive. This information included 'in particular' details of discharge authorisations granted both for black and grey list substances, the results of the inventory of discharges of black list substances which the member states must draw up pursuant to Article 11 of the directive, and information on the pollution reduction programmes they must establish for grey list substances under Article 7, paragraph 1. Finally, Article 13, paragraph 1 mentioned among the specified items of information to be provided 'the results of monitoring by the national network'. Yet no other provision of the directive refers to any such network or imposes any specific monitoring obligations on the member states. Monitoring of surface water quality is however required by all the daughter directives of Directive 76/464/EEC[336] as well as under some other Community instruments.[337]

It should be noted that, unlike many other environmental directives, neither Directive 76/464/EEC nor its daughter directives originally contained clauses explicitly requiring the member states to send periodical reports to the Commission on their own initiative. The information referred to in Article 13, paragraph 1 was to be provided only at the Commission's express request, which, it is stipulated, was 'to be submitted in each case.'[338] The relevant provisions in the daughter directives did not actually impose additional obligations on the member states independently of Article 13, paragraph 1 of the framework directive, but only referred to that clause and further specified what information was to be regarded as 'necessary' for its purposes. In fact, the daughter directives only put *the Commission* under a periodical reporting obligation: the Commission was required to make a 'comparative assessment' of the implementation of the different daughter directives by the member states 'on the basis of the information supplied to it by them pursuant to Article 13 of Directive 76/464/EEC at its request'[339] and to forward the results of this assessment to the Council every five years.[340]

[336] See, eg Dir 86/280/EEC, Art 5.

[337] See, eg Council Decision 77/795/EEC of 12 Dec 1977 establishing a common procedure for the exchange of information on the quality of surface fresh water in the Community, OJ No L334, 24.12.1977, p 29; Council Dir 79/869/EEC of 9 Oct 1979 concerning the methods of measurement and frequencies of sampling and analysis of surface water intended for the abstraction of drinking water in the Member States, OJ No L271, 29.10.1979, p 44.

[338] Dir 76/464/EEC, Art 13, para 1. See also eg Dir 86/280/EEC, Art 6, para 1: '. . . at its request, *which it must submit case by case* . . .' (emphasis added).

[339] Dir 86/280/EEC, Art 6, para 1 and similar provisions in the other daugther directives.

[340] Dir 86/280/EEC, Art 6, para 2 and similar provisions in the other daugther directives.

No such assessments have been submitted to the Council so far. As a matter of fact, it was only *in October 1988* that the Commission first applied Article 13 and asked the member states to supply information on the implementation of Directives 82/176/EEC, 84/156/EEC, 83/513/EEC, 84/491/EEC and 86/280/EEC and on the inventories of discharges of the substances regulated by those directives.[341] It is on the basis of information thus received from the member states that the Commission intended to prepare and submit to the Council 'the comparative assessment of the implementation of each of the specific directives.'[342] Although 'model forms' were drawn up and circulated to the competent national authorities to facilitate the collection and harmonise the presentation of the relevant data,[343] the Commission indicated in January 1992 that only two member states had provided 'satisfactory information' in response to its request.[344]

As part of a comprehensive effort to 'standardize and rationalize' the reporting obligations of the member states under environmental directives, Article 13, paragraph 1 of Directive 76/464/EEC and the corresponding provisions in the daughter directives were amended and made uniform in 1991.[345] The new provisions, which were to be transposed by 1 January 1993, now explicitly require member states to report to the Commission every three years and to provide the specific information stipulated in a questionnaire to be established through a comitology procedure.[346] The questionnaire for the various water directives was adopted by a Commission Decision of 27 July 1992[347] and amended by another Commission Decision[348] three years later. This questionnaire is designed

> to clarify the reporting obligations imposed on the Member States and to ensure that information provided to the Commission by the Member States are [*sic*] comprehensive, consistent and comparable.[349]

[341] Answer of the Commission to Written Question No 1494/91, OJ No C202, 10.8.1992, p 7. See also Answer of the Commission to Written Question No 1495/91, OJ No C78, 30.3.1992, p 13; Answer of the Commission to Written Question No 146/90, OJ No C266, 22.10.1990, p 18.

[342] Answer of the Commission to Written Question No 1495/91, OJ No C78, 30.3.1992, p 13.

[343] *Ibid.*

[344] Answer of the Commission to Written Question No 1494/91, OJ No C202, 10.8.1992, p 7.

[345] Council Dir 91/692/EEC of 23 Dec 1991 standardising and rationalising reports on the implementation of certain Directive relating to the environment, OJ No L377, 31.12.1991, p 48.

[346] *Ibid*, Art 2. See also Answer of the Commission to Written Question No 2201/95, OJ No C40, 12.2.1996, p 14.

[347] Commission Decision 92/446/EEC of 27 July 1992 concerning questionnaires relating to directives in the water sector, OJ No L247, 27.8.1992, p 10.

[348] Commission Decision 95/337/EC of 25 July 1995 amending Decision 92/446/EEC concerning questionnaires relating to directives in the water sector, OJ No L200, 24.8.1995, p 1.

[349] *Ibid*, 8th preambular para.

The first member state reports, covering the period 1993–1995, were due by 30 September 1996, and the Commission itself was to publish its first comprehensive report on the implementation of the water directives by 30 June 1997.[350] At the time of writing, this report has not yet been published.

Meanwhile, however, specific reports on the implementation of Directive 76/464/EEC and its daughter directives, apparently based on information received by the Commission prior to the introduction of standardised questionnaires, were prepared by consultants on behalf of the Commission. The first, although completed in December 1993,[351] was published only in 1996; it reviews the state of legislation and administrative structures for the implementation of the directives in the member states.[352] The second was completed in October 1995 and assesses the actual impact of the directives on surface water quality, focusing on black list substances.[353] A third, similar report, focusing on grey list substances, was finalised in June 1996.[354] The latter two reports, containing mostly information of a scientific, factual nature, will be taken into account in my overall discussion of the effectiveness of normative efforts for the control of emissions of toxic substances in chapter 17. In this chapter, I shall only discuss the first report, which provides information on legislative and administrative measures taken in the member states for the purpose of implementing Directive 76/464/EEC and its daughter directives.

This report analyses the formal transposition of the directives into national legislation, the administrative mechanisms established in the member states for granting discharge permits, the member states' 'control strategies' for both black and grey list substances, their systems for the monitoring of discharges of dangerous substances, including the different analytical methods used, and finally the resources required for the implementation of the directives at the national and subnational level. Based on their rather superficial analysis, the authors draw some conclusions about what they call 'key issues . . . regarding the viability of the systems introduced by Directive 76/464/EEC and its daughter directives.'[355] According to the report, the directives have been transposed in all the member states,

[350] Dir 91/692/EEC, Art 2.

[351] Answer of the Commission to Written Question No 2851/95, OJ No C91, 27.3.1996, p 16.

[352] European Commission, *Administrative Structures and Implementation of the Community Directives on the Dangerous Substances Discharged into the Aquatic Environment*, Office for Official Publications of the European Communities, Luxembourg, 1996 (hereafter referred to as *Administrative Structures*).

[353] RIZA, *Impact of Directive 76/464/EEC and its 'daughter' directives on the most important surface waters in the Community*, vol I: Main Report, Oct 1995.

[354] RIZA & Delft Hydraulics, *Evaluation of the Directive 76/464/EEC regarding List II substances on the quality of the most important surface waters in the Community*, vol I: Main Report, June 1996.

[355] *Administrative Structures*, above n 352, p 42.

though with considerable delay in some of them, due in part to 'a certain lack of compatibility between existing national systems and the requirements of the directives.'[356] However, the report stresses that while formal transposition is 'largely complete', this 'does not mean that the implementation of the directives is also complete.'[357]

Confirming the conclusions that the Commission itself had already drawn when it attempted to obtain information from the member states on their implementation of Article 7 of Directive 76/464/EEC, the report notes that control strategies for grey list substances and candidate black list substances are considerably less developed than those for the 17 black list substances covered by the daughter directives. This seems to be due to a variety of reasons, but mainly to 'the absence of solid data' on, and the often diffuse nature of, discharges of grey list substances or the real or perceived lack thereof.[358] Permit requirements for effluent discharges exist in all member states,[359] but the report does not examine whether these authorisation systems actually guarantee that all discharges of both black and grey list substances are subject to emission standards as required by Directive 76/464/EEC. Given the findings concerning the underdeveloped state of control strategies for grey list substances, it seems likely that the answer to this question, had it been explicitly addressed, would have been negative.

On-the-ground monitoring of emissions of dangerous substances is another important element of the emission control policies required by Community law. The report finds that 'Member States attach varying levels of significance to the monitoring of industrial discharges.'[360] Monitoring efforts by public authorities seem quite limited in most member states, due to lack of resources and/or coordination, and analytical methods used vary from member state to member state. The report notes a marked preference for self-monitoring of industrial discharges by permit-holders in many member states.[361] Finally, the report discusses resource issues affecting the implementation of the directives, which it notes 'requires considerable technical and administrative resources' in the member states.[362] Lack of adequate resources appears to be a problem faced by many of the public authorities entrusted with implementing the directives at the national or subnational level.

The report concludes that 'the very wide range in the rate and level of implementation of the directives . . . reflects widely differing background

[356] *Ibid*, p 3.
[357] *Ibid*.
[358] *Ibid*, p 18.
[359] *Ibid*, p 21.
[360] *Ibid*, p 28.
[361] *Ibid*, p 32.
[362] *Ibid*, p 39.

conditions in Member States in terms of administrative and legal systems resources' and that 'successful implementation . . . still appears to be some way off' in all member states.[363] It notes the feeling expressed by authorities in some member states that 'the approach adopted by the directives is increasingly obsolete and needs to be reviewed'[364] in the light of other developments in environmental policy both at Community and national level, in particular the move towards integrated pollution control and permitting systems, which they feel 'offer more efficient control systems and streamline resource and administrative requirements.'[365] Thus, the report's conclusions seem to lend support to the Commission's shift in policy with respect to the control of toxic emissions to water and its subsequent proposal to repeal Directive 76/464/EEC, which will be further discussed below.

To revert to the issue of compliance with existing Community law, as opposed to developments *de lege ferenda*, the most striking aspect of the report is the fact that its authors apparently made no effort to review current administrative *practice* with regard to discharge authorisations in the member states and to examine what, from a legal point of view, are the most relevant indicators of compliance with the directives, ie the *actual permits* delivered by the competent authorities of the member states and the discharge conditions laid down in those permits. The conclusions of the report seem to be based mainly on secondary sources of information and on aggregate data of uneven quality gathered through interviews with member state officials. One does not have the impression that the Commission's consultants actually examined a single discharge permit. In view of the fact that some of the daughter directives apply only to a very small number of industrial plants throughout the Community, it would not have been an insurmountable task to do so and to verify whether the emission standards laid down in the applicable permits actually conform with the emission limit values fixed by those directives. Considering the pivotal role of the prior authorisation requirement and the individual emission standards in the regulatory system established by Directive 76/464/EEC, it is most surprising that the Commission apparently did not instruct its consultants to look into this.

There is also other evidence that the Commission actually *has no interest* in monitoring practical compliance with the directives, or what it calls 'correct application' in its annual reports to the European Parliament, as opposed to formal implementation. This evidence can be found in the above-mentioned questionnaires established by the Commission pursuant to Directive 91/692/EEC. The questionnaire relating to Directive

[363] *Administrative Structures*, above n 352, p 43.
[364] *Ibid*, p 42.
[365] *Ibid*, p 43.

76/464/EEC and its daughter directives requires member states to answer the following question for each of the black list substances:

What emission standards have been laid down *in general for* the authorizations for direct discharges into [surface] waters?[366]

An explanatory note further stipulates that only a 'range of values' must be provided, 'based on/derived from existing national/regional standards or EEC directives,'[367] while another explains that member states 'should summarize the range of emission standards permitted.'[368] Likewise, a similar question concerning the time limits laid down in authorisations is to be answered 'in general' and, where it refers to the 'period of validity of individual authorizations', the member states are instructed to 'give *average* and/or range only.'[369]

Both questions are ambiguously worded. The question on emission standards could be interpreted as referring only to the standards laid down *for* the relevant authorisations in national implementing legislation or regulations, and not to the actual emission standards fixed *in* individual authorisations, which, from the legal point of view, are the most relevant ones.[370] Indeed, Directive 76/464/EEC provides that '*the authorization* shall lay down emission standards' for black list substances[371] and that these standards 'must not exceed' the relevant limit values established by the Council.[372] Thus, in order to verify compliance with these obligations, the

366 Decision 95/337/EC, above n 348, Annex, Part I ('Outline questionnaire on Dir 76/464/EEC and daughter directives'), Heading A ('Measures referring to List I substances of Dir 76/464/EEC'), Question 3 (emphasis added).

367 *Ibid*, note (a) *sub* 'NB'.

368 *Ibid*, App 3 ('Explanatory note to the questionnaire of Dir 76/464/EEC and daughter directives'), p 18.

369 *Ibid*, Question 5 (emphasis added).

370 See also the quite explicit explanatory note for a similarly though not identically worded question relating to the emission standards for grey list substances to be set by the member states pursuant to Art 7, para 2 of Dir 76/464/EEC:

'The emission standards to be indicated refer to national or regional compulsory or recommended values given by the competent/legislative/statutory authorities . . . , *not to the values set in the permit* given by competent/local authorities. Where numerous individual standards exist, it is *not necessary to record the individual values of the authorizations* given by the competent authority, *but to summarize the range of emission standards contained in such authorizations.*' *Ibid*, App 3, pp 19–20 (emphasis added).

The actual question refers to 'emission standards . . . laid down *in general as a basis for consideration and prior authorization* for direct discharges into waters in relation to quality objectives'. *Ibid*, Annex, Part I, Heading B ('Measures referring to List II substances'), Question 3 (emphasis added). Or does this difference in wording indicate that the question relating to emission standards for List I substances should be interpreted *a contrario* as referring to the actual standards contained in the authorisations? At any rate, the wording of the questionnaire is unclear and indicates that the Commission is not especially eager to obtain legally accurate information.

371 Dir 76/464/EEC, Art 3, para 2 (emphasis added).

372 *Ibid*, Art 6, para 1.

Commission needs detailed information on the emission standards laid down *in individual permits*, not 'summarized' information on the norms laid down 'in general' *for* such permits in 'existing national/regional standards'. The emission standards 'permitted' by national or regional implementing legislation or regulations may well formally be in accordance with the Community limit values, but if the standards in the actual permits do not conform the member state concerned will not have fulfilled its Community obligations.

Similar observations can be made with respect to the question pertaining to 'deadlines for authorizations and/or emissions.'[373] It seems that two different obligations arising from Directive 76/464/EEC and the daughter directives are being confused in this question. Article 3, paragraph 3 of the 1976 Directive provides that authorisations for existing discharges shall 'stipulate' a 'period' within which the conditions laid down in them, in particular the emission standards, must be complied with, while Article 6, paragraph 4 mandates the Council to lay down in each daughter directive 'deadlines' which these periods may not exceed. Article 3, paragraph 4, for its part, stipulates that authorisations 'may be granted for a limited period only' but 'may be renewed', taking into account any changes in Community limit values. This provision is complemented by the requirement, laid down in each daughter directive, that 'authorizations shall be reviewed at least every four years.'[374]

One part of the question seems to address the periods referred to in Article 3, paragraph 3 (deadlines for compliance with emission standards), another the periods referred to in Article 3, paragraph 4 (periods of validity of individual authorisations). Legally speaking, these are two different requirements which must both be complied with in national legislation as well as, most importantly, in *each* individual permit. From a legal point of view, the 'average' period of validity of authorisations is obviously irrelevant. The relevant question is whether all permits are effectively granted for a limited period only and actually reviewed at least every four years. The answers given by the member states to the questions as phrased in the questionnaire will not provide the Commission with the specific information required to enable it to verify compliance with the distinct obligations laid down by Community law.

Infringement Proceedings and the Case-law of the Court of Justice

According to the information contained in its annual reports to the European Parliament on the application of Community law, the Commission

[373] Decision 95/337/EC, above n 348, Annex, Part I, Heading A, Question 5.
[374] See, eg, Dir 86/280/EEC, Art 3, para 3.

has initiated a series of infringement proceedings against member states for various failures to comply with their obligations under Directive 76/464/EEC and related directives. Until 1987 these proceedings exclusively concerned formal non-compliance. Article 226 letters were routinely sent to member states which had failed to communicate national implementing measures upon expiry of the term laid down in the relevant directive. This probably explains why the framework directive, contrary to its daughter directives, was not mentioned at all in the synoptic tables of infringements published by the Commission:[375] since Directive 76/464/EEC does not contain a provision requiring the member states to communicate national measures before a particular date, the routine administrative system for compliance monitoring, based as it is on checking the formal notification of implementing measures by the end of the specified period, could not 'catch' cases of non-compliance with this directive.

Most of the Article 226 proceedings initiated for failures to communicate national measures for the implementation of daughter directives were discontinued by the Commission as soon as the member state concerned had provided evidence of formal transposition into national law. Only three cases, against Italy, Germany and Portugal, resulted in a judgment of the Court of Justice. In the Italian case, which concerned non-transposition of the 1983 cadmium Directive, the Court found that by not adopting within the prescribed time limit all the legislative and administrative provisions needed to transpose Directive 83/513/EEC 'fully and correctly' into its national law, Italy had failed to fulfil its obligations under the Treaty.[376] Since the defendant member state did not seriously dispute the infringement, the judgment contains little of legal interest.[377] The same applies to

[375] Cf above n 332.

[376] Case C–70/89, *Commission v Italian Republic*, [1990] ECR I–4817.

[377] To complete the picture of the Court's case-law concerning Dir 76/464/EEC and its daughter directives, a recent, related Art 234 case on a referral by an Italian lower court, the *Pretura circondariale di Vicenza*, should also be mentioned. Case C–168/95, *Luciano Arcaro*, [1996] ECR I–4705.

The questions referred to the Court of Justice arose in criminal proceedings against an industrialist named Luciano Arcaro, who was prosecuted under Italy's long overdue implementing legislation, a legislative decree (*decreto legislativo*) of Jan 1992, for having discharged cadmium-containing effluent into the Bacchiglione river without a permit. The Italian court requested a preliminary ruling from the Court of Justice on three rather nebulously worded questions of interpretation of Community law, one of which, as understood by the Court, was whether Dir 76/464/EEC and 83/513/EEC should be interpreted as requiring prior authorisation for any discharges of cadmium, even those from existing plants.

The Court found that this was indeed the correct interpretation of the directives, which allow no exceptions whatsoever to the prior authorisation requirement for discharges of black list substances. Under Italian law, however, discharges from existing installations such as Mr Arcaro's plant, for which no Community emission limit values were laid down in Dir 83/513/EEC, appear to be exempted from the authorisation requirement as long as national emission standards for them have not been fixed by a ministerial decree based on the 1992 legislative decree.

the case against Portugal, which concerned the transposition of Directives 86/280/EEC and 88/347/EEC.[378]

The German case involved failure to transpose no fewer than five different daughter directives of Directive 76/464/EEC. The only significant legal issue in these proceedings was a long-standing 'generic' question of contention between the Commission and the Federal Republic which had already been litigated earlier with respect to other environmental directives, namely, the validity of transposition of Community law by purely administrative measures. Germany claimed to have fully implemented the directives through administrative instructions and circulars (*allgemeine Verwaltungsvorschriften*), but the Court, reaffirming its long-established case-law,[379] held that binding provisions of domestic law were required and that Germany had consequently failed to comply with its obligations under the Treaty, notwithstanding its assertion that material compliance with all the substantive provisions of the relevant directives had in fact been fully achieved.[380]

The initial focus on formal implementation of the directives as opposed to practical application is no special feature of the Commission's enforcement policy in this particular field, but a standard attitude prevailing in all areas of the Commission's rather cursory supervision of compliance with Community environmental law.[381] Anyone remotely familiar with water pollution problems in Europe will find the Commission's statement that in the water sector, as opposed to other sectors of environmental policy, 'problems of correct application [of Community directives] are rare, but they often take time to settle'[382] rather puzzling. The Commission services themselves have not made any real effort to monitor the practical application of Community law on the ground and to take legal action where necessary to force member states to apply water directives correctly. Occasionally, the Commission may initiate infringement proceedings in a case of inadequate

The other two questions raised by the *Pretura* address the consequences of this legal situation for Mr Arcaro's criminal liability and do not directly concern the interpretation of the directives. Reaffirming its established case-law on the general issue of the legal effect of directives in the absence of full and correct transposition into national law, the Court held that the provisions of the relevant directives in and of themselves cannot be a basis for imposing criminal liability on an individual, since national authorities cannot invoke provisions of Community law which they have failed to implement against private individuals.

As it clearly appears from the *Pretura*'s factual findings and the Court of Justice's judgment in the *Arcaro* case that, at the time when criminal proceedings were brought against Mr Arcaro, Dir 83/513/EEC had not yet been fully transposed into Italian law, one may wonder why the Commission did not initiate Art 228 proceedings against the Italian Republic for failure to comply with the Court's earlier ruling.

378 Case C–213/97, *Commission v Portuguese Republic*, [1998] ECR I–3289.

379 See, eg Case C–131/88, *Commission v Federal Republic of Germany*, [1991] ECR I–825.

380 Case C–262/95, *Commission v Federal Republic of Germany*, [1996] ECR I–5729.

381 On this question, see generally Pallemaerts (1991).

382 11th Annual report on monitoring the application of Community law (1993), OJ No C154, 6.6.1994, at p 47.

application of Community law, but when this does occur it is generally the result of a complaint against a member state lodged by a private individual rather than of the existence of a consistent monitoring and enforcement policy on the part of the Commission services.

The first such case concerning the discharge of dangerous substances in the aquatic environment is mentioned in the Commission's annual report for the year 1988. It concerned the pollution of the Gallego river in Spain by effluents and waste from a pesticide production plant, discharged in violation of 'a number of directives on hexachlorocyclohexane.'[383] According to the official notice announcing the initiation of proceedings in the Court of Justice,[384] these directives did not, surprisingly enough, include Directive 84/491/EEC on HCH emissions into the aquatic environment. This case did not culminate in a judgment, as it was eventually settled out of court. In the 1992 annual report, the Commission announced that it had initiated infringement proceedings against the United Kingdom over releases of dangerous substances from an abandoned mine in Cornwall in violation of Directives 80/68/EEC and 76/464/EEC.[385] To my knowledge, this case did not result in a judgment either.

In 1995, the Commission instituted proceedings before the Court of Justice against Greece for its failure to draw up pollution reduction programmes for specific polluted lakes, rivers and coastal waters and to implement a prior authorisation system for discharges of dangerous substances as required by Directive 76/464/EEC.[386] These proceedings led to the first Court judgment addressing issues of practical application of Directive 76/464/EEC.[387] Though largely based on factual considerations peculiar to the particular case at hand, the judgment has some legal implications of a more general relevance, especially as regards the interpretation of the member states' obligations with respect to pollution by grey list substances.

The action against Greece was triggered by complaints submitted to the Commission concerning the pollution of specific surface waters subject to the provisions of Directive 76/464/EEC, Lake Vegorritis, the Soulos River and the Gulf of Pagasi. The judgment provides no information about the exact nature and source of the pollution complained of, but discharges of grey list substances were involved, since the Commission's main pleas were

[383] 6th Annual report on monitoring the application of Community law (1988), OJ No C330, 30.12.1989, p 25, para 153. See also Commission Press Release IP(88)703, 15 Nov 1988.

[384] Case C–21/89, *Commission v Spain*, OJ No C45, 24.2.1989, p 13.

[385] 10th Annual report on monitoring the application of Community law (1992), OJ No C233, 30.8.1993, p 55, para 2.12.3.

[386] 13th Annual report on monitoring the application of Community law (1995), OJ No C303, 14.10.1996, p 52.

[387] Joined Cases C–232/95 and C–233/95, *Commission v Hellenic Republic*, [1998] ECR I–3343.

based on Article 7 of the Directive. The Commission alleged that Greece had infringed the provisions of Article 7, paragraph 1 by failing to establish pollution reduction programmes for the waters in question and those of Article 7, paragraph 2 by failing to make effluent discharges liable to contain grey list substances subject to a requirement of prior authorisation. The Court refused to consider the latter plea on the grounds that it was subsumed into the former, arguing that where no programmes, as required by Article 7, paragraph 1 have been established, it is a fortiori impossible to grant authorisations in accordance with Article 7, paragraph 2, since these authorisations must lay down emission standards based on the quality objectives established in the relevant programmes.[388] But the Commission's first plea was held to be well-founded and the Court ruled that Greece had failed to fulfil its obligations under Article 7 of the Directive 'by failing to establish programmes including quality objectives and setting deadlines for their implementation' with a view to reducing pollution of the waters in question by grey list substances.

The Directive does not define what constitutes a programme within the meaning of Article 7. In its defence, Greece referred to domestic legislation laying down water quality objectives and emission standards and to a number of general programmes for the quantitative and qualitative management of water resources in the areas in question, implying that these measures satisfied the requirements of the Directive. However, the Court found that the measures invoked by the defendant member state lacked the specificity required by Article 7 of Directive 76/464/EEC, because Greece had not shown that the existing programmes on which it relied 'relate specifically to the substances mentioned in List II.'[389]

The Court stressed that the objective of the Directive is 'more specific' than merely achieving a reduction of water pollution generally.[390] The Court particularly emphasised the importance of the establishment of quality objectives as an essential element of the regulatory regime for grey list substances laid down in Article 7. The Greek measures did not meet the requirements of Article 7 because they also failed to 'indicate the quality objectives on the basis of which the pollution caused by [grey list] substances is to be reduced.'[391] The mere existence of regulations fixing discharge limits for certain substances is not sufficient if those limits 'are not *based on* any quality objectives for the reduction of existing pollution which are defined *within the framework of specific programmes*.'[392] Thus, the judgment clearly affirms the fundamental nature of the member states' obligation to

[388] Joined Cases C–232/95 and C–233/95, *Commission v Hellenic Republic*, [1998] ECR I–3343, paras 27–29.
[389] *Ibid*, para 36.
[390] *Ibid*, para 35.
[391] *Ibid*.
[392] *Ibid*, para 41 (emphasis added).

draw up programmes specifically aimed at reducing pollution by grey list substances and the crucial function, within those programmes, of quality objectives as a basis for all other measures.

Apart from these few cases addressing specific instances of non-compliance in individual member states, the Commission, in recent years, has also of its own initiative launched an across-the-board effort to enforce the provisions of Article 7 of Directive 76/464/EEC in a systematic and horizontal manner.[393] Through this action, which the Commission itself has termed 'a comprehensive operation,'[394] it is trying to compel all member states to draw up and implement pollution reduction programmes for grey list substances. As a result of this Commission initiative, some member states have reportedly taken measures to comply with their obligations,[395] but in most cases the Commission has had to pursue the matter before the Court of Justice. The Court has already rendered judgment in a number of these cases, against Luxembourg,[396] Belgium,[397] Spain,[398] Italy,[399] Germany,[400] Greece,[401] Portugal[402] and the Netherlands.[403]

While the Greek case discussed above related to pollution of specific waters, the Commission's plea in this series of proceedings (which includes a second case against Greece) was formulated in much more general terms, addressing the overall implementation of Article 7 of Directive 76/464/EEC in these member states. To circumvent the difficulties resulting from the fact that List II of the Directive does not in fact contain a comprehensive, agreed list of grey-list substances but a number of rather loosely defined categories of substances subject to interpretation, the Commission resorted to some creative legal reasoning to remedy this relative indeterminacy of the member states' obligations under Article 7. It decided to focus its enforcement efforts initially on one particular category of List II substances. As the first indent of List II provides that substances belonging to the categories in List I (ie black list substances) for which no Community limit values have yet been laid down shall be treated as grey list substances, it was possible to produce a specific list of grey list substances out of the list of 129 black list

[393] Answer of the Commission to Written Question No 1496/91, OJ No C202, 10.8.1992, p 7. See also the 7th Annual Report of the Commission on monitoring the application of Community law (1989), OJ No C232, 17.9.1990, p 25, para 157.

[394] Answer of the Commission to Written Question No 3068/93, OJ No C317, 14.11.1994, p 15.

[395] 10th Annual report on monitoring the application of Community law (1992), OJ No C233, 30.8.1993, p 56, para 3.3.3.

[396] Case C–206/96, *Commission v Luxembourg*, [1998] ECR I–3401.

[397] Case C–207/97, *Commission v Belgium*, [1999] ECR I–275.

[398] Case C–214/96, *Commission v Spain*, [1998] ECR I–7661.

[399] Case C–285/96, *Commission v Italy*, [1998] ECR I–5935.

[400] Case C–184/97, *Commission v Germany*, [1999] ECR I–7837.

[401] Case C–384/97, *Commission v Hellenic Republic*, [2000] ECR I–3823.

[402] Case C–261/98, *Commission v Portugal*, [2000] ECR I–5905.

[403] Case C–152/98, *Commission v Netherlands*, [2001] ECR I–3463.

substances annexed to the 1982 Commission Communication[404] and endorsed by the Council in its resolution of 7 February 1983.[405] By subtracting the 'confirmed' black list substances for which daughter directives have been adopted, as well as the substances for which the Commission proposed in 1990 to fix limit values 'on a priority basis',[406] the Commission arrived at a list of 99 grey list substances. The exclusion of the latter group of substances seems rather arbitrary, in view of the fact that the Commission's 1990 proposal was never adopted by the Council and that no limit values have in fact been set for these substances. Moreover, the proposal in question was formally withdrawn in 1993.[407] Also, one may wonder why the Commission did not include in its list those grey list substances such as metals that are individually identified in List II.[408]

The Commission's choice to focus its claims on this list of 99 substances, despite its incomplete nature, seems to have been a strategic one. While this litigation strategy has the disadvantage of restricting the potential reach of enforcement action and not exploiting the full scope of the member states' obligations under Article 7, it has the advantage of being able to elicit an unequivocal and enforceable ruling by the Court of Justice instead of a holding which, in reaffirming the full extent of member state obligations with respect to the whole category of grey list substances, merely replicates the indeterminacies of the directive itself. In its applications against Luxembourg and the Netherlands, as opposed to the other defendant member states, the Commission did not actually limit its claim to the list of 99 substances. In the first case, this seems to have been an unintended error rather than a deliberate difference of strategy, since the reasoned opinion referred only to the 99 substances in question. Thus the Court, on procedural grounds, declared inadmissible that part of the application which related to substances other than those listed in the reasoned opinion, and the ruling against Luxembourg, as in most other cases,[409] is specifically restricted to

[404] Communication of the Commission to the Council of 22 June 1982 on dangerous substances which might be included in List I of Council Dir 76/464/EEC, OJ No C176, 14.7.1982, p 3.

[405] Council Resolution of 7 Feb 1983 concerning the combating of water pollution, OJ No C46, 17.2.1983, p 17.

[406] Proposal for a Council Directive amending Dir 76/464/EEC on pollution caused by certain dangerous substances discharged into the aquatic environment of the Community, OJ No C55, 7.3.1990, p 7, Art 2.

[407] As Advocate-General J Mischo observes in paras 4 and 37 of his opinion in Case C–152/98. He concludes that there are consequently 114 'priority substances' identified in the 1982 Communication which are to be treated provisionally as grey list substances.

[408] In Case C–152/98, however, the Commission also specifically claimed and the Court held that the Netherlands had not complied with its obligations under Art 7 of Dir 76/464/EEC inter alia by failing to lay down water quality objectives for the grey list metals borium, tellurium, silver, uranium and titanium in the Scheldt River basin.

[409] Except, oddly, in Cases C–384/97, *Commission v Hellenic Republic*, and C–261/98, *Commission v Portugal*, where the Court's verdict refers generally to 'substances falling within the first indent of List II', even though the scope of the Commission's application was restricted to the 99 substances. The judgment provides no explanation for what seems to be an *ultra petita* ruling.

the 99 substances.[410] In the case against the Netherlands, however, the Commission's application seems to have been deliberately broader in scope, as it referred to an infringement of the provisions of Article 7 of the Directive as a result of the Dutch authorities' failure to establish pollution reduction programmes and set water quality objectives for Annex II substances in the Scheldt basin generally. The Court, in its dictum, held that the Netherlands had failed to comply with its Community obligations by not taking all necessary measures for the implementation of Article 7, without specifying with respect to what substances. But in its reasoning, the Court implied that the obligation to establish quality objectives in fact only applies to the candidate black list substances identified by the Commission in its 1982 Communication which effectively occur in the waters of the Scheldt basin.[411] These ambiguities in the position of the Commission and the Court indicate some uncertainty as to the exact scope of the member states' obligations under Article 7.

The first important question to be settled in this litigation was that of the accuracy of the Commission's contentions regarding the legal effects of the list of candidate black list substances in the 1982 Commission communication on member state obligations with respect to grey list substances under Article 7 of the Directive. It is by no means self-evident that a list laid down in a Commission communication, a non-binding document reflecting the view of a single institution and merely endorsed 'as a basis for further work' by a Council resolution, another non-binding instrument, can have such far-reaching legal consequences. In the first case that it ruled on, that against Luxembourg, the Court accepted without any discussion the Commission's view of the imperative nature of the list of 99 substances. In fact, it was not forced to address this issue because the defendant member state refrained from raising it.[412] It was in the proceedings against Belgium that the Court was compelled explicitly to address the issue of the validity of the list as a basis for determining the scope of the member states' legal obligations under Article 7 of Directive 76/464/EEC. Having already implicitly accepted the validity of the list in an earlier judgment, the

[410] Case C–206/96, *Commission v Luxembourg*, [1998] ECR I–3401, para 15.

[411] Case C–152/98, *Commission v Netherlands*, [2001] ECR I–3463, para 34. The Court approvingly cited para 36 of the Advocate-General's opinion, referring to 114 substances. In para 37 of that same opinion, the Advocate-General expressed some surprise at the fact that the Commission did not limit the scope of its action against the Netherlands to these substances, while it alleged infringement only with respect to 99 substances in similar actions against other member states.

[412] The only, rather implausible defence raised by Luxembourg was that there were no discharges of waste water containing any of the 99 substances in its territory and that, consequently, there was no need for it to establish any programmes. However, this assertion was easily countered by the Commission with a list of industrial activities which necessarily discharge some of the substances in question, forcing Luxembourg to admit that some of these substances must indeed be discharged in its surface waters. *Ibid*, para 22. The Court stressed that the obligation to establish pollution reduction programmes extends to all surface waters affected by pollution, as defined in the Directive. *Ibid*, para 20.

Court did not come to a different conclusion in this case, but explicated its reasoning.

In its defence, the Belgian government contended that the list of 99 substances on which the Commission based its action was not of a legally binding nature, having been adopted by a mere Council resolution without legal force, a resolution which moreover indicates that the list is to serve 'as a basis for further work'. In these circumstances, Belgium alleged, the list in question cannot have the immediate effect of creating, for the member states, the specific obligations relied on by the Commission, all the more so since Directive 76/464/EEC is a framework directive requiring further implementing measures.

The Court held that:

> the point at issue in the present case is not the legal nature, binding or not, of the resolution in question, but the question whether the 99 substances belong to the families and groups of substances in List I of the Annex to the Directive and whether more specific legislative provision is required before they can be treated as List II substances.[413]

The first question is a factual one, and the Court further noted that:

> it is not in dispute that the 99 substances belong scientifically to the families and groups of substances in List I and were identified in the course of research undertaken by the Commission with the help of representatives of the Member States.[414]

The Commission communication and subsequent Council resolution are to be viewed as the culmination of a fact-finding process which recognised that the substances in question met the criteria for black list substances laid down in Directive 76/464/EEC and should be the subject of further measures in the framework of that Directive. Thus the Council resolution is not to be regarded as a normative act, but as an authoritative interpretation of the scientific categories referred to in the Directive. It is on this basis that the Court, like the Commission, accepted the resolution as evidence that the 99 substances in question belong to List I.

As regards the framework nature of the Directive, the Court made it clear that this applies only to the establishment of Community emission limit values and quality objectives under Article 6. Indeed, further legislative action in the form of implementing directives is required for the adoption of the specific measures envisaged for black list substances for the 99 substances identified in the Council resolution. However, the enforcement action brought by the Commission does not relate to these measures, whose absence is obviously not the member states' responsibility, but rather to the alternative measures provided in the directive pending the adoption of

[413] Case C–207/97, *Commission v Belgium*, para 32.
[414] *Ibid*, para 33.

further Community measures. The directive provides that the provisions of Article 7 are to be applied provisionally to all identified black list substances for which no Community emission limit values and quality objectives have yet been laid down. The Court pointed out that 'there is absolutely no need for more specific legislative provision before the substances in question, which have been identified, are to be treated as List II substances by the Member States', and pollution reduction programmes similar to those for grey list substances are to be established for them.[415] The judgment emphasised that 'the Directive cannot be regarded as a framework-directive so far as that obligation is concerned.'[416]

Having established in principle the obligation of the member states to apply the provisions of Article 7 to each of the 99 substances at issue, the Court then has to clarify the precise scope of the specific obligations under those provisions and evaluate the extent of each member state's compliance with them. The obligations *in concreto* of each member state will in the first place depend on factual circumstances concerning the discharges of hazardous substances in its territory. The obligation to draw up pollution reduction programmes is not an absolute one, but depends on the existence of discharges of the substance concerned in the member state's territory. This point was clarified in several judgments. In the Luxembourg case, the defendant government first argued that there was no need to draw up any programmes since there were no industries processing and discharging any of the substances in question. However, although Luxembourg had never replied to Commission requests for a list of those substances discharged in the aquatic environment under its jurisdiction, the Commission was able to show that industries discharging some of the 99 substances existed in Luxembourg, and the defendant government eventually acknowledged as much. The judgment specifies that the obligation to establish programmes extends to all waters affected by discharges of the substances in question, and implies that programmes must only be drawn up for those substances which are effectively discharged.[417] Similarly, in its judgment against the Netherlands, the Court responded to the defendant's argument that Annex II potentially covers tens of thousands of substances by stating that the obligations resulting from Article 7 apply only to those substances included in the Commission's list of candidate black list substances which can actually be found in the surface waters concerned.[418] This was also confirmed in the ruling against Belgium, in which the Court held that the member states were obliged to establish programmes 'at least in the case of pollution caused by any of the substances at issue which is likely to be present in waste

[415] *Ibid*, para 35.
[416] *Ibid*.
[417] Case C–206/96, *Commission v Luxembourg*, paras 20–21.
[418] Case C–152/98, *Commission v Netherlands*, para 34.

discharged in their territory.'[419] The terms of the judgment imply that the first step to be taken by member states in complying with their obligations under Article 7 is in fact to determine 'which substances are relevant in the national context,'[420] inter alia through 'analyses of the waters affected.'[421]

This does not, however, mean that the member states have discretion to decide whether or not to take measures pursuant to Article 7 depending on their own assessment as to whether their surface waters can be considered 'polluted' by the substances in question, as the German government has argued. According to Germany, the obligation to draw up pollution reduction programmes exists only where there is evidence of 'pollution'. In its view, the national measures it had taken to restrict discharges of all black and grey list substances had been so effective that no 'pollution' within the meaning of the directive could be said to exist, and hence it had no obligation to set quality objectives and establish pollution reduction programmes pursuant to Article 7. This argument was forcefully rejected by the Court in the following terms:

> under the directive the obligation on Member States to draw up programmes including quality objectives is conditioned not by a finding of actual water pollution by List II substances, governed by Article 7 of the directive, but by discharges of those substances into the aquatic environment.[422]

The several defendant member states, in their attempts to demonstrate compliance with the provisions of Article 7, generally relied on a variety of existing national measures which they claimed should be considered equivalent to the 'programmes' referred to in those provisions. None of these defences was found convincing by the Court, which in its case-law insisted on a rather rigorous interpretation of the directive. Already in the first Greek case, analysed above, the Court had rejected a number of general measures relied on by Greece as insufficient and stressed the importance of the requirement that the programmes should relate specifically to the substances in question and should be based on water quality objectives.[423] This line of argument is further amplified in subsequent judgments. Spain referred to a royal decree establishing quality objectives for some 30 List II substances and to legislation requiring the establishment of further water quality objectives in river basin management plans. Belgium, for its part, relied on existing legislation establishing both quality objectives and sectoral emission standards for a number of grey list substances and on measures for the reduction of discharges of certain substances taken pursuant to commit-

[419] Case C–207/97, *Commission v Belgium*, para 35.
[420] *Ibid*, para 43.
[421] *Ibid*, para 41.
[422] Case C–184/97, *Commission v Germany*, para 61.
[423] Joined Cases C–232/95 and C–233/95, *Commission v Hellenic Republic*, para 36. This was confirmed in Case C–384/97, *Commission v Hellenic Republic*.

ments made by Belgium within the framework of the North Sea Conferences. The Spanish and Belgian measures were dismissed by the Court as 'only a series of *ad hoc* legislative measures which cannot amount to an organised and coordinated system of quality objectives relating to specific watercourses or bodies of standing water,'[424] and 'merely *ad hoc* measures, not comprehensive and coherent programmes for pollution reduction, based on studies of the waters affected and setting quality objectives,'[425] respectively. In its judgment against Belgium, the Court spelt out, in the following general terms, the requirements for Article 7 programmes:

> What is specific to the programmes in question is the fact that they must embody a comprehensive and coherent approach, covering the entire national territory of each Member State and providing practical and coordinated arrangements for the reduction of pollution caused by any of the substances in List II which is relevant in the particular context of the Member State concerned, in accordance with the quality objectives fixed by those programmes for the waters affected. They differ, therefore, both from general purification programmes and from bundles of *ad hoc* measures designed to reduce water pollution.[426]

Germany asserted that its national system of regulation of discharges is more stringent than that called for by the directive and effectively meets all the substantive requirements of Community law, so that no useful purpose would be served by the establishment of the pollution reduction programmes referred to in Article 7. The German system makes no distinction between black and grey list substances and subjects all discharges to prior authorisation and stringent emission limit values. Germany argued that since the basic purpose of the directive is ultimately to ensure that emission limit values are set and enforced with a view to the reduction and elimination of pollution, and since this purpose is met, the establishment of programmes fixing quality objectives becomes redundant. It also maintained that, as appears from the dual system set up by the directive itself, emission limit values are by definition more stringent and environmentally protective than quality objectives and that the constant improvement of water quality in Germany testifies to that. Having thus exercised its right, laid down in Article 10 of the Directive, to take more stringent measures, Germany alleged that it was no longer required to establish programmes under Article 7.

The Court rejected Germany's argument that the setting of stringent emission limit values dispenses it from the establishment of pollution reduction programmes comprising quality objectives.[427] It noted that, in the

[424] Case C–214/96, *Commission v Spain*, para 30.
[425] Case C–207/97, *Commission v Belgium*, para 45.
[426] *Ibid*, para 40. This is now referred to by the Court itself as 'settled case-law'. See Case C–384/97, *Commission v Hellenic Republic*, para 40.
[427] Case C–184/97, *Commission v Germany*, para 29.

scheme of the directive, water quality objectives are an essential instrument, their establishment being provided for both for black list substances (at Community level) and grey list substances (at member state level).[428] Emission limit values are not by definition more stringent; that depends entirely on the level at which they are set.[429] Moreover, emission limit values, as opposed to quality objectives, are inadequate to deal with pollution from diffuse sources, which the Court says must also be covered by the pollution reduction programmes.[430] Finally, these programmes are indispensable to enable the Commission to verify compliance by the member states and undertake the comparative appraisal of implementation with a view to harmonisation provided for in Article 7, paragraph 7.[431] The Court rejected both Germany's plea that it is under no obligation to draw up programmes, as well as its alternate plea that its existing system of regulation effectively amounts to a programme within the meaning of Article 7. In terms similar to those of the judgments against Belgium and Spain, the Court again stressed that programmes must necessarily comprise quality objectives, which are missing in the German system:

> Consequently, neither general rules nor *ad hoc* measures adopted by a Member State which, though comprising a wide range of water-protection standards, none the less do not lay down quality objectives relating to a given watercourse or area of water cannot [*sic*] be deemed to constitute a programme within the meaning of Article 7 of the directive.[432]

The Court's recent case-law has clarified the precise extent of the obligations of member states under Article 7 of the Directive with respect to grey list substances and black list substances which are to be treated provisionally as grey list substances pending the adoption of Community emission limit values and quality objectives. Since the latter category in fact comprises the vast majority of black list substances, Article 7 has by default become one of the most important substantive provisions of the directive. The Court has made it clear that the obligation to draw up pollution reduction programmes is to be taken seriously and requires purposeful implementation. A programme is to be established specifically for each identified individual grey list substance discharged in the aquatic environment of the member state concerned. All attempts by member states to present a series of general and incidental measures as implied programming have been

[428] Case C–184/97, *Commission v Germany*, para 34.
[429] *Ibid*, paras 39–40.
[430] *Ibid*, para 36.
[431] *Ibid*, paras 31–32.
[432] *Ibid*, para 58. It appears from the original German language version of the judgment that there is a translation error in para 58 of the English version: for 'cannot be deemed' one should obviously read 'can be deemed'.

rejected. Programmes must reflect a 'comprehensive and coherent approach' and must cover the entire national territory.[433]

As to the substantive content of the programmes, the Court has primarily stressed the fundamental nature of the quality objectives to be 'laid down in the shape of a programme intended for specific watercourses and bodies of standing water.'[434] These quality objectives are to 'serve as the point of reference for calculating the emission standards specified in the prior authorisations,'[435] thus ensuring the 'uniform application' of these authorisations.[436] A system of emission limit values which is not based on quality objectives does not satisfy the requirements of Article 7. The quality objectives are also to serve as a point of reference for measures to reduce pollution from diffuse sources. But beyond that, and pointing out that the programmes shall provide 'practical and coordinated arrangements for the reduction of pollution,'[437] the Court does not give further guidance as to their content. Member states thus retain a considerable measure of discretion in this respect, as well as in determining the actual level of the quality objectives and the deadlines for implementation referred to in the directive.

An interesting question not answered by this case-law is whether the member states, having set their quality objectives, also have an obligation to ensure that these are actually achieved within the deadlines they have freely determined. There is some recent, unrelated case-law in which the Court has held that member states have an obligation of result to ensure Community water quality objectives are met in those areas they have designated for this purpose.[438] It would not stretch the *effet utile* doctrine very far to suggest that the same might apply to the quality objectives to be established pursuant to Article 7 of Directive 76/464/EEC. All in all, the potential implications of the case-law on Article 7 are very important, were the Commission to choose to pursue a rigorous enforcement strategy. It is important to note here that while most of the judgments rendered concern only the 99 substances on which the Commission chose to focus its claim, the obligations upheld by the Court in these cases apply potentially to a much wider range of substances and could be enforced in a similar way.[439]

[433] Case C–207/97, *Commission v Belgium*, para 40. See also Case C–261/98, *Commission v Portugal*, para 29.

[434] Case C–214/96, *Commission v Spain*, para 29.

[435] Case C–207/97, *Commission v Belgium*, para 41. See also Joined Cases C–232/95 and C–233/95, *Commission v Hellenic Republic*, para 28.

[436] Case C–214/96, *Commission v Spain*, para 29.

[437] Case C–207/97, *Commission v Belgium*, para 40.

[438] Case C–198/97, *Commission v Germany*, [1999] ECR I–3257, para 35; Case C–307/98, *Commission v Belgium*, [2000] ECR I–3933, para 49.

[439] This can be inferred from Case C–152/98, *Commission v Netherlands*, [2001] ECR I–3463, in which the Commission did not limit its claim to 99 substances, and the Court held

prevention and control[442] was submitted to the Council. This proposal, the Commission's main legislative initiative in the field of industrial pollution control under the 5th Action Programme, was inspired by an OECD Recommendation[443] and recent developments in regulatory policy in some member states.[444] It was eventually adopted, in a substantially modified form, by the Council in September 1996.

A New Framework for Industrial Pollution Control

The stated aim of the IPPC Directive, as set out in its preamble, is 'to modify and supplement existing Community legislation concerning the prevention and control of pollution from industrial plants' in order to achieve 'an integrated approach' to pollution prevention and reduction. The two pieces of existing Community legislation identified in the preamble of the Directive as in need of reform are Directive 76/464/EEC on water pollution by dangerous substances[445] and Directive 84/360/EEC, its air pollution counterpart.[446] In order to fully appreciate the implications and significance of the IPPC Directive, it is necessary to analyse its provisions against the background of these two existing directives, which both introduced a regime of prior authorisation for certain kinds of polluting activities. The provisions of Directive 76/464/EEC have been analysed in detail earlier in this chapter. Those of Directive 84/360/EEC will be summarised here only to the extent relevant to my argument.

In contrast with Directive 76/464/EEC, whose scope of application is not fixed by reference to a specific list of industrial processes but covers all discharges of dangerous substances into the aquatic environment, whatever their source, Directive 84/360/EEC applies only to specific categories of industrial plants, listed in its Annex I. The operation or 'substantial alteration' of all plants belonging to these categories requires a prior authorisation from the competent national authority.[447] Such authorisation may only be issued if 'the use of the plant will not cause significant air pollution *particularly from the emission of substances referred to in Annex II*' and

[442] Proposal for a Council Directive on integrated pollution prevention and control, OJ No C311, 17.11.1993, p 6.

[443] OECD Council Recommendation C(90)164 on Integrated Pollution Prevention and Control.

[444] Such as the United Kingdom's Environmental Protection Act (1990). See Gibson (1991); Emmott & Haigh (1996); Irwin (1989).

[445] Council Dir 76/464/EEC of 4 May 1976 on pollution caused by certain dangerous substances discharged into the aquatic environment of the Community, OJ No L129, 18.5.1976, p 23.

[446] Council Dir 84/360/EEC of 28 June 1984 on the combating of air pollution from industrial plants , OJ No L188, 16.7.1984, p 20 (hereafter referred to as Dir 84/360/EEC).

[447] Dir 84/360/EEC, Art 3, paras 1–2.

all appropriate preventive measures against air pollution have been taken, including the application of the *best available technology*, provided that the application of such measures *does not entail excessive costs*.[448]

Annex II lists the 'most important polluting substances' whose emissions must be controlled by the member states.[449]

While the Directive does not explicitly require the competent national authorities to lay down emission standards for each of the specific air pollutants listed, it does subject the granting of an authorisation to the condition that 'none of the emission limit values *applicable* will be exceeded.'[450] This language can be taken to refer both to any limit values which may have been laid down nationally and to those which may be imposed by Community law. Article 8 of the Directive indeed provides for the possibility of fixing 'emission limit values based on the *best available technology not entailing excessive costs*' at Community level 'if necessary.'[451] Such limit values have in fact been established only for a limited number of categories of industrial plants.[452] However, regardless of the existence or not of applicable Community limit values, Directive 84/360/EEC does entail a general obligation for the member states to require the application of 'best available technology not entailing excessive costs' (BATNEEC) when authorizing any new plants[453] and to take appropriate measures 'for the gradual adaptation of existing plants' to such technology.[454] In practice, emission standards are the instrument most likely to be used by member states to fulfil these obligations.

The IPPC Directive is designed to establish a single regulatory regime for the prevention and control of pollution from major point sources which, ultimately, is intended to replace the existing sectoral regimes laid down in Directives 76/464/EEC and 84/360/EEC. This appears from the transitional provisions in Article 19, which in essence stipulate that those earlier directives will no longer apply to installations which have been authorised pursuant to the IPPC Directive. The change from one regime to the other is not a purely formal matter but entails important substantive changes for the plants in question. While the scope of application of the IPPC Directive is considerably wider than that of Directives 76/464/EEC and 84/360/EEC put together and the new Directive introduces detailed requirements for a

[448] *Ibid*, Art 4 (emphasis added).
[449] Some of these air pollutants, such as eg heavy metals, are also important water pollutants listed in the annex to Dir 76/464/EEC and have been shown to reach the marine environment through the atmosphere.
[450] *Ibid*, Art 4(3)
[451] *Ibid*, Art 8, para 1 (emphasis added).
[452] So far, 'daughter' directives of Dir 84/360/EEC have been adopted only for large combustion plants (Dir 88/609/EEC), new and existing municipal waste incinerators (Dirs 89/369/EEC and 89/429/EEC) and hazardous waste incinerators (Dir 94/67/EC).
[453] Dir 84/360/EEC, Art 4(1).
[454] *Ibid*, Art 13.

whole range of industrial activities which were not hitherto subject to specific provisions of Community law, my main purpose in this section is to analyse the implications of the IPPC Directive for those activities which were already covered by the sectoral authorisation regime of the 1976 Directive. I first compare various key provisions of the IPPC Directive with existing legal requirements under Directive 76/464/EEC and, where relevant as a point of comparison, Directive 84/360/EEC, and then discuss the legal implications of the transitional provisions.

Permitting Requirements for Industrial Plants

Unlike Directive 76/464/EEC, the IPPC Directive does not focus on a particular category of pollutants such as dangerous substances. Its scope of application is circumscribed by reference to specific 'categories of industrial activities' listed in its Annex I. When a particular activity falls under one of these categories and is therefore subject to the IPPC regime, the integrated approach implies that *all* 'emissions in the air, water and land' must be controlled 'in order to achieve a high level of protection for the environment taken as a whole.'[455] This general requirement applies to all substances likely to cause pollution,[456] but Annex III of the directive contains an 'indicative list of the main polluting substances to be taken into account if they are relevant for fixing emission limit values'. This list was drawn up based on the existing lists of pollutants in the annexes to Directives 76/464/EEC and 84/360/EEC.[457] However, the new list is of a purely 'indica-

[455] IPPC Directive, Art 1.

[456] 'Pollution' is defined in a manner consistent with the precautionary principle in Art 2(2).

[457] In the Commission's original proposal, Annex III was basically a combination of Annex II of Dir 84/360/EEC and the black and grey lists of Dir 76/464/EEC lumped together into a single list of 'most important' water pollutants. The Council made a number of changes in this list, some of an essentially editorial nature, and others with substantive implications. While the black and grey lists numbered 8 entries each, the new combined list of water pollutants has only 12 entries in all. A number of categories which were divided up between the black and grey list have been combined into a single category since there is no longer any differentiation between substances whose emissions must be reduced and others whose discharge is to be eliminated altogether. Thus, for instance, mercury and cadmium and their compounds, which are included in the black list of Dir 76/464/EEC, while other heavy metals appear in the grey list, have now been subsumed into the general category of 'metals and their compounds'. The most important substantive change is the extension of the category of carcinogenic substances to include compounds which have 'mutagenic properties or properties which may affect reproduction' as well. It should also be noted that non-persistent mineral oils and hydrocarbons, which figure in the grey list of Dir 76/464/EEC, are no longer mentioned in Annex III of the IPPC Directive, while the black list category of 'persistent mineral oils and hydrocarbons of petroleum origin' has been extended to cover not only persistent hydrocarbons in general but also other 'persistent and bioaccumulable organic toxic substances'. Finally Annex III includes 'substances which contribute to eutrophication' as a new category in its own right, while the grey list refers only to 'inorganic compounds of phosphorus and elemental phosphorus', as well as another, entirely new category, 'substances which have an unfavourable influence on the oxygen balance' of the receiving waters.

tive' nature and the substances listed have no special status different from other, unlisted pollutants. They are subject to the same general requirement that measures should be taken 'to prevent or, where that is not practicable, to reduce emissions' in all environmental media.[458] There is no special obligation to *eliminate* pollution by certain particularly hazardous pollutants, as required for black list substances under Directive 76/464/EEC. The Commission actually objected to amendments proposed by the European Parliament which would have reinstated the aim 'to eliminate pollution' in the relevant provisions of the IPPC Directive.[459]

According to the IPPC Directive, permits issued under its rules shall include emission limit values for pollutants, in particular those listed in Annex III to the Directive, which are 'likely to be emitted from the installation concerned *in significant quantities*.'[460] The Commission's original proposal referred to pollutants '*other than those emitted only in trace amounts and which cannot cause pollution*'. The wording chosen by the Council is manifestly intended to extend member state discretion in selecting the pollutants to be regulated even further. Moreover, the IPPC Directive also authorises member states to lay down emission limit values 'for certain groups, families or categories of substances', as opposed to individual substances,[461] and to replace limit values by 'equivalent parameters or technical measures,'[462] whatever that means.

With respect to emissions of dangerous substances into the aquatic environment, the existing provisions of Directive 76/464/EEC on permitting requirements do not leave the member states as much latitude. Under those provisions, which apply to a list of substances and groups of substances which largely overlaps that laid down in Annex III of the IPPC Directive,[463] member states are bound to lay down in the permits they issue emission standards for 'discharges of *any* such substance,'[464] ie any substance belonging to the groups or families of substances whose emission is regulated by Directive 76/464/EEC, without any qualification. For black list substances, these emission standards shall not exceed limit values laid down at Community level, 'taking into account the best technical means available,'[465] unless a member state demonstrates that it can ensure compliance with environmental quality standards through other measures. For all other substances listed in the annex, for which no emission limit values and quality standards have been fixed at Community level, the emission standards in

[458] IPPC Directive, Art 1.
[459] See Re-examined proposal for a Council Directive on integrated pollution prevention and control, EC Doc COM(96) 306 final, 24 June 1996, p 3.
[460] IPPC Directive, Art 9, para 3 (emphasis added).
[461] *Ibid*, Art 2(6).
[462] *Ibid*, Art 9, para 3.
[463] Cf above n 457.
[464] Dir 76/464/EEC, Art 3(1) (emphasis added).
[465] *Ibid*, Art 6, para 1 *in fine*.

the discharge permits shall be based on nationally established water quality objectives.

The IPPC Directive contains no equivalent, equally specific requirements as to the setting of emission standards for discharges of particular water pollutants. Its provisions on permit conditions contain no explicit reference to environmental quality standards nor to uniform limit values established at Community level. They only provide that emission limit values shall be laid down in the permit by the competent national authority for those pollutants whose emissions it deems 'significant' and that such limit values shall 'be based on the best available techniques' and shall be established 'taking into account the technical characteristics of the installation concerned, its geographical location and the local environmental conditions.'[466]

Best Available Techniques

The definition of the concept of 'best available techniques' (BAT), which is pivotal in the regulatory system established by the IPPC Directive, was the subject of protracted negotiations in the Council, resulting in several amendments to the Commission's proposal. This proposal, as the Commission points out in its explanatory memorandum, was 'substantially based on definitions in international conventions.'[467] At the time of drafting of the Commission proposal, three multilateral conventions containing a virtually identical definition of 'best available technology' or 'best available techniques' had recently been concluded: the 1992 Helsinki Convention on the Protection and Use of Transboundary Watercourses and International Lakes,[468] the 1992 Helsinki Convention on the Protection of the Marine Environment of the Baltic Sea Area[469] and the 1992 Paris Convention for the Protection of the Marine Environment of the North-East Atlantic.[470] This definition was itself directly inspired by that contained in a PARCOM Recommendation of June 1989,[471] which describes 'best available technology' as:

> the latest stage of development (state of the art) of processes, of facilities or of methods of operation which indicate the practical suitability of a particular measure for limiting emissions.

The 1989 recommendation further specifies that, in determining what constitutes BAT 'in general or individual cases', 'special consideration' should

[466] IPPC Directive, Art 9, para 4.
[467] EC Doc COM(93) 423 final, 14 Sept 1993, p 13.
[468] See Annex I.
[469] See Annex II, Reg 3.
[470] See App 1, para 2.
[471] PARCOM Recommendation 89/2 of 22 June 1989 on the Use of Best Available Technology, cf above ch 4.

be given to, inter alia, 'the economic feasibility of such technology' and the precautionary principle.

In its 1993 IPPC proposal, the Commission elaborated on these earlier definitions by adding separate sub-definitions of the terms 'best', 'available' and 'techniques' and further expanding the list of factors to be given 'special consideration'. While earlier texts generally used the term 'best available technology', the Commission in its proposal, following the example set by the 1992 Paris Convention, substituted the broader and semantically more accurate concept 'best available *techniques*' which refers not only to the actual technology used but also to 'the way in which the installation is designed, built, maintained, operated and decommissioned'.

The Council made changes in most components of the definition as proposed by the Commission, so as to water it down even further, extend the range of factors that may be taken into consideration in determining what constitutes BAT for any specific installation, and thus maximise national discretion. While the Commission had proposed that BAT should constitute '*the basis of* emission limit values for preventing or, where that is not practicable, *minimizing* emissions to the environment as a whole,'[472] the Council considerably lowered the level of ambition and underscored the relativity of the BAT concept by referring instead to its suitability

> for providing *in principle* the basis for emission limit values designed to prevent and, where that is not practicable, *generally to reduce* emissions and the impact on the environment as a whole.[473]

Similarly, in defining what is to be regarded as 'best' techniques, the Council found it necessary to substitute 'a high *general* level of protection of the environment as a whole' for 'a high level of protection', as proposed by the Commission, as the test of a given technique's effectiveness. These changes in language are intended to dilute whatever objectivity the BAT concept may possibly have and justify a considerable measure of flexibility in its application. Emission limit values set in individual permits must only 'in principle' be based on BAT. Emissions must only be 'generally reduced' rather than 'minimized', let alone eliminated. A high level of protection must not necessarily be achieved in all individual cases, as long as the 'general' level of protection remains sufficiently high.

According to the definition of BAT set out in Article 2(11) of the IPPC Directive, techniques are considered 'available' when they are 'developed on a scale which allows implementation in the relevant industrial sector, *under economically and technically viable conditions, taking into consideration the costs and advantages*.'[474] Thus, in determining what techniques are 'economically viable', member states are entitled to perform

[472] Commission proposal, above n 442, Art 2(10) (emphasis added).
[473] IPPC Directive, Art 2(11) (emphasis added).
[474] *Ibid* (emphasis added).

some sort of cost/benefit calculus. This results not only from the core definition of BAT itself, but is emphasised once more in Annex IV to the Directive, which lists the various

> considerations to be taken into account *generally or in specific cases* when determining best available techniques . . . *bearing in mind the likely costs and benefits of a measure* and the principles of precaution and prevention.[475]

The Commission actually considers the explicit reference to costs and benefits an 'essential' element of the definition of BAT, and objected to European Parliament amendments deleting it on the grounds that, without such reference, 'there would be no proportionality to the controls.'[476] The Directive does not, however, specify *whose* costs and benefits should be taken into consideration. The application of stringent emission controls will rarely be to the advantage of the operator. Should these private costs be weighed against the public benefits of pollution prevention or reduction? The emphatic reference to economic viability almost calls for individualised cost-benefit analyses to justify permit conditions.

The list of 'considerations to be taken into account' in Annex IV of the Directive is substantially longer than in the corresponding provisions of the above-mentioned PARCOM Recommendation and international conventions. This stems in part from the integrated approach to pollution control, which requires that equal attention be given to all forms of emissions and waste production, as opposed to an approach that focuses exclusively on the protection of the aquatic environment. Thus, for instance, the Commission proposed and the Council agreed to include among the relevant factors listed in Annex IV the consumption of raw materials, energy efficiency and the promotion of recovery and recycling, factors which are not mentioned in any of the earlier international definitions of BAT formulated in a water pollution context. This certainly broadens the concept of BAT and makes it consistent with an integrated approach to the protection of the environment as a whole, but at the same time also confuses it, as some of the criteria mentioned in Annex IV may well lead to conflicting conclusions when applied simultaneously, all the more so since these criteria are not listed in any order of priority.

When different techniques are available for a given activity, should preference be given to 'the use of low-waste technology'[477] or to a technology which guarantees waste recovery? Is the use of hazardous substances in an industrial process acceptable if they are effectively recycled, or should priority in all circumstances be given to 'the use of less hazardous substances,'[478] when available? Does BAT vary according to the 'commission-

[475] IPPC Directive, Annex IV, heading (emphasis added).

[476] Cf the explanatory memorandum to the Re-examined proposal, EC Doc COM(96) 306 final, 24 June 1996, p 3.

[477] IPPC Directive, Annex IV, item 1.

[478] *Ibid*, item 2.

ing date'[479] of the installation? May a plant commissioned before a certain date be exempted from the requirement to apply an available technique, even if its application is economically feasible? Is a determination of BAT that takes into account not only the 'nature and volume of the emissions', as proposed by the Commission, but also their 'effects', as decided by the Council,[480] consistent with 'the principles of precaution and prevention' referred to in the heading of Annex IV and, for that matter, in Article 174, paragraph 2 of the Treaty? Can the lack of full scientific evidence as to the 'effects' of particular emissions be invoked to justify exemptions from the use of available and economically feasible emission reduction techniques? Clearly, the multiplicity and range of criteria that may be taken into account is such that the prescriptive value of the concept of BAT is effectively nullified. Decisions as to what constitutes BAT are likely to be made on a case-by-case basis by permitting authorities, rather than on the basis of any common conception.

Local Environmental Conditions and Environmental Quality Standards

Not only is the very concept of BAT, as defined in the Directive, plagued by its innate indeterminacy, but the obligation of member states to base emission limit values on BAT when issuing permits is itself subject to significant qualifications. The Commission's proposal contained a provision stipulating that:

> if environmental quality standards . . . are being met by lower emission requirements than those achievable by the use of best available techniques, the competent authority *may allow more emissions than would have resulted from the application of the best available techniques* on condition that:
> (a) only a negligible increase in pollution is likely to result; and
> (b) no contribution to transboundary and/or global pollution is likely to occur.[481]

In its explanatory memorandum, the Commission justifies this clause by pointing out that 'BAT may not be required if the local environmental quality is very good and the substances released from the installation will not add unacceptable pollution,'[482] thus effectively endorsing the classical British argument against harmonised emission limit values. This provision was, however, vigorously opposed in the Council by those member states which have traditionally been proponents of uniform, technology-based emission standards throughout the Community as a means of achieving the highest possible level of environmental protection while equalising the conditions of competition within the internal market.

[479] *Ibid*, item 7.
[480] *Ibid*, item 6.
[481] Commission proposal, above n 442, Art 9, para 3 (emphasis added).
[482] Explanatory memorandum, EC Doc COM(93) 423 final, 14 Sept 1993, p 17.

Yet the wording that was eventually adopted by the Council, while not as explicit as that initially proposed by the Commission, has essentially the same effect of allowing national authorities to derogate from the BAT standard and impose less stringent permit conditions whenever they consider this justified by the 'geographical location' of the installation and the 'local environmental conditions.'[483] Indeed, the reference to plant location and environmental conditions is manifestly designed to qualify the general requirement that emission limit values 'shall be based on the best available techniques'. This clause is likely to be invoked by permit applicants and permitting authorities as a basis for derogating from BAT-based standards when the condition of the environment at the site of the installation is such that it can absorb more pollution without there being any risk of infringement of applicable environmental quality standards.

As a matter of fact, the wording of Article 9, paragraph 4 of the Directive could be read as not only *allowing* member states to take local environmental conditions into account, but even *requiring* them to do so. This, at any rate, seems to be the Commission's construction of this provision, as it opposed the European Parliament's amendment to the Council's common position aimed at deleting the reference to geographical location and environmental conditions on the grounds that '[t]he *obligation* to consider local environmental conditions . . . is essential to produce the optimised pollution control solution which is the goal of the Directive' and that removing it 'would fundamentally distort the integrated approach.'[484] Thus, surprisingly, the Commission has now become the most adamant advocate of local flexibility in standard-setting. Its interpretation of Article 9, paragraph 4 is, however, not shared by all member states, as the Council adopted a preambular clause which rather indicates the *optional* nature of derogations from the BAT standard by stipulating that

> it is *for the Member States to determine* how the technical characteristics of the installation concerned, its geographical location and local environmental conditions *can, where appropriate*, be taken into consideration.[485]

Whatever interpretation ultimately prevails, it is certainly ironic that, 20 years after the adoption of Directive 76/464/EEC, which introduced the principle of Community-wide emission limit values but allowed member states, as an *exception* to this principle, not to apply those limit values if they could demonstrate that less stringent permit conditions were sufficient to ensure compliance with water quality standards fixed at Community level, the IPPC Directive now effectively legitimises the environmental

[483] IPPC Directive, Art 9, para 4.

[484] Cf the explanatory memorandum to the Re-examined proposal, EC Doc COM(96) 306 final, 24 June 1996, p 3 (emphasis added).

[485] IPPC Directive, 18th preambular para (emphasis added).

quality-based approach to emission control by subsuming it under the general rule, rather than treating it as an exception to it.

The Commission's original proposal contained a general obligation for the member states—in addition to the requirement that emission standards shall be based on BAT—'to ensure that emission limit values are set with the aim of ensuring that environmental quality standards are not breached.'[486] This provision is reminescent of similar clauses in Directive 76/464/EEC, which prescribes that emission standards for grey list substances 'shall be based on . . . quality objectives' to be fixed by the member states,[487] and in Directive 84/360/EEC, which provides that industrial plants may only be authorised if the competent national authority is 'satisfied that . . . all the air quality limit values applicable will be taken into account.'[488]

The final version of the IPPC Directive contains no such clause, but merely provides that 'where an environmental quality standard requires stricter conditions than those achievable by the use of the best available techniques, additional measures shall in particular be required in the permit.'[489] The primary obligation of member states under the Directive is to base standards on BAT, taking into account local environmental conditions where appropriate. The Directive apparently assumes that compliance with this primary obligation will normally be sufficient to ensure that environmental quality standards are respected. It is only in exceptional cases, where this is not so, that the implicit secondary obligation to avoid infringement of EQS comes into play to require member states to take 'additional measures' and impose 'stricter conditions' in the permit.

It should be noted that the term 'environmental quality standards' as defined in the IPPC Directive refers only to standards 'set out in Community legislation.'[490] One wonders why standards laid down by national legislation are thus excluded from the ambit of the obligation set out in Article 10 of the IPPC Directive, especially as some Community legislation, such as Article 7 of Directive 76/464/EEC relating to grey list substances, expressly requires member states to establish EQS at the national level even in the absence of Community-wide standards.

Community Emission Limit Values

While the provisions of Article 9 of the IPPC Directive and the definition of 'best available techniques' in Article 2(11) leave the member states

[486] Commission proposal, above n 442, Art 9, para 1.
[487] Dir 76/464/EEC, Art 7, para 2.
[488] Dir 84/360/EEC, Art 4(4).
[489] IPPC Directive, Art 10.
[490] *Ibid*, Art 2(7).

virtually unfettered discretion in determining emission limit values for any given installation, the Directive contains a provision on 'Community emission limit values' which may potentially lead to some measure of harmonisation in the future and thus eventually limit national discretion in a number of cases. Article 18 provides that the Council will set emission limit values at Community level for certain categories of installations and pollutants '*for which the need for Community action has been identified.*'[491] A second paragraph stipulates that in the absence of such Community limit values fixed pursuant to this provision, emission limit values already laid down in existing Community legislation 'shall be applied as minimum emission limit values' for the purposes of the IPPC Directive.

This paragraph refers to a number of existing directives, mostly daughter directives of Directives 76/464/EEC and 84/360/EEC, establishing water and air emission standards for specific pollutants and sectors of industry. Thus, by virtue of Article 18, paragraph 2 of the IPPC Directive, these standards will continue to apply for all installations in the sectors concerned, even for new installations authorised pursuant to the IPPC Directive. Article 18, paragraph 2 effectively limits the discretion of competent authorities under Article 9, paragraph 4, in that they will not be free to invoke 'local environmental conditions' to prescribe less stringent emission standards for the installations in question than those laid down in existing Community legislation.

In addition to affirming the continued validity of emission standards set out in earlier Community legislation, Article 18 of the IPPC Directive also provides for new Community emission limit values to be established by the Council, acting on a proposal from the Commission, 'in accordance with the procedures laid down in the Treaty'. While this provision does not actually confer on the Council any powers which it did not already have by virtue of the Treaty itself, it does give the Commission an explicit mandate for a future legislative programme aimed at harmonising emission limit values in some of the industrial sectors covered by the IPPC Directive. Ironically, it is a mandate that the Commission itself did not really seek, as its original proposal did not contain any similar provision, but only referred to emission limit values 'which *have been* set at Community level,'[492] ie those already laid down in existing legislation.

In drafting the IPPC proposal, the Commission seems to have given up much of its earlier belief in the virtues of uniform Community-wide emission standards as an instrument for achieving a high level of environmental protection as well as harmonising the conditions of competition in the internal market. To justify its proposal in terms of the principle of subsidiarity, the Commission, in its explanatory memorandum, repeatedly

[491] IPPC Directive, Art 18, para 1 (emphasis added).
[492] Commission proposal, above n 442, Art 8, para 2 (emphasis added).

stresses that the proposed Directive will only lay down a general legal framework for integrated pollution control but that it will be for the member states to determine the actual emission limit values to be imposed in individual permits.[493] It emphasises that 'the setting of emission limit values can generally best be done at local level' and that 'where broadly comparable limits are set across the Community and where the effect on competitiveness is minimal . . . there may not always be a need for harmonization at Community level.'[494] In objecting to a European Parliament amendment which would have introduced a recital calling for 'special attention' to be given to the establishment of Community limit values, the Commission likewise argued that 'produc[ing] uniform emission limit value directives in every case . . . would again distort the potential for local optimisation.'[495] In its zeal to tune its discourse to the prevailing political mood within the Council and advocate 'local optimisation', has the Commission not in fact implicitly renounced the ostensible *ratio legis* of Directive 76/464/EEC and all its daughter directives, ie the harmonisation of national standards for discharges of hazardous substances in order to avoid distortions of competition?

The Commission does not, however, altogether rule out the possibility of future initiatives to harmonise emission limit values in certain sectors. As a matter of fact, the Commission proposed provisions specifically designed to enable it to monitor the standard-setting practices of national authorities through a regular exchange of information between it and the member states on the emission limit values laid down by such authorities 'and the best available techniques from which those values are derived.'[496] The explanatory memorandum states that the results of this exchange of information may be used by the Commission as a basis for formulating possible future proposals for the harmonisation of emission standards at Community level in some 'priority sectors', should it find substantial disparities among member states in the interpretation and application of BAT.[497] However, it is significant that, while the explanatory memorandum refers to this possibility, the Commission's draft directive did not contain any explicit provision to this effect and that such provision was actually added at the Council's initiative.

The proviso that Community emission limit values shall only be set for those categories of installations and pollutants '*for which the need for Community action has been identified*, on the basis, in particular, of the exchange

[493] Explanatory memorandum, EC Doc COM(93) 423 final, 14 Sept 1993, p 8.

[494] *Ibid*, p 12.

[495] Explanatory memorandum to the re-examined proposal, EC Doc COM(96) 306 final, 24 June 1996, p 3.

[496] Commission proposal, above n 442, Art 15, para 1.

[497] Explanatory memorandum, EC Doc COM(93) 423 final, 14 Sept 1993, pp 4, 12 and 18.

of information'[498] was apparently included to appease the subsidiarity concerns of some member states. The explicit reference to the information exchange procedure which, in accordance with the Commission's proposal, was included in Article 16 of the IPPC Directive as a basis for any standard-setting at Community level, effectively put off the possible establishment of any Community limit values for several years. Indeed, the first data to be supplied by the member states for information exchange purposes were not due before the end of 1999.

The provisions of Article 16 are in fact interpreted by industry and some governments as practically pre-empting further Community legislative activity to establish technology-based emission limit values for specific pollutants and sectors of industry. In this regard, it is highly significant that UNICE, the confederation of European industry, expresses a strong preference for the IPPC Directive as 'a central reference point' for future BAT standard-setting efforts not only at EU level, but also within the framework of the Paris Commission, whose measures in UNICE's view 'must be fully consistent with EU legislation on industrial pollution control.'[499]

Periodical Review of Permit Conditions

'Best available techniques', as defined in the IPPC Directive, is a dynamic, evolutionary concept, which is expected to change over time. Annex IV expressly provides that 'technological advances and changes in scientific knowledge and understanding' are one of the considerations to be taken into account in determining what constitutes BAT for any given installation. Article 11 requires member states to ensure that their competent authorities are informed of 'developments in best available techniques'. This is necessary not only in order to be able to determine BAT-based emission standards whenever new permits are to be issued, but also to revise the permit conditions of existing installations. Article 13 imposes an obligation on competent authorities to 'periodically reconsider and, where necessary, update permit conditions' and, more specifically, requires them to reconsider conditions 'in any event' whenever 'substantial changes in the best available techniques make it possible to reduce emissions significantly without imposing excessive costs.'

It should be noted that a periodical review of permit conditions is also required under some existing Community legislation. For instance, authorisations for discharges of black list substances pursuant to Directive 76/464/EEC may be granted for a limited period only, and several daugh-

[498] IPPC Directive, Art 18, para 1.
[499] UNICE Statement to the Fourth North Sea Conference, Esbjerg, 8–9 June 1995, para 4.

ter directives setting emission limit values for specific sectors and substances require such permits to be reviewed at least every four years. The Commission proposed to specify a minimum frequency for the reconsideration of permit conditions under the IPPC Directive, requiring competent authorities to reconsider permits at least once every 10 years, but the Council preferred to leave this entirely at the member states' discretion.

Implications for Discharges Authorised Pursuant To Directive 76/464/EEC

What will be the legal position of installations previously authorised pursuant to Directive 76/464/EEC once the IPPC Directive will have been fully transposed and applied? As has been pointed out above, the scope of application of the two directives overlaps but is by no means identical. Therefore it was not possible simply to replace Directive 76/464/EEC by the new IPPC Directive. The Commission noted in its explanatory memorandum that, because there are processes discharging dangerous substances into surface waters which are not covered by the IPPC proposal and whose emissions must continue to be controlled, it was not possible to repeal Directive 76/464/EEC immediately, although 'future proposals may be necessary' to deal with this issue.[500] However, from the outset, it was the Commission's intention that the IPPC Directive become the only legal instrument at Community level for the regulation of all emissions from the industrial activities listed in its Annex I, including their aquatic emissions of dangerous substances which are currently regulated by Directive 76/464/EEC. That is why the Commission proposed that the provisions of that Directive and its daughter directives concerning permit requirements should no longer apply to installations authorised pursuant to the IPPC Directive. It should be stressed, though, that not *all* provisions of those earlier directives have been made redundant by the IPPC Directive. The actual quality standards and emission limits set for individual black list substances in the daughter directives of Directive 76/464/EEC will continue to apply, though not indefinitely, since the Commission in its explanatory memorandum already announced its intention to review the 'future need for these daughter Directives.'[501] The transitional provisions proposed by the Commission were, however, slightly amended by the Council.

Article 20, paragraph 1 provides that the 'provisions concerning authorization systems' of Directive 76/464/EEC and its daughter directives shall no longer apply to those installations once 'the measures required pursuant to Article 5' of the IPPC Directive have been taken with respect to them. Article 5 lays down the obligations of member states with respect to

[500] Explanatory memorandum, EC Doc COM(93) 423 final, 14 Sept 1993, p 19. As to these 'future proposals' see below.
[501] *Ibid.*

existing installations: the competent authorities shall ensure that such installations 'operate in accordance with the requirements' of the IPPC Directive not later than eight years after the date on which it is brought into effect, either by issuing a new permit in accordance with the procedure and substantive requirements of the IPPC Directive, or 'by reconsidering and, where necessary, by updating' the conditions of their existing permits. Once a previously authorised installation has thus been granted a new permit or has had its existing permit reconsidered, the provisions of Articles 3, 5, 6, paragraphs 3 and 7, paragraph 2 of Directive 76/464/EEC shall no longer apply to it.

A distinction must be made between installations discharging black list substances for which Community emission limit values have been established by daughter directives, and those discharging grey list substances, including black list substances for which no Community standards have been set. In the latter case, the only relevant provision of Directive 76/464/EEC applying to such installations is Article 7, paragraph 2, which requires a permit laying down emission standards for the discharge of *any* grey list substance and furthermore requires those standards to be based on nationally determined water quality objectives. Under the provisions of the IPPC Directive, national authorities are required to establish limit values only for those substances whose emissions they deem 'significant' and there is no obligation to base limit values on specific water quality objectives. In principle, limit values must be based on BAT, but this obligation is qualified by references to plant location and local environmental conditions, which confer substantial discretion on national authorities.

So the shift from the existing regime of Directive 76/464/EEC to the new regime of the IPPC Directive entails disparate consequences. On the one hand, the IPPC Directive has the effect of substantially increasing member state discretion as to the choice of the substances whose emission is to be controlled. This may result in a lowering of the level of environmental protection. On the other hand, the shift from environmental quality-based emission standards under Directive 76/464/EEC to BAT-based emission standards under the IPPC Directive may arguably limit national discretion and lead to higher standards, though not necessarily, as the wording of Article 9, paragraph 4 of the IPPC Directive still allows competent authorities to take environmental quality into account when determining permit conditions.

In the case of installations discharging black list substances and covered by one of the daughter directives, the relevant provisions of Directive 76/464/EEC which would no longer apply are those of Articles 3, 5 and 6, paragraph 3. These are the provisions which require prior authorisation for *all* discharges of *any* dangerous substance, which stipulate that such authorisation can only be granted for a limited period, and which lay down the obligations of competent authorities with respect to setting emission standards. As mentioned earlier, these shall not exceed the limit values established at Community level unless the member state concerned can show that Community water quality objectives can be met by less stringent permit conditions. The Council did not follow the Commission's proposal to declare inapplicable Article 6 of Directive 76/464/EEC as a whole, since paragraphs 1, 2 and 4 of this provision do not directly concern the authorisation system as such but only mandate the Council to establish emission limit values and quality objectives for black list substances at Community level.

Article 20, paragraph 1 of the IPPC Directive also provides that, in addition to the specified provisions of Directive 76/464/EEC, 'the relevant provisions concerning authorization systems' of the daughter directives will no longer apply either. These provisions were initially identified in Annex II of the Commission's proposal, but the Council chose only to list the directives concerned, without specifying their relevant provisions. The Council effectively postponed the arduous task of removing any overlaps or inconsistencies between the IPPC Directive and earlier legislation, as Article 20, paragraph 3 provides that the relevant provisions of the directives listed in Annex II shall later be amended 'where necessary . . . in order to adapt them to the requirements of [the IPPC] Directive'. Taking as a guide the Commission's initial proposal, the main substantive provisions of the daughter directives whose application will be suspended as a result of Article 20, paragraph 1 appear to be those which require authorisations to be reviewed at least every four years and provide that permits for new plants may be granted

> only if those plants apply the standards corresponding to the *best technical means available* when that is necessary for the elimination of pollution . . . or for the prevention of distortion of competition.[502]

As pointed out above, however, the actual emission limit values set by the 'daughter' directives would continue to apply by virtue of Article 18, paragraph 2 of the IPPC Directive. As to the continued validity of the environmental quality objectives laid down in daughter directives pursuant to Article 6, paragraph 2 of Directive 76/464/EEC, the legal position is not entirely clear. A specific transitional provision in Article 20, paragraph 3 of the IPPC Directive stipulates that 'the exception provided for in Article 6(3) of Directive 76/464/EEC', authorising member states to derogate from Community emission limit values provided those quality objectives are complied with, shall no longer apply to both existing and new installations which have either been granted a permit or whose permit conditions have

[502] See eg Council Dir 84/156/EEC of 8 Mar 1984 on limit values and quality objectives for mercury discharges by sectors other than the chlor-alkali electrolysis industry, OJ No L74, 17.3.1984, p 49, Art 3, para 4.

been updated or which have notified a change in operation in accordance with the IPPC Directive. However, the explanatory memorandum as well as the wording of the Commission's original proposal for Annex II indicate that it did envisage a continued role for these quality objectives in the new IPPC scheme, as a secondary basis for determining emission limit values. In the Council's version of the IPPC Directive, environmental quality standards only play a role in the context of Article 10, ie as a basis for imposing 'additional measures' beyond BAT when BAT-based emission standards appear not to be sufficient to meet environmental quality standards. The notion of 'environmental quality standards', as defined in Article 2(7), would seem to encompass the quality objectives set out in the daughter directives of Directive 76/464/EEC.

As in the case of installations discharging grey list substances, the first consequence of the new IPPC provisions for plants emitting black list substances is to give national authorities discretion to determine whether or not the quantity emitted is 'significant' enough to warrant the imposition of emission limit values. As the pollutants in question have been considered of sufficient concern to justify the establishment of uniform standards at Community level, it can be assumed that it is rather unlikely that emissions from plants specifically covered by such standards will be deemed 'insignificant'. Once a competent authority has decided to lay down an emission limit value for the substance concerned, it will be bound by virtue of Article 18, paragraph 2 of the IPPC Directive to apply the Community limit value laid down in the relevant daughter directive as a minimum standard. Since Article 6, paragraph 3 of Directive 76/464/EEC no longer applies, member states will not be free, as they were under that provision, to derogate from the Community limit value even if they can achieve compliance with the relevant quality objectives by other means. In that respect, the provisions of the IPPC Directive are more restrictive of national discretion than those of the 1976 Directive.

In all other respects, however, the new Directive will have the effect of relaxing legal constraints on emissions of black list substances. The important principle that permits for discharges of such substances may be granted for a limited period only will no longer apply, since the IPPC Directive imposes no restrictions at all as to the duration of permits. It only requires competent authorities to '*periodically* reconsider and, *where necessary*, update permit conditions.'[503] The specific obligation to review permits at least every four years which was imposed by all daughter directives of Directive 76/464/EEC will be made inapplicable by virtue of the transitional provisions of the IPPC Directive. So will the requirement laid down in all but one of the daughter directives that permits for new plants shall be granted only if they 'apply the standards corresponding to the best technical means

[503] IPPC Directive, Art 13, para 1 (emphasis added).

available', without any qualification as to cost. This requirement was arguably more demanding than the corresponding requirement in Article 9, paragraph 4 of the IPPC Directive that standards shall be based on BAT, as defined in that Directive, with its multiple references to economic feasibility and cost-benefit assessment.

Discharges of Dangerous Substances from Small Installations: Need for a Special Regime?

Once it had been decided that Directive 76/464/EEC would partly be superseded by the new regulatory system of the IPPC Directive, the Commission was forced to reconsider its policy with respect to the remainder of the 1976 Directive, which was increasingly being regarded as an 'outdated' piece of legislation. As the IPPC Directive applies only to the largest industrial point sources within the scope of Directive 76/464/EEC, the latter would not automatically become redundant altogether, and the future of its provisions relating to other point sources and diffuse sources of toxic emissions had to be addressed. When it adopted its proposal for the IPPC Directive in 1993, the Commission indicated its intention to submit further proposals to deal with the issue of aquatic emissions of dangerous substances from activities not covered by that directive, which would, at least provisionally, continue to be subject to the provisions of Directive 76/464/EEC. At first, the possibility of amending Directive 76/464/EEC to transform it into an adequate complement of the proposed new legislation was considered. While the draft IPPC Directive was still under consideration by the Council, and at about the same time as the Commission's proposal for a directive on the ecological quality of water[504] was being finalised for submission to the Council, the Commission services were also working on a complementary draft proposal for amendments to Directive 76/464/EEC.[505] Two versions of this draft proposal were presented to two successive meetings of national experts and a consultation meeting with industry associations and environmental organisations in 1994, but were not warmly received. The Commission then opted for a different approach, focusing on multi-media pollution controls for small and medium-sized industrial point sources not covered by the IPPC Directive, rather than a comprehensive reform of Directive 76/464/EEC. In August 1996, soon after the Council had reached political agreement on the final version of the IPPC Directive, the Commission services issued a 'consultation paper' in which they outlined their

[504] See above n 70.

[505] *Council Directive of . . . 199. modifying Council 76/464/EEC of 4 May 1976 on pollution caused by certain dangerous substances discharged into the aquatic environment of the Community*, unpublished Commission document presented to the 21st National Experts Meeting on Dir 76/464/EEC, Brussels, 24–25 May 1994.

strategy and policy intentions with respect to emissions from 'smaller installations.'[506]

It is symptomatic of the current trends in Community environmental policy that the Commission was trying to 'sell' its initiative to develop a new legal instrument for such installations by invoking a deregulation rationale. Referring to the objectives of general Community policy in favour of small and medium-sized enterprises and to the Molitor Group's criticism of the 'inflexible, inefficient and costly' procedures of Directive 76/464/EEC,[507] the Commission argued that 'industries remaining under 76/464/EEC would be subject to more stringent administrative procedures than those under the proposed IPPC Directive' and pointed out that this 'would of course contradict the objective to simplify administrative burdens on [smaller installations].'[508]

The Commission, as though uncomfortable about the fact that its argument, taken to its logical conclusion, might just as well be used to advocate the outright abolition of Community emission control requirements for smaller industries, then proceeded to justify its proposal for a Community legislative initiative in terms of the subsidiarity principle by invoking the 'potential long range effects' of emissions of dangerous substances and the need for 'coordination at Community level' with a view to 'a concerted effort to minimise their impact at both European and global level.'[509] The Commission concluded that 'a new Directive is needed, which would *simplify the requirements of Directive 76/464/EEC, increase its flexibility of application* and expand its scope towards a more integrated approach', addressing emissions of dangerous substances into all environmental media as opposed to the aquatic environment alone.[510] The consultation paper went out of its way to stress that 'the Community *should only provide a frame for action*, indicating simple basic essential rules, leaving to Member States the flexibility to adapt their legislation.'[511] It further pointed out that emission-oriented measures targetting smaller industries can only be one part of a broader strategy which also incorporates product control legislation and the use of market-based instruments.

506 *A Community strategy for the integrated control of emissions of dangerous and long-range effects substances from smaller installations*, Consultation paper of the Commission Services, Aug 1996 (hereafter referred to as 'Consultation paper').

507 Consultation paper, paras 22 and 37. A summary of the report of this 'group of independent experts' on the 'simplification' of regulation was published as EC Doc COM(95) 288 final, 21 June 1995.

508 Consulation paper, para 38. In fact, the comparison of administrative requirements under Dir 76/464/EEC and the IPPC Directive given in Table 1 to substantiate the Commission's claim is at least in part legally incorrect.

509 Consultation paper, para 29.

510 *Ibid*, para 45 (emphasis added).

511 *Ibid*, para 46 (emphasis added).

Finally, the paper provided an outline of what the Commission considered the 'key elements' of the envisaged proposal for a directive on the control of emissions of dangerous and long-range-effect substances from smaller installations. The scope of the proposed directive would be limited to those smaller point sources which release dangerous substances 'of concern at European level'. Such 'priority substances' would have to be identified through a risk assessment process taking as a starting point the indicative list of substances annexed to the IPPC Directive.[512] A permit requirement, linked to emission limit values and quality objectives, would remain 'the core concept' of the proposed new regulatory system, but the authorisation process should be an integrated one, resulting in a 'one stop shop' permit for the smaller industries concerned. The permitting procedures and permit conditions should be '*simpler than currently foreseen in* the . . . IPPC Directive and *the existing 76/464/EEC*.'[513] The concept of 'best available techniques' as defined in the IPPC Directive would also be applied in determining operating conditions for smaller installations.[514]

The environmental regulation of small and medium-sized enterprises was the main topic of the informal meeting of EU environment ministers organised by the Dutch presidency in April 1997. The President's conclusions of this meeting stressed that:

> Environmental requirements should be related to the nature and magnitude of environmental pollution and not to the size of the enterprise. Therefore, in principle, similar requirements should apply to larger and smaller enterprises. Also, a European policy should be based upon an integral approach.[515]

The ministers nevertheless recognised that special treatment of smaller companies may be justified 'as far as administrative procedures are concerned', but expressed a preference for an integrated, 'comprehensive strategy' rather than one focusing mainly on emissions of dangerous substances, as envisaged by the Commission. In view of the member states' apparent lack of enthusiasm for the approach proposed in its consultation paper, the Commission decided to shelve that initiative for 'further consideration' and to deal with the question of toxic emissions from non-IPPC

[512] *Ibid*, para 62.

[513] *Ibid*, para 58 (emphasis added). This argument is remarkable in view of the fact that Art 7 of Dir 76/464/EEC *does not actually contain any procedural requirements* for the delivery of permits for discharges of grey list substances and black list substances for which no Community emission limit values have been laid down pursuant to Art 6. It merely provides that such discharges 'shall require prior authorization . . . in which emission standards shall be laid down' and that these standards shall be based on national water quality objectives. It leaves member states totally free to determine the actual authorisation procedure and even to provide for a simplified procedure and integrated permit for small entreprises if they so wish.

[514] Consultation paper, para 60.

[515] President's Conclusions, Informal Meeting of EU Environment Ministers, Amsterdam, 18–20 Apr 1997, para 3.

installations instead by what it calls 'a quicker and simpler way of achieving the same objective', namely by including, in its proposal for a framework directive on water policy, additional provisions on Community action to address pollution by selected hazardous substances.[516]

The Framework Directive on Water Policy: Implications for Toxic Emissions

In the introductory section of this chapter, I discussed the general structure of Directive 2000/60/EC and the main features of the regulatory system for the control of water pollution that it establishes. I will now analyse the implications of this system for the regulation of toxic emissions and examine a number of specific provisions on pollution by hazardous substances which were included in the Directive as a substitute for the provisions of Directive 76/464/EEC that are due to be repealed. The inclusion of these provisions is very much the result of pressure from the European Parliament, which insisted that the Framework Directive should provide the same level of protection against toxic water pollution as the 1976 Directive. Unconvinced by the initial efforts made by the Commission and the Council to accommodate these concerns, the Parliament adopted a series of amendments to the common position, which resulted in further substantial changes to the text during the conciliation procedure. As we shall see, it remains doubtful that the requirements of Directive 2000/60/EC with respect to emissions of hazardous substances are really equivalent to those of Directive 76/464/EEC. There are also a number of significant inconsistencies between the provisions of the Framework Directive and the legal and political commitments made by the Community and its member states within the framework of the regional marine environment protection regimes to which they are parties.

The Objective of 'Good Chemical Status': the Return to Environmental Quality Standards

As discussed above, the main substantive obligation of the member states under Article 4 of Directive 2000/60/EC is to implement a series of measures 'with the aim of achieving good surface water status', which implies the achievement of both 'good ecological status' and 'good chemical status'. A water body will be deemed to fulfil the 'good chemical status' requirement if the concentrations of pollutants

[516] Amendment to the proposal for a Council Directive establishing a framework for Community action in the field of water policy, EC Doc COM(97) 614 final, 26 Nov 1997, Explanatory memorandum, p 2.

do not exceed the environmental quality standards established in Annex IX and under Article 16(7), and under other relevant Community legislation setting environmental quality standards at Community level.[517]

Annex IX refers to the environmental quality objectives for certain black list substances laid down in the daughter directives of Directive 76/464/EEC. The phrase 'other relevant Community legislation' is presumably meant to refer to the 1970s directives establishing quality objectives for water intended for specific uses, but the reference to those directives in the definition of 'good chemical status' is somewhat puzzling as the Framework Directive actually *repeals* all of them, except Directive 76/160/EEC on bathing waters, either seven or thirteen years after the date of its entry into force. Article 16, paragraph 7, of the Framework Directive provides for the establishment at a later stage, ie by subsequent Community legislation, of quality standards for certain 'priority substances' which are yet to be identified.

As we have seen, Annex V of Directive 2000/60/EC also requires member states to set, independently of further Community legislative action, environmental quality standards for specific synthetic and non-synthetic pollutants as part of the physico-chemical criteria determining the 'ecological status' of surface waters. Such standards shall be established for all 'priority substances' identified as being discharged into the body of water concerned as well as for other pollutants 'discharged in significant quantities', thus leaving the member states considerable discretion in the choice of substances to be covered by these standards. In view of the detailed provisions of Annex V concerning the setting of environmental quality standards by the member states, it is surprising that no explicit reference to these standards is to be found anywhere in the substantive provisions of the directive spelling out the obligations of the member states.[518] Article 4, paragraph 1(a) stipulates in general terms that the environmental objectives are to be achieved 'in accordance with the provisions laid down in Annex V', but the definition of 'good surface water chemical status' in Article 2(24) contains no reference at all to Annex V. The definition of 'good surface water chemical status' refers only to environmental quality standards established at Community level but not to the standards set by the member states pursuant to Annex V of Directive 2000/60/EC itself. This would seem to imply that the latter standards are irrelevant for the determination of a surface water's 'chemical status'. However, as the achievement of 'good surface water status' also requires that the criteria for 'good ecological

[517] European Parliament and Council Dir 2000/60/EC of 23 Oct 2000 establishing a framework for Community action in the field of water policy, OJ No L327, 22.12.2000, p 1, Art 2(24) (hereafter referred to as 'Framework Directive').

[518] Except, as we have noted above, in the transitional provisions concerning the application of the IPPC Directive.

status' are met, the environmental quality standards for specific pollutants set for this purpose would nevertheless have to be complied with under this heading.

At any rate, it is evident that the EQS-based definition of 'good chemical status' is highly inadequate, since it can be interpreted as implying that only those pollutants for which water quality standards have actually been established by Community law are relevant for the 'chemical status' of a body of water. In other terms, a water body which is highly polluted by dangerous substances for which no such EQS exist could nonetheless legally be considered as meeting the 'good chemical status' requirement. And a body of water which fails to comply with an EQS set by the competent member state under Annex V of the Directive would equally qualify for 'good chemical status' designation, even though it would fail to meet the criteria for 'good ecological status'. Apart from the paradoxical conclusions to which the technical definition of 'good chemical status' inevitably leads, the very fact that the achievement of the Framework Directive's 'environmental objectives' is to be judged primarily by reference to environmental quality criteria indicates that the new instrument has adopted what is essentially an EQS-based approach to water pollution, *including pollution by dangerous substances*, which represents a significant departure from the approach laid down in Directive 76/464/EEC.

Obligation of Result?

Moreover, it is not even clear that member states positively have an obligation of result to achieve 'good surface water status', however inadequately defined, by the deadline laid down in the Framework Directive. In the Commission's initial proposal, the ultimate achievement of this objective was clearly envisaged as an obligation of result, as member states were to be required to:

> prevent deterioration of ecological quality and pollution of surface waters and restore polluted surface waters, *in order to achieve good surface water status* in all surface waters by 31 December 2010.[519]

But this requirement was watered down into an almost meaningless obligation of means in the Council's common position, whose relevant provision merely stipulated that member states 'shall aim to achieve' this 'environmental objective' through 'phased implementation' of their programmes of measures,[520] which were to be drawn up 'with the aim of moving progressively towards achieving the objectives established under Article 4.'[521] The European Parliament adopted an amendment which

[519] EC Doc COM(97) 49 final, 26 Feb 1997, Art 4, para 1(a) (emphasis added).
[520] Common position, Art 4, para 1.
[521] *Ibid*, Art 11, para 1.

would have re-introduced an unconditional obligation to achieve 'good surface water status' within a 10-year period.[522] The final text of the Directive, as agreed between Council and Parliament within the framework of the conciliation procedure, reflects an ambiguous compromise between both positions. It provides that 'in making operational the programmes of measures', which are to be established for each river basin district '*in order to achieve* the objectives established under Article 4,'[523]

> Member States *shall protect, enhance and restore* all bodies of surface water . . . *with the aim of achieving good surface water status* at the latest 15 years after the entry into force of this Directive.[524]

Would a member state which failed to achieve 'good surface water status' in all its surface waters, despite having made every possible effort to implement the relevant programmes of measures which it had drawn up in good faith in order to achieve this objective, be found to be in breach of its obligations under the Directive? Does the Directive state an obligation of result or merely one of means? No one could confidently predict how the Court of Justice would answer this question. The Court has recently held that compliance with quality objectives for bathing water established under Directive 76/160/EEC is an obligation of result,[525] but the relevant language of that Directive is more categorical than that of the Framework Directive. On the other hand, the fact that the Framework Directive explicitly makes provision for a number of exceptional cases in which member states 'will not be in breach of this Directive' when failing to achieve 'good status' in certain bodies of water[526] could be interpreted *a contrario* as implying that failure to achieve 'good surface water status' at the expiry of the relevant time period in all other circumstances *does* constitute a breach of the Directive. Another of its provisions, which requires member states to take certain remedial action 'in order to achieve those objectives' when it becomes apparent 'that the objectives set under Article 4 for the body of water are unlikely to be achieved,'[527] would also tend to support the interpretation that Article 4 states obligations of result.

Specific Measures for the Control of Toxic Emissions

Having examined the implications of the 'environmental objectives' laid down in Article 4 of the Framework Directive, I shall now analyse what actual measures for the control of toxic emissions from point and diffuse sources member states are expected to take to achieve these objectives. As

522 EP Legislative Resolution of 16 Feb 2000, amendment 24.
523 Framework Directive, Art 11, para 1 (emphasis added).
524 *Ibid*, Art 4, para 1(a)(ii) (emphasis added).
525 Case C–198/97, *Commission v Germany*, [1999] ECR I–3257, para 35.
526 Framework Directive, Art 4, para 6.
527 *Ibid*, Art 11, para 5.

discussed, the basic requirement under the Directive is to establish a 'programme of measures' for each river basin district including a number of mandatory 'basic measures' and a number of optional 'supplementary measures'. The basic measures do not comprise any measures targetted specifically at reduction of emissions of hazardous substances, other than the implementation of Community measures for priority substances which may later be adopted under Article 16. Other than that, there is a general requirement to introduce 'emission controls' for 'point source discharges liable to cause pollution', either through a system of prior authorisation, or prior registration based on generally binding rules,[528] or through other forms of regulation 'such as a prohibition on the entry of pollutants into water'. These controls are to be 'periodically reviewed and, where necessary updated.'[529] The Directive leaves the nature and level of the emission controls at the discretion of the member states. In fact, it appears from the definition of the notion of 'emission controls' that these are not necessarily emission limit values but may also include 'conditions on the effects . . . of an emission.'[530] The member states' discretion is constrained only by the general provision in Article 11, paragraph 1, that the programmes of measures shall be established 'in order to achieve the objectives established under Article 4'.

The programmes of measures shall also contain 'measures to prevent or control the input of pollutants' from 'diffuse sources liable to cause pollution'. As for point sources, the exact nature of these measures is left at the member states' discretion. The Framework Directive only lists a range of options such as authorisation or registration systems or other forms of prior regulation, 'where such a requirement is not otherwise provided for under Community legislation', thus stressing the subsidiary nature of its requirements vis-a-vis existing legal requirements for certain diffuse sources under other directives—for example, the Nitrates Directive.

Under Article 10 of Directive 2000/60/EC, member states also have a general obligation to ensure that certain discharges into surface waters from both point and diffuse sources, specified in other Community legislation, are controlled according to the so-called 'combined approach'. The 'combined approach' implies that where compliance with any water quality standards established pursuant to the Framework Directive (which presumably includes those established by the member states pursuant to Annex V) or to other Community legislation (including the environmental quality objec-

[528] The Commission explains that it has introduced this new option because it has 'been used in many Member States as an administratively more convenient mechanism of controlling pollution from small installations than full permits'. See Amendment to the proposal for a Council Directive establishing a framework for Community action in the field of water policy, EC Doc COM(97) 614 final, 26 Nov 1997, Explanatory memorandum, p 7.

[529] Framework Directive, Art 11, para 2(g).

[530] *Ibid*, Art 2(41).

tives for selected black list substances set by the daughter directives of Directive 76/464/EEC) require stricter discharge conditions than those referred to in the general provisions of Article 10, more stringent emission controls shall be applied. The general requirement under Article 10 for the relevant sources is to implement either 'emission controls based on best available techniques' or 'the relevant emission limit values' already laid down under a number of existing directives or later to be adopted pursuant to Article 16 of the Framework Directive, and for diffuse impacts, 'best environmental practices' or other controls. Thus, additional, more stringent measures will have to be taken if they are necessary to meet the applicable EQS.

This 'combined approach' provision is reminescent of a similar requirement in Article 10 of the IPPC Directive, discussed above. As a matter of fact, the IPPC Directive is referred to in Article 10, paragraph 2 of the Framework Directive; discharges within its scope are subject to the 'combined approach' not only under the IPPC Directive itself but also under the Framework Directive. The implication of this seems to be that a broader range of EQS will be relevant for triggering the application of the 'combined approach'. Under the IPPC Directive only those EQS 'set out in' Community legislation are relevant, whereas Article 10, paragraph 3 of the Framework Directive also refers to EQS 'established pursuant to' its own provisions or to any other Community legislation. This would include the EQS set by member states pursuant to Annex V of Directive 2000/60/EC and even those established by them pursuant to Article 7 of Directive 76/464/EEC.[531] Other sources of toxic emissions subject to the provisions of Article 10 include the point sources and significant 'multiple and diffuse sources' of certain black list substances regulated under the daughter directives of Directive 76/464/EEC, which are listed in Annex IX of the Framework Directive and are not repealed by it. In this respect, the legal effect of Article 10 is to require all member states, including those that have not opted for the EQO approach under Directive 76/464/EEC, to ensure that the EQO fixed by the daughter directives are complied with, if necessary by setting 'more stringent emission controls' for the relevant point and diffuse sources than already required under those directives. The further implications of Article 10 of the Framework Directive for toxic emissions are difficult to gauge, since its overall scope of application will depend on future implementing directives for 'priority substances' to be adopted pursuant to Article 16.

[531] This provision is to remain in force until 13 years after the entry into force of the Framework Directive, subject to certain transitional arrangements. *Ibid*, Art 22, paras 2 and 3. At any rate, there is no reason why the eventual repeal of Directive 76/464/EEC should necessarily affect the national standards established pursuant to it while it was in force.

Priority Substances

As we have seen, Directive 2000/60/EC does not focus on hazardous substances or on any other particular category of water pollutants, but deals with water pollution generally, leaving member states considerable freedom in selecting the specific pollutants to be targeted in their river basin management plans and programmes of measures, both in terms of setting environmental quality standards and establishing emission controls. Annex VIII of the Directive contains an 'indicative list of the main pollutants' which is essentially the same as in Annex III of the IPPC Directive,[532] but this list is not referred to specifically in any of the operative provisions concerning environmental objectives or programmes of measures. However, Article 16 of the Directive lays down a general framework for the subsequent adoption, through implementing Community legislation, of a list of 'priority substances', including 'priority hazardous substances', for which additional 'specific measures' shall be taken. During the legislative process this provision was continuously redrafted and its final version was an important point of contention in the conciliation procedure between the Council and the Parliament.

From the start, the Commission felt a political need to show, in response to the European Parliament's critical comments on its 1996 communication on water policy,[533] that it had not altogether relinquished the special concern for toxic water pollutants which underlay the development of much of the Community's existing water pollution control legislation. Though its initial proposal for the framework directive did not contain any specific provision on hazardous substances, it included a generally worded Article 21 which allowed for the elaboration by the Commission, at a later stage, of 'strategies against pollution of water by individual pollutants or groups of pollutants.' The Commission argued, in its explanatory memorandum, that the 'emission limit value part' of Directive 76/464/EEC would become 'redundant' as a result of the adoption of the proposed framework directive and implementation of the emission control provisions of the IPPC Directive.[534] The 'only significant remaining elements' of the 1976 Directive which the Commission considered 'worth retaining' were the pollution reduction programmes for grey list substances and the mechanism for adopting EQOs at Community level.[535] It claimed that the programmes in question would also be 'overtaken' by the new, integrated 'programmes of measures', while the existing EQOs for black list substances had been incor-

[532] For an analysis of this annex and its relationship with the black and grey lists of Dir 76/464/EEC see above n 457.

[533] EP Opinion of 23 Oct 1996.

[534] EC Doc COM(97) 49 final, 26 Feb 1997, Explanatory memorandum, p 12.

[535] *Ibid.*

porated in the definition of 'good chemical status.'[536] Further Community EQOs for specific pollutants or groups of pollutants could be adopted later, 'as appropriate', within the framework of the pollution control 'strategies' referred to in Article 21 of the proposal.[537]

Following the lukewarm reception of its consultation paper on a new strategy for emission controls for small installations, and anticipating criticism that the proposed framework directive would not provide a level of protection of surface waters against emissions of dangerous substances equivalent to that of Directive 76/464/EEC and its daughter directives, the Commission decided to amend its initial proposal in order to include additional and more detailed provisions on pollution by dangerous substances, explicitly designed to replace those of Directive 76/464/EEC.[538] It did so in November 1997, even before receiving the European Parliament's opinion on first reading; procedurally, this is a rather unusual step. The amendments are presented as 'a simplified and updated version of the existing controls on small installations under Directive 76/464/EEC.'[539] The Commission went out of its way to stress that its amended proposal 'take[s] over the essential provisions of Directive 76/464/EEC'[540] and, on this basis, proposed to repeal the 1976 Directive altogether.

Where the initial version only stipulated that the Commission 'may' prepare 'strategies' to deal with particular pollutants, the strengthened version of Article 21 provided at the outset that 'the Council *shall adopt specific control measures* against pollution of water by individual pollutants or groups of pollutants *presenting an unacceptable risk to the environment*.'[541] The Commission, in its amended proposal, also proposed to introduce an additional 'environmental objective', inspired by the language of Directive 76/464/EEC, namely to '*eliminate* pollution of the waters by *certain pollutants*.'[542] The pollutants in question would be specific hazardous substances identified in the framework of the 'strategies' provided for in Article 21. The amended proposal further required the Commission to submit a proposal for a 'first priority list of substances' by a certain deadline.[543]

The Commission's initiative was designed to reintroduce, in its proposal, the objective of elimination of pollution by specified hazardous substances,

[536] Cf Draft framework directive, Art 1(23) & Annex IX, as amended by COM(97) 614 final.

[537] EC Doc COM(97) 49 final, 26 Feb 1997, Explanatory memorandum, p 12.

[538] Amendment to the proposal for a Council Directive establishing a framework for Community action in the field of water policy, EC Doc COM(97) 614 final, 26 Nov 1997.

[539] *Ibid*, Explanatory memorandum, p 2.

[540] *Ibid*, p 3.

[541] Draft framework directive, Art 21, para 1, as amended by COM(97) 614 final (emphasis added).

[542] *Ibid*, Art 4, para 1(d), as amended by COM(97) 614 final (emphasis added).

[543] *Ibid*, Art 21, para 2, as amended by COM(97) 614 final.

while narrowing down the open-ended scope of the black and grey lists of Directive 76/464/EEC through the concept of a priority list. The explanatory memorandum indicated the Commission's intention to propose a first priority list of 'around 30 substances', arguing that it 'is essential for the success and credibility of any programme on dangerous substances that the substances be tackled in manageable tranches'. According to the Commission, the difficulties in implementing Directive 76/464/EEC must be ascribed to 'the lack of any means of identifying priority substances for action.'[544] That is why it proposed a risk assessment scheme to select and prioritise hazardous substances 'on the basis of risk to or via the aquatic environment.'[545]

The Council, in its common position, endorsed the Commission's revised proposal for a control strategy for 'priority' hazardous substances without major changes.[546] Significantly, however, it refused to include any explicit reference to the elimination of pollution by any substances in the provisions specifying the 'environmental objectives' to be achieved by the member states. The common position only reluctantly recognised the notion of a specific objective for certain pollutants by mentioning, in an introductory article stating the general 'purpose' of the directive in terms without any immediate legal implications, that the framework it establishes is also intended to contribute, inter alia, to the '*progressive reduction* of emissions of hazardous substances'.[547]

This was insufficient to satisfy the European Parliament, which insisted on mandatory provisions stating the ultimate aim of eliminating pollution by toxic substances and adopted several amendments inspired by the language of the toxics phase-out objectives proclaimed at the Esbjerg North Sea conference and OSPAR ministerial meeting.[548] The final compromise agreed between Parliament and Council was to include in the Framework Directive the objective of 'ceasing or phasing out' emissions, but only for a smaller list of 'priority hazardous substances' to be identified within the overall list of 'priority substances' that is to be established by future legislative action. The relevant provisions are further analysed below.

In its final form, Article 16 of Directive 2000/60/EC provides that the European Parliament and the Council, through the regular legislative procedure, shall adopt 'specific measures' against water pollution by 'individual pollutants or groups of pollutants presenting *a significant risk* to or

[544] EC Doc COM(97) 614 final, 26 Nov 1997, Explanatory memorandum, p 3.

[545] Draft framework directive, Art 21, para 2, as amended by COM(97) 614 final. These procedures are based on those used for the assessment of risks from 'existing chemicals' under Council Regulation (EEC) No 793/93 on the evaluation and control of the risks of existing substances, OJ No L 84, 5.4.1993, p 1.

[546] Common position, Art 16.

[547] *Ibid*, Art 1 *in fine* (emphasis added).

[548] EP Legislative Resolution of 16 Feb 2000, amendments 10, 14, 24, 58, 93 and 61.

via the aquatic environment'. It further specifies that these measures 'shall be aimed at *progressively reducing and, for priority hazardous substances . . . at ceasing or phasing out* discharges, emissions and losses.'[549] Compared to the Commission's proposal, which referred to 'an unacceptable risk' and did not indicate the objective of the measures to be taken, this language both lowers the threshold for and increases the level of ambition of Community action. A similarly worded reference to 'the aim of progressively reducing pollution from priority substances and ceasing or phasing out emissions, discharges and losses of priority hazardous substances' was inserted in the key provisions of Article 4 on 'environmental objectives', but its context makes clear that this objective places no obligation on member states other than to implement the specific Community measures which are later to be adopted pursuant to Article 16.[550] It should be noted that the word 'elimination', which was used in the European Parliament's amendments,[551] occurs nowhere in the operative provisions of the Directive, where it was replaced by the phrase 'ceasing or phasing out,'[552] but only in a preambular clause which provides that 'the *ultimate aim* of this Directive is to achieve the elimination of priority hazardous substances.'[553]

Procedure for Further Legislative Action on 'Priority Substances'

The first step in the process outlined shall be the submission by the Commission of a proposal for a list of 'priority substances' for which measures are to be taken. It is spelled out that 'substances shall be prioritised for action on the basis of risk to or via the aquatic environment'. The preferred risk assessment procedure is the standard procedure for existing substances laid down under Regulation No 793/93, but in order to speed up the assessment and focus it on the specific purposes of the Directive that procedure may be 'targeted' by focusing it solely on aquatic ecotoxicity and human toxicity via the aquatic environment. Where even a targeted risk assessment proves impracticable within the timescale provided, a 'simplified risk-based assessment procedure' may be followed. Within this overall list of 'priority substances', the Commission shall identify the 'priority hazardous substances'. Hazardous substances are defined in the Directive as:

549 Framework Directive, Art 16, para 1 (emphasis added).

550 *Ibid*, Art 4, para 1(a)(iv).

551 EP Legislative Resolution of 16 Feb 2000, amendment 24.

552 Except in Art 1, where it merely describes the objective of international agreements on marine pollution, and oddly, in Art 11, para 3(k), where the Conciliation Committee seems to have forgotten to adapt the language to that of Art 16, but since this clause is to be applied 'in accordance with action taken pursuant to art. 16', this apparent omission should not have legal consequences.

553 Framework Directive, recital 27 (emphasis added).

substances or groups of substances that are toxic, persistent and liable to bio-accumulate, and other substances or groups of substances which give rise to an equivalent level of concern.[554]

In selecting 'priority hazardous substances' for the purposes of Directive 2000/60/EC, the Commission is to take into account substances of concern already identified within the framework of 'relevant Community legislation regarding hazardous substances' and 'relevant international agreements'. The list of priority substances is to be adopted by the European Parliament and the Council and will become Annex X of the Directive. It will be subject to review at least every four years.

The inclusion of a substance on the priority list entails the obligation for the Commission to submit to Council and Parliament 'proposals of controls' on point and diffuse sources[555] as well as proposals for environmental quality standards for concentrations of the substance in question in water, sediments or biota.[556] As far as emission controls for point sources and EQS are concerned, such proposals are to be submitted no later than two years from the date of inclusion of the substance on the list.[557] These Commission proposals are, of course, only the starting point of a process which should eventually lead to the adoption of measures. The proposals will have to be adopted by Parliament and Council in accordance with the standard legislative procedure, and Directive 2000/60/EC explicitly envisages the possibility that agreement at Community level cannot be reached within as long as six years of its date of entry into force, in which case member states will be under an obligation to take measures at the national level for the substances in question.[558]

Depending on the status of the substance concerned, the control measures to be proposed by the Commission shall be aimed either at the 'progressive reduction' or at the 'cessation or phasing out' of discharges, emissions and losses. In the latter case, the proposals shall also include an 'appropriate timetable' for the achievement of this objective, which shall not exceed 20 years.[559] This corresponds roughly with the target date of 2020 agreed within the framework of OSPAR. The elaboration of the Commission proposals themselves is likely to be a complex task, as Article 16 places an obligation on the Commission to identify

the appropriate cost-effective and proportionate level and combination of product and process controls for both point and diffuse sources and take account of Community-wide uniform emission limit values for process controls.[560]

[554] Framework Directive, Art 2(29).
[555] *Ibid*, Art 16, para 4.
[556] *Ibid*, Art 16, para 5.
[557] *Ibid*, Art 16, para 6.
[558] *Ibid*.
[559] *Ibid*, Art 16, para 4.
[560] *Ibid*.

This effectively requires the Commission to compile detailed information for each substance on the different sources and their respective contributions to water pollution and on various control options and their cost-effectiveness. A balance has to be struck between product and process controls in order to select, as the Commission points out in its explanatory memorandum, 'the most advanced techniques and technologies for pollution reduction *which are justified in terms of the proportionality between their cost and the reduction achieved*.'[561] Member states are likely to closely scrutinise Commission proposals from this angle.

After their adoption by the European Parliament and the Council, the agreed control measures for substances identified under Article 16 will eventually have to be implemented by the member states in the framework of the 'programmes of measures' which they are to establish for each river basin district. The 'basic measures' required under these programmes include specific reference to action under Article 16.[562]

The First List of 'Priority Substances'

As action against hazardous substances was perceived as essential to the political credibility of the Framework Directive, the Commission worked hard to submit a first proposal for a *list of priority substances* to the Council prior to the final adoption of the Directive itself. This proposal, listing 32 substances, was finalised in February 2000.[563] As it was completed before the final text of the Directive was agreed between Council and Parliament, it did not take into account the distinction between 'priority substances' and 'priority hazardous substances' and the other new provisions introduced as a result of the Parliament's amendments. Following the adoption of Directive 2000/60/EC, the Commission amended its proposal to make it conform with these provisions and to identify, within the overall list of substances, those it proposed to designate as 'priority hazardous substances.'[564] In a rather unusual move under the co-decision procedure, the Council adopted the Decision establishing the list of priority substances at first reading, incorporating all the amendments proposed by the European Parliament in its opinion. The final list, as adopted, comprises 33 substances or groups of substances. Eleven of them are identified as 'priority hazardous substances', and a further fourteen are designated as 'under review' for such classification; the Commission is to make a proposal for final classification of these substances within one year from the adoption of the list. The number of substances in this intermediate category was increased as a result

[561] EC Doc COM(97) 614 final, 26 Nov 1997, Explanatory memorandum, pp 4–5 (emphasis added).

[562] *Ibid*, Art 11, para 3(k).

[563] EC Doc COM(2000) 47 final, 7 Feb 2000.

[564] EC Doc COM(2001) 17 final, 16 Jan 2001.

of the Parliament's amendments. The legislative process leading to the adoption of the Decision seems to reflect some sense of urgency as to the need for further action to regulate hazardous water pollutants. The Commission was, somewhat reluctantly, forced to accelerate its pace of work, especially owing to political pressure from the European Parliament.

Ironically, the explanatory memorandum of the initial Commission proposal points out that frequent revisions of the priority list are not to be contemplated and that the Council common position's provision for review once every six years lays down an appropriate timeframe. The adoption and implementation of control measures for the substances on the initial list, it is argued, has to take precedence over any expansion of the list. More frequent revisions of the priority list would not be 'realistic' in terms of workload for the Commission and the member states.[565] However, the European Parliament, in its amendments to the common position, insisted on a higher frequency of reviews and, as a result, the six-year timeframe which the Commission cited approvingly in its explanatory memorandum was shortened to four years.[566] In its revised proposal for a list of priority substances, the Commission of course took this shortened review period into acount, and proposed that a final decision on the classification of the hazardous substances 'under review' be made within the framework of the first normally scheduled review of the list of priority substances, ie after four years.[567] The Commission was again forced by the Parliament to speed up the process, as a footnote to the list of priority substances, as eventually adopted by Decision 2455/2001/EC,[568] provides that it is to make a proposal for final classification of the substances identified as 'under review' not later than 12 months after adoption of the list. After the final decision on classification, the Commission will, however, still have a normal period of two years to formulate proposals for controls for the substances in question.

The first list of priority substances adopted in November 2001, which now forms Annex X of Directive 2000/60/EC, is based on the 'simplified' risk assessment procedure, which according to the Commission was the only one feasible in view of time constraints. Priority substances of concern were identified through a combination of monitoring data and modelling techniques to determine their relative risk to the aquatic environment. Ranked working lists of substances were developed based on monitoring data for water and sediments and on modelling of potential environmental exposure based on production and use data. Based on the working lists

565 EC Doc COM(2000) 47 final, Explanatory memorandum, para 70.

566 Framework Directive, Art 16, para 4.

567 EC Doc COM(2001) 17 final, Explanatory memorandum, para 13.

568 European Parliament and Council Decision 2455/2001/EC of 20 Nov 2001 establishing the list of priority substances in the field of water policy and amending Dir 2000/60/EC, OJ No L331, 15.12.2001, p 1 (hereafter referred to as Decision 2455/2001/EC).

derived through the different methods a final list of priority substances was elaborated in consultation with member state experts and stakeholders. It should be noted that the method used did not take into account data on the marine environment and groundwater.[569] In the explanatory memorandum of its initial proposal, the Commission argued, somewhat surprisingly, that the marine environment was not covered as such in the Framework Directive,[570] but that the priority list might later be expanded if ongoing work in OSPAR indicates that additional substances must be targeted for the protection of the marine environment.[571] The extensive debate on the implications of the directive for the marine environment in the European Parliament forced the Commission to pay more attention to this aspect. In identifying 'priority hazardous substances' for the purpose of its amended proposal, the Commission took into account the ongoing work under OSPAR Convention, as the explanatory memorandum makes clear.[572] As a result of the Parliament's amendments, several preambular references to OSPAR and other relevant international agreements for the protection of the marine environment were added to Decision 2455/2001/EC, including one which provides that all substances identified as hazardous by OSPAR are to be considered in the selection process for the next review of the priority list due to take place in four years.[573]

An Inappropriate Instrument for the Protection of the Marine Environment

The question of the criteria for the selection of priority substances raises the more general issue of the Framework Directive's application to the marine environment and its compatibility with the regional marine

[569] EC Doc COM(2000) 47 final, Explanatory memorandum, paras 65–66.

[570] This is legally incorrect given the directive's coverage of coastal waters. In the original Commission proposal COM(97)49 final, the scope of application of the proposed framework directive was limited to groundwater, surface fresh waters, estuaries and coastal waters. The revised Commission proposal COM(97)614 final extended the scope to territorial waters and other marine waters. In the final version of the Directive, 'surface water' is defined as comprising not only 'inland waters except groundwater' but also 'transitional waters and coastal waters, except in respect of chemical status for which it shall also include territorial waters'. 'Transitional waters' are 'bodies of surface water in the vicinity of river mouths which are partly saline in character as a result of their proximity to coastal waters but which are substantially influenced by freshwater flows'. 'Coastal waters' within the meaning of the directive are in fact a portion of the territorial sea as defined in international law: they comprise all marine waters up to a distance of 1 nautical mile from the baseline from which the breadth of the territorial sea is measured. See Framework Directive, Art 2. Thus, in the final analysis the regulatory system established by the Framework Directive applies fully to the marine environment up to 1 mile from the baseline, and partly to the territorial sea as a whole, in so far as it concerns the 'chemical status' of water.

[571] EC Doc COM(2000) 47 final, Explanatory memorandum, para 65.

[572] EC Doc COM(2001) 17 final, Explanatory memorandum, para 11.

[573] Decision 2455/2001/EC, recital 17.

environment protection regimes to which the Community and most member states have subscribed. Directive 2000/60/EC was obviously primarily designed as an instrument for river basin management. Its overall approach is based on a regulatory philosophy, concepts and instruments developed and tested in a context of management of freshwater resources. In its eagerness to propose a comprehensive framework instrument covering all aspects of water management, in order to replace all existing Community legislation in the field, the Commission, almost as an afterthought, decided to extend its scope of application to the marine environment,[574] without giving much consideration to the special nature and context of marine pollution control, or to how the proposed new Community legislation would fit in with existing non-Community instruments in the field.

Indeed, the geographical scope of the Framework Directive substantially overlaps that of the 1992 OSPAR Convention, the 1992 Helsinki Baltic Sea Convention and the Land-Based Sources Protocol to the 1976 Barcelona Mediterranean Convention. By introducing a separate legal concept with no equivalent in these other instruments, 'coastal waters', it in fact establishes a different legal regime for coastal waters, the rest of the territorial sea and the marine environment beyond the limit of the territorial sea, which, from a marine pollution control perspective, is unnecessary and appears incompatible with the regional seas conventions' integrated approach to the marine environment as a whole (which, as defined in those conventions, also includes internal marine waters on the landward side of the baseline and estuaries up to the freshwater limit). The territorial and substantive overlap between the provisions of Directive 2000/60/EC and international marine pollution control law raises issues concerning the consistency of the regulatory approach and objectives of the two regimes and how the member states concerned will apply them concurrently.

When one examines the substance and justification of those amendments, it becomes painfully obvious that this matter was overlooked by the Commission in its haste to amend its 1997 proposal for a framework directive. In order to establish a link between the new directive's regulatory system and the protection of the marine environment, the Commission proposed that one of the 'environmental objectives' to be pursued by the member states through their 'programmes of measures' should be:

> to *prevent*, *reduce and control* pollution of the marine environment from any source, using for this purpose the *best practicable means* at their [ie the member states'] disposal and *in accordance with their capabilities*.[575]

[574] The main reason for this extension was to 'match' the geographical scope of Dir 76/464/EEC, which also applies to the marine environment, in order to convince the Council and the European Parliament that the Framework Directive would be a full and adequate substitute for the 1976 Directive and thus pave the way for the latter's repeal. See EC Doc COM(97) 614 final, Explanatory memorandum, p 5.

[575] *Ibid*, Art 4, para 1(e), as amended by COM(97) 614 final (emphasis added).

This language, described by the Commission in its explanatory memorandum as 'the objective in relation to marine waters to which Member States have committed themselves in the context of the United Nations Convention on the Law of the Sea,'[576] was copied verbatim from Article 194 of that Convention, an outdated provision which states in very general terms the obligations of states with respect to the protection of the marine environment and falls far short of the more specific obligations with respect to pollution from land-based sources to which the Community and member states have subscribed under the pertinent regional instruments. Strikingly, the explanatory memorandum contains no reference at all to the 1992 Paris and Helsinki conventions or the revised Athens Protocol, which between them cover all the European sea areas under the jurisdiction of EU member states. Did the Commission deliberately opt for lowest-common-denominator international language which carefully avoids the use of the verb 'eliminate' as well as the concept of 'best available techniques', both of which are common to those regional instruments? The reference to states' 'capabilities' was obviously included in the 1982 UN Convention to accommodate the concerns of developing countries, and hardly seems relevant in an EC context.

The Commission's serious lack of attention to regional marine pollution control standards was at least in part repaired by the Council and the European Parliament. The latter in particular tried hard to ensure consistency between the Framework Directive and the toxics phase-out policy of OSPAR, but did not entirely succeed, due to the opposition of some member states within the Council. Both in the Council's common position and in the final text of Directive 2000/60/EC, the preamble acknowledges that the Community and member states are party to the above-mentioned international agreements 'containing important obligations on the protection of marine waters from pollution' and affirms that 'this Directive is to make a contribution towards enabling the Community and Member States to meet those obligations.'[577] The Council did not follow the Commission's proposal to include an explicit reference to the protection of the marine environment, albeit a very inadequately worded one, in the provisions of Article 4 on 'environmental objectives'. Instead, it chose to mention 'the protection of territorial and marine waters' and 'achieving the objectives of relevant international agreements including those which aim to prevent and eliminate pollution of the marine environment' among the secondary aims to which the Framework Directive is intended merely to 'contribute' in the introductory article entitled 'Purpose', which does not directly impose any

[576] Amendment to the proposal for a Council Directive establishing a framework for Community action in the field of water policy, EC Doc COM(97) 614 final, 26 Nov 1997, Explanatory memorandum, p 6. Here, the Commission glosses over the fact that not all EU member states have yet ratified the UN Convention.

[577] Common position, recital 19; Framework Directive, recital 21.

obligation on the member states.[578] A cross-reference to this provision was inserted in Article 4, to the effect that the 'environmental objectives' for surface waters shall be 'without prejudice to the relevant international agreements referred to in Article 1 for the parties concerned,'[579] implicitly recognising that these agreements may impose more far-reaching obligations in respect of the marine environment, but only for the 'parties concerned', which presumably underscores the fact that not all member states are party to the agreements in question (although the Community is).

As a result of the conciliation procedure, the provisions in Article 1 of the Framework Directive were strengthened by further specifying that the objectives in relation to the marine environment would be pursued

> by Community action under Article 16(3) to cease or phase out discharges, emissions and losses of priority hazardous substances, with the ultimate aim of achieving concentrations in the marine environment near background values for naturally occurring substances and close to zero for man-made synthetic substances.[580]

The wording of this 'ultimate aim' is taken literally from the Esbjerg Declaration and OSPAR Hazardous Substances Strategy. As we have seen above, a reference to the cessation or phasing out of emissions of 'priority hazardous substances', but not to the 'ultimate aim' specified in Article 1, was also added to the legally more important provisions of Article 4.[581]

The question that arises is whether the objectives of the regional agreements and those of the Framework Directive with respect to the protection of the marine environment have in fact been made fully consistent through these provisions, so that the Directive will indeed, as its preamble and Article 1 claim, contribute to enabling the Community and the member states to meet their obligations under those agreements. Closer scrutiny shows that the provisions of the Directive are in fact contradictory and that serious inconsistencies remain.

Under the Framework Directive the ultimate obligation of the member states with respect to the quality of transitional waters and coastal waters would be to implement measures to achieve 'good surface water status' as defined in the Directive, ie both 'good chemical status' and 'good ecological status'. The obligations relating to 'chemical status' also apply to territorial waters beyond the limit of the coastal waters,[582] although technically, territorial waters, unlike coastal waters, are not to be assigned to any river basin district and as a consequence need not be covered by programmes of measures.

578 Framework Directive, Art 1.
579 *Ibid*, Art 4, para 1(a) *in fine*.
580 *Ibid*, Art 1, final indent.
581 *Ibid*, Art 4, para 1(a)(iv). See also recital 27.
582 *Ibid*, Art 2(1).

As explained above, the notion of 'good chemical status' is based on environmental quality standards established at Community level. At present such standards exist only for a limited number of black list substances for which they have been laid down by implementing directives of Directive 76/464/EEC. Additional Community EQS are later to be established for 'priority substances' identified pursuant to Article 16 of the Framework Directive. The chemical status of marine or transitional waters would be deemed 'good' as long as concentrations of the pollutants in question do not exceed those standards.[583] This approach seems to be at odds with the political objective agreed under the marine pollution conventions and now incorporated as a secondary objective in Article 1 of the Framework Directive itself, where the 'ultimate aim' is to achieve concentrations of hazardous substances in the marine environment *near background values* for naturally occurring substances and *close to zero* for man-made synthetic substances. The only way to avoid this contradiction would be to set Community EQS at levels near background values or close to zero for the substances concerned, which is not presently the case with the existing EQS for black list substances.

The contradiction is even more obvious when one looks at the 'normative definitions' of 'ecological status' in Annex V of the Framework Directive. For coastal waters and transitional waters, the objective of reaching 'good ecological status' also applies. As we have seen, this notion, as defined in Annex V, comprises physico-chemical quality elements, including EQS for significant pollutants. The definition in fact requires member states to establish environmental quality standards for coastal waters and transitional waters on the basis of toxicity to aquatic organisms, which would tolerate the presence of certain concentrations of hazardous synthetic and non-synthetic pollutants. By contrast, the definition of 'high ecological status'—the category above 'good ecological status'—refers to concentrations of synthetic pollutants 'close to zero and at least below the limits of detection' and concentrations of non-synthetic pollutants 'within the range normally associated with undisturbed conditions (background levels).'[584] Thus, it is the definition of 'high ecological status' and not that of 'good ecological status' that corresponds with the 'ultimate aim' referred to in Article 1 of Directive 2000/60/EC and laid down in the international instruments on marine pollution. By requiring member states only to achieve 'good ecological status', Article 4 of the Framework Directive effectively legitimises a lower level of protection of the marine environment than aimed at under the relevant regional legal instruments and corresponding ministerial declarations and under Article 1 of the Directive itself.[585]

583 *Ibid*, Art 2(24).

584 *Ibid*, Annex V, table 1.2.4.

585 While the 'environmental objectives' for surface waters in Art 4 contain a reference to the aim of ceasing or phasing out *emissions* of 'priority hazardous substances', they do not mention the 'ultimate aim' in terms of *concentrations* in the marine environment stated in

To be sure, Article 16 of the Framework Directive provides for specific action to be taken at Community level aimed at the cessation or phasing out of emissions, discharges and losses of 'priority hazardous substances' from both point and diffuse sources. Article 1 specifies that the 'ultimate aim' of such action is to achieve 'concentrations in the marine environment near background values for naturally occurring substances and close to zero for man-made synthetic substances.' It is certainly positive that these ambitious objectives, which thus far had been proclaimed only in soft law texts, have for the first time been laid down in a legally binding instrument. But this has been achieved at the expense of a limitation of their substantive scope, since under Directive 2000/60/EC these phase-out objectives apply only to a selected list of 'priority hazardous substances', whereas in their original form they applied to *all* hazardous substances. Moreover, as the above analysis shows, the toxics phase-out objective, which was added at a late stage in response to political concerns, appears to be out of tune with the overall thrust and philosophy of the Framework Directive, which makes the Community's commitment to it somewhat equivocal. Indeed, the Directive's heavy reliance on the use of environmental quality standards and its highly selective approach to the control of hazardous substances differ significantly from the strategies for the elimination of marine pollution by hazardous substances adopted under the regional marine conventions.

Comparison with the Regime of Directive 76/464/EEC

When it proposed to add to Article 4 of the draft framework directive the objective to eliminate pollution by certain pollutants, the Commission asserted that this provision, inspired by Article 2 of Directive 76/464/EEC, was 'essential to show that the Community's policy towards dangerous substances remains the same' as under that Directive.[586] Are the provisions of the Framework Directive on emission control and pollution reduction programmes for hazardous substances really equivalent to those of Directive 76/464/EEC? We have already seen in our discussion of the implications of the IPPC Directive how the new, integrated permitting system for large industrial point sources introduced by that Directive gives member states more regulatory flexibility with respect to aquatic emissions of black list substances from these sources than they previously enjoyed under Directive 76/464/EEC. For emissions from point sources subject to the IPPC Directive, the Framework Directive essentially refers to the requirements of the

Art 1. So the provision in Art 4, para 2 that specifies that 'where more than one of the objectives under paragraph 1 relates to a given body of water, the most stringent shall apply' seems incapable of obviating the perverse effects of the definition of 'good surface water status'.

[586] *Ibid.*

IPPC Directive. The only additional requirement it provides for is the extension of the 'combined approach', which already applied for Community EQS under the IPPC Directive, to include compliance with EQS established by the member states pursuant to the Framework Directive. Once these EQS are in force, this could, in occasional cases, lead to a tightening of emission controls for some IPPC installations.

It is, however, primarily for emission sources not covered by the IPPC Directive that the Framework Directive was presented as a modern substitute for the 'obsolete' provisions of Directive 76/464/EEC. For point sources, the new requirements of the Framework Directive are a watered-down version of the existing provisions in Article 7 of Directive 76/464/EEC, which require prior authorisation and emission standards for *all* discharges of grey list substances (including black list substances for which no Community standards have been set). Under these provisions, member states also have a duty to draw up and implement national pollution reduction programmes fixing water quality objectives for all of these substances. The new provisions on 'programmes of measures' per individual river basin enable member states to exempt from any controls discharges which they regard as not 'liable to cause pollution', to make certain discharges subject to prior registration only, and to substitute other, unspecified 'emission controls' for emission limit values. They would also allow member states to fix the actual level of any controls on a largely discretionary basis, where Directive 76/464/EEC provides that pollution reduction programmes 'shall take into account the latest economically feasible technical developments.'[587] Under the 1976 Directive, control of diffuse sources is optional, whereas under the Framework Directive it is in principle part of the mandatory 'basic measures' to be implemented, at least in so far as member states consider these sources as 'liable to cause pollution'. But here too, the relevant new provision leaves member states almost total freedom in the choice of means.[588]

Most importantly, however, the new Directive considerably enlarges the range of discretion of the member states in selecting pollutants to be made subject to quality standards and emission controls and determining the ultimate objectives to be achieved. The black and grey lists and the previously unconditional duty respectively to eliminate and reduce pollution by particular substances will be abolished and replaced by vaguely formulated 'environmental objectives'. It is only for a small number of 'priority substances' that specific, more prescriptive measures aimed at emission reduction or phase-out, to be laid down by subsequent Community legislative

[587] Dir 76/464/EEC, Art 7, para 4. The only obligation in Art 11, para 3(g) of the Framework Directive which did not exist under Art 7 of the 1976 Directive is that of periodical reconsideration and, 'where necessary', updating of authorisations.

[588] Framework Directive, Art 11, para 3(h).

action, 'taking into account all significant sources *and the cost-effectiveness and proportionality of the available reduction options*,'[589] may eventually limit national discretion.

With the Framework Directive, the centre of gravity of Community water policy unmistakably shifts to an effects-oriented approach primarily based on risk assessment and quality standards. Indeed, effects- and risk-based criteria will play a decisive role in determining the scope and extent of member states' pollution control obligations. The 'status' of water bodies which triggers many of these obligations is determined *by reference to environmental quality standards largely established by the member states themselves*. These standards shall be based on an assessment of risks of adverse effects on aquatic organisms. Any emission control measures beyond those required to ensure that EQS are complied with are conditioned on a finding, at Community level, of 'significant risk to or via the aquatic environment'.

Repeal of Directive 76/464/EEC and Transitional Provisions

Directive 76/464/EEC as a whole will not be repealed immediately, but only 13 years after the date of entry into force of Directive 2000/60/EC, ie one year after the 'programmes of measures' for each river basin district have to be made operational by the member states.[590] However, Article 6 of the 1976 Directive is to be rescinded immediately upon entry into force of the Framework Directive. This article is the provision that mandates the Council to adopt harmonised emission limit values and environmental quality objectives for black list substances. As this legislative programme was abandoned years ago, the abrogation of this provision will not have any practical consequences.[591] The actual limit values and quality objectives established by the various daughter directives of Directive 76/464/EEC will remain in force and 'shall be considered emission limit values and environmental quality standards for the purposes' of the Framework Directive, as Annex IX and the various provisions referring to it make clear. But the special status given to these daughter directives is only temporary, as Article 16 of Directive 2000/60/EC provides that they shall be 'reviewed' by the Commission in the course of its preparation of future proposals for control strategies for 'priority substances'. If the black list substance to which the

[589] Framework Directive, recital 42 (emphasis added).

[590] Framework Directive, Art 21, para 2, last indent.

[591] Apart from the repeal of the legal basis of the 'dual approach' in para 3 of Art 6 of Dir 76/464/EEC. This is the provision authorising member states opting for the EQO approach not to apply the harmonised emission limit values if they can demonstrate compliance with the EQO. However, as we have seen above, the application of this provision for discharges from installations subject to the IPPC Directive had already been suspended by Art 20, para 3 of that Directive. Yet the EQOs for black list substances will continue to apply, *in addition to* the emission limit values rather than as an alternative to them, under the 'combined approach' of Art 10 of the Framework Directive.

daughter directive relates is selected as a 'priority substance' under the Framework Directive, the Commission shall propose a 'revision' of the existing standards. If not, the Commission shall 'propose the appropriate measures including the possible repeal of the controls' laid down in the daughter directives.[592] This indicates clearly that the Framework Directive is ultimately to prevail over all earlier Community legislative action with respect to discharges of toxic substances in the aquatic environment.

During the transition period prior to the complete repeal of Directive 76/464/EEC, important transitional provisions will apply which will affect the further implementation and enforcement of Article 7 of the 1976 Directive. Upon adoption of the list of 'priority substances' pursuant to Article 16 of Directive 2000/60/EC, that list automatically replaces the list of 129 'candidate' black list substances laid down in the Commission communication of 22 June 1982,[593] which has recently successfully been used by the Commission as an instrument for the enforcement of the member states' obligations under Article 7 of Directive 76/464/EEC. A further transitional clause provides that for the purposes of meeting those obligations, 'Member States *may* apply the principles for the identification of pollution problems and the substances causing them, the establishment of quality standards, and the adoption of measures' laid down in the Framework Directive.[594] These transitional provisions are of great importance in view of the large number of recent judgments of the Court of Justice in which member states have been condemned for failing to comply with their obligations under Article 7 of Directive 76/464/EEC with respect to 99 hazardous substances.[595]

The immediate implications of the first transitional provision are quite clear: since the adoption of Decision 2455/2001/EC, member states are required to establish pollution reduction programmes and quality objectives for a much smaller number of substances than under the previous legal regime. Instead of 99 substances (and potentially an even larger number), only 33 have to be regulated. The consequences of the second transitional provision are less self-evident. It seems that member states are given the option either to apply the actual provisions of Article 7 of Directive 76/464/EEC or to apply a number of rather ill-defined 'principles' deriving from the new provisions of Directive 2000/60/EC. The latter alternative is

[592] Framework Directive, Art 16, para 10. The following substances for which emission limit values and quality objectives have been laid down pursuant to Art 6 of Dir 76/464/EEC have not been listed as 'priority substances' in Annex X of Dir 2000/60/EC, as established by Decision 2455/2001/EC: carbon tetrachloride, DDT, aldrin, dieldrin, endrin, isodrin, trichloroethylene and perchloroethylene.

[593] *Ibid*, Art 21, para 3(a).

[594] *Ibid*, Art 21, para 3(b) (emphasis added).

[595] The insertion of this transitional provision, which was not actually proposed by the Commission, is probably the direct result of those infringement proceedings and the concern of a number of defendant member states to reduce the burden of compliance with the Court judgments.

certainly intended to authorise member states to use the risk assessment procedure laid down in Annex V of the Framework Directive for the purpose of establishing EQS pursuant to Article 7 of Directive 76/464/EEC. It presumably also aims to give them the possibility of choosing from the range of regulatory options for point sources provided in Article 11, paragraph 1(g) of the Framework Directive instead of requiring them to strictly apply a system of prior authorisations and emission standards, as the 1976 provisions do. But the implications of the reference to 'the principles for the identification of pollution problems and the substances causing them' are not entirely clear. Is it intended to allow member states to use the methods for the 'identification of pressures' and 'assessment of impact' laid down in Annex II of the Framework Directive to determine 'significant' sources of pollution[596] and the 'likelihood that surface water bodies . . . will fail to meet the environmental quality objectives,'[597] ie to establish whether a 'pollution problem' exists? Does it imply that pollution reduction measures will only have to be taken for those water bodies and substances for which failure to meet EQS is found to be likely? At any rate, these transitional provisions introduce a considerable measure of legal uncertainty in the further implementation of Article 7 of Directive 76/464/EEC during the transition period.

As the above analysis has shown, the Framework Directive on Community water policy fails to impose meaningful substantive constraints on the member states' policies for the control of toxic emissions into the aquatic environment. Despite the Commission's rhetorical smokescreen and the efforts of the European Parliament to salvage the objective of eliminating hazardous substances, the new legislation is clearly less demanding than Directive 76/464/EEC as far as control of these substances is concerned. Of course, final judgment must be reserved until the planned additional legislative action on specific measures for 'priority substances' has been taken. The adoption of the list of priority substances in itself has no immediate legal implications other than narrowing the range of the member states' remaining obligations under the 1976 Directive. The real test will be the subsequent elaboration of concrete emission control measures. It remains to be seen whether these will effectively match the proclaimed objective of cessation or phasing out of discharges, emissions and losses of 'priority' hazardous substances. After 25 years, Community policy appears to have come full circle: the legislative process has brought the institutions and the member states back to square one. The legal and policy discourse has changed but, in terms of implementing a toxics phase-out, they appear to be no further along than they were in 1976.

[596] Framework Directive, Annex II, s 1.4.
[597] *Ibid*, s 1.5.

9

The Interaction Between International Law and European Community Law: the Participation of the European Community in International Conventions Concerning Emissions of Dangerous Substances in the Aquatic Environment

AS APPEARS FROM the preceding chapters, there is a substantial measure of overlap in both geographical scope and substantive terms between the various conventional regimes for the control of marine pollution from land-based sources and pollution of international rivers on the one hand and the provisions of European Community law regulating toxic emissions in the aquatic environment on the other hand. In our specific field of enquiry, there is considerable interaction between conventional international law and European Community law. The influence runs both ways. For example, the regulatory regime for black and grey list substances established by the 1974 Paris Convention substantially inspired the provisions of Directive 76/464/EEC, and these instruments together in turn served as a model for the 1976 Rhine Convention and the 1980 Athens Protocol to the Barcelona Convention. The definition of BAT first elaborated in the framework of the Paris Commission and later codified in the 1992 Paris Convention was effectively 'adopted' by the European Commission and copied almost verbatim in its proposal for the IPPC Directive, and that convention's definitions of BAT and BEP were both incorporated in the EC Commission's subsequent proposal for a directive on the ecological quality of water. Several decisions and recommendations of the Paris and Rhine Commissions with respect to hazardous substances were modelled on EC directives, while, conversely, some internal EC measures were taken in response to Paris Commission recommendations.

The interaction between international law and EC law is not, however, limited to benign mutual cross-fertilisation. The relationship between the two has been formalised in international legal terms through the EC's status as a contracting party in its own right to the different marine and river pollution conventions. The co-existence of formally distinct yet interlocking legal regimes and institutional frameworks purporting to regulate the same activities has caused political conflicts over issues of competence and precedence and raised intricate legal problems about the respective authority of the Community and individual member states as contracting parties to these conventions in their relations with third parties. As a result, the standard-setting activities of treaty bodies like the Paris Commission have been delayed and constrained in certain areas. These problems, which notwithstanding their legal overtones in fact also reflect political differences about the policy-making autonomy of the Community and its member states and the relative importance of a high level of environmental protection and the integrity of the internal market, will be analysed in this chapter.

THE LEGAL FRAMEWORK OF THE COMMUNITY'S EXTERNAL COMPETENCE IN THE ENVIRONMENTAL FIELD

Until its amendment by the Single European Act (SEA), the EEC Treaty contained no specific provisions on environmental policy nor, a fortiori, any provisions expressly conferring on the Community the power to enter into international agreements concerning the protection of the environment. Yet this did not prevent the development of a Community policy on the environment and the adoption of numerous legal acts in this field. From the outset, the Commission was keen to give this policy an important external dimension and to assert the Community's role as a major actor in international environmental cooperation at the regional and global level.[1] The Commission's eagerness to promote the participation of the EC in international environmental fora and agreements was guided at least as much by symbolic considerations of political recognition and prestige as by practical concerns about ensuring the effectiveness of environmental policies at the Community and wider international level. The member states somewhat half-heartedly followed the Commission, by unanimously agreeing within the Council to allow the EC to become a contracting party to a number of

[1] See the 1st Programme of Action of the European Communities on the Environment, Annex to the Declaration of the Council of the European Communities and of the Representatives of the Governments of the Member States meeting in the Council of 22 Nov 1973 on the programme of action of the European Communities on the environment, OJ No C112, 20.12.1973, pp 11, 47–49.

environmental conventions, while at the same time remaining reluctant to relinquish their role as independent actors in international environmental fora. The legal formula of the 'mixed agreement,'[2] whereby both the Community and the member states can be contracting parties to a treaty with third states, made it possible to reconcile these two apparently conflicting objectives.

Prior to the entry into force of the SEA, the practice of Community participation in international environmental conventions was based on the legal theory developed by the Court of Justice that the external competence of the Community parallels its internal competence.[3] In a series of cases, beginning with the famous *ERTA* case,[4] the Court of Justice held that the Community has the authority to enter into international agreements not only where this is expressly provided for in the Treaty, but also pursuant to the provisions of the Treaty granting internal legislative powers and the measures adopted by Community institutions based on those provisions. Thus the Community's external competence flows implicitly from its internal competence when the conclusion of an international agreement is necessary to attain the objectives for which these internal competences have been provided. The treaty-making power of the Community exists whenever there is a corresponding internal legislative power, regardless of whether or not this internal power has effectively been used for the purpose of adopting internal measures.[5] In the pre-SEA period, Council decisions concluding international environmental agreements on behalf of the Community were routinely based on Article 235 EEC, the implied powers clause of the Treaty, which was also used as a legal basis for internal environmental measures that were not directly related to the establishment and functioning of the common market and therefore did not fall within the ambit of Article 100 EEC.

The external competence of the Community in the field of environmental policy was given an explicit legal basis by the SEA, which introduced in the EEC Treaty a provision stipulating that:

> *Within their respective spheres of competence*, the Community and the Member States shall cooperate with third countries and with the relevant international organizations. The arrangements for Community cooperation may be the subject of agreements between the Community and the third parties concerned. . . .

[2] See the definition by Schermers (1983), p 25. On the concept of mixed agreement, see also MacLeod, Henry & Hyett (1996), pp 142–44.

[3] For a more detailed discussion of the development of the Community's external environmental powers in the light of the case-law, see Nollkaemper (1987), pp 63–66.

[4] Case 22/70, *Commission v Council*, [1971] ECR 263.

[5] Joined Cases 3, 4 and 6/76, *Cornelis Kramer*, [1976] ECR 1279; *Draft Agreement establishing a European laying-up fund for inland waterway vessels*, Opinion 1/76, [1977] ECR 741.

The previous paragraph shall be *without prejudice to Member States' competence* to negotiate in international bodies and to conclude international agreements.[6]

While this provision codifies existing practice with respect to the external competence of the Community as it had developed prior to the SEA, it does not clarify the division of competence between the Community and its member states, which has proved to be the main area of contention and cause of problems in external fora. Indeed, the wording of Article 130r, paragraph 5 EEC (now Article 174, paragraph 4 EC) was criticised by an authoritative commentator for being 'so unclear that it provides few answers as regards the Community's external powers in the environmental field.'[7] The apparent desire to preserve the existing legal ambiguities was evidenced by a declaration annexed to the final act of the intergovernmental conference which negotiated the SEA, stressing that the reference to the competence of the member states was not intended to affect the case-law of the Court of Justice in the *ERTA* case.[8] Thus the precise extent of respective external competences is left to be determined on a case-by-case basis in accordance with the rather vague general principles enunciated by the Court of Justice through political bargaining between the Commission and the Council, with the Court as a potential umpire.[9]

In practice, all multilateral environmental conventions to which the Community is a contracting party, whether concluded before or after the entry into force of the SEA, are in the form of 'mixed agreements.'[10] Depending on their subject matter and geographical scope, either some or all member states are also contracting parties, in addition to the Community, and are represented in their individual capacity in the bodies established under those conventions. This concurrent representation in treaty bodies, which has the political advantage of 'allowing the Member States to exercise competence, while at the same time protecting the sphere of action of the Community,'[11] leads to legal difficulties whenever a formal vote has to be taken, as the conventions generally do not allow the Community and the member states parties to exercise their voting rights simultaneously.[12] From

[6] Art 130r, para 5 EEC (emphasis added). This provision was not modified by the TEU, but renumbered as Art 130r, para 4 EC. It became Art 174, para 4 as a result of the Treaty of Amsterdam. For a detailed discussion of this clause and its implications for the external environmental competence of the Community, see Krämer (1990), pp 81–86.

[7] *Ibid*, p 82.

[8] Yet, as Krämer points out, both the existing practice and the wording of Art 130r, para 5 are actually 'incompatible with the principles enunciated in the [ERTA] judgment'! Krämer (1990), p 84.

[9] Although the Court of Justice has never yet been called upon to rule on the extent of the Community's treaty-making power in the environmental field, it has occasionally done so in other fields. See, eg, Case C-268/94, *Portugal v Council*, [1996] ECR I–6207.

[10] Krämer (1995), p 86; MacLeod, Henry & Hyett (1996), p 329.

[11] Neuwahl (1991), p 739.

[12] On the issue of the exercise of voting rights by the Community and its member states within the framework of international organisations, see generally Frid (1995) and Sack (1995).

the point of view of Community law, recourse to the mixed agreement formula implies that the convention in question covers matters which are partly within the sphere of competence of the Community and partly within that of the member states. Exactly *where* the boundary between national and Community competence lies is, of course, the crucial question. And while it is quite possible to conclude a mixed agreement without answering that question,[13] it is bound to return to haunt the parties in the course of implementation, as experience with some of the conventions which are the subject of the present study indicates.

THE LEGAL POSITION OF THE EC AS A CONTRACTING PARTY IN INTERNATIONAL CONVENTIONS CONCERNING TOXIC EMISSIONS

The European Community is a contracting party to the 1974 Paris Convention, the 1974 and 1992 Helsinki Baltic Conventions, the 1976 Bonn Convention, the 1976 Barcelona Convention and its 1980 Athens Protocol, as amended in Syracuse in 1996, the 1987 Danube Convention, the 1990 Elbe Convention, the 1992 Helsinki Rivers Convention, the 1992 Paris Convention, the 1994 Sofia Danube Convention and the 1996 Oder Convention, and has recently also concluded the new 1999 Berne Rhine Convention, which has yet to enter into force. In these conventions, the Community is or will become a party alongside those of its member states which have a direct interest in their subject matter as riparian states of the sea or river concerned, and the European Commission participates in the activities of the regulatory bodies established under them as the Community's representative, alongside the national delegations of the member states. The division of powers between the Community and its member states with respect to the implementation of these conventions and, more specifically, with respect to negotiating and voting powers within these bodies, has been a source of problems between the Commission and the member states, as well as between the Community and third states which are also contracting parties to the conventions in question.

Marine Environment Protection Conventions

The EC was involved in the negotiations leading to the conclusion of the 1974 Paris Convention. In the text of the Convention, special provision was

[13] In fact, as one commentator has noted, the popularity and increasing use of the 'mixed agreement' formula seems to be associated 'very often with *an avoidance of the exact delimitation of the respective powers* of Community institutions and those of the Member States'. Simmonds (1989), p 37 (emphasis added).

made for the Community to become a contracting party as well as for the sharing of voting rights between the Community and its member states. Article 19 of the Convention provides:

> Within the areas of its competence, the European Economic Community is entitled to a number of votes equal to the number of its member States which are Contracting Parties to the present Convention. The European Economic Community shall not exercise its right to vote in cases where its member States exercise theirs and conversely.

The Community formally became a contracting party to the Paris Convention by a Council Decision of 3 March 1975, which at the same time designated the Commission to represent the Community in the Paris Commission.[14] The Commission, however, was not given an unconditional mandate: it is to put forward the Community's position 'in accordance with such Directives as the Council may give it.'[15] The provisions of Article 19 of the 1974 Convention were incorporated in Article 20, paragraph 2 of the 1992 Paris Convention without any material alteration, other than the addition of a reference to hypothetical 'other regional economic integration organisations', which may also become contracting parties to the new convention under the same conditions as the EC.

The new Paris Convention was signed on behalf of the Community on 22 September 1992 but was only formally concluded by the Council five years later.[16] The Commission's proposal for conclusion, submitted to the Council on 6 January 1995,[17] ie after the entry into force of the TEU, resulted in a protracted argument between the Commission and the Council about their respective competences within the framework of the new Convention. Invoking the new provisions of Article 228 EC (now Article 300 EC), as amended by the TEU,[18] the Commission requested the Council to authorise it to approve, on behalf of the Community, decisions made by OSPAR Commission pursuant to Article 13 of the 1992 Convention, as well as amendments to the Convention's annexes and the adoption of new appendices to the Convention resulting from the amendment of an annex.[19] Under Article 300, paragraph 4 EC, the Council may give the Commission a mandate to approve 'modifications' to agreements concluded by

[14] Council Decision 75/437/EEC of 3 Mar 1975 concluding the Convention for the prevention of marine pollution from land-based sources, OJ No L194, 25.7.1975, p 5.

[15] *Ibid*, Art 3. Although the term 'Directives' is capitalised in this provision, it is presumably to be understood as directives for negotiation (as in Art 133, para 3 EC) and not as Directive in the sense of formal acts of the Council within the meaning of Art 249 EC.

[16] Council Decision 98/249/EC of 7 Oct 1997 on the conclusion of the Convention for the protection of the marine environment of the North-East Atlantic, OJ No L104, 3.4. 1998, p 1.

[17] EC Doc COM(94)660 final, 6 Jan 1995.

[18] For a general discussion of the impact of the TEU on the legal framework of the external relations of the EC, see eg Konstadinidis (1996).

[19] EC Doc COM(94)660 final, 6 January 1995, Proposal for a Council Decision, Art 3.

the Community pursuant to Article 300, paragraph 2, 'where the agreement provides for them to be adopted by a simplified procedure or by a body set up by the agreement', thus avoiding the need for a formal Council decision for the approval of every such 'modification'.

In its explanatory memorandum, the Commission gave a very extensive and questionable interpretation of the concept of 'modification', as referred to in Article 300, paragraph 4, stretching it to include acts of the Paris Commission which, though having legal effects under the provisions of the 1992 Convention, can hardly be regarded as 'modifications' of that convention. The Commission simply lumped decisions of the Paris Commission together with amendments to annexes and appendices under the general category of 'procedures resulting in a modification of the Convention', arguing merely that such decisions are 'of a rather technical nature.'[20] While the amendment of annexes and the adoption of appendices pursuant to, respectively, Article 17 and 18 of the Paris Convention can be considered as modifications of the convention adopted by a simplified procedure, the same cannot be said of decisions of the Paris Commission, which cannot modify but only *implement* the provisions of the convention itself. The term 'modifications' in Article 300, paragraph 4 must be interpreted as a synonym of 'amendments' and does not seem intended to cover every act adopted by a body set up by an agreement, whatever its legal effect.[21] At any rate, the Council rejected the Commission's request for such an open-ended mandate and its expansive interpretation of Article 300, paragraph 4, as the eventual Council decision concluding the 1992 Paris Convention contains no preambular reference to that provision and merely mandates the Commission to represent the Community in the Paris Commission 'as regards matters within the sphere of Community competence.'[22] Consequently, when a new Annex to the Convention, concerning the protection of marine biodiversity, was adopted in 1998, a formal Council decision was required to enable the Community to approve it.[23]

Together with its Mediterranean member states Spain, France, Italy and Greece, the EC is also a contracting party to the Barcelona Convention, which it concluded by a Council Decision of 25 July 1977.[24] Article 19 of the Convention, concerning the exercise of voting rights in the organs of the Convention and its protocols, contains provisions which are virtually

[20] *Ibid*, Explanatory memorandum, para 12.
[21] MacLeod, Henry & Hyett (1996), p 105.
[22] Decision 98/249/EC, above n 16, Art 3.
[23] Council Decision 2000/340/EEC of 8 May 2000 concerning the approval, on behalf of the Community, of the new Annex to the Convention for the protection of the marine environment of the North-East Atlantic on the protection and conservation of the ecosystems and biological diversity of the maritime area, the corresponding Appendix 3 and the Agreement on the meaning of certain concepts in the new Annex, OJ No L118, 19.5.2000, p 44.
[24] Council Decision 77/586/EEC of 25 July 1977 concluding the Convention for the protection of the Mediterranean Sea against pollution, OJ No L240, 19.9.1977, p 1.

identical to those of Article 19 of the 1974 Paris Convention. In 1983, the Community became a party to the Athens Protocol. The Council Decision concluding the Protocol refers in its preamble, inter alia, to Directive 76/464/EEC.[25] Without awaiting action by the member states concerned, the Community in 1999 formally accepted the amendments to the Barcelona Convention and the Athens Protocol adopted, respectively, in 1995 and 1996.[26]

The 1974 Helsinki Convention did not contain any provision enabling the EC to become a contracting party. The Community was not involved in the negotiation of that Convention, though the Commission had expressed an interest in participating on a similar basis as in the other regional marine pollution conventions. It later tried to convince the contracting parties to open negotiations on an amendment to the 1974 Convention with a view to permitting its accession.[27] Initially, this effort was not successful due to political objections on the part of some contracting parties to the Helsinki Convention, but in 1991, following the political changes in Eastern Europe, the Helsinki Commission finally accepted the principle of EC participation.[28] This was eventually achieved both through a technical amendment to the 1974 Convention enabling the Community to accede to it, as originally proposed by the Commission, and by the invitation extended to the Community to participate in the negotiations leading to a complete revision of the 1974 Convention in 1992. Though it was stipulated that the 1974 Convention would cease to apply as soon as the new 1992 Helsinki Baltic Convention became effective, the EC's accession to the first convention remained necessary to enable it to participate as a full contracting party in the activities of the Helsinki Commission during the transitional period between the adoption and entry into force of the 1992 Convention—which, as it turned out, lasted eight years. This is why, on 21 February 1994, the Council simultaneously adopted two decisions, the first to formalise the Community's accession to the 1974 Convention,[29] and the second to conclude the 1992

[25] Council Decision 83/101/EEC of 28 Feb 1983 concluding the Protocol for the protection of the Mediterranean Sea against pollution from land-based sources, OJ No L67, 12.3.1983, p 1.

[26] Council Decision 1999/802/EC of 22 Oct 1999 on the acceptance of amendments to the Convention for the Protection of the Mediterranean Sea against Pollution and to the Protocol for the Prevention of Pollution by Dumping from Ships and Aircraft (Barcelona Convention), OJ No L322, 14.12.1999, p 32; Council Decision 1999/801/EC of 22 Oct 1999 on accepting the amendments to the Protocol for the protection of the Mediterranean Sea against pollution from land-based sources (Barcelona Convention), OJ No L322, 14.12.1999, p 18.

[27] See Johnson & Corcelle (1990), p 299.

[28] See the Report of the Twelfth Meeting of the Commission held in Helsinki, 19–22 Feb 1991, *Baltic Sea Environment Proceedings*, No 37, p 19.

[29] Council Decision 94/156/EC of 21 Feb 1994 on the accession of the Community to the Convention on the Protection of the Marine Environment of the Baltic Sea Area 1974 (Helsinki Convention), OJ No L73, 16.3.1994, p 1.

Convention,[30] which had been signed on behalf of the Community on 24 September 1992.[31]

River Pollution Conventions

The Convention for the protection of the Rhine against chemical pollution was concluded in 1976 between all riparian states of the Rhine and the EEC, which a few months earlier had adopted Directive 76/464/EEC, containing very similar provisions. The Convention effectively provides a legal framework for involving a third state, Switzerland, in a regime for combating pollution inspired by Directive 76/464/EEC. The legal implications of the Community's participation in the Convention are spelled out in its Article 16, which provides:

> For the purposes of applying this Convention, the European Economic Community and its Member States shall act in their respective areas of competence.

In order to enable the Community to participate in the International Commission for the Protection of the Rhine against Pollution, the body entrusted with the implementation of the Convention, an Additional Agreement was concluded, amending the 1963 Agreement by which that Commission was originally established. The Additional Agreement contains a provision on voting rights similar in substance to Article 19 of the 1974 Paris Convention, enabling the Community to vote 'in those areas coming within its jurisdiction'. The Convention and Additional Agreement were both concluded by a Council Decision of 25 July 1977.[32] On 12 April 1999, the Community, together with the riparian member states, signed the new Berne Convention on the Protection of the Rhine. A decision authorising the conclusion of the Berne Convention was adopted by the Council on 7 November 2000.[33] Under Article 10, paragraph 3 of the new Convention, the Community will exercise voting rights in the Rhine Commission in lieu

[30] Council Decision 94/157/EC of 21 Feb 1994 on the conclusion, on behalf of the Community, of the Convention on the Protection of the Marine Environment of the Baltic Sea Area (Helsinki Convention as revised in 1992), OJ No L 73, 16.3.1994, p 19.

[31] A Proposal for a Council Decision concerning the approval, on behalf of the Commission, of the amendments to the Annexes to the Convention on the protection of the marine environment of the Baltic Sea area (Helsinki Convention), was withdrawn by the Commission in Dec 2001. See EC Doc COM(1999) 128 final.

[32] Council Decision 77/586/EEC of 25 July 1977 concluding the Convention for the protection of the Rhine against chemical pollution and an Additional Agreement to the Agreement, signed in Berne on 29 Apr 1963, concerning the International Commission for the Protection of the Rhine against Pollution, OJ No L240, 19.9.1977, p 35.

[33] Council Decision 2000/706/EC of 7 Nov 2000 concerning the conclusion, on behalf of the Community, of the Convention for the Protection of the Rhine, OJ No L289, 16.11.2000, p 30.

of its member states whenever it is competent for the implementation of the recommended action to be decided upon.

Since the late 1980s, a significant number of new multilateral conventions for the protection of international rivers against pollution were concluded. Whenever the riparian parties involved included one or several member states and at least one non-member state of the EC,[34] the Community participated in the elaboration of these agreements and became a contracting party to them.

On 22 March 1990, the Council approved a tripartite cooperation agreement between Germany, the EEC and Austria, at that time still a non-member state, on the management of water resources in the Danube Basin.[35] This agreement covers both the quantitative and qualitative aspects of water management and establishes a Standing Committee on the Management of Water Resources, which was given the power inter alia to make recommendations on 'minimum requirements in respect of discharges to the aquatic environment.'[36] Upon signing the agreement, the FRG and the EEC made a joint declaration indicating 'the present areas of competence of the European Economic Community within the scope of the Agreement' by reference to a list of Community legal instruments in force at the time, which includes Directive 76/464/EEC and its daughter directives.[37]

In the wake of the political changes in Central and Eastern Europe, Germany initiated negotiations with its neighbours to conclude comprehensive basin agreements for the Elbe and Oder rivers. The Commission was mandated by the Council to participate in these efforts. The Convention between Germany, the Czech and Slovak Federal Republic and the EEC establishing the International Commission for the Protection of the Elbe was signed in Magdeburg on 8 October 1990 and concluded by the Community by a Council Decision of 18 November 1991.[38] The

[34] This explains why the Community is not a party to the Agreement on the Protection of the Meuse and the Agreement on the Protection of the Scheldt, both concluded in Charleville-Mézières on 26 Apr 1994, between France, the Netherlands and the three Regions of Belgium. No non-member states are parties to these Agreements. However, the European Commission was granted observer status in the respective international commissions established under them. An unofficial English translation of the Agreements appears at 34 ILM 851 (1995).

[35] Council Decision 90/160/EEC of 22 Mar 1990 concerning the conclusion of the Agreement between the Federal Republic of Germany and the European Economic Community, on the one hand, and the Republic of Austria, on the other, on cooperation on management of water resources in the Danube Basin, OJ No L90, 5.4.1990, p 18.

[36] Agreement between the Federal Republic of Germany and the European Economic Community, on the one hand, and the Republic of Austria, on the other, on cooperation on management of water resources in the Danube Basin, Regensburg, 1 Dec 1987, Art 7, para 3 (a).

[37] Declaration by the Federal Republic of Germany and the European Economic Community, OJ No L90, 5.4.1990, pp 24–25.

[38] Council Decision 91/598/EEC of 18 Nov 1991 concerning the conclusion of the Convention on the International Commission for the Protection of the Elbe, OJ No L321, 23.11.1991, p 24.

Convention calls, inter alia, for 'the application of state-of-the-art techniques for the reduction of emissions'[39] and empowers the Commission it establishes to 'propose specific action for the reduction of discharges of harmful materials from point sources . . . and from diffuse sources,'[40] including 'limit values for the discharge of effluent.'[41] Article 8 on decision-making procedures within the Elbe Commission provides that each delegation shall have one vote and further stipulates:

> Negotiations and decisions within the framework of this Convention as well as its implementation shall be conducted by the European Economic Community and the Federal Republic of Germany within their respective fields of competence. The European Economic Community shall not exercise its right to vote in cases in which the Federal Republic of Germany is competent and vice versa.[42]

The same provision can be found in the Convention on the International Commission for the Protection of the Oder, which was concluded in Wroclaw on 11 April 1996 between Germany, Poland, the Czech Republic and the EC.[43] As the contracting parties to this agreement, except Poland, are the same as in the Elbe Convention, and Germany was the driving force behind its negotiation as well as the only EU member state involved, it is not surprising that the Wroclaw agreement is very similar in both form and substance to that earlier convention. The institutional framework and mandate of the Oder Commission is modelled on that of the Elbe Commission. A decision authorising the Community to ratify the Oder agreement was taken by the Council in March 1999.[44]

The development of international river conventions for specific river basins was given an additional impetus by the adoption of a multilateral framework convention on the subject under the auspices of the United Nations Economic Commission for Europe (ECE) in Helsinki in March 1992.[45] This convention, which was concluded by the EC by a Council Decision of 24 July 1995,[46] contains both a set of general provisions applicable to all contracting parties and a set of special provisions which apply

[39] Convention on the International Commission for the Protection of the Elbe, Magdeburg, 8 Oct 1990, Art 1, para 3.

[40] *Ibid*, Art 2, para 1 (f).

[41] *Ibid*, Art 2, para 1 (b).

[42] *Ibid*, Art 8, para 2.

[43] Convention on the International Commission for the Protection of the Oder, Wroclaw, 11 Apr 1996, OJ No L100, 15.4.1999, p 20, Art 8, para 2.

[44] Council Decision 1999/257/EC of 29 Mar 1999 concerning the conclusion of the Convention on the International Commission for the Protection of the Oder, OJ No L100, 15.4.1999, p 20.

[45] Convention on the Protection and Use of Transboundary Watercourses and International Lakes, Helsinki, 17 Mar 1992, 31 ILM 1312 (1992) (hereafter referred to as 1992 Helsinki Rivers Convention). For a discussion of this Convention, see above ch 7.

[46] Council Decision 95/308/EC of 24 July 1995 on the conclusion, on behalf of the Community, of the Convention on the protection and use of transboundary watercourses and international lakes, OJ No L186, 5.8.1995, p 42 (hereafter referred to as Decision 95/308/EC).

between 'Riparian Parties' of particular transboundary watercourses and encourage them to conclude bilateral or multilateral cooperation agreements, additional to the convention itself, governing the management of these specific watercourses. The notion of 'Riparian Parties' is defined as 'the Parties bordering the same transboundary waters,'[47] and these parties may include:

regional economic integration organizations constituted by sovereign States members of the Economic Commission for Europe to which their member States have transferred competence over matters governed by this Convention, *including the competence to enter into treaties in respect of these matters.*[48]

So far, the EC is the only regional organisation party to the Convention; as a matter of fact it is the only existing organisation in the ECE region which fulfils these criteria.

As regards voting rights within the Conference of the Parties, the convention contains a clause modelled on the now classic formula pioneered by the 1974 Paris Convention.[49] It should be noted, however, that Article 25 of the Helsinki Rivers Convention contains further, original provisions governing the respective legal position under the Convention of regional economic integration organisations and their member states. It provides that:

the organization and its member States shall decide on their respective responsibilities for the performance of their obligations under this Convention. In such cases, the organization and its member States shall not be entitled to exercise rights under this Convention concurrently.[50]

Regional economic integration organisations are also specifically required to 'declare the extent of their competence with respect to the matters governed by this Convention' in their instrument of approval and to inform the depositary of 'any substantial modification' which may subsequently occur.[51] Pursuant to this obligation, the Community, upon depositing its instrument of approval, made a formal declaration of competence, the content of which was explicitly approved by the Council and annexed to its Decision concluding the Convention.[52] It will be interesting to see whether the other contracting parties to the Convention will be satisfied with the EC's declaration; it is ambiguously worded, in terms arcane to anyone unfamiliar with the technicalities of the law on the external relations of the Community, which are clearly the result of a compromise between the Community institutions. It simply lists a series of directives,

[47] 1992 Helsinki Rivers Convention, Art 1, para 4.
[48] *Ibid*, Art 23 (emphasis added).
[49] *Ibid*, Art 18, para 2.
[50] *Ibid*, Art 25, para 3.
[51] *Ibid*, Art 25, para 4.
[52] Decision 95/308/EC, above n 46, Art 2 and Annex II.

including Directive 76/464/EEC and its daughter directives, under which 'the Community is competent for international matters', while stressing at the same time that 'the Member States of the European Community also have *international competence which applies equally* to matters covered by the [Helsinki Rivers] Convention', matters which are not further specified. The declaration concludes by pointing out that the list of relevant directives '*may be subject to change* with the amendment or repeal of existing texts or the adoption of new texts.'[53]

Finally, a Convention on Cooperation for the Protection and Sustainable Use of the Danube River was signed in Sofia on 29 June 1994 by all the riparian states of the Danube and the EC and concluded by the Community on 24 November 1997.[54] This Convention, which is very broad in scope and covers all aspects of 'sustainable water management', both quantitative and qualitative, is not intended to replace the 1987 Regensburg agreement between Germany, Austria and the EC but rather to establish a broader framework for cooperation involving all basin states and the Community, inspired by the 1992 Helsinki Rivers Convention. According to Article 4(2) of the Statute of the International Commission for the Protection of the Danube River, annexed to the Convention, the Community 'within the areas of its competence, is entitled to a number of votes equal to the number of its Member States which are Contracting Parties' but 'shall not exercise its right to vote in cases where its Member States exercise theirs and conversely'.

LEGAL AND POLITICAL PROBLEMS OF EC PARTICIPATION

This situation of concurrent jurisdiction between the Community and its member states has led to frequent problems between the Commission and national delegations and delayed decision-making in bodies such as the Paris Commission, much to the frustration of the other contracting parties. In the Second Environmental Action Programme, the Commission explained that its main concern in participating in international conventions was to ensure that any rules agreed in international fora 'are in

[53] *Ibid*, Annex II (emphasis added).

[54] Council Decision 97/825/EC of 24 Nov 1997 on the conclusion of the Convention on cooperation for the protection and sustainable use of the Danube River, OJ No L342, 12.12.1997, p 18. This decision, which is based on Art 130s, para 1 in conjunction with Art 228 of the Treaty, was unsuccessfully challenged by Spain in annulment proceedings before the Court of Justice. The claimant argued that the Council decision should have been based on Art 130s, para 2 instead of 130s, para 1, as the Sofia Convention deals with the 'management of water resources', but the Court rejected this claim on the grounds that the main purpose of the convention is the protection and improvement of the water quality of the Danube basin, and that it deals with quantitative water management only in an incidental manner. Case C–36/98, *Spain v Council*, [2001] ECR 779.

conformity with the rules of the Treaties and with the environmental protection measures taken at Community level.'[55] This has led the Commission to adopt a rather conservative attitude within the organs of international conventions, generally refusing to endorse any measure on which the Community has not yet reached agreement internally.

Conflict in the Paris Commission

A few examples from Paris Commission practice will illustrate the attitude of the EC and the problems to which it has given rise.[56] In 1985, the EC Commission objected to the adoption by the Paris Commission of measures to control pollution by cadmium from diffuse sources, on the grounds that such measures were not provided for in the Directive 83/513/EEC.[57] At the same meeting of the Paris Commission, the EC Commission also held up the adoption of a decision on the prohibition of PCBs and PCTs, arguing that the Community could not commit itself because the matter was under discussion internally.[58] In 1990, the Commission entered a reservation to the adoption of a Paris Commission decision on the reduction of mercury and cadmium discharges from batteries, another matter which was the subject of a proposed directive under discussion in the Council.[59] The reservation was maintained in 1991[60] because of 'discrepancies' between the proposed PARCOM decision and Directive 91/157/EEC, which had meanwhile been adopted by the EC Council.[61] The adoption of a Paris Commission decision on the phasing out of uses of cadmium in applications other than batteries was also delayed due to the fact that the issue was under consideration within the EC. Finding itself unable to make progress in the field as long as the decision-making process within the Community was not completed, the Paris Commission at its 1990 meeting could do no more than to invite the EC to 'speed up its work in this field.'[62]

More recently, in 1996, a direct clash occurred between the EC legislative process and the standard-setting work of PARCOM, when the

[55] Second Action Programme, para 45.

[56] On the participation of the EC in the Paris Commission, see generally IJlstra (1990).

[57] PARCOM Doc 7/13/1–E, June 1985, para 5.5.

[58] *Ibid*, para 5.13. The internal decision-making process within the Community resulted in the adoption, a few months later, of Council Dir 85/467/EEC of 1 Oct 1985, OJ No L 269, 11.10.1985, p 56.

[59] PARCOM Doc 12/13/1–E, June 1990, para 5.31.

[60] PARCOM Doc 13/9/1–E, June 1991, para 4.23.

[61] Council Dir 91/157/EEC of 18 Mar 1991 on batteries and accumulators containing certain dangerous substances, OJ No L78, 26.3.1991, p 38.

[62] PARCOM Doc 12/13/1–E, June 1990, para 5.34. The relevant directive, imposing restrictions on a variety of uses of cadmium within the Community, was eventually adopted one year later. See Council Dir 91/338/EEC of 18 June 1991, OJ No L 186, 12.7.1991, p 59.

Commission sought and obtained from the Council a mandate[63] to renegotiate two PARCOM decisions adopted in 1992 and 1993 and restricting the use of HCE in the non-ferrous metal industry,[64] in order to bring them into line with the provisions of a proposed EC directive allowing derogations for small aluminium foundries.[65] As a result of this incident, in which the Community found itself in the politically awkward position of having to call for reconsideration of international commitments entered into by a large group of its member states a few years earlier, the Commission now systematically requests a negotiating mandate from the Council in order to exercise the Community's voting rights in the Paris Commission and thus prevent member states from voting individually on proposals for measures under the Paris Convention on matters which it considers to be within the sphere of Community competence.

In its efforts to justify these requests to the Council, the Commission puts considerable emphasis on its concern to avoid any 'disruption' or 'fragmentation' of the internal market by international measures which would bind member states individually.[66] It is clear that the European Commission, instead of welcoming enhanced regional cooperation for the protection of the marine environment, primarily views the norm-setting activities of the Paris Commission as a potential threat to the integrity of the internal market and an unwelcome interference in the Community's own legislative process. It is significant in this respect that the Commission, in its request for a negotiating mandate for the 1997 meeting of PARCOM, recommended that the Community's position should be to seek postponement of the adoption of all proposed measures to restrict the marketing and use of hazardous substances and to demand that all proposals for PARCOM decisions on BAT and emission limit values for industrial sectors be transformed into non-binding recommendations.[67]

[63] EC Doc SEC(95) 2174 final, 15 Dec 1995.

[64] PARCOM Decision 92/4 on the phasing out of the use of hexachloroethane (HCE) in the secondary aluminium industry and in the primary aluminium industry with integrated foundries, Sept 1992; PARCOM Decision 93/1 on the phasing out of the use of hexachloroethane (HCE) in the non-ferrous metal industry, OSPAR Doc 15/13/1–E, June 1993, Annex 7. On these decisions see also above ch 4.

[65] Amended proposal for a European Parliament and Council Directive amending for the 16th time Dir 76/769/EEC on the approximation of the laws, regulations and administrative provisions of the Member States relating to restrictions on the marketing and use of certain dangerous substances and preparations, OJ No C12, 17.1.1996, p 12. This proposal was adopted as European Parliament and Council Dir 97/16/EC of 10 April 1997 amending for the 15th time Dir 76/769/EEC on restrictions on the marketing and use of certain dangerous substances and preparations, OJ No L116, 6.5.1997, p 31. Following the adoption of this directive, the Council formally approved the revised PARCOM Decision 96/1 on the phasing out of the use of hexachloroethane in the non-ferrous metal industry. See Council Decision 98/24/EC of 23 Mar 1998, OJ No L96, 28.3.1998.

[66] See EC Doc SEC(95) 2174 final, 15 Dec 1995, Explanatory memorandum, para 5; EC Doc SEC(96) 1024 final, 7 June 1996, Explanatory memorandum, para 5; EC Doc SEC(97) 1195 final, 2 July 1997, Explanatory memorandum, para 4.

[67] See EC Doc SEC(97) 1195 final, 2 July 1997.

The relevant provisions of the 1974 and 1992 Paris Conventions[68] are based on the assumption that the division of jurisdiction between the EC and its member states is clearcut, with either the Community or its member states being competent for a given issue and thus entitled to vote on that issue. Sometimes the voting system within the Paris Commission operates as envisaged. For example, when the Commission formally adopted its programmes and measures for the reduction of mercury and cadmium pollution in 1985, the Community cast its vote on behalf of its member states.[69] In this case the Community's competence was undisputed because the proposed PARCOM Decision covered exactly the same field as previous EEC Directives,[70] on whose provisions it was in fact based. But in many other instances, the division of powers between the Community and its member states is not quite as clearcut and may even become a matter of contention between the Commission and individual member states. In such instances, the Commission, representing the Community, and individual member states express separate and sometimes even divergent positions on matters under discussion within the Paris Commission.

For example, when the EC Commission objected to the adoption of a Paris Commission decision on PCBs in 1985, several EC member states expressed their disagreement with the Commission's position that the EC had exclusive competence in the field due to the earlier adoption of an EEC Directive and said they were prepared to adopt the proposed Paris Commission decision.[71] The EC Commission and the EC member states thus openly quarrelled about the extent of the Community's jurisdiction in an external forum.

On other occasions, even though open conflict is avoided, the attitudes of the Commission and certain member states indicate ambiguity as to the extent of Community competences. For instance, when the EC Commission in 1990 made a reservation to the adoption of a PARCOM Decision on the reduction of mercury and cadmium in batteries, the United Kingdom entered a reservation in its own right.[72] Such a situation, whereby both the Community and one of its member states formally take a position about a matter before the Paris Commission, was clearly inconsistent with the provisions of Article 19 of the 1974 Paris Convention in force at that time, which, like their successor provisions in the 1992 Convention, imply that one acts to the exclusion of the other.

The ambiguous positions of the EC Commission and the EC member states about their respective competences and recurrent arguments about

[68] 1974 Paris Convention, Art 19; 1992 Paris Convention, Art 20, para 2.

[69] Paris Commission, *Procedures and Decisions Manual*, C5.3/89–E, 1/14, para 3.

[70] Dir 82/176/EEC, 83/513/EEC and 84/156/EEC.

[71] PARCOM Doc 7/13/1–E, June 1985, para 5.14. For a more detailed account of the discussion on PCBs, see IJlstra (1990), pp 388–390.

[72] PARCOM Doc 12/13/1–E, June 1990, para 5.31.

the matter, holding up the decision-making process within the Paris Commission, have confused and irritated its non-EC members and led to calls for clarification of the situation.[73] At its 4th meeting in 1982, the Paris Commission discussed the question of its relations with the EC. Informal consultations had been held between officers of the Paris Commission and officials of the EC Commission, which had led to agreement that the two bodies should pursue a 'parallel or joint approach to dealing with common problems, ie that where progress is made in one forum, this could be used as a basis for making progress in the other'. At the Paris Commission meeting, the delegation of the EC Commission confirmed that the EC had 'no intention to act as a bloc to impede progress'. It also pointed out that even though the Community had acquired competence in certain areas relating to the implementation of the Paris Convention through the adoption of Community measures, 'there would be nothing to prevent the EEC Member States from adopting more stringent measures either individually *or collectively in bodies such as the Paris Commission*.'[74]

However, when the question of Community competence was again discussed in the Paris Commission in 1985, the EC Commission stressed the exclusive nature of EC competence in matters which are the subject of an EEC Directive. The delegation of the EC Commission stated 'its view that on matters where Community competence exists, it would be for the EEC delegation to negotiate on behalf of the Community and its Member States when proposals for decisions were discussed within the framework of the Paris Commission *since such decisions could affect Community law*.'[75] The EC Commission also qualified its earlier statement with respect to the right of EC member states to agree on more stringent measures within the framework of the Paris Commission. While confirming 'that the provisions of Directive 76/464/EEC do allow for Member States to take more stringent measures than those prescribed in the Directive', it pointed out 'that acceptance of *obligations at international level* in respect of such measures is a matter which concerns the Community as a whole,'[76] thus questioning the right of the member states to assume international obligations with respect to more stringent measures in the framework of the Paris Convention independently of the Community.

However, this assertion of exclusive Community competence did not go unchallenged. Again, the EC Commission openly clashed with EC member states in the forum of the Paris Commission. One national delegation

[73] IJlstra (1990), p 390, speaks of 'un certain malaise'. For a detailed critical account of the behaviour of the EC within the Paris Commission, from a Norwegian perspective, see Saetevik (1988), ch 9.

[74] *Fourth Annual Report on the Activities of the Paris Commission*, London, 1982, pp 7–8, paras 37–39.

[75] PARCOM Doc 7/13/1–E, June 1985, para 4.6 (emphasis added).

[76] *Ibid*, para 4.5 (emphasis added).

actually went on record stating that it 'disagreed with the interpretation of the European Commission regarding its claim for exclusive competence.'[77] The discussion remained inconclusive and the Swedish and Norwegian delegations, in frustration, resorted to the rather unusual move of entering a formal statement in the record of the meeting expressing their concern that the 'unclear situation regarding the competence of the EEC in relation to its individual Member States' was interfering with the effective implementation of the Paris Convention.[78] The EC responded with a similar statement undertaking to 'clarify matters relating to the competence of the Community' by the next meeting of the Paris Commission.[79] Such clarification, however, was never actually provided.

Indeed, the Community declined to respond in writing to questions regarding its competence which were formally put to it by the Chairman of the Paris Commission following the discussion at the 1985 PARCOM meeting.[80] The EC representative explained at the next meeting in 1986 that it was 'not yet possible' to do so because the Paris Commission had 'asked for precise answers' on matters which were still 'in a process of evolution.'[81] He made an oral statement which merely reiterated a number of generalities and avoided addressing the fundamental question, stressing instead that 'the precise division of responsibilities between the Community and its Member States *is an internal matter for the Community*.'[82] With an undeniable sense of irony, the EC delegation expressed 'its wish to see progress made as rapidly as possible' in the work of the Paris Commission, while at the same time stressing that the Commission in its work should bear in mind the fact that the Community's internal decision-making procedures 'can take a long time.'[83]

It should be noted that the European Commission's position on the competence of the individual member states to assume international obligations which are more stringent than those imposed by Community law has not

[77] PARCOM Doc 7/13/1–E, June 1985, para 4.4.

[78] *Ibid*, para 4.9.

[79] *Ibid*, para 4.10.

[80] See the letter of 18 Oct 1985 from D Tromp, Chairman of the Paris Commission, to AJ Fairclough, Acting Director General for the Environment, Consumer Protection and Nuclear Safety, Commission of the European Communities, reproduced *in extenso* in Saetevik (1988), pp 170–73 (App 5).

[81] PARCOM Doc 8/12/1–E, June 1986, para 3.2.

[82] *Ibid*, para 3.3 (emphasis added). This statement by the Commission echoes a ruling of the Court of Justice on the compatibility of the IAEA Convention on the Physical Protection of Nuclear Materials with the EAEC Treaty, in which the Court, in discussing the division of powers between the Community and its member states, stated that 'the exact nature of that division is a domestic question in which third parties have no need to intervene'. Ruling 1/78, [1978] ECR 2151, at para 35. See Simmonds (1989), pp 38–39. A similar statement describing the division of powers as a 'purely internal matter' was also made on behalf of the Community by one of its member states during the final stage of the negotiations on the UN Convention on the Law of the Sea in 1982. See Simmonds (1989), p 122.

[83] PARCOM Doc 8/12/1–E, June 1986, para 3.7 & 3.9.

always been consistent. It has already been pointed out above that the Commission's attitude on this question within PARCOM has changed over time. Moreover, its assertion in the Paris Commission in 1985 that Article 10 of Directive 76/464/EEC, while it does authorise member states to take more stringent measures at the national level, does not apply to the acceptance of international obligations, directly contradicted the position it took five years earlier in the context of the proposed adoption by the Community of a measure for the control of mercury emissions under the Convention on the Protection of the Rhine against Chemical Pollution, which was more stringent than a similar measure proposed by the Commission in implementation of Directive 76/464/EEC.

On that occasion, the Commission, in an explanatory memorandum to the Council, had affirmed that the Rhine measure was

> compatible with Directive 76/464/EEC, Article 10 of which provides that 'where appropriate, one or more Member States may individually or jointly take more stringent measures than those provided for under this Directive'.[84]

It is worth recalling that in this instance the Commission probably saw the stronger measures recommended by the ICPR as instrumental in its efforts to break the deadlock in the Council negotiations over its own proposal for a directive on mercury emissions. One has a strong impression that the Commission's position on the respective powers of the Community and the member states is determined more by opportunistic political considerations than by legal principles.

The Community's External Competence According to the Case-law of the Court of Justice

When the Community became a contracting party to the 1974 Paris Convention, it had not yet adopted any internal measures for the control of water pollution, let alone marine pollution.[85] However, in the preamble of its decision concluding the Convention, the Council, referring to the First Environmental Action Programme in which the *intent* to adopt such

[84] Proposal for a Council Decision supplementing Annex IV to the Convention on the Protection of the Rhine against Chemical Pollution, EC Doc COM(80) 319 final, 18 June 1980, Explanatory memorandum, p 6.

[85] Thus, contrary to what is frequently asserted in the literature, Community treaty-making in the environmental field did not always *follow* the exercise of internal legislative powers. Cf McGoldrick (1997), p 196; MacLeod, Henry & Hyett (1996), p 326 n 17. The latter authors mention both the conclusion of the 1974 Paris Convention and that of the 1976 Barcelona Convention as examples of the 'few occasions' on which the Community became a contracting party to an environmental convention despite the absence of internal rules covering the subject matter. This assertion is incorrect as far as the Barcelona Convention is concerned, since the adoption of Dir 76/464/EEC predates the conclusion of that convention.

measures was announced, considered that it was necessary to conclude the Paris Convention in order to attain one of the objectives of the Community and based its decision on Article 235 of the Treaty.[86] After the adoption of Directive 76/464/EEC, the legal basis of the Community's external competence in the field of the control of water pollution became more firmly established. The subsequent Council decisions concluding the 1976 Rhine Convention, the Barcelona Convention and the Athens Protocol all refer to Directive 76/464/EEC in their preamble.

The Community's competence to conclude these various conventions cannot be disputed. What is at issue is whether the Community's external competence in the field of regulation of emissions of dangerous substances into the aquatic environment has become exclusive. As noted above, in all the relevant conventions the Community is a contracting party alongside one or several of its member states. The fact that these conventions were concluded as mixed agreements, as a matter of EC law, implies that jurisdiction over their subject matter is shared between the Community and the member states.

Exclusive vs Shared Competence

Nevertheless, the European Commission has claimed that the Community's external competence in the field of environmental protection is exclusive in those areas in which internal Community measures have been adopted. It relies on the case-law of the Court of Justice as a basis for its claim of exclusive competence within the Paris Commission. As early as 1978, the Commission, referring to the Court's decision in the *ERTA* case, mentioned Directive 76/464/EEC as an example of an internal Community measure giving rise to exclusive external competence for the Community, in a reply to a parliamentary question about the extent of its external competences. The Commission claimed that the member states no longer have the competence to undertake international obligations in the field covered by this Directive, regardless of whether the Community had in fact exercised its external competence or not.[87]

In recent years, the Commission has based its claim of exclusive competence not only on Directive 76/464/EEC and its daughter directives, but also on other internal measures. Thus, for instance, it has often relied on Directive 76/769/EEC, the legal framework for the harmonization of restrictions on the marketing and use of certain dangerous substances at Community level.[88] This Directive, originally based on Article 100 EEC, requires the

[86] Council Decision 75/437/EEC of 3 Mar 1975 concluding the Convention for the prevention of marine pollution from land-based sources, OJ No L194, 25.7.1975, p 5.

[87] Answer by the Commission to Written Question No 174/77, OJ No C56, 6.3.1978, p 1.

[88] Dir 76/769/EEC of 27 July 1976 on the approximation of the laws, regulations and administrative provisions of the Member States relating to restrictions on the marketing and use of certain dangerous substances and preparations, OJ No L262, 27.9.1976, p 201.

member states to restrict the placing on the market and/or use of specific hazardous substances listed in its annex. The restrictions in question either amount to a complete ban on marketing and use, or to the prohibition of particular uses which are deemed hazardous for human health or the environment. Once a particular substance has been listed and made subject to restrictions under Directive 76/769/EEC, these restrictions can be amended by the Commission in consultation with a technical adaptation committee.[89] Adding a new substance to the annex, however, requires a Council directive. Arguing that 'any dangerous substance or preparation can be added to this Directive by an amendment',[90] and stressing the need to ensure the application of the risk assessment criteria and procedures laid down in EC law,[91] the Commission claims that the Community has exclusive competence to vote on proposals for international measures to regulate the marketing or use of hazardous substances.[92]

Another argument recently invoked by the Commission in support of its claims of Community competence[93] is that a particular substance which a convention body proposes to control is subject to a risk assessment procedure within the framework of Regulation (EEC) No. 793/93 on the evaluation and control of the risks of existing substances.[94] This regulation does not actually regulate the placing on the market of particular substances but merely institutes a Community procedure for the systematic evaluation of the health and environmental risks of substances that were on the market before 1981. This procedure may or may not eventually lead to the formulation of a Commission proposal for measures to restrict the marketing and use of the substance in question under Directive 76/769/EEC.[95] However, the provisions of Regulation 793/93 in and of themselves have no legal effect on the marketing or use of any substance in the Community. Finally, the Commission's allegation that external Community competence for substances for which no Community provisions have as yet been laid down results from Directive 83/189/EEC[96] seems altogether spurious, as we shall see below.

The 'possible development of a BAT document' under the recent IPPC Directive has also been cited as a basis of Community competence with respect to proposed PARCOM measures regarding BAT and emission limit

89 *Ibid*, Art 2a.

90 EC Doc SEC(97) 1195 final, 2 July 1997, Explanatory memorandum, para 8.

91 *Ibid*, para 9.

92 *Ibid*, paras 8, 10. See also EC Doc SEC(95) 2174 final, 15 Dec 1995, Explanatory memorandum, para 7; EC Doc SEC(96) 1024 final, 7 June 1996, Explanatory memorandum, para 8.

93 See EC Doc SEC(97) 1195 final, 2 July 1997, Explanatory memorandum, paras 10–11; EC Doc SEC(96) 1024 final, 7 June 1996, Explanatory memorandum, para 10.

94 Council Regulation (EEC) No 793/93 of 23 Mar 1993 on the evaluation and control of the risks of existing substances, OJ No L84, 5.4.1993, p 36.

95 *Ibid*, Art 11, para 3.

96 See EC Doc SEC(96) 1024 final, 7 June 1996, Explanatory memorandum, para 8.

values for specific industrial sectors.[97] The notion of 'BAT document' is nowhere to be found in the provisions of Directive 96/61/EC. It is true that Article 18 of this Directive provides for the establishment by subsequent legislative measures of binding 'Community emission limit values' when 'the need for Community action has been identified', but the Commission has thus far made no proposals for such measures. Instead, it has entrusted a technical bureau within the EC Joint Research Centre with the elaboration of non-binding 'reference documents' on BAT for various activities subject to the IPPC Directive. These documents are intended merely as a guide for competent national authorities issuing permits for such activities.

Case-law No Basis for Claim of Exclusive Competence

The controversy about the respective competences of the EC and its member states in the Paris Commission must be analysed in the context of the case-law of the Court of Justice on the external competences of the Community. It is questionable whether this case-law actually bears out the Commission's far-reaching claims of exclusive Community competence. Indeed, as the Community's powers in the field of environmental policy are not exclusive, the member states in principle still have the capacity to undertake international obligations in this field. The basic position, as clearly stated by the Court of Justice in a case concerning another area of non-exclusive Community competence (development aid), is that in such areas the member states 'are accordingly entitled to enter into commitments themselves vis-à-vis non-member States, either collectively or individually, or even jointly with the Community.'[98]

However, this right is not absolute; it is subject to certain limitations deriving from the existence of secondary Community law in the field in question. The fundamental rule on the limits of the member states' autonomous treaty-making powers was formulated by the Court in its classic *ERTA* judgment, in which it held that whenever the Community

> adopts provisions laying down common rules, whatever form these may take, the Member States no longer have the right, acting individually or even collectively, to undertake obligations with third countries which *affect those rules*.[99]

As the Court refers to *obligations* vis-à-vis third countries, the *ERTA* doctrine can only apply to the conclusion of legally binding international instruments. Indeed, international commitments made by member states in a non-binding form[100] are intrinsically incapable of affecting legally binding

[97] See EC Doc SEC(97) 1195 final, 2 July 1997, Explanatory memorandum, paras 12, 15.
[98] Case C–316/91, *Parliament v Council*, [1994] ECR I–653 at 661, para 26.
[99] Case 22/70, *Commission v Council*, [1971] ECR 263, at 274, para 17 (emphasis added).
[100] Such as, for instance, recommendations of treaty bodies such as the Paris Commission or Helsinki Commission.

rules of Community law. In so far as legally binding commitments are involved, the key test is whether or not the international obligations assumed by the member states can *affect* the Community rules, rather than whether they have the same subject matter. This will depend on the exact nature of both the 'common rules' laid down under Community law and the international obligations undertaken by the member states.

It is important to note that, contrary to what the Commission often implies in its representations to the Council, the mere *power* of Community institutions to legislate in a particular area is not sufficient to deprive the member states of their external competence. In 1976, the Court of Justice ruled in the *Kramer* case that where Community law confers certain powers on Community institutions and those institutions have not yet fully exercised those powers, the power of the member states to assume international commitments in this field remains unaffected.[101] This was confirmed by the Court in its 1994 opinion on the Community's competence to conclude the WTO agreements on trade in services (GATS) and trade-related intellectual property rights (TRIPs), in which it again ruled that 'the Community's exclusive external competence does not automatically flow from its power to lay down rules at internal level.'[102] Unequivocally rejecting the Commission's claim of exclusive external competence on the basis of the Community's legislative authority under Article 100a of the Treaty, the Court held:

> As regards Article 100a, it is undeniable, that where harmonizing powers *have been exercised*, the harmonization measures thus adopted *may* limit, or even remove, the freedom of the Member States to negotiate with non-member countries. *However, an internal power to harmonize which has not been exercised in a specific field cannot confer exclusive external competence in that field to the Community.*[103]

It is only 'as and when common rules *which could be affected* . . . come into being' that the member states lose their right to contract external obligations in the field concerned.[104] It is not the mere existence of 'common rules' that is decisive, but whether they are capable of being 'affected' within the meaning of the *ERTA* doctrine.

There are differences of opinion in the literature as to the exact interpretation to be given to this term. According to some authors, Community rules will be 'affected' only if the international obligations contracted by the member states are inconsistent with these rules.[105] Other commentators, however, consider that such inconsistency is not required, and that

[101] Joined Cases 3, 4 and 6/76, *Cornelis Kramer*, [1976] ECR 1279, at 1312, para 39.

[102] Opinion 1/94 of 15 Nov 1994, [1994] ECR I–5267, at 5411, para 77. For a scathing critique of this opinion, see Bourgeois (1995).

[103] *Ibid*, p 5414, para 88 (emphasis added).

[104] *Ibid*, p 5411, para 77 (emphasis added).

[105] Tridimas & Eeckhout (1994), p 165.

potential interference of member states' external commitments with an ongoing Community harmonisation process in the same field is sufficient for the '*ERTA* effect' to occur.[106] Whether one subscribes to the former or latter view, the starting point for any enquiry into the exclusive or non-exclusive character of the Community's external competence is an analysis of the scope and nature of the internal rules of Community law in the field in question. In both cases, an examination of the substantive content of the international rules will also be necessary, if only to determine whether their subject matter coincides with that of the relevant Community rules.

As to the kind of common rules which may give rise to exclusive external Community competence, the Court of Justice has stated in an opinion of 19 March 1993 concerning the competence of the Community to conclude ILO Convention No 170 concerning safety in the use of chemicals at work:

> The exclusive or non-exclusive nature of the Community's competence does not flow solely from the provisions of the Treaty but may also depend on *the scope of the measures which have been adopted* by the Community institutions for the application of those provisions *and which are of such a kind as to deprive Member States of an area of competence which they were able to exercise previously* on a transitional basis.[107]

As commentators have pointed out, the Court's recent case-law on external relations has taken a rather restrictive view of the exclusive nature of external Community competence.[108] Indeed, in both its *ILO* and *WTO* opinions, the Court rejected the Commission's far-reaching claims of exclusive Community competence and instead advanced the concept of 'joint competence' or 'shared powers' to denote the division of authority between the Community and the member states.[109] This approach has been variously perceived as 'pragmatic' by some commentators[110] and as 'a step back' from earlier case-law by others.[111] At any rate, it is now firmly established that 'the presumption lies with concurrent competence' and that exclusive Community competence is an exception to this general rule, which may arise as a result of the use that the Community has made of its internal legislative competence in a given field.[112]

[106] Frid (1995), p 101; Auvret-Finck (1995), p 455; CWA Timmermans, Case note on Opinion 2/91, *Sociaal-Economische Wetgeving* 1994, p 626.

[107] Opinion 2/91 of 19 March 1993, *Re ILO Convention 170*, [1993] ECR I–1061, para 9 (emphasis added). See also the annotations by N Neuwahl, *Common Market Law Review* 30 (1993), pp 1185–1195; N Emiliou, *European Law Review* 19 (1994), pp 76–86; Timmermans, above n 106.

[108] Frid (1995), p 109, notes a 'general recent trend in Community law . . . to restrict the matters which come within the ambit of the Community's external exclusive competence'.

[109] See generally Neuwahl (1996).

[110] Tridimas & Eeckhout (1994), p 160.

[111] Bourgeois (1995), pp 780–81.

[112] Tridimas & Eeckhout (1994), pp 154–155.

Influence of Secondary Law on Member States' External Competence

The capacity of member states to undertake international obligations independently of the Community will be pre-empted where secondary Community law has laid down common rules which have the effect of strictly limiting the freedom of action of the member states, where Community legislation has fully 'occupied' the field in question. The degree of harmonisation aimed at and the extent of the member states' residual legislative competence will be decisive. Where Community law only lays down minimum requirements and leaves member states free to impose more stringent standards at the national level, as is the case with all environmental measures based on Article 175 EC, the Community does not as a rule acquire exclusive external competence.[113]

To judge whether the Community's external competence has become exclusive, it is necessary to determine whether, under the common internal rules laid down pursuant to the Treaty, the member states have in fact *transferred their powers* to the Community in respect of the matters concerned[114] or, as the Court put it in its *ILO* opinion, whether these rules 'are of such a kind as *to deprive Member States of an area of competence*'. According to the Court, it is only where 'very detailed rules'[115] have been laid down in Community harmonising measures based on Article 94 or 95 of the Treaty, which establish 'more than minimum requirements'[116]—in other words, where Community law is aimed at *complete harmonization*[117]—that the member states have relinquished their competence to undertake international commitments 'outside the framework of the Community institutions.'[118]

Against this background, I shall now examine the actual content of the various Community rules relied on by the European Commission in support of its claim to exclusive Community competence in international bodies, to establish whether they meet the tests applied by the Court in determining whether internal legislation gives rise to exclusive external competence. Logically, this enquiry starts with Directive 76/464/EEC and its daughter directives, the main set of 'common rules' invoked by the Commission.

[113] MacLeod, Henry & Hyett (1996), p 327.

[114] Kapteyn & VerLoren van Themaat (1989), p 774; Frid (1995), p 99.

[115] Opinion 2/91, above n 107, at para 23.

[116] *Ibid*, para 23.

[117] Opinion 1/94, above n 102, at para 96.

[118] *Ibid*, para 26. In its opinion on ILO Convention No 170 the Court found that only the provisions in Part III of that convention, relating to the classification, packaging and labelling of chemical substances and preparations, an area 'covered to a large extent by Community rules progressively adopted since 1967 with a view to achieving an ever greater degree of harmonization', were capable of 'affecting' the existing Community rules in this area within the meaning of the *ERTA* judgment. *Ibid*, paras 25–26.

As we have seen in the previous chapter, Directive 76/464/EEC does not in fact lay down detailed rules with respect to all emissions of dangerous substances in the aquatic environment, but only establishes a legal framework pursuant to which standards relating to emissions of particular black list substances may be laid down by the Council, on the one hand, and a set of general rules governing discharges of grey list substances to be implemented by the member states in their national legislation and administrative practice, on the other hand. The Directive provides that the Council shall fix emission limit values and quality objectives for selected black list substances. While it confers the power to fix such values on the Council, it should be recalled that, as shown in this study, the Council has only very partially exercised those powers. It has adopted limit values for only a limited number of substances, and has failed to lay down anything like an exhaustive set of Community rules in the field of emissions of dangerous substances.

Directive 76/464/EEC is not an instrument whereby the member states have actually transferred their powers in the field of regulation of emissions of dangerous substances to the Community.[119] It does not deprive them of their competence in this field. The member states have retained the power to fix emission standards in individual discharge permits. These standards may not exceed the limit values established by the Council, but the Directive expressly provides that member states may take more stringent measures than those resulting from the provisions of the Directive.[120] As regards the regulation of discharges of grey list substances, the Directive in fact relies entirely on national measures. It instructs the member states to establish pollution reduction programmes and fix national quality objectives and emission standards for discharges of those substances.[121]

Directive 76/464/EEC establishes only minimum requirements and stops far short of achieving complete harmonisation of the rules relating to discharges of dangerous substances in the aquatic environment. Thus it is hard

[119] It should be noted, however, that the Community specifically mentioned Dir 76/464/EEC and its daughter directives in the formal declaration it made upon signing the UN Convention on the Law of the Sea pursuant to Art 2 of Annex IX of that Convention, which required it to specify the matters governed by the Convention 'in respect of which competence has been transferred to [the Community] by its member States . . . and the nature and extent of that competence.' The declaration states that, with regard to the protection of the marine environment, 'the Member States *have transferred to the Community competences* as formulated in provisions adopted by the Community', such as Dir 76/464/EEC, and its implementing directives 82/176/EEC, 84/513/EEC and 84/156/EEC. Declaration of the European Economic Community on Signature of the Convention, reprinted in Simmonds (1989), App I, pp 158–160 (emphasis added). For a detailed discussion of this declaration, see Simmonds (1986).

[120] Dir 76/464/EEC, Art 10. This provision was recently given an extensive interpretation by the Court of Justice in Case C-232/97, *L. Nederhoff & Zn. v Dijkgraaf en hoogheemraden van het Hoogheemraadschap Rijnland*, [1999] ECR I-6385, paras 51–61.

[121] The establishment of further Community provisions in this field under Art 7, para 7 is envisaged only in exceptional cases and no such provisions have in fact been adopted. Cf above ch 8.

to see how acceptance by individual member states of decisions of an international body providing for specific measures to reduce pollution by dangerous substances could 'affect' the rules laid down in Directive 76/464/EEC. Quite to the contrary, the acceptance of toxics reduction obligations under regional marine pollution conventions is entirely consistent with the Community provisions, since these actually require member states to take similar measures at the national level.

In its comments made before the Paris Commission, quoted above, the EC Commission recognised that member states had the power to take more stringent measures nationally but objected to their capacity to enter into international commitments with respect to such measures because such commitments were a matter which 'concerned the Community as a whole'. Yet the Commission failed to explain precisely *how* commitments entered into by the member states might affect internal Community rules within the meaning of the *ERTA* ruling. This question is explored in some detail in a joint opinion from the legal services of the Commission and Council of the EC of 1986. It appears from this opinion that the main concern of the Community institutions is that the acceptance by member states at the international level of norms which are more stringent than those laid down by Community law might restrict the Community's freedom of action and in particular its ability to fix a maximum standard which is less stringent than the international one. The opinion also points out that 'the commitment to a more severe international norm could in certain circumstances generate pressure on the Community to raise the internal standard.'[122]

These objections do not actually relate to the fact that *existing* Community law might be affected, but rather to the fact that the Community's discretion with respect to future *changes* in Community law may be constrained.[123] As Lammers points out, these objections, which are more of a political than legal nature, find no basis in the *ERTA* judgment, which was only concerned with the effect of international obligations on *existing* Community rules.[124] This interpretation of the *ERTA* ruling was confirmed by the Court's 1993 opinion on the ILO Convention, which refers specifically to the necessary limitations on the freedom of member states 'to enter into international commitments containing rules capable of affecting *rules already adopted*' by Community institutions.[125] The reference in the above-mentioned 1986 opinion of the legal services to the risk of 'pressure' on the Community betrays the primary motive of the Commission's insistence on

[122] EC Council Doc 9591/86, 9 Dec 1986, quoted in Lammers (1989a), p 41.
[123] Cf Krämer (1995), p 85, who also considers that the fact that more stringent measures subscribed to by individual member states in international fora 'might rule out a subsequent compromise at Community level' is not a sufficient reason to deny them the right to enter into international commitments of this sort.
[124] Lammers (1989a), pp 41–42.
[125] Opinion 2/91, above n 107, at para 11 (emphasis added).

exclusive competence in international bodies such as the Paris Commission: the Commission is reluctant to accept that the legislative process in the Community may be influenced by decisions of non-EC bodies. But in its 1993 opinion, the Court of Justice explicitly rejected this argument, as raised by the Commission:

> Difficulties, such as those referred to by the Commission, which might arise for the legislative function of the Community cannot constitute the basis for exclusive Community competence.[126]

Those commentators who have discussed the external competence of the Community in the context of Directive 76/464/EEC seem to agree that this competence is by no means exclusive. Timmermans considers that the external competence of the Community with respect to the subject matter of Directive 76/464/EEC is only partly exclusive, ie to the extent that the Directive lays down detailed mandatory rules, such as those relating to the requirement of prior authorisation for discharges of black list substances. However, most provisions of the Directive, which require further Community action, allow for competing national external powers to be exercised. The *ERTA* doctrine cannot be applied to those provisions to the effect of displacing the external competence of the member states. Referring to Article 10 of the Directive, Timmermans also points out that the implementing measures of the Directive would leave room for residual national powers both internally and externally.[127]

Leenen also rejects the Commission's claim for exclusive external competence. He argues that:

> it seems impossible to consider the EEC's external powers to be exclusive in cases in which the internal competences have been established by directives in which the Member States have preserved the right to fix more stringent measures.[128]

Mastellone, for his part, considers that the Community's external powers will only become exclusive once limit values and quality objectives have been laid down for all substances referred to in Directive 76/464/EEC, although the member states 'will retain the freedom to conclude international agreements fixing more stringent measures.'[129] Finally, Nollkaemper, who has examined the issue most thoroughly, views the Commission's claim to exclusive Community competence with great scepticism, considering that the test whether Community law is 'affected' must be applied literally. He concludes, referring specifically to Directive 76/464/EEC as an example, that:

126 Opinion 2/91, above n 107, para 20.
127 Timmermans (1981), pp 19, 21.
128 Leenen (1984), p 103.
129 Mastellone (1981), p 113.

in all cases where Community powers are based on minimum-directives, Member States can be supposed to possess a reserved power to take more stringent measures on the international plane independently.[130]

The reasons why no exclusive external Community competence results from Directive 76/464/EEC apply a fortiori to Directive 96/61/EC on integrated pollution prevention and control. This Directive is based on Article 130s EC (now Article 175) and consequently, by virtue of Article 130t EC (now Article 176), can establish only minimum requirements. As we have seen above in chapter 8, the IPPC Directive in fact provides for an even lesser degree of harmonisation than Directive 76/464/EEC and actually increases the discretionary powers of member states with respect to the establishment of emission standards for dangerous substances. It does not, for that matter, contain any specific provisions regulating emissions of such substances differently from other pollutants. While it contains detailed rules on *procedures* for the authorisation of the activities falling within its scope of application, it leaves the member states almost unfettered discretion in determining the *substantive* pollution control requirements to which these activities shall be subjected. To be sure, the IPPC Directive allows for the establishment of Community emission limit values for pollutants 'for which the need for Community action has been identified,'[131] but no such values are likely to be established any time soon. In these circumstances, it is implausible that the rules of Directive 96/61/EC could be 'affected' by OSPARCOM decisions defining BAT and laying down emission limit values for particular sectors of industry, even if these are subject to its provisions.

The situation is different, however, when it comes to commitments to restrict the marketing or use of particular hazardous substances. Under Community law, this matter is governed by the provisions of the above-mentioned Directive 76/769/EEC, which was originally based on Article 100 EEC and aims at complete harmonisation.[132] This is made clear in its preamble, which notes that differences in national provisions relating to the marketing and use of dangerous substances 'constitute an obstacle to trade and directly affect the establishment and functioning of the common market' and that this obstacle should be removed by 'approximating the laws governing the matter in the Member States'.

The provisions of Directive 76/769/EEC do not merely establish minimum requirements: where the placing on the market and use of a substance is not altogether prohibited, the obligation of the member states to

[130] Nollkaemper (1987), p 84. In a recent study focusing on EC external competence in the field of the control of marine pollution from shipping, the same author also concludes that the ECJ case-law provides 'frail legal support for grand ambitions'. See Nollkaemper (1997).

[131] Dir 96/61/EC, Art 18, para 1.

[132] Since the entry into force of the SEA, amendments to Dir 76/769/EEC have been based on Art 100a EC (now Art 95).

ensure that the regulated substances 'may only be placed on the market or used subject to the conditions specified' in the annex to the Directive[133] implies that member states are not free to prevent any marketing or use of the substances in question which complies with the conditions laid down at Community level.[134] Once a substance or preparation has been listed in the annex to Directive 76/769/EEC, the conditions of its marketing and use are determined by Community law and cannot be derogated from by national law, save when authorised by the Commission under Article 95, paragraph 6 EC. The Directive lays down detailed common rules under which the member states have in effect transferred their regulatory powers to the Community with respect to the products concerned. As a result, the *ERTA* doctrine applies and member states no longer have the right to assume international obligations to restrict the marketing or use of the substances in question, independently of the Community.

This limitation of the external competence of the member states, however, does not apply to dangerous substances and preparations generally, but only to those listed in the annex to Directive 76/769/EEC, for which specific Community provisions have been laid down. Indeed, in the absence of such common provisions, member states remain free, by virtue of the rule of reason, to regulate the marketing and use of any substance at the national level. Consequently, there is nothing to prevent them from undertaking international obligations in this field. Contrary to what the Commission has repeatedly asserted, the mere fact that any substance *can* at any time be added to the annex of Directive 76/769/EEC is not sufficient to deprive member states of their external competence. As the Court of Justice has stressed in its *WTO* opinion, 'an internal power to harmonize which has not been exercised' cannot confer exclusive external competence on the Community.[135] It is only as and when common rules have been laid down with respect to a particular substance that the *ERTA* doctrine comes into play.

For the same reasons, the Commission's claim that the existence of Regulation (EEC) No 793/93, which provides for a Community risk assessment procedure for existing chemicals, operates to restrain the freedom of member states to commit themselves internationally to restrict the use of any such chemicals, appears unfounded. The Regulation lays down common rules on risk *assessment*, not on risk reduction as such. While it

[133] Dir 76/769/EEC, Art 2.

[134] It should be noted here, however, that, in a recent judgment, the Court of Justice has held that Art 10 of Dir 76/464/EEC must be interpreted as allowing member states to apply national measures which have the effect of making the actual use of a dangerous substance, which may lead to its discharge into the aquatic environment, impossible or altogether exceptional, even if the use of that same substance is merely *restricted* under the relevant provisions of Dir 76/769/EEC. Case C–232/97, above n 120, para 65.

[135] Opinion 1/94, above n 102, at para 88.

does provide for the development, in appropriate cases, of risk reduction strategies at Community level, which may result in Commission proposals for restrictions on marketing and use within the framework of Directive 76/769/EEC[136]—and thus reflects a preference for a Community approach—there is nothing in the Regulation that excludes the possibility of member states taking unilateral regulatory measures with respect to existing substances subject to its risk assessment procedure.[137]

Directive 83/189/EEC on technical standards and regulations,[138] also invoked by the Commission in one of its requests for negotiating mandates, cannot possibly be a basis for external Community competence with respect to the regulation of chemicals which are not subject to Directive 76/769/EEC. The same applies to its successor instrument, Directive 98/34/EC.[139] These directives merely introduce a duty for member states to notify proposals for national regulatory measures relating to products, which may affect the free movement of goods, in order to enable the Commission and the other member states to formulate objections to any such planned measures which may be inconsistent with Community law. Far from entailing any transfer of national powers to the Community or any form of harmonisation, they in fact explicitly recognise the regulatory competence of individual member states but subject its exercise to a number of procedural obligations designed to safeguard Community interests and to ensure compliance with Community law. The mere fact that member states contemplating unilateral measures to restrict the marketing or use of particular hazardous substances in their territory are under a Community obligation to notify such planned measures and delay their entry into force until the Commission and other member states have had the opportunity to comment or object, as for any other product standards or technical regulations, does not imply that such measures fall within the sphere of the Community's exclusive external competence, but quite the contrary.

[136] Reg (EEC) No 793/93, above n 94, Art 11.

[137] This has been explicitly confirmed by the Court of Justice in Case C–473/98, *Kemikalieinspektionen v Toolex Alpha AB*, [2000] ECR I–5681.

[138] Council Dir 83/189/EEC of 28 Mar 1983 laying down a procedure for the provision of information in the field of technical standards and regulations, OJ No L109, 1983, p 8.

[139] European Parliament and Council Dir 98/34/EC of 22 June 1998 laying down a procedure for the provision of information in the field of technical standards and regulations, OJ No L204, 21.7.1998, p 37.

Part III

Toxic Substances in International Trade: The Regulation of International Trade in Pesticides

10

Health and Environmental Effects in the Third World of Inadequately Regulated Pesticide Trade and Use: The Problem and Its Perception

WHILE THE FIRST part of this study focused mainly on the regulation of the toxic effluents of industrial production *processes*, a classic concern of pollution control legislation, this second part looks at the health and environmental impact of industrial production from a different angle: that of the effects of the use of and trade in a particular, highly controversial category of *products* of the chemical industry, pesticides.

The need to protect human health and the environment against the effects of the ever-increasing use of pesticides worldwide has given rise to a variety of regulatory responses in many countries. As the health and environmental problems linked to the production, trade and use of pesticides transcend the national level, due to the strongly multinational character of the agrochemical industry, the growing international trade in pesticides, and the intricacies of the global food economy, national governments have perceived a need to address certain regulatory issues at the international level. This has resulted in discussions and negotiations on some aspects of pesticide control within the framework of international organisations, leading to the development of international regulatory instruments of various kinds.

International regulatory efforts first focused on problems arising from disparities in national regulation. For example, since the 1960s, the Codex Alimentarius Commission, a joint body of the World Health Organization (WHO) and the Food and Agriculture Organization of the United Nations (FAO), has been trying to establish internationally accepted standards for pesticide residues in food. This effort was prompted by the expanding international trade in foodstuffs and the concern of countries exporting agricultural products that the sale of their products may be impeded because they do not meet the pesticide residue standards of the importing countries. Within the Codex Alimentarius Commission, governments are attempting to agree international minimum standards, coupled with an undertaking not to prevent the importation of products which meet those minimum standards.[1]

Another area of early international regulatory activity is the harmonisation of national regulations concerning the pre-marketing registration, packaging and labelling of pesticides. At the World Food Conference in Rome in 1974, the pesticide industry proposed that the FAO arrange intergovernmental consultations on the standardisation of regulatory procedures and criteria for the registration of pesticides. The divergence between national regulations has always been a major industry concern because it increases development, testing and marketing costs. In response to the industry initiative, a series of intergovernmental meetings on the 'harmonization of pesticide registration requirements' have been held under the auspices of the FAO since 1975. The primary aim of those FAO consultations has not been to achieve the highest possible uniform international standards for the protection of human health and the environment, but rather to cut costs and remove technical trade barriers for the benefit of the pesticide industry. The FAO consultations have produced elaborate recommendations but, as industry itself complains, few concrete results.

In the limited regional context of the EC, efforts to harmonise pesticide regulations have been more successful, because of the overriding economic imperatives of the internal market. In the 1970s, the EC Council adopted directives banning the marketing and use throughout the Community of certain pesticides[2] and laying down uniform packaging and labelling standards for pesticides which are applicable in all EC member states.[3] After an initial failure to adopt a Commission proposal to this effect in the late 1970s,[4] the Council, as part of its pre-1992 push to complete the establishment of the internal market, in 1991 adopted a directive establishing a harmonized and uniform registration system for agricultural pesticides at Community level.[5] This was followed in 1998 by a similar directive on the

[1] See generally Kay (1976). At the EC level, reference must be made to: Council Dir 76/895/EEC of 23 Nov 1976 relating to the fixing of maximum levels of pesticide residues in and on fruit and vegetables, OJ No L340, 9.12.1976, p 26; Council Dir 86/362/EEC of 24 July 1986 on the fixing of maximum levels for pesticide residues in and on cereals, OJ No L221, 7.8.1986, p 37; Council Dir 86/363/EEC of 24 July 1986 on the fixing of maximum levels for pesticide residues in and on foodstuffs of animal origin, OJ No L221, 7.8.1986, p 43.

[2] Council Dir 79/117/EEC of 21 Dec 1978 prohibiting the placing on the market and use of plant protection products containing certain active substances, OJ No L 33, 8.2.1979, p 36.

[3] Council Dir 78/631/EEC of 26 June 1978 on the approximation of the laws of the Member States relating to the classification, packaging and labelling of dangerous preparations (pesticides), OJ No L206, 29.7.1978, p 13.

[4] Proposal for a Council Directive on the marketing of pesticides authorised for the European Community, OJ No C212, 9.9.1976, p 3.

[5] Council Dir 91/414/EEC of 15 July 1991 concerning the placing of plant protection products on the market, OJ No L230, 19.8.1991, p 1.

placing on the market of biocides for non-agricultural use.[6] These EC directives on pesticides are primarily designed to ensure the free movement of goods and equal conditions of competition throughout the Community both for the professional users of pesticides and for the chemical companies which produce them.

Notwithstanding the ongoing efforts to harmonise national regulations regarding residue levels in food and requirements for the registration of pesticides, the problem which has dominated the agenda of international regulatory activity in the field of pesticides since the late 1970s is that of the human and environmental costs of indiscriminate use of pesticides in the Third World, and in particular the export of banned or severely restricted pesticides to developing countries.[7]

In 1973, an obscure expert committee of the World Health Organization (WHO) published a technical report which contained a short sentence that had far-reaching, unanticipated and certainly unintended consequences. It stated that 'it seems possible that the number of cases of accidental poisoning due to pesticides may be of the order of half a million a year.'[8] That fact took a number of years to percolate from the paper flood of the UN bureaucracy, but by the end of the 1970s it had caught media attention, sent investigative reporters flying around the globe to document corporate 'dumping' of hazardous pesticides in the Third World, sparked off an international campaign by environmental, consumer and development activists questioning the legitimacy of the business practices of the agrochemical industry, triggered a flurry of political debates and regulatory activity in various international organisations, and caused grave concern in the corporate boardrooms of the handful of multinational chemical companies which dominate the global pesticides trade. So controversial and wide-ranging were the political implications of the WHO's findings on pesticide poisoning in the Third World that the organisation, unaccustomed to so much publicity, later sought to disclaim responsibility by qualifying its conclusions and complaining that they had been 'often widely quoted out of context.'[9]

[6] European Parliament and Council Dir 98/8/EC of 16 Feb 1998 concerning the placing of biocidal products on the market, OJ No L123, 24.4.1998, p 1.

[7] See generally Weir & Shapiro (1981); Norris (1982); Bull (1982).

[8] World Health Organization, *Safe Use of Pesticides*, 20th Report of the WHO Expert Committee on Insecticides, WHO Technical Report Series No 513, Geneva, 1973, p 42.

[9] FAO Panel of Experts on Pesticide Specifications, Registration Requirements, and Application Standards, Group on Pesticide Registration Requirements, Report of the 4th Meeting, FAO Doc AGP:1982/, p 8. It seems that the only policy initiative taken by the WHO itself in reponse to the Expert Committee's report was a resolution of the organisation's Executive Board which requested the Director-General to 'take steps to develop a tentative classification of pesticides which would distinguish between the more and less hazardous forms of each pesticide' and 'invited Member States to submit annual reports on morbidity data on pesticide poisoning'. WHO Executive Board Res EB52.R11, May 1973. This initiative resulted in the adoption by the World Health Assembly in May 1975 of the WHO Recommended

According to a survey conducted by the FAO in the early 1980s, some 80 developing countries were not thought to have legislation to control the marketing and use of pesticides.[10] As this figure includes countries on whose legislation no information is available, the actual number of countries which completely lack regulation was probably lower. At about the same time, GIFAP, the international trade association of the pesticide industry, for its part reported that there were only five countries where no regulations at all existed.[11] However, industry apparently used a much broader definition of regulation, which included very informal control and testing procedures as well as import restrictions based not on health and environmental criteria but on lack of foreign exchange. In any event, whether or not legislation exists on the books is not the most relevant question. The real problem is that many Third World countries lack the technical and administrative capacity to effectively control the import, marketing and use of pesticides and to enforce what scant regulation they may have.

The other side of the problem is that the stringent regulations of the industrialised countries which manufacture and export most pesticides do not apply to products intended for export. Taking advantage of this legal vacuum, the agrochemical industry exports hazardous pesticides which have not been registered or whose use is banned or subject to severe safety restrictions in their country of manufacture, to developing countries where their use cannot adequately be controlled. As a result, highly toxic or persistent pesticides are used indiscriminately throughout the Third World, causing massive poisoning of the rural population and widespread environmental contamination. Based on the rather limited epidemiological data available, the latest comprehensive WHO study estimates that there are more than one million cases of unintentional acute pesticide poisoning in the world annually, about 20,000 of them fatal.[12] Acute pesticide poisoning is described as a 'major problem . . . particularly in developing countries', where risks of intensive exposure and fatality rates are higher.[13] Extrapolating from data on the size of the population at risk, the same study concludes that there could in fact be as many as five million cases of unin-

Classification of Pesticides by Hazard, based on acute toxicity to humans, and of a recommendation to member states, other international agencies and regional bodies to make use of this classification in their respective activities. World Health Assembly Res. WHA28.62, May 1975. This classification is regularly updated and still in use today. See WHO Recommended Classification of Pesticides by Hazard and Guidelines to Classification 1996–1997, WHO Doc WHO/PCS/96.3.

[10] Bates (1982), p 98.

[11] GIFAP, *International Regulation of Pesticides*, Doc C.11959, Brussels, Mar 1984, p 23.

[12] World Health Organization, *Public Health Impact of Pesticides Used in Agriculture*, Geneva, 1990, p 85 and Table 26.

[13] *Ibid*, p 104.

tentional pesticide poisoning, including both mild and severe poisonings, in developing countries alone each year.[14]

Alarming data on the health effects of pesticides in developing countries and moral outrage over the 'dumping' by transnational corporations of banned hazardous chemicals in the Third World and the 'double standards' applied by exporting countries have focused attention on serious gaps in existing regulation and have prompted governments to address the issue of international trade in banned and severely restricted pesticides in a variety of international fora.

This second wave of international regulatory activity has centred not on problems arising from *disparities* in national regulation, but on those arising from the *lack or inadequacy* of pesticide control legislation in a large number of developing, pesticide-importing countries. In contrast with the earlier phase, when the agenda was set mainly by industrial and trade interests, this new phase in regulatory activity was fueled by political concern about the health and environmental effects of growing pesticide use in developing countries.

Although most of the debate has focused on the 'dumping' in developing countries of hazardous pesticides whose use is prohibited in industrialised countries, this is by no means the only aspect of the problem. A substantial part of the damage can be ascribed to pesticides which are not actually banned in the exporting countries but are still being used in those countries, subject to a number of restrictions. The problem is that the safety restrictions to which highly toxic pesticides are subject in producing countries cannot adequately be enforced or are unrealistic in Third World conditions. Much environmental damage is also caused by pesticides which may not intrinsically be particularly hazardous but which are being misused, ie applied indiscriminately and uneconomically, thus inflicting unnecessary harm on the environment. Finally, it should not be overlooked that exports from industrialised countries are not the only source of pesticides in the Third World. As the Bhopal accident has tragically illustrated, a number of developing countries now have sizeable domestic production and formulation facilities.

Though it is only one aspect of a much wider complex of interrelated issues, the problem of international trade in banned and severely restricted pesticides has been the focus of international regulatory initiatives since the beginning of the 1980s, probably because of its controversial moral implications and political appeal. It is also symptomatic of the tension between free trade and health and environmental protection policies, a tension which raises interesting legal issues concerning the relationship between the law of international trade and international environmental law. As a matter of

[14] *Ibid*, p 86.

fact, the export notification and prior informed consent procedures which have been developed to regulate exports of banned or severely restricted chemicals are one of the first examples of trade-related environmental measures, both at the international level and at the level of the European Community,[15] long before the potential conflict between environmental regulation and international trade liberalisation policies emerged in all its acuity as one of the key issues on the international political agenda in the run-up to the United Nations Conference on Environment and Development.

The international regulatory process designed to address the problems associated with international trade flows of hazardous chemicals is in essence an attempt to define and delineate the respective responsibilities of exporting countries, importing countries and the private sector. What is the responsibility of a country which allows the export of chemicals it considers unsafe for domestic use to other countries which may be unaware of the hazards and lack the means to adequately protect their population and environment against the effects of those chemicals? Can the transnational agrochemical industry rely on this legal vacuum to legitimise exports of hazardous pesticides which have not been registered, or whose use is banned or subject to severe safety restrictions in their country of manufacture, to developing countries where their use cannot adequately be controlled? On the other hand, to what extent must countries which import chemicals assume responsibility for the protection of their own citizens and natural resources through the establishment and enforcement of adequate standards, and how far can they rely on exporting countries to assist them?[16]

The international regulatory debate on the regulation of trade in banned and severely restricted pesticides can be seen as an attempt to counterbalance some of the deficiencies of an international regime for the regulation of the trade and use of chemicals which essentially remains based on national product regulation and free trade. The various actors in the debate are seeking to reach a compromise somewhere on a spectrum of measures ranging from virtual laissez-faire to strict control, trying to accommodate the conflicting interests of exporting countries and their agrochemical industry, and importing countries and a variety of non-governmental public interest groups. As the regulators attempt to deal with these transnational, product-related effects of chemical production, they are faced with limitations resulting from the international economic order and free trade regimes, and are forced to devise 'solutions' which do not fundamentally challenge the freedom of production and trade as such.

[15] For a general analysis of the concept of trade-related environmental measures and their legal implications under European Community law, see Demaret (1993).

[16] On the issue of allocation of responsibility, see generally Ashford & Ayers (1985), pp 888–90; Handl & Lutz (1989), pp 49–51.

On the laissez-faire end of the regulatory spectrum, one finds measures which do not affect the prevailing principle that exported chemicals are exempt from national regulation by the exporting country and that their control is the exclusive responsibility of the importing countries. These measures are designed to assist importing countries to adopt their own regulations by providing them with certain information. Such information is provided by producing countries on a voluntary basis either directly to importing countries or through international organisations.

Next in the gradation of possible measures are variations of export notification systems. Unlike notifications of control actions, which are not addressed to any particular importing country or tied to a specific export transaction, export notifications are directly related to actual exports of pesticides. The principle is that whenever a banned or severely restricted pesticide is exported, the government of the importing country must be informed of the export shipment and of the regulatory restrictions to which the pesticide is subject in the exporting country.

However, export notifications can also be one element of a more restrictive system of export control, in which the export of a banned or severely restricted pesticide is only allowed under certain specific conditions. One alternative is to permit the export only if the government of the importing country has been properly notified and has not *objected* to the export within a certain period of time following notification. This system has been dubbed 'prior informed choice', the 'choice' made by the importing country being a tacit one, as opposed to explicit consent. Indeed, another alternative is to allow the export only if the importing country government, having received notification, has expressly *consented* to the export. This option is known as 'prior informed consent' (PIC in short), and has been the subject of much debate in international organisations.[17]

On the restrictive end of the spectrum of possible measures, an outright prohibition of the export and production of domestically banned pesticides should logically be considered. However, this option has so far received no serious consideration in the ongoing international regulatory debate and

[17] The concept of 'prior informed consent' was first coined in the context of international trade in hazardous chemicals, but its relevance is not limited to that particular context. Though the term 'prior informed consent' is not actually used in the 1989 Basel Convention, the procedure for the control of transboundary movements of hazardous wastes laid down in that convention is based on the same principle and has also been referred to in the literature as a 'prior informed consent procedure'. See Kummer (1995), pp 65–70. Similar procedures have also been developed for regulating the transboundary transfer of genetically modified organisms in the Cartagena Protocol on Biosafety, but the use of the term 'advance informed agreement' instead of 'prior informed consent' in that Protocol reveals the reluctance of governments to acknowledge the analogy and thus lend support to the emergence of a general principle. Cartagena Protocol on Biosafety to the Convention on Biological Diversity, signed in Montreal, 29 Jan 2000, UN Doc UNEP/CBD/ExCOP/1/3, 20 Feb 2000, p 42. Some authors indeed view the 'principle of prior informed consent' as an emerging principle of customary international law. See Birnie & Boyle (1992), pp 334, 336; Kummer (1995), p 24.

has been dismissed by industry and most governments as extreme and irresponsible, on the grounds that such a ban would infringe the sovereignty of importing countries and their freedom to make their own risk/benefit assessments and regulatory decisions. Ironically, concern about 'environmental imperialism' and the sovereignty of importing countries has not been voiced primarily by the developing countries whose sovereignty is supposedly at stake, but mostly by pesticide-exporting companies and countries.

The international regulatory regime for hazardous pesticides examined in this study is part of a broader regime governing international trade in banned and severely restricted *chemicals* generally. However, this study focuses on pesticides because the vast majority of the chemicals subject to the regime are pesticides and the regime developed primarily in response to international concern about the health and environmental effects of banned and severely restricted pesticides exported to developing countries. As we shall see in the following chapters, it is the evidence of these effects which propelled the issue onto the international agenda and set the international normative process in motion. Most of the international regulatory debate has focused on pesticides; regulation of trade in other hazardous chemicals has tended to be ancillary to that of pesticides. The environmental problems are most acute with pesticides because these chemicals, contrary to most others, are produced for the very purpose of their deliberate release into the environment. Problems associated with the use of industrial chemicals are rather seldom addressed by prohibiting or severely restricting their use, but rather through process standards designed to limit their emission into the environment and to reduce worker exposure to them. Pesticides are a typical case of *product* rather than process regulation[18] and are generally more 'densely' regulated than other chemicals, both at the national and international level. The number and variety of regulatory instruments applicable to them and the diverse institutional fora in which these instruments have been developed make the regulation of international trade in pesticides a particularly interesting subject for the study of the international normative process.

The following chapters trace the development of the international regulatory regime which emerged to address the lack of any transnational norms of health and environmental protection in a global pesticides market governed by principles of free trade and territorial chemical safety regulation. The normative process can be seen as an attempt to graft some international standards onto what basically remains a territorially fragmented regulatory system. These standards gradually evolved from a voluntary

[18] The distinction between product and process regulation in environmental law is of crucial importance in the debate on the legitimacy of trade-related environmental measures under the law of international trade. See generally Lee (1994); Walker (1993), pp 29–30.

information exchange regime to a more restrictive, legally binding prior informed consent regime which, while preserving national regulatory sovereignty and free trade principles, imposes some responsibilities on exporting states. So far, the international normative process has shunned more interventionist modes of international regulation involving direct controls on the production and export of hazardous pesticides.

In chapters 12 to 14, the three successive stages of the regulatory efforts of intergovernmental organisations, focusing first on export notification schemes, then on voluntary prior informed consent procedures and finally on the development of a legally binding instrument, are analysed. Faced with political pronouncements in favour of the principle of prior informed consent, the main chemical-exporting countries took the lead in elaborating their own internationally agreed guidelines on information exchange through the OECD, in order to forestall the development of more restrictive international regulations within the framework of Third World dominated UN organisations. Thus, in the international regulatory debate on international trade in banned and severely restricted pesticides, a fragile consensus first emerged on some form of institutionalised export notification scheme, while controversy continued to centre on the desirability and effectiveness of prior informed consent as a possible additional form of export regulation. In a second phase, prior informed consent gained acceptance as the international standard, but its modalities of implementation were deliberately designed to minimise direct effects on trade. The prior informed consent regime was initially laid down exclusively in soft law instruments. In its third stage, the normative process focused on the development of a legally binding international instrument, as the regime was transformed from soft law into hard law. Paradoxically, however, this transformation was accomplished at the expense of a weakening of some of the substantive elements of the existing, non-binding regime.

To place the transnational normative process in its broader context, the relationship and interaction between national and transnational regulation is discussed at both the beginning and end of this case study. Chapter 11 describes and discusses the United States legislation on export notification, which served as a model for the early development of international instruments. Against the background of the international normative process, chapter 15 examines how the European Union and its member states have responded to transnational normative efforts and contributed to them. In the final chapter of this part, chapter 16, the further evolution of national law and policy in the United States in the wake of international regulatory activities is studied in order to assess whether emerging international standards on trade in hazardous chemicals have had any impact.

In concluding this introduction, it should be mentioned that the problem of international trade in banned and severely restricted pesticides is part of a broader issue, that of the transboundary transfer of environmental risks.

Related issues which are also the subject of international regulatory efforts are the transboundary movement of hazardous wastes and the transfer of hazardous production technologies. These issues raise similar legal problems and are sometimes addressed in a generic manner in the literature.[19] It has even been argued that it is possible to infer from the law and practice in these different areas an emerging general principle of international law requiring prior notification of transboundary environmental risks.[20] This question is not addressed in the present study, which is not concerned with the analysis of general principles of international law but with the effectiveness of the international regulatory law developed specifically to deal with the particular issue of international trade in hazardous pesticides. The transboundary movement of wastes is the subject of a distinct international regulatory regime, based on the 1989 Basel Convention[21] and a number of related regional instruments, which has been analysed in great detail by other authors.[22] Even though there are similarities between the two regimes, there are also important differences in that one deals with products and the other with wastes and that the two forms of hazardous exports are regulated by separate, specific international instruments developed independently of each other in different international fora.[23]

[19] See Handl & Lutz (1989); Rublack (1994).

[20] Partan (1990); Kummer (1995), pp 23–24. Cf Gündling (1989).

[21] Basel Convention on the Control of Transboundary Movements of Hazardous Wastes and their Disposal, Basel, 22 Mar 1989, 28 ILM 657 (1989).

[22] See, in particular, the comprehensive study by Kummer (1995).

[23] There is, however, one exception at the regional level. The OAU's Bamako Convention equates with hazardous wastes 'hazardous substances which have been banned, cancelled or refused registration by government regulatory action, or voluntarily withdrawn from registration, in the country of manufacture, for human health or environmental reasons' and subjects these substances to the same legal regime as hazardous wastes, ie a ban on their importation into Africa and restrictions on their movement within Africa. Bamako Convention on the Ban of the Import into Africa and the Control of Transboundary Movement and Management of Hazardous Wastes within Africa, Bamako, 30 Jan 1991, 30 ILM 775 (1991), Art 2, para 1(d). For a more detailed analysis of the Bamako Convention, see generally Kummer (1995), pp 99–107; Baender (1991).

11

The 'Soft' Response Model: United States Legislation on the Export of Banned and Severely Restricted Pesticides

THE UNITED STATES was the first country to enact legislative provisions imposing certain conditions on the export of pesticides,[1] even before the export of banned and severely restricted chemicals really emerged as an issue on the international political agenda.[2] Having anticipated international policy-making in this field, the US was able to exert a strong influence on the international regulatory debate and, at least initially, to impose its 'soft' regulatory approach, based on notification requirements, as a model for the development of international standards. Before analysing the international normative process which is the focus of the second part of this study, it is therefore appropriate to start off with a discussion of relevant US legislation.

The statutory framework for the regulation of the production, marketing and use of pesticides in the United States is laid down in the Federal Insecticide, Fungicide and Rodenticide Act (FIFRA), which was one of several major federal environmental statutes passed by Congress in the early 1970s. The FIFRA was enacted on 21 October 1972 and, notwithstanding a number of amendments in 1973, 1975, 1978, 1979, 1988, and 1991, has remained unchanged in its basic structure until today. The federal government agency responsible for regulating pesticides under the act is the US Environmental Protection Agency (EPA). No pesticide may be distributed or sold in the United States unless it has been registered by the EPA pursuant to FIFRA.[3] Registration shall be granted if, after an elaborate screening procedure of the pesticide based on extensive data to be supplied by the

[1] It should be mentioned, however, that Germany banned the production, use and export of one pesticide, DDT, in 1972. See below ch 15.

[2] On US law and policy concerning hazardous exports, see generally Schulberg (1979); Azevedo (1985); Shuman (1983); Scherr (1987).

[3] 7 USC 136a (a).

applicant, the EPA determines that 'when used in accordance with widespread and commonly recognized practice it will not generally cause unreasonable adverse effects on the environment.'[4] For the purposes of the FIFRA, 'environment' is defined as including 'water, air, land, and all plants and man and other animals living therein, and the interrelationships which exist among these.'[5] Thus, hazards to human health are covered by the notion 'adverse effects on the environment'. In determining whether adverse effects are 'unreasonable', the EPA must perform a cost-benefit assessment, 'taking into account the economic, social, and environmental costs and benefits of the use' of the pesticide.[6]

It should be noted that registration under the FIFRA is use-specific, ie the effects on the environment are assessed by the EPA taking into account the specific uses for which the pesticide is proposed by the applicant, and registration is valid only for those uses. When registering a pesticide, the EPA will classify it as being either for 'general use' or for 'restricted use' or for both.[7] A 'restricted use' classification implies that the pesticide, even when used in accordance with its directions for use, 'may generally cause, *without additional regulatory restrictions*, unreasonable adverse effects on the environment, including injury to the applicator,'[8] and may therefore only be used by or under the direct supervision of 'certified applicators', ie specially trained persons, or subject to other special restrictions.[9] But even registration of a pesticide for general use is not to be regarded as a general license to market and use the pesticide for any purpose.[10]

It is clear that the act vests a considerable amount of administrative discretion in the EPA. The agency has wide-ranging powers under the FIFRA to prohibit or restrict the marketing and use of pesticides. The EPA's regulatory decisions pursuant to the FIFRA can take a variety of forms: denial of registration upon application,[11] cancellation of registration at the agency's initiative or upon expiry of a certain period,[12] suspension of registration pending cancellation in the event of an 'imminent hazard,'[13] and voluntary cancellation at the request of the registrant.[14] Each of those actions is subject to specific procedural requirements and to administrative and/or judicial review. As a matter of fact, decisions to deny, cancel or

[4] 7 USC 136a (c) (5) (D).
[5] 7 USC 136 (j).
[6] 7 USC 136 (bb).
[7] 7 USC 136a (d) (1) (A).
[8] 7 USC 136a (d) (1) (C) (emphasis added).
[9] 7 USC 136i.
[10] See the 'unlawful acts' specified in 7 USC 136j (a), especially subsections (1) (E) and (2) (G).
[11] 7 USC 136a (c) (6).
[12] 7 USC 136d (a) (1).
[13] 7 USC 136d (c).
[14] 7 USC 136d (f)(1).

suspend registration of a pesticide are often highly controversial and the subject of extensive administrative hearings and litigation in federal courts.

In its original 1972 version, section 17 (a) of the FIFRA exempted from the requirements of the Act all pesticides 'intended solely for export to any foreign country and prepared or packed according to the specifications or directions of the foreign purchaser.'[15] By exempting exported products from domestic regulation and deferring to 'the specifications of the foreign purchaser', the US legislator acted consistently with the prevailing international regulatory order, still essentially based on the national and territorial character of health and environmental product regulations and its corollary, free international trade.

However, it appears that the US Congress, when legislating to establish an elaborate system of regulatory controls on the distribution and use of pesticides for the protection of human health and the environment in the United States, at the same time implicitly recognised the limitations of that prevailing order and acknowledged the international responsibility of the United States as a major chemical-producing and trading nation by creating a mechanism for the international diffusion of information on US regulatory decisions. Indeed, since as early as 1972, section 17 (b) of the FIFRA has provided that the Administrator of the EPA has a duty to notify foreign governments and international organisations of certain regulatory decisions:

> Whenever a registration, or a cancellation or suspension of the registration of a pesticide becomes effective, or ceases to be effective, the Administrator shall transmit through the State Department notification thereof to the governments of other countries and to appropriate international agencies.[16]

Through section 17 (b) of the FIFRA, the United States unilaterally introduced a notification procedure which later provided a model for the development of international notification schemes. Of all the measures conceivable to bridge the regulatory gap between exporting and importing countries, this form of notification, which later became known internationally as 'notification of control action'—as opposed to actual export notification—is the least intrusive on free trade, the furthest removed from any form of trade regulation. Notification is provided in a general manner, to the international community at large, and not specifically to directly concerned trading partners who import the products which are the subject of the control actions notified. Any link with actual trade in those products is carefully avoided.

[15] Pub L No 92–516, 86 Stat 995, § 2.
[16] 7 USC 136o (b).

As part of a series of amendments to the FIFRA passed by Congress in 1978,[17] section 17 of the Act was modified to introduce specific measures with respect to pesticide exports on top of the existing general requirement of notification of regulatory measures to foreign governments laid down in section 17 (b). The amendments to section 17 were partly the result of a general congressional review of US policy regarding hazardous exports, which was prompted by a public controversy about the lack of statutory authority to prohibit the export to other countries of certain consumer goods banned by the US Consumer Product Safety Commission in 1977.[18]

In July 1978, the Commerce, Consumer, and Monetary Affairs Subcommittee of the Committee on Government Operations of the House of Representatives held a series of hearings on the export of hazardous products banned by US regulatory agencies. The Subcommittee not only addressed the export of consumer products, but also reviewed the situation with respect to exports of pesticides, food, pharmaceuticals and medical devices.[19] Based on the Subcommittee's findings, the House Committee on Government Operations issued a report with recommendations for the development of a comprehensive national policy on hazardous exports.[20] This report provides an interesting background for understanding the premises on which the US regulatory approach to the issue is based, the conflicting views which this approach tried to accommodate and the policy choices that were made by the US legislator when it adopted the FIFRA amendments in late 1978. Although it reflects what was, at that time, an essentially domestic policy debate,[21] the congressional panel's report already articulates and considers most of the issues around which the subsequent regulatory debate in international fora would later revolve.

In its recommendations, the House Committee sought to strike a balance between the responsibility of the exporting country and the sovereignty of the importing country. As one official put it in her testimony to the Committee, US policy-makers had to confront 'the need to balance the

[17] Federal Pesticide Act of 1978, Pub L No 95–396, 92 Stat 833.

[18] The controversy did not initially arise over pesticides, but over children's sleepwear treated with a carcinogenic flame retardant chemical (TRIS). However, in the subsequent congressional inquiry the issue of exports of pesticides banned in the US was specifically addressed. See Norris (1982), pp 84–88.

[19] See United States House of Representatives, *US Export of Banned Products*, Hearings before a Subcommittee of the Committee on Government Operations, 95th Cong, 2d Sess, 11–13 July 1978.

[20] United States House of Representatives, *Report on Export of Products Banned by US Regulatory Agencies*, 34th Report by the Committee on Government Operations, HR Rep 95–1686, 95th Cong, 2d Sess, 4 Oct 1978.

[21] Although it appears from the report (*ibid*, p 12) that the House Committee was aware of the 1977 and 1978 UNEP Governing Council decisions (see below ch 12), the congressional initiatives in 1978 were prompted by public concern in the United States rather than by international pressure. At that time, those UNEP decisions were no more than isolated recommendations of a low-profile UN body and the international policy debate on exports of banned and severely restricted substances had not yet really started.

morality and sovereignty issues.'[22] The congressional panel, declaring itself 'in substantial agreement' with this official's assessment of the issue, came to the conclusion that the US 'has a significant responsibility for the safety of the goods it sells abroad', but also that 'this responsibility must be exercised in a way which *respects the sovereignty of other nations* and accounts for differing conditions which may affect judgments of health and safety.'[23]

Accordingly, the Committee rejected what it called 'the two extreme positions': prohibiting all exports of products banned from the US domestic market or allowing such exports without any restrictions. Interestingly, the Committee apparently never considered a ban on the *production* of products which may not be sold in the US as one of a range of conceivable policy alternatives. What it eventually recommended was an expansion and strengthening of notification and labelling requirements coupled with the introduction of a statutory basis for export controls based on the principle that 'no product which is banned from the domestic market should be allowed to be exported *without a determination from the appropriate regulatory agency*' in the United States that the export is justified.[24] According to the Committee's recommendations, authorisation to export should be granted only if a foreign government has formally requested that export be allowed; if, in the competent US regulatory agency's discretionary judgement, special circumstances in the importing country make the product safe for use there; or if, upon an application for permission to export, the same US agency determines that the export meets other criteria to be established by statute or regulation.[25] It should be noted that the Committee did not go so far as to recommend that the formal *consent* of the government of the importing country be required. The concept of 'prior informed consent' is not mentioned in the report. But consent is implied when the foreign government requests the export or presumed when the exporter provides evidence 'that the product conforms to the specifications of the foreign purchasers' and 'that the government of the importing country has received notification of the US regulatory action.'[26]

The Committee's report makes it quite clear that, in its view, a notification policy alone is not sufficient. The US State Department is harshly criticised for its position, expressed during the congressional hearings, which 'sees information exchange as the only component of a US policy on the export of hazardous products', 'as the maximum effort the United

[22] United States House of Representatives, *Report on Export of Products Banned by US Regulatory Agencies*, above n 20, p 31 (Statement of E Peterson, Special Assistant to the President for Consumer Affairs).

[23] *Ibid* (emphasis added). See also p 3, paras 2 & 3.

[24] *Ibid*, pp 6, 31 (emphasis added).

[25] *Ibid*, p 6.

[26] *Ibid*, p 31.

States should make', and 'ignores the reality of US technical and scientific superiority.'[27] For its part, the congressional panel took the view that:

while notification to foreign governments of US agency action is a critical element of an export policy . . . the ability of an agency to *exercise a unilateral judgment* must also be included in such a policy.[28]

Accordingly, it recommended that the provisions of relevant US statutes, including the FIFRA, be amended to establish export permit procedures 'to assure that only essential and reasonable exports of these [banned] products are allowed'[29] and to provide authority for the competent US agency to control exports and even 'to totally prohibit export of a product so dangerous that no reasonable argument could be made for its consumption anywhere in the world.'[30] The report is striking for the confidence it places in the wise use of administrative discretion by government agencies.

In the end, however, Congress did not entirely follow the House Committee's recommendations. It seems not to have been convinced of the desirability of enabling US regulatory agencies to exercise their 'unilateral judgment' as proposed by the Committee. Instead of conferring discretionary authority on the EPA to control exports of unregistered pesticides, the new measures enacted in 1978 were based exclusively on the *caveat emptor* principle. The amended section 17 (a) of the FIFRA provides for a form of export-related notification for exports of pesticides not registered for use in the US and requires compliance with certain minimal labelling requirements for all exported pesticides. To strengthen the existing provisions on the notification of control actions, an additional clause was added to section 17 (b) which requires the EPA to provide, upon request by a recipient of a notification of a control action, information on the rationale for the control action and on alternative pesticides which are available for the same use.

Section 17 (a) (2) stipulates that pesticides not registered for use in the US may only be exported

if, prior to export, the foreign purchaser has signed a statement acknowledging that the purchaser understands that such pesticide is not registered for use in the United States and cannot be sold in the United States . . . A copy of that statement shall be transmitted to an appropriate official of the government of the importing country.[31]

Section 17 (a) (1) provides that all pesticides for export must comply with most of the labelling requirements applicable within the US. In particular, the label must state the active ingredients and the name and address of

[27] United States House of Representatives, *Report on Export of Products Banned by US Regulatory Agencies*, above n 20, p 24.
[28] *Ibid*, p 3, para II.6 (emphasis added).
[29] *Ibid*, p 5, para III.1.
[30] *Ibid*, p 6, para III.3 (e).
[31] 7 USC 136o (a) (2).

the manufacturer, include warning statements and precautionary information as well as instructions for treatment in case of poisoning, and may not make any false representations.[32] Unregistered pesticides must be marked conspicuously as '*Not Registered for Use in the United States of America*.'[33]

Although section 17 (a) does not explicitly provide this, the EPA has interpreted the statute as requiring bilingual labelling. All relevant information must appear in the language of the importing country as well as in English.[34] This interpretation is based on another provision of FIFRA which specifies that all information on pesticide labels must be 'in such terms as to render it likely to be read and understood by the ordinary individual under customary conditions of purchase and use.'[35] According to the EPA's 1980 policy statement, the 'EPA interprets this passage to apply to ordinary individuals in the importing country as well as in the United States.'[36] However laudable, this administrative interpretation still fails to take account of the fact that the 'ordinary individual under customary conditions of use' in the Third World is likely to be illiterate and thus unable to 'read and understand' the information on the label. The EPA has also made clear that section 17 (a) labelling requirements are minimal standards which are to be complied with regardless of the importing country's requirements.[37]

Having examined the relevant statutory provisions and their legislative history, it is most interesting to consider their actual interpretation and implementation by the administrative agencies concerned. In 1975, ie prior to the 1978 FIFRA amendments, the EPA issued a statement of its policy on the implementation of section 17 (b), in which it narrowly construed its notification duty.[38] It reviewed the legislative history and concluded that the congressional intent was not to require notification of every registration, cancellation or suspension action, but only when 'some useful purpose would be served.'[39] The EPA announced that it would notify only such regulatory actions which are 'determined to have national or international significance' and 'may have, in the opinion of the Administrator, widespread environmental, economic or political implications.'[40]

In 1978, the US General Accounting Office (GAO) investigated the EPA notification practice under Section 17 (b). It found that the Agency took a

[32] 7 USC 136o (a) (1).

[33] 7 USC 136 (q) (1) (H).

[34] EPA, 'Statement of Policy on the Labelling Requirements for Exported Pesticides, Devices and Pesticide Active Ingredients and the Procedure for Exporting Unregistered Pesticides', *Federal Register* 45 (1980), p 50274, at p 50275 (hereafter referred to as 1980 EPA Statement of Policy).

[35] 7 USC 136 (q) (1) (E).

[36] 1980 EPA Statement of Policy, above n 34, p 50278.

[37] *Ibid*, pp 50275, 50279.

[38] EPA, 'Notification to Foreign Governments of Certain Pesticide Actions', *Federal Register* 40 (1975), p 20987.

[39] HR Rep No 1540, 92d Cong, 1st Sess 33, 1972.

[40] EPA, above n 38.

very narrow view of the 'international significance' of its regulatory decisions and, between 1972 and 1978, had notified only five out of 14 cancellation, suspension or restriction measures.[41] For example, the EPA had not informed foreign governments of the cancellation of chlordane and heptachlor, which were at that time two of the most widely used pesticides in the world.[42] Moreover, notwithstanding the express language of the statute, the EPA as a matter of policy did not notify suspensions, but only certain cancellations.[43] The GAO criticised the EPA's 'international significance' criterion:

> In its attempts to identify significant actions, EPA has overlooked the need to notify foreign nations of several pesticide cancellations of importance that affect human health.[44]

It also appeared from the GAO investigation that the few notifications that were actually issued often did not reach the appropriate officials in the country of destination.[45] One US embassy official who was in charge of transmitting these notices admitted that he never forwarded them because 'it might adversely affect US exporting.'[46] In this context, the GAO observed that '*instructions supplied to Embassy officials may be ambiguous*, leading them to believe that pesticide notifications are discretionary.'[47] These findings, which were reported to Congress by a senior GAO official testifying in the congressional hearings of July 1978, *before* the export provisions of the FIFRA were amended a few months later, cast serious doubt on the effectiveness of notification procedures as a solution to the problem of exports of hazardous pesticides. It is ironic that the US Congress, notwithstanding the evidence already available at that time about the deficiencies and limitations of notification mechanisms, nevertheless chose to enact new statutory notification requirements instead of actual export control measures, and that the US government actively promoted the US notification approach as a model for the subsequent standard-setting efforts of various international agencies.

Like the provisions of section 17 (b) on the notification of US control actions to foreign governments, the new export-related notification requirements of section 17 (a), which were added to the FIFRA in 1978, have also been interpreted restrictively by the EPA. Although there is no basis for this in the language of the statute, the Agency ruled in its 1980 official inter-

[41] US General Accounting Office, *Better Regulation of Pesticide Exports and Pesticide Residues in Imported Food is Essential*, GAO Rep No CED-79-43, 22 June 1979, p 62 (hereafter cited as 1979 GAO Report).

[42] *Ibid*, p 64.

[43] *Ibid*.

[44] *Ibid*, p 67.

[45] *Ibid*, p 104.

[46] US House of Representatives, *US Export of Banned Products*, above n 19, p 81.

[47] *Ibid* (emphasis added).

pretation of the Act that purchaser acknowledgement statements are only required *for the first shipment of each year*. Consequently, the government of the importing country only receives notice of those statements on an annual basis as well. The rationale for the EPA's decision was that 'repetitive notices would be of only marginal value, and in cases of a high volume of exports to a foreign country, might result in a flood of paper' and that annual notification was sufficient to fulfil the purpose of the statute.[48]

Although the purchaser acknowledgement statement must have been received by the exporter and transmitted to the EPA prior to shipment, the statute does not require that the authorities of the importing country be notified *before* the export.[49] In fact, in most cases, due to delays in transmission through the State Department, the notice is received long after the shipment has arrived. In the EPA's view, this is not inconsistent with the statutory intent:

> The Agency believes that the purpose of the purchaser acknowledgement statement is to advise foreign governments that pesticides which have been judged by the United States to be hazardous to human health or the environment, or pesticides for which no hazard assessment has been made, are being exported by US producers to their country. . . . *The Agency does not consider that the acknowledgement statement is primarily intended to serve as preshipment notification to foreign governments in order that they may intercept shipments of such pesticides.*[50]

Yet the EPA does prescribe that the acknowledgement statement to be notified to the foreign government should contain certain information which would enable that government to control imports if it so desires, such as the name and address of the exporter and importer and the exact destination of the shipment.[51] The EPA has made clear that purchaser acknowledgement statements are required even for pesticides which are officially registered in the importing country, and has also rejected a suggestion by the industry that 'non-commercial transactions', ie intra-company transfers such as shipments of active ingredients from a company's US production facility to its formulation plants abroad, should be exempt from the section 17 (a) notification requirements.[52]

Section 17 (a) requires a purchaser acknowledgement statement for 'any pesticide other than a pesticide registered under [FIFRA]'. This includes all pesticides which have never been submitted for registration, whose registration has been denied because of 'unreasonable adverse effects' on humans or the environment, or which are exported for uses for which their registration has been cancelled or denied.[53] According to the EPA, section 17 (a)

48 1980 EPA Statement of Policy, above n 34, p 50276.
49 *Ibid*.
50 *Ibid* (emphasis added).
51 *Ibid*, p 50277.
52 *Ibid*, p 50278.
53 *Ibid*, p 50276.

does not apply to pesticide products which are only 'minor variations' on registered products, ie the same active ingredient but a different formulation.[54] The major loophole in the provision is that it does not cover pesticides which were initially registered but were later found to be hazardous and *voluntarily* withdrawn from the market *by the manufacturer* to avoid impending EPA cancellation action. By doing so, the manufacturer can both avoid the bad publicity of a cancellation and evade the FIFRA restrictions on exports.[55] Furthermore, no export notification is required for pesticides registered only for 'restricted use.'[56]

In parallel with the parliamentary initiatives which resulted in the 1978 FIFRA amendments, the Carter Administration also initiated an across-the-board executive review of US hazards export policy. To this effect, an Interagency Working Group on Hazardous Substances Export Policy was established in 1978. After an extensive two-year study, it recommended a number of refinements in existing notification procedures under the FIFRA and other statutes, and a limited system of export controls for certain particularly dangerous products.[57] Interestingly, the Working Group expounded a foreign policy rationale for export controls:

> If the United States does not exercise special vigilance over the export of certain extremely hazardous banned or significantly restricted products which represent a substantial threat to human health or safety or the environment, *our economic and diplomatic ties with other countries could be jeopardized.* Citizens and governments of foreign countries receiving these products, or being affected indirectly as innocent bystanders, *may develop increasingly hostile attitudes towards this country and its products.*[58]

The group advocated an international 'leadership role' for the US in the regulation of hazardous exports, which would be 'consistent with the President's human rights themes and will enhance our trading position.'[59] Enlightened self-interest was the motto.

A few days before leaving office, President Carter signed an Executive Order implementing the recommendations of the Interagency Working Group.[60] The order was based on existing statutory authority under the

[54] 1980 EPA Statement of Policy, p 50275. On the enforcement difficulties faced by the EPA as a result of this similarity exemption, see Crowe (1992), pp 344–50.

[55] SJ Scherr, Natural Resources Defense Council, Statement before the House Committee on Agriculture, Subcommittee on Department Operations, Research and Foreign Agriculture, concerning Exports of Banned Pesticides, 22 July 1981, pp 13–14.

[56] 7 USC 136a (d) (1) (C).

[57] See generally 'Background Report on the Executive Order on Federal Policy Regarding the Export of Banned or Significantly Restricted Substances', *Federal Register* 46 (1981), p 7806 (hereafter referred to as HSEP Report).

[58] *Ibid*, p 7812 (emphasis added).

[59] *Ibid*, p 7815.

[60] Executive Order No 12264, *Federal Register* 46 (1981), p 4659.

Export Administration Act of 1979,[61] which empowers the President to regulate the export of goods for foreign policy and national security purposes. The administration took the view that controlling the export of hazardous substances was a legitimate 'foreign policy' objective within the meaning of this Act.[62]

The main feature of the Executive Order was the compilation of a 'Commodity Control List' of 'extremely hazardous substances', 'which represent a substantial threat to human health and the environment' and 'the export of which would cause clear and significant harm to the foreign policy interests of the United States.'[63] The export of such substances would require an export licence, which would be granted only in 'exceptional cases'[64] with the informed consent of the government of the importing country.[65] The order further improved existing notification procedures, by channelling all communications through the State Department[66] and requiring the publication of an annual summary of US regulatory actions on hazardous products which would be distributed to foreign governments and interested international organisations.[67] Finally, all US agencies concerned were directed to encourage and participate actively in international regulatory efforts.[68] It was envisaged that these efforts might ultimately lead to an international convention governing international trade in hazardous substances.[69]

The order would not significantly have affected existing notification practices under the FIFRA, although it also applied to restricted-use pesticides, but only 'to the extent not inconsistent with applicable law.'[70] Practically, this probably authorised an extension of Section 17 (b) notification procedures to restricted pesticides, but not of section 17 (a) acknowledgement statement requirements.

The Carter Executive Order was very short-lived and was never actually implemented. A few weeks after its promulgation, it was revoked by President Reagan in an Executive Order entitled 'Federal Exports and Excessive Regulation.'[71] In a memorandum accompanying his Executive Order, President Reagan requested the Secretaries of State and Commerce to review the hazardous substances export policy and propose revisions of

[61] 50 USC 2401.
[62] See Memorandum from L Ulman, Deputy Assistant Attorney-General, to E Peterson, Special Assistant to the President for Consumer Affairs, reprinted in *Federal Register* 45 (1980), p 53768.
[63] Executive Order No 12264, s 1-301.
[64] *Ibid.*
[65] *Ibid*, s 1-306.
[66] *Ibid*, s 1-201.
[67] *Ibid*, s 1-401–1-403.
[68] *Ibid*, s 1-501.
[69] HSEP Report, above n 57, p 7815.
[70] Executive Order No 12264, ss 1-101 (m) (1) (B), 1–201.
[71] Executive Order No 12290, *Federal Register* 46 (1981), p 12943.

relevant statutes and regulations to make them 'more consistent and cost-effective.'[72] The main recommendation resulting from this review with regard to pesticide exports was the elimination of export-specific notifications.[73] The Secretaries' report asserts that:

> export-specific notification is a burdensome regulatory procedure that fails to achieve its intended purpose. . . . Many developing countries . . . lack sufficient scientific or technical capability to use effectively the export-specific notices. . . . [The procedure] *focuses attention on the source rather than on the nature of the product.*[74]

This statement turns the main rationale for export notification on its head, using it as an argument against the procedure, and clearly reveals the Reagan administration's overriding concern for the 'source of the product', ie US industry.

The amendment of section 17 (a) of the FIFRA suggested by the report was never formally proposed to Congress. The administration apparently lost interest in the issue, having made its ideological point. In June 1981, the National Agricultural Chemicals Association hitched on to the deregulation bandwagon and unsuccessfully lobbied for amendments to the FIFRA which would have eliminated government-to-government notification and put the exporter in charge of informing the importing country directly.[75] Eventually, even the industry dropped its active opposition to section 17 (a) and indeed, on occasion, commented favourably on the notification procedure. This seems to confirm that export notifications have not harmed pesticide manufacturers, ie that they have not resulted in any significant curb on exports of banned hazardous pesticides to the Third World. In 1983 congressional hearings, representatives of the EPA testified in favour of maintaining the notification requirement and denied that it had adversely affected US industry.[76]

At the end of part II of this study, when discussing the impact of international regulatory initiatives on the domestic policy and law of pesticide-exporting countries, I shall examine to what extent US policy has changed as a result of emerging international standards.

[72] Memorandum from the President to the Secretary of Commerce and the Secretary of State, 17 Feb 1981, reprinted in *US Export Weekly* 17 (1982), p 339.

[73] Secretary of State & Secretary of Commerce, Report to the President on the Review of US Hazardous Substances Export Policy, 10 May 1982, reprinted in *US Export Weekly* 17 (1982), pp 336, 338.

[74] *Ibid*, p 338 (emphasis added).

[75] Norris (1982), p 31.

[76] US House of Representatives, *Regulation of Pesticides: Hearings before the Subcommittee on Department Operations, Research and Foreign Agriculture of the House Committee on Agriculture*, 98th Cong, 1st Sess, 1983, vol 4, p 333.

12

The First Phase of International Regulatory Efforts: The Focus on Export Notification

THE PIONEERING ROLE OF THE UNITED NATIONS ENVIRONMENT PROGRAMME

It is through two United Nations bodies, the General Assembly and the Governing Council of the United Nations Environment Programme (UNEP), that the issue of international trade in banned and severely restricted chemicals was put on the international agenda and became the subject of international normative efforts. UNEP was the first international forum in which developing countries aired their concerns about exports of banned hazardous products from industrialised countries. With its broad environmental mandate, its technical expertise in the field of chemicals management and its coordinating role within the UN system,[1] UNEP was perceived to be the most appropriate international agency to deal with the problem of regulating exports of pesticides and other hazardous chemicals.

International Register of Potentially Toxic Chemicals

Since its inception, UNEP has been involved in the international collection and exchange of information on the environmental effects of toxic chemicals. The 1972 United Nations Conference on the Human Environment, which led to the establishment of UNEP, had recommended the creation of an 'International Registry of Data on Chemicals in the

[1] UNGA Res 2997 (XXVII) of 15 Dec 1972, which established UNEP and laid down its mandate, specifically entrusted UNEP Governing Council with the task of 'provid[ing] general policy guidance for the direction and *co-ordination of environmental programmes within the United Nations system*' (para I, 2(b)). However, this coordinating role was somewhat tempered by the explicit recognition, in the resolution's preamble, of 'the *sectoral responsibilities* of the organizations in the United Nations system' (5th preambular para).

Environment.'[2] Following this recommendation, UNEP formally established the International Register of Potentially Toxic Chemicals (IRPTC) in 1975, 'to serve as an essential tool in optimizing the use of chemicals for human well-being while at the same time providing a global early warning system of undesirable environmental side effects.'[3]

The IRPTC, based in Geneva, functions primarily as a scientific data bank, collecting information on the environmental and toxicological effects of chemicals through a network of national correspondents, and responding to specific inquiries from governments regarding particular chemicals. The expert group which elaborated the original plan for the IRPTC had proposed that one of the main functions of the Register should be to provide information on regulatory measures which could serve as a basis or model for developing countries in drafting their own chemicals control legislation. However, another UNEP-appointed expert group found that the compilation and distribution of legislative and regulatory information would be too complex a task, beyond the resources of the IRPTC, and recommended instead that the Register act only as a referral system in this field.[4]

Consequently, the provision of information on regulatory measures became a relatively low-priority objective in the original mandate of the IRPTC as approved by UNEP Governing Council in 1975.[5] Although as early as 1973, at its first meeting, the Governing Council had decided 'to assess the feasibility of, and if appropriate to create, a global "early warning" system to provide notice to countries . . . the health of whose populations may be affected by the export of environmentally harmful substances,'[6] the IRPTC was not initially set up and equipped to perform this role. It did not provide notice to individual governments of hazards associated with particular exports of chemicals. It routinely distributed only general, as opposed to export-related, information on chemicals. Third World governments may of course use the IRPTC to obtain information on specific chemicals they are importing, but the initiative is entirely theirs. The IRPTC was primarily set up to provide information on request, not to alert importing countries to potential hazards on its own initiative.[7]

[2] Report of the United Nations Conference on the Human Environment, UN Doc A/CONF.48/14, Recommendation 74, para (e).

[3] UNEP Governing Council Dec 29 (III), para 8, UN Doc A/10025, 1975, p 96.

[4] Alston (1978), pp 397, 421 and n 107.

[5] See UN Doc UNEP/WG.96/2, 20 Jan 1984, p 4.

[6] UNEP Governing Council Dec 1 (I), para 12 (d) (ii), 28 UN GAOR Supp (No 25), UN Doc A/9025, 1973, p 41.

[7] On the background and activities of the IRPTC, see generally Alston (1978), pp 418–22; *The state of information on potentially harmful chemicals in international trade*, UN Doc UNEP/WG.96/2, 20 Jan 1984; *Exchange of information on banned hazardous chemicals and unsafe pharmaceutical products*, UN Doc A/36/255, 1981, Annex I.

Governing Council Decisions

It is through UNEP, however, that international trade in banned and severely restricted chemicals emerged as an issue on the international political agenda. During a debate on the IRPTC's activities at the 5th meeting of UNEP Governing Council in 1977, Kenya's Minister for Water Development made a strong statement condemning exports of banned hazardous products to the Third World and calling for international regulations to prevent such exports. As quoted in the Kenyan press, the minister declared that 'Kenya detests the use of developing countries as experimental or dumping grounds for chemical products that have been banned or have not been adequately tested.'[8] The official account of his intervention in the 'sanitized' UN language of the proceedings of the Governing Council carefully avoids the term 'dumping' and does not quite convey the same sense of urgency and moral outrage:

> One delegation emphasized that IRPTC was of great interest to developing countries, as purchasers of chemicals, pharmaceuticals and food products from the developed countries. Frequently the use of such products was controlled in the exporting countries because the products did not meet their safety standards, yet they were sold in the developing countries' markets.[9]

Kenya introduced a draft for a Governing Council decision which, after noting 'that certain developing countries have been used without their consent as testing grounds for various types of chemicals and drugs, and as dumping grounds for unfit foods', would have

> urge[d] governments to ensure that exporters of drugs, chemicals, cosmetics and foods take necessary measures to ensure that untested and unapproved commodities are *not exported without the express consent* of the appropriate government authorities in the recipient country.[10]

After some North-South discussions between the members of the Governing Council, a compromise proposal was tabled jointly by Belgium and Kenya, which somewhat toned down the language of the original Kenyan proposal but retained the key message. This new draft decision recognised that 'there have been unethical practices' with respect to hazardous exports and that there was a 'need for harmonious co-operation between manufacturers . . . , exporters and importing countries.'[11] Accordingly, it recommended that:

[8] Statement of Dr Gikonyo Kiano, Minister for Water Development, Kenya, as quoted in Weir & Shapiro (1981), pp 66, 96 n 1, citing as a source the Nairobi daily *The Standard*, 11 May 1977, p 3.

[9] UNEP, Report of the Governing Council on the work of its 5th session, 32 UN GAOR Supp (No 25), UN Doc A/32/25, 1977, p 27.

[10] UN Doc GC(V)/SC.1/CRP.19, 19 May 1977 (emphasis added).

[11] UN Doc GC(V)/SC.1/CRP.25, 20 May 1977.

those concerned with the export of chemicals, foods, drugs and cosmetics take necessary measures *which have been elaborated internationally* to ensure that such commodities are not *introduced without the express consent* of the appropriate government authorities into the recipient country.[12]

This language stressed the need for international normative efforts and avoided any express reference to export controls by laying the emphasis on the 'introduction' of the products 'into the recipient country'. After further discussion, this draft decision was combined with another draft decision calling for international cooperation for the protection of human and environmental health within the framework of the UN system, and addressing not only UNEP but also the WHO and FAO,[13] and the Governing Council eventually adopted a decision in which it

urges Governments to take steps to ensure that potentially harmful chemicals, in whatever form or commodity, which are unacceptable for domestic purposes in the exporting country, *are not permitted to be exported without the knowledge and consent of appropriate authorities in the importing country.*[14]

It is surprising that the final version of the decision again laid greater emphasis on the responsibility of exporting countries and on the need to control exports of hazardous chemicals, and that such an unambiguous endorsement of export controls and what later became known as the principle of *prior informed consent* was adopted by consensus. In 1977, the issue was not yet as politically sensitive as it became during the ensuing debates in the UN General Assembly, and the industrialised countries probably felt they could easily make a statement of good intentions to appease the Third World without really committing themselves, since no concrete implementing measures had been proposed. Perhaps they hoped the issue would fade from international attention. However, this proved to be a miscalculation; as the problem remained high on the Third World's political agenda, the industrialised countries became increasingly cautious, as appears from the subsequent decisions of UNEP Governing Council.

The subject was again debated at the following meeting of the Governing Council,[15] which adopted another decision in which it 'strongly reaffirm[ed]' its earlier pronouncement, while at the same time substantially qualifying it. In this decision, the Governing Council:

appeals to the countries exporting potentially harmful chemicals, in whatever form or commodity, to *prevent the export* of items which are restricted, or not registered

[12] UN Doc GC(V)/SC.1/CRP.25, 20 May 1977, 2nd operative para (emphasis added).
[13] UN Doc GC(V)/SC.1/CRP.8, 18 May 1977.
[14] UNEP Governing Council Dec 85 (V), UN Doc A/32/25, 1977, p 116 (emphasis added).
[15] UNEP, Report of the Governing Council on the work of its 6th session, 33 UN GAOR Supp (No 25), UN Doc A/33/25, 1978, at pp 19, 54.

for use in the countries of origin *until the exporting countries have ascertained that the results of tests and evaluations* on the effects of these chemicals on the health of people and the environment (as well as detailed instructions in mutually agreed languages for the safe use of these products) *have been provided to the designated authorities in the recipient countries*, so as to make it possible for these authorities to make fully informed decisions on the import and utilization of the products.[16]

The wording of this recommendation signifies a retreat from the position the Governing Council expressed in 1977, in that the consent of the importing country is no longer required; simple notification is now regarded as sufficient. However, some notion of export control still applies: notification must occur prior to export and export may not be permitted unless and until notification has been made.

Consistent with its recommendation on exports of banned and severely restricted chemicals, UNEP also decided to strengthen the role of the IRPTC in the exchange of information on such chemicals, instructing it

to give priority to providing countries with information on legal and administrative limitations, bans and regulations placed on potentially toxic chemicals in the producing countries.[17]

Pursuant to this decision, the IRPTC prepared legal files on the regulatory status of 400 chemicals in 12 different countries. This information was later used in the preparation of the UN's Consolidated List of products whose consumption and/or sale have been banned, withdrawn, severely restricted or not approved by Governments; it has also been published separately and is available directly to governments on request.[18]

Towards the Development of an International Normative Instrument

It was soon recognised that these general recommendations of the Governing Council and the existing information exchange arrangements of the IRPTC were insufficient to solve the problem, and that a more detailed international instrument would be necessary. The elaboration of such an instrument was undertaken by UNEP in the scope of its ongoing programme for the development of international environmental law. In 1981, UNEP convened an *Ad Hoc* Meeting of Senior Government Officials Expert in

[16] UNEP Governing Council Dec 6/4, *ibid*, p 129 (emphasis added).

[17] UNEP Governing Council Dec 6/3 B, para 6, *ibid*, p 128.

[18] International Register of Potentially Toxic Chemicals, *IRPTC Legal File 1986*, IRPTC Data Profile Series No 7, United Nations Environment Programme, Geneva, 1987, vols I and II. See also *The state of information on potentially harmful chemicals in international trade*, UN Doc UNEP/WG.96/2, 20 Jan 1984, p 7.

Environmental Law, in Montevideo, Uruguay, which adopted a 'Programme for the development and periodic review of environmental law', which was later approved by the Governing Council.[19] This programme, known as the Montevideo Programme, includes as one of its objectives:

> to *control international trade* in hazardous or inadequately tested chemicals, particularly where the sale of such substances has already been banned or restricted in the producing country.[20]

It provides that this objective is to be achieved by the 'preparation of guidelines at the global level as a first step towards a global convention' and the 'development and implementation of internationally harmonized practices, in particular for the gathering and dissemination of information.'[21]

Pursuant to this recommendation, the Governing Council decided in 1982 to convene a meeting of government experts 'to consider guidelines or principles on . . . the *exchange of information relating to trade* in and use and management of potentially harmful chemicals in particular pesticides.'[22] The specific reference to pesticides was added at the proposal of the Federal Republic of Germany,[23] which was at that time in the process of drafting national legislation on pesticide exports.[24] Although the Governing Council decision in its preamble refers to the trade control objective laid down in the Montevideo Programme, it narrows the mandate of the expert meeting to information exchange. This subtle but significant shift in focus was acknowledged by UNEP Secretariat in the following terms:

> The Governing Council by Decision 10/24 *re-oriented* the proposed principles or guidelines towards 'the exchange of information relating to trade', rather than towards the more ambitious objective 'to control international trade' as originally formulated in the 1982 Montevideo Programme. . . . *This new focus is indeed narrower than the two earlier Governing Council decisions* on the subject, which called for an export ban unless importing countries had obtained the required information (Decision 6/4 of 1978) or had actually given their consent (Decision 85/V of 1977).[25]

Thus, as it moved from the level of general principles to the level of practical implementation, UNEP retreated from its strong position in favour of

[19] UNEP Governing Council Dec 10/21, UN Doc UNEP/GC.10/14, 1982, p 100.

[20] Report of the Ad Hoc Meeting of Senior Government Officials Expert in Environmental Law, UN Doc UNEP/GC.10/5/Add.2, 1982, Annex, p 7 (emphasis added).

[21] *Ibid.*

[22] UNEP Governing Council Dec 10/24, para 1 (c), UN Doc UNEP/GC.10/14, 1982, p 102 (emphasis added).

[23] Draft Guidelines for the Exchange of Information on Trade and Management of Potentially Harmful Chemicals (in Particular Pesticides) in International Trade, UN Doc UNEP/WG.96/4, 15 Nov 1983, p 8 (hereafter referred to as Draft Guidelines).

[24] See below ch 15.

[25] Draft Guidelines, above n 23, pp 8–9, para 18 (emphasis added).

export controls to a vague concept of information exchange, through a series of small, incremental shifts in discourse which gradually narrowed the scope of the debate. However, in parallel to the work of UNEP Governing Council, a political debate on hazardous exports and possible policy responses to the issue was also being conducted in the UN General Assembly.

THE RESOLUTIONS OF THE UNITED NATIONS GENERAL ASSEMBLY

In view of the issue's obvious political appeal and wider implications in terms of North-South relations, international trade, consumer protection and the role of transnational corporations, the developing countries also turned to the General Assembly to focus attention on the problem and increase the political pressure on industrialised countries to respond favourably to their calls for international regulation. Ironically, while UNEP's approach was gradually becoming more moderate and technical than suggested by its initial political response in 1977, the General Assembly, in a series of successive resolutions, seemed to be moving in the opposite direction, from a relatively weak pronouncement on information exchange in 1979[26] to a strong, albeit not unambiguous, call for export controls and informed consent in 1982.[27] It was as though the Third World sought to compensate UNEP's blunting edge by a surge in rhetoric in the General Assembly.

Early Resolutions on Information Exchange and the Debate on Transnational Corporations

Two years after Kenya's initiative led to the issue of international trade in hazardous products being debated in UNEP, Kenya brought up the matter in the United Nations General Assembly. As a result, at its 1979 session, the General Assembly adopted, without a vote, a resolution based on a Kenyan proposal, which

> urges Member States to *exchange information* on hazardous chemicals and unsafe pharmaceutical products that have been banned in their territories, and to *discourage*, in consultation with importing countries, the exportation of such products to other countries.[28]

[26] UNGA Res 34/173, below n 28.
[27] UNGA Res 37/137, below n 65.
[28] UNGA Res 34/173, 17 December 1979, 34 UN GAOR Supp (No 46), UN Doc A/34/46, p 189 (emphasis added).

While this resolution did not explicitly call for an export ban, the term 'discourage' does connote some form of government intervention. The proviso 'in consultation with importing countries' was apparently added to underscore that the ultimate decision should rest with the government of the importing country. Furthermore, the notion of consultation also implies some form of government-to-government communication on exports. By its references to consultation and information exchange, the resolution lent support to the concept of export notification which was further elaborated in later General Assembly resolutions and other international instruments. Finally, it called on the Secretary-General of the United Nations to submit a report to the General Assembly at its 35th session 'about the experience of Member States and United Nations agencies and bodies concerned.'[29]

The Secretary-General failed to present the report in question at the 35th session of the General Assembly as requested. Initially, there seemed to be little enthusiasm for dealing with the issue within the UN Secretariat. The General Assembly adopted a resolution 'noting with regret' the Secretary-General's failure to report and urging him to submit the report at the next session.[30] More significantly, the resolution refers to the role of transnational corporations, and

> mindful of the importance of objective information about banned hazardous chemicals and unsafe pharmaceutical products . . . requests the Commission on Transnational Corporations to study . . . the ways and means *within the information system on transnational corporations* to improve the exchange of information on banned hazardous chemicals and unsafe pharmaceutical products, with a view to formulating appropriate recommendations.[31]

This paragraph gave rise to some controversy and was only adopted by a vote in which most Western chemical-exporting countries, except the Netherlands, abstained.[32] The United States delegation, explaining its abstention in committee, stated that 'it did not believe that the Commission on Transnational Corporations was the appropriate body to deal with the subject' and that 'an issue so complex would best be left to more appropriate United Nations agencies such as the World Health Organization.'[33] The United Kingdom also objected that this 'very specialized topic' was 'not within the province of the Commission on Transnational Corporations.'[34]

[29] UNGA Res 34/173, 17 December 1979, 34 UN GAOR Supp (No 46), UN Doc A/34/46, para 2.

[30] UNGA Res 35/186, 15 Dec 1980, 35 UN GAOR Supp (No 48), UN Doc A/35/48, pp 202–203.

[31] *Ibid* (emphasis added).

[32] UN Doc A/35/PV.96, 1980, p 59.

[33] UN Doc A/C.3/35/SR.72, 1980, pp 8, 9.

[34] *Ibid*, p 9.

This opposition to Commission involvement can be ascribed to the general hostility of Western countries towards the Commission and Centre on Transnational Corporations (UNCTC), which they view as politically biased organs. In the General Assembly, their strategy was to resist the politicisation of the issue by defining it as a purely technical problem to be dealt with by specialised agencies further removed from public scrutiny, in which the West, through the sheer weight of its technical expertise, has greater influence. In an article criticising UN regulatory efforts in the environmental, health and safety and other fields, former US Permanent Representative to the United Nations Jeane Kirkpatrick charges that 'the people who shape the negotiations and the debates concerning regulation almost invariably utterly lack technical expertise about the matters . . . to be regulated' and that 'political concerns dominate.'[35] According to her:

> The process of goal-setting and problem-defining is governed not by consideration of what is technically necessary, desirable, or feasible, but quite simply by the politics of the blocs, in the political culture of the international class struggle.[36]

Apart from the institutional issue of the UNCTC's involvement, the US also resented the preambular language of the resolution, which suggested that transnational corporations cannot be relied upon to furnish 'objective' information to importing countries and the resolution's general accusatory focus on multinationals. The US delegate pointed out in committee that 'the issue of hazardous substances involved more than just transnational corporations.'[37] This statement apparently reflects the same concern as expressed by Ambassador Kirkpatrick when she denounced the UN's focus on transnational corporations as 'a very crude kind of anticapitalist ideology' which views 'punitive regulation of transnational corporations' as 'a kind of good in itself.'[38]

The more specific reasons for Western opposition to the involvement of the UNCTC in the exchange of information on banned hazardous chemicals become obvious when one considers the report prepared by the UNCTC in response to Resolution 35/186. The Centre had been asked to study the 'ways and means' by which it could contribute to the improvement of this exchange of information and in its report recommended that 'the exchange also may include information on . . . the principal producers and distributors of identified toxic and hazardous products'[39] and that the

[35] Kirkpatrick (1983), p 19.
[36] *Ibid.*
[37] UN Doc A/C.3/35/SR.72, 1980, p 8.
[38] Kirkpatrick (1983), p 21.
[39] *Role of the information system on transnational corporations regarding the exchange of information on banned hazardous chemicals and unsafe pharmaceuticals*, UN Doc E/C.10/90, 20 July 1981, p 19.

Centre's role, supplementary to that of the other agencies involved, could be 'the identification of transnational corporations involved in the production and marketing of products considered sufficiently toxic or hazardous for inclusion in the existing information systems,'[40] 'especially where transnational corporations are important or principal actors.'[41] Obviously, the main chemical-producing countries were not keen on the UNCTC performing this investigative function and identifying specific chemical companies as responsible for exports of banned hazardous chemicals to the Third World.[42]

The Secretary-General's report, submitted to the General Assembly in 1981, was quite different in tone from that of the UNCTC. It reviewed existing information exchange systems, in particular UNEP International Register of Potentially Toxic Chemicals and the WHO Certification Scheme on the Quality of Pharmaceutical Products, and advocated continued reliance on them,[43] although it acknowledged that they 'may not be a completely adequate response to the problem'[44] and that some improvements 'may be envisaged with a view to providing more oriented and responsive systems of information exchange.'[45]

The report, however, did not suggest any specific reforms. It did not endorse the controversial proposals made by the UNCTC in its earlier report. While it recognised that 'consideration might . . . be given to determining whether more elaborate international control systems would be needed,'[46] the report's position on export control and even notification schemes appears very reserved, if not negative. It described export restrictions as 'in some cases a hindrance to the freedom of choice of chemical or pharmaceutical goods by the importing country'[47] and stressed the need to 'avoid any implication of imposing unilateral restrictions.'[48] As for export notification, it stated that

> one of the constraints on the *utility* of such a system is the limited facilities of many recipient importing countries for digesting the voluminous, highly technical information and taking action on it in good time.[49]

This argument runs counter to the basic logic of the previous General Assembly resolutions, which viewed the deficient technical capabilities of

[40] *Role of the information system on transnational corporations regarding the exchange of information on banned hazardous chemicals and unsafe pharmaceuticals*, UN Doc E/C.10/90, 20 July 1981, p 21.

[41] *Ibid*, p 20.

[42] Cf the US objections to the inclusion of manufacturer information in the Consolidated List. See below.

[43] *Exchange of information on banned hazardous chemicals and unsafe pharmaceutical products*, Report of the Secretary-General, UN Doc A/36/255, 22 May 1981, p 9.

[44] *Ibid*, p 8.

[45] *Ibid*, p 9.

[46] *Ibid*.

[47] *Ibid*, p 8.

[48] *Ibid*, p 9.

[49] *Ibid*, p 6 (emphasis added).

importing countries as the very *raison d'être* of information exchange systems such as export notification. While the developing countries' technical inability to protect themselves adequately against toxic imports indeed impairs the full *effectiveness* of notification systems, the *utility* of such systems is precisely that they are aimed at providing information to remedy this inability and enhance the regulatory capacity of importing countries. By a subtle distortion, the report transforms the main rationale for export notification schemes into an argument against them.

However, the General Assembly, in its Resolution 36/166, did not endorse the report's approach. In fact, it implicitly rejected the Secretary-General's reservations about national export control measures by 'invit[ing] Member States to deal with this subject through appropriate means, *including possible legislation at the national level*, where they do not yet exist.'[50] The resolution furthermore called for 'technical assistance to the developing countries . . . to help them establish an adequate system for monitoring the import of . . . banned hazardous chemicals.'[51] Finally, the Assembly, ostensibly unsatisfied with the Secretary-General's 1981 report,[52] 'once again request[ed]' him 'to consult Member States on the existing information systems' and to submit another report.[53]

General Assembly Resolution 37/137: Endorsing Prior Informed Consent

The climax of the General Assembly's work on exports of hazardous products came at the 37th session in 1982. The Group of 77 pursued the issue with great vigour, introducing it through the Economic and Social Council (ECOSOC), and caught the producing countries, which presumably assumed that further consideration of the question had effectively been postponed until the 38th session,[54] somewhat by surprise.[55] Going beyond the relatively harmless and noncommittal language of the previous resolutions, the General Assembly broke the precarious consensus which had prevailed until then.

[50] UNGA Res 36/166, 16 Dec 1981, 36 UN GAOR Supp (No 51), UN Doc A/36/51, p 193 (emphasis added).

[51] *Ibid*, para 6.

[52] See above n 43.

[53] UNGA Res 36/166, above n 50, para 8.

[54] Para 8 of Resolution 36/166 indeed called on the Secretary-General to report to the 38th session.

[55] In its official report on the 37th session of the General Assembly, the Netherlands Ministry of Foreign Affairs noted that the Venezuelan initiative was quite unexpected, though it wrongly asserted that the issue was altogether new on the UN agenda. 'In de zomerzitting 1982 van ECOSOC diende de vertegenwoordiger van Venezuela *tot ieders verrassing* een ontwerp-resolutie in over een onderwerp *dat nieuw was* voor de discussie in de Verenigde Naties.' Ministerie van Buitenlandse Zaken, *Verslag van de 37ste zitting van de Algemene Vergadering van de Verenigde Naties*, Den Haag, 1983, p 193 (emphasis added).

The Third World floor leader this time was Venezuela, which, along with sponsors of previous resolutions such as Kenya and Argentina, introduced in the ECOSOC a draft resolution entitled 'Protection against harmful or potentially harmful products.'[56] The Council decided to transmit this draft resolution to the General Assembly for consideration,[57] notwithstanding the opposition of the Western countries.[58] The draft, in the most radical language ever adopted by any intergovernmental body on the hazardous exports issue,

> urges all countries that have prohibited the consumption, use, and/or sale of harmful or potentially harmful products to ensure that these are *not produced or exported* by corporations or individuals that have their main seat of business in their territory, *or are otherwise liable to their jurisdiction*.[59]

Not only did this text call for an outright export and production ban, it also advocated the exercise of extraterritorial jurisdiction by home countries to restrict the foreign operations of their multinationals,

> cognizant of the fact that almost all these products are manufactured and exported by corporations that have their main seat of business in a limited number of industrialized countries.[60]

Naturally, such explicit attribution of responsibility and drastic measures were unpalatable to industrialised countries. In a joint statement to the ECOSOC, the EC countries objected to the draft resolution on the grounds that products banned in one country may be acceptable in another due to different conditions, that it would be impracticable to institute a system of export permits, and that industries could easily evade any restrictions by relocating to other countries.[61] The latter argument of course ignored the resolution's reference to extra-territorial jurisdiction, which was designed precisely to cope with the problem of relocation.

When the text transmitted by the ECOSOC was discussed in the General Assembly's Second Committee, the Third World sponsors of the resolution realised that their draft as it stood was unrealistic and again set out to negotiate a compromise which would be acceptable to Western countries. During informal consultations, a consensus was eventually reached with all

[56] UN Doc E/1982/L.46, 21 July 1982.

[57] ECOSOC Dec 1982/180, 1982 UN ESCOR Supp (No 1A), UN Doc E/1982/82/Add 1, p 33.

[58] According to news agency reports, the industrialised countries rejected a revised compromise proposal put forward by the sponsors following negotiations with other delegations. In the end, the ECOSOC decided simply to refer the original draft, without endorsing it, to the General Assembly for consideration. C Raghavan, 'United Nations to Consider Action against Harmful Products', Inter Press Service report, Geneva, 30 July 1982.

[59] UN Doc E/1982/82/Add 1, p 33 (emphasis added).

[60] *Ibid*, preamble.

[61] Ministerie van Buitenlandse Zaken, above n 55, p 194.

members of the General Assembly but the United States,[62] which led the Venezuelan delegate to denounce 'the rigid attitude displayed by one delegation.'[63]

On 17 December 1982, the General Assembly adopted Resolution 37/137 on 'Protection against products harmful to health and the environment' by a vote of 146 to 1, with the United States as the lone dissenter.[64] In this resolution, the General Assembly:

1. *Agrees* that products that have been *banned* from domestic consumption and/or sale because they have been judged to endanger health and the environment should be sold abroad by companies, corporations or individuals only when a request for such products is received from an importing country or when the consumption of such products is *officially permitted* in the importing country;
2. *Agrees* that all countries that have *severely restricted* or have not approved the domestic consumption and/or sale of specific products, in particular pharmaceuticals and pesticides, should make available *full information* on these products with a view to safeguarding the health and environment of the importing country, including clear labelling in a language acceptable to the importing country.[65]

Furthermore, the resolution requested the Secretary-General 'to prepare and regularly update a consolidated list of products whose consumption and/or sale have been banned, withdrawn, severely restricted or, in the case of pharmaceuticals, not approved by Governments.'[66]

The accusal of transnational corporations, which had been so explicit in the draft, was couched in more disguised terms in a preambular paragraph which stated only 'that almost all of these products are at present manufactured and exported from a limited number of countries', while another preambular paragraph recognised 'that the primary responsibility for consumer protection rests with each State.'[67]

In opposing the resolution, the US delegation used mainly budgetary arguments. It objected to the cost of compiling the 'consolidated list' called for by the resolution, which would necessitate an increase in the overall UN

[62] At the time of the debate in the UN General Assembly, the Reagan administration was in the process of reviewing US regulatory requirements with respect to exports of hazardous products and considering proposals for deregulation. For obvious reasons, a UN call for a strengthening of export controls was most unwelcome at that time. The US delegation was instructed to oppose the draft resolution or at least ensure 'that it does not call for a new "code" of international "regulations" to govern the export of hazardous substances.' The delegation was under instructions to 'avoid any categoric statements about U.S. policy at this time' and not to accept 'any language that would commit us to a specific export policy.' US State Department Memorandum on Agenda Item 12(29) of the 37th Session of the UN General Assembly, 7 Oct 1982.

[63] UN Doc A/C.2/37/SR.47, 1982, p 7.

[64] UN Doc A/37/PV.109, 1982, p 52.

[65] UNGA Res 37/137, 17 Dec 1982, 37 UN GAOR Supp (No 51), UN Doc A/37/51, pp 112–13 (emphasis added).

[66] *Ibid.*

[67] *Ibid*, preamble.

budget, which the US opposed as a matter of general policy. The US pressed for an amendment that would have required the list to be produced 'within existing resources', but this amendment was rejected in committee.[68] When a US congressional subcommittee expressed concern about the American vote against the resolution, the State Department went out of its way to assure the committee that 'the negative US votes were cast on the basis of our overall financial policy in the UN'[69] but that the US was in 'agreement with the basic approach of the resolution.'[70] Nevertheless, the State Department admitted that while 'the US vote was based *primarily* on the unacceptable financial implications of the text,'[71] the US also had 'reservations regarding the substance of the resolution.'[72]

Indeed, Ambassador Kirkpatrick, in an article published a few weeks after the adoption of Resolution 37/137, denounced the resolution as 'another example of this new wave of paternalistic regulation.'[73] The US delegation deplored 'categorical and unfounded judgments' and 'ambiguities' in the resolution[74] and labelled it 'very poorly drafted.'[75] More specifically:

> We believe that each importing country should have the freedom to decide whether it wants to import a specific product, and that the United Nations should not seek to impose a universal policy on all countries . . . Thus, we objected to categoric judgments in this resolution that suggested that use of a product banned in one country, under the particular conditions and circumstances of that country, is automatically harmful or damaging in another country.[76]

The 'ambiguities' complained of concerned the meaning of the terms 'non-approved' and 'severely restricted' which were considered inconsistent with US regulatory categories.[77] Notwithstanding all these objections, the US delegation still pretended that it 'fully endorsed [the resolution's] underlying principles and approach, as also the opinion expressed in the seventh preambular paragraph that the primary responsibility for consumer protection rested with each state.'[78]

[68] UN Doc A/C.2/37/SR.47, 1982, pp 7, 9.

[69] US House of Representatives, *Regulation of Pesticides*, Hearings before the Subcommittee on Department Operations, Research and Foreign Agriculture, 98th Cong, 1st Sess, 1983, vol 2, p 143 (Statement of MR Hughes, Dy Asst Sec of State for Environment, Health and Natural Resources).

[70] *Ibid*, p 142.

[71] *Ibid*, vol 4, p 294 (Letter from J Blanchard, Acting Director, Office of Environment and Health, Dept of State, to CM Benbrook, Staff Director, Subcommittee on Department Operations, Research and Foreign Agriculture) (emphasis added).

[72] *Ibid*, vol 2, p 143 (Statement of MR Hughes).

[73] Kirkpatrick (1983), p 21.

[74] UN Doc A/C.2/37/SR.47, 1982, p 9.

[75] *Regulation of Pesticides*, above n 69, vol 4, p 295.

[76] *Ibid*.

[77] UN Doc A/C.2/37/SR.47, 1982, p 9. See also below for a further discussion of the definitional issues.

[78] *Ibid*, p 9.

It was obvious, however, that the US had quite a different view of the 'underlying principles' of the resolution than its Third World sponsors. While the US refrained from explicitly rejecting the principle of export controls and informed consent laid down in the first operative paragraph, its objections to some of the language of the resolution could be interpreted as implicitly dismissing the underlying notion that, in principle, products banned domestically should not be exported. Instead, US statements consistently emphasised the responsibility of the importing country and information exchange as the principal prescriptions of the resolution. For their part, however, the developing countries made it clear that they regarded export restrictions and the abolition of double standards as the fundamental principles. When introducing the resolution in committee, the representative of Venezuela said:

> The resolution acknowledged that the primary responsibility for consumer protection rested with each State. *Nevertheless, the countries producing those products*, which had taken steps to protect their own populations by prohibiting their consumption, use or sale within their own borders, *were called upon to cease their manufacture for export to other countries, particularly the developing countries.*[79]

It is probably the ambiguity of the term 'officially permitted' in the first operative paragraph[80] which led the US not to expressly oppose this paragraph, and enabled the member states of the EC and other producing countries to vote in favour of the resolution without really committing themselves. Legally speaking, what is not prohibited is permitted, and exporting countries would argue, as indeed some have, that where the use of a pesticide is not positively banned by law in the importing country, or even where the importing country has no legislation at all regarding pesticides, the product in question is 'officially permitted'[81] and may be exported under the terms of the resolution without any need for an official request from the government of the importing country. Besides, the resolution does not explicitly specify that the request should be made by a *governmental authority*;[82] thus, an order from a commercial importer could arguably be regarded as a 'request' within the meaning of the first operative paragraph.

Whatever its ambiguities, Resolution 37/137 increased the political pressure on governments of chemical-exporting countries and specialised international organisations to take measures to address the concerns first raised

[79] *Ibid*, p 4 (emphasis added).

[80] This ambiguity is also noted by Harland (1985), p 228.

[81] Harland's more optimistic interpretation, according to which the phrase 'officially permitted' 'appears to contemplate more than simply requiring that the sale of the product be lawful' and 'is presumably meant to refer to situations where the product is one which complies with registration provisions or a relevant safety standard in the importing country' (*ibid*) is certainly not the only plausible one.

[82] Although Harland reads the concept of 'request' as implying 'governmental involvement' (*ibid*, p 227) this is not obvious from the actual wording of the relevant clause.

by developing countries through UNEP a few years earlier. It established broad-based support in the international community for increased information exchange but also for some form of regulatory action based on the principles of prior informed consent and of shared responsibility of exporting countries. A specific measure directly called for by the resolution was the establishment by the UN secretariat of a 'consolidated list' of banned and severely restricted products. The practical implementation and significance of this initiative, designed to promote organised information exchange, will be further discussed below. But first I shall focus on the actual normative work, which was not pursued through the General Assembly but in other, more specialised fora. The organisation that took the lead in elaborating standards, long before UNEP was ready to move from statements of principle to practical questions of regulatory design, was a regional body, the Organization for Economic Co-operation and Development (OECD).

SEIZING THE INITIATIVE: THE OECD AS A VEHICLE FOR THE REGULATORY AGENDA OF THE INDUSTRIALISED COUNTRIES

In 1978, the OECD launched a Special Programme on the Control of Chemicals,[83] which became the main forum for international consultation and cooperation among Western industrialised nations on matters of chemical safety.[84] This programme, aimed at the improvement and harmonisation of the regulatory practices of the OECD member states, effectively functions as the primary channel of communication and coordination mechanism between the US, Europe and Japan on chemical regulatory issues. One of its main objectives is 'to prevent the creation of non-tarriff barriers to trade in chemicals.'[85]

It is no surprise, therefore, that the main chemical-producing and exporting countries chose the OECD as their preferred forum to address the issue of international trade in hazardous chemicals when it emerged on the international environmental policy agenda as a result of political pressure from Third World countries exerted through United Nations bodies. The OECD was the first intergovernmental organisation to consider the issue at the 'technical' level and to elaborate detailed, internationally agreed standards on information exchange and notification procedures. By taking the lead in this manner, the 'club' of Western industrialised nations was initially successful in pre-empting the development of more restrictive international

[83] OECD Council Decision C(78)127, 21 Sept 1978.

[84] On the activities of OECD in the field of chemicals regulation, see generally Schweitzer (1983). See also the OECD brochure *The OECD Chemicals Programme*, OECD, Paris, 1993.

[85] OECD Council Decision C(78)127, 21 Sept 1978, Art 1.

regulations in the framework of United Nations organisations with a majority constituency of developing countries.

The work of the OECD on the exchange of information relating to exports of hazardous chemicals was initiated within the framework of the then newly established Special Programme on the Control of Chemicals. In December 1979, the Management Committee of the Programme approved a project on 'Information Needs Associated with Exports of Chemicals' and appointed Canada as the 'lead country.'[86] In October 1980, based on a paper prepared by the lead country which identified export notification procedures as 'the key question' to be considered in the scope of the OECD project,[87] the Committee decided to set up an Expert Group on Information Exchange Related to the Export of Chemicals. In doing so, it 'took note' of the 'important' Decision 85 (V) of UNEP Governing Council of May 1977.[88] The Expert Group was mandated to prepare guidelines and to consider, among other subjects, '*the extent to which exporting countries can intervene* in the export of hazardous chemicals'[89] and 'the respective roles of government and industry in Member Countries in relation to such export.'[90]

Seminar on 'Control of Chemicals in Importing Countries'

In order to provide an opportunity for an exchange of views among the various parties concerned and some input into the work of the Expert Group, the OECD organised a seminar on 'Control of Chemicals in Importing Countries', which was hosted in Dubrovnik in April 1981 by the government of Yugoslavia, at that time an associate member of the OECD. The seminar was attended by representatives of most OECD member states, a number of developing countries, the chemical industry, and other international organisations such as the EC, UNEP and the FAO.[91] The title of the seminar was quite significant and indicative of the general thrust of the OECD's approach to the problem. It identifies the importing country as the primary locus of control and de-emphasises control of exports. During the seminar it was made clear that for all practical purposes 'importing countries' was synonymous with 'developing countries.'[92]

[86] OECD Doc ENV/CHEM/MC/79.M/2.

[87] OECD Doc ENV/CHEM/MC/80.8, 16 Sept 1980, p 1.

[88] Report of the 5th Meeting of the Management Committee, Paris, 22–23 Oct 1980, OECD Doc ENV/CHEM/MC/M/80.2, para 9. For UNEP Governing Council Dec 85 (V), see above n 14.

[89] OECD Doc ENV/CHEM/MC/M/80.2, para 10 (i) (emphasis added).

[90] *Ibid*, para 10 (iii).

[91] The proceedings of the seminar are published in *Control of Chemicals in Importing Countries*, OECD, Paris, 1982 (hereafter referred to as *Control of Chemicals*).

[92] *Ibid*, p 103.

One of the most striking features of the policy debate at this seminar was the notable difference in attitude between the European and American chemical industry representatives. The European industry view was articulated by a speaker from a German trade association, who said that the German chemical industry:

> views with increasing concern the attempts within the OECD as well as other international organisations such as the UN to subject the exportation of chemical products to further restrictions and thus . . . to distort it in an inadmissible way.[93]

He objected to any form of export control, including notification, alleging that

> the rigorous application of such a notification system would lead to an unimaginable new bureaucracy. The importing countries would be flooded with notifications that they would probably be unable to handle.[94]

He stressed that most problems resulted from misuse of chemicals and advocated training programmes to help importing countries.[95]

Another industry representative from the Netherlands also opposed export notification systems, evoking the spectre of 'burdensome extensive paperwork and time-consuming bureaucracy' and 'trade restrictions and protectionist measures'[96] and citing problems of confidentiality and the protection of intellectual property rights in the provision of information.[97] He emphasised direct transfer of information from the industry to users through proper labelling as the appropriate solution.[98] However, he was less adamant in his opposition to export notification than his German colleague and was reluctantly willing to accept it 'should such a system be considered absolutely indispensable', provided the notification requirement was limited to chemicals 'either legally banned or legally subject to very significant restrictions.'[99]

By contrast, the US chemical industry spokesman did not object to the notification systems already in force in the US, although he opposed any additional legislation[100] and laid great emphasis on the responsibility of governments for the lack of user education and training.[101] The US government representative, for his part, basically commended the existing export noti-

[93] B. Broecker, 'Specific Problems of Exported Chemicals', in *ibid* p 147.
[94] *Ibid*, p 149.
[95] *Ibid*, p 150.
[96] L De Reeder, 'Industry's Approach to the Control of Chemicals in Importing Countries', in *ibid*, p 123.
[97] *Ibid*, pp 127–28.
[98] *Ibid*, pp 125–26.
[99] *Ibid*, p 123.
[100] G Dominguez, 'Exportation of Hazardous Chemicals—A U.S. Chemical Industry Perspective', in *ibid*, p 142.
[101] *Ibid*, pp 143–144.

fication provisions of the FIFRA and other US statutes as a model for an international solution,[102] while the official delegate from Germany seemed willing to accept a notification system for 'the most serious cases', ie banned chemicals, on an experimental basis.

The seminar did not formulate precise recommendations, but rather produced a set of conclusions enumerating a number of factors for consideration by the Expert Group.[103] Those conclusions were rather ambiguous with regard to the concept of a notification system and the responsibilities of exporting countries. They did recognise that 'in view of the needs of importing countries, the flow of information on trade in specific chemicals between exporting and importing countries should be expanded.'[104] On the other hand, they echoed some of the industry arguments against export notification, noting that: 'Small and medium-sized countries may have very limited or no established mechanisms for dealing with such information'[105] and that 'Notifications of control actions are often misunderstood in other countries, leading to over-reaction or inconsistent action.'[106] Finally, labelling was presented as a form of information exchange on a par with export notification: 'Labelling is an effective means of providing information which can be put to immediate use in importing countries.'[107] The latter conclusion, which might give the impression that labelling was considered an adequate substitute for government-to-government notification, apparently reflects the views expressed by industry representatives.

Elaboration of Voluntary Guidelines on Information Exchange

The OECD approach to the issue of international trade in hazardous chemicals, as it emerged from this seminar and the subsequent work of the Expert Group, proceeds from an analysis of the respective responsibilities of exporting and importing countries. In a background paper prepared for the Expert Group, those responsibilities are described as 'complementary to each other' and 'difficult to demarcate . . . in legal terms.'[108] While the 'primary responsibility' is viewed as resting with importing countries, it is recognised that exporting countries have a 'complementary

[102] Bracken, 'Export Policy of a Producing Country', in *ibid*, p 158.

[103] The Expert Group itself pointed out in the report of its first meeting that it 'was not bound by all the conclusions of the Seminar, but that the conclusions provided useful guidance', in particular as to 'the needs of importing countries'. OECD Doc ENV/CHEM/MC/81.4, 21 May 1981, p 3, para 5.

[104] Conclusions of the Seminar, in *Control of Chemicals*, above n 91, p 16, para 7.

[105] *Ibid*, p 17, para 13.

[106] *Ibid*, p 20, para 32.

[107] *Ibid*, p 19, para 30.

[108] Unpublished, unnumbered OECD document on file with the author.

responsibility.'[109] Consequently, the Expert Group saw it as its task to develop appropriate mechanisms through which this complementary responsibility could be assumed.

In the background paper, various 'possible governmental responses'[110] to the export of hazardous chemicals were identified for consideration, ranging from controls on production or exports of specific hazardous chemicals to 'export advices to importing countries', possibly coupled with a requirement of 'import acceptance' on the part of authorities in the importing countries—the term 'prior informed consent' had not yet been coined—and the provision of additional information to those authorities upon request. The first set of 'draft principles' recommended that exporting countries 'should consider taking one or more' of those different possible measures.[111]

But although a range of regulatory options was thus initially explored, the Expert Group, favouring a restrictive reading of its mandate, made a clearcut political choice to focus on export notification procedures as the most appropriate response to the problem, following the example set by the United States. Notwithstanding the reference originally made to UNEP Governing Council Decision 85 (V) on its establishment, the Expert Group was adamant

> to make clear that the thrust of this project is to propose guidelines on *information exchange* which will give an importing country the opportunity to determine its need for action, *rather than to impose controls on exports*.[112]

The 'consent' portion of UNEP recommendations was thus quite deliberately ignored.

Most of the negotiations in the Expert Group revolved around two issues: the *procedural aspects* of notification and the *scope of application* of the notification requirements, ie the criteria for the selection of chemicals that should be subject to them. The group eventually agreed on a two-step information exchange process, applying to 'banned or severely restricted chemicals' and involving a one-time-only export notification and possible additional information to be supplied at the request of the importing country.[113] On this basis, it drew up 'Proposed Guiding Principles on Information Exchange Related to Export of Hazardous Chemicals,'[114] which were submitted to the OECD Council for adoption through the Management Group of the Chemicals Programme and the Environment

[109] Unpublished, unnumbered OECD document on file with the author.

[110] *Ibid.*

[111] *Ibid*, Annex IV, para 2.

[112] *Report of the Expert Group on Information Exchange Related to the Export of Hazardous Chemicals*, OECD Doc ENV/CHEM/MC/82.1, Aug 1982, p 4 (hereafter referred to as Expert Group Report) (emphasis added).

[113] *Ibid*, p 9, paras 25–27.

[114] *Ibid*, Annex 1.

Committee. The OECD's standard-setting work was completed in April 1984, when the Council formally adopted a recommendation based on the Expert Group's proposals, in which it:

> Recommends that if a chemical is exported which is banned or severely restricted in the exporting Member country, *information be provided* from that country to the importing country to enable the latter to make timely and informed decisions concerning that chemical.[115]

The recommendation further endorses the Guiding Principles elaborated by the experts and invites both the OECD member states and non-member countries to apply the procedure for information exchange set out in that document.

The OECD Guiding Principles on Information Exchange Related to Export of Hazardous Chemicals

The basic operative provisions of the OECD Guiding Principles are the following:

> If an export of a banned or severely restricted chemical occurs, the exporting Member country should ensure that necessary steps are taken to provide the importing country with relevant information so as to alert it to that fact. . . . The provision of such information to the importing country would be *on a one-time basis* when the first export following the control action in the exporting Member country occurs.[116]

It is further specified that the Guiding Principles 'apply to exports from one Member country to another as well as to exports to non-Member countries' of the OECD.[117] Considerable emphasis is laid on the fact that '*importing countries have the primary responsibility* for protection of health and the environment from risks associated with imports of chemicals which have been banned or severely restricted for use in the exporting countries'[118] and that the Guiding Principles 'do not deal with the control of export of such chemicals.'[119] In other words, as the OECD Secretary-General put it in an explanatory note to the organisation's Council, while the OECD

[115] Recommendation of the Council Concerning Information Exchange Related to Export of Banned or Severely Restricted Chemicals, OECD Doc C(84)37(Final), 4 Apr 1984, reprinted in 23 ILM 664 (1984) (emphasis added).

[116] Guiding Principles on Information Exchange Related to Export of Banned or Severely Restricted Chemicals, OECD Doc C(84)37(Final), 4 April 1984, Appendix, paras 5, 7, reprinted in 23 ILM 666 (1984) (emphasis added) (hereafter cited as OECD Guiding Principles).

[117] *Ibid*, para 2 (iii).

[118] *Ibid*, para 1 (emphasis added).

[119] *Ibid*, para 2 (i).

approach recognises that exporting countries have a responsibility to provide assistance to importing countries, it is also based on the assumption that such assistance 'should take the form of information and not of control of exports.'[120] To underscore this point, a clause which did not figure in the Expert Group's original draft was added to the final version of the Guiding Principles to emphasise 'that the procedures of the exporting country *should not be such as to delay or control the export*.'[121] As we will see below, this provision was later literally copied by UNEP in its Provisional Notification Scheme.

The Guiding Principles also accommodate other industry concerns aired at the Dubrovnik seminar and echoed by the Expert Group in its report. Thus, one clause recognises that

> the provision of information by the exporting Member country must take into account the protection of the confidentiality of data in the importing country and the protection of proprietary rights.[122]

Furthermore, the Guiding Principles contain a final provision which states:

> Any control measures applied to an imported chemical for which information has been received within the framework of the Guiding Principles should not be more restrictive than those applied to the same chemical produced domestically or imported from a country other than the one that supplied the information.[123]

The origin of this clause can be traced back to the alleged danger of 'protectionist measures' invoked by industry as an argument against export notification. The Expert Group considered this problem and

> recognized that the information could be used in the importing country to discriminate against imported chemicals or between chemicals from different exporting countries. It was the consensus that it should be clearly stated that information sent to an importing country should not be used in a manner which would be inconsistent with the General Agreement on Tariffs and Trade (GATT).[124]

Accordingly, the group proposed the inclusion of an explicit reference to the GATT in the Guiding Principles.[125] Though the language eventually adopted by the Council does not explicitly mention the GATT, the implicit reference to the principles of national treatment and most-favoured-nation treatment is plain enough.

Let us now examine the procedural aspects of the notification system recommended in the OECD Guiding Principles. First of all, it is clearly stipulated that export notification is to be provided 'on a one-time basis'.

120 OECD Doc C(84)37, 13 Mar 1984, p 2, para 6.
121 *Ibid*, para 5, *in fine* (emphasis added).
122 OECD Guiding Principles, para 9.
123 *Ibid*, para 13.
124 Expert Group Report, above n 112, p 13.
125 *Ibid*, p 18, para 9.

Although several members of the Expert Group had favoured more frequent notifications, eg on an annual basis, consensus could only be reached on a one-time notification which, however, 'would not preclude a more frequent information exchange if desired by the *exporting* country.'[126]

The information to be included in the export notification is minimal: the notice need only mention the identity of the chemical, the regulatory restrictions to which it is subject and 'the fact that an export is expected or about to occur.'[127] Indication of the reasons for the control action is optional, and the notification need not contain any further details which would be required for the importing country to take action to stop the import if it so desired. As the Expert Group's report points out, consensus could not be reached on the inclusion of such details:

> Several experts favoured the inclusion of the name and address of the exporter and importer, the quantity shipped and the proposed date of entry. Many experts stated that the [export notice] should be kept as simple as possible in order to make it workable and in view of resource implications and questions of confidentiality.[128]

The eventual compromise was that such details could be supplied as additional information at the request of the importing country and subject to the discretion of the exporting country.[129] This compromise is reflected in a clause which states that the additional information which could be requested comprises 'such information surrounding the circumstances of the export/import transaction *as may be agreed upon by the exporting and importing countries*.'[130]

Perhaps the most significant procedural provision is that which states that the Guiding Principles 'may be implemented by countries through public *or private* entities designated or authorized by them to do so.'[131] This clause must be seen in the context of the Expert Group's statement that 'the proposed guiding principles are designed to be flexible, cost-effective and *to keep any governmental involvement to the minimum*.'[132] It appears that, in response to French and British objections to government involvement in the information exchange process, the Guiding Principles were deliberately drafted in a flexible way so as to allow governments to delegate their responsibilities to industry:

> There was considerable discussion of the extent to which a government regulatory agency should be involved in the information exchange. It was the consensus that

126 Expert Group Report, above n 112, p 12 (emphasis added).
127 OECD Guiding Principles, para 6.
128 Expert Group Report, above n 112, p 10.
129 *Ibid*, p 13.
130 OECD Guiding Principles, para 10 (ii) (emphasis added).
131 *Ibid*, para 2 (iv) (emphasis added).
132 Expert Group Report, above n 112, p 12 (emphasis added).

the government in each exporting country would determine how the [export notice] should be sent to the importing country.[133]

This understanding was made explicit in a preliminary statement to the proposed Guiding Principles, which was not reproduced in the final version adopted by the Council but instead replaced by the more ambiguous clause cited above. According to this statement,

[the] terms 'exporting country' and 'importing country' are *not intended to refer exclusively to the government* of the exporting country or the importing country but may refer to non-governmental organisations in either.[134]

The exporter may thus be entrusted with the issuance of the export notice,[135] and the importer may be the recipient, unless the importing country officially designates some governmental agency as the entity to which export notifications must be addressed. Practically speaking, this means, for example, that Germany would be in compliance with the Guiding Principles if Bayer notified its own subsidiary in Peru that an insecticide being exported to Peru to be marketed locally by the subsidiary is banned by German law.

The scope of application of the OECD scheme is carefully circumscribed. The Guiding Principles apply to 'banned or severely restricted chemicals', which are defined as

any chemical that is the subject of a control action taken by a competent authority in the exporting Member country:

i) to ban or severely restrict the use or handling of the chemical in order to protect human health or environment domestically; or

ii) to refuse a required authorisation for a proposed first time use based upon a decision in the exporting Member country that such use would endanger human health or the environment.[136]

There was extensive discussion in the Expert Group on the scope of the Guiding Principles and the definition of 'banned or severely restricted chemicals'. Several experts favoured a broader definition, which would have included all unapproved chemicals, even where there had been no affirmative denial of registration, while others wanted a more specific definition. Eventually, the above compromise definition was agreed, on the grounds that 'it would be impractical (if not impossible) to arrive at a precise or scientific definition' and that 'a broad definition is necessary' to give effect to

[133] Expert Group Report, above n 112, p 11.
[134] *Ibid*, p 16 (emphasis added).
[135] *Ibid*, p 11.
[136] OECD Guiding Principles, para 3.

the 'underlying principle' of the Guiding Principles.[137] However, in his note to the Council recommending adoption of the Guiding Principles, the Secretary-General of the OECD, as if to reassure member governments, candidly noted that 'the number of chemicals banned or severely restricted in Member countries is small relative to the total number of chemicals subject to national regulation'[138] and stressed that 'Member countries would exercise discretion' with respect to the scope of the notification system through their 'interpretation of the phrase "banned or severely restricted" . . . within the framework of national law and administrative practice.'[139] He also pointed out that the proposed definition did not cover chemicals voluntarily withdrawn from the market or produced solely for export.[140]

Through the early elaboration of its 'Guiding Principles on Information Exchange Related to Export of Banned or Severely Restricted Chemicals', which were ready in draft form in March 1982, ie before either UNEP or the FAO had even formally decided to elaborate instruments of their own, the OECD exerted a decisive influence on the subsequent regulatory efforts of both these organisations. By first circumscribing the notion of 'banned or severely restricted chemicals', promoting notification procedures as the most adequate response to the problems arising from international trade in such chemicals, and delegitimating alternative approaches such as export control measures, the OECD and its membership effectively managed, at least initially, to dictate the terms and limit the scope of the international policy debate in other intergovernmental organisations, as appears from the rest of this chapter.

UNEP PROVISIONAL NOTIFICATION SCHEME: THE FIRST STAGE IN THE DEVELOPMENT OF SOFT LAW AT THE GLOBAL LEVEL

The '*Ad Hoc* Working Group of Experts for the Exchange of Information on Potentially Harmful Chemicals (in Particular Pesticides) in International Trade,'[141] established by UNEP Governing Council in 1982, did not actually meet before March 1984, when the substantive work of the OECD on the same issue was already completed. At its first meeting, held in

[137] Expert Group Report, above n 112, p 7. It is interesting to note that the United States did not object to the use of the terms 'banned or severely restricted' in the OECD Guiding Principles, whereas it found those same terms 'vague' and 'ambiguous' when used in UN resolutions.

[138] OECD Doc C(84)37, 13 Mar 1984, p 2, para 9.

[139] *Ibid*, para 10.

[140] *Ibid*, p 3, para 11.

[141] The group was originally named '*Ad Hoc* Working Group for the Exchange of Information on Trade and Management of Potentially Harmful Chemicals (in Particular Pesticides) in International Trade', but was later renamed.

Noordwijkerhout in the Netherlands, the working group had before it 'Draft Guidelines for the Exchange of Information on Trade and Management of Potentially Harmful Chemicals in Particular Pesticides', prepared by UNEP Secretariat.[142] These draft guidelines consisted of a set of 'legal elements', which were 'presented as an annotated checklist of basic provisions rather than a comprehensive draft agreement.'[143]

According to the Secretariat, the proposed guidelines were to fulfil a purpose quite different from that of the proposed International Code of Conduct on the Distribution and Use of Pesticides, which was under development within the framework of the FAO at the same time, as we shall see below. The key difference was the draft guidelines' 'emphasis on improved information exchanges between Governments' and the fact that they were 'addressed to Governments rather than to manufacturers or users.'[144] UNEP conceded that voluntary codes of conduct may 'serve a useful complementary function'[145] but it dismissed them as insufficient on the grounds that they did not 'meet the specific requirements of mandatory information exchange as postulated by UNEP Governing Council.'[146]

The draft guidelines essentially reflected the principles of the 1978 Governing Council decision[147] and further elaborated on them. They provided for a general obligation for states to exchange information on regulatory measures relating to 'potentially harmful chemical products', as well as relevant scientific and technical information concerning their management.[148] In addition, a specific obligation to notify 'designated national authorities' in importing countries of exports of 'banned or severely restricted chemical products' was proposed.[149] Such exports were to be subject to 'prior authorization', which would be conditional on export notification.[150] Such notification should contain a 'summary of regulatory restrictions in use' in the country of export and the reasons for such restrictions, as well as precautionary information and details permitting the identification of the shipment.[151] Chemicals not registered for use in the exporting country, though not subject to notification, were to be labelled as 'not registered for use in country of origin.'[152] Finally, all 'potentially harmful chemical products' destined for export were to be subject to packaging and labelling standards 'no less stringent' than those applicable in the exporting country.[153]

[142] Draft Guidelines, above n 23.
[143] *Ibid*, p 5.
[144] *Ibid*, p 9.
[145] *Ibid.*
[146] *Ibid.*
[147] UNEP Governing Council Dec 6/4, above n 16.
[148] Draft Guidelines, above n 23, para 3 (a).
[149] *Ibid*, paras 3(c), 9(b).
[150] *Ibid*, para 9(a)–(b).
[151] *Ibid*, para 10(b)(vii), (ix).
[152] *Ibid*, para 8.
[153] *Ibid*, para 7.

From Export Authorisation to Mere Information Exchange

The most controversial aspect of the draft guidelines, not surprisingly, was the export authorisation requirement. In its commentary to the guidelines, UNEP Secretariat had made a strong case for this system:

> Considering the potential health and environmental risks created by exports in other States . . . and considering the international responsibility of States for such risks . . . , *a system of mandatory export authorizations should be introduced at the national level*, at least for those products which are subject to total bans or severe restrictions within the country of export and hence are known to present risks to human health or the environment. This is not a new procedure, and there are a number of precedents for the requirement of export permits regarding other products in the interest of national public policy.'[154]

The commentary also stressed that more restrictive options were 'conceivable', including a requirement of express consent, and argued that the guidelines were really a moderate solution

> which would ensure mandatory notification of the country of destination without imposing a trade ban, thus leaving it up to the country of destination to follow up with trade controls if required.[155]

The Secretariat went out of its way to reassure industrialised countries that the guidelines were not intended to impede international trade:

> The secretariat explained that UNEP was not a regulatory body, and had no intention of seeking to regulate international trade. The objective of the draft guidelines was to establish a mandatory linkage between exports of chemicals and the provision of information thereon, not to institute a trade control mechanism.[156]

The commentary even stated that one of the aims of the guidelines was

> *to facilitate international trade*, to avoid the risk of conflicting and/or excessive restrictions due to a legitimate concern of Governments to protect their national environmental and health interests.[157]

Yet even the minor element of trade control in the proposed mandatory notification system was unacceptable to the representatives[158] of exporting countries and manufacturers at the working group meeting. According to the industry observer 'the emphasis in the draft guidelines on mandatory import and export controls was incompatible with information exchange,

154 *Ibid*, p 18 (emphasis added).
155 *Ibid*, p 19.
156 *Ad Hoc* Working Group of Experts for the Exchange of Information on Potentially Harmful Chemicals (in Particular Pesticides) in International Trade, Report of the First Session, UN Doc UNEP/WG.96/5, 2 May 1984, p 6 (hereinafter cited as Working Group Report).
157 Draft Guidelines, above n 23, p 6 (emphasis added).
158 Although the Working Group formally was composed of 'government experts participating in their personal capacity' it is clear that they all spoke on behalf of their governments.

and could lead to unwarranted disruption of trade'.[159] A number of government experts 'questioned the appropriateness of export authorization'[160] and warned of 'the potential problems of practical implementation if notification always had to be sent prior to import.'[161] Some experts even proposed dropping the export-specific notification requirement altogether.[162]

On the other hand, Third World representatives were equally unhappy with the draft guidelines, which they saw as reflecting too great a laissez-faire approach: 'Some experts from developing countries were of the view that the guidelines should not be confined to information exchange; *an element of trade regulation was also required*.'[163] They proposed to strengthen the guidelines by adding a provision requiring the express consent of the importing country but met with strong opposition.[164]

As no agreement could be reached on the draft guidelines as proposed by the Secretariat, an industrialised country representative tabled revised draft guidelines largely modelled on, and partly even literally copied from, the draft OECD Guiding Principles on Information Exchange Related to Export of Banned and Severely Restricted Chemicals, themselves largely inspired by existing US legislation, which 'the Working Group agreed to take as the basis of its further consideration.'[165] By this move, the OECD countries effectively managed to dictate the terms of the negotiation and to limit its scope. The revised draft guidelines considerably watered down the notification requirement, by introducing a two-tier notification system: 'notification of control action', ie general notice to all countries of regulatory measures taken, unrelated to any particular export, and a one-time 'notification of export', ie export-specific notification to the importing country at the time of the first export of a particular banned or severely restricted chemical to that country.

The Provisional Notification Scheme as an Interim Solution

Faced with persistent disagreement, the OECD countries made another smart procedural move:

'The representative of EEC, supported by other experts, noted a wide measure of consensus on the objectives of revised draft guidelines 9 and 10 [ie those dealing

159 Working Group Report, above n 156, at p 5.
160 *Ibid*, p 10.
161 *Ibid*, p 11.
162 *Ibid*.
163 *Ibid*, p 3 (emphasis added).
164 *Ibid*, p 11.
165 *Ibid*, p 10.

with notification requirements], and suggested the early implementation of those objectives *as a first step*.[166]

This proposal eventually led to the adoption of a 'Provisional Notification Scheme,'[167] reflecting the minimal consensus, and to the deferral of the resolution of outstanding substantive issues. No final version of the guidelines was formally agreed by the meeting, but instead the Secretariat was requested to

ensure the preparation of revised draft guidelines, in the light of the comments and discussions during the first session of the Working Group, and on the basis of those elements on which consensus has been reached.[168]

For all its 'provisionality', the Provisional Notification Scheme seemed quite likely to predetermine the ultimate outcome of the negotiations by precluding other options. The proponents of the Provisional Notification Scheme obviously hoped that, by the time the *Ad Hoc* Working Group would reconvene to finalise the guidelines, the scheme would be so firmly established that alternative solutions would have become almost unthinkable. Thus, the 'provisional' scheme was clearly intended to become definitive.

The negotiating success achieved by the OECD countries appears from a comparative analysis of the key provisions of the Provisional Notification Scheme with the corresponding provisions of the original draft guidelines. These were the following:

(a) Exports or re-exports of banned or severely restricted chemical products should be subject to *prior authorization by the competent authorities of the country of export*.
(b) Authorization to export or re-export banned or severely restricted chemical products *should not be granted unless* due notification has been given to the designated national authority of the country or countries of destination.[169]

The Provisional Notification Scheme reduced the notification requirement to its most elementary form. The relevant provision reads as follows:

If an export or re-export of a banned or severely restricted chemical occurs, the country of export should ensure that necessary steps are taken to provide the designated national authority of the country of import with relevant information.[170]

It is noteworthy that the Provisional Notification Scheme even avoids the use of the term 'notification' with regard to exports.[171] In the first draft of

[166] *Ibid*, p 11 (emphasis added).
[167] Provisional Notification Scheme for Banned and Severely Restricted Chemicals, UN Doc UNEP/WG.96/5, 2 May 1984, Annex (hereafter referred to as Provisional Notification Scheme).
[168] Working Group Report, above n 156, p 14.
[169] Draft Guidelines, above n 23, para 9(a)–(b) (emphasis added).
[170] Provisional Notification Scheme, para 4(a).
[171] Cf the semantic argument in the European Parliament, see below ch 15.

the scheme prepared by the Secretariat, the section in question was entitled 'Notification of export,'[172] but the working group changed this title to 'Information regarding export,'[173] which sounds less formal and mandatory. The report of the working group openly acknowledges that 'the terminology was brought into line with the draft "guiding principles" of OECD.'[174] Even more significant is another amendment to the Secretariat's draft, apparently made to dispel any lingering fear of disguised export controls:

> It is the intention that, *so far as possible*, the information should be provided prior to export, but it is recognized that this may not always be possible, and that the procedures of the country of export *should not be such as to delay or control the export.*[175]

This language was taken verbatim from the OECD Guiding Principles.

The Provisional Notification Scheme also considerably restricted the range of information to be provided to the importing country. Whereas the original draft guidelines contained detailed provisions concerning the contents of the notification (which were to include, inter alia, the name and address of exporter and importer, expected date and mode of shipment, quantities to be shipped, intended use), the 'minimum information' required under the Provisional Notification Scheme merely consists of

> (i) A copy of, or reference to, the information provided at the time of the notification of control action;
> (ii) Indication that an export of the chemical concerned is expected or about to occur.[176]

The information provided at the time of the control action is meant to include the chemical identification of the product, the regulatory restrictions to which it is subject and the reasons for them.[177] However, if it only refers to an earlier notification of control action, the actual export notification is not likely to be very effective, since the relevant information may have been transmitted years before the export. In any event, the notification would not provide any of the information that would be necessary to enable the importing country to intercept the shipment.

The labelling and packaging provisions of the draft guidelines turned out not to be quite as controversial as those on notification. In its commentary on the draft guidelines, UNEP Secretariat had made a strong plea for making national standards applicable to exports:

[172] UN Doc UNEP/WG.96/L.1/Add.2, 29 Mar 1984, Annex, p 2.
[173] UN Doc UNEP/WG.96/5, 2 May 1984, Annex, p 2.
[174] *Ibid*, p 14.
[175] *Ibid*, Annex, p 2 (emphasis added).
[176] Provisional Notification Scheme, para 4(c) (emphasis added).
[177] *Ibid*, para 3(c).

[A] number of exporting countries, as well as the European Economic Community . . . currently apply *'double standards'*, whereby products intended for export to third countries are exempt from stricter provisions applicable to locally marketed products. In view of the environmental risks of global transfer and the special risks for developing countries, *such double standards are difficult to justify*. While importing countries may indeed impose their own standards of classification, packaging and labelling, they should be considered as additional requirements and not as a reason to drop any stricter domestic standards of the country or region of export.[178]

At the Noordwijkerhout meeting, this provoked some controversy. One expert, apparently irritated by the use of the term 'double standards' and the implied moral stigma, argued that:

the fact that chemicals were regulated for national use, but not for export, was not a double standard, but a recognition of international legal practice and of the right of importers to establish their own standards.[179]

Obviously, there was also industry opposition to the proposed labelling and packaging standard, which was alleged to be 'unworkable in practice,'[180] while another government expert wished to have it 'clearly stated that the classification, labelling and packaging should be governed mainly by the legislation of the importing country.'[181] Notwithstanding these reservations, the Secretariat proposal was not rejected altogether, though it was not included in the Provisional Notification Scheme, which only covered notification procedures. The Secretariat maintained its proposal on labelling standards in the revised draft guidelines which it issued in November 1984 as a basis for further discussion in the *Ad Hoc* Working Group following the adoption of the Provisional Notification Scheme by UNEP Governing Council.[182]

Despite the express mandate given by the Governing Council, experts from a number of countries initially suggested that pesticides should be excluded from the scope of the guidelines, since they properly belonged in the domain of the FAO.[183] They argued that UNEP should not interfere with the ongoing elaboration, by the FAO, of a voluntary code of conduct on pesticides, 'which would deal more comprehensively with all aspects of the issue.'[184] These reservations led to a reference in the draft report of the

[178] Draft Guidelines, above n 23, p 16 (emphasis added).
[179] UN Doc UNEP/WG.96/5, 2 May 1984, p 10.
[180] *Ibid*, p 5.
[181] *Ibid*, p 9.
[182] The proposal was reformulated in the following terms: 'States should ensure that potentially harmful chemicals exported or re-exported from their territories are subject to no less stringent requirements of classification, packaging and labelling than comparable products destined for use in the country of export.' Revised Draft Guidelines for the Exchange of Information on Potentially Harmful Chemicals in International Trade, Text prepared by UNEP Secretariat, UN Doc UNEP/WG.112/3, 23 Nov 1984, p 6, para 7(b).
[183] Working Group Report, above n 156, pp 3, 5, 11 and 13.
[184] *Ibid*, p 3.

meeting to the need for the working group 'to reconsider its mandate with regard to specific categories of chemicals' at the next meeting.[185] However, this reference was deleted from the final report, as the OECD countries probably did not feel it necessary to pursue the point when it turned out that the guidelines would be even less restrictive than the latest draft of the FAO code. It was agreed that pesticides would remain within the scope of the guidelines 'for the moment.'[186]

At its 12th meeting in May 1984, UNEP Governing Council formally adopted the Provisional Notification Scheme and 'call[ed] upon all Governments and the Executive Director to take the necessary steps to bring the Scheme into effect as soon as possible.'[187] One government would have preferred the Governing Council simply to 'take note' of the Provisional Notification Scheme, rather than formally adopting it.[188] But several other countries expressed support for the immediate adoption of the Scheme, and one was so satisfied that it recommended that the Scheme be 'adopted without further initiatives', thereby concluding UNEP's work on the subject.[189] However, the Council did not accept the latter proposal, but instead mandated the *Ad Hoc* Working Group to continue its work with a view to the eventual adoption of more comprehensive guidelines by the Governing Council.[190] At Noordwijkerhout, the working group had considered that the question of a convention, as originally contemplated in the Montevideo Programme, was 'premature' and 'not within [its] mandate' and 'should be left to the Governing Council.'[191] However, the prospect of a convention was not given any consideration by the 1984 session of the Council either and seemed put off to a distant and uncertain future.

By settling for the weak compromise of the Provisional Notification Scheme, the Third World had gained nothing—since the scheme only reflected what the exporting countries had already unilaterally committed themselves to in the framework of the OECD—and lost the political momentum created by the earlier resolutions of the Governing Council and the General Assembly, whose strong principles were superseded by the virtually meaningless provisions of the Provisional Notification Scheme.

Referring to UN General Assembly Resolution 37/137, the representative of the UNCTC at the *Ad Hoc* Working Group meeting in the Netherlands had, in vain, made a strong plea for consistency:

[185] UN Doc UNEP/WG.96/L.1/Add.1, 29 Mar 1984, p 6.
[186] Working Group Report, above n 156, p 4.
[187] UNEP Governing Council Dec 12/14, pt II, para 5, UN Doc UNEP/GC.12/19, 1984, Annex I, p 26.
[188] *Ibid*, p 13.
[189] *Ibid*, p 54.
[190] UNEP Governing Council Dec 12/14, above n 187, pt II, para 2.
[191] Working Group Report, above n 156, p 12.

Those General Assembly resolutions constituted an important initiative at the international level, and the guidelines should consequently be elaborated within the principles and structures agreed upon by the Assembly.[192]

The working group, however, clearly ignored the principle of informed consent established in the General Assembly resolution and opted for the least restrictive solution of one-time notification without export controls. It is quite surprising therefore that the Secretary-General of the United Nations, in a 1984 report to the General Assembly, stated that the Provisional Notification Scheme 'represents an important step towards the harmonization of positions' in regard to the responsibilities of the exporting countries.[193] Rather than 'harmonizing' conflicting positions, 'more restrictive' versus 'less restrictive,'[194] UNEP had in fact completely espoused the latter and dismissed the former. Through UNEP, the OECD countries had gained unqualified Third World endorsement for their minimal notification system. In this instance, UNEP obviously functioned as 'an extension arm to the developing countries for OECD deliberations', to quote the words of a former EPA official.[195] The pre-empting of the global regulatory debate in UNEP by the OECD initiative was paralleled by similar developments in the second specialised organisation that addressed the issue at the universal level, albeit from a somewhat different angle, the Food and Agricultural Organization of the United Nations (FAO).

THE FAO INTERNATIONAL CODE OF CONDUCT ON THE DISTRIBUTION AND USE OF PESTICIDES

The FAO and Pesticides: Some Background

In order to put our analysis of the FAO's role in the development of international pesticides regulation in the proper perspective, it is useful to take a brief look at this agency's overall policy with respect to agricultural development in general and to chemical pest control in particular. Indeed, this determined the context in which the FAO came to address the regulatory issues related to international trade in pesticides.

The FAO is the intergovernmental organisation with the longest-standing institutional interest in pesticides. In accordance with the organisation's constitutional mandate to promote 'the adoption of improved methods of agricultural production,'[196] the FAO Plant Protection Service has

[192] *Ibid*, p 5.
[193] UN Doc A/39/290, 18 June 1984, p 34.
[194] *Ibid.*
[195] Schweitzer (1983), p 41.
[196] Constitution of the Food and Agriculture Organization of the United Nations, Art I, para 2(c).

long been involved in promoting pesticide use in the Third World, as part of the overall 'Green Revolution' package of modern agricultural methods to increase agricultural productivity. FAO technical assistance has been instrumental in the introduction and expansion of chemical pest control in many developing countries, thus opening up the Third World as a major growth market for the agrochemical industry.

It should always be borne in mind, therefore, that the FAO's concern with the health and environmental effects of pesticides and the regulation and control of pesticide use is only incidental to its priority objective of increasing agricultural production.[197] The interest of the FAO in problems resulting from disparities in national regulation of pesticides and the development of international standards is relatively recent and, ironically, largely industry-inspired. As we shall see below, industry influence was instrumental in shaping the FAO's early policy agenda in the field of pesticides regulation. It is not surprising therefore that the FAO has, as one commentator put it, 'usually been the international agency within the UN grouping least distrusted by industry.'[198]

The close association of the FAO with multinational agribusiness has been the subject of much controversy in the past. The heyday of the FAO-industry relationship was in the late 60s and early 70s, when a liaison unit staffed by agribusiness executives was set up within the FAO Secretariat to promote industry involvement in FAO-sponsored agricultural development projects and other forms of collaboration between the UN system and the private sector. This unit, the Industry Cooperative Programme (ICP), functioned as 'a link, through the FAO, between multinational agribusiness firms and developing countries,'[199] which led critics to denounce the FAO as an 'industry broker.'[200] As a result of such criticism,[201] the FAO's privileged relationship with industry eventually became a political liability for the organisation and in 1978 the Director General of the FAO decided to terminate the ICP.[202]

Although the ICP was no longer in existence at the time the FAO decided to elaborate an international code of conduct as its response to the problems associated with the marketing and use of hazardous pesticides in developing countries, the agrochemical industry, through the early work of the ICP, has had a lasting influence in determining the overall direction and phi-

[197] For a quasi-official statement of the FAO policy and activities with regard to pesticides, see Bates (1982). For a general analysis and critique of the FAO pesticides policy, see Dinham (1991). For a critique of FAO pest eradication projects in Africa, see Linear (1985), ch 4.

[198] Boardman (1986), p 103. See also Paarlberg (1993), p 319, who notes that, in the international regulatory debate, 'FAO's sympathies were clearly with industry'.

[199] Solomon (1977), p 71.

[200] Weir & Shapiro (1981), p 52.

[201] The most articulate and well-known indictment of the FAO-industry cooperation, which provoked the political controversy, is to be found in George (1976), ch 9.

[202] *Ibid*, p 214.

losophy of the FAO's pesticides policy. A brief historical account of the ICP activities in the 1970s is therefore relevant as a background to a proper analysis and understanding of the FAO regulatory policy. It should also be noted that, notwithstanding the demise of the ICP, the pesticides industry continues to participate actively in FAO meetings as an observer, through its global trade association, the Global Crop Protection Federation (GCPF), previously known as the International Group of National Associations of Manufacturers of Agrochemical Products (GIFAP).

The activities of the ICP cannot be more aptly described than by quoting the words of one of its apologists:

> The ICP is a unique effort intended to *bring multinational business inside the United Nations system*, specifically the FAO, with the primary objective of stimulating agro-industrial expansion in the developing world. . . . *Multinational business uses the ICP as a lobbying organization to gain access for industry's positions and ideas in the world political system.* The prime focus of this type of activity, which began in 1972 at the United Nations Conference on the Human Environment, has been on the pesticides industry.[203]

A few examples suffice to illustrate the influence the agrochemical industry was able to exert on the policy of governments and international organisations through the ICP. At the Stockholm Conference in 1972, the ICP distributed industry propaganda on pesticides in the form of an official FAO document.[204] The FAO country representatives in the Third World have provided free advice and assistance to the ICP's corporate members, alerting them to business opportunities.[205] Industry staff have worked as advisers in FAO pest control projects.[206] The ICP Pesticides Working Group, in cooperation with the FAO Plant Protection Service, has organised training seminars 'on the safe and efficient use of pesticides in agriculture and public health' for government officials in developing countries of Africa, Asia and Latin America.[207] According to the above-quoted advocate of the ICP:

> The seminars have stimulated countries to seek FAO technical assistance and increase their pesticide programs. National representatives, after being informed of the work done by industry prior to marketing a product, became more appreciative of the need to reach a balance appropriate to developmental priorities between the need for pesticide use and the desire to avoid possible environmental dangers.[208]

[203] Solomon (1977), pp 71, 72, 74 (emphasis added).

[204] *Ibid*, p 75.

[205] *Ibid*, p 73.

[206] In Tanzania, for example, the German chemical company Hoechst was put in charge of supervising a FAO spraying programme. Weir & Shapiro (1981), p 53.

[207] *Ibid*, p 79. See also George (1976), p 224, noting that these seminars provided the ICP member companies with an 'opportunity to push their products with governments.' Paradoxically, this leading critic of ICP also refers to its Pesticides Working Group as one of the few 'positive aspects' of the programme. *Ibid*, p 221.

[208] Solomon (1977), p 80.

In addition to its participation in such technical assistance and training projects, the ICP was instrumental in setting the agenda for the FAO's initial involvement in the area of pesticides regulation. At the 1974 World Food Conference, the ICP engineered a major lobbying effort to gain international recognition of pesticides as an essential tool in the struggle against hunger and governmental endorsement of the agrochemical industry's international legislative agenda. Evoking the spectre of a shortage of pesticides in developing countries, the Conference adopted a resolution drafted with the 'assistance' of industry representatives,[209] in which it called on the FAO 'to convene on an urgent basis an *ad hoc* consultation, including member governments *and industry*' to consider, inter alia, 'the standardization of regulatory procedures and environmental rules' for pesticides.[210] Disparities in national regulation were perceived as an obstacle to increasing pesticide production and use. As Boardman notes, the 'moves towards greater harmonisation of the registration schemes for pesticides' initiated at the World Food Conference 'were to rest on assumptions of their value and benefits rather than of their hazards.'[211]

The World Food Conference resolution set the 'intellectual framework' for and determined the direction of the ensuing FAO activities on international regulation of pesticides.[212] Pursuant to this resolution, the FAO convened the *Ad Hoc* Government Consultation on Pesticides in Agriculture and Public Health, which met in Rome in April 1975, hardly half a year after the World Food Conference.[213] The ICP and the GIFAP coordinated the active industry presence at the conference and some of their representatives served as chairmen and rapporteurs of subcommittees.[214] The meeting, in its resolutions, acknowledged 'the need for a continuing flow of pesticides'[215] (*sic*) and recognised that the divergence in national registration requirements 'may increase the cost of new pesticides and inhibit the development or limit the availability of critically needed pest control materials.'[216] To keep the pesticides 'flowing', it recommended that the FAO call another consultation 'to analyze and discuss the basis for harmonizing the requirements for registration of pesticides in different countries.'[217] The resolution also stressed that 'representatives of the pesticides industry . . . should be encouraged to attend and participate'.

209 Solomon (1977), p 76.

210 Res X, Report of the World Food Conference, UN Doc E/CONF.65/20, 1974, pp 11–12 (emphasis added).

211 Boardman (1986), p 104.

212 *Ibid*, p 103. See generally *ibid*, pp 103–09 and Cockerill (1979), pp 119–25.

213 'Consultations' may be convened by the Conference, Council or Director-General of FAO under Art VI, para 5 of the FAO Constitution.

214 Solomon (1977), p 77.

215 Res XIII, Report of the Ad Hoc Government Consultation on Pesticides in Agriculture and Public Health, FAO Doc 1975/M/3, p 3.

216 Res XII, *ibid*, p 2.

217 *Ibid.*

Early FAO Work on the Harmonisation of Pesticide Registration Requirements

The recommendations of the 1975 meeting were endorsed by the FAO Council and Conference, and the proposed *Ad Hoc* Government Consultation on International Standardization of Pesticide Registration Requirements was accordingly held in Rome in October 1977. This meeting was prepared by a special Group of Experts on Pesticide Registration Requirements and also received direct input from industry in the form of proposals submitted by the GIFAP in an official background paper.[218] It was made clear at the outset that the development of international standards would be aimed at harmonisation, rather than unification of national regulations.[219] As an FAO officer put it:

> The risk/benefit judgement involved in pesticide registration may differ from country to country and it would be wrong to establish the same value judgement for the use of a pesticide for *all* countries. Thus there cannot be harmonization of registration itself but only harmonization of the requirements for registration, as recognized by FAO in its programme. . . . Developed countries should avoid imposing their value judgements on other countries and if at all possible, while working out their judgements, bear in mind the consequences of such judgements beyond their national boundaries.[220]

It is thus clear that the main goal of the FAO's early work on the harmonisation of pesticide registration requirements was not to achieve the highest possible international standards for the protection of human health and the environment, but rather to facilitate the penetration of the multinational agrochemical industry into national markets by removing technical barriers to trade. As the conference report states: 'A major objective of the Consultation was *to reduce costs of agricultural production* through harmonizing and *simplifying* the requirements of pesticide registration.'[221]

Industry's main concerns were the harmonisation of pesticide testing methods, to ensure that test results from one country would be accepted for registration in another,[222] and the international protection of the confidentiality of proprietary data submitted for registration, to avoid

[218] GIFAP Submission to FAO for the Ad Hoc Government Consultation on Pesticides in Agriculture and Public Health, FAO Doc AGP:PRR/77/BP.9, 1977; see also Cockerill (1977), pp 120–21.

[219] *Report of the Ad Hoc Government Consultation on International Standardization of Pesticide Registration Requirements*, FAO Doc AGP:1977/M/9, p 3

[220] Bates (1982), p 97 (emphasis in original).

[221] *Report of the Ad Hoc Government Consultation on International Standardization of Pesticide Registration Requirements*, FAO Doc AGP:1977/M/9, p 28 (emphasis added).

[222] Cockerill (1979), p 120.

competitive use of such data by other registrants.[223] The GIFAP was largely successful in implementing its agenda. The Government Consultation recommended the elaboration of guidelines on pesticide evaluation methods by an expert panel, specifically for the evaluation of environmental hazards,[224] and also recommended that another expert group be set up

to investigate ways and means of reconciling the public interest in data submitted to registration authorities . . . with the manufacturers' interest in having some of the information treated as confidential.[225]

Finally, the meeting called for the harmonisation of labelling requirements and proposed the development of 'Guidelines on Good Labelling Practice.'[226]

However, the 1977 Government Consultation did not consider the problem of international trade and information exchange on regulatory measures as such. The report merely notes that some developing countries

have delayed taking action towards registration, with the result that they experience a high incidence of accidental poisoning due to the general availability of highly toxic compounds, mostly without proper labelling and warning notices.[227]

Towards a Code of Conduct: the FAO Response to the Hazardous Exports Issue

A Second Government Consultation on International Harmonization of Pesticide Registration Requirements was held in October 1982 to review the progress achieved since the 1977 meeting. At that time, the export issue had aroused such international public and political concern that it could no longer be ignored, even by the FAO. Moreover, the question was being debated in other international organisations and the FAO probably feared that its position as the 'lead agency' in the field of pesticides would be threatened if it did not act. Addressing an OECD seminar in April 1981, an FAO plant protection officer had already suggested as much:

FAO has expressed concern about the large number of organizations involving themselves directly or indirectly in the subject of pesticides registration. Apart from duplication of effort . . . there is always a risk of conflicting recommendations. . . . What is most urgently needed is an effort to clearly identify and define the role and con-

[223] *Report of the Ad Hoc Government Consultation on International Standardization of Pesticide Registration Requirements*, FAO Doc AGP:1977/M/9, p 4 (Statement of the Director-General of GIFAP).
[224] *Ibid*, p 12 (Res II), 20 (Res V).
[225] *Ibid*, p 32.
[226] *Ibid*, p 24–26 (Res VI).
[227] *Ibid*, p 28.

tribution of each organisation in this subject and to improve the cooperation between those concerned.[228]

The FAO Group of Experts on Pesticide Registration Requirements, which met in May 1982 to prepare the subsequent Government Consultation, discussed the question of control of exports of pesticides and 'was of the opinion that this subject might best be dealt with by the preparation of a Code of Practice.'[229] Initially, the idea of a voluntary code of conduct for the pesticides industry was apparently conceived as a means of staving off the threat of export controls. The code of conduct would fill the legislative vacuum in developing countries and be a substitute for regulation by exporting countries:

A best way to exercise control is by the importing country but, where the infrastructure to operate a registration scheme had not been developed, the Group felt that the Code of Conduct would provide a worthwile contribution. . . . The role of the country exporting the pesticides was discussed and although some assistance to the importing country could be given, the Group felt that for a variety of reasons this would very often be of limited effectiveness.[230]

As recommended by the expert group, the question of a code of conduct was considered by the Government Consultation in 1982 and was the subject of considerable debate. This time, both the GIFAP representatives and observers from the Pesticides Action Network (PAN), a recently established coalition of non-governmental environmental, development and consumer groups, actively participated. The industry organisation's position was that, although it did not consider a code of conduct necessary, it was nevertheless willing to cooperate if the FAO thought a code was desirable. However, it strongly opposed the inclusion of international trade and information exchange in the list of topics to be covered by the code. Due to strong NGO lobbying, industry this time did not prevail. The concept of a code dealing inter alia with the export issue received strong support from Third World government delegates and from the representative of UNEP.[231] The meeting endorsed the proposed code in the following terms:

Until a country has the infrastructure and resources to manage the restrictions on pesticides usually required to control the supply, the elaboration of an internationally agreed Code of Conduct in the Distribution and Use of Pesticides could offer a major contribution to the safe and efficient use of pesticides.[232]

228 Bates (1982), pp 98–99.

229 FAO Panel of Experts on Pesticide Specifications, Registration Requirements and Application Standards, Group on Pesticide Registration Requirements, *Report of the 4th Meeting*, FAO Doc AGP:1982/, p 8.

230 *Ibid.*

231 D Bull, FAO Code of Conduct on Pesticides, 20 Dec 1983 (unpublished discussion paper for the Pesticides Action Network International Meeting, Feb. 1984), p 2.

232 *Report of the 2nd Government Consultation on International Harmonization of Pesticide Registration Requirements*, FAO Doc AGP:1982/M/5, p 22.

In its report, it specially stressed the responsibility of the importing country and the industry, while somewhat downplaying that of the exporting country.

In the absence of an effective pesticide registration process and infrastructure controlling the availability of pesticides, an importing country must depend heavily on the pesticide industry . . . to promote the safe and sensible distribution and use of pesticides working with whatever infrastructure that exists in a country. . . . The role of the exporting country is yet another factor to be considered. Considerable emphasis has been given recently to the desirability of regulating pesticide exports from producing countries. While no company should trade in pesticides without evaluating the risks, the fact that a product is not registered in an exporting country is not necessarily a valid reason for that country refusing to allow exports of the pesticide.[233]

Nonetheless, the problem of exports is referred to in the list of topics recommended for inclusion in the code, which comprises: 'User information including labelling, storage and disposal; *International trade and information exchange*; Advertising and marketing; Restriction of availability; Training and education of users; Packaging.'[234]

The GIFAP strongly objected to the participation of NGOs in the further drafting process of the code.[235] The Government Consultation, however, did not accept that a private group representing trade interests, while taking its own involvement for granted, should consider that of other NGOs representing the public interest as somehow less legitimate. Leaving the door open for a consultative role for NGOs, the Consultation:

recommend[ed] that the Director-General of FAO, in consultation with the appropriate UN organizations and bodies and *international organizations outside [the] UN System*, draft a Code of Conduct in the Distribution and Use of Pesticides.[236]

In June 1983, the FAO Council endorsed this recommendation and specifically stressed the need for close cooperation with UNEP, thereby acknowledging the intention of that organisation to develop general rules addressing the question of information exchange on banned and severely restricted chemicals.[237] The actual drafting work in the FAO was initiated before the fist meeting of UNEP *Ad Hoc* Working Group of Experts in March 1984.

233 FAO Doc AGP:1982/M/5, p 21.
234 *Ibid*, p 22 (emphasis added).
235 Bull, above n 231, p 2.
236 *Report of the 2nd Government Consultation on International Harmonization of Pesticide Registration Requirements*, FAO Doc AGP: 1982/M/5, p 23 (emphasis added).
237 Report of the Council of FAO, 83rd Sess, Rome, 13–24 June 1983, FAO Doc CL83/REP, p 14.

The Drafting Process of the FAO Code of Conduct

In early 1983, the FAO Secretariat started working on the preparation of the 'International Code of Conduct on the Distribution and Use of Pesticides', as the instrument was officially entitled. The Code went through a great number of drafts, which were elaborated taking into account inputs from NGOs and industry, discussed at a UN interagency meeting, and finally officially circulated to member governments for comments in September 1984. A final draft[238] was put before the FAO Committee on Agriculture for consideration in March 1985. The Code was eventually submitted through the FAO Council to the organisation's Conference for adoption in November 1985. It has the legal status of a recommendation to member states 'for consideration by them with a view to implementation by national action' pursuant to Article IV, paragraph 3 of the FAO Constitution. An analysis of the successive drafts reveals an intricate process of interest accommodation and compromise.

Their evolution reflects a continuous wavering between a document setting standards for voluntary compliance by industry and a recommendatory instrument for implementation by governments through national legislation. In the early drafts, the emphasis was on a voluntary code addressed to industry. The 5th draft contained an introductory note which stated that:

> A Code of Conduct should be recognised as a *self-commitment* by the industry concerned and by all those engaged in trade. Thus, it addresses the responsibilities of manufacturers and traders and *complements the international measures taken in the field of relations between governments.*[239]

The preamble 'entreat[ed] all those engaging in the distribution and use of pesticides . . . to commit themselves *morally* to this Code and undertake *voluntarily* to support its implementation.'[240] Several provisions of the draft code made clear that it was addressed primarily to industry[241], yet others were ambiguous[242] or referred explicitly to the responsibilities of governments, stating that the code was 'designed to encourage the introduction and enforcement of the necessary regulatory measures.'[243]

[238] International Code of Conduct on the Distribution and Use of Pesticides, FAO Doc COAG/85/9, Feb 1985 (hereafter referred to as 1985 Draft).

[239] FAO Code of Conduct on the Distribution and Use of Pesticides, 5th Draft, unnumbered FAO Doc, 14 Aug 1983 (emphasis added) (hereafter referred to as 1983 Draft).

[240] *Ibid*, p 4 (emphasis added).

[241] *Ibid*, Arts 2.1, 6.2, 6.3.

[242] *Ibid* Arts 1.1, 11.1.

[243] *Ibid* Art 2.5; see also Arts 6.1, 7.

In later drafts, the emphasis shifted to governments as the primary addressees of the code. The provisions of the 7th draft were very explicit in this respect, stressing the responsibility of governments in terms which could be interpreted as applying even beyond the limits of their territorial jurisdiction:

This Code is to establish *international standards of conduct for Governments in the exercise of their jurisdiction* over public and private enterprises engaged in the manufacture, trade and use of pesticides of all types and for all purposes *everywhere*. . . . The Code is specifically addressed to governments and *through them* to manufacturers, commercial enterprises, [etc.] . . . Governments should *enjoin* their own pesticide industry to adhere strictly to the provisions of this Code . . . particularly in countries where pesticides are not otherwise regulated or controlled.[244]

While that draft attributed primary responsibility to governments, it also provided for a kind of subsidiary responsibility on the part of industry:

Governments have full responsibility to give effect to the Code and should take legislative and other appropriate action to ensure that it is fully implemented. . . . *Pending such implementation, the pesticide industry is urged to conform willingly to the principles and ethics of the Code.*[245]

The shift in emphasis was apparently a move on the part of the FAO to hedge against a charge by UNEP Secretariat that a voluntary code was somehow of a lesser normative quality than the proposed UNEP Guidelines which would be addressed to governments. At the first UNEP *Ad Hoc* Working Group meeting, one expert supported the FAO by pointing out that 'contrary to the impression given by [the comments of UNEP Secretariat], that code would be addressed to Governments and not only to pesticide manufacturers and users.'[246]

In the final episode of this soul-searching exercise, the pendulum swung back to a voluntary code with multiple addressees, probably in response to comments from governments and industry, which naturally preferred a non-binding code.[247] The final version provides:

The objectives of this Code are to set forth responsibilities and establish *voluntary* standards of conduct for all public and private entities engaged in or affecting the distribution and use of pesticides, *particularly where there is no or an inadequate national law to regulate pesticides*.[248]

[244] International Code of Conduct on the Distribution and Use of Pesticides, unnumbered FAO Doc, June 1984, Arts 1.1, 1.3, 3.2 (emphasis added) (hereafter referred to as 1984 Draft).

[245] *Ibid*, Arts 12.1, 12.4 (emphasis added).

[246] UN Doc UNEP/WG.96/5, 1984, p 4.

[247] See GIFAP, *FAO Code of Conduct on the Distribution and Use of Pesticides*, Draft GIFAP Version, GIFAP Doc C.14074, 16 Oct 1984, especially Arts 1.1, 1.2, 3.1, 4.1, 12.1, 12.2.

[248] FAO Code of Conduct, Art 1.1 (emphasis added).

The Code specifically calls for 'collaborative action' on the part of governments, intergovernmental organisations and industry in order to ensure the implementation of its provisions.[249]

Scope and Content of the FAO Code of Conduct: a General Overview

Consistent with overall FAO policy with respect to pest control, the Code is premised on the assumption that the need for increased food production cannot be met without a 'steady increase in the worldwide use of pesticides'[250] and consequently sees it as its main objective to 'ensure efficient and safe use' of pesticides 'while minimizing health and environmental concerns due to improper handling or use.'[251] The provisions of the Code reflect a risk management philosophy based on the concept of 'shared responsibility', ie the notion that 'many segments of society' should 'work together' to minimise the environmental and health risks associated with an ever-increasing use of pesticides, which is viewed as 'necessary and acceptable.'[252] Thus, unlike the classical recommendations of intergovernmental organisations addressed primarily to governments, the Code is a hybrid document with a wide range of addressees:

> The entities which are addressed by this Code include international organizations; governments of exporting and importing countries; industry, including manufacturers, trade associations, formulators and distributors; users; and public-sector organizations such as environmental groups, consumer groups, and trade unions.[253]

The FAO Code is much broader in scope than the OECD Guiding Principles and UNEP Provisional Notification Scheme and subsequent Guidelines. It deals comprehensively with all aspects of pesticide distribution and use, not just with information exchange on banned and severely restricted pesticides in international trade. It is useful to give a brief general outline of

[249] *Ibid*, Art 12.1.
[250] FAO Conference Res 10/85, 1st & 2nd preambular paras.
[251] FAO Code, Art 1.3.
[252] *Ibid*, Art 1.2.
[253] *Ibid*, Art 1.4. Indeed, the code even purports to set standards for the conduct of NGOs. Art 5.4 specifically provides: 'To avoid unjustified confusion and alarm among the public, public-sector groups should consider all available facts and try to distinguish between major differences in levels of risk among pesticides and uses.' This industry-inspired provision, which tends to distract attention from the irresponsible marketing practices of the pesticides industry in the Third World by spreading the blame and suggesting that NGOs act irresponsibly too, is no doubt related to the educational pretentions which the code claims in its introduction, where it states that 'the strong public pressure for banning or restricting the use of some effective and much needed pesticides often stems from *a lack of understanding* of the many important issues involved. This document is designed, therefore, also to provide the general public with some basis guidance on these issues' (emphasis added).

the Code's content before proceeding to a detailed discussion of its trade provisions. In doing so, I shall also highlight some limitations of the Code as a regulatory instrument.

Article 3 lays down the general principles of what the Code calls 'pesticide management'. It provides that, while governments 'have the overall responsibility . . . to regulate the distribution and use of pesticides in their countries,'[254] 'manufacturers and traders should observe the . . . practices' recommended in the Code, 'especially in countries without legislation or means of implementing regulations.'[255] The substantive provisions spell out in some detail the responsibilities of industry, governments and other parties concerned with respect to such questions as testing of pesticides (Article 4), measures to reduce health hazards (Article 5), regulatory and technical requirements for the marketing of pesticides (Article 6), restriction of pesticide availability and use (Article 7), domestic distribution and trade (Article 8), labelling and packaging (Article 10) and advertising (Article 11).

In most of these areas, specific recommendations are addressed both to public authorities and to private parties, in accordance with the underlying principle of 'shared responsibility'. While these recommendations are ostensibly intended to complement each other, the dividing line between public and private responsibilities is often not very clear. When a recommendation has different addressees or does not explicitly identify its addressee, the concept of 'shared responsibility' tends to confuse or dilute responsibilities rather than clarify them. The provisions regarding restrictions on the availability and use of pesticides, whose ambiguity is anything but accidental, are a case in point. Those provisions were systematically watered down during the drafting process.

The 5th draft contained a provision on the special responsibility of industry when marketing pesticides in the Third World, which disappeared from later drafts:

> The industry must undertake to market only tested and innocuous products which are designed to meet the needs of small farmers in the poor countries. Strict attention must be given to the true ethics of such trade and due consideration must be given to measures that reduce the possibility of adverse effects on unsophisticated users.[256]

In the same draft, it was further specified that:

> [i]n countries where adequate regulations and technical services are lacking, pesticide formulations falling in . . . WHO Hazard Classes 1a and 1b ['very highly toxic' and 'highly toxic'] should normally not be available for use.[257]

[254] FAO Code, Art 3.1.
[255] *Ibid*, Art 3.4.
[256] 1983 Draft, above n 239, Art 6.2.
[257] *Ibid*, Art 8.7.

In the 7th draft, this provision was moved to an explanatory note at the back of the code[258]—which did not form part of the code itself—and replaced by a more vaguely worded clause absolving industry of any direct responsibility:

> *Governments should be prepared to ban* the availability and use of a very highly toxic product if control measures cannot be enforced to the extent that safety in the use of the product can be assured.[259]

This recommendation was further qualified in the final version of the Code, in which it is worded as follows:

> Prohibition of the importation, sale and purchase of an extremely toxic product *may be desirable* if control measures or good marketing practices are insufficient to ensure that the product can be used safely. However, this is a matter for decision *in the light of national circumstances*.[260]

Thus, what originated as a principle of corporate social responsibility ended up as a vague recommendation to governments couched in contextual language. The Code eventually stopped short of recommending that industry should refrain from marketing highly toxic compounds in developing countries; it even stopped short of recommending in unambiguous terms that governments should prohibit this practice.

The ambiguity of the 'shared responsibility' approach appears most clearly in the interpretation of those provisions of the Code that lack any specific addressee. What, for example, is one to make of Article 3.5, which provides that:

> pesticides whose handling and application require the use of uncomfortable and expensive protective clothing and equipment should be avoided, especially in the case of small-scale users in tropical climates?

Who bears primary responsibility for the implementation of this principle? Should *industry* voluntarily refrain from marketing such pesticides for use by small farmers in tropical countries? Is it the responsibility of the *governments* of those countries to prohibit the use of such pesticides? Or is it a recommendation addressed directly to *users* themselves, although it is obvious that 'small-scale users in tropical climates' more often than not lack the necessary information and freedom of action to comply with it?

The Trade Provisions of the Code

The introduction to the Code, which explains its history and purpose, reveals how prominent the export issue was among the concerns which

258 1984 Draft, above n 244, Annex, p 5 (Note 7).
259 *Ibid*, Art 7.3 (emphasis added).
260 FAO Code, Art 7.5 (emphasis added).

prompted its development and how central that issue was to the policy debate during its drafting process. The Code's concept of 'shared responsibility' is presented as the most appropriate policy response to pesticide-related problems in developing countries and as the proper alternative to regulation by exporting countries. Indeed, most of the introduction reads almost like a manifesto against export controls, and some of its language seems directly inspired by industry publications.

Noting the 'intensive discussions on whether the exporting country should assume responsibility' for the marketing and used of banned or severely restricted pesticides in developing countries, the introduction stresses that because the 'climatic, ecological, agronomic, social, economic and environmental conditions and . . . pest problems' in those countries are different, 'the government of the exporting country is . . . in no position to judge' whether those products are suitable and safe for use in the importing countries. In what seemed like a candid admission of the strength of industry influence in the drafting process, the introduction to the 1984 draft went on to say that

> such a judgement must, therefore, be made *by the industry* in the light of the scientific evaluation it has made and a detailed knowledge of the conditions prevailing in the country of proposed use.[261]

Although this last passage was amended in the final version to refer to the judgement of 'the responsible authority in the importing country *in consultation with industry* and other government authorities', the general thrust of the introduction remained unchanged.[262]

While the drafters of the Code did not go as far as to deny any responsibility on the part of exporting countries, an attempt was made in early drafts to differentiate that responsibility as it relates to pesticides banned on environmental grounds, as opposed to those banned for toxicological reasons:

> It is essential to note that when pesticides are banned it is generally for toxicological, environmental *or political* reasons. Valid and adequate toxicological reasons justifying banning a product are of concern, though not necessarily of equal importance, to most countries. Consequently, such products should not be exported or imported without careful consideration of the toxicological implications for those likely to be exposed. Environmental conditions and criteria may differ considerably from country to country due to differing ecological conditions and use patterns, and also due to different risk/benefit considerations resulting from differing socio-economic conditions. *Reasons for banning a pesticide on ecological grounds in one country may therefore not be valid in another.*[263]

[261] 1984 Draft, above n 244, pp 1–2 (Introduction) (emphasis added).
[262] 1985 Draft, above n 238, p 2 (Introduction) (emphasis added).
[263] 1983 Draft, above n 239, Art 5.3 (emphasis added); cf 1984 Draft, above n 244, p 2 (Introduction) and Annex p 6 (Note 8); 1985 Draft, above n 238, p 2 (Introduction).

The reference to 'political reasons' was added in the 5th draft, apparently at the suggestion of the industry, which views certain regulatory decisions as politically motivated, induced by misguided public pressure and based on scientifically unsound reasons.[264] The implication was that exporting countries should not impose their value judgements on other countries and that such ill-founded bans and restrictions certainly should not be extended to exports.

These introductory considerations were reflected in the provisions on trade and information exchange of the 5th draft, which recommended notifications of control actions and one-time export notifications for all pesticides banned or severely restricted 'in order to protect health or the environment'[265] but required the consent of the importing country only for exports of pesticides 'banned or severely restricted *for toxicological reasons*.'[266]

This distinction was dropped in the 7th draft, which, presumably in response to comments from Third World governments on earlier drafts, contained stronger trade provisions requiring prior informed consent for exports of *all* banned or severely restricted pesticides, regardless of whether the motives of the regulatory measures were toxicological or environmental:

> Governments of pesticide exporting countries which take action to ban or severely restrict the use or handling of a pesticide in order to protect health or the environment domestically should take appropriate measures to ensure that . . . *no export takes place . . . without prior notification* to the importing country government advising of the domestic regulatory status of the pesticide and the hazard which led to such restrictions [and] *without the explicit consent of the importing country*.[267]

However, this apparent endorsement of the principle of prior informed consent was conditional.[268] In an explanatory note for governments, the FAO Secretariat pointed out that these provisions were only provisional and would 'be amended in the next draft to incorporate revised wording agreed at UNEP *Ad Hoc* Working Group Meeting' of March 1984.[269] Indeed, in the final draft submitted to the FAO Committee on Agriculture a few months later, the trade and information exchange provisions of the Code

[264] This language was somewhat toned down in the final version of the Code. The last two sentences disparaging environmental regulation of pesticides were dropped, and the phrase 'political reasons' was replaced by the more neutral phrase 'social reasons'.

[265] 1983 Draft, above n 239, Art 10.2 and 10.3.

[266] *Ibid*, Art 9.9 (1) (emphasis added).

[267] 1984 Draft, above n 244, Art 9.1 (emphasis added).

[268] It should be noted that the wording used did not specify in what form or at what time the 'explicit consent' of the importing country was to be given. It did not necessarily imply consent on a shipment-by-shipment basis.

[269] 1984 Draft, above n 244, Annex I, para 1.

of Conduct were completely brought into line with UNEP Provisional Notification Scheme agreed at that meeting—in turn inspired by the OECD Guiding Principles—providing only for notifications of control actions and one-time export notifications.[270] The requirement of explicit consent was deleted. In this way, the FAO, which under pressure from NGOs and its Third World member states had somewhat strayed from its traditional pro-pesticides course, was brought back into the fold.

The Final Adoption of the Code: Conflict and Compromise

When the watered-down final draft of the code was presented to the political organs of the FAO for formal adoption in 1985, a year after the endorsement of the Provisional Notification Scheme by UNEP Governing Council, many developing countries expressed dissatisfaction with the weak nature of the instrument, and especially the deletion of the principle of prior informed consent. However, the opposition was not strong enough to overcome the political pressure for early adoption of the Code by consensus and to force substantial amendments to the Secretariat's draft.

The draft was first considered by the Committee on Agriculture, which 'gave broad general acceptance' to the Code and stressed that its adoption should not be delayed. The report of the Committee meeting notes, however, that some members 'expressed concern at the non-inclusion of the "prior consent" clause in Article 9 on Information Exchange'. Nevertheless,

> most members, although wishing to see stronger provisions in the Code, agreed that a realistic and practical approach would be to accept the Code in its present form, in the spirit of cooperation and goodwill among all concerned.[271]

Based on the discussions in the Committee on Agriculture, the Director-General submitted the draft Code to the FAO Council in a virtually unchanged form and recommended that 'as a whole the text should remain unchanged.'[272] In his introductory statement to the Council, the Director-General called for consensus to be maintained and commended the draft in the following terms:

> It inevitably represents a compromise between conscientious interests of all kinds, and even of zealous extremes. . . . It will fully satisfy neither the bluest blood of free enterprise nor the greenest sap of environmentalism. In this hard world, however, nothing is perfect.[273]

[270] 1985 Draft, FAO Doc COAG/85/9, Feb 1985, above n 238, Art 9.
[271] FAO Doc COAG/85/REP 5, 1985, paras 7 and 10.
[272] FAO Doc CL/87/9-Sup 1, May 1985.
[273] Statement by Mr Edouard Saouma, Director-General of the Food and Agriculture Organization of the United Nations to the 87th Session of the FAO Council, Rome, 17 June 1985, p 15.

Notwithstanding the Director-General's strong plea for consensus, many developing countries intervened in the Council to criticise the draft and call for amendments. The Philippines proposed that, as a minimum, the clause copied from the OECD Guiding Principles stating that it may not be 'possible' to provide information prior to export and that procedures in the exporting country 'might not be such as to permit delay or control the export'[274] be deleted. This proposal was supported by most developing countries and recommended by the Council for consideration by the Director-General.[275] With this and a few other recommendations for minor amendments, the Council recommended that the draft Code be submitted to the FAO Conference for adoption.

The amendments recommended by the Council were incorporated in the ultimate draft submitted by the Director-General to the Conference,[276] but this was insufficient to satisfy the concerns of the developing countries, which continued to call for further amendments. At the opening of the discussions on the Code, Ecuador and the Philippines intervened to call for the reinstatement of the principle of PIC into the Code. The Philippines proposed an amendment to Article 9 of the Code providing that export should take place 'only following the explicit written consent of the importing country.'[277] This provoked a new round of discussion on PIC. Of the forty-odd countries who spoke on the Code, the vast majority, most of them developing countries, supported the proposed amendment.

The Third World feeling was well summarised by the Ethiopian delegate, when he said: 'We believe that if a pesticide is dangerous, it should be banned and not exported.'[278] Support for the amendment was not limited to developing countries, however. The Netherlands, for instance, stated that it agreed 'in essence' with the proposal to reinsert PIC but doubted that the issue could be reconsidered at such a late stage. It therefore suggested that, as a compromise, the Code be adopted without changes, but subject to incorporation of PIC within two years.[279] A similar compromise was proposed by Colombia.[280]

Most exporting countries, such as the United States, the United Kingdom and Japan, opposed last-minute amendments and stressed that they were only prepared to adopt the Code without further changes.[281] Notwithstanding the overwhelming support expressed for prior informed consent, it was clear that no agreement could be reached on the proposed amendment. No country was willing to assume responsibility for delaying

[274] FAO Doc CL/87/9-Sup 1, May 1985, p 12, para 9.6.
[275] FAO Doc CL 87/DC/9, May 1985, p 3, para 14.
[276] FAO Doc C 85/25, Sept 1985.
[277] FAO Doc C 85/II/PV, p 371.
[278] *Ibid*, p 372.
[279] *Ibid*, pp 391–92.
[280] *Ibid*, p 373.
[281] *Ibid*, pp 398–99.

adoption of the Code. In the end, the Chair obtained consensus on the basis of the compromise proposal suggested by Colombia and the Netherlands.[282]

The Code was adopted without substantive changes, in the form submitted by the Director-General, but a statement was inserted in the report of the Conference to reflect the support expressed for PIC and the need for incorporation of this principle to be reconsidered in the near future:

> While recognizing the significant improvements introduced in the text, the majority expressed deep concern that the principle of 'Prior Informed Consent' no longer appeared in the present version of the Code. . . . These members, however, recognized the need not to delay the adoption of the Code and accordingly, urged that the principle of 'Prior Informed Consent' be considered for inclusion in any future first revision of the Code.[283]

It is to be noted that this reference to PIC is worded in relatively noncommittal terms. It is not recorded as a decision of the Conference, but only as a position taken by a majority of the members. The wording used does not actually mandate inclusion of PIC in the Code, but only reconsideration of the issue. The report is even less precise as regards the timing of the suggested revision. While it does recognise the 'dynamic nature' of the Code and the need for 'periodical revisions', and records the wish of 'most members' that there be a first revision 'within the next biennium', it also recommends that revisions be made 'after some experience had been gained in the implementation of the Code.'[284] This wording later allowed opponents of an early revision of the Code to argue against it on the grounds that insufficient experience had been gained in its implementation. In the meantime, the as yet inconclusive debate between advocates and opponents of more stringent regulation of international trade in banned and severely restricted chemicals continued in UNEP.

CONSOLIDATING THE 'PROVISIONAL' NOTIFICATION SCHEME: THE COMPLETION OF UNEP GUIDELINES

Following the adoption of the Provisional Notification Scheme (PNS) by the Governing Council in 1984, further work on the draft UNEP guidelines had proceeded rather slowly. The interest of governments in UNEP exercise decreased substantially, as is apparent from the reduced attendance at the second meeting of the *Ad Hoc* Working Group, held in Rome in January 1985. Indeed, a number of countries continued to question the need for more elaborate guidelines, expressing their support for the provisions 'pro-

[282] FAO Doc C 85/II/PV, p 409.
[283] FAO Doc C 85/REP/8, p 16, para 44.
[284] *Ibid*, para 45.

visionally' agreed by the Governing Council and opposing any modification of the Provisional Notification Scheme.[285] However, the Secretariat had prepared revised draft guidelines on the basis of the discussions at the first meeting, and this revised draft was submitted for discussion at the Rome meeting. It should be noted that this meeting was held in the wake of the Bhopal disaster, which had led to enhanced public concern about the hazards of pesticide production. In Rome, India proposed that the *Ad Hoc* Working Group seek a broader mandate from UNEP Governing Council, to enable it to consider health and safety issues related to the transfer of chemical production technology and also to formulate guidelines on this matter, but this suggestion was rejected by many other countries on the grounds that the working group was not the appropriate forum for such an effort. In view of the lack of support, India had no option but to withdraw its proposal.[286]

In respect of export notification, the revised draft guidelines prepared by the Secretariat were not materially different from the Provisional Notification Scheme. In fact, their language is almost identical. The only difference is that the revised draft guidelines included some bracketed text 'on which no consensus was reached.'[287] Thus, the provision on export notification read as follows:

> When an export or re-export of a banned or severely restricted chemical occurs, the country of export should ensure that necessary steps are taken to provide the designated national authority of the country of import with relevant information [and no such export or re-export takes place without the explicit consent of the importing country].[288]

This reflected the unresolved disagreement at the first working group meeting and identified informed consent as an issue for further debate.

The Rome meeting made no substantive progress on the controversial issue of prior informed consent, choosing not to re-open discussion on those provisions of the guidelines which were based on the PNS. One expert pointed out that the bracketed clause requiring the 'explicit consent of the importing country' for exports of banned or severely restricted chemicals was not an agreed provision of the PNS and suggested its deletion, but others stressed that this clause had been advocated by many at the first session. The substantive discussion was once again deferred to a later meeting and the text remained unchanged, including the bracketed phrase.[289]

[285] UN Doc UNEP/WG.112/5, p 7, para 26.
[286] *Ibid*, p 18, para 65.
[287] Revised Draft Guidelines, UN Doc UNEP/WG.112/3, 23 Nov 1984, p 2.
[288] *Ibid*, para 9(c) (brackets in original).
[289] UN Doc UNEP/WG.112/5, 8 May 1985, p 14, para 53.

There was some discussion, however, on the issue of chemicals not registered for use in the country of export. The Secretariat's draft included a provision, inspired by US legislation, requiring that chemicals not registered for use in the country of export be specifically labelled as such. One expert proposed to add to this provision a special notification requirement for such chemicals. However, the majority of participants objected to specific provisions for this category of chemicals, arguing that most of them were already included in the definition of banned or severely restricted chemicals and were thus already subject to a notification requirement under the PNS.[290] This was not entirely accurate, however, since only those chemicals which had been refused registration were covered, but not those which had never been submitted for registration. Nevertheless, this argument prevailed and the provision in question was deleted.

In the context of the discussions on the implementation of the PNS, disagreement appeared as to the extent of governmental involvement required in the notification procedure. Indeed, several OECD countries claimed that it would be possible to comply with the notification provisions 'by way of delegating certain functions to the exporting industries concerned'. Those countries were interpreting the provisions of the PNS in accordance with those of the OECD Guiding Principles, which explicitly mention the possibility of delegating to 'private entities'. However, there was no similar provision in UNEP Provisional Notification Scheme, and many experts objected to this approach, invoking the need for governmental supervision to 'ensure actual compliance.'[291]

The language of the relevant provision of the OECD Guiding Principles does not require the governmental authorities of the country of export to carry out the export notification procedure themselves, but only to 'ensure that the necessary steps are taken', which leaves open the possibility of delegating this responsibility to the private parties involved. When UNEP adopted the same language for its PNS, non-OECD countries may not have been aware of the liberal interpretation given to it in the OECD context. It is thus not surprising that the assertion of the freedom to delegate the duty of notification provoked a response from those countries in UNEP forum. However, the issue was not resolved. The working group did not attempt to reach agreement on a particular interpretation. The provisional nature of the scheme was invoked as a reason to defer consideration of the issue until a later meeting, when 'practical experience' would have been gained.[292]

The Rome meeting was unable to finalise the draft guidelines and transmit them to the Governing Council for adoption. Instead it recommended

[290] UN Doc UNEP/WG.112/5, 8 May 1985, p 14, para 51.
[291] *Ibid*, p 7, para 25. See also p 3, para 11.
[292] *Ibid*, p 7, para 25.

that an additional meeting be convened in order to complete the work, but without any sense of urgency. In fact, the meeting and the adoption of the guidelines by the Governing Council did not occur until two years later. Following the Rome meeting, UNEP Secretariat prepared a second revised draft of the guidelines,[293] which was widely circulated to governments, intergovernmental and non-governmental organisations for comments in 1986. Together with those comments, the second revised draft was submitted to the third session of the *Ad Hoc* Working Group, held in London in February 1987.[294]

The Finalisation of the London Guidelines on the Exchange of Information on Chemicals in International Trade

In the second revised draft, the provisions on notification of control actions and export notification were identical to those of the Provisional Notification Scheme. The provision relating to the consent of the importing country, which still appeared in square brackets in the first revised draft, had now been deleted altogether, presumably as a result of the discussion at the Rome meeting, although this deletion had not formally been decided at the time. However, in their comments, a number of NGOs had suggested that a prior informed consent clause be reinserted in the guidelines. While the Secretariat probably hoped to avoid reopening the discussion on this issue, the stage was set once more for a replay of the confrontation between proponents and opponents of prior informed consent.

The meeting was under strong pressure from its British chair and UNEP Secretariat to reach consensus on a final text of the guidelines so that these could be submitted to UNEP Governing Council for formal adoption in June 1987. This created an unfavourable context for in-depth discussion of major substantive issues. The vast majority of OECD countries participating in the meeting argued for the adoption of the provisions in the Secretariat's draft based on the PNS. It was clear that their main objective was to formalise and give permanent status to the OECD-inspired information exchange provisions of the PNS, thus putting an end to the regulatory debate in UNEP and other international fora and foreclosing discussion of additional regulatory measures beyond information exchange. In opposing any departure from the PNS provisions, they constantly argued for consistency between UNEP Guidelines and the information exchange provisions of the FAO Code of Conduct, which had meanwhile been formally adopted by the FAO Conference in November 1985. Those FAO Code provisions, like the PNS, were directly inspired by the OECD Guiding

[293] UN Doc UNEP/WG.112/6, 27 Jan 1986.
[294] UN Doc UNEP/WG.155/2, 12 Nov 1986.

Principles. The OECD countries' effort to obtain early UNEP endorsement of those provisions was clearly part of a strategy to prevent any revision of the FAO Code which could be forced onto the agenda of the 1987 FAO Conference as a result of the uneasy compromise reached in that forum in 1985.

However, a number of experts from developing countries criticised the PNS as insufficient and insisted that the guidelines include provisions on prior informed consent.[295] They were supported by the Netherlands, which had recently introduced a voluntary PIC scheme in cooperation with industry at the national level. The Netherlands' concern was to ensure that, even if no consensus could be achieved on PIC, the final text of UNEP Guidelines would leave room for, even encourage, such national initiatives.

The opponents of PIC prevailed, arguing that UNEP Guidelines 'should not extend beyond information exchange, especially as there was as yet little practical experience of such exchange.'[296] They considered it premature to change the provisions of the PNS before sufficient experience had actually been gained in their implementation. The meeting eventually decided to limit the scope of the guidelines to information exchange, as in the PNS, but a few concessions were made to appease the proponents of PIC. First, the provision taken verbatim from the OECD Guiding Principles stipulating that the 'procedures of the country of export should not be such as to delay or control the export' was deleted from the final text of the guidelines, thus creating some room for individual countries to introduce export control measures if they so desired. However, a proposal to delete the provision specifying that information should be provided prior to export only 'in so far as possible' was rejected, even though a similar provision had been deleted from the FAO Code of Conduct in 1985. It was argued by experts from OECD countries that it would be unrealistic to expect that information could always be provided prior to export and that the information regarding exports was not to be considered as a mechanism for controlling trade.

Even though the actual provisions of UNEP Guidelines were strictly limited to information exchange, the working group agreed that countries would be free to go beyond mere information exchange. Thus, a paragraph was added to the introductory clauses of the guidelines to make clear that they:

> do not preclude States from instituting broader and more frequent information exchange or other systems involving consultation with importing countries on banned or severely restricted chemicals designed to *gain experience with alternative procedures*.[297]

[295] UN Doc UNEP/WG.155/6, 10 Feb 1987, p 9, para 30.
[296] *Ibid*, p 9, para 31.
[297] *Ibid*, Annex I, p 1, para 4 (emphasis added).

The concept of 'systems involving consultation with importing countries' actually refers to prior informed consent. It was necessary to use that circumlocution because the United States objected to any mention of the term 'prior informed consent' in the guidelines. Finally, in a separate recommendation, which is not part of the actual guidelines, the working group recommends that 'States additionally consider other ways of meeting the objectives of these guidelines' and suggests a few 'alternative procedures' which could be envisaged to this effect,

> *inter alia*, more frequent or extensive information exchange, consultation with importing States, *or various forms of prior consent*, recognizing that some forms may go beyond information exchange.[298]

Here again, the reference to prior informed consent is 'diluted'. It is presented, not as a clear-cut alternative, but as only one of many options. Moreover, by referring to 'various forms' of prior consent, the wording suggests that 'a common understanding of this concept was lacking', as the report of the meeting notes.[299] Depicting prior informed consent as an ill-defined concept tends to downplay its significance.

In addition to their core provisions on notification, the London Guidelines contain provisions on other aspects of information exchange, which apply to chemicals generally, as opposed to banned and severely restricted chemicals only. Thus, for example, the guidelines impose a general duty on states exporting chemicals to

> ensure that, where appropriate, information, advice and assistance is provided to States of import concerned regarding the sound management of such chemicals, including appropriate precautionary information.[300]

It is specified that 'as far as practicable, precautionary information should be provided in the principal language or languages of the State of import'. The guidelines also recognise the need to provide information directly to the end-user through adequate labelling and provide that exporting states have some responsibility in this respect. The relevant provision stipulates that

> States should recognize . . . that it is desirable that chemicals exported from their territories are subject to no less stringent requirements of classification, packaging and labelling than comparable products destined for use in the State of export.[301]

The language was watered down from the original draft, which actually required exporting states to 'ensure' that exported chemicals comply with these requirements, instead of merely recognising that this is 'desirable.'[302]

[298] *Ibid*, p 11, para 37(h) (emphasis added).
[299] *Ibid*, p 8, para 29.
[300] London Guidelines, para 13 (b).
[301] *Ibid*, para 14 (a).
[302] UN Doc UNEP/WG.155/2, 12 Nov 1986, p 54, para 15 (b).

Nevertheless, this provision, which has no equivalent in the FAO Code, is quite significant for its implicit recognition that responsibility in this field does not rest solely with importing states. The cautious language reflects the general reluctance of exporting countries to accept special labelling requirements for exported chemicals. This was even more apparent in the rejection of a clause that would have required exported chemicals not registered for use in the country of export to bear a label stating 'not registered for use in country of origin.'[303] Following some initial discussion at the Rome meeting, this clause was placed in square brackets; in London, it was deleted altogether. It is noteworthy that the US opposed this provision, even though a similar requirement exists in US law.[304]

The introduction to the London Guidelines contains a paragraph clarifying the relationship between them and other international instruments:

> These guidelines are complementary to existing instruments developed by the UN and WHO and to the FAO International Code of Conduct on the Distribution and Use of Pesticides, which is the primary guidance for the management of pesticides internationally. These guidelines should be implemented in a non-duplicative manner for the different classes of chemicals covered by existing instruments.

This paragraph primarily reflects concerns expressed by the United States and other OECD countries about the overlap between UNEP Guidelines and the FAO Code in the field of pesticides. From time to time, during the negotiations within UNEP, proposals had been made to exclude pesticides from the scope of the guidelines, on the grounds that they were adequately dealt with in the FAO Code of Conduct, which had been finally adopted prior to the conclusion of the negotiations within UNEP. However, no agreement was ever reached to this effect, and pesticides continued to be included within the ambit of the guidelines. There was concern on the part of some OECD countries that UNEP, under pressure from developing countries, might eventually recommend export control measures going beyond the fragile consensus reached in the FAO and prompting reconsideration of that consensus.

In an effort to consolidate the status of the FAO Code, the United States proposed to add an elaborate annex to UNEP Guidelines on the relationship between the two instruments.[305] The United States wanted to see the Code recognised as 'the principal guidance for the management of pesticides internationally' and, effectively, to subordinate the application to pesticides of UNEP Guidelines to consistency with the relevant Code provisions. Referring specifically to the information exchange procedures, the draft annex provided that 'all other activities in this field should be carried

[303] UN Doc UNEP/WG.155/2, 12 Nov 1986, para 15 (d).
[304] See above ch 11.
[305] UN Doc UNEP/WG.155/2, 12 Nov 1986, pp 57 *et seq*.

out consistent with provisions of the FAO Code.'[306] It was expressly stipulated that the FAO Code provisions would prevail over UNEP Guidelines:

As duplication of notification and information exchange is to be avoided, actions taken consistent with the FAO Code should be deemed consistent with the provisions of UNEP Guidelines.[307]

The language that was eventually included in the introduction to the London Guidelines does not go quite as far as the American proposal. It does recognise the FAO Code as 'primary guidance', as suggested by the United States, but does not explicitly state that the Code shall prevail over UNEP Guidelines. It only calls for 'non-duplicative' implementation of the guidelines, which dispenses with the need for states to run two parallel notification procedures for pesticides but does not in principle rule out the application of additional, complementary measures under UNEP Guidelines. As it turned out, this question was never of more than theoretical interest, since the provisions of UNEP Guidelines remained essentially the same as those of the FAO Code. However, the debate was symptomatic of the perpetual tension between the two organisations and illustrates the way in which negotiations in one forum were influenced by the other and arguments of 'consistency' and 'coordination' were systematically used as a negotiating tactic by some governments.

THE IMPLEMENTATION OF RESOLUTION 37/137: CONTROVERSY OVER THE UNITED NATIONS CONSOLIDATED LIST OF BANNED OR SEVERELY RESTRICTED PRODUCTS

In a parallel effort to the mainstream regulatory debate in UNEP, the OECD and the FAO aimed at establishing non-binding international standards for multilateral and bilateral information exchange on hazardous chemicals in international trade, the United Nations Secretariat was involved in the implementation of a multilateral information scheme on banned and severely restricted products mandated by the UN General Assembly in its Resolution 37/137. This exercise, which raised a number of issues of interest for ongoing normative efforts, will be analysed in the concluding section of this chapter.

The compilation and publication of the Consolidated List, as called for by General Assembly Resolution 37/137, proved a difficult and controversial task for the UN Secretariat. The list was first issued in a preliminary form on 30 December 1983, one year after the adoption of the

[306] *Ibid.*
[307] *Ibid*, p 58.

resolution.[308] It covers four categories of products: pharmaceuticals, pesticides, industrial chemicals and consumer products. In the following discussion, I shall concentrate on issues relevant to pesticides, which are the focus of this study.

As mandated by the General Assembly,[309] the Secretariat first collected information available within the UN system, information which had been compiled by various specialised agencies in the scope of their ongoing programmes. To supplement this information, the Secretary-General sent out a note to member states in May 1983 requesting them to provide information for inclusion in the list, as called for in Resolution 37/137.[310] In all, only 45 governments replied to the Secretary-General's request for information, and some of those that responded actually declined to provide the requested information, invoking technical and conceptual difficulties with the list.[311] Other governments simply ignored the Secretary-General's request altogether.

The United States, for instance, did not supply any information at all, arguing that the 'terminology in the proposed listing . . . is not compatible with national laws and procedures' and that, as a result, there was a 'possibility of misleading potential users of the list as to the true meaning of actions taken by individual Member Governments.'[312] In its reply to the Secretary-General's note, the US government expressed its 'belief . . . that an attempt to list products in vaguely defined categories would oversimplify technically complex issues and not provide Governments with usable information.'[313] The US dismissed the list altogether as 'inadequate for publication.'[314]

Other pesticide-exporting countries responded in an equally negative or evasive manner to the Secretary-General's inquiries. Their comments reflected a general distrust of UN regulatory intrusion in what they regard as a 'technical issue' and a fear of having their products and chemical companies blacklisted by the UN. It was argued that the list 'would not satisfy sound scientific criteria,'[315] was a 'duplication of work',[316] or even 'in some

[308] *Consolidated list of products whose consumption and/or sale have been banned, withdrawn, severely restricted or not approved by Governments*, 1st issue, 30 Dec 1983 (unnumbered UN Secretariat document) (hereafter referred to as *1983 Consolidated List*). A revised first issue was published in 1984: *Consolidated list of products whose consumption and/or sale have been banned, withdrawn, severely restricted or not approved by Governments*, 1st rev issue, June 1984, UN Doc DIESA/WP/1 (hereafter referred to as *1984 Consolidated List*).

[309] See UNGA Res 37/137, above n 65, para 4.

[310] *1984 Consolidated List*, above n 308, pp ii, iii, iv.

[311] *Ibid.*

[312] *1984 Consolidated List*, above n 308, Annex III ('Comments received from Governments concerning conceptual aspects of the consolidated list of products requested by the General Assembly in operative paragraph 4 of resolution 37/137'), p 267 (Comments of the United States).

[313] *Ibid.*

[314] *Ibid.*

[315] *Ibid*, p 259 (Comments of Switzerland).

[316] *Ibid.*

cases . . . could be positively harmful.'[317] The UK extensively criticised the concept of a negative list:

It would . . . be wrong to assume, as could happen from the list envisaged by the United Nations, that substances not used or prohibited in the United Kingdom were automatically harmful. . . . The United Kingdom considers that one of the most serious dangers in producing a negative list is that it carries the implication that if a substance is not on the prohibited list it must be safe, a wholly unwarranted and unwise assumption.[318]

Both the UK and the Federal Republic of Germany provided only information on 'banned' products, under the pretext that 'severely restricted' was not adequately defined.[319] The FRG said it would be willing to provide further information when 'a more precise definition' of the concept 'severely restricted' had been elaborated by the UN.[320]

A special concern of all chemical-producing countries was the provision in Resolution 37/137 that the Consolidated List should contain brand names and the names of manufacturers, as well as chemical names and regulatory information.[321] Governments appeared very reluctant to provide such commercial information: only four countries, none of them major exporters, did supply names of manufacturers.[322] Most of the manufacturer information published in the list was compiled by the UNCTC from chemical trade publications.[323] The US objected that 'use of manufacturer information on a UN list is . . . likely to be incomplete, uninformative, and potentially discriminatory against manufacturers whose names are used,'[324] while Britain contended that 'publication of brand names would be biased against those countries where such information was readily available.'[325]

Struggling with Definitions

One of the major problems encountered by the UN Secretariat in compiling the Consolidated List, as well as a subject of continuing contention and debate within UN organs in the early years of the list's existence, was the question of how to define the categories of products to be included in the list. Resolution 37/137 only defines those categories in the most general

[317] *Ibid*, p 262 (Comments of the United Kingdom).
[318] *Ibid*, pp 262–263.
[319] *Ibid*, pp 267, 262.
[320] Antwort der Bundesregierung auf die Kleine Anfrage der Abgeordneten Frau Dr. Hickel und der Fraktion Die Grunen, Deutscher Bundestag, Doc 10/695, 29 Nov 1983, p 4.
[321] UNGA Res 37/137, above n 65, para 5.
[322] *1984 Consolidated List*, above n 308, p viii n 10.
[323] *Ibid*, p vi.
[324] *Ibid*, p 272.
[325] *Ibid*, p 265.

terms, as 'products whose consumption and/or sale have been banned, withdrawn, severely restricted or, in the case of pharmaceuticals, not approved by Governments'. The legal imprecision of the terms used in the resolution is a consequence of the fact that it was drafted as a political document, not as a regulatory instrument, and that its authors, in aiming for inclusiveness, were forced to generalise in view of the broad scope of the text, which covers different types of products and a wide variety of regulatory contexts.

In order to execute the mandate given to it by the General Assembly, the Secretariat was forced to make policy choices in interpreting and operationalising the terms of that mandate. In its introduction to the first issue of the list, the Secretariat noted that the wording used in Resolution 37/137 'raises a number of conceptual difficulties, particularly regarding the application of the term "severely restricted"', which 'has not been defined either in a legal or scientific context', and concluded that 'it is therefore *a question of judgement as to the degree of restriction* which warrants the inclusion of a particular product in the consolidated list.'[326] However, the criteria used by the Secretariat in making this judgement were not made explicit at that time.

The lack of clarity in this respect provided a convenient excuse for some governments to justify their reluctance to provide information for inclusion in the Consolidated List. Thus, the United States challenged the conceptual basis of the list by drawing subtle semantic distinctions between the language used in the resolution and that of its domestic legislation. Basically, the US argument was that 'banned' and 'severely restricted' are regulatory categories which do not exist in US law, and that therefore it is not possible to draw up lists of products which fall under these headings. In the US, so the argument goes, there is no negative list of 'banned' and 'severely restricted' pesticides, but only a positive list of registered pesticides authorised for specific uses.[327] For anyone familiar with US legislation on the registration and use of pesticides,[328] this semantic argument sounds quite artificial. For it is clear that, although the terms 'banned' and 'severely restricted' are not used as such in the FIFRA, these notions do have equivalents in the US regulatory system.

The point can easily be illustrated by quoting from the reply of the US government to the Secretary-General's request for information and pointing out the inconsistencies in its argumentation:

Under FIFRA, EPA cannot take action to 'ban' a pesticide; but EPA does have the authority to cancel or suspend the registration of a pesticide. Since pesticides are

[326] *1983 Consolidated List*, above n 308, p 7. See also *Products harmful to health and the environment*, Report of the Secretary-General, UN Doc A/39/452, 7 Sept 1984, para 21 (emphasis added).

[327] *1983 Consolidated List*, above n 308, Annex III, p 13.

[328] Cf above ch 11.

registered by use, cancellation or suspension action is tied to specific uses and not to specific compounds.[329]

What else is a pesticide whose registration is cancelled or suspended for all uses, but a banned pesticide? Yet the US government goes on to conclude: 'For these reasons, the EPA terms are inconsistent with the term "banned" as used in resolution 37/137.'[330] It rather appears that this conclusion is inconsistent with the terms of the FIFRA.[331]

With respect to the concept 'severely restricted', the US similarly contended:

The term 'severely restricted' is difficult to use in relation to pesticides. Under FIFRA, the term 'restricted' has a very specific and different meaning.... In the context of the U.S. regulatory scheme, *restriction represents a decision that a pesticide can be safely used if applied properly.* Consequently, it is doubtful whether the 37/137 'severely restricted' category should be construed to include such products.[332]

Yet, according to the relevant US statutory provisions, a pesticide classified for 'restricted use' is a pesticide which

when applied in accordance with its directions for use, warnings and cautions and for the uses for which it is registered ... may generally cause, without additional regulatory restrictions, unreasonable adverse effects on the environment, including injury to the applicator.[333]

Thus, a use restriction under US law amounts to a decision that a pesticide can only safely be used if applied by properly qualified persons or, conversely, that the product in question is unsafe when improperly used by unqualified persons. In this context, it is hard to understand the logic of the argument that the meaning of the term 'restricted' in US law is fundamentally 'different' from the meaning of the same term in Resolution 37/137.

At any rate, the definitional arguments raised by the US and other governments in reaction to the invitation to submit information to the UN Secretariat for the preparation of the Consolidated List highlighted the need for developing proper definitions of the concepts used in circumscribing the scope of the list. At the time the UN list was first issued, there were no internationally agreed definitions of the terms 'banned' and 'severely restricted'. The only international forum in which the question of

[329] *1984 Consolidated List*, above n 308, p 270.

[330] *Ibid.*

[331] According to the relevant provisions of FIFRA, 'it shall be unlawful for any person ... to distribute or to sell to any person ... any pesticide that is not registered' under FIFRA. 7 USC 136j (a) (1).

[332] *1984 Consolidated List*, above n 308, p 271. (emphasis added).

[333] FIFRA § 3 (d), 7 USC 136a (d) (1) (C). Pesticides classified for restricted use may normally only be applied by certified, ie specially trained, applicators or under the direct supervision of certified applicators.

definitions and criteria for the selection of chemicals had already been addressed—in the context of the drafting of an international regulatory instrument—was the OECD. The UN Secretariat was aware of the efforts of the OECD expert group to define 'significant regulatory action' for the purpose of developing information exchange procedures in connection with exports of hazardous chemicals.[334]

The OECD's experts had come to the conclusion that 'it would be impractical (if not impossible) to arrive at a precise and scientific definition' and had eventually agreed on a tentative, broad definition of 'significant regulatory action' as 'a control action taken [by a public authority] in the exporting country to ban or severely restrict the use or handling of chemicals in order to protect health or the environment', including 'the refusal of a proposed first-time use.'[335] This language served as a basis for a tautological definition of 'banned or severely restricted chemical'[336] adopted by the OECD Council in its April 1984 Guiding Principles on Information Exchange Related to Export of Banned or Severely Restricted Chemicals and later copied by UNEP in the Provisional Notification Scheme endorsed by its Governing Council in May 1984. It is quite significant that the United States, which was an active and influential participant in the work of the OECD expert group, accepted the use of the vague concept 'banned or severely restricted chemical' in the OECD recommendations, while it found the very same concept objectionable in the context of a UN General Assembly resolution.

The lack of a clear and widely accepted definition of the concepts 'banned' and especially 'severely restricted' did not, as we saw, prevent the publication of the first edition of the Consolidated List in 1983. The Secretariat adopted a casuistic approach, without explicit criteria, and exercised its discretionary judgement as to whether or not particular regulatory actions taken by individual governments qualified a product or substance for inclusion in the list. In his first report to the General Assembly on the implementation of Resolution 37/137 following the first issue of the list, the Secretary-General, in an apparent attempt to defend the Consolidated List in the face of persistent criticism from certain governments, somewhat downplayed the significance of what he called 'these problems of definition', asserting that they

[334] *1983 Consolidated List*, above n 308, p 7 & n 6.

[335] OECD, *Report of the Expert Group on Information Exchange Related to Export of Hazardous Chemicals*, Paris, Aug 1982, p 7.

[336] 'A banned or severely restricted chemical includes any chemical that is the subject of a control action taken by a competent authority in the exporting . . . country . . . to ban or severely restrict the use or handling of the chemical in order to protect human health or environment domestically'. Guiding Principles on Information Exchange Related to Export of Banned or Severely Restricted Chemicals, OECD Doc C(84)37(Final), Appendix, para 3.

have not been a major hindrance for the preparation of the list and it has proved possible to use the terms specified in the resolution for the collection of information.[337]

Nevertheless, before embarking on the production of the second edition of the list, the UN Secretariat, together with the other UN entities involved, reviewed the criteria for the inclusion of products and agreed on working definitions, which were circulated to governments for comment in July/August 1985.[338] It was proposed to define a 'severely restricted' chemical as:

a substance that is approved by a competent national authority following thorough analysis of the risk/benefit situation, *subject to restrictions that strictly define the conditions of its uses* in a given situation.[339]

In response to comments from governments which pointed out the risk of inconsistency with the concept of 'severely restricted pesticide', as defined in the draft FAO Code of Conduct, which had just been approved by the FAO Council,[340] this definition was narrowed down to:

A product for which *virtually all uses have been prohibited* nationally in one or more countries by final government regulatory action because of health or environmental reasons, but for which *certain specific uses remain authorized*.[341]

Similarly, for the purpose of the second issue of the list, a 'banned' chemical was defined as:

A product that has been *prohibited for all uses* nationally in one or more countries by final government regulatory action because of health or environmental reasons.[342]

Thus, the Consolidated List definitions were brought into line with those of the FAO Code of Conduct. The revised definitions were also consistent with those of the OECD Guiding Principles and UNEP Provisional Notification Scheme, which, though worded differently (and tautologically), are very similar in substance. In his 1986 report to the General Assembly, the Secretary-General indicated that the criteria for chemical products were

[337] *Products harmful to health and the environment*, Report of the Secretary-General, UN Doc A/39/452, 7 Sept 1984, p 7, para 23.

[338] *Products harmful to health and the environment*, Report of the Secretary-General, UN Doc A/41/329, 23 May 1986, p 5, para 9.

[339] 'Summary of arrangements agreed upon for the production of the consolidated list of products whose consumption and/or sale have been banned, withdrawn, severely restricted or not approved by Governments', 10 June 1985, p 6, para 24 (unnumbered UN Secretariat document) (emphasis added).

[340] See *International Code of Conduct on the Distribution and Use of Pesticides*, FAO Doc C 85/25-Rev. 1, Nov 1985, pp 5, 7.

[341] UN Doc A/41/329, 23 May 1986, Annex, p 13, para B.2. (emphasis added).

[342] *Consolidated list of products whose consumption and/or sale have been banned, with-*

'modif[ied] slightly . . . in order to ensure that they are consistent with recently developed policy instruments adopted in other intergovernmental forums.'[343] In the introduction to the second edition of the Consolidated List it is noted that, although these criteria have 'significantly facilitated the screening of information for the list', 'the interpretation by Governments of the criterion "severely restricted", in particular, continues to vary widely, *leading to considerable unevenness in the reporting on national restrictive regulatory measures.*'[344]

The Consolidated List Under Political Scrutiny

Pursuant to its decision 'to keep under review the format of the consolidated list with a view to its possible improvement,'[345] the General Assembly reviewed progress at its 38th session in 1983. The Assembly had before it the new report prepared by the Secretary-General in response to Resolution 36/166.[346] This report reviewed the use made by member states of the existing international information systems on toxic chemicals, such as the IRPTC and the ILO/WHO International Programme for Chemical Safety. It found that less than half the countries which replied to the enquiry had used those systems 'to obtain information on imported chemicals . . . and to check if they are banned or proposed to be banned in the producing country or in any other country.'[347] Most of them 'considered those schemes adequate to meet the requirements of their legislation', though one country found them 'not . . . fully adequate.'[348] The report concluded that 'the international information systems available are not being used to the fullest extent'[349] and that 'the consolidated list . . . will supplement existing mechanisms within the United Nations system and provide a further means for assisting importing countries to protect themselves.'[350] That statement was apparently intended to refute the contention of some Western governments that the publication of the Consolidated List was superfluous duplication of work and impinged on the jurisdiction of specialised agencies.

drawn, severely restricted or not approved by Governments, 2nd issue, 1986, UN Doc ST/ESA/192 (hereafter referred to as *1986 Consolidated List*), Annex II (Criteria for inclusion of pharmaceutical and chemical products in the Consolidated List), p 641 (emphasis added).

[343] *Products harmful to health and the environment*, Report of the Secretary-General, UN Doc A/41/329-E/1986/83, 23 May 1986, p 5, para 10.

[344] *1986 Consolidated List*, above n 342, p iv (emphasis added).

[345] UNGA Res 37/137, above n 65, para 6.

[346] *Exchange of information on banned hazardous chemicals and unsafe pharmaceutical products*, Report of the Secretary-General, UN Doc A/38/190, 27 May 1983.

[347] *Ibid*, p 5.

[348] *Ibid.*

[349] *Ibid*, p 6.

[350] *Ibid*, p 7.

The resolution adopted by the General Assembly following consideration of this report was once more an artful compromise. While the original draft tabled by Pakistan called on the Secretary-General to 'disseminate widely' the Consolidated List,[351] the final version only requested him to 'make [it] available.'[352] The Secretary-General was asked to prepare further reports, but a proposed emphasis on 'the labelling and advertising practices of manufacturers and distributors of pharmaceutical and chemical products'[353] was found too controversial and deleted in committee. Instead, the Secretary-General was given a mandate no more specific than to recast for the third time his report 'on the exchange of information on banned hazardous chemicals and unsafe pharmaceutical products' and to report 'on the implementation of Assembly resolution 37/137.'[354] Finally, a request to non-governmental organisations to 'provide information for inclusion in the list'[355] was edited into the following bizarre paragraph:

> [The General Assembly] urges non-governmental organizations to extend cooperation to the Secretary-General regarding the preparation of the consolidated list, particularly *in the identification of potential sources of information among national Governments and in obtaining governmental information on relevant regulatory actions.*[356]

It is indeed ironic that an intergovernmental organisation should have to rely on NGOs to obtain official governmental information from its member states. But it certainly was an ingenious ploy to overcome the uncooperative attitude of some member governments. This explains the misgivings of the US, which were not entirely appeased by this representation of NGOs as purveyors of government information, as mere intermediaries between national governments and the UN Secretariat, rather than providers of information in their own right. 'The United States continued to have reservations about paragraph 6 of the draft resolution concerning cooperation with non-governmental organizations', said the US delegate in committee, and he stressed that 'the information in the list should clearly be based only on official sources.'[357] Apparently the US was afraid of what Jeane Kirkpatrick saw as an

> 'iron triangle' uniting nongovernmental organisations, third world representatives (particularly of the radical third world countries) and ideologically sympathetic international bureaucrats in quest of restrictive international health and safety regulations.[358]

351 UN Doc A/C.2/38/L.28/Rev 1, 1983.
352 UNGA Res 38/149, 38 UN GAOR Supp (No 47), UN Doc A/38/47, p 120.
353 UN Doc A/C.2/38/L.28/Rev 1, 1983.
354 UNGA Res 38/149, above n 352, paras 7, 8.
355 UN Doc A/C.2/38/L.28/Rev 1, 1983.
356 UNGA Res 38/149, above n 352, para 6 (emphasis added).
357 UN Doc A/C.2/38/SR.53, 1983, p 3.
358 Kirkpatrick (1983), p 21.

Nevertheless, the US apparently did not regard Resolution 38/149 as sufficiently threatening to bother to vote against it, and did not prevent its adoption by consensus.

The situation was quite different at the next session of the General Assembly, where the Consolidated List again became the subject of acrimonious discord. The two reports submitted by the Secretary-General pursuant to Resolution 38/149 did not contain much that was new. One of them once again surveyed the activities of various UN agencies and other international organisations in the field of information exchange on hazardous substances, largely copying a similar survey published by UNEP a few months earlier,[359] while the other, reviewing the implementation of Resolution 37/137, basically recommended staying the course and maintaining the Consolidated List in its existing form.[360] The latter report reiterated that the list 'complements existing information mechanisms' because it 'presents in a unified manner information on important restrictive regulatory decisions.'[361] These conclusions were, of course, intended to refute the major objections formulated by Western governments. The Secretary-General further recommended expanding the coverage of the list to include

> fuller information . . . regarding the regulatory context in which measures are taken by governments, the nature of limitations imposed regarding the manufacture, import, sale and use of products and the health or environmental reasons for which regulatory measures are taken.[362]

Echoing the recommendations of the Secretary-General, Venezuela proposed a resolution which would have instructed him to develop the list further 'with particular emphasis on the legal, public health and commercial context of the regulatory actions' and to 'strengthen the existing organizational arrangements to provide capabilities for legal analysis, risk assessment, commercial marketing analysis' etc.[363] Naturally, such a major expansion of a UN programme which they already viewed with considerable scepticism and suspicion was not acceptable to Western governments. A compromise was eventually hammered out by Sweden, but it proved impossible once again to get the US to join the consensus.

The compromise resolution, which was adopted by a vote of 147 to 1, with the US voting against,[364] essentially cut costs by reducing the frequency

[359] *Exchange of information on banned hazardous chemicals and unsafe pharmaceutical products*, Report of the Secretary-General, UN Doc A/39/290, 18 June 1984. Cf *Survey of programmes and activities for the exchange of information on potentially harmful chemicals (in particular pesticides) in international trade*, UN Doc UNEP/WG.96/3, 15 Dec 1983.

[360] *Products harmful to health and the environment*, Report of the Secretary-General, UN Doc A/39/452, 7 Sept 1984.

[361] *Ibid*, p 2 (emphasis added).

[362] *Ibid*, p 8.

[363] UN Doc A/C.2/39/L.25, 1984.

[364] UN Doc A/39/PV.104, 3 Jan 1985, p 29.

of publication of different language versions of the list and deferred for consideration in a 'continuing review' any substantive change in the contents of the list.[365] Notwithstanding these concessions by the Third World, the US stood firm in its opposition to the resolution. The Soviet Union seized this opportunity to score a few easy propaganda points, by deploring the fact that 'the work of the United Nations was being hampered by the efforts of some Western States to protect their monopolies.'[366]

In opposing the proposed resolution, the US rehashed its familiar arguments about bureaucratic jurisdictional boundaries:

> Resolution 37/137 had brought to the surface a serious problem regarding the respective spheres of responsibility of the United Nations Secretariat and of the secretariats of other agencies in the United Nations system.

The US delegate recognised that there may be 'room for improvement' in the information exchange programmes of the specialised agencies, but, he said, 'it was quite another matter for the United Nations Secretariat to duplicate the expertise and functions of other agencies.'[367] He further criticised the quality of the information in the Consolidated List:

> *Sketchy information*, as contained in the current consolidated list, *was inappropriate as well as dangerous* because it could be used as a substitute for a proper review of the complete information already available and thus lead to faulty decision-making.[368]

Reading this statement, one almost has the impression that it is not so much the products themselves as the information about them which is hazardous. In order to make this 'dangerous' information harmless, the US proposed that the Consolidated List be 'transformed into a document which would direct inquirers to the appropriate sources of full and complete information.'[369] At one stage, this suggestion was reflected in a draft compromise resolution, apparently in an attempt to accommodate the objections of the United States. The draft provided that the review of the list should

> give due consideration to the possible advantages and disadvantages of streamlining its content, so that users, when alerted to the potential hazards of a product, may be directed to sources of more complete information.[370]

When it appeared that this concession was insufficient to sway the US, the Third World reneged on the compromise and the clause was eventually deleted from the final text of the resolution.[371]

[365] UNGA Res 39/229, 18 Dec 1984, UN Doc A/RES/39/229.
[366] UN Doc A/C.2/39/SR.58, 1984, p 3 (Statement of Mr Reshetnyak, Ukrainian SSR).
[367] *Ibid*, p 5.
[368] *Ibid* (emphasis added).
[369] *Ibid.*
[370] UN Doc A/C.2/39/L.125, 1984, para 5 (d).
[371] UN Doc A/39/789/Add. 1, 1984, p 6.

It is noteworthy that the US received no support from the European Community in its opposition to the Consolidated List during the 39th session of the General Assembly. The EC countries supported the resolution 'because they had always been in favour of the concept of a consolidated list,'[372] quite a surprising statement in view of the negative comments on the list which some Community member states had sent to the Secretary-General a little over one year earlier. The EC endorsement of the list was however not wholly unqualified:

> The list complemented existing information mechanisms within the United Nations system and *the question as to how it could relate to them in a manner that did not involve duplication was an open one.*[373]

In the light of the experience with the first issue of the Consolidated List and the ongoing debate in the ECOSOC and the General Assembly, the Secretary-General initiated an internal administrative review of the criteria and procedures for compiling the list in early 1985, prior to the publication of the second edition. Consultations between the various UN agencies involved resulted in new arrangements for the production of the Consolidated List, whereby responsibility for the collection and analysis of information was delegated by the UN Secretariat to the WHO and UNEP/IRPTC. As noted above, this review also resulted in the formulation of explicit criteria for the selection of products for inclusion in the list. The preparation of the second issue of the Consolidated List in accordance with the new arrangements was in process when the Secretary-General reported to the ECOSOC and the 41st session of the General Assembly in 1986.[374]

The United States seized this opportunity to introduce a draft resolution at the second regular session of the ECOSOC in July 1986 which, while 'commending' the Secretary-General for his efforts 'towards improvement of the list' and for his 'constructive and appropriate delegation of responsibility' to UNEP/IRPTC and the WHO, proposed to 'keep the criteria under continuing review' and, more importantly, to exclude from future editions of the list all data on brand names and manufacturers of the listed products.[375] Under the memoranda of understanding concluded between the various UN agencies involved, the collection and analysis of such commercial data, which was to be published as a separate reference list, was to be the responsibility of the UNCTC.[376] Thus, the US initiative

[372] UN Doc A/C.2/39/SR.58, p 4 (Statement of Mr Murray, Ireland, on behalf of the States members of the European Community).

[373] *Ibid* (emphasis added).

[374] *Products harmful to health and the environment*, Report of the Secretary-General, UN Doc A/41/329-E/1986/83, 23 May 1986.

[375] UN Doc E/1986/C.3/L.19, 15 July 1986.

[376] UN Doc A/41/329-E/1986/83, 23 May 1986, p 7, para 16 and p 8, para 21.

was also aimed at terminating any UNCTC involvement in the production of the Consolidated List.[377]

The American proposal provoked a strong response from developing countries, who pointed out that the exclusion of commercial information from the Consolidated List would be contrary to the explicit mandate of the General Assembly in Resolution 37/137. Amendments to the US draft resolution were tabled by Venezuela and Peru, who proposed that the list 'shall continue to be published as one document, including brand names, manufacturers and all other relevant commercial information.'[378] Those amendments were adopted by the ECOSOC in a slightly modified form,[379] and eventually the United States was forced to vote against its own resolution, as amended by the G77 countries. On 8 December 1986, the General Assembly endorsed the ECOSOC resolution by an overwhelming majority,[380] with the US casting the sole negative vote. Again, the United States received no support from the European Community. Only one EC member state, the Federal Republic of Germany, abstained.

In its explanation of its vote, the US delegation stated that it was 'particularly pleased' with the new arrangements for the production of the Consolidated List and, in particular, the 'wise and highly important delegations of authority to WHO and UNEP' and that, in view of those, it had been 'prepared not to oppose continued production of the list, even though [it] had voted against the resolutions which created the list'. The US claimed that it had been forced to vote against by the attitude of 'other Assembly members insist[ing] to bring forward another confrontation on this issue' and the ECOSOC decision to include in the list 'the discriminatory commercial data' produced by the UNCTC, which discriminates against Western manufacturers 'who are open with their commercial and regulatory data' and 'serves to protect manufacturers in socialist and developing countries.'[381]

This was the last rearguard action of the United States in the General Assembly to oppose the full implementation of Resolution 37/137. The importance of the UN General Assembly as a forum for international political debate on trade in banned and severely restricted products waned as attention shifted to the negotiations on regulatory instruments in UNEP and the FAO, which were about to enter a new phase with the breakthrough on prior informed consent in UNEP Governing Council and the FAO Conference in 1987.

[377] According to the draft resolution, 'work done in connection with the list should be performed *exclusively*' by UNEP and WHO. UN Doc E/1986/C.3/L.19, 15 July 1986, para 5 (emphasis added).

[378] UN Doc E/1986/C.3/L.22, 16 July 1986.

[379] ECOSOC Res 1986/72, 23 July 1986.

[380] UNGA Dec 41/450, 8 Dec 1986.

[381] United States Mission to the United Nations, Press Release USUN 183-(86), 8 Dec 1986.

13

The Second Phase of International Regulatory Efforts: Towards a Consensus on Prior Informed Consent

BEYOND EXPORT NOTIFICATION: THE REVISION OF THE LONDON GUIDELINES FOR THE EXCHANGE OF INFORMATION ON CHEMICALS IN INTERNATIONAL TRADE

With the adoption of the London Guidelines and their referral to UNEP Governing Council for its formal endorsement in February 1987, it seemed for a while that the international regulatory debate on trade in banned and severely restricted chemicals had come to a conclusion. A consensus had been reached both in UNEP and the FAO on an international notification system, and notwithstanding continued pressure from advocates of more stringent regulation, in particular prior informed consent, it did not seem possible to move the consensus further in that direction. The discussions on PIC in the *Ad Hoc* Working Group of Experts had not resulted in any substantive change in the notification provisions of the PNS. The OECD countries had prevailed in this technical forum and succeeded in imposing the OECD Guiding Principles as a universal prescription. They expected that the formal adoption of the London Guidelines by UNEP Governing Council would lay the issue to rest, at least for a number of years.

The Debate in UNEP Governing Council: a Breakthrough for Prior Informed Consent

In spite of these expectations, the May 1987 meeting of UNEP Council became a turning point in the international debate. The developing countries, which had been overwhelmed and outnumbered in the technical working groups, strongly reasserted their viewpoint in this political forum. The OECD countries, which were taken by surprise, were compelled to make substantial concessions which they had previously successfully resisted and forced to accept a new round of negotiations.

The Governing Council had before it a draft decision elaborated through informal consultations among member governments within the Committee of Permanent Representatives to UNEP. This draft was largely based on the recommendations from the London meeting but included some additional language intended to give PIC slightly more prominence than in those recommendations, in an apparent effort to accommodate the concerns of developing countries. Indeed, the draft contained a preambular paragraph 'taking into account that prior informed consent may be an important additional means of ensuring that hazardous substances will not be imported in ignorance of the risks' and requested the Executive Director 'to develop modalities of prior informed consent and other modalities which could usefully supplement the modalities of the London Guidelines.'[1] This language did not actually give the Executive Director a mandate to initiate negotiations with a view to amending the London Guidelines, but would have allowed him to further explore the issue of PIC at his discretion and to come back to the Governing Council with proposals and a possible request for further authority at a later stage. The draft decision did not in fact envisage any review of the London Guidelines by the Governing Council in order to consider 'whether there is a need to elaborate or modify them' before 1991.

This compromise did not satisfy the developing countries, which demanded that the principle of prior informed consent be further elaborated and incorporated into the London Guidelines *before* their adoption. They pointed out that the Guidelines, as adopted in London, fell short of the original intent of the Governing Council, as expressed in its Decision 85(V), which stressed the need not only to provide information but also to obtain the consent of importing countries. Indeed it seemed that after 10 years of discussions on the issue of banned and severely restricted chemicals, UNEP had not made any progress, but had actually retreated from its original recommendations.[2]

As an alternative to the text submitted by the Committee of Permanent Representatives, Senegal introduced a draft decision which, referring to Decision 85(V), stated that the London Guidelines should go beyond the information exchange provisions of the PNS and

> that further measures are called for to allow importing countries either to accept or to reject the import of such chemicals and that it is therefore necessary to include in the London Guidelines the principle of prior consent.[3]

[1] UN Doc UNEP/GC.14/CW/L.4, 26 May 1987, p 5.
[2] UN Doc UNEP/GC.14/CW/L.6/Add. 9, 13 June 1987, pp 6–7.
[3] UN Doc UNEP/GC.14/CW/CRP.5, 11 June 1987.

The Senegalese proposal included a series of amendments to the London Guidelines designed to incorporate PIC provisions. These amendments were submitted for immediate adoption by the Governing Council.

The Senegalese proposal provoked extensive discussion in the Governing Council and received overwhelming support from developing countries. The industrialised countries, which had pressed for adoption of the London Guidelines without further changes and opposed an early review on the grounds that some experience with their implementation was first needed, were forced to re-evaluate their position. They continued to reject an immediate amendment of the Guidelines without referral back to a technical working group but indicated that they were prepared to accept further discussions on PIC in a working group. A compromise was eventually reached along these lines.

In its Decision 14/27,[4] the Governing Council adopted the London Guidelines but at the same time implicitly recognised that they are insufficient and provided for their early amendment. The Governing Council recalled its earlier Decision 85(V) and noted that the London Guidelines 'constitute an important step towards full implementation of decision 85(V)', especially of its objective of information exchange. Thus, while the London Guidelines constitute a first step, the Governing Council considered 'that additional measures are required to enable importing countries to give or withhold their consent to particular exports following receipt of adequate information from exporting countries' and that 'such measures, based on the principle of prior informed consent, should be incorporated in the London Guidelines, as expeditiously as possible.'

To this end, the Governing Council instructed the Executive Director to convene an *Ad Hoc* Working Group of Experts with a view to 'developing modalities of prior informed consent and other approaches which could usefully supplement the modalities of the London Guidelines'. In describing the terms of reference of the working group, the Governing Council took language from the original draft submitted by the Committee of Permanent Representatives, which presents PIC as a concept to be further developed and considered alongside 'other approaches'. However, the preambular paragraphs as well as the explicit instruction to the working group to 'recommend measures for incorporating the principle of prior informed consent into the Guidelines' left little doubt as to the intended result of the exercise. While the working group was free to consider 'other approaches', in any event it had to incorporate PIC into the Guidelines.

The constraining terms of reference of the working group were difficult to accept for a number of delegations, because they effectively precluded

[4] UNEP Governing Council Dec 14/27, 17 June 1987, Report of the Governing Council on the work of its 14th session, June 1987, pp 83–85.

further dilatory tactics. The decision of the Governing Council was adopted by consensus, but the United Kingdom and the United States felt the need to make formal statements for the record indicating their reluctant acceptance of the new agenda for negotiations. The United Kingdom 'expressed doubts about the practicality of establishing a satisfactory system of prior informed consent', while the United States deplored that some language in the decision 'appeared to prejudge the outcome of the work of the *Ad Hoc* Working Group.'[5]

The Governing Council had made a political decision to incorporate the 'principle of prior informed consent' into the London Guidelines but had not given a clear definition of what that principle entailed, other than by referring to the very general terms of Decision 85(V). The language of the Governing Council decision, by referring to 'modalities' of prior informed consent, in fact implied that the concept needed further elaboration and that various ways and means of implementing the general principle of prior informed consent were conceivable. So, while the Governing Council had reached consensus on a principle, that consensus was very shallow and did not extend to the actual implications of the principle. To the contrary, the consensus was premised on the understanding that the principle was open to different interpretations. One of the aspects on which the various actors still widely diverged was the extent to which PIC implied export control. The countries which had initially opposed PIC realised that the terms of the Governing Council decision left considerable room for manoeuvre and proceeded to redefine the concept of PIC according to their own terms in the course of the ensuing new round of negotiations.

From Principle to Procedure: Redefining Prior Informed Consent

In order to prepare for the first meeting of the *Ad Hoc* Working Group of Experts, UNEP Secretariat convened an advisory panel for an exploratory round of discussions in December 1987. At the beginning of this meeting, the United States, in what was apparently a rearguard action by die-hard opponents of PIC, attempted to sidetrack the discussions by reinterpreting the mandate given by the Governing Council. Exploiting the reference to 'other approaches' in the Governing Council decision, the United States suggested that the working group should address PIC only as one of a range of possible options. This suggestion, however, received no support from other participants and the negotiations subsequently focused on elaborating the 'modalities' of PIC.

The Secretariat had prepared a discussion paper in which it outlined various possible definitions of the concept of PIC and identified a series

[5] UNEP Governing Council Dec 14/27, 17 June 1987, Report of the Governing Council on the work of its 14th session, June 1987, paras 109–10.

of aspects which would have to be considered in elaborating 'modalities' of PIC.[6] The paper contrasted a 'classic' concept of PIC, whereby explicit consent would be required on a shipment-specific basis, with other, more flexible approaches. The first of these approaches was the so-called 'prior informed choice' system, inspired by the draft regulation of the Commission of the EC,[7] whereby exports would be allowed to proceed unless the importing country had actually objected to them. Under this system, lack of response would be equated with tacit consent. The paper also proposed consideration of voluntary PIC systems, which would apply only to exports to those countries which had expressed their desire to participate in PIC. In all those approaches, the PIC procedure is linked with actual export shipments.

The most innovative feature of the Secretariat's proposal was the suggestion that the application of PIC might be de-linked from export transactions and linked instead with notifications of control actions. In what it called 'intensified information exchange on control actions', the Secretariat proposed that a response procedure might be tagged on to the existing notification procedure of the London Guidelines. Following receipt of a notification of control action, importing countries would have the opportunity to indicate in advance whether or not they would accept imports of the chemical in question. The advantage of this system, according to the Secretariat, would be to 'separate the concept of prior informed decision-making from the *ad hoc*, shipment-by-shipment nature of the export trade.'[8] The decision of the importing country to consent to or refuse import would not be taken with reference to a specific shipment, but in a general way, in advance of actual exports:

> By *de-coupling the prior informed consent decision from the export process*, import countries would be able to make across-the-board decisions without the time pressure of a pending shipment.[9]

Another suggestion raised in the Secretariat's paper was that an international list of pesticides could be developed for the purpose of determining those compounds subject to PIC requirements. This could take the form, either of a positive list ('essential pesticides list') of pesticides exempt from PIC, or of a 'blacklist' of banned or severely restricted pesticides subject to PIC.[10] In the absence of an international list, it would be for each exporting country individually to apply the definitions in the London Guidelines to determine which chemicals were to be regarded as 'banned or severely restricted' for the purpose of implementing PIC. Thus, the chemicals

[6] UN Doc UNEP/WG.184/3, 9 Dec 1987.
[7] See below ch 15.
[8] UN Doc UNEP/WG.184/3, 9 Dec 1987, p 4.
[9] *Ibid* (emphasis added).
[10] *Ibid*, p 5, para 5(a).

subject to PIC would vary from exporting country to exporting country, and exporting countries with laxer standards would actually enjoy an export advantage because they would only have to apply PIC to those chemicals which *they* regarded as banned or severely restricted. An international list would harmonise PIC requirements; the application of PIC would thus be made independent of the regulatory situation in the exporting country.

The Secretariat's discussion paper provided the elements of a PIC procedure around which consensus could eventually be built. In particular, the suggestion to 'de-couple' the PIC procedure from the export process proved instrumental in breaking the deadlock around PIC and developing a 'modality' of PIC which would be acceptable to exporting countries. The linking of PIC with notifications of control actions transformed PIC into an extension of the information exchange procedures rather than a mechanism for export control. The proposed development of an international list of chemicals subject to PIC provided a means of removing the fear of discrimination between exporting countries. The voluntary nature of the PIC procedure was also seen as a way of ensuring that it would not be too restrictive of international trade and that PIC would not be applied to importing countries which showed no interest in the procedure.

The report of the advisory panel which considered the Secretariat's discussion paper does not contain clear proposals but rather identified those aspects around which future discussion would revolve. The report lists all possible modalities and 'variables' of PIC and a set of objectives and criteria against which these are to be evaluated. In particular, the report notes the need to consider 'control-action-driven' modalities of PIC versus 'shipment-driven' modalities. It also recommends further consideration of developing a list as a means of identifying chemicals subject to PIC. The need to further refine the definitions of 'banned' and 'severely restricted' chemicals as criteria for drawing up such a list is mentioned, as is the possibility of implementing a PIC modality on a voluntary basis in terms of participation by exporting and importing countries.[11]

Identifying Chemicals Subject to Prior Informed Consent: Towards an International List

In preparing for the PIC negotiations, UNEP Secretariat further sounded out support for various PIC modalities and in particular for the concept of an international list of chemicals subject to PIC. UNEP Executive Director submitted the issue of PIC to a panel of 'senior advisers on environmental law', which endorsed the idea of elaborating what they called a 'red flag'

[11] UN Doc UNEP/WG.184/4, 16 Dec 1987.

international list of chemicals for which PIC would apply. As a simple criterion for drawing up this list, the advisers suggested the number of countries having banned or severely restricted the chemical in question. The list would be circulated to all countries together with detailed information on the chemicals in question, as a basis for countries to make decisions on imports.[12] The concept of the 'red flag' list featured prominently in the note which the Executive Director, apparently encouraged by the support of the senior advisers, submitted to the first meeting of the *Ad Hoc* Working Group for its consideration.[13] In order to stimulate discussion on this proposal, the Executive Director also provided an indicative list of some 70 chemicals banned or severely restricted in five or more countries, based on the information readily available to the IRPTC.[14]

Two meetings of the '*Ad Hoc* Working Group of Experts on Prior Informed Consent and Other Modalities to Supplement the London Guidelines for the Exchange of Information on Chemicals in International Trade' were required to fulfil the mandate assigned to it by the 1987 Governing Council decision. The first was held in Dakar in September 1988 and the second in New York in February 1989. The outcome of the negotiations, in the form of formal amendments to the London Guidelines, was eventually submitted by UNEP Executive Director to the 15th session of the Governing Council for endorsement in May 1989.

Negotiations in the *Ad Hoc* Working Group initially focused on the list concept. Agreement was reached at an early stage on the desirability of developing a 'red flag' list as a basis for the PIC procedure. Exporting countries which had initially opposed the idea because they feared that it would be perceived as a 'blacklist' eventually accepted it when they realised it would be a means of limiting the number of chemicals subject to PIC and of avoiding trade discrimination between exporting countries. Once consensus was reached on the list concept, the key question became that of the criteria for inclusion of chemicals on the list. The discussion on this question set proponents of a comprehensive list including as many banned or severely restricted chemicals as possible against advocates of a more restrictive approach, favouring the use of strict criteria to limit the number of chemicals on the list in order to keep it 'manageable'.

The two sides agreed that the starting point for the establishment of the list should be control actions notified by governments but differed as to whether all control actions should be taken at face value and would automatically qualify a chemical for inclusion on the list or whether chemicals should be selected based on additional criteria. Various selection criteria were proposed, such as review by an international expert group to

[12] UN Doc UNEP/WG.187/5, 22 Apr 1988, p 3, para 11.
[13] UN Doc UNEP/WG.188/2, 25 May 1988.
[14] UN Doc UNEP/WG.188/2/Add. 1, 15 Sept 1988.

determine whether the reasons for the control action could be considered 'internationally significant' or whether the chemicals 'meet a specific set of toxicological and environmental criteria which indicated them to be potential hazards in countries other than the one which had banned or severely restricted them.'[15] It was clear that such a review process based on largely discretionary criteria would involve a lot of work and place a heavy responsibility on the experts in charge of it. It would not be simple for an *ad hoc* expert panel to evaluate the complex scientific and technical background of regulatory decisions taken by national governments.

Instead of instituting a substantive international review process for national control actions, the negotiators opted for the objective, though admittedly rather arbitrary, criterion proposed by the Executive Director, namely the number of countries having banned or severely restricted the chemical. However, an element of review was included in the process, though on limited, more formal grounds. In fact, a compromise was struck between international review of control actions and automatic selection based on the number of countries in which the chemical is banned or severely restricted. It was agreed that chemicals banned or severely restricted by 10 or more countries would be automatically placed on the list, while those banned or severely restricted by more than five but less than 10 countries would be submitted to an 'informal consultation to determine whether they meet the definitions of banned or severely restricted for health or environmental reasons' as laid down in the London Guidelines.[16] Thus the scope and stated reasons of the control actions notified by governments would be examined to determine whether they actually constituted bans or severe restrictions for 'health or environmental reasons' within the meaning of the London Guidelines. This still involves a measure of discretionary judgement, though less than the more substantive criteria initially proposed.

The selection process described above would be applied to draw up an initial 'red flag' list based on control actions taken by governments in the past. However, for control actions notified after the entry into force of the PIC procedure, no threshold number of countries would have to be reached. Chemicals banned or severely restricted by any single country would be placed on the list of chemicals subject to PIC. The same 'informal consultative process' would be used to assess whether the control action meets the definitions of the London Guidelines. This distinction between past and future control actions was clearly the result of a political compromise, since there is no objective reason to attach more weight to future national regulatory decisions than to past ones.

[15] UN Doc UNEP/WG.188/5, 10 Oct 1988, p 13, para 48.
[16] *Ibid*, p 14, para 50(b)(ii).

Designing the Prior Informed Consent Procedure

After having agreed on the mode of selection of chemicals subject to PIC, the expert group considered the actual procedure through which the consent of importing countries should be obtained. Following the course charted during the preliminary consultations undertaken by UNEP Secretariat, the discussion centered on control-action-driven modalities versus shipment-linked modalities. Most exporting countries reiterated their firm opposition to shipment-linked consent and argued for the PIC mechanism to be dissociated from individual shipments. It was argued that shipment-linked procedures 'did not allow sufficient time for decision-making, might result in trade distortions, could be environmentally ineffective, and would be administratively burdensome.'[17] Whatever the merit of these arguments, it was clear that the main concern was to remove PIC from a trade control context. It was stressed that action taken by importing countries under the PIC procedure 'should apply to the chemical generically, to both domestic production and all sources of import, and not to individual shipments.'[18] This called for PIC decisions to be taken at an early stage, in response to notifications of control actions, instead of export notifications. On these grounds, UNEP opted for a control-action-linked PIC system.

It was also agreed that, since the PIC system was designed to assist importing countries which lacked effective regulatory procedures, participation by importing countries would be on a voluntary basis. All countries would be invited by UNEP to indicate whether they wished to participate in the system and to designate a competent national authority for this purpose. It would be assumed that countries which failed to designate a national authority for PIC purposes did not wish to participate in the procedure. However, the regular information exchange provisions of the London Guidelines would continue to apply to those countries. There would be no special prerequisites for participation by exporting countries. All exporting countries would be expected to comply with the PIC decisions of participating importing countries.

The PIC procedure would be triggered by the communication to participating countries of the initial list of chemicals subject to PIC and subsequent notices of additional chemicals becoming subject to PIC as a result of control actions notified. For each chemical subject to PIC, a 'decision guidance document' would be drawn up, providing background information on the chemical, its effects, the national prohibitions and restrictions to which it is subject and reasons for them, and available alternatives. Based on this information, each designated national authority would be expected

[17] *Ibid*, Annex I, p 3.
[18] *Ibid*.

to decide whether or not to consent to future imports of the chemical. A response would have to be sent to UNEP within 90 days and could take several forms. It could either be a final decision to consent unconditionally to importation or subject to certain stated conditions or to refuse importation, or an interim decision requesting additional information or indicating that the matter was under review, with the option of suspending importation pending a final decision. Responses from participating importing countries would be compiled by UNEP and communicated to all countries.

In this way, the PIC procedure would in fact amount to little more than an extended information exchange system, whereby information is exchanged not only about control actions taken unilaterally by countries but also about decisions taken pursuant to the international PIC procedure. These decisions simply become an additional category of information about the regulatory status of chemicals to be exchanged internationally. The compromise formula for PIC on which consensus was reached within UNEP was not very clear as regards the trade implications of the PIC procedure. What use was to be made of this information? What consequences would have to be drawn from PIC decisions?

Responsibilities for Implementation: What Obligations for Exporting Countries?

In deciding what the consequences would be if a participating importing country failed to respond, UNEP struck a compromise between an approach requiring explicit consent and an approach equating no response with tacit consent ('prior informed choice'). It was agreed that:

> if a country does not make a response or responds with less than a final decision, the *status quo* with respect to importation of the chemical should continue. This means that the chemical should not be exported without the explicit consent of the importing country, unless it is a pesticide which is registered in the importing country or is a chemical the use of which has been allowed by other governmental action of the importing country.[19]

This carefully crafted compromise is ambiguous, its language even potentially contradictory. The notion of status quo implies that the chemical would continue to be exported if it had previously been exported to the country in question prior to the implementation of the PIC system, and that no exports would be initiated to non-responding countries which had not previously imported the chemical. However, the second sentence places

[19] UN Doc UNEP/WG.188/5, 10 Oct 1988, p 17.

further restrictions on exports in that it states as a rule that there should be no exports in the absence of explicit consent, subject to two well-defined exceptions. It is not clear what should happen where a chemical had previously been exported to a country without being registered or otherwise allowed by governmental action. The notion of 'governmental action' does not necessarily refer to regulatory decisions but is deliberately vague and allows for different interpretations. An extensive interpretation would regard the involvement of any governmental agency in the import transaction as a form of tacit consent under this rule.

At the second meeting of the *Ad Hoc* Working Group several countries tried to stretch the interpretation of this clause even further by putting an interpretative statement on record to the effect that they regarded the phrase 'the use or importation of which has been allowed by other governmental action of the importing country' as 'includ[ing] previous legal importation.'[20] This could cover situations where no governmental action at all was involved. In countries without any legislation on the import of chemicals, importation would indeed have been legal, not as a result of any governmental action but rather as a result of governmental *inaction*. The divergent interpretations of this provision illustrate that there was in fact hardly any consensus on the rule that would apply in case of no response.

Another contentious issue was that of the responsibility of exporting countries for enforcement of PIC procedures. The debate on this question opposed those who felt exporting countries had a responsibility to take export control measures to prevent exports in violation of PIC decisions and those who rejected any reference to export controls and insisted that enforcement was the sole responsibility of importing countries. Exporting countries such as the United States claimed they had no legal authority to control exports. Initially the only responsibility imposed on exporting countries was to 'transmit' information on PIC decisions to their industry. Thus the PIC system would have relied on voluntary compliance by exporters.

After protracted argument a clause was eventually inserted which requires governments of exporting countries to 'implement appropriate procedures, *within their authorities*, to *help* ensure that exports do not occur contrary to the decisions of participating importing countries.'[21] Thus, exporting countries would only be required to take whatever measures they deemed 'appropriate' and 'within their authorities'. The United States made it clear that it had no intention of seeking legislative authority to control exports of chemicals subject to PIC. After further discussion at the second meeting of the working group, the language of this provision was slightly

[20] UN Doc UNEP/PIC.WG.2/4, 16 Feb 1989, p 6, para 29.
[21] UN Doc UNEP/WG.188/5, 10 Oct 1988, p 17 (emphasis added).

amended to refer to 'appropriate procedures, within their *authority*, *designed* to ensure that exports do not occur.'[22] The implications of these amendments are not entirely clear but could be interpreted as strengthening the case for export controls. While 'authorities' was apparently meant to refer to existing domestic statutory authorities, thus enabling an exporting state to rely on deficiencies in its domestic law as an excuse for failing to control exports, 'authority' could be interpreted as synonymous with 'jurisdiction'. There can be little doubt that under international law it is well within the jurisdiction of an exporting country to take measures to regulate its exports. Moreover, the procedures referred to should actually be 'designed' to prevent exports in violation of PIC decisions rather than merely 'help' to do so.

Specifying the Concept of 'Severely Restricted Chemical'

With the perspective of the expansion of the information exchange procedures of the London Guidelines to include PIC, the question of the definition of 'banned and severely restricted' chemicals acquired a new importance. While these notions had been rather vaguely defined in the first version of the Guidelines, on the understanding that countries would necessarily exercise a certain measure of discretion in determining what chemicals would come under the information exchange procedures, tighter definitions were perceived to be essential for the application of a more consequential procedure like PIC. This became apparent in the discussion on the criteria for the selection of chemicals subject to PIC, where one of the central concerns became the question of determining whether national control actions which form the basis for this selection are in accordance with the definitions in the London Guidelines.

At the first meeting of the *Ad Hoc* Working Group, several countries drew attention to the difference between the definitions of 'banned and severely restricted' in the London Guidelines and the FAO Code of Conduct. They urged that the definition in the Guidelines be brought into line with that in the Code, which is also used in the UN Consolidated List, not only for the sake of consistency but also because the latter definition was seen as more precise, 'more explicit' than the former.[23] This was not just a question of wording and style, however; it also had important substantive implications.

The original definition of 'banned or severely restricted chemical' referred to:

[22] London Guidelines, as amended 1989, para 12(c)(iv), UN Doc UNEP/PIC.WG.2/4, 16 Feb 1989, p 20.

[23] UN Doc UNEP/WG.155/5, p 14, para 51.

any chemical that is the subject of a control action taken by a competent governmental authority in the State of export . . . to ban or severely restrict the use *or handling* of the chemical in order to protect human health or the environment domestically.[24]

By contrast, the FAO Code definition of 'severely restricted' covers pesticides 'for which virtually all registered uses have been prohibited by final government regulatory action but specific registered uses remain authorized.' The original London Guidelines definition is broader in that it recognises that relevant regulatory restrictions on pesticides may relate not only to the *purpose* for which they are used but also to their handling, ie the *manner* in which they are used. The FAO definition, which equates a severe restriction with a limited ban, is more restrictive. Pesticides whose use is authorised but whose handling is restricted to specially trained and equipped applicators would not be covered by the FAO definition, while they arguably fall under the original UNEP definition.

A number of developing countries stressed the fact that acutely toxic pesticides subject to handling restrictions in industrialised countries were a special hazard in the Third World, where such handling restrictions cannot be observed. For this reason, they were reluctant to narrow the definition of 'severely restricted' to exclude handling restrictions. No consensus was reached on the proposed change in definition at the first meeting; the matter of definitions was referred to a small sub-group of legal experts, which was instructed to formulate proposals for the next meeting of the working group.[25]

A number of alternative options were considered by the working group at its second meeting, based on a working paper elaborated by the legal experts. Apart from the two main options of leaving the original definitions unchanged or aligning them with those of the FAO Code, one of the options proposed was to adopt the definitions from the FAO Code and Consolidated List but expand them to include the category of pesticides which, for health or environmental reasons, are 'restricted by final government action to be used only by [specially trained, equipped] licensed or registered applicators' or by 'special classes of users.'[26] This would have covered pesticides subject to certain handling restrictions by defining them more precisely, thus overcoming objections to the 'circular' nature of the original definition in the London Guidelines.

The definitional issue, crucial as it was in determining the scope of the PIC procedure, was not easily resolved. Exporting countries were reluctant

[24] London Guidelines, UN Doc UNEP/GC.14/17, 2 Apr 1987, Annex IV, p 2, para 1(b) (emphasis added).

[25] UN Doc UNEP/WG.155/5, p 15, para 52.

[26] Working paper on definitions of banned and severely restricted chemicals, UN Doc UNEP/WG.PIC.2/3, 7 Jan 1989, p 2 (original brackets).

to include a whole new category of pesticides in the definition of 'severely restricted', and the term 'handling' in the original definition was criticised as being 'too general to provide clear guidance on what chemicals should be included in the PIC procedure.'[27]

Eventually, a compromise was reached whereby a mechanism was developed to deal with the issue of acutely toxic pesticides otherwise than by generally including handling restrictions in the definition of 'severely restricted'. The definition was brought into line with the FAO definition and the reference to handling deleted, but a special procedure was developed to bring within the scope of PIC certain pesticides which, though not 'severely restricted' according to the new definition, were considered to pose special hazards in developing countries.[28] It was agreed that, in the context of the procedure for establishing the initial list of chemicals subject to PIC, an expert group would review pesticide formulations containing active ingredients classified as 'extremely hazardous' by the WHO (Class Ia) to determine if 'there are acutely hazardous pesticide formulations of concern to developing countries which are not already included in the PIC procedure.'[29] Any such pesticides would be included in the PIC procedure in addition to those selected on the basis of bans or severe restrictions. Though the wording of the compromise did not prejudge whether this process would actually result in an additional list of chemicals subject to PIC—the experts were still to determine 'if there exists a need for a list'—it clearly recognised the problem of acutely toxic pesticides and mandated UNEP to consider it even though it was beyond the scope of 'banned and severely restricted' chemicals *stricto sensu*.

Initially, the category of acutely toxic pesticides to be considered for inclusion on the PIC list was restricted to those classified as 'extremely hazardous' in the WHO Recommended Classification of Pesticides by Hazard. The mandate of the expert group as outlined in Annex II of the London Guidelines did not extend beyond a review of the compounds in the WHO Class Ia. However, there are pesticides in lower hazard classes which also pose problems to developing countries owing to their acute toxicity. At the Governing Council meeting which adopted the amended London Guidelines, Kenya stressed the importance of the issue of acutely toxic pesticides and urged that they be comprehensively covered by PIC procedures. At the initiative of Kenya, some language was added to the Governing Council decision adopting the Guidelines to expand the mandate of the expert group with respect to acutely toxic pesticides. The Governing Council instructed the group to 'keep the issue of acutely hazardous pesticide formulations under continuing review' after consideration of the Class Ia compounds

27 UN Doc UNEP/PIC.WG.2/4, 16 Feb 1989, p 6, para 25.
28 *Ibid.*
29 *Ibid*, p 26.

'with a view to formulating any recommendations for additional action in this regard.'[30] Thus the expert group would also be able to propose the inclusion on the PIC list of acutely toxic pesticides not listed in the WHO Class Ia.

Information to be Provided to Importing Countries

The information that would be provided to participating importing countries along with the list of chemicals subject to PIC or subsequent qualifying control actions was of crucial importance since it would serve as a basis for the importing country's decision with respect to future importation of the chemical. For the PIC procedure to be effective, it is essential that importing countries receive adequate information which they can use to make informed decisions. For this purpose, more information should be provided than a mere account of the control actions which have made the chemical subject to PIC. It was agreed that, for each chemical subject to PIC, UNEP, in cooperation with the FAO for pesticides, would draw up a 'chemical data sheet', later renamed 'decision guidance document', with comprehensive information to assist countries in making their PIC decisions. In view of the importance of these documents, their content, which was the subject of some discussion during the negotiations, is outlined in Annex III to the amended London Guidelines. The document is to contain information both about the control action or control actions which have led to the inclusion of the chemical on the PIC list and about the chemical itself. The latter category of information includes data on the chemical and physical properties of the chemical, its toxicological characteristics, environmental effects, exposure potential, etc, as well as precautionary information and recommendations about packaging and labelling, storage and disposal.

The decision guidance document must also contain information about 'alternatives considered effective replacements by the country taking the control action, including, eg, integrated pest management and non-chemical alternatives'. There was considerable discussion about the feasibility and desirability of providing such information. The representatives of industry, a number of producing countries and the FAO claimed it would be impossible to provide general information on alternatives for each chemical and use because available alternatives would vary according to local conditions, and listing specific alternative products could therefore be misleading and discriminatory from a commercial point of view. However, experts from developing countries insisted that information on alternatives

[30] UNEP Governing Council Dec 15/30, 25 May 1989, UN Doc UNEP/GC.15/12, Annex I, pp 160–62, para 6.

was essential. The wording that was eventually agreed puts the responsibility for providing information about alternatives on the country notifying the control action. It relieves UNEP of any responsibility for gathering such information. Information is to be included in the decision guidance document only to the extent that it has been provided with the notification of control action. It was also agreed to stress the limited validity of the information about alternatives by adding a disclaimer to the effect that: 'Other pesticides registered for this use may exist in other countries; all pesticides should be assessed or tested as appropriate under local conditions.'[31]

With its 1987 political decision to revise the London Guidelines and incorporate in them the principle of prior informed consent, UNEP had again seized the initiative and moved first to take the international regulatory debate forward. The FAO followed a little later, reconsidering the issue at its 1987 Council and Conference meetings and taking a similar decision to proceed with an amendment of the FAO Code of Conduct in November 1987. The decision-making process in the FAO, conducted largely in parallel with that in UNEP, is analysed below.

THE REVISION OF THE FAO INTERNATIONAL CODE OF CONDUCT ON THE DISTRIBUTION AND USE OF PESTICIDES

It was clear from the wording of the compromise reached at the 1985 FAO Conference that it would be a point of contention whether the revision of the Code would make it on to the agenda of the next Conference. The language in the report was worded to accommodate conflicting positions, which were to clash again in 1987. Countries opposed to PIC apparently hoped that the developing countries, appeased by the symbolic recognition of their concerns in the Conference report, would lose interest in the PIC issue and would not actually press for a revision of the Code in 1987. Some proponents of PIC too confidently assumed that the issue would automatically come up for reconsideration in 1987 and did not actively pursue it for a while. The Secretariat, concerned as ever about maintaining consensus on the Code and reluctant to reopen the debate on a contentious issue, far from taking any initiative to promote a revision of the Code actually manoeuvered to keep it off the 1987 Conference agenda.

In a progress report on the implementation of the Code submitted to the FAO Council meeting in November 1987,[32] immediately prior to the 1987 Conference, the Secretariat presented the results of a questionnaire sent to member states and pointed out that the implementation of the Code

[31] UN Doc UNEP/WG.188/5, 10 Oct 1988, p 19.

[32] Progress Report on the Implementation of the International Code of Conduct on the Distribution and Use of Pesticides, FAO Doc CL 92/2, Sept 1987.

was still at a very early stage. The report did not address the issue of PIC and referred to possible revision of the Code only in the most general terms, echoing the 1985 Conference report, stating that it was the intention 'to put forward such revisions for consideration after the necessary experience has been gained in the implementation of the Code.'[33] The implicit message of the report that any revision of the Code in 1987 would be premature was explicitly confirmed by the Assistant Director-General in his introductory statement to the Council: 'More experience of member countries in its adoption and wide use is required before revisions can be contemplated.'[34]

The Secretariat's attitude, and in particular the fact that the progress report had been presented to the Council 'for information' only, provoked an angry reaction from developing countries, who recalled the compromise of 1985 and insisted that the issue of PIC be fully considered at the 1987 Conference. The Federal Republic of Germany, the United States, Australia, Japan and the United Kingdom reiterated the familiar arguments against PIC and argued that the way forward was in implementation of the Code and the provision of technical assistance to developing countries. The Secretariat joined them in pointing out that the experience acquired so far was too limited and proposed that a 'more detailed assessment of progress and problems in the implementation of the Code of Conduct', including consideration of the need for revisions, be initiated through the Committee on Agriculture in 1989.[35] This would have effectively deferred any decision on the principle of PIC for another two years. However, the Council could not ignore the strong pressure from the majority of members for early reconsideration of the PIC issue and eventually decided to place the question on the agenda of the Conference.[36]

The Debate and Decision at the 1987 FAO Conference

Having been forced to accept a debate at the Conference for which it was not prepared, the Secretariat again made a rather heavy-handed effort to influence the discussion. In his introductory statement, the Assistant Director-General dwelled at great length on the long consensus-building process that went into the elaboration of the Code, claimed that the Secretariat's survey indicated that the information exchange provisions of the Code were effective in meeting the concerns of developing countries, and echoed a number of arguments against PIC advanced by the OECD

[33] *Ibid*, para 46.
[34] FAO Doc CL 92/PV/2, Nov 1987, p 13.
[35] *Ibid*, p 30.
[36] *Ibid*, p 34.

countries, stating, for instance, that 'it seems that PIC might be incompatible with the GATT's regulations', as had been asserted by the United States. He suggested that importing countries concerned about imports of banned and severely restricted pesticides were free to introduce PIC requirements unilaterally through national legislation.[37]

Notwithstanding the Secretariat's effort to set the tone of the discussion by an intervention strongly biased against PIC, the developing countries came out in a coordinated manner in favour of a revision of the Code. The stage was set for difficult negotiations by Zambia, which tabled a draft resolution, co-sponsored by Colombia, Ecuador, Lesotho, the Philippines and Venezuela, to amend Article 9 of the Code immediately at the Conference.[38] The preambular paragraphs of the draft resolution referred to the report of the 1985 Conference and to the 1987 decision of UNEP Governing Council to incorporate the principle of PIC in the London Guidelines. The debate on the draft resolution was strongly polarised along North-South lines. However, it was significant that a number of industrialised countries which had earlier opposed PIC, such as Australia and Spain, expressed support for the draft resolution.[39] On the other hand, it was surprising that the Netherlands, which was already implementing a PIC scheme unilaterally, though reiterating its support for the principle, did not support the draft resolution but actually endorsed the view of the FAO Secretariat that the immediate inclusion of PIC in the Code would be inappropriate.[40]

The stalemate was broken by the mediating role of the Nordic countries, which proposed a compromise formula on which consensus was eventually reached. Norway, speaking on behalf of the Nordic group early in the debate, expressed at the outset support for the intent of the Zambian resolution to incorporate the principle of PIC into the Code. While the Nordic countries were prepared to accept the proposed amendment to the Code, they stressed the need for a 'thorough preparation of the text at the technical level' in order to 'reach a general consensus.'[41] In order to accommodate the concerns of the Secretariat and a number of industrialised countries, they proposed that the principle of incorporation of PIC into the Code be accepted immediately but that the actual amendment of the text be deferred until the next Conference, following full consideration of the issue by a technical working group. Norway put forward an amendment to the Zambian draft resolution along these lines. The Norwegian compromise proposal was that the Conference would decide that the principle of PIC 'should be incorporated' into the Code and would call on the Secretariat 'to arrange for the establishment of a working group to consider the issues involved in the incorporation of PIC into the Code, including

[37] FAO Doc C 87/I/PV/15, 20 Nov 1987, p 5.
[38] FAO Doc C 87/LIM/39, Nov 1987.
[39] FAO Doc C 87/I/PV/16, 20 Nov 1987, pp 11, 32.
[40] *Ibid*, p 22.
[41] *Ibid*, p 2.

those of implementation', which would report to the following Conference. This proposal tried to strike a delicate balance between the desire of developing countries to obtain immediate satisfaction on their point of principle and the reluctance of most industrialised countries to amend the Code without thorough preparation at the technical level.[42]

The United States, which was reluctant to yield on the point of principle but willing to contemplate further consideration of the issue in a technical working group, proposed that the wording of the Nordic proposal be amended to state that the principle of PIC 'could be incorporated' into the Code. They argued that the Nordic proposal was contradictory because it prejudged the outcome of the technical discussion by deciding that the principle should be incorporated before its implications had been fully studied. The United States went out of its way to emphasise that it did not reject PIC a priori but only wanted to give the working group an open-ended rather than imperative mandate:

> Our point is simply that we are willing to state that it 'could' be included in the Code if, after further study by a group of experts, strong convincing reasons are presented that it is both workable and in the best interests of all member countries to have the principle included in the Code.[43]

These attempts to appease Third World concerns, however, could not hide the fact that the American proposal would have effectively put off the political decision on the principle of incorporating PIC in the Code. This is what it was all about, and precisely what was unacceptable to the developing countries, who perceived it as a mere dilatory tactic. As Zambia put it: 'I think the strategy appears to be to continue to defer PIC indefinitely, *ad infinitum*.'[44] When it became clear that the sponsors of the PIC resolution would not accept any further postponement of the decision, negotiations again centred on the Nordic compromise proposal, which was eventually adopted without major changes.

In its final form, Resolution 5/87 of the FAO Conference, 'considering that it is necessary to include the principle of "prior informed consent" into the provisions of the Code dealing with information exchange', decided that the principle '*should* be incorporated *within the next biennium*', thus recognising that this incorporation was not to be the immediate effect of the Conference resolution but the result of a process to be completed within two years. The second operative paragraph instructed the Director-General to convene

> a working group to consider the issues involved in the incorporation of the 'prior informed consent' principle in the Code, including those of implementation, in order to advise member countries on how best to give effect to the principle.

[42] *Ibid*, p 43.
[43] *Ibid*, p 44.
[44] *Ibid*, p 51.

It provides that the results are to be presented to the next session of the Conference.[45]

Having failed to amend the substance of the resolution, Germany, the United States, Japan, Switzerland, France, the United Kingdom and Italy entered a formal reservation in the record of the Conference to the first operative paragraph of the Resolution 'because this text prejudged any decision to be taken by the Twenty-fifth Session of the Conference'. This reservation, similar to those made by the United Kingdom and the United States in UNEP Governing Council a few months earlier, irritated the developing countries who answered it with a formal statement accusing it of going 'against the spirit of the Code'. This rhetorical posturing was quite symptomatic of the strongly polarised positions on the issue and of the far-reaching political implications of the Resolution. Indeed, the Resolution, coming only a few months after a similar UNEP decision, signalled a decisive turn in the international regulatory debate on trade in banned and severely restricted chemicals. In two international fora, the OECD countries, which had previously successfully controlled this debate through their pre-emptive strategy, had lost the political initiative to the Third World and been forced to accept a new round of negotiations and confront a new set of demands from developing countries on a question which they had assumed to be settled.

Incorporating the Prior Informed Consent Procedure in the FAO Code of Conduct

In its effort to fulfil the mandate given to it by the Conference, the FAO Secretariat had to find ways of bridging the deep differences between North and South on the PIC issue and of restoring consensus on the Code. In doing so, it had to take account of the parallel negotiations going on in UNEP and try to ensure consistency between developments in both fora in an effort to uphold the FAO's 'lead role' in the field of pesticides. As a matter of fact, negotiations on PIC in UNEP and the FAO were closely linked, with alternating meetings, and developments in one forum had direct repercussions in the other. Throughout the negotiations, close contacts were maintained between the respective secretariats of the two organisations, which also laid the basis for their later cooperation in implementing PIC.

To prepare the ground for a 'government consultation', ie a technical meeting of member governments at which amendments to the Code could be elaborated for submission to the organisation's political organs, the Secretariat first arranged an informal 'expert consultation' in March 1988, in which a number of experts nominated by governments, industry and non-

[45] FAO Conference Resolution 5/87 (emphasis added).

governmental organisations were invited to participate in their personal capacity. As during the first round of consultations in UNEP, the United States made an attempt to call into question the explicit mandate given by the Conference and suggest another approach to the problem. In a letter sent to all participants prior to the meeting, the expert from the US Environmental Protection Agency suggested that the meeting

> will be most productive, I believe, if we *restructure the nature of the debate* which has been taking place. Instead of beginning with discussions on the acceptability and modalities of PIC, it would seem more productive if we could clearly identify the nature and importance of the problems needing attention. Then *evaluating a range of alternatives* designed to come to grips with the problems rather than beginning with a solution.[46]

Though he realised the Conference resolution required PIC to be implemented, he suggested that the experts should 'study and recommend other alternatives and *possible reconsideration of the PIC decision.*'[47] Clearly, the US was very reluctant to participate in a debate which had not been structured on its own terms and still hoped that some way could be found, through the 'technical' bodies, to undo the controversial political decision taken by the Conference.

However, the US attempt to change the FAO's agenda was not successful. Faced with unambiguous instructions from its highest governing body, the Secretariat would not allow the debate to be sidetracked. In his introductory statement to the expert meeting, the Assistant Director-General made it very clear that the Conference resolution could not be misunderstood and that the end result of the exercise would have to be incorporation of PIC into the Code. However, he did stress that, in order to restore consensus and ensure the effectiveness of the Code, it would be 'particularly important to overcome the concerns of countries who reserved their position' on PIC, referring to the United States and other OECD countries that had expressed a formal reservation at the 1987 Conference. As significant issues which would have to be addressed, he referred in particular to the fear of 'unfair trade restriction on exporting countries with strong registration systems' and that 'PIC may result in additional and possibly burdensome administrative procedures.'[48] He suggested that establishing a uniform list of pesticides subject to PIC and avoiding excessive bureaucratic involvement in the PIC procedures in both importing and exporting countries might be ways to overcome these objections.

[46] Letter from Edwin L Johnson, Director, Developing Countries Staff, US Environmental Protection Agency, to participants in the FAO Expert Consultation on PIC, Mar 1988 (emphasis added).

[47] *Ibid* (emphasis added).

[48] Report of the Expert Consultation on the Introduction of 'Prior Informed Consent' in Art 9 of the International Code of Conduct on the Distribution and Use of Pesticides, 23–25 Mar 1988, FAO Meeting Report AGP:1988/, pp 1–2.

Shift from Export Control Towards Information Exchange

Though the debate was not 'restructured' in the sense intended by the US, ie by focusing on approaches other than PIC, the effort to accommodate the concerns of exporting countries encouraged by the Secretariat actually led to a 'restructuring' of the approach to PIC itself, to a shift away from export control and towards information exchange. The report specifically notes that 'PIC was seen by some as a mechanism for reinforcing the exchange of information.'[49]

The experts agreed on a provisional working definition of PIC, which is described as meaning 'that no international shipment of a [banned or severely restricted pesticide] . . . should proceed without the prior consent of the competent national authority in the importing country.'[50] The reference to shipments is somewhat misleading because it seems to connote a shipment-linked PIC procedure. In fact, the report indicates that the experts did not actually see this as an essential element of PIC, but actively explored non-shipment-linked procedures as a way of overcoming the objections of exporting countries.

The meeting considered in detail the possible procedures whereby the consent of importing countries could be obtained and the categories of pesticides to which the PIC system should apply. It did not formulate a specific proposal but rather identified a range of possible options. As regards the consent procedure, the experts identified three possible options: decisions of importing countries could be made at the time of receipt of a notification of control action, upon receipt of an international list of pesticides subject to PIC, or in response to an export notification. The meeting did not express a preference for a particular option but indicated that these options were not necessarily exclusive of one another and could possibly be combined. The report is vague as regards the implications of the PIC procedure for exporting countries. It notes the existence of 'a wide range of views on the appropriate role of governments, especially those of exporting countries.'[51] It does mention, however, that

> there is some obligation on the part of the exporting country to ensure that no shipment is made unless it is convinced that the importing country has given its consent in the appropriate manner.[52]

As regards the scope of the PIC system, the experts 'suggested that an internationally agreed list would be necessary under a PIC system' and listed a series of criteria which could be used in drawing up such a list. Apart from

[49] FAO Meeting Report AGP:1988/, p 8.
[50] *Ibid*, p 10.
[51] *Ibid*, p 15.
[52] *Ibid*, p 17.

national control actions and a possible threshold number of countries, they also mentioned other significant criteria such as 'pesticides which may cause special hazards in developing countries' and 'unregistered pesticides and/or those withdrawn due to health or environmental concerns.'[53] The latter category was repeatedly mentioned as requiring attention both in the UNEP and the FAO, but neither organisation managed to develop a mechanism to deal with it.

The problem of acutely toxic pesticides posing special hazards in developing countries, first signalled by the FAO expert group, was later addressed in the context of the process for establishing the initial list. The importance of an adequate definition of 'severely restricted' pesticides for the purpose of assessing national control actions was also discussed. Diverging views were expressed as to the adequacy of the definition in the FAO Code, and it was recommended that the FAO Secretariat examine the national interpretations of this definition to ascertain that it covered all relevant control actions.[54] The Secretariat, however, was reluctant to reopen the debate on definitions and never reported back on this question. The definitions in the FAO Code were left unchanged and were later even adopted by UNEP as well.

Preserving the FAO's Turf and Coordinating with UNEP

The 'FAO Government Consultation on the Inclusion of Prior Informed Consent in the International Code of Conduct on the Distribution and Use of Pesticides' was held in January 1989, a few months after the first meeting of UNEP *Ad Hoc* Working Group of Experts. The negotiations in the FAO were heavily influenced by the results of UNEP meeting. In fact, the proposal for a PIC procedure submitted to the Government Consultation by the Secretariat was essentially the same as the procedure provisionally agreed by UNEP experts, with a few minor differences. The proposal was more directly inspired by the results of UNEP meeting than by the recommendations made by the FAO's own expert consultation.

The proposal consisted of two parts: a set of draft amendments to the Code laying down the basic provisions relating to PIC, and more detailed guidelines on the operation of the PIC procedure to supplement the provisions of the Code.[55] It is more interesting to examine the differences between the FAO proposal and UNEP scheme than their similarities. First of all, not suprisingly, the FAO seeks to affirm its jurisdiction in the field of

[53] *Ibid*, p 13.
[54] *Ibid*, p 14.
[55] FAO Doc AGP:GC/89/WP.2, Jan 1989.

pesticides and claims primary responsibility for the implementation of PIC. The proposal states that, in view of its 'expertise', 'FAO will operate the PIC scheme as far as pesticides are concerned'. It is mentioned in passing that this will be done 'in cooperation with UNEP', but the role of UNEP is given far less prominence than in the London Guidelines.[56] Like UNEP scheme, the FAO proposal provides for a review of pesticides which have already been subject to national control actions in the past in order to determine if they should be subject to PIC, but it does not specify the criteria to be used, other than conformity with the definitions. There is no reference to a threshold number of control actions as a condition for inclusion on the list. Finally, the FAO proposal differs as regards the consequences of a lack of response. It contains a different definition of the 'status quo' which should continue in the event of no response. It provides that exports may proceed 'if importation and/or local production is allowed', but does not explicitly require 'governmental action' to this effect, as does UNEP.

As the participants in the consultation were mainly representatives of national agriculture departments, it is not surprising that the FAO's claim for primary responsibility in the field of pesticides was supported. Most delegations supported the idea that the PIC procedure for pesticides should be operated by the FAO, but even the FAO's own constituency did not uncritically endorse the organisation's lead role. Indeed, the report notes that 'the Consultation stressed the importance of close cooperation with UNEP and other relevant organizations to avoid duplication of effort and promote most effective use of scarce resources.'[57]

Criteria for Selection of Pesticides Subject to Prior Informed Consent

There was extensive discussion on the criteria for the selection of pesticides for inclusion in the PIC procedure. Some countries suggested that a ban or severe restriction in a single country should be sufficient to include a pesticide on the initial list. France and Japan insisted that numerical criteria relating to the number of countries having taken control action were not adequate and that scientific criteria should be applied. They called for 'scientific validation' of national control actions. The FAO Secretariat was reluctant to take such a responsibility upon itself and stressed that it did not have sufficient resources to perform an in-depth evaluation of national control actions. Instead, it proposed to apply a numerical threshold of

[56] FAO Doc AGP:GC/89/WP.2, Jan 1989, p 1.

[57] Report of the Government Consultation on the Principle of Prior Informed Consent in the International Code of Conduct on the Distribution and Use of Pesticides, FAO Doc COAG/89/8, Feb 1989, p 9, para 54.

five countries as agreed in UNEP and to review control actions only for conformity with definitions.

The discussion then focused on the number of national control actions that would be required to trigger the PIC procedure. There was a lot of support for a lower threshold than agreed by UNEP, but also some pressure for raising the threshold, including for future control actions. Where UNEP system provides that in future a single control action would make a pesticide subject to PIC, the United Kingdom proposed that no pesticide should be subject to PIC unless it had been banned or severely restricted in at least five countries. Eventually, it was agreed to fix the threshold 'initially' at five countries and to apply it only for past control actions.[58] However, the report notes that many delegates 'were of the view that a smaller number of countries should be sufficient to trigger the PIC procedure.'[59] In the end, the same criteria for the selection of pesticides subject to PIC were agreed in the FAO as in UNEP, the only difference being that the wording of the FAO guidelines does not *preclude* consideration of pesticides banned or severely restricted in less than five countries for inclusion in the initial list.

Notwithstanding the reluctance of the Secretariat to reconsider the definitions in the FAO Code, as recommended by the expert consultation, several delegations raised the issue at the Government Consultation. A number of developing countries urged that the definition of 'severely restricted' pesticides in the Code be revised, as it did not adequately cover acutely toxic pesticides subject to handling restrictions. The United Kingdom and other industrialised countries objected to this proposal on the grounds that it was not within the terms of reference of the Consultation to review the definitions in Article 2 of the Code, but only the information exchange provisions in Article 9.

This rather spurious argument did not succeed in preventing substantive discussion, since the term 'severely restricted' is used only in Article 9 of the Code and is directly relevant to the PIC procedure. The Philippines put forward a proposal to amend the definition to include pesticides 'governed by strict handling regulations'[60] but did not manage to have it included in the amendments proposed by the Consultation. Since no consensus could be reached, the proposal was mentioned in the report for further consideration by the Committee on Agriculture. The report reflects the conflicting viewpoints on the issue, noting on the one hand that 'it was strongly emphasized that handling restrictions of pesticides should also be considered', and on the other that a number of countries had argued that this could complicate the implementation of the PIC scheme 'as virtually all pesticides had specific handling restrictions.'[61]

[58] *Ibid*, p 32.
[59] *Ibid*, p 9, para 55.
[60] *Ibid*.
[61] *Ibid*.

The matter was again discussed by the Committee on Agriculture, after UNEP working group had found a way of dealing with the problem of acutely toxic pesticides through a review of the WHO Class Ia compounds for possible inclusion on the PIC list. Instead of changing the definition of 'severely restricted', the Committee decided to adopt the same solution as UNEP.[62] Notwithstanding this compromise, there was persistent dissatisfaction among developing countries about the scope of the PIC scheme. During the final discussion on the Code amendments at the Conference, several proposals for additional categories of pesticides to be considered for inclusion in the PIC procedure were formulated.

Special concern was expressed about unregistered pesticides and those voluntarily withdrawn by the manufacturer for health or environmental reasons, two categories which had already been mentioned at the expert consultation. The Philippines proposed that, as a minimum measure to address the problem of unregistered pesticides, member countries should be required to notify to the FAO 'any pesticide that is not registered in their country but is still traded'. Another proposal was made to broaden the mandate of the expert panel in charge of the elaboration of the initial list to enable it to keep the issue of acutely toxic pesticides 'under continuing review' and to consider substances which are not in the WHO Class Ia, as agreed by UNEP Governing Council.[63] However, in the interest of consensus, the Conference decided not to accept any additional amendments and merely recorded them in its report for possible future consideration.[64]

Responsibilities of Importing and Exporting Countries

The Secretariat's original proposal was amended by the Consultation as regards the consequences of a lack of response by a participating importing country. The Secretariat had initially explained the concept of the *status quo* with respect to importation as follows:

> This means that if a pesticide is registered in the country or if importation and/or local production is allowed, importation will not be banned.[65]

Several developing countries argued against any presumption of tacit consent, while a number of exporting countries opposed what they called 'prohibition by default'. This led to a proposal to adopt compromise language similar to that agreed in UNEP, whereby continued exports are allowed if

[62] FAO Doc COAG/89/REP.6, May 1989, p 4, para 169.
[63] FAO Doc C 89/REP, paras 117–18.
[64] *Ibid*, para 119.
[65] FAO Doc AGP:GC/89/WP.2, Jan 1989, p 5.

the exporter has evidence that it is a pesticide that is registered in the importing country or is a pesticide the use of which has been allowed *by other governmental action* of the importing country.

At the last moment, however, a British proposal to delete the reference to 'governmental action' was accepted, thus making the FAO provision weaker than the corresponding UNEP provision. No governmental action is required, and exports would be permitted to continue whenever the use of the pesticide had been 'allowed' in the past, no matter on what account. This is confirmed by the statement in the report of the meeting which explains the wording as 'permitting trade to continue where it had existed in the past, but that it not be initiated without the consent of the importing country.'[66] In the Committee on Agriculture, two delegations put on record their interpretation of the provision to the effect that 'in the absence of a response from an importing country, chemicals previously legally imported can continue to be imported.'[67] This would apply to situations where imports are legal not as a result of any affirmative governmental action, but simply as a result of the lack of any regulation.

A related, much-debated question is that of the responsibility of exporting countries for the enforcement of PIC decisions. The discussion on this point was largely determined by the compromise reached at UNEP meeting. Developing countries were pressing for more explicit recognition of the responsibility of exporting countries to take export control measures, while exporting countries were unwilling to accept any commitments going beyond the compromise language agreed within UNEP. The Government Consultation adopted virtually the same language as UNEP, recommending that exporting countries 'implement appropriate procedures, *within their authority*, to ensure that exports do not occur contrary to the decision of participating importing countries.' After additional negotiations in the Committee on Agriculture, it was eventually agreed to amend this to read '*take* appropriate *measures*, within their authority *and legislative competence*, *designed* to ensure . . .'[68]

At issue is the extent to which governmental authorities in the exporting country have the legal authority to control exports. A number of exporting countries have made it clear that they do not have such authority under their national legislation and have no intention to seek it. They interpret the clause 'within their authority' as exempting them from taking measures not within their existing statutory authority. Developing countries, however, find it objectionable that exporting countries should be able to rely on their domestic legislation to justify their failure to prevent exports in violation

[66] FAO Doc COAG/89/8, Feb 1989, p 9, para 57.
[67] FAO Doc COAG/89/REP.6, May 1989, p 3, para 168.
[68] *Ibid*, para 167 (emphasis added).

of the PIC procedure. It is also possible to interpret the clause as synonymous with 'within their jurisdiction' in an international legal sense. Under international law, there can be little doubt that exporting countries have jurisdiction to regulate their own exports. The addition of a reference to 'legislative competence' can be seen as strengthening this interpretation. Indeed, where existing national legislation does not provide a legal basis for controlling exports of pesticides subject to PIC, it is well within the exporting country's competence to legislate to that effect.

Another concern expressed with respect to enforcement of the PIC procedure and Code provisions in general relates to the non-binding nature of the Code. The report of the Conference notes the concern of 'many member nations' that, because of its voluntary character, the Code may not be fully effective in achieving its objectives. In view of this, some support was expressed at the Conference for transforming the Code into a binding legal instrument. However, no agreement could be reached on such a course of action, and it was merely recorded in the report that 'it was proposed that the Secretariat should explore the possibility of establishing a legally binding instrument.'[69] This was not an explicit instruction given by the Conference to the Secretariat, but simply a proposal made by members. Thus, it was basically left to the Secretariat's discretion whether or not to follow up on this suggestion.

The adoption by the FAO Conference in November 1989 of Resolution 6/89, which formally amends Articles 2 and 9 of the Code of Conduct and at the same time endorses complementary Guidelines on the operation of the PIC procedure, effectively concluded the second round of international normative efforts, resulting in broad consensus on a voluntary PIC procedure for banned and severely restricted pesticides and other chemicals, to be implemented in a coordinated manner by UNEP and the FAO. The final section of this chapter examines the joint practice of the two organisations in implementing the non-binding PIC scheme established in 1989.

IMPLEMENTING THE VOLUNTARY PRIOR INFORMED CONSENT PROCEDURE: UNEP-FAO COOPERATION

The PIC procedures adopted by UNEP and the FAO in 1989 afford these international agencies an important role in their implementation. The choice of a multilateral PIC system based on a single international list of PIC chemicals and central record of PIC decisions, rather than on bilateral communication between importing and exporting countries, implies a crucial clearing-house function for UNEP and the FAO. The operation of

[69] FAO Doc C 89/REP, para 116.

the PIC procedures requires an international focal point for the collection and dissemination of information.

However, the role assigned to the international organisations is more than a purely technical one of maintaining communication and acting as a clearing-house. Important policy decisions about the operation of the PIC system, and in particular about the selection of chemicals subject to the procedure, have in effect been delegated to them, where they have been instructed to review national control actions to verify their conformity with definitions, with the assistance of an expert group or what is described as an 'informal consultative process'. The political discretion and substantive role of this expert group is even more manifest in the procedure for the review of acutely toxic pesticides to determine those which pose a special hazard in developing countries warranting their inclusion on the PIC list. Moreover, the preparation of the 'decision guidance documents' on the chemicals subject to PIC also involves a considerable measure of discretion in the selection and presentation of the information that will be used as a basis for decision-making in importing countries.

From Competition to Cooperation: Managing Conflicts of Competence

In view of the important role accorded the secretariats of UNEP and the FAO in implementing the PIC procedure, it is not surprising that the organisations have struggled over the division of operational responsibilities between them. From the beginning of the negotiations on information exchange on banned and severely restricted chemicals, there have been recurrent differences between the two organisations, both eager to preserve or enhance their jurisdiction and control over the policy area of pesticides regulation. The FAO, in particular, has always been reluctant to accept the development of an autonomous policy role by UNEP in the field of pesticides regulation, a field which it tends to consider as its reserved domain. However, UNEP, in view of its coordinating role and environmental mandate, certainly has a legitimate interest in the pesticides issue and became involved in the international regulatory debate precisely because certain aspects of the problem had been disregarded by the FAO.

UNEP's decision to develop guidelines on the exchange of information on banned and severely restricted chemicals in international trade was taken before the FAO's initiative to develop an international code of conduct on pesticides. The FAO has always resented the fact that UNEP independently undertook to develop guidelines which are applicable to pesticides as well as industrial chemicals as an usurpation of its traditional 'lead role'. The underlying issue in this jurisdictional dispute is, of course, the extent to which pesticides regulation should be governed by agricultural or environmental considerations. However, repeated attempts to exclude pesticides from the scope of application of UNEP Guidelines on the grounds that they are more appropriately dealt with by the FAO Code of Conduct have remained unsuccessful. With the support of many governments who view the involvement of an environmental agency in the field as important, UNEP has managed to resist efforts to restrict the scope of its regulatory initiatives and has preserved and further developed its independent policy-making role. In fact, the presence of UNEP on the scene as a 'competitor' has proven to be a strong incentive to prompt the FAO into action and has probably forced the FAO to go further in its regulatory efforts than it would have done of its own initiative. For instance, were it not for the 1987 UNEP Governing Council decision, it is doubtful that the FAO Conference would ever have decided to incorporate the principle of PIC into the FAO Code.

While pesticides remained within the scope of the London Guidelines, the concerns of the FAO and some governments about duplication of efforts were calmed by a statement in the preamble to those guidelines that they were to be implemented in a 'non-duplicative manner' alongside the FAO Code. In view of the overlapping field of application of the two instruments, there was a real possibility that different or even conflicting provisions might be adopted and that separate PIC procedures might be developed by the two organisations which would be very confusing, if not impossible, for governments to implement in a parallel fashion. To avoid this situation, an effort was made throughout the negotiations on the PIC procedure to maintain consistency between UNEP and the FAO provisions. This pressure for consistency created a strong interdependence between the two negotiating fora, which was exploited as a tactical advantage by some negotiators, using advances in one forum to force the other to follow suit.

When it became clear that UNEP and the FAO PIC procedures would be compatible, UNEP proposed that they be implemented jointly, as a single procedure. UNEP *Ad Hoc* Working Group of Experts, meeting shortly after the FAO Government Consultation in early 1989, recommended 'that UNEP and FAO share the operational responsibility for the implementation of the PIC procedure and jointly manage and implement common elements.'[70] At the same time, however, UNEP stressed that its willingness to share operational responsibility with the FAO did not imply a readiness to relinquish its political responsibility and a recognition of a preferential role for the FAO in the field of pesticides. The report of the meeting notes the understanding 'that the sharing of operational responsibilities . . . is without prejudice to the scope of the Guidelines.'[71] This statement, which must be understood against the background of the recurrent discussions about the

[70] UN Doc UNEP/PIC.WG.2/4, 16 Feb 1989, p 7, para 33(c).
[71] *Ibid*, para 34.

scope of UNEP Guidelines, is illustrative of UNEP's sensitivity to the jurisdictional dispute with the FAO.

The acuity of this dispute is patent from the position taken by the representative of the FAO at UNEP meeting. Notwithstanding UNEP's proposal to share operational responsibilities, he felt it necessary to formally record his 'concern' in the report of the meeting that UNEP's view of the sharing of responsibilities may 'not [be] in line with the consensus reached at the FAO Government Consultation.'[72] Indeed, it should be recalled that the Government Consultation had considered it obvious that in view of its expertise, 'FAO will operate the PIC scheme as far as pesticides are concerned.'[73] Thus, the FAO was still claiming exclusive or at least primary responsibility and was not satisfied with the sharing arrangement offered by UNEP. Notwithstanding this posturing, once final political decisions had been reached and compatible PIC procedures adopted in both organisations, UNEP and the FAO secretariats actually did come to terms and establish cooperative arrangements for the joint implementation of their PIC procedures.

The Role of the Joint Group of Experts on Prior Informed Consent

This 'Joint FAO/UNEP Programme for the Operation of Prior Informed Consent' involves the establishment of a joint data base and information exchange system for chemicals included in the PIC procedure and a single network of designated national authorities, as well as cooperation in the preparation of decision guidance documents. The most important element from a substantive point of view is the joint mechanism established by the FAO and UNEP for the selection of chemicals subject to the PIC procedure. For this purpose, a 'Joint Group of Experts on PIC' was established, at least according to UNEP's interpretation.[74] However, the status of this group is not entirely unambiguous. The FAO proposed that the task of reviewing chemicals for inclusion in the PIC procedure, since it involved mainly pesticides, should be entrusted to an existing FAO expert panel, the 'FAO Panel of Experts on Pesticide Specifications, Registration Requirements and Application Standards', in which a few additional experts designated by UNEP would be invited to participate. Thus, in the FAO's view, this group was not a new joint body set up specifically for the implementation of the PIC procedure, but an expanded FAO body. This was an oblique way for the FAO to reassert its 'supremacy' in the field.

[72] *Ibid*, p 6, para 27.
[73] FAO Doc COAG/89/8, Feb 1989, p 31.
[74] UN Doc UNEP/PIC.WG.3/5, 14 Sept 1990, p 3.

UNEP clearly perceived it that way, and in order not to have its participation subordinated to the existing FAO panel, proceeded to establish a new 'UNEP Group of Experts on PIC' as a counterpart to the FAO panel. Together with the FAO panel, UNEP group forms what UNEP has labelled the 'FAO/UNEP Joint Group of Experts on PIC'. UNEP group of experts is in fact a ficticious entity, which has never met separately but was formally created only to enable UNEP to participate on an equal footing with the FAO in the joint group. It is symptomatic, however, that the FAO initially did not use the term 'Joint Group' but rather presented the first meeting of the panel, which it hosted in Rome in December 1989, as the 8th session of the FAO Panel of Experts, 'held jointly with UNEP Expert Group.'[75] The FAO thus seemed reluctant to recognise that both organisations participate as equal partners in an expert group for the implementation of their joint PIC procedure. The petty squabbling over the status of the expert panel indicates that the competition between UNEP and the FAO still marks their cooperative efforts. Notwithstanding the attempts of UNEP to maintain some balance at the formal level, the FAO's view is probably closer to reality. Indeed, in the beginning, the Joint Group was dominated by the FAO-appointed experts, most of them representatives of national pesticide registration authorities, who constituted the majority of its members.

The first step in the operation of the PIC procedure[76] was the designation of competent national authorities by participating countries. At about the same time, the Executive Director of UNEP and the Director General of the FAO, in a coordinated move, sent official notes to governments inviting them to designate a national authority for the purpose of participating in the PIC procedure. UNEP already had a network of designated national authorities set up for the purpose of the notification procedures of the London Guidelines. Thus, it informed those governments which had already designated authorities in the past of the expanded responsibilities of those authorities under the PIC procedure and requested them to confirm their designations. The FAO, for its part, approached its member governments for the first time, suggesting that it would be most 'effective' if they were to designate 'a government department or office responsible for broad national policy on agricultural pesticides.'[77] The fact that each agency addressed its own constituency separately—UNEP primarily environment

[75] FAO Panel of Experts on Pesticide Specifications, Registration Requirements and Application Standards (Group on Pesticide Registration Requirements) & UNEP Group of Experts on Prior Informed Consent, *Report of the Eighth Session, held jointly with UNEP Expert Group*, Rome, 18–21 Dec 1989, FAO Meeting Report AGP:1990/.

[76] For a more detailed analysis of the practical operation of the voluntary PIC procedure and the work of the FAO/UNEP Joint Group of Experts on PIC, see Victor (1998).

[77] Circular letter from the Director General of FAO to member governments, Ref No G/AGP-13, 31 Oct 1989.

ministries and the FAO agriculture departments—was bound to lead to jurisdictional conflicts at the national level as well. It was envisaged that countries could designate more than one competent authority, eg one for pesticides and another for industrial chemicals. In practice, several countries made different designations to the FAO and to UNEP, nominating two or more 'designated national authorities', each claiming competence for the implementation of PIC with respect to pesticides.[78] Thus, in some countries, the international PIC procedure was used by government departments to affirm or undermine domestic attributions of competence. This put UNEP and the FAO in a delicate position, forcing them to seek clarification of the respective competences of the designated authorities with respect to the PIC procedure.

Establishing the Initial List of Chemicals Subject to Prior Informed Consent

The second step in the implementation of the procedure, and the most important task for the Joint Group, was to establish the initial list of chemicals subject to PIC. What was originally conceived as a rather simple exercise turned out to be a long and complex process, considerably delaying the start-up of the PIC scheme. As a basis for the compilation of the PIC list, the IRPTC provided an inventory of control actions previously notified by governments under the London Guidelines, supplemented with data contained in the UN Consolidated List. While Annex II of the London Guidelines provided that any chemicals banned or severely restricted in ten or more countries would be 'immediately' placed on the PIC list, while those controlled in five or more countries would first have to be screened for conformity with definitions, the expert group did not actually apply this distinction but proceeded to review all control actions to determine whether they met the definitions. The equivalent provision in the FAO Guidelines on the Operation of Prior Informed Consent makes no similar distinction based on the number of national bans or restrictions, but provides for all control actions to be evaluated as to their conformity with the definitions. The group chose to apply the FAO provisions, effectively setting aside the conflicting UNEP rules.

Once they had opted for a substantive review of all control actions, the experts noted that the information compiled by UNEP contained 'many deficiencies' and was difficult to interpret. Indeed, UNEP had made no attempt to check whether the control actions notified to it complied with the definitions. Often, the information supplied by governments in their notifications of control actions was insufficient to determine whether the

[78] See UN Doc UNEP/PIC.WG.3/6, 19 Oct 1990, p 14, para 49.

action had been taken 'for health or environmental reasons' within the meaning of UNEP and the FAO definitions.[79] It thus became necessary to request many governments to supply additional information about their control actions and the reasons for them. Designated national authorities were invited to submit updated inventories of control actions. A considerable amount of information had to be verified before decisions could be made on the inclusion of chemicals on the PIC list.[80]

In the process of drawing up the initial list, the expert group also had to further refine the criteria for the selection of chemicals, and in the process made significant substantive decisions about the types of control actions that would be deemed relevant for the purposes of PIC. The interpretative decisions made by the group remained significant after the establishment of the initial list of chemicals subject to PIC, as they have also been used as criteria for the review of new control actions, to determine whether the chemicals subject to these actions are to be included in the PIC procedure. It is from this perspective that the criteria developed by the Joint Group have been included in the official document elaborated jointly by UNEP and the FAO to provide guidance to governments on the operation of the PIC procedure, including guidance on the types of control actions to be reported and information to be provided under the procedure.[81]

The Joint Group first clarified certain aspects of the definitions which had been addressed during the earlier discussions in UNEP and the FAO and on which some consensus had emerged, though it had not been explicitly recorded in the provisions of UNEP Guidelines and the FAO Code. Thus, for example, the experts confirmed that the concept of 'banned or severely restricted' pesticides would cover not only restrictions of use resulting from government regulatory action but also voluntary withdrawals by companies, provided there is 'clear evidence' that the withdrawal is for health or environmental reasons.[82] The FAO Guidelines on the operation of PIC make reference to voluntary withdrawals,[83] and the question was also discussed in UNEP. However, the requirement of 'clear evidence' was added by the expert group. It may in fact be very difficult to appreciate the reasons for a withdrawal, because one would have to rely on whatever information is voluntarily made available by the company. In view of the implications, it would not be in any company's interest to provide information about its motives for withdrawing a pesticide from the market. Where government

[79] FAO Meeting Report AGP:1990/, p 3.

[80] Thus, the inclusion of 34 pesticides on the initial list was delayed because 'national inventories must be updated before a final decision is taken'. UN Doc UNEP/PIC/WG.1/2/2, 27 Mar 1991, p 2.

[81] *Guidance for Governments*, Joint FAO/UNEP Programme for the Operation of Prior Informed Consent, FAO/UNEP, Rome/Geneva, 1991, pp 37 *et seq.*

[82] FAO Meeting Report AGP:1990/, p 5.

[83] FAO Doc COAG/89/8, Feb 1989, p 31.

action is involved, the group agreed that only final regulatory action would be taken into account, ie action resulting in actual cessation of use. Provisional regulatory action which is still subject to domestic review would not qualify to bring a chemical under the PIC procedure.[84] These interpretations of the definitions were quite in line with the discussions in the FAO and UNEP during the negotiations on PIC and did not really break any new ground.

The same can be said of the confirmation by the Joint Group that pesticides which are subject to special handling restrictions, or 'restrictions that are essentially use directions', such as 'prohibition of use by women of child-bearing age' or 'restrictions limiting use to certain types of trained or certified applicators' are not to be considered as 'severely restricted' for the purpose of PIC. However, the group recognised that these pesticides were of concern and recommended that control actions of this nature should be notified under the regular information exchange procedures.[85] The latter recommendation is significant because the experts thereby implicitly recognised the inadequacy of the definitions. Indeed, the suggestion of drawing a distinction between control actions for the implementation of the PIC procedure on the one hand and notification procedures on the other is not really consistent with the provisions of the FAO Code or London Guidelines, which make no such distinction and contain a single definition of 'banned or severely restricted'. If a pesticide is regarded as 'banned or severely restricted' for the purpose of the notification procedure, it is equally so for the purpose of the PIC procedure and vice-versa.

The group's effort to mitigate the consequences of its policy of construing definitions restrictively betrays some apprehension about those consequences. This appears clearly from a statement in the report of the second meeting, in which the group

> expressed once more its concern about the fact that strict interpretation of the definitions for bans and severe restictions would lead to the elimination from the PIC procedure of many notifications received so far and considered that *this would counter the original intention* of both the International Code of Conduct and the London Guidelines.[86]

This statement was intended to justify the recommendation that disqualified control actions should continue to be notified through the information exchange procedure. However, one may wonder why the group chose to make this recommendation to mitigate the consequences of its own interpretation of the definitions, which it itself admits are contrary to the original intention of UNEP and the FAO instruments, instead of using its

[84] FAO Meeting Report AGP:1990/, p 4.
[85] *Ibid*, p 5.
[86] UN Doc UNEP/PIC.WG.3/5/Add. 1, p 3, para 11 (emphasis added).

discretion to interpret the definitions in a less restrictive way. The group's attitude is quite puzzling and contradictory.

Indeed, although the experts have manifestly had second thoughts about the implications of excluding certain pesticides from the PIC procedure, they have nevertheless chosen to use their discretion conservatively and to interpret the definitions in a restrictive way. In particular, they have given a very restrictive interpretation of what is to be understood by 'health or environmental reasons'. The experts have recommended that this should be interpreted to mean that

> the control action should be based upon data, information or analysis which indicate that use *under the expected conditions in the country* may give rise to an *unacceptable risk* to human health or the environment.[87]

The notion of 'unacceptable risk', which implies a rather high threshold, does not occur in the actual definitions as laid down in the London Guidelines and FAO Code of Conduct. Neither does the requirement that risk assessment should be related to the actual local conditions of use, which places a rather heavy burden on the country notifying the control action.

The Joint Group has generally taken a narrow view of what constitutes a control action for 'health or environmental reasons'. For instance, they decided that control actions taken because of pest resistance problems could not be regarded as taken for environmental reasons.[88] Yet the development of pest resistance is undeniably an adverse ecological effect and the resulting increase in pesticide use is bound to have environmental consequences. Equally disputable is the decision that control actions to restrict the use of certain pesticides in proximity to waterways or aquifers will not be taken into account;[89] the pollution of ground and surface water by pesticides is clearly an environmental and potential health risk. Countries such as Germany and the United States have taken a number of control actions in recent years to restrict the use of certain pesticides in order to reduce the risk of water pollution. From a public health perspective, the experts' decision not to take into account bans or severe restrictions of pesticides imposed 'solely on the basis of . . . acute toxicity ranking' or 'solely because a less toxic alternative is available'[90] is also questionable. It implies that a policy of banning the use of certain pesticides because of their high acute toxicity, in order to avoid the resulting risk to human health under conditions of use in developing countries, is not a policy based on legitimate health considerations.

The expert group also decided that 'the banning/non-registration of a pesticide solely on the basis of control actions taken in other countries,

[87] *Guidance for Governments*, above n 81, p 10 (emphasis added).
[88] *Ibid*, p 38.
[89] *Ibid* See also FAO Meeting Report AGP:1990/, p 6.
[90] *Guidance for Governments*, above n 81, p 39.

without national analysis indicating that use under expected conditions in the country may give rise to unacceptable risk to human health or the environment' will not be taken into account.[91] This applies regardless of the reasons for those control actions taken in other countries. The experts' apparent concern here was to avoid a snowball effect resulting from the PIC procedure. This is why they decided to recognise only regulatory decisions which countries have taken independently, following a *national* risk analysis based on local conditions of use. This implies that most control actions taken by importing countries as a result of the PIC procedure will be disqualified on the grounds that they are based only on information provided under that procedure and not on an independent national risk analysis. This negates the very rationale of the PIC procedure, which is to enable countries which lack the capacity to perform independent risk analysis to rely on risk evaluations made in other countries.

Another aspect of the definition of 'severely restricted' pesticide which gives rise to interpretation problems is the question of determining when 'virtually all registered uses' of a pesticide can be considered to have been banned. For the application of this provision, the experts decided to distinguish between 'major' and 'minor' uses and to apply a quantitative criterion. Thus, a pesticide for which a large number of minor uses have been banned 'while major uses remain authorized' would not be regarded as severely restricted. Conversely, 'banning of only a few uses that comprised the major portion of the quantity used or area treated would be considered a severe restriction, even if several minor uses remained.'[92] In order to determine whether a use must be considered 'major' or 'minor', it would be necessary to obtain quantitative use information from the country notifying the control action. This may make it very difficult to appreciate certain control actions, as such information may not be readily available. Many companies regard details on the quantities of pesticides marketed for specific uses as confidential business information. Again, one must wonder why the group chose a criterion which is of doubtful practical applicability and may lead to the exclusion of a number of significant control actions.

The Question of Acutely Toxic Pesticide Formulations

However, the Joint Group did not take an equally restrictive view of its mandate to review acutely toxic pesticide formulations. It will be be recalled that there was some inconsistency on this question between UNEP and the FAO provisions. While the FAO provisions called only for the review of pesticides in the WHO's Class Ia, UNEP Governing Council had

[91] *Ibid*, p 38.
[92] FAO Meeting Report AGP:1990/, p 5.

somewhat expanded the mandate of the expert group by instructing it to keep the problem of acutely toxic pesticides 'under continuing review'. It had been proposed to introduce a similar clause in the decisions of the FAO Conference. The Conference, however, had decided not to adopt this proposal or any other last-minute proposals which had not been discussed at the 'technical' level in the Government Consultation or in the Committee on Agriculture, in order not to jeopardise the consensus reached on PIC. Instead, it had referred these proposals to the expert group for its consideration, with a view to their possible adoption at the next Conference, following a more thorough discussion. When the expert group discussed this proposal at its first meeting, it agreed that the FAO instrument, too, should provide for a 'continuing review' of acutely toxic pesticide formulations, including those in other hazard categories than the WHO Class Ia, which it acknowledged may also cause problems during use in developing countries.[93]

As a matter of fact, the expert group did not wait for a formal amendment of the FAO Guidelines on the Operation of PIC along the lines of UNEP Governing Council decision before considering acutely toxic pesticides without regard to their formal WHO hazard classification. It actually operated in accordance with the broader UNEP mandate from the beginning, requesting the FAO Secretariat to collect information from governments on all pesticides, 'regardless of the hazard category', which cause special problems due to their acute toxicity.[94] At its second meeting, the Joint Group confirmed that

> all pesticides listed in WHO Class Ia *and any other pesticides which may create problems under conditions of use in developing countries* [would] be reviewed for inclusion in the PIC procedure.[95]

It also agreed on a priority list of 11 pesticides for review in this category, including one, paraquat, which is listed in the WHO Class II.[96]

It should be noted that this priority list was of pesticides *to be considered for inclusion* in the PIC list; no positive decision to include them in the list had yet been made. Indeed, the mandate given to the expert group required it first to determine that certain pesticides 'cause significant problems under conditions of use in developing countries' before deciding to include them on the list. This involved the collection and review of information which was not readily available to UNEP or the FAO under the existing information exchange procedures. The group recommended that a special data collection programme be initiated to identify such pesticides. Information was gathered from governments and international organisa-

[93] FAO Meeting Report AGP:1990/, p 12.
[94] *Ibid.*
[95] UN Doc UNEP/PIC.WG.3/5/Add. 1, p 2, para 4 (emphasis added).
[96] UN Doc UNEP/PIC/WG.1/2/2, p 2, para 4.

tions, as well as from industry, non-governmental organisations and the scientific literature.[97]

The Prior Informed Consent Procedure in Operation

No fewer than three meetings of the FAO/UNEP Joint Group of Experts on PIC were required between 1989 and 1991 before agreement could be reached on an initial list of 18 pesticides and five industrial chemicals to which the PIC procedure shall apply.[98] However, the adoption of this list was only the first step in making the procedure operational for the chemicals in question. Before participating countries can be formally requested to communicate their decisions on the future importation of any PIC chemical, a 'decision guidance document' (DGD) for that chemical has to be drafted, reviewed, approved, translated and, finally, circulated to designated national authorities of participating countries. The first set of DGDs, for the first six pesticides on the PIC list, was circulated in November 1991.[99] This marked the official start of the operation of the voluntary PIC procedure, as participating countries for the first time were given the opportunity to make and communicate decisions pursuant to the procedure. Further DGDs for additional chemicals were circulated in 1993 and 1997.[100] Six years elapsed between the adoption of the initial list and the circulation of DGDs for all the chemicals on it. As of early 1998, only 17 pesticides and five industrial chemicals were effectively subject to the PIC procedure.[101]

At the same time, 127 chemicals for which control actions have been notified to UNEP/FAO were still under consideration for inclusion in the PIC procedure.[102] These include chemicals banned or severely restricted in five or more countries prior to the start-up of the voluntary PIC procedure or in one or more countries after that date.[103] Indeed, according to the provisions of the London Guidelines and the FAO Code, from the moment the PIC procedure became operational, a control action taken for health or environmental reasons by any single country and notified to UNEP or the FAO is in principle sufficient to warrant making a chemical subject to the procedure. These chemicals have been included in a list of 'candidate chemicals' undergoing further review before a decision is taken to prepare DGDs with a view to their effective inclusion in the PIC procedure. This review

[97] *Ibid*, p 3, para 11.

[98] Report of the 3rd FAO/UNEP Joint Meeting on Prior Informed Consent, 1991, p 25, Table 1.

[99] UN Doc UNEP/FAO/PIC/INC.1/4, 19 Dec 1995, p 4, Table 1.

[100] UN Doc UNEP/FAO/PIC/INC.5/INF/3, 3 Mar 1998, p 2, Table 1.

[101] *Ibid.*

[102] Report of the 8th FAO/UNEP Joint Meeting on Prior Informed Consent, 1995, p 10.

[103] The cut-off date agreed by the Joint Group of Experts is 1 Jan 1992.

process involves clarifying the reasons and legal status of control actions and verifying that the chemicals in question are still being produced and used.

By the end of 1995, a total of 144 countries had designated national authorities for participating in the voluntary PIC procedure.[104] These authorities are expected to complete an 'importing country response form' for each chemical for which a DGD has been circulated, indicating whether or not imports of the chemical are allowed. About half the number of participating countries have effectively communicated responses to the FAO/UNEP for at least some PIC chemicals.[105] These import responses are compiled by the secretariat and officially distributed to designated national authorities of participating countries every six months. The first such circular was sent out in August 1992.

[104] UN Doc UNEP/FAO/PIC/INC.1/4, 19 Dec 1995, p 2, para 8.
[105] UN Doc UNEP/FAO/PIC/INC.1/6, 19 Dec 1995, p 4, para 17.

14

The Third Phase of International Regulatory Efforts: From 'Hard' Soft Law to 'Soft' Hard Law?

THE DEBATE ABOUT THE NEED FOR FURTHER REGULATORY INITIATIVES IN UNEP AND FAO

Following the amendment of UNEP London Guidelines and the FAO Code of Conduct in 1989, the two organisations, in addition to implementing the voluntary PIC procedure, continued to consider what further regulatory action to take with respect to chemicals, respectively pesticides. The 1989 FAO Conference report already contained a reference to the possibility of converting the FAO Code of Conduct into a binding legal instrument. This possibility was to be further investigated by the secretariat and also considered by the expert group on the implementation of the PIC procedure. In UNEP, the question of elaborating a convention on chemicals, building on the non-binding London Guidelines, came under active consideration in 1990. It should be noted that the 1989 Governing Council decision amending the London Guidelines also contained an explicit mandate to the Executive Director of UNEP to reconvene an *Ad Hoc* Working Group of Experts to monitor the implementation of the amended Guidelines, review 'other activities related to the production and use of chemicals' and prepare a report for the 1991 session of the Governing Council 'on any further steps which should be taken to supplement the amended London Guidelines, *including the possible further need for a convention*'.[1]

Towards a Legally Binding Instrument?

The possibility of transforming the London Guidelines into a legally binding instrument was first raised during the negotiations leading up to their initial

[1] UNEP Governing Council Dec 15/30, 25 May 1989, UN Doc UNEP/GC.15/12, Annex I, pp 160–62, para 11(c) (emphasis added).

adoption in 1987. Since there was no consensus on the need for a convention on information exchange on chemicals in international trade, consideration of this question was deferred until after the resolution of the highly contentious issue of prior informed consent. The 1989 Governing Council decision, referring to 'the possible further need for a convention', did not prejudge the outcome of the deliberations of the newly established *Ad Hoc* Working Group of Experts instructed to consider 'further steps' to be taken by UNEP.

However, opponents of the early development of an international legal instrument prevailed at the first session of the *Ad Hoc* Working Group, held in Nairobi in October 1990. Instead of recommending further consideration of the need for a legally binding instrument prior to the 1991 meeting of the Governing Council, the working group recommended that the Executive Director of UNEP:

> start preparations, in consultation with all parties concerned, for the development of *an international code of ethics* for use by industries, related to their management of and international trade in chemicals, as a complement to the amended London Guidelines and other internationally agreed codes.[2]

While the working group thus expressed a strong preference for a further soft law approach in this area, the idea of a convention was nevertheless not altogether abandoned; the working group recommendations included a suggestion that the Governing Council 'request further action ... *possibly including the development of a convention* when enough experience has been gained in the implementation of the amended London Guidelines.'[3]

By referring in general terms to 'the management of chemicals' in its recommendations on both the proposed 'international code of ethics' and the still hypothetical future convention, the working group acknowledged that its mandate was by no means confined by the scope of the amended London Guidelines, which deal only with information exchange on chemicals in international trade. Indeed, the working group had been instructed by the Governing Council to review all relevant activities 'related to *the production and use* of chemicals,'[4] not just questions related to trade and information exchange.

After its 1990 Nairobi meeting, the *Ad Hoc* Working Group of Experts met again in Geneva in April 1991 to finalise its recommendations for submission to UNEP Governing Council at its 16th session in May 1991. While the first meeting of the expert group had put off the possible development of a convention to a more distant future and instead given prefer-

[2] UN Doc UNEP/PIC.WG.3/6, p 16 (emphasis added).
[3] *Ibid* (emphasis added).
[4] UNEP Governing Council Dec. 15/30, above n 1, para 11(b) (emphasis added).

ence to the development of a code of ethics, the second meeting came to quite different conclusions.

The tone was set by the opening statement delivered on behalf of the Executive Director of UNEP by the Director of the IRPTC. Apparently quite disappointed with the results of the first session, the Executive Director openly called on the working group 'to amend and supplement the recommendations of the first session as necessary'. In an implicit criticism of the weakness of those recommendations, he called the working group's attention to a decision on the environmentally sound management of chemicals adopted by the second session of the Preparatory Committee of the UNCED, which urged, inter alia, that work should be expedited to 'strengthen the legal basis' of prior informed consent.[5]

Several representatives from developing countries and non-governmental organisations strongly criticised the recommendations of the first session, and in particular the recommendation to develop a 'code of ethics', arguing that there was already more than enough soft law in the field of international management of chemicals and that it was time for UNEP to start work on a legally binding instrument, instead of committing resources to the development of yet another set of non-binding rules. This feeling was shared by a number of industrialised countries. In the end, a consensus emerged to rewrite the recommendation on the code of ethics in such a way as to reduce UNEP's commitment to this initiative and place the primary responsibility for it on industry. The revised recommendation called on the Executive Director of UNEP:

> to invite the various private sector parties involved in the international trade in chemicals to enter into commitments aimed at achieving the objectives laid down in the amended London Guidelines and to prepare a code of ethics on the international trade in chemicals in consultation with the international organizations concerned.[6]

The overall thrust of this recommendation differs significantly from that of the initial recommendation adopted in Nairobi in 1990. Instead of committing UNEP to drafting a code in collaboration with industry, as a clear *alternative* to the development of a convention, it calls on industry to enter into commitments for the implementation of the PIC procedure and to develop a code of ethics of its own initiative. UNEP thus recovered its freedom to consider other approaches without being constrained by negotiations with industry on a code of ethics.

The *Ad Hoc* Working Group then proceeded to reconsider the possibility of developing a convention. More support was expressed for the idea than at the previous meeting. Malaysia introduced a proposal 'to start

[5] PREPCOM Decision 2/17.

[6] UN Doc UNEP/PIC/WG.1/2/4, 13 Apr 1991, p 18, para 81(c).

preparations immediately, in consultation with all parties concerned, for the development of a global convention on chemicals.'[7] Many industialised countries opposed the early development of a convention, arguing that more experience was needed and that the work on a convention would distract scarce resources from the implementation of the voluntary PIC procedure. Though the discussion revolved around essentially the same arguments as the earlier discussion at the Nairobi meeting, the case for a convention was strengthened by the introductory comments of the Executive Director and the recommendations of the UNCED Preparatory Committee. It was also argued that there was no incompatibility between the development of a convention by UNEP and the development of a code of ethics by industry.

After long discussion, consensus was eventually reached on a compromise recommendation which called on the Governing Council to:

> request further urgent action by the *Ad Hoc* Working Group, including work on *strengthening the legal basis of the amended London Guidelines . . . through the development of a convention,* taking into consideration, *inter alia*, experience gained in the implementation of the amended London Guidelines and the PIC procedure, the ongoing work of the Preparatory Committee of the United Nations Conference on Environment and Development with regard to the development of an international framework for the environmentally sound management of toxic chemicals, and other relevant international instruments and activities.[8]

By referring to the broad agenda of the UNCED preparatory work, the recommendation suggested that the scope of the proposed convention need not necessarily be the same as that of the London Guidelines, but could be substantially broader.

Notwithstanding the apparent consensus reached at the Geneva meeting, the proposed development of a global convention on chemicals by UNEP remained a highly controversial issue. The decision taken by the Governing Council at its 16th session in May 1991 indicated that opposition to such a convention was still strong. As it turned out, proponents of a convention did not manage to consolidate the ground gained in Geneva but suffered a substantial setback as the Governing Council did not follow the working group's recommendation, but amended it significantly at the initiative of the United States and the United Kingdom. As a consequence, the Governing Council merely requested the Executive Director

> to re-convene the *Ad Hoc* Working Group for further urgent action, including work on strengthening the legal basis of the amended London Guidelines, taking into consideration, *inter alia*, experience gained in the implementation of the Guidelines and the prior informed consent procedure.[9]

[7] UN Doc UNEP/PIC/WG.1/2/CRP.2, 10 Apr 1991.
[8] UN Doc UNEP/PIC/WG.1/2/4, p 19 (emphasis added).
[9] UNEP Governing Council Dec 16/35, 31 May 1991, para 8.

In an apparent effort to narrow down the scope of any further action by UNEP, the 1991 Governing Council decision no longer referred explicitly to the development of a convention and to the UNCED agenda.

CHEMICAL SAFETY ISSUES ON THE AGENDA OF THE UNITED NATIONS CONFERENCE ON ENVIRONMENT AND DEVELOPMENT (UNCED)

The management of toxic chemicals was one of many topics addressed by the UNCED in 1992 and dealt with in Agenda 21, the global action plan for environment and sustainable development adopted by the Rio Conference.

Chapter 19 of Agenda 21 covers the 'environmentally sound management of toxic chemicals, including prevention of illegal international traffic in toxic and dangerous products'. It contains a series of recommendations for national and international action in six programme areas which it identifies as requiring priority attention, including inter alia 'information exchange on toxic chemicals and chemical risks' and 'prevention of illegal international traffic in toxic and dangerous products'.

The origin of the attention given to 'prevention of illegal international traffic in toxic and dangerous products' can be traced back to resolutions on this topic adopted by the United Nations General Assembly.[10] As explained in Agenda 21, the notion of illegal traffic 'refers to traffic that is carried out in contravention of a country's laws or relevant international legal instruments.'[11] Though illegal traffic may be a problem for some countries, one may wonder whether it really deserves the special attention it has received from the General Assembly and the UNCED. Indeed, most problems caused by the export of banned or severely restricted chemicals to developing countries were not the result of illegal traffic but rather of *legal* traffic, due precisely to the legal vacuum which exists both in exporting and importing countries and the lack, at the time, of any binding international instruments restricting such trade. The UNCED apparently recognised this in Agenda 21, noting that its concern 'also relates to transboundary movements of those products that are not carried out in accordance with applicable internationally adopted guidelines and principles,'[12] thus referring to traffic in contravention of applicable soft law rules, which is not 'illegal' in the technical sense. At any rate, the measures recommended in Agenda 21 to deal with the problem of 'illegal traffic' essentially relate to the reinforcement of national regulatory and enforcement capacities, a

[10] UNGA Resolutions 42/183 and 44/226.
[11] Agenda 21, para 19.66.
[12] *Ibid*, para 19.66.

matter which, though important, is not directly relevant to the development of international environmental law as such and will therefore not be further discussed here.

Under the heading 'information exchange on toxic chemicals and chemical risks', Agenda 21 deals mainly with the implementation of the amended London Guidelines, particularly the PIC procedure. The main political issue addressed by the UNCED in this context, in the wake of the earlier, inconclusive debate in UNEP, was the desirability of elaborating a legally binding international instrument in this field. The relevant provisions of Agenda 21 reflected persistent disagreement on this matter within the international community. The objective formulated by the UNCED in 1992 was

> to achieve by the year 2000, as feasible, full participation in and implementation of the PIC procedure, including *possible mandatory applications through legally binding instruments* contained in the Amended London Guidelines and in the FAO International Code of Conduct, taking into account the experience gained within the PIC procedure.[13]

This rather cryptic language is obviously the result of a compromise between advocates and opponents of a binding instrument. Making the application of the PIC procedure mandatory through the elaboration of a legally binding instrument is mentioned as a possibility, while the reference to the London Guidelines and the FAO Code is probably intended to stress that, were the development of such an instrument to be undertaken, it should be based on existing soft law and not be broader in scope. However, the suggestion that a possible future binding instrument be 'contained in' the London Guidelines and the FAO Code of Conduct legally does not make any sense, as both the Guidelines and the Code are non-binding instruments. Another provision of Agenda 21 calls on governments to:

> implement the PIC procedures as soon as possible and . . . invite relevant international organizations, such as UNEP, GATT, FAO, WHO and others, in their respective area of competence, to *consider* working expeditiously towards the conclusion of legally binding instruments.[14]

While this recommendation strengthened the position of proponents of a binding instrument, it remained sufficiently non-committal to be acceptable to opponents, especially as it did not give a clear mandate to any particular organisation and left ample room for dilatory argument about the 'respective area of competence' of the various 'relevant international organizations'. The UNCED manifestly refrained from taking a political decision on this controversial issue and chose to refer the matter back to other fora for further consideration.

[13] *Ibid*, para 19.38 (b) (emphasis added).
[14] *Ibid*, para 19.39 (d) (emphasis added).

POST-RIO INITIATIVES: A NEW REGULATORY AGENDA FOR THE INTERNATIONAL COMMUNITY

A few months after the Rio Conference, UNEP convened an informal expert meeting to advise the Executive Director on the issue of a legal instrument and prepare the next plenary meeting of the *Ad Hoc* Working Group of Experts, which was scheduled for January 1993. The informal preparatory meeting, held in November 1992, did not resolve the controversy but instead recommended that a task force be established to consider elements of a possible legally binding instrument for the mandatory application of PIC *and* the development of a code of ethics on international trade in chemicals.

The Third Session of UNEP *Ad Hoc* Working Group of Experts on the Implementation of the Amended London Guidelines met in Geneva in January 1993. The group continued its work in accordance with the mandate given to it by UNEP Governing Council in May 1991. As mentioned above, the group's terms of reference included, inter alia, 'work on strengthening the legal basis of the amended London Guidelines'. Although these terms of reference were laid down prior to the UNCED, the group, in carrying out its mandate, also took into account the relevant provisions of chapter 19 of Agenda 21, quoted above.

At its third meeting, the group revisited the now familiar argument between proponents and opponents of the early elaboration of a binding legal instrument, which had already occupied much of the first two meetings. The opponents, mostly experts from developed countries, 'stated that more experience would be needed in the implementation of the [London] Guidelines' before the development of a binding instrument could be considered,[15] while the advocates of a convention, mostly developing countries representatives, stressed 'the urgent need for preventing illegal international traffic in hazardous chemicals', 'stated that enough experience had been gained from the PIC procedure to demonstrate its feasibility' and concluded that 'it was time to ensure application of the PIC procedure by developing a legally binding instrument.'[16]

In a joint proposal, the United States and the member states of the EC suggested that an informal group be established to 'evaluate aspects of the PIC procedure where the application of a legally binding instrument would enhance the operation of the procedure, and *develop draft convention language, if appropriate.*'[17] Eventually, in a compromise between both sides, the group recommended to the Governing Council the establishment of a 'task force . . . to consider modalities for a legally binding instrument for

[15] UN Doc UNEP/PIC/WG.1/3/5, 23 Apr 1993, para 93.
[16] *Ibid*, para 102.
[17] *Ibid*, para 101 (emphasis added).

the mandatory application of the PIC procedure', while stressing that 'the scope of a legally binding instrument should, for the time being, be limited to the PIC procedure.'[18]

The development of a 'code of ethics' on the international trade in chemicals, which was proposed at the second meeting of the *Ad Hoc* Working Group and endorsed in principle by UNEP Governing Council in 1991, was given considerably less attention by the group at its third meeting than the elaboration of a legal instrument. The group merely took note of the outcome of two informal consultative meetings with industry arranged by UNEP Secretariat in 1992 and recommended that UNEP 'continue to facilitate the work for preparing a code of ethics on the international trade in chemicals.'[19] The level of government interest in this initiative did not appear to be very high, as most governments were focusing their attention on the work of the task force on a legally binding instrument. The establishment of this task force was welcomed by the members of the Governing Council at its 17th session in May 1993 and a high priority was accorded to this initiative during the Council's discussion of the future activities of UNEP in the field of the development of international environmental law.

Preparing the Ground for Negotiations on a Legally Binding Instrument

The first meeting of the task force, in September 1993, agreed on a set of 'elements which might be included in a legally binding instrument for the mandatory application of the prior informed consent procedure.'[20] Like the existing voluntary PIC procedure, the instrument to be elaborated would cover 'banned and severely restricted chemicals and hazardous pesticide formulations which may be causing problems under conditions of use in developing countries.' The elements set out in the task force report were closely modelled on the existing provisions of the London Guidelines and the FAO Code, and included hardly anything new. The only questions not yet covered by the voluntary instruments which were to be addressed in the proposed legally binding instrument were measures to deal with non-compliance and a financial mechanism to finance technical assistance and 'incremental costs' to developing countries arising from 'the full implementation of the PIC procedure'. It was also proposed to elaborate trade-related provisions to deal with such matters as control of trade with non-parties, matters which are only superficially addressed in the existing instruments.

[18] UN Doc UNEP/PIC/WG.1/3/5, para 103.11–12.
[19] *Ibid*, para 103.4.
[20] UN Doc UNEP/PIC/TF.1/4, 29 Sept 1993, Annex, p 7.

UNEP Secretariat was invited to circulate the task force report to governments and interested organisations for comment and to further 'refine' the elements identified in the report for consideration by a second meeting of the task force, followed by another full session of the *Ad Hoc* Working Group. On the whole, the task force stuck very closely to the working group's instruction not to extend the scope of the proposed legal instrument beyond the PIC procedure. Whereas, as pointed out above, some support had been expressed at the second meeting of the *Ad Hoc* Working Group for the elaboration of a more comprehensive, global convention, dealing with more aspects of the management of chemicals than just PIC, this idea seemed to have been abandoned in 1993.

Significantly, the recommendations of the working group suggested that the formal political decision to initiate negotiations on a legal instrument should not be taken by UNEP Governing Council but rather by the UN Commission on Sustainable Development (CSD), which was to consider the management of chemicals at its meeting scheduled for May 1994, to which the *Ad Hoc* Working Group urged the Executive Director of UNEP to report. At the group's third meeting, the representative of the FAO, in what was obviously a bid to assert his organisation's jurisdiction and reduce UNEP's control over the negotiating process, expressed reservations about the choice of UNEP as a forum for such negotiations, pointing out that the proposed legal instrument on PIC 'would have consequences for environment, agriculture, trade, health and industry'. He suggested that the matter should be submitted to the UN General Assembly or the CSD, which could decide to establish a special negotiating committee, whose secretariat would be controlled jointly by 'the agencies most closely involved.'[21] The task force, in which not only the FAO, but also the ILO, the WHO, the GATT and the European Commission participated, endorsed this approach, and urged UNEP to convene an interagency meeting 'to strengthen the collaboration among relevant organizations identified in chapter 19 of Agenda 21, in particular FAO', prior to the 1994 meeting of the CSD.[22]

UNEP's work proceeded at a rather slow pace in 1994, with a second meeting of the task force, followed by the fourth session of the *Ad Hoc* Working Group of Experts on the Implementation of the Amended London Guidelines. The task force further elaborated the 'elements which might be included in a legally binding instrument' and reported to the *Ad Hoc* Working Group that it considered its task completed. It recommended that the outcome of its work be used as a basis for drafting legal language for the proposed instrument.[23] The working group discussed the elements elaborated by the task force and further refined them. While industry

[21] UN Doc UNEP/PIC/WG.1/3/5, para 100.
[22] UN Doc UNEP/PIC/TF.1/4, para 25(d).
[23] UN Doc UNEP/PIC/TF.2/4, 10 Mar 1994, para 24(a).

representatives continued to express their scepticism about the need for a legally binding instrument on PIC, there was a growing consensus among governments that the development of such an instrument was desirable and that the elements elaborated by the task force, as amended by the working group, constituted a suitable basis for commencing negotiations. The meeting noted, however, that there was as yet 'no clear mandate for the development and subsequent negotiations for a legally binding instrument' and that 'guidance' from the Commission on Sustainable Development and/or the UN General Assembly would be necessary in this regard.[24] Accordingly, the working group recommended that the Executive Director of UNEP report to the second session of the CSD in May 1994 and seek its guidance.[25]

Waiting for a Mandate from Governments

The CSD considered this matter as part of its review of the implementation of the recommendations in chapter 19 of Agenda 21. The Commission 'welcome[d]' the progress achieved by UNEP *Ad Hoc* Working Group and:

> recommend[ed] that UNEP, *together with FAO and in close consultation with other international organizations*, continue to evaluate and address problems with the implementation of the voluntary PIC procedure and *to develop effective legally binding instruments concerning the PIC procedure*.[26]

Contrary to the expectations of the *Ad Hoc* Working Group, the CSD did not, however, provide a clear mandate to UNEP for initiating formal negotiations nor decide on the forum, procedure and timeframe of such negotiations and on the role of other interested UN agencies such as the FAO in the process. Nor did the Commission recommend that the General Assembly take the ultimate decision, as suggested earlier by the FAO representative at the third meeting of the *Ad Hoc* Working Group in 1993.

The high-level meeting of the Commission rather added to the confusion by suggesting that the matter of a legally binding instrument should be considered by 'the inter-sessional meeting of the Intergovernmental Forum on Chemical Safety and other relevant bodies.'[27] Moreover, the Chairman's summary of the meeting also notes the 'strong sentiment . . . expressed by participants' that the proposed instrument should not only make the PIC procedure legally binding, but '*subsequently ban* the export of domestically

[24] UN Doc UNEP/PIC/WG.1/4/5, 15 Apr 1994, para 85.
[25] *Ibid*, para 89(d).
[26] UN Doc E/CN.17/1994/20, para 165 (emphasis added).
[27] *Ibid*, p 53, para 11.

prohibited chemicals' from OECD to non-OECD countries.[28] This seemed to signal a new round of discussion on the proper *scope* of the proposed legal instrument, which UNEP *Ad Hoc* Working Group had agreed in 1993 should be limited to the PIC procedure.[29]

The indecision of the CSD left the whole issue floating in mid-air until December 1994, when UNEP and the FAO jointly organised an 'informal consultative meeting' of government experts and representatives of various intergovernmental and non-governmental organisations to consider the substantive and procedural issues involved in the development of a legally binding instrument and formulate recommendations for submission to the next regular session of UNEP Governing Council in May 1995. Meanwhile, the FAO Council, at its November 1994 session, had endorsed cooperation with UNEP for the purpose of elaborating an international legal instrument for the application of the PIC procedure.[30] The informal consultative meeting recommended that the Executive Director of UNEP seek a formal mandate from UNEP Governing Council to start negotiations 'with a view to the conclusion of such an instrument possibly by 1997.'[31]

The Code of Ethics on the International Trade in Chemicals: a Sideshow

Meanwhile, the drafting of a Code of Ethics on the International Trade in Chemicals had been completed in April 1994. This effort had been undertaken under the auspices of UNEP pursuant to its Governing Council Decision 16/35 of 31 May 1991, with subsequent endorsement by the UNCED in chapter 19 of Agenda 21.[32] In this instance, UNEP acted as a facilitator of voluntary self-regulation by the private sector. Indeed, the code was not formally adopted by any organ of UNEP but is the result of informal consultations between the 'various private sector parties involved in the international trade in chemicals' which, according to the terms of Decision 16/35, were 'invited' by the Executive Director of UNEP to 'enter into commitments'.

In accordance with the instructions of the Governing Council, the Executive Director invited representatives of various national and international chemical industry associations to an informal meeting in Geneva in May 1992 to consider the modalities for the development and adoption of a code of ethics. The industry associations responded positively and requested

[28] *Ibid* (emphasis added).
[29] UN Doc UNEP/PIC/WG.1/3/5, para 103.12.
[30] Report of the Council of FAO, 107th Session, Rome, 15–24 Nov 1994, FAO Doc CL 107/REP, p 8, para 48.
[31] UN Doc UNEP/PIC/CONS.5/L.1/Rev. 1, para 58.
[32] Agenda 21, para 19.50(a).

UNEP to 'continue to provide an *international forum for consultation by private sector parties* concerned with the preparation of the code.'[33] Accordingly, three further meetings were hosted by UNEP from 1992 to 1994. At the conclusion of the fourth and final meeting in Geneva in April 1994, the Code of Ethics 'was considered agreed upon *by the parties that had participated in its preparatory process*.'[34] It was then communicated by UNEP Executive Director to the second meeting of the Commission on Sustainable Development in May 1994, which 'appreciate[d]' it and 'stress[ed] that it should be widely applied by industry in all countries without delay.'[35]

The Code of Ethics on the International Trade in Chemicals[36] is intended as a complement to the London Guidelines for the Exchange of Information on Chemicals in International Trade. While the latter are addressed to governments and focus on information exchange and prior informed consent procedures, the former is addressed to industry and other private sector parties and is broader in scope, covering 'the production and management of chemicals in international trade, taking into account their entire life cycle'. Thus, the nature of UNEP Code of Ethics also differs fundamentally from that of the FAO International Code of Conduct on the Distribution and Use of Pesticides, which, although addressed to industry as well, includes many recommendations primarily aimed at governments. As defined in the Code of Ethics, the concept 'private sector parties' covers not only industry but also 'workers and their representatives, environmental and consumer groups and other non-governmental organizations, and the public.'[37] However, by their very nature, most guidelines in the code are addressed primarily to industry. A footnote stipulates that, in countries with a government-owned chemical industry, the terms 'industry' and 'private sector parties' may be read as referring to 'enterprises'. It should be noted that representatives of state-owned chemical industries, eg from China, also participated in the drafting of the code.

Private sector parties are invited to subscribe voluntarily to the Code of Ethics, more specifically to 'make a commitment to undertake self-regulatory measures to meet the standards of conduct set out' in the code,[38] independently of any legal obligations and government policies. The introduction stresses that adhering to the code 'is *a voluntary action* of the private sector parties' and does not require any government approval.[39]

[33] UN Doc UNEP/PIC/CONS.2/1/4, 7 May 1992, p 10, para 39(e) (emphasis added).

[34] UN Doc UNEP/PIC/CONS.2/4/3, 8 Apr 1994, p 3, para 15 (emphasis added).

[35] UN Doc E/CN.17/1994/20, para 166.

[36] Code of Ethics on the International Trade in Chemicals, UN Doc UNEP/PIC/CONS.2/4/3, 8 Apr 1994, Annex, pp 4–16.

[37] *Ibid*, para 2(d).

[38] *Ibid*, para 4.

[39] *Ibid*, para 11 (emphasis added).

In making such a voluntary commitment, the private sector recognises its 'shared responsibility, along with the governments of chemical exporting and importing countries, for the protection of human health and the environment.'[40] Parties subscribing to the code shall publish a written statement to this effect and notify UNEP of their decision. UNEP will maintain and regularly publish a list of those private sector parties that have entered into a commitment to apply the code.[41]

The core of the Code of Ethics consists of a set of 'general principles' followed by 'standards of conduct' providing 'guidance' for their implementation. The basic substantive principle requires private sector parties:

> to take appropriate actions to protect human health and the environment from adverse effects from the production and management of chemicals in international trade.[42]

More specifically, industry should 'develop management systems to enable the proper production and management of chemicals, taking into account their entire life cycle' and, 'to the extent practicable', do business only with other private sector parties 'who meet applicable safety, health and environmental criteria.'[43] The first set of standards of conduct relates to risk reduction. Chemical producers have a general responsibility 'to minimize adverse health and environmental effects from chemicals being manufactured and managed'[44] and are required to 'voluntarily take corrective action' when 'safe manufacture and management of a chemical . . . does not seem possible'[45] and to 'halt manufacturing and trade, and recall products when appropriate', whenever there are 'unacceptable risks associated with the product.'[46] These provisions are somewhat ambiguous, as they suggest that production and trade must not necessarily be stopped when it is impossible to ensure the safety of a chemical, but that other, unspecified 'corrective action' may suffice as long as the risk is not judged to be 'unacceptable'.

The provisions of the Code of Ethics relating to quality assurance implicitly condemn double standards in the production of chemicals by requiring producers and formulators to:

> ensure, *to the extent possible*, that chemicals manufactured or formulated by a subsidiary company or a contract manufacturer meet *appropriate* human

[40] *Ibid*, para 5.
[41] *Ibid*, para 38(a). The list of the parties which have subscribed to the Code of Ethics is published on UNEP website.
[42] *Ibid*, para 11.
[43] *Ibid*, para 12.
[44] *Ibid*, para 18(a)(i).
[45] *Ibid*, para 18(b).
[46] *Ibid*, para 18(c).

health and environmental requirements which are consistent with the requirements of the country of manufacture *as well as those of the parent or contracting company*.[47]

Though somewhat tempered by the proviso 'to the extent possible' and the qualification 'appropriate', this provision imposes a special responsibility on transnational corporations.

The Code of Ethics also spells out the responsibilities of industry with respect to the provision of information about chemicals. The basic principle is that producers and formulators should 'provide information and instructions in a form and language which will ensure safe and effective use of a chemical' to all parties concerned, including transporters, traders, occupational users, consumers and government authorities.[48] In particular, industry is expected to 'make reasonable efforts to ensure that the information relevant to health and environmental protection from harmful effects of chemicals reaches the occupational users or traders in importing countries'[49] and to provide, on request, to government authorities in such countries, information 'concerning banned or severely restricted chemicals and alternatives to such chemicals.'[50] It should be noted in this connection that another provision[51] specifically requires industry to cooperate with government authorities 'in order to ensure implementation of the export notification procedures for banned or severely restricted chemicals, where applicable' and, as regards those chemicals subject to the PIC procedure, to comply with the PIC decisions of importing countries.

THE NEGOTIATION OF AN INTERNATIONAL LEGALLY BINDING INSTRUMENT FOR THE APPLICATION OF THE PRIOR INFORMED CONSENT PROCEDURE

Defining the Mandate of UNEP/FAO Intergovernmental Negotiating Committee

At its 18th session in May 1995, UNEP Governing Council decided to launch formal intergovernmental negotiations for the purpose of elaborating an international legally binding instrument for the application of the PIC procedure. It acted on the recommendations of the *Ad Hoc* Working Group of Experts on the Implementation of the Amended London Guidelines, which had completed its work in 1994. The FAO Council had already

[47] UN Doc UNEP/PIC/CONS.2/4/3, para 23(b) (emphasis added).
[48] *Ibid*, para 27(a)–(b).
[49] *Ibid*, para 28(a).
[50] *Ibid*, para 28(b).
[51] *Ibid*, para 19.

given its go-ahead to the FAO Secretariat to 'proceed with the preparation of a draft legally-binding instrument on the operation of the PIC procedure as part of the joint FAO/UNEP programme on PIC' at its 107th session in November 1994,[52] but a formal decision of UNEP governing body was still lacking. Thus, UNEP Governing Council Decision 18/12 of 26 May 1995 was the ultimate step in the excruciatingly slow consensus-building process described above, which took six years altogether. It provided the formal authority for the establishment of a negotiating committee, defined its mandate and determined a timetable for the conduct of the negotiations, thus effectively confirming UNEP's role as the lead agency in the process of developing a convention on PIC.

While the Governing Council decided to authorise the Executive Director of UNEP to convene, together with the FAO, 'an intergovernmental negotiating committee with a mandate to prepare an international legally binding instrument for the application of the prior informed consent procedure for certain hazardous chemicals in international trade,'[53] the exact scope of the instrument to be negotiated remained controversial. An apparent consensus not to go beyond making mandatory the application of the PIC procedure as it was then laid down in the voluntary UNEP and FAO instruments, which had emerged from the deliberations of UNEP *Ad Hoc* Working Group and task force in 1993 and 1994, was shattered during the 1994 meeting of the CSD, where, as we saw above, many countries urged that in the process of developing a legally binding instrument, consideration should be given to the option of *banning* the export of domestically prohibited chemicals.

The same demand was forcefully reiterated at the 1995 Governing Council meeting by the Group of 77, led by Malaysia, which tabled an amendment to the draft Governing Council decision stipulating that the proposed international instrument should include provisions banning 'the export of domestically prohibited chemicals, including pesticides.'[54] In the ensuing negotiations, a compromise was finally reached on a 'double-track' approach: while the mandate of the negotiating committee remained limited to the PIC procedure, it was agreed that, in parallel with the activities of that committee, a group of experts would be convened, also in cooperation with the FAO, to:

> consider . . . and recommend what *further measures* are needed to reduce the risks from a limited number of hazardous chemicals, *either within or beyond the scope of the existing prior informed consent procedure*.[55]

[52] Report of the Council of FAO, 107th Session, Rome, 15–24 Nov 1994, FAO Doc CL 107/REP, p 8, para 48.

[53] UNEP Governing Council Dec. 18/12, 26 May 1995, para 1.

[54] UN Doc UNEP/GC.18/PC/CRP.24.

[55] UNEP Governing Council Dec 18/12, para 2 (emphasis added).

This group was instructed to report to the next session of the Governing Council, in January 1997, which would then:

give consideration to the need to develop further measures . . . including the possibility that the mandate of the intergovernmental negotiating committee . . . *be extended to provide a basis for such measures.*[56]

Thus, while the committee initially had no mandate to consider anything beyond PIC, the possibility of reconsidering its mandate was explicitly envisaged in the 1995 decision of the Governing Council, which was bound to revisit this controversial issue at its 1997 meeting. The decision also set out a timeframe for the negotiating process: the intergovernmental committee was to begin its work as soon as possible and a diplomatic conference for the adoption and signing of the instrument was to be convened 'preferably not later than early 1997'. This extremely tight schedule did not really seem to take seriously into account the eventuality of a Governing Council decision to extend the mandate of the committee in January 1997. Countries opposed to a more comprehensive convention were keen to press for an early conclusion of the negotiations; those in favour of 'further measures' seemed to have an interest in slowing down the negotiation process on PIC in order to obtain a postponement of the final diplomatic conference and thus to ensure that the negotiating committee would have sufficient time following the January 1997 Governing Council meeting to incorporate additional measures in the convention should it be given a mandate to do so.

Scope of the Instrument: Beyond Prior Informed Consent?

The first two meetings of the 'Intergovernmental Negotiating Committee for an International Legally Binding Instrument for the Application of the Prior Informed Consent Procedure for Certain Hazardous Chemicals in International Trade' (INC/PIC), convened jointly by UNEP and the FAO, were held respectively in Brussels and in Nairobi in March and September 1996. During these meetings, the European Union effectively asserted itself as one of the chief actors in those negotiations, as the European Commission, given the existence of internal EC legislation on PIC,[57] had obtained a mandate from the Council to negotiate on behalf of the European Community and its member states.

Argument about the desirable scope of the PIC instrument mobilised most of the negotiators' attention during the first meeting of the INC. However, the debate took on a somewhat different form from what might have been

[56] UNEP Governing Council Dec 18/12, para 3 (emphasis added).
[57] See below ch 15.

expected based on earlier discussions in the CSD and UNEP Governing Council. There was no coordinated G77 position, and none of the countries that had supported the call for an export ban on previous occasions argued that the legally binding instrument should contain provisions banning the export of domestically prohibited chemicals from OECD to non-OECD countries. Instead, the debate focused on whether or not the instrument under negotiation should be a framework convention broader in scope than the existing voluntary PIC scheme as laid down in the London Guidelines and the FAO Code of Conduct and, more specifically, on the desirability of including provisions on export notification for banned or severely restricted chemicals and a mechanism for adopting further control measures, including possible provisions for eventually phasing out or banning the *production*, rather than merely the export, of certain hazardous chemicals.

However, this time the call for extending the scope of the instrument beyond PIC came not from the G77 but from European countries. In his opening speech at the Brussels meeting, the Belgian environment minister suggested that the legally binding instrument, in addition to the actual PIC provisions, should also provide a legal framework for the adoption of more drastic international action with respect to certain hazardous chemicals, including global production phase-out measures, as and when an international consensus on such measures emerged. He referred specifically to the measures under consideration in UNEP and the IFCS for phasing out certain persistent organic pollutants (POPs) and proposed that the instrument under negotiation in the INC/PIC should provide a legal basis for such measures.[58] He was, however, promptly rebuked by the Executive Director of UNEP, who stressed in her address to the opening session that, while 'it was agreed that additional actions at the international level in addition to PIC were required to ensure the continued safe and sustainable use of chemicals', the INC should 'focus on achieving unanimity on the PIC convention itself.'[59]

While not being quite as specific about possible further measures as the Belgian minister, the EU at the start of the negotiations took the position that the scope of the instrument should not be strictly limited to the PIC procedure but should be flexible, in order to accommodate future developments. It proposed that the legally binding PIC instrument should to this end contain a framework provision providing a basis for the negotiation and adoption of additional protocols to the instrument at a later stage. This

[58] Report of the Intergovernmental Negotiating Committee for an International Legally Binding Instrument for the Application of the Prior Informed Consent Procedure for Certain Hazardous Chemicals and Pesticides in International Trade on the Work of its First Session, UN Doc UNEP/FAO/PIC/INC.1/10, 21 Mar 1996, p 2, para 5 (hereafter referred to as 'Report INC I').

[59] *Ibid*, para 10.

view was strongly opposed by the United States, Australia, Canada and some other OECD countries, who argued that the INC should strictly stick to its mandate and not attempt to elaborate any provisions going beyond the application of the existing PIC procedure.

At the expert meeting on 'further measures', held in Copenhagen in April 1996, pursuant to the 1995 compromise decision of UNEP Governing Council, the Netherlands and Belgium jointly introduced a proposal to develop an integrated international legal instrument for the application of the PIC procedure, the phasing out of persistent organic pollutants (POPs) and any later additional international measures to promote chemical safety.[60] Since the Copenhagen meeting was not a negotiating session for the PIC instrument, the Commission was not mandated to represent a formal EU position. Those EU member states that participated in the meeting acted in their own capacity. While no consensus could be reached on a formal recommendation to the Governing Council to consider the integrated approach, as proposed by the Netherlands and Belgium, due primarily to opposition from the United States and Australia, the report of the meeting invited the Executive Director of UNEP to request the views of governments on such an approach and submit them to the 19th session of the Governing Council for consideration.[61]

The controversy over the scope of the PIC instrument was not resolved during the second session of the INC/PIC in Nairobi. The EU reiterated and further formalised its position by proposing that the objective and scope of the instrument be formulated in general terms and that provision be made for the possible adoption of protocols containing additional measures to achieve this objective. The United States and like-minded OECD countries continued to oppose any extension of the objective and scope of the instrument beyond PIC. The G77, which had not taken any clear position on this issue during the first meeting, remained reluctant to enter the fray and did not directly address the EU proposal. It did, however, indicate that the PIC procedure per se was insufficient and that the instrument should therefore include a reference to the more general objective of promoting the environmentally sound management of chemicals, especially in developing countries, in accordance with the principle of 'common but differentiated responsibility.'[62] Thus formulated, the objective of the instrument would justify the inclusion of detailed provisions on capacity-building and techni-

[60] UN Doc UNEP/PIC/EG/1/CRP.1, 16 Apr 1996.

[61] Report of the Government-designated Group of Experts on Further Measures to Reduce the Risks from a Limited Number of Chemicals, UN Doc UNEP/GC.19/INF.7, 21 Nov 1996, p 9, para 47.

[62] Report of the Intergovernmental Negotiating Committee for an International Legally Binding Instrument for the Application of the Prior Informed Consent Procedure for Certain Hazardous Chemicals and Pesticides in International Trade on the Work of its Second Session, UN Doc UNEP/FAO/PIC/INC.2/7, 12 Nov 1996, p 5, para 19 (hereafter referred to as 'Report INC II').

cal assistance, which seemed to be the primary goal of the G77. However, the concept of 'environmentally sound management of chemicals' is sufficiently broad to be able to encompass measures additional to the PIC procedure, as envisaged by the EU.

Leaving aside the fundamental political controversy with respect to the scope of the PIC Convention, the early work of the INC/PIC also showed that, even within the narrow confines of the PIC procedure, a number of contentious points remained. The most controversial question was that of export notification. All developing countries that spoke on the issue, as well as the EU, strongly supported the inclusion of export notification provisions in the PIC Convention, while the United States, Australia, Canada and Japan argued that such provisions, though included in the existing voluntary UNEP and FAO instruments, were 'not appropriate for discussion in this forum'[63] because they are not part of the PIC procedure *stricto sensu*. Export notification mechanisms were also criticised for being potentially trade-restrictive.

The US position on this issue was somewhat puzzling, since export notification requirements for pesticides not registered for use in the United States and for certain other toxic chemicals subject to regulatory restrictions have been in force under US domestic law since the late 1970s, as discussed in chapter 11.[64] Apparently, the United States did not want to assume any international obligations in this field unless it could be assured that other exporting parties would be subject to equally onerous notification requirements. The US felt that export notification, as currently practiced by the US, places a disproportionate burden on American exporters, since the EU requires export notification only for those chemicals banned or severely restricted *under EC law*, while a large number of hazardous chemicals subject to bans or restrictions in individual EU member states are not covered by any export notification requirements.

The EU, for its part, showed a similar concern about ensuring a 'level playing field' in another area of the negotiations. While, under the 1992 EEC Regulation, which will be discussed in chapter 15, exporters are legally required to comply with PIC decisions of importing countries participating in the voluntary PIC procedure,[65] there is no similar legislation in other OECD member states thus far. Thus, the EC had not only a political but also a direct trade interest in making sure that the PIC convention would require all exporting parties to impose the same compliance obligation on exporters under their jurisdiction. Countries which view the PIC procedure as essentially an information exchange mechanism and consider that the

[63] Report INC I, above n 58, p 7, para 29.

[64] Toxic Substances Control Act (TSCA), s 12(b), 15 USC 2611(b); Federal Insecticide, Fungicide and Rodenticide Act (FIFRA), s 17(a), 7 USC 136o(a).

[65] Council Regulation (EEC) No 2455/92, Art 5(4).

enforcement of PIC decisions is the sole responsibility of importing countries were reluctant to commit themselves to any form of export control. This is apparently why the United States, at the first meeting of the INC, opposed the inclusion in the PIC convention of a provision requiring exporting parties to take appropriate enforcement measures. At the end of the second meeting, however, the EC's view seemed to prevail, as a wide consensus began to emerge on draft language committing each exporting party to 'take appropriate legislative and/or administrative measures to ensure compliance by exporters of prior informed consent chemicals in its territory.'[66]

Review of the Negotiations in Progress and Consideration of Related Chemical Safety Issues by the 19th Session of UNEP Governing Council

At the 19th session of UNEP Governing Council held in Nairobi in early 1997 there was considerable debate on the relationship between the PIC negotiating process and other chemical safety issues on the international agenda. Acting on behalf of the EU, the Dutch presidency tabled a draft decision on chemicals management in which it proposed to initiate 'an expeditious assessment process on the advantages and disadvantages of a framework convention on chemicals based on chapter 19 of Agenda 21'. The EU draft decision also called for an early conclusion of the negotiations on the PIC instrument and for the establishment of an intergovernmental negotiating committee to develop an international legally binding instrument on persistent organic pollutants (POPs), and urged that both the PIC and POPs conventions should have 'the necessary flexibility to allow for easy adaptation in view of future developments relating to the different instruments on the safe and environmentally sound management of chemicals'.[67] After protracted negotiations, the Governing Council reached a compromise on a package of four distinct but inter-related decisions on chemicals management issues.

The EU failed in its bid to have the Governing Council direct the INC/PIC to incorporate 'the necessary flexibility' in the PIC instrument. Instead, the Governing Council 'confirm[ed] the present mandate' of the INC, while at the same time 'recogniz[ing] that *additional elements* relating to the prior informed consent procedure are under consideration' in the Committee,[68] thus avoiding any direct reference to the notion of 'further measures' as referred to in its earlier Decision 18/12 and in the report of the Copenhagen expert meeting. However, the Governing Council adopted a separate deci-

[66] Report INC II, above n 62, p 19, Art 10 (c).
[67] UN Doc UNEP/GC.19/CW/CRP.3, 28 Jan 1997.
[68] UNEP Governing Council Dec 19/13A, 7 Feb 1997, paras 1 and 3 (emphasis added).

sion on 'further measures to reduce the risks from a limited number of hazardous chemicals', in which it endorsed most of the recommendations of the Copenhagen meeting, while merely *noting* those concerning 'possible bans or phase-outs' but nevertheless inviting the IFCS to 'consider taking action, as appropriate, to implement them and to report on such action' to the 1999 session of the Governing Council.[69]

The third Governing Council decision 'concludes that international action, including a global legally binding instrument, is required to reduce the risks to human health and the environment arising from the release' of a number of specific POPs and requests the Executive Director to convene a new intergovernmental negotiating committee with a mandate to prepare such an instrument.[70] While the Governing Council notes, in the preamble of this decision, 'that many of the persistent organic pollutants . . . are currently subject to the voluntary prior informed consent procedure' and further states that UNEP activities in the field of chemicals 'should be carried out in a coordinated manner to ensure that the international instruments being developed in this field are fully coherent and complementary', it fails to draw the logical conclusion that the phase-out of the production and use of POPs and the regulation of international trade in hazardous chemicals might better be addressed through the development of a single, integrated international instrument. The reluctance of governments to envisage the establishment of a common legal framework for the regulation of international trade in and production and use of hazardous chemicals—in which PIC could become a prelude to more drastic measures, including, ultimately, a production ban—led the Governing Council to reject any formal linkage between the PIC and the POPs negotiations.

As a token concession to the EU, however, the Council adopted a separate, fourth decision on 'enhanced coherence and efficiency among international activities related to chemicals', providing for further consideration of these issues at its next regular session in 1999. For this purpose, UNEP's Executive Director was instructed to submit a report to the Governing Council 'outlining options of both a legal and administrative nature' for achieving 'enhanced coherence' between the PIC instrument, the future POPs convention, and other intergovernmental activities within the framework of chapter 19 of Agenda 21.[71] One of the 'options' to be examined in the Executive Director's report, though not explicitly mentioned, is obviously the EU's proposal for a framework convention, but the legal and institutional difficulty of developing such an instrument was bound to become even greater after the signing of the PIC convention and the launching of negotiations on a separate POPs convention. Eventually both negotiations

[69] UNEP Governing Council Dec 19/13B, 7 Feb 1997, para 3.
[70] UNEP Governing Council Dec 19/13C, 7 Feb 1997, para 8.
[71] UNEP Governing Council Dec 19/13D, 7 Feb 1997, para 1.

proceeded separately and led to the adoption of two different conventions: the Rotterdam Convention on the Prior Informed Consent Procedure for Certain Hazardous Chemicals and Pesticides in International Trade, which will be examined in detail below, and the Stockholm Convention on Persistent Organic Pollutants, which will not be further considered in this study.

THE CONVENTION ON THE PRIOR INFORMED CONSENT PROCEDURE FOR CERTAIN HAZARDOUS CHEMICALS AND PESTICIDES IN INTERNATIONAL TRADE

Following the first and second session in 1996 and UNEP Governing Council meeting in early 1997, three further sessions of the INC/PIC were required to finalise negotiations on the PIC Convention. The third session was held in Geneva in May 1997, the fourth in October of the same year at the FAO Headquarters in Rome, and the fifth and final negotiating session in March 1998 in Brussels, hosted by the European Commission.[72] The Convention on the Prior Informed Consent Procedure for Certain Hazardous Chemicals and Pesticides in International Trade,[73] as drafted by the INC, was formally adopted and opened for signature at a diplomatic conference hosted by the Netherlands in Rotterdam on 10–11 September 1998. This section analyses the provisions of the Rotterdam Convention as they finally took shape.

Scope of the Convention

The scope of the Convention, like that of the voluntary PIC procedure, covers two categories of chemicals: banned or severely restricted chemicals and 'severely hazardous pesticide formulations'. The latter category is the Convention's equivalent to the 'acutely hazardous pesticide formulations of concern to developing countries', which were first identified as a group of chemicals deserving to be made subject to the PIC procedure in the amended London Guidelines. However, in negotiating the scope of the Convention, this category was not only renamed but also redefined. As now defined in the Convention, it refers to:

[72] The reports of the third and fourth meeting of the INC/PIC and the resulting drafts of the convention are respectively to be found in UN Doc UNEP/FAO/PIC/INC.3/2, 26 June 1997 (hereafter referred to as 'Report INC III') and UN Doc UNEP/FAO/PIC/INC.4/2, 4 Nov 1997 (hereafter referred to as 'Report INC IV').

[73] Convention on the Prior Informed Consent Procedure for Certain Hazardous Chemicals and Pesticides in International Trade, Rotterdam, 11 Sept 1998, UN Doc UNEP/FAO/PIC/CONF/2, 15 July 1998 (hereafter referred to as Rotterdam Convention or PIC Convention).

a chemical formulated for pesticidal use that produces severe health *or environmental* effects observable *within a short period of time* after single or multiple exposure, *under conditions of use*.[74]

Even though this new definition no longer refers explicitly to products 'of concern to developing countries', Article 6 of the Rotterdam Convention does stipulate that only 'a *developing country* or a *country with an economy in transition* . . . that is experiencing problems caused by a severely hazardous pesticide formulation *under conditions of use in its territory*' may propose such a pesticide for inclusion in the list of chemicals subject to the PIC procedure. Nevertheless, the new category is broader than the corresponding one referred to in the London Guidelines and the FAO Code of Conduct and used for the application of the voluntary PIC procedure, because it covers not only pesticides acutely toxic to human health but also those causing severe *environmental* effects, albeit effects 'observable within a short period of time'.

The definition is, in effect, a compromise between the positions of the EU, which proposed to extend the scope of the Convention to '*chemicals* causing *severe* health *or environmental* effects under conditions of use in developing countries or in countries with economies in transition,'[75] and the US, which initially opposed any extension of the category beyond *acutely* hazardous *pesticide* formulations, as referred to in the London Guidelines and the FAO Code, and consequently any reference to non-acute hazards and to *environmental* effects.[76] The agreed definition allows for consideration of environmental effects and of effects due to multiple as opposed to single exposure, but implicitly retains some notion of acuity through its reference to 'a short period of time'.

Compared with the existing definitions of these concepts in the London Guidelines and the FAO Code, some substantive changes were also made in the definitions of 'banned chemical' and 'severely restricted chemical' laid down in the Convention. Banned chemicals within the meaning of the Convention include chemicals which have been:

withdrawn by industry either from the domestic market or from further consideration in the domestic approval process and where there is clear evidence that such action has been taken in order to protect human health or the environment.[77]

For severely restricted chemicals, the new definition refers to chemicals 'virtually all *use* of which within one or more categories has been prohibited by final regulatory action in order to protect human health or the

[74] Rotterdam Convention, App I, Art 2 (d) (emphasis added).

[75] See Art 3, para 1 (b) in the European Community's 'Proposed Text' for the 3rd Session of the INC, May 1997.

[76] See UN Doc UNEP/FAO/PIC/INC.5/CRP.2, 9 Mar 1998, Art 2 (d) & n 6–8.

[77] Rotterdam Convention, Art 2 (b).

environment,'[78] whereas the existing definitions were based on the prohibition of 'virtually all *uses*'. The reference to 'use' instead of 'uses' in the plural makes it possible to take into account the *volume* of prohibited use compared to the overall volume of use of the chemical, as opposed to the mere *number* of prohibited *uses* relative to the number of remaining uses which are still allowed. A proposal by the EU to define a severely restricted chemical by reference to the extent of overall environmental or health risk reduction achieved by the regulatory restrictions, rather than either the number of prohibited uses or the volume of prohibited use, was strongly opposed by the US, Canada, Australia and like-minded countries.

Criteria and Procedure for the Selection of Chemicals

The core of the PIC Convention consists of the provisions relating to the criteria and decision-making procedure governing identification of the chemicals that are to be made subject to PIC. The criteria and procedure are different for 'banned or severely restricted chemicals' and 'severely hazardous pesticide formulations'. Chemicals already subject to the voluntary PIC procedure and for which decision guidance documents have been circulated under that procedure prior to the opening for signature of the Convention are listed in Annex III to the Convention and will automatically become subject to the legally binding PIC procedure as soon as the Convention enters into force. The criteria and procedures laid down in the Convention are to be applied for identifying *additional* PIC chemicals and adding them to Annex III after its entry into force.

The process for listing banned or severely restricted chemicals will be triggered by the parties' notifications of national regulatory actions to the Convention secretariat. Parties will be under a legal obligation to notify the secretariat 'as soon as possible' and in any event no later than 90 days after a final regulatory action banning or severely restricting a chemical within the meaning of the Convention has become effective.[79] Annex I to the Convention lists the information to be provided by parties with each notification of control action. The secretariat will verify whether all information required has been provided and, if so, circulate to all parties a summary of this information. If the information is incomplete, the notifying party will be invited to provide the missing information.[80]

In the process of transforming the voluntary PIC procedure into a legally binding one, states have perceived a need to further elaborate and formalise both the substantive and procedural provisions governing the listing of PIC

[78] Rotterdam Convention, Art 2 (c) (emphasis added).
[79] *Ibid*, Art 5, para 1.
[80] *Ibid*, Art 5, para 3.

chemicals. In this process, there was a strong tendency, encouraged by some chemical-exporting countries, to raise the threshold for the inclusion of chemicals by increasing the number of procedural steps and the amount of data to be provided, introducing additional substantive and formal criteria and maximising the room for discretionary review of national regulatory decisions which may qualify a chemical for PIC listing.

The first important change from the voluntary procedure which significantly raises that threshold is that, under the Rotterdam Convention, a notification of regulatory action from a single country will no longer be sufficient to trigger consideration of a chemical for inclusion in the PIC list. At least two notifications from two different 'PIC regions' will be required. This minimum number and regional criterion were included in the Convention because the negotiators considered that regulatory action by a single country, or even by more than one country within a single geographical region, would not provide 'a sufficiently broad basis to merit listing of the chemical in Annex III.'[81] Also, once the Convention has entered into force, only notifications from *contracting parties* will be eligible for consideration.

The conference of the parties to the PIC Convention will, at its first meeting, establish a 'Chemical Review Committee' (CRC) composed 'of a limited number of government designated experts in chemicals management . . . appointed on the basis of equitable geographical distribution, including ensuring a balance between developed and developing Parties.'[82] This committee will be in charge of reviewing the final regulatory actions notified by contracting parties in accordance with the criteria laid down in Annex II to the Convention and, on this basis, recommending to the conference of the parties whether or not to list a chemical in Annex III.[83] A chemical will be put on the CRC's agenda for consideration as soon as the secretariat has received two notifications, from at least two regions, which meet the information requirements of Annex I.[84]

The criteria for the inclusion of banned or severely restricted chemicals in the PIC procedure are set out in Annex II to the Rotterdam Convention. A much-debated issue during the negotiations was whether or not national control actions should be based on a full risk assessment or a more limited risk/hazard evaluation to warrant the listing of the chemical concerned under the Convention. The agreed provisions of Annex II stipulate that the CRC shall not only 'confirm that the final regulatory action has been taken in order to protect human health or the environment,'[85] but also:

[81] *Ibid*, Annex II, para (c).
[82] *Ibid*, Art 18, para 6.
[83] *Ibid*, Art 5, para 6.
[84] *Ibid*, Art 5, para 5.
[85] *Ibid*, Annex II, para (a).

establish that the final regulatory action has been taken as a consequence of a risk evaluation . . . based on a review of scientific data in the context of the conditions prevailing in the Party in question.[86]

It is further specified that the documentation provided by the notifying party shall demonstrate that data have been generated and reviewed according to, respectively, 'scientifically recognized methods' and 'generally recognized scientific principles and procedures.'[87] The information requirements for notifications of national regulatory actions, as spelled out in Annex I, provide that the data submitted shall not only include the 'reasons for the final regulatory action'[88] and a 'summary of the hazards and risks presented by the chemical,'[89] but also 'indication of whether the final regulatory action was taken on the basis of a risk or hazard evaluation and, if so, information on such evaluation.'[90] The key notions of 'risk evaluation' and 'hazard evaluation' are not otherwise defined in either Annex I or Annex II, nor in any other provision of the convention, but the report of the fifth session of the INC/PIC contains a statement to the effect that:

The term 'risk evaluation' used in Annex I and II is understood by the Intergovernmental Negotiating Committee not to be a risk assessment, but rather an evaluation of intrinsic toxicological and ecotoxicological properties and actual or expected relevant exposure, including actual incidents and scientific evidence of hazard.[91]

At any rate, it is quite clear that the level of detail and the amount of scientific data and evidence required will make it almost impossible for any regulatory actions taken by developing countries to qualify for consideration as a basis for including chemicals in the PIC list.[92] Furthermore, the criteria for inclusion, as formulated in Annex II, involve a substantial measure of discretionary judgement on the part of the CRC, not only in relation to the adequacy of any risk or hazard evaluation but also in so far as they provide for consideration of whether the national regulatory action 'provides a sufficiently broad basis to merit listing of the chemical in Annex III.'[93] In doing so, the CRC is to 'take into account', *inter alia*,

whether the considerations that led to the final regulatory action being taken are applicable only in a limited geographical area or in other limited circumstances.[94]

[86] Rotterdam Convention, para (b).
[87] *Ibid*, subparas (i) and (ii).
[88] *Ibid*, Annex I, para 2(a)(v).
[89] *Ibid*, para 2(a)(vi).
[90] *Ibid*, para 2(a)(iv).
[91] UN Doc UNEP/FAO/PIC/INC.5/3, 17 Mar 1998, p 12, para 82.
[92] The report of the 4th session of the INC/PIC notes 'the apprehensions of the developing countries regarding their ability to meet the criteria . . . , in particular those relating to scientific data.' Report INC IV, above n 72, p 12, para 53.
[93] Rotterdam Convention, Annex II, para (c).
[94] *Ibid*, subpara (iii).

Thus, even if a regulatory action meets all the scientific and 'risk evaluation' criteria, the CRC may still consider that it is inappropriate to make the chemical subject to the PIC procedure because the reasons for its regulation are not of sufficient international relevance. An earlier draft of the relevant provision would have required regulatory actions to be 'sufficiently applicable *in a global context*,'[95] but the threshold was eventually set a little lower, given that the requirement of at least two notifications from two different regions before any chemical can be considered for PIC listing already guarantees some level of international significance.

The procedure and criteria for inclusion in Annex III of 'severely hazardous pesticide formulations' are laid down in Article 6 and Annex IV of the PIC Convention, respectively. The initiative of proposing the listing of any pesticide falling within the scope of the definition of 'severely hazardous pesticide formulation' will have to be taken by a contracting party to the Convention which is either a developing country or a country with an economy in transition 'experiencing problems . . . under conditions of use in its territory.'[96] At one stage during the negotiations, it was proposed that non-governmental organisations also be given the possibility of submitting documented proposals for the listing of hazardous pesticides in Annex III, but a provision to that effect was later deleted from the draft Convention, though the final version of Article 6, paragraph 1 does specify that parties proposing any pesticide formulations for inclusion 'may draw upon technical expertise from any relevant source'. Detailed information will have to be submitted by the proposing party to the secretariat, as set out in part I of Annex IV to the Convention, including 'a clear description of incidents related to the problem, including the adverse effects and the way in which the [pesticide] formulation was used.'[97] After receiving 'adequate' initial documentation from the proposing party, it will be up to the secretariat to collect additional information on the chemical in question, as specified in part 2 of Annex IV,[98] and to forward the proposal with all relevant information to the CRC for its consideration.[99]

The actual decision on the inclusion of any chemical in the PIC list is to be taken through a two-tiered decision-making process. First, as we have already seen, the matter will be considered by the CRC, a subsidiary body of the conference of the parties composed of experts, which will review the information submitted and, on the basis of the above-mentioned criteria, make a recommendation to the conference of the parties and draft a 'decision guidance document' for its consideration.[100] The final decision on

[95] Report INC IV, above n 72, p 43 (emphasis added).
[96] Rotterdam Convention, Art 6, para 1.
[97] *Ibid*, Annex IV, part 1, item (g).
[98] *Ibid*, Art 6, para 3.
[99] *Ibid*, Art 6, para 4.
[100] *Ibid*, Art 7, para 1.

whether or not to include a chemical in Annex III and to approve the 'decision guidance document' will not, however, be taken by this subsidiary body, but rather by the conference of the parties itself.[101]

The most controversial issue in this context was to what extent decisions at both levels would have to be taken by consensus. There was agreement that consensual decision-making is desirable whenever possible, but opinions differed as to whether there should be provision for some form of voting if it proves impossible to reach consensus. Eventually, the negotiators reached agreement on a formula which provides that the CRC 'shall make every effort to make its recommendations by consensus' but allows it to have recourse to a two-thirds majority vote 'as a last resort' if all efforts to reach consensus have failed,[102] while the formal decision by the conference of the parties to add a chemical to Annex III will have to be made by consensus.[103] Some countries which were reluctant to accept majority decision-making made it quite clear during the negotiations that, if anything less than consensus were to be provided for at the level of the conference of the parties, 'a ratification clause for the adoption of annexes [listing PIC chemicals] would be required.'[104]

It is evident from the above analysis that the process for making chemicals subject to the PIC procedure under the Rotterdam Convention will be a protracted one, much more formalised and subject to explicit political discretion than the current, rather informal process under the existing, voluntary UNEP/FAO PIC scheme.[105] Some participants in the negotiations would no doubt have preferred the legally binding PIC procedure to start all over again from square one, setting aside the *acquis* of the six years of operation of the voluntary UNEP/FAO scheme. If all the chemicals subject to that scheme would have to go through a new screening process, in accordance with the new criteria and procedures of the convention, it would take several years even after its entry into force before any chemicals could actually become subject to the hard-won legally binding PIC procedure. Eventually, however, the INC/PIC agreed that all the chemicals for which decision guidance documents had already been circulated under the voluntary procedure would be included from the outset in Annex III of the PIC Convention, without reconsideration of their status. Thus, the PIC procedure will become operational and legally binding immediately for 27 chemicals upon the entry into force of the Rotterdam Convention.

[101] Rotterdam Convention, Art 7, para 2.

[102] *Ibid*, Art 18, para 6(c).

[103] *Ibid*, Art 22, para 5(b). Amendments to Annex III, however, will not require subsequent ratification by the contracting parties, but will enter into force on a date to be specified by the conference of the parties in its decision. *Ibid*, para 5(c).

[104] Report INC IV, above n 72, p 6, para 23.

[105] As UNEP/FAO secretariat euphemistically put it in a note submitted to the 4th session of the INC/PIC, the voluntary procedure is 'less subject to government scrutiny'. UN Doc UNEP/FAO/PIC/INC.4/INF/1, 9 Oct 1997, p 5, para 18.

Ensuring the Transition from the Voluntary Prior Informed Consent Procedure

However, there are still an important number of 'candidate chemicals' in the 'pipeline' of the voluntary procedure, for which decision guidance documents have not yet been circulated. Their fate also depends on the arrangements governing the transition from the voluntary scheme to the legally binding PIC procedure, which were only considered at a relatively late stage in the Convention negotiations. At its Geneva meeting, the INC/PIC requested UNEP/FAO secretariat to prepare a background paper on questions related to the transition from the voluntary procedure to the legally binding procedure.[106] This paper proposed that the decision on transitional arrangements be made in the form of a resolution of the diplomatic conference adopting the PIC Convention[107] and suggested that 'the current voluntary PIC procedure may continue for a limited period of time' after the signing of the Convention, either in accordance with the existing provisions of the London Guidelines and FAO Code of Conduct, or in accordance with the new provisions of the Convention, with or without the possibility of adding new chemicals to the PIC list before its entry into force.[108] The Rome meeting of the INC agreed to recommend to the governing bodies of both UNEP and FAO that the Rotterdam diplomatic conference be mandated to amend the voluntary procedure as necessary, pending the entry into force of the Convention.[109]

At its final meeting, the INC approved a draft resolution on interim arrangements[110] that was formally adopted without any changes by the Rotterdam diplomatic conference together with the Convention itself. It provides for the establishment of a voluntary 'interim PIC procedure' based on the new substantive provisions of the PIC Convention, which is effective from the date of the Convention's adoption and will cease to operate on a date to be decided by the conference of the parties to the Convention at its first meeting following entry into force. Pending entry into force, additional chemicals meeting the criteria laid down in the Convention can still be made subject to the interim PIC procedure by the INC/PIC, which will continue to meet regularly during the transitional period. The Convention itself contains a 'grandfather clause' which provides that the conference of the parties, at its first meeting, 'shall decide . . . to list . . . in Annex III' any

[106] Report INC III, above n 72, p 7, para 36.
[107] UN Doc UNEP/FAO/PIC/INC.4/INF/1, 9 Oct 1997, p 5, para 18.
[108] *Ibid*, para 19.
[109] Report INC IV, p 10, above n 72, para 47. The Governing Council of UNEP agreed in advance to accept the changes in the voluntary PIC procedure decided by the Conference of Plenipotentiaries at its 5th special session in May 1998. See UNEP Governing Council Dec SS.V/5, 22 May 1998, UN Doc UNEP/GCSS.V/7, p 28.
[110] UN Doc UNEP/FAO/PIC/CONF/4, 15 July 1998.

chemicals not initially listed in Annex III but made subject to the voluntary PIC procedure before the date of that meeting, 'provided that it is satisfied that all the requirements for listing in that Annex have been fulfilled.'[111] Though the conference of the parties, technically speaking, will have some discretion in making this decision, the chance that any chemicals 'PIC-listed' during the interim period would eventually not be included in Annex III seems, from a political point of view, rather small.

Obligations of Exporting Parties

The obligations of exporting parties with respect to exports of PIC chemicals are spelled out in Article 11 of the Rotterdam Convention. As demanded by the EU, each exporting party will have a duty to 'take appropriate legislative or administrative measures to *ensure that exporters within its jurisdiction comply* with [PIC] decisions' of importing countries no later than six months after these decisions are communicated to all parties by the Convention secretariat.[112] Even where importing parties have failed to provide a response under the PIC procedure, exporting parties will have a limited duty to control exports, in accordance with the *status quo* principle already laid down in the amended London Guidelines and the FAO Code of Conduct since 1989. Article 11, paragraph 2 provides that each party shall ensure that no chemical listed in Annex III is exported from its territory to any importing party

> that, in exceptional circumstances, has failed to transmit a response or has transmitted an interim response that does not contain an interim decision, unless:
> (a) It is a chemical that, at the time of import, is registered as a chemical in the importing Party; or
> (b) It is a chemical for which evidence exists that it has previously been used in, or imported into, the importing Party . . . ; or
> (c) Explicit consent to the import has been sought and received by the exporter through a designated national authority of the importing Party. . . .'

It should be noted, however, that this provision, though inspired by the *status quo* provisions of the existing voluntary instruments, differs from them in a number of significant respects. In the London Guidelines, the corresponding provision was not clearly formulated in terms of an obligation of exporting *states*. It merely provided that 'the *status quo* with respect to importation of the chemical *should* continue' and that the chemical '*should* not be exported' unless a number of conditions were met.[113] Not only was this clause formulated in merely recommendatory terms, but its addressee

[111] Rotterdam Convention, Art 8.
[112] Rotterdam Convention, Art 11, para 1(b) (emphasis added).
[113] Amended London Guidelines, para 7.3 (d) (emphasis added).

was not identified. There was no explicit reference to any responsibility of governmental authorities in exporting states; the recommendation could also be interpreted as being addressed directly to exporters. Article 11 of the PIC Convention now clearly places an *obligation* on exporting *parties* to ensure that export does not occur unless one of the three exceptions applies. In this respect, the Convention plainly strengthens the obligations of exporting countries.

In other respects, however, the original language of the London Guidelines has been weakened. This language allowed export only with 'the explicit consent of the importing country' or when the chemical in question 'is a *pesticide* which is registered in the importing country or is a *chemical* the use or importation of which has been *allowed by other governmental action of the importing country*.'[114] The new provisions of the Rotterdam Convention will allow exportation not only of pesticides, but also of *other chemicals* which are 'registered' in the importing party, and also whenever there is evidence that the exported chemical has previously been used in or imported by the country of destination, even where this previous use or importation has not been explicitly allowed by any *governmental action* of the importing state.

Export Notification and Other Information Exchange Provisions

By recognising in February 1997 that 'additional elements' were duly under consideration in the PIC negotiations, UNEP Governing Council strengthened the negotiating position of the EU and the developing countries favouring the inclusion of provisions on export notification in the PIC Convention, but long negotiations still proved necessary within the INC to reach agreement on the precise nature, form and timing of the export notification requirements. At the Geneva meeting immediately following the Governing Council decision, African countries were still calling for notification on a shipment-by-shipment basis, while many OECD countries expressed preference for a one-time-only notification requirement covering all future exports to the same importing country. At the end of the Rome meeting, annual notification seemed to be gaining ground as a compromise formula. At the final meeting of the INC, consensus was eventually reached on the provisions of Article 12 of the Convention relating to export notification, which represent a compromise between the demands of importing countries and the concerns of some exporting countries to minimise any interference with trade.

Only chemicals banned or severely restricted *by the exporting party* (as opposed to PIC chemicals) will be subject to export notification

[114] *Ibid* (emphasis added).

requirements. Notification shall be provided 'prior to the first export following adoption of the corresponding final regulatory action' to ban or severely restrict the chemical in question and, thereafter, on an annual basis, before the first export in each calendar year.[115] One repeat notification will have to be made by the exporting party if the importing country fails to acknowledge receipt of the first notification.[116] These export notification requirements will cease to apply for each specific chemical and importing party, once the chemical in question has been included in Annex III and the party concerned has made a formal PIC decision on its importation pursuant to the Convention.[117] The provisions of Article 12 effectively allow the EC to continue its existing practice of providing a single export notification covering all exports of the same chemical to the same importing state from the Community as a whole. The US eventually dropped its demand that the Community commit itself to making a separate export notification for each of its member states exporting the chemical.[118]

In addition to the PIC procedure proper and the export notification mechanism for chemicals banned or severely restricted in exporting parties, the PIC Convention also contains provisions on other forms of information exchange between the parties. These provisions can be found in Articles 13 and 14. Article 13, paragraph 1 provides that the conference of the parties 'shall encourage the World Customs Organization to assign specific Harmonized System customs codes' to PIC chemicals, and that, when such codes have been assigned, parties shall require that they be mentioned on shipping documents accompanying exported chemicals. Initially, it was proposed by some participants in the negotiations that PIC chemicals also bear a special label which would facilitate their identification, but no consensus could be reached on this proposal; as the report of the Rome meeting notes, 'most representatives agreed that a specific label for PIC chemicals was not warranted.'[119]

However, Article 13 contains other requirements concerning the labelling of chemicals. The EU, which, as shall be further explained in chapter 15 below, already has provisions on the labelling and packaging of chemicals destined for export to third countries in a 1992 Regulation, strongly pushed for similar provisions to be included in the PIC Convention, in order to place non-EU exporters of chemicals under equivalent obligations and ensure a level playing field for all exporting parties, but it was only partly successful. The Convention provides that parties shall require that

[115] Rotterdam Convention, Art 12, para 2.

[116] *Ibid*, Art 12, para 4.

[117] *Ibid*, Art 12, para 5.

[118] See Comments of the United States of America, UN Doc UNEP/FAO/PIC/INC.4/CRP.1, 20 Oct 1997, p 16, n 49 & Art 11, para 4bis of the Text of the Draft Articles in Report INC IV, above n 72, Annex II, p 27.

[119] Report INC IV, above n 72, p 7, para 26.

both PIC chemicals and chemicals banned or severely restricted in their territories

> are, when exported, subject to labelling requirements that ensure adequate availability of information with regard to risks and/or hazards to human health or the environment, taking into account relevant international standards.[120]

Furthermore, other chemicals subject to domestic environmental or health labelling requirements in the exporting party *may* be made subject to similar requirements when exported.[121] Both provisions are 'without prejudice to any requirements of the importing Party'. The same chemicals that are subject to mandatory labelling requirements when exported shall also be accompanied by 'a safety data sheet that follows an internationally recognised format' when they are destined 'to be used in the workplace or for other occupational purposes.'[122] Finally, Article 13 provides that both the information on the label and that in the safety data sheet 'should, as far as practicable, be given in one or more of the official languages of the importing Party.'[123]

In addition to these specific provisions on labelling and safety data sheets, the PIC Convention also contains a general provision on 'the exchange of scientific, technical, economic and legal information concerning the chemicals within the scope of this Convention, including toxicological, ecotoxicological and safety information', which parties undertake to 'facilitate.'[124] This includes 'the provision of publicly available information on domestic regulatory actions relevant to the objective of this Convention.'[125] This clause is apparently designed to apply to regulatory actions which fall short of banning or severely restricting a chemical within the meaning given to those terms by the Convention and consequently are not subject to the mandatory notification requirements of Article 5, but which may nevertheless be of interest to other parties.

The reference to 'publicly available information' indicates a certain reluctance on the part of some parties to disclose all relevant information, some of which may be regarded as confidential under their domestic law. This explains why the Convention also contains a clause stipulating that 'Parties that exchange information pursuant to [the] Convention shall protect any confidential information as mutually agreed.'[126] Such protection may, however, not be claimed for *all* information exchanged under the Convention, since the same article also lays down a list of basic information which

[120] Rotterdam Convention, Art 13, para 2.
[121] *Ibid*, Art 13, para 3.
[122] *Ibid*, Art 13, para 4.
[123] *Ibid*, Art 13, para 5.
[124] *Ibid*, Art 14, para 1(a).
[125] *Ibid*, Art 14, para 1(b).
[126] *Ibid*, Art 14, para 2.

'shall not be regarded as confidential for the purposes of [the] Convention'. This non-confidential information includes all the information provided in notifications of final regulatory actions, proposals for the inclusion of 'severely hazardous pesticide formulations' and safety data sheets, as well as information on precautionary measures and 'the summary results of the toxicological and ecotoxicological tests.'[127]

The developing countries were not particularly successful in their demands for strong provisions on financial and technical assistance to be included in the PIC Convention. The Convention does contain one article entitled 'Technical assistance' and a number of other, scattered provisions in other articles providing for various forms of assistance to developing country parties, but all in all these provisions are rather non-committal compared to the corresponding provisions on 'new and additional financial resources' and transfer of technology in many recent global environmental conventions. The parties to the Rotterdam Convention merely commit themselves to 'cooperate in promoting technical assistance for the development of the infrastructure and the capacity necessary to manage chemicals to enable implementation of this Convention.'[128] More specifically, parties 'with more advanced programmes for regulating chemicals *should* provide technical assistance' to developing countries and transition countries.[129] Another clause in another article of the Convention requires exporting parties to provide advice and assistance to importing parties, 'upon request and as appropriate', to help them 'strengthen their capacities and capabilities to manage chemicals safely during their life-cycle.'[130] Despite some discussion on the matter during the early meetings of the INC,[131] in the end no specific provisions on financial assistance were included in the Convention.

The Debate on Trade-related Issues

One of the most contentious issues during the final stages of the negotiations in the INC was the question of the trade implications of the legally binding PIC procedure and the relationship between the provisions of the PIC Convention and the rules of the WTO's multilateral trading system. The debate on this issue in the INC/PIC was closely related to the general controversy on the potential conflict between multilateral environmental

[127] Rotterdam Convention, Art 14, para 3.
[128] *Ibid*, Art 16.
[129] *Ibid* (emphasis added).
[130] *Ibid*, Art 11, para 1(c)(ii).
[131] An appendix to the report of the Rome meeting outlines a variety of possible options for further consideration, but these were not taken up again in the final stages of the negotiations. See Report INC IV, above n 72, p 47.

agreements and the WTO rules which has been plaguing international normative efforts in the field of environmental protection since the early 1990s. Even before the trade versus environment debate emerged as a major item on the international agenda, the question of the compatibility of the regulation of trade in hazardous chemicals with multilateral trade disciplines had already received some attention in the mid-1980s, during the development of the first non-binding international instruments in the OECD, UNEP and the FAO.

Referring to this earlier consideration of the issue, UNEP *Ad Hoc* Working Group of Experts which prepared the groundwork for the negotiations on the PIC Convention suggested in its final report that 'trade-related provisions may be incorporated on the basis of the relevant provisions of the amended London Guidelines and the FAO Code of Conduct.'[132] The working group also stressed, however, that 'progress made since their adoption in addressing linkages between environmental and trade policies' should be taken into account, and that the parties' obligations should also be formulated so as to 'ensur[e] that [their] ability to take measures to protect human health and the environment is fully maintained.'[133] More specifically, the group's final report, referring inter alia to Article XX (b) and (g) of the GATT, contained a rather cryptically formulated suggestion that the new international instrument to be elaborated should recognise 'that government authorities have the right to take actions that might [discriminate] [restrict trade] in some circumstances and certain conditions to protect health and the environment.'[134]

At the first meeting of the INC/PIC, where the 'elements' proposed by the *Ad Hoc* Working Group were first discussed,[135] several delegations expressed their sensitivity to the trade policy aspects of the proposed PIC Convention by stressing that 'the trade implications of any provisions proposed for inclusion in the legally binding instrument had to be considered in the light of existing trade agreements . . . in order to avoid duplication and overlap.'[136] These delegations also argued that the importance of 'environment and trade policies being mutually supportive and complementary

[132] UN Doc UNEP/PIC/WG.1/4/5, 15 Apr 1994, p 26, para 69.

[133] *Ibid*, pp 26–27.

[134] *Ibid*, p 27, para 69(a). The original brackets in the report apparently reflect some disagreement as to the use of the terms 'discriminate' and 'restrict trade', as para 70 notes that 'exact wording is under review'.

[135] Several governments that had submitted written comments to UNEP Secretariat prior to the 1st meeting of the INC had already 'pointed to the need to take fully into account the relevant rights and obligations under GATT/WTO rules'. See UN Doc UNEP/FAO/PIC/INC.1/3, 8 Dec 1995, p 12, para 45. Presumably in response to those comments, the Secretariat had prepared a background note on 'Trade-related issues' for the 1st meeting of the INC, based in part on the conclusions of a UNEP Expert Group on International Environmental Agreements and Trade, chaired by Ambassador W Lang of Austria. UN Doc UNEP/FAO/PIC/INC.1/8, 22 December 1995.

[136] UN Doc UNEP/FAO/PIC/INC.1/10, 21 Mar 1996, p 6, para 26.

. . . should be considered in any trade provisions' and that '*any measures taken pursuant to the legally binding instrument should be least trade-restrictive* and non-discriminatory.'[137] These discussions struck other delegations as rather surrealistic, given that the very purpose of a PIC Convention, in their view, was to restrict trade in hazardous chemicals.

Prompted by the discussion at the INC's first session, the chairperson of the INC/PIC included a number of relevant provisions in her 'Tentative draft key articles' submitted to the second session.[138] These provisions formed the basis for further consideration of the subject. The first clause, a paragraph to be inserted in an article on 'General obligations', provided:

> The Parties shall ensure that measures taken to regulate the chemicals under this Convention do not create unnecessary obstacles to and/or constitute a means of arbitrary or unjustifiable discrimination or disguised restrictions on international trade.[139]

Additionally, she proposed to include in the article on obligations of importing parties a provision stipulating that 'each Party shall ensure that import decisions apply uniformly to all sources of import and to domestic production of chemicals for domestic use.'[140] Finally, a special article on 'Control of trade with non-Parties' was proposed, which provided:

> Non-Parties that are in compliance with the substantive provisions of this Convention should, as far as the application of trade measures is concerned, be treated on an equal basis with Parties that are in compliance.[141]

None of these draft provisions survived the later sessions of the INC unscathed. There was strong opposition to the inclusion of any provision on trade with non-parties at the second[142] and third[143] meeting, and the draft article in question was eventually deleted from the negotiating text at the fourth meeting.[144] The other trade-related provisions were substantially rewritten during the negotiations, though some of their basic principles were retained in a modified form in the final version of the Rotterdam Convention.

At the second session of the INC, an alternative, expanded formulation of the non-discrimination principle was inserted into the article of the draft convention relating to obligations of importing parties:

[137] UN Doc UNEP/FAO/PIC/INC.1/10, 21 Mar 1996, p 12, para 56 (emphasis added). This language seems inspired by para 39.3(d) of Agenda 21.

[138] UN Doc UNEP/FAO/PIC/INC.2/6, 30 July 1996.

[139] *Ibid*, p 5, Art 4, para 5.

[140] *Ibid*, p 8, Art 9, para 7.

[141] *Ibid*, p 10, Art 14.

[142] See UN Doc UNEP/FAO/PIC/INC.2/7, 12 Nov 1996, p 7, para 31.

[143] See UN Doc UNEP/FAO/PIC/INC.3/2, 26 June 1997, p 26, n 50.

[144] See UN Doc UNEP/FAO/PIC/INC.4/2, 4 Nov 1997, p 7, para 30 & p 29, n 37.

A Party shall ensure that a decision to prohibit or restrict the importation of a product is not applied so as to afford *protection to domestic production*, does not constitute a means of *arbitrary or unjustified discrimination* between Parties where the same conditions apply, does not constitute an *unnecessary obstacle to trade* and is not a *disguised barrier to international trade*.[145]

This draft provision laid down no less than four trade-related conditions, manifestly inspired by language from various GATT/WTO instruments, to be complied with by parties deciding to prohibit the import of chemicals, and thus would have provided as many grounds to challenge such regulatory decisions. The references to 'arbitrary or unjustified discrimination' and 'disguised barriers to international trade' are reminescent of the *chapeau* of GATT Article XX, while the prohibition of 'unnecessary obstacles to trade' can be found in Article 2.2 of the 1994 WTO Agreement on Technical Barriers to Trade. The use of these terms was apparently designed to incorporate by reference into the PIC Convention all of their technical meanings and interpretations in international trade law.

This language did not meet with general approval and, at the third meeting, the US submitted an alternative proposal, inspired by language originally taken from the OECD Guiding Principles which was later incorporated in the London Guidelines and the FAO Code of Conduct:

Each Party shall ensure that its actions pursuant to this Article with regard to an imported chemical are *not more restrictive* than with regard to the same chemical produced domestically for domestic use or imported from any other country.[146]

Eventually, however, consensus was reached on a wholly different formulation, which imposes *positive* rather than negative obligations on importing parties and seems more appropriate in view of the environmental and health protection rationale of the Rotterdam Convention. The final version of the relevant provision reads:

A Party that . . . takes a decision not to consent to importation of a chemical or to consent to its importation only under specified conditions shall, if it has not already done so, simultaneously prohibit, or make subject to the same conditions,
(a) Importation of the chemical concerned from any source; and
(b) Domestic production of the chemical for domestic use.[147]

145 UN Doc UNEP/FAO/PIC/INC.2/7, 12 Nov 1996, p 19, Art 9, para 7.

146 US Comments on PIC INC 3 Negotiating Text, 25 Apr 1997, p 10 (emphasis added).

147 Convention on the Prior Informed Consent Procedure for Certain Hazardous Chemicals and Pesticides in International Trade, Rotterdam, 11 Sept 1998, UN Doc UNEP/FAO/PIC/CONF/2, 15 July 1998, Art 10, para 10 (hereafter referred to as Rotterdam Convention or PIC Convention). This wording is based on a proposal made by the EC at the 3rd session of the INC. See UN Doc UNEP/FAO/PIC/INC.3/2, 26 June 1997, p 21, Art 9, para 7. Canada expressed a preference for the earlier formulation over both the US and EC proposals, on the grounds that it was 'consistent with our obligations under GATT/WTO rules', but recognised that 'it may not be palatable to countries who are not signatories to the GATT/WTO'. UN Doc UNEP/FAO/PIC/INC.3/CRP.3, 26 May 1997, p 16.

Although this provision translates the most-favoured nation and national treatment principles of the GATT in the specific context of the PIC procedure and should provide adequate protection to chemical-exporting countries against discriminatory use of that procedure, it was not perceived by all of them as sufficient to meet their trade concerns. They therefore continued to press for the inclusion in the convention of a general 'savings clause' which, though not referring specifically to the GATT/WTO rules, would ensure that such rules would prevail in the event of any conflict in the application of the provisions of the PIC convention. This clause, inspired by similar language in the 1992 Convention on Biological Diversity[148] and the 1994 UN Convention to Combat Desertification,[149] essentially provided that those provisions 'shall not affect the rights and obligations of any Party deriving from any existing international agreement.'[150]

A provision to this effect had already been suggested by UNEP *Ad Hoc* Working Group in its 1994 'elements' paper, in order to clarify the relationship between the future PIC instrument and existing international conventions relevant to chemicals management, such as the Basel Convention and a number of ILO conventions. The language proposed by the working group was not unqualified, however, as it provided that rights and obligations under existing agreements would not be affected '*except* where the exercise of those rights and obligations *would be in contravention to the purpose*' of the PIC instrument.[151] The inclusion of such a proviso was not uncontroversial, however; the corresponding phrase in the article entitled 'Relationship with other agreements' which was inserted into the draft convention at the third session of the INC and which referred more specifically to 'serious damage or threat *to human health or the environment*' was bracketed and remained so throughout the negotiations, as was the qualifier 'existing' before the term 'international agreement.'[152] In the end, no such article was included in the Rotterdam Convention at all.

Even though the draft 'savings clause', as it appeared in the consolidated negotiating text, contained no explicit reference to trade agreements and had in fact originally been proposed by the *Ad Hoc* Working Group to address the relationship between the PIC instrument and other international

[148] Convention on Biological Diversity, signed in Rio de Janeiro, 5 June 1992, 31 ILM 818 (1992), Art 22, para 1.

[149] United Nations Convention to Combat Desertification in those Countries Experiencing Serious Drought and/or Desertification, Particularly in Africa, signed in Paris, 17 June 1994, UN Doc A/AC.241/27, 12 Sept 1994, Art 8, para 2.

[150] UN Doc UNEP/FAO/PIC/INC.3/2, 26 June 1997, p 31, Art 19 bis.

[151] UN Doc UNEP/PIC/WG.1/4/5, 15 Apr 1994, p 27, para 73. The working group explicitly referred to Art 22, para 1 of the Convention on Biological Diversity, where the corresponding phrase reads 'except where the exercise of those rights and obligations would cause a serious damage or threat to biological diversity'.

[152] UN Doc UNEP/FAO/PIC/INC.3/2, 26 June 1997, p 31, Art 19 bis (emphasis added). See also UN Doc UNEP/FAO/PIC/INC.4/2, 4 November 1997, p 31, Art 19 bis & UN Doc UNEP/FAO/PIC/INC.5/2, 15 Jan 1998, p 14, Art 18.

environmental conventions, it was clearly perceived by the INC as in fact designed to govern the new convention's relationship to international trade law and referred to an informal contact group on trade issues, together with the other above-mentioned trade-related provisions. The US strongly pressed for the inclusion of the 'savings clause', without the final qualifying phrase, which it argued was 'unnecessary' and would 'create confusion.'[153] The EU, for its part, advocated deletion of this draft article on the grounds that it 'introduces a hierarchy between international Conventions' by 'giv[ing] priority to the provisions of any international agreement over the provisions contained in the PIC Convention.'[154] After extensive negotiations in the contact group, a compromise was reached between these opposing positions by deleting the 'savings clause', as well as the draft paragraph on 'arbitrary or unjustifiable discrimination' and 'unnecessary obstacles to trade', from the body of the Convention, and addressing the issue through the following preambular language:

> *Recognizing* that trade and environmental policies should be mutually supportive with a view to achieving sustainable development;
> *Emphasizing* that nothing in this Convention shall be interpreted as *implying in any way a change in the rights and obligations of a Party* under any existing international agreement *applying to chemicals in international trade or to environmental protection;*
> *Understanding* that the above recital *is not intended to create a hierarchy* between this Convention and other international agreements; . . .[155]

The first of the three recitals is legally rather innocuous 'boilerplate' language from Agenda 21 and various later policy declarations on trade and environment, which only serves as a political backdrop for the other two recitals. The second recital is legally the most significant one: it sets out a rule of interpretation, which is part of the 'context' to be taken into account, in accordance with Article 31 of the Vienna Convention on the Law of Treaties, in interpreting the provisions of the PIC Convention. Its formulation is softer than the various wordings of the 'savings clause' which were under consideration. The preambular language does not actually say that the provisions of the Rotterdam Convention 'shall not affect' provisions of other treaties in force relating to the same subject matter, nor imply that they are 'subject to' such other treaties within the meaning of Article 30, paragraph 2 of the Vienna Convention.

Much to the disappointment of a number of delegations, the preamble does not refer explicitly to any WTO instruments, but the general reference

[153] See UN Doc UNEP/FAO/PIC/INC.5/CRP.2, 9 Mar 1998, Art 18 and n 51. See also UN Doc UNEP/FAO/PIC/INC.4/CRP.1, 20 Oct 1997, p 21, n 65.

[154] UN Doc UNEP/FAO/PIC/INC.4/CRP.4, 21 Oct 1997, p 15, n 21. See also UN Doc UNEP/FAO/PIC/INC.5/CRP.3, 9 Mar 1998, p 17.

[155] Rotterdam Convention, preamble, 8th, 9th & 10th recital (emphasis added). See the proposal of the contact group in UN Doc UNEP/FAO/PIC/INC.5/CRP.48, 12 Mar 1998.

to agreements '*applying to chemicals in international trade*' nevertheless clearly includes the relevant rules of international trade law applicable to trade in goods, including chemicals. The reference, in the same sentence, to international *environmental* agreements seems designed to stress once more that these preambular clauses are not intended to confer any special status on international trade law. The third recital, obviously inspired by the EU's rejection of any implied hierarchical relationship between international trade law and international environmental law, apparently serves a similar purpose.

The outcome of the negotiations on the relationship between the Rotterdam Convention and the law of international trade seems legally rather ambiguous. One side had come to Brussels quite determined to seek affirmation in the Convention's provisions, albeit in a thinly disguised way, of the primacy of international trade law over international environmental law. The other side adamantly opposed, as a matter of principle, the inclusion in the Convention of any explicit provisions on the subject, arguing that the general rules of treaty interpretation were quite sufficient.[156] The former side can claim that the preamble recognises that the Convention is not intended to prevail over the existing rights and obligations of parties under WTO agreements. The opposite side, for its part, can be satisfied that the PIC Convention contains no explicit reference to any WTO instruments or trade law principles and will be able to assert, on the basis of the preambular provisions, that the Convention rejects the very idea of any subordination of international environmental law to international trade law. But the relevant provisions are so ambivalent that neither side can be sure what the exact legal position would be in the event of a trade dispute involving a conflict between the application of the PIC Convention and trade disciplines. At the same time, ironically, both sides ostensibly agree that the provisions of the Rotterdam Convention are fully consistent with the relevant WTO rules.

The Trade Implications of the Rotterdam Convention: a Future Battleground?

While the overt controversy between environmental advocates and free trade pundits was settled by this ambiguous compromise, it should be noted that other provisions of the Rotterdam Convention may, somewhat paradoxically, have the effect of strengthening the legal position, under international trade law, of chemical-exporting nations vis-à-vis importing countries taking regulatory action to prohibit or restrict the importation and use of chemicals in their territory. It is not a coincidence that a further

[156] See UN Doc UNEP/FAO/PIC/INC.4/CRP.4, 21 Oct 1997, p 15, n 21.

preambular paragraph, proposed by the European Community, which would have 'recogniz[ed] that any State has the sovereign right to ban or restrict the importation, production, and use in its territory of hazardous chemicals and pesticides, including those banned or restricted in other States',[157] was left out of the preamble after other delegations in the INC objected that it had trade implications and would upset the delicate compromise on trade-related issues reflected in the three recitals carefully drafted by the contact group.

As is well-known, the United States and Canada successfully used the WTO's dispute settlement mechanism to challenge the EC's ban on the importation of hormone-treated beef on the grounds that it violates the provisions of the WTO's 1994 Agreement on Sanitary and Phytosanitary Measures (SPS Agreement).[158] Similar provisions in the 1994 TBT Agreement could conceivably be used to challenge regulatory measures taken by a country to prevent the importation and use of particular hazardous chemicals.

Under the Rotterdam Convention, any contracting party that decides to ban or severely restrict the use of a hazardous chemical in its territory in order to protect human health or the environment is under a legal obligation to notify the Convention secretariat of such final regulatory action and to provide it with the information specified in Annex I to the Convention.[159] The Convention secretariat, in turn, 'shall forthwith forward to all Parties a summary of the information received.'[160] This notification requirement differs fundamentally from that for '*proposed* technical regulations' under Article 2.9 of the 1994 TBT Agreement, in that it applies only *a posteriori* to '*final* regulatory actions' which have already become effective and is not designed to enable other parties whose trade interests might be jeopardised to submit comments *before* the notifying party adopts the action in question. But it is not inconceivable that the information which is to be provided under the PIC Convention might nevertheless be used to challenge national regulatory actions *a posteriori* under other provisions of the TBT Agreement.

Article 2.2 of that Agreement provides that 'technical regulations shall not be more trade-restrictive than necessary to fulfil a legitimate objective, *taking account of the risks non-fulfilment would create*' and further specifies that 'relevant elements' to be considered 'in assessing such risks' include 'available scientific and technical information'. One of the items of information to be provided under Annex I of the PIC Convention is:

[157] UN Doc UNEP/FAO/PIC/INC.5/CRP.3/Corr. 2, 11 March 1998, p 2. See also UN Doc UNEP/FAO/PIC/INC.5/CRP.45, 12 March 1998, p 2, where the language was revised to refer, more accurately, to 'any Party' instead of 'any State'.

[158] See *EC Measures Concerning Meat and Meat Products (Hormones)*, Report of the Appelate Body, WTO Doc WT/DS26/AB/R—WT/DS48/AB/R, 16 January 1998.

[159] Rotterdam Convention, Art 5, para 1.

[160] *Ibid*, Art 5, para 3.

Indication of *whether* the final regulatory action was taken on the basis of a risk or hazard evaluation and, if so, information on such evaluation, covering a reference to the relevant documentation.[161]

Answering this question in the negative virtually amounts to pleading guilty to a charge of infringement of the TBT Agreement, which can be read as requiring WTO members to demonstrate that their technical regulations are based on some form of balancing their trade-restrictive character against an assessment of the risk entailed by non-fulfilment of legitimate environmental or health protection objectives.[162]

The PIC Convention compels its contracting parties to provide detailed information on their regulatory actions, including a statement of the health or environmental reasons for them, a 'summary of the hazards and risks presented by the chemical' concerned, and even information on 'the expected effect' of these actions.[163] Moreover, the Convention institutes an international process for the scrutiny of national regulatory measures by a Chemical Review Committee, composed of 'a limited number of government-designated experts in chemicals management,'[164] which is mandated to review the notifications submitted by individual parties in order to determine whether the inclusion of the banned or severely restricted chemical in Annex III of the Convention is warranted.[165]

The criteria to be used in making this determination, as set out in Annex II of the Rotterdam Convention, directly address the motives and scientific basis of the regulatory action. At the first meeting of the INC, the working group that produced the first draft of these criteria stressed that the international expert group that would apply them 'would not perform a peer review of the national bans or severe restrictions and the basis for it.'[166] But in actual fact, as the final provisions of the Convention stand, the Chemical Review Committee will do precisely that: review national bans and severe restrictions of particular chemicals. And if, following such review, it does *not* 'confirm that the final regulatory action has been taken in order to protect human health or the environment'[167] or 'establish that [it] has been taken as a consequence of a risk evaluation . . . based on a review of scientific data in the context of the conditions prevailing in the Party in question'[168] or find that it did not actually 'result in a significant reduction

[161] Rotterdam Convention, Annex I, para 2(a)(iv) (emphasis added).

[162] As argued by Canada in its recent WTO action against the EC challenging the French ban on asbestos. See *European Community—Measures Affecting Asbestos and Asbestos-Containing Products*, Report of the Panel, WTO Doc WT/DS135/R, 18 Sept 2000. For procedural reasons, neither the Panel, nor the Appelate Body addressed the merits of the Canadian arguments based on the TBT Agreement.

[163] Rotterdam Convention, Annex I, para 2(a)(v)–(vi).

[164] *Ibid*, Art 18, para 6(a).

[165] *Ibid*, Art 6, para 5.

[166] UN Doc UNEP/FAO/PIC/INC.1/10, 21 Mar 1996, p 29, para 21.

[167] Rotterdam Convention, Annex II, para (a).

[168] *Ibid*, Annex II, para (b).

of risk for human health or the environment',[169] not only will the chemical not be included in the list of PIC chemicals, but the Committee's decision will considerably strengthen the legal position of any chemical-exporting country that would wish to use the WTO dispute settlement mechanism to challenge the regulatory action of the notifying party as being in violation of the TBT Agreement.

The WTO Appelate Body, in its recent *Hormones* report, rejected the American and Canadian contention that the term 'risk assessment', as used in the SPS Agreement,[170] implied that specific scientific methods or procedural requirements had to be followed and that absolute scientific certainty of the existence of a significant risk was required. It stressed that the SPS Agreement's requirement that sanitary measures be 'based on' a risk assessment only means that there should be 'a rational relationship between the measure and the risk assessment.'[171] More importantly, the report also points out that:

> the risk that is to be evaluated in a risk assessment . . . is not only risk ascertainable in a science laboratory operating under strictly controlled conditions, but also *risk in human societies as they actually exist, in other words, the actual potential for adverse effects on human health in the real world where people live and work and die.*[172]

The question arises as to whether states which are members of the WTO and also become parties to the Rotterdam Convention do not thereby accept stricter substantive and procedural limitations on their right to take regulatory action to ban or severely restrict hazardous chemicals than those resulting directly from the TBT Agreement itself, if the latter is construed in a similar way as the WTO Appelate Body has interpreted the relevant provisions of the SPS Agreement in the *Hormones* case. In that case, for instance, the Appelate Body also held that these provisions did not

> insist that a Member that adopts a sanitary measure shall have carried out *its own* risk assessment. . . . The SPS measure might well find its objective justification *in a risk assessment carried out by another Member, or an international organization.*[173]

The Rotterdam Convention, however, refers in two different places to an evaluation of the risk under the 'prevailing conditions *within the Party taking the* [regulatory] *action*.'[174] Consequently, a regulatory measure taken solely on the basis of a risk assessment performed in another country or by

[169] *Ibid*, Annex II, para (c)(ii).

[170] It should be noted here that the terms of the 1994 SPS Agreement are not exactly the same as, but are similar to, those of the corresponding provisions in the 1994 TBT Agreement. For a more detailed analysis of these provisions see Wirth (1994a).

[171] *EC Measures Concerning Meat and Meat Products (Hormones)*, above n 158, p 78, para 193.

[172] *Ibid*, p 75, para 187 (emphasis added).

[173] *Ibid*, p 77, para 190 (emphasis added).

[174] Rotterdam Convention, Annex II, para (b)(iii) (emphasis added). See also the chapeau of para (b), and the reference to 'the environment *of the Party that submitted the notification*' in para (c)(ii).

an international organisation does not qualify a chemical for inclusion in the list of chemicals subject to the PIC procedure.

Though the trade law implications of the provisions of the PIC Convention remain to be fully explored, it is already clear that the new instrument may have consequences not only for international trade in banned or severely restricted chemicals, but also for the domestic regulatory policies of contracting parties. At any rate, it seems that the legal implications of the PIC Convention, when applied in conjunction with relevant WTO rules, are likely to be a subject of great interest to international trade lawyers in the future.

Consequences of the Entry into Force of the Rotterdam Convention

The Rotterdam Convention will enter into force three months after the deposit of the 50th instrument of ratification, acceptance, approval or accession,[175] a process which is likely to take a few years. As it allows both the European Community and its individual member states to become contracting parties, the EC could make a significant contribution towards early entry into force of the Convention if all its member states were to ratify it speedily.[176] When it becomes effective, the PIC Convention will make compliance with PIC decisions of importing parties and export notification requirements legally binding for all chemical-exporting parties, but it is by no means obvious that the transformation of the voluntary PIC procedure into a mandatory one will enhance its effectiveness in achieving the objective of promoting chemical safety in developing countries. As appears from the above analysis, the formal 'hardening' of the PIC regime through its incorporation in a legally binding instrument in fact masks a significant 'softening' of some of its substantive features. In particular, the formalisation of the procedure and criteria for making a chemical subject to the regime will hamper its further development. It is likely to take years for any additional chemicals to be added to Annex III, as the cumbersome procedure, restrictive criteria prone to discretionary political interpretation and consensus decision-making within the conference of the parties all tend to make the listing of chemicals much more difficult than it already is under the voluntary procedure. Moreover, as we have seen above, the provisions of the Rotterdam Convention may even have certain perverse effects in conjunction with the WTO rules relating to technical barriers to trade, in that they may facilitate the mounting of trade law challenges to national regulatory actions to ban or severely restrict chemicals.

175 Rotterdam Convention, Art 26, para 1.

176 However, the acceptance of the convention by the Community itself will not count as additional to ratification by EC member states for the purposes of entry into force. *Ibid*, Art 26, para 3.

15

The Implementation of International Norms by the European Community: Community Regulation of Hazardous Chemical Exports

IN THIS CHAPTER, we shall examine how the European Community, as a major trading power and supranational legislator, has responded to internal and external pressures to regulate its exports of banned and severely restricted pesticides. The EC's normative activities in this area, unlike those of the United States, which predated and considerably influenced the development of norms at the international level, were initiated after the start of the regulatory efforts in intergovernmental fora like the United Nations, the OECD and the FAO, and largely in response to them. After it became involved in the transnational normative process, the EC inevitably began to exercise an influence of its own as an important political and institutional actor on the international scene endowed with independent rule-making authority.

In order to put the development of EC legislation on chemical exports in perspective, one first needs to briefly analyse the evolution of the Community's internal legislation concerning the marketing and use of pesticides, which has sought to harmonise national regulations in force in EU member states. These harmonisation efforts first addressed agricultural pesticides, which are referred to as 'plant protection products' in Community law, and were later extended to pesticides for non-agricultural use, for which the legal term 'biocidal products' was coined. The necessary use of this particular legal terminology in this chapter, alongside other terms used throughout this study, may unintentionally cause some confusion, as the notions of pesticide and biocide are often used as synonyms in non-EC terminology.

THE REGULATION OF PESTICIDES UNDER EUROPEAN COMMUNITY LAW

The Early Harmonisation Measures of the 1970s

The Community's involvement in the regulation of the marketing and use of pesticides is one aspect of its overall effort to remove obstacles to the free movement of goods within the internal market. Differences in the laws and regulations of the member states with respect to the distribution and use of pesticides can be an impediment to intra-Community trade in plant protection products, as well as to the free movement of the agricultural products in whose production they are used. In order to reduce such disparities in national standards, the Community has taken several harmonisation measures in the field of pesticides since the mid-1970s.

The first area of regulation to be harmonised, because it interfered directly with the establishment of the common market for agricultural products, was that of pesticide residue levels in such products.[1] Although the Commission submitted its first proposal for Community legislation on the matter in 1968,[2] it took eight years for the Council to reach agreement. It was only in November 1976 that the Council finally adopted the first Directive fixing maximum pesticide residue levels for fruit and vegetables.[3] This Directive ensures the free movement of goods by requiring member states not to prohibit the marketing of any products which comply with Community maximum residue levels. However, since it sets residue standards for only a small portion of the total number of pesticides in use in the Community, it did not achieve total harmonisation. Indeed, the Court of Justice has since ruled that member states remain free to fix national limit values for residues of pesticides for which no Community values exist and to prohibit the placing on the market of products which exceed those national limits.[4] The residue standards laid down in the 1976 Directive have been regularly updated since then, and limit values for new substances have been added to its Annex II. Similar directives fixing maximum residue levels for other categories of agricultural products have also been adopted.

The harmonisation of maximum residue levels, while facilitating intra-Community trade in agricultural products, did not remove obstacles to the free movement of plant protection products themselves, as member states remained free to determine the requirements for the placing on the market and use of pesticides within their territory. In order to harmonise legisla-

[1] See generally Krämer (1986), pp 236–39.

[2] OJ No C139, 1968, p 19.

[3] Council Dir 76/895/EEC of 23 Nov 1976 relating to the fixing of maximum levels of pesticide residues in and on fruit and vegetables, OJ No L340, 9.12.1976, p 26.

[4] See Case 94/83, *Officier van Justitie v Albert Heijn BV*, [1984] ECR 3263; Case 54/85, *Ministère Public v Mirepoix*, [1986] ECR 1067.

tion in this field, the Commission submitted to the Council in August 1976 a draft directive concerning the placing on the market of 'EEC-accepted' pesticides.[5] This proposal, based on what was then Article 100 of the EEC Treaty, did not provide for a total harmonisation of pesticide registration requirements but rather for the creation of a legal category of 'EEC-accepted' pesticides which could be freely marketed throughout the Community. The proposal recognised that many plant protection products were primarily intended for local or regional commerce and use and that it would be appropriate for member states to continue to regulate these products nationally, in accordance with local and regional agricultural and environmental conditions and requirements.

Only those pesticides containing active substances listed in an annex to the proposed directive would be eligible for 'EEC-accepted' status.[6] Applications for acceptance would have to be submitted in a single member state, which would determine whether the product met the conditions for acceptance as laid down in the directive. The other member states and the Commission were to be notified of any applications and any approvals granted. Any pesticide having obtained 'EEC-accepted' status in a single member state could in principle be freely marketed in the entire Community. The proposal allowed for limited derogations from this principle, subject to authorisation through a comitology procedure, where a member state could show that a product accepted by another member state would not meet efficacy, safety or environmental requirements in the conditions prevailing within its territory. Finally, the proposed directive laid down detailed labelling and packaging standards for 'EEC-accepted' pesticides. Owing to opposition from certain member states which were not prepared to accept the restrictions on national regulatory authority which would have resulted from the proposed 'EEC-acceptance' system, the Commission's 1976 proposal was never adopted by the Council.

Having failed to gain approval for this ambitious harmonisation scheme, the Commission formulated proposals for partial approximation measures which turned out to be more successful. The question of packaging and labelling standards was addressed separately from that of the pre-marketing authorisation of pesticides. In June 1978, the Council adopted a Directive on the approximation of the laws of the member states relating to the classification, packaging and labelling of pesticides.[7] This

[5] Proposal for a Council Dir concerning the placing of EEC-accepted plant protection products on the market, OJ No C212, 9.9.1976, p 3.

[6] Annex I to the proposal included most active ingredients on the market at the time it was drafted. Interestingly, the criteria for inclusion of substances in this list were not stated in the proposal. The only criteria mentioned were those for the evaluation of the end-use products (preparations).

[7] Council Dir 78/631/EEC of 26 June 1978 on the approximation of the laws of the Member States relating to the classification, packaging and labelling of dangerous preparations (pesticides), OJ No L206, 29.7.1978, p 13 (hereafter referred to as Dir 78/631/EEC).

Directive 78/631/EEC classifies pesticide preparations into different categories ('very toxic', 'toxic', and 'harmful') according to their acute toxicity and establishes labelling standards corresponding to these categories. It also lays down uniform packaging standards for all pesticides.

Directive 78/631/EEC provides for full harmonisation in that it explicitly precludes member states from prohibiting or restricting, on grounds of classification, packaging or labelling, the placing on the market of pesticides which satisfy the requirements laid down in its provisions. However, it does not affect the power of the member states with respect to the *authorisation* of pesticides. Several of the Directive's provisions actually refer to decisions to be taken by competent national authorities for pesticides subject to authorisation.[8] One of these provisions provides that the exercise of such national regulatory authority shall be 'subject to Community rules on the authorization of pesticides,'[9] rules which did not exist at the time of adoption of Directive 78/631/EEC. But its preamble indicates the intention of the Council to adopt such rules at a later stage, where it notes that 'it will in addition [to Directive 78/631/EEC] be necessary to include in later Directives special provisions concerning the authorization, distribution and use of . . . pesticides.'[10]

While the goal of uniform Community-wide rules on the pre-marketing authorisation of pesticides remained elusive, the Commission, faced with a growing number of disparate regulatory measures in the member states, pursued a more modest objective of minimal harmonisation of measures *prohibiting* the sale and use of certain particularly hazardous pesticides. If the member states could not agree on a uniform *positive* list of pesticides whose use might be *authorised* throughout the Community, it was thought they should at least be able to agree on a lowest-common-denominator *negative* list of pesticides whose use would be *banned* in all member states. The Commission thus took a legislative initiative which led to the adoption on 21 December 1978 of a Council Directive prohibiting the placing on the market and use of plant protection products containing certain active substances.[11]

This Directive initially banned the marketing and use of 13 persistent organochlorine and mercury-based pesticides throughout the Community, subject only to the possibility of temporary derogations for specific well-defined uses. Additional active substances were later added to the negative list through a series of subsequent amendments. Directive 79/117/EEC provides that an active substance shall be included in this list

[8] OJ No L206, 29.7.1978, Art 6, paras 2(b), 3, 4 and 5.

[9] *Ibid*, Art 6, para 5.

[10] *Ibid*, 8th recital.

[11] Council Dir 79/117/EEC of 21 Dec 1978 prohibiting the placing on the market and use of plant protection products containing certain active substances, OJ No L33, 8.2.1979, p 36 (hereafter referred to as Dir 79/117/EEC).

if, even when properly applied for the purpose intended, its use gives rise or is likely to give rise to:
(a) harmful effects on human or animal health;
(b) unreasonable adverse effects on the environment.[12]

However, this Community list of banned active substances clearly remained a lowest common denominator of the prohibitions in force in individual member states.

Even though amendments can be made by a qualified majority since the entry into force of the Single European Act,[13] the Commission has been reluctant to propose amendments unless there is a consensus among the member states that a substance should be added to the list.[14] There are many pesticides for which national bans are in force in several member states but which are not subject to a Community-wide prohibition under Directive 79/117/EEC. The Court of Justice has held that, since the Directive 'does not . . . pursue complete harmonization of national rules concerning the marketing and use of plant protection products', Articles 29 and 30 of the EC Treaty do not preclude national legislation prohibiting the sale or use of other pesticides than those listed in the annex to the Directive, even when such legislation has the effect of impeding intra-Community trade.[15]

Like most product standard directives adopted under the approximation of laws provisions of the Treaty, both Directives 78/631/EEC and 79/117/EEC contain an exemption clause for pesticides intended for export to third countries.[16] The rationale for this exemption is spelled out in the preamble of Directive 79/117/EEC, which states that 'it is not appropriate to apply Community provisions to plant protection products intended for export to third countries *since in general these countries have their own regulations*.'[17] Though the export exemption could be viewed as a standard and logical feature of any *internal* market instrument, the justification given for it appears questionable in view of the fact that many developing countries lack effective national legislation on pesticides.

The 1991 Directive on Plant Protection Products

As part of its pre-1992 push towards the completion of the internal market, the Commission made a second and this time successful attempt to

[12] Dir 79/117/EEC, Art 6, para 6.
[13] Dir 79/117/EEC was originally based on Art 100 EEC. Amendments can now be adopted under Art 95 EC.
[14] On Commission policy with respect to proposed additions to the list, see Krämer (1986), pp 218–20.
[15] Case 125/88, *Officier van Justitie v Nijman*, [1989] ECR 3533. See the commentary by Krämer (1993b), pp 347–55.
[16] Dir 78/631/EEC, Art 1, para 2 (c); Dir 79/117/EEC, Art 5 (b).
[17] Dir 79/117/EEC, above n 11, preamble (emphasis added).

establish a harmonised system for registration of agricultural pesticides in the Community. The Commission's second proposal, announced in the White Paper on the Internal Market as a necessary measure for the removal of the remaining barriers to intra-Community trade in plant protection products, was presented to the Council in 1989.[18] On 15 July 1991, after two years of difficult negotiations, the Council adopted Directive 91/414/EEC concerning the placing of plant protection products on the market[19] by a qualified majority decision, against the vote of Denmark, on the basis of Article 43 of the Treaty.

The choice of this provision (now Article 37 EC), which provides the necessary powers for the implementation of the common agricultural policy, as the legal basis for a measure whose primary motives, as reflected in its preamble, are the completion of the internal market and the protection of public health and the environment, has been criticised by the European Parliament and was only reluctantly accepted by some member states. Even though the preamble also refers to the importance of pesticides in agricultural production, as well as to the potential obstacles to trade in agricultural products which may result from differences in national pesticide regulations, the Directive's link with the common agricultural policy is tenuous at best and the measure would have been more appropriately based on Article 100a (now Article 95) of the Treaty. As we have seen, previous Community legislation concerning pesticides was in fact based on the approximation of laws clause. The choice of Article 43 in this case appears to have been prompted by political considerations such as the desire to place this field of Community law firmly in the hands of agricultural policymakers and to limit the influence of the European Parliament in the legislative process, by avoiding the cooperation procedure as it was then prescribed by Article 100a.

The Directive establishes a two-tier registration system for the marketing of pesticides in the Community. The first tier provides for the screening and registration of active substances at Community level and their inclusion on a single Community list of 'active substances authorized for incorporation in plant protection products' (Annex I of the Directive). The second tier is the authorisation of actual plant protection products or preparations, which remains in the hands of individual member states but is made subject to the application of uniform principles and criteria and of the principle of mutual recognition. Plant protection products shall not be placed on the market nor used in the territory of a member state unless they have been authorised by the competent national authority. Member states shall only authorize plant protection products whose active substances are included in the Community list.

[18] OJ No C 89, 10.4.1989, p 22.
[19] OJ No L 230, 19.8.1991, p 1 (hereafter referred to as Dir 91/414/EEC).

The two-tier system is the crucial difference between Directive 91/414/EEC and the Commission's unsuccessful 1976 proposal. Under that proposal, the granting of 'EEC-acceptance' by a single member state would automatically have resulted in free market access in all member states, without any requirement for a further administrative decision in any other member state. Under Directive 91/414/EEC, the power of each member state to authorise the placing on its market of any pesticide is *formally* preserved, though the actual possibility for a member state to refuse authorisation for a product authorised by another member state in accordance with the Directive is strictly limited and subject to review by Community institutions.

The Directive provides that active substances shall be included in the Community list if their use can be expected 'in the light of current scientific and technical knowledge' not to 'have any harmful effects on human or animal health or any unacceptable influence on the environment.'[20] This shall be determined on the basis of a dossier submitted by the applicant, containing detailed information specified in Annex II of the Directive. This information is to be reviewed and a decision reached through a procedure which provides for decision-making by qualified majority and thus makes it possible for objections by individual member states to be overruled.[21] A central role is given to the Standing Committee on Plant Health, a body composed of national experts designated by the member states.[22]

The Commission first assesses the information and then submits it to this Committee, together with a proposal for a decision. The Committee delivers its opinion on the proposal by qualified majority. If the Committee agrees with the Commission, the latter may formally adopt the proposed measure. If the Committee is of a different opinion, the matter shall be referred to the Council, which shall decide by qualified majority. If the Council fails to reach a decision within three months, the Commission can decide in its place.[23] The inclusion of a substance on the list shall be subject to review at least once every 10 years or at any time if there are indications that the authorisation criteria are no longer fulfilled.[24]

Authorisations for the marketing and use of plant protection products shall be granted by the competent authorities of the member states, within the legal framework laid down by the Directive.[25] In addition to the general requirement that authorised products shall only contain active substances included in the Community list, the Directive contains a detailed list of

[20] *Ibid*, Art 5, para 1.
[21] *Ibid*, Art 6, para 1.
[22] This committee was established by Commission Decision 78/436/EEC, OJ No L124, 12.5.1978, p 16.
[23] Dir 91/414/EEC, Art 19.
[24] *Ibid*, Art 5, para 5.
[25] *Ibid*, Art 3, para 1.

criteria with which products must be shown by the applicant to comply.[26] The criteria are similar to but more detailed than those applying to active substances. Pesticide products may only be registered if they have 'no harmful effect' on human or animal health or on groundwater[27] and 'no unacceptable influence' on the environment.[28] Another requirement is that their residues 'can be determined by appropriate methods in general use'[29] and that maximum residue levels in agricultural products have been established.[30] Some criteria of course leave ample room for interpretation, and member states inevitably differ in their assessment of what constitutes, eg, 'unacceptable influence' on the environment. In order to promote consistency in the application of the criteria for authorisation, the Directive provides for the adoption of 'uniform principles for the evaluation of plant protection products.'[31] These uniform principles were not adopted simultaneously with Directive 91/414/EEC itself, but later, through a separate implementing directive which added an Annex VI to the original 1991 Directive.[32]

The most important provisions in terms of the internal market objective of the Directive are those relating to mutual recognition of authorisations. Article 10 imposes an obligation on member states to authorise the placing on the market in their territory of pesticide products containing active substances inscribed in the Community list and authorised by another member state 'to the extent that agricultural, plant health and environmental conditions relevant to the use of the product are comparable in the regions concerned.' Thus member states are only entitled to refuse authorisation if the relevant conditions are not comparable. But even in such cases, the Directive considerably limits the discretionary power of national authorities

[26] Dir 91/414/EEC, Art 4, para 1.

[27] *Ibid*, Art 4, para 1(b)(iv).

[28] *Ibid*, Art 4, para 1(b)(v).

[29] *Ibid*, Art 4, para 1(d).

[30] *Ibid*, Art 4, para 1(f).

[31] *Ibid*, Art 23, para 1 and annex VI.

[32] Council Dir 94/43/EC of 27 July 1994 establishing Annex VI to Dir 91/414/EEC concerning the placing of plant protection products on the market, OJ No L227, 1.9.1994, p 31. It should be noted that Dir 94/43/EC, which was adopted on the legal basis of Art 18, para 1 of Dir 91/414/EEC, was annulled by the Court of Justice at the request of the European Parliament on 18 June 1996. The Court found that the Parliament's prerogatives had been disregarded by the Council in that the contested 1994 Directive, adopted without consultation of the Parliament, was inconsistent with the provisions of the 1991 Directive with respect to the conditions for authorisation of plant protection products. The Court's judgment held that 'by not taking account of the effects which plant protection products may have on all groundwater, the contested directive specifically failed to observe one of the essential elements of the matter expressly laid down in the basic directive.' Case C–303/94, *European Parliament v Council*, [1996] ECR I–2943, para 31. See the case note by V Heyvaert in *Tijdschrift voor Milieurecht*, 1996, pp 450–53. Following the annulment of Dir 94/43/EC, a new, slightly modified Annex VI was adopted by the Council in 1997. Council Dir 97/57/EC of 22 Sept 1997 establishing Annex VI to Dir 91/414/EEC concerning the placing of plant protection products on the market, OJ No L265, 27.9.1997, p 87.

because it provides for decisions refusing authorisation to be reviewed by Community institutions.

The final decision 'as to whether or not comparability exists' shall be taken by the Commission or Council on the opinion of the Standing Committee on Plant Health in accordance with the same qualified majority procedure as applies to the approval of active substances at Community level.[33] In this way, under the scheme instituted by the Directive, member states can be forced to accept the placing on the market of certain pesticides in their territories against their will. The application of the Directive could even compel certain member states to allow the re-introduction of pesticides which they had earlier banned, provided a qualified majority exists to include the chemicals in question on the Community list of authorised substances.

It is quite striking that, under the scheme of Directive 91/414/EEC, the logic of harmonisation does not operate as effectively to force member states with laxer standards to remove from the market pesticides which cannot meet the requirements for inclusion in the Community list. Indeed, the Directive allows member states to authorise, during a period of 12 years from the date of notification of the Directive, the placing on the market of products containing unlisted active substances, provided these products are already on the market at the time the Directive becomes effective.[34] This long transitional period was instituted to allow the Commission and the Standing Committee to review all active substances which are already on the market and decide whether or not they meet the criteria for inclusion in the Community list. In the event of a negative decision, a period will be prescribed within which existing authorisations will have to be withdrawn. However, the Community institutions may also decide to extend the transition period for certain active substances for as long as they need to come to a final decision.

At the demand of a number of environmentally concerned member states, a 'safeguard clause' has been included in the Directive, which allows a member state to 'provisionally restrict or prohibit the use and/or sale' of an authorised pesticide on its territory when it has 'valid reasons' to consider that it constitutes a risk for health or the environment.[35] However, such decisions shall be reviewed by the Commission in conjunction with the Standing Committee on Plant Health and may be overruled by a qualified majority decision of the Community institutions.

In sum, Directive 91/414/EEC entails a substantial transfer of power from national authorities to Community institutions in the field of pesticides regulation. It contains mechanisms which could potentially lead to some

[33] Dir 91/414/EEC, Art 10, para 3.
[34] *Ibid*, Art 8, para 2.
[35] *Ibid*, Art 11.

measure of deregulation in environmentally progressive member states. Whether or not this actually occurs depends on the interpretation of the environmental criteria in the Directive by the institutions charged with establishing the list of authorised active substances. So far, the process of implementation of Directive 91/414/EEC and listing of active substances has been proceeding very slowly.

The 1998 Biocides Directive

Directive 91/414/EEC applies only to plant protection products, ie pesticides for agricultural use. As another legislative initiative for the completion of the internal market, the Commission submitted to the Council in July 1993 a proposal for a directive aimed at setting up a harmonised Community system for the authorisation of pesticides for non-agricultural use, to complement the system established by Directive 91/414/EEC.[36] On the basis of this proposal, the European Parliament and the Council on 16 February 1998 adopted Directive 98/8/EC, which regulates the placing on the market of this category of products referred to as biocides.[37]

This Directive establishes an authorisation system closely modelled on that of Directive 91/414/EEC for a broad range of products described as 'biocidal products', ie products intended to prevent the occurrence or action of harmful organisms or otherwise render them harmless. This general category includes 23 'product types' exhaustively listed in an annex to the directive, including such products as disinfectants, rodenticides, avicides, molluscicides, insecticides, wood protection products, and antifouling paints, but excludes products covered by other directives, such as cosmetics, food additives, pharmaceuticals and agricultural pesticides or 'plant protection products', as defined in Directive 91/414/EEC.

Like Directive 91/414/EEC, Directive 98/8/EC provides for the establishment of a Community list of active substances authorised for use in biocide products. The inclusion of substances in this list is to be decided by the Commission or by the Council, based on the opinion of a 'Standing Committee on Biocidal Products' composed of representatives of the member states.[38] Decision-making in this committee or in the Council, as the case may be, is by qualified majority, except in certain cases where the Council may reject the Commission proposal by a simple majority.[39] The decision shall be taken on the basis of an assessment carried out by

[36] COM(93) 351 final—SYN 465, OJ No C 239, 3.9.1993, p 3.

[37] European Parliament and Council Dir 98/8/EC of 16 Feb 1998 concerning the placing of biocidal products on the market, OJ No L123, 24.4.1998, p 1 (hereafter referred to as Dir 98/8/EC).

[38] *Ibid*, Art 11, para 4.

[39] *Ibid*, Art 28.

the competent authority of the member state where the application for registration of the substance in question was filed.[40] This application must include comprehensive technical, toxicological and ecotoxicological data, as laid down in an annex to the Directive.

Directive 98/8/EC provides that authorisation for the placing on the market of individual *products*, as opposed to the approval of active *substances*, shall be given by the competent national authority of the member state concerned, subject to compliance with the conditions stipulated in Article 4 of the Directive and in accordance with the 'common principles' laid down in its Annex VI.[41] These conditions include the absence of 'unacceptable' effects on human or animal health, non-target organisms, groundwater and surface waters, including estuarine and marine waters, and other environmental compartments. The annex containing the 'common principles' was not included in the Commission's initial proposal but was proposed to be adopted in a later implementing directive, like the 'uniform principles' of Directive 91/414/EEC, but the European Parliament, mindful of this unsavoury precedent, refused to consider the Commission's proposal as long as it had not been completed by an annex establishing those principles. The Commission was thus forced to submit an amended proposal in 1995[42] before the Parliament agreed to give its opinion on first reading in 1996.[43]

Like Directive 91/414/EEC, Directive 98/8/EC provides for mutual recognition of authorisations, with every member state bound to allow the placing on its market of biocides already authorised by another member state, provided the active ingredient is listed in the Community list.[44] The Directive also includes a list of 'low-risk biocidal products' which may be marketed subject only to 'registration' by the competent authorities of the member states concerned, pursuant to a simplified procedure.[45]

Like Directive 91/414/EEC, Directive 98/8/EC is marked by an imbalance between the level of constraint it places on member states with a view to guaranteeing the free movement of goods and that designed to protect health and the environment. This appears from several of its provisions. For instance, individual member states are still allowed, on a provisional basis and subject to certain conditions, to authorise the marketing and use in their territory of products containing active substances not included in the Community list for a period not exceeding three years, pending a decision on the inclusion of these substances in the list,[46] or even for a

[40] *Ibid*, Art 11, para 2.
[41] *Ibid*, Art 5, para 1.
[42] COM(95) 387 final—COD 465, OJ No C 261, 6.10.1995, p 5.
[43] European Parliament opinion of 18 Apr 1996, OJ No C141, 13.5.1996, p 191.
[44] Dir 98/8/EC, Art 4.
[45] *Ibid*, Art 3, para 2.
[46] *Ibid*, Art 15, para 2.

transitional period of up to 10 years after the implementation date of the directive, if the active substance in question was already on their market at that time.[47]

When an application for inclusion of an active substance on the Community list of authorised substances is denied, member states shall be required to cancel any existing authorisations or registrations of products containing the substance in question 'as appropriate,'[48] but the Directive does not impose any deadline for this, while it does stipulate that in the converse case, when an application for Community listing is granted, member states which had not yet allowed the use in their territory of products containing the listed substance will be required to do so within 120 days of the filing of an application to this effect when such products are authorised in another member state.[49] Where an active substance which was initially included in the Directive's positive list is later found to have unacceptable effects and a decision is consequently taken at Community level to remove it from the list, the Directive surprisingly stipulates that such a decision 'shall not have immediate effect but shall be delayed for a period of up to a maximum of four years from the date of that decision.'[50]

Directive 98/8/EC is obviously based on a rather unbalanced reading of the principle of subsidiarity, proceeding from the assumption that action at Community level is more justified when national measures threaten to *restrict* access to the market than when such access is *allowed*. This gives the impression that Community action is more important when unilateral national measures for the protection of human health or the environment threaten the smooth functioning of the internal market than when a lax national authorisation policy endangers human health or the environment in the Community.

THE DEVELOPMENT OF A COMMUNITY POLICY ON PESTICIDE EXPORTS

As the above review indicates, regulation of pesticides by the European Community was originally concerned exclusively with the internal market. The exclusion of pesticides intended for export from the scope of Community legislation was no more than a logical consequence of this internal market approach and was not perceived as a political issue until the early 1980s. As a result, the development of a Community policy on exports of pesticides was slow. The Commission initially did not regard such a policy as necessary. The earliest political initiatives in this field were actually taken

[47] Dir 98/8/EC, Art 16, para 1.
[48] *Ibid*, Art 16, para 3.
[49] *Ibid*, Art 4, para 1.
[50] *Ibid*, Art 10, para 5(iii).

by the European Parliament against Commission opposition. It is only in the mid-1980s that the Commission, confronted not only with political pressure from the Parliament but also from a number of member states contemplating unilateral national measures, as well as with the regulatory activities of intergovernmental organisations such as the OECD, UNEP and the FAO, changed its position and eventually submitted a proposal for legislation to the Council in 1986.

Early Commission Policy

Prior to its 1986 legislative initiative, the Commission consistently opposed regulation of pesticide exports on the grounds that 'it should be for the importing country to lay down its own rules for trade in these products'[51] and that these rules 'may differ from Community provisions for sound and objective reasons.'[52] Yet the Commission's policy was not entirely without contradictions. When questioned in 1981 about possible exports of banned hazardous consumer products from the United States to the European Community it stated:

> The Commission feels that every country engaged in international trade must ensure that any products liable to be a direct hazard to users or consumers should not be exported.[53]

However, it was apparently not prepared to apply the same principle to the Community's own pesticide exports. To rationalise this double standard, the Commission relied on the familiar argument that local conditions in developing countries may lead to a different risk/benefit assessment:

> A decision to ban a pesticide must be based on an assessment of the comparative risks and advantages of their use in a given climate, agricultural or ecological situation. The balance may swing one way in Europe and another in a developing country. The use of DDT for malaria control is one example. To try and impose Community rules on non-member countries or deny them supplies of pesticides they need could cause vexed political problems.[54]

Originally, the Commission was even opposed to the idea of export notification. It argued that the hazardous pesticides banned by Community law

[51] Answer of the Commission to Written Question No 648/82 of Mrs Poirier, OJ No C245, 20.9.1982, p 10.
[52] Answer of the Commission to Written Question No 1082/82 of Mr Rogers, OJ No C339, 27.12.1982, p 10.
[53] Answer of the Commission to Written Question No 1370/80 of Mr Glinne, OJ No C49, 9.3.1981, p 15.
[54] Written Question No 648/82, above n 51.

have been the subject in recent years of many exhaustive scientific and official publications throughout the world. The Commission considers that their properties and possible adverse effects are now sufficiently well-known internationally that a special system of information and notification is unnecessary.[55]

Later, however, the Commission, while still unwilling to take any action to amend Community directives, expressed some support for the concept of organised information exchange, but deferred to the initiative of other international organisations in this field. It recognised that

the developing countries must have sufficient access to the information they need to draw an informed conclusion about different pesticides. This can best be achieved by an international agreement under the aegis of international agencies such as the WHO or FAO.[56]

In particular, the Commission seemed to favour the FAO as the most appropriate forum to address the issue, and it participated in the consultations on the FAO Code of Conduct.[57] In its statements about the desirability of international information exchange arrangements for hazardous products generally, the Commission continued to place heavy emphasis on the 'observance of [the] sovereign rights of each state', stressing 'that it is up to each country to decide whether a product may be imported or not.'[58]

It is worth mentioning that information exchange on hazardous products and notification of regulatory actions were not alien concepts in EC law. In fact, the Community in 1984 established an internal emergency information exchange system on dangerous consumer products.[59] Under this scheme, member states which decide to impose urgent restrictions on the marketing or use in their territory of particular consumer products because of serious and immediate risks for the health or safety of consumers are obliged to notify the Commission immediately.[60] The Commission, in turn, is required to forward such information to the designated national authorities of the other member states.[61] However, notwithstanding the existence of this internal notification system for dangerous consumer products, the Commission remained opposed to a Community legislative initiative to regulate exports of hazardous chemicals until 1985.

[55] Answer of the Commission to Written Question No 1778/79 of Mr Muntingh, OJ No C156, 1980, p 49.

[56] Written Question No 648/82, above n 51.

[57] Written Question No 1082/82, above n 52; see also Deb European Parliament, OJ 1983, Ann No 1–304, p 240 (Statement of Commissioner Narjes).

[58] Answer of the Commission to Written Question No 2162/80 of Mr Michel, OJ No C140, 10.6.1981, p 15.

[59] Council Decision 84/113/EEC of 2 March 1984 introducing a Community system for the rapid exchange of information on dangers arising from the use of consumer products, OJ No L70, 13.3.1984, p 16.

[60] *Ibid*, Art 1 (1).

[61] *Ibid*, Art 1 (3).

The Political Debate in the European Parliament

The European Parliament first considered the issue of exports of banned hazardous pesticides in 1981, in response to a petition submitted by a number of Dutch environmental groups requesting the Parliament to recommend an export ban. The Parliament's Committee on the Environment, Public Health and Consumer Protection issued an opinion generally endorsing the Commission's views and rejecting the petition on the grounds that it was 'premature' and that

> banning exports of insecticides whose use is banned or limited . . . is not acceptable so long as research has not come up with effective and inexpensive substitute products for the developing countries.[62]

Shortly thereafter, the issue was put back on the Parliament's agenda by the introduction, on behalf of the Socialist Group, of a motion for a resolution calling for a full inquiry by the Environment Committee and regulation of EC pesticide exports.[63] This motion was debated for over two years in the Environment Committee[64] and in the Committee on Development and Cooperation. The Environment Committee eventually adopted a report recommending that exports of banned pesticides from the EC be made subject to notification and the express consent of the importing country and that all exported pesticides be made to comply with EC packaging and labelling standards.[65] The Committee on Development and Cooperation, for its part, issued an opinion in which it

> emphasises that the ultimate decision-taking and control must rest within the sovereignty of the importing country and believes that the ILO, WHO and FAO Guidelines and Code of Conduct must command the greatest support from the European Economic Community.[66]

The report did not, however, explicitly criticise the notion of notification and prior informed consent.

On 14 October 1983, the full Parliament unanimously but for one abstention adopted the resolution proposed by the Environment Committee. This resolution, in essence,

[62] EP Doc PE 69.433/rev, 14 Jan 1981, pp 5, 6.

[63] Motion for a resolution on the export of dangerous substances and preparations and the desirability of increasing the protection of workers and consumers in the importing countries and of the European consumer of exotic foodstuffs, EP Doc 1–903/80, 12 Feb 1981.

[64] See Working Document, EP Doc PE 77.668, 1982.

[65] Report drawn up on behalf of the Committee on Environment, Public Health and Consumer Protection on the export of various dangerous substances and preparations (Rapporteur: Mrs Squarcialupi), EP Doc 1–458/83, 27 June 1983.

[66] Committee on Development and Cooperation, Opinion, EP Doc PE 82.811/fin., 28 March 1983, p 3.

1. Regrets that important Directives—in particular 78/631/EEC and 79/117/EEC—provide no safeguards for pesticides exported to other countries;
2. Calls therefore on the Commission of the European Communities to amend Directives 79/117/EEC and 78/631/EEC so that pesticides can be exported under the following conditions:
(a) that the government of the importing country is informed of the particular nature of the product and of the restrictions to which it is subject in the exporting country and the reasons for such restrictions;
(b) *that the government of the importing country, having received such notification, explicitly requests the purchase;*
3. Believes that legislative and market conditions must be urgently established to ensure that the export of all pesticides destined for the developing countries are subject to the following conditions:
(a) that it is packaged and labelled as described in Directive 78/631/EEC;
(b) that the directions for use are written in the most common language of the country of destination, preferably accompanied by diagrams, unless specified otherwise by the importing countries.[67]

Furthermore, the Parliament urged the Commission to de-emphasise chemical pest control and to give priority to integrated pest management in Community aid programmes, and to provide assistance to developing countries to enhance their own regulatory capacity.

The most contentious part of the resolution in the plenary debate was operative paragraph 2 and in particular subparagraph 2 (b) requiring prior informed consent. The Christian-Democrats tried to have subparagraph 2 (b) deleted and introduced an amendment to this effect.[68] Their spokesperson defended the amendment with the following argument:

We do not feel that the governments of importing countries should explicitly declare that they are importers. This would tend to create a bureaucratic world market in which bureaucracy would be the clear winner. This would be an infringement of the sovereignty of all importing countries, and we feel that it is up to the purchaser, and not to his government, to decide, in full knowledge of the facts, whether or not a given product should be accepted.[69]

This amendment was rejected, however, as was another amendment tabled by the Socialist Group, which aimed to tighten export restrictions by adding, as an additional condition for export, that the government of the importing country 'provides proof that the import of the product is essential to the importing country for reasons of health policy.'[70]

[67] European Parliament Res on the export of various dangerous substances and preparations, 14 Oct 1983, OJ No C307, 14.11.1983, p 109 (emphasis added).
[68] Amendment No 4, EP Doc 1–458/4, 6 Oct 1983.
[69] Deb EP, Sess 1983–84, OJ 1983, Ann No 1–304, p 236 (Remarks of Mrs Lentz-Cornette).
[70] Amendment No 3, EP Doc 1–458/3, 6 Oct 1983.

During the plenary debate in Parliament, the Commissioner in charge of environmental affairs criticised the resolution for seeking to force EC standards on other countries and reiterated the Commission's position that:

> If we really were to try and impose Community legislation unilaterally on third countries, this would have numerous political and legal implications, as the autonomy and the principle of respect of the sovereign rights of these third countries would thereby be affected, and these countries must and can make their own decisions concerning the safety and health of their citizens.[71]

This comment applied to both paragraphs 2 and 3 of the resolution, notwithstanding the fact that only paragraph 3 could conceivably be viewed as advocating extra-territorial regulation. Although the Commissioner thus implicitly rejected a notification scheme, he nevertheless stated the Commission was prepared to give the importing countries 'any form of information . . . imaginable'[72] and 'wishes to concentrate all its efforts on international cooperation,'[73] referring in particular to the FAO Code of Conduct as a possible solution. In response, the rapporteur pointed out the inconsistency in the Commission's position, criticising it for failing to make the distinction between export notification, which is aimed precisely at providing information, and application of Community standards to exports.[74] 'We use the word "notification" because it seems more official, while you use the word "information" which I would say was less official.'[75]

In 1983, the European Parliament resolution was the clearest pronouncement thus far by a political institution from a group of pesticide-exporting countries in favour of a system of export controls based on the principle of prior informed consent. However, the resolution had no immediate effect on the position of the Commission, which continued to oppose any export regulation by the Community. It was only two years later that the Commission changed its mind and proposed legislation to the Council.

Developments in Individual Member States

Together with political pressure from the European Parliament, national legislative and administrative measures in a number of individual member states were an important factor which eventually prompted policy change at the EC level. Germany, the United Kingdom and the Netherlands

[71] Deb EP, Sess 1983–84, OJ 1983, Ann No 1–304, p 240 (Remarks of Commissioner Narjes).

[72] *Ibid.*

[73] *Ibid.*

[74] *Ibid.*

[75] *Ibid.*

legislated on hazardous exports prior to the adoption of the first Community legislation on the subject. All three of these member states belong to the top ten pesticide-exporting countries in the world, accounting respectively for 17.6 per cent, 10.9 per cent and 4.7 per cent of world exports in 1995.[76] In 1987, their respective shares of overall EC pesticide exports to the Third World amounted to 31.1 per cent, 19.5 per cent and 7.4 per cent.[77]

Germany

In principle, under German law, as in most other jurisdictions, pesticides destined for export are exempt from the authorisation requirement which applies to pesticides for domestic sale.[78] As an exception to this rule, however, a special statute enacted in 1972 bans not only the sale and use, but also the *production* and *export* of DDT and DDT formulations.[79] In the 1970s, Germany hoped that this export and production ban would set an example for other countries and lead to a worldwide phase-out of DDT.[80] The German government noted in the early 1980s that the fact that this had not occurred and that DDT was still being manufactured on a large scale in developing countries demonstrated that unilateral measures by Germany could not effectively influence international trade in pesticides.[81] In any event, the German ban on DDT production and export remained a unique and isolated measure.

In 1983, while the international regulatory debate on trade in banned and severely restricted chemicals was developing in the OECD and the United Nations, the federal government submitted to parliament a bill to amend the Plant Protection Act (*Pflanzenschutzgesetz*).[82] In response to this mounting international pressure for action, it included in this bill a number of provisions concerning pesticides intended for export from Germany.[83]

Although pesticides for export would remain exempt from compliance with most national standards,[84] the government proposed to make them

[76] 1995 International Trade Statistics Yearbook, vol II, United Nations, New York, 1996, UN Doc ST/ESA/STAT/SER.G/44, p 106.

[77] Based on figures published by the Central Statistical Office of the Netherlands in 1990. Centraal Bureau voor Statistiek, *Kwartaalbericht Milieu*, 1990/1, p 26, table 6.6.

[78] See *Pflanzenschutzgesetz*, 1968 (as amended 1975), § 7 (1) (1); *Pflanzenschutzgesetz*, 1986, § 11 (1) (1).

[79] *Gesetz über den Verkehr mit DDT*, § 1 (1), BGBl. 1972 I 1385.

[80] It is only recently that discussions on a total phase-out of DDT have started in both regional and global fora, as part of the development of international legal instruments on persistent organic pollutants (POPs).

[81] Antwort der Bundesregierung auf die Kleine Anfrage der Abgeordneten Frau Dr Hickel und der Fraktion Die Grünen, Deutscher Bundestag, Doc 10/695, 29 Nov 1983, p 2.

[82] Entwurf Gesetz zum Schutz der Kulturpflanzen (Pflanzenschutzgesetz), Bundesrat, Doc 355/83, 26 Aug 1983. On the reform of pesticides legislation in Germany, see generally Rehbinder (1983).

[83] See Rehbinder (1983), pp 255–56.

[84] Entwurf Gesetz, above n 82, §§ 18 (3), 19.

subject to certain minimum labelling requirements[85] and to require them to be accompanied by directions for use including information on appropriate use, possible adverse effects on health and the environment, emergency treatment in cases of poisoning, and safe disposal.[86] Furthermore, the government proposed in its bill to grant discretionary authority to certain federal ministers to ban, by executive regulation, the export of specific pesticides in exceptional circumstances.[87]

Some committees of the *Bundesrat*, unsatisfied with the export provisions proposed by the government, recommended an amendment to the government's bill which would in principle have prohibited the export of pesticides containing active substances banned in Germany but would have authorised the same ministers to grant exemptions and permit the export of such pesticides in particular cases 'if their application is necessary in other countries for the prevention of substantial damage.'[88] However, the plenary of the *Bundesrat* rejected this recommendation and forwarded the bill to the *Bundestag* without proposing any amendments to its export provisions.[89] The bill was eventually adopted by the *Bundestag* in 1986, without major changes in these provisions. The only significant amendment inserted language requiring German exporters of pesticides to 'take into account' the FAO Code of Conduct on the Distribution and Use of Pesticides.[90]

The main export provision, § 20 (3) of the *Pflanzenschutzgesetz*, as enacted in 1986, provides that:

> so far as necessary for the prevention of substantial danger to human or animal health or other danger, in particular to ecosystems, which cannot be averted by other means, the Federal Minister for Food, Agriculture and Forestry . . . is empowered to prohibit the export of particular pesticides or of pesticides containing certain substances.[91]

It should be noted, however, that the new Plant Protection Act does not provide for any form of export notification and does not empower the German federal government to institute such a system. Instead, it assumes

[85] *Ibid*, § 20 (2).

[86] *Ibid*, § 20 (1) (1).

[87] *Ibid*, § 20 (3).

[88] Empfehlungen der Ausschusse zum Entwurf eines Gesetzes zum Schutz der Kulturpflanzen (Pflanzenschutzgesetz), Bundesrat, Doc 355/1/83, 27 Sept 1983, p 22.

[89] See Deutscher Bundestag, Doc 10/1262 (1984).

[90] Beschlussempfehlung und Bericht des Ausschusses für Ernährung, Landwirtschaft und Forsten (10. Ausschuss) zu dem von der Bundesregierung eingebrachten Entwurf eines Gesetzes zum Schutz der Kulturpflanzen (Pflanzenschutzgesetz—PflSchG), Deutscher Bundestag, Doc 10/4618, 2 Jan 1986, p 22. Moreover, a technical amendment was made in the provision granting statutory authority to ban exports, to the effect that this authority would apply only to exports to non-member states of the EC. *Ibid*, p 23.

[91] *Pflanzenschutzgesetz*, 1986, § 20 (3) (author's translation).

that labelling and directions for use are an adequate and sufficient means of providing information to the importing country, ie directly to the importer and users, not to that country's governmental authorities. It is significant that the information which must be supplied through labelling and use directions does not include the domestic regulatory status of the exported pesticide, which is precisely the key information that notification systems are designed to transmit.

The German law's reliance on labelling and user information is surprisingly close to the position of the German chemical industry, as presented to the 1982 OECD Seminar on Control of Chemicals in Importing Countries.[92] The federal government argued in 1984 that its legislative proposals were 'sufficient' to comply with the OECD Guiding Principles.[93] It had, however, already been observed by a leading German legal scholar in 1983 that the export provisions of the Plant Protection Act, by failing to provide full information on exported pesticides, and especially on their domestic regulatory status, to importing countries, fell short of the requirements of UN General Assembly Resolution 37/137.[94] Yet the German legislature eventually preferred to rely on the goodwill of industry to comply voluntarily with the provisions of the FAO Code of Conduct.

As if to compensate for this lacuna in the *Pflanzenschutzgesetz* and to demonstrate the seriousness of its commitment to the 'soft' approach to export notification, the German chemical industry association *Verband der Chemischen Industrie* adopted a voluntary code of conduct for the export of dangerous chemicals, in which its member companies undertook to inform the German federal authorities, on an annual basis, of any exports of chemicals banned or severely restricted in Germany and of their countries of destination.[95] This voluntary information scheme was designed to enable the German authorities to comply with the export notification provisions of the OECD Guiding Principles, the London Guidelines and the FAO Code of Conduct, without any need for legislation.

United Kingdom

In the early 1980s, the UK was the only advanced industrialised country which did not have a statutory pesticides registration scheme. The evaluation and clearance for use of pesticides in Britain was governed by the Pesticides Safety Precautions Scheme (PSPS), a voluntary, non-statutory

[92] See above ch 12.
[93] Antwort der Bundesregierung auf die Kleine Anfrage des Abgeordneten Dr Ehmke und der Fraktion Die Grunen, Deutscher Bundestag, Doc 10/1443, 5 May 1984, p 3.
[94] Rehbinder (1983), p 256.
[95] Verband der Chemischen Industrie e.V., *Verhaltenscodex für die Ausfuhr von gefährlichen Chemikalien.*

agreement between manufacturers and the government. The Scheme did not apply to 'products intended solely for introduction overseas'.

In 1984, the government introduced a bill aimed at providing a legal basis for a fully fledged statutory pesticides registration and control system. This led to the enactment of the Food and Environment Protection Act 1985 which, inter alia, empowered the Minister of Agriculture and the Secretary of State to prohibit or regulate the importation, sale, supply or use, but not the exportation, of pesticides.[96] However, the Act also contains a clause which provides that the Minister:

> may require the provision of such information by importers, exporters, manufacturers, distributors or users of a pesticide as he considers to be necessary . . . for the fulfilment by the government of the United Kingdom of any international obligation to supply information.[97]

When the government's bill was discussed in the House of Lords, these provisions were considered unsatisfactory; in committee, there was all-party support for an amendment which would have given the Ministers the power to prohibit the export of pesticides as well.[98] In order to pre-empt this move, the government pointed out that it already had the power to prohibit or regulate the export of any products under the Import, Export and Customs Powers (Defence) Act 1939[99] if it so desired, but that it did not consider export controls on pesticides appropriate. The Lords withdrew their amendment and eventually adopted the government's language, with a technical amendment.

In a consultative document on the implementation of the Food and Environment Protection Act, issued in November 1985, the Ministry of Agriculture, Fisheries and Food indicated that the measures the British government intended to take with respect to exports of banned or severely restricted pesticides would be strictly based on UNEP's 1984 Provisional Notification Scheme—which, as we have seen in chapter 12 above, the United Kingdom initiated. The British government would notify other countries of any action taken to ban or severely restrict the use of particular pesticides in the UK. British companies exporting any of these would be requested to inform the government, which in turn would notify the government of the importing country and refer it to the original notification of control action.

[96] Food and Environment Protection Bill, HL 49/2 (1984), cl 15 (1) (a)–(c).

[97] Food and Environment Protection Act 1985, s 16.

[98] Oxfam Public Affairs Unit, *Food & Environment Protection Bill, Part III: Pesticides, Briefing Paper on Export Control Aspects for Members of the House of Commons*, Oxford, Feb 1985, p 4.

[99] 2 & 3 Geo 6, ch 69, s 1 (1).

The consultation paper made it quite clear that the British authorities had no intention of interfering with exports. Their intervention would be limited to a one-time notification for which they 'expect[ed] to obtain the voluntary co-operation of exporters'. The use of the statutory powers contained in section 16 of the Food and Environment Protection Act would only 'be considered if the voluntary approach does not prove satisfactory.'[100] In July 1986, the Department of Trade and Industry sent a circular to manufacturers, distributors and traders of chemicals in the UK, referring to UNEP Provisional Notification Scheme and to the OECD Guiding Principles and the FAO Code of Conduct and inviting them voluntarily to provide information to the Department on the first export of any chemical banned or severely restricted in the UK to any particular country, in order to enable it to notify the appropriate authorities of that country on a one-time-only basis. The circular assured British exporters that the notification sent to the foreign government 'will not bear the name of the exporting company.'[101]

The statutory powers provided by section 16 of the Food and Environment Protection Act were never formally used.

The Netherlands

In the mid-1980s, the Netherlands was in the process of reforming its legislation on toxic chemicals. While existing Dutch laws allowed the unrestricted export of pesticides whose use is banned or severely restricted in the Netherlands,[102] a new Act on Environmentally Harmful Substances (*Wet Milieugevaarlijke Stoffen*), was enacted in 1985 and entered into force on 1 February 1986.

This Act confers broad discretionary powers on the government to regulate, inter alia, the export of chemical substances,[103] if there is a 'reasonable' likelihood of 'undesirable effects on man or the environment.' The relevant provisions of the Act allow the government to issue regulations banning the export of certain pesticides,[104] instituting export licensing or imposing other conditions on exports,[105] or requiring export notification.[106]

[100] Ministry of Agriculture Fisheries and Food, *Implementing Part III of the Food and Environment Protection Act 1985*, Consultative Document, London, Nov 1985, p 45.

[101] Department of Trade and Industry, *The Export of Banned or Severely Restricted Chemicals*, Circular to manufacturers, distributors and traders of chemicals, London, July 1986, para 7.

[102] Bestrijdingsmiddelenwet (1962, as amended 1975), Art 2 (3), *Staatsblad van het Koninkrijk der Nederlanden*, 1962, 288.

[103] Wet Milieugevaarlijke Stoffen (1985), *Staatsblad van het Koninkrijk der Nederlanden*, 1986, 10, Art 24 (1).

[104] *Ibid*, Art 24 (2) (a).

[105] *Ibid*, Art 24 (2) (c).

[106] *Ibid*, Art 24 (2) (b).

The Act was amended by parliament to limit the government's discretion and ensure that certain minimum conditions are imposed on exports. One provision specifies that export notification shall be mandatory 'at least for substances and preparations whose application causes a serious danger to man or the environment.'[107] A list of such substances is to be laid down by regulation.[108] The export is to be notified prior to shipment, both to the responsible government authorities in the Netherlands and in the importing country. The information to be provided to the importing country shall be determined by government regulation.[109] The exporter must prove that the authorities of the importing country, having received this information, have consented to the import of the product. If this requirement is not satisfied, the Minister of Environment has the power to ban the export.[110] With this new legislation, the Netherlands assumed a leadership position on pesticide exports within the EC. Ironically, however, the export provisions of the Act were never formally implemented.

In a note submitted to parliament in November 1985,[111] the Minister of Environment gave an outline of the regulations the government *intended* to issue in implementation of the export provisions of the *Wet Milieugevaarlijke Stoffen*. The note announced that the export control regime would apply to 22 listed chemicals. If the government of the importing country were to object in writing in response to an export notification the export would not be permitted, but it would be allowed if the importing country failed to react to the notification. In its note, the government also indicated, however, that it did not intend to issue regulations immediately, but would first await the outcome of an anticipated EC legislative initiative, to ensure that any Dutch regulatory scheme would be compatible with EC law. In 1986, however, the government and the Dutch chemical industry association agreed on a voluntary notification scheme along the lines set out in the minister's 1985 note to parliament and applying to the 22 chemicals in question. The industry undertook to refrain voluntarily from exporting any such chemicals to any country that would make known its objection to import.[112]

As in Germany and the UK, this voluntary scheme was later superseded by Community legislation, and no formal export regulations under the *Wet Milieugevaarlijke Stoffen* were ever adopted.[113] The normative debate in Europe moved back from national legislatures to the EC institutions.

[107] *Ibid*, Art 29 (1).
[108] *Ibid*.
[109] *Ibid*, Art 29 (2).
[110] *Ibid*, Art 29 (3).
[111] Uitvoer van gevaarlijke stoffen en preparaten, Tweede Kamer, Sess 1985–1986, Doc 19310, nrs 1–2.
[112] Vrijwillige regeling export gevaarlijke stoffen en preparaten, *Staatscourant* 1986, 102.
[113] See generally Jukkema (1988).

THE 1988 EEC REGULATION CONCERNING EXPORT FROM AND IMPORT INTO THE COMMUNITY OF CERTAIN DANGEROUS CHEMICALS

Towards an EEC Regulation on Exports of Banned and Severely Restricted Chemicals

As the political interest in the issue of chemical exports increased both within the Community's own member states and at the international level, the Commission's negative attitude towards regulation of international trade in banned and severely restricted chemicals began to change, prompted by several factors. First of all, political pressure from other Community institutions certainly played a role. Apart from the strong position taken by the European Parliament in its resolution of 14 October 1983, there were also indications of support for Community action in the Council.

In June 1983, the Dutch government, in an attempt to prod the Commission into action, put the pesticides export issue on the Council agenda as a 'miscellaneous' item and submitted a memorandum suggesting 'that Community rules be adopted regarding the export of specified pesticides to countries outside the Community'. This memorandum noted that since the Community accounts for some 60 per cent of world pesticide exports 'it bears a special responsibility in the matter' and proposed that Community rules should cover exchange of information, export notification procedures, labelling and packaging as well as 'monitoring of compliance with export rules.'[114] Recognising the inadequacy of existing Community legislation, the Netherlands note mentions the need for 'adapting existing rules accordingly', referring specifically to Directive 79/117/EEC.

It should be pointed out here that the Netherlands did not explicitly recommend that Community rules should incorporate the principle of prior informed consent although, by referring to compliance monitoring, it did imply that some form of export control would be desirable. In response to this Dutch initiative, the Council decided in June 1983 to request the Commission to prepare a report on the issue and referred the matter to the Committee of Permanent Representatives for further discussion.[115] One year later, in a more general resolution of 3 October 1984 requesting the Commission 'to submit any appropriate proposals to the Council as soon as possible' in order to 'integrate the environmental dimension in development

[114] Memorandum from the Netherlands delegation, EC Council Doc 7289/83 (Annex), 30 May 1983.

[115] *Toxic Substances Control Newsletter*, Autumn 1983, p 2.

aid', the Council recalled that it had 'already held an exchange of views . . . on whether to exercise greater control over exports of pesticides' to developing countries.[116]

Apart from the Council request and the European Parliament resolution, other motives which seem to have incited the Commission to act are the fact that EC member states took a common position in the UN General Assembly in favour of Resolution 37/137 and that, as we have seen above, several member states were in the process of enacting national legislation on exports of chemicals. The taking of unilateral legislative action by a number of member states, providing statutory authority for national measures to regulate exports of banned or severely restricted chemicals, was perceived as a potential source of trade distortions and therefore became a strong incentive for Community action.

Nevertheless, the Commission still took a long time to elaborate concrete proposals for Community action. Initially, it merely observed developments in international fora passively and waited for the outcome of the ongoing negotiations in UNEP and the FAO before taking any initiative of its own. The Commission did participate in UNEP and the FAO negotiations, but acted as a follower rather than a leader in the international regulatory debate. Its position in these negotiations was essentially conservative, as it joined some EC and other OECD member states in their efforts to ensure that the emerging international standards for the responsibility of exporting countries did not go beyond mere information exchange.

In the FAO, the Commission's primary concern did not even relate to the substance of the proposed Code of Conduct but was to obtain international recognition of the Community's prerogatives with regard to the regulation of pesticides through the insertion of a clause making the Community a 'party' to the Code in its own right. For this purpose, the Commission sought but did not obtain a formal mandate from the Council authorising it to participate in the FAO negotiations on behalf of the Community and to express the EC's views concerning those areas of the Code falling within the Community's competence.[117] Clearly, the member states did not attach as much importance as did the Commission to affirming the Community's legal and institutional position in the context of a non-binding international instrument.

[116] Resolution of the Council and of the representatives of the Governments of the Member States of the European Communities, meeting within the Council, of 3 Oct 1984, on the link between the environment and development, OJ No C 272, 12.10.1984, p 1, 4th preambular para *in fine*.

[117] Recommendation for a Council decision authorising the Community to participate in the working of the FAO Conference to draw up an International Code of Conduct on the Distribution and Use of Pesticides, EC Doc COM(85) 541 final, 15 Oct 1985.

Although it initially opposed the principle of PIC both in the FAO and UNEP, the Commission eventually changed its position on this question as well and moved closer to the European Parliament's view that regulation of exports of banned and severely restricted chemicals had to be based on that principle. This important shift in the Commission's position was prompted by discussions in the OECD on controlling transboundary movements of waste. In March 1985, an OECD ministerial conference adopted a recommendation urging member states not to allow the export of hazardous waste, in particular to developing countries, unless the importing country has given its formal consent and possesses 'adequate' disposal facilities.[118] Thus, the member states of the OECD, which in 1984 explicitly rejected export controls with respect to banned and severely restricted chemicals, agreed in 1985 that hazardous waste should not be shipped abroad without the consent of the importing country. According to the Commission, this indicated that 'the present work of the OECD is moving towards a strengthening of notification procedures.'[119]

The Commission acted quickly to translate the OECD recommendation on waste exports into Community law. As early as October 1985, it submitted a proposal to the Council to amend an existing 1984 Directive on transfrontier shipments of waste[120] so as to make exports to third countries subject to prior informed consent as recommended by the OECD. This proposal was adopted by the Council in June 1986.[121] Barely two weeks later, the Commission officially put before the Council its proposal for a regulation concerning exports of dangerous chemicals,[122] in which it proposed to make such exports subject to the principle of 'prior informed choice'. In explaining this proposal, the Commission established a clear parallel between the regulation of the export of banned and severely restricted chemicals and that of hazardous waste, by referring in its explanatory memorandum to the OECD recommendations of 1985.

While the Commission deserves credit for trying to be consistent in its approach to hazardous exports, its interpretation of the OECD recommendation as signalling an overall shift in OECD policy towards PIC is debatable. The economic interests at stake in the chemical trade are entirely

[118] Conclusions and Recommendations of the OECD Conference on International Co-operation concerning Transfrontier Movements of Hazardous Wastes, Basel, Switzerland, 26–27 Mar 1985.

[119] EC Doc COM(86) 362 final, p 21.

[120] Council Dir 84/631/EEC of 6 Dec 1984 on the supervision and control within the European Community of the transfrontier shipment of hazardous waste, OJ No L326, 13.12.1984, p 31.

[121] Council Dir 86/279/EEC of 12 June 1986 amending Council Dir 84/631/EEC, OJ No L181, 4.7.1986, p 13.

[122] Proposal for a Council Regulation concerning export from and import into the Community of certain dangerous chemicals, EC Doc COM(86) 362 final, 25 June 1986, OJ No C 177, 1987, p 5.

different from those involved in waste export operations, and the fact that the OECD member governments subscribed to the principle of prior informed consent in the context of waste shipments in 1985 did not necessarily indicate that they were prepared to accept the same standard for exports of chemicals. As a matter of fact, the preamble of a later OECD recommendation on exports of hazardous waste explicitly refutes the analogy by stressing 'the particular nature of wastes and *the distinction between wastes and products which are traded internationally*.'[123]

The Legal Basis Issue

As the Commission changed its political position with respect to the desirability of controlling exports of banned and severely restricted chemicals, it also had to modify its legal discourse concerning the Community's competence to take such measures. In its initial opposition to the European Parliament resolution, the Commission had accused the Parliament of trying to 'impose Community legislation unilaterally on third countries.'[124] By misrepresenting export controls as extra-territorial legislation, as an extension of Community standards to non-member states, the Commission implied that there was no legal basis in the EEC Treaty for regulating exports of hazardous products to third countries. As we saw above, early Community legislation with regard to pesticides and other chemical products, such as Directives 78/631/EEC and 79/117/EEC, was based on Article 100 (now Article 94) of the Treaty, which authorises directives laying down product standards for the Community's internal market but contains no reference to external trade with non-member states.

Even if, narrowly construed, Article 100 did not provide authority for Community measures regulating the export of pesticides, a sufficient legal basis for such measures could nevertheless be found in another provision of the EEC Treaty, even before the entry into force of the Single European Act. When the Commission became interested in taking a legislative initiative, it changed its legal discourse and suddenly 'discovered' a legal basis in the Treaty. It no longer stressed the limitations of the powers granted by Article 100 but found authority for Community action in Article 113 (now Article 133 EC). This article confers broad powers on the Community in the field of the 'common commercial policy', which covers all aspects of external trade with non-member countries, including, *inter alia*, '*export policy*'.

[123] OECD Council, Decision-Recommendation on Exports of Hazardous Wastes from the OECD Area, C(86)64(final) (5 June 1986) (emphasis added).

[124] Debates of the European Parliament, Sess 1983–84, OJ 1983, Annex 1–304, p 240 (Statement of Commissioner Narjes).

While it is true that the overall thrust of the common commercial policy is towards 'the progressive abolition of restrictions on international trade,'[125] including restrictions on exports, the 1962 Community Programme of Action for the implementation of the common commercial policy[126] did recognise that certain export restrictions might remain necessary for reasons such as those listed in Article 36 (now Article 30) of the Treaty, which include 'the protection of health and life of humans, animals or plants'. The Programme of Action provided for the unification at Community level of such export restrictions through decisions of the Council based on Article 113. This clearly implied that Article 113 empowers the Council to institute Community export controls.

In an important opinion on the scope of the common commercial policy, the Court of Justice of the European Communities later gave an extensive interpretation of the terms of Article 113, which easily accommodates measures to regulate external trade in hazardous products:

> Although it may be thought that at the time when the Treaty was drafted liberalization of trade was the dominant idea, the Treaty nevertheless does not form a barrier to the possibility of the Community's developing a commercial policy aiming at a regulation of the world market for certain products rather than at a mere liberalization of trade.[127]

In the same opinion, the Court also stressed the importance of a uniform regime governing external trade from the viewpoint of the functioning of the common market:

> A restrictive interpretation of the concept of common commercial policy would risk causing disturbances in intra-Community trade by reason of the disparities which would then exist in certain sectors of economic relations with non-member countries.[128]

The Commission first invoked Article 113 as a legal basis for Community action to regulate exports of banned or severely restricted chemicals in 1985, when it requested a mandate from the Council to participate in the negotiations on the FAO Code of Conduct on the Distribution and Use of Pesticides. The Commission based its request on Article 113, arguing that 'the Code's principle concern is trade policy, responsibility for which has been transferred by the member states to the Community.'[129] It should be noted though that, while the FAO Code does contain provisions concerning international trade in pesticides, most of its provisions deal with other aspects of pesticide distribution and use, and the Commission's claim

[125] EC Treaty, Art 133 (former Art 113 EEC).
[126] Programme d'action en matière de politique commerciale commune, JO 1962, p 2357.
[127] Opinion 1/78, *International Agreement on Natural Rubber*, [1979] ECR 2909.
[128] *Ibid.*
[129] EC Doc COM(85) 541 final, 15 Oct 1985, p 2.

that the instrument's 'principle concern' is trade policy was somewhat exaggerated.

The Commission probably did not really intend to claim that the entire subject matter of the Code fell within the ambit of the common commercial policy, but only those provisions designed to regulate exports of pesticides. However, the Council apparently felt that this was not a sufficient basis to give the Commission a formal negotiating mandate, since it did not accept the proposal. Nevertheless, the Commission did not depart from its view that Community measures to regulate exports of banned and severely restricted chemicals should properly be taken within the scope of the common commercial policy. Accordingly, the proposal for a regulation concerning export from and import into the Community of certain dangerous chemicals, which the Commission submitted to the Council in 1986,[130] was also based on Article 113. The choice of this legal basis was apparently so self-evident to the Commission that it did not deem it necessary to explain the reasons for it in its explanatory memorandum.

When the Commission formulated this proposal and chose to base it on Article 113, the proposed use of a trade policy instrument for environmental protection purposes was not entirely unprecedented. Indeed, since the early 1980s the Commission had submitted to the Council several proposals for trade-related environmental measures (TREMs) based on Article 113.[131] However, in each of these cases, the Council invariably rejected Article 113 and opted instead for Article 235 (now Article 308 EC) as the legal basis. The Commission nevertheless persisted in its view that Article 113 was the proper legal basis for such measures and consistently continued to base all proposals for TREMs on this provision of the Treaty.[132] The 1986 proposal for a regulation concerning the export and import of dangerous chemicals was one of them.

Notwithstanding the Council's reluctance to accept Article 113 as a legal basis for environmentally motivated trade measures, the Commission could find support for its interpretation of Article 113 in the rejection of a restrictive interpretation of the concept of 'common commercial policy' by the Court of Justice in Opinion 1/78. The subsequent development of the case-law of the Court confirms that the Commission's choice of legal basis was well-founded. In 1990, the Court of Justice ruled that Article 113

[130] EC Doc COM(86) 362 final, 25 June 1986.

[131] For a comprehensive overview and analysis of trade-related environmental measures (TREMs) in Community law, see Demaret (1993). The early measures referred to here all concerned restrictions on trade in wildlife: Regulation 348/81 banning the importation of whale products, Regulation 3626/82 implementing CITES, Dir 83/129/EEC banning the importation of seal skins and derived products. For further details, see Demaret (1993), pp 320–29.

[132] For further examples, see *ibid*, pp 330–31, 345–55. Only once did the Council follow the Commission and adopt an environmental measure with effects both within the Community and on external trade (Regulation (EEC) No 3254/91) on the combined legal basis of Art 113 and Art 130s.

constituted an 'appropriate legal basis' for a regulation restricting the import into the Community of radioactively contaminated agricultural products from third countries, adopted by the Council in the wake of the Chernobyl nuclear accident.[133]

This regulation had been challenged by Greece on the grounds that its purpose 'is not protection of trade but rather the protection of public health' and that it therefore could not be validly adopted under Article 113 of the Treaty. However, the Court upheld the regulation. It found that since the regulation 'is intended to regulate trade between the Community and non-member countries', the mere fact that its adoption was prompted by public health concerns was not sufficient to 'remove [it] from the sphere of the common commercial policy.'[134] The Court invoked the provisions of what was then Article 130r, paragraph 2 EC, according to which 'environmental protection requirements shall be a component of the Community's other policies,'[135] in support of its view that a measure taken under Article 113 may legitimately pursue other than purely commercial objectives.

The Commission's proposal for a regulation on the export of certain dangerous chemicals was drafted and submitted to the Council before the entry into force of the SEA. At that time, there could be little doubt that Article 113 was the appropriate, and probably only, legal basis for such a measure in the EEC Treaty. However, the situation had changed at the time of adoption of the proposal by the Council, as a result of the coming into force of the SEA. Indeed, the new provisions of Title VII, introduced into the EEC Treaty by the SEA, conferred broad environmental powers on the Community, which could also be relied on as a legal basis for measures to control exports of hazardous chemicals.

Article 130r, paragraph 1, as it stood following the entry into force of the SEA, provided for Community action 'to preserve, protect and improve the quality of the environment', without any limitation as to the territorial scope of the environment concerned. It further stipulated that Community action relating to the environment shall also have as an objective 'to contribute towards protecting human health'. Thus, since the SEA, the regulation of exports of banned and severely restricted chemicals with a view to protecting human health and the environment in third countries clearly falls within the ambit of the objectives of Community environmental policy as laid down in Article 130r. This is even more so after Maastricht, as the

[133] Case C–62/88, *Hellenic Republic v Council*, [1990] ECR I–1545. This judgment is often cited as *Chernobyl I*.

[134] *Ibid*.

[135] This integration requirement was introduced by the SEA and further strengthened by the TEU and the Treaty of Amsterdam. In its current form, Art 6 EC provides that 'environmental protection requirements must be integrated into the definition and implementation of [other] Community policies and activities . . . , in particular with a view to promoting sustainable development.'

international dimension of the Community's environmental policy was explicitly recognised by the TEU, which added to the list of environmental policy objectives in Article 130r, paragraph 1 (now Article 174, paragraph 1 EC) the promotion of 'measures at international level to deal with regional or worldwide environmental problems'. Consequently, since 1 July 1987, Article 130s (now Article 175, paragraph 1 EC) provides an alternative legal basis for the adoption of measures to regulate hazardous exports. This was the legal basis chosen by the Council when it adopted the regulation in 1988.

The Council's choice of legal basis in this case and its general reluctance to base TREMs on Article 133 EC has been criticised by the Commission and by commentators.[136] It is true that Community measures to regulate exports of hazardous chemicals to third countries are, per definition, 'intended to regulate trade between the Community and non-member countries', as understood by the Court in its *Chernobyl I* judgment, and must therefore prima facie be regarded as trade policy measures. In general, the Court has held that the choice of legal basis cannot depend only on the subjective intent of the institution concerned as to the purpose of a given measure, but 'must be based on objective factors which are amenable to judicial review.'[137] The effect of an export control measure on trade with third countries is certainly an 'objective factor' to which considerable weight must be given. As Article 6 of the Treaty stipulates that environmental protection requirements shall be integrated in other Community policies, it is perfectly legitimate for a measure taken within the framework of the common commercial policy to pursue an environmental objective, and such an objective does not disqualify it as a trade measure. Referring to the principle of integration, the Court of Justice has repeatedly stressed that a measure does not automatically come under Article 175 merely by reason of the fact that it pursues environmental protection objectives in conjunction with other objectives.[138]

[136] Based on his analysis of the case-law of the Court of Justice, Demaret (1993), pp 356–68, cogently argues that, notwithstanding the Council's consistent practice to the contrary, Art 113 (now Art 133) remains the proper legal basis for TREMs in the EC Treaty. He indicates, however, that the situation may be changed 'in borderline cases' as a result of the Maastricht amendments.

[137] Case 45/86, *Commission v Council*, [1987] ECR 1493, para 11.

[138] Case C–62/88, *Hellenic Republic v Council*, [1990] ECR I–1545, para 20. See also the *Titanium dioxide* judgment of 11 June 1991, Case C-300/89, *Commission v Council*, [1991] ECR I–2867, para 22. In this case the Court held that a measure which simultaneously pursues environmental protection objectives and the harmonisation of conditions of competition within the internal market should be based on Art 100a instead of Art 130s. However, the Court seems to have somewhat retreated from this view in more recent judgments. In its ruling of 17 Mar 1993 on the dispute between the Commission and the Council concerning the legal basis of Dir 91/156/EEC on waste, Case C–155/91, *Commission v Council*, [1993] ECR I–939, the Court of Justice held that the mere fact that a measure has an effect on the internal market does not, in and of itself, imply that it should be based on Art 100a. The use of Art 100a as a legal basis is not justified when the Community act only *incidentally* results in

Analysis of the 1986 Commission Proposal

The Commission's original proposal for what eventually became Regulation (EEC) No 1734/88 concerning export from and import into the Community of certain dangerous chemicals, even though it was substantially amended by the Council, is worth analysing in some detail, in view of the originality of the 'informed choice' system proposed by the Commission. Even though this system was not endorsed by the Council, the proposal nevertheless constituted an important political decision of the Commission of the European Communities and a significant contribution to the international regulatory debate in its own right. The Commission itself underscored the political significance of its proposal by describing the issue of hazardous exports as 'one of the most important political issues of the moment in respect to environmental matters and international trade.'[139]

After its initial reluctance to get involved in the regulation of chemical exports, the Commission realised that the Community as a major trading power could not ignore this issue and that the common commercial policy was the most appropriate framework for addressing it. At the time it was formulated, the proposed regulation was the most far-reaching and interventionist international regulatory proposal, contrasting sharply with the minimalist approach which had initially prevailed in other international fora. The measures proposed by the Commission were more stringent than anything contained in the recommendatory instruments developed by the

harmonisation of the conditions of competition. In this case, the Court found that the *primary purpose* of Dir 91/156/EEC was the protection of the environment, that it only had an incidental effect on the conditions of competition and trade, and that it was therefore properly based on Art 130s.

This case-law was confirmed in the judgment of 28 June 1994, Case C–187/93, *European Parliament v Council*, [1994] ECR I–2857, in which the Court ruled on the validity of the legal basis of Regulation (EEC) No 259/93 on the supervision and control of movements of waste within, into and out of the Community. This act, which regulates both intra-Community trade and external trade in waste, was based by the Council on Art 130s, while both the Commission and the Parliament considered that the proper legal basis was Art 100a combined with Art 113. The Court upheld the Council's choice of Art 130s as opposed to Art 100a on similar grounds as in Case C-155/91 but did not address the merits of the Parliament's claim that the regulation should also have been based on Art 113. Indeed, as this provision of the Treaty does not provide for parliamentary participation in the legislative process, the selection of Art 130s as the legal basis in lieu of Art 113 could not possibly have affected the Parliament's prerogatives. Consequently, the Court ruled out the claim as inadmissible insofar as it was based on Art 113. However, one has the impression that the Court, had it actually addressed the merits of this issue, would probably have rejected Art 113 as a legal basis just as it rejected Art 100a, since the primary purpose of the regulation's external trade provisions is not to promote free trade, but rather to *limit* exports and imports of wastes in order to ensure the protection of the environment both within the Community and outside its borders.

[139] Proposal for a Council Regulation concerning export from and import into the Community of certain dangerous chemicals, EC Doc COM(86) 362 final, 25 June 1986, Explanatory memorandum, p 4.

OECD, UNEP and the FAO at that time. The Commission's initiative was also especially significant as the first proposal for a *binding* legal instrument to regulate exports of banned and severely restricted chemicals. Notwithstanding the eventual rejection of its innovative provisions by the Council, the 1986 proposal did give a new and important impetus to the ongoing debate on prior informed consent in other international fora.

The legal form of the proposed Community measures, a regulation instead of a directive, was consistent with the Commission's choice to regard them, from a legal point of view, as trade policy measures. In order to ensure the uniformity of the rules governing external trade, most common commercial policy instruments based on Article 133 EC are regulations, which are preferred over directives because of their direct applicability.

The Commission proposed to introduce restrictions on the export of dangerous chemicals in two stages. In a first stage, it aimed to 'bring Community practice into line with existing international codes' by establishing a mandatory export notification procedure, which would ensure the application of those existing international standards 'at Community level and in a uniform manner.'[140] Recognising the need for the EC to improve on the information exchange measures recommended by the OECD, UNEP and the FAO, the Commission proposed to apply the principle of prior informed consent, or rather 'informed choice', as it preferred to call it, in a second stage:

> The Commission has felt it politically essential to introduce in the proposed regulation the principle of 'informed choice', which allows an importing third country, within a certain time limit, to give its consent or not to the importation of a dangerous chemical which is subject to a Community regulation.[141]

The 'informed choice' system, as proposed by the Commission, would only have come into effect two years after the entry into force of the regulation. The Commission hoped that UNEP and the OECD could in the meantime be convinced to include the same system in their respective instruments, and it requested a mandate from the Council to further negotiate on behalf of the EC in those organisations.

The Commission opted for a rather restrictive interpretation of the concept of 'banned or severely restricted chemicals', by proposing to limit the scope of application of the draft regulation to a limited list of chemicals banned or severely restricted under Community law. The need for a single list of chemicals for application of the regulation results from the proposal's objective to achieve a uniform regime for the export of hazardous chemicals from the Community, in order to avoid trade distortions. If the

[140] *Ibid*, p 2 (Communication from the Commission to the Council).
[141] *Ibid*.

Community instrument were to leave the interpretation of the concept of 'banned or severely restricted chemicals' to the member states, different chemicals would be subject to the regulation's provisions in each member state and the objective of instituting a uniform regime would be jeopardised.

It should be noted, however, that the mode of selection of chemicals proposed by the Commission reflected the lowest common denominator of the regulatory decisions of the member states. With respect to pesticides, for instance, the Commission proposed to apply export regulations to those substances whose marketing and use in the Community is prohibited by Directive 79/117/EEC. As was pointed out at the beginning of this chapter, this Directive only lists those pesticides which member states unanimously agree must be banned for environmental reasons. There are, however, many more pesticides that are banned or severely restricted under national law in one or more member states. To comply fully with relevant OECD, FAO and UNEP recommendations, all pesticides banned or severely restricted at the national level would need to be covered by export notification requirements. In the absence of complete harmonisation of pesticide controls within the EC, a uniform Community export notification scheme would not be sufficient to provide to importing third countries all the information they are entitled to under the applicable OECD, FAO and UNEP guidelines.

Under the proposed regulation, the export notification procedure would have been centralised at Community level. The Commission, and not the national authorities of the member states, would have been in charge of notifying importing countries. According to the Commission, 'this simplifies considerably the procedure envisaged by UNEP which requires double notification—at the moment of enactment of national laws and at the moment of export—for each of the twelve Member States.'[142] As noted, this 'simplification' is not of a purely procedural nature but also has significant substantive implications.

The Commission would have been in charge both of notifications of control actions and export notifications. The export notification procedure to be implemented during the first stage would have involved both the designated national authority of the member state and the Commission. Before exporting any listed chemicals, the exporter would have been required to inform the designated authority of the member state from which the product is to be exported and provide it with certain information concerning the shipment, including the country of destination and the chemical identity of the substance or preparation concerned. This information was to be forwarded by this national authority to the Commission, which in turn would have notified the government of the importing country, providing it with the information submitted by the exporter, as well as with 'a

[142] EC Doc COM(86) 362 final, 25 June 1986, Explanatory memorandum, p 8.

summary of regulatory restrictions in the Community relating to the chemical concerned.'[143]

Although, during the first stage, exports were not conditioned on the consent of the importing country, the draft regulation nevertheless provided that the Commission would inform the member state authority of 'any relevant reaction from the country of destination' to the export notification.[144] The national authority would have been required to communicate this information to the exporter. The Commission presumably hoped that exporters would exercise voluntary self-restraint in the event of a negative reaction from an importing country.

In the second stage, however, which was to take effect two years after the entry into force of the proposed regulation, additional restrictions would be imposed on exports of listed chemicals. Under the 'informed choice' system proposed by the Commission, the export from the Community of the chemicals covered by the regulation would have required an authorisation, to be issued by the designated authority of the member state of exportation. Article 4, paragraph 3 of the draft regulation provided that an authorisation should 'in no case . . . be given if the country of destination informs the Commission that it does not consent to the import of the chemical concerned'. However, the export authorisation would have been issued not only 'if the country of destination consents to the import of the chemical concerned', but also '*if no communication is received from that country within 60 days* of the date on which notification was sent by the Commission'.[145] Once issued, the export permit would have been valid for one year.

The system proposed by the Commission was a somewhat imperfect implementation of the principle of prior informed consent. The *explicit* consent of the importing country, which was called for in the 1983 European Parliament resolution, would not actually have been required. If the importing country did not react within 60 days, its silence would have been interpreted as *tacit* consent. This is probably why the Commission chose to label its proposed system 'informed choice' instead of using the more explicit terminology 'prior informed consent'.

It should be noted that the draft regulation was a compromise between various departmental interests within the Commission. The Directorate-General for Environment devised the 'informed choice' formula as a means of giving importing countries some opportunity to prevent unwanted shipments of hazardous chemicals without actually conditioning exports on their express consent. One of the main industry arguments against prior informed consent was that such a scheme would be impracticable because

[143] *Ibid*, Art 3, para 3.
[144] *Ibid*.
[145] *Ibid*, Art 4, para 2 (emphasis added).

developing countries lack the technical and administrative capacity to adequately deal with incoming export notifications and would simply fail to respond, thus holding up exports, even if they wished to import the chemical in question.

The Commission's proposal, which would have allowed exports to proceed if the importing country did not react, went some way towards meeting these objections. However, even this watered-down version of PIC was accepted with great reluctance by the Directorate-General for Industry, which feared that the proposed regulation would impose cumbersome bureaucratic constraints on EC exporters and thus put them at a competitive disadvantage vis-à-vis non-EC companies unhampered by similar export restrictions. This is why the informed choice system was not to be introduced immediately, as proposed in earlier drafts of the regulation, but only after two years, in the hope that other chemical-exporting countries could in the meantime be convinced to follow suit.

As a corollary of the compromise reached within the Commission on the 'informed choice' formula, the Commission's proposal also comprised a recommendation for a Council decision authorising the Commission to negotiate on behalf of the Community within the framework of the OECD and UNEP. Having at last endorsed some form of informed consent, the Commission proposed to take the lead in the international regulatory debate and to try and 'export' the informed choice formula to other international fora. The Commission's objective in these fora was to seek to ensure that exporters in other countries would be subject to similar constraints as those to be imposed on EC exporters. In the negotiating directives which it requested the Council to endorse, the Commission described its aim as to achieve

> a modification of existing notification procedures comprising essentially the introduction of the principle of prior informed choice of the authorities of the importing country *by means of a swift procedure.*[146]

The Commission was apparently convinced of the intrinsic value of its 'informed choice' system as a reasonable compromise between the interests of exporting and importing countries, especially in view of its 'swiftness', and saw this minimalist version of PIC as a model for a solution at the international level. It is somewhat surprising that the Commission proposal did not refer to the FAO as one of the international fora in which to pursue a Community initiative, notwithstanding the strong support expressed for PIC at the 1985 FAO Conference. Perhaps this was due to the Council's earlier refusal to grant the Commission a formal mandate to participate in the FAO Code of Conduct negotiations.

[146] EC Doc COM(86) 362 final, 25 June 1986, Recommendation for a Council Decision, Annex, para 1 (emphasis added).

The 1988 Export Notification Regulation

On 16 June 1988, two years after the submission of the original proposal by the Commission, the Council adopted Regulation (EEC) No 1734/88 concerning export from and import into the Community of certain dangerous chemicals.[147] In its final form, as adopted by the Council, the Regulation was substantially weaker than the Commission's initial proposal.

As mentioned above, the Regulation was based on Article 130s of the Treaty, instead of Article 113 as originally proposed by the Commission. The Council did not follow the Commission in considering the Regulation as a trade policy measure, but chose to treat it as an environmental policy measure under Article 130s, in view of its objective of protecting health and the environment. This choice was probably based primarily on political considerations related to the decision-making procedure. Apparently, member states were reluctant to accept the decision-making by qualified majority which would have resulted from the choice of Article 113 EEC as the legal basis, and opted instead for Article 130s because, at that time, it provided for unanimity.

The rejection of Article 113 as the legal basis may perhaps also to some extent have been motivated by the general reluctance of some member states to recognise that environmental protection can be a legitimate trade policy objective and to allow environmental considerations to 'contaminate' the Community's common commercial policy. The Commission argued strongly that Article 113 was the proper legal basis for this measure, and entered a formal statement in the minutes of the Council criticising the Council's decision to change the legal basis to Article 130s and reserving the right to challenge that decision in Court.[148] It did not, however, carry out this threat to initiate annulment proceedings against the Regulation.

The Council did not accept the 'informed choice' procedure proposed by the Commission, but opted instead for a minimal notification system modelled on the OECD Guiding Principles and corresponding FAO and UNEP provisions. The only reference to 'informed choice' is to be found in the preamble to the Regulation, which provides that the Council would consider, before 1 July 1990, 'the possibility of introducing into this Regulation the principle of prior informed choice'. This was to be done on the basis of a report on the implementation of the notification provisions followed by a proposal from the Commission. In fact, the Council rejected the Commission's view that the EC should take the lead internationally in

[147] Council Regulation (EEC) No 1734/88 of 16 June 1988 concerning export from and import into the Community of certain dangerous chemicals, OJ No L155, 22.6.1988, p 2 (hereafter referred to as Regulation 1734/88).

[148] *Agence Europe*, No 4673, 4 Dec 1987.

applying PIC and try to convince other international bodies to do the same. The Council did not wish to risk imposing on Community exporters a competitive disadvantage but chose to await further developments at the international level before taking any far-reaching regulatory initiatives.

Together with the Regulation, the Council adopted a resolution which, referring implicitly to the Dutch initiative to introduce PIC at the national level, welcomed 'action by Member States to test the practical value' of PIC and invited the Commission:

> to examine this question in greater detail and to submit, where necessary, in the light of the information supplied by the Member States *and developments in relevant international practices*, appropriate proposals with a view to the possible adjustment of the Community instrument.[149]

This resolution, which also noted the Commission's intention to participate in UNEP negotiations on PIC, clearly indicated that developments in other international fora would be a key determinant of further action by the Community. Thus the Community elected to remain a follower rather than become a leader.

The Regulation aims to establish 'a common system of notification and information.'[150] The preamble refers to the need for what it describes as 'uniform Community procedures' for the implementation of the recommendations of various international organisations on exports of banned and severely restricted substances. The system instituted by the Regulation is uniform in that it applies to a common list of banned and severely restricted chemicals governed by Community law and provides for a single export notification for the EC as a whole. As explained above, this implied that third countries would in fact receive less information from the Community and its member states than they would be receiving if each member state were to implement the international notification schemes individually. However, the common notification system established by the Regulation was not necessarily intended to be exclusive of other measures, since Article 8 explicitly envisages the possibility for member states to apply national notification systems to substances not covered by the Regulation. Actually, this provision implicitly recognised the limited scope of the Community notification scheme and its deficiencies with regard to the international recommendations, in view of the fact that there are many chemicals banned or severely restricted under national law in one or more member states which are not subject to notification requirements under the Regulation.

The responsibility for the implementation of the common notification procedure under the Regulation is assigned to the member states, which are

[149] Council Resolution of 16 June 1988, OJ No C170, 29.6.1988, p 1 (emphasis added).
[150] Reg 1734/88, Art 1.

to designate a competent national authority for this purpose.[151] In this respect, the Council did not follow the Commission's original proposal, which was to entrust the task of notifying third countries on behalf of the Community to the Commission. The provisions of the Regulation leave the designated national authority considerable discretion as to how notification will be effected. It only provides that the designated authority of the exporting member state 'shall take the necessary measures to ensure that the appropriate authorities of the country of destination receive notification.'[152] This language, which is very similar to and apparently inspired by that of the OECD Guiding Principles, does not explicitly require that the designated authority *itself* give notification. It would be possible for a member state to delegate that responsibility to the exporter, provided it can ensure that the notification requirement is effectively complied with. This is explicitly envisaged in a footnote to Annex II of the Regulation, which specifies the information to be given 'where the designated authority provides that the notification be made *by the exporter*'.

The Regulation itself does not impose any obligation directly on exporters. National implementing legislation seems required to this effect. This is somewhat unusual for a regulation, which in principle is directly applicable and should not require any national legislative measures to be effective. In this case, it is hard to see how the Regulation could be applied without additional national legislation specifying the obligations of exporters, either to notify third countries in accordance with the Regulation or to inform the designated authority in the exporting country of intended exports in order to enable it to carry out the notification. Indeed, the designated authority would need to be informed by exporters in order to be able to comply with its obligations under the Regulation. Normally, such a duty of information should have been imposed on exporters by the Regulation itself. It was perfectly possible to do so, and it is hard to understand why the Council did not include such provision. The instrument is worded more like a directive than a regulation. It almost seems as if the Council had in fact intended to adopt a directive in the form of a regulation.

The actual notification requirements introduced by the Regulation are rather minimal. It is only stipulated that the notification 'shall as far as possible take place prior to export' and shall contain the information listed in Annex II of the Regulation.[153] This includes details on the chemical identity of the substance, safety information and a 'summary of regulatory restrictions and reasons for them'. The only shipment-specific information to be provided is the expected date of export and the

[151] *Ibid*, Art 3.
[152] *Ibid*, Art 4, para 1.
[153] *Ibid*.

exporting country.[154] No details must be given about the identity of the exporter or importer. The information in the notification clearly is not intended to enable the importing country to prevent the shipment in question should it so desire, and seems quite inadequate for that purpose.

The Regulation additionally imposes a restriction on the transmission of information to importing countries, where it provides that this 'shall take into account the need to protect the confidentiality of data and ownership.'[155] Presumably this means that confidential, proprietary data shall not be transmitted as part of the notification procedure, though it is hard to see how the limited information required to be supplied pursuant to Annex II could contain such data. Some of the toxicological data developed by the manufacturer for registration purposes, which have been provided to national authorities and may have been used as a basis for imposing regulatory restrictions, could conceivably be of a proprietary nature. However, the Regulation requires information on reasons for regulatory restrictions to be provided only in summary form, which should make it easy to comply with the notification requirement without releasing confidential data.

The Regulation provides that notification shall be required only for the first export of a chemical listed in Annex I from the Community to a given third country. This single notification covers 'every subsequent export of the chemical concerned from the Community to the same third country.'[156] In order to enable exporters in other member states to know whether a particular chemical has already been notified to a particular country, the Regulation provides for the Commission to act as a clearing-house. Designated authorities are to send copies of all notifications to the Commission, which shall assign a reference number to them and distribute them to designated authorities in other member states. The reference numbers shall also be published in the *Official Journal* of the EC. Subsequent exports of the same chemical to the same country must be 'accompanied by a reference to the number of the notification published in the *Official Journal*.'[157] Such reference, however, is unlikely to be of much use to importing countries, which cannot be expected to read the *Official Journal*. It is doubtful whether the reference number can serve as a reminder of the earlier notification anyway, since it does not occur on that notification when originally received by the importing country but is assigned to it by the Commission *ex post facto*. It seems to be essentially a formal requirement designed to enable customs authorities to check compliance with notification procedures.

In principle, notification is given to each third country only once. The Council has opted for one-time-only export notification, like the OECD,

[154] Reg 1734/88, Annex II.
[155] *Ibid*, Art 4, para 5.
[156] *Ibid*, Art 4, para 3.
[157] *Ibid*.

instead of 'periodical' notification as recommended by UNEP. The Regulation does provide, however, that 'notification must be given afresh, whenever major changes are made to the rules concerning the substances in question.'[158] This would apply only in the event of a change in *Community* rules relating to the substance in question, since Community law forms the basis of the common notification system.

The Council's lack of concern for the effectiveness of the Regulation appears not only from the incomplete nature of its provisions from the viewpoint of direct applicability and the shortcomings of the notification procedure both as regards frequency and content of the notification, but also from the fact that the Council even watered down those provisions in the Commission proposal which were designed to promote voluntary compliance by exporters. While the Regulation does not require the consent of importing countries, it is not to be excluded that a country receiving a notification may nevertheless respond to it and object to the intended export. The Regulation contemplates this eventuality where it provides that designated national authorities shall inform the Commission of 'any significant reaction from the country of destination.'[159] This information is then to be communicated to all member states by the Commission. But the Regulation does not specify what use is to be made of it. The provision in the Commission's original proposal which required the designated authority of the member state of export to inform the exporter of the response from the country of destination was deleted by the Council.

An interesting question is whether a member state which has been informed of an objection from an importing country would be free to prohibit the export under national law should it wish to do so, notwithstanding the fact that the export is not banned by the Regulation. This is not a purely hypothetical situation, as some member states, notably the Netherlands and Germany, have national legislation providing authority to ban exports of pesticides. The problem of residual national powers in the field covered by the Regulation has apparently been envisaged more explicitly by the Commission in its original proposal than by the Council.[160] As mentioned above, Article 8 of the Regulation reserves the possibility for member states to apply at the national level 'similar *information* procedures' to those laid down in the Regulation with respect to substances not covered by the Community notification system, but the provision does not refer to the possibility of national measures other than information procedures, such as, eg export control measures.

[158] *Ibid*, Art 4, para 4.

[159] *Ibid*, Art 4, para 2.

[160] On the question of residual national powers with respect to TREMs, see also Demaret (1993), pp 368–81.

However, the Commission proposal explicitly recognised that, by virtue of the general provisions of Regulation (EEC) No 2603/69 establishing common rules for exports,[161] member states retained the right to take national measures prohibiting the export of specific chemicals for health or environmental reasons. Indeed, its preamble noted that the regulation 'authorize[s] Member States to adopt or apply export . . . prohibitions . . . on grounds inter alia of protection of health and life of humans, animals or plants', while Article 4, paragraph 7 of the Commission proposal stipulated that

> any decision taken by a Member State in accordance with Article 11 of Regulation (EEC) No 2603/69 affecting the export of chemicals shall be communicated forthwith to the Commission which shall inform the other Member States.

No similar provision is contained in the Regulation as finally adopted by the Council, but it would seem that, even in the absence of an express provision to that effect, Regulation (EEC) No 1734/88 should not be interpreted as intending to derogate from the general provisions of the 1969 Regulation in respect of the residual powers of the member states.

As a form of information exchange additional to the export notification, the Regulation imposes labelling requirements on the exported chemicals that are subject to the notification system. In this respect, the Council adopted the Commission's original proposal virtually unchanged. Article 5 provides that these chemicals shall comply with the same packaging and labelling requirements as are applicable within the Community, 'without prejudice to any specific requirements of the importing country'. Thus, Community packaging and labelling standards shall apply to the extent that they are not incompatible with any requirements existing in the importing country. The Community standards have a subsidiary function in the absence of standards in the importing country. These provisions on packaging and labelling are a rather original feature of the EEC Regulation. No similar provisions are to be found in the OECD Guiding Principles or in the FAO Code of Conduct. Only UNEP's London Guidelines recognise the 'desirability' of imposing minimum labelling requirements on exported chemicals, whether banned or severely restricted or not.

The Implementation of the 1988 Regulation

Article 7 of the Regulation required member states to provide the Commission with information on the implementation of the notification requirements. Based on this information, the Commission was to report 'regularly'

[161] Reg (EEC) No 2603/69 of the Council of 20 Dec 1969 establishing common rules for exports, OJ Spec Ed 1969 (II), p 590, Art 11.

to the Council and the European Parliament. The preamble stipulated that the first report should be compiled before 1 January 1990 and thereafter every two years. However, the Commission did not submit any report before March 1993, ie after Regulation 1734/88 had already been repealed and replaced by a new Regulation in 1992. Significantly, the explanatory memorandum of the Commission proposal leading to the adoption of this new Regulation did not contain any information about the operation of Regulation 1734/88 and the experience that could be drawn from it.

According to the 1993 Commission report, in a period of over three years, ie from the entry into force of the Regulation until 1 November 1992, not more than 60 export notifications were effectuated pursuant to it for the Community as a whole. Only six member states reported notifications to the Commission. The other six confirmed to the Commission that, 'to their knowledge', they did not export any of the products covered by the Regulation.[162] Of the 21 substances or groups of substances listed in Annex I to the Regulation, only eight were the subject of notifications. In all, notifications were addressed to some 30 importing countries.[163] Whether due to non-compliance or to other causes, the small number of notifications, products and third countries of destination involved indicates the limited practical significance of Regulation 1734/88.

THE 1992 REGULATION CONCERNING EXPORT AND IMPORT OF CERTAIN DANGEROUS CHEMICALS: INCORPORATING THE PRINCIPLE OF PRIOR INFORMED CONSENT

In a compromise between advocates and opponents of PIC among the member states, the Council, when it adopted Regulation (EEC) No 1734/88, had undertaken to reconsider the introduction of a PIC procedure at Community level two years later, and invited the Commission to submit appropriate proposals before July 1990. The Commission, in a formal statement recorded in the Council minutes, had expressly 'dissociated itself' from the Council decision not to translate the principle of 'informed choice' into EC law immediately, as it had originally proposed in 1986. It had solemnly reaffirmed its commitment to this principle as 'the only acceptable basis for the Community's exports of chemical products whose use is banned or strictly limited in the Community', noting 'growing international pressure for its adoption.'[164] One could say that there was in fact a political understanding between the Council and the Commission that the matter

[162] Report of the Commission on the Implementation of Regulation (EEC) No 1734/88, EC Doc COM(93) 121 final, 31 Mar 1993, p 3.

[163] *Ibid*, Annex A2.

[164] *Agence Europe*, No 4673, 4 Dec 1987.

would be reconsidered on the basis of the outcome of the negotiations on PIC that were then going on in UNEP and the FAO.

The Commission closely followed those negotiations and, as soon as agreement on a PIC scheme started taking shape in those international fora, began to draft proposals for amending Regulation 1734/88. It is symptomatic of the recognised inadequacy of that Regulation that proposals for amending it were being drafted even before it had entered into force on 22 June 1989.[165] Nevertheless, the Commission did not manage to meet the target date of 1 July 1990 mentioned in the preamble of the 1988 Regulation; it submitted its proposal to the Council a few months later, on 17 December 1990.[166] The new Regulation concerning Community exports and imports of certain dangerous chemicals, Regulation (EEC) No 2455/92, was eventually adopted by the Council on 23 July 1992.[167] It entered into force on 29 November 1992 and replaced Regulation 1734/88, which it formally repealed.[168]

Regulation 2455/92 considerably expands on Regulation 1734/88 by supplementing the Community export notification scheme, in force since 1989, with a PIC procedure based on the recommendations contained in the amended London Guidelines and the FAO Code of Conduct. Apart from introducing the PIC procedure, the 1992 Regulation also makes a number of improvements in the existing export notification procedure, thus filling a substantial legal vacuum and removing certain ambiguities inherent in the provisions of the 1988 Regulation, and rendering the notification system potentially more effective and uniformly applicable throughout the Community.

Expanded Obligations of Exporters and Designated National Authorities

The new Regulation specifies that the designated national authority of the member state of export shall itself notify the country of destination, and that the exporter is under an obligation to provide it with the information necessary to that effect, no later than 30 days before export is due to take place. Under the 1988 Regulation, member states could delegate the duty of notification to the exporters themselves and were only required to 'take the necessary measures to ensure' that the notification 'as far as possible take place prior to export.' The 1992 Regulation provides that the export

[165] A first draft proposal for amendments was presented by the Commission to national experts at the first meeting of the designated authorities for the application of Council Regulation No 1734/88 on 22–23 June 1989, see EC Doc XI/155/89-Rev 1.

[166] Proposal for a Council Regulation (EEC) concerning export and import of certain dangerous chemicals, EC Doc COM(90) 591 final, OJ C 17, 25.1.1991, p 16.

[167] Council Reg (EEC) No 2455/92 of 23 July 1992 concerning exports and imports of certain dangerous chemicals, OJ No L 251, 29.8.1992, p 13 (hereafter referred to as Reg 2455/92).

[168] *Ibid*, Art 12, para 1.

notification 'shall as far as possible take place at least 15 days before export.'[169] However, the notification requirements 'may be waived wholly or partly at the discretion of the designated authority of the exporting Member State' in 'an emergency situation in which any delay may endanger public health or the environment in the importing country'. The export notification procedure, originally introduced by the 1988 Regulation, continues to apply to chemicals banned or severely restricted under Community law, as listed in Annex I of Regulation 2455/92. Three pesticides which were banned under Community law between 1988 and 1990[170] were added to this list of chemicals subject to export notification requirements.

Strengthened Packaging and Labelling Requirements

The new Regulation also strengthens the packaging and labelling requirements for exported chemicals, initially introduced by Article 5 of Regulation 1734/88. These requirements now apply not only to chemicals banned or severely restricted under Community law, as provided in the 1988 Regulation, but generally to all 'dangerous chemicals . . . intended for export' which would be subject to Community provisions relating to packaging and labelling if they were marketed within the EC.[171] However, the requirement of compliance with EC packaging and labelling standards is qualified by the proviso that 'this obligation shall be without prejudice to any specific requirements of the importing country' and that

> the label need comply with only the requirements of the importing third country if such requirements ensure the label has all the health, safety and environment related information which EEC use would require.[172]

This provision emphasises the priority to be given to the standards of the importing country and stresses the complementary function of EC standards. Another new provision requires that label information be given in the language of the country of destination 'as far as practicable.'[173]

Mandatory Application of the Prior Informed Consent Procedure

The most important provisions of Regulation 2455/92 are those relating to the PIC procedure. Article 5, paragraph 4 of the 1992 Regulation

[169] *Ibid*, Art 4, para 1.
[170] Nitrofen, 1,2-dibromoethane and 1,2-dichloroethane.
[171] *Ibid*, Art 7, para 1. It should be noted that the Council went beyond the Commission's initial proposal in making the labelling and packaging requirements applicable to *all* exported dangerous chemicals. The Commission had originally proposed that they should apply only to the chemicals listed in Annexes I and II of the Regulation, ie those subject to the export notification and/or PIC procedure. Cf Commission proposal, above n 166, Art 6, para 1.
[172] *Ibid*, Art 7, para 1.
[173] *Ibid*, Art 7, para 2.

explicitly provides that 'the exporter shall be required to comply with the decision of the country of destination participating in the PIC procedure'. Contrary to the ambiguous regime of Regulation 1734/88, Regulation 2455/92 thus imposes obligations directly on exporters. The necessary information for the application of the PIC procedure in the Community is to be incorporated in Annex II of the Regulation. According to Article 5, paragraph 3, this Annex shall include the international list of banned and severely restricted chemicals subject to the PIC procedure, as established jointly by UNEP and the FAO, the list of countries participating in UNEP/FAO voluntary scheme and the decisions taken by these countries regarding the import of the listed chemicals. The purpose of including all this information in an annex to the Regulation is to make the international PIC procedure enforceable as part of European Community law.

When the Regulation was formally adopted in July 1992, however, Annex II was left blank. In the text of Regulation 2455/92 as published in the *Official Journal*, Annex II bears the heading 'Chemicals subject to the international PIC procedure and the PIC decisions of importing countries' but contains no entries. The reason for this is that, at the time the Commission submitted its proposal to the Council, UNEP/FAO scheme was not yet operational: the initial list of chemicals subject to PIC had not yet been established by the competent UNEP/FAO Joint Group of Experts; consequently, participating countries had not yet been able to take any official decisions on the importation of those chemicals under the PIC procedure either. Although a first list of 20 chemicals subject to the international PIC scheme had been drawn up by UNEP/FAO expert group[174] by the time Regulation 2455/92 was adopted by the Council, no effort was made to include this information in Annex II at that time. It is only in January 1994 that the first entries in Annex II were formally adopted.[175]

By imposing a direct obligation on exporters to comply with explicit PIC decisions of importing countries, the EC acted in accordance with the relevant provisions of the FAO Code of Conduct and the amended London Guidelines which require exporting countries to take appropriate measures to ensure that exports do not occur contrary to the decisions of participating importing countries. However, the actual enforcement measures to be taken were left at the discretion of the member states, as Article 6 of the 1992 Regulation only provides that they 'shall take appropriate legal or administrative action in case of infringement'. The Commission had initially proposed the imposition of 'severe or dissuasive sanctions . . . on persons exporting chemicals subject to the international PIC procedure . . .

[174] See *Report of the Third FAO/UNEP Joint Meeting on Prior Informed Consent*, Rome, 3–7 June 1991, Annex 2.

[175] See below n 181.

contrary to the PIC decision of the country of destination,'[176] but that requirement apparently proved too specific for some member states.

In contrast with the language in Article 5, paragraph 4, the provisions of Article 5, paragraph 5 dealing with exports to countries participating in the PIC procedure but which have not taken a formal PIC decision with respect to a particular chemical listed in Annex II, are not formulated in an imperative manner. In conformity with the corresponding clauses in the London Guidelines and the FAO Code of Conduct, these provisions state that in such case:

> the *status quo* with respect to importation of the chemical should continue. This means that the chemical *should* not be exported without the explicit consent of the importing country, unless it is a pesticide which is registered in the importing country or is a chemical the use or importation of which has been allowed by other governmental action of the importing country.[177]

It would be hard to read these provisions as imposing a positive obligation on exporters in the same manner as Article 5, paragraph 4. The Commission apparently did not consider this necessary, since its original proposal did not include any specific provisions dealing with such cases.[178]

As the delay in the adoption of the first entries in Annex II indicates, the procedure for including all information relating to the PIC procedure in Annex II of the Regulation is bound to cause problems with the application of the PIC system by the Community. Indeed, changes in this information are communicated by UNEP/FAO every six months, as new chemicals are added to the PIC list and new PIC decisions are taken by participating importing countries. This is a routine matter since the PIC procedure became fully operational. However, under Article 11, paragraph 2 of the Regulation, any such changes require a formal amendment of Annex II to become applicable at Community level. This provision stipulates that the 'amendments initiated by UNEP and FAO' to the information in Annex II 'shall be adopted' in accordance with a qualified-majority comitology procedure laid down in the 1967 Directive on the classification, packaging and labelling of dangerous substances.[179] This rather cumbersome procedure, which is clearly designed to give the member states a share of decision-making authority, is quite inappropriate in this case, since it seems to imply that 'adoption' of these amendments is a discretionary decision of the relevant Community institutions. In fact, however, such amendments should be a mere formality since, under the

[176] Commission proposal, above n 166, Art 5, para 4.
[177] Reg 2455/92, Art 5, para 5 (emphasis added).
[178] Commission proposal, above n 166, Art 5, para 4.
[179] Council Dir 67/548/EEC of 27 June 1967 on the approximation of laws, regulations and administrative provisions relating to the classification, packaging and labelling of dangerous substances, OJ No L196, 16.8.1967, p 1, Art 21.

international PIC procedure, changes to the list of chemicals subject to PIC and PIC decisions of importing countries are not actually within the Community's jurisdiction. Exporting countries have no discretion whether or not to 'adopt' these changes but are committed to apply the PIC list as established by UNEP/FAO and to respect the decisions of importing countries. The procedure laid down in Regulation 2455/92 results in unnecessary delay and could lead third countries to doubt the Community's intention to comply faithfully with the international PIC scheme.

Responsibilities of the Commission

Article 3, paragraph 2 of the Regulation provides that the Commission 'shall act as common designated authority' on behalf of the Community as far as its participation in the international PIC procedure is concerned. This implies that the Commission shall act as the focal point for the receipt of information from UNEP/FAO on the application of the PIC procedure, as well as for the communication of decisions on the importation of chemicals subject to the PIC procedure taken by the Community in accordance with the relevant provisions of Regulation 2455/92 and other Community legislation. In addition, Article 5, paragraph 1 of the Regulation stipulates that the Commission shall notify to UNEP/FAO the chemicals banned or severely restricted in the Community, as listed in Annex I, providing all the information required under the relevant international instruments.

The Regulation deals not only with the export of dangerous chemicals from the Community, but also with action to be taken with respect to the import of chemicals subject to the PIC procedure *into* the Community. In this respect, Article 5, paragraph 2 provides that 'the Commission shall evaluate in close cooperation with the Member States the risks posed by the chemicals' notified by UNEP/FAO as subject to PIC, and shall take a decision on the future import of these chemicals in accordance with the comitology procedure of Directive 67/548/EEC. If the chemical in question is not already banned or severely restricted by Community law, import permission 'shall not normally be refused'. However, based on the information received, the Commission may in this case decide to make a proposal to the Council to ban or severely restrict the chemical in question and may then impose 'interim import conditions' pending a decision by the Council.

It is expressly stipulated that, in any event, the Commission 'shall ensure that the response [it gives to PIC notifications received from UNEP/FAO] does not conflict with existing Community legislation.'[180]

[180] Reg 2455/92, Art 5, para 2.

These provisions are clearly based on the assumption that existing Community law is generally adequate to control imports of chemicals into the Community and shall not be superseded by the PIC procedure, but that information received under the PIC procedure may be taken into account in revising Community law. Where a chemical subject to PIC is banned or severely restricted by national legislation in one or several member states, but not at Community level, the Commission shall take this into account in formulating the Community's response to UNEP/FAO.

Implementation and Amendment of the 1992 Regulation

The first amendment to Regulation 2455/92 was made in January 1994, by a Commission Regulation[181] which finally laid down the first entries in Annex II, listing a number of chemicals subject to the PIC procedure and decisions of a series of participating importing countries with respect to those chemicals. As a result of this Regulation, which entered into force on 12 February 1994, Community exporters became legally required to comply with the decisions of a number of third countries banning the import of such pesticides as aldrin, dieldrin, DDT, dinoseb, fluoroacetamide and HCH. These decisions, taken within the framework of the voluntary UNEP/FAO PIC scheme, were officially notified to all governments and the European Community by FAO on 25 August 1992.

Thus, it was one and a half year after the adoption of Regulation 2455/92 that the Community actually took the necessary legislative action to make the PIC provisions of the regulation operational. Ironically, in May 1993, the Commission published a brochure on the Community's policy with respect to exports of banned or severely restricted chemicals,[182] boasting that Regulation 2455/92 'makes the PIC procedure mandatory for the export of chemicals from the Community to participating countries' and 'could serve as a model for a workable international PIC system'. However, the brochure fails to mention that, at the time of its publication, the Community's much-hailed mandatory PIC procedure was not yet operational for lack of any entries in Annex II of the regulation.

It should also be noted that the 1994 Commission Regulation, covering six substances only, was insufficient for the Community to fulfil its commitments under the FAO/UNEP scheme, as no fewer than 17 chemicals had already been made subject to the PIC procedure internationally and PIC

[181] Commission Reg (EC) No 41/94 of 11 Jan 1994 amending Annex II of Council Reg (EEC) No 2455/92 concerning the export and import of certain dangerous chemicals, OJ No L8, 12.1.1994, p 1.

[182] Commission of the European Communities, *Informing the Importer—Guide to Council Regulation EEC/2455/92 concerning the export and import of certain dangerous chemicals*, Luxembourg, May 1993.

decisions of a large number of participating countries concerning those chemicals formally notified by the FAO/UNEP. Moreover, the first version of Annex II, as laid down by the Commission Regulation of January 1994, did not contain a full list of countries participating in UNEP/FAO PIC scheme, as required by Article 5, paragraph 3(b) of Regulation 2455/92, but only listed those participating countries which had notified their PIC decisions with respect to the six chemicals concerned. As a result of this omission, the provisions of Article 5, paragraph 5 relating to the *status quo* in regard to exports of chemicals to non-responding participating countries could not be applied. Annex II was updated and completed only two and a half years later.[183]

Another amendment of Regulation 2455/92 was adopted by the Council in December 1994. It added a number of pesticides (including PCP, ethylene oxide, dinoseb, captafol, and dicofol) and industrial chemicals to the list of chemicals banned or severely restricted in the Community in Annex I of Regulation 2455/92. This was the result of a Commission proposal of March 1993,[184] which was itself a direct consequence of internal Community measures to ban or severely restrict the substances in question agreed by the Council in 1990 and 1991. One may wonder why the Commission waited until March 1993 to propose the necessary amendments to Annex I resulting from those measures, which were all taken *before* the adoption of Regulation 2455/92 by the Council on 23 July 1992, instead of inviting the Council at that time to incorporate them in Annex I at once. Fifteen more chemicals were added to the list in December 1994.[185]

The delays in the adoption, respectively amendment of Annexes I and II are symptomatic of a certain lack of diligence on the part of the Commission and the Council in making Regulation 2455/92 fully effective.

In July 1995, the European Commission, in cooperation with the European Parliament, organised a three-day 'Conference on International Trade in Dangerous Chemicals' in Brussels. This conference was intended to assess the effectiveness of Regulation 2455/92, to analyse the chemicals management situation in developing countries and the role of information exchange and PIC procedures in improving it, and to formulate recommendations for future measures and policy in this field. It was attended by

[183] Commission Reg (EC) No 1492/96 of 26 July 1996 amending Annexes II and III of Council Reg (EEC) No 2455/92 concerning the export and import of certain dangerous chemicals, OJ No L189, 1996, p 19. A further update was made by Commission Reg (EC) No 1237/97 of 27 June 1997 amending Annex II of Council Reg (EEC) No 2455/92 concerning the export and import of certain dangerous chemicals, OJ No L173, 1.7.1997, p 37.

[184] Proposal for a Council Regulation amending for the first time Annex I of Council Reg (EEC) No 2455/92 concerning the export and import of certain dangerous chemicals, EC Doc COM(93) 120 final, 25 Mar 1993.

[185] See Council Reg (EC) No 3135/94 of 15 Dec 1994 amending Annex I of Council Reg (EEC) No 2455/92 concerning the export and import of certain dangerous chemicals, OJ No L332, 22.12.1994, p 1.

representatives of all interested parties, including government representatives from EU member states and non-EU countries, in particular chemical-importing developing countries, as well as representatives of various intergovernmental organisations with an interest in chemical safety, of industry, trade unions and NGOs.

In preparation for the conference, the Commission had commissioned the German aid agency GTZ to conduct a survey of designated national authorities in importing countries and other interested actors to evaluate the impact of the EU's export notification and PIC procedures. This survey showed that many public authorities in importing third countries were not familiar with the EC measures of which they are the supposed primary beneficiaries, that notifications often did not reach the competent authorities and that the information provided in export notifications was inadequate to meet the needs of importing countries.

During the conference it was stressed by all participants that information exchange and PIC procedures were not in themselves sufficient to ensure chemical safety in developing countries and that more efforts should be devoted to training and capacity building. Several suggestions were formulated by participants for improving the existing EU measures: providing more information in export notifications, especially information concerning the port of entry and identity of the importer, developing provisions for more effective control of shipments in cooperation with customs authorities, extending export notification requirements to all chemicals subject to PIC, including those which are not banned or severely restricted under EC law, etc. Participants also called on the EU to contribute actively to the development of a global, legally binding instrument on PIC.

In his closing statement, the representative of the Commission agreed that a revision of Regulation 2455/92 was necessary and announced that a proposal to this effect would be prepared as soon as possible. Indeed, some amendments to Annex III of the Regulation, which lists the information to be provided to importing countries in export notifications, were adopted in July 1996.[186] More information must now be supplied in the notifications, including the identity of the importer. However, no further revisions of the Regulation were proposed prior to the adoption of UNEP/FAO PIC Convention. As soon as the Rotterdam Convention had been signed, the Commission started working on a proposal for a new regulation designed to bring Community law in line with the provisions of the Convention. This proposal was submitted to the Council in early 2002.[187]

[186] Commission Reg (EC) No 1492/96, above n 183.

[187] Proposal for a Council Regulation concerning the export and import of dangerous chemicals, EC Doc COM (2001) 803 final, OJ C126E, 28.5.2002, p 291.

16

The Implementation of International Norms by the United States: The Evolution of National Law and Policy

IN CHAPTER 11, I have analysed the development of national legislation on pesticide exports in the United States in the 1970s, which preceded and strongly influenced the development of international standards, especially in the 1980s. In order to assess the effectiveness of international normative efforts in this area, it is necessary to take a look at the subsequent evolution of national law and policy in the United States, to see whether the various international instruments adopted in the 1980s and 1990s have had any effect on the law and practice of the United States, which remains an important exporter of pesticides in the world market.

The existing labelling and export notification provisions of the FIFRA have repeatedly been criticised in the US Congress as insufficient and ineffective, and there have been a number of proposals to regulate exports more strictly by requiring the express consent of the importing country. According to a leading congressional advocate of stringent export controls:

> *Notification is not control.* What we need is a mechanism for controlling these exports—for saying that, as a matter of public policy, they will not be permitted except under limited circumstances.[1]

Yet, notwithstanding frequent congressional and public criticism of the notification system and the numerous proposals which have been made from all sides for changing it in one sense or the other, Section 17 of the FIFRA has remained unchanged to this day. Several bills to amend its provisions were introduced in the 1980s and 1990s,[2] but Congress did not adopt any of them.

[1] 126 Cong Rec H1234 (daily ed 25 February 1980) (Statement of Rep Barnes) (emphasis added).

[2] See, eg, HR 6587, 96th Cong, 2nd Sess (1980), 126 Cong Rec H1243 (daily ed, 25 Feb 1980); HR 2439, 97th Cong, 1st Sess (1981); HR 3254, 98th Cong, 1st Sess (1983); HR 1416, 99th Cong, 1st Sess (1985); HR 2580, 99th Cong, 1st Sess (1985); HR 4364, 99th Cong, 2nd Sess (1986); S 2227, 101st Cong 2nd Session (1990); S 898, 102nd Cong, 1st Sess (1991).

As we have seen in chapter 12, the export notification system introduced by the FIFRA served as a model for the development of the first generation of international soft law instruments designed to promote the exchange of information on banned and severely restricted chemicals in international trade. However, the provisions of these instruments were not in all respects identical to the American system. For instance, there is a difference in scope between the export provisions of the FIFRA and the voluntary notification schemes recommended by the OECD, UNEP and the FAO in the mid-1980s. The scope of application of the provisions of section 17 (a) of the FIFRA is not determined by reference to the concept of 'banned or severely restricted' pesticides as defined in various international instruments, but rather by reference to the notion of pesticides not 'registered' for use in the United States.

The EPA has always asserted that the 'purchaser acknowledgement statement' system, as it has existed under the FIFRA since 1978, is sufficient for the US to comply with the export notification requirements laid down in the relevant recommendations of the OECD, UNEP and the FAO.[3] The accuracy of this assertion hinges on how one interprets the definition of a 'severely restricted' chemical or pesticide under these voluntary instruments. As discussed in chapter 12, it can be argued that at least some 'restricted use' pesticides, which are not subject the FIFRA's export notification requirements under the terms of section 17 (a), must be regarded as 'severely restricted chemicals' within the meaning of the early OECD and UNEP definitions of this concept and should therefore be subject to those requirements. This, however, has consistently been denied by the US government, which found support for its more restrictive definition in the FAO Code of Conduct, which equates a 'severe restriction' with a ban on 'virtually all uses' of a pesticide. On the other hand, in another respect the scope of the FIFRA's export provisions is broader than that of the international instruments, in that they also apply to pesticides which were never submitted for registration in the United States, even when such pesticides are not covered by the international definitions of 'banned' and 'severely restricted' chemicals.

In the mid-1980s, the EPA carried out an evaluation of the effectiveness of the FIFRA notification provisions, in which an EPA official visited a number of African countries to find out what use was made of notifications from the United States in the receiving countries. The conclusion of this field research was 'that most of the information provided was adequate—but that almost none of it was reaching people who could effectively use it.'[4] The author of the study also expressed her opinion that 'the costs of

[3] See 'OECD Committee to Seek Council Action on Guidance Affecting Chemical Exports', *US Export Weekly* 19 (1983), p 417.

[4] Halter (1984), p 1. See also Lindsay (1985).

requiring importing nations to give prior consent for certain export shipments are likely to outweigh the potential benefits.'[5] It should be noted, however, that this was not an official statement of the EPA's position and that this view was expressed before the United States reluctantly joined in the international consensus that the principle of prior informed consent should be incorporated in the provisions of UNEP London Guidelines and the FAO Code of Conduct. Another important review of US policy was carried out a few years later by the United States General Accounting Office, which issued a highly critical report in April 1989 in which it accused the EPA of not adequately monitoring compliance by pesticide manufacturers with the FIFRA's export notification requirements.[6]

In response to these criticisms, and ostensibly also in response to the evolution of the international normative process on hazardous exports in the late 1980s, the EPA began to devote more attention to enforcement action[7] and announced a review of its official policy on the implementation section 17 of the FIFRA in early 1990.[8] According to the EPA's announcement, the purpose of the review was to make the notification programme 'more responsive to the concerns of the US public, international organisations and representatives of other countries about international trade in and use of pesticides.'[9] By the end of the 1980s, the EPA had reached the 'conclusion that improving notification procedures is not enough.'[10] Referring explicitly to the emerging international consensus on PIC, the Agency indicated that one of its new aims was 'to bring US activities into conformity with recently developed international procedures' and announced its intention to implement the voluntary PIC procedure 'to the extent possible under its current legislative authority.'[11] The policy review was actually only completed three years later,[12] and its eventual outcome fell well short of full implementation of the PIC procedure.

In fact, the main changes introduced in the EPA's policy relate to the interpretation of the labelling requirements for exported pesticides and of the categories of 'unregistered' pesticides subject to export notification requirements under section 17 (a), and the information provided in, and procedures for the transmission of, notifications of control actions pursuant

[5] Halter (1987), p 36.

[6] United States General Accounting Office, *Export of Unregistered Pesticides Is Not Adequately Monitored by EPA*, Report to the Chairman, Environment, Energy, and Natural Resources Subcommittee, Committee on Government Operations, House of Representatives, No GAO/RCED-89-128, Apr 1989, 40 pp.

[7] See Crowe (1992).

[8] EPA, 'Pesticide Export Policy Review', *Federal Register* 55 (12 Feb 1990), pp 4956–4967.

[9] *Ibid*, p 4956.

[10] *Ibid*, p 4957.

[11] *Ibid*, p 4959.

[12] EPA, 'Pesticide Export Policy—Final Policy Statement', *Federal Register* 58 (18 Feb 1993), pp 9062–9090.

to section 17 (b). The labelling requirements have been clarified and expanded. Additional warnings are required for highly toxic pesticides, and the information on the label is to be provided in multilingual form, ie in English and 'an acceptable language of the country of import,'[13] including the statement 'Not Registered for Use in the United States of America', to which additional explanatory text may be added to explain the regulatory status of the pesticide in the US.[14] The exemption of some unregistered pesticides from export notification requirements on technical grounds, which resulted from the EPA's earlier, rather liberal interpretation of section 17 (a), was narrowed.[15]

As regards the procedures for export notification, the EPA partially retreated from the interpretation *contra legem* which it had adopted in its 1980 statement of policy,[16] to the effect that section 17 (a) 'purchaser acknowledgement statements' were not required for every single export shipment, but only for the first shipment in each calendar year. As a rule, per-shipment statements are now required prior to each shipment, unless the exporter explicitly opts for an 'annual summary reporting' system and follows special procedures to this effect. In such case, a purchaser acknowledgement statement will be required only for the first export of each calendar year, but the exporter will be under an additional obligation to submit to the EPA an 'annual summary report' listing the dates of all shipments of the same pesticide to the same foreign purchaser during the same year.[17] The information to be included in the purchaser acknowledgement statement was expanded to include 'the country or countries of final destination of the export shipment . . . if different from the country of the foreign purchaser's address.'[18] This information is intended to allow the EPA to notify each of the intended countries of final destination.[19]

Changes were also made in the procedures for the transmission of both 'purchaser acknowledgement statements' and section 17 (b) notifications of regulatory actions to foreign governments. These are now transmitted directly by the EPA to 'the appropriate government official' in each country concerned, rather than through diplomatic channels. The EPA had found that 'the current process often delays receipt by foreign governments of information about US pesticide actions'[20] and had agreed with the State

[13] 40 CFR Ch 1 § 168.65(b)(4).

[14] *Ibid*, § 168.75(b)(3)(i).

[15] *Ibid*, § 168.75(b).

[16] EPA, 'Statement of Policy on the Labelling Requirements for Exported Pesticides, Devices and Pesticide Active Ingredients and the Procedure for Exporting Unregistered Pesticides', *Federal Register* 45 (1980), p 50274.

[17] 40 CFR Ch 1 § 168.75(c)(2)(ii).

[18] 40 CFR Ch 1 § 168.75(c)(1)(iv).

[19] 40 CFR Ch 1 § 168.75(d).

[20] EPA, 'Pesticide Export Policy—Final Policy Statement', *Federal Register* 58 (18 Feb 1993), p 9082.

Department that it was desirable to avoid 'overburdening formal diplomatic channels with technical information.'[21]

All these changes, whatever their inherent merits, had nothing to do with the implementation of the voluntary PIC procedure as adopted by UNEP and the FAO in 1989. The changes presented by the EPA as actually designed to implement UNEP and the FAO recommendations are minimal. The format of the FIFRA section 17 (b) notices of US regulatory action is to be made consistent, to the extent possible, with that of the 'notification of control action forms' set out in the Amended London Guidelines and the FAO Code of Conduct. Moreover, the EPA announced that it 'will also notify the FAO/UNEP Secretariat, using notification of control action forms, of all final actions which meet the internationally-agreed upon definitions of "banned and severely restricted for health or environmental reasons" ',[22] thus implicitly admitting that its earlier notification practice under the FIFRA section 17 (b) did not fully meet the requirements of UNEP and the FAO instruments. At the same time, the Agency indicated that this notification to the FAO/UNEP Secretariat would substitute for the direct government-to-government notification of all relevant US regulatory actions which fall within the scope of both UNEP/FAO and the FIFRA section 17(b) notification requirements, 'to avoid possible confusion to those receiving and managing duplicative information.'[23]

Significantly, however, no measures were taken to ensure that no pesticides are exported from the United States to countries participating in the voluntary PIC procedure in violation of decisions made by those countries pursuant to the procedure. As we have seen in chapter 13, this is one of the most important recommendations addressed to governments of exporting countries in the Amended London Guidelines and the FAO Code of Conduct. The EC has implemented it by imposing an obligation of compliance with PIC decisions directly on all exporters subject to the jurisdiction of its member states under Regulation (EEC) No 2455/92. No similar action has so far been taken by the United States.

In an official notice regarding US participation in the voluntary PIC procedure, the EPA described that procedure as 'an international *information-sharing* program sponsored by the United Nations' and merely announced that it would regularly publish information on PIC decisions of importing countries in the *Federal Register* with a view to '*informing the public*', but carefully avoided suggesting any form of export control.[24] Indeed, the Agency currently lacks statutory authority under FIFRA to prohibit exports

[21] EPA, 'Pesticide Export Policy Review', *Federal Register* 55 (12 Feb 1990), p 4965.
[22] EPA, 'Pesticide Export Policy—Final Policy Statement', *Federal Register* 58 (18 Feb 1993), p 9082.
[23] *Ibid*, p 9083.
[24] EPA, 'Prior Informed Consent Information-Sharing Program; Notice of Participation', *Federal Register* 57 (9 Dec 1992), pp 58390–91 (emphasis added).

of pesticides subject to the PIC procedure[25] and merely noted in its 1993 policy statement that it 'agrees that FIFRA should be amended to provide EPA with statutory authority to implement PIC fully.'[26] In 1994, the US representative in UNEP *Ad Hoc* Working Group of Experts on the Implementation of the Amended London Guidelines announced that her government 'had prepared a proposal for a new regulatory framework to control export of pesticides banned for uses within the United States,'[27] but so far this proposal has not materialised.

As appears from the above overview of developments since the mid-1980s, the international normative process seems to have had only a marginal impact on domestic policy and legislation in the United States thus far. It seems likely that any legislative reforms will be delayed until the administration decides to submit the 1998 PIC convention to the US Senate for its 'advice and consent' to ratification.

[25] It should be mentioned, however, that, even though the EPA cannot act under the FIFRA as it currently stands, the President already has the authority, under ss 3(13) and 6(a)(1) of the Export Administration Act of 1979, as amended by the Export Administration Amendments Act of 1985 (reprinted in 24 ILM 1370 (1985)), to prohibit or 'curtail' the export of 'goods and substances banned or severely restricted for use in the United States in order to foster public health and safety and to prevent injury to the foreign policy of the United States as well as to the credibility of the United States as a responsible trading partner'.

[26] EPA, 'Pesticide Export Policy—Final Policy Statement', *Federal Register* 58 (18 Feb 1993), p 9083.

[27] UN Doc UNEP/PIC/WG.1/4/5, 15 Apr 1994, p 7, para 45. See also p 11, para 87.

Part IV

Overview and Conclusions

17

The Regulation of Toxic Emissions in the Aquatic Environment: A Regime Appraisal

IN THIS CHAPTER, I will attempt to synthesise the development and substance of the international regime for the regulation of toxic emissions in the aquatic environment, with a view to evaluating its effectiveness mainly from the angle of the normative force of the prescriptions resulting from the international normative process, and assessing the extent to which the evidence in this issue-area matches the instrumental model which underlies the development of transnational environmental law.

This will involve an analysis of how the object and purpose of transnational regulation has been defined and what regulatory instruments have been developed in the course of the normative process. We shall examine the respective role of hard law and soft law, of international law and European Community law, and the interaction between these different normative orders. The impact of the normative system on the behaviour of states and non-state actors and its adequacy in terms of environmental goal achievement will be explored.

REGIME OVERVIEW

Emissions of toxic substances into the European aquatic environment, both inland and marine, are regulated under a complex set of partly overlapping and interlocking legal regimes of both international law and EC law. These include three separate though similar international conventional regimes governing marine pollution from land-based sources respectively for the North Sea and North East Atlantic, the Baltic Sea and the Mediterranean. These regimes developed in the 1970s and were consolidated in the 1990s through the adoption of a second generation of legal instruments: the 1992 Paris Convention, the 1992 Helsinki Convention and the amendments to the 1976 Barcelona Convention and its 1980 Athens Protocol, adopted in 1995 and 1996. The second relevant normative order is that of EC environmental law, in particular a 1976 Directive on discharges of dangerous substances into the aquatic environment, both freshwater and marine, and the more recent 1996 Directive on integrated pollution prevention and control and 2000 Framework Directive on water policy. Some discharges into international rivers in Europe are also subject to a third international legal regime laid down in river basin agreements between the riparian states, such as the 1976 Bonn Convention on the protection of the Rhine against chemical pollution.

Notwithstanding differences in wording and detail, the objectives, basic thrust and regulatory philosophy of these multiple legal instruments are essentially the same. States have undertaken to prevent and combat water pollution by hazardous substances, which were initially defined by reference to two lists of families and groups of substances hazardous to the aquatic environment due to their toxicity, persistence and tendency to bio-accumulate. Pollution by the most hazardous substances—black list substances—is to be eliminated, that by other hazardous substances—those of the grey list—to be reduced or strictly limited. In order to achieve these objectives, a number of regulatory instruments are to be applied by states. All discharges of hazardous substances shall be subject to administrative authorisation. Authorisations shall impose emission standards to be fixed by national authorities based on best available technology and/or environmental quality objectives. International harmonisation of policies for the control of toxic water pollution is to be pursued through the adoption of common programmes and measures, including common emission limit values and environmental quality objectives. Though the basic objective and principles of this legal arsenal seem relatively straightforward, closer analysis reveals that the intended result has not been achieved and that the legal machinery has not functioned as intended.

First of all, there appears to be a considerable measure of indeterminacy in the formulation of the basic objective itself, due to the way in which pollution is defined and the pollutants subject to the regime are identified. In the elaboration of the legal instruments, language was crafted that accommodates diverging views of states on crucial substantive questions: which are the hazardous substances causing pollution which is to be eliminated? On what basis should emission standards be determined? Should they be uniform or vary from place to place depending on environmental and economic circumstances? States have retained a substantial margin of discretion and the mechanisms for further specification of their obligations have only partly been used to limit that discretion. The various marine pollution and river basin conventions all provide for institutional mechanisms for further decision-making on implementation measures, which can be used to flesh out the obligations of the parties. Some of them even allow the adoption of legally binding measures. But, where it exists, this possibility has only rarely been used and practice shows a clear preference for recommendatory instruments and overall national resistance to further norm specification. Common measures for a number of hazardous substances and source sectors have been adopted, but their scope remains narrow relative to the magnitude of the problems to be addressed and the level of ambition of the ultimate objectives. The painstaking haggling over the technicalities of implementation measures has tended to deflect attention from the basic regime obligations and detract from whatever independent normative force they may have.

Instead of pursuing with greater diligence the implementation of the existing hard law instruments, governments have found it politically more attractive to initiate a parallel normative process through ministerial conferences producing new commitments in the form of political declarations. This has resulted in the adoption of soft law instruments containing quantified emission reduction commitments and timetables, like the successive North Sea ministerial declarations and the Rhine Action Plan, proclaiming ever more ambitious objectives. The growing importance of soft law is paradoxical from the perspective of the instrumental model which associates soft law with early, 'immature' stages of the normative process. There is as yet no evidence that this soft law will ultimately be translated into hard law. On the contrary, overall, the revision of the existing legal instruments in the 1990s has not resulted in an increase in their normative force but rather tended to preserve and even enlarge the room for national discretion. While most states have complied with their principal formal obligations—like the introduction of an administrative permit system for discharges—few seem to have made a purposeful effort to put into effect obligations of a programmatic nature aimed at the actual elimination of pollution by hazardous substances.

TOXIC SUBSTANCES IN INTERNATIONAL WATERS: DEFINING THE PROBLEM AND THE OBJECT OF TRANSNATIONAL REGULATION

In defining the substances whose direct or indirect release into the marine environment is to be made subject to control under its provisions, the 1974 Paris Convention for the Prevention of Marine Pollution from Land-Based Sources builds on the 'black list'/'grey list' system introduced by the 1972 Oslo and London waste dumping conventions.[1] By transforming the black and grey lists, initially devised for the purpose of regulating dumping, into the object of a legal regime designed to control water pollution generally, the reach of transnational toxics regulation and its potential economic implications for states were vastly expanded. This is why the signing of the

[1] Convention for the Prevention of Marine Pollution by Dumping from Ships and Aircraft, Oslo, 15 Feb 1972, 11 ILM 262 (1972); Convention on the Prevention of Marine Pollution by Dumping of Wastes and Other Matter, London, Mexico City, New York, Washington, 29 Dec 1972, 18 ILM 510 (1979).

1974 Paris Convention was a momentous step in the evolution of international environmental law.

The Paris Convention further articulates the criteria for the selection of target substances, which were initially formulated in the Oslo and London Conventions. Persistence, toxicity 'or other noxious properties' and 'tendency to bio-accumulation' are explicitly mentioned as the criteria according to which substances have been allocated to the different annexes. Though 'exhibiting similar characteristics', grey list substances are distinguished from black list substances on the grounds that 'they seem less noxious or are more readily rendered harmless by natural processes.'[2] A few months earlier, the riparian states of the Baltic Sea had signed the 1974 Helsinki Convention, which was the first international legal instrument to coin the term 'hazardous substances' in a marine pollution context. However, this Convention somewhat deviated from the general 'black list'/'grey list' model by ascribing to that term a narrow technical meaning, distinguishing it from the broader category of 'noxious substances.'[3]

It is European Community law that can be credited with having crystallised the legal category of 'dangerous substances' into a unifying concept for the regulation of toxic emissions in the aquatic environment, both marine and inland. The hazardous properties of substances—toxicity, persistence and bio-accumulation—which were initially identified as justifying measures to prevent or control their release into the marine environment were judged to be equally relevant to the protection of the freshwater environment, and consequently served as a basis for determining the pollutants targetted by Directive 76/464/EEC, a legal instrument for the control of discharges to both marine and inland surface waters. The black and grey lists in the annex to this directive, essentially a further elaboration of the lists annexed to the 1974 Paris Convention, were in turn adopted, with or without modifications, by the drafters of subsequent regional instruments such as the 1976 Rhine Chemical Convention and the 1980 Athens Protocol, as well as a number of other land-based sources protocols concluded within the framework of UNEP's Regional Seas Programme.

Thus a category of pollutants variously labelled as 'dangerous', 'hazardous', 'noxious' or 'toxic' substances gradually developed into a specific object of international environmental regulation. This incremental process of definition did not, however, produce an unequivocally circumscribed category. Indeed, the main feature of the concept of 'dangerous substances', as defined in the above-mentioned instruments, is its open-ended nature. While it may seem clear-cut to lawyers who are unfamiliar with basic notions of environmental chemistry and ecotoxicology, the concept of 'dangerous substances' as a legal category is actually tainted with considerable

[2] 1974 Paris Convention, Annex A, Part II.
[3] 1974 Helsinki Convention, Annexes I and II. See above ch 5.

indeterminacy. It is a polymorphous concept, whose inner core is readily identifiable[4] but whose outer contours are ill-defined and ever-shifting,[5] as scientific knowledge on the hazardous properties of individual substances in the aquatic environment evolves.

This inherent indeterminacy makes the concept at the same time attractive and perilous for international environmental policy-makers. Attractive because the ambiguity of the definition leaves a lot of flexibility to states in the interpretation and implementation of their international commitments with respect to toxic emissions. Perilous because the scope of these commitments is never cast in concrete but always at the mercy of the unpredictable evolution of scientific knowledge relating to the toxicological and environmental risks of an ever-increasing number of pollutants, which may suddenly be found to meet the criteria for inclusion within the regulated category.

DETERMINING THE OBJECTIVE OF THE INTERNATIONAL REGULATORY EFFORTS

Any evaluation of the effectiveness of the international normative process involves ascertaining to what extent international regulatory efforts have achieved their objective. This objective may not always have been explicitly stated by the norm-makers, but where it has been, the stated purpose of the norm is obviously the first point of reference for assessing goal achievement.

When toxic pollution of the marine environment was first recognised as a problem to be addressed by international law, ie when the Oslo and London dumping conventions were negotiated, the objectives of these international legal instruments were formulated in very general terms, if at all. Neither convention in fact contains an explicit statement of its objective, but the aim of the contracting parties in concluding these treaties can be inferred from a number of preambular and operative provisions setting forth in general terms the basic undertakings of the parties. These provisions refer to the parties' intention to 'prevent' or 'combat' marine pollution generally and pollution by the dumping of toxic wastes specifically. However, at the same time, these conventions explicitly acknowledged that dumping was only one of many sources of toxic inputs and that the regulation of this activity would not be sufficient per se to achieve the overall objective of preventing marine pollution. Interestingly, the preambular provisions of both 1972 conventions also contain a clause setting forth, in

[4] Ie individually listed substances or definite categories such as 'mercury and its compounds'.

[5] Ie vaguely defined categories such as 'substances in respect of which it has been proved that they possess carcinogenic properties in or via the aquatic environment'.

soft language, what sounds like a second-order, longer-term objective, viz the development of 'products and processes which will minimize the amount of harmful waste requiring disposal.'[6]

Given the historical continuity in the development of the regional marine environment protection regime in the Northeast Atlantic area, it is not suprising that the objectives of the 1974 Paris Convention are formulated in terms very similar to those of the Oslo Convention. The declared objective of the contracting parties to the Paris Convention is to 'prevent' marine pollution generally and to 'combat' pollution from land-based sources in particular. Their most specifically formulated collective design is to 'eliminate' marine pollution from land-based sources by black list substances and to 'limit strictly' and 'reduce' that by grey list substances. Unlike the Oslo and London Conventions, however, the 1974 Paris Convention contains no explicit reference to the development of cleaner products and processes as a long-term objective. The 1974 Helsinki Convention's stated goal is to 'control and minimize' land-based pollution of the Baltic marine environment and that of the 1976 Barcelona Convention to 'prevent, abate and combat' pollution of the Mediterranean caused by land-based sources. This latter goal is further specified in the 1980 Athens Protocol, which formulates specific objectives with respect to land-based pollution by black and grey list substances in virtually the same terms as the 1974 Paris Convention.

The early instruments regulating toxic emissions into the freshwater environment use very similar terms in stating their objectives. The stated purpose of Directive 76/464/EEC is to 'protect the aquatic environment of the Community from pollution', and in particular to 'eliminate' pollution of inland surface waters and coastal waters by black list substances and to 'reduce' pollution by grey list substances. The 1976 Bonn Convention on the chemical pollution of the Rhine, concluded in the wake of the 1976 EEC Directive, goes one step beyond the twin goals of pollution 'elimination' and 'reduction', respectively, by professing to aim for 'the gradual elimination of *discharges*' of black list substances. However, both Directive 76/464/EEC and the Bonn Convention qualify their stated goals by stressing that their respective provisions are only a 'first' or 'initial' step towards the achievement of these ambitious objectives.

The second wave of legal instruments for the protection of the aquatic environment, elaborated in the 1990s, brought some change in the language used in the various explicit or implicit statements of regulatory purpose. Despite these changes, resulting in greater uniformity, there also appears to be a significant overall measure of continuity. The general objective of the 1992 Paris Convention with respect to land-based sources is now

[6] Oslo Convention, 4th preambular para, *in fine*. Cf London Dumping Convention, 5th preambular para, *in fine*.

to 'prevent *and eliminate*' pollution, without any distinction between pollution caused by black list and grey list substances. I have already argued in chapter 4 that the generalisation of the use of the verb 'eliminate' tends to attenuate its specific meaning, and that some other provisions of the new Paris Convention suggest that this verb does not necessarily imply *full* elimination.

Essentially the same terminology is used in the 1992 Helsinki Baltic Convention, where the goal to 'prevent and eliminate' pollution, including pollution by harmful substances from land-based sources, is explicitly linked to the ambitious long-term aim of 'ecological restoration' of the Baltic Sea. As to the 1995 amendment to the Barcelona Convention, it adds to that Convention's original aim 'to prevent, abate and combat' marine pollution the new general objective of '*eliminating*' pollution 'to the fullest possible extent' and the specific objective of '*reduction and phasing out*' of toxic substances. The new formulation of the objective of the Mediterranean land-based sources protocol, as amended in Syracuse in 1996, goes even further by aiming for the '*elimination*' of pollution from land-based sources and activities generally, while omitting the qualification 'to the fullest possible extent', and for the 'phasing out' of *inputs* of hazardous substances specifically.

While there is a clear trend towards greater, albeit less focused, use of the verb 'eliminate' in the marine pollution conventions, the second-generation instruments which apply primarily to inland water pollution, like the 1992 Helsinki Rivers Convention and the 1996 IPPC Directive, seem to be heading in the opposite direction, by *avoiding* the use of that very same term. As mentioned in chapter 8, Directive 96/61/EC merely aims 'to prevent or, where that is not practicable, to *reduce* emissions' of pollutants in all environmental media 'in order to achieve a high level of protection of the environment taken as a whole',[7] and the Commission deliberately blocked an attempt by the European Parliament to reintroduce the term 'eliminate' into the language of EC pollution control law. The goal of the Helsinki Rivers Convention, for its part, is to 'prevent, control and reduce' pollution of transboundary watercourses generally and, more specifically, to 'prevent, control and reduce the *release* of hazardous substances into the aquatic environment.'[8]

Different verbs, ranging from 'control' to 'eliminate', are used in the formulation of the basic objectives of the various, interrelated international legal instruments reviewed above. Formulations such as to 'control', 'combat' or even 'limit' pollution are the most ambiguous: the first two

[7] Dir 96/61/EC, Art 1 (emphasis added). See also the 8th preambular para, which states explicitly that the 'objective' of the IPPC is to prevent or '*minimise*' emissions into air, water and soil.

[8] 1992 Helsinki Rivers Convention, 3rd preambular para (emphasis added).

terms could even be interpreted as mere obligations of *means* rather than obligations of result, while the latter term, though it seems more definite, in fact says nothing about the *level* at which pollution is to be 'limited' and thus does not necessarily preclude a further *increase* in pollution, provided some upper limit is ultimately set at some indefinite moment. The terms 'reduce', 'abate' and certainly 'eliminate' imply a higher level of ambition in the formulation of objectives. At any rate, they would all seem to preclude any increase in pollution and to entail, if not the elimination of pollution, then at least some measure of reduction.

The verb 'minimise', though also suggesting reduction, actually implies that pollution is to be kept as low *as possible*, ie that some level of pollution is inevitable, and involves discretion in judging what is or is not possible. Finally, the objective to 'prevent' pollution, though sounding ambitious, may also be ambiguous, depending on context, especially in relation to *existing* pollution. Prevention could either be seen as an equivalent of elimination, ie where *any* form of pollution is effectively prevented, or as closer to pollution control or limitation, eg where new or increased pollution is prevented but without necessarily reducing or eliminating existing levels of pollution.

Of all the formulations encountered in the first-generation legal instruments of the 1970s, the most far-reaching and specific objective seems to be that of 'eliminating' pollution by black list substances. However, whatever subtle semantic distinctions might be implied by the use of particular verbs rather than others in such formulations of purpose, their actual substantive meaning is ultimately contingent on what is to be regarded as 'pollution'. As noted in chapter 4, the standard definition of pollution used in the 1970s—prior to the emergence of the precautionary principle—involves positive evidence of actual harmful effects resulting from the release of substances in the aquatic environment. In view of the scientific uncertainty that is pervasive in many areas of ecotoxicology, this definition is in fact prone to divergent interpretations and leaves states considerable room for discretionary judgement in deciding whether or not the introduction of particular toxic substances in the environment constitutes pollution within the meaning ascribed to this term by the relevant international instruments. The exact location of this threshold above which pollution shall be deemed to exist, was uncertain and a matter of contention between governments.

Consequently, in the 1970s and most of the 1980s, there was a considerable measure of legal indeterminacy in any formulation of the purpose of the transnational legal regulation of toxic emissions which used the term 'pollution'. The only wording which avoided the use of this term was that found in the 1976 Rhine Convention, where it referred to its purpose as the 'gradual elimination of *discharges*' of black list substances. As we saw in chapter 8, a provision formulated in similar terms was contained in the

Commission's proposal for what eventually became Directive 76/464/EEC, but this wording was not adopted by the Council, which preferred to refer instead to the elimination of *pollution* by black list substances.

The new, precautionary definition of pollution, which was incorporated in all the second-generation legal instruments of the 1990s, obviously has substantive implications for their statements of purpose. Inputs of toxic substances into the aquatic environment are now to be regarded as pollution not only where they have been proved to cause harmful effects, but also whenever such effects are 'likely'. But the implications of this broadening of the notion of pollution should not be overrated. The recognition of the precautionary approach has not actually displaced the free play of sovereign discretion; it has only shifted the boundaries within which it can be exercised. Instead of exploiting the scientific uncertainty surrounding cause/effect relationships, dilatory arguments aimed at forestalling or postponing regulatory intervention will now focus on relative risk assessment and priority-setting.[9] By vastly increasing the potential incidence of 'pollution', the precautionary principle necessitates the use of discretion in targetting national and international regulatory efforts.

CONCEPTUALISING THE SOLUTION: DEVISING THE REGULATORY INSTRUMENTS

Having thus defined the problem and proclaimed the objective, what solution did the transnational environmental regulators conceive and what instruments did they consider appropriate for achieving it? Given the regulatory regimes they have designed, the most plausible answer that leaps to mind is: *technology plus administrative law*. The first and foremost common feature of those regimes is their reliance on a system of prior administrative authorisation of discharges of toxic effluents from point sources. This system is designed as a procedural means of bringing those discharges under public control and making them subject to certain substantive conditions aimed at limiting their impact on the aquatic environment, conditions which are to be met through the use of appropriate technological means of emission control.

It is clear from the way in which transnational environmental law developed in this area that regulators initially concentrated most of their attention on industrial point sources of hazardous substances. While the contribution of diffuse sources to toxic inputs to the aquatic environment was not ignored, early normative approaches to this phenomenon were rather rudimentary. It is only at a later stage of their development that the various regulatory regimes became more sophisticated in dealing with

[9] On the proceduralisation of the precautionary principle, see generally Ladeur (1994a).

non-point source pollution. My analysis will therefore focus first on the normative process with respect to point sources.

Ostensibly, the administrative licensing system for discharges of effluents containing hazardous substances is not an end in itself but only an instrumental legal framework for the regulation of all identifiable individual point sources. Within this framework, administrative decisions are to be made by competent national authorities as to the nature and quantities of toxic substances whose emission into the aquatic environment is authorised. Emission standards are viewed as the main legal form in which such decisions are to be expressed. Up to this point, the various transnational legal instruments for the control of toxic emissions are almost totally concordant. From a substantive point of view, however, the key question is by whom and *on what basis* emission limit values are to be established. This is where the divergence starts.

In the early stages of the international normative process, the rift is between those states favouring an approach whereby emission standards are to be derived on a case-by-case basis from environmental quality objectives for the aquatic environment, and those in favour of uniform technology-based emission standards to be applied across the board regardless of the quality of the receiving waters. For the former, there is no need for international harmonisation of emission standards. The only form of harmonisation that may be justified is that of environmental quality standards for particularly hazardous substances. Such standards should be established on the basis of scientific research designed to determine the level of concentration of the relevant pollutants in the aquatic environment at which no adverse effects are observed, thus taking into account the 'assimilative capacity' of the environment. The 'elimination' of pollution involves nothing more than ensuring that this acceptable level of contamination is not exceeded.

For the latter category of states, harmonised emission standards should be fixed internationally on the basis of the best available technology, in order to avoid distortions of competition resulting from disparities in national emission control policies. Pollution is to be 'eliminated' by gradually tightening emission limit values in pace with the evolution of technology, thus continuously reducing emissions of toxic substances to the lowest possible level. To accommodate these two conflicting perspectives on the control of toxic emissions, international law and European Community law merely establish a neutral legal framework which preserves national discretion to adopt either approach and does not prejudge the substantive content of any harmonised norms that may eventually be adopted. The normative force of such a framework is obviously low.

Directive 76/464/EEC provides a procedural mechanism for the establishment of the obligations of member states with respect to the regulation of discharges of black list substances, to be further specified through the adoption of emission limit values and EQOs for individual substances at Community level. No similar harmonisation is envisaged for grey list substances; the directive in this respect merely provides a very general Community legal framework within which national discretion is to be freely exercised. The relevant international legal instruments of the same generation, such as the 1974 Paris Convention, the 1974 Helsinki Convention, the 1980 Athens Protocol and the 1976 Bonn Convention also establish little more than a vague general framework for individual and collective action by their contracting parties. Notwithstanding some differences of terminology, the basic outline of this framework is essentially the same in all conventions. They all provide for the adoption and implementation by the parties, both jointly and individually, of 'programmes and measures', common 'objectives', 'guidelines', 'regulations', 'standards' or 'criteria' with a view to achieving their stated objectives of 'eliminating', 'reducing' or 'limiting' pollution by hazardous substances. The instruments to be used for this purpose invariably include discharge permits, emission standards and EQOs, separately or in combination with each other, as well as more vaguely described product and process standards.

The actual impact of the international normative process on the ground depends to a large extent on the emission standards that are imposed through the administrative permitting system that it prescribes. The setting of these standards involves the exercise of political discretion either at the international level, whenever harmonised emission limit values are fixed within the institutional framework established by the relevant instruments, or at the national level, when no common standards exist for a particular substance and competent national authorities remain free to set whatever emission standards they deem appropriate in the individual permits they issue. The international regulatory framework is not very specific with respect to the basis on which such standards are to be established. Other than the general objective of pollution reduction, the only guidance provided is in the form of some reference to technological and economic criteria.

The concept of 'best available technology' (BAT) as it is currently defined was not as such part of the early regulatory discourse. The first-generation instruments use other language to denote what nevertheless seems like essentially the same notion. They variously refer to the 'best technical means available,'[10] the 'latest economically feasible technical developments,'[11] the 'latest technical developments'[12] and the 'availability and feasibility' of treatment processes, re-use methods and low-waste technologies,[13] but

[10] Dir 76/464/EEC, Art 6, para 1 and Bonn Convention, Art 5, para 2.
[11] Dir 76/464/EEC, Art 7, para 4.
[12] 1974 Paris Convention, Art 4, para 3.
[13] 1980 Athens Protocol, Art 6, para 3 and Annex III, section D.

merely to require member states or states parties to take these *into account*, either when establishing emission limit values at the international level, or when setting standards in individual permits, or both. The notion of 'best available technology' was first explicitly defined in a 1989 recommendation of the Paris Commission. This definition was later transposed into hard law in the 1992 Paris Convention as well as in the other second-generation water pollution conventions of the 1990s. It also inspired the definition of 'best available techniques' in the 1996 IPPC Directive. As pointed out in chapter 4, the 'modern' definition of BAT involves so many contextual factors prone to divergent interpretations that its normative force is extremely weak.

Yet this equivocal concept has now—together with the twin concept of 'best environmental practice' (BEP)—become the primary standard in terms of which the obligations of states with respect to discharges of dangerous substances are expressed under the different land-based sources and river pollution regimes. In the early international legal instruments, the primary, and most specific, obligation of states was to 'eliminate' pollution by black list substances and to 'reduce' pollution by grey list substances, and BAT and related concepts were merely viewed as a means to this end. In the new generation of conventions, the duty to 'define' and 'apply' BAT for point sources has in fact become the most specific obligation, as the former duty to eliminate pollution by a specific category of hazardous substances has been subsumed under a vague general obligation to 'prevent and eliminate' pollution and thus watered down.

The regulators' view of how to deal with non-point sources of hazardous substances was initially not very developed. There was a general awareness of the existence of important diffuse sources of pollution, but regulatory instruments to tackle them had not been conceptualised to the same degree as for point sources. The early provisions on the subject were rather scant, both in conventional international law and EC law. The first-generation international legal instruments contain merely a few scattered general references to the possible use of product standards as regulatory tools for the control of water pollution.[14] Directive 76/464/EEC, for its part, addresses the problem of diffuse sources only with respect to grey list substances, where it provides that national pollution reduction programmes for such

[14] Art 6, para 2 of the 1974 Helsinki Convention refers to the adoption of measures concerning 'products containing [noxious] substances and materials and their use'. Art 4, para 3 of the 1974 Paris Convention provides for the adoption of 'specific regulations or standards governing . . . the composition and use of substances and products'. Art 5, para 3 and 7, para 1 of the 1980 Athens Protocol respectively refer to 'standards for use' of black list substances and 'the control and progressive replacement of products . . . causing significant pollution of the marine environment'. Finally, Art 6, para 6 of the 1976 Bonn Convention contains exactly the same wording as Art 7, para 4 of Dir 76/464/EEC.

substances '*may* also include specific provisions governing the composition and use of substances or groups of substances and products.'[15] It is only ten years later that Directive 86/280/EEC actually requires member states to 'draw up specific programmes' of measures to eliminate diffuse-source pollution by all black list substances for which daughter directives have been adopted, through 'the replacement, retention and/or recycling' of these substances.[16] Occasionally, Community measures to restrict the placing on the market and/or use of specific products which cause diffuse pollution of the aquatic environment are adopted within the framework of Directive 76/769/EEC.

Eventually, the growing awareness of the significance of diffuse sources and the work of the INSC and PARCOM on the subject led to the development of a new regulatory concept, that of 'best environmental practice'. In trying to formulate, in abstract general terms, a standard for national and international action against pollution from non-point sources, PARCOM produced a 'definition' of the BEP concept whose prescriptive content is minimal, as we have seen in chapter 4. Nevertheless, this vague concept has now been enshrined, alongside its counterpart BAT, in the provisions of all the second-generation water pollution conventions as one of the key determinants of their contracting parties' substantive obligations with respect to toxic emissions.

ASSESSMENT OF THE EFFECTIVENESS OF TRANSNATIONAL NORMATIVE EFFORTS

All of the international legal instruments considered provide for 'dual-track' implementation: implementation at the international level through the further specification of general obligations by the adoption of common standards, whether binding or non-binding, in their respective institutional frameworks, and direct implementation of these same primary general obligations, or implementation of secondary obligations resulting from common standards, if any, by individual states. In the absence of such common standards, the track of direct implementation, as we have seen, leaves governments—the primary addressees of the international normative process—virtually unfettered discretion in determining the concrete substantive obligations of the secondary addressees, ie individual polluters under their jurisdiction. Whatever secondary obligations have been established under the various legal regimes are in and of themselves totally insufficient to achieve the stated objective of elimination of toxic water pollution, as we shall now see.

[15] Dir 76/464/EEC, Art 7, para 4 (emphasis added).
[16] Dir 86/280/EEC, Art 5.

European Community Law

Directive 76/464/EEC has been labelled a framework directive because the achievement of its objective of eliminating water pollution by black list substances requires the elaboration of additional, implementing legislation at Community level. The regulatory scheme it establishes for the control of toxic emissions into the aquatic environment is premised on the adoption of emission limit values and environmental quality objectives for individual black list substances through 'daughter directives' and their subsequent transposition into national law by the member states. As we have seen in chapter 8, only a small number of such implementing directives have actually been adopted by the Council, regulating discharges of no more than 17 substances out of a total of 129 priority substances qualifying for inclusion in the black list, identified by the Commission in 1982. Efforts to implement Directive 76/464/EEC as originally planned, ie through the elaboration of secondary obligations in the form of daughter directives, were abandoned by the Commission in the early 1990s. And such Community standards for individual black list substances as have actually been set fall short of the objective of eliminating pollution and have not been reviewed and strengthened since their adoption, as though there had been no technological advances since the 1980s. Overall, the secondary obligations of member states resulting from the implementation process of Directive 76/464/EEC are very limited in scope and have failed to achieve the directive's ambitious goals.

What has been the actual effect of Directive 76/464/EEC and its daughter directives on emissions of hazardous substances in Community surface waters? In the mid-1990s, the Commission contracted some Dutch research institutes to carry out studies to answer this question. Two separate studies were undertaken, one dealing with black list substances[17] and the other with grey list substances,[18] with a common methodological approach. To evaluate the impact of the directives, the researchers, in consultation with the Commission, made a selection of black and grey list substances and of river basins on which to focus their analysis. Thus, the scope of the study was deliberately limited in order to keep it 'manageable'. Sixteen national and international river systems in 11 member states were selected, mostly on the basis of availability of data. The sample of 14 black list substances selected for the study includes the two heavy metals (mercury and cadmium) and most of the chlorinated organic compounds for which emission limit

[17] RIZA, *Impact of Dir 76/464/EEC and its 'daughter' directives on the most important surface waters in the Community*, vol I Main Report, Oct 1995.

[18] RIZA & Delft Hydraulics, *Evaluation of the Dir 76/464/EEC regarding List II substances on the quality of the most important surface waters in the Community*, vol I Main Report, June 1996.

values and quality objectives have been laid down by daughter directives. As regards grey list substances, 16 of them were selected, including a number of heavy metals, nutrients, pesticides, PAHs and other organic micropollutants. For each of the river basins under consideration, the researchers examined the state of transposition of the directives and collected all available data on water quality and industrial discharges for the substances concerned, tried to identify the 'driving forces' leading to improvement of water quality and on this basis drew conclusions as to the effectiveness of Directive 76/464/EEC.

The study on black list substances concludes that Directive 76/464/EEC and its daughter directives are 'one of the important factors that have contributed to the improvement in water quality of a number of main surface waters in the past 10–12 years,'[19] though their impact varies from member state to member state and river to river. The data on which this conclusion is based are rather ambiguous, which probably explains the relatively cautious terms in which the conclusion is formulated. The researchers in fact found that sufficient data on both water quality and discharges were available only for three of the 16 rivers investigated. Complete data sets for *all* the substances under consideration were available only for the Rhine. For two other rivers, the available data were sufficient to identify trends for only a few substances. For the rest of the surface waters studied, data gaps made it impossible to draw any definite conclusions at all. The most serious gaps were found in the area of discharge information. In spite of Article 11 of Directive 76/464/EEC, which requires member states to draw up an inventory of discharges of black list substances, most member states were unable to provide any information on such discharges for the vast majority of the substances concerned.

For about half the rivers selected, the study had to conclude that 'given the available information, an evaluation of the impact of Directive 76/464/EEC cannot be made'. For the other rivers, the often very incomplete data available on some black list substances generally showed a declining trend over time in both pollutant concentrations and discharges. But the evidence compiled in the study seems insufficient to demonstrate that this gradual improvement in water quality is actually *due to* Directive 76/464/EEC and its daughter directives. Even for the Rhine, the river for which the most complete information is available, the conclusions are formulated in qualified terms: it is concluded that the directive is one of the 'driving forces leading to the reduction of discharges by industries and municipalities' alongside other instruments such as the 1976 Bonn Chemical Pollution Convention and the Rhine Action Programme.[20] Though it

[19] RIZA, *Impact of Dir 76/464/EEC and its 'daughter' directives on the most important surface waters in the Community*, vol I Main Report, Oct 1995, pp 6–1.

[20] *Ibid*, p C–7.

argues that Directive 76/464/EEC played an 'important role', the study also points out 'that no single convention, treaty or Directive is responsible for quality improvement of the river Rhine.'[21]

The simple fact that pollution by some black list substances has decreased does not prove that this is the result of the implementation of Community law. Positively demonstrating the effect of the directive would require data about the proportion, in the relevant river basin, of the overall load of each particular black list pollutant originating from industries for which emission limit values have been established at Community level, their emission levels prior to the implementation of the directive, and the emission levels resulting from the imposition of the Community limit values in their discharge permits. This kind of detailed information about the emissions of specific sectors and their actual permit conditions is not presented in the study. It does, however, contain some information which seems to contradict the validity of the instrumental assumptions about the functioning of Community law. In the Rhine basin, discharges of 1,2-dichloroethane were reduced by more than 95 per cent in the period 1985–1992. However, the relevant daughter directive setting emission limit values for this black list substance, Directive 90/415/EEC, was only adopted in 1990 and did not require actual compliance with these values before 1993. Thus, most, if not all of the emission reduction occurred *before* the directive had to be implemented and is clearly not the *result* of its implementation. The study regards this as evidence that 'even discussions leading to Directives may have a positive impact on discharge reductions', suggesting that governments and industry actually anticipated the adoption of the directive.[22] The Commission's proposal for what became Directive 90/415/EEC was indeed made in 1988 and was under consideration in the Council for two years prior to its adoption. But the fact that 1,2-dichloroethane was identified as a priority substance under the Rhine Action Programme in 1987 may have been equally, if not more, important.

The study's overall conclusions on the impact of Directive 76/464/EEC are also based on the state of formal transposition in the member states, which was found to be 'complete', and on the fact that in most of the basins considered, a prior authorisation requirement for black list substances was only introduced after the adoption of the directive. Thus, the directive is 'often the most important driving force with regard to management actions to implement a permit system.'[23] Of course, the mere introduction of a permit system is not sufficient to ensure pollution reduction; that depends on the *use* that is made of it, on the actual emission standards that are imposed on individual pollution sources, their enforcement and periodical

[21] Main Report, Oct 1995, pp 6–1.
[22] *Ibid.*
[23] *Ibid.*

review and strengthening. The study hardly provides any information on these aspects, which are nevertheless crucial to any serious assessment of effectiveness.

The results of the second study, that relating to grey list substances, also fail to demonstrate the effectiveness of Directive 76/464/EEC. The problems of data availability encountered by the researchers, both as regards water quality and emissions, were similar to those faced in the first study. Due to lack of data, no conclusions could be drawn for half the rivers studied.[24] Partial or more or less complete data on a small number of substances, mostly heavy metals and nutrients, was available for the other half of the sample. Where sufficient information for identifying trends could be found, it generally indicated a gradual improvement in water quality. Overall, reliable discharge information was very scarce, as for black list substances. Very little useful information at all was available for pesticides and other organic micropollutants.

The most important conclusion reached by the study is that none of the member states have in fact fully complied with Article 7 of Directive 76/464/EEC and implemented a pollution reduction programme for grey list substances as specified in that provision. According to the researchers and the national experts they interviewed, it is not actually possible to implement Article 7 as intended and to establish both EQO and emission standards on an individual substance basis. There are thousands of grey list substances and the technical ability to analyse all of them does not exist. Therefore, it is considered 'not realistic' to define an emission standard for each grey list substance as required.[25] Also, the methodology for deriving emission standards from EQO, as prescribed by Article 7, cannot be applied in practice because it requires quantification of all emissions, including those from diffuse sources, which, according to the study, is technically 'not feasible.'[26]

Instead of establishing water quality objectives for each individual grey list substance and deriving emission limit values from them, member states have in fact applied what the study calls 'alternative measures': they have followed an 'emission approach' to the control of pollution by these substances quite similar to that prescribed by the directive for black list substances, except that in this case there are no Community emission limit values restricting their regulatory discretion.[27] While most member states have established water quality standards for a number of grey list substances considered relevant in their specific conditions, these standards have

[24] RIZA & Delft Hydraulics, *Evaluation of the Dir 76/464/EEC regarding List II substances on the quality of the most important surface waters in the Community*, vol I Main Report, June 1996, p 6–5, Table 6.1.

[25] *Ibid*, p 4–5.

[26] *Ibid*, p 4–4.

[27] *Ibid*, p 6–1.

not directly been used as a basis for regulating emissions. Instead, emission standards have been set independently of them, based on a national interpretation of best available technology.

Somewhat paradoxically, the study concludes that Directive 76/464/EEC is 'probably one of the driving forces' for the introduction of these alternative measures, which 'do not necessarily consider individual List II substances specifically but rather consider them as part of a general policy and procedure for water pollution control.'[28] Rather than assessing the effectiveness of the directive itself, the study in fact evaluates the effectiveness of the alternative measures and concludes that, 'in most cases' it is these measures which 'have had the most direct impact on the water quality of the surface waters.'[29] With respect to those substances and river systems for which data are available, it finds evidence that the alternative measures have generally resulted in water quality improvements. But in these cases, the impact, if any, of Directive 76/464/EEC is at best indirect. The study identifies other 'driving forces' which have prompted member states to develop their own pollution control strategies, including various international agreements and national political and economic developments, and points out that it is impossible to quantify their relative contribution.[30]

These studies indicate that the effectiveness of Directive 76/464/EEC is questionable. Pollution by black list substances in general has not been eliminated. However, in so far as the available data allow judgements to be made, there is some evidence that pollution by a number of black and grey list substances has been reduced since the adoption of the directive, although it is often unclear to what extent this can effectively be attributed to its provisions. At any rate, as far as grey list substances are concerned, the provisions of the directive have not been implemented the way they were intended to be. By its own standards, Article 7 has clearly been ineffective. Its impact on discharges of grey list substances has been indirect at best, where it has prompted member states to regulate emissions of some of these substances, albeit by other means than those actually prescribed by the directive. As to the provisions on black list substances, they have only been implemented for a small number of substances, and where emission reductions of these substances have actually occurred, the extent to which this is due to the application of the Community emission limit values in those few sectors for which they have been established remains in doubt.

Directive 76/464/EEC has undoubtedly had an impact on law and administrative procedures,[31] especially in those member states which did not have

[28] Main Report, June 1996, p 6–5, Table 6.1.

[29] *Ibid.*

[30] *Ibid*, p 6–2.

[31] See also European Commission, *Administrative Structures and Implementation of the Community Dirs on the Dangerous Substances Discharged into the Aquatic Environment*, Office for Official Publications of the European Communities, Luxembourg, 1996.

a permit system for discharges of hazardous substances prior to its adoption and which have introduced one pursuant to the directive. The implementation studies report that transposition has been completed in all the member states under consideration. Thus, the directive has enhanced the legal and administrative *means* of controlling emissions of toxic substances, but this has not automatically led to the intended *result* in terms of pollution reduction, let alone elimination, being achieved. In fact, the instrumental relationship between the instruments provided by Community law (permits, emission standards, quality objectives) and the observed improvements in water quality for some black and grey list substances is far from obvious. Paradoxically, there are some indications that where Community law has had an impact, it is otherwise than through the actual implementation of the rules and procedures it lays down, often in oddly non-legal ways, eg by raising governmental awareness of dangerous substances as a category of pollutants requiring action and prompting national authorities to take certain pollution control measures, though different from those actually prescribed by Directive 76/464/EEC, based on their peculiar national strategies and priorities.

As discussed in chapter 8, the new provisions of Directive 96/61/EC on integrated pollution prevention and control, which are designed to supersede the emission control provisions of Directive 76/464/EEC, substantially increase the discretionary power of the member states with respect to the authorisation of discharges of hazardous substances. The specification of the new directive's vague BAT standard through the fixing of emission limit values at Community level is envisaged only in exceptional cases. The Commission's new legislative policy since the early 1990s gives priority to the elaboration of framework legislation consisting mainly of vague general principles and procedural provisions, rather than to the harmonisation of substantive environmental standards. The new Framework Directive on water policy, Directive 2000/60/EC, introduces a new, though ill-defined, instrument for toxics reduction, the so-called Community 'strategies against pollution of water', but such strategies are designed to address only a limited number of pollutants, to be identified through a cumbersome 'risk assessment' procedure. It will be a matter of years before any specific obligations will be imposed on member states as a result of these strategies. The added value of this new instrument over and above the instruments already provided for in Directive 76/464/EEC is doubtful.

International Conventions and Soft Law

Regional regimes for the protection of the marine environment have become an object of fascination for political scientists and regime theorists, ever since Sunneva Saetevik and Peter Haas published their well-known monographs[32] analysing the development and operation of the North Sea and Mediterranean environmental regimes from a political science perspective.

In his 1990 book *Saving the Mediterranean*, a classic of the now prolific literature on international environmental regimes, Haas asserts that UNEP's Mediterranean Action Plan and its legal offspin, the Barcelona Convention and its protocols, is 'widely acclaimed as the most successful example of international environmental collaboration' and that, without it, 'the Mediterranean would be much more polluted than it is now.'[33] In a 1993 article on international cooperation for the protection of the marine environment of the North Sea and Baltic Sea, the same author provides an equally sanguine account of what he describes as the 'increasing institutional effectiveness' of the Oslo, Paris and Helsinki Commissions,[34] which he lumps together analytically as 'a single international institution which is responsible for developing a single policy system and a set of legally binding rules for both the Baltic and North seas.'[35]

Saetevik, however, concluded from her rather more thorough assessment of the first decade of international environmental cooperation within the framework of the Paris Commission that the outcomes of this cooperation 'are characterized by few binding decisions and rather more recommendations often couched in terms inferring little in the way of obligations.'[36] In fact, she even found it appropriate to coin the term 'non-decision' to denote a typical kind of policy outcome of the Paris Commission's activities, where technical studies and expert discussions on possible measures remain inconclusive and do not lead to any formal decision due to the opposition of some contracting parties.[37] Another, more recent policy study of the effectiveness of the Paris Convention, notes that 'in the initial and main phase of PARCOM cooperation, the relative improvement in relation to status quo seems rather marginal' but also points out that, especially since the Second North Sea Conference in 1987, 'effectiveness seems to have improved somewhat . . . quite probably leading to *reduced* pollution of the North Sea.'[38]

While, as Haas demonstrates in his 1993 article, the Oslo Commission has undeniably been effective in phasing out the direct dumping of waste at sea in the North East Atlantic region, the evidence he presents to substantiate his conclusions as to the effectiveness of the normative activities of the Paris and Helsinki Commissions in the field of *pollution from land-*

[32] Saetevik (1988); Haas (1990).
[33] Haas (1990), p xx.
[34] Haas (1993), p 134.
[35] *Ibid*, pp 133–34.
[36] Saetevik (1988), p 134.
[37] For an overview of such 'non-decisions', see *ibid*, pp 49–51.
[38] Wettestad & Andresen (1991), pp 62–63 (original italics).

based sources is less convincing.[39] The mere increase in the average number of decisions and recommendations adopted annually by the Commissions[40] is not, in and of itself, an adequate measure of effectiveness, but, at best, only an indicator of activity.[41] Any serious assessment of effectiveness also requires a thorough examination of the substantive *content* of the relevant decisions and recommendations, which is lacking in Haas' article.[42] In fact, Haas himself seems to be aware of this flaw in the empirical basis of his generalisations, where he refers in his introduction to the 'increasing activity and *probable* effectiveness' of the regional regulatory institutions[43] and elsewhere asserts, in what sounds like a direct contradiction of his overall conclusion, that 'only a small number of PARCOM's actions may be said to significantly influence existing practices.'[44]

Our analysis of the substantive outcome of the international normative process within the framework of the Paris Commission and the North Sea Conferences in chapter 4 indicates that the actual collective action taken by the contracting parties pursuant to the 1974 Paris Convention falls well short of full implementation of the Convention's mandate for reduction and elimination of pollution by hazardous substances. The Paris Commission has adopted 'programmes and measures' within the meaning of the Convention for only a limited number of black list and grey list substances and has not often made use of its power to adopt them in the form of legally binding decisions, opting instead for non-binding recommendations. The normative force of the concepts of 'best available technology' and 'best environmental

[39] Haas' assertion that 'virtually all the issues that were on the original agendas of the black and gray lists were subsequently treated by . . . PARCOM and HELCOM' (Haas (1993), p 170) is very much open to dispute, considering that both commissions have adopted measures with respect to only a fraction of the hazardous substances within the scope of these lists. For example, while there are hundreds of persistent organic compounds, only a few of them have actually been regulated. It should also be recalled that PARCOM's original mandate, as laid down in the 1974 Paris Convention was to *eliminate* pollution by black list substances.

[40] Haas notes that the number of PARCOM decisions and recommendations increased from an average of 3.8 per year before 1986 to 5.7 per year since 1986, while the average annual number of HELCOM recommendations on land-based sources rose from 2.5 prior to 1988 to 3.5 since that year. Haas (1993), pp 152, 160.

[41] Wettestad and Andresen, though reaching conclusions similar to those of Haas as regards the positive influence of the INSC process on the regulatory efforts of the Paris Commission, are more cautious in their assessment of the ultimate effectiveness of those efforts: '*Assuming that there is a certain connection between PARCOM measures and decreasing pollution*, [the increased activity of PARCOM] indicates that goal achievement has increased somewhat in the latter part of the 80's.' Wettestad & Andresen (1991), p 59 (emphasis added).

[42] The normative output of PARCOM and HELCOM with respect to land-based sources is examined only superficially, and with a number of legal inaccuracies. Thus, for example, Haas' summary of the distinction between PARCOM decisions and recommendations in terms of both the procedure for their adoption and their legal effects under the 1974 Paris Convention is plainly wrong. Haas (1993), p 144.

[43] *Ibid*, p 134 (emphasis added).

[44] *Ibid*, p 152.

practice', which have become the centerpiece of PARCOM's regulatory strategy since the late 1980s, is low, even when further 'defined' in specific sectoral recommendations, owing to the many contextual factors and unquantified parameters included in such definitions and descriptions of BAT and BEP. The normative output of the Paris Commission overall does not significantly restrict the discretion of the national permitting authorities which are ultimately responsible for regulating polluting industrial activities. PARCOM so far has refrained from banning the *production* of any toxic substance and has only occasionally adopted measures with a view to prohibiting the *use* of particular substances in specific industrial processes.

It is striking that, notwithstanding significant differences in structure and content between the framework provisions of the 1974 Paris Convention and those of the Helsinki Convention signed the same year, the implementing measures for the protection of the Baltic marine environment against pollution from land-based sources adopted by the Helsinki Commission are quite similar in scope and substance to those elaborated by the Paris Commission for the North Sea and North East Atlantic. On the whole, and notwithstanding a number of variations attributable to objective differences in environmental conditions, pollution sources and economic circumstances in the two regions, many of the same pollutants and industrial sectors have been addressed by specific measures in both commissions, though not necessarily at the same time and in identical terms.[45] The concepts of BAT and BEP were first elaborated in the form of HELCOM and PARCOM recommendations and later incorporated in the new provisions of the 1992 Helsinki Baltic Convention, as in those of the 1992 Paris Convention.

The common measures adopted by the contracting parties to the Athens Protocol are much more limited in number and scope than those elaborated by the Paris and Helsinki Commissions. As appears from the detailed discussion in chapter 6, very few measures to eliminate or reduce pollution by black and grey list substances as envisaged in the Athens Protocol have been taken so far. In implementing the Protocol, contracting parties have shown a marked preference for environmental quality standards over emission standards and product standards. Common emission standards have in fact been adopted for only two black list substances, mercury and cadmium. Thus the actual practice of the contracting parties is very far removed from the full implementation of the provisions of Article 5 of the Protocol, which provide for standards to be set for each black list substance and periodi-

[45] Though these and other similarities and interactions between the two regimes exist, these factors and the overlapping membership of both regimes do not, however, seem sufficient to warrant the conclusion, drawn by Haas (1993), that the Helsinki Commission, the Paris Commission and the North Sea Conferences in fact constitute nothing less than a single international institution. The historical background of the Helsinki and Paris conventions and the political conditions in which the Baltic and North Sea marine environment protection regimes developed are significantly different.

cally reviewed. The fixing of an environmental quality objective for just one organochlorine compound can hardly be regarded as a comprehensive programme of measures to eliminate pollution by such compounds.

Overall, the joint measures adopted thus far under the Athens Protocol are not likely to have more than a marginal impact on the conditions of industrial production and emissions of hazardous substances in the Mediterranean region. The evidence clearly contradicts Peter Haas' optimistic reading of the Athens Protocol as actually 'set[ting] limits on industrial, municipal, and agricultural emissions into the Mediterranean, as well as controlling wastes transmitted by rivers and through the atmosphere'[46] and 'banning a number of agricultural compounds used as fungicides, biocides, and pesticides.'[47] As a matter of law, the Protocol itself does not even come close to setting specific limits on any emissions from land-based sources and prohibiting the use of specific hazardous substances, and the few common implementing measures adopted by the parties are absolutely insufficient to achieve its ambitious objectives of pollution reduction and elimination. In actual fact, most of the provisions of the Athens Protocol have turned out to be just as 'exhortatory' as those of the Barcelona Convention itself.[48] My own assessment of the effectiveness of the regime established under the Convention and Protocol in curbing pollution of the Mediterranean by hazardous substances leads to similar conclusions as the overall evaluation of the Mediterranean Action Plan by Skjaerseth, who found no hard evidence that the MAP had been successful in achieving its stated goal of 'enhancing the marine environment.'[49] His analysis of regime implementation highlights the 'widespread lack of effective and precise decision-making' by the meetings of the parties, the general absence of focus and priority-setting and the influence of 'non-environmental motivations.'[50] Skjaerseth does not dismiss the political significance of Mediterranean environmental cooperation, but describes it more realistically than Haas as 'a political success without much substantial environmental impact.'[51]

THE ROLE OF SOFT LAW: ENHANCING THE EFFECTIVENESS OF HARD LAW?

According to Haas, the enhanced 'institutional effectiveness' of the Paris and Helsinki Commissions is primarily to be ascribed to 'institutional

46 Haas (1990), p 67.

47 *Ibid*, p 110. Haas refers specifically to organohalogens and organic compounds of tin and phosphorus.

48 Haas contrasts the protocol's 'specific guidelines for selected substances' with the framework provisions of the Barcelona Convention, which he calls 'exhortatory'. *Ibid*, pp 68, 118.

49 Skjaerseth (1993), p 321.

50 Skjaerseth (1996), pp 48, 51.

51 Skjaerseth (1993), p 321.

change', ie the introduction of ministerial conferences as new, high-level and high-profile policy-making structures in the existing institutional network.[52] The new political forum provided by the International Conferences on the Protection of the North Sea since 1984 significantly increased the public visibility of North Sea policy-making and hence the pressure on 'laggard states' to accept more far-reaching measures than they had previously been prepared to commit themselves to in the less visible, technical forum of the Paris Commission.[53] The North Sea Conference process, initiated in Bremen in 1984, has also been hailed by other authors as an example of regional environmental cooperation, as a source of 'political impetus' for the further development of national, European Community and international law in the area of marine pollution control.[54] The apparently successful North Sea model was later copied in the Baltic region, where the first ministerial conference on marine pollution was held in 1988.

Though it is undeniable that the ministerial meetings have given a new political impetus to the work of the Paris and Helsinki Commissions, their impact should not be overrated. Indeed, as I have demonstrated in chapter 4, a close substantive scrutiny of the recommendations and decisions adopted by the Paris Commission since the start of the North Sea conference process indicates that increased activity should not uncritically be equated with enhanced effectiveness. Neither the Paris Commission nor the European Community has been particularly successful in implementing INSC recommendations concerning the reduction of inputs of hazardous substances.

In the first place, while the provisions of the successive North Sea ministerial declarations with respect to the reduction of inputs of hazardous substances into the North Sea have gradually become more specific, they nevertheless still contain many substantive ambiguities and leave considerable room for national discretion in their interpretation and implementation. Not only are the political commitments entered into by the signatories of the declarations not as unequivocal as they seem, they are also, to a significant extent, little more than a reaffirmation of earlier undertakings, of a more general, yet legally binding nature, made by the riparian states of the North Sea in becoming contracting parties to the 1974 Paris Convention and adopting Directive 76/464/EEC.

It is also clear that the INSC process has largely failed in its proclaimed intent of providing political impetus to the further development of *binding* rules of international and European Community law and of promoting a more effective implementation of those rules. Indeed, with a few exceptions, the policy guidelines laid down in the North Sea declarations have not effec-

[52] Haas (1993), pp 177–79.
[53] *Ibid*, pp 173–74.
[54] See eg Ehlers (1990).

tively been translated into legally binding international measures by the Paris Commission and the EC. The INSC process has certainly had an impact on political discourse in these other fora, but has not really stimulated the production of substantive legal norms.

In other words, the political impetus from the INSC process seems highly overrated in terms of its effect on the development of transnational environmental law. In the final analysis, the INSCs appear to be essentially a political exercise. The fact that the participants in the INSC process are a lot more reluctant to assume legal obligations than to subscribe to political statements of intent indicates that the self-congratulatory tone of the North Sea declarations is not entirely justified.

All the regional marine environment protection regimes are characterised by a wide gap between law and practice, between political rhetoric and concrete action, between international commitments and actual national policies. What is puzzling is that this gap does not seem to be perceived as a political liability by policy-makers. Notwithstanding their acknowledged failure to achieve the quantified reduction targets for inputs of toxic substances first laid down in the London Declaration in 1987 and later confirmed by the Hague Declaration in 1990, North Sea states subscribed to even more ambitious objectives at PARCOM ministerial meeting in Paris in 1992 and again raised their pledge at the Esbjerg North Sea Conference in 1995.

Where the London Declaration called for a 'substantial' input reduction 'of the order of 50%' by 1995,[55] the Hague Declaration pledged reductions 'of 50% or more' by the same deadline for 36 toxic pollutants as a matter of priority, and reductions 'of the order of 70% or more' for some of them.[56] Where the 1992 Paris Declaration recommended the reduction of toxic emissions 'to levels that are not harmful' by the year 2000 'with the aim of their elimination,'[57] the 1995 Esbjerg Declaration proclaimed nothing less than 'the target of their cessation within one generation (25 years),'[58] though also noting in passing that earlier reduction targets set in the Hague Declaration were 'not expected to be fully met.'[59] These successive ministerial declarations convey the impression of a perpetual rhetorical flight forward: the North Sea states appear to be aiming for a moving target that never quite seems to be reached but is systematically moved forward further into the future as the deadline approaches. Indeed, the

[55] Ministerial Declaration, Second International Conference on the Protection of the North Sea, London, 24–25 Nov 1987 (hereafter referred to as London Declaration), para XVI.2.

[56] Final Declaration, Third International Conference on the Protection of the North Sea, The Hague, 7–8 Mar 1990 (hereafter referred to as Hague Declaration), paras 2–3.

[57] Final Declaration of the Ministerial Meeting of the Oslo and Paris Commissions, Paris, 21–22 Sept 1992, Part III, 4th indent.

[58] Ministerial Declaration of the Fourth International Conference on the Protection of the North Sea, Esbjerg, 8–9 June 1995 (hereafter referred to as Esbjerg Declaration), para 17.

[59] Esbjerg Declaration, para 20.

periodic reiteration of ambitious environmental rhetoric through high-level political declarations may well be attractive to governments precisely as a convenient, symbolical means of creating and maintaining the illusion of progress where little substantive progress is actually made.

A similar trend in political discourse, albeit somewhat less pronounced, can be observed in the Baltic region. Where the 1988 ministerial declaration recommended a 'substantive reduction' of toxic inputs 'for example in the order of 50 per cent of the total discharges,'[60] the 1990 Baltic Sea Declaration, adopted by a summit conference of the heads of government of the riparian states, called for emission reductions to levels compatible with the ultimate objective of 'ecological restoration of the Baltic Sea' and recognised that the 50 per cent target was only 'a first step' to this end.[61]

THE EFFECT OF THE EUROPEAN COMMUNITY'S PARTICIPATION IN THE BROADER INTERNATIONAL NORMATIVE PROCESS

In an article on the external environmental policy of the EC, a senior Commission official, backed by the authority of a leading scholar in international environmental law, once asserted:

> Il est bien évident que par l'efficacité de ses moyens d'action, sans pareil en dehors de ceux des Etats, la Communauté peut intensifier l'effet des règles internationales, voire en accélérer la mise en oeuvre. Les expériences, très positives dans ce sens, ne manquent pas.[62]

The experience of Community participation in international conventions for the protection of the marine and riverine environment, as described in chapter 9 above, quite clearly contradicts this optimistic assertion. There is little evidence that the involvement of the EC has enhanced the effectiveness of these particular international instruments. Quite the contrary: it appears that recurring arguments about the division of powers between the Community and its member states have hampered the work of bodies like the Paris Commission and the Rhine Commission, and that the obstructionist attitude of the Commission of the EC has actually *slowed down* the implementation of these conventions.

[60] Declaration on the Protection of the Marine Environment of the Baltic Sea Area, Helsinki, 15 Feb 1988, reprinted in: Intergovernmental Activities in the Framework of the Helsinki Convention 1974–1994, *Baltic Sea Environment Proceedings*, No 56, Annex 3, p 187, 1st operative para

[61] Baltic Sea Declaration by Heads of Governments and High Political Representatives of the Baltic Sea States, Norway, the Czech and Slovak Federal Republic and the Representative of the Commission of the European Communities assembled at Ronneby, Sweden, 2–3 Sept 1990, reprinted in *Yearbook of International Environmental Law*, vol 1 (1990), p 424, paras 1 and 3.

[62] Brusasco & Kiss (1989), p 710.

In her study published more than 10 years ago, Sunneva Saetevik already noted 'the negative effects of the EC Commission's behaviour on the Paris Commission's ability to achieve binding decisions.'[63] Peter Haas too has observed that the role of the EC in the Paris Commission 'has exercised a major restraint on agenda-setting and international decision making.'[64] Indeed, the European Commission's main concern as representative of the Community in the Paris Commission has been to assert the external competence of the Community and to prevent individual EC member states from entering into international commitments within the framework of the Paris Convention with respect to matters which it considers to be within the Community's sphere of competence. These jurisdictional concerns are evidence of a growing tension between the normative activities of regional environmental bodies such as PARCOM and EC economic law.

It seems that the European Commission, instead of welcoming enhanced regional cooperation for the protection of the marine environment, rather views the norm-setting activities of PARCOM primarily as a potential threat to the integrity of the internal market and an unwelcome interference with the Community's own legislative process. In his 1993 article, Haas suggested that the 'OSPARCOM may serve as a smaller vanguard body in which leader countries can mobilize support for more stringent EC measures.'[65] It appears to be the European Commission's intent to avoid precisely such strategic use of external fora by environmentally progressive member states, and it is not unlikely that this concern will also eventually determine its policy with respect to normative efforts in the framework of the Helsinki Convention.

The very fact that the Commission's position on the respective external competences of the Community and the member states in the field of the regulation of toxic emissions into the aquatic environment has fluctuated in the service of tactical political objectives confirms that political considerations are paramount. The rather indeterminate nature of the relevant rules of law creates ample room for political maneuvering. As Nollkaemper has pertinently noted,

> since the Community is still maturing, it is inevitable that the specific boundaries of the Community's powers for a particular topic are often unclear at a given moment. *In this grey area, legal and political elements entwine.*[66]

The policy of the Commission as the official representative of the Community in the organs of international environmental conventions seems to have been concerned more with the formal recognition of the Community's institutional status and external prerogatives in these international fora, and

[63] Saetevik (1988), p 135.
[64] Haas (1993), p 140.
[65] *Ibid*, p 163.
[66] Nollkaemper (1987), p 56 (emphasis added).

as a corollary, the enhancement of its own power and influence, than with the achievement of environmental policy objectives through the effective implementation of those conventions.[67] The jurisdictional problems in the relations between the Community and its member states have also provided a convenient 'legal' pretext to delay regulatory action under those conventions for member states which are not so eager to implement them diligently. Conversely, member states which are frustrated by the slow pace of environmental decision-making within the Community look upon other international fora as a means of accelerating the development of environmental norms and putting pressure on the Community and are therefore determined to assert their residual external powers. Neither side has any real interest in a firmer delimitation of the jurisdictional boundaries. Viewed from this perspective, the never-ending argument about the respective external competences of the Community and its member states in the environmental field is seen for what it truly is: 'a political contest within legal boundaries.'[68]

[67] See Haigh (1991), p 174.
[68] Nollkaemper (1987), p 91.

18

The Regulation of International Trade in Pesticides: A Regime Appraisal

THIS CHAPTER PROVIDES an overall appraisal of the regime for the regulation of international trade in pesticides which formed the subject of the case study in Part III of this book. Like the previous chapter, it seeks to evaluate the adequacy of the normative instruments developed by the international community for the achievement of their stated policy objectives and draw some conclusions regarding the validity of the instrumental model of transnational regulation in a particular issue-area.

REGIME OVERVIEW

The international normative process with respect to the international trade in banned and severely restricted pesticides started in the late 1970s with the adoption, by the United Nations General Assembly and the Governing Council of UNEP, of a number of resolutions calling for international regulation. In the early 1980s the first soft law instruments providing for organised information exchange on national regulatory measures and export notification requirements for exports of banned or severely restricted chemicals were elaborated in the framework of the OECD, UNEP and the FAO. Despite the sweeping declarations of principle made in the United Nations political fora in the 1970s, the soft regulatory instruments negotiated in the 1980s were symptomatic of the unwillingness of exporting countries to assume any international legal obligations with respect to their exports of banned or severely restricted pesticides and of their determination to confine international standard-setting strictly to the area of information exchange as opposed to export control.

The first hard law instrument to be adopted, the 1988 EEC export notification regulation, still reflected the same reluctance to move beyond information exchange. The implementation of the OECD, UNEP and FAO recommendations in Community law was achieved at the expense of a loss of substance, as the scope of application of the EC's mandatory export notification requirements was much narrower than that of the international soft law instruments they purported to implement.

Continued political pressure for a strengthening of those instruments led to a continuation of the international normative process and to the acceptance of the prior informed consent procedure as the new international standard in 1989. In this process, prior informed consent (PIC), originally conceived as an export control mechanism, was transformed into essentially another form of information exchange. The normative force of the amended soft law instruments remained weak in certain crucial areas, especially as regards the criteria for the selection of the substances to be made subject to the regime and the responsibilities of exporting states.

The PIC procedure was again first transformed from soft law into hard law by the EC, which adopted a PIC regulation in 1992, but then failed to make it fully effective before 1994. In what is so far the latest stage in the international normative process, UNEP and the FAO decided in 1995 to transform the voluntary PIC procedure, which they had been implementing jointly since its adoption in soft law form in the late 1980s, into a legally binding international instrument. This led to the signing of a global PIC convention, the Rotterdam Convention, in 1998. But again, the transformation of soft law into hard law was achieved at the expense of certain important substantive features of the existing voluntary regime. The threshold for making substances subject to the PIC procedure has been raised substantially. The coverage of the regime will be reduced as political commitments *erga omnes* are transformed into legal obligations *inter partes*. And the provisions of the Rotterdam Convention further entrench and isolate PIC as a purely procedural form of transnational regulation.

TOXIC SUBSTANCES IN INTERNATIONAL TRADE: DEFINING THE PROBLEM AND THE OBJECT OF TRANSNATIONAL REGULATION

It was public and governmental concern with the serious human and environmental costs of the largely uncontrolled use of hazardous pesticides in developing countries that propelled the issue of international trade in banned and severely restricted chemicals onto the international political agenda in the late 1970s and transformed this category of chemicals into the object of a transnational normative process. However, pesticide problems in the Third World are not caused *exclusively* by imported chemicals whose use is either banned or subject to severe regulatory restrictions in exporting countries. Pesticides which *can* be legally marketed and applied in industrialised countries may nevertheless cause health or environmental problems under specific conditions of use in developing countries, and some developing countries with burgeoning chemical industries have become not only users but also important *producers* of pesticides in their own right.

The fact that the problem to be addressed by transnational law has from the outset been defined as *international trade* in *banned and severely restricted* pesticides and that international normative efforts have focused largely on this dimension of what is in fact a larger issue—one linked to a particular overall pattern of agricultural development in the Third World, which is heavily reliant on genetically uniform, high-yielding crop varieties and high inputs of agrochemicals—can be attributed to the conceptual prism of interstate relations and territorial regulatory jurisdictions through which government policy-makers and international lawyers have viewed and analysed this issue. This approach, focusing on a particular epiphenomenon, necessarily imposes limitations on the potential effectiveness of transnational regulatory intervention in addressing more fundamental, underlying problems.

When UNEP Governing Council first brought the toxic trade problem to the attention of the international community in 1977, it described the problem category rather vaguely as 'potentially harmful chemicals, in whatever form or commodity, which are *unacceptable for domestic purposes* in the exporting country.'[1] The description became somewhat more precise in a subsequent Governing Council decision, which referred to chemicals 'which are *restricted, or not registered for use*, in the countries of origin.'[2] The UN General Assembly used similar language in its resolutions stigmatising 'products whose consumption and/or sale have been *banned, withdrawn, severely restricted* or . . . *not approved*' because they 'have been judged to endanger health and the environment.'[3] These resolutions, drafted as political statements rather than regulatory instruments and intended to apply to a variety of product categories, including not only pesticides, but also industrial chemicals, consumer products and pharmaceuticals, were necessarily marked by some terminological imprecision.

In its first attempt to elaborate an operational regulatory instrument, the OECD delineated its scope of application by reference to the concept of 'banned or severely restricted chemical', a concept defined rather tautologically as including 'any chemical that is the subject of a control action taken by a competent authority in the exporting . . . country . . . to ban or severely restrict the use or handling of the chemical in order to protect human health or environment domestically' or to refuse 'authorisation for a proposed first time use' for similar reasons.[4] As a result, 'banned or severely restricted

[1] UNEP Governing Council Dec 85 (V) (emphasis added).

[2] UNEP Governing Council Dec 6/4 (emphasis added).

[3] UNGA Res 37/137, 37 UN GAOR Supp (No 51), UN Doc A/37/51, 1982, pp 112–13 (emphasis added).

[4] Guiding Principles on Information Exchange Related to Export of Banned or Severely Restricted Chemicals, OECD Doc C(84)37(Final), Appendix, para 3.

chemical' became a term of art, which was used in most subsequent international instruments. UNEP Governing Council, though it had initially called for the development of guidelines on international trade in products more broadly described as 'potentially harmful chemicals, in particular pesticides,'[5] later adopted the OECD terminology in the Provisional Notification Scheme it endorsed in 1984. In the 1985 FAO Code of Conduct on the Distribution and Use of Pesticides, the definition of 'banned' and 'severely restricted' pesticides was further narrowed down by specifying that a 'severe restriction' is the equivalent of a prohibition of '*virtually all* registered uses' and eliminating any reference to handling restrictions.

Yet, many pesticides which are not banned but merely subject to stringent handling restrictions in industrialised countries, have proved to be particularly hazardous under prevailing conditions of use in developing countries. Of seven pesticides identified by NGOs in 1989 as responsible for serious health problems in the Third World,[6] none are banned in a majority of industrialised countries.[7] When the FAO Code was renegotiated in 1989, some developing countries unsuccessfully proposed amending the definition of 'severely restricted' pesticides to include pesticides 'governed by strict handling regulations.'[8] Similar proposals were made during the amendment process of UNEP's London Guidelines. As a compromise, a new category of chemicals was eventually identified as a legitimate object of international regulatory attention within the scope of the prior informed consent procedures introduced by both UNEP and the FAO in 1989: '*acutely hazardous pesticide formulations* of concern to developing countries, which are not already included in the PIC procedure.'[9]

The definitions of 'banned' and 'severely restricted' pesticides and 'acutely hazardous pesticide formulations', as laid down in the FAO Code of Conduct and UNEP London Guidelines, both as amended in 1989, were subject to further interpretation and refinement at the international level in the process of implementing the voluntary PIC procedure. The expert panel established jointly by the FAO and UNEP to determine which chemicals should be made subject to this procedure generally gave a rather restrictive interpretation of what is to be understood by national regulatory

[5] UNEP Governing Council Dec 10/24, para 1 (c), UN Doc UNEP/GC.10/14, 1982, p 102.

[6] Carbofuran, dichlorvos, methamidophos, methomyl, methyl parathion, monocrotophos, phosphamidon. See *The FAO Code: Missing Ingredients, Pesticides Trust*, London, Oct 1989, p 99.

[7] Consolidated list of products whose consumption and/or sale have been banned, withdrawn, severely restricted or not approved by Governments, UN Doc ST/ESA/239, August 1994, pp 211–12, 294, 308–09, 299, 315.

[8] Report of the Government Consultation on the Principle of Prior Informed Consent in the International Code of Conduct on the Distribution and Use of Pesticides, FAO Doc AGP:1989/M/2, p 9, para 55.

[9] UN Doc UNEP/PIC.WG.2/4, p 26 (emphasis added).

measures taken for 'health or environmental reasons' and subjected such national measures as had been notified pursuant to the FAO Code and UNEP Guidelines to strict scrutiny. As a result, only 22 pesticides were identified for inclusion in the list of PIC chemicals between 1990 and 1997.

As a general rule, any strengthening of the substantive obligations of exporting states with respect to exports of banned or severely restricted chemicals has been accompanied by a narrowing of the category of chemicals subject to these obligations. This happened, as we saw, in the transformation of the soft law instruments from a mere export notification regime to a prior informed consent regime. The same has occurred in the process of translating the voluntary international export notification regime into legally binding provisions of EC law, whose scope of application was limited to those chemicals banned or severely restricted at the Community level. And the recent transformation of UNEP-FAO voluntary PIC regime into a legally binding instrument resulted in a similar narrowing of its scope. Even though the general definitions of 'banned' and 'severely restricted' chemicals and 'hazardous pesticide formulations' have remained roughly the same, the data requirements for consideration of national measures have been vastly expanded, the criteria qualifying products for PIC listing made more stringent, and the international decision-making process for listing chemicals has become considerably more formal, slow and cumbersome.

DETERMINING THE OBJECTIVE OF THE INTERNATIONAL REGULATORY EFFORTS

There has never been a single, universally recognised statement of the purpose of transnational regulatory activity in the field of international trade in banned and severely restricted pesticides. Many attempts to formulate this objective have apparently had some difficulty in actually distinguishing ends from means. A typical example is Article 1 of Regulation (EEC) No 2455/92, entitled 'Objectives', which provides that this instrument's purpose is:

> to establish a common system of notification and information for imports from and exports to third countries of certain chemicals which are banned or severely restricted on account of their effects on human health and the environment and to apply the international notification and 'prior informed consent' (PIC) procedure established by [UNEP and FAO].

One has to search in the preamble for some statement of what these procedures are actually intended to achieve. The most specific pertinent recital says no more than that 'measures are necessary for the protection of man and the environment, in both the Community and third countries.'[10] A similarly vague formulation of purpose can be found in UNEP's London Guidelines, which also amalgamate ends and means in declaring their objective of 'increasing chemical safety in all countries through the exchange of information on chemicals in international trade.'[11] Thus, aims are either stated in extremely vague and general terms which effectively make them indistinguishable from the goal of any form of international cooperation relating to the management of hazardous chemicals, or in very specific terms which reflect the means to be used—information exchange—rather than the actual aim pursued by their use. This lack of any explicit statement of the objective of international normative activity can be explained by the absence of real consensus between governments on what the ultimate aim of regulating international trade in banned and severely restricted chemicals actually is.

When the Governing Council of UNEP and the United Nations General Assembly first called for measures to address the issue of international trade in banned or severely restricted chemicals in the late 1970s, they expressed their special concern about the human health and environmental health effects of the use of such chemicals in importing developing countries. The international measures called for were to be aimed primarily at 'safeguarding the health and environment of the importing country'[12] by 'discourag[ing] the *exportation* of banned products'[13] and 'ensur[ing] protection against risks associated with potentially harmful chemicals caused by lack of awareness' in importing countries.[14] International regulatory action was needed to 'search for a solution to problems arising from the *production and export* of banned or severely restricted substances.'[15] There was a rather strong focus on the responsibilities of producing and exporting countries and the need to control exports of banned and severely restricted chemicals. A group of senior governmental experts in environmental law, meeting under the auspices of UNEP in 1982, formulated the objective of UNEP's future normative efforts in this area as '*to control international trade* in hazardous or inadequately tested chemicals, particularly where the sale of such substances has already been banned or restricted in the producing country.'[16]

But this early emphasis on export control was soon watered down to a focus on information exchange procedures. As we saw in chapter 12, the OECD Guiding Principles, the first soft law instrument to be drafted,

[10] Regulation (EEC) No 2455/92, 11th preambular para.
[11] London Guidelines, Introduction, para 1.
[12] UNGA Res 37/137.
[13] UNGA Res 34/173 (emphasis added).
[14] UNEP Governing Council Dec 6/4.
[15] UNGA Res 36/166 (emphasis added).
[16] Report of the *Ad Hoc* Meeting of Senior Government Officials Expert in Environmental Law, UN Doc UNEP/GC.10/5/Add 2, 1982, Annex, p 7 (emphasis added).

defined its objective specifically as to 'assist . . . importing countries to make timely and *informed* decisions about chemicals entering their territories,'[17] while stressing that the 'the protection of man and the environment from the hazards associated with [such] chemicals' was 'the primary responsibility' of importing countries.[18] The OECD was particularly keen to emphasise that 'the procedures of the exporting country should not be such as to delay or control the export.'[19] It even explicitly gave its normative intervention an additional economic and free trade rationale, when professing to 'support national efforts to control the hazards associated with chemicals *while minimising competitive and trade distortions*.'[20] So did the FAO Director-General in his preface to the International Code of Conduct on the Distribution and Use of Pesticides, where he described the aim of the FAO's standard-setting activities in the field of pesticides as 'to increase international confidence in the availability, regulation, marketing and use of pesticides for the improvement of agriculture, public health and personal comfort.'[21]

The various rather disparate statements of the objective of international normative efforts also reflect a number of implicit assumptions about the *causes* of the problem these efforts seek to address. In the London Guidelines, the 'serious and costly health and environmental problems' resulting from the export and use in developing countries of chemicals banned or severely restricted in industrialised countries are ascribed 'to *ignorance about the risks* associated with the use of chemicals.'[22] The FAO Code, for its part, refers to 'improper handling or use' of pesticides[23] due to the lack of effective national regulatory controls as the main cause of health and environmental effects in developing countries. The Code is consequently designed 'to set forth responsibilities and establish voluntary standards of conduct for all public and private entities . . . particularly *where there is no or an inadequate national law to regulate pesticides*'[24] and thus to 'promote practices which encourage the safe and efficient use of pesticides, including minimizing adverse effects on humans and the environment and preventing accidental poisoning from improper handling.'[25]

With respect specifically to international trade in banned and severely restricted chemicals, the objective pursued by the various international regulatory instruments is 'enhancing the sound management of chemicals *through the exchange of scientific, technical, economic and legal*

17 OECD Guiding Principles, 11th preambular para (emphasis added).
18 *Ibid*, 10th preambular para.
19 *Ibid*, para 5 *in fine*.
20 *Ibid*, 12th preambular para (emphasis added).
21 FAO Code of Conduct, Preface, p 1.
22 UNEP London Guidelines, Introduction, para 8 (emphasis added).
23 FAO Code of Conduct, Art 1.3.
24 *Ibid*, Art 1.1 (emphasis added).
25 *Ibid*, Art 1.5.3.

information.'[26] Information exchange is perceived as the main means to enable competent authorities in importing countries 'to *assess the risks* associated with the pesticide and *to make timely and informed decisions* as to the importation and use of the pesticides covered,'[27] to '*strengthen the national capacities of developing countries to protect themselves* from the consumption and/or sale of banned, withdrawn, severely restricted or . . . non-approved products.'[28] Thus, the purpose of international normative activity is clearly seen as merely supportive of *national* decision-making and *national* regulation of hazardous chemicals by importing countries and not as a substitute for it.

When international consensus finally emerges on prior informed consent procedures, those procedures are also presented primarily as 'a mechanism for importing countries to formally record and disseminate *their* decisions,'[29] that is, as just another form of information exchange rather than an export control mechanism. This philosophy is confirmed and made explicit in the most recent and authoritative statement of purpose of the PIC procedure, which describes the objective of the Rotterdam Convention as:

> to promote shared responsibility and cooperative efforts among Parties in the international trade of certain hazardous chemicals in order to protect human health and the environment from potential harm and to contribute to their environmentally sound use, by *facilitating information exchange* about their characteristics, by providing for a *national* decision-making process on their import and export and by disseminating these decisions to Parties.[30]

CONCEPTUALISING THE SOLUTION: DEVISING THE REGULATORY INSTRUMENTS

We have seen how the problem of the use of banned and severely restricted pesticides in developing countries has been diagnosed as essentially due to 'ignorance', to 'lack of awareness' of the risks associated with these chemicals, ie to inadequate information, as well as to 'inadequate national law' and the absence of an effective regulatory infrastructure in importing countries. The proposed remedy fits the diagnosis: the main objective of international normative efforts should be the provision of adequate information to these countries, together with other forms of assistance, in order to strengthen their capacity to 'protect themselves', to make their own 'informed decisions' about imported chemicals. The solution as conceptualised is one that is premised on the 'primary responsibility' of the

[26] London Guidelines, Introduction, para 2 (emphasis added).
[27] FAO Code, Art 9.2 (emphasis added).
[28] UNGA Res 37/137, para 3 (emphasis added).
[29] London Guidelines, Introduction, para 5 (emphasis added).
[30] Rotterdam Convention, Art 1 (emphasis added).

importing country and does not interfere with the fragmented, territorial structure of regulatory law and the basic principles of free trade. The regulatory instruments designed to operationalise this approach are organised information exchange about national regulatory actions and export notification mechanisms for banned and severely restricted chemicals. At first, the responsibility of exporting states is explicitly delineated as not extending beyond the provision of information.

In a second stage of the normative process, the principle of 'prior informed consent' gains recognition as the basic international standard, one that is still fully consistent with the primary responsibility and regulatory sovereignty of importing countries. It further institutionalises some measure of shared responsibility on the part of exporting countries. In addition to providing information, they are now formally committed to respecting the 'informed decisions' of importing countries which are officially recorded through an international mechanism, although the exact implications of this commitment remain somewhat hazy. Initially conceived by its advocates as a shipment-specific administrative export control mechanism to be administered by exporting countries, the PIC 'principle' is transformed into a formalised PIC 'procedure' disconnected from actual trade transactions. In essence, it becomes a mechanism for formally 'recording' national regulatory decisions of importing countries at the international level and 'disseminating' them to the international community at large, ie an additional form of information exchange.

It is only most reluctantly that exporting countries have accepted some sort of subsidiary responsibility for enforcement. Under the voluntary procedure of the FAO Code and the London Guidelines, there was no unambiguous commitment on the part of exporting countries to actually prohibit any exports in violation of importing countries' decisions not to consent to importation of particular PIC chemicals. Many exporting countries still considered that PIC decisions should be enforced at the point of importation. The EC, however, did unilaterally impose such a prohibition on exporters subject to its jurisdiction through Regulation (EEC) No 2455/92, but then failed to take the necessary implementing action to make this prohibition fully effective until early 1994. It was not without some difficulty that the EC managed to level the playing field by obtaining the insertion in the Rotterdam Convention of a clause requiring all parties to take appropriate legislative or administrative measures to ensure that exporters subject to their jurisdiction comply with other parties' PIC decisions.

ASSESSMENT OF THE EFFECTIVENESS OF TRANSNATIONAL NORMATIVE EFFORTS IN THE FIELD OF TOXIC TRADE

If the objective of the international normative process is narrowly defined as the promotion of the exchange of information on banned and severely restricted chemicals in international trade, this process can be considered to have been relatively effective. Through the establishment of a network of designated national authorities and of mechanisms for the notification of national regulatory actions as well as export notification, the amount of information exchanged internationally and potentially available to regulatory authorities in importing countries has no doubt increased considerably since the mid-1980s. But it is by no means self-evident that this has resulted in a commensurate reduction of health and environmental risks from pesticides in the developing world.

The assumption—explicitly or implicitly made in many of the statements of purpose of the international regulatory efforts quoted above—that the importation by developing countries of pesticides which are banned or severely restricted in industrialised countries is due only to 'ignorance' or lack of full information about the real nature and hazards of those substances and their regulatory status in exporting countries, and that the provision of adequate information will be sufficient to stop such importation, is highly questionable. The mere provision of information simply does not necessarily result in policy changes in importing countries: if the social and economic arrangements in a developing country are such that the sale and use of hazardous pesticides will enable a small group of people to reap substantial economic benefits while inflicting any risks on others, better governmental awareness of those risks will not automatically lead to a different risk/benefit assessment and regulatory policy.

But even if the importation and use of hazardous pesticides *is* actually the result of lack of information in importing countries, the mere provision of information to their authorities through international notification procedures will not in itself be sufficient to end such importation and use. This strategy will only be effective if these authorities also have the political will, necessary regulatory instruments and means of enforcement to prevent these activities.[31] If only the latter are lacking, PIC procedures may be helpful, provided that exporting countries are prepared to provide enforcement assistance by controlling exports of chemicals subject to PIC to ensure that they do not violate decisions of importing countries. But as we have seen, the drafting history of the various international regulatory instruments indicates a considerable reluctance on the part of many exporting countries precisely to take such enforcement action. The relevant provision of the PIC Convention will, when it eventually enters into force, impose a legal obligation on all exporting parties to take 'appropriate legislative and/or administrative measures' to ensure compliance by exporters under their jurisdiction with PIC decisions of other parties. It remains to be seen

[31] An analysis of pesticide regulatory policy in Mexico, for example, reveals that the problem is not lack of legislation but lack of sufficient political consensus and resources to enforce it. See Goodman (1987).

whether this provision will be more effective than those of the existing voluntary instruments.

As a matter of fact, David Victor, a political scientist who has studied the implementation of the voluntary PIC procedure by UNEP and the FAO and questioned the need for a legally binding instrument to make it more effective, has asserted that this procedure is 'highly successful' because 'there is not a single documented case of a firm exporting a PIC substance contrary to the PIC procedure.'[32] Compliance with the voluntary PIC procedure is very hard to verify, however, because it does not actually provide any organised mechanism for monitoring compliance. There are no reporting obligations for either exporting or importing countries nor any other system for gathering information about actual trade in PIC chemicals. The FAO/UNEP Joint Group of Experts on PIC, which supervises the operation of the voluntary procedure, has no mandate to scrutinise compliance by individual countries.[33] There is some evidence from NGO sources, however, that indicates that certain banned or severely restricted pesticides, including compounds subject to the voluntary PIC procedure, are still widely used in developing countries.[34] This does not necessarily imply, of course, that the products in question have been exported to those countries in violation of the PIC procedure; the importing country may have consented to their importation or they may be produced locally.

It should be kept in mind that the PIC procedure is neutral from a substantive point of view: it only serves to elicit and formally record decisions freely made by national authorities about the future importation of PIC chemicals. To the extent that it merely formalises and registers the status quo, the application of the PIC procedure will not result in any improvement of the situation from a public health and environmental point of view. The procedure is in fact explicitly biased towards the status quo, as it provides that existing trade patterns may continue where an importing country fails to make a PIC decision.

Where it does no more than entrench the status quo, the institutionalisation of notification and consent procedures at the international level may have perverse effects. In a way, notification systems and even, in the final analysis, prior informed consent, amount to little more than a sophisticated way of legitimating the continued export of certain banned and severely restricted pesticides by establishing a set of procedures and channels of

[32] Victor (1998), p 250. This claim is apparently based on a number of interviews with national and international officials involved in the administration of PIC and experts from industry and NGOs, not on a detailed review of empirical evidence.

[33] It is somewhat confusing, therefore, that Victor describes the role of the Joint Group as 'implementation review'. *Ibid*, p 260. It seems to me that its actual role is more akin to policy-making.

[34] *The Pesticide Trail: The impact of trade controls on reducing pesticide hazards in developing countries*, The Pesticides Trust, London, Jan 1995.

information.[35] They fail to address the underlying substantive issues while conveying the impression that something is being done about them. Is not the essential effect of export notification—and, in a similar way, of the provision of detailed hazard information in the form of PIC decision guidance documents—to shift the full burden of responsibility to the importing country? The transfer of information effectively relieves the exporting country of responsibility. Prior informed consent merely completes the process of exoneration of responsibility. Indeed, the consenting recipient country knowingly assumes the risk and can no longer rely on lack of information to excuse its failure to guard against the hazard. As the legal maxim goes: *Volenti non fit iniuria.*

A more meaningful standard by which to judge the effectiveness of the PIC procedure, rather than formal compliance with PIC decisions, is whether the procedure actually results in a reduction in the production, trade and use of banned and severely restricted pesticides. Even though UNEP and the FAO have gone out of their way, in PIC decision guidance documents, to stress that the inclusion of a chemical in the PIC list is not to be viewed as a recommendation to ban that chemical, the vast majority of governments participating in the PIC procedure have used it to prohibit the import of the chemicals on which they were invited to make PIC decisions.[36] But the actual impact of international regulatory procedures on trade is extremely difficult to assess due to a lack of publicly accessible information. Import and export statistics normally contain only aggregate information on pesticides in general, or on broad subcategories such as insecticides, fungicides and herbicides, but provide no figures on trade in individual compounds. This makes it impossible to distinguish exports of banned and severely restricted substances from overall pesticide exports. Whatever information can be found is of a fragmentary nature, often the result of occasional studies carried out by intergovernmental or non-governmental institutions.

One study of pesticide exports from the United States, based on a detailed analysis of customs shipping records, found that the volume of identifiable exports of banned and restricted pesticides from US ports increased by 28.5 per cent between 1992 and 1996.[37] These figures include pesticides that

[35] Thus also Ward (1994a), p 88: 'A trade perspective might account for the utility of information exchange and prior informed consent in terms which emphasise *their potential to promote principled international trade in chemicals*, within the boundaries of international trade law, *even when chemicals are banned or severely restricted somewhere in the international market.*' (emphasis added)

[36] See Victor (1998), p 252, Table 6.2, for an overview of the import responses made by participating countries pursuant to the PIC procedure for each chemical.

[37] Foundation for Advancements in Science and Education, *Exporting Risk: Pesticide Exports from US Ports*, 1995–1996, FASE Research Report, Los Angeles, 1998, p 9. The figures include only those pesticides whose chemical identity was mentioned in the shipment records, ie 36% of total exports in 1995–1996. *Ibid*, p 20, n 35. See also Smith & Root (1999).

were never registered in the US, pesticides that were previously registered but were banned by regulatory action, pesticides regarded as severely restricted by US authorities and, finally, 'restricted use' pesticides which, though not regarded as severely restricted by US authorities and not subject to export notification requirements under the FIFRA, arguably fall into that category. Most of the export growth was in the 'restricted use' category. The aggregate volume of exports of the first three categories of pesticides remained more or less stable during the period under consideration. However, the most recent published data from the same source, covering the period 1997–2000, indicate that, while the overall export volume for the same three categories taken together shows no declining trend, the relative share of exports in the second and third category has recently diminished, while that in the first category has considerably increased (more than doubled compared to 1992).[38] No explanation is provided for these trends. At any rate, it seems that the application of the FIFRA export notification requirements to pesticides never registered for use in the United States has no noticeable impact on US exports of those products. As for the recent decline in exports of banned or severely restricted pestidices, apparent only since 1998—20 years after the introduction of US export notification requirements and six years after the voluntary PIC procedure became operational—its cause is not evident.

Similar quantitative information is not available for exports from the European Community. However, the reports published by the European Commission on the implementation of the 1988 and 1992 EEC Regulations on the export of hazardous chemicals contain some information on export notifications which provides a very rough picture of actual trade. As was already mentioned in chapter 15, the number of notifications made pursuant to the 1988 Regulation between 1989 and 1992 was rather small: only 60 export notifications were made in all, covering exports of eight chemicals banned or severely restricted in the Community to some 30 different countries of destination.[39] Since export notification is required only for the first export from the Community to any third country, the number of notifications does not reflect the total number of export transactions, nor provide any indication as to the quantities of exported chemicals. Since the entry into force of the 1992 Regulation, the total number of export notifications has risen to 488 and the number of countries of destination to 99.[40] The Commission reports that 'the effectiveness of the Regulation was in general considered to be very satisfactory' and asserts that the fact that 'the

[38] Smith (2001), p 8.

[39] *Report from the Commission on the operation of Regulation (EEC) No 1734/88 concerning export from and import into the Community of certain dangerous chemicals*, EC Doc COM(93) 121 final, 31 Mar 1993.

[40] *Report from the Commission on the operation of Regulation (EEC) No 2455/92 of 23 July 1992 concerning the export and the import of certain dangerous chemicals*, EC Doc COM(1998) 245 final, 28 Apr 1998, pp 18–19.

number of export notifications sent to third countries has increased 8 fold' between 1992 and 1997 constitutes 'significant progress.'[41]

If this increased number of notifications reflected a proportional increase in the export of banned and severely restricted chemicals from the Community, the Commission's view of the effectiveness of Regulation 2455/92 would be surprising. However, as pointed out above, no direct inference about the volume of trade can be made from the number of notifications, as a single notification from a single member state covers all subsequent exports of the same chemical to the same third country. In referring to 'progress', the Commission probably saw the increase in the number of notifications as evidence of a higher rate of compliance by exporters than under the 1988 Regulation. Indeed, in its 1993 report about the implementation of that earlier regulation, the Commission had expressed some doubts as to whether the low number of export notifications really matched actual exports.[42] Contrary to Regulation 2455/92, its predecessor, Regulation 1734/88, did not impose any obligations directly on exporters, but only on member states. Anyway, the number of notifications indicates that, despite the existence of an export notification requirement in the Community since 1989 and the subsequent adoption of the PIC procedure, there are still substantial exports of a number of chemicals banned or severely restricted under Community law. On the other hand, the fact that no notifications at all were recorded for over half of the 39 substances and groups of substances listed in Annex I to the 1992 Regulation[43] suggests that more than half of the entries in Annex I are largely symbolic, in that these products, when they were formally made subject to export notification requirements, were in fact no longer produced or traded in the Community.

A global survey of international trade in 'widely prohibited chemicals' was carried out by UNEP and the FAO in 1995 as part of the preparatory process of the negotiations on a legally binding PIC instrument. A questionnaire was sent out to all governments requesting information on the production, export and import during the period 1990–1994 of all chemicals subject to the voluntary PIC procedure, as well as other chemicals listed in Annex I of EEC Regulation 2455/92, which are considered as candidate PIC chemicals as they are banned or severely restricted in 15 countries. Information was provided by 60 countries, representing about 75 per cent of the global chemicals trade. Though the data collected are not comprehensive, the study provides some indications on the status of trade in banned and severely restricted chemicals worldwide. These indications are ambiguous, however.

[41] EC Doc COM(1998) 245 final, 28 Apr 1998, pp 9, 13
[42] EC Doc COM(93) 121 final, p 4, para 2.1.2.
[43] EC Doc COM(1998) 245 final, p 20.

On the one hand, the study suggests a decline in the number of widely prohibited chemicals that are still in production. In 1990, 22 of the 47 chemicals selected for the study were still being manufactured; in 1994, only 10 of them were reportedly still in production.[44] The production of six PIC chemicals was discontinued between 1990 and 1994,[45] for some of them even *before* they formally became subject to the voluntary PIC procedure. For the remaining PIC chemicals which are still being produced, 'production quantities appear to have remained stable or decreased by 1994.'[46] On the other hand, the number of chemicals traded seems to have increased during the same period. In 1994, 35 chemicals were reported as being exported, as opposed to only 23 in 1990.[47] The corresponding figures for imports are 40 in 1994 versus 30 in 1990.[48] Every single chemical on the PIC list was still being imported into South America in 1994, mostly without any clear declining trend in quantities.[49]

The authors of the study, while emphasising the limitations of the available data, conclude that:

> the study does suggest that, on a global level, trade in banned and severely restricted chemicals still occurs, although production appears to have undergone a sharp decline in 1994 as compared with 1990.[50]

They do not venture to draw any conclusions as to the relationship between the observed decrease in production and international regulatory efforts. Were these efforts instrumental in halting the production of a number of PIC chemicals? Or was their impact only marginal, as these chemicals had already reached the end of their commercial life anyway? The evidence of continuing trade in banned and severely restricted chemicals suggests that the international normative process has not yet had a major impact on such trade.

If export notification and prior informed consent schemes are viewed as part of a broader process of capacity-building in developing countries—as they indeed are in many policy statements—their effectiveness in promoting chemical safety will to a large extent be conditioned by that of the other elements of this process. The provision of information is only one element; other essential elements include such matters as the development of national legislation, regulatory infrastructure and enforcement capacity and the education and training of users and public officials.

[44] *Report on study on international trade in widely prohibited chemicals*, UN Doc UNEP/FAO/PIC/INC.1/Inf.1, 16 Feb 1996, p 3, para 8.
[45] *Ibid*, pp 8–9, Table 1.
[46] *Ibid*, p 3, para 8
[47] *Ibid*, p 4, para 13.
[48] *Ibid*, p 5, para 18.
[49] *Ibid*, pp 17–20, Table 3.
[50] *Ibid*, p 6, para 25.

The FAO Code of Conduct, for one, places considerable emphasis on these elements. The surveys carried out by the FAO in an attempt to evaluate the impact of the Code have produced some interesting information on these aspects. The first results published in 1987 indicated that a quarter of the developing countries responding to the questionnaire did not have 'legislative authority to regulate the distribution and use of pesticides' nor operational registration and control schemes.[51] The vast majority of the respondents also complained that government resources allocated to the regulation and management of pesticide use in their countries were insufficient.[52] Two years later, the responses, covering a larger number of developing countries, were still roughly the same: 84 per cent of those countries reported that government resources available for this purpose were 'not adequate to control pesticides'.[53] Roughly two thirds of them also specifically responded that they did not have operational internal systems to analyse data on imported pesticides prior to their import.[54]

Ten years after the adoption of the FAO Code, another review of implementation came to the conclusion that:

> The main area of progress was on pesticide legislation and regulations on availability, distribution and use. . . . Only very few countries remain without legislation. . . . *Although the government regulatory framework may gradually have improved in some situations, in general the distribution, trade and use practices showed only limited improvement.*[55]

Thus, although there seems to have been progress in the formal implementation of the Code's provisions on national regulatory policies, this has not proved to be effective in actually improving the situation on the ground. This is also the conclusion reached by one of the rare academic studies of the effectiveness of the FAO Code of Conduct and international regulatory efforts in the field of pesticides management generally. According to Paarlberg:

> UNEP and FAO have devoted enormous energy to the issue of international pesticide trade. This is the issue of greatest political interest to international industry and the NGOs, but it is not the main source of unsafe use problems in poor countries. . . . *Even if this PIC experiment succeeds on its own terms, its actual impact on pesticide exports may at first be scarcely noticeable.*[56]

[51] Progress report on the implementation of the International Code of Conduct on the Distribution and Use of Pesticides, FAO Doc CL 92/2, Sept 1987, p 3, paras 13–14.

[52] *Ibid*, p 4, para 19.

[53] International Code of Conduct on the Distribution and Use of Pesticides: analysis of responses to the questionnaire by Governments, FAO Doc AGP:GC/89/BP.1, Jan 1989, p 6.

[54] *Ibid*, p 9.

[55] Review of the implementation of the International Code of Conduct on the Distribution and Use of Pesticides, FAO Doc COAG/95/8, Jan 1995, pp 2, 3, paras 12, 16 (emphasis added).

[56] Paarlberg (1993), p 344.

It should be added that the political focus on the 'dumping' of banned and severely restricted pesticides in developing countries is also convenient for Third World governments. It is much easier to blame transnational agrochemical companies and Northern governments for chemical safety problems in the South than to change domestic policies which also contribute to these problems. This, too, may explain the emphasis of the international normative process on what is, in reality, an epiphenomenon of well-entrenched agricultural and industrial development strategies.

19

Transnational Environmental Law between Legal Instrumentalism and Legal Symbolism

HAVING SUMMARISED MY findings on the international normative process in the field of toxic emissions in the aquatic environment and toxic substances in international trade, I shall now attempt to draw a number of general conclusions, and, in so doing, highlight a number of striking similarities between the two case studies presented.

THE PRIMACY OF PROCESS OR THE PERPETUAL DEFERRAL OF SUBSTANTIVE OBLIGATIONS

The foremost common feature of the normative processes in both areas is the propensity of transnational environmental law to transform substance into process.[1] As we have seen above, after having apprehended the problem, the international normative process focuses on the development of regulatory instruments to address it. In doing so, it has proved to be much more productive in developing procedural obligations for states and non-state actors than in establishing actual substantive standards to govern their conduct.

The problem of toxic discharges to the aquatic environment can be tackled through several kinds of substantive legal norms. The type of norm most frequently used in both domestic and transnational law is the emission standard. However, as the discussion in chapters 4 and 8 amply illustrates, environmental quality standards are another possible form of indirect substantive regulation of emissions from point sources. Where releases into the environment are caused by diffuse sources, product standards are an appropriate instrument. Such standards can take different forms, from the outright prohibition of the production, marketing or use

[1] On the propensity of international legal discourse to transform substance into process, see generally Kennedy (1987).

of hazardous products and their substitution by less harmful products, to less drastic measures designed merely to limit pollution caused by the use of the products in question. Direct regulation of production processes could also be envisaged, either through the proscription of environmentally unsound processes or the prescription of particular process changes or the use of certain add-on pollution reduction and control technologies. Transnational law will effectively constrain the discretion of national regulators only to the extent that it actually mandates the application of such specific substantive standards. As we have seen, the international normative process is far from reaching this level of specificity in respect of most toxic pollutants and their emission sources.

Even where it seems to establish what, at first sight, may appear to be a powerful substantive regime, such as the obligation to eliminate pollution by black list substances, international and EC law in fact turns out to provide little more than a procedural framework for national and international measures that remain to be specified. Let us take Directive 76/464/EEC as an example. This framework directive itself sets no real substantive environmental standards but merely enunciates a number of general obligations with respect to the reduction and elimination of water pollution to be further specified through decision-making processes at the Community and national level. The only hard obligations of the member states are to subject discharges of black and grey list substances to a permit system, to establish emission limit values for individual discharges through this system, to lay down national water quality objectives for grey list substances and to draw up national pollution reduction programmes for those substances—programmes whose substantive content is left entirely at their discretion. In essence, these are all merely procedural obligations, which do not as such guarantee any environmental result.

It is only at the end of a protracted Community decision-making process on individual black list substances that Community law actually may impose on member states the obligation to apply specific emission limit values or environmental quality objectives to specific discharges. As we have seen, this process has proved so cumbersome that such specific substantive obligations have been laid down for only a very limited number of substances and sources. For many years, there seems to have been a tacit understanding between the Commission and the member states that the 'framework' nature of Directive 76/464/EEC implied little in the way of substantive obligations other than those specifically laid down in a small number of daughter directives. The Commission therefore refrained from using the interpretative power of the Court of Justice as a means of putting flesh on the bones of the general Community law obligations to eliminate pollution by certain substances and reduce it by others. It is only recently that the Commission, in a remarkable moment of institutional schizophrenia, decided to seek judicial enforcement of the provisions on pollution reduction programmes, at the same time as it proposed to the Council to repeal those very same provisions and replace them with new procedural provisions contained in a framework directive on the management of water resources. Meanwhile, the emission control provisions of Directive 76/464/EEC are being superseded by those of the IPPC Directive, which represents the ultimate triumph of process over substance.

The various land-based sources and river pollution regimes established under international law present a very similar picture. They rely on the same regulatory techniques and instruments—national and international plans, programmes and measures, administrative licensing systems, emission standards, quality objectives, product standards—as Community law. They impose on their contracting parties few concrete substantive obligations per se, but mostly lay down only a set of general principles and objectives, as well as a procedural framework for their implementation at the national and international level. One finds that the moment of substantive regulation is continually deferred and, at any rate, failing international agreement on how to translate these objectives and principles into concrete practical standards, remains firmly located at the national level.

In a global survey of the state of international law with respect to marine pollution from land-based sources published in 1990, Michael M'Gonigle found that 'specific categorical obligations of a substantive nature' were 'notably absent' and concluded that:

> the international regulation produced by [regional] agreements has been *largely procedural in nature*, leaving it up to new 'technical' negotiating bodies to set substantive standards at the international level. Overall, therefore, *the major control strategy has been to recast a general obligation into an imprecise institutional one.*[2]

More than a decade later, notwithstanding the second generation of regional instruments for the control of marine pollution that have been developed in Europe, the situation has not materially changed. OSPAR Commission, for example, is mandated by the 1992 Paris Convention to draw up 'plans for the reduction and phasing out of substances that are toxic, persistent and liable to bioaccumulate arising from land-based sources.'[3] The Convention contains no quantified emission reduction targets, nor specific deadlines for implementation. In effect, the actual determination of the substantive content of the parties' obligations under OSPAR Convention is referred to a process of future decision-making on the selection of substances to be made subject to regulation—through ecological risk assessment—and on the identification of 'best available techniques' and 'best environmental practice' for particular sources of pollution and the formulation

[2] M'Gonigle (1990), p 202 (emphasis added).
[3] 1992 Paris Convention, Annex I, Art 3(a).

of specific programmes and measures at the national and international level—through contextual interest balancing based on open-ended environmental, technological and economic criteria. This process is left to the parties themselves, acting both individually and collectively, through the Commission.

Much like the framework provisions of the United Nations Convention on the Law of the Sea (UNCLOS) on the protection of the marine environment, which do not contain much in the way of substantive rules to control the various sources of marine pollution but merely refer to unspecified 'internationally agreed rules, standards and recommended practices and procedures,'[4] the Paris Convention and its counterpart instruments for the Baltic Sea and Mediterranean, as regards the regulation of emissions from land-based sources, ultimately also end up 'refer[ring] the reader to later co-operation which will be limited by vague standards.'[5] The UNCLOS refers to other international instruments for substantive rules and standards on land-based pollution, but these instruments themselves, upon close scrutiny, hardly fulfil the promise of substantive regulation any better than the United Nations Convention itself. Viewing the different regional international legal instruments on land-based sources as a truly substantive regulatory regime, just as much as UNCLOS itself, requires 'faith in the applicability of principles, the working out in practice and the redemption of substance by process.'[6] These instruments are classic example of what Martti Koskenniemi has described as 'the strategy of environmental treaties . . . to treat the substance of the environmental conflict by referring its normative regulation elsewhere.'[7]

The fundamental substantive question raised by international trade in toxic chemicals—should international law prohibit the *production* and *export* of pesticides banned or severely restricted in producing countries for human health and environmental reasons?—is studiously avoided by the international normative process in this field, which, not surprisingly, has focused on the development of procedural rules and arrangements. The first area of normative activity has been the development of international information exchange procedures, initially of a general, non-regulatory nature and later supplemented by procedures linked to actual trade flows such as export notification requirements. In a following stage, further pressure for substantive regulation resulted in the development of an international, voluntary prior informed consent procedure, which was later transformed into a legally binding, conventional regime.

[4] United Nations Convention on the Law of the Sea, Art 207, para 1, on pollution from land-based sources. For a discussion of this provision and its current relevance, see Franckx (1998).

[5] To quote David Kennedy's semantic analysis of UNCLOS. Kennedy (1987), p 243.

[6] *Ibid*, p 206.

[7] Koskenniemi (1991), p 78.

But, again, what was originally envisaged as a way of giving effect to a substantive obligation not to allow exports of banned or severely restricted pesticides unless the competent authorities of the importing state, being duly informed, expressly consent, was transformed into an elaborate information exchange procedure only faintly related to any form of export control. The development of the PIC procedure is another typical example of the 'proceduralization of substance'[8] by the international normative process. It is only at the very end of a complex and drawn-out set of procedures—notification of national control actions, review of these actions by an international panel, listing of chemicals subject to the procedure, elaboration and approval of decision guidance documents, notification of these documents to participating states, communication of national responses to an international clearing-house, compilation and dissemination of these responses to participating states—that a substantive obligation to prevent exports may eventually arise. And the very existence of this ultimate obligation—long disputed by certain exporting states—has only recently been affirmed in hard law.

THE CREATIVE USE OF AMBIGUITY, THE PERVASIVENESS OF NORMATIVE INDETERMINACY AND THE LOW NORMATIVE FORCE OF TRANSNATIONAL ENVIRONMENTAL LAW

It has been noted that 'functional ambiguity' is a basic characteristic of the language of international law.[9] In the two substantive areas under consideration, we have indeed found a lot of evidence that ample use has been made of deliberate ambiguity as a legislative strategy. Frequently, states have chosen to resort to the use of indeterminate terms in formulating normative texts as a way of papering over substantive disagreement. Ambiguity is prevalent at all stages of the normative process: in the definition of the object of regulation, in the formulation of the goals pursued by regulation and in the elaboration of the substantive obligations of states and non-state actors. Ambiguity in legal texts 'is neither accidental nor incidental'. On the contrary, political scientists regard it as 'the most useful attribute of legal language.'[10] Legal scholars as well have observed that indeterminacy is a 'structural property of international legal language itself.'[11]

As regards both toxic emissions and toxic trade, the object of international normative efforts has never been determined in unambiguous terms. The conceptual categories used—'dangerous substances' and 'banned or severely restricted chemicals'—have no fixed boundaries: their delimitation

[8] Kennedy (1987), p 218.
[9] Balekjian (1981), p 358.
[10] Edelman (1985), p 141.
[11] Koskenniemi (1989), p 44.

is in a constant state of flux and states have very different views as to whether particular substances belong to them and are a legitimate target of regulatory efforts. But the very existence of such vaguely defined categories has also made it possible for states to agree on basic principles and objectives of international regulation while at the same time retaining a significant measure of national discretion in determining their actual substantive reach.

A good example of the creative use of ambiguity in the formulation of regulatory objectives is that of the stated goal of eliminating pollution, as found in most of the international instruments on land-based sources and river pollution analysed in Part II of this book. The relative indeterminacy of the notion of 'pollution', as defined prior to the emergence of the precautionary principle, in view of the scientific uncertainty about the causation of harm, allowed states to formulate what seemed to be highly ambitious objectives of pollution reduction and elimination, whose implementation was in fact implicitly conditioned on proof of actual environmental harm. The goal of eliminating pollution, as interpreted in the 1970s, was in effect so conveniently vague that it allowed advocates of pollution control through environmental quality standards and proponents of technology-based emission limitation to rally around a common objective. This is a clear case in which substantive disagreement was 'disguised behind a layer of terms and clauses which are intentionally, that is functionally, ambiguous.'[12]

As to the means to be used by states to achieve such generally worded objectives, the provisions purporting to prescribe their substantive obligations use terms which are often as indeterminate as those used to formulate the objectives themselves. The substantive obligations of the riparian states of the North East Atlantic under the relevant provisions of the 1992 Paris Convention are a case in point. In essence, they require contracting parties to 'prevent and eliminate' pollution from land-based sources by adopting 'programmes and measures' providing for the application of 'best available techniques' and 'best environmental practice,'[13] two concepts whose definition in Appendix 1 of the Convention is so vague as to lack any prescriptive quality. Much the same can be said about the corresponding provisions in other international legal instruments for the protection of the marine and freshwater environment and in relevant EC directives such as the 1996 IPPC Directive.

Functional ambiguity as a normative technique is not, however, necessarily ineffective, as it offers 'the possibility to use a term in an initially rather indeterminate way, until such time as common agreement may promote its elaboration or also definite fixation.'[14] Initially indeterminate

[12] Balekjian (1981), p 363.
[13] 1992 Paris Convention, Art 2, para 3, Art 3, and Annex I, Art 1, para 1.
[14] Balekjian (1981), p 361.

norms may later be specified through further normative activity, thereby progressively acquiring what has been called 'process determinacy'. Indeed that seems to have been the legislative strategy which the drafters of most of the water pollution instruments had in mind, as they all provide for some institutional and procedural mechanism through which more specific common rules can be further elaborated during the course of implementation. In his comprehensive overview of the legal regime for transboundary water pollution, Nollkaemper notes a 'continuous drive to defining increasingly specifically the obligations of states.'[15] But as we have seen in Part II, attempts to make more specific the international and Community obligations of European states with respect to the control of toxic emissions into the aquatic environment have not proved particularly successful. Nollkaemper argues that, somewhat paradoxically, flexible rules may in fact be more effective in certain circumstances.[16]

Overall, the analysis in this book leads to the conclusion that the normative force of existing international norms in the area of transnational toxics regulation tends to be rather low. As regards toxic emissions, most of the existing general norms are little more than policies or principles from which it is difficult to infer specific behavioural prescriptions for the norm addressees. Even where such norms may seem rather determinate to the uninformed reader—for example, the obligation to 'eliminate' pollution by certain hazardous pollutants—it turns out upon closer scrutiny that there is in fact a substantial measure of normative ambiguity and often an explicit or implicit common understanding between the individual states concerned as well as the collective bodies they have put in charge of certain aspects of rule specification and implementation to regard them as mere policies and principles which do not, in and of themselves, mandate specific action in the absence of further elaboration and clarification. In the field of the regulation of international trade in banned and severely restricted pesticides, states have thus far retained considerable discretion in interpreting the rather vague criteria under which particular substances are to be made subject to export notification and prior informed consent regimes and in deciding what action, if any, to take beyond mere information exchange.

The two case studies in this book provide plenty of evidence of the strategic use of ambiguity in the international normative process. In many instances, the cost of agreement has been a considerable measure of indeterminacy of language. Thus, the experience in this area directly contradicts the assertion that 'clarity and precision of the treaty's regulations' is an 'important prerequisite' for their 'universal acceptance.'[17] Rather the exact opposite seems true: it is not clarity and precision, but rather ambiguity that

[15] Nollkaemper (1993a), p 4.
[16] *Ibid*, p 19. Thus also Victor, Raustiala & Skolnikoff (1998), pp 684–89.
[17] Beyerlin & Marauhn (1997), p 151.

is a prerequisite of successful treaty-making. This is not typical of transnational toxics law alone but reflects a general trend in international environmental law 'to use international instruments, which in the past served as the vehicle to generate binding rules of international law, as mere programmatic political documents.'[18] The question of the prescriptive force of international rules leads us to analyse the balance between national discretion and international constraint in transnational environmental law.

THE ALLOCATION OF THE POWER OF SUBSTANTIVE DECISION-MAKING AND THE LOCUS OF INTEREST-BALANCING IN TRANSNATIONAL ENVIRONMENTAL LAW

International law has been described by scholars viewing it from a policy-oriented perspective as a 'global process of authoritative decision' designed to, inter alia,

> identify authoritative decision-makers, state and specify basic community policies, establish appropriate structures for the making of decisions . . . and authorize procedures for the making of the different necessary kinds of decisions.[19]

Who are the 'authoritative decision-makers' identified by transnational environmental law and what structures and procedures does it provide for making substantive regulatory decisions with respect to toxic emissions and toxic trade?

There can be no doubt that authoritative decision-making remains first and foremost in the hands of sovereign states, both in international environmental law and European Community environmental law. To be sure, international law and Community law have created international and supranational 'decision-makers', respectively, and endowed them with some normative powers in the environmental field, but the use these have made of such powers has, on the whole, restricted national regulatory discretion only to a limited extent. National sovereignty is constrained only by a number of rather vague principles and policies and by a set of more or less detailed procedural rules, but, as we have seen, by very few real *substantive* norms. Within the normative framework of the policies, principles and procedures laid down by transnational law, the bulk of the power of actual *substantive* decision-making remains firmly rooted at the national level. Whatever substantive rules exist are generally of such a studiedly ambiguous nature that, in view of the fact that states are also the prime interpreters of their own international obligations,[20] these rules' constraining effect on national regulatory sovereignty is limited.

[18] Székely (1997), p 174.
[19] McDougal & Reisman (1983), p 107. See also Higgins (1994), pp 2–12.
[20] On this question, see generally Gross (1953), pp 59–88.

Under the international legal regimes governing marine pollution from land-based sources and river pollution, it is primarily states who interpret what constitutes 'pollution' and decide what substances are 'dangerous'. While international commissions have been established with the power to develop common interpretations and thus further specify the vague general obligations laid down in international legal instruments, their normative pronouncements are in most cases not legally binding, and the substantive scope of such specific norms as have been developed is invariably very narrow relative to the overall size of the problems which the legal instruments seek to address. And, of course, the decision-making power in these treaty bodies itself remains in the hands of states and is often constrained by explicit or implicit rules of unanimity or consensus. Thus, much the same can be said of the international pollution control conventions as of the UNCLOS, which itself refers to such specialised regional conventions as sources of substantive norms:

> The Convention displaces its own role as establisher of the substantive legal fabric *onto the agents whose behavior it was meant to order*—creating an international legal order by self-effacement.[21]

This 'self-effacement' of the international legal order is even more evident in the outcomes of the international normative process regarding international trade in banned and severely restricted pesticides. Far from superimposing substantive international norms on national law (or non-law) in exporting and importing states, the relevant international instruments merely institute an international procedural framework for communication between national legal orders, thus reproducing and consolidating the existing territorial fragmentation of regulatory authority over a transnational industry.[22] Ultimately, the only authoritative decision-maker recognised by international law and policy is the importing state, with the exporting state in a reluctant auxiliary role—that of spreading information about and possibly helping to enforce the sovereign regulatory decisions of the competent authority of the importing state. In their own way, the international export notification and prior informed consent regimes are a perfect illustration of how 'modernist international law continually recapitulates the territorial nation-state.'[23]

It is quite symptomatic to what extent the international political and legal discourse on international trade in banned and severely restricted substances revolves around the question of national sovereignty. The most frequently heard argument against substantive international regulation is that

[21] Kennedy (1987), p 221 (emphasis added).

[22] For an interesting general analysis of the implications of the territorial allocation of prescriptive jurisdiction over the environmental effects of transnational corporate activities, see Rubin (1994).

[23] Kennedy (1987), p 230.

industrialised countries should not control exports of pesticides and set standards for exported chemicals because this would infringe the sovereignty of the importing countries and their freedom to determine their own standards. Terms like 'global paternalism'[24] and 'environmental imperialism'[25] have been coined in this context. Arguments about sovereignty are a common feature of international politico-legal debates, but what makes this particular debate so surreal is the reversal of roles that characterises it. The charges of 'paternalism' and 'imperialism' are not made by those nations whose sovereignty is supposedly at stake, but by the other side. Ironically, we witness an alliance of industrialised countries and transnational corporations vigorously upholding the sovereignty of developing countries which they are so reluctant to recognise on other occasions.

The substantive vacuity and argumentative manipulability of fuzzy doctrinal concepts such as sovereignty has been brilliantly demonstrated by Martti Koskenniemi, who concluded that 'anything can be explained as in accordance with or contrary to sovereignty.'[26] When the concept of sovereignty has outlived its usefulness as a rhetorical device, the actors of course quickly fall back into their traditional roles. If an importing country actually decides to exercise its sovereignty and to restrict the free sale of hazardous chemicals within its jurisdiction, exporting industries and countries will promptly challenge the exercise of the very sovereignty which they so keenly defended just a short while earlier.

In the Community legal order, with its supranational institutional structures, one would expect the decision-making power of the member states to be more constrained than in the international legal order. The first *caveat* that should temper our enthusiasm is that, in the first 15 years of EC environmental policy, normative instruments in the field of environmental law could only be adopted by a unanimous decision of the Council. The introduction of Article 100a in the EC Treaty in 1987 first opened the possibility of the adoption of some environmental legislation by a qualified majority vote, but the member states long resisted the Commission's attempts to prompt the Council to make the most extensive possible use of these new powers. The Maastricht Treaty further expanded the reach of qualified majority decision-making in the environmental policy area by instituting the cooperation procedure as the standard legislative procedure under Article 130s, paragraph 1 EC, and the supranational character of the Community legislative process was again strengthened when the Treaty of Amsterdam entered into force and substituted the codecision procedure for the cooperation procedure in this provision, now renumbered as Article 175, paragraph 1 EC. But the new emphasis on subsidiarity,

24 Kirkpatrick (1983), pp 17, 19.

25 'Environmental Imperialism', *Wall Street Journal*, 17 Dec 1984, p 34, col 1 (editorial).

26 Koskenniemi (1989), p 206.

another consequence of the TEU, has markedly tempered the effects of these treaty changes on the Community's legislative policy in the environmental field.

The allocation of the power of substantive decision-making of course depends not only on the Community's institutional structures and legislative procedures, but also on the substantive content of Community environmental law. In the area of toxic emissions, one finds that most of the relevant norms of Community law have hardly any more substance than the corresponding norms of international law. The framework provisions of Directive 76/464/EEC impose mainly procedural obligations, and member states have strongly resisted and ultimately brought to a halt the Commission's ambitious programme to complement them with substantive provisions laying down emission limit values and water quality objectives for well over a hundred individual hazardous substances. By doing so, member states were in fact seeking to preserve their own power of authoritative substantive decision-making on both the identification of specific water pollutants to be regulated and the fixing of emission standards in individual discharge permits. This power, which was threatened by the Commission's initially rather assertive interpretation and implementation of Directive 76/464/EEC, was fully restored and further buttressed by the vague procedural provisions of the IPPC Directive, which amount to a full restoration of national regulatory sovereignty in the field of industrial emission control.

Another feature of the Community legal order which is potentially threatening to national powers of substantive decision-making is the role of the Court of Justice. The Court is indeed the ultimate 'authoritative decision-maker' in the Community, as it has the exclusive power to decide on the authoritative interpretation of Community law. In the field of environmental law, the Court's far-reaching powers of interpretation and 'judicial activism' have turned out to be a kind of 'wild card' which may suddenly upset the delicately crafted political compromises negotiated within the Council underlying ambiguous Community norms and drastically reduce the member states' room for self-interpretation. The Commission is all too well aware of this fact, as appears from its rather cautious enforcement policy in the environmental field generally and in the area of toxic emissions in the aquatic environment specifically. In fact, the Commission seems wary to relinquish its own power of 'first-order' interpretation of Community law and of strategic political compliance bargaining with the member states to the Court, perhaps out of fear that it might act like a judicial 'elephant' in a political china-shop.

Thus far, in our search for authoritative decision-makers, we have only considered the role of states and of the international and supranational institutions established by them. In international law, the sovereign nation-state is of course, in Koskenniemi's words, the 'transcendental condition from which discourse proceeds.'[27] The international legal order, but also the Community legal order, is premised on the ultimate legislative authority of the territorial sovereign. But, in environmental matters, the prime actors whose activities are to be regulated are not states, but non-state actors, mainly private companies. In the end, transnational environmental law is about influencing not public, but *private* decisions in matters such as investment, technological choices, production and consumption patterns and trade. It mainly seeks to do so through the medium of national regulatory authority—though the European Community can also exercise direct legislative authority to regulate the behaviour of legal subjects under the jurisdiction of its member states, and some international soft law instruments such as, for example, the FAO International Code of Conduct on the Distribution and Use of Pesticides, also have private entities among their primary norm addressees.

Another question that must be raised is to what extent environmental law, whether national or transnational, really substitutes authoritative public decisions—norms resulting from democratically legitimised processes of social choice—for private decisions, or at least influences such decisions. In free market economies, environmental regulators are compelled to walk a tightrope between the public interest in environmental protection and the economic and political feasibility of imposing costly environmental constraints on private enterprise. This dialectic between public environmental interests and private economic interests manifests itself in the formulation and implementation of environmental legislation, through various interest-balancing mechanisms.

At the international level, the tension between environmental protection and economic development is further enhanced by a parallel tension between national sovereignty and the responsibility of states vis-á-vis each other and the international community as a whole for the protection of the global environment. As a consequence, international environmental regulators are forced to show deference both to private economic interests (be they national or transnational) and to national sovereignty (often a cover for private economic interests at the national level). This is no doubt one explanation for the low prescriptive force of many outcomes of the international normative process in the environmental field, which can be seen as so many half-hearted efforts to accommodate national economic and political imperatives with transnational ecological constraints.

The balancing of environmental and economic interests in the normative process can take place at several levels. At the international level, where treaty bodies are empowered to elaborate on general policies and vague principles and derive more specific norms from them, such as eg the role of

[27] Koskenniemi (1989), p 107.

OSPAR Commission in the 'definition' of best available technology or best environmental practice for particular industrial sectors or activities. In so doing, it is expressly mandated by the 1992 Paris Convention to take into account a whole range of contextual environmental, technological and economic factors. As appears from many of the decisions and recommendations on BAT and BEP analysed in chapter 4, BAT and BEP are often themselves 'defined' in rather ambiguous terms, thus leaving to individual states a considerable measure of discretion in applying them. Consequently, the actual *locus* of interest-balancing—which was ostensibly raised to the international level by the development of international regulatory regimes—is shifted back again from the international to the national level.

Our case studies of transnational toxics regulation have revealed a marked preference of states for the use of what Jonas Ebbeson, in his typology of international pollution control obligations, has termed 'balancing norms'. In international law such norms effectively leave states considerable latitude in determining the strictness of their own obligations. As Ebbeson points out, the degree of international environmental governance provided by such norms is low:

> [A]s a means of international environmental governance, defining obligations in terms of balancing norms too often implies an overly ineffective approach. . . . Wide discretion is left to the parties themselves to determine not only how to proceed, but also what to achieve. A common attribute is the low degree of legal restraint and the lack of assessable criteria for what constitutes implementation compatible with the international regulations.[28]

International balancing norms are frequently also translated into balancing norms in domestic law. At the national level, the power of interest-balancing in regulatory law is most often vested in administrative authorities, operating within the confines of generally rather vague statutory mandates given to them by the legislature. In the regulation of discharges of toxic substances into the aquatic environment, the defining moment and the ultimate *locus* of interest-balancing is most often the fixing of emission standards in individual discharge permits, a power delegated to supposedly objective regulatory bureaucracies charged with interpreting and applying the rules laid down by the legislator.[29] International normative efforts attempting to limit their discretion through the fixing of harmonised emission limit values have met with strong resistance and had only limited success. More recent developments in international and especially Community law have tended towards a retreat from substantive harmonisation towards the formulation of elaborate procedural prescriptions which merely empower and entrench national regulatory discretion. Thus,

[28] Ebbeson (1996), p 135.

[29] For a critique of this approach to regulation and the use of discretion by regulatory bureaucracies, see generally Frug (1984).

Community environmental law, like the international law of the sea, 'merely registers the process by which the determination will be made, referring us to what will be the origin or source of the determination,'[30] ie the member states and their administrative authorities. And the recent tendency of industrial pollution control law to set only general objectives and performance standards, as epitomised by the British philosophy of 'integrated pollution control' and its European offspring 'integrated pollution prevention and control', explicitly designed as it is to leave 'management decisions which are rightly the preserve of managers firmly in their hands,'[31] effectively delegates much substantive decision-making to the private sector. Are business executives the new 'authoritative decision-makers' empowered by EC environmental law?

THE COMPARATIVE EFFECTIVENESS OF EUROPEAN COMMUNITY LAW AND INTERNATIONAL LAW

It is generally assumed that the unique features of the Community legal order tend to make EC law considerably more effective than classical international law.[32] The supranational nature and autonomous legislative authority of the Community institutions, their power to impose legal obligations on member states without unanimous consent in a substantial number of policy areas (including, to a large extent, environmental policy) and the special legislative instruments available to them, whose legal effect is not conditional on national ratification, all concur to endow the European Community with far-reaching regulatory powers unmatched by any intergovernmental organisation, let alone by conventional treaty-making processes. The supervisory and enforcement powers conferred on the Commission, an independent supranational body with an express mandate to ensure the application of Community law, and the existence of a Court of Justice whose jurisdiction is recognised as compulsory by all the member states, and which, since the entry into force of the TEU, can even impose financial penalties on them in certain circumstances, are powerful devices to guarantee the member states' compliance with their obligations. Last but not least, the well-established supremacy of Community law over national law, the doctrine of direct effect and the Community's elaborate system of judicial protection of individual rights also have the potential to contribute significantly to the effectiveness of Community law.

[30] Kennedy (1987), p 220.

[31] Slater (1994), p 22.

[32] See, eg Schermers & Waelbroeck (1992), p 278: 'The Communities enforce their rules more effectively than other international organizations, in particular as result of the greater homogeneity of their Members and their stronger institutional structure.'

After the substantive analysis of international normative efforts in Parts II and III, the question which must now be answered is: does the evidence indeed indicate that EC law is more effective than international law as an instrument of environmental policy in the issue areas under consideration?

The limitations inherent in the requirement of unanimity during the formative stages of EC environmental law in the 1970s and most of the 1980s have already been mentioned above, so I need not dwell on them here. These constraints were partly removed in 1987 by the SEA, and the unanimity rule in Article 130s abolished in 1993 by the TEU, at least for most areas of environmental policy. Another key factor is the nature of the Community legal instruments available to the institutions. The strongest and potentially most effective of them, the regulation, was never used in the area of toxic emissions but was chosen as the most appropriate instrument for the regulation of exports of hazardous substances. Interestingly, the Commission and the Council were at first rather reluctant to make full use of the possibility offered by this instrument to impose obligations directly on exporters. Regulation 1734/88 was drafted more like a directive than a regulation and refrained from making use of the possibility to lay down directly applicable obligations for legal subjects other than the member states themselves. Regulation 2455/92 does contain provisions addressed directly to exporters, but it is quite symptomatic that the Commission was not particularly keen on making these fully effective as early as possible, as it adopted the necessary implementing measures with considerable delay.

Where directives are used as a legislative instrument and member states fail to take the necessary transposition measures, some of their provisions may nevertheless have direct effect in the legal order of the member states and be enforced through national courts. Directive 76/464/EEC and its daughter directives contain a number of provisions which meet the requirements for direct effect laid down by the Court of Justice. However, the doctrine of direct effect can only have its full impact where directives are aimed at conferring *rights* on individuals and those individuals are willing and able to enforce those rights through national courts. In the regulation of industrial pollution, the main purpose of Community environmental law is not to grant rights but rather to impose *obligations* on polluters through the medium of national law. If member states fail to transpose such obligations fully into their domestic legal order, Community law cannot bind the polluters directly.

The theoretical superiority of Community law in constraining national discretion can only materialise to the extent that its relevant substantive provisions have sufficient normative force. In chapters 8 and 15 of this book I have presented considerable evidence of the low normative force of the relevant EC legal instruments. Directives 76/464/EEC, 96/61/EC and, last but not least, 2000/60/EC are not examples of far-reaching substantive harmonisation, but rather exemplify the general trend noted by Francis Snyder, who observes that 'much contemporary European Community legislation . . . serves primarily as a supranational umbrella, beneath which the European Community increasingly recognises the validity of diverse national policies.'[33] In fact, many provisions of these directives could be considered as containing merely *principles* or even *policies*, rather than rules, within the meaning of Van Dijk's typology of norms.[34]

It could be argued that Article 2 of Directive 76/464/EEC, which provides for the elimination of pollution by black list substances and the reduction of it by grey list substances, only states a *policy*, ie an objective to be attained, without any underlying consensus on the ways and means to be used for realising it. At most, it could be regarded as a *principle*, as it is formulated in abstract terms, requiring member states to 'take appropriate steps' but refraining from specifying what those steps should be, what specific behaviour is required of them. The framework nature of the directive itself has been interpreted by member states as implying that its provisions needed further elaboration and specification before concrete obligations for them would arise. But the procedures for norm specification envisaged in Directive 76/464/EEC—the adoption of emission limit values and quality objectives for individual sectors and pollutants through daughter directives—have proved too cumbersome to be really effective.

The Community legal order also provides judicial mechanisms for norm interpretation and specification, but these have so far played a negligible role in the field of regulation of toxic emissions. While member states and even the Commission itself regard most provisions of Directive 76/464/EEC as mere policies or principles, the Court of Justice, with its *effet utile* doctrine, has a tendency to use its powers of interpretation to maximise the effectiveness of Community law (and, at the same time, its own power) and in the past has not shrunk from deriving very concrete legal effects from rather abstractly formulated norms of primary or secondary Community law. After all, if general Treaty provisions on the elimination of *customs duties* were deemed capable of direct effect, is there any reason why provisions of a framework directive prescribing the elimination of particular forms of *water pollution* should not be capable of producing similar effects? If the Court of Justice were given the opportunity to interpret the relevant provisions of Directive 76/464/EEC through a referral from a national court under Article 234 EC, it might well give them new life. But such an opportunity is not very likely to occur, in view of the problems of standing encountered by potential claimants in national courts.

[33] Snyder (1990), p 18.
[34] Cf above ch 2.

The Commission, too, could ask the Court of Justice to rule on a member state's compliance with the framework provisions of Directive 76/464/EEC. But, as we have seen in chapter 8, the Commission has shown little interest in scrutinising the administrative practice of member states beyond the formal implementation of Community law. As I indicated earlier, the Commission may well have political reasons not to do so. At any rate, it clearly lacks a true enforcement strategy in the field of toxic emissions and has not systematically exploited all the potentialities of the relevant directives. It prefers to devote its resources to the production of new water legislation of rather doubtful normative quality rather than focus on using all the legal means at its disposal to promote the effectiveness of the existing instruments. The fact that the Commission, after years of procrastination, suddenly launched Article 226 proceedings against most member states for their failure to implement Article 7 of Directive 76/464/EEC on grey list substances is certainly to be applauded, but how is it to be squared with the fact that, at about the same time, the Commission also decided to propose the repeal of the provisions it is now ostensibly trying to enforce?

The greatest weakness of Article 226 infringement proceedings as an instrument for the enforcement of EC law is the discretionary nature of their initiation by the Commission. The Commission enjoys full political discretion in deciding whether or not to bring legal action against member states and may be guided by considerations which have little to do with the concern to ensure the effectiveness of Community environmental law. For example, the Commission may consider that not jeopardising member state support for important legislative proposals under consideration in the Council is more important than enforcing existing legislation which is no longer in tune with its current policy priorities. The introduction into the Treaty of a provision which enables the Commission to ask the Court to impose financial penalties on member states which have failed to comply with an earlier Court judgment is not likely to fundamentally alter this state of affairs, as the use of this new possibility is just as discretionary as the infringement proceedings themselves. Where the Commission for whatever reason chooses not to pursue judicial enforcement, no sanctions can be imposed by the Court. However, if the Commission is determined to enforce a particular directive, the threat of financial penalties may be more effective than that of a merely declaratory judgment, and it may considerably strengthen the Commission's bargaining position in compliance negotiations with the member states. But, notwithstanding this important new development, the fact remains, as Francis Snyder has pointed out, that:

> Neither the Commission and the Court of Justice taken together as institutions, nor negotiation and adjudication taken together as processes, despite their merits, are

sufficient alone to ensure the effectiveness of Community law in the broader social sense . . .[35]

THE INTERACTION BETWEEN SOFT LAW AND HARD LAW AND THEIR COMPARATIVE EFFECTIVENESS

The two case studies in Parts II and III both demonstrated the importance of soft law in the international normative process and confirmed that it is impossible to study international environmental hard law in isolation from soft law. In both cases under consideration, however, soft law appears to have somewhat different functions.[36]

Soft law did not play any significant role in the initial stages of the international normative process for the regulation of emissions of hazardous substances into the aquatic environment. Apart from a few very general recommendations of the Stockholm Conference and regional bodies like the Council of Europe, international legal instruments for the control of marine pollution from land-based sources and transboundary river pollution were developed without much preliminary recourse to non-binding instruments. Somewhat paradoxically, the importance of soft law seems to increase as these regimes develop. This is partly by design, where the relevant conventions have established international regulatory bodies with the power to address recommendations to the contracting parties designed to further elaborate on and specify their obligations, which are only formulated in very general terms in the binding instruments themselves.

But even where treaty bodies have explicitly been given the competence to adopt legally binding measures, they have turned out to be rather reluctant to use it, preferring to have recourse to non-binding recommendations instead, as the early practice of the Paris Commission and the more recent adoption of the Rhine Action Programme as a substitute for binding emission limit values demonstrate. In certain cases, such as the North Sea land-based sources regime, one could argue that hard law has effectively abdicated to soft law, where riparian states have deliberately decided to bypass the formal institutional structures and legal instruments through the establishment of a high-profile informal political forum which produces a considerable volume of soft law in the form of periodical ministerial declarations. Ironically, these soft law instruments are considered more effective than hard law by many of the politicians and officials involved in this process.

The empirical evidence, as we saw in chapter 4, does not warrant such categorical judgements. But there is some evidence that high-level political

[35] Snyder (1993a), p 53.

[36] For an overview of the different functions of soft law in international environmental policy, see Beyerlin & Marauhn (1997), pp 7–10.

meetings have provided a fresh impetus to the activities of the formal treaty bodies and resulted in the adoption of a number of legally binding instruments by them. However, a large gap between political rhetoric and positive international law persists, because participating states have by no means been prepared to translate all the political commitments made at ministerial conferences into primary or secondary treaty obligations. Thus, soft law has proved only partly successful in its role as a precursor of hard law. In many cases, it has played a different role: it has functioned as a complement to or even substitute for hard law, where there exists a political will of governments to cooperate, but not to subscribe to legally binding commitments. This is well-evidenced by the North Sea land-based sources regime, which has been aptly described by Nollkaemper as consisting of 'coexistent normative orders of non-legal and legal norms, with some movement from the first to the second order.'[37] Such movement does not automatically result in increased effectiveness, as 'the potential legal effects of crossing the threshold may in part be undone by a loss of substance.'[38] Non-binding norms are not necessarily ineffective and may have effects otherwise than through their transformation into hard law. Indeed, as Nollkaemper points out, 'the legal nature [of a] norm is only one of many—and certainly not a decisive determinant in explaining effectiveness.'[39]

In the field of the regulation of international trade in banned and severely restricted substances, soft law appears to have performed its precursor function more effectively, though extremely slowly. It took more than 20 years for the international normative process in this area to produce a global legally binding instrument, albeit one that has not yet entered into force. Initially, there was a great reluctance on the part of the main chemical-producing and exporting nations to accept any international obligations with respect to their exports of domestically banned or restricted products. The sweeping declarations of principle to which they had reluctantly subscribed in UN political fora soon gave way to a defensive, 'pragmatic' approach leaning strongly toward the laissez-faire end of the regulatory spectrum. In response to political pressure from developing, chemical-importing countries and non-governmental organisations, the industrialised countries first accepted only the development of non-binding information exchange and export notification schemes—which they themselves initiated within the framework of the OECD as a model for subsequent soft law instruments by UN bodies such as UNEP and the FAO—and some of them enacted national legislation providing for such export notification, as an alternative to stronger forms of export control.

[37] Nollkaemper (1998), p 360.
[38] *Ibid*, p 367.
[39] *Ibid*, p 370.

The first legally binding international instrument to be adopted was EEC Regulation 1734/88, which imposed uniform export notification requirements on EEC member states, in response to the soft law instruments elaborated by the OECD, UNEP and the FAO in the mid-1980s. The European Community again acted to translate soft law into hard law in the early 1990s, after the non-binding instruments of UNEP and the FAO had been amended in 1989 to incorporate a voluntary prior informed consent procedure for international trade in certain banned and severely restricted chemicals. But it was only in 1995 that the international community reached consensus on the necessity of elaborating a universal, legally binding international instrument on the subject, which was completed in early 1998 after two years of negotiations and formally adopted and opened for signature at a diplomatic conference in Rotterdam in September 1998. Ostensibly, the Rotterdam Convention purports to transform the existing non-binding PIC procedure into hard law, in order to make it more effective. Paradoxically, however, it is by no means certain that this transformation will actually result in greater effectiveness,[40] as the negotiation of the new convention resulted in watering down a number of important substantive features of the existing voluntary procedure. This development too, challenges common assumptions about the effectiveness of the international normative process.

INSTRUMENTAL AND SYMBOLIC FUNCTIONS OF TRANSNATIONAL ENVIRONMENTAL LAW

The different findings of this study call into question the validity of the mainstream instrumentalist model of the development of transnational environmental law which I outlined in chapter 2. They also cast serious doubt on the effectiveness of transnational law as an instrument of international policies to regulate toxics in the environment and indicate that the international normative process has other than purely instrumental functions. A symbolic, value-expressive social function definitely seems to be one of them.

The normative process in both areas studied here does not fully match the instrumental model on which it is implicitly based. By the standards of that model, it has not achieved what it set out to achieve. The norms result-

[40] See also Victor (1998), pp 257–60, who questions the assumption of governments that a legally binding PIC regime will be more effective than the voluntary one and criticises the decision to launch negotiations on a PIC convention, which 'stymied implementation' of the voluntary procedure. This author argues that 'compliance with the nonbinding regulatory commitments in PIC . . . has been perfect' and that the voluntary PIC procedure 'worked well in part because its nonbinding legal form permitted high flexibility and learning by doing'. *Ibid*, pp 258, 264.

ing from the norm-making process mostly do not go beyond policies and principles and lack the specificity and determinacy required to exercise a strong 'compliance pull' on states. Those policies and principles have not systematically been translated into specific behavioural prescriptions for states and non-state actors. To the extent that such prescriptions exist, that concrete rules have been laid down, they are most often of a purely procedural nature and lack substantive normative force. Transnational toxics law, like international legal discourse generally, 'points constantly away from material choice.'[41]

It could be argued that the international normative process is merely incomplete and that, over time, it will eventually reach full maturity and result in sufficiently specific, unambiguous and legally binding norms to address the environmental problems it is trying to tackle. While it is clear that the normative process is an ongoing one and that further development will no doubt occur, it is not obvious, however, that such development will proceed in the direction that the instrumental model indicates. The recent evolution of both European Community law and international legal regimes for water pollution control rather points in another direction: a *retreat* from a regulatory strategy based on the further development of legally binding, increasingly specific and prescriptive substantive norms. In EC law, the relevant norms, while still legally binding, tend to become less specific and are directed at procedural rather than substantive harmonisation. In the treaty regimes, notwithstanding their recent reform, the trend in implementation is towards increasing use of soft law instruments and vague regulatory concepts such as BAT and BEP. As regards the regulation of toxic trade, while there has been a recent move towards hard law at the global level, the development of a legally binding international instrument has been at the cost of a narrowing of the existing soft law regime's substantive reach and has further entrenched prior informed consent as a purely procedural form of transnational regulation.

So far, transnational law has had only a marginal impact on the modes of production which are at the root of the 'toxification' of the global environment by industrial activity.[42] Such norms as have been developed may affect the trade in and consumption of certain hazardous products and the control and disposal of toxic effluents from certain industrial production processes, but, with few exceptions, they rarely directly address industrial production itself. Like domestic pollution control law, transnational law has focused on what Peter Yeager has termed the 'politics of circulation', but stayed aloof from the 'politics of production.'[43] It has regulated

[41] Koskenniemi (1989), p 456.

[42] The term is taken from World Resources Institute, *World Resources 1994–95* (Oxford University Press, New York/Oxford, 1994), ch 12.

[43] Yeager (1991), p 160.

international trade in certain toxics but refrained from banning their production. It has limited or sometimes banned the *use* of other toxic substances which may result in pollution of the aquatic environment but has again stopped short of prohibiting their *production*. It has prescribed the use of add-on pollution control technology in certain industrial sectors and fixed emission standards to limit discharges of toxics in the aquatic environment. But, thus far, it has only occasionally, almost incidentally, either proscribed or prescribed the use of particular production *processes*.

The pivotal regulatory concepts developed by the international normative process in the two relevant areas, 'best available technology' and 'prior informed consent', are in fact remarkably non-prescriptive as far as their impact on both national regulatory discretion and industrial production is concerned. These concepts have gradually evolved from soft law into hard law to become the linchpin of the international legal obligations of states with respect to, respectively, toxic emissions and toxic trade. But, in substance, they barely affect sovereign discretion, as they confirm the sovereign state in its legal role as the sole authoritative substantive decision-maker. Thus transnational toxics law, much like the law of the sea, effectuates the 'progressive displacement of a national sovereignty by international regulation, *itself procedurally implemented by states*.'[44] Indeed, in the end, it is states that determine what constitutes 'best available technology' for polluting industrial processes and whether or not to grant their 'prior informed consent' for imports of banned or severely restricted chemicals, within the framework of the procedures established by international law.

What is the true normative force of a concept like BAT which, in substance, merely provides that states shall lay down environmental standards for industrial production activities on an *ad hoc* basis, based on a contextual interest-balancing process which shall take into account the environmental impacts to be reduced, the state of technological development and the economic feasibility of emission control measures? Is this not what states in actual practice already do anyway? How can law function as an instrument of social change if it merely prescribes what technology and economics dictate? Similarly, does not the principle of PIC, as procedurally implemented by states, merely legitimise the existing state of things, as dictated by free trade and territorial regulatory sovereignty,[45] leaving the chemical industry free to continue the production and export of hazardous chemicals within this legal framework?

Martti Koskenniemi has poignantly analysed how international law 'is constantly lapsing either into what seems like factual description or politi-

[44] Kennedy (1987), p 224 (emphasis added).

[45] Indeed, as Lothar Gündling has noted, territorial sovereignty is 'the legal foundation of prior consent'. Gündling (1989), p 65. See also Ward (1994a), p 88 (referring to PIC as 'a formalised affirmation of a country's territorial sovereignty').

cal prescription.'[46] In so far as it merely restates and consolidates national sovereignty and political discretion, international legal discourse is only descriptive and apologetic, not normative. And where it pretends to be normative, to project a substantive legal order which transcends the sovereign state, it becomes utopian and political, not legal. Koskenniemi argues that international law 'is *unable to fulfil any functions* unless it has a degree of autonomy from particular State behaviour, will and interests.'[47] I would submit, however, that transnational law, notwithstanding its lack of autonomy, is perfectly capable of fulfilling at least one function, ie a *symbolic* function, and may in fact to a significant extent be designed to fulfil precisely that function.

Indeed, as Kratochwil has pointed out, 'certain functions of norms cannot be analyzed in terms of merely instrumental rationality.'[48] Various sociological perspectives on domestic environmental law suggest that this law is not as instrumental as it may seem, but also fulfils an important *symbolic* function in social and political life by granting recognition to certain social values and defusing social and political conflict. In Thurman Arnold's words:

> It is part of the function of 'Law' to give recognition to ideals representing the exact opposite of established conduct. 'Law' is primarily a great reservoir of emotionally important social symbols.[49]

These observations were made in a domestic law context, but there is no *a priori* reason why normative phenomena at the international level could not, *mutatis mutandis*, fulfil a similar function. The symbolic dimension of European Community law, for instance, has already been noted in Francis Snyder's work on various aspects of Community law in the field of agriculture and food aid:

> The letter of the law usually, if not always, provides at best only a very uncertain guide to the actual operation of legislation. . . . *Its main import*, in addition to its putative function as a formal channel for allocating power to make political and economic decisions, *can be viewed most usefully perhaps as symbolic, ideological and expressive*. To the wider public, legislation signals both incremental shifts and broad changes of direction in particular state policies, at least in so far as these policies are encapsulated in legislative form.[50]

The signal that transnational toxics law conveys to society is that concerted efforts are being made by governments to eliminate pollution by toxic substances and curb international trade in banned and severely restricted

[46] Koskenniemi (1989), p 1.
[47] *Ibid*, pp 4–5 (emphasis added).
[48] Kratochwil (1989), p 260.
[49] Arnold (1969), p 49.
[50] Snyder (1990), p 169 (emphasis added).

pesticides. Some progress has no doubt been made in these areas, but the regulatory instruments that have been developed at the international level have thus far not been effective in achieving the environmental objectives they purport to pursue, because they have stopped short of directly addressing the unsustainable modes of production which are at the root of the problem. And to the limited extent that it *does* work, the international normative process apparently does not work in the way in which it is intended to, ie by elaborating, implementing and enforcing increasingly specific rules of conduct for states, and, through them, the individual legal subjects whose activities are the actual target of regulation. The instrumental power of law as a preventive and regulatory tool of international environmental governance, as a means for the articulation and enforcement of ever more precise and constraining action-guiding prescriptions directed at the achievement of well-defined and rationally determined policy objectives, appears to be overrated by lawyers and policy-makers alike.

But it would be wrong to assess the social function and effectiveness of law merely from the perspective of instrumental rationality. The prevailing 'notion that the main function of law is one of "constraint" in order to arrive at determinate choices' has rightly been criticised as flawed.[51] It is important to take into account not only the manifest function of law as an instrument of social engineering, but also its latent function as a means of social and political communication.[52] Instrumental ineffectiveness should not be viewed as a mere dysfunction of the normative system. Instrumentally ineffective norms are not necessarily wholly devoid of social effects. Law may have an influence on social behaviour otherwise than through inducing compliance. Although it may fail in its instrumental function, the normative process may nevertheless be effective in its symbolic function, through the 'dissemination of symbolic satisfactions'[53] and the 'institutionalization' of 'symbolic reassurances'[54] to political demands. In a national public law context, this phenomenon has been referred to by legal sociologists as the 'symbolic effectiveness of law.'[55] Law is increasingly being used for non-legal ends, as a form of symbolic reformist discourse in which the creation of norms becomes an end in itself, divorced from their application in practice.[56] The rhetoric of legal reformism serves as a convenient substitute for actual social change.

The case studies in this book provide evidence that the latent, symbolic function of norms is also an important driving force of international normative activity in the environmental field. The secret of transnational envi-

[51] Kratochwil (2000), p 47.
[52] Garcia Villegas (1995), pp 158–61.
[53] Edelman (1985), p 39.
[54] *Ibid*, p 171.
[55] Garcia Villegas (1995).
[56] *Ibid*, pp 175–76.

ronmental law's political success may well lie in its peculiar ability to create an illusion of substantive progress where in fact little such progress is actually made. As the 'language of international law conveys a certain interpretation of social reality,'[57] in doing so it may in fact obfuscate certain aspects of social reality. The image conveyed by the prevailing international regulatory approaches to the control of emissions of toxic substances into the aquatic environment and international trade in banned and severely restricted pesticides is one of responsible national governments which will ensure, through administrative systems of regulation based on an objective assessment of environmental, technological and economic factors, that private polluters use the 'best available technology' to prevent toxic emissions, and which, if provided with sufficient information on hazards and alternatives, will halt the importation and use of hazardous chemicals in agriculture. This image obfuscates the fact that, in reality, national governments have no real control over the direction of industrial development and the choice of products and production technologies, nor over the transnational economic and social processes which stimulate the spread throughout the world of unsustainable modes of agricultural production that are increasingly reliant on the use of hazardous pesticides. In a way, the frenetic international law-making activity in the environmental field, through which states assert their formal position as the primary actors in the international legal system, may serve as a form of symbolic compensation for the declining effective regulatory power of the nation state in a globalising economy.

This critical assessment of legal symbolism should not be taken as an argument to dismiss the international normative efforts that have been analysed in this book as irrelevant. While the normative process seems to have had a limited effectiveness from a purely instrumental perspective, this does not mean that it has not served any social purpose. As we have seen, law-making is capable of having effects on society otherwise than by prescribing behavioural constraints which are effectively complied with. This certainly applies to transnational environmental law-making as well. As Edith Brown Weiss has pointed out: 'One of the main functions of international law is to provide *a process for legitimating norms*.'[58] The formulation of norms at the international level confers legitimacy and authority on environmental values, principles and policy objectives, however vaguely defined. It also serves to articulate a common conceptual framework for policy development at the national level. One of the effects of transnational normative activity has been to identify certain categories of hazardous chemicals, such as toxic, persistent and bio-accumulative substances and banned and severely restricted pesticides, as legitimate objects of

[57] Koskenniemi (1989), p xxiii.
[58] Brown Weiss (1998), p 15 (emphasis added).

international concern. Even though the relevant international norms themselves do not impose significant substantive constraints on their addressees, their mere existence has transformed their objects into a focus of attention not only for national and international policy-makers, but also for national and international research and monitoring efforts as well as action by non-governmental organisations and other stakeholders. There is evidence that this form of 'stigmatisation' has indirect effects on the behaviour of the responsible target groups.

Another important consequence of transnational normative activity, as regime theory tells us, is the institutionalisation of collective action. Even where regime norms lack immediate problem-solving effectiveness, the process of their formulation institutionalises international cooperation in a given issue-area. As we have seen in chapter 2, there is no sharp qualitative distinction in regime analysis between substantive, procedural and institutional norms. The institutional dimension of international regimes often deserves as much attention as their instrumental, problem-solving capacity. It has been noted by one observer of international environmental regimes that in some cases 'regime establishment started with the adoption of framework conventions that lacked substantive cooperation.'[59] Institution-building is often, though not always, a precursor of substantive action. In the field of toxics, one of the results of transnational normative activity has no doubt been the establishment of institutional structures and procedures for international cooperation and communication. Where such activity has failed to produce substantive normative prescriptions which effectively constrain the behaviour of states, the resulting structures and procedures nevertheless serve as a framework for loose, non-constraining policy coordination. Ineffective norms may provide longer-term policy guidance, a function of regimes which has been described as 'policy orientation'—a function distinct from and in fact incompatible with that of 'realistic prescription.'[60]

Binding norms laying down specific behavioural prescriptions are only one component of multi-layered, dynamic normative systems for transnational environmental governance. The instrumentalist model tends to attach great importance to the elaboration of such legally binding rules as the most effective regulatory strategy at the international level. But, as this study shows, the legal force of norms is by no means a guarantee of their effectiveness. Clearly, excessive confidence in the power of transnational law as an instrument for the achievement of environmental policy objectives is unwarranted. The role of legally non-binding norms in international environmental governance processes is at least equally important and common instrumentalist assumptions about the relative effectiveness of soft law and

[59] Gehring (1994), p 350.
[60] *Ibid*, p 439.

hard law are not supported by much empirical evidence. Norms of various kinds are part of a continuum of discourse and practice in the international community and should be analysed in this context. In international environmental policy, the instrumental capacity of normative prescriptions of any kind, whatever their legal nature, effectively to constrain and guide state behaviour is limited and their symbolic function all the more real. But both are not mutually exclusive and the interplay and balance between them should be seen as inherent features of the phenomenon of transnational environmental governance.

Bibliography

AALDERS, M (1984) *Industrie, milieu en wetgeving: de Hinderwet tussen symboliek en effectiviteit* (Kobra, Amsterdam)

AARHUS, K (1995) 'Rhetoric and Reality in European Pollution Control Policy', *International Environmental Affairs* 7 pp 111–26

AGEGE, CO (1985) 'Dumping of Dangerous American Products Overseas: Should Congress Sit and Watch?', *Journal of World Trade Law* 19 pp 403–10

ALLOTT, A (1981) 'The Effectiveness of Law', *Valparaiso University Law Review* 15 pp 229–42

ALSTON, P (1978) 'International Regulation of Toxic Chemicals', *Ecology Law Quarterly* 7 p 397

ANDRESEN, S and WETTESTAD, J (1995) 'International Problem-Solving Effectiveness: The Oslo Project Story So Far', *International Environmental Affairs* 7 pp 127–49

ARNOLD, TW (1969) 'Law as Symbolism', in Aubert, V (ed), *Sociology of Law* (Penguin Books, Harmondsworth)

ASHFORD, NA and AYERS, C (1985) 'Policy Issues for Consideration in Transferring Technology to Developing Countries', *Ecology Law Quarterly* 12 p 871

ASHWORTH, J and PAPPS, I (1992) 'Should Environmental Legislation Set the Rules Constraining Polluters? Defining the Ends and Assessing the Means of Environmental Policy: An Examination of the EC Mercury Directive', *International Review of Law and Economics* 12 pp 79–93

AUSSANT, J (1987) 'Conventions régionales contre la pollution marine: contenu et problèmes, participation de la Communauté', *Revue du Marché Commun* pp 14–24

AUVRET-FINCK, J (1995) 'L'Avis 2/91 relatif à la Convention n° 170 de l'OIT', *Cahiers de droit européen* 31 pp 443–60

AYRES, RU and SIMONIS, UE (1994) (eds), *Industrial Metabolism: Restructuring for Sustainable Development* (United Nations University Press, Tokyo/New York/Paris)

AZEVEDO, MP (1985) 'Trade in Hazardous Substances: An Examination of U.S. Regulation', in Ives, JH (ed), *The Export of Hazard: Transnational Corporations and Environmental Control Issues* (Routledge & Kegan Paul, Boston/London/Henley)

BAENDER, MB (1991) 'Pesticides and Precaution: The Bamako Convention as a Model for an International Convention on Pesticides Regulation', *New York University Journal of International Law and Policy* 24 pp 557–609

BALEKJIAN, WH (1981) 'The Language of International Law: Linguistic Considerations Involved in the Drafting and Interpretation of International Legal Instruments', in: *Memoria del X Congreso Mundial Ordinario de Filosofia del Derecho y Filosofia Social*, Vol. V, Universidad Nacional Autonoma de Mexico, Mexico, pp 357–63

BATES, J (1982) 'Pesticides—Constraints and Controls in Importing Countries', in *Control of Chemicals in Importing Countries* (OECD, Paris)

BAUGHEN, S (1995) 'Multinationals and the Export of Hazard', *Modern Law Review* 58 pp 54–71

BENNETT, G (1990) 'The Implementation of EC Environmental Directives: the Gap between Law and Practice', *Milieu*, pp 174–78

BERNAUER, T (1995) 'The Effect of International Environmental Institutions: How We Might Learn More', *International Organization* 49 pp 351–77

BEYERLIN, U and MARAUHN, T (1997) *Law-Making and Law-Enforcement in International Environmental Law after the 1992 Rio Conference* (Erich Schmidt Verlag, Berlin)

BIRNIE, P (1992) 'International Environmental Law: Its Adequacy for Present and Future Needs', in Hurrell, A and Kingsbury, B (eds), *The International Politics of the Environment: Actors, Interests and Institutions* (Clarendon Press, Oxford)

BIRNIE, PW and BOYLE, AE (1992) *International Law and the Environment* (Clarendon Press, Oxford)

BLECHSCHMIDT, FL (1989) 'The Control of Pollution of Inland Waters: A Necessary Impulse for the British Approach?', *Environmental Policy & Law* 19 pp 17–23

BOARDMAN, R (1986) *Pesticides in World Agriculture: The Politics of International Regulation* (Macmillan, London)

BOCZEK, B (1978) 'International Protection of the Baltic Sea Environment against Pollution: A Study in Marine Regionalism', *American Journal of International Law* 72 pp 782–814

BOEHMER-CHRISTIANSEN, S (1990a) 'Environmental Quality Objectives versus Uniform Emission Standards', in Freestone, D and IJlstra, T (eds), *The North Sea: Perspectives on Regional Environmental Co-operation* (Graham & Trotman/Nijhoff, London/Dordrecht/Boston)

——(1990b) 'Emerging International Principles of Environmental Protection and their Impact on Britain', *The Environmentalist* 10 pp 95–113

BOISSON DE CHAZOURNES, L (1995) 'La mise en oeuvre du droit international dans le domaine de l'environnement: enjeux et défis', *Revue Générale de Droit International Public* 99 pp 37–76

BOSSO, CJ (1987) *Pesticides and Politics: The Life Cycle of a Public Issue* (University of Pittsburgh Press, Pittsburgh)

BOTHE, M (1980) 'Legal and Non-Legal Norms—A Meaningful Distinction in International Relations?', *Netherlands Yearbook of International Law* 11 pp 65–95

——(1989) 'Fresh Water Management in Europe—International Legal Issues', in *Preserving the Global Environment*, Proceedings of the 18th Annual Conference of the Canadian Council on International Law (Canadian Council on International Law, Ottawa)

BOUMAN, N (1996) 'A New Regime for the Meuse', *Review of European Community and International Environmental Law* 5 pp 161–68

BOURGEOIS, JHJ (1995) 'The EC in the WTO and Advisory Opinion 1/94: An Echternach Procession', *Common Market Law Review* 32 pp 763–87

BOYLE, A (1985) 'Marine Pollution under the Law of the Sea Convention', *American Journal of International Law* 79 pp 347–72

——(1990) 'The Law of the Sea and International Watercourses: An Emerging Cycle', *Marine Policy* 14 pp 151–57

——(1991) 'Saving the World? Implementation and Enforcement of International Environmental Law through International Institutions', *Journal of Environmental Law* 3 pp 229–46

BOOTH, H and GREEN, A (1976) 'The European Community Environmental Programme and United Kingdom Law', *European Law Review* 1 pp 535–53

BROWN WEISS, E (1998) 'The Changing Structure of International Law', in Prieur, M and Lambrechts, C (eds), *Mankind and the Environment: What Rights for the Twenty-First Century?* (Editions Frison-Roche, Paris)

BROWNLIE, I (1981) 'The Reality and Efficacy of International Law', *British Yearbook of International Law* 52 pp 1–8

BRUNNÉE, JA (1992) 'The Jigsaw Puzzle of International Environmental Protection: International Approaches to Atmospheric Pollution and the Baltic Sea Area', *International Journal of Legal Information* 20 pp 1–17

BRUSASCO-MACKENZIE, M and KISS, A (1978) 'Quelques réflexions sur l'action des Communautés européennes en matière de protection de l'environnement', *Revue du Marché Commun* 21 pp 310–20

——(1989) 'Les relations extérieures des Communautés européennes en matière de protection de l'environnement', *Annuaire Français de Droit International* 35 pp 702–10

BULL, D (1982) *A Growing Problem: Pesticides and the Third World Poor* (OXFAM, Oxford)

BURCHI, S (1977) 'International Legal Aspects of Pollution of the Sea from Rivers', *Italian Yearbook of International Law* 3 pp 115–42

BUTLER, WE (1991) (ed), *Control over Compliance with International Law* (Martinus Nijhoff, Dordrecht/Boston/London)

BYRNE, CD (1989) *Community Water Quality Policy for the Nineties* (Commission of the European Communities, Report EUR 12156 EN, Brussels)

CALDWELL, LK (1990) *International Environmental Policy: Emergence and Dimensions*, 2nd edn (Duke University Press, Durham/London)

CAMERON, J (1996) 'Compliance, Citizens and NGOs', in Cameron, J, Werksman, J and Roderick, P (eds), *Improving Compliance with International Environmental Law* (Earthscan Publications, London)

CAMERON, J, WERKSMAN, J and RODERICK, P (1996) (eds), *Improving Compliance with International Environmental Law* (Earthscan Publications, London)

CARBONNIER, J (1988) *Flexible droit: pour une sociologie du droit sans rigueur*, 6e édn, (Librairie Générale de droit et de jurisprudence, Paris)

CARSON, R (1994) *Silent Spring* (Houghton Mifflin Company, New York)

CASHMAN, L (1991) 'La réglementation communautaire en matière d'eau: une vision d'ensemble', *Aménagement-Environnement*, n° spécial, pp 34–41

CHARNOVITZ, S (1991) 'Exploring the Environmental Exceptions in GATT Article XX', *Journal of World Trade* 27 pp 37–55

——(1992) 'GATT and the Environment: Examining the Issues', *International Environmental Affairs* 4 pp 203–33

——(1994) 'Green Roots, Bad Pruning: GATT Rules and their Application to Environmental Trade Measures', *Tulane Environmental Law Journal* 7 pp 299–352

CHAYES, AH and CHAYES, A (1989) 'From Law Enforcement to Dispute Settlement: A New Approach to Arms Control Verification and Compliance', *International Security* 14 pp 147–64

——(1993) 'On Compliance', *International Organization* 47 pp 175–205

——(1995) *The New Sovereignty: Compliance with International Regulatory Agreements* (Harvard University Press, Cambridge/London)

CHEMILLIER-GENDREAU, M (1995) *Humanité et souverainetés: essai sur la fonction du droit international* (Editions La Découverte, Paris)

CHURCHILL, RR and GIBSON, J (1990) *The Implementation of the North Sea Declarations by the United Kingdom—An Assessment* (Greenpeace International, Amsterdam)

COCKERILL, CP (1979) 'Agricultural Pesticides: The Urgent Need for Harmonization of International Regulation', *California Western International Law Journal* 9 pp 111–38

COMMONER, B (1990) *Making Peace with the Planet* (Pantheon Books, New York)

COPLIN, WD (1966) *The Functions of International Law: An Introduction to the Role of International Law in the Contemporary World* (Rand McNally & Company, Chicago)

CROSS, FB and WINSLETT, BJ (1987) '"Export Death": Ethical Issues and the International Trade in Hazardous Products', *American Business Law Journal* 25 pp 487–521

CROWE, A (1992) 'Breaking the Circle of Poison: EPA's Enforcement of Current FIFRA Export Requirements', *Georgetown International Environmental Law Review* 4 pp 319–59

D'AMATO, A (1985) 'Is International Law Really "Law"?', *Northwestern University Law Review* 79 pp 1293–1314

DÉJEANT-PONS, M (1990) *La Méditerranée en droit international de l'environnement*, (Economica, Paris)

DEKKER, RH (1983) 'Zwarte lijststoffen: stand van zaken in de Europese Gemeenschappen', *H_2O* 16 pp 274–79

DEKKER, RH and DE VILLENEUVE, CHV (1995) 'Internationale aspecten', in van den Berge, AP Groen, K, Havekes, HJM, Hofstra, MA and Teulings, JHA (eds), *Bestrijding van de watervervuiling—Vijfentwintig jaar WVO* (Ministerie van Verkeer en Waterstaat/Unie van Waterschappen, Den Haag)

DEMARET, P (1993) 'Environmental Policy and Commercial Policy: The Emergence of Trade-Related Environmental Measures (TREMs) in the External Relations of the European Community', in Maresceau, M (ed), *The European Community's Commercial Policy after 1992: The Legal Dimension* (Kluwer, London/Dordrecht/Boston)

DE VILLENEUVE, CHV (1996) 'Western Europe's Artery: The Rhine', *Natural Resources Journal* 36 pp 441–54

DE YTURRIAGA BARBERAN, JA (1975) 'Convenio de Paris de 1974 para la prevencion de la contaminacion marina de origen terrestre', *Revista de Instituciones Europeas* 2 pp 49–71

——(1979) 'Regional Conventions on the Protection of the Marine Environment', *Recueil des Cours de l'Académie de Droit International*, vol 162, p 321

DINHAM, B (1991) 'FAO and Pesticides: Promotion or Proscription?', *The Ecologist* 21 pp 61–5

DOEHRING, K (1984) 'Effectiveness', in Bernhardt, R (ed), *Encyclopedia of Public International Law*, vol 7 (North-Holland, Amsterdam/New York/Oxford)
DOWDESWELL, E (1994) 'International Environmental Law', *Global Environmental Law Annual* 2 pp 65–72
DUNLAP, TR (1981) *DDT: Scientists, Citizens and Public Policy* (Princeton University Press, Princeton)
DUPUY, P-M (1991) 'Soft Law and the International Law of the Environment', *Michigan Journal of International Law* 12 pp 420–35
EBBESON, J (1994) 'Substantive Requirements in International and National Environmental Law', in *Law and Ecology*, Special Issue of *Retfaerd* (The Academic Press, Copenhagen)
——(1996) *Compatibility of International and National Environmental Law* (Kluwer Law International, London/The Hague/Boston)
EDELMAN, M (1985) *The Symbolic Uses of Politics* (University of Illinois Press, Urbana/Chicago)
EHLERS, P (1990) 'The History of the International North Sea Conferences', in Freestone, D and IJlstra, T (eds), *The North Sea: Perspectives on Regional Environmental Co-operation* (Graham & Trotman/Nijhoff, London/Dordrecht/Boston)
——(1993) 'The Helsinki Convention, 1992: Improving the Baltic Sea Environment', *International Journal of Marine and Coastal Law* 8 pp 191–214
EMMOTT, N and HAIGH, N (1996) 'Integrated Pollution Prevention and Control: UK and EC Approaches and Possible Next Steps', *Journal of Environmental Law* 8 pp 301–11
FALK, R (1989) 'The Capacity of International Law to Respond to the Environmental Challenge', in *Preserving the Global Environment*, Proceedings of the 18th Annual Conference of the Canadian Council on International Law (Canadian Council on International Law, Ottawa)
——(1995) 'Environmental Protection in an Era of Globalization', *Yearbook of International Environmental Law* 6 pp 3–25
FARQUHAR, JT (1983) 'The Policies of the European Community towards the Environment—the "Dangerous Substances" Directive', *Journal of Planning Law* pp 145–55
FAURE, M (1999) 'Community Environmental Law and the Harmonisation of Conditions of Competition: An Economic Perspective', *Law & European Affairs* 9 pp 327–37
FISHER, R (1981) *Improving Compliance with International Law* (University Press of Virginia, Charlottesville)
FITZMAURICE, M (1992) *International Legal Problems of the Environmental Protection of the Baltic Sea* (Graham & Trotman/Nijhoff, London/Dordrecht/Boston)
——(1993) 'The 1992 Convention on the Baltic Sea Environment', *Review of European Community and International Environmental Law* 2 pp 24–30
FRANCIONI, F (1991) 'Exporting Environmental Hazard through Multinational Enterprises: Can the State of Origin be Held Responsible?', in Francioni, F and Scovazzi, T (eds), *International Responsibility for Environmental Harm* (Graham & Trotman/Nijhoff, London/Dordrecht/Boston)
FRANCK, TM (1990) *The Power of Legitimacy Among Nations* (Oxford University Press, New York/Oxford)

FRANCKX, E (1998) 'Regional Marine Environment Protection Regimes in the Context of UNCLOS', *International Journal of Marine and Coastal Law* 13 pp 307–24
FRID, R (1995) *The Relations between the EC and International Organizations: Legal Theory and Practice* (Kluwer Law International, The Hague/London/Boston)
FRIED, JHE (1968) 'How Efficient is International Law?', in Deutsch, KW and Hoffmann, S (eds), *The Relevance of International Law—Essays in Honor of Leo Gross* (Schenkman Publishing Company, Cambridge)
FRIEDMANN, W (1964) *The Changing Structure of International Law* (Columbia University Press, New York)
——(1970) *De l'efficacité des institutions internationales* (Librairie Armand Colin, Paris)
FROSCH, RA (1996) 'Toward the End of Waste: Reflections on a New Ecology of Industry', *Daedalus* 13/19 pp 199–212
FRUG, GE (1984) 'The Ideology of Bureaucracy in American Law', *Harvard Law Review* 97 pp 1276–388
GARCIA VILLEGAS, M (1995) 'Efficacité symbolique et pouvoir social du droit', *Revue interdisciplinaire d'études juridiques* 34 pp 155–80
GEHRING, T (1990) 'International Environmental Regimes: Dynamic Sectoral Legal Systems', *Yearbook of International Environmental Law* 1 pp 35–56
——(1994) *Dynamic International Regimes: Institutions for International Environmental Governance* (Peter Lang Verlag, Frankfurt)
GEORGE, S (1976) *How the Other Half Dies: The Real Reasons for World Hunger* (Penguin Books, Harmondsworth/New York)
GIBSON, J (1991) 'The Integration of Pollution Control', in Churchill, R, Warren, L and Gibson, J (eds), *Law, Policy and the Environment* (Blackwell, Oxford/Cambridge)
GIBSON, J and CHURCHILL, RR (1990) 'Problems of Implementation of the North Sea Declarations: A Case Study of the United Kingdom', in Freestone, D and IJlstra, T (eds), *The North Sea: Perspectives on Regional Environmental Co-operation* (Graham & Trotman, London/Dordrecht/Boston)
GINJAAR, L (1988) 'Towards a New EC Water Policy', *Environmental Policy and Law* 18 pp 210–19
GOLUB, J (1994) *The Pivotal Role of British Sovereignty in EC Environmental Policy* (European University Institute, Working Paper RSC No. 94/17, Florence)
——(1996) *Sovereignty and Subsidiarity in EC Environmental Policy* (European University Institute, Working Paper RSC No. 96/2, Florence)
GOODMAN, LW (1987) 'Foreign Toxins: Multinational Corporations and Pesticides in Mexican Agriculture', in Pearson, CS (ed), *Multinational Corporations, Environment, and the Third World: Business Matters* (Duke University Press, Durham)
GORE, A (1993) *Earth in the Balance: Ecology and the Human Spirit* (Plume, New York)
GREENE, O (1996) 'Environmental Regimes: Effectiveness and Implementation Review', in Vogler, J and Imber, MF (eds), *The Environment and International Relations* (Routledge, London/New York)
——(1998) 'Implementation Review and the Baltic Sea Regime', in Victor, DG, Raustalia, K and Skolnikoff, EB (eds), *The Implementation and Effectiveness of*

International Environmental Commitments: Theory and Practice (MIT Press, Cambridge/London)

GRESSER, J, FUJIKURA, K and MORISHIMA, A (1981) *Environmental Law in Japan* (MIT Press, Cambridge/London)

GRIJNS, LC and MOSTERT, E (1991) *The Rhine after 1992: Towards a Method for Comparing and Weighing Two Conflicting Interests* (Centre for Comparative Studies on River Basin Administration, Delft)

GROSS, L (1953) 'States as Organs of International Law and the Problem of Auto-interpretation', in Lipsky, GA (ed), *Law and Politics in the World Community* (University of California Press, Los Angeles)

GÜNDLING, L (1989) 'Prior Notification and Consultation', in Handl, G and Lutz, RE (eds), *Transferring Hazardous Technologies and Substances: The International Legal Challenge* (Graham & Trotman/Martinus Nijhoff, London/Dordrecht/Boston)

GUNNINGHAM, N (1974) *Pollution, Social Interest and the Law* (Martin Robertson, London)

GURTNER-ZIMMERMANN, A (1998) 'The Effectiveness of the Rhine Action Programme', *International Environmental Affairs* 10 pp 241–66

GURUSWAMY, LD (1982) 'Laws Controlling Mercury Pollution: Issues and Implications for the United Kingdom', *Lloyd's Maritime and Commercial Law Quarterly* pp 611–35

——(1984) 'EEC Legislation Controlling Dangerous Substances: Legal Odyssey or Unchartered Voyage of Discovery?', *Lloyd's Maritime and Commercial Law Quarterly* pp 465–80

GURUSWAMY, LD, PAPPS, I and STOREY, DJ (1983) 'The Development and Impact of an EEC Directive: The Control of Discharges of Mercury to the Aquatic Environment', *Journal of ommon Market Studies* 22 pp 71–100

HAAS, PM (1990) *Saving the Mediterranean: The Politics of International Environmental Cooperation* (Columbia University Press, New York)

——(1993) 'Protecting the Baltic and North Seas', in Haas, PM, Keohane, RO and Levy, MA (eds), *Institutions for the Earth: Sources of Effective International Environmental Protection* (MIT Press, Cambridge/London)

HAAS, PM, KEOHANE, RO and LEVY, MA (1993) (eds), *Institutions for the Earth: Sources of Effective International Environmental Protection* (MIT Press, Cambridge/London)

HAIGH, N (1984) *EEC Environmental Policy and Britain*, 1st edn (Environmental Data Services, London)

——(1986) Comparative Report: Water and Waste in Four Countries—A Study of the Implementation of the EEC Directives in France, Germany, Netherlands and the United Kingdom, *European Community Environmental Policy in Practice*, vol 1 (Graham & Trotman, London)

——(1990) *EEC Environmental Policy and Britain*, 2nd rev edn (Longman, London)

——(1991) 'The European Community and International Environmental Policy', *International Environmental Affairs* 3 pp 163–80

——(1994) (ed), *Manual of Environmental Policy: the EC and Britain* (Catermill Publishing, London)

HAKAPÄÄ, K (1981) *Marine Pollution in International Law* (Suomalainen Tiedeakatemia, Helsinki)

HALTER, FL (1984) 'How to Improve International Information Exchange about Pesticides to Meet the Needs of Developing Countries: A Case Study', unpublished paper presented to the Annual Conference of the Association for the Advancement of Policy, Research and Development, 14–16 November 1984

——(1987) 'Regulating Information Exchange and International Trade in Pesticides and Other Toxic Substances to Meet the Needs of Developing Countries', *Columbia Journal of Environmental Law* 12 pp 1–37

HANDL, G (1990) 'Environmental Security and Global Change: The Challenge to International Law', *Yearbook of International Environmental Law* 1 pp 3–33

——(1994) 'Controlling Implementation of and Compliance with International Environmental Commitments: The Rocky Road from Rio', *Colorado Journal of International Environmental Law and Policy* 5 pp 305–31

——(1997) 'Compliance Control Mechanisms and International Environmental Obligations', *Tulane Journal of International and Comparative Law* pp 29–49

HANDL, G and LUTZ, RE (1989) 'The Transboundary Trade in Hazardous Technologies and Substances from a Policy Perspective', in Handl, G and Lutz, RE (eds), *Transferring Hazardous Technologies and Substances: The International Legal Challenge* (Graham & Trotman/Martinus Nijhoff, London/Dordrecht/Boston)

HARLAND, D (1985) 'Legal Aspects of the Export of Hazardous Products', *Journal of Consumer Policy* 8 pp 209–38

HAWKINS, K (1984) *Environment and Enforcement—Regulation and the Social Definition of Pollution* (Clarendon Press, Oxford)

HAYS, SP (1987) *Beauty, Health and Permanence: Environmental Politics in the United States, 1955–1985* (Cambridge University Press, Cambridge/New York)

HAYWARD, P (1990) 'The Oslo and Paris Commissions', in Freestone, D and IJlstra, T (eds), *The North Sea: Perspectives on Regional Environmental Co-operation* (Graham & Trotman/Martinus Nijhoff, London/Dordrecht/Boston)

HENKIN, L (1968) *How Nations Behave: Law and Foreign Policy* (Praeger, New York/Washington/London)

——(1995) *International Law: Politics and Values* (Martinus Nijhoff, Dordrecht/Boston/London)

HEY, E (1991) 'The Precautionary Approach: Implications of the Revision of the Oslo and Paris Conventions', *Marine Policy* 15 pp 244–54

HEY, E, IJLSTRA, T and NOLLKAEMPER, A (1993) 'The 1992 Paris Convention for the Protection of the Marine Environment of the North-East Atlantic: A Critical Analysis', *International Journal of Maritime and Coastal Law* 8 pp 1–49

HIGGINS, R (1994) *Problems and Process: International Law and How We Use It* (Clarendon Press, Oxford)

HILF, J (1995) 'The Convention for the Protection of the Marine Environment of the North-East Atlantic–New Approaches to an Old Problem?', *Zeitschrift für ausländisches öffentliches Recht und Völkerrecht* 55 pp 580–603

HOWARTH, W (1992) 'New Strategies for Water Directives', *European Environmental Law Review* pp 117–21

IJLSTRA, T (1988) 'Regional Cooperation in the North Sea: An Inquiry', in Vukas, B (ed), *The Legal Regime of Enclosed or Semi-Enclosed Seas: The Particular Case of the Mediterranean* (University of Zagreb, Institute of International and Comparative Law, Zagreb)

——(1990) 'L'action communautaire dans les Commissions de Paris et d'Oslo' in Lebullenger, J and Le Morvan, D (eds), *La Communauté européenne et la mer* (Economica, Paris)

——(1994) 'The 1993 Copenhagen Intermediate Ministerial Meeting: North Sea Co-operation at a Turning Point?', *International Journal of Marine and Coastal Law* 9 pp 173–80

INGRAM, P (1983) 'Effectiveness', *Archiv für Rechts- und Sozialphilosophie* 69 pp 484–503

IRWIN, FH (1989) 'Integrated Pollution Control', *International Environmental Affairs* 1 pp 255–74

JACOBSON, HK and BROWN WEISS, E (1995) 'Strengthening Compliance with International Environmental Accords: Preliminary Observations from a Collaborative Project', *Global Governance* 1 pp 119–48

JACOBSON, HK and KAY, DA (1983) (eds), *Environmental Protection: The International Dimension* (Allanheld Osmun, Totowa)

JADOT, B (1991) 'Les objectifs de qualité des eaux de surface en droit communautaire et en droit interne', *Aménagement-Environnement*, n° spécial, pp 3–12

JANS, JH (1990) 'De kwaliteit van de Europese milieuregelgeving', *Sociaal-Economische Wetgeving* 38 pp 503–26

——(1995) *European Environmental Law* (Kluwer Law International, London/The Hague/Boston)

JASANOFF, S (1985) 'Remedies Against Hazardous Exports: Compensation, Products Liability and Criminal Sanctions' in Ives, JH (ed), *The Export of Hazard: Transnational Corporations and Environmental Control Issues* (Routledge & Kegan Paul, Boston/London/Henley)

JESSURUN D'OLIVEIRA, HU (1987) 'De vervuiling van de Rijn—een nieuwe aflevering van het feuilleton: Sandoz en institutionele fricties tussen IRC en EEG', in Aalders, MVC and Koeman, NSJ (eds), *Ontwikkelingen in het milieurecht* (Tjeenk Willink, Zwolle)

JOHNSON, SP (1983) *The Pollution Control Policy of the European Communities* (Graham & Trotman, London)

JOHNSON, SP and CORCELLE, G (1990) *The Environmental Policy of the European Communities* (Graham & Trotman, London/Dordrecht/Boston)

——(1995) *The Environmental Policy of the European Communities*, 2nd edn (Kluwer Law International, London/The Hague/Boston)

JOHNSTON, DM (1981) 'The Environmental Law of the Sea: Historical Development', in Johnston, DM (ed), *The Environmental Law of the Sea* (Erich Schmidt Verlag, Berlin)

JUKKEMA, JW (1988) 'De uitvoer van gevaarlijke produkten naar landen van de Derde Wereld', *Nederlands Juristenblad* 63 pp 1238–41

JUSTE, J (1993) 'La Convention pour la protection du milieu marin de l'Atlantique Nord-Est', *Revue générale de Droit international public* 97 pp 365–93

KAMMINGA, M (1978) 'Who Can Clean up the Rhine: The European Community or the International Rhine Commission?', *Netherlands International Law Review* 25 pp 63–79

KAPTEYN, PJG and VERLOREN VAN THEMAAT, P (1989) *Introduction to the Law of the European Communities*, 2nd edn (Kluwer, Deventer)

KAY, DA (1976) *The International Regulation of Pesticide Residues in Food, Studies in Transnational Legal Policy No. 13* (West Publishing Company, St. Paul)

KENNEDY, D (1987) *International Legal Structures* (Nomos Verlagsgesellschaft, Baden-Baden)

KEUNE, H (1978) 'Kollision rechtlicher, politischer und wirtschafts-psychologischer Gesichtspunkte bei der Auswahl der Stoffe für die Liste I der EG-Gewässerschutz-Richtlinie', *Zeitschrift für Wasserrecht* 17 pp 193–204

KIRKPATRICK, JJ (1983) 'Global Paternalism: The UN and the New International Regulatory Order', *Regulation* 7(1) pp 17–22

KISS, A (1987a) 'The Protection of the Rhine Against Pollution', in Utton, AE and Teclaff, LA (eds), *Transboundary Resources Law* (Westview Press, Boulder/London)

——(1987b) '"Tchernobâle" ou la pollution accidentelle du Rhin par les produits chimiques', *AFDI* 33 pp 719–27

——(1980) 'Mechanisms of Supervision of International Environmental Rules', in Kalshoven, F, Kuyper, PJ and Lammers, JG (eds), *Essays on the Development of the International Legal Order* (Sijthoff & Noordhoff, Alphen aan den Rijn/Rockville)

KISS, A and SHELTON, D (1991) *International Environmental Law* (Transnational Publishers/Graham & Trotman, New York/London)

KOH, HH (1996) 'Transnational Legal Process', *Nebraska Law Review* 75 pp 181–207

KOSKENNIEMI, M (1989) *From Apology to Utopia: The Structure of International Legal Argument* (Lakimiesliiton Kustannus, Helsinki)

——(1991) 'Peaceful Settlement of Environmental Disputes', *Nordic Journal of International Law* 60 pp 73–92

——(1992) 'Breach of Treaty or Non-Compliance? Reflections on the Enforcement of the Montreal Protocol', *Yearbook of International Environmental Law* 3 pp 123–62

KONSTADINIDIS, SV (1996) 'The New Face of the Community's External Relations: Recent Developments on Certain Controversial Issues', in Konstadinidis, SV (ed), *The Legal Regulation of the European Community's External Relations after the Completion of the Internal Market* (Dartmouth, Aldershot/Brookfield/Singapore/Sydney)

KRÄMER, L (1986) *EEC Consumer Law* (Story-Scientia, Brussels)

—— (1988) 'Du contrôle de l'application des directives communautaires en matière d'environnement', *Revue du Marché commun* pp 22–8

——(1989) 'The Open Society, its Lawyers and its Environment', *Journal of Environmental Law* 1 pp 1–9

——(1990a) *EEC Treaty and Environmental Protection* (Sweet & Maxwell, London)

——(1991) 'The Implementation of Community Directives within Member States: Some Implications of the Direct Effect Doctrine', *Journal of Environmental Law* 3 pp 39–56

——(1992) *Focus on European Environmental Law* (Sweet & Maxwell, London)
——(1993a) 'Freshwaters and Community Law', in Kiss, A and Shelton, D (eds), *Manual of European Environmental Law* (Grotius Publications, Cambridge)
——(1993b) *European Environmental Law—Casebook* (Sweet & Maxwell, London)
——(1995) *E.C. Treaty and Environmental Law*, 2nd edn (Sweet & Maxwell, London)
KRATOCHWIL, FV (1983) 'Is International Law "Proper" Law? The Concept of Law in the Light of an Assessment of the "Legal" Nature of Prescriptions in the International Arena', *Archiv für Rechts- und Sozialphilosophie* 69 pp 13–46
——(1984) 'Trasymmachos Revisited: On the Relevance of Norms and the Study of Law for International Affairs', *Journal of International Affairs* 37 pp 343–56
——(1989) *Rules, Norms and Decisions* (Cambridge University Press, Cambridge/New York)
——(2000) 'How Do Norms Matter?', in Byers, M (ed), *The Role of Law in International Politics* (Oxford University Press, Oxford)
KROMAREK, P (1988) 'La protection des eaux douces en droit communautaire', in Bocken, H (ed), *Milieurecht—recente ontwikkelingen/Droit de l'environnement—développements récents*, Vol. I (E Story-Scientia, Brussel)
KUMMER, K (1995) *International Management of Hazardous Wastes: The Basel Convention and Related Legal Rules* (Clarendon Press, Oxford)
KUWABARA, S (1984) *The Legal Regime of the Protection of the Mediterranean against Pollution from Land-Based Sources* (Tycooly, Dublin)
LADEUR, K-H (1994a) 'Zur Prozeduralisierung des Vorsorgebegriffs durch Risikovergleich und Prioritätensetzung', *Jahrbuch des Umwelt- und Technikrechts* pp 297–331
——(1994b) 'Von der Gefahrenabwehr zum Risikomanagement im stoffbezogenen Umweltrecht', in Winter, G (ed), *Risikoanalyse und Risikoabwehr im Chemikalienrecht: Interdisziplinare Untersuchungen* (Werner Verlag, Düsseldorf)
LAMMERS, JG (1980) 'New International Legal Developments Concerning the Pollution of the Rhine', *Netherlands International Law Review* 27 pp 171–93
——(1984) *Pollution of International Watercourses: A Search for Substantive Rules and Principles of Law* (Martinus Nijhoff, Boston/The Hague/Dordrecht/Lancaster)
——(1989a) 'Milieuverdragen en de externe bevoegdheden van de Europese Economisch Gemeenschap', in *Europees Milieurecht* (T.M.C. Asser Instituut, 's-Gravenhage)
——(1989b) 'The Rhine: Legal Aspects of the Management of a Transboundary River', in Verwey, WD (ed), *Nature Management and Sustainable Development* (IOS Press, Amsterdam)
——(1991) 'International and European Community Law Aspects of Pollution of International Watercourses', in Lang, W, Neuhold, H and Zemanek, K (eds), *Environmental Protection and International Law* (Graham & Trotman/Martinus Nijhoff, London/Dordrecht/Boston)
LANG, W (1984) 'Die Verrechtlichung des internationalen Umweltschutzes': vom "soft law" zum "hard law"', *Archiv des Völkerrechts* 22 pp 283–305
——(1992) 'Diplomacy and International Environmental Law-Making: Some Observations', *Yearbook of International Environmental Law* 3 pp 108–22

——(1996) 'Compliance Control in International Environmental Law: Institutional Necessities', *Zeitschrift für ausländisches öffentliches Recht und Völkerrecht* 56 pp 685–95

LAVRYSEN, L (1992) 'De Europese wetgeving op de bescherming van de oppervlaktewateren', *Tijdschrift voor Milieurecht* pp 2–12

LEE, JR (1994) 'Process and Product: Making the Link between Trade and the Environment', *International Environmental Affairs* 6 pp 320–47

LEENEN, A (1984) 'Participation of the EEC in International Environmental Agreements', *Legal Issues of European Integration Legal Issues of European Integration* 1 pp 93–111

LEFEVERE, JGJ (1996) 'State Liability for Breaches of Community Law', *European Environmental Law Review* 5 pp 237–42

LE MORVAN, D (1988) 'L'action des Communautés européennes en matière de protection de la Mer Méditerranée', in Vukas, B (ed), *The Legal Regime of Enclosed or Semi-Enclosed Seas: The Particular Case of the Mediterranean* (University of Zagreb, Institute of International and Comparative Law, Zagreb)

——(1990) 'La pratique des Communautés européennes au regard des dispositions "environnementales" de la Convention des Nations Unies sur le droit de la mer', in Vukas, B (ed), *Essays on the New Law of the Sea 2* (University of Zagreb, Institute of International and Comparative Law, Zagreb)

LEOPOLD, JH (1990) (ed), *Milieuwetgeving—Internationale regelingen verontreiniging zee en rivieren*, vol. Ib (Tjeenk Willink, Zwolle)

LINDSAY, A (1985) 'The Faith Halter Report', *Chemistry and Industry* pp 656–59

LINEAR, M (1985) *Zapping the Third World: The Disaster of Development Aid* (Pluto Press, London)

LOMAS, O (1988) 'Environmental Protection, Economic Conflict and the European Community', *McGill Law Journal* 33 pp 507–39

MCDOUGAL, MS and REISMAN, WM (1983) 'International Law in Polict-Oriented Perspective', in Macdonald, RSJ and Johnston, DM (eds), *The Structure and Process of International Law: Essays in Legal Philosophy, Doctrine and Theory* (Marinus Nijhoff, The Hague/Boston/Lancaster)

MCGOLDRICK, D (1997) *International Relations Law of the European Union* (Longman, London/New York)

MACLEAN, RM (1989) 'The Proper Function of International Law in the Determination of Global Behaviour', *Canadian Yearbook of International Law* 27 pp 57–79

MACLEOD, I, HENRY, ID and HYETT, S (1996) *The External Relations of the European Communities* (Clarendon Press, Oxford)

MCMANUS, RJ (1983) 'Ocean Dumping: Standards in Action', in Jacobson, H and Kay, D (eds), *Environmental Protection: The International Dimension* (Allanheld Osmun, Totowa)

MACRORY, R (1992) 'The Enforcement of Community Environmental Laws: Some Critical Issues', *Common Market Law Review* 29 pp 347–69

——(1996) 'Community Supervision in the Field of the Environment', in Somsen, H (ed), *Protecting the European Environment: Enforcing EC Environmental Law* (Blackstone Press, London)

MAJONE, G (1982) 'The Uncertain Logic of Standard Setting', *Zeitschrift für Umweltpolitik* 4 pp 305–23

MASSIN, JM (1990) 'Les implications de la Conférence de Londres sur la protection de la Mer du Nord ou une convention environnement sur la Mer du Nord: un luxe ou une nécessité?', in Lebullenger, J and Le Morvan, D (eds), *La Communauté européenne et la mer* (Economica, Paris)

MASTELLONE, C (1981) 'The External Relations of the EEC in the Field of Environmental Protection', *International & Comparative Law Quarterly* pp 104–17

MENG, Q-N (1987) *Land-Based Marine Pollution: International Law Development* (Graham & Trotman/Nijhoff, London/Dordrecht/Boston)

M'GONIGLE, RM (1990) '"Developing Sustainability" and the Emerging Norms of International Environmental Law: The Case of Land-Based Marine Pollution Control', *Canadian Yearbook of International Law* 28 pp 169–225

MICKLITZ, HW (1992a) 'International Regulation and Control of the Production and Use of Chemicals and Pesticides: Perspectives for a Convention', *Michigan Journal of International Law* 13 pp 653–97

——(1992b) 'International Regulation on the Export and Import of Banned and Severely Restricted Chemicals and Pesticides', *Milieu en Recht* pp 207–15

MINCKE, C (1998) 'Effets, effectivité, efficience et efficacité du droit: le pôle réaliste de la validité', *Revue interdisciplinaire d'études juridiques* 40 pp 115–51

MINGST, KA (1981) 'The Functionalist and Regime Perspective: The Case of River Rhine Cooperation', *Journal of Common Market Studies* 20 pp 161–73

MITCHELL, RB (1993) 'Compliance Theory: A Synthesis', *Review of European Community and International Environmental Law* 2 pp 327–34

——(1994) *Intentional Oil Pollution at Sea: Environmental Policy and Treaty Compliance* (MIT Press, Cambridge/London)

——(1996) 'Compliance Theory: An Overview', in Cameron, J, Werksman, J and Roderick, P (eds), *Improving Compliance with International Environmental Law* (Earthscan Publications, London)

MÖBS, H (1978) 'Die Richtlinienpolitik der Europäischen Gemeinschaften im Gewässerschutz—Massstäbe für die Ausfüllung, Auslegung und den Vollzug gemeinschaftsrechtlicher Emissionsgrenzwerte un Gewässergüteziele', *Recht der Wasserwirtschaft* 21 pp 13–30

MOL, APJ (1995) *The Refinement of Production: Ecological Modernization Theory and the Chemical Industry* (Van Arkel, Utrecht)

NEUWAHL, NA (1991) 'Joint Participation in International Treaties and the Exercise of Power by the EEC and its Member States: Mixed Agreements', *Common Market Law Review* 28 pp 717–40

——(1996) 'Shared Powers or Combined Incompetence? More on Mixity', *Common Market Law Review* 33 pp 667–87

NOLLKAEMPER, A (1987) 'The European Community and International Environmental Co-operation: Legal Aspects of External Community Powers', *Legal Issues of European Integration* 2 pp 55–91

——(1990a) 'The European Community and State Practice—A Case-Study on Land-Based Marine Pollution', in Vukas, B (ed), *Essays on the New Law of the Sea 2* (University of Zagreb, Institute of International and Comparative Law, Zagreb)

——(1990b) 'Toezichthoudende mechanismen in het internationale milieurecht', in van Buuren, PJJ, Betlem, G and IJlstra, T (eds), *Milieurecht in stelling* (Tjeenk Willink, Zwolle)

——(1990c) 'The Rhine Action Programme: A Turning-Point in the Protection of the North Sea?', in Freestone, D and IJlstra, T (eds), *The North Sea: Perspectives on Regional Environmental Co-operation* (Graham & Trotman/Martinus Nijhoff, London/Dordrecht/Boston)

——(1992a) 'Marine Pollution from Land-Based Sources: Towards a Global Approach', *Marine Pollution Bulletin* 24 pp 8–12

——(1992b) 'On the Effectiveness of International Rules', *Acta Politica* 27 p 49

——(1993a) *The Legal Regime for Transboundary Water Pollution: Between Discretion and Constraint* (Martinus Nijhoff/Graham & Trotman, Dordrecht/Boston/London)

——(1993b) 'Progressie en stagnatie in het internationale regime voor grensoverschrijdende waterverontreiniging', *Milieu en Recht* pp 11–23

——(1997) 'The External Competence of the Community with Regard to the Law of Marine Environmental Protection: The Frail Legal Support for Grand Ambitions', in Ringbom, H (ed), *Competing Norms in the Law of Marine Environmental Protection—Focus on Ship Safety and Pollution Prevention* (Kluwer Law International, London/The Hague/Boston)

——(1998) 'The Distinction between Non-Legal and Legal Norms in International Affairs: an Analysis with Reference to International Policy for the Protection of the North Sea from Hazardous Substances', *International Journal of Marine and Coastal Law* 13 pp 355–71

Norris, R (1982) (ed), *Pills, Pesticides & Profits: The International Trade in Toxic Substances* (North River Press, Croton-on-Hudson)

O'Connell, ME (1992) 'Enforcing the New International Law of the Environment', *German Yearbook of International Law* 35 pp 293–332

Ogus, A (1994) 'Standard Setting for Environmental Protection: Principles and Processes', in Faure, M, Vervaele, J and Weale, A (eds), *Environmental Standards in the European Union in an Interdisciplinary Framework* (MAKLU, Antwerpen/Apeldoorn)

Okuwaki, N (1996) 'The Changing Nature of International Obligations: Effectiveness of International Law and Compliance', *Proceedings of the American Society of International Law* 90 pp 348–53

Paarlberg, RL (1993) 'Managing Pesticide Use in Developing Countries', in Haas, PM, Keohane, RO and Levy, MA (eds), *Institutions for the Earth: Sources of Effective International Environmental Protection* (MIT Press, Cambridge/London)

Pallemaerts, M (1991) 'De toepassing van het Europees milieurecht in België: praktische uitvoering versus formele omzetting', in Centrum voor Beroepsvervolmaking in de Rechten (ed), *Rechtspraktijk en milieubescherming* (Kluwer, Antwerpen)

——(1992a) 'International Environmental Law from Stockholm to Rio: Back to the Future?', *Review of European Community and International Environmental Law* 1 pp 254–66

——(1992b) 'Van Stockholm tot Rio: hoe "duurzaam" is de ontwikkeling van het internationaal milieurecht?', *Tijdschrift voor Milieurecht* pp 58–66

——(1992c) 'Is benzeen een gevaarlijke stof waarvan de lozing verboden is behoudens uitdrukkelijke bepaling in de lozingsvergunning ingevolge het Algemeen Lozingsreglement en Richtlijn 76/464/EEG?', *Tijdschrift voor Milieurecht* pp 25–7

——(1994) 'Van de stranden van Blackpool tot de moerassen van Santoña: plaatsgebonden verplichtingen in het Europees milieurecht', *Tijdschrift voor Milieurecht* pp 19–24

——(1995a) 'La conférence de Rio: grandeur ou décadence du droit international de l'environnement?', *Revue Belge de Droit International* pp 175–223

——(1995b) 'De opkomst van het begrip "duurzame ontwikkeling" in het internationaal juridisch en politiek discours: een conceptuele revolutie?', *Recht en Kritiek* 21 pp 380–97

——(1996) 'International Environmental Law in the Age of Sustainable Development: A Critical Assessment of the UNCED Process', *Journal of Law and Commerce* 15 pp 623–76

——(1999) 'The Decline of Law as an Instrument of Community Environmental Policy', *Law & European Affairs* 9 pp 338–54

PALMER, G (1992a) 'The Earth Summit: What Went Wrong at Rio?', *Washington University Law Quarterly* 70 pp 1005–28

——(1992b) 'New Ways to Make International Environmental Law', *American Journal of International Law* 86 pp 259–83

PARTAN, DG (1990) 'The "Duty to Inform" in International Environmental Law', in Baram, MS and Partan, DG (eds), *Corporate Disclosure of Environmental Risks: U.S. and European Law* (Butterworth Legal Publishers, Salem)

PLATE, F (1991) 'European Water Policy: Water Quality and Quantity Aspects in an International Setting', in Soons, A (ed), *Implementation of the Law of the Sea Convention through International Institutions* (Law of the Sea Institute, Honolulu)

PRAT, J-L (1990) 'La C.E.E. et la protection de la Mer du Nord', in Lebullenger, J and Le Morvan, D (eds), *La Communauté européenne et la mer* (Economica, Paris)

PRAVDIC, V (1988) 'The Link between Natural Sciences and the Legal Regime of the Seas', in Vukas, B (ed), *The Legal Regime of Enclosed or Semi-Enclosed Seas: The Particular Case of the Mediterranean* (University of Zagreb, Institute of International and Comparative Law, Zagreb)

PRECHAL, S (1995) *Directives in European Community Law* (Clarendon Press, Oxford)

RAFTOPOULOS, EG (1990) 'The Mediterranean Action Plan: A Paradigm for Rethinking International Law', in Vukas, B (ed), *Essays on the New Law of the Sea 2* (University of Zagreb, Institute of International and Comparative Law, Zagreb)

——(1992) 'The Barcelona Convention System for the Protection of the Mediterranean Sea against Pollution: An International Trust at Work', *International Journal of Estuarine and Coastal Law* 7 pp 27–41

REHBINDER, E (1983) 'Umweltschutz und Pflanzenschutzrecht', *Natur und Recht 5* p 249

——(1985) 'Environmental Protection and the Law of International Trade', in Dupuy, RJ (ed), *The Future of the International Law of the Environment* (Graham & Trotman/Martinus Nijhoff, Dordrecht/Boston/Lancaster)

——(1994) 'Concept for a Regulation of Material Flows', in Gebers, B and Jendroska, J (eds), *Environmental Control of Products and Substances* (Peter Lang Verlag, Frankfurt)

REHBINDER, E and STEWART, RB (1985) *Environmental Protection Policy*, Integration Through Law: Europe and the American Federal Experience, vol 2 (Walter de Gruyter, Berlin/New York)

RENGELING, H-W (1989) *Umweltvorsorge und ihre Grenzen im EWG-Recht* (Carl Heymanns Verlag, Köln)

RICHARDSON, G, OGUS, A and BURROWS, P (1982) *Policing Pollution—A Study of Regulation and Enforcement* (Clarendon Press, Oxford)

RINGIUS, L (1995) *The Environmental Action Plan Approach: A Milestone in Pollution Control in the Baltic Sea* (Centre for International Climate and Environmental Research, Oslo, Working Paper 1)

ROSE, G (1992) 'Prior Informed Consent: Hazardous Chemicals', *Review of European Community and International Environmental Law* 1 pp 64–8

RUBIN, AP (1994) 'The Impact of Changing International Institutions on Environmental Law and Corporate Responsibility', in Urbani, EJ, Rubin, CP and Katzman, M (eds), *Transnational Environmental Law and its Impact on Corporate Behavior* (Transnational Juris Publications, Irvington-on-Hudson)

RUBLACK, S (1993) *Der grenzüberschreitende Transfer von Umweltrisiken im Völkerrecht* (Nomos Verlagsgesellschaft, Baden-Baden)

——(1994) 'Völkerrecht und Umweltrisikenexport', *Archiv des Völkerrechts* 32 pp 54–98

SACHARIEW, K (1991) 'Promoting Compliance with International Environmental Standards: Reflections on Monitoring and Reporting Mechanisms', *Yearbook of International Environmental Law* 2 pp 31–52

SACK, J (1995) 'The European Community's Membership of International Organizations', *Common Market Law Review* 32 pp 1227–56

SADOWSKI, S (1997) 'Protection of the Marine Environment of the North Sea: the "Russian Doll" Effect', in Ringbom, H (ed), *Competing Norms in the Law of Marine Environmental Protection—Focus on Ship Safety and Pollution Prevention* (Kluwer Law International, London/The Hague/Boston)

SAETEVIK, S (1988) *Environmental Cooperation between the North Sea States: Success or Failure?* (Belhaven Press, London/New York)

SAND, PH (1990) *Lessons Learned in Global Environmental Governance* (World Resources Institute, Washington)

——(1992) (ed), *The Effectiveness of International Environmental Agreements: A Survey of Existing Legal Instruments* (Grotius Publications, Cambridge)

——(1996) 'Institution-Building to Assist Compliance with International Environmental Law: Perspectives', *Zeitschrift für ausländisches öffentliches Recht und Völkerrecht* 56 pp 774–95

SANDS, P (1991) 'The Role of Non-Governmental Organizations in Enforcing International Environmental Law', in Butler, WE (ed), *Control over Compliance with International Law* (Martinus Nijhoff, Dordrecht/Boston/London)

——(1993) 'Enforcing Environmental Security', in Sands, P (ed), *Greening International Law* (Earthscan Publications, London)

——(1995) *Principles of International Environmental Law*, vol 1 (Manchester University Press, Manchester/New York)

——(1996) 'Compliance with International Environmental Obligations: Existing International Legal Arrangements', in Cameron, J, Werksman, J and Roderick, P (eds), *Improving Compliance with International Environmental Law* (Earthscan Publications, London)

SANKEY, J (1989) 'Domestically Prohibited Goods and Hazardous Substances—A New GATT Working Group is Established', *Journal of World Trade* 23(6) pp 99–108

SCHACHTER, O (1991) *International Law in Theory and Practice* (Martinus Nijhoff, Dordrecht/London/Boston)

SCHALLY, HM (1996) 'The Role and Importance of Implementation Monitoring and Non-Compliance Procedures in International Environmental Regimes', in Lang, W (ed), *The Ozone Treaties and their Influence on the Building of International Environmental Regimes*, Österreichische aussenpolitische Dokumentation (Bundesministerium für auswärtige Angelegenheiten, Vienna)

SCHERMERS, HG (1983) 'A Typology of Mixed Agreements', in O'Keeffe, D and Schermers, HG (eds), *Mixed Agreements* (Kluwer, Deventer)

SCHERMERS, H-G and WAELBROECK, D (1992) *Judicial Protection in the European Communities*, 5th edn (Kluwer Law & Taxation, Deventer/Boston)

SCHERR, SJ (1987) 'Hazardous Exports: U.S. and International Policy Developments', in Pearson, CS (ed), *Multinational Corporations, Environment, and the Third World: Business Matters* (Duke University Press, Durham)

SCHEUER, H (1981) 'Les travaux de la Commission de la C.E.E. concernant la pollution transfrontière du Rhin', *Revue Juridique de l'Environnement* pp 314–24

SCHULBERG, F (1979) 'United States Exports of Products Banned for Domestic Use', *Harvard International Law Journal* 20 p 331

SCHWEBEL, SM (1971) (ed), *The Effectiveness of International Decisions* (Sijthoff/Oceana Publications, Leiden/Dobbs Ferry)

SCHWEITZER, GE (1983) 'Toxic Chemicals: Steps Toward Their Evaluation and Control', in Jacobson, H and Kay, D (eds), *Environmental Protection: The International Dimension* (Allanheld Osmun, Totowa)

SHUMAN, E (1983) 'Potentially Hazardous Merchandise: Domestic and International Mechanisms for Consumer Protection', *Vanderbilt Journal of Transnational Law* 16 pp 179–229

SIMMONDS, KR (1986) 'The Community's Declaration upon Signature of the UN Convention on the Law of the Sea', *Common Market Law Review* 23 pp 523–44

——(1989) 'The European Economic Community and the New Law of the Sea', *Recueil des Cours de l'Académie de Droit International* 218 pp 9–166

SKALA, A (1982) *Internationale Technische Regeln und Standards zum Umweltschutz: Ihre Entstehungsarten und rechtliche Wirkungen* (Carl Heymanns Verlag, Köln)

SKJAERSETH, JB (1993) 'The "Effectiveness" of the Mediterranean Action Plan', *International Environmental Affairs* 5 pp 313–34

——(1996) 'The 20th Anniversary of the Mediterranean Action Plan: Reason to Celebrate?', *Green Globe Yearbook* pp 47–53

——(1999) *The Making and Implementation of North Sea Pollution Commitments: Institutions, Rationality and Norms* (University of Oslo, Department of Political Science, Oslo)

SLATER, D (1994) 'The Role of Her Majesty's Inspectorate of Pollution', in Boyle, AE (ed), *Environmental Regulation and Economic Growth* (Clarendon Press, Oxford)

SLAUGHTER BURLEY, A-M (1993) 'International Law and International Relations Theory: A Dual Agenda', *American Journal of International Law* 87 pp 205–39

SLOUKA, ZJ (1982) 'International Law-Making: A View from Technology', in Onuf, NG (ed), *Law-Making in the Global Community* (Carolina Academic Press, Durham)

SMITH, C (2001) 'Pesticide Exports from U.S. Ports, 1997–2000', *Global Pesticide Campaigner* 11(3) pp 1, 8–10

SMITH, C and ROOT, D (1999) 'The Export of Pesticides: Shipments from U.S. Ports, 1995–1996', *International Journal of Occupational and Environmental Health* 5 pp 141–50

SNYDER, F (1990) *New Directions in European Community Law* (Weidenfeld & Nicholson, London)

——(1993a) 'The Effectiveness of European Community Law: Institutions, Processes, Tools and Techniques', *Modern Law Review* 56 pp 19–54

——(1993b) *Soft Law and Institutional Practice in the European Community* (European University Institute, Working Paper LAW No. 93/5, Florence)

SOHN, LB (1976) 'The Effectiveness of International Law', in Nawaz, MK (ed), *Essays on International Law in Honour of Krishna Rao* (Sijthoff, Leiden)

SOLOMON, LD (1977) 'Industry Cooperative Programme of the Food and Agriculture Organization of the United Nations: A Catalytic Organization Bridging Multinational Agribusiness Corporations and Developing Countries', *Texas International Law Journal* 13 pp 69–93

SOMERS, E and MAES, F (1989) *The Implementation of the North Sea Declarations—A Belgian Assessment* (Rijksuniversiteit Gent, Gent)

SOMSEN, H (1991) 'The Regionalization of EC Marine Pollution Law: The Example of the Mediterranean Sea', *International Journal of Estuarine and Coastal Law* 6 pp 229–37

——(1996) (ed), *Protecting the European Environment: Enforcing EC Environmental Law* (Blackstone Press, London)

STEINER, HJ and VAGTS, DF (1986) *Transnational Legal Problems* (Foundation Press, New York)

SYBESMA-KNOL, N (1994) 'De Europese Gemeenschap als deelnemer in het werk van andere internationale organisaties: een aanwinst?', in *Liber Amicorum Paul De Vroede* (Kluwer Rechtswetenschappen België, Antwerpen)

SZASZ, PC (1992) 'International Norm-Making', in Brown Weiss, E (ed), *Environmental Change and International Law: New Challenges and Dimensions* (United Nations University Press, Tokyo)

SZÉKELY, A (1997) 'Non-Binding Commitments: A Commentary on the Softening of International Law Evidenced in the Environmental Field', in *International Law on the Eve of the Twenty-First Century: Views from the International Law Commission* (United Nations, New York)

TAYLOR, D, DIPROSE, G and DUFFY, M (1986) 'EC Environmental Policy and the Control of Water Pollution: the Implementation of Directive 76/464 in Perspective', *Journal of Common Market Studies* 24 pp 225–45

TIMMERMANS, C (1981) 'Division of External Powers between Community and Member States in the Field of Harmonization of National Law—A Case Study', in Timmermans, C and Volker, E (eds), *Division of Powers between the European Communities and their Member States in the Field of External Relations* (Kluwer, Deventer)

TOMCZAK, M (1984) 'Defining Marine Pollution: A Comparison of Definitions Used by International Conventions', *Marine Policy* 8 pp 311–22

TRIDIMAS, T and EECKHOUT, P (1994) 'The External Competence of the Community and the Case-Law of the Court of Justice: Principle versus Pragmatism', *Yearbook of European Law* pp 143–77

TULOKAS, M (1981) 'The Baltic Sea and Pollution', *Scandinavian Studies in Law* 25 pp 207–21

VAN DER BURGT, C (1984) 'Naissance d'un traité', in *Les Commissions d'Oslo et de Paris-La première décennie: Coopération internationale pour la protection de notre environnement marin* (Oslo and Paris Commissions, London)

VAN DER MENSBRUGGHE, Y (1990) 'Legal Status of International North Sea Conference Declarations', in Freestone, D and IJlstra, T (eds), *The North Sea: Perspectives on Regional Environmental Co-operation* (Graham & Trotman/Martinus Nijhoff, London/Dordrecht/Boston)

VAN DER VEEN, C (1977) 'Waterbeheer en de Europese Gemeenschap', *Milieu en Recht* pp 112–18

VAN DIJK, P (1987) 'Normative Force and Effectiveness of International Norms', *German Yearbook of International Law* 30 pp 9–35

VAN DUNNÉ, JM (1991) (ed), *Transboundary Pollution and Liability: the Case of the River Rhine* (Koninklijke Vermande, Lelystad)

VAN HOUTTE, H (1990) 'Health and Safety Regulations in International Trade', in Sarcevic, P and Van Houtte, H (eds), *Legal Issues in International Trade* (Graham & Trotman/Martinus Nijhoff, London/Dordrecht/Boston)

VENNEKENS-CAPKOVA, J (1990) 'Dangerous Substances: Chameleons in Water Policy', in Freestone, D and IJlstra, T (eds), *The North Sea: Perspectives on Regional Environmental Co-operation* (Graham & Trotman/Martinus Nijhoff, London/Dordrecht/Boston)

VICTOR, DG (1998) '"Learning by Doing" in the Nonbinding International Regime to Manage Trade in Hazardous Chemicals and Pesticides', in Victor, DG, Raustiala, K and Skolnikoff, EB (eds), *The Implementation and Effectiveness of International Environmental Commitments: Theory and Practice* (MIT Press, Cambridge/London)

VICTOR, DG, RAUSTIALA, K and SKOLNIKOFF, EB (1998) (eds), *The Implementation and Effectiveness of International Environmental Commitments: Theory and Practice* (MIT Press, Cambridge/London)

VON MOLTKE, K (1988) 'International Commissions and Implementation of International Environmental Agreements', in Carroll, JE (ed), *International Environmental Diplomacy: The Management and Resolution of Transfrontier Environmental Problems* (Cambridge University Press, Cambridge/New York)

VUKASOVIC, V (1988) 'Barcelona Convention as an Important Component of the Mediterranean Action Plan', in Vukas, B (ed), *The Legal Regime of Enclosed or Semi-Enclosed Seas: The Particular Case of the Mediterranean* (University of Zagreb, Institute of International and Comparative Law, Zagreb)

WÄGENBAUER, R (1991) 'The European Community's Policy on Implementation of Environmental Directives', *Fordham International Law Journal* 14 pp 455–77

WALKER, SL (1993) *Environmental Protection versus Trade Liberalization: Finding the Balance* (Publications des Facultés universitaires Saint-Louis, Bruxelles)

WALLS, MP (1988) 'Chemical Exports and the Age of Consent: The High Cost of International Export Control Proposals', *New York University Journal of International Law and Politics* 20 pp 753–75

WARD, H (1994) 'Trade and Environment Issues in the Multilateral Regulation of International Trade in Chemicals', in Gebers, B and Jendroska, J (eds), *Environmental Control of Products and Substances* (Peter Lang Verlag, Frankfurt)

WEIR, D and SHAPIRO, M (1981) *Circle of Poison: Pesticides and People in a Hungry World* (Institute for Food and Development Policy, San Francisco)

WELLENS, KC and BORCHARDT, GM (1989) 'Soft Law in European Community Law', *European Law Review* 14 pp 267–321

WETTESTAD, J (1989) 'Uncertain science and matching policies: science, politics and the organization of North Sea environmental cooperation', in Andresen, S and Ostreng, W (eds), *International Resource Management: the Role of Science and Politics* (Belhaven Press, London/New York)

——(1992) 'The "Effectiveness" of the Paris Convention on Marine Pollution from Land-Based Sources', *International Environmental Affairs* 4 pp 101–21

WETTESTAD, J and ANDRESEN, S (1991) *The Effectiveness of International Resource Cooperation: Some Preliminary Findings* (Fridtjof Nansen Institute, Oslo)

WILLIAMS, R (1994) 'The European Commission and the Enforcement of Environmental Law: an Invidious Position', *Yearbook of European Law* 14 pp 351–99

WINTER, G (1986) (ed), *Grenzwerte: Interdisziplinäre Untersuchungen zu einer Rechtsfigur des Umwelt-, Arbeits- und Lebensmittelschutzes* (Werner Verlag, Düsseldorf)

——(1996) 'On the Effectiveness of the EC Administration: The Case of Environmental Protection', *Common Market Law Review* 33 pp 689–717

WIRTH, DA (1994a) 'The Role of Science in the Uruguay Round and NAFTA Trade Disciplines', *Cornell International Law Journal* 27 pp 817–59

——(1994b) 'Reexamining Decision-Making Processes in International Environmental Law', *Iowa Law Review* 79 pp 769–802

WOLF, R (1986) *Der Stand der Technik* (Westdeutscher Verlag, Opladen)

WOLFF, A (1987) 'Peter Hansen: Orchestrator of the Directory', *European Environment Review* 1 p 32

WCED (1987) World Commission on Environment and Development, *Our Common Future* (Oxford University Press, Oxford/New York)

YEAGER, PC (1991) *The Limits of Law—The Public Regulation of Private Pollution* (Cambridge University Press, Cambridge/New York)

YOUNG, O (1979) *Compliance and Public Authority: A Theory with International Applications* (Johns Hopkins University Press, Baltimore/London)

YOUNG, O and VON MOLTKE, K (1994) 'The Consequences of International Environmental Regimes: Report from the Barcelona Workshop', *International Environmental Affairs* 6 pp 348–70

Index